COMPANY LAW

COMPANY LAW

LEE ROACH

LLB, PhD, FHEA

Senior Lecturer in Law,
University of Portsmouth

OXFORD
UNIVERSITY PRESS

OXFORD
UNIVERSITY PRESS

Great Clarendon Street, Oxford, OX2 6DP,
United Kingdom

Oxford University Press is a department of the University of Oxford.
It furthers the University's objective of excellence in research, scholarship,
and education by publishing worldwide. Oxford is a registered trade mark of
Oxford University Press in the UK and in certain other countries

© Oxford University Press 2019

Public sector information reproduced under Open Government Licence v3.0
(http://www.nationalarchives.gov.uk/doc/open-government-licence/open-government-licence.htm)

Published in the United States of America by Oxford University Press
198 Madison Avenue, New York, NY 10016, United States of America

British Library Cataloguing in Publication Data
Data available

Library of Congress Control Number: 2018960299

ISBN 978–0–19–878663–4

Printed in Great Britain by
Bell & Bain Ltd., Glasgow

To Tom and Sandra Roach

Preface

When OUP first approached me to write a new company law textbook, I was initially reluctant. Company law is not a subject that suffers from a shortage of excellent texts, and my initial concern was whether there was space for a new text in an already crowded market. Such a text would have to try and offer something a little different and, to that end, the aims of this text are:

- to provide a fresh, modern, and accessible account of the UK's company law and corporate governance systems;
- to explain the practical application and effectiveness of the law using a range of helpful pedagogic features;
- to provide a range of online features that complement the text and allow students to stay up-to-date as regards legal developments; and
- to explain the relationship between company law and corporate governance recommendations.

The last bullet point is an important one. In my opinion, it is becoming impossible to view company law and corporate governance as distinct topics. Instead, to obtain a holistic understanding of how companies operate (or how they should operate), it is important to discuss company law and corporate governance alongside one another (although this text remains primarily a company law text). Accordingly, this text has no corporate governance chapter and instead integrates corporate governance coverage into the discussion of the relevant company law topics. This will hopefully better allow you to understand the relationships between company law and corporate governance principles.

I would like to express my thanks to the publishing team at OUP, notably Tom Young, Caroline Mitchell, Lucy Hyde, Jessica Lehmani, Guy Jackson, Fiona Barry, Hayley Buckley, and Kimberley Payne. I would also like to thank the numerous reviewers (listed on p xvii) whose invaluable feedback helped improve this book immeasurably.

I hope you find this book useful. If you have any feedback, then please feel free to get in touch either by sending a message through the accompanying website (www.companylawandgovernance.com) or by sending me a message on the accompanying Twitter account (https://twitter.com/UKCompanyLaw).

The law is stated, as it is understood to me, as of January 2019. Several legal developments in December 2018 occurred too late to be included within the main text, but have been explained in the 'Latest news' section at p xviii.

LRR,
Portsmouth,
January 2019

Guide to the book

This book includes a range of features that are designed to support and strengthen your understanding of company law and corporate governance. This guided tour will show you how to get the most out of this textbook and your studies.

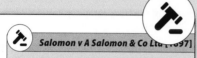

Case boxes Key cases are succinctly summarized in these boxes, providing an account of the facts decision, judgments and, where appropriate, commentary on the case.

Diagrams and tables Tables and figures are presented throughout the book. These will help your understanding and revision, graphically presenting some of the key concepts and principles to be considered in your study of company law.

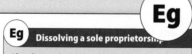

Example boxes Legal principles are applied to fictional example scenarios, clearly demonstrating the purpose behind the law and the application of it in practice.

'Law in action' boxes Relevant, real-world examples of company law and corporate governance in action give you invaluable insight into the reality of the corporate legal world.

BC Group. Taking into account revenue,
mpany in the UK and in Europe (and the
revenue of $51.4 billion, made a profit of
me of writing, its **market capitalization**
yees in over 70 countries.

➡ **market capitalization**: the amount of shares a company has multiplied by its current share price

'At a glance' icons These icons, indicating key provisions, casenotes, links, and definitions, make the book easy to navigate and highlight key information.

FURTHER READING

Stuart R Cross, 'Limited Liability Partnerships Act 2000: Problems A
• Discusses the background and operation of the LLPA 2000 and
  that will impede the general usefulness of LLPs.

David Kershaw, *Company Law in Context: Text and Materials* (2nd e
• Discusses the corporate agency problem and looks and explair

Further reading In the penultimate part of the chapter, you will find a further reading section that recommends a variety of sources to deepen your understanding.

SELF-TEST QUESTIONS

1. Define the following terms:
  • think small first;
  • sole proprietorship;
  • partnership;

Self-test questions Each chapter finishes with a set of questions, allowing you to apply your new-found knowledge to consolidate your learning.

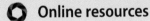 ## Online resources

www.oup.com/uk/roach-company/

This book is accompanied by a suite of online resources, including:

- A chapter on insider dealing and market abuse
- Answers to the end-of-chapter self-test questions
- Multiple-choice questions to test your understanding
- Extended further reading lists
- A glossary of hundreds of legal terms used in this text
- A guide to referencing sources using OSCOLA

For updates, please follow **https://twitter.com/UKCompanyLaw** on Twitter, run by the author, and visit his blog at **www.companylawandgovernance.com** for a repository of company law and corporate governance resources, as well as blog posts from the author on developments in the law.

Contents in brief

PART VI: CORPORATE RESCUE, RESTRUCTURING, AND INSOLVENCY

Detailed contents

Acknowledgements

The author and Oxford University Press would like to thank the following people for their invaluable contributions during the development of this title: Dr Simisola Akintoye, Lecturer, De Montfort University; Greg Allan, Lecturer, University of Leicester; Dr Femi Arnao, Senior Lecturer, University of Sussex; Dr Stelios Andreadakis, Senior Lecturer, Brunel University; Anil Balan, Principal Lecturer, University of East London; Dr Vivienne Bradwell, Senior Teaching Fellow, SOAS University of London; Professor Iris Chiu, Lecturer, University College London; Nick Dearden, Faculty Head of Education, Manchester Metropolitan University; Julian Dobson, Senior Lecturer, University of Winchester; Kieran Durcan, Senior Lecturer, University of Lincoln; Mark Edwards, Principal Lecturer, Sheffield Hallam University; Dr Ama Eyo, Lecturer, Bangor University; Ross Fletcher, Senior Lecturer, Northumbria University; Dr David Gibbs, Lecturer, University of East Anglia; Victoria Roper, Senior Lecturer, Northumbria University; Keith Gompertz, Senior Lecturer, Coventry University; Dr Suren Gomtsian, Lecturer, University of Leeds; Professor Nicholas Grier, Lecturer, Abertay University; Aled Griffiths, Honorary Research Fellow, Bangor University; Dr Sabine Hassler, Senior Lecturer, University of the West of England; Dr Johanna Hoekstra, Lecturer, University of Greenwich; Professor Andrew Johnston, Lecturer, University of Sheffield; Ian King, Lecturer, University of Salford; Kathrin Kuehnel-Fitchen, Lecturer, Robert Gordon University; Dr Mark Leiser, Lecturer, University of Leicester; Larry Mead, Principal Lecturer, University of Derby; James Mendelsohn, Senior Lecturer, University of Huddersfield; Professor David Milman, Lecturer, Lancaster University; Viviana Mollica, Lecturer, University of East Anglia; Scott Morrison, Senior Lecturer, Middlesex University; Dr Rachael Ntongho, Lecturer, University of Bolton; Dr Adaeze Okoye, Senior Lecturer, University of Brighton; Kathleen O'Reilly, Lecturer, University of South Wales; Dr Onyeka Osuji, Reader, University of Essex; Brian Pillans, Lecturer, Glasgow Caledonian University; Dr Renginee G. Pillay, Université Paris III—Sorbonne-Assas International Law School, Mauritius; Dr Pavel Repyeuski, Senior Lecturer, Leeds Beckett University; Kevin Rogers, Deputy Head of Law, University of Roehampton; Navajyoti Samanta, Lecturer, University of Sheffield; Tom Serby, Lecturer, Anglia Ruskin University; Dr Chris Taylor, Senior Lecturer, University of Bradford; Chris Umfreville, Lecturer, University of Aston; Sue Warnock, Senior Lecturer, Bournemouth University; Professor Sally Wheeler, Head of Law, Queen's University Belfast; Lorraine Wilson, Teaching Fellow, University of Stirling; Saba Yousif, Senior Lecturer, University of Gloucestershire; Dr Daoning Zhang, Lecturer, Canterbury Christ Church University.

Latest news

Several legal developments in December 2018 and January/February 2019 occurred too late for inclusion in the main text. These developments have been noted here, and this 'Latest news' section is referenced at the relevant points in the main text.

The Kingman Review of the FRC

In April 2018, the government launched an independent review of the Financial Reporting Council (FRC),[1] to be undertaken by Sir John Kingman.[2] In May 2018, a report by the BEIS and Work and Pensions Select Committees on the collapse of Carillion plc (discussed in the main text at 8.1.5) was highly critical of the FRC,[3] with the Committees stating that:

> The FRC was far too passive in relation to Carillion's financial reporting. It should have followed up its identification of several failings in Carillion's 2015 accounts with subsequent monitoring. Its limited intervention … clearly failed to deter the company in persisting with its over-optimistic presentation of financial information. The FRC was instead happy to walk away after securing box-ticking disclosures of information. It was timid in challenging Carillion on the inadequate and questionable nature of the financial information it provided and wholly ineffective in taking to task the auditors who had responsibility for ensuring their veracity.[4]

When the Kingman Review published its final report in December 2018,[5] it was critical of the FRC's effectiveness and remit, stating that:

- the FRC has, unlike other meaningful regulators, no statutory base;
- it is not fully independent and its funding structure is not appropriate;
- the FRC's powers are 'clearly deficient' and its work does not carry the same credibility as other regulators;
- the UK Stewardship Code has not been effective in practice.[6]

It was therefore unsurprising that the Review described the FRC as 'a rather ramshackle house, cobbled together with all sorts of extensions over time. The house is – just – serviceable, up to a point, but it leaks and creaks, sometimes badly. The inhabitants of the house have sought to patch and mend. But in the end, the house is built on weak foundations,'[7] before going on to state that '[i]t is time to build a

---

[1] See https://www.gov.uk/government/news/government-launches-review-of-audit-regulator accessed 10 January 2019.

[2] Sir John Kingman is the chair of Legal & General plc and the chair of UK Research & Innovation.

[3] See https://publications.parliament.uk/pa/cm201719/cmselect/cmworpen/769/76902.htm accessed 10 January 2019.

[4] ibid para 149.

[5] 'Independent Review of the Financial Reporting Council' (2018), available from https://www.gov.uk/government/news/independent-review-of-the-financial-reporting-council-frc-launches-report accessed 10 January 2019.

[6] ibid paras 11–12.

[7] ibid para 4.

new house'[8] and replace the FRC with a new independent statutory regulator. The Kingman Review recommended that this new regulator be called the Audit, Reporting and Governance Authority, and its duties should be:

- to set and apply high corporate governance, reporting and audit standards;
- to regulate and be responsible for the registration of the audit profession;
- to maintain and promote the UK Corporate Governance Code and the UK Stewardship Code, reporting annually on compliance with the Codes;
- to maintain wide and deep relationships with investors and other users of financial information;
- to monitor and report on developments in the audit market, including trends in audit pricing, the extent of any cross-subsidy from non-audit work and the implications for the quality of audit; and
- to appoint inspectors to investigate a company's affairs where there are public interest concerns about any matter that falls within the Authority's statutory competence.[9]

The government has confirmed that it accepts the recommendations of the Kingman Review and so will seek to replace the FRC with a new regulator with stronger statutory powers.[10] The FRC has also welcomed the recommendations of the Kingman Review.[11] At the time of writing, no timeframe has been put on the creation of this new regulator.

Audit reforms

Part 19.4 of the text discusses the role of the auditor and examine several issues relating to audit quality, audit market concentration, and auditor independence. Several developments have occurred in relation to the audit function that are noted here.

The CMA market study[12]

The chairman of the Competition and Markets Authority (CMA), Andrew Tyrie, noted that the Kingman Review's recommendation to create a new regulator for auditors was a step in the right direction in addressing concerns relating to the quality of statutory audits, but the concerns could only be fully addressed if an examination of the audit market (notably looking at competition in the audit market) was also carried out. Accordingly, as noted at 19.4.1, in October 2018, the CMA announced that it was undertaking a market study into the effectiveness of the statutory audit market.[13]

In December 2018, the CMA published an update paper in which it proposed a raft of reforms for consultation,[14] of which four are especially noteworthy. The first is that

---

[8] ibid para 5.

[9] ibid para 112.

[10] See https://www.gov.uk/government/news/independent-review-of-the-financial-reporting-council-frc-launches-report accessed 10 January 2019.

[11] See https://www.frc.org.uk/news/december-2018-(1)/frc-comment-on-sir-john-kingman-s-independent-revi accessed 10 January 2019.

[12] See https://www.gov.uk/cma-cases/statutory-audit-market-study accessed 10 January 2019.

[13] See https://www.gov.uk/government/news/cma-launches-immediate-review-of-audit-sector accessed 10 January 2019.

[14] CMA, 'Statutory Audit Services Market Study: Update Paper' (CMA 2018), available from https://assets.publishing.service.gov.uk/media/5c17cf2ae5274a4664fa777b/Audit_update_paper_S.pdf accessed 10 January 2019.

FTSE 350 audit committees should be subject to regulatory requirements and obligations, including:

- a requirement that audit committees report directly to an independent regulator (likely the FRC's replacement) before, during and after a tender selection process;
- a requirement that audit committees report to the regulator throughout the audit engagement; and
- the regulator would be empowered to issue public reprimands and direct messages to shareholders.[15]

The second proposed reform is the introduction of mandatory joint audits.[16] This would require FTSE 350 companies to appoint two auditors and both would need to sign off on the company's accounts. The company would choose which two auditors to appoint but, in order to promote more competition amongst the audit market of FTSE companies, the CMA proposes that one of the auditors should be a challenger firm (i.e. a firm not part of the Big Four).

The third proposed reform is the introduction of a market share cap,[17] which would involve limiting the market share of Big Four firms by stating that a certain percentage of the audit market must be reserved for challenger firms. Whilst the CMA is of the opinion that this could increase the number of challenger firms obtaining larger audits, it stated that it believed that this goal would be better achieved via the introduction of mandatory joint audits (indeed, the CMA views joint audits and a market share cap as alternative reforms).

The fourth reform is to require a full split between audit and non-audit services in Big Four firms (and possibly others).[18] Currently, audit firms can provide non-audit services to their audit clients, subject to several prohibitions and limitations. The CMA proposes that audit and non-audit services be split either:

- structurally, so that certain audit firms would be prohibited from providing non-audit services, or;
- operationally, so that firms could provide both services, but would need to separate the audit and non-audit businesses (i.e. each business would need its own board, staff, assets etc).

At the time of writing, the reforms are being consulted on and, given the impact that some of the reforms would have on the audit market, it is likely that there will be opposition. The CMA's market study continues, and it has stated that it is likely to make recommendations to government for legislation to be passed implementing whatever reforms it recommends.

The Brydon Review into UK Audit Standards

In December 2018, the government launched an independent review into standards in the UK audit market.[19] The Brydon Review into UK Audit Standards[20] will consider:

---

[15] ibid paras 4.7–4.25.

[16] ibid paras 4.26–4.60.

[17] ibid paras 4.61–4.87.

[18] ibid paras 4.112–4.137.

[19] See https://www.gov.uk/government/news/government-takes-next-step-in-improving-standards-of-uk-audit-market-with-new-independent-review-into-audit-standards accessed 10 January 2019.

[20] Named after the head of the review, Donald Brydon, who is chair of the Sage Group plc and the former chair of the London Stock Exchange Group plc.

- how far audit can and should evolve to meet the needs of investors and other stakeholders, putting the UK at the forefront;
- how auditors verify information they are signing off on;
- how to manage any residual gap between what audit can and should deliver; and
- what are the public's expectations from audit.

The review's terms of reference were published in February 2019.

Reform of limited partnership law

In April 2018, the government published a consultation on the reform of limited partnership law. The consultation came about due to a concern that limited partnerships did not operate in a transparent manner and could be used for illegal activities (e.g. money laundering). In December 2018, the government published a response to its consultation,[21] in which it proposed a series of reforms, notably:

- persons who wish to apply to register a limited partnership will need to demonstrate that they are registered with an anti-money laundering supervisory body;
- applications to register a limited partnership must state a proposed principal place of business that is in the UK;
- limited partnerships should be required to file a confirmation statement at least every 12 months; and
- the Registrar of Companies will be given the power to strike off limited partnerships that are dissolved or not carrying on business (and, as a result of this, a restoration process will also be introduced).

A revised UK Stewardship Code

As noted at 14.5.2, the UK Stewardship Code has not been updated since 2012. In January 2019, the FRC launched a consultation on a revised UK Stewardship Code.[22] A notable difference is the change in structure. The 2012 Code consisted of seven Principles with accompanying guidance. The proposed 2019 Code[23] follows a structure that is more similar to the UK Corporate Governance Code and consists of 14 Principles which are accompanied by 33 Provisions that provide more detail. Additional guidance is also provided at the rear of the proposed 2019 Code.

In terms of content, the key proposed changes[24] to the revised 2019 Code are:

- Signatories to the Code must develop their organizational purpose and disclose how their purpose, strategy, values, and culture enable them to fulfil their stewardship objectives.

---

[21] The consultation document and the government's response can be found at https://www.gov.uk/government/consultations/limited-partnerships-reform-of-limited-partnership-law accessed 10 January 2019.

[22] See https://www.frc.org.uk/getattachment/dff25bf9-998e-44f6-a699-a697d932da60/;.aspx accessed 30 January 2019.

[23] The proposed revised Code can be found at https://www.frc.org.uk/getattachment/bf27581f-c443-4365-ae0a-1487f1388a1b/Annex-A-Stewardship-Code-Jan-2019.pdf accessed 30 January 2019.

[24] A summary of the changes between the 2012 Code and the proposed 2019 Code can be found at https://www.frc.org.uk/getattachment/b11e40ec-7d2e-4acb-9619-ae210fc9ac18/Annex-B-Proposed-Revisions-to-the-UK-Stewardship-Code-2012-vs-2019-Jan-2019.pdf accessed 30 January 2019.

- Signatories to the Code are expected to take into account environmental, social, and governance factors when fulfilling their stewardship responsibilities.
- The Code's Provisions differentiate between the different types of person that the Code is aimed at (e.g. asset owners, asset managers, service providers). So, whilst some Provisions apply universally, other Provisions provide a version that applies to asset owners and a different version that applies to asset managers.
- The 2010 and 2012 Codes largely focused on stewardship in relation to the exercise of listed equities. The proposed 2019 Code expects investors to exercise stewardship across a wider range of asset classes (e.g. bonds).

The FRC proposes that the revised Code will be published and will come into effect on 16 July 2019 (although this may change depending on the responses to the consultation). The first list of signatories to the 2019 Code will be published in the first quarter of 2020.

The FCA as the UK Listing Authority

As noted at 18.1.2.1, the FCA acts as the UK Listing Authority (UKLA). In February 2019, the FCA stated that commentators and members of the public did not know what the UKLA did and whether it was a separate body from the FCA. Accordingly, in order to provide clarity, the FCA announced that it has decided to phase out the use of the term 'UK Listing Authority' from its website and external communications.[25] However, the FCA will not be phasing out the term completely as it will still accept documents from issuers that use the term (although the FCA would prefer that the terms 'the Financial Conduct Authority' or 'the FCA' be used).

---

[25] FCA, *Primary Market Bulletin* (February 2019/No 20) 1, available from https://www.fca.org.uk/publication/newsletters/primary-market-bulletin-20.pdf accessed 14 February 2019.

Table of cases

Page numbers in bold indicate a case that is discussed in a case box.

UK cases

Cases of the Court of Justice of the European Union

Cases of the European Court of Human Rights

Cases from other countries

Australia

Canada

United States

Table of legislation and other rules

Table of subordinate legislation

Table of codes, standards, and rules

List of abbreviations

4AMLD	Fourth Anti-Money Laundering Directive
5AMLD	Fifth Anti-Money Laundering Directive
6AMLD	Sixth Anti-Money Laundering Directive
ABI	Association of British Insurers
AGM	annual general meeting
AIM	Alternative Investment Market
art/Art	article (domestic law)/Article (EU/international law)
BEIS	Department for Business, Energy and Industrial Strategy
BERR	Department for Business, Enterprise and Regulatory Reform
BIS	Department for Business, Innovation and Skills
CA 1862	Companies Act 1862
CA 1867	Companies Act 1867
CA 1929	Companies Act 1929
CA 1948	Companies Act 1948
CA 1980	Companies Act 1980
CA 1981	Companies Act 1981
CA 1985	Companies Act 1985
CA 1989	Companies Act 1989
CA 2006	Companies Act 2006
CARD	Consolidated Admission and Reporting Directive
CDDA 1986	Company Directors Disqualification Act 1986
CEO	chief executive officer
CFO	chief finance officer
CHS	Companies House Service
CIC	Community Interest Company
cl	clause
CLR	Company Law Review
CLRSG	Company Law Review Steering Group
CMA	Competition and Markets Authority
CMCHA 2007	Corporate Manslaughter and Corporate Homicide Act 2007
CMO	chief marketing officer
COO	chief operating officer
CPR 1998	Civil Procedure Rules 1998
CRO	chief risk officer
CSO	chief security officer
CUR	current annuity rate
CVA	company voluntary arrangement
DEPP	Decision Procedure and Penalty
DTI	Department of Trade and Industry
DTR	Disclosure Guidance and Transparency Rules
EA(GPGI)R 2017	Equality Act 2010 (Gender Pay Gap Information) Regulations 2017

EC	European Community
ECHR	European Convention on Human Rights
ECJ	European Court of Justice
ECtHR	European Court of Human Rights
EEA	European Economic Area
EEC	European Economic Community
EGM	extraordinary general meeting
EPS	earnings per share
ERRA 2013	Enterprise and Regulatory Reform Act 2013
EU	European Union
EUI	Euroclear UK and Ireland Ltd
FCA	Financial Conduct Authority
FRC	Financial Reporting Council
FSA	Financial Services Authority
FSMA 2000	Financial Services and Markets Act 2000
FTSE	Financial Times Stock Exchange
GAR	guaranteed annual rate
GDP	gross domestic product
GLO	Group Litigation Order
HMRC	Her Majesty's Revenue and Customs
IA 1986	Insolvency Act 1986
IAS	International Accounting Standard
ICAEW	Institute of Chartered Accountants in England and Wales
ICAS	Institute of Chartered Accountants in Scotland
ICSA	Institute of Chartered Secretaries and Administrators
IoD	Institute of Directors
IPO	initial public offering
IR 2016	Insolvency (England and Wales) Rules 2016
ISA	International Standard on Auditing
ISC	Institutional Shareholders' Committee
LIBOR	London interbank offered rate
LLA	liability limitation agreement
LLP	limited liability partnership
LLPA 2000	Limited Liability Partnerships Act 2000
LR	Listing Rules
LSE	London Stock Exchange
Ltd	private limited company
NAPF	National Association of Pension Funds
NASDAQ	National Association of Securities Dealers Automated Quotations
NED	non-executive director
OFT	Office of Fair Trading
ONS	Office for National Statistics
PA 1890	Partnership Act 1980
PIE	public interest entity
PIRC	Pensions and Investment Research Consultants

plc	public limited company
PR	Prospectus Rules
PSC	person/people with significant control
Pt	Part
PwC	PricewaterhouseCoopers
r/rr	rule/rules
reg	regulation
RIE	recognized investment exchange
s/ss	section/sections
SA	*Société Anonyme*
SAIL	single alternative inspection location
SBEEA 2015	Small Business, Enterprise and Employment Act 2015
Sch	Schedule
SE	*Societas Europeae*
SEC	Securities and Exchange Commission
SIC	Standard Industrial Classification of Economic Activities
SID	senior independent director
SIP 16	Statement of Insolvency Practice 16
SME	small and medium-sized enterprises
SUP	*Societas Unius Personae*
TFEU	Treaty on the Functioning of the European Union
UKLA	United Kingdom Listing Authority
USR 2001	Uncertificated Securities Regulations 2001

PART I

Introduction

Part I of this text provide an introduction to company law and corporate governance. The chapters in Part I provide a foundation that will better allow you to understand the substantive company law rules and recommendations that are discussed in subsequent chapters. Part I consists of two chapters, namely:

CHAPTER 1 INTRODUCTION

A full understanding of company law rules can only be obtained if you appreciate what company law aims to do. Accordingly, Chapter 1 begins by looking at the aims of company law and corporate governance. It is also important to appreciate the importance of the company as a business structure, but such an appreciation can only be obtained if you understand how the company compares to other business structures. Accordingly, Chapter 1 provides a brief discussion of the other key business structures, namely the sole proprietorship, partnership, and limited liability partnership.

CHAPTER 2 SOURCES OF COMPANY LAW AND CORPORATE GOVERNANCE

A thorough understanding of company law and corporate governance is only possible if you are fully aware of, and comfortable dealing with, the various sources of company law and corporate governance. Today, companies are regulated by a wide range of rules and recommendations, and so this chapter provides a detailed discussion of these sources. It is also important that you understand the relationship between company law rules and corporate governance recommendations as there is an increasing link between the two.

1 Introduction

- The aims of company law and corporate governance
- Company law in practice
- Other business structures

INTRODUCTION

This textbook discusses and examines the regulation of the company, undoubtedly one of the most important institutions ever devised. In 1911, Nicholas Murray Butler, then President of Colombia University, stated that '[t]he limited liability corporation is the greatest single discovery of modern times . . .. Even steam and electricity are far less important than the limited liability corporation, and they would be reduced to comparative impotence without it.'[1] In 1973, the Confederation for British Industry stated that '[o]ur style of life is largely determined by the activities and style of business; and the style of business is largely determined by the activities and style of our companies.'[2] Clearly, it is vital that such an important, powerful and influential institution is regulated appropriately.

But institutions with such power also tend to be regarded with suspicion. Concerns regarding the role of companies have existed since the seventeenth century with the growth of the great chartered companies such as the East India Company. Over the past few decades, these concerns have intensified. As Sir Adrian Cadbury noted:

> Societal concerns over corporate activities are now wider in scope and more in evidence. While instances of fraud and failure may have sparked off corporate governance enquiries, as they did in Britain, an underlying unease over the role of companies in society was already surfacing and was a focus of media attention to a considerably greater degree than in the past.[3]

The spate of corporate scandals that have occurred over the past thirty years (many of which are discussed at various points in this text) has exacerbated this unease. The result has been a renewed focus on how companies are governed. Again, quoting Cadbury, '[w]hat remains

---

[1] Quoted in S Bainbridge, 'Abolishing Veil Piercing' (2001) 26 J Corp L 479, 479.
[2] CBI, 'The Responsibilities of the British Public Company' (CBI 1973) 8.
[3] Adrian Cadbury, *Corporate Governance and Chairmanship: A Personal View* (OUP 2002) 13.

astonishing is the rapidity with which corporate governance has moved from an arcane technical term to figuring on the agenda of the G8 Summit'.[4] This is a company law text, but it is impossible to have a complete understanding of company law without also understanding its relationship with corporate governance. It could be argued that company law is largely concerned with what a company can do, whereas corporate governance focuses more on what a company should do. Effective management of a company requires both law and governance to be taken seriously. The relationship between company law and corporate governance is discussed more in Chapter 2.

Corporate governance is not a new subject. As Tricker notes '[c]orporate governance is old, only the phrase is new'.[5] Despite its relative newness, however, the phrase 'corporate governance' has become 'one of the most commonly used phrases in the current global business vocabulary'.[6] Whilst the origins of the subject are legal, corporate governance now transcends the law and is relevant to all business disciplines. This breadth is reflected in the Cadbury Committee's definition of corporate governance as 'the system by which companies are directed and controlled'.[7] This text, however, cannot and does not seek to provide a thorough account of corporate governance as a topic.[8] Rather, it focuses on company law and discusses governance as and when it becomes relevant. The close relationship between company law and corporate governance is demonstrated by the fact that both subjects have overlapping aims.

1.1 The aims of company law and corporate governance

There is no single overriding objective behind our system of company law and governance. Instead, UK company law has to balance a series of aims, not all of which align. The principal aims of our system of law and governance are set out below. How the law attempts to fulfil these aims is discussed throughout this text.

1.1.1 Accountability

Company law and governance should provide for a system whereby companies should be free to partake in appropriate risk-taking activity that benefits society but, at the same time, it should be done in such a way that ensures companies, directors, and managers remain accountable. However, bearing this in mind, consider the following example of one of the world's largest companies.

---

[4] ibid 236.

[5] Bob Tricker, *Corporate Governance: Principles, Policies, and Practices* (3rd edn, OUP 2015) 4.

[6] Jill Solomon, *Corporate Governance and Accountability* (4th edn, Wiley 2013) 3.

[7] Committee on the Financial Aspects of Corporate Governance, 'The Report of the Committee on the Financial Aspects of Corporate Governance' (Gee Publishing Ltd 1992) para 2.5.

[8] For more detailed discussion of corporate governance, see Ronald AG Monks and Nell Minow, *Corporate Governance* (5th edn, Wiley 2011); Jill Solomon, *Corporate Governance and Accountability* (4th edn, Wiley 2013); Bob Tricker, *Corporate Governance: Principles, Policies, and Practices* (3rd edn, OUP 2015); Marc Moore and Martin Petrin, *Corporate Governance: Law, Regulation and Theory* (Palgrave 2017); Christine A Mallin, *Corporate Governance* (6th edn, OUP 2018).

HSBC Holdings plc

HSBC Holdings plc is the holding company for the HSBC Group. Taking into account revenue, profits, assets held, and market value, it is the largest company in the UK and in Europe (and the seventeenth largest in the world).[9] In 2017, it generated revenue of $51.4 billion, made a profit of $21 billion, and held assets worth $2.5 trillion.[10] At the time of writing, its **market capitalization** is over £131 billion. It employs more than 250,000 employees in over 70 countries.

➡ **market capitalization**: the amount of shares a company has multiplied by its current share price

The question that has proved so difficult to answer is how we can make such massive entities accountable. Size gives a company power, and that power demands regulation. As companies grow, their ability to affect those around them also grows. Today's companies have grown to a massive scale, with many of the largest companies generating revenues that dwarf the gross domestic products of many countries. BP plc is the largest revenue-generating company in the UK—in 2017, the BP group's revenues amounted to $244.5 billion.[11] Of the 200 countries ranked in terms of gross domestic product (GDP) by the World Bank, only 43 had a GDP higher than BP group's revenue.[12] Only 23 countries have a higher GDP than the $500.3 billion revenue that Walmart generated in 2017–18.[13] How such massive entities can be effectively regulated is a central challenge of company law and governance.

The laws and mechanisms that exist to hold such companies accountable are discussed throughout the text. Monks and Minow, in discussing the US system of regulation, place the responsibility for regulating companies firmly on the government,[14] through the use of legislation. In the UK, there is no doubt that legislation establishes a number of very important accountability mechanisms, from general meetings to directors' duties, to disclosure obligations. But, in relation to the regulation of larger companies, the UK also places strong reliance on a series of codes and reports, which do not establish mandatory rules, but instead establish best practice recommendations. These codes and reports provide for the appointment of non-executive directors and the creation of board committees, and lay down principles regarding board composition. To appreciate the UK system of company law and governance, one must look at the law and the relevant codes and reports. But company law and governance are not merely concerned with regulating large public companies. They must also provide a framework of accountability that is flexible enough to cater for smaller companies too.

1.1.2 Flexibility

Whilst the business community desires laws that are certain and predictable (as noted at 1.1.3 when the aim of certainty is discussed), it is also important that the law is flexible so that it can react to evolving and novel corporate practices. The problem that arises

---

[9] Rankings are derived from the Forbes Global 2000, www.forbes.com/global2000/list.

[10] HSBC Holdings plc, 'Annual Report and Accounts 2017' (HSBC 2018) 2.

[11] BP, 'Annual Report and Form 20-F 2017' (BP 2018) 125.

[12] World Bank, 'Gross Domestic Product 2017' (World Bank 2016), http://data.worldbank.org/data-catalog/GDP-ranking-table.

[13] Walmart, '2018 Annual Report' (Walmart 2018) 7.

[14] Robert AG Monks and Nell Minow, *Corporate Governance* (5th edn, Wiley 2011) 18.

is that laws that are predictable are often inflexible, and laws that are flexible are often unpredictable, but the businessman 'wishes to have his cake and eat it; to be given predictability on the one hand and flexibility to accommodate new practices and developments on the other'.[15] Striking a balance between predictability and flexibility is a difficult task and one that Parliament and the courts are not always best placed to undertake. This explains why, despite the length of the Companies Act 2006 (CA 2006), a lot of areas of company activity are not covered by prescriptive rules, and instead companies can draft their own rules by inserting/amending provisions in their articles of association. Companies subject to the UK Corporate Governance Code are not bound to comply with its recommendations.

 The articles of association are discussed at 5.3.

The task is made more difficult by the breadth of companies that must be regulated. Companies can range from a small, one-person private company with a tiny revenue to a massive, multinational corporate group with hundreds of thousands of employees and revenues in the billions. Our system of company law must be flexible enough to effectively regulate all types of company, whilst also recognizing the differences that exist between such companies. Unfortunately, it is true to say that UK company law (and textbooks) have often focused too much on the needs of large companies. Certainly, the Companies Act 1985 was 'structured around the needs of larger, publicly owned companies'.[16] But public companies are a notable minority—of the 3.8 million companies in the UK, only 5,836 are public companies.[17] Accordingly, the Company Law Review Steering Group recommended the adoption of a 'think small first' approach, under which the focus would be on 'minimising complexity and maximising accessibility',[18] thereby ensuring that the law would better cater for smaller companies. The following example demonstrates how the 'think small first' approach works in practice.

Annual general meetings and 'think small first'

It has long been acknowledged that, in smaller companies, annual general meetings ('AGMs') are often pointless, as the directors and members are usually the same people. Despite this, successive Companies Acts required all companies to hold an AGM every year. Section 366(1) of the CA 1985 stated that all companies had to hold an AGM, but s 366A provided that a private company could dispense with this requirement by passing an elective resolution.[19] Clearly, this is not an approach that thinks small first. A public company would only need to know the base requirement in s 366, whereas a private company would need to also know of the exception in s 366A and the provisions relating to elective resolutions. It would then need to pass an elective resolution. Accordingly, the law was more complex and cumbersome for smaller companies. Conversely, the CA 2006 simply provides that public companies must hold an AGM,[20] and generally makes no mention of private companies, meaning that private companies do not need to hold an AGM, but can if they so wish without the need to pass any resolutions to opt in or out of the rules relating to AGMs.

In terms of governance, the focus has been almost exclusively on large, listed companies, with the UK Corporate Governance Code expressly stating that it applies to all companies

---

[15] Roy Goode, 'The Codification of Commercial Law' (1988) Mon LR 135, 150.

[16] CLRSG, 'Modern Company Law for a Competitive Economy: The Strategic Framework' (1999) para 5.2.3.

[17] Companies House, 'Incorporated Companies in the UK, July to September 2018 (2018) Tables 1a and 1b.

[18] CLRSG, 'Modern Company Law for a Competitive Economy: The Strategic Framework' (1999) 'Executive Summary'.

[19] Under s 379A of the CA 1985, passing an elective resolution required the consent of all the members.

[20] CA 2006, s 336(1).

with a premium listing. This is unsurprising given that the corporate scandals that have propelled corporate governance into the spotlight have mostly involved large, listed companies. Further, most of the important governance mechanisms (e.g. non-executive directors, board committees, etc) would be of no use to smaller companies. However, that is not to say that governance is not relevant to unquoted companies, and the Code's focus on listed companies became the subject of criticism following the collapse of BHS Ltd. As a result, a set of governance principles has been devised for large private companies.

∽ Premium listings are discussed at 18.4.1.2.

∽ The governance of private companies is discussed at 2.2.2.2.

1.1.3 Certainty

As Lord Mansfield has stated '[i]n all mercantile transactions, the great objective should be certainty . . '.[21] Corporate transactions can require a significant amount of planning and it is important that business persons can engage in transactions without undue fear that those transactions will be set aside. In order for this to be the case, company law and governance must exhibit several characteristics:

- The law must be clear. If a statute, such as the CA 2006, is drafted poorly or if the reasoning behind a legal judgment is vague, ambiguous, or misguided, then directors, members, and other relevant persons will be reluctant to rely on it.
- The law must be applied consistently and set aside sparingly. Whilst the law must be free to develop to evolving situations, companies must be free to act on the basis that settled law will not be changed without due reason. This is especially true of fundamental company law principles, such as corporate personality, which the courts have been extremely wary of unduly interfering with.

Litigation is expensive and predictable law helps companies and directors organize their activities so as to avoid costly legal breaches. Should a dispute arise, predictable law helps the dispute be resolved more speedily and cheaply. In some cases, however, applying the law in a predictable fashion may lead to an unfair result being imposed on one or both of the parties. In such a case, should fairness or predictability be the dominant consideration?

1.1.4 Transparency

Companies and directors cannot be held accountable if they conduct their business in secret. Famously, Louis Brandeis, a former Justice of the US Supreme Court, stated that '[s]unlight is said to be the best of disinfectants'[22] and, in echoing this, Nordberg stated that:

> Disclosure is something like sunlight and fresh air. It either kills germs or lets us see where they might be lurking, so we can clean them up. It also prevents them from growing in the first place, because people are more careful about what they do in the first place when they know everyone else can see.[23]

This is certainly true in the case of corporate activity and, as will become evident throughout this text, the UK system of company law and governance places great emphasis on the value of corporate transparency. Companies (especially public and quoted companies) are subject to significant disclosure obligations across the range of their activities. This disclosed information is relied upon by numerous persons:

- Investors will use financial information in order to determine whether to purchase shares. Increasingly, investors will also look at the company's environmental and social impact

---

[21] *Vallejo v Wheeler* (1774) 1 Cowp 143, 153.

[22] Louis D Brandeis, *Other People's Money and How the Bankers Use It* (Frederick A Stokes Co 1914).

[23] Donald Norberg, *Corporate Governance: Principles and Issues* (Sage 2011) 196.

when making investment decisions, and non-financial reporting is viewed as increasingly important.

- Creditors will look to the company's accounts before deciding whether to provide or extend credit to the company.
- Suppliers will want to investigate the company prior to contracting with the company, especially if goods or services are supplied on credit.
- Information disclosed will be used by the market to accurately determine share price.
- The media will use publicly available information when reporting on the company's activities.

Such information is only of use if it is easily accessible. Fortunately, much of the information that companies disclose must be made available to the public (most of it for free). Significant amounts of information can be obtained from the company's registered office or its website. Further, the public register of information on companies maintained by Companies House is now freely available online.[24]

Unfortunately, the effectiveness of these disclosure obligations can be reduced in two ways. First, as is discussed at 19.1, annual reports and accounts are becoming increasingly lengthy and complex, which can put people off using them. Second, and more worryingly, are those instances where the directors disclose information that presents a deceptive picture of the company's state of affairs. Typically, this will involve a company engaging in creative and deceptive accounting and business practices in order to portray the company as being much more financially healthy than it actually is. The following infamous example provides a demonstration of this, and also how the safeguards to prevent such fraud failed.

 Enron and Arthur Andersen LLP

In the late 1990s, Enron appeared to experience a massive growth in revenue (from $13.3 billion in 1996 to $100.8 billion in 2000), and its share price nearly quadrupled over that period. Enron portrayed itself as an extremely profitable company (its 2000 financial accounts showed a healthy profit of $979 million) and it boasted proudly of its corporate values. A year later, the company would be filing for bankruptcy amidst allegations of fraud.

Enron had, for a number of years, been using 'special purpose entitles' to hide large losses from the market. In effect, Enron was portraying itself as profitable when it was in fact making significant losses. To make matters worse, Enron's auditor, Arthur Andersen LLP, was found to have been complicit in the deception by destroying documentation that proved Enron's fraud. In October 2001, Enron declared a loss of $1 billion, and in December 2001 it filed for bankruptcy. Arthur Andersen was subsequently convicted of obstructing justice and collapsed soon after.[25] A number of Enron's directors were imprisoned.

Sadly, this type of practice has become alarmingly common over the past twenty years. Doubtless, a number of the directors involved in such fraudulent activity do so because they fear being sacked or are concerned their performance-related pay might be adversely affected. This leads us onto another aim of company law and governance, namely to avoid the misalignment of interests.

---

[24] See https://beta.companieshouse.gov.uk.

[25] The US Supreme Court reversed Andersen's conviction in 2006, but this was too late to be of aid to the firm.

1.1.5 Avoiding misalignments of interests

The company is a separate person at law, but it can only operate through human intermediaries. These intermediaries may be tempted to engage in activities that do not benefit the company, but benefit themselves. This is especially problematic in the case of the company's directors. The directors are agents of the company, but they may be tempted to use their considerable managerial power to act in a manner that benefits themselves. This problem has long been recognized. Writing in 1838, Adam Smith stated:

The directors of such companies however being the managers of other people's money than of their own, it cannot well be expected that they should watch over it with the same anxious vigilance which the partners in private copartnery frequently watch over their own .... Negligence and profusion, therefore, must always prevail, more or less in the management of the affairs of such a company.[26]

The directors position as agents is discussed at 6.3.

One of the aims of company law is to try and ensure that negligence and profusion do not prevail and that misalignments of interests are avoided or minimized by focusing stakeholders on a common goal (usually, the company's interests).

1.1.6 Efficiency

Company law and best-practice recommendations must take into account the cost and impact they will have on the company's efficiency. Laws that unduly impede efficiency or impose excessive costs will face stiff opposition, and companies will seek to avoid them. Company law also needs to acknowledge that some laws are not suitable for some companies on efficiency grounds, and exceptions must be provided for.

The 'small companies regime'

The CA 2006 acknowledges that some of its requirements are, in practice, of little use to smaller companies and would be prohibitively costly to implement. Accordingly, small companies are, via what is known as the 'small companies regime', excluded from certain requirements such as the need to have their accounts audited, the need to provide full accounts or group accounts, and the need to prepare a strategic report.

Small companies are discussed at 19.3.1.3.

The UK Corporate Governance Code is also conscious of efficiency concerns, which is why it operates on a comply-or-explain basis. A company to whom the Code applies may decide not to implement a recommendation of the Code on the ground that it would unduly impede efficiency—this is perfectly permissible providing that, if the company is listed, it explains why it has decided not to follow the relevant recommendation.

1.1.7 Avoiding disaster

Breaches of company law can have disastrous consequences for a company, be it in the form of punitive fines, significant compensation payments, or a loss of reputation (which can be especially disastrous). Poor corporate governance can cause a company to sustain heavy losses or worse, as the following demonstrates.

---

[26] Adam Smith, *An Inquiry into the Nature and Causes of the Wealth of Nations* (Ward Lock 1838) 586.

The rise of the 'rogue trader'

Over the past 30 years, we have seen an increasing number of cases involving 'rogue traders'. A common theme amongst rogue trader cases is that the trader is only able to engage in the unlawful conduct due to the presence of poor governance mechanisms and weak oversight. Examples of prominent rogue trader incidents include the following:

- Nick Leeson's unauthorized trading activities caused one of London's most established banks, Barings, to collapse in 1992 after he engaged in unauthorized trades that resulted in losses of £827 million.
- In 1996, Yasuo Hamanaka, a trader at the Japanese Sumitomo Corporation engaged in unauthorized trading over a ten-year period that cost the company 285 billion yen (around $2.6 billion).
- Jerome Kerviel whose unlawful trading activities between 2006 and 2008 at French banking company Societé Generale cost the bank €4.9 billion. Kerviel was unsurprisingly dismissed by the company, but later successfully claimed for wrongful dismissal on the ground that the company knew of his unlawful activities long before he was dismissed.
- Kweku Adeboli was based in the London branch of Swiss bank UBS. In 2011, he engaged in a number of fraudulent trades that cost the bank $2.3 billion, and wiped $4.5 billion off its share price.

The collapse of Barings Bank is discussed more at 10.5.1.

Poor governance in a company can bring the company down. Poor governance in a sector can have more wide-ranging consequences. Sir David Walker, in his review of banks and financial institutions following the 2008–9 financial crisis, identified that:

> serious deficiencies in prudential oversight and financial regulation in the period before the crisis were accompanied by major governance failures within banks. These contributed materially to excessive risk taking and to the breadth and depth of the crisis. The need is now to bring corporate governance issues closer to centre stage.[27]

Not all disasters are avoidable and, every year, thousands of companies find themselves struggling to such an extent that the company's existence comes under threat. As discussed in Chapter 21, company law (or insolvency law if you regard the subjects as distinct) also establishes mechanisms designed to help struggling companies. For those companies that are beyond help, or for whom such help is unsuccessful, company law also provides mechanisms for the orderly liquidation and dissolution of the company.

1.2　Company law in practice

The laws, recommendations, and principles discussed in this text do not exist solely in the classroom, or on the page of a text. The laws and recommendations discussed set out the framework by which millions of companies are governed—companies that range from a small, single-person private company to a massive multinational company. It is vital to appreciate why these laws exist as they do and how they are applied in practice.

---

[27] 'A Review of Corporate Governance in UK Banks and Other Financial Institutions' (2009) 9.

To that end, this text utilizes two boxed features that demonstrate the importance, aims, and application of the law.

1.2.1 Example boxes

Example boxes provide fictional examples following a fictional corporate group (the 'Dragon Group'), as set out in Figure 1.1.

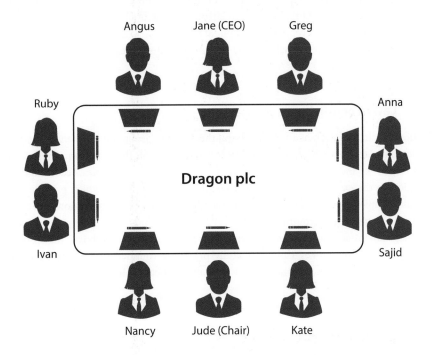

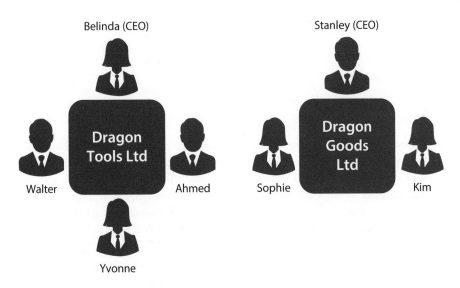

FIGURE 1.1 The Dragon Group

The Dragon Group will be used to demonstrate how the law is applied in practice. We will also see the origins of the group and how it evolves over time. In this chapter, we will see how Jane Dragon commences business as a sole proprietor, how she then enters into partnership with someone else, and how she eventually incorporates her business as a limited liability partnership. In Chapter 3, we will see Jane promote her business, before incorporating as a private company (Dragon Ltd) and, as it grows, we will see it re-register as a public company (Dragon plc). Eventually, Dragon plc will list its shares on the London Stock Exchange and it will set up subsidiaries (Dragon Tools Ltd and Dragon Goods Ltd). In the final chapters of the book, we will see Dragon plc struggle financially and eventually be liquidated and dissolved. And in the chapters in between, the Dragon Group will be used to show why the law exists as it does, and how it is applied in practice.

1.2.2 Law in action boxes

Fictional examples such as those involving the Dragon Group are excellent in helping to demonstrate the application of the law, but to understand the importance, relevance, and impact of the law, nothing beats an actual, real-world example. Accordingly, in addition to the example boxes, this text uses law in action boxes, which provide real-world examples of situations that demonstrate the importance and operation of the law/corporate governance recommendations.

These law in action boxes, along with example boxes, and case boxes that provide details of some of the key cases, hopefully provide a rounded understanding of the importance and relevance of the law, as well as its practical application.

1.3 Other business structures

A person, such as Jane Dragon, who wishes to engage in some form of business activity will need to do so via some form of business structure. Whereas some countries allow for the creation of dozens of forms of business structure, UK businesses primarily operate through one (or more) of four business structures:

1. the sole proprietorship;
2. the partnership;
3. the limited liability partnership (LLP); and
4. the company.

Obviously, this text is concerned with the company, but in order to understand how useful the company as a business structure is, it is important to briefly consider the other business structures available. It should also be noted that many UK businesses do not conduct business through a company, indicating that the company will be an unsuitable vehicle in certain cases. However, as Figure 1.2 demonstrates, in recent years, the percentage of businesses operating through a company has increased, whilst the use of other business structures has decreased.

Understanding the advantages and disadvantages that companies have over other business structures (and vice versa) is essential.

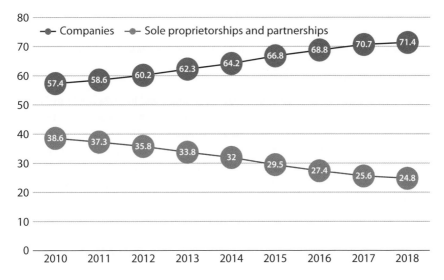

FIGURE 1.2 Trends in business structure usage (%)

Source: Office for National Statistics, 'UK Business: Activity, Size and Location 2018' (ONS 2018).

1.3.1 **Sole proprietorship**

Consider the following.

> **Eg** **Sole proprietorship**
>
> Jane Dragon is a qualified lawyer and accountant. She wishes to set up her own business providing consultancy services to local businesses. She is not planning on taking on any employees: she wishes to have total control over the business, and wants to be entitled to all the profits that the business generates. She has never run her own business before, so she is looking for a simple business structure with little formality and regulation.

The business structure that seems to best meet Jane's needs is the sole proprietorship, the simplest UK business structure. A sole proprietor is normally defined as a sole individual carrying on some form of business activity (i.e. a self-employed person). However, this definition can be slightly misleading in that, whilst a sole proprietorship will be run largely for the benefit of the sole proprietor, sole proprietorships are free to take on employees (although the vast majority do not). The key point to note is that the business is not incorporated, nor does the sole proprietor undertake business activity in partnership with anyone. Sole proprietorships come in two forms:

1. Where the sole proprietor is a professional (as Jane is), then she will be known as a 'sole practitioner'.

2. Where the sole proprietor is not a professional, then he/she will be known as a 'sole trader'. Although it is common to refer to all single-person businesses as sole traders, sole practitioners are not actually sole traders.

Unlike incorporated business structures, there is no separation between a sole proprietor and his business, and sole proprietorships are not legal persons. Therefore, Jane will own all of the assets of the business and will be entitled to all of the profits that the business generates.

1.3.1.1 Formation

Setting up business as a sole proprietor is extremely simple and involves less formality than setting up other forms of business. All that Jane need do to commence business as a sole proprietor is register herself with HM Revenue and Customs (HMRC) as self-employed. Sole proprietors are required to complete their own tax returns (although many will engage an accountant for this), so Jane should ensure that she keeps clear and accurate records of all sales and purchases, so that the process of self-assessment can be completed quickly and easily.

Jane will need to choose a name for her business. She could use her own name and call the sole proprietorship 'Dragon', or 'J Dragon', or 'Jane Dragon'. If she wishes to use any other name, then this will be classified as a 'business' name,[28] and is subject to limitations and statutory regulation. Jane decides to call the sole proprietorship 'J Dragon' so no further issues arise.

 The regulation of business names is discussed at 3.2.3.1.

1.3.1.2 Finance

Jane may struggle to finance her new business as sole proprietorships are at a disadvantage compared with other business structures. A partnership can raise finance by admitting new partners or acquiring additional funds from existing partners; a company (especially public companies) can raise finance by selling shares. Neither of these options is available to Jane if she wishes to remain a sole proprietor. She will either need to invest her own money into the business (and risk losing it if the business fails), persuade others to invest (in which case, they may demand a share of the profits, which Jane does not want), or obtain a loan. Given that many sole proprietorships are small affairs, banks are cautious when lending to them, and obtaining large sums of **debt capital** is usually impossible.

➡ **debt capital**: capital raised through borrowing

1.3.1.3 Liability

The principal disadvantage of carrying on business as a sole proprietorship is that Jane's liability is personal and unlimited. Whereas partnerships and companies can be limited, it is impossible to create a limited sole proprietorship. All of Jane's assets (including private assets, such as her house, car, and bank accounts) can be seized and sold in order to satisfy the debts and liabilities of the sole proprietorship.

1.3.1.4 Dissolution

Consider the following.

> **Eg** **Dissolving a sole proprietorship**
>
> After a few months, it is clear that Jane's business is not making enough money to be sustainable as she cannot find enough clients (it transpires that Angela Smith, a local sole proprietor who also provides consultancy services, has cornered the market). Jane tries to sell her business as a going concern but, due to its lack of profit and the presence of Angela's business, she cannot secure a buyer. Accordingly, she decides to dissolve the sole proprietorship.

---

[28] CA 2006, s 1192.

Dissolution of a sole proprietorship is very easy. The first step is for Jane to cease acquiring any new business. She can then tie up any loose ends, such as collecting any debts owed, paying off creditors, laying off employees, etc. Any money left over belongs to Jane. She should then inform HMRC that she is no longer self-employed. This will bring the sole proprietorship to an end.

1.3.2 **Partnership**

Consider the following.

> **Partnership**
>
> Angela Smith approaches Jane. She informs Jane that she wishes to expand her business and therefore asks Jane if she wishes to work with her. Angela and Jane will have equal say in management, and any profits generated by the new business will be split equally between them. Jane and Angela decide to set up business as a partnership, called Smith & Dragon.

A partnership is defined as 'the relation which subsists between persons carrying on a business in common with a view of profit'.[29] This seemingly straightforward definition contains a number of words and phrases that have proven deceptively complicated to define in practice and have spawned a mass of case law. An examination of this is beyond the scope of this text,[30] but the key point to note here is that the phrase 'relation which subsists' indicates that a partnership is based upon the relationship between the partners. Whereas the creation of an LLP or company requires permission from the state (usually through registration), a partnership is created simply by Jane and Angela agreeing to enter into business as partners. This agreement need not take any particular form: it may be written, oral, or implied through conduct. However, in order to avoid future disputes, it is advisable for the partnership agreement to be in writing, and the majority of partnership agreements are usually executed by deed and will contain written terms stating how the partnership is to be run.

Defining a partnership as a form of contractual relationship makes clear that Smith & Dragon will not enjoy legal personality[31] and therefore cannot acquire rights or incur obligations in its own name, nor can it own assets. It also means that, from a liability point of view, the partners occupy a vulnerable position for several reasons:

- Jane and Angela are agents of Smith & Dragon and of each other,[32] meaning that the actions of Jane/Angela can contractually bind the firm and Angela/Jane.

- Jane can be **vicariously liable** for the wrongful acts or omissions of Angela, and vice versa.[33] Accordingly, if Angela were to commit a tort in the course of the firm's business, Jane could also be liable.

- Jane and Angela are jointly liable for the debts and obligations of Smith & Dragon, incurred whilst they are partners.[34]

➡ **vicarious liability:** where a person is liable for the unlawful acts or omissions of another person

---

[29] Partnership Act 1890, s 1(1).

[30] For more, see Geoffrey Morse, *Partnership and LLP Law* (8th edn, OUP 2015) ch 1.

[31] Unlike in Scotland, where a partnership is 'a legal person distinct from the partners of whom it is composed' (PA 1890, s 4(2)).

[32] PA 1890, s 5.   [33] ibid s 10.   [34] ibid s 9.

As in a sole proprietorship, the liability of partners is personal and unlimited, so Jane and Angela could find themselves being declared bankrupt if Smith & Dragon's debts or liabilities are substantial. It is, however, possible for a partner to limit his liability through a special form of partnership known as a limited partnership.

1.3.2.1 Limited partnership

The Limited Partnerships Act 1907 provides for the ability to register a business as a limited partnership, the partners of which are not subject to the unlimited levels of liability to which general partners are subject. Instead they are liable to contribute such capital as is stipulated in the registration documents[35] and no more.[36]

Limited partnerships are extremely rare, largely because limited liability is more readily obtainable by incorporating the business as an LLP or company. For several reasons, a limited partnership would not be suitable for Jane and Angela:

- There must be at least one general partner, whose liability will be unlimited.[37] Accordingly either Jane or Angela would have unlimited liability.
- Limited partners are not permitted to take part in the management of the firm, nor do they have the power to bind the firm.[38] A limited partner who does take part in management will be liable for the debts and liabilities of the firm as if he were a general partner. This will be of no use as Jane and Angela both wish to be involved in the business's management.

For these reasons, limited partnerships are rare and would be of little aid to Jane and Angela. What would be of use is a partnership that allowed both Jane and Angela to limit their liability. Such a structure now exists, namely the limited liability partnership.

1.3.3 Limited liability partnerships

Consider the following.

 Eg | **Limited liability partnerships**

Angela was sued for providing negligent advice to a client. Fortunately, an exclusion clause in the contract meant that the client's claim failed. However, this has caused Jane and Angela to become concerned about their level of potential liability. They therefore decide that they wish to adopt a business structure that limits their liability, whilst retaining some of the advantages of a partnership (especially in terms of taxation). Accordingly, they dissolved Smith & Dragon and incorporated Smith & Dragon LLP.

Limited liability partnerships ('LLPs'), created under the Limited Liability Partnerships Act 2000 ('LLPA 2000'), are often described as a 'hybrid' business structure, because they combine the characteristics of a partnership and a company. Whilst this is true, there is little doubt that LLPs have more in common with registered companies than

---

[35] Limited Partnerships Act 1907, s 8A(2)(d).

[36] Although until this amount is contributed, the partner will remain a general partner (*Rayner & Co v Rhodes* (1926) 24 Ll L Rep 25 (KB)).

[37] Limited Partnerships Act 1907, s 4(2).   [38] ibid s 6(1).

TABLE 1.1 The differences between an ordinary partnership and an LLP

	Ordinary partnership	LLP
Formation	Can be formed informally by two or more persons agreeing to carry on business in partnership	Formally incorporated by registering certain documents with the Registrar of Companies (just like a company)
Has corporate personality	No	Yes (just like a company)
Regulated by	Partnership law, notably the PA 1890	Company law, unless the LLPA 2000 states otherwise
Partners known as	The partners of an ordinary partnership are simply known as 'partners'	The partners of an LLP are known as 'members' (just like a company has members)
Liability of partners	The partners of an ordinary partnership are jointly liable for the debts of the partnership and are jointly and severally liable for its liabilities	The members of an LLP are not generally liable for the debts and liabilities of an LLP—the LLP itself is liable (just like a company is liable for its own debts and liabilities)
Disqualification	The partners of an ordinary partnership cannot be disqualified from acting as a partner of an ordinary partnership	The members of an LLP can be disqualified from acting as a member of an LLP (just as directors can be disqualified from a company)

with partnerships. In fact, their resemblance to companies is so apparent that it has been argued that describing LLPs as partnerships is 'misleading'.[39] Table 1.1 demonstrates the numerous differences between LLPs and ordinary partnerships (and also shows how similar LLPs are to companies).

Section 1(2) of the LLPA 2000 provides that an LLP shall be a body corporate, meaning that, like a company, it will have a legal personality separate from that of its members. Accordingly, the LLP itself will be liable for its debts and will be vicariously liable for the acts of its agents, meaning that John and Angela will only be liable for such sums as have been agreed amongst themselves.[40] Further, there may be tax advantages as LLPs are tax transparent, meaning that the LLP itself is ignored and each partner is taxed personally based on their share of the LLPs income (just like an ordinary partnership). However, Jane and Angela will need to bear a few disadvantages in mind:

● Like a registered company, an LLP is formed through incorporation by registration with the Registrar of Companies,[41] and so is not as easy to establish as a sole proprietorship or ordinary partnership.

● LLPs are, unless otherwise stated, not subject to partnership law,[42] but are instead subject to the LLPA 2000 (and regulations passed under it) and company law. They are, therefore, subject to much more regulation than sole proprietorships or ordinary partnerships.

---

[39] Paul L Davies and Sarah Worthington, *Gower's Principles of Modern Company Law* (10th edn, Sweet & Maxwell 2016) 6.

[40] Insolvency Act 1986, s 74. Note that this applies to LLPs by virtue of reg 5 of the Limited Liability Partnerships Regulations 2001, SI 2001/1090.

[41] LLPA 2000, ss 2 and 3.   [42] ibid s 1(5).

The above discussion indicates that the LLP was never designed to be a business structure of mass appeal and, certainly, it was not intended to be a vehicle for small businesses, as some at the time argued that it could be. It was created mainly to cater for the needs of those who lobbied for it—namely, large professional firms. This is indicated by the fact that, as of September 2018, there were only 50,532 LLPs registered in the UK.[43] Virtually all large accountancy and solicitors' firms have adopted LLP status.

CHAPTER SUMMARY

- Company law should (i) hold companies and directors to account; (ii) be flexible enough to respond to novel and evolving practices; (iii) provide certainty; (iv) promote transparency; (v) help to avoid misalignment of interests; (vi) promote corporate efficiency, and; (vii) help avoid corporate disaster.

- Other than companies, the principal business structures are the sole proprietorship, the partnership, and the limited liability partnership.

- A sole proprietorship is a sole individual carrying on some form of business activity (i.e. a self-employed person). A sole proprietor is entitled to all the profit that the business generates, but the sole proprietor is personally liable for all the debts and liabilities of the business.

- Two or more persons who wish to engage in business together can form an ordinary partnership. The liability of the partners is personal and unlimited.

- Limited liability partnerships were created to provide suitable business structures for large, professional firms. In many respects, limited liability partnerships resemble companies.

FURTHER READING

Stuart R Cross, 'Limited Liability Partnerships Act 2000: Problems Ahead' [2003] JBL 268.
- Discusses the background and operation of the LLPA 2000 and highlights a number of problems that will impede the general usefulness of LLPs.

David Kershaw, *Company Law in Context: Text and Materials* (2nd edn, OUP 2012) ch 5.
- Discusses the corporate agency problem and looks and explains the costs that non-aligned interests impose upon the company.

Geoffrey Morse, *Partnership and LLP Law* (8th edn, OUP 2015).
- Provides a detailed account of the law relating to partnerships and LLPs.

Bob Tricker, *Corporate Governance: Principles, Policies, and Practices* (3rd edn, OUP 2015) ch 1.
- Looks at the growth of interest in corporate governance as a topic.

SELF-TEST QUESTIONS

1. Define the following terms:
- think small first;
- sole proprietorship;
- partnership;

---

43 Companies House, 'Incorporated Companies in the UK, July to September 2018' (2018) Table 1c.

- limited partnership;
- limited liability partnership.

2. State whether each of the following statements is true or false and, if false, explain why:

   - The company is the most popular business structure.
   - A sole proprietor is a self-employed person.
   - All forms of partnership are brought into existence by the partners agreeing to conduct business through a partnership.
   - The liability of all the partners in a limited partnership is limited.
   - Limited liability partnerships are generally regulated by partnership law.
   - The company is the only business structure that has separate legal personality.

3. What are the aims of company law? Provide examples of how the law seeks to fulfil these aims.

4. Jane Dragon and Angela Smith decide that they wish to work together, but are unsure as to which business structure would be most appropriate. They seek your advice regarding which business structure would be most suitable, bearing in mind:

   - they wish to avoid significant levels of formality and regulation;
   - they want to have flexibility in establishing the procedures by which the business is to be run;
   - they want to be able to run their own affairs;
   - they want to avoid personal liability for the debts and liabilities of the business;
   - the process of creating the business should be relatively cheap and quick;
   - they do not want to invest significant amounts of their own capital in setting up the business and will probably wish to raise capital from outside sources;
   - they wish to take on employees.

   Discuss to what extent each of the various business structures fulfil all, or some, of these aims and advise Jane and Angela which business structure would be most suitable for their business.

 ONLINE RESOURCES

This book is accompanied by online resources to better support you in your studies. Visit www.oup.com/uk/roach-company/ for:

- answers to the self-test questions;
- further reading lists;
- multiple-choice questions;
- glossary.

Updates to the law can be found on the author's Twitter account (@UKCompanyLaw) and further resources can be found on the author's blog (www.companylawandgovernance.com).

2 | Sources of company law and corporate governance

- Sources of company law
- Sources of corporate governance principles

INTRODUCTION

Before this text delves into the various laws and best practice recommendations that govern companies, it is important to understand the structure of the UK's company law and governance framework. Historically, company law texts did this by discussing the various sources of company law. However, as corporate governance has become a more prominent topic, an increasing body of corporate governance principles have also been established. There are some corporate topics that are governed purely by law, and other topics that have very little established law and are governed largely by best practice recommendations. However, increasingly, company law and corporate governance are becoming intertwined and to obtain a holistic understanding of an issue, recourse must be had to company law and corporate governance recommendations. Directors' remuneration is an excellent example of a topic that involves both company law requirements and corporate governance recommendations.

 Directors' renumeration is discussed in more detail at 8.1.5.

 Institutional investors are discussed at 14.5.1.

> ### Directors' remuneration
>
> Who determines the remuneration of the directors is a matter for the company's articles. Aside from that, the law does not generally interfere in the process by which pay is determined. However, the UK Corporate Governance Code establishes several recommendations relating to the determination of pay, notably the establishment of a remuneration committee. The Companies Act 2006 (CA 2006) requires companies to disclose details regarding the directors' pay packages and service contracts and, in quoted companies, the members are given the right to vote on aspects of the directors' remuneration. Institutional investors have been especially active in this area, so the UK Stewardship Code is of relevance too.

This chapter discusses the various sources of company law. It then moves on to summarize the key sources of corporate governance and how they have developed.

2.1 Sources of company law

Companies are legal creatures. They exist only because the law provides for their existence. The law grants them powers, places limitations upon those powers, imposes obligations, and sets out the processes by which companies are created, operated, and dissolved. In order to understand what company law states, it is important to first understand from where company law derives. Whilst our system of company law largely revolves around a central piece of company law legislation, the sources of company law are extremely diverse. This section discusses these legal sources, beginning with the principal source, namely legislation.

2.1.1 Legislation

Lord Halsbury LC stated that 'a limited company owes its existence to the Act of Parliament, and it is to the Act of Parliament one must refer to see what are its powers, and within what limits it is free to act'.[1] This indicates that legislation forms the principal source of company law in the UK, with the principal legislative provisions being found in the Companies Acts.

2.1.1.1 The Companies Acts and the Company Law Review

The UK system of company law has, for over 150 years, been built around a central Companies Act (although, as is discussed at 2.1.1.3 more recently, specific areas of company law have been hived off into separate Acts of Parliament). A detailed exposition of the evolution of company law legislation need not be undertaken here.[2] However, Figure 2.1 sets out the timeline of the Companies Acts and amending Acts.

As Figure 2.1 indicates, the current Companies Act is the CA 2006—an Act that has been described as 'the product of the most extensive revision of company law since 1856'.[3] Accordingly, before looking at the 2006 Act, a discussion of the eight-year process that led to its enactment will be of help. In 1998, Margaret Beckett, then President of the Board of Trade, stated that:

> Our current framework of company law is essentially constructed on foundations which were put in place by the Victorians in the middle of the last century. There have been numerous additions, amendments and consolidations since then, but they have created a patchwork of regulation that is immensely complex and seriously out of date.[4]

Accordingly, the government decided to 'embark on a fundamental review of the framework of core company law'[5] and, to that end, the Company Law Review (CLR) was set up, headed by a Steering Group (CLRSG). In its opening consultation document, the CLRSG identified numerous problems with the then system of regulation, namely that it was outdated, used overly formal language, was excessively detailed, contained obsolete

---

[1] *Ooregum Gold Mining Co of India Ltd v Roper* [1892] AC 125 (HL) 133.

[2] For a detailed discussion of the evolution of companies legislation, see Geoffrey Morse, *Palmer's Company Law* (Sweet & Maxwell 2018) Ch 1.1.

[3] Sarah Worthington, *Sealy & Worthington's Text, Cases & Materials in Company Law* (11th edn, OUP 2016) 4.

[4] CLRSG, 'Modern Company Law for a Competitive Economy' (1998) Foreword.

[5] ibid para 1.1.

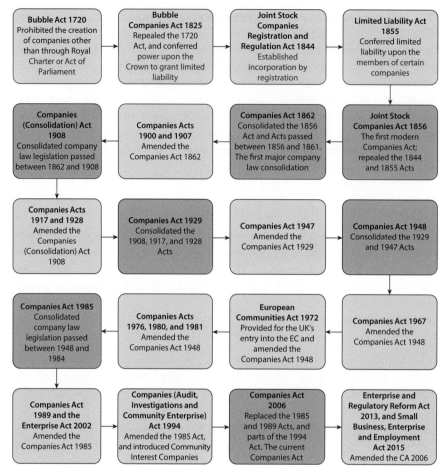

*Boxes in grey represent the free-standing Companies Acts that establish the broad regulatory system. Boxes in purple signify amending Acts, or other notable Acts.

FIGURE 2.1 The Companies Acts and amending legislation

and ineffective provisions, imposed unnecessary costs upon companies, and had failed to adapt to an increasingly globalized marketplace.[6] The CLR was tasked with, *inter alia*, making recommendations which would modernize our company law system 'in order to provide a simple, efficient and cost-effective framework for carrying out business activity which:

- permits the maximum amount of freedom and flexibility to those organising and directing the enterprise;

- at the same time protects, through regulation where necessary, the interests of those involved with the enterprise, including shareholders, creditors and employees; and

- is drafted in clear, concise and unambiguous language which can be readily understood by those involved in business enterprise.'[7]

---

[6] ibid paras 3.1–3.4 and 4.4.
[7] ibid para 5.2. This paragraph sets out the CLRSG's full terms of reference.

The CLRSG published a two-volume Final Report, which contained a set of detailed recommendations and draft clauses.[8] The government responded by publishing two White Papers,[9] both of which produced draft clauses that were broadly in line with the CLR's recommendations. Due to the length of time it was taking to produce a Bill, it was decided that some reforms would be implemented piecemeal via statute prior to the Bill's introduction into Parliament.[10] Eventually, in November 2005, the Company Law Reform Bill (later changed to the Companies Bill) was introduced into Parliament. However, due to the bulk of amendments made to the Bill (it is reported that it underwent over 3,000 amendments during its passage through Parliament),[11] the Bill did not receive Royal Assent until November 2006.

2.1.1.2 **The Companies Act 2006**

The CA 2006 received Royal Assent on 8 November 2006 and is reportedly the lengthiest piece of legislation ever passed by Parliament. When originally passed, it consisted of 1,300 sections and 16 Schedules (more sections and Schedules have been added since). The Act is divided into 47 Parts, with each Part focusing on a specific aspect of company law (e.g. Pt 2 deals with company formation). Each Part usually consists of a number of sections,[12] with larger Parts often being divided up into Chapters. Eighteen Schedules at the end of the Act provide further details on relevant provisions (e.g. Sch 1A provides further details on when a person will be regarded as a 'person with significant control' over the company).

Although the Act was enacted on 8 November 2006, only 29 sections of the Act came into force on that day.[13] It would take eight Commencement Orders over the course of nearly three years[14] for the rest of the Act to come into effect (and several original provisions are still not yet fully in force).[15] During this three-year implementation period, around 80 statutory instruments were passed which amended the Act. Further significant additions and amendments have derived from the Enterprise and Regulatory Reform Act 2013 (ERRA 2013) and the Small Business, Enterprise and Employment Act 2015 (SBEEA 2015). Consequently, the Act now contains over 100 more sections than when first enacted.

These additions and amendments have come at a cost, namely length. Successive Companies Acts have become increasingly bulky (the CA 2006 is nearly double the length of the CA 1985). To offset this increased length, the CLR stated that company law legislation should be 'drafted in clear, concise and unambiguous language which can be readily understood by those involved in business enterprise'.[16] Unfortunately, a survey conducted by the Department for Business Innovation and Skills (BIS) in 2010 found

---

[8] The Final Report, along with the CLRSG's consultation documents can be found at https://webarchive. nationalarchives.gov.uk/20070402095949/http://www.dti.gov.uk/bbf/co-act-2006/clr-review/page22794.html accessed 10 January 2019.

[9] DTI, *Modernising Company Law* (Cm 5553, 2002); DTI, *Company Law Reform* (Cm 6456, 2005).

[10] For example, the rules relating to Community Interest Companies (CICs) were introduced by the Companies (Audit, Investigations and Community Enterprise) Act 2004. CICs are discussed at 3.3.4.1.

[11] Geoffrey Morse, *Palmer's Company Law* (Sweet & Maxwell 2018) para 1.140.

[12] Though not all. For example, Pt 29 (which concerns fraudulent trading) consists of only one section (namely s 993).

[13] CA 2006, s 1300(1).   [14] The Act was almost fully in force by the 1 October 2009.

[15] Namely ss 22(2), 327(2)(c), and 330(6)(c).

[16] CLRSG, 'Modern Company Law for a Competitive Economy' (1998) para 5.2.

that only 20 per cent of those questioned were of the opinion that the CA 2006 had simplified the law (compared to 34 per cent who felt it had not).[17]

The frequent amendments to the Act also increase the likelihood of relevant parties lacking awareness of the law. Unsurprisingly, awareness of changes introduced by the CA 2006 correlated with company size, with larger companies (who have the resources to engage specialist advisors) demonstrating greater awareness. The 2010 BIS survey noted above found that 94 per cent of respondents from quoted companies were aware of the changes, compared to only 40 per cent of respondents from small private companies.[18]

Complexity of company law legislation is further increased by the fact that the Companies Acts are no longer the sole company law enactment. In recent years, laws that were traditionally located within a Companies Act have been split off into other Acts.

2.1.1.3 Other notable Acts of Parliament

Historically, the vast bulk of statutory company law would be found in the Companies Acts. However, this is no longer the case and, beginning in the 1980s, a process began that would see several important company law topics hived off from the Companies Acts. 1986 was an especially important year as that year saw several major company law topics placed into three distinct Acts of Parliament:

- **Insolvency Act 1986**: historically, corporate insolvency law was governed by the Companies Acts. In 1982, the Cork Report[19] recommended that insolvency law (both individual and corporate) should be placed into a single piece of legislation. Unfortunately, this recommendation was not immediately acted upon and corporate insolvency law provisions were split between the CA 1985 and a newly enacted Insolvency Act 1985. However, on the day that the Insolvency Act 1985 came into force, it, and the insolvency law provisions in the CA 1985, were repealed and re-enacted in the form of the Insolvency Act 1986 (IA 1986).[20] The IA 1986, along with its supporting subordinate legislation,[21] now provides the framework for corporate insolvency law.

- **Company Directors Disqualification Act 1986**: the ability to disqualify a director was first introduced by s 75 of the Companies Act 1928. Subsequently, the law relating to director disqualification was contained in successive Companies Acts and the Insolvency Act 1976. The Cork Report recommended that the law relating to disqualification should be placed into a single statute but it was instead originally split across the CA 1985 and the Insolvency Act 1985. However, these provisions were repealed and re-enacted by the provisions now found in the Company Directors Disqualification Act 1986 (CDDA 1986).

- **Financial Services and Markets Act 2000**: prior to 1986, financial services were effectively self-regulated. A government-commissioned report in 1984[22] recommended placing the regulation of financial services into a statutory framework, and the result was the passing of the Financial Services Act 1986. This Act has now been repealed and has been superseded by the Financial Services and Markets Act 2000 (FSMA 2000).

---

[17] Infogroup and BIS, 'Evaluation of the Companies Act 2006: Volume One' (Infogroup, 2010) 181.

[18] ibid 35. Across all company types, average awareness levels stood at a healthy 85 per cent.

[19] *Report of the Review Committee on Insolvency Law and Practice* (Cm 8558, 1982).

[20] Except the provisions in the Insolvency Act 1985 that dealt with the disqualification of directors. These were not placed into the IA 1986, but were instead repealed and re-enacted in the form of the Company Directors Disqualification Act 1986.

[21] Notably the Insolvency (England and Wales) Rules 2016, SI 2016/1024.

[22] *Review of Investor Protection* (Cmnd 9125, 1984).

2.1.1.4 **Subordinate legislation**

The importance of subordinate legislation is often overlooked, but it fulfils four extremely important roles within the UK company law system. First, there are numerous areas of company law where an Act of Parliament establishes the basic rules and framework, but the technical details are set out in subordinate legislation. For example, Pt 15 of the CA 2006 sets out the basic legal rules regarding a company's annual reports and accounts. The detailed rules regarding what should be included in the annual reports and accounts are, however, found in several pieces of subordinate legislation.[23] Linked to this are the extensive powers granted to the Secretary of State by the CA 2006 to pass regulations that flesh out the provisions in the Act. For example, the CA 2006 provides that if a company does not register its own set of articles, then the relevant set of model articles will apply.[24] The Act, however, does not provide for model articles, but instead states that the Secretary of State is empowered to make regulations that provide for a model set of articles that companies may use (namely the Companies (Model Articles) Regulations 2008).[25]

Annual reports and accounts are discussed at 19.3.

The model articles are discussed at 5.3.1.3.

Second, subordinate legislation can be used to amend existing legislation, as the following example demonstrates.

Subordinate legislation and tax evasion

Section 657 of the CA 2006 empowers the Secretary of State to make regulations that amend Pt 17 of the Act (which establishes rules regarding a company's share capital). Section 641 of the Act allows a company to reduce its share capital. A takeover usually occurs where a company (the bidder) purchases existing shares in another company (the target). **Stamp duty** is payable on a transfers of shares. Companies sought to avoid paying stamp duty by having the target reduce its share capital to nil and then issuing new shares to the bidder, thereby avoiding stamp duty as no transfer of shares had occurred. To curtail this form of tax evasion, the Secretary of State exercised the s 657 power and made regulations[26] amending s 641 to prohibit any scheme whereby a reduction of capital is effected in order to allow a person to acquire all the shares in a company.[27]

Reducing share capital is discussed at 17.1.1.

→ **stamp duty**: a tax payable on documents that effect transfers of certain assets or property (e.g. shares)

A significant amount of subordinate legislation may be passed under an Act. For example, at the time of writing, 129 statutory instruments have been enacted under the CA 2006 that serve to flesh out, or amend, the provisions of the Act.

Third, subordinate legislation (in the form of Commencement Orders) is used to bring into effect legislative provisions that do not come into effect immediately upon an Act's passing. For example, as noted, only a small number of the CA 2006's provisions came into force when it was enacted, with the remainder being brought into force via eight Commencement Orders. Commencement Orders often also provide for transitional provisions that will operate in the period leading up to the provisions coming into force.

Finally, subordinate legislation is often used to implement EU law, with examples including:

- the Companies (Shareholders' Rights) Regulations 2009,[28] which implemented the Shareholders Rights Directive;

---

[23] Namely the Small Companies and Groups (Accounts and Directors' Report) Regulations 2008, SI 2008/409, and the Large and Medium-Sized Companies and Groups (Accounts and Reports) Regulations 2008, SI 2008/410.

[24] CA 2006, s 20(1).   [25] SI 2008/3229.

[26] Companies Act 2006 (Amendment of Part 17) Regulations 2015, SI 2015/472.

[27] CA 2006, s 641(2A)–(2C).   [28] SI 2009/1632.

- the Statutory Auditors and Third Country Auditors Regulations 2016[29] and 2017,[30] which implemented the Audit Directive and amended domestic law to make it consistent with the Audit Regulation;
- the Financial Services and Markets Act 2000 (Market Abuse) Regulations 2016,[31] which implemented the Market Abuse Regulation.

2.1.1.5 Department for Business, Energy and Industrial Strategy

As noted above, the Secretary of State is granted significant powers in terms of passing subordinate legislation and, as is discussed throughout the text, is also empowered under statute to exercise a wide range of other company law powers (e.g. the power to seek a disqualification order against a director, or accept a disqualification undertaking). This leads us to ask which Secretary of State the legislation refers to. Historically, the responsibility of company law regulation was placed upon the Board of Trade, a committee of the Privy Council that was established in the seventeenth century. In 1970, the Board was merged with the Ministry of Technology to form the Department of Trade and Industry (DTI). Since then, this department has undergone several changes in name and jurisdiction. In 2007, it was changed to the Department for Business, Enterprise and Regulatory Reform (BERR), before changing again in 2009 to the Department for Business, Innovation & Skills (BIS). Upon Theresa May's appointment as Prime Minister in 2016, she reshuffled the government departments and BIS was merged with the Department of Energy and Climate Change to form the current Department for Business, Energy and Industrial Strategy (BEIS).[32] Accordingly, when company law legislation refers to the Secretary of State, it is referring to the Secretary of State for BEIS.

2.1.1.6 Rules with legislative backing

 The official list and the FCA's role is discussed at 18.4.

Certain rules are not legislative per se, but have legislative backing and, if breached, can result in a breach of legislation. Such rules, in practice, therefore have the force of legislation. For example, companies that wish to admit their shares onto the official list must comply with the provisions found in Pt VI of the FSMA 2000. The FSMA 2000 empowers the Financial Conduct Authority (FCA) to make rules relating to the listing of securities,[33] and these rules are known as the Listing Rules.[34] If the FCA considers that an issuer of listed securities or an applicant for listing has breached the Listing Rules, then it can impose a financial penalty of such an amount as it considers appropriate.[35]

The Listing Rules and Prudential plc

On 27 February 2010, media outlets reported that Prudential plc was planning a takeover bid of AIA Group Ltd ('AIA'). On 1 March 2010, Prudential announced its intent to acquire AIA in a $35.5 billion deal (Prudential later withdrew from the deal). The Financial Services Authority ('FSA', the FCA's predecessor) was not informed of the proposed acquisition until after it had been leaked to the media on 27 February. Listing Principle 6 of the Listing Rules required listed companies to deal

---

[29] SI 2016/649.   [30] SI 2017/516.   [31] SI 2016/680.

[32] For more, see www.gov.uk/government/organisations/department-for-business-energy-and-industrial-strategy accessed 10 January 2019.

[33] FSMA 2000, s 73A(1).   [34] ibid s 73A(2).   [35] ibid s 91(1).

with the FSA 'in an open and co-operative manner'.[36] The FSA ruled that Prudential should have informed it of the proposed acquisition well before 27 February. In failing to do so, Prudential had breached Listing Principle 6 and a penalty of £14 million was imposed.[37] Prudential's failure to inform the FSA also breached Principle 11 of the FSA's Principles of Business,[38] for which Prudential was fined a further £16 million.[39] Prudential's chief executive officer (CEO) was also censured.

There are other bodies that are empowered to make rules with statutory backing, including:

- The Takeover Panel is empowered to make rules (namely, the City Code on Takeovers and Mergers) regulating takeovers, mergers, and other transactions that can have an effect upon the ownership of companies.[40]
- The Financial Reporting Council is empowered to determine technical standards and other standards on professional ethics and internal quality control of statutory auditors and statutory audit work.[41]

2.1.2 Case law

Although legislation constitutes the primary source of company law to date, the relevant legislation does not aim to provide an exhaustive company law code, and case law still has an extremely important role to play in four respects.

First, despite the bulk and broad coverage of company law legislation, there are areas of company law that have little or no legislative involvement. In such cases, vast swathes of law may be entirely judge-made. For example, the law relating to those instances where the actions of the directors can be attributed to the company was created by judges to resolve certain difficulties created by a company's separate personality. In some cases, case law can even override statutory principles. For example, statute grants companies corporate personality, yet the courts have devised instances (albeit highly limited ones) where they will set that corporate personality aside.

Attribution is discussed at 6.5.4.

Second, legislation often grants the courts[42] a significant supervisory jurisdiction and empowers them to make a wide range of orders, award civil remedies, and impose criminal sanctions. For example, the courts are empowered to alter a company's constitution (or prevent an alteration),[43] set aside certain transactions involving the company[44] or its directors,[45] rectify company registers[46] or order a company to allow for their inspection,[47] grant or deny permission for a derivative claim to continue,[48] order

---

[36] Today, this rule can be found in Listing Principle 2 (see Listing Rules, LR 7.2.1).

[37] For full details, see the Final Notice issued by the FSA at www.fca.org.uk/publication/final-notices/fsa-pru-plc.pdf accessed 10 January 2019.

[38] Principle 11 (which remains the same today) requires firms to deal with regulators in an open and cooperative way and disclose to regulators anything relating to the firm that the regulator would expect notice.

[39] For more, see www.fca.org.uk/publication/final-notices/fsa-prudential-plc.pdf accessed 10 January 2019.

[40] CA 2006, s 943(1) and (2).

[41] Statutory Auditors and Third Country Auditors Regulations 2016, SI 2016/649, regs 2 and 3.

[42] Section 1156 of the CA 2006 provides that, in England and Wales, 'the court' refers to the High Court or the County Court.

[43] CA 2006, s 996(2)(d).   [44] See e.g. CA 2006, s 40(6); IA 1986, s 244(4).

[45] CA 2006, ss 190 and 195(2).   [46] ibid s 125.   [47] ibid s 162(8).   [48] ibid s 261.

the preparation of revised accounts,[49] prevent a variation of class rights,[50] relieve a director from certain liabilities,[51] disqualify directors,[52] appoint an administrator,[53] and (perhaps the most drastic power) wind up a company.[54] Where a criminal offence has been committed by the company (e.g. corporate manslaughter)[55] or some other person (e.g. insider dealing),[56] then the courts can impose criminal penalties, such as fines and imprisonment.

Third, legislation must be interpreted and applied.[57] While the CA 2006 is a detailed piece of legislation, it is not exhaustive and some provisions are left purposefully vague in order to provide the courts with flexibility in their application. For example, s 994 of the CA 2006 allows a member to apply to the court for a remedy if he feels that his interests have been unfairly prejudiced. However, the Act provides no guidance whatsoever as to how conduct is to be judged as unfair and prejudicial, so the task has been left entirely to the courts. Occasionally, statute acknowledges the interpretative function of case law. For example, one of the most noteworthy reforms in the CA 2006 is the codification of directors' duties. However, the duties have not been exhaustively codified and much of the detail is to be found in case law. The Act acknowledges this by stating that 'regard shall be had to the corresponding common law rules and equitable principles in interpreting and applying the general duties'.[58]

> The unfair prejudice remedy is discussed at 15.3.

Finally, well-established case law principles often form the basis of future legislation, and many provisions in company law legislation are derived from case law. The codification of directors' duties is a good example as each duty is based on a common law predecessor. Indeed, s 170(3) of the CA 2006 expressly acknowledges this by stating that the duties 'are based on certain common law rules and equitable principles as they apply in relation to directors and have effect in place of those rules and principles as regards the duties owed to a company by a director'.

2.1.3 The constitution of the company

> The consitution of a company is discussed in more detail in Chapter 5.

Just as some countries will have a constitution that sets out the powers, rights, and obligations of its government and citizens, a company also has a constitution that sets out the powers of the company and its board, and provides rules for the internal operation of the company. In many aspects, the CA 2006 is a permissive piece of legislation that allows companies considerable discretion to create their own internal rules through their constitution. For example, the CA 2006 says very little about the process for appointing directors, preferring to leave this as a matter for the company to decide via its articles. In some cases, the CA 2006 will often establish default rules that apply to all companies, but the Act will then allow companies to modify (or even completely exclude) those rules if their constitutions so provide. For example, existing shareholders of a company are usually granted the right of first refusal (known as a pre-emption right) when a new batch of shares are allotted,[59] but in private companies, pre-emption rights can be completely excluded if the articles so provide.[60]

> Pre-emption rights are discussed at 16.4.4.

---

[49] ibid s 456.   [50] ibid ss 633–4.   [51] ibid s 1157.
[52] Company Directors Disqualification Act 1986.   [53] IA 1986, Sch B1, paras 1(1) and 2(a).
[54] ibid s 122.   [55] Corporate Manslaughter and Corporate Homicide Act 2007, s 1.
[56] Criminal Justice Act 1993, s 52.
[57] For an ageing, but still important, discussion on this, see David Milman, 'The Courts and the Companies Acts: the Judicial Contribution to Company Law' [1990] LMCLQ 401.
[58] CA 2006, s 170(4).   [59] ibid s 561.   [60] ibid s 567.

Persons subject to the constitution who fail to comply with its provisions may find themselves in breach of the *ultra vires* rules[61] or in breach of contract,[62] and directors who do not act in accordance with the constitution may find themselves in breach of duty.[63]

2.1.4 Contract

As noted at 1.1.2, one of the aims of company law is to provide sufficient flexibility and autonomy so that companies can be run based on their own needs and characteristics. On a day-to-day basis, it follows that contract is one of the most important sources of law governing companies as companies will, on a regular basis, enter into contacts with members, directors, suppliers, creditors, service providers (such as auditors and lawyers), and customers and clients. As many companies will contract based on standard terms they have themselves drafted, such agreements will be governed by legally binding rules created by the company itself. Of course, these contracts are governed by general contract law (which is outside the scope of this text), but there are occasions when company law provides for specific rules relating to certain contracts (all of which are discussed in this text):

- The CA 2006 provides that the company's constitution forms a contract (i) between the company and its members; and (ii) between the members themselves.[64]
- As a company is a legal person, it cannot provide a signature or 'sign on the dotted line'. Instead the Act lays down special rules regarding how companies enter into contracts.[65]
- Special rules exist regarding contracts entered into on behalf of companies that have not yet been incorporated.[66]
- The Act provides that directors' service contracts must be made available for inspection,[67] and that service contracts of a certain length must have member approval.[68]

2.1.5 European Union law

Although it is true that the majority of UK company law is home-grown, it is also important to acknowledge the significant impact that EU law has had upon our company law system. Indeed, it has been argued that the EU is a primary driver of company law reform (although the continued relevance of this argument will be affected by the UK's withdrawal from the EU):

The UK's withdrawal from the EU is discussed at 2.1.5.3.

> The focus for company law reform in Europe is provided by the European Union, it is no longer the Member States. This goes for legislation but also the most important court decisions are now made at the European level. The European Court of Justice has become the most important company law court in Europe. It now hears more company law cases, proportionally speaking, in a year than any other supreme court in Europe.[69]

As is discussed in subsequent chapters, there are notable areas of UK company law legislation that exist to implement EU law. The law relating to company formation,

---

[61] ibid ss 39 and 40. However, as discussed at 6.2, the *ultra vires* doctrine has lost much of its force.

[62] ibid s 33.   [63] ibid s 171(1).   [64] ibid s 33 (discussed at 5.3.4).

[65] ibid ss 43–52 (discussed at 6.1).   [66] ibid s 51 (discussed at 3.2.7).

[67] ibid s 228 (discussed at 8.1.5.3).   [68] ibid s 188 (discussed at 11.4.1).

[69] Mads Andenas, 'European Company Law Reform and the United Kingdom' (2000) 21 Co Law 36, 36.

pre-incorporation contracts, *ultra vires*, market abuse, auditor regulation, the maintenance of capital, prospectuses, the regulation of listed companies, corporate transparency, and shareholder rights has been greatly influenced by EU law. More recently, EU law is increasingly focusing on corporate governance issues too, such as directors' remuneration and board diversity. Accordingly, EU law is now one of the most important sources of UK company law (although, as is discussed later, for how long this will remain the case is currently unclear).

2.1.5.1 Right of establishment

English company law has long recognized companies incorporated in other countries. Speaking in 1933, Lord Wright stated, 'English courts have long since recognised as juristic persons corporations established under foreign law . . .'.[70] However, statutory recognition only came following our entry into the EU in 1973. Article 26 of the Treaty on the Functioning of the European Union (TFEU) commits the EU to establishing an internal market, within which there should be freedom of goods, persons, services, and capital. Key to achieving this is the right of EU nationals to establish themselves anywhere in the EU and so Art 49 of the TFEU prohibits restrictions on the freedom of establishment, which includes the right to 'set up and manage undertakings, in particular companies or firms . . .'. Article 54 then goes on to provide:

> Companies or firms formed in accordance with the law of a Member State and having their registered office, central administration or principal place of business within the Union shall, for the purposes of this Chapter, be treated in the same way as natural persons who are nationals of Member States.

There are two principal ways in which a company can establish a presence in another EU Member State. First, a company could simply incorporate a subsidiary in another Member State. However, the company might not wish to go through the formality of setting up a subsidiary, or it might not wish to be subject to the full force of that State's company law. There might also be tax concerns. Fortunately, setting up a subsidiary is not necessary as Art 49 provides that the prohibitions on restrictions of freedom of establishment 'shall also apply to restrictions on the setting-up of agencies, branches or subsidiaries by nationals of any Member State established in the territory of any Member State'. So, for example, a company based in France could engage in business in the UK by simply establishing a UK branch (which will not be subject to the full force of UK company law), rather than incorporating a subsidiary. However, this does afford companies the opportunity to avoid domestic company law by incorporating in one State and setting up a branch in another, as the following case demonstrates.

 The law relating to overseas companies is discussed at 3.3.4.2.

 See Paul J Omar, 'Freedom of Movement for Companies and the Avoidance of Regulation' (1999) 10 ICCLR 286.

⚖️ **Case C-212/97 *Centros Ltd v Erhvervs-og Selskabsstryrelsen* [1999] ECR I-1459**

FACTS: Danish law required companies to have a minimum paid-up share capital, whereas UK law imposes no such requirement upon private companies. Mr and Mrs Bryde, both Danish citizens, set up a UK private company, Centros Ltd. Centros had a nominal share capital of £100, but this was never paid up. Further, Centros never engaged in any business in the UK. Mrs Bryde

---

[70] *Lazard Bros v Midland Bank Ltd* [1933] AC 289 (HL) 297.

applied to the Danish authorities (referred to as 'the Board') for permission to establish a branch of Centros in Denmark (this branch, unlike Centros itself, would engage in business). The Board rejected her application because, in choosing to incorporate in the UK and set up a branch in Denmark, she was acting so as to avoid the Danish share capital laws. Centros commenced proceedings, contending that its right to establishment has been unlawfully restricted. The Board argued that Centros was in fact abusing the right to establishment. The Danish court referred the matter to the European Court of Justice (ECJ).

HELD: The Court rejected the Board's argument stating that:

> a national of a Member State who wishes to set up a company chooses to form it in the Member State whose rules of company law seem to him the least restrictive and to set up branches in other Member States cannot, in itself, constitute an abuse of the right of establishment.[71]

Accordingly, the Court held that the Board's refusal to register the branch amounted to a breach of the right of establishment.

COMMENT: EU Member States tried to mitigate the effect on the *Centros* ruling by permitting the registration of the branch, but then imposing additional requirements or limitations upon the branch if it is where the business primarily operates. Unsurprisingly, the EU courts generally view this as a breach of the right to establishment.[72]

Second, a company based in one Member State could re-locate to another Member State. The key issue here is whether a company based in Member State A can relocate to Member State B, but still remain subject to Member State A's company laws. The following case provided the answer.

Case C-201/06 *Cartesio Oktato es Szogáltató bt* [2008] ECR I-9641

See Thomas Biermeyer, 'Bringing Darkness into the Dark: European Cross-Border Mobility in Re Cartesio' (2009) 16 MJ 251.

FACTS: Cartesio was formed as a limited partnership under Hungarian law, and its seat of business was registered as being in Hungary. It wished to relocate its seat of business to Italy, but still wanted to be subject to Hungarian law. Accordingly, instead of dissolving the partnership and establishing a new business in Italy, Cartesio simply applied to a Hungarian court to have its seat of business transferred to Italy. The court rejected the application on the ground that Hungarian law did not allow a company incorporated in Hungary to transfer its seat of business abroad, whilst continuing to be subject to Hungarian law. Cartesio appealed, and the issue was referred to the ECJ.

HELD: The ECJ held that the Hungarian court was entitled to reject the transfer application. It said that, in the absence of EC rules setting out which companies enjoy a right of establishment on the basis of a single connecting factor (such as location of the seat of business), the Member State's national law will determine the issue. Thus:

> a Member State has the power to define both the connecting factor required of a company if it is to be regarded as incorporated under the law of that Member State and, as such, capable of enjoying the right of establishment, and that required if the company is to be able subsequently to maintain that status.[73]

---

71 [1999] ECR-I 1459, para 27.

72 Case C-167/01 *Kamer van Koophandel en Fabrieken voor Amsterdam v Inspire Art Ltd* [2003] ECR I-10155.

73 [2008] ECR I-9641, para 110.

Cartesio involved a situation where a Member State's laws prevented a business from remaining subject to the law of the State where it was relocating from. In the following case (whose facts are almost exactly opposite to *Cartesio*), the ECJ ruled on a situation where a company wanted to change legal systems but was prevented from doing so by the law of the State it was relocating to.

 See Mathias Krarup, 'VALE: Determining the Need for Amended Regulation Regarding Free Movement of Companies Within the EU' (2013) 24 EBL Rev 691.

Case C-378/10 *VALE Epitesi kft* [2012] 3 CMLR 41

FACTS: VALE Construzioni Srl ('VALE'), an Italian company, wished to discontinue business in Italy and re-register as a company in Hungary. Accordingly, VALE requested for its name to be removed from the Italian commercial register. This request was granted and an entry was made on the register stating that 'the company had moved to Hungary'. Nine months later, the managing director of VALE attempted to set up a company in Hungary ('VE') and applied to register it on the Hungarian commercial register. The application stated that VALE was the predecessor of VE. The Hungarian court refused to register VE on the ground that, under Hungarian law, a company which is not Hungarian cannot be identified as a predecessor. VE commenced proceedings and the Hungarian court referred the case to the ECJ.

HELD: The ECJ held that, in preventing non-Hungarian companies from being recognized as predecessors, the relevant Hungarian Law treated companies differently depending on whether the conversion was domestic or cross-border. It stated that such a law 'is likely to deter companies which have their seat in another Member State from exercising the freedom of establishment laid down by the Treaty and, therefore, amounts to a restriction with the meaning of arts 49 and 54 TFEU'.[74] In other words, whilst Member States are free to establish rules regarding conversions and re-registrations, those rules must not discriminate against foreign companies. If they do, as in *VALE*, a breach of EU law will be established.

COMMENT: Here, a company wished to change the laws that it was subject to by re-registering in another Member State. Some Member States allow companies to do this by simply re-registering in that jurisdiction, but the CA 2006 does not provide rules relating to cross-border re-registration. However, the Companies (Cross-Border Mergers) Regulations 2007[75] (which implemented the Cross-Border Merger Directive) can be used to achieve the same outcome. For example, a country in France could create a new company in the UK. It would then simply merge the French company into the UK company, and dissolve the French company.

Whilst the right to establishment is provided for in the TFEU, it is EU case law that provides the vast bulk of the detail on the extent and application of this right. The law in this area, whilst sometimes lacking in clarity, does provide companies with significant mobility in terms of where to base themselves and which State's law they will be governed by. It should be remembered, however, that freedom of establishment is but one pillar of the single market. In order for an effective single market to operate, it is also important that laws of EU Member States do not differ too radically.

2.1.5.2 **The harmonization programme**

Article 50(2)(g) of the TFEU provides that attaining freedom of establishment involves 'coordinating to the necessary extent the safeguards which, for the protection of the interests of members and others, are required by Member States of companies

---

[74] [2012] 3 CMLR 41, para 36.   [75] SI 2007/2974.

or firms . . . with a view to making such safeguards equivalent throughout the Union'. To that end, the EU embarked upon a programme that aimed to better harmonize company law across EU Member States.

The TFEU provides that attaining freedom of establishment shall be carried out 'by means of directives'[76] and so the EU harmonization programme has been conducted via a series of directives. These directives are numbered (e.g. the First Company Law Directive, etc) and, of the 14 harmonization directives that have been proposed this far, 11 have been passed into law.[77] Directives are advantageous in that they set out the aims and then leave the implementation of those aims up to the Member State, thereby providing a notable measure of flexibility. This flexibility is enhanced as most company law directives provide for 'minimum harmonization' (i.e. the directive establishes minimum standards, but Member States can implement more exacting standards if they so wish). In practice, however, flexibility is reduced for two reasons. First, most company law directives are highly detailed, which naturally reduces the scope for flexible implementation. Second, in more recent years, more use is being made of 'maximum harmonization' directives (e.g. the Prospectus Directive), which set out minimum standards which must be implemented, whilst also prohibiting Member States from implementing more exacting standards than those found in the directive. A detailed discussion of harmonization directives is not needed here,[78] but Figure 2.2 sets out a timeline of these directives, and other notable pieces of EU harmonization legislation.

It is evident from Figure 2.2 that the 1970s and 80s witnessed a flurry of activity, but the harmonization programme then stalled. It took several prominent corporate scandals (notably Parmalat and Enron) to once again re-ignite the EU's interest in company law reform, with a 2002 report noting that 'EU company law has not kept up with the developments which shape its role and application . . .'.[79] Crucially, the report was critical of the process of harmonization, stating that it had 'lost sight of what the Group believes to be the primary purpose of company law: to provide a legal framework for those who wish to undertake business activities efficiently, in a way they consider to be best suited to attain success'.[80]

In 2003, the European Commission published an Action Plan,[81] which stated '[n]ow is the right time to give a fresh and ambitious impetus to the EU company law harmonization process'.[82] The Plan put forward 23 measures to be implemented and, although notable directives were passed in relation to cross-border mergers, shareholder rights, and the regulation of auditors, most the Action Plan's measures were never acted upon. As a result, it was decided that several measures announced in the 2003 Action Plan that had not yet been implemented would be withdrawn. The focus would be on 'better regulation',

---

[76] TFEU, Art 50(1).   [77] The Fifth, Ninth, and Fourteenth Directives were abandoned.

[78] More detail on the directives can be found in John Birds et al, *Boyle & Birds' Company Law* (9th edn, Jordan 2014) 30–8.

[79] 'Report of the High Level Group of Company Law Experts on a Modern Regulatory Framework for Company Law in Europe' (2002) 1, http://www.ecgi.org/publications/documents/report_en.pdf accessed 10 January 2019.

[80] ibid 29.

[81] European Commission, 'Modernising Company Law and Enhancing Corporate Governance in the European Union—A Plan to Move Forward' (Communication) COM (2003) 284 final. For more, see Theodor Baums, 'European Company Law beyond the 2003 Action Plan' (2007) 8 EBOR 143.

[82] European Commission, 'Modernising Company Law and Enhancing Corporate Governance in the European Union—A Plan to Move Forward' (Communication) COM (2003) 284 final, para 1.2.

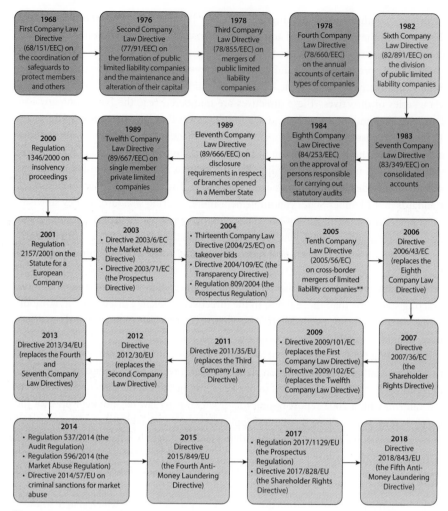

* Boxes in grey represent EU legal acts currently in force, whereas boxes in purple represent EU legal acts that have been repealed and replaced.
** This directive was originally proposed in 1984 but, due to difficulties in reaching agreement between Member States, it was only adopted in 2005 (which explains why the numbering is out of sequence).

FIGURE 2.2 The principal EU harmonization legal acts

and the 'simplification of key existing legislation . . .'.[83] The reasons behind this move towards simplification were that the administrative costs of complying with EU company law were particularly high, and the older company law directives were in need of updating.[84] As a result, subsequent years were characterized by little new law and instead (as Fig. 2.2 indicates) the directives that were passed focused on repealing, consolidating, and replacing existing directives with new directives that contained simplified law.

---

[83] Directorate General for Internal Market and Services, 'Consultation on Future Priorities for the Action Plan on Modernising Company Law and Enhancing Corporate Governance in the European Union' (EU Commission, 2005) 3.

[84] European Commission, 'Communication from the Commission on a Simplified Business Environment for Companies in the Areas of Company Law, Accounting and Auditing' (Communication) COM (2007) 394 final 2–3.

In 2012, a new Action Plan was launched on the ground that 'new developments have taken place since that require in the Commission's view further action'.[85] In particular, the Plan noted shortcomings in the EU's corporate governance framework (which had become especially notable during the financial crisis) and therefore identified three main areas of action, namely enhancing transparency, engaging shareholders, and supporting companies' growth and their competitiveness.[86] However, perhaps the most noteworthy proposal within the Action Plan is the recommendation that existing EU Company Law Directives should be merged, with the Commission proposing that major company law directive be merged into a single instrument.[87] At the time of writing, a proposal has been adopted by the Commission that would merge many of the existing Company Law Directives into a single Directive (although it would not seek to amend them).[88]

2.1.5.3 The UK's withdrawal from the EU

On the 23 June 2016, a referendum took place in the UK to decide whether the UK should remain an EU Member State. By 51.9 per cent to 48.1 per cent, the referendum was won by those who wished to leave. The referendum was not binding,[89] but the government confirmed that the UK will leave the EU, and subsequently stated that the UK will also not seek to retain its membership of the single market (which has become known as 'hard Brexit'). The process for leaving the EU (provided for by Art 50 of TFEU) was triggered on 29 March 2017 meaning that, in the absence of Art 50 being revoked or the UK seeking and being granted an extension to the Art 50 process, the UK will leave the EU by 29 March 2019.

In terms of the impact that Brexit will have upon UK company law, Parliament has now enacted the European Union (Withdrawal) Act 2018 which, in its current form,[90] will have several effects:

- It will repeal the European Communities Act 1972 on the date the UK exits the EU.[91]
- As a result of the 1972 Act's repeal, directly applicable EU law (such as EU Regulations) would cease to apply in the UK, thereby leaving large gaps in our system of company law (e.g. the UK's market abuse regime largely derives from the Market Abuse Regulation). To avoid this, the Act will convert directly applicable EU law into UK law on the date the UK exits the EU.[92]
- EU laws that are not directly applicable (e.g. directives) must be implemented via domestic legislation. Acts of Parliament that implement EU law will remain in force when the UK leaves the EU. However, as noted at 2.1.1.4, much EU company law has been implemented via subordinate legislation, the bulk of which was created under the 1972 Act. This subordinate legislation will cease to have effect once the 1972 Act is repealed, so the Act will preserve all UK laws passed that implement EU obligations.[93]

---

[85] European Commission, 'Action Plan: European Company Law and Corporate Governance—A Modern Legal Framework for More Engaged Shareholders and Sustainable Companies' (Communication) COM (2012) 740 final 2.

[86] ibid 4–5.   [87] ibid 15.

[88] European Commission, 'Proposal for a Directive of the European Parliament and of the Council Relating to Certain Aspects of Company Law (Codification)' COM (2015) 616 final.

[89] This follows from the fact that the European Union Referendum Act 2015 makes no mention of the referendum being binding in any way.

[90] It is possible that the Act could be amended prior to exit day so that these effects are amended.

[91] European Union (Withdrawal) Act 2018, s 1.

[92] ibid s 3(1).   [93] ibid s 2.

- EU law-derived rights, powers, liabilities, obligations, restrictions, remedies, and procedures that can be enforced, allowed, or followed in a UK domestic court will be recognized and available under UK law.[94]

- Historic EU case law will not bind any UK court or tribunal, nor will UK courts be able to
refer cases to the Court of Justice of the EU.[95]

The clear effect of the Act is to preserve EU law at the point that the UK withdraws from
the EU, meaning that the impact of Brexit on UK company law would be minimal in the
short term. However, post Brexit, Parliament will determine which EU-derived laws it
wishes to keep and repeal, meaning that, over the medium-to-long term, the impact of
Brexit on UK company law might be much more substantial.[96] The UK system of company law is predominantly home-grown and so a hard Brexit may potentially affect specific areas of company law only, including the listing regime, the market abuse regime,
the regulation of auditors, and the law relating to cross-border mergers and insolvencies.
Of course, barriers would arise in relation to the ability of UK companies to establish and
do business in the EU. One notable concern is the effect a hard Brexit would have upon
the UK's financial services industry and London's status as Europe's financial capital.

Brexit and the UK financial services industry

In February 2018, the Governor of the Bank of England warned that Brexit could lead to banks
leaving London.[97] A report by PricewaterhouseCoopers (PwC) warned that 70,000–100,000
financial services jobs could be lost by 2020 as a result of Brexit.[98] There is significant concern as
to whether UK companies will lose their passporting rights. The European Banking Authority, the
London-based independent EU Authority that regulates the banking sector, will relocate to Paris.

Passporting is discussed at 18.5.3.1.

Finally, it should be noted that, until the UK formally leaves the EU, it will remain fully
subject to its EU law obligations and EU law will apply in full (and depending on the
terms of the withdrawal agreement (if one is agreed), it may remain subject to EU law in
some form post-Brexit).

2.1.6 Human rights laws

It might be assumed that companies are not protected by human rights laws, as they
are not human, but this is not the case as the European Convention on Human Rights
(ECHR) applies to persons as well as humans.[99] As the company is a person, it is protected by certain human rights provisions that can apply to companies. Sometimes
the ECHR expressly provides for this. For example, art 1 of the First Protocol of the
ECHR states that 'every natural or legal person is entitled to peaceful enjoyment of his

---

[94] ibid s 4.   [95] ibid s 6(1).

[96] For more discussion of the potential effects of Brexit on UK company law, see the accompanying
blog post at https://companylawandgovernance.com/2016/07/02/company-law-and-brexit accessed 10
January 2019.

[97] See www.theguardian.com/politics/blog/live/2016/mar/08/boris-johnson-abandons-city-hall-eu-
referendum-gag-after-hypocrisy-claim-politics-live 10 January 2019.

[98] PwC, 'Leaving the EU: Implications for the UK Financial Services Sector' (PwC 2016) 1.

[99] For more, see Marius Emberland, The Human Rights of Companies: Exploring the Structure of EHCR
Protection (OUP 2006).

possessions'. As corporate human rights protection derives from corporate personality, it will be discussed in more detail at 4.3.9 when corporate personality is discussed.

2.2 Sources of corporate governance principles

Legislation is largely absent from our UK corporate governance system, with the vast majority of corporate governance principles and recommendations deriving from a series of reports and codes (the principal examples of which are set out in Figures 2.3 and 2.4).

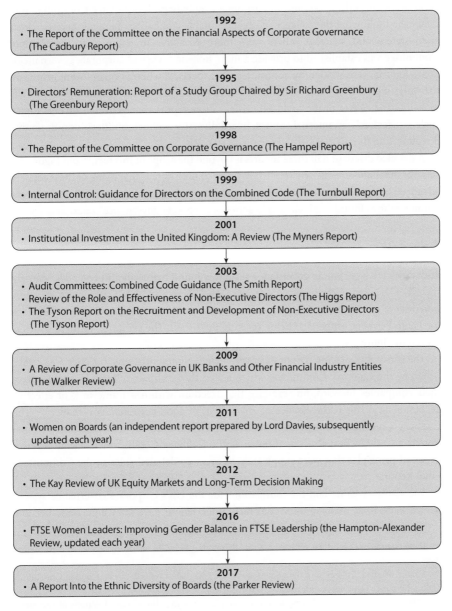

FIGURE 2.3 Corporate governance reports

Within the past three decades, there have been a notable number of such reports and codes, so many in fact that a detailed study of all of them is beyond the scope of this text. However, an understanding of the principal reports and codes is essential if one wishes to understand how the current corporate governance regime came into being. Accordingly, here the principal reports and codes are discussed, beginning with the main corporate governance reports.

2.2.1 Reports

Over the past 25 years, there have been a notable number of reports examining aspects of corporate governance. These reports have been extremely varied in their nature. Some were created in response to corporate events (e.g. the Cadbury Committee was established following the collapse of several notable companies that had received clean audit statements), whereas others were more proactive in nature (e.g. the Hampel Committee was established to provide a more holistic review of corporate governance). Some reports were written by committees of experts,[100] whereas others were primarily the work of prominent individuals in the business world (e.g. the Walker Review, which looked at the causes of the financial crisis). These reports have covered diverse topics such as directors' pay, internal control, board diversity, audit committees, non-executive directors, and the reasons behind the financial crisis.

A detailed discussion of these reports is beyond the scope of this text,[101] but Figure 2.3 sets out the main reports. The important point to note here is that many of these reports advanced best practice recommendations, and the more generally accepted of these recommendations found their way into a series of corporate governance codes.

2.2.2 Codes

Today, the UK's corporate governance system is found primarily in two codes (namely the UK Corporate Governance Code, and the UK Stewardship Code), with an additional set of governance principles (namely the Wates Corporate Governance Principles for Large Private Companies) being recently published. The evolution of these codes is set out in Figure 2.4.

The concept of placing corporate governance recommendations in a code was established by the Cadbury Committee, which stated that companies 'must be free to drive their companies forward, but exercise that freedom within a framework of effective accountability. This is the essence of any system of good corporate governance.'[102] The Cadbury Committee sought to provide such a framework by appending to its Final Report a Code of Best Practice (known as the Cadbury Code), which set out a series of broad principles that were supplemented by more detailed rules in the Committee's Final Report.

The Cadbury Code laid the foundations for the UK's corporate governance system in two ways. First, many of the Code's recommendations have since gone on to become

---

[100] These committees (and their reports) are usually referred to by the name of the person who chaired them.

[101] A more detailed discussion of the various corporate governance reports can be found at Christine A Mallin, *Corporate Governance* (6th edn, OUP 2018) ch 3.

[102] Committee on the Financial Aspects of Corporate Governance, 'The Financial Aspects of Corporate Governance: Draft Report' (Gee Publishing Ltd 1992) para 1.1.

1992
• The Code of Best Practice (The Cadbury Code)

1998
• The Combined Code on Corporate Governance

2000
• The Combined Code on Corporate Governance (first update)

2003
• The Combined Code on Corporate Governance (second update)

2006
• The Combined Code on Corporate Governance (third update)

2008
• The Combined Code on Corporate Governance (fourth update)

2010
• The UK Corporate Governance Code (replaced the Combined Code)
• The UK Stewardship Code

2012
• The UK Corporate Governance Code (first update)
• The UK Stewardship Code (first update)

2014
• The UK Corporate Governance Code (second update)

2016
• The UK Corporate Governance Code (third update)

2018
• The UK Corporate Governance Code (fourth update)
• The Wates Corporate Governance Principles for Large Private Companies

2019
• The UK Stewardship Code (second update)

FIGURE 2.4 Corporate governance codes

standard corporate governance practices. Second, perhaps more importantly, the Committee recommended that the Code should not have statutory backing. Instead it recommended that listed companies should include a 'statement of compliance' as part of their annual report, which would state whether or not the company had complied with the Code of Practice and, if the Code has not been complied with, the company should provide clear reasons for its non-compliance. This recommendation was adopted and made part of the Stock Exchange's *Yellow Book*.[103] This approach has become known as the 'comply-or-explain' approach and is now regarded as 'the trademark of corporate governance in the UK'.[104]

The comply-or-explain approach is discussed at 2.2.2.1.

The Cadbury Code was pioneering but, as the Cadbury Committee focused on the financial aspects of corporate governance, the Cadbury Code was not a general corporate

---

[103] The *Yellow Book* was the predecessor of the Listing Rules.
[104] FRC, 'The UK Corporate Governance Code' (FRC 2016) 4.

governance code. The Hampel Report noted that the Cadbury Code, and the recommendations advanced in the Greenbury Report, were 'responses to things which were perceived to have gone wrong . . . We are equally concerned with the positive contribution which good corporate governance can make.'[105] Accordingly, the Hampel Committee sought to identify 'a small number of broad principles . . . which we hope will command general agreement'.[106] These principles were placed into a draft Code of Practice, which was then passed to the London Stock Exchange for approval. Following some minor amendments, it was published as the Combined Code on Corporate Governance in 1998.

The Combined Code adopted many of the recommendations found in the Cadbury and Greenbury Reports, but also strengthened some and established brand-new recommendations. Like the Cadbury Code, it also operated on a comply-or-explain basis. Between 2000 and 2008, the Code was updated four times. The fifth update, in 2010, renamed the Code as the UK Corporate Governance Code.

2.2.2.1 The UK Corporate Governance Code

The UK Corporate Governance Code was first published in 2010 and the most recent set of best practice corporate governance recommendations can be found in the 2018 version of the Code. The Code consists of a series of 18 broad Principles (numbered A to R), which are fleshed out by 41 slightly more detailed Provisions. This principles-based approach means that the Code is written in a much more readable and accessible manner than statute, and contains much less technical detail. More detailed guidance can be found in supporting guidance documents published by the Financial Reporting Council (FRC), notably its Guidance on Board Effectiveness.[107]

The Code is broken down into five sections, with each section focusing on a broad governance topic, namely:

1. board leadership and company purpose;
2. division of responsibilities;
3. composition, succession, and evaluation;
4. audit, risk, and internal control; and
5. remuneration.

The 2016 version of the Code stated that '[i]ts fitness for purpose in a permanently changing economic and social business environment requires its evaluation at appropriate intervals'.[108] Responsibility for updating the Code currently lies with the FRC and, to date, the Code has been updated four times (in 2012, 2014, 2016, and 2018). Following the 2016 update, the FRC stated that it did not intend to update the Code again until at least 2019 but, in light of the government's corporate governance reform Green Paper,[109] the FRC announced a 'fundamental review'[110] of the Code in 2017, which led to an updated Code being published in July 2018. The 2018 update to the Code is the most significant update to date, as it completely reworked the Code's structure and notably shortened the Code to provide additional clarity. The 2018 Code applies to accounting periods beginning on

The Kingman Review of the FRC is discussed at xviii.

---

[105] Committee on Corporate Governance 'Final Report' (Gee Publishing Ltd 1998) para 1.7.
[106] ibid para 1.20.   [107] FRC, 'Guidance on Board Effectiveness' (FRC 2018).
[108] FRC, 'The UK Corporate Governance Code' (FRC 2016) 1.
[109] Department for Business, Energy and Industrial Strategy, *Corporate Governance Reform: Green Paper* (BEIS, 2016).
[110] Financial Reporting Council, 'Plan & Budget and Levies 2017/18' (FRC 2017) 4.

or after the 1 January 2019, so companies will begin reporting on the 2018 Code in 2020 (meaning that, in 2019, companies will still report on the 2016 Code).

The Code operates on a comply-or-explain basis. This means that, compliance with the Code's Provisions is not mandatory (which is why it is incorrect to state that the Provisions 'require' a particular course of action), except where the Code's Provisions mirror a legal requirement.[111] Even listed companies are not required to comply with the Code's Provisions, but a company with a premium listing is required to include in its annual report a statement setting out how it applied the Principles of the Code, and:

- a statement as to whether the company has complied with all the relevant Provisions of the Code; or
- a statement identifying which Provisions were not complied with, the period within which they were not complied with, and the reasons for non-compliance.[112] It is worth noting that, historically, the quality of explanations for non-compliance was low. This prompted the FRC to issue guidance on what amounts to an explanation.[113] However, in some cases, the quality of explanations is still weak. For example, only 31 per cent of FTSE 350 companies provide good or detailed explanations as to how they engage with shareholders.[114]

The rationale behind the comply-or-explain approach is primarily the need to provide companies with flexibility. As the FRC states:

A regulatory framework that aims to improve standards of corporate governance is more likely to succeed if it recognises that governance should support, not constrain, the entrepreneurial leadership of the company, while ensuring risk is properly managed. This requires a degree of flexibility in the way companies adopt and adapt governance practices. . . . To be effective it needs to be implemented in a way that fits the culture and organisation of the individual company. This can vary enormously from company to company depending on factors such as size, ownership structure and the complexity of its activities.[115]

This flexibility allows companies to implement the Code's Provisions in their own way, or to not implement them if there are good reasons for not doing so. Amongst the largest companies, the Code's recommendations have mostly become standard practice, resulting in strong levels of compliance. In 2018, 72 per cent of FTSE 350 companies declared full compliance with the Code.[116] Ninety-five per cent of FTSE 350 companies reported that they either complied with all, or all but one or two, of the Code's provisions.[117] Figure 2.5 sets out the compliance levels of FTSE 100, 250, and 350 companies between 2010 and 2018.

The high levels of compliance amongst larger companies is not surprising, as the Code's Introduction states that it is 'applicable to all companies with a premium listing, whether incorporated in the UK or elsewhere'. However, of the 3.8 million companies in the UK, only 1275 have a premium listing.[118] The important question therefore is to

---

[111] For example, Provision 24 recommends that the board of a company should establish an audit committee (discussed at 19.4.4). Article 39(1) of the Audit Directive (2006/43/EC) requires that each public interest entity (which includes listed companies) must have an audit committee.

[112] Listing Rules, LR 9.8.6(6).

[113] FRC, 'What Constitutes an Explanation Under "Comply or Explain?"' (FRC 2012).

[114] Grant Thornton LLP, 'Corporate Governance Review 2018' (Grant Thornton 2018) 6.

[115] FRC, 'The UK Approach to Corporate Governance' (FRC 2010) 6.

[116] Grant Thornton LLP, 'Corporate Governance Review 2018' (Grant Thornton 2018) 33.   [117] ibid.

[118] As of December 2018. Statistics derived from the website of the Financial Conduct Authority (see https://marketsecurities.fca.org.uk/officiallist accessed 10 January 2019).

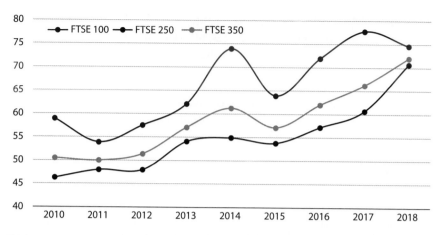

FIGURE 2.5 UK Corporate Governance Code FTSE compliance levels (%)

what extent the Code applies to other companies. The Code does provide some conces-sions for 'smaller companies',[119] which the Code defines as those outside the FTSE 350 throughout the year immediately prior to the reporting year. The 2016 Code stated that companies below the FTSE 350 'may nonetheless consider that it would be appropriate to adopt the approach in the Code and they are encouraged to do so',[120] but this encour-agement is not present in the 2018 Code.

The Code does not apply to unlisted companies (although there is nothing stop-ping such companies from choosing to adopt the Code's provisions if they so wish). The result is that the Code (and indeed the UK's corporate governance system) has, until very recently, focussed almost exclusively on large listed companies. This is unsurprising given that the major corporate scandals that propelled corporate gov-ernance into prominence all involved large listed companies. It is, however, a nota-ble weakness of our corporate governance system, especially given the contribu-tion made by unlisted companies. As a former Director General of the Institute of Directors noted:

> unlisted enterprises lie at the heart of the UK economy. They account for a sig-nificant proportion of its GDP and employment. Furthermore, they are a key source of dynamism and entrepreneurial spirit. Their potential contribution to any economic recovery should not be underestimated.[121]

As a result, there has been increased focus on devising a set of governance principles for other types of company.

2.2.2.2 The Wates Corporate Governance Principles

Governance scandals involving private companies can be just as damaging as those involving large listed companies, as the controversy surrounding the collapse of BHS demonstrates.

---

[119] Although it is worth noting that the number of such concessions is reduced in the 2018 Code when compared to the 2016 Code.

[120] FRC, 'The UK Corporate Governance Code' (FRC 2016) 4.

[121] Institute of Directors and ecoDa, 'Corporate Governance Guidance and Principles for Unlisted Companies in the UK' (IoD 2010) 5.

BHS Ltd and the governance of private companies

Sir Philip Green purchased British Home Stores plc in 2000 for £200 million, and converted it to a private company, BHS Ltd. Over the next few years, BHS Ltd paid out hundreds of millions in dividend payments (most of which went to Monaco-based companies controlled by Green's wife) which were often in excess of the company's profits. A parliamentary inquiry concluded that 'the Green family became incredibly wealthy ... but in doing so reduced the capacity of the company to invest and succeed'.[122] This resulted in BHS being unable to compete and it started sustaining losses. Desperate to offload the company, Green sold it to Retail Acquisitions Ltd ('RAL') in 2015 for £1. However, Dominic Chappell, the owner of RAL, was described as a 'manifestly unsuitable purchaser'[123] who had a record of corporate failure. Unsurprisingly, he was unable to rescue BHS and in April 2016, it was placed into administration. The company's debts totalled £1.3 billion, and its pension fund deficit stood at £571 million. An attempt to find a buyer for the company failed and the company went into liquidation, with the loss of 11,000 jobs.

A parliamentary inquiry into BHS called into question the governance of the various companies involved. The inquiry noted that, whilst most of BHS's competitors were subject to the Code, BHS was not, as it was a private company.[124] The inquiry concluded:

Sir Philip chose to run these companies as his own personal empire, with boards taking decisions with reference to a shared understanding of his wishes rather than the interests of each individual company. Boards had overlapping memberships and independent non-executive directors did not participate in key decisions. We saw meagre evidence of the type of constructive challenge that a good board should provide. These weak governance arrangements allowed the overarching interests of the Green family to prevail and facilitated the flow of money off shore to the ultimate beneficial owner of the parent company, Lady Green. . . . These weaknesses in corporate governance contributed substantially to the ultimate demise of BHS.[125]

Following the publication of the inquiry's report, Frank Field MP, the co-chair of the inquiry, stated that '[s]afeguards for important private companies may need to be reviewed'.[126] The question was whether the UK Corporate Governance Code should be expanded to cover other types of company, or whether a separate code should be created. Whilst some bodies recommended expanding the scope of the current Code,[127] the government in its Green Paper on corporate governance reform noted that the Code was 'designed primarily with Premium Listed companies in mind and some of its provisions will not be appropriate for privately-held businesses'.[128] In its response to the Green Paper, the government therefore invited several relevant bodies (e.g. the FRC, the Confederation of British Industry (CBI), the Institute of Directors (IoD)) to set up a Coalition Group under the chairmanship of James Wates that would develop a voluntary set of corporate governance principles for large private companies.[129]

---

[122] Business, Innovation and Skills Committee, 'The Sale and Acquisition of BHS Inquiry' (2016) para 3.

[123] ibid. [124] ibid para 125. [125] ibid paras 135 and 137.

[126] See http://news.sky.com/story/bhs-crisis-spurs-call-for-tough-director-test-10514130 accessed 10 January 2019.

[127] See e.g. www.icsa.org.uk/about-us/press-office/news-releases/icsa-proposes-changes-to-the-governance-of-private-companies accessed 10 January 2019.

[128] BEIS, 'Corporate Governance Reform: Green Paper' (BEIS 2016) para 3.11.

[129] BEIS, 'Corporate Governance Reform: The Government Response to the Green Paper Consultation' (BEIS 2017) 41, Action 10.

In December 2018, the Group published its final report,[130] which set out a set of six principles, as shown in Table 2.1.

TABLE 2.1 The Wates Corporate Governance Principles for Large Private Companies

Principle one: purpose and leadership	An effective board develops and promotes the purpose of a company, and ensures that its values, strategy and culture align with that purpose.
Principle two: board composition	Effective board composition requires an effective chair and a balance of skills, backgrounds, experience and knowledge, with individual directors having sufficient capacity to make a valuable contribution. The size of a board should be guided by the scale and complexity of the company.
Principle three: director responsibilities	The board and individual directors should have a clear understanding of their accountability and responsibilities. The board's policies and procedures should support effective decision-making and independent challenge.
Principle four: opportunity and risk	A board should promote the long-term success of the company by identifying opportunities to create and preserve value, and establishing oversight for identification and mitigation of risks.
Principle five: remuneration	A board should promote executive remuneration structures aligned to the sustainable long-term success of a company, taking into account pay and conditions elsewhere in the company.
Principle six: stakeholder relationships and engagement	Directors should foster effective stakeholder relationships aligned to the company's purpose. The board is responsible for overseeing meaningful engagement with stakeholders, including the workforce, and having regard to their views when taking decisions.

The Wates Principles operate on an 'apply-and-explain' basis, namely:

- A company that adopts the Wates Principles should follow them in a way that is most appropriate to their organisation. The board should apply each Principle by considering them independently within the context of the company's specific circumstances. They should explain in their own words how they have addressed the Principles in their governance practices. Companies should provide a supporting statement that gives an understanding of how their corporate governance policies and processes operate to achieve the desired outcome for each Principle.

- The guidance that accompanies each Principle does not need to be reported on.

To facilitate this, the Principles are written in a very broad, high-level manner and, accordingly, are capable of being applied in a range of different ways. The rationale behind this flexibility is that, in large private companies, '[d]iffering management and ownership structures means that a one-size-fits-all approach to corporate governance in large private companies is not appropriate'.[131]

The Wates Principles themselves do not state to which type of companies they apply. Instead, the Companies (Miscellaneous Reporting) Regulations 2018[132] have inserted a new Pt 8 into Sch 7 of the Large and Medium-Sized Companies and Groups (Accounts and Reports) Regulations 2008 that will apply to any company that is not subject to DTR 7.2 and:

---

[130] FRC, 'The Wates Corporate Governance Principles for Large Private Companies' (FRC 2018).
[131] ibid 8.   [132] SI 2018/860.

- has more than 2,000 employees; and/or
- has a turnover of more than £200 million and a balance sheet total of more than £2 billion.[133]

DTR 7.2 is discussed at 19.3.2.3.

Such companies will be required to include in their directors' report a 'statement of corporate governance arrangements' that states:

- which corporate governance code, if any, the company applied in that financial year;
- how the company applied the code; and
- if the company departed from the code, its reasons for doing so.[134]

The Wates Principles (along with the UK Corporate Governance Code) would be a code against which companies could report in their statement of corporate governance arrangements. The Wates Principles, along with the new rules relating to the statement of corporate governance arrangements, will apply to financial years starting on or after 1 January 2019, so reporting on the Wates Principles will begin in 2020.

2.2.2.3 The UK Stewardship Code

The UK Stewardship Code is discussed in more detail at 14.5.2. The 2019 update is discussed in the 'Latest news' section at xviii.

The UK Corporate Governance Code and the Wates Principles predominantly establish recommendations relating to the conduct of companies and their directors. However, as is discussed throughout this text, the company's members also play an extremely important role in promoting governance. The issue that arises is that members (especially large shareholders) have not been especially active, and mechanisms that rely on member involvement (such as general meetings) tend to be ineffective. This lack of member engagement was a contributory factor to the financial crisis, with the Walker Review stating that 'board and director shortcomings . . . would have been tackled more effectively had there been more vigorous scrutiny and engagement by major investors acting as owners'.[135] In an effort to encourage greater investor engagement, the FRC published the UK Stewardship Code in 2010, and an updated version in 2012. In January 2019, the FRC published a consultation on a revised Stewardship Code, which is due to come into effect in July 2019.

CHAPTER SUMMARY

- The principal sources of company law are legislation, case law, the constitution of the company, contract, EU law, and human rights law.
- Legislation is the principal form of UK company law, with the Companies Act 2006 being the most important piece of company law legislation. Other notable Acts include the Insolvency Act 1986 and the Financial Services and Markets Act 2000.
- Subordinate legislation is also important as it can flesh out or amend provisions found in Acts of Parliament, bring legislative provisions into force, and implement EU law.

---

[133] Large and Medium-Sized Companies and Groups (Accounts and Reports) Regulations 2008, Sch 7, para 23(3).
[134] ibid Sch 7, para 26(1).
[135] 'A Review of Corporate Governance in UK Banks and Other Financial Industry Entities: Final Recommendations' (HM Treasury, 2009) [5.11].

- Companies are, to a degree, permitted to create their own internal rules via their constitution. Companies can also create their own law by drafting their own standard terms for use in contracts.
- EU law has been a significant source of company law, but the UK is due to leave the EU by 29 March 2019.
- Corporate governance best practice recommendations are found in a series of reports and codes, with the two principal codes being the UK Corporate Governance Code and the UK Stewardship Code. Both codes operate on a comply-or-explain basis, under which certain persons much comply with the code or explain their reasons for non-compliance. The Wates Corporate Governance Principles for Large Private Companies were published in December 2018.

FURTHER READING

Brenda Hannigan, *Company Law* (5th edn, OUP 2015) 23–41.
- Provides a readable, but detailed, account of the influence that EU law has upon UK company law.

Christine A Mallin, *Corporate Governance* (6th edn, OUP 2018) ch 3.
- Discusses the development of corporate governance codes.

John Armour and Wolf-Georg Ringe, 'European Company Law 1999–2010: Renaissance and Crisis' (2011) 48 CML Rev 127.
- Discusses why the EU company law harmonization programme stalled, and looks at the impact of the financial crisis on EU company law.

Joseph A McCahery and Erik PM Vermuelen, *Corporate Governance of Non-Listed Companies* (OUP 2008).
- Discusses the expansion of corporate governance practices to unlisted companies, and provides suggestions for reform.

Reinier R Kraakman et al, *The Anatomy of Corporate Law: A Comparative and Functional Approach* (OUP 2004).
- Discusses the objectives of company law, and provides a comparative discussion of company law systems.

www.gov.uk/government/organisations/department-for-business-energy-and-industrial-strategy.
- The website of the Department for Business, Energy and Industrial Strategy, the government department responsible for company law reform.

https://frc.org.uk.
The website of the Financial Reporting Council, the body responsible for updating the UK Corporate Governance Code and the UK Stewardship Code.

SELF-TEST QUESTIONS

1. Define the following terms:
- right of establishment;
- comply or explain;
- apply and explain.

2. State whether each of the following statements is true or false and, if false, explain why:
- All company law legislation is contained in the CA 2006.
- The CA 2006 provides a set of model articles that companies may use.

- The Department for Business, Energy and Industrial Strategy is the governmental department responsible for company law reform.
- The UK Corporate Governance Code applies to public companies.
- Companies have human rights.

3. 'The vast bulk of UK company law is home-grown and so leaving the EU will only have a minimal effect on UK company law.' Discuss this quote.

4. 'The comply-or-explain approach has failed to bring about a sufficient increase in corporate governance standards, and it is time that Parliament passed a Corporate Governance Act.' Do you agree with this quote? Provide reasons for your answer.

 ONLINE RESOURCES

This book is accompanied by online resources to better support you in your studies. Visit www.oup.com/uk/roach-company/ for:

- answers to the self-test questions;
- further reading lists;
- multiple-choice questions;
- glossary.

Updates to the law can be found on the author's Twitter account (@UKCompanyLaw) and further resources can be found on the author's blog (www.companylawandgovernance.com).

PART II
The formation and nature of the company

Part II of this text discusses how companies are created and some of the fundamental issues regarding the nature of the company. Part II consists of four chapters, namely:

CHAPTER 3 INCORPORATION

This chapter discusses the various ways by which a company can be brought into existence and the different types of company that can be created. Throughout this text, it will be seen that different types of company are regulated in very different ways and so it is vital to understand the differences between the various types of company.

CHAPTER 4 CORPORATE PERSONALITY

Chapter 4 looks at one of, if not the defining characteristic of the company, namely its corporate personality. A company is a person and this has profound effects in terms of what the company can do and how it is regulated. Determining when a company's corporate personality can be disregarded is one of the most important company law issues (and one that has caused the courts considerable difficulty), and so it is discussed in depth in this chapter.

CHAPTER 5 THE CONSTITUTION OF THE COMPANY

To a significant degree, companies can create their own rules via their constitution. This chapter looks at the various sources of a company's constitution (notably the articles of association), how the constitution is amended and interpreted, and how the constitution can be enforced.

CHAPTER 6 CORPORATE CAPACITY AND LIABILITY

As the company is a legal person and cannot act of its own accord, the law has developed complex rules regarding who can act on behalf of the company, and how liability can be imposed on the company for the actions of others. This final chapter in Part II discusses these rules.

PART II

3 Incorporation

- Unregistered companies
- Incorporation by registration
- Classifications of company
- Re-registration

INTRODUCTION

The ability to conduct a business through a company has contributed hugely to the world's financial, social, and technological development. In 1911, Nicholas Murray Butler, then President of Columbia University, stated in a much-quoted passage 'the limited liability corporation is the single greatest discovery of modern times . . .. Even steam and electricity are far less important than the limited liability corporation, and would be reduced to comparative impotence without it.'[1] It is therefore no surprise that the company is by far the most popular business structure in the UK (as demonstrated by Figure 1.2 at 1.3).

This chapter focuses on the process by which companies are created, and the different types of company that can be created. The creation of a company brings about the existence of a 'body corporate' and so the process of creating a company is known as 'incorporation'. There are four principal methods of incorporating a company, namely:

1. incorporation by royal charter;
2. incorporation by Act of Parliament;
3. incorporation by delegated authority;
4. incorporation by registration.

The general rule is that the Companies Act 2006 (CA 2006) only applies to registered companies[2] (i.e. companies incorporated by registration). However, in order to prevent unregistered companies (i.e. companies incorporated by the other three methods) being under-regulated and having an unfair advantage over registered companies, the CA 2006 provides that the Secretary of State may pass regulations that set out how the CA 2006 is applied to unregistered companies.[3] Such regulations have been passed[4] and provide that large parts of the 2006 Act will apply to unregistered companies. This chapter starts by looking at how unregistered companies are created.

---

[1] Nicholas Murray Butler, *Why Should We Change Our Form of Government?* (Girvin Press 2007) 82.
[2] CA 2006, s 1(1).   [3] ibid s 1043.
[4] Unregistered Companies Regulations 2009, SI 2009/2436.

3.1 Unregistered companies

Compared to registered companies, there are very few unregistered companies—of the 3.8 million companies in the UK, only 901 are unregistered.[5] However, unregistered companies still occupy an important role in our company law system, and those that are created are often notable. Accordingly, it is important to understand how unregistered companies can be created.

3.1.1 Incorporation by royal charter

➡ **royal charter:** a document issued by, or on behalf of, the monarch that grants certain rights to a person, place, or body

The Crown, through the exercise of the royal prerogative, has the power to create a company through the granting of a **royal charter** and such companies are known as 'chartered companies'. Such companies are rare (only 1,023 chartered companies have been created since the thirteenth century).[6] Between the sixteenth and nineteenth centuries, royal charters were granted to trading companies engaged in activities that the monarch or government wished to encourage (for example, exploration, colonization, and overseas trade). Virtually all of the early joint-stock companies (e.g. the East India Company (1600), and the South Sea Company (1711)) were created by royal charter.

With the introduction of incorporation by registration, the number of companies created by royal charter every year has fallen considerably (and in 2018, no chartered companies were created), and charters are no longer granted to trading companies—charters are now almost exclusively granted to bodies engaged in areas such as:

- charitable activities (e.g. the National Society for the Prevention of Cruelty to Children, the Royal British Legion);
- educational activities (e.g. the British Broadcasting Corporation, the Open University);
- professional and regulatory activities (e.g. the Bank of England, the Institute of Chartered Secretaries and Administrators).

3.1.2 Incorporation by Act of Parliament

Parliament may create a company by passing an Act of Parliament. Today, very few such companies exist—no companies have been created by Act of Parliament since 2013, and there are currently only 42 such companies on the register of companies.[7] The exact nature of the company would often depend upon whether the Act was public or private.

3.1.2.1 Public Act of Parliament

➡ **public Act:** an Act that deals with matters of public interest that affect the general population

Companies created as the result of a **public Act** were usually created to serve some public need and are usually of national importance or benefit. Examples of such companies

---

[5] Companies House, 'Company Register Activity in the United Kingdom 2017–18' (Companies House 2018) Table C1.

[6] A full list of all charters granted since 1231 is available from the website of the Privy Council Office at https://privycouncil.independent.gov.uk/royal-charters/chartered-bodies accessed 10 January 2019.

[7] Companies House, 'Company Register Activity in the United Kingdom 2017–18' (Companies House 2018) Table B3.

include the Post Office[8] and the National Assembly of Wales.[9] The organization of the 2012 London Olympic and Paralympic Games was the responsibility of the Olympic Delivery Authority—a company created by a public Act of Parliament.[10] A number of nationalized industries were, historically, run by companies created by a public Act (examples include British Telecommunications,[11] British Gas Corporation,[12] British Steel Corporation,[13] and British Railways).[14] Most of these industries have since been privatized and so very few companies created by public Act remain.

3.1.2.2 Private Act of Parliament

Persons may petition Parliament to pass a **private Act** that will create a company that facilitates that person's commercial dealings, and such companies are known as 'statutory companies'. Historically, most statutory companies were created in order to run newly privatized industries. However, most of those statutory companies have since become standard registered companies under the CA 2006, so few statutory companies remain.

➡ **private Act:** an Act that affects specific groups of persons, organizations, or localities

3.1.3 Incorporation by delegated authority

Legislation may confer upon specified persons or bodies the ability to create a company. For example, the Open-Ended Investment Company Regulations 2001[15] empower the Financial Conduct Authority (FCA) to make an authorization order which brings into existence an open-ended investment company.

3.2 Incorporation by registration

Petitioning for a royal charter or the creation of an Act of Parliament is not the most accessible or efficient way to create a company. In 2017/18, 620,285 new companies were incorporated in the UK.[16] This many companies could never be created by the mechanisms discussed above. Accordingly, to meet demand, a simple, quick, and efficient method of incorporation was required. With the passing of the Joint Stock Companies Act 1844, such a method was created—namely, incorporation by registration. Today almost all new companies are created by registration under the CA 2006.

Persons who wish to incorporate a company by registration (such persons are known as 'promoters') must subscribe their names to a memorandum of association and comply with the CA 2006's requirements regarding registration.[17] These requirements involve registering certain documents with Companies House. Compliance with these requirements is important, lest the application for incorporation be rejected. Companies House has revealed that 8 per cent of online applications and almost 53 per cent of paper applications are rejected due to non-compliance with the legal requirements.[18]

---

[8] Post Office Act 1969, s 6.   [9] Government of Wales Act 1998, s 1.

[10] London Olympic Games and Paralympic Games Act 2006, s 3(1).

[11] British Telecommunications Act 1981, s 1.   [12] Gas Act 1972, s 1.

[13] Iron and Steel Act 1975, s 1.

[14] Transport Act 1947, s 1 (originally known as the British Transport Commission).   [15] SI 2001/1288.

[16] Companies House, 'Companies Register Activities in the UK 2017-18' (Companies House 2018) Table A.1.

[17] CA 2006, s 7(1).

[18] See https://companieshouse.blog.gov.uk/2017/08/21/successfully-register-a-company-with-companies-house accessed 10 January 2019.

3.2.1 **The registration documents**

In order to incorporate a company by registration, the promoters must provide the requisite 'registration documents' to Companies House. Companies House is an executive agency, sponsored by the Department for Business, Energy and Industrial Strategy (BEIS). As an executive agency, it is not funded by BEIS, but instead derives its income from the fees it charges for the services it provides. These fees include incorporating and dissolving companies, storing information of companies in the register of companies, and making such information available to the public.

The registration documents required to incorporate a company consist of the memorandum of association, the application for registration and accompanying documentation, and the statement of compliance.[19] These registration documents will now be discussed.

3.2.2 **The memorandum of association**

🔗 The memorandum is discussed in more detail at 5.2.

Historically, the memorandum of association was one of the company's most important constitutional documents. However, under the CA 2006, the memorandum has lost much of its importance, but all companies must have a memorandum and so one must be provided alongside the application for registration.[20]

Those persons (or a single person) who wish to form a company must subscribe their names to a memorandum of association,[21] which must state that those subscribers (i) wish to form a company under the CA 2006; and (ii) agree to become members of the company and, in the case of a company that is to have a share capital, to take at least one share each.[22] The memorandum must be set out in a prescribed form[23] and must be authenticated by each subscriber.[24] The subscribers of a company's memorandum will, upon incorporation, become the company's first members.[25]

3.2.3 **The application for registration and accompanying documentation**

The memorandum must be accompanied by an application for registration, which must also be accompanied by specified documentation.[26] For many filing activities, Companies House provides standard forms that comply with the relevant statutory requirements. Form IN01[27] is the standard application for registration form. The application for registration requires the promoters to provide certain basic information concerning the company such as whether the company will be public or private;[28] and whether the liability of the members will be limited or unlimited (and, if liability is to be limited, whether it will be limited by shares or guarantee).[29] The rest of the information required in the application is slightly more complex and so each piece of required information will be discussed individually.

---

[19] CA 2006, s 9.   [20] ibid s 9(1).   [21] ibid s 7(1)(a).   [22] ibid s 8(1).
[23] The prescribed forms can be found in Schs 1 and 2 of the Companies (Registration) Regulations 2008, SI 2008/3014.
[24] CA 2006, s 8(2).   [25] ibid s 112(1).   [26] ibid s 9.
[27] See www.gov.uk/government/uploads/system/uploads/attachment_data/file/534915/IN01_V7.pdf accessed 10 January 2019.
[28] CA 2006, s 9(2)(d).   [29] ibid s 9(2)(c).

3.2.3.1 **The proposed name of the company**

The application for registration must state the company's proposed name.[30] The regulation of company names is notable in terms of what words or phrases must and cannot be used. It is important that third parties know what type of company they are dealing with, so most companies must include a specified designation at the end of their name to indicate their company type, as Table 3.1 indicates.

TABLE 3.1 Company designations

Company type	Designation	Exceptions
Private limited company	'Ltd' or 'limited'[31]	Private companies that are charities, or companies subject to existing exemptions,[32] and community interest companies[33]
Public company	'plc' or 'public limited company'[34]	Community interest companies[35]
Community interest company	'cic' or 'community interest company' if private.[36] If public, 'community interest public company' or 'community interest plc'[37]	None
Societas Europeae	'SE'[38]	None

Historically, all companies needed to have their names approved by the Board of Trade[39] (later the DTI) prior to incorporation. The Companies Act 1981[40] amended this so that pre-approval was no longer generally required (subject to some exceptions discussed below), and instead companies could use any name unless it was prohibited. This system continues today, and the law imposes numerous limitations upon what names can be used:

- Companies House is required to keep an index of the names of all UK-registered companies, unregistered companies to which the CA 2006 applies, and overseas companies that have registered their particulars with Companies House.[41] A company generally cannot choose for its name the same name as another company listed on the index.[42]

- The Secretary of State can direct a company to change its name if in his opinion the company name is the same as, or too similar to, a company name on the index.[43]

- A person (the applicant) can object to a company name on the grounds that (i) it is the same as a name associated with the applicant in which he has goodwill; or (ii) that it is

---

[30] ibid s 9(2)(a).   [31] ibid s 59(1).   [32] ibid ss 60(1), 61, and 62.   [33] ibid s 59(4).

[34] ibid s 58(1).   [35] ibid s 58(3).

[36] Companies (Audit Investigations and Community Enterprises) Act 2004, s 33(1).   [37] ibid s 33(4).

[38] Council Regulation (EC) 2157/2001 of 8 October 2001 on the Statute for a European Company (SE) [2001] OJ L294/1, art 11.

[39] Companies Act 1948, s 17 (now repealed).   [40] Companies Act 1981, s 22 (now repealed).

[41] CA 2006, s 1099(1) and (2). This index must also list the names of limited partnerships and LLPs (s 1099(3)).

[42] ibid s 66(1). In determining whether a name is the same as one listed on the index, more detailed rules are found in Sch 3 of the Company, Limited Liability Partnership and Business (Names and Trading Disclosures) Regulations 2015, SI 2015/17.

[43] CA 2006, ss 67 and 68.

sufficiently similar to such a name that its use in the UK would be likely to mislead by suggesting a connection between the company and the applicant.[44] The objection will be heard by a company names adjudicator[45] and, if the objection is upheld, the adjudicator may make an order requiring the company to change its name.[46]

● The Secretary of State may pass regulations that set out which characters (e.g. letters, numbers, punctuation marks, symbols, etc.) can be used in a company's name.[47] These regulations also provide that a company's name cannot be longer than 160 characters.[48]

● A company name must not be registered if, in the opinion of the Secretary of State, the use of that name would constitute an offence.[49] So, for example, it is an offence for a company that is not a building society to use any name that indicates it is a building society.[50]

● There are restrictions on using the names of companies that have gone into insolvent liquidation.[51]

● A company name must not be registered if, in the opinion of the Secretary of State, it is offensive.[52]

 Offensive company names

Following a successful freedom of information request by the BBC,[53] Companies House revealed a list of company names that were rejected on the grounds of being potentially offensive, with examples including Titanic Holdings Ltd, Stylish Bitch Ltd, and Blue Arsed Fly Designs Ltd.

In some cases, the requirement for approval still exists and permission will need to be obtained to use certain words and phrases in a company name:

● If a company wishes to use a name that would give the impression that the company is connected with certain governmental bodies (e.g. Her Majesty's Government, local authorities), then approval is required from the Secretary of State.[54]

● Certain 'sensitive words or expressions' require the approval of the Secretary of State.[55] Examples of such words include 'British', 'NHS', 'Parliament', and 'Regulator'.[56]

● Certain words and phrases can only be used if permission is obtained from certain persons. For example, a company that wishes to use the word 'insurance' in its name must obtain a letter of non-objection from the FCA.[57]

---

[44] ibid s 69(1). A company with a name that is the same as, or too similar to, another might also have committed the tort of passing off.

[45] ibid ss 69(2) and 70.   [46] ibid s 73(1)(a).

[47] ibid s 57(1). See reg 2 and Sch 1 of the Company, Limited Liability Partnership and Business (Names and Trading Disclosures) Regulations 2015.

[48] Company, Limited Liability Partnership and Business (Names and Trading Disclosures) Regulations 2015, reg 2(4).

[49] CA 2006, s 53(a). A list of such words, whose use can constitute an offence, can be found at Companies House, 'Incorporation and Names' (2016) Annex C.

[50] Building Societies Act 1986, s 107(1) and (11).

[51] IA 1986, s 216 (discussed at 23.3.5).   [52] CA 2006, s 53(b).

[53] See www.bbc.co.uk/news/uk-wales-politics-42016501 accessed 10 January 2019.

[54] CA 2006, s 54(1). A list of words and phrases that could fall within s 54(1) can be found in Sch 4 of the Company, Limited Liability Partnership and Business (Names and Trading Disclosures) Regulations 2015.

[55] CA 2006, s 55(1).

[56] The full list can be found in Sch 1, Pt 1 of the Company, Limited Liability Partnership and Business Names (Sensitive Words and Expressions) Regulations 2014, SI 2014/3140.

[57] Companies House, 'Incorporation and Names' (2016) Annex A. This annex provides a list of such words and phrases.

Upon incorporation, the company must display its registered name at its registered office, any inspection place,[58] and any other location where it carries on business.[59] Its registered name must also be disclosed on the company's website,[60] and on documents such as business letters, cheques, and all other forms of business correspondence and documentation.[61] Failure to comply with these rules, without reasonable excuse, is a criminal offence.[62]

Following incorporation, a company may voluntarily change its name either by passing a **special resolution**,[63] or by some other means provided for by the company's articles.[64] In both cases, notice of the change of name must be given to Companies House (using Form NM01) and the registrar will then issue a new certificate of incorporation.[65] The new name has effect from the date of the certificate's issue,[66] but it is important to note that a change of name will not affect any rights or obligations that the company has, nor will it affect any legal proceedings brought against the company.[67]

➡ **special resolution:** a vote of the members which is passed by a majority of not less than 75 per cent

3.2.3.2 The registered office

Every company must at all times have a registered office, to which all communications and notices may be addressed.[68] The application for registration must state whether the company's registered office is to be situated in (i) England and Wales (or in Wales); (ii) Scotland; or (iii) Northern Ireland.[69] Given that these represent the three legal systems in the UK, this information is useful in order to determine which courts will have jurisdiction, which system of law will apply, and where the company is domiciled.[70]

As is discussed throughout this text, certain persons have the right to inspect, or deposit, certain documents at the company's registered office. Further, a document is deemed to be served to the company if it is left at, or sent by post to, the registered office.[71] Accordingly, the application for registration must also provide a statement of the intended address of the company's registered office.[72] Upon incorporation, the company must disclose the address of its registered office on all its business letters, order forms, and its websites.[73] A company may change the address of its registered office by giving notice to Companies House (see Form AD01).[74]

3.2.3.3 Statement of capital and initial shareholdings

If the proposed company is to have a share capital, then the application for registration must include a statement of capital and initial shareholdings,[75] which must state:

- the total number, and the aggregate value, of shares to be taken by the subscribers upon the company's formation;[76]

---

[58] Company, Limited Liability Partnership and Business (Names and Trading Disclosures) Regulations 2015, reg 21(1).

[59] ibid reg 22.   [60] Ibid reg 24(2).   [61] ibid reg 24(1).   [62] ibid reg 28.

[63] CA 2006, ss 77(1)(a) and 78.   [64] ibid ss 77(1)(b) and 79.   [65] ibid s 80(3).

[66] ibid s 81(1).   [67] ibid s 81(2) and (3).

[68] ibid s 86.   [69] ibid s 9(2)(b).

[70] *Gasque v Commissioners of Inland Revenue* [1940] 2 KB 80 (KB).

[71] CA 2006, s 1139(1).   [72] ibid s 9(5)(a).

[73] Company, Limited Liability Partnership and Business (Names and Trading Disclosures) Regulations 2015, reg 25(1) and (2)(c).

[74] CA 2006, s 87(1).   [75] ibid s 9(4)(a).   [76] ibid s 10(2)(a) and (b).

nominal value: the fixed value attached to shares in a limited company (discussed at 16.2.1)

share premium: the amount paid for a share in excess of its nominal value (discussed at 16.2.2)

- the aggregate amount (if any) to be unpaid on those shares (whether on account of their **nominal value** or by way of **premium**);[77]

- for each class of shares, particulars of the rights attached to those shares, the total number of shares of that class, and the aggregate nominal value of shares of that class;[78]

- the name and address of each subscriber to the memorandum[79] and the number, nominal value, and class of shares to be taken by each subscriber on formation;[80] and

- for each subscriber, the amount to be paid up and the amount (if any) to be unpaid on each share (whether on account of their nominal value or by way of premium).[81]

This statement only provides a snapshot of capital and shareholdings upon incorporation. Whenever a company allots new shares, it must provide Companies House with an updated statement of capital (see Form SH01).[82]

3.2.3.4 Statement of guarantee

If the proposed company is to be limited by guarantee, the application must contain a statement of guarantee,[83] which must state:

- the name and address of each subscriber to the memorandum;[84]

- that each member undertakes that if the company is wound up while he is a member, or within one year after he ceases to be a member, he will contribute to the assets of the company such amount (not exceeding a specified amount) as may be required for (i) payment of the debts and liabilities of the company contracted before he ceases to be a member; (ii) payment of the costs, charges, and expenses of winding up; and (iii) adjustment of the rights of the contributories among themselves.[85]

3.2.3.5 Statement of the company's proposed officers

The application must contain a statement of the company's proposed officers,[86] which must provide required particulars (e.g. name, nationality, date of birth)[87] of the first director(s) of the company and, if applicable, the first company secretary (or joint secretaries).[88] The statement must also include a statement by the subscribers to the memorandum that each of the persons named as a director, as secretary, or as one of the joint secretaries, has consented to act in the relevant capacity.[89]

3.2.3.6 Statement of initial significant control

PSCs and the PSC register are discussed at 13.3.2.

The application must contain a statement of initial significant control,[90] which identifies whether, on incorporation, there will be any persons with significant control (PSCs) over the company.[91]

3.2.3.7 Articles of association

The articles of association can be submitted alongside the application for registration and are discussed further at 5.3.

The articles of association provide the internal rules by which a company is run, and all companies must have a set of articles.[92] Promoters are free to draft their own articles, but it can be burdensome and requires a sound knowledge of company procedures.

---

[77] ibid s 10(2)(ba).　　[78] ibid s 10(2)(c).
[79] ibid s 10(3) and Companies (Registration) Regulations 2008, reg 3.
[80] CA 2006, s 10(4)(a).　　[81] ibid s 10(4)(b).　　[82] ibid s 555.　　[83] ibid s 9(4)(b).
[84] ibid s 11(2) and Companies (Registration) Regulations 2008, reg 4.
[85] CA 2006, s 11(3).　　[86] ibid s 9(4)(c).
[87] The full list of particulars can be found in ss 162–64 of the CA 2006.
[88] CA 2006, s 12(1).　　[89] ibid s 12(3).　　[90] ibid s 9(4)(d).　　[91] ibid s 12A(1).
[92] ibid s 18(1).

Accordingly, statute has long provided a set of model articles[93] that promoters can use if they so wish. Unless the proposed company wishes to adopt the model articles, the application for registration must contain a copy of the proposed articles of association.[94] If no articles are submitted alongside the application, then the company will be governed by the model articles.[95]

3.2.3.8 Statement of company type and business activities

The application must contain a statement of the type of company it is to be and its intended business activities.[96] Information on business activities should be disclosed based on the Standard Industrial Classification of Economic Activities (SIC) 2007,[97] which sets out the different types of economic activity and assigns each one a classification code. So, for example, the code for 'manufacture of motor vehicles' is 29100.[98]

3.2.3.9 Election as to where to keep registers

Public companies are required to keep certain statutory registers, but private companies may elect to (i) keep their own registers; or (ii) instead require Companies House to keep the applicable information on its central register. If the latter option is chosen, notice of this election must be provided to Companies House when the registration documents are delivered.[99]

> ∞ The statutory registers and the election available to private companies are discussed further at 19.2.

3.2.4 Statement of compliance

The application for registration must be accompanied by a statement of compliance,[100] which states that the requirements of the CA 2006 as to registration have been complied with.[101] Companies House may accept this statement as sufficient evidence of compliance.[102]

3.2.5 Submission of the registration documents, and registration

At the time of writing, the registration documents can be submitted in hard copy or electronically, but Companies House is committed to becoming a fully digital organization. The registration documents should be submitted to the registrar of companies[103] that is responsible for the country in which the registered office is to be based, namely, (i) the registrar of companies for England and Wales; (ii) the registrar of companies for Scotland; or (iii) the registrar of companies for Northern Ireland.[104]

The registrar in question will examine the registration documents to make sure they are completed properly and fully. Note that, as a company cannot be formed under the CA 2006 for an unlawful purpose,[105] the registrar is free to refuse a registration if the company is being formed for such a purpose. The following case provides such an example.

---

[93] These can be found in the Companies (Model Articles) Regulations 2008, SI 2008/3229.
[94] CA 2006, s 9(5)(b).   [95] ibid s 20(1).   [96] ibid s 9(5)(c).   [97] ibid s 9(5A).
[98] Companies House, 'Standard Industrial Classification of Economic Activities (SIC) 2007' (2007) 9.
[99] CA 2006, ss 128B, 167A, 279A, and 790X. The Secretary of State has the power to extend this election to public companies, but has not yet chosen to do so.
[100] ibid s 9(1).   [101] ibid s 13(1).   [102] ibid s 13(2).
[103] In the CA 2006, the responsibilities of Companies House are stated as being those of 'the registrar'. For the sake of clarity, duties of the registrar will be referred to as duties of Companies House.
[104] CA 2006, s 9(6).   [105] ibid s 7(2).

***R v Registrar of Joint Stock Companies* [1931] 2 KB 197 (CA)**

FACTS: Registration documents were submitted to register a proposed company called the Irish Hospitals (Sweeps) Ltd. A proposed object of the company was to sell in England or elsewhere tickets for a lottery that was run in the then Irish Free State. The registrar refused to register the registration documents on the ground that this purpose was unlawful.

HELD: Section 41 of the Lotteries Act 1823 prohibited the sale of tickets in any lottery, except those that were or shall be authorized by an Act of Parliament. When the 1823 Act was passed, Ireland was part of the UK, but was not at the time of this case (1931). The Court held that, whilst there was an Act that authorized the sale of the tickets,[106] it was an Act passed by the Irish Parliament. As the Irish Parliament had no jurisdiction in England, it followed that the sale was not authorized for the purposes of the 1823 Act, and so the company was formed for an unlawful purpose. Accordingly, the registrar was entitled to refuse the registration.

COMMENT: Today, companies are no longer required to have an **objects clause**, so it is more difficult for Companies House to determine whether a company is being set up for an unlawful purpose. However, in practice, cases involving such companies are very rare.

➡ **objects clause:** a clause in a company's articles that sets out the purposes for which the company was formed (discussed at 6.2.1).

If the registration documents are acceptable, the registration fee must be paid, and the fee payable depends on how the registration documents were submitted and whether same-day registration is wanted. Companies House strongly encourages online registration via its pricing model (i.e. paper registration is considerably more expensive than online registration).[107]

Upon payment of the fee, the registration documents will be registered.[108] The company will be allocated a registration number[109] (useful for distinguishing between companies with similar names) and a certificate of incorporation will be issued.[110] This certificate provides conclusive proof that the requirements for registration have been met and that the company is registered under the CA 2006.[111] From the date of registration (which will also be stated on the certificate), the company's corporate personality comes into being, its subscribers becomes its members (and shareholders if the company has a share capital), and its officers are formally appointed to their respective offices.[112]

It was noted above that the registrar can refuse to register a company being formed for an unlawful purpose. However, what if the registrar does, through error or negligence, register such a company? Can such a company be 'de-incorporated'? Under the CA 2006, there is no mechanism to repeal the registration of a company and so the registration of such a company would normally stand.[113] However, the CA 2006 does not bind the Crown and so the Attorney General, acting on behalf of the Crown, may issue proceedings for judicial review, as occurred in the following case.

---

106 Namely the Public Charitable Hospital (Temporary Provisions) Act 1930.

107 See Sch 1, para 8 of the Registrar of Companies (Fees) (Companies, Overseas Companies and Limited Liability Partnerships) Regulations 2012, SI 2012/1907.

108 CA 2006, s 14.   109 ibid s 1066(1).   110 ibid s 15(1).

111 ibid s 15(4).   112 ibid s 16.

113 *Bowman v Secular Society Ltd* [1917] AC 406 (HL).

R v Registrar of Companies, ex p Attorney General [1991] BCLC 476 (DC)

FACTS: The objects clause of Lindi St Claire (Personal Services) Ltd[114] provided that the company was set up for carrying on the business of prostitution and, although this was an unlawful purpose, the company was registered by the registrar in 1979. The Attorney General applied for a judicial review of the registrar's decision to register the company.

HELD: Ackner LJ stated that the carrying on of the company's trade would involve it entering into contracts that were sexually immoral and therefore illegal. Accordingly, the court granted judicial review of the registrar's decision, the company's registration was quashed, and it was struck off the register.

3.2.5.1 **Trading certificate**

A private company can commence business as soon as its certificate of incorporation is issued. Conversely, a public company cannot commence any business or exercise any borrowing powers until it has been additionally issued with a trading certificate.[115] A trading certificate will only be issued if Companies House is satisfied that that the additional registration requirements for public companies have been complied with (chiefly the requirements as to minimum share capital discussed at 16.3). If a public company commences business or exercises borrowing powers without a trading certificate, then an offence is committed by the company and every officer in default.[116] If a public company has been registered and it has not been issued with a trading certificate within one year of registration, it may be wound up by the court.[117]

3.2.6 **'Off-the-shelf' companies**

Registration of the required documents is not an unduly burdensome process—but it does require a relatively serious layperson's knowledge of the procedures by which a company is run. Further, preparation of the documents can be time-consuming, especially if the promoters require bespoke articles that cater for the particular needs of the proposed company. Persons who lack such knowledge or wish to gain access to the benefits of incorporation quickly may prefer to purchase an 'off-the-shelf' company.

There are businesses and individuals (known as 'incorporation agents', or 'company formation agents') that specialize in creating and selling companies. They will register the necessary documents with Companies House and then leave the company 'on the shelf' until it is purchased. When this occurs, the incorporation agent will notify Companies House of the relevant changes, for example, change of directors, registered office, etc. It has been estimated that incorporation agents are responsible for around 60 per cent of all new company formations.[118]

---

[114] Prior to this company name being accepted by the registrar, he rejected several previous proposed names such as 'Prostitute Ltd', 'Hookers Ltd', and 'Lindi St Claire (French Lessons) Ltd'.

[115] CA 2006, s 761(1).

[116] ibid s 767(1).

[117] Insolvency Act 1986 (IA 1986), s 122(1)(b).

[118] Company Law Review Steering Group, 'Modern Law for a Competitive Economy: Developing the Framework' (DTI 2000) para 11.32.

The use of an incorporation agent brings several benefits, chief amongst them being speed and reduced expense. Many incorporation agents operate online only and can provide purchasers with an off-the-shelf company for under £20 (although this is not likely to include hard copies of the relevant documentation). There is, however, one major drawback to purchasing an off-the-shelf company: because the company was created months, or even years, before it was purchased, it will not be tailored to meet the needs of the new business. If the promoters are willing to spend more money and wait a little longer, incorporation agents will create a bespoke company that meets their needs.

3.2.7 **Pre-incorporation contracts**

Prior to obtaining the certificate of incorporation, persons acting on behalf of the unformed company (or their agents)[119] may need to enter into contractual agreements with third parties in order to cater for the needs of the unformed company (e.g. rent premises, purchase supplies, hire workers, etc.). Until the company is fully incorporated, it will not exist as a separate entity and so will have no capacity to enter into contracts. Are such pre-incorporation contracts void or, because they are clearly for the benefit of the unformed company, are they regarded as valid? Historically, the common law provided the answer, but it was based on determining the intent of the parties, as revealed in the contract.[120] This process was notoriously difficult and resulted in significant confusion in the law and a perception that cases in this area could turn based on complex and technical distinctions. For an example, contrast the cases of *Kelner v Baxter*[121] and *Newborne v Sensolid (Great Britain) Ltd*.[122] In *Kelner*, the promoter signed the contract 'on behalf of' the unformed company, and it was held that a binding contract existed between the promoter and the third party. In *Newborne*, the promoter signed the contract using the company's name and added his own signature underneath. It was held that the contract was purportedly between the promoter and the unformed company and, as the company had no contractual capacity, no contract existed.

As a consequence of the UK's entry into the European Union (EU), it was obliged to implement Art 7 of the First EU Company Law Directive,[123] which states:

> If, before a company has acquired legal personality (that is, before being formed) action has been carried out in its name and the company does not assume the obligations arising from such action, the persons who acted shall, without limit, be jointly and severally liable therefore, unless otherwise agreed.

This has been implemented by s 51(1) of the CA 2006, which states:

> A contract that purports to be made by or on behalf of a company at a time when the company has not been formed has effect, subject to any agreement to the contrary, as one made with the person purporting to act for the company or as agent for it, and he is personally liable on the contract accordingly.

Accordingly, where s 51(1) applies,[124] a promoter will be personally liable for a pre-incorporation contract, irrespective of how he expresses his signature. This obviously

---

[119] In this section, these persons are referred to collectively as 'promoters'.

[120] *Phonogram Ltd v Lane* [1982] QB 938 (CA).

[121] (1866) LR 2 CP 174.   [122] [1954] 1 QB 45 (CA).   [123] Council Directive 68/151/EEC.

[124] Section 51 will not apply where (i) a company was bought off the shelf after the contract was entered into, but was in existence at the time the contract was entered into; or (ii) where the company once existed but has since been dissolved (*Cotronic (UK) Ltd v Dezonie* [1991] BCC 200 (CA)).

benefits third parties, because they will now be able to sue the promoter—but can the promoter enforce the contract against the third party? The Court of Appeal has stated that the promoter can enforce the contract,[125] but the fact that clarification was required from the courts is an indication of a flaw in the drafting of s 51.

3.2.7.1 Agreements to the contrary

As s 51 operates 'subject to any agreement to the contrary', it follows that a promoter will not be liable on a pre-incorporation contract if there exists an agreement providing that he will not be liable. This agreement need not be in the actual contract itself, although in practice it usually will be.[126] Simply acting as a promoter for an unformed company will not be enough to establish the existence of a contrary agreement.[127] The courts will require such an agreement to 'either be made explicitly . . . or must be capable of being clearly and unambiguously inferred from the other terms of the contract'.[128] The following case also demonstrates that the parties must have intended to exclude s 51 in the agreement.

Royal Mail Estates Ltd v Maple Teesdale [2015] EWHC 1890 (Ch)

FACTS: A contract was entered into under which Royal Mail Estates Ltd ('RME') agreed to sell a piece of property to Kensington Gateway Holdings Ltd ('Kensington') for £20 million. The contract provided that the word 'Buyer' would refer to Kensington and it was signed 'for an on behalf of the Buyer' followed by 'Maple Teesdale pp Buyer'. It transpired that, at the time the contract was entered into, Kensington had not yet been incorporated, but neither RME nor Maple Teesdale (the promoter of Kensington) knew this. Teesdale decided not to go ahead with the sale and so RME sued, claiming that under s 51,[129] Teesdale was personally liable on the contract. Teesdale stated that cl 24.1 of the contract stated that 'the benefit of the contract is personal to the Buyer' and that this constituted an agreement to the contrary under s 51. Teesdale sought to have the case summarily dismissed.

HELD: The court stated that 'there is only a contrary agreement . . . if there is found to be an agreement between the parties by which they intended to exclude the [s 51] Effect'.[130] As neither RME nor Teesdale knew that Kensington had not been incorporated at the time of the contract, it followed that they could not have had in mind s 51 when they agreed the words in cl 24.1. Accordingly, cl 24.1 did not amount to an agreement to the contrary and so Teesdale's application for summary judgment was refused.

3.2.7.2 Binding the company

It will be noted that Art 7 permits a company to 'assume the obligations' of the pre-incorporation contract, but s 51 confers no such power on the company, and the courts

---

[125] *Braymist Ltd v Wise Finance Co Ltd* [2002] EWCA Civ 127, [2002] Ch 273.

[126] *Royal Mail Estates Ltd v Maple Teesdale* [2015] EWHC 1890 (Ch), [2016] 1 WLR 942 [40] (Jonathan Klein).

[127] *Phonogram Ltd v Lane* [1982] QB 938 (CA).

[128] Geoffrey Morse, *Palmer's Company Law* (Sweet & Maxwell 2018) para 3.007.1.

[129] The case, in fact, concerned the predecessor to s 51, namely s 36C of the CA 1985.

[130] [2015] EWHC 1890 (Ch), [2016] 1 WLR 942 [51].

have clearly stated that a company cannot, following its incorporation, ratify or adopt a pre-incorporation contract.[131] A number of commentators have argued that this is an omission and that companies should, upon incorporation, be free to adopt pre-incorporation contracts.[132]

If a company does wish to be bound by the terms of a pre-incorporation contract, this could occur in several ways:

- the pre-incorporation contract could contain a term which provides that, upon incorporation, the promoter will cease to be liable under the contract providing that the company enters into a contract with the third party on the same terms as the pre-incorporation contract; or
- following incorporation, the company, the promoter, and the third party could enter into a tripartite agreement which provides that the pre-incorporation contract will be discharged, and a new agreement will be entered into between the company and the third party (this is known as 'novation').

The courts will require clear evidence of novation.[133] Novation will not occur simply because a company acts on the pre-incorporation contract as if it were bound.[134] However, novation need not be express and novation may be inferred based on the conduct of the parties (e.g. where the company and third party agreed to modify the agreement),[135] although this will be rare.

3.3 Classifications of company

The CA 2006 allows for a number of different company types that can suit a wide array of businesses from small, single-person companies to multinational companies with hundreds of thousands of employees and shareholders.[136] However, the actual number of company types on offer is quite small, as essentially company type is based on three characteristics, namely:

- Is the company public or private? Public companies can be further broken down into those whose shares are traded on a stock exchange and those who are not.
- Does the company have a share capital or not?
- Is the liability of the company's members limited or unlimited?

Public companies must be limited and must have a share capital. Private companies can be limited or unlimited, and may or may not have a share capital. Accordingly, there are only five types of registrable standard company,[137] and when completing Form IN01, the promoter must choose which type of company to incorporate. The relevant extract of Form IN01, which sets out the five types of standard company, is found in Figure 3.1.

---

[131] *Re Northumberland Avenue Hotel Co Ltd* (1886) 33 ChD 16 (CA).

[132] See e.g. RR Pennington, 'The Validation of Pre-Incorporation Contracts' (2002) 23 Co Law 284, 285.

[133] *Bagot Pneumatic Tyre Co v Clipper Pneumatic Tyre Co* [1901] 1 Ch 196 (Ch).

[134] *Re Northumberland Avenue Hotel Co Ltd* (1886) 33 ChD 16 (CA).

[135] *Howard v Patent Ivory Manufacturing Co* (1888) 38 ChD 156 (Ch).

[136] In this sense, an important distinction is between micro-entities, small, medium-sized, and large companies. However, as this distinction only arises in relation to a company's accounts and reports, it is discussed at 19.3.1.3.

[137] There are several types of specialized company that are discussed at 3.3.4.

IN01
Application to register a company

A4	Company type❶	

Please tick the box that describes the proposed company type and members' liability (only one box must be ticked):

☐ Public limited by shares
☐ Private limited by shares
☐ Private limited by guarantee
☐ Private unlimited with share capital
☐ Private unlimited without share capital

❶ **Company type**
If you are unsure of your company's type, please go to our website: www.gov.uk/companieshouse

FIGURE 3.1 Standard company types

Despite there only being five types of standard company, they can cater for an extremely wide range of business types. We start by looking at the most notable characteristic, namely whether the company is public or private.

3.3.1 **Public and private companies**

When creating a company, its promoters are required to state whether the company is to be registered as a public company or a private company,[138] so it is important that promoters choose the type of company that best suits the needs of their business. Section 4 of the CA 2006 defines public and private companies as follows:

- A public company is a company limited by shares, or limited by guarantee and having a share capital, the certificate of incorporation of which states that it is a public company.[139]

- A private company is any company that is not a public company.[140]

These definitions are not especially useful as they do not help us understand the differences between the two company types. Section 4(4) does go on to state that there are 'two major differences' between public and private companies, which are set out in Pt 20 of the Act. These are:

1. A public company is so called because it can offer to sell its shares to the public at large and, to facilitate this, it may offer to sell its shares on a stock market (although it is worth noting that the majority of public companies do not place their shares on a stock exchange). This is a notable advantage because issuing shares allows public companies to potentially obtain large amounts of capital. Private limited companies may not offer to sell their shares to the public at large,[141] and no private company (limited or unlimited) can list its shares.[142]

2. Whilst private companies can be created with a trivial amount of capital, public companies are required to have a minimum allotted share capital of £50,000.[143]

A public company's minimum share capital requirement is discussed in more detail at 16.3.

In reality, there are numerous noteworthy differences between public and private companies, as Table 3.2 indicates.

---

[138] CA 2006, s 9(2)(d). For a discussion of how the public/private distinction arose, see Derek French, Stephen Mayson, and Christopher Ryan, *Mayson, French & Ryan on Company Law* (34th edn, OUP 2017) 60–1.

[139] CA 2006, s 4(2).   [140] ibid s 4(1).

[141] ibid s 755(1). From this, it follows that an unlimited company may offer to sell its shares to the public.

[142] Financial Services and Markets Act 2000 (FSMA 2000), s 75(3) and Financial Services and Markets Act 2000 (Official Listing of Securities) Regulations 2001, SI 2001/2956, reg 3(a).

[143] CA 2006, s 763(1)(a).

TABLE 3.2 The differences between a public company and a private company

	Public	Private
Required to have a share capital	Yes	No
Limited or unlimited liability of members	Limited only	Limited or unlimited
Can offer to sell shares to the public at large	Yes	No (unless unlimited)
Can trade shares on a stock exchange	Yes	No
Minimum capital requirement	£50,000	No minimum capital requirement
Minimum number of directors	Two	One
Suffix	'plc' or 'public limited company'	'Ltd' or 'Limited' if limited. No suffix if unlimited
Must hold AGM	Yes	No (unless the articles state otherwise)
Can use written resolution procedure	No	Yes
Required to appoint a company secretary	Yes	No (unless the articles state otherwise)
Can be classified as micro-entity, small or medium-sized	No	Yes
Requires a trading certificate	Yes	No
Level of regulation	The CA 2006 regulates public companies much more stringently than private companies	

Source: Roach, *Concentrate Company Law* (5th edn, OUP 2018).

Private companies vastly outnumber public companies—as of September 2018, there were 3,843,514 companies incorporated in the UK, of which only 5,836 were public.[144] The reason for this is that public companies are regulated much more heavily than private companies and have many more formalities to comply with (e.g. the requirement to hold an AGM). In many private companies, the directors and members are the same people and will wish to keep control of the company—they will therefore have no desire to sell shares to the public, so there is little reason to incorporate as a public company.

3.3.1.1 Quoted, listed, and traded companies

As noted, public companies can trade their shares on a stock exchange and such companies are often referred to as listed or quoted companies. There is an important difference between these two terms:

The official list is discussed at 18.4.

- The glossary to the FCA Handbook provides that a listed company is a company that has a class of its securities listed on the UK's official list. At the time of writing, 15,298 securities are listed on the official list.[145]

---

[144] Companies House, 'Incorporated Companies in the UK, July to September 2018' (Companies House 2018) Tables 1a and 1b.

[145] See www.fca.org.uk/markets/ukla/listing-applications/official-list accessed 29 October 2018. Note that this does not mean that 15,298 companies are listed, as many companies list multiple classes of security (e.g. HSBC Bank plc has 1,550 different types of security listed on the official list).

- A quoted company is a company whose share capital (i) has been included on the official list;[146] or (ii) is officially listed in a European Economic Area (EEA) State; or (iii) is admitted to dealing on the New York Stock Exchange or National Association of Securities Dealers Automated Quotations (NASDAQ).[147] A company that is not a quoted company is known as an unquoted company.[148]

The distinction between a listed and quoted company

- The shares of Vodafone Group plc are listed on the official list, so Vodafone will be a listed company and a quoted company.
- The shares of Facebook Inc are not listed on the UK's official list, but they are listed on NASDAQ. Accordingly, Facebook is a quoted company, but it is not a listed company.
- A2D Funding plc only has debt securities listed on the official list. Accordingly, it is a listed company, but as it has no share capital listed, it is an unquoted company.
- The shares of ASOS plc are placed on the AIM (formerly the 'Alternative Investment Market'). As AIM is not part of the official list and does not fall within the definition of a quoted company, it follows that ASOS is not a listed company and is an unquoted company.

To complicate matters, the CA 2006 also refers to a 'traded company', which is defined as a company with any shares that (i) carry rights to vote at general meetings; and (ii) are admitted to trading on a regulated market in an EEA State by or with the consent of the company.[149] In practice, most companies with listed/quoted shares will also be traded companies.

Certain rules and best practice recommendations do not apply to all listed/quoted/traded companies, but only to those who are part of the Financial Times Stock Exchange (FTSE) 100, 250, or 350. For example, the recommendations of the Hampton-Alexander Review, which is looking at how to improve gender diversity in the boardroom, only apply to FTSE 350 companies. Accordingly, it is important to know how the FTSE indexes operate. The FTSE Indexes are a series of tables that measure companies by reference to their market capitalization (as this is how the investment community measures company size). A company's market capitalization is determined by multiplying a company's share price by the number of shares it has. Accordingly, a company's market capitalization (and possibly its position in the FTSE indexes) will fluctuate as its share price and the number of shares it has fluctuate.

The Hampton-Alexander Review is discussed at 8.3.1.1.

There are hundreds of FTSE indexes covering companies all over the world, but in the UK, the principal three indexes are the FTSE 100, the FTSE 250, and the FTSE 350. The difference between them is as follows:

- **FTSE 100**: The largest 100 companies on the London Stock Exchange in terms of market capitalization form the FTSE 100. As of November 2018, FTSE 100 companies have a combined market capitalization of over £1.8 trillion, which represents about 80 per cent of the value of shares listed on the London Stock Exchange's Main Market.

---

[146] From this, it follows that most listed companies will also be quoted companies (but see A2D Funding plc example in the Law in Action box below).
[147] CA 2006, s 385(2).   [148] ibid s 385(3).
[149] ibid s 360C.

- **FTSE 250**: The next 250 companies after the FTSE 100 (i.e. the 101st largest to the 350th largest) form the FTSE 250. As of November 2018, the combined market capitalization of FTSE 250 companies was just over £344 billion.
- **FTSE 350**: Companies in the FTSE 100 and FTSE 250 collectively form the FTSE 350.

3.3.2 **Share capital**

Laypersons tend to assume that all companies have shares, but this is not the case. Company promoters (except those creating a public company) are free to determine whether their company will have a share capital or not. The vast majority of companies in the UK have a share capital—of the 3.8 million companies on the register, only 147,516 do not have a share capital.[150]

Shares and share capital are discussed in more detail in Chapter 16.

Public companies must have a share capital,[151] whereas private companies need not (although the vast majority do). Remember, if a company does not have share capital, then it will not have shareholders—it will have members.

3.3.3 **Limited and unlimited companies**

The terms 'limited' and 'unlimited' do not refer to the company itself, but to the liability of its members, and the application for registration must state whether the liability of the members is to be limited or not.[152] As noted, the liability of the members of a public company must be limited,[153] whereas the liability of a private company's members can be limited or unlimited. The vast majority of UK companies are limited companies. Of the 3.8 million companies in the UK, only 4,624 were unlimited.[154]

3.3.3.1 **Limited companies**

A company will be a limited company if 'the liability of its members is limited by its constitution'.[155] As companies have separate corporate personality, it follows that the members are normally not liable for the debts of the company. As Lord Cranworth stated:

> There is no doubt that the direct remedy of a creditor is solely against the incorporated company. He has no dealing with any individual shareholder, and if he is driven to bring any action to enforce any right he may have acquired, he must sue the company, and not any of the members of whom it is composed.[156]

This does not, however, mean that the members contribute nothing, as the law provides that the members are liable to contribute to the company. However, their liability to contribution is limited (hence limited liability), with the method of limitation depending primarily upon whether the company has a share capital or not:

- A limited company without a share capital is said to be 'limited by guarantee'[157] and the liability of the members is limited to the amount they have undertaken to contribute in

---

[150] Companies House, 'Companies Register Activity in the United Kingdom 2017–18' (Companies House 2018) Table C1.
[151] CA 2006, s 4(2).   [152] ibid s 9(2)(c).   [153] ibid s 4(2).
[154] Companies House, 'Companies Register Activity in the United Kingdom 2017–18' (Companies House 2018) Table C1.
[155] CA 2006, s 3(1).
[156] *Oakes v Turquand and Harding* (1867) LR 2 HL 325 (HL) 357.
[157] Before 22 December 1980, it was possible to create, or become, a company limited by guarantee with a share capital, but this is no longer the case (CA 2006, s 5(1)).

the event of its being wound up.[158] This amount will be stated in the statement of guarantee and, in practice, it is very small and is usually set at £1. This is because many companies limited by guarantee are not-for-profit companies or are engaged in some form of community-driven activity and so it is important to ensure that the members are not exposed to excessive liability upon liquidation.

The statement of guarantee is discussed at 3.2.3.4.

- A limited company with a share capital is said to be 'limited by shares', and the liability of its members will be limited to the amount that is unpaid on their shares.[159] This means that members who have fully paid for their shares prior to liquidation are generally not liable to contribute any more to the company upon its liquidation.[160] This is a notable difference between companies limited by guarantee and companies limited by shares—in the former, the member is only liable to contribute in the event of the company's liquidation, whereas in the latter, the unpaid amount remains a debt that the company can call on anytime and the members usually pay fully for their shares prior to liquidation. Accordingly, in most companies limited by shares, the members have nothing to contribute upon liquidation.

Companies limited by shares vastly outnumber companies limited by guarantee—at the end of 2017/18, there were just over 3.8 million companies on the register, of which only 147,266 were limited by guarantee.[161] Accordingly, this text will focus largely on companies limited by shares. The following example demonstrates this form of limited liability in action.

Eg **Limited liability by shares**

Jane Dragon decides to incorporate a company, Dragon Ltd. A month later, she decides to create a wholly-owned subsidiary called Dragon Supplies Ltd ('DS'). DS has an issued share capital of £100, consisting of 100 shares with a nominal value of £1 each. The terms of subscription state that shares may be (i) fully paid up immediately; or (ii) subscribers may pay half of their value now and remain liable for the remainder. Dragon Ltd chooses the second option and pays £50 for the 100 shares. A year later, before Dragon Ltd has fully paid for the shares, Jane decides to wind up DS Ltd following the disastrous launch of a new product that failed to live up to sales expectations and used up all the company's capital. The liquidator will be able to recover from Dragon Ltd the amount that has yet to be paid on the shares (£50). Had Dragon Ltd fully paid for the shares when first issued (as is usually the case in private companies), or subsequently paid the remainder prior to liquidation, the liquidator would not be able to recover any monies from Dragon Ltd.

Limited liability is one of the most important advantages of conducting business through a company. As one commentator stated '[t]he limited liability corporation is the greatest single discovery of modern times . . .. Even steam and electricity are far less important than the limited liability corporation, and they would be reduced to comparative impotence without it.'[162] Limited liability is essential in order to encourage investment, as people would be reluctant to invest in companies (especially those investing small amounts) if their personal assets were at risk. It is argued that limited liability minimizes

---

[158] ibid s 3(3); IA 1986, s 74(3).
[159] CA 2006, s 3(2).   [160] IA 1986, s 74(2)(d).
[161] Companies House, 'Companies Register Activity in the United Kingdom 2017–18' (Companies House 2018) Table C1.
[162] Quoted in S Bainbridge, 'Abolishing Veil Piercing' (2001) 26 J Corp L 479, 479.

or eliminates this risk.[163] However, other commentators disagree and instead argue that limited liability does not minimize member risk, but instead 'results in uncompensated risk being imposed on creditors who deal with the company'.[164] Consider the following example.

Eg   **Limited liability and risk**

Prior to DS's liquidation (see the previous example box), it borrowed £10,000 from Welsh Bank plc to be paid back in one year's time with an APR of 4.5 per cent. That money was invested in promoting and launching a new product that proved to be a commercial disaster, and left DS with no capital or assets. Accordingly, before the loan was paid back, Dragon Ltd decided to wind up DS. The member of DS (namely Dragon Ltd) is only liable for the amount unpaid on the shares (£50 in the example above), whereas Welsh Bank plc will likely receive very little of the monies owed to it.

Accordingly, it has been argued that limited liability shifts the risk of corporate failure from the members onto the creditors.[165] However, there are those who disagree with Prentice's assertion that this risk is uncompensated as, through the interest rate charged, '[v]oluntary creditors receive compensation in advance for the risk that the firm will be unable to meet its obligations'.[166] It should be noted that not all creditors occupy a strong enough bargaining position to insist upon a higher interest rate and smaller trade creditors may not be able to negotiate an interest rate that offsets the risk of non-payment. Some creditors (e.g. involuntary creditors, such as tort creditors) have no bargaining power at all.

3.3.3.2 **Unlimited companies**

As noted, only a tiny minority of companies are unlimited. The reason why there are so few unlimited companies is simple: in an unlimited company, the liability of its members is unlimited.[167] However, their liability is different to other persons whose liability is unlimited (e.g. the partners of a partnership). Sole proprietors and partners of an ordinary partnership can be sued directly by creditors of the sole proprietorship and partnership. As a company has separate personality, the creditors of an unlimited company cannot directly sue the members, but must instead sue the company. If the company's assets are insufficient to pay the creditors' claims, the creditors would be likely to seek to have the company wound up. The liquidator could then require the members to contribute to the debts of the company, and there is no limit on the amount that the liquidator can seek (subject to the maximum amount required to pay off the company's debts and the costs of liquidation).

The obvious question is why anyone would set up an unlimited company. Unlimited companies do not need to file their accounts with Companies House,[168] although they

---

[163] Henry Manne, 'Our Two Corporation Systems: Law and Economics' (1967) 53 Va L Rev 259, 259.

[164] DD Prentice, 'Corporate Personality, Limited Liability and the Protection of Creditors' in R Grantham and C Rickett (eds), *Corporate Personality in the Twentieth Century* (Hart 1998) 104.

[165] RA Posner, *Economic Analysis of Law* (4th edn, Little, Brown 1992) 394.

[166] Frank H Easterbrook and Daniel R Fischel, 'Limited Liability and the Corporation' (1985) 52 Univ Chicago LR 89, 105.

[167] CA 2006, s 3(4).   [168] ibid s 448(1).

will still need to furnish their members with copies of the accounts. A number of provisions in the CA 2006 only apply to limited companies, so unlimited companies will be exempt (e.g. the prohibition on a private company offering its shares to the public only applies to limited companies).[169] Accordingly, unlimited companies are subject to slightly fewer formalities and limitations and have more privacy than limited companies—but this is unlikely to be a fair trade-off for the loss of limited liability.

3.3.4 Specialized company types

The five company types noted in Figure 3.1 (see 3.3) are standard company types. There are also a few specialized company types.

3.3.4.1 Community interest companies

Community interest companies (CICs) were established as a vehicle for businesses that engage in social, charitable,[170] or community-driven activities.

Community interest companies

CICs engage in a wide range of community-driven activities. The following are some examples:

- Little Fish Theatre CIC puts on theatre productions that tackle social issues such as homophobia, drug use, street crime, and sexual rights.
- Warm Wales CIC helps people to gain access to improved heating and insulation, and to ensure homes have affordable warmth whilst reducing their carbon footprint.
- Blues and Beers CIC organizes an annual festival in Wallingford which brings live music to the town, and provides a showcase for local food and drink producers.
- Bookdonors CIC sells second-hand books on behalf of charities, libraries, and other organizations. A portion of the money raised is returned to the book suppliers, whilst the rest is used to provide training and employment to disabled persons and the long-term unemployed.

Any limited company can be formed as, or become, a CIC.[171] CICs are formed in the same manner as other registered companies, but once the registration documents have been submitted to Companies House, they will be sent to the Regulator of Community Interest Companies.[172] The Regulator will determine whether the proposed CIC meets the community interest test, namely whether a reasonable person might consider that the company's activities are being carried on for the benefit of the community.[173] If the Regulator is satisfied that this test has been satisfied, he will communicate this to Companies House, who will complete the registration process.[174] CICs are subject to the CA 2006, but are subject to additional limitations regarding distributions of assets.[175]

---

[169] ibid s 755(1).

[170] It should be noted that a CIC cannot be registered as a charity (Companies (Audit, Investigations and Community Enterprise) Act 2004, s 26(3)).

[171] CA 2006, s 6(1); Companies (Audit, Investigations and Community Enterprise) Act 2004, s 26(1).

[172] Companies (Audit, Investigations and Community Enterprise) Act 2004, s 36(3)(a).

[173] ibid s 35(2).   [174] ibid s 36A.

[175] Community Interest Company Regulations 2005, SI 2005/1788, regs 17–25.

CICs have not proven to be especially popular. By the end of 2017/18, there were only 14,254 CICs on the register.[176] However, the number of new CICs incorporated each year is steadily increasing—when CICs were first available in 2004/05, only 208 were created that year, whereas in 2017/18, 2,844 new CICs were incorporated.[177] Unfortunately, it is also the case that a notable number of CICs are dissolved each year, with 1,631 (11.4 per cent of the overall number) being dissolved in 2017/18.[178]

3.3.4.2 Overseas companies

In an increasingly globalized world, companies incorporated outside the UK may wish to engage in business within the UK. Such companies can, of course, simply incorporate a subsidiary in the UK, and many larger multinationals do this. However, it is not necessary to do so, and some companies may simply wish to establish a presence in the UK without formally incorporating here. If such companies are classified as 'overseas companies', then the CA 2006 (and accompanying subordinate legislation) imposes certain requirements upon them.

An overseas company is a company incorporated outside the UK.[179] Once such a company opens a 'branch' or 'establishment' in the UK, it must register certain particulars with Companies House.[180] The problem that arises is that the CA 2006 provides that a 'branch' means a branch within the meaning of the Eleventh Company Law Directive,[181] but that Directive does not define what a branch is, so reference must be made to EU case law on this issue. The particulars that must be registered include basic details regarding the overseas company (e.g. name, legal form, list of officers, etc.) and the UK establishment (e.g. address, date of opening, business carried on, etc.).[182] Failure to register the required particulars is a criminal offence.[183] As of March 2018, 11,941 overseas companies had registered particulars with Companies House.[184]

3.3.4.3 European companies

Mention should be made of two types of company under EU law, namely the *Societas Europeae* and the *Societas Unius Personae*. The idea of creating a Europe-wide company structure has been around since before the creation of the EU.[185] After decades of debate, the idea finally became a reality in 2001 with the passing of the Statute for a European Company.[186] When originally passed it was designed to facilitate cross-border mergers by, *inter alia*, allowing companies in different EU Member States to merge to form a new company called a *Societas Europeae* (SE). SEs are governed primarily by EU law,[187] rather

---

[176] Regulator of Community Interest Companies, 'Annual Report 2017–2018' (2018) 15.

[177] ibid.   [178] ibid.   [179] CA 2006, s 1044.

[180] CA 2006, s 1046; Overseas Companies Regulations 2009, SI 2009/1801, regs 3–11.

[181] CA 2006, s 1046(3). Regulation 2 of the Overseas Companies Regulations 2009 provides that the word 'establishment' has the same meaning.

[182] Overseas Companies Regulations 2009, regs 6 and 7. For more, see Companies House, 'Overseas Companies Registered in the UK' (Companies House 2015).

[183] CA 2006, s 1054.

[184] Companies House, 'Companies Register Activity in the United Kingdom 2017–18' (Companies House 2018) Table C1.

[185] For more, see Vanessa Edwards, 'The European Company—Essential Tool or Eviscerated Dream?' (2003) 40 CML Rev 443.

[186] Council Regulation 2157/2001/EC of 8 October 2001 on the Statute for a European Company (SE) [2001] OJ L294/1.

[187] Namely Council Regulation 2157/2001/EC and Council Directive 2001/86/EC.

than national law, but the relevant EU law is not exhaustive[188] and the 2001 Statute does regularly refer to national law. The result is that the law applicable to SEs is not uniform throughout the EU. As a result of this, and the fact that the right of establishment and the cross-border directive means that reliance on a SE is often not needed, the take-up of SEs has not been strong. As of December 2018, there are only 3,124 SEs established in the EU, of which 49 are based in the UK.[189]

In 2008, a proposal for a European Private Company Law Statute was published, in which it was noted that, although small and medium-sized enterprises (SMEs) accounted for 99 per cent of companies in the EU, only 8 per cent of them engaged in cross-border trade.[190] Accordingly, it was proposed that a European private company (*Societas Privata Europeae*) be created to facilitate SMEs that wished to engage in cross-border trade. Due to a lack of political agreement, the proposal was withdrawn in 2014, but shortly before its withdrawal, a new proposal was published for a single-member private company called the *Societas Unius Personae*.[191] However, the proposal was rejected by the European Economic and Social Committee,[192] and no progress has been made since.

3.4 Re-registration

A company may begin life in one form, but the needs of the business may necessitate or encourage a change in the company's status (e.g. a private company may grow and wish to re-register as public). Part 7 of the CA 2006 sets out the process for re-registration as a means of altering the company's status. It should be noted that whilst Pt 7 allows for most types of re-registration, there are some omissions—for example, there is no process for a company limited by guarantee to re-register as a company limited by shares.

The exact process for re-registration depends on the type of status being altered:

- The most common re-registration is for a private company to re-register as a public company (typically to enable the company to raise more capital by offering shares to the public). This is done by the private company passing a special resolution, delivering certain documents to Companies House (see Form RR01), and complying with certain conditions (e.g. the conditions placed upon public companies as to minimum share capital).[193]

- A public company may wish to re-register as private (e.g. to free up capital, or to reduce its regulatory burden) by passing a special resolution and delivering certain documents to Companies House.[194] Given that this form of re-registration may result in the company's shares being less transferable (as they can no longer be sold to the public or placed on a stock exchange), a process exists that allows the members to cancel the special resolution and prevent the re-registration.[195]

---

[188] For a more detailed discussion of the regulation of SEs, see Companies House, 'The European Company: Societas Europeae (SE)' (Companies House 2016), and http://ec.europa.eu/internal_market/company/societas-europaea/index_en.htm accessed 10 January 2019.

[189] Statistics derived from http://ecdb.worker-participation.eu accessed 10 January 2019.

[190] Proposal for a Council Regulation on the Statute for a European Private Company COM (2008) 396 final 2.

[191] Proposal for a Directive of the European Parliament and of the Council on Single Member Private Limited Liability Companies COM (2014) 212 final.

[192] Opinion of the European Economic and Social Committee on the Proposal for a Directive of the European Parliament and of the Council on Single Member Private Limited Liability Companies (2014).

[193] CA 2006, s 90.   [194] ibid s 97 (see Form RR02).   [195] ibid s 98.

- A private limited company can re-register as unlimited if all the members of the company assent to the re-registration, and if certain documents are delivered to Companies House.[196] Note that a company that was unlimited and then re-registered as limited cannot subsequently re-register back as an unlimited company.[197]

- An unlimited private company can re-register as a limited company by passing a special resolution and delivering certain documents to Companies House.[198] Note that a company that was previously limited and then re-registered as unlimited cannot subsequently re-register back as a limited company.[199]

- A public company can re-register as an unlimited private company with a share capital if all the members of the company assent to the re-registration, and if certain documents are delivered to Companies House.[200] Note that the re-registration will not be permitted if the company has previous re-registered as limited or unlimited.[201]

Where relevant, the company may be required to change its name and articles so as to comply with the requirements of its new status (e.g. change its designation from 'Ltd' to 'plc', or change the applicable model articles). In all cases, a re-registration fee is payable[202] and a new certificate of incorporation will be issued upon re-registration.[203]

CHAPTER SUMMARY

- The process of creating a company is known as 'incorporation'.

- A company can be incorporated by (i) royal charter; (ii) Act of Parliament; (iii) delegated authority; or (iv) registration.

- The vast majority of companies are incorporated by registration, which involves registering specified documents with the registrar of Companies House.

- The information required in the application for registration includes the company's proposed name, its registered office, a statement of capital or guarantee, a statement of the company's proposed officers, and a statement identifying the company type and business activities.

- A promoter who enters into a contract on behalf of a company not yet incorporated will be bound by that contract (as will the other party), but the company will not usually be bound.

- Public companies are so called because they can offer to sell their shares to the public at large and can trade them on a stock exchange. Private companies cannot sell their shares to the public or trade them on a stock exchange.

- Public companies must be limited and must have a share capital. Private companies can be limited or unlimited, and may or may not have a share capital (most are limited and do have a share capital).

- Companies can change their status (e.g. from private to public) by a process called re-registration.

---

[196] ibid s 102(1) (see Form RR05). [197] ibid s 102(2). [198] ibid s 105(1) (see Form RR06).
[199] ibid s 105(2). [200] ibid s 109(1) (see Form RR07). [201] ibid s 109(2).
[202] Registrar of Companies (Fees) (Companies, Overseas Companies and Limited Liability Partnerships) Regulations 2012, Sch 1, para 8.
[203] CA 2006, ss 96, 101, 104, 107, and 111.

FURTHER READING

Frank H Easterbook and Daniel R Fischel, 'Limited Liability and the Corporation' (1985) 52 Univ Chicago LR 89.
* Provides an excellent, detailed discussion of the rationale for limited liability, and the effect limited liability has upon various types of creditors.

Robert R Pennington, 'The Validation of Pre-Incorporation Contracts' (2002) 23 Co Law 284.
* Compares the common law and statutory rules regarding pre-incorporation contracts.

www.gov.uk/government/organisations/companies-house/about/statistics accessed 10 January 2019.
* Companies House statistics webpage. Provides a range of statistics relating to company incorporations and the number and type of companies incorporated in the UK.

www.gov.uk/government/collections/companies-house-guidance-for-limited-companies-partnerships-and-other-company-types accessed 10 January 2019.
* Companies House provides a range of guidance documents on issues discussed in this chapter and other chapters in the book.

www.gov.uk/government/uploads/system/uploads/attachment_data/file/534915/IN01_V7.pdf accessed 10 January 2019.
* This webpage links to Form IN01, the application form that must be completed to incorporate a company by registration.

SELF-TEST QUESTIONS

1. Define the following terms:
* unregistered company;
* royal charter;
* trading certificate;
* off-the-shelf company;
* market capitalization;
* overseas company.

2. State whether each of the following statements is true or false and, if false, explain why:
* The CA 2006 only generally applies to registered companies.
* The application to register a company must be submitted electronically.
* A company cannot be bound by a contract entered into before it was incorporated.
* A public company must be limited and must have a share capital.
* A listed company is also a quoted company.
* The largest 250 companies, in terms of market capitalization, are known as the FTSE 250.
* A company limited by guarantee cannot re-register as a company limited by shares.

3. 'The process for incorporating a company is complex, expensive, and is not designed to be accessible for laypersons'. Do you agree with this quote? Provide reasons for your answer.

4. Before Jane decides to incorporate her business, she seeks your advice regarding the following:
* She wants to know the advantages and disadvantages of conducting business through a company, as opposed to conducting business through a partnership.
* If she did decide to incorporate, she wants to know whether creating a company is a simple and inexpensive process.

- She is unsure as to what type of company to create and seeks your advice on this. She has told you that she wishes to retain control of the company, but she is open to selling shares to others to raise capital in order to fund her expansion plan for the business (although she feels she will probably need to borrow capital too). Given her lack of experience of running a company, she is also keen to keep the administrative requirements placed upon the company to a minimum.

Advise Jane on the above matters.

 ONLINE RESOURCES

This book is accompanied by online resources to better support you in your studies. Visit www.oup.com/uk/roach-company/ for:

- answers to the self-test questions;
- further reading lists;
- multiple-choice questions;
- glossary.

Updates to the law can be found on the author's Twitter account (@UKCompanyLaw) and further resources can be found on the author's blog (www.companylawandgovernance.com).

4 Corporate personality

INTRODUCTION

The doctrine of corporate personality has been described as 'one of the cornerstones of modern company law'[1] and 'the outstanding legal characteristic that currently distinguishes the company from most other forms of business organisation.'[2] At its most basic level, the doctrine of corporate personality simply provides that the company is a person. As such, it is able to do many things that humans are able to do, including own property, enter into contracts, and be subject to legal rights, duties, and obligations. However, the artificial nature of corporate personality, and the fact that it can be abused, means that a significant body of law has developed in this area. Before looking at the law relating to corporate personality, it is important to briefly discuss some of the terminology that is often used in this area.

4.1 A note on terminology

Throughout the course of this chapter (and indeed this text), certain terminology will be used in relation to a company's corporate personality. Accordingly, it is worth briefly explaining the use of this terminology at this point.

4.1.1 The veil of incorporation, and piercing the veil

The law in this area abounds with metaphors, of which the principal metaphor is the 'veil of incorporation' (or the 'corporate veil'), which is used by commentators, lawyers,

---

[1] Paddy Ireland, 'The Conceptual Foundations of Modern Company Law' (1987) J L & Soc 149, 149.
[2] Geoffrey Morse, *Palmer's Company Law* (Sweet & Maxwell 2018) para 1.002. The word 'most' is used because certain other business organizations, notably limited liability partnerships, also have corporate personality.

and judges to refer to corporate personality. Upon the company's incorporation, a veil is created which generally shields those behind it (notably the directors and members) from liability, as the following example demonstrates.

Eg   The corporate veil

In January 2018, Dragon plc incorporates a new wholly-owned subsidiary, namely Dragon Research Ltd ('DR'). This company is set up to engage in market research and will be funded by selling its research findings to various parties, including Dragon plc. To fund its start-up costs, it borrows £100,000 from Welsh Bank plc, with repayment due within a year. However, the company finds it difficult to attract employees with the requisite research and technical skills and, as a result, it is not able to engage in any commercially viable research in its first year. Come January 2019, SR has only paid back £30,000 to Welsh Bank, and so Welsh Bank obtains a court order winding up DR. DR's corporate personality means that it is liable for its debts and liabilities, not DR's members (namely Dragon plc) or its directors. Accordingly, Welsh Bank can usually only seek payment from DR and not Dragon plc or DR's directors.

As is discussed at 4.5, there are times when the law sets aside a company's separate personality, and this is often referred to as 'piercing' or 'lifting' the veil. However, these terms have often been used, rather confusingly, to refer to different things. Indeed, the use of such unclear expressions has been criticized on the ground that it can 'risk causing confusion and uncertainty in the law'.[3] Accordingly, in this chapter, setting aside a company's corporate personality will be referred to as 'disregarding' corporate personality, except where a quote still refers to 'piercing' or 'lifting' the veil.

4.1.2 **Individuals and persons**

Statute and case law regularly refer to 'individuals' and 'persons' and it is important to understand the distinction between them. In an Act of Parliament, unless a contrary intention appears,[4] then the word 'person' includes a body of persons corporate or unincorporated.[5] In other words, the word 'person' includes both natural persons and bodies corporate (such as companies and limited liability partnerships (LLPs)). Conversely, the word 'individual' refers to natural persons only. The offence of insider dealing provides a good example of the practical significance of this distinction.

Individuals and persons

Section 52(2)(a) of the Criminal Justice Act 1993 provides that an *individual* who has information as an insider will be guilty of insider dealing if he encourages another *person* to deal in price-affected securities, irrespective of whether that *person* knew they were price affected (italics added). From this, it follows that a company cannot be guilty of insider dealing under s 52(2)(a), but it does not matter whether the person encouraged to deal was a natural person or a company.

---

[3] *VTB Capital plc v Nutritek International Corp* [2013] UKSC 5, [2013] 2 WLR 398 [124](Lord Neuberger).
[4] A good example of such a contrary intention is s 156A of the Companies Act 2006 (CA 2006) (which, at the time of writing, is not in force), which provides that a director must be a natural person, even though s 250 states that the word 'director' includes any *person* occupying the position of director, by whatever name called.
[5] Interpretation Act 1987, s 5 and Sch 1, para 1.

In this text, the word 'individual' will be used to refer to a natural person only, and the word 'person' will be used to refer to both natural persons and bodies corporate, unless otherwise stated.

4.1.3 Legal and natural persons

It is also important to distinguish between natural persons (i.e. human beings) and legal persons (e.g. companies, LLPs). However, the accuracy of this distinction depends upon how the phrase 'legal person' is defined. If the phrase 'legal person' is defined as 'a person created by the law', then clearly the distinction is valid, as a company would be such a person and a human would not. However, if one defines a 'legal person' as 'a person who enjoys, and is subject to, rights and duties at law',[6] then the distinction falls apart as both humans and companies are legal persons. In this text, in order to avoid this confusion, the phrase 'legal person' will be avoided. Instead, when distinguishing the different types of person, humans will be referred to as 'natural persons', and companies will be referred to as 'bodies corporate' (as this is the term used in statute to describe the corporate entity).

4.2 The company as a person

Unincorporated business structures consist of either an individual (in the case of a sole proprietorship) or a group of persons (in the case of a partnership), whereas a 'corporation is not a mere aggregate of shareholders',[7] but is instead regarded by the law as a person in itself. This person is referred to in the CA 2006 as a 'body corporate' and it comes into existence upon the company's registration.[8] This person does not have a physical existence, but is simply a legal creation or, as Lord Selbourne stated, 'a mere abstraction of law'.[9] Accordingly, it is often referred to as a 'legal' or 'juridical' person (although, as noted at 4.1.3, there are problems with this label).

The specific consequences of corporate personality are discussed in more detail at 4.3, but it is worth noting here that the broad consequence of corporate personality is that it creates a separation between the interests, rights, property, and liabilities of the company, and the interests, rights, property, and liabilities of others. As Lord Sumner stated:

> Between the investor, who participates as a shareholder, and the undertaking carried on, the law interposes another person, real though artificial, the company itself, and the business carried on is the business of that company, and the capital employed is its capital and not in either case the business or the capital of the shareholders.[10]

The interposing of corporate personality has numerous consequences, many of which are commercially beneficial. However, it is also possible to interpose a company for nefarious purposes (e.g. to avoid a legal obligation, as in *Gilford*, discussed at 4.5.1.1) and both statute and the courts are empowered to set aside corporate personality and remove the separation that exists between the company and other persons.

---

[6] Mick Woodley, *Osborn's Concise Law Dictionary* (12th edn, Swett & Maxwell 2013) 254.

[7] *Re Exchange Banking Co* (1882) 21 ChD 519 (CA) 536 (Cotton LJ).

[8] CA 2006, s 16(1) and (2). Unregistered companies also have corporate personality.

[9] *Great Eastern Railway Co v Turner* (1873) LR 8 Ch App 149, 152.

[10] *Gas Lighting Improvement Co Ltd v Commissioners of Inland Revenue* [1923] AC 723 (HL) 741.

As persons, companies can do many of the things that natural persons can do, but a company has no physical existence. In that sense, 'a corporation is an artificial being, invisible, intangible, and existing only in operation of law'.[11] The artificial nature of the company means that certain laws must be modified to apply to companies, or cannot apply to companies at all.

The company as a legal person

As the company is not a natural person, it follows that certain rights, statuses, and punishments that can only apply to natural persons cannot apply to companies, such as:

- A company cannot undertake certain roles that require performance from a natural person, such as a television entertainer or author.[12]
- Certain rights that protect natural persons may not be applicable to companies (e.g. the right to freedom from torture under Art 3 of the ECHR).
- A company may not be found guilty of certain criminal acts that only a natural person can undertake (e.g. a company cannot be convicted of certain driving offences, as, currently, only natural persons can drive).[13]
- As a company cannot be imprisoned, a company cannot be convicted of an offence for which the only punishment is imprisonment (e.g. murder).[14]

Before looking in detail at the consequences of corporate personality, it would help to briefly discuss the history of corporate personality, as this will help to better understand the seminal case in this area, namely *Salomon*.

4.2.1 A brief history of corporate personality

The concept of separate personality has existed for over 750 years. It is widely regarded that the concept of the *persona ficta* ('fictitious person') was devised in the mid-thirteenth century by Pope Innocent IV in order to grant separate personality to certain ecclesiastical bodies.[15] In terms of company law, corporate personality was bestowed upon chartered companies and companies incorporated by Act of Parliament. However, as discussed at 3.2, for most business persons, neither of these methods of incorporation was accessible or practical.

Accordingly, businesses sought to mimic the corporate form by creating partnerships that had many of the features of a company, of which the notable example was the deed-of-settlement company (more commonly referred to as a 'joint-stock company'). A deed-of-settlement company was actually a partnership created under a deed, with the deed providing that persons would hold transferable shares in the firm's capital and that management would be undertaken by a core group of persons, usually known as a committee of directors. Whilst deed-of-settlement companies resembled companies, they suffered from three notable problems:

---

[11] *Trustees of Dartmouth College v Woodward* (1819) 17 US (4 Wheat) 518, 636 (Marshall CJ).

[12] *Newstead (Inspector of Taxes) v Frost* [1980] 1 WLR 135 (HL) 139 (Viscount Dilhorne).

[13] *Richmond Upon Thames LBC v Pinn & Wheeler* [1989] RTR 354 (DC). With the advent of driverless cars, it will be interesting to see if/how this principle evolves.   [14] *R v ICR Haulage* [1944] KB 551.

[15] For more, see Maximilian Koessler, 'The Person in Imagination or Persona Ficta of the Corporation' (1949) 9 La L Rev 435.

1. the law never regarded them as anything more than a specialized form of partnership, to whom partnership law applied;

2. they often had hundreds or thousands of members, and partnership law, being based on a personal relationship between the partners, was not designed to regulate such entities, and;

3. deed-of-settlement companies did not have corporate personality.

It soon became clear that deed-of-settlement companies were an unsuitable alternative to the company and could not be effectively regulated by partnership law. The answer to this problem was to provide for deed-of-settlement companies to acquire formal company status. This was achieved via the passing of the Joint Stock Companies Act 1844, which allowed for the creation of companies by registration, with such companies having corporate personality. Corporate personality became much more readily available,[16] although notably limitations were put in place that still placed corporate personality outside the range of many businesses (notably the 25-member minimum, and the burdensome requirement for provisional registration).[17] Fortunately, the Joint Stock Companies Act 1856 did away with provisional registration and reduced the minimum number of members to seven. As time passed, these barriers were further reduced and today, creating a company with corporate personality can be a quick and inexpensive affair, and modern companies only require at least one member. As a result of this, the company has become the dominant business structure,[18] and so the majority of businesses in the UK enjoy corporate personality.

The process of incorporating a company by registration is discussed at 3.2.

However, it has been argued that the availability of incorporation by registration 'seemed to have relatively little impact'[19] and that 'the courts were still invoking partnership principles to resolve company law problems'.[20] Essentially, all that the 1844 Act did was to permit deed-of-settlement companies to acquire corporate personality. It was only with the case of *Salomon* that the courts took this to its logical conclusion and fully appreciated the true significance of corporate personality.

4.2.2 The case of *Salomon*

The case of *Salomon v A Salomon & Co Ltd* is regarded by many as an 'unyielding rock'[21] and 'probably the most famous case in company law'.[22] In a 2015 poll by the Incorporated Council of Law Reporting, *Salomon* was voted as the most significant case between 1865 and 1914, and one of the top 15 most significant cases since 1865.[23]

As discussed above, whilst the concept of corporate personality existed long before *Salomon* (it is common for students to mistakenly believe that *Salomon* established the concept), it was only with the House of Lords' judgment in *Salomon* that the courts finally grasped the full significance of what corporate personality entails.

---

[16] The 1844 Act sought to force larger deed-of-settlement companies to incorporate by registration by prohibiting partnerships from having large numbers of partners.

[17] It is also worth noting that companies incorporated by registration could not offer limited liability until the passing of the Limited Liability Act 1855.   [18] As noted at 1.3, 71.4 per cent of businesses are companies.

[19] Ross Grantham, 'The Doctrinal Basis of the Rights of Company Shareholders' (1998) 57 CLJ 554, 559.

[20] ibid. Indeed, the principal company law text of the day was Lindley, *Treatise on the Law of Partnership, Including its Application to Companies* (Sweet & Maxwell 1860).

[21] Lord Templeman, 'Forty Years On' (1990) 11 Co Law 10, 10.

[22] Derek French, Stephen Mayson, and Christopher Ryan, *Mayson, French & Ryan on Company Law* (33rd edn, OUP 2016) 127.

[23] See https://www.iclr.co.uk/news-and-events/150-years-of-case-law-on-trial accessed 10 January 2019.

Salomon v A Salomon & Co Ltd [1897] AC 22 (HL)

FACTS: Salomon was a sole trader engaged in the business of bootmaking. He decided to incorporate the business and, to that end, he created a company and sold the bootmaking business to this newly-created company in return for £39,000. This payment came via (i) 20,000 £1 shares; (ii) £10,000 worth of debentures, secured by a floating charge over all of the assets of the company; and (iii) the balance in cash. Legislation at the time[24] required that a company have a minimum of seven members. Accordingly, the company's 20,007 shares were divided up, with Salomon holding 20,001[25] shares, and his wife and five children each holding one share. Shortly thereafter, the business failed and went into liquidation. The company owed money to several creditors, including Salomon himself (the £10,000 in debentures). As Salomon had secured his loan (via a floating charge), he enforced this and claimed the £10,000 that he was owed. Unfortunately, this meant that there were no more assets to pay the other creditors (whose debts were unsecured). The liquidator, arguing on behalf of the other creditors, stated that, instead of taking money from the company, Salomon should be personally liable for its debts.

At first instance, Vaughan Williams J held that the company was Salomon's agent and that he was therefore liable for its debts. Salomon appealed, but the Court of Appeal[26] dismissed his appeal, with Lopes LJ stating that '[t]he Act contemplated the incorporation of seven independent bona fide members, who had a mind and a will of their own, and were not the mere puppets of an individual who, adopting the machinery of the Act, carried on his old business in the same way as before, when he was a sole trader'.[27] Lindley LJ agreed, stating that, by appointing six 'dummy' shareholders, the company was formed 'contrary to the true intent and meaning of the Companies Act 1862'[28] and was therefore a 'sham'[29] and 'a device to defraud creditors'.[30] The Court held that the company acted as a trustee for Salomon and he should be liable for its debts. Salomon appealed to the House of Lords.

HELD: The appeal was allowed. As regards the first-instance decision branding the company as Salomon's agent, Lord Herschell stated:

> a company may in every sense be said to carry on business for and on behalf of its shareholders; but this certainly does not in point of law constitute the relation of principal and agent between them or render the shareholders liable to indemnify the company against debts which it incurs.[31]

As regards the Court of Appeal decision, the House of Lords adopted a much more literal approach to interpreting the CA 1862. Lord Macnaghten stated '[t]here is nothing in the Act requiring that the subscribers to the memorandum should be independent or unconnected, or that they or any one of them should take a substantial interest in the undertaking, or that they should have a mind and will of their own . . .'.[32] The fact that the company was effectively controlled by one person was not a reason to ignore the company's separate personality. Again, quoting Lord Macnaghten '[t]he company attains maturity on its birth. There is no period of minority—no interval of incapacity. I cannot understand how a body corporate thus made "capable" by statute can lose its individuality by issuing the bulk of its capital to one person . . .'.[33] Accordingly, Salomon had complied fully with the requirements for incorporation and therefore the company was liable for its debts, and not Salomon himself.

---

[24] Companies Act 1862, s 6 (now repealed).
[25] The 20,000 £1 shares plus the one share to which he subscribed when he registered the company.
[26] [1895] 2 Ch 323 (CA).   [27] ibid 341.   [28] ibid 340.   [29] ibid 339.
[30] ibid.   [31] [1897] AC 22 (HL) 43.   [32] ibid 50–1.   [33] ibid 51.

Salomon is regarded by many as the most important case in company law, for three reasons:

1. The House clearly stated that a validly incorporated company could legitimately be used to shield its members from liability (although this had been recognized previously)[34] or, as Palmer put it, it helped facilitate business persons (especially small traders) to 'escape the tyranny of unlimited liability'.[35]

2. It implicitly recognized the validity of the 'one-person company' (that is, a company run only by one person, with a number of dormant nominee shareholders) almost a century before it was possible to formally create a one-person company in 1992.

3. It recognized the fact that a person holding shares in a company (even all of the shares) is not enough to establish a relationship of agency or trusteeship.

Salomon represented 'a fundamental paradigm shift'[36] in that it moved the registered company away from being viewed as akin to a partnership, and instead viewed it like a chartered company or company created by Act of Parliament. This 'radically reformulated the corporate concept',[37] but led to criticism that it inappropriately opened up access to corporate personality. Famously, the House of Lords decision in *Salomon* was branded as 'calamitous'[38] by Kahn-Freund who argued that the rigid approach in *Salomon* combined with the ease with which companies can be registered, resulted in businesses that would usually operate through partnerships instead operating through companies. This in itself would not be an issue if company law adequately protected creditors, but Kahn-Freund felt this was not the case and that creditors were 'exposed to grave injury owing to the timidity of the Courts and of the Companies Act'.[39] Accordingly, as a result of *Salomon*, he felt that the company became 'a means of evading liabilities and concealing the real interests behind the business'.[40] It is certainly true that corporate personality can be abused and it has been described as an ideal vehicle for fraud. However, both statute and the courts can set aside a company's corporate personality in certain cases. Before this can be discussed, it is important to discuss the consequences of corporate personality.

4.3 Consequences of corporate personality

Having discussed the fact of corporate personality, it is important to understand the consequences of a company having corporate personality. Some of the most notable consequences were discussed when *Salomon* was examined. Here, a range of other consequences are set out. It is worth noting that the consequences of corporate personality set out in *Salomon* largely benefitted the company and, whilst many consequences are beneficial, it is also possible for corporate personality to work against a company (e.g. by rendering the company liable for breaches of the law).

In many ways, a company can do many of the things, and has many of the same rights, as a natural person. However, because it is not natural and has 'no soul to be saved and

---

[34] See *Re Baglan Hall Colliery Co* (1870) LR 5 Ch App 346, 356, where Giffard LJ said that the ability 'to form a limited company, in order to avoid incurring further personal liability . . . was the policy of the Companies Act . . .'

[35] Francis B Palmer, *Private Companies: Their Formation and Advantages and the Model of Converting a Business into a Private Company* (11th edn, Stevens 1901) 6.

[36] Ross Grantham, 'The Doctrinal Basis of the Rights of Company Shareholders' (1998) 57 CLJ 554, 561.

[37] ibid.   [38] O Kahn-Freund, 'Some Reflections on Company Law Reform' (1944) 7 MLR 54, 55.

[39] ibid.   [40] ibid.

no body to be kicked',[41] it follows that the law does treat companies differently to natural persons in some respects. An example of this lies in relation to a company's nationality.

4.3.1 **Nationality, domicile, and residence**

Just like a natural person, a company has a nationality. The country where a company is registered determines its nationality[42] and where it is domiciled.[43] However, unlike a natural person, a company cannot change its nationality or domicile, nor can it have dual nationality or domicile.[44] What can be changed is a company's residence and, just like a natural person, a company may have multiple residences simultaneously, and may reside in a country different to its nationality. Determining a company's residence is more difficult than determining its nationality or domicile, as it is based on where a company 'really keeps house and does business',[45] with business being carried out 'where the central management and control actually abides'.[46] Thus, a company that was registered in the UK, but was managed and controlled from Cairo, was resident in Egypt.[47] In practice, a company's residence is only important in terms of determining its tax liabilities.

4.3.2 **Perpetual succession**

As the company is not a natural person, it is not subject to the physical weaknesses that natural persons endure and so companies can be effectively immortal.

Long-living companies

The oldest existing registered company in the UK is unclear. Many believe that it is the Marine and General Mutual Life Assurance Society which, it has been argued, was registered in 1852 and has the registered number 00000006. However, Companies House records indicate the company was actually incorporated in 1862 and that the oldest existing company appears to be Ashford Cattle Market Co Ltd, which was incorporated in 1856, but its registered number is 00000118.

The vast majority of companies do not exist anywhere near this length of time— the average age of companies on the register of companies is 8.4 years.[48] The important point to note is that members, directors, and employees may come and go, but the company can continue (this can be contrasted with a partnership, which may be dissolved upon the death of a partner), and this is referred to as 'perpetual succession'.[49] In one notable Australian case, a company was able to survive the death of all its members[50] and a private company's ability to continue following the death of all of its members is provided for under art 17(2) of the model articles for private companies.

---

[41] *Stepney Corporation v Osofsky* [1937] 3 All ER 289 (CA) 291 (Greer LJ).

[42] *Janson v Driefontein Consolidated Mines Ltd* [1902] AC 484 (HL).

[43] *Gasque v Inland Revenue Commissioners* [1940] 2 KB 80 (KB).

[44] Compare this to SEs, which can change domiciles amongst EU Member States whenever they wish.

[45] *De Beers Consolidated Mines Ltd v Howe* [1906] AC 455 (HL) 458 (Lord Loreburn LC).   [46] ibid.

[47] *Egyptian Delta Land and Investment Co Ltd v Todd* [1929] AC 1 (HL).

[48] Companies House, 'Companies Register Activity in the United Kingdom 2015/16' (Companies House 2016) Table A9.

[49] *Trustees of Dartmouth College v Woodward* (1819) 17 US 4 Wheat) 518, 636 (Marshall CJ).

[50] *Re Noel Tedman Holdings Pty Ltd* [1967] Qd R 561.

4.3.3 **Contractual capacity**

The company, as a person, has capacity to enter into contracts (in largely the same way as a natural person can) with those outside and within the company, as the following case demonstrates.

 The extent of a company's contractual capacity is discussed at 6.2.

Lee v Lee's Air Farming Ltd [1961] AC 12 (PC)

FACTS: Lee was employed as a pilot by a company in which he held 2,999 shares (out of a total of 3,000) and of which Lee was the only director. Whilst engaged on company business, his plane crashed and he was killed. His widow sought compensation for his death from the company which, under the relevant legislation, was payable to the widows of deceased employees. The company's insurers argued that Lee was not an employee of the company, on the basis that he was synonymous with the company and the contract of employment had been made with himself (which is not permissible, since an agreement requires two parties).

HELD: Lee's widow was entitled to compensation. Lee had not made a contract with himself; rather, he had made a contract with the company, which was a separate entity. The fact that he owned virtually all of the shares and was the only director did not change the fact that the company was the employer and he was its employee.

COMMENT: This was a Privy Council case involving a New Zealand company, but the principle in *Lee* was affirmed by the Court of Appeal in *Secretary of State for Business, Enterprise and Regulatory Reform v Neufeld*.[51] However, in that case, the Court did acknowledge the possibility that a contract of employment between a company and a director/shareholder might be a sham, in which case, the contract would not be regarded as valid (although this was not the case in *Neufeld*).

4.3.4 **Ownership of assets**

A company is capable of owning property. A consequence of this is that the company's property 'belongs beneficially to the company itself and in no sense belongs, either in law or in equity, to the shareholders, who have no interest of any nature, whether proprietary or otherwise, in its assets'.[52] This allows for a clear delineation between the property of the company and the property of other persons (notably members), as the following case demonstrates.

Macaura v Northern Assurance Co Ltd [1925] AC 619 (HL)

FACTS: Macaura owned a timber yard. He set up a company, Irish Canadian Sawmills Ltd ('ICS'), and transferred all of the timber to this new company, in return for which he obtained 42,000 fully paid-up shares in ICS. He then took out an insurance policy, in his own name, with Northern Assurance Co Ltd ('NA') against loss caused to the timber by fire. A fortnight later, the timber was destroyed in a fire and NA refused to pay out. Macaura sued.

HELD: Macaura's claim failed. In order to claim successfully, the insured party must have an insurable interest in the property in question. Macaura had no such interest, because the property did not belong to him; it belonged to ICS.

---

[51] [2009] EWCA Civ 280, [2009] BCC 687.

[52] *Prest v Prest* [2012] EWCA Civ 1395, [2013] 2 WLR 557 [101] (Rimer LJ).

It is important to be able to determine which property belongs to the company because any capital borrowed by the company will likely be secured against the company's assets, not the assets of the members/directors. If the company then fails to repay the loan, the creditors can bring claims against the assets of the company, but cannot generally claim against the assets of the members/directors. Similarly, a freezing injunction brought against a director of a company will not apply to the assets of that company.[53]

4.3.5 **A company cannot be owned**

It is common to hear certain persons (usually majority shareholders) described as 'the owners of a company', but this is actually incorrect. A person may own a majority or all the shares in a company (and may even be the only director), but that does not mean that he owns the company itself—all it means is that he owns his shares. The company itself cannot be owned because persons cannot be owned.

4.3.6 **The company's business**

Whatever business is being undertaken by the company is the company's business, and not that of its members. As Lord Sumner stated 'the business carried on is the business of the company . . .. the idea that [the company] is mere machinery for effecting the purposes of the shareholders is a layman's fallacy.'[54] The following case demonstrates this.

 Cristina v Seear [1985] 2 EGLR 128 (CA)

FACTS: Mr and Mrs Cristina ('the Cristinas') were tenants of a property, out of which they ran a company in which they owned all the shares. When the tenancy expired, the landlord sought to terminate the tenancy, but the Cristinas sought to rely on legislation which provided security of tenure to tenants 'where the property comprised in the tenancy is or includes premises which are occupied by the tenant and are so occupied for the purposes of a business carried on by him'.[55]

HELD: The business was carried on by the company, and not the Cristinas. Accordingly, the premises were not occupied for the purposes of a business carried on by the tenants (i.e. the Cristinas), and so the legislation in question did not apply.

4.3.7 **Commencing and defending legal proceedings**

Determining who can sue in cases involving unincorporated businesses (especially partnerships) has historically proven to be an extremely troublesome issue. No such problems exist in relation to companies, because it is clear that where a company is wronged, the company, as an entity, is able to sue (and, as a consequence, the members generally cannot sue on its behalf). Thus, when a member falsely claimed that the company was insolvent and dishonestly carrying on business, the company was able to successfully sue that member for libel.[56]

---

[53] *Group Seven Ltd v Allied Investment Corporation Ltd* [2013] EWHC 1509 (Ch), [2014] 1 WLR 735.
[54] *Gas Lighting Improvement Co Ltd v Commissioners of Inland Revenue* [1923] AC 723 (HL) 741.
[55] Landlord and Tenant Act 1954, s 23(1).
[56] *Metropolitan Saloon Omnibus Co Ltd v Hawkins* (1859) 4 Hurl & N 87.

Where the company commits a wrong, the company can be sued for a civil wrong (e.g. negligence, breach of contract), and can also be found guilty of a criminal offence. As the company can only act through human actors, complex rules have developed regarding how the actions of certain persons (e.g. directors, manager, employees) can be attributed to the company.

The rules regarding the liability of a company are discussed at 6.5.

4.3.8 Capacity to create, and participate in, other business structures

Being a person, a company is generally free to form other business structures. A company can incorporate another company[57] or LLP,[58] or form a partnership with other persons. However, a company cannot be a sole proprietor.

A company can also participate in other businesses. For example, a company can be a member of another company,[59] or it can act as another company's company secretary. A company can, at the time of writing, act as a director of another company, but when s 156A of the CA 2006 comes into force, corporate directors will be generally prohibited (subject to some—as of yet unspecified—exceptions). In some cases, a company is prohibited from participating in some forms of business (e.g. a company cannot act as an insolvency practitioner).[60]

4.3.9 'Human' rights

The title of the European Convention on Human Rights (ECHR) would seem to indicate that the protection it affords is limited to natural persons, thereby excluding bodies corporate such as companies.[61] However, this is not the case and, unlike other human rights regimes,[62] certain rights embodied in the ECHR can also apply to bodies corporate. The ECHR may state this overtly, as is the case with Art 1 of the First Protocol, which states '[e]very natural or legal person is entitled to the peaceful enjoyment of his possessions'. Other provisions do not expressly include companies, but state that the protection is afforded to 'everyone'. Article 34, which identifies which parties can petition the European Court of Human Rights (ECtHR), provides that '[t]he Court may receive applications from any person, non-governmental organisation or group of individuals claiming to be the victim of a violation . . . of the rights set forth in the Convention or the protocols thereto'. For the purposes of Art 34, a company qualifies as a non-governmental organization[63] and therefore can petition the ECtHR.

Not all of the rights contained in the ECHR will apply to companies. For example, Art 3 (which prohibits torture) clearly cannot apply to a company. In practice, human rights cases involving companies tend to concentrate around a few key provisions of the

---

[57] CA 2006, s 7(1) refers to the ability of 'one or more persons' to form a company.

[58] LLPA 2000, s 2(1) refers to 'two or more persons' subscribing their names on the incorporation document.

[59] Although a subsidiary cannot generally be a member of its own holding company (CA 2006, s 136(1).

[60] Insolvency Act 1986 (IA 1986), s 390(1).

[61] For more on the human rights of companies, see Marius Emberland, *The Human Rights of Companies: Exploring the Structure of ECHR Protection* (OUP 2006).

[62] The United Nations' International Bill of Human Rights applies only to natural persons, as does the US Convention on Human Rights.

[63] *Verein 'Kontakt-Information-Therapie' (KIT) and Hagen v Austria* (1988) 57 DR 81. Companies would qualify as persons, were it not for the fact that the authentic French text of Art 34 refers to a *personne physique* ('physical person').

ECHR, namely Art 6 (the right to a fair trial), Art 10 (freedom of expression), and Art 1 of the First Protocol (peaceful enjoyment of property). The following case, the first ECtHR case involving a corporate applicant, demonstrates how a company's 'human' rights can be protected.

Sunday Times v UK (1980) 2 EHRR 245

FACTS: In the wake of the Thalidomide tragedy, parents of those children born with defects due to the drug issued legal proceedings against Distillers Company (Biochemicals) Ltd ('Distillers', the company that manufactured and marketed the drug). Whilst these proceedings were ongoing, *The Sunday Times* stated that it was to publish an article looking at how the tragedy occurred. The Attorney General applied for an injunction restraining the publication of the article, which was granted on the ground that it would constitute contempt of court. *The Sunday Times* filed an application in the ECtHR, claiming that the injunction interfered with its right to freedom of expression, as protected under Art 10 of the ECHR.

HELD: The ECtHR held that, whilst Art 10(2) permitted restrictions on freedom of expression 'as are prescribed by law and are necessary in a democratic society . . . for maintaining the authority and impartiality of the judiciary', the restriction of publication 'did not correspond to a social need sufficiently pressing to outweigh the public interest in freedom of expression . . .'[64] and, as such, was not 'necessary'. Accordingly, the ECtHR held that *The Sunday Times'* Art 10 rights had been infringed.

Clearly, corporate personality results in some powerful consequences and it has long been evident that the consequences of corporate personality are capable of being abused. Accordingly, the law provides for a number of ways in which a company's corporate personality can be set aside. These will now be examined, beginning with setting aside corporate personality under statute.

4.4 Disregarding corporate personality under statute

Section 16(2) of the CA 2006 provides that, upon incorporation, a body corporate comes into existence (i.e. corporate personality is bestowed upon companies by statute). As Lord Diplock stated '[t]he "corporate veil" in the case of companies incorporated under the Companies Acts is drawn by statute and it can be pierced by some other statute if such other statute so provides . . .'.[65] Numerous examples exist of statutory provisions that disregard corporate personality. Many such provisions set aside corporate personality in order to impose liability on those behind the corporate veil for a breach of the law,[66] such as:

> The trading certificate is discussed at 3.2.5.1.

- if a public company does business or exercises any borrowing powers prior to being issued with a trading certificate, then every officer in default will have committed an offence;[67]

---

[64] (1980) 2 EHRR 245, 282.

[65] *Dimbleby and Sons Ltd v National Union of Journalists* [1984] 1 WLR 427 (HL) 435.

[66] Although it could be argued that, as these provisions impose personal liability on those behind the corporate veil, no disregarding of corporate personality occurs, nor is needed.   [67] CA 2006, s 767(1).

- persons found to have engaged in fraudulent trading will have committed a criminal offence,[68] and may be ordered to contribute to the assets of the company;[69]
- persons found to have engaged in wrongful trading can be ordered to contribute to the assets of the company;[70]
- where a body corporate is found to have traded with the enemy, then any director, officer, or manager can be found guilty of an offence if the trading was committed with his consent or connivance, or can be attributed to his neglect.[71]

Other provisions are not predicated upon a breach of the law and simply disregard corporate personality for some other valid justification. For example, the shareholders of a company that is part of a corporate group will want to know how the entire group is performing, and not just the company in which they hold shares. Accordingly, the CA 2006 provides that parent companies must prepare group accounts[72] which set out the consolidated financial details of the parent and all its subsidiaries.[73] By consolidating the accounts in this way, the separate personalities of the companies in the group are disregarded.

⊘ Group accounts are discussed at 19.3.1.4.

Many of the statutory provisions that disregard corporate personality impose personal liability on the directors and other officers. As a result, it could be argued that the concept of corporate personality is perhaps more beneficial to those persons upon whom statute does not normally impose liability, notably the members.

4.5 Disregarding corporate personality under common law

As corporate personality is granted via statute, it is understandable that disregarding corporate personality under the common law (i.e. where no statutory authority to disregard it exists) is controversial and the courts have, accordingly, always used such power sparingly. It is worth noting that the law in this area has been almost completely reshaped by the case of *Petrodel Resources Ltd v Prest*.[74] However, in order to understand the impact of *Prest* (and why certain Justices felt the need to reformulate the law so notably), it is important to look at the law pre-*Prest*.

4.5.1 Piercing the corporate veil pre-*Prest*

The courts' reluctance to disregard a company's corporate personality is demonstrated in the following case.

Adams v Cape Industries plc [1990] Ch 433 (CA)

FACTS: A corporate group was engaged in the mining, marketing, and selling of asbestos. The parent company, Cape Industries plc ('Cape'), was based in England. The asbestos was mined by a subsidiary company based in South Africa, and was marketed and sold by two other subsidiaries, namely NAAC (based in Illinois, USA) and Capasco (based in England). The asbestos was sold to a

📖 See Stephen Griffin, 'Holding Companies and Subsidiaries: The Corporate Veil' (1991) 12 Co Law 16.

---

[68] ibid s 993 (discussed at 23.3.3.2).   [69] IA 1986, ss 213 and 246ZA (discussed at 23.3.3.1).
[70] ibid ss 214 and 246ZB (discussed at 23.3.4).   [71] Trading with the Enemy Act 1939, s 10.
[72] CA 2006, s 399.   [73] ibid s 404.   [74] [2013] UKSC 34, [2013] 3 WLR 1.

factory in Texas, the employees of which subsequently developed medical conditions caused by exposure to asbestos. A number of actions were initiated against Cape, Capasco, and NAAC, and were settled out of court for around US$20 million.

Cape then decided to place NAAC in liquidation and a new company (CPC) was set up to continue NAAC's work. This new company was not a subsidiary of Cape, but did receive financial support from Cape. A further 206 claimants from the Texas factory initiated proceedings against Cape and Capasco, and a US court ordered that damages of just over US$15 million be paid. The claimants therefore sought to enforce the judgment in the UK against Cape and Capasco. The only way in which this could be achieved was if these companies were held to be present in the US. The claimants argued that Cape and Capasco were present in the US through their subsidiaries, NAAC and CPC. For this argument to succeed, the separate corporate personalities of each company would need to be disregarded, and Cape, Capasco, and NAAC/CPC treated as one entity.

HELD: The US subsidiaries were separate and distinct from their English parent. Accordingly, Cape and Capasco were not present in the US, and so the US judgment could not be enforced against them. The reason why Cape had created subsidiaries in the US was so that liability would fall on those subsidiaries. *Salomon* recognized that this was a valid use of the company and nothing in the case convinced the Court that the principle in *Salomon* should not be followed.

In *Adams*, the claimants put forward four arguments in favour of disregarding Cape's corporate personality, namely (i) the company was a fraud, or a sham; (ii) a relationship of agency existed between Cape and its subsidiaries; (iii) Cape and its subsidiaries should be treated as a 'single economic unit'; and (iv) Cape's corporate personality should be disregarded in the interests of justice. All these arguments failed on the facts, and the Court of Appeal strongly reaffirmed the principle in *Salomon* and indicated that a company's corporate personality will not be lightly cast aside. To fully understand how *Prest* has significantly altered the law in this area, it is useful to briefly look at these four arguments.

4.5.1.1 Abuse of the corporate form

In *Adams*, Slade LJ stated that 'there is one well recognised exception to the rule prohibiting the piercing of the "corporate veil"'.[75] This was where the company was used to perpetrate a fraud, or where the company was a 'mere façade concealing the true facts'.[76] A common theme amongst these cases is that the company is used to evade a contractual obligation, or even to avoid the sole purpose of a contract entirely, as the following cases demonstrate.

Gilford Motor Co Ltd v Horne [1933] Ch 935 (CA)

FACTS: Horne was the managing director of Gilford Motor Co Ltd ('Gilford'). His employment contract contained a restrictive covenant that provided that, upon leaving Gilford's employment, he would not attempt to solicit any of its customers. Horne's contract was terminated, but he convinced his wife to set up a company in her name, which was nonetheless under Horne's control. This new company competed directly with Gilford. Gilford sought an injunction to enforce the restrictive covenant and prevent the new company from soliciting its customers. Horne argued that the covenant was binding on him only, not on the new company.

---

[75] [1990] Ch 433 (CA) 539.   [76] *Woolfson v Strathclyde Regional Council*, 1978 SLT 159 (HL) 161 (Lord Keith).

HELD: Lord Hanworth MR stated that the new company was 'formed as a device, a stratagem, in order to mask the effective carrying on of a business of [Horne]'.[77] Accordingly, an injunction was granted that prevented Horne and the new company from soliciting Gilford's customers.

 ### Jones v Lipman [1962] 1 WLR 832 (Ch)

FACTS: Lipman agreed to sell a piece of land to Jones for £5,250. Prior to the sale being completed, Lipman decided he did not wish to proceed with the sale, and transferred the piece of land to Alamed Ltd. Lipman and one other person were the sole directors and members of Alamed. Lipman's solicitors informed Jones of the sale of the land to Alamed and offered £250 by way of compensation for breach of contract. Jones sued, seeking a court order compelling the sale.

HELD: Russell J stated that Alamed was 'a creature of [Lipman's], a device and a sham, a mask which he holds before his face in an attempt to avoid recognition by the eye of equity'.[78] Accordingly, an order for specific performance was granted compelling the sale of the land to Jones.

COMMENT: Russell J described Alamed as a 'sham', and this word is often used in cases of this type. However, it is argued that this word is inappropriate, as the companies in these cases were not shams—they were validly incorporated and their existence was not called into doubt. The veil was not pierced in *Jones* because Alamed was a sham, but because its corporate personality was abused. This is why it is preferable to refer to these cases as examples of 'abuse of the corporate form',[79] rather than the somewhat dramatic language used in some of the cases.[80]

4.5.1.2 Agency

As discussed at 6.3, where two parties are involved in an agency relationship, the principal is generally responsible for the authorized acts of the agent. In the corporate context, a relationship of agency can arise where the company is regarded as an agent of a member, so that the member, as principal, is liable for the acts of the company (i.e. the company's corporate personality is ignored and the member made liable). However, *Salomon* emphatically established that the mere fact of incorporation does not cause a relationship of agency to be created between the company and its members, although an agency relationship between the company and a member can arise on the particular facts of a case, as the following case demonstrates.

 ### Smith, Stone and Knight Ltd v Birmingham Corporation [1939] 4 All ER 116 (QB)

FACTS: Smith, Stone and Knight Ltd ('SSK') manufactured paper. It acquired a partnership that was involved in the waste paper business. SSK set up a subsidiary company to run this waste paper business, but never transferred ownership of the business to the subsidiary. SSK also retained ownership of the land upon which the subsidiary operated. This land was compulsorily

---

[77] [1933] Ch 935 (CA) 956.　　[78] [1962] 1 WLR 832 (Ch) 836.

[79] CM Schmitthoff, '*Salomon* in the Shadow' [1976] JBL 305.

[80] Indeed, in *Prest*, Lord Sumption stated ([2013] UKSC 34 [28]) that '[r]eferences of a "façade" or "sham" beg too many questions to provide a satisfactory answer'.

purchased by Birmingham Corporation ('Birmingham'), who planned to pay the subsidiary compensation for the loss of the land and the disturbance caused to the business. SSK contended that it was entitled to the compensation. Birmingham argued that, because the subsidiary was a separate entity, it should receive the compensation.

HELD: The subsidiary was the agent of SSK and, as such, SSK recovered the compensation. The crucial factor in the court's decision was the level of domination that SSK exhibited over the subsidiary. SSK owned the subsidiary's business, the land upon which it conducted business, and it also owned 497 of the subsidiary's 502 shares (with nominees of SSK holding the remaining five shares).

Cases such as *Smith, Stone & Knight* are rare (and *Smith* itself has been subject to criticism on the ground that the cases cited did not provide authority for the decision to find that a relationship of agency existed).[81] In *Adams*, the Court stressed that, in the absence of an express agreement of agency,[82] it is highly unlikely that a relationship of agency will exist between a parent and subsidiary.[83] Simply owning a majority shareholding will not by itself establish a relationship of agency. As Cohen LJ stated, '[u]nder the ordinary rules of law, a parent company and a subsidiary company, even a 100 per cent subsidiary company, are distinct legal entities, and in the absence of an agency contract between the two companies, one cannot be said to be the agent of the other'.[84] Unfortunately, whilst the courts have stated what does not amount to agency, they have been unable to clearly establish a test or an accepted set of factors to determine if a relationship of agency does exist in the corporate context.

It should be noted that, following *Prest*, cases involving an agency relationship are no longer regarded as examples of disregarding corporate personality (although finding the existence of an agency relationship will usually have a similar effect).

4.5.1.3 Single economic unit

It is common for larger companies to carry out their various functions via a number of smaller subsidiary companies. Are the various companies to be regarded as having separate corporate personalities or are they to be treated as one 'single economic unit'? The answer was provided by Roskill LJ, who stated that it was 'long established and now unchallengeable by judicial decision . . . that each company in a group of companies . . . is a separate legal entity possessed of separate legal rights and liabilities'.[85] This statement was designed to affirm the principles established in *Salomon* and to ensure that the law in this area remained certain. Unfortunately, the following case introduced a measure of unwelcome uncertainty into the law.

 See D Hayton, 'Contractual Licenses and Corporate Veils' (1977) 36 CLJ 12.

 DHN Food Distributors Ltd v Tower Hamlets London Borough Council **[1976] 1 WLR 852 (CA)**

FACTS: DHN Food Distributors Ltd ('DHN') was a holding company that included two other wholly owned subsidiaries. One of the subsidiaries, Bronze Investments Ltd ('Bronze'), did not

---

[81] Murray A Pickering, 'The Company as a Separate Legal Entity' (1968) 31 MLR 481, 494.
[82] For a case in which an express agreement existed, see *Southern v Watson* [1940] 3 All ER 439 (CA).
[83] *Adams v Cape Industries plc* [1990] Ch 433 (CA) 545–9 (Slade LJ).
[84] *Ebbw Vale Urban District Council v South Wales Traffic Area Licensing Authority* [1951] 2 KB 366 (CA) 370.
[85] *The Albazero* [1977] AC 774 (HL) 807.

carry on any business activity, but it did own the land upon which DHN carried out business (DHN occupied the land as a **bare licensee**). The local authority compulsorily purchased this land and £360,000 was paid to Bronze, as the owner of the land. DHN could not find alternative premises, so all three companies went into liquidation, thereby entitling the holder of a legal or equitable interest in the land to receive compensation for disturbance to the business. DHN argued that it was entitled to such compensation. The local authority argued that Bronze Investments owned the land, that Bronze's business had not been disturbed, and that DHN was not entitled to any compensation for disturbance because it had no legal or equitable interest in the land (a bare licence not conferring such an interest).

HELD: DHN was entitled to compensation for the disturbance to the business that the compulsory purchase caused. In a much-criticized passage, Lord Denning MR stated:

> The subsidiaries are bound hand and foot to the parent company and must do just what the parent company says . . .. This group is virtually the same as a partnership where all the three companies are partners . . .. The three companies should, for present purposes, be treated as one, and the parent company, DHN, should be treated as that one.[86]

COMMENT: Although the judges involved were unanimous that the three companies should be treated as one, there was no clear test established to determine when groups of companies should be regarded as one single economic unit. Denning MR's passage above indicates the lack of clarity, because he described the subsidiaries as 'bound hand and foot' before going on to describe them as 'partners'. A subsidiary that 'must do just what the parent company says' cannot realistically be regarded as a 'partner'.

> **bare licensee:** someone who is permitted to be present on another's land, but is required to leave if the owner withdraws permission

The validity of DHN was questioned by subsequent courts. For example, in Adams, Slade LJ stated:

> The relevant parts of the judgment in the *DHN* case must . . . be regarded as decisions on the relevant statutory provisions for compensation, even though these parts were somewhat broadly expressed, and the correctness of the decision was doubted by the House of Lords in *Woolfson v Strathclyde Regional Council*.[87]

Whilst *DHN* has not been specifically overruled (it was simply distinguished in *Woolfson*), following *Prest*, it is highly unlikely that *DHN* now provides good law. However, there are still areas of the law where groups of companies are regarded by the courts as a single unit. For example, Art 101 of the Treaty on the Functioning of the European Union (TFEU) prohibits agreements and decisions between undertakings that restrict or distort competition. A parent and its subsidiaries would not be treated as separate undertakings under Art 101, and are instead usually regarded as a 'single economic unit'.[88]

4.5.1.4 In the interests of justice

Several judges have contended that the court should have a general power to ignore a company's corporate personality where justice demands. For example, in *Re a Company*,[89] the Court of Appeal stated that 'the court will use its powers to pierce the corporate veil if it is necessary to achieve justice'.[90] In *VTB Capital plc v Nutritek*

---

[86] [1976] 1 WLR 852 (CA) 860.   [87] *Adams v Cape Industries plc* [1990] Ch 433 (CA) 536.
[88] Case C-73/95 P *Viho v Commission* [1996] ECR I-5457, para 16.   [89] [1985] BCLC 333 (CA).

International Corps,[91] Lord Neuberger stated that 'it may be right for the law to permit the veil to be pierced in certain circumstances in order to defeat injustice'.[92] However, he exhibited a much more restrictive approach in *Prest* (even though it was only decided a few months later) and it is now accepted that, following *Prest*, the courts cannot pierce the veil in the interests of justice alone. The reason for this was stated by Davis LJ in *R v Boyle Transport (Northern Ireland) Ltd*,[93] who stated that '[s]o vague an approach would be unprincipled and would give rise to great uncertainty and inconsistency in decision making'.[94]

Prest is now the leading case in this area and is discussed next.

4.5.2 The modern approach: *Prest v Petrodel Resources Ltd*

The decision of the Court of Appeal in *Adams v Cape Industries plc* clearly indicates that the courts were not quick to disregard the corporate veil and the number of grounds upon which the veil could be disregarded was limited. However, the law relating to when the courts would disregard the veil was still unacceptably vague and the established instances lacked clarity and definition. As Easterbrook and Fischel stated, disregarding the corporate veil 'seems to happen freakishly. Like lightning, it is rare, severe, and unprincipled.'[95] Fortunately, the Supreme Court in *Prest* has now clarified when the courts can disregard the veil. However, it has done this by taking a very restrictive approach, by stating that there is only one instance in which the veil can be disregarded and, even in that instance, the veil will only be disregarded if it is necessary to do so.

See Ernest Lim, 'Salomon Reigns' (2013) 129 LQR 480.

Petrodel Resources Ltd v Prest [2013] UKSC 34

FACTS: The case involved a divorce settlement between Mr and Mrs Prest. The High Court had awarded Mrs Prest a settlement totalling £17.5 million,[96] but much of Mr Prest's assets were tied up in companies that were solely owned and controlled by him. Section 24(1)(a) of the Matrimonial Causes Act 1973 grants courts the power to 'order that a party to the marriage shall transfer to the other party . . . property to which the first mentioned party is entitled . . .'. The High Court utilized this power to disregard the corporate personalities of these companies and order the relevant properties to be transferred to Mrs Prest. Mr Prest appealed, questioning whether the court had the power to do this given that the properties did not belong to Mr Prest, but to his companies. The Court of Appeal, in allowing Mr Prest's appeal, held that the companies' corporate personalities could not be disregarded in these circumstances and so the High Court had no jurisdiction to make the order under s 24(1)(a). Mrs Prest appealed.

HELD: The appeal was unanimously allowed, but not on the ground that the companies' corporate personalities could be disregarded. The Supreme Court held that the properties were held on trust by the companies for the benefit of Mr Prest and, as such, they could form part of the divorce settlement. More importantly for present purposes, the Court unanimously refused to disregard the corporate veil and stated that there was only one instance in which the courts could disregard the veil, namely where 'a person is under an existing legal obligation or liability or subject to an

---

[90] ibid 337–8.   [91] [2013] UKSC 5, [2013] 2 AC 337.   [92] ibid [127].
[93] [2016] EWCA Civ 19, [2016] 2 WLR 63.   [94] ibid [88].
[95] Frank H Easterbrook and Daniel R Fischel, 'Limited Liability and the Corporation' (1985) 52 Univ Chicago LR 89, 89.
[96] *Prest v Prest* [2011] EWHC 2956 (Fam).

existing legal restriction which he deliberately evades or whose enforcement he deliberately frustrates by interposing a company under his control'.[97] Further, a court could only disregard the veil in this instance if 'all other, more conventional, remedies have proved to be no assistance'.[98]

COMMENTS: *Prest* is discussed in more detail below, but two points are worth noting here. First, as the case was decided on the basis of the existence of a trust, it follows that the Justices' comments regarding the disregarding of the corporate veil are *obiter* (although, as discussed at 4.5.2.4, Lord Sumption's approach has been followed and will likely continue to be). Second, as will be seen, whilst the decision may have been unanimous, there was a considerable disagreement amongst the Justices as to the reformulation of the law relating to disregarding the corporate veil.

Before looking at the Court's approach to disregarding corporate personality, it is worth noting that the Court did discuss whether the courts should have such a power at all. Ultimately, the Court concluded that such a power should exist. Lord Sumption, who delivered the leading judgment, stated that 'the recognition of a limited power to pierce the corporate veil in carefully defined circumstances is necessary if the law is not to be disarmed in the face of abuse'.[99] The Court then set about establishing what these 'carefully defined circumstances' are.

4.5.2.1 Redefining the disregarding of corporate personality

Lord Sumption began by stating what disregarding corporate personality means:

> Properly speaking, it means disregarding the separate personality of the company. There is a range of situations in which the law attributes the acts or property of a company to those who control it, without disregarding its separate legal personality. The controller may be personally liable, generally in addition to the company, for something that he has done as its agent or as a joint actor. Property legally vested in a company may belong beneficially to the controller, if the arrangements in relation to the property are such as to make the company its controller's nominee or trustee for that purpose . . . But when we speak of piercing the corporate veil, we are not (or should not be) speaking of any of these situations, but only of those cases which are true exceptions to the rule in *Salomon* . . . i.e. where a person who owns and controls a company is said in certain circumstances to be identified with it in law by virtue of that ownership and control.[100]

Accordingly, it is clear that Lord Sumption does not regard many cases discussed in 4.5.1 as situations in which corporate personality was actually disregarded. Indeed, Lord Neuberger went even further, stating 'there is not a single instance in this jurisdiction where the doctrine [of the court disregarding corporate personality] has been invoked properly and successfully'.[101] However, the Justices were not unanimous regarding which prior cases were true examples of disregarding corporate personality. For example, Lord Sumption and Lady Hale held the opinion that *Gilford Motor Co Ltd v Horne* and *Jones v Lipman* were cases where corporate personality was disregarded.[102] Conversely, Lord Neuberger did not regard these cases as examples of disregarding corporate personality,

Gilford and *Jones* are discussed at 4.5.1.1.

---

[97] [2013] UKSC 34, [2013] 3 WLR 1 [35].
[98] ibid [62].   [99] ibid [27].   [100] ibid [16].   [101] ibid [64].   [102] ibid [29]–[30], and [91].

stating that the decision in *Gilford* could be justified on the ground that the company was Horne's agent,[103] and, in *Jones*, Alamed Ltd could have been compelled to sell the land to Jones without disregarding corporate personality at all.[104]

It is clear that many older cases involving disregarding corporate personality must no longer be regarded as examples of instances where corporate personality was disregarded. This leads us to ask when the courts will disregard a company's corporate personality. To answer this, the 'concealment' and 'evasion' principles must be discussed.

4.5.2.2 The 'concealment' and 'evasion' principles

Lord Sumption drew a distinction between the 'concealment' and 'evasion' principles (although both may be present in a case) and noted that, in pre-*Prest* case law, 'much confusion has been caused by failing to distinguish between them'.[105] As noted above, Lord Sumption regarded many prior cases as not actually involving disregarding corporate personality at all, but instead, these cases were often examples of the concealment principle, which provides that 'the interposition of a company or perhaps several companies so as to conceal the identity of the real actors will not deter the courts from identifying them, assuming that their identity is legally relevant'.[106] For Lord Sumption, the concealment principle is 'legally banal and does not involve piercing the veil at all'.[107] Instead, all that the court is doing is 'looking behind [the company's corporate personality] to discover the facts which the corporate structure is concealing'.[108]

According to Lords Sumption and Neuberger, the 'evasion principle' is the only instance where corporate personality can be disregarded by the courts, and occurs 'where a person is under an existing legal obligation or liability or subject to an existing legal restriction which he deliberately evades or whose enforcement he deliberately frustrates by interposing a company under his control.'[109] In such a case, the court may 'pierce the corporate veil [...] only for the purpose of depriving the company or its controller of the advantage that they would otherwise have obtained by the company's separate legal personality'.[110] We can see that to disregard corporate personality and impose liability on a person (*X*), three conditions must be satisfied. First, there must be an existing legal obligation, liability, or restriction that is placed upon *X*. As the following case demonstrates, if the obligation is not placed upon *X*, but is placed upon someone else (e.g. the company that *X* is acting for), the company's corporate personality will not be disregarded.

 See Jennifer Payne, 'Reaching the Man Behind the Company' (1998) 2 CFILR 147.

➡ **charterparty:** a contract for the hiring of a ship

Yukong Line Ltd of Korea v Rendsburg Investment Corps of Liberia **[1998] 1 WLR 294 (QB)**

FACTS: Rendsberg Investments Corp of Liberia ('Rendsburg') chartered a ship from Yukong Line Ltd ('Yukong'). Yamvrias, a broker acting on behalf of Rendsburg, signed the **charterparty**. Before the ship was delivered, Yamvrias informed Yukong that Rendsburg would be unable to perform the charterparty. On the same day the charterparty was repudiated, the funds in Rendsburg's bank accounts were transferred to Ladidi Investments Corps ('Ladidi'). It transpired that Yamvrias was the beneficial owner of Rendsburg and a co-owner of Ladidi. Yukong sought damages from Yamvrias, arguing that the corporate personalities of Rendsburg and Ladidi should be disregarded so that Yamvrias could be regarded as party to the charterparty.

---

[103] ibid [70]–[72].   [104] ibid [73].   [105] ibid [28].   [106] ibid [28].
[107] ibid.   [108] ibid.   [109] ibid [35].   [110] ibid.

HELD: The Court dismissed Yukong's action. The Court had no doubt that Yamvrias, in transferring the funds from Rendsburg to Ladidi, did so for his own financial benefit by placing the funds out of the reach of Yukong. However, the obligation in this case (to pay the charter rate) was placed upon Rendsburg—it was not placed upon Yamvrias, and the Court could therefore see no reason why he should be made party to the charterparty.

Second, *X* must interpose a company in order to evade or frustrate the obligation or liability in question. For example, in *Gilford*, Horne interposed the company in order to avoid a restrictive covenant he was subject to. Similarly, in *Jones*, Lipman interposed Alamed Ltd in order to avoid his obligation to sell a piece of land.

Third, the company being interposed must be under *X*'s control. This does not mean that the person need be a director or major shareholder (although this may very well be the case, as in *Jones*). For example, in *Gilford Motor Co Ltd*, Horne was not a director or member of the company, yet he was clearly in control of it.

One question remains regarding the evasion principle, namely where *X* interposes a company to evade or frustrate an existing contractual obligation he has with a third party, will a contract exist between *X* and the third party? In *Antonio Gramsci Shipping Corp v Stepanovs*,[111] Burton J stated that a contract entered into by a 'puppet company' could be enforced against the company and *X*. However, in the following case, the Supreme Court overruled *Antonio Gramsci* on this point and held that *X* would not be bound.

VTB Capital plc v Nutritek International Corp [2013] UKSC 5

See Christopher Hare, 'From Salomon to Spiliada: Orthodoxy and Uncertainty in the Supreme Court' (2013) 72 CLJ 280.

FACTS: VTB Capital plc ('VTB') lent US$225 million to Russagroprom LLC ('RAP'), which RAP intended to use to purchase a number of Russian companies from Nutritek. RAP defaulted on the loan. VTB alleged that it was induced into entering into the loan agreement with RAP based on fraudulent misrepresentations made by Nutritek. VTB alleged that representations were made indicating that RAP and Nutritek were not under common control, whereas the truth of the matter was that both companies were controlled by Malofeev, a Russian entrepreneur. VTB commenced proceedings against Nutritek, Malofeev, and several other companies that were involved, alleging that they were liable for RAP's breach of contract. In order for this claim to succeed, the corporate personality of RAP would need to be pierced and VTB argued that the veil should be pierced on the ground that Malofeev and his associated companies were using RAP as a puppet company to orchestrate a fraud against VTB. VTB claimed that once the veil was pierced, the defendants would become party to the original loan agreement between VTB and RAP, and so would be liable on it.

HELD: The Supreme Court refused to pierce the corporate veil. Lord Neuberger stated that, to find the defendants liable on the loan agreement would involve an extension of the circumstances in which the veil could be pierced. It would, in effect, result in Malofeev becoming a co-contracting party with RAP under the loan agreement. He refused to do this on the ground that:

> where B and C are the contracting parties and A is not, there is simply no justification for holding A responsible for B's contractual liabilities to C simply because A controls B and has made misrepresentations about B to induce C to enter into the contract. This could not be said to result in unfairness to C: the law provides redress for C against A, in the form of a cause of action in negligent or fraudulent misrepresentation.[112]

---

[111] [2011] EWHC 333 (Comm), [2012] 1 All ER (Comm) 293.   [112] [2013] UKSC 5, [2013] 2 WLR 398 [139].

In *Prest*, the Justices were not unanimous in their treatment of the concealment and evasion principles:

- Lord Neuberger agreed with the principles as stated by Lord Sumption but, as noted, disagreed on which cases were examples of the evasion principle in practice.
- Lady Hale (with whom Lord Wilson agreed) was not convinced that 'it is possible to classify all of the cases in which the courts have been or should be prepared to disregard the separate legal personality of a company neatly into cases of either concealment or evasion'.[113]
- Lord Mance broadly supported Lord Sumption's approach, but seemed not to agree that evasion was the only instance where corporate personality should be disregarded and that it would be 'dangerous'[114] to foreclose all possible future situations where veil-piercing might occur.
- Lord Walker welcomed Lord Sumption's analysis, but did not comment specifically on the concealment or evasion principles.
- Lord Clarke stated that Lord Sumption's exposition of the concealment and evasion principles may be correct, but stated that the distinction was not discussed in argument and should not be adopted until the court has heard detailed submissions on it.[115]

Accordingly, only two of the seven Justices involved expressly endorsed the concealment and evasion approach. There was also disagreement as to whether the evasion principle was the only instance in which corporate personality could be disregarded. Clearly, Lords Sumption and Neuberger believed this to be the case, but other Justices (namely Lords Mance and Clarke) were open to the idea, albeit with Lord Mance stating that such instances would be 'novel and very rare'.[116]

4.5.2.3 **A remedy of last resort**

Establishing the applicability of the evasion principle is not enough in itself to justify disregarding a company's corporate personality, as Lord Neuberger stated that the court should only disregard corporate personality 'when all other, more conventional, remedies have proved to be of no assistance . . .',[117] while Lord Sumption stated that 'if it is not necessary to pierce the corporate veil, it is not appropriate to do so . . .'.[118] This indicates that disregarding a company's corporate personality should be a remedy of last resort and that if alternative remedies are available, or if the court can achieve a desired result without disregarding corporate personality, then the company's corporate personality should not be disregarded, even if the evasion principle is applicable. It has been argued that this, along with the narrowness of the evasion principle means that 'it seems unlikely that the doctrine could ever be invoked properly and successfully in the future'.[119] Accordingly, it is important to look at post-*Prest* case law to see to what extent Lord Sumption's approach has been adopted, or whether the limitations in *Prest* render the courts' ability to disregard corporate personality as a 'vacant power'[120] that is unlikely to ever be exercised.

4.5.2.4 **Post-*Prest* case law**

Given that the Justices' comments in *Prest* relating to disregarding corporate personality were *obiter*, they are not binding and it was open to future courts to refuse to follow

---

113 [2013] UKSC 34, [2013] 3 WLR 1 [92].   114 ibid [100].

115 ibid [103].   116 ibid [100].   117 ibid [62].   118 ibid [35].

119 Derek French, *Mayson, French & Ryan on Company Law* (35th edn, OUP 2018) 121.

120 Laura Stockin, 'Piercing the Corporate Veil: Reconciling R v Sale, Prest v Petrodel Resources Ltd and VTB Capital plc v Nutritek International Corp' (2014) 35 Co Law 363, 365.

the approach advocated by Lord Sumption. Unsurprisingly, however, post-*Prest* cases have unanimously adopted the approach set out by Lord Sumption. For example, in the following case, the Court of Appeal clearly accepted the distinction between concealment and evasion.

R v Sale [2013] EWCA Crim 1306[121]

FACTS: Sale was the managing director and sole shareholder of Sale Service and Maintenance Ltd ('SSM'). Sale bribed a manager of Network Rail who, in return, arranged for a number of valuable contracts to be awarded to SSM. Sale was convicted of corruption and fraud and was given a suspended sentence. Confiscation proceedings were brought to recover the proceeds of Sale's criminal acts. The question was whether this amount would be calculated by reference to the amount that Sale had benefitted, or the amount that SSM had been paid by Network Rail.

HELD: The gain acquired by Sale should be determined by reference to the amount that SSM had benefitted,[122] even though they were separate persons. Where, as was the case here, a person is the sole controller of a company and there is a very close interrelationship between the criminal activities of that person and the steps taken by the company in advancing those criminal acts, then the activities of that person and the company 'are so interlinked as to be indivisible. Both entities are acting together in the corruption.'[123] However, in coming to this conclusion, the Court did not disregard SSM's corporate personality. Treacy LJ stated that Lord Sumption's evasion principle did not apply here because there was no legal obligation that was frustrated or evaded by the interposition of SSM.[124] Instead, the Court was simply looking behind the corporate veil in order to 'discover the facts which the existence of the corporate structure would otherwise conceal so as properly to identify [Sale's] true benefit'.[125] The Court noted that this was clearly an application of Lord Sumption's concealment principle.[126]

See Laura Stockin, 'Piercing the Corporate Veil: R v Sale, Prest v Petrodel Resources Ltd and VTB Capital plc v Nutritek International Corp' (2014) 35 Co Law 363.

Despite the belief that the evasion principle is so narrow that it is 'almost entirely mythical',[127] there have been a number of post-*Prest* cases in which corporate personality has been disregarded. In all these cases, the courts have invoked the evasion principle in order to justify disregarding a company's corporate personality.

Wood v Baker [2015] EWHC 2536 (Ch)

FACTS: In 2005, a bankruptcy order was made against Baker.[128] Bankrupts are required to disclose to their trustee in bankruptcy details regarding any property acquired, or any increase in income, following the commencement of the bankruptcy order.[129] In 2015, following an investigation by Her Majesty's Revenue and Customs (HMRC), a number of Baker's associates were arrested on

---

[121] See also *R v Boyle Transport (Northern Ireland) Ltd* [2016] EWCA Crim 19, [2016] 4 WLR 63.

[122] It should be noted that the Court of Appeal did hold that the amount covered under the order at first instance (£1.9 million) was disproportionate, and reduced it to £197,683.

[123] [2013] EWCA Crim 1306, [2014] 1 WLR 663 [40] (Treacy LJ).

[124] ibid [39].   [125] ibid [43].   [126] ibid [40].

[127] Derek French, Stephen Mayson, and Christopher Ryan, *Mayson, French & Ryan on Company Law* (33rd edn, OUP 2016) 125.

[128] For other cases where the evasion principle was applied, see *Pennyfeathers Ltd v Pennyfeathers Property Co Ltd* [2013] EWHC 3530 (Ch), and *JSC BTA Bank v Solodchenko* [2015] EWHC 3680 (Comm). It is interesting to consider whether disregarding corporate personality might occur more often now that the courts have clearer rules regarding when corporate personality can be disregarded.   [129] IA 1986, s 333.

suspicion of money-laundering and tax fraud (Baker was later arrested too). Baker's associates stated that Baker had been using a series of companies that he controlled in order to hide his assets and place them out of the control of the trustee in bankruptcy. He had also been using the assets of these companies to pay for lavish benefits for himself (such as a £5,000 birthday dinner at a Michelin-starred restaurant). He had not provided the trustee with sufficient details of these companies and Judge Hodge QC stated that there had been 'a consistent and long-standing history of concealment by the bankrupt of his businesses and assets and evasion on his part of his bankruptcy obligations'.[130] The trustee applied for a court order freezing the business and assets of these companies.

HELD: The trustee's application was granted. More importantly for our purposes, the Court stated Baker had 'demonstrated a way of working which involves interposing front men, or front companies, between his trustees and his business affairs . . .'.[131] This interposition of the companies to avoid his obligations to the trustees was a clear example of the evasion principle, and so the corporate personalities of the various companies were disregarded.[132]

Cases such as *Wood* are likely to be rare and in most post-*Prest* cases, the courts have refused to disregard a company's corporate personality[133] or have achieved a result akin to disregarding corporate personality through an application of the concealment principle, or through other more conventional means.[134] Indeed, prior to *Prest*, there were examples of courts utilizing conventional legal principles in order to achieve a result akin to disregarding corporate personality without actually disregarding it, often by finding that a duty of care existed.

4.5.2.5 A duty of care

In the following notable case, the Court held that a parent company was liable to an employee of its subsidiary without disregarding its corporate personality by finding that the parent company owed the employee a duty of care.

 See Andrew Sanger, 'Crossing the Corporate Veil: The Duty of Care Owed by a Parent Company to the Employees of its Subsidiary' (2012) 71 CLJ 478.

Chandler v Cape Industries plc [2012] EWCA Civ 525

FACTS: Chandler was, for periods between April 1959 to February 1962, an employee of Cape Building Products Ltd (CBP), a subsidiary of Cape plc. In 2007, Chandler discovered that he had contracted asbestosis as a result of being exposed to asbestos whilst working for CBP. He sought to obtain compensation, but CBP had been dissolved many years before and, during Chandler's period of employment, CBP had no insurance policy in place which would indemnify Chandler for his loss. Accordingly, Chandler commenced proceedings against the parent, Cape plc.

HELD: In appropriate cases, the law could impose upon a parent company responsibility for the health and safety of its subsidiary's employees. These circumstances included where:

- the businesses of the parent and subsidiary are in a relevant respect the same;
- the parent has, or ought to have, superior knowledge on some relevant aspect of health and safety in the particular industry;

---

130 [2015] EWHC 2536 (Ch), [2015] BPIR 1524 [18].   131 ibid [18].   132 ibid [30]–[33].

133 See e.g. *R v Boyle Transport (Northern Ireland) Ltd* [2016] EWCA Crim 19, [2016] 4 WLR 63; *Persad v Singh* [2017] UKPC 32, [2017] BCC 779.

134 See e.g. *Lakatamia Shipping Co Ltd v Su* [2014] EWCA Civ 636, [2015] 1 WLR 291.

- the subsidiary's system of work is unsafe as the parent company knew, or ought to have known; and
- the parent knew or ought to have foreseen that the subsidiary or its employees would rely on it using that superior knowledge for the employees' protection.[135]

In such cases, the parent would have assumed a responsibility towards the employees of the subsidiary and so liability could be imposed upon it. The Court held that the above circumstances were present here and so Cape plc had assumed a responsibility Chandler, and so it was ordered to pay him damages.

COMMENT: *Chandler* is an important case, but it is important to understand its impact. The Court 'emphatically'[136] rejected any suggestion that the imposition of liability on Cape plc involved the disregarding of Cape's corporate personality. The Court stated clearly that the duty was based on Cape assuming a responsibility towards Chandler, which it had breached. The Court was also keen to stress that the duty of care owed by a parent company to the employees of its subsidiaries did not arise automatically, and would only occur where the three-stage test in *Caparo Industries plc v Dickman* was met (which would not be the case in most companies).[137] Accordingly, whilst *Chandler* is not an example of the courts disregarding corporate personality, it does demonstrate that liability can be imposed on a parent for the actions of its subsidiary without having to disregard the parent's corporate personality.

It has been argued that liberal use of the principle on *Chandler* could 'make significant inroads into the separate entity rule'.[138] To date, such liberal use has not occurred, and the courts have generally ruled that the parent company does not owe a duty of care to persons affected by the acts of its subsidiary. Three Court of Appeal cases in particular are worthy of note. In each case, the issue was whether a UK-registered parent company was liable for the acts of an overseas subsidiary:

- In *Lungowe v Vedanta Resources plc*,[139] the claimants alleged that Vedanta (a UK-registered company) was liable for the damage caused by the discharge of toxic materials from a mine run by one of its Zambian subsidiaries. The Court had to determine whether the claimants' case could be heard in an English court and held that it could. The issue of whether Vedanta owed a duty to the claimants was not determined in the case, but will be if the case proceeds to trial. At the time of writing, the case is subject to appeal.

- In *Okpabi v Royal Dutch Shell plc*,[140] the claimants alleged that Shell was liable for the environmental damage caused by oil leaks from a pipeline run by one of its Nigerian subsidiaries. The Court held that Shell did not owe the claimants a duty of care, as there was insufficient proximity and it would not be fair to impose a duty.

- In *AAA v Unilever plc*,[141] following elections in Kenya, a group of protesters invaded a plantation run by a subsidiary of Unilever. The protesters raped and murdered the employees of the plantation, and destroyed property. It was argued by 218 employees of the subsidiary that Unilever should be liable as it should have foreseen the risk of such violence and should have done more to protect the claimants. The Court held that, due to a lack of proximity, Unilever did not owe the claimants a duty of care.

---

[135] [2012] EWCA Civ 525, [2012] 1 WLR 3111 [80] (Arden LJ).   [136] ibid [69].

[137] See *Thompson v The Renwick Group plc* [2014] EWCA Civ 635, [2014] 2 BCLC 97, for a case where a duty of care was not established.

[138] Pey Woan Lee, 'The Enigma of Veil-Piercing' (2015) 26 ICCLR 28, 33.

[139] [2017] EWCA Civ 1528, [2018] 1 WLR 3575.   [140] [2018] EWCA Civ 191, [2018] Bus LR 1022.

[141] [2018] EWCA Civ 1532. [2018] 7 WLUK 50.

No clear principles derive from these cases, but it is clearly an evolving area of the law and it is hoped that when the Supreme Court examines this issue in the *Lungowe* appeal, it will provide greater clarity as to exactly when a duty of care will exist.

4.6 Circumventing corporate personality via contract

Corporate personality shields those behind the corporate veil from liability. However, such persons may contract away this protection and render themselves personally liable. This often occurs where creditors lend money to smaller companies. Such creditors will often seek to ensure repayment of the loan by requiring the directors or members (who are often the same persons) to contractually agree to guarantee the loan (i.e. if the company defaults on the loan, the guarantors become liable for the remaining amount).

CHAPTER SUMMARY

- Humans are natural persons and are referred to as 'individuals' (although they are also 'persons'). A company is a legal person (i.e. is not an individual) and has its own separate personality.

- The case of *Salomon* is still important today as it recognized that (i) a company can be used to legitimately shield its members from liability; and (ii) holding shares in a company (even all the shares) is not enough per se to establish an agency relationship.

- The consequences of corporate personality include (i) a company has capacity to enter into contracts; (ii) a company can own assets; (iii) a company can commence and defend legal proceedings; and; (iv) a company can create, and participate in other businesses.

- Corporate personality is bestowed upon a company by statute, so it follows that statute can take away a company's separate personality.

- Lord Sumption in *Petrodel Resources Ltd v Prest* stated that the courts can only disregard corporate personality where a person who is under an existing legal obligation seeks to deliberately evade that obligation by interposing a company under his control. This is known as the 'evasion principle'.

- Even if the evasion principle is present, the court will only disregard a company's corporate personality if other conventional remedies have proved to be of no assistance.

- One conventional remedy that can produce results similar to disregarding corporate personality is where the courts hold that a parent company owed a duty of care to an employee of a subsidiary (as occurred in *Chandler v Cape Industries plc*).

FURTHER READING

Tan Cheng-Han, 'Veil-Piercing–A Fresh Start' [2015] JBL 20.
- Discusses *Petrodel Resources Ltd v Prest* in detail and argues that the approach adopted by Lord Sumption in *Prest* is welcome.

William Day, 'Skirting Around the Issue: The Corporate Veil after Prest v Petrodel' [2014] LMCLQ 269.

- Discusses *Petrodel Resources Ltd v Prest* and looks at alternative remedies under which company operators can be made liable.

O Kahn-Freund, 'Some Reflections on Company Law Reform' (1944) 7 MLR 54.

- Discusses corporate personality and argues that *Salomon* was a poor decision that unduly harms the interests of creditors.

Martin Petrin, 'Assumption of Responsibility in Corporate Groups: Chandler v Cape plc' (2013) 76 MLR 603.

- Discusses *Chandler v Cape plc* and argues that the test established in that case is too broad.

Murray A Pickering, 'The Company as a Separate Entity' (1968) 31 MLR 481.

- Despite its age, this article provides a useful and detailed discussion of the nature and extent of a company's corporate personality.

SELF-TEST QUESTIONS

1. Define the following terms:

- corporate veil;
- piercing the veil;
- individual;
- legal person;
- evasion principle.

2. State whether each of the following statements is true or false and, if false, explain why:

- A company's separate personality was established in the case of *Salomon v A Salomon & Co Ltd*.
- A company cannot be owned.
- A company can set up another company.
- The *ratio* of *Petrodel Resources Ltd v Prest* is that the courts can only disregard corporate personality where a person is under an existing legal obligation or liability or subject to an existing legal restriction which he deliberately evades or whose enforcement he deliberately frustrates by interposing a company under his control.
- The courts can only disregard a company's corporate personality where other conventional remedies have proved to be of no assistance.
- A parent company does not owe a duty of care to persons harmed by the actions of its subsidiary.

3. 'Whilst *Petrodel Resources Ltd v Prest* has helped clarify the law relating to piercing the corporate veil, the approach advocated by Lord Sumption is far too restrictive.' Discuss the case of *Prest* and analyse the approach put forward by the Supreme Court.

4. Dragon Tools Ltd ('DT'), a subsidiary of Dragon plc, wishes to build a new factory. In order to fund this, DT borrows £200,000 from Dragon plc, and this money is used to purchase a piece of land upon which the factory will be built. DT purchases the land, but then discovers that it does not have planning permission. Fortunately, HouseBuild Ltd, a local property developer, has offered DT £220,000 for the land and so DT and HouseBuild enter into a contract for the sale of the land. A few days later, however, Sajid (a director of Dragon plc and a member of the local council) indicates to the directors of DT that if it applied for planning permission, it would certainly be granted. Accordingly, before the sale of the land is completed, DT transfers the land to Dragon plc, and argues that the contract with HouseBuild is no longer valid as DT does not own the land. DT obtains the planning permission and begins plans to construct the factory.

The factory is to be used to build a new piece of machinery that is currently in a prototype stage. The research and development of this machine is being conducted by Dragon Research Ltd ('DR'), another subsidiary of Dragon plc. All of the directors of DR are either directors of Dragon plc or are nominated by Dragon plc. The R&D work is being funded by DR selling shares, all of which have been purchased by Dragon plc, but this funding is insufficient. The directors of Dragon plc tell the directors of DR to find ways to reduce costs, and this is done by stopping research on what materials are best used to house the machine's internal components. However, as a result of this, the machine's housing suffers from a structural weakness and, when tested for the first time, the machine explodes injuring several of DR's employees. A short time later, these employees commence proceedings against DR, but DR has since been voluntarily wound up by Dragon.

The directors of Dragon plc and DT seek your advice regarding any possible liability that Dragon and DT might face.

 ONLINE RESOURCES

This book is accompanied by online resources to better support you in your studies. Visit www.oup.com/uk/roach-company/ for:

- answers to the self-test questions;
- further reading lists;
- multiple-choice questions;
- glossary.

Updates to the law can be found on the author's Twitter account (@UKCompanyLaw) and further resources can be found on the author's blog (www.companylawandgovernance.com).

5

The constitution of the company

- Defining the constitution
- The memorandum of association
- The articles of association
- Resolutions and agreements
- Other constitutional documents
- Shareholders' agreements

INTRODUCTION

Despite being the largest piece of legislation ever passed, the Companies Act 2006 (CA 2006) does not seek to exhaustively regulate the internal affairs of companies. Much is left to the companies themselves, who will usually create their own internal rules via the company's constitution. A company's constitution largely fulfils the same function as the constitutions that some countries have, namely to set out the powers, rights, and obligations of those who are subject to the constitution. Accordingly, a company's constitution aims to set out the powers, rights, and obligations of the company's members and directors, and also to lay down certain rules regarding how the company is to be run.

This chapter begins by looking at what constitutes a company's constitution. As will be seen, the CA 2006 introduced some major reforms in this area.

5.1 Defining the constitution

Unlike prior Companies Acts, the CA 2006 seeks to define (albeit not exhaustively) what the constitution is, and it is clear that the CA 2006's conception of the constitution is much different than under prior Companies Acts. Prior to the passing of the CA 2006, a company's constitution consisted primarily of the memorandum of association and the articles of association. Section 17 of the CA 2006 now provides that a company's constitution will include the company's articles, and resolutions and agreements affecting the company's constitution. As s 17 uses the word 'include', it is clear that it does not provide an exhaustive definition and other documents will also form part of a company's constitution. Other provisions within the CA 2006 broaden the s 17 definition:

⚮ These 'constitutional documents' are discussed at 5.5.

- Section 32 provides the members with a right to request 'constitutional documents', which will include the matters referred to in s 17, but will also include a range of other documents (such as the certificate of incorporation, statement of capital, and statement of guarantee).

- Section 257 provides that references to a company's constitution in Pt 10 of the Act will include the matters mentioned in s 17 along with (a) any resolution or other decision come to in accordance with the constitution; and (b) any decision by the members of the company, or a class of members, that is treated by virtue of any enactment or rule of law as equivalent to a decision by the company.

Each of the principal constitutional documents will now be discussed.

5.2 The memorandum of association

The constitutional status of the memorandum is unclear. The memorandum is not expressly stated as forming part of the constitution, leading some academics to conclude that 'the memorandum of association no longer features as part of the company's constitution.[1] However, other commentators note that the CA 2006's definition of the constitution is not exhaustive and that 'the memorandum of association would also be considered to be a constitutional document'.[2] Ultimately, given the reduced importance of the memorandum under the CA 2006, it probably matters little whether it forms part of the constitution or not.

What is clear is that, prior to the CA 2006, the memorandum was of fundamental importance and formed one of the two principal constitutional documents. The Company Law Review Steering Group (CLRSG) stated that '[t]here is a case, in the interests of simplification, for ending the distinction between the Memorandum and the Articles, and providing instead for a single constitutional document as a number of other jurisdictions do'.[3] The CLRSG included such a recommendation in its Final Report,[4] and this was accepted by the government in its 2002 White Paper.[5] Unfortunately, this recommendation was absent from the second White Paper in 2005[6] (indeed, this White Paper never referred to the company's memorandum) and was never acted upon. Accordingly, the CA 2006 still requires all companies to have a memorandum,[7] but the content and importance of the memorandum have been greatly reduced, and it no longer forms a principal constitutional document. Table 5.1 demonstrates the reduced importance of the memorandum under the CA 2006.

⚮ The application for registration is discussed at 3.2.3.

It is clear that much of the information that was contained in the pre-2006 memorandum would now be included within the company's application for registration. As regards those companies that were incorporated under the CA 1985 and prior Companies Acts, the information in their memoranda will be regarded as forming part of the articles, except the information required under s 8.[8]

---

[1] Paul L Davies and Sarah Worthington, *Gower & Davies' Principles of Modern Company Law* (9th edn, Sweet & Maxwell 2012) 68.

[2] Brenda Hannigan, *Company Law* (5th edn, OUP 2018) 97.

[3] CLRSG, 'Modern Company Law for a Competitive Economy: The Strategic Framework' (1999) para 5.3.11.

[4] CLRSG, 'Modern Company Law for a Competitive Economy: Final Report' (2001) para 9.4.

[5] Department of Trade and Industry (DTI), *Modernising Company Law* (Cm 5553-I, 2002) para 2.2.

[6] DTI, *Company Law Reform* (Cm 6456, 2005) 33–6.   [7] CA 2006, s 7(1)(a).   [8] ibid s 28(1).

TABLE 5.1 The memorandum under the Companies Acts 1985 and 2006

Companies Act 1985	Companies Act 2006
Sections 1(3)(a) and 2 of the CA 1985 (now repealed) provided that the memorandum must state: <ul><li>if the company is public, the memorandum must state that the company is public;</li><li>the name of the company;</li><li>whether the company is to be situated in England and Wales, or in Scotland;</li><li>the objects of the company;</li><li>whether or not the liability of the members is limited, and the method of limitation, and;</li><li>details concerning the company's share capital and the subscribers of the company's first shares.</li></ul>	Section 8 of the CA 2006 provides that the memorandum must state that the subscribers: <ul><li>wish to form a company under the Act, and;</li><li>agree to become members of the company and, in the case of a company with a share capital, to take at least one share each.</li></ul> This is often known as the 'association clause'.

5.3 The articles of association

With the reduced importance of the memorandum, the articles now form a company's principal constitutional document. Every company must have a set of articles[9] and promoters are free to draft their own articles that suit the needs of their particular business requirements, and submit them upon registration, or they can simply rely on a set of model articles (or a combination of the two).

The model articles are discussed at 5.3.1.3.

The CA 2006 is silent as regards a number of key company law issues (e.g. how directors are appointed, the balance of power between the board and the members, how dividends are to be declared), preferring to let the company itself determine the rules in these areas. Even where the CA 2006 does establish rules, a number of these rules are default rules only, and can be modified, or even completely disapplied, by the articles. Accordingly, the articles are as important a source of law as the CA 2006 and, in some areas of law, arguably more important. Our discussion of the articles begins by looking at what typically goes into a company's articles.

5.3.1 Content

As the articles form the most important constitutional document of the company, it follows that their content is of paramount importance. Companies are generally free to draft their own articles, and so can include whatever provisions they wish, subject to some requirements, exceptions, and limitations, including:

- the articles must be contained in a single document, and must be divided into paragraphs numbered consecutively;[10]

- article provisions cannot exclude or modify rights provided for under statute, unless the statute so provides;

- articles cannot deprive a company of powers conferred to it under statute, unless the statute so provides. So, as is discussed later, the articles cannot deprive the company of the ability to amend the articles.

---

[9] ibid s 18(1).   [10] ibid s 18(3).

5.3.1.1 **Provisions formerly in the memorandum**

As discussed, following the emasculation of the memorandum under the CA 2006, certain provisions that used to form part of the memorandum will now form part of the articles.[11] So, for example, if a company incorporated under the CA 1985 retained its objects clause, then this will now be regarded as a provision of the company's articles.

⌘ The objects clause is discussed at 6.2.1.

5.3.1.2 **Internal rules**

The articles set out the internal rules that, in conjunction with statute and case law, govern the rights, obligations, and powers of the company, members, and directors, and the relationship that exists between them. Typical matters covered in the articles include rules relating to:

- the extent to which the model articles apply;
- the powers and responsibilities of the directors;
- the conduct of board meetings;
- the appointment of directors, and when directors must vacate office;
- the issuing of shares, and the payment of dividends;
- the transfer and transmission of shares;
- increasing and reducing capital;
- the exercise of borrowing powers;
- the calling and running of general meetings.

As can be seen, the above rules are extremely important and, therefore, a company's articles are just as important a source of law as the CA 2006 or case law. It is therefore very important to draft appropriate and effective articles. Thankfully, the law offers a helping hand by providing sets of model articles.

5.3.1.3 **Model articles**

Drafting articles can be a complex and technical task and many promoters (especially promoters of smaller companies) may lack the knowledge or time required to draft suitable articles. Accordingly, since the Joint Stock Companies Act 1856, successive Companies Acts have empowered the Secretary of State to create sets of model articles that companies may use.[12] Although these provisions allow the Secretary of State to create different sets of model articles for different types of company, this power was restricted under prior Companies Acts. For example, the CA 1985 specified which types of company could have model articles[13] and, for example, provided that one set of model articles (known as Table A) should be made available for all companies limited by shares.[14] The CLRSG was of the opinion that a specific set of model articles should be designed for private companies.[15] Accordingly, the CA 2006 simply states that '[d]ifferent model articles may be prescribed for different descriptions of company'.[16] The CA 2006 is accompanied by the Companies (Model Articles) Regulations 2008, which provides model articles for private companies limited by shares (found in Sch 1), private companies limited by guarantee (found in Sch 2), and public companies (found in Sch 3). Unlimited companies, being very rare, are not provided with a set of model articles and will need to draft and register their own articles.

---

[11] ibid s 28.   [12] The current relevant provision is s 19 of the CA 2006.   [13] CA 1985, s 8 (now repealed).
[14] ibid s 8(1) and (2) (now repealed). Table A can be found in Sch 1 of the Companies (Tables A to F) Regulations 1985, SI 1985/805.
[15] CLRSG, 'Modern Company Law for a Competitive Economy: Developing the Framework' (2000) para 7.73.
[16] CA 2006, s 19(2).

Where the promoters of a limited company do not submit their own articles upon registration, the applicable model articles will form the company's articles.[17] Even if the promoters do register their own articles, the relevant model articles will still form part of the company's articles, insofar as they do not modify or exclude the relevant model articles.[18] The result of this is that companies are free to use only their own articles, adopt the relevant model articles in full (on their own or alongside a bespoke set of articles), or adopt specific provisions of the model articles. In fact, as s 19(3) allows a company to 'adopt all or any of the provisions of the model articles', a company can, alongside the application for registration, submit a document that sets out its own bespoke article provisions, but which also states that specified provisions of the model articles will also apply. This makes it easy to pick and choose which provision of the model articles apply, and also makes it clear how the bespoke articles differ from the model articles (thereby excluding such model provisions). In practice, larger companies almost always adopt their own bespoke articles, and will often expressly state in their articles that the relevant model articles are excluded.[19] Smaller companies tend to adopt the model articles (especially if the company is bought off-the-shelf), with some modifications to cater for their particular needs.

'Off-the-shelf' companies are discussed at 3.2.6.

Companies incorporated under prior Companies Acts that are governed by the old model articles will be governed by their existing model articles, but can adopt the new model articles if they so choose.

5.3.2 Interpretation of the articles

The articles, like any other document, need to be interpreted,[20] and the courts may be required to interpret the provisions of the articles in order to resolve a dispute, as the following case demonstrates.

Rayfield v Hands [1960] Ch 1 (Ch)

FACTS: Article 11 of the company's articles provided that '[e]very member who intends to transfer shares shall inform the directors who will take the said shares equally between them at a fair value . . .'. Rayfield wished to transfer his shares, so he notified the directors, but the directors refused to purchase the shares. The directors argued that there was a difference between the words 'shall' and 'will', with the former creating an obligation, but the latter merely providing an option. Accordingly, as art 11 stated that the directors 'will take the said shares', they were not under an obligation to do so, but merely had the option to do so if they wished. Rayfield sued the directors and sought an order compelling the directors to purchase his shares at fair value.

HELD: The Court stated that the words 'will take the said shares' indicated a 'resultant prospective eventuality, in which the member has to sell his shares and the directors have to buy them . . .'[21] Accordingly, art 11 imposed an obligation upon the directors to purchase Rayfield's shares, and the court ordered that they be bought at fair value.

---

17 ibid s 20(1)(a).   18 ibid s 20(1)(b).

19 A common provision in the articles of larger companies is for art 1 to state that '[n]o regulations set out in any statute, or in any statutory instrument or other subordinate legislation made under any statute, concerning companies shall apply as the regulations or articles of the company'.

20 As the model articles are provided for under statute, it follows that the Interpretation Act 1978 applies to the interpretation of the model articles and to articles which partly adopt the model articles (*Fell v Derby Leather Co Ltd* [1931] 2 Ch 252 (Ch)).

21 [1960] Ch 1 (Ch) 3 (Vaisey J).

As the articles constitute a contract, they will usually be interpreted in line with general contractual principles of interpretation, but specific rules have been established relating to the interpretation of the articles. In *Re Hartley Baird Ltd*,[22] Wynn-Parry J stated that, when interpreting the articles, the maxim **ut res magis valeat quam pereat** should be applied, meaning that the courts will attempt to interpret the articles in such a way as to produce a workable result, and to avoid an unreasonable result. As Jenkins LJ stated:

➡ *ut res magis valeat quam pereat*: 'it is better for a thing to have effect than to be made void'

> the articles of association of the company should be regarded as a business document and should be construed so as to give them reasonable business efficacy, where a construction tending to that result is admissible on the language of the articles, in preference to a result which would or might prove unworkable.[23]

The interpretive power of the courts is notable. Indeed, in *Thompson v Goblin Hill Hotels Ltd*,[24] Lord Dyson stated that the plain and obvious meaning of the words used in the articles may be rejected if it produces a 'commercial absurdity'.[25] The courts have also confirmed that they will add words to avoid an absurdity.[26]

There are, however, notable limits upon the courts' ability to interpret the articles, including:

- when interpreting an amendment to the articles, the courts cannot consider the effect that the amendment was meant to have;[27]
- the court is not empowered to rectify the articles, even if it can be established that they do not give effect to the wishes of the parties;[28]
- the courts cannot add terms to make the articles fairer or more reasonable[29] (although, as noted, they can add words to existing article provisions).

Although the courts cannot add terms to the articles, they can imply terms into the articles. One might assume that the implication of a term would constitute an addition, but this is not the case. Instead, as Lord Hoffmann stated 'the implication of the term is not an addition to the instrument. It only spells out what the instrument means.'[30] Historically, the courts were of the opinion that 'the implication of terms is, in essence, an exercise in interpretation'.[31] However, the Supreme Court has recently appeared to move away from this, with Lord Neuberger stating that 'construing the words used and implying additional words are different processes governed by different rules'.[32] Accordingly, the implication of terms will be considered separately.

5.3.2.1 Implication of terms

There is little doubt that the courts are able to imply terms into the articles, as the following case demonstrates.

---

[22] [1955] Ch 143 (Ch).   [23] *Holmes v Keyes* [1959] Ch 199 (CA) 215.
[24] [2011] UKPC 8, [2011] 1 BCLC 587.   [25] ibid [18].
[26] *Folkes Group plc v Alexander* [2002] EWHC 51 (Ch), [2002] 2 BCLC 254.
[27] *Rose v Lynx Express Ltd* [2004] EWCA Civ 447, [2004] 1 BCLC 455.
[28] *Scott v Frank F Scott (London) Ltd* [1940] Ch 794 (CA).
[29] *Attorney General of Belize v Belize Telecom Ltd* [2009] UKPC 10, [2009] 1 WLR 1988.
[30] ibid [18].
[31] *Stena Line Ltd v Merchant Navy Ratings Pension Fund Trustees Ltd* [2010] EWHC 1805 (Ch), [2011] Pens LR 223 [36] (Arden LJ).
[32] *Marks & Spencer plc v BNP Paribas Securities Services Trust Co (Jersey) Ltd* [2015] UKSC 72, [2016] AC 742 [26].

Equitable Life Assurance Society v Hyman [2002] 1 AC 408 (HL)

FACTS: Around 90,000 policyholders had taken out a specific life assurance policy with Equitable Life ('EQ').[33] This policy entitled them to an **annuity**, which was increased by the payment of bonuses. Policyholders could choose to receive the annuity at a guaranteed annual rate ('GAR'), or at a current annuity rate ('CAR') that would fluctuate with the market. From 1993 onwards, the CAR fell below the GAR, which proved extremely expensive for EQ. Accordingly, EQ started issuing lower bonuses to policyholders who took their annuity at the GAR, and higher bonuses to those on the CAR. Although this was contrary to the terms of the policy, EQ justified it on the basis that art 65 of EQ's articles stated that the amount of the bonus payment was at the absolute discretion of the directors. A number of policyholders (of whom Hyman was chosen a representative) commenced proceedings against EQ.

HELD: Lord Steyn stated that it was 'necessary to distinguish between the processes of interpretation and implication'.[34] He noted that there was no express restriction in art 65 that prevented the directors from amending the bonus payments in the way they had and, therefore, this was not an issue of interpretation.[35] The critical question was whether a relevant restriction could be implied into art 65. In determining this, Lord Steyn stated that the determining factor was whether the implication of a term was strictly necessary. On this, he stated 'the self-evident commercial object of the inclusion of guaranteed rates in the policy is to protect the policyholder against a fall in market annuity rates by ensuring that if the fall occurs he will be better off than he would have been with market rates.'[36] Taking this into account, he felt that it was strictly necessary to imply a term providing that the art 65 power would not be exercised in a way that conflicted with the policyholders' contractual rights or in a manner that 'was designed to deprive the relevant guarantees of any substantial value.'[37] Accordingly, the House held that the directors had breached art 65.

See Alan Berg, 'Equitable Life Assurance Society v Hyman—the Extrinsic Facts Issue' [2002] JBL 570.

➡ **annuity**: a yearly payment of a sum of money

However, the courts' ability to imply terms is limited. For example, the courts cannot imply terms into the articles based on extrinsic circumstances.[38] The following case is regarded as the leading case in this area, although, as is discussed below, it has been subject to criticism from the Supreme Court.

Attorney General of Belize v Belize Telecom Ltd [2009] UKPC 10

FACTS: The share capital of Belize Telecommunications Ltd ('BTC') was divided into three classes of share, namely two classes or ordinary shares (known as B and C), and a single preference share (known as the 'special share'). BTC's articles provided for the appointment of eight directors, with four of those being appointable by a majority of the C shareholders. The articles provided

See Kelvin FK Low and Kelry CF Loi, 'The Many "Tests" for Terms Implied in Fact: Welcome Clarity' (2009) 125 LQR 561.

---

[33] Each policyholder was also a member of Equitable Life.

[34] [2002] 1 AC 408 (HL) 458.

[35] It should be noted that whilst Lord Cooke did come to the same conclusion as Lord Steyn (i.e. the policyholders should succeed), he did view the case as one involving interpretation, and came to the conclusion that a restrictive interpretation of art 65 did not entitle the directors to act as they did.

[36] [2002] 1 AC 408 (HL) 459.   [37] ibid.

[38] *Bratton Seymour Service Co Ltd v Oxborough* [1992] BCC 471 (CA).

that if the holder of the special share also owned at least 37.5 per cent of the issued capital in C shares, then that person could appoint or remove two of the four directors allocated to the C shareholders. Belize Telecom Ltd ('BT') acquired the special share and a majority of the C shares, and so it appointed two directors. However, shortly thereafter, BT lost a number of C shares and its holding was reduced below the 37.5 per cent figure. The issue that arose was that the only person who could remove such directors was a special shareholder who held at least 37.5 per cent of the C shares, but no such person now existed. Accordingly, the Attorney General contended that there should be an implied term in the articles providing that the two directors would vacate office if the special shareholder lost the requisite number of C shares.

HELD: Lord Hoffmann began by looking at the power of the courts to imply terms, and stated that:

> The court has no power to improve upon the instrument which it is called upon to construe, whether it be a contract, a statute or articles of association. It cannot introduce terms to make it fairer or more reasonable. It is concerned only to discover what the instrument means. However, that meaning is not necessarily or always what the authors or parties to the document would have intended. It is the meaning which the instrument would convey to a reasonable person having all the background knowledge which would reasonably be available to the audience to whom the instrument is addressed.[39]

Applying this to the facts, Lord Hoffmann stated that the two directors were there by virtue of BTC holding the special share and the requisite C shares. If those criteria were subsequently not met, there would be no one who could remove the two directors, and they could remain in office indefinitely. In order to avoid this absurdity, Lord Hoffmann stated that it was necessary to imply into the articles a term providing that the two directors would cease to hold office if the special shareholder lost the requisite shareholding.

Despite the fact that *Belize* was generally well received and has been described as 'a remarkable little gem of a judgment',[40] concern did exist that it unduly relaxed the test for the implication of terms by moving from a test based on necessity to one based on reasonableness (even though Lord Hoffmann did state clearly that reasonableness alone was not enough). The Supreme Court denied this, stating:

> the notion that a term will be implied if a reasonable reader of the contract, knowing all its provisions and the surrounding circumstances, would understand it to be implied is quite acceptable, provided that (i) the reasonable reader is treated as reading the contract at the time it was made and (ii) he would consider the term to be so obvious as to go without saying or to be necessary for business efficacy. . . . The second proviso is important because otherwise Lord Hoffmann's formulation may be interpreted as suggesting that reasonableness is a sufficient ground for implying a term. . . . It is necessary to emphasise that there has been no dilution of the requirements which have to be satisfied before a term will be implied.[41]

---

[39] [2009] UKPC 10, [2009] 1 WLR 1988 [16].

[40] Kelvin FK Low and Kelry CF Loi, 'The Many "Tests" for Terms Implied in Fact: Welcome Clarity' (2009) 125 LQR 561, 561.

[41] *Marks & Spencer plc v BNP Paribas Securities Services Trust Co (Jersey) Ltd* [2015] UKSC 72, [2016] AC 742 [23]-[24] (Lord Neuberger PSC).

In a parting swipe, Lord Neuberger PSC stated that Lord Hoffmann's observations should be regarded as 'a characteristically inspired discussion rather than authoritative guidance on the law of implied terms'.[42] However, given that Lord Neuberger PSC emphasized many of the same points as Lord Hoffmann, it has been argued that Lord Neuberger's dismissal of Lord Hoffmann's approach is 'a little baffling'.[43] It is also worth noting that other Justices were more praiseworthy, with Lord Carnwath stating:

> while I accept that Lord Hoffmann's judgment has stimulated more than usual academic controversy, I would not myself regard that as a sufficient reason to question its continuing authority. On the contrary, properly understood, I regard it as a valuable and illuminating synthesis of the factors which should guide the court.[44]

5.3.3 Amending the articles

As a company, or the market within which it operates, evolves, it may become necessary or desirable for the company to amend its articles. There are three principal ways in which a company's articles can be amended:

1. The court or some other relevant authority may alter the company's articles if empowered to do so. For example, if a public company passes a resolution re-registering itself as a private company, the members may apply for that resolution to be cancelled.[45] The court may then make an order confirming or cancelling the resolution and may also alter the company's articles in consequence of the order made.[46]

2. A company may amend its articles by passing a special resolution,[47] (subject to the rules regarding entrenchment).

Entrenchment is discussed at 5.3.3.3.

3. If all of the members agree to an amendment (irrespective of whether a resolution is passed), then the amendment will be valid.[48] In practice, this method will only be appropriate or practical in smaller companies.

Here, we are concerned primarily with the second method which, from a governance point of view, is notable as it allows the majority to alter the terms of the articles against the wishes of the minority (and provides an example of how the s 33 statutory contract differs to a standard contract). However, it should be noted that the ability to alter the articles is not limitless and both statute and the common law impose restrictions on the ability to amend the articles.

The s 33 contract is discussed at 5.3.4.

5.3.3.1 Statutory restrictions

Statute may restrict a company's ability to alter its articles, or may restrict the effect that an alteration has. The following are examples of such restrictions:

- The ability to alter the articles is limited by the provisions of the Companies Acts.[49] For example, a company is able to entrench article provisions, thereby making them more difficult to alter.

---

[42] ibid [31].   [43] Edwin Peel, 'Terms Implied in Fact' (2016) 132 LQR 531, 534.

[44] [2015] UKSC 72, [2016] AC 742 [74].   [45] CA 2006, s 98(1).   [46] ibid s 98(3), (4), and (5)(b).

[47] ibid s 21(1). It should be noted that where an amendment involves a variation of class rights (discussed at 16.6), then ss 630 and 631 set out the rules regarding amendment.

[48] *Cane v Jones* [1980] 1 WLR 1451 (Ch).

[49] *Allen v Gold Reefs of West Africa Ltd* [1900] 1 Ch 656 (CA).

- Unless he agrees to the alteration in writing, a member is not bound by any alteration to the articles made after he became a member if the effect of the alteration (i) is to require him to take or subscribe for more shares than the amount he had at the date of the alteration; or (ii) in any way increases his liability as at that date to contribute to the company's share capital; or (iii) otherwise to pay money to the company.[50]

In other cases, statute empowers the courts to prohibit alterations of the articles without the court's consent. For example, if the members apply to the court to object to a public company re-registering as private, then the court may make an order requiring the company not to make any, or any specified, amendments to the articles without the leave of the court.[51]

5.3.3.2 Common law restrictions

The common law imposes a number of restrictions upon a company's ability to alter its articles, including the following:

- An amendment will not be valid if it deprives a member of a right that has already accrued, unless the member agrees to the amendment.[52]

- A company cannot contract out of the statutory ability to alter it articles (e.g. by placing a provision in its articles that seeks to render any part of the articles unalterable).[53] However, it is possible to make a company's articles effectively unalterable if all of the members (or enough of them to defeat a special resolution) enter into a shareholders' agreement under which they agree not to exercise their ability to alter the articles. Note, though, that if the company is party to such an agreement, it will not be bound.[54]

 Shareholders' agreements are discussed at 5.6.

- In some cases, amendment of the articles may end up breaching a separate contract that exists between the company and some other person (often a director). Whilst a company is not prevented from amending its articles in a way that would amount to a breach of contract, an action for breach of contract can result from such an amendment, for which the company may be liable, as the following case demonstrates.

Southern Foundries (1926) Ltd v Shirlaw [1940] AC 701 (HL)

FACTS: Southern Foundries (1926) Ltd ('Southern') entered into a service contract with one of its directors, Shirlaw, under which Shirlaw was appointed to the post of managing director for ten years. Southern's shares were acquired by Federated Foundries Ltd ('Federated') and Federated amended Southern's articles to provide that Federated's board could remove Southern's directors. Four years into his role as managing director, the board of Federated exercised this power and removed Shirlaw as a director. As Southern's articles stated that only a director of the company could be managing director, this meant that Shirlaw's tenure as managing director was also terminated. Shirlaw contended that this amounted to a breach of his service contract.

HELD: The House held that the amendment of the articles had caused Shirlaw's service contract to be breached by Southern, for which he was entitled to damages. Lord Porter stated that '[a] company cannot be precluded from altering its articles thereby giving itself power to act upon

---

[50] CA 2006, s 25.   [51] ibid s 98(6).

[52] *James v Buena Ventura Nitrate Grounds Syndicate Ltd* [1896] 1 Ch 456 (CA).

[53] *Walker v London Tramways Co* (1879) 12 ChD 705 (Ch).

[54] *Russell v Northern Bank Development Corp Ltd* [1992] 1 WLR 588 (HL) (discussed at 5.6.1).

the provisions of the altered articles—but so to act may nevertheless be a breach of contract if it is contrary to a stipulation in a contract validly made before the alteration'.[55]

COMMENT: One might assume that as it was Federated that voted to amend the articles and exercised the power to remove Shirlaw, it should be liable for breach, but it was Southern that was held liable. This was because it is only the company that has the right to amend its own articles (albeit through a special resolution of its members) and so Southern had granted Federated the right to dismiss Shirlaw.

Undoubtedly, the most important common law limitation on a company's ability to amend its articles was laid down by Lindley MR in *Allen v Gold Reefs of West Africa Ltd*,[56] who stated that the power to alter the articles must:

> like all other powers, be exercised subject to those general principles of law and equity which are applicable to all powers conferred on majorities and enabling them to bind minorities. It must be exercised, not only in the manner required by law, but also bona fide for the benefit of the company as a whole . . .[57]

The application of the bona fide test involves answering two questions. The first question that arises is what we mean by 'the company'. This phrase has been described as 'a Delphic term employed by different judges in different circumstances to signify different things'.[58] In one case, Evershed MR stated that the company 'does not . . . mean the company as a commercial entity distinct from the corporators: it means the corporators as a general body'.[59] However, the bulk of case law disagrees and provides that the company refers to the body corporate.[60] In many cases, the distinction matters little, as what benefits the company and its members will often coincide. However, an amendment that exists to benefit the shareholders, but not the company, will be deemed invalid.

 Dafen Tinplate Co Ltd v Llanelly Steel Co (1907) Ltd [1920] 2 Ch 124 (Ch)[61]

FACTS: The shareholders of Llanelly Steel Co (1907) Ltd ('Llanelly') were primarily involved in manufacturing tinplates. They were originally invited to become shareholders in Llanelly on the understanding that the steel bars used to make these tinplates would be purchased from Llanelly (although they were under no legal obligation to do so). Dafen Tinplate Co Ltd ('Dafen') was one such shareholder, and it decided to stop purchasing steel bars from Llanelly and instead purchased them from a rival steel company. Llanelly asked to purchase Dafen's shares, but Dafen refused. Accordingly, the majority shareholders of Llanelly inserted a new provision in the articles

---

[55] [1940] AC 701 (HL) 740–1.   [56] [1900] 1 Ch 656 (CA).   [57] ibid 671.

[58] FG Rixon, 'Competing Interests and Conflicting Principles: An Examination of the Power of Alteration of Articles of Association' (1986) 49 MLR 446, 454.

[59] *Greenhalgh v Arderne Cinemas Ltd* [1951] Ch 286 (CA) 291.

[60] *Allen v Gold Reefs of West Africa Ltd* [1900] 1 Ch 656 (CA) 671 (Lindley MR); *Sidebottom v Kershaw Leese & Co Ltd* [1920] 1 Ch 154 (CA) 165–66 (Sterndale MR); *Shuttleworth v Cox Brothers & Co (Maidenhead) Ltd* [1927] 2 KB 9 (CA) 23 (Scrutton LJ).

[61] See also *Brown v British Abrasive Wheel Co Ltd* [1919] 1 Ch 290 (Ch).

which stated that the company could pass a resolution compelling any shareholder (except one named shareholder) to sell their shares to the board or other persons as determined by the board at fair value. Dafen commenced proceedings, alleging that the new article provisions were invalid.

HELD: The amendment to the articles was invalid as it was not bona fide for the company's benefit. Peterson J stated:

> It may be for the benefit of the majority of the shareholders to acquire the shares of the minority, but how can it be said to be for the benefit of the company that any shareholder, against whom no charge of acting to the detriment of the company can be urged, and who is in every respect a desirable member of the company, and for whose expropriation there is no reason except the will of the majority, should be forced to transfer his shares to the majority or to anyone else? Such a provision might in some circumstances be very prejudicial to the company's interest.[62]

COMMENT: Peterson J was not stating that expropriation clauses cannot be for the benefit of the company. His principal issue with this clause was that it was too wide and that '[t]o say that such an unrestricted and unlimited power of expropriation is for the benefit of the company appears to me to be confusing the interests of the majority with the benefit of the company as a whole'.[63] From this, it follows that an expropriation clause can be valid if it operates in narrower circumstances that benefit the company (e.g. where the power can only be invoked to purchase the shares of a shareholder who is competing with the company).[64]

The second question that arises is when an amendment will be bona fide for the benefit of the company. This is a complex issue, largely because the test imposed by Lindley MR, whilst flexible enough to grant the court a wide discretion, is rather vague, to the extent that the High Court of Australia described it as 'almost meaningless'.[65] What is clear is that the test established by Lindley MR is subjective, meaning that if the majority shareholders honestly believed that the alteration was for the company's benefit as a whole, then the alteration would be valid, even if the court disagrees with the majority's assessment. As Scrutton LJ stated '[i]t is not the business of the Court to manage the affairs of the company. That is for the shareholders and directors.'[66] However, the subjective beliefs of the majority shareholders cannot be the sole factor that determines the validity of an amendment and, accordingly, the courts have introduced a number of other factors to help determine the validity of an amendment. The following case indicates that, whilst the bona fide test is subjective, the reasonableness of the amendment is also relevant.

Shuttleworth v Cox Brothers & Co (Maidenhead) Ltd [1927] 2 KB 9 (CA)

FACTS: The company's articles provided that its directors (one of whom was Shuttleworth) would hold office for as long as they wished, unless they became disqualified by virtue of one of six specified events. Shuttleworth engaged in a financial irregularity, but it did not fall within one of the six specified events. The other directors used their majority shareholdings to pass a special

---

[62] [1920] 2 Ch 124 (Ch) 141.   [63] ibid.
[64] *Sidebottom v Kershaw Leese & Co Ltd* [1920] 1 Ch 154 (CA).
[65] *WCP Ltd v Gambotto* (1993) 30 NSWLR 385 (High Court of Australia) 388 (Meagher JA).
[66] *Shuttleworth v Cox Brothers & Co (Maidenhead) Ltd* [1927] 2 KB 9 (CA) 23.

resolution altering the articles by adding a seventh event, namely that a director must resign if all the other directors required him to. Following the alteration, Shuttleworth's co-directors demanded his resignation. Shuttleworth challenged the alteration.

HELD: Bankes LJ confirmed that Lindley MR's test was subjective, but went on to ask what criteria the court should use to ascertain the opinion of the shareholders in question. He stated:

> The alteration may be so oppressive as to cast suspicion on the honesty of the persons responsible for it, or so extravagant that no reasonable men could really consider it for the benefit of the company. In such cases the Court is, I think, entitled to treat the conduct of shareholders as it does the verdict of a jury, and to say that the alteration of a company's articles shall not stand if it is such that no reasonable men could consider it for the benefit of the company.[67]

Applying this, he stated that 'it seems to me impossible to say that the action of these defendants was either incapable of being for the benefit of the company or such that no reasonable men could consider it for the benefit of the company'.[68] Accordingly, Shuttleworth's challenge failed and the amendment was deemed to be valid.

One other factor that was relevant in *Shuttleworth* was that there was not 'a trace of any vindictiveness or wrong motive'[69] on behalf of the defendants, and the courts have stated that if the articles are fraudulently or maliciously amended, then this will not be bona fide.[70]

One difficulty that arises is that Lindley MR's test was formulated to deal with situations where the interests of the company and its members conflicted, and provided that the company's interests prevailed. Where an amendment does not affect the company, but instead affects the rights of differing shareholders, it has been argued that Lindley MR's test is 'inappropriate, if not meaningless'.[71] This has been branded as a 'major defect'[72] of the rule and has resulted in the courts, in such cases, moving their focus towards the effect the amendment had upon the shareholders.

Greenhalgh v Arderne Cinemas Ltd [1951] Ch 286 (CA)

FACTS: Greenhalgh was a minority shareholder of Arderne Cinemas Ltd ('Arderne'), the articles of which provided that a shareholder should not sell his shares to an outsider if an existing shareholder was willing to purchase them. Mallard, the managing director and majority shareholder of Arderne, wished to sell his shares to an outsider. He therefore (in his capacity as a shareholder) amended the articles to permit the selling of shares to an outsider without first offering them to an existing shareholder, provided that it was approved by an ordinary resolution (which would be a certainty, given that he owned the majority of Arderne's shares). Greenhalgh challenged the alteration, on the ground that it was not for the benefit of Arderne as a whole.

HELD: Evershed MR stated that 'the phrase, "the company as a whole", does not (at any rate in such a case as the present) mean the company as a commercial entity, distinct from the corporators:

---

[67] ibid 18.   [68] ibid 19.   [69] ibid 17.

[70] *Sidebottom v Kershaw Leese & Co Ltd* [1920] 1 Ch 154 (CA) 163 (Sterndale MR).

[71] *Peters' American Delicacy Co Ltd v Heath* (1939) 61 CLR 457 (High Court of Australia) 512 (Dixon J).

[72] FG Rixon, 'Competing Interests and Conflicting Principles: An Examination of the Power of Alteration of Articles of Association' (1986) 49 MLR 446, 469.

it means the corporators as a general body'.[73] He then stated that 'the case may be taken of an individual hypothetical member and it may be asked whether what is proposed is, in the honest opinion of those who voted in its favour, for that person's benefit'.[74] In determining whether the amendment benefitted this hypothetical member, the court would ask whether 'the effect of it were to discriminate between the majority shareholders and the minority shareholders, so as to give to the former an advantage of which the latter were deprived'.[75] Applying this, the Court held that, if an outsider wished to purchase the shares of a hypothetical member, it might well be in that member's benefit to sell his shares directly to an outsider. Further, the advantage obtained by Mallard was also obtained by all the other shareholders, so the amendment was not discriminatory. Accordingly, the amendment was deemed valid.

In the following case, the Privy Council confirmed that, in cases where a company has no interest in the amendment, some other test is required. Unfortunately, the Privy Council declined to devise such a test.

 See Richard Williams, 'Bona Fide in the Interest of Certainty' (2007) 66 CLJ 500.

Citco Banking Corp NV v Pusser's Ltd [2007] UKPC 13

FACTS: The share capital of Pusser's Ltd consisted primarily of Class A shares, with each share carrying one vote. Twenty-eight per cent of these shares were controlled by Tobias, Pusser's' chair, whilst 13 per cent were controlled by Citco Banking Corp NV. The remaining shares were widely held. The articles were amended to provide that (i) 2,000 Class B shares should be issued, with each one carrying 50 votes; and (ii) 2,000 of the Class A shares held by Tobias should be converted to Class B shares. The resolution was passed by just under 1.126 million votes to 183,000 votes (all the dissenting votes came from Citco). Tobias stated that the resolution was passed in order to raise capital to expand Pusser's' business. Citco argued that the purpose of the amendment was to give Tobias indisputable control over Pusser's, and so was not bona fide in the company's interests.

HELD: Lord Hoffmann, giving the judgment of the Board, began by approving the test in *Allen* and confirming its subjectivity as held in *Shuttleworth*. Applying the test in *Shuttleworth*, namely 'whether reasonable shareholders could have considered that the amendment was for the benefit of the company',[76] the Board held that it would have been reasonable for the shareholders to accept in good faith the arguments put forward by Tobias as to why the amendment was in Pusser's' interests. Accordingly, the amendment was held to be valid.

COMMENT: Although *Citco* was decided based upon the traditional bona fide test, Lord Hoffmann did acknowledge that this test:

> will not enable one to decide all cases in which amendments of the articles operate to the disadvantage of some shareholder or group of shareholders. Such amendments are sometimes only for the purpose of regulating the rights of shareholders in matters in which the company as a corporate entity has no interest, such as the distribution of dividends or capital or the power to dispose of shares.[77]

In such a case, '[s]ome other test of validity is required'.[78] Lord Hoffmann did note the 'hypothetical member' test used in *Greenhalgh*, but stated that '[s]ome commentators have not found this

---

[73] *Greenhalgh v Arderne Cinemas Ltd* [1951] Ch 286 (CA) 291.   [74] ibid.
[75] ibid.   [76] [2007] UKPC 13, [2007] Bus LR 960 [24].   [77] ibid [18].   [78] ibid.

approach entirely illuminating . . .'.[79] Unfortunately, as the case was decided based on the bona fide test, Lord Hoffmann did not consider what 'other test of validity' should be applied in cases where the bona fide test was not suitable.

Accordingly, a lacuna in the law does remain. However, it has been argued that this might not be an issue as minorities are more protected today than they were, notably via the unfair prejudice remedy. This remedy did not exist when many of the above cases were decided, and the existence of this remedy provides a much more useful source of minority shareholder redress. For example, Hannigan argues that if *Greenhalgh* were to take place today, Greenhalgh would surely have obtained a remedy on the ground that his affairs were unfairly prejudiced (although the article amendment would not have been set aside).[80]

The unfair prejudice remedy is discussed at 15.3.

In the case of *Re Charterhouse Capital Ltd*,[81] Sir Terence Etherton stated that the following principles could be derived from the relevant case law:

- The limitations on the exercise of the power to amend a company's articles arise because, as in the case of all powers, the manner of their exercise is constrained by the purpose of the power and because the framers of the power of a majority to bind a minority will not, in the absence of clear words, have intended the power to be completely without limitation.

- A power to amend will be validly exercised if it is exercised in good faith in the interests of the company.

- It is for the shareholders, and not the court, to say whether an alteration of the articles is for the benefit of the company, but it will not be for the benefit of the company if no reasonable person would consider it to be such.

- The view of shareholders acting in good faith that a proposed alteration of the articles is for the benefit of the company, and which cannot be said to be a view which no reasonable person could hold, is not impugned by the fact that one or more of the shareholders was actually acting under some mistake of fact or lack of knowledge or understanding. In other words, the court will not investigate the quality of the subjective views of such shareholders.

- The mere fact that the amendment adversely affects, and even if it is intended adversely to affect, one or more minority shareholders and benefit others does not, of itself, invalidate the amendment if the amendment is made in good faith in the interests of the company.

- A power to amend will also be validly exercised, even though the amendment is not for the benefit of the company because it relates to a matter in which the company as an entity has no interest but rather is only for the benefit of shareholders as such or some of them, provided that the amendment does not amount to oppression of the minority or is otherwise unjust or is outside the scope of the power.

- The burden is on the person impugning the validity of the amendment of the articles to satisfy the court that there are grounds for doing so.[82]

5.3.3.3 Entrenched provisions

As noted, a company cannot formally make its articles unalterable.[83] Prior to the CA 2006, companies would try to entrench certain constitutional provisions by placing

---

[79] ibid. [80] Brenda Hannigan, *Company Law* (5th edn, OUP 2018) 107.
[81] [2015] EWCA Civ 536, [2015] BCC 574. [82] ibid [90].
[83] Although, this could be indirectly achieved in practice by putting in place a shareholders' agreement (discussed at 5.6), under which the shareholders agreed not to exercise their power to amend the articles.

them in the objects clause, instead of the articles (because alteration of the objects was more difficult than alteration of the articles).[84] The CLRSG considered whether companies should be able to entrench provisions in the articles, and argued that:

> It can be argued that entrenchment unduly restricts the future freedom of members (including those who were not members when the memorandum and articles were drawn up) and should be prohibited. But we incline to the contrary view, believing that entrenchment has a role to play in enabling those who establish companies to opt to protect particular interests.[85]

Consequently, the CA 2006 introduced the ability for companies to entrench article provisions at any time.[86] Entrenched provisions are not rendered unalterable, but they can only be amended or repealed 'if certain conditions are met, or procedures are complied with, that are more restrictive than those applicable in the case of a special resolution'.[87] This could include requiring a higher majority or unanimity instead of the usual special resolution, or by requiring the alteration to be approved of by certain specified members[88] or other persons.

In order to prevent abuse, the Act does impose several safeguards, notably that entrenchment will not prevent alteration where all of the members agree to an alteration, or where the court orders an alteration be made.[89] A company must also inform Companies House (i) if the articles contain provision for entrenchment upon formation, or if the articles are amended to include an entrenched provision;[90] or (ii) if the articles are amended to remove entrenched provisions.[91] The company must also provide a statement of compliance certifying that the amendment was made in accordance with the company's articles.[92]

5.3.3.4 Notification to Companies House

If a company amends its articles, then it must send a copy of the amended articles to Companies House not later than 15 days after the amendment takes effect.[93] Failure to do so is a criminal offence,[94] and Companies House is empowered to send notice to the company requiring it to send a copy of the amended articles within 28 days of the notice being issued.[95] If the company complies, no criminal proceedings will be brought in respect of the original failure to comply.[96] If the company does not comply, then criminal proceedings may be brought and the company will be liable to an additional civil penalty of £200.[97]

---

[84] Pre-CA 2006, the objects clause was found in the memorandum, and alteration of the objects required a special resolution and court confirmation (CA 1985, s 4). Provisions that were entrenched in a company's memorandum will now be regarded as forming part of the articles (CA 2006, s 28(2)).

[85] CLRSG, 'Modern Company Law for a Competitive Economy: Developing the Framework' (2000) para 7.71.

[86] Section 22(2) provides that provisions may be entrenched when the company is first formed, or the company may amend its articles post-incorporation to include an entrenched provision providing that all the members of the company agree to the amendment. However, s 22(2) has not yet been brought into force, largely due to the fear that it could operate to prevent the creation or amendment of class rights.

[87] CA 2006, s 22(1).

[88] As occurred in *Russell v Northern Bank Development Corp Ltd* [1992] 1 WLR 588 (HL) (discussed at 5.6.1).

[89] CA 2006, s 22(3).   [90] ibid s 23(1).   [91] ibid s 23(2).   [92] ibid s 24.

[93] ibid s 26(1). If the articles were amended by special resolution under s 21, then a copy of the resolution must also be sent to Companies House within 15 days of it being passed (CA 2006, s 30(1)).

[94] ibid s 26(3).   [95] ibid s 27(1) and (2).   [96] ibid s 27(3).   [97] ibid s 27(4).

Upon receipt of the amended articles, Companies House must publish in **The Gazette**[98] a notice stating (i) the name and registered number of the company; (ii) a description of the document; and (iii) the date the document was received.[99] The amendment to the articles and the text of the amended articles must also be provided to *the Gazette*.[100] If the company fails to comply with these rules, then it cannot rely on the article amendment against any other person until the amendment has been officially notified, or if it can demonstrate that the other person knew of the amendment.[101]

The Gazette: the UK's official public record

5.3.4 Enforcing the constitution

The courts have long held that a company's articles form a contract between a company and its members, and between the members themselves.[102] Section 33(1) of the CA 2006 expands upon this to cover the constitution in general, by providing that '[t]he provisions of a company's constitution bind the company and its members to the same extent as if there were covenants on the part of the company and of each member to observe those provisions'. Accordingly, the company's constitution forms a contract (often known as the 'statutory contract' or a 'relational contract'), and, as the articles constitute the principal constitutional document, it is appropriate to discuss the statutory contract here. The s 33 contract can impose obligations upon:

- the company when dealing with its members;
- the members when dealing with the company; and
- the members when dealing with each other.

Breach of certain provisions of the company's constitution may therefore constitute breach of contract, thereby allowing the non-breaching party to commence a personal action and obtain a remedy. However, as will be discussed, not all of the constitution's provisions will amount to terms of the s 33 contract. Before discussing the extent to which the s 33 contract can be enforced, it is important to note the ways in which the s 33 contract differs from a standard contract.

5.3.4.1 The s 33 statutory contract

The s 33 contract is a highly unusual one and, in several important ways, it differs from a standard contract and is not subject to certain standard contractual rules. Table 5.2 demonstrates the principal differences between a standard contract and the s 33 contract.

5.3.4.2 A contract between the company and its members

As the constitution forms a contract between the company and its members, it follows that both parties can enforce compliance with the terms of the constitution against the other, as demonstrated in the following two cases. In the first case, the company enforced the constitution against one of its members, whereas in the second, a member enforced the constitution against the company.

---

[98] Section 1116 of the CA 2006 does allow the Secretary of State to make regulations providing for alternative means of publication, but no such regulations have been passed, probably because *The Gazette* is easily available online (www.thegazette.co.uk accessed 10 January 2019).

[99] CA 2006, s 1077(1) and (2).   [100] ibid s 1078(2).   [101] ibid s 1079(1) and (2)(a).

[102] *Re Tavarone Mining Co* (1873) LR 8 Ch App 956.

TABLE 5.2 The statutory contract and a standard contract

	A standard contract	The s 33 contract
Source of binding force	Derives its binding force from the agreement between the parties	Derives its binding force from s 33 of the CA 2006
Alteration of terms against a party's wishes	Terms cannot usually be altered against the wishes of the parties	As the articles can be altered by passing a special resolution, the majority can alter the terms of the statutory contract against the wishes of the minority
Regulation of unfair terms	Subject to the provisions of the Unfair Contract Terms Act 1977	Not subject to ss 2 and 3 of the Unfair Contract Terms Act 1977[103]
Enforcement by a third party	Generally, third parties cannot enforce a standard contract, but can do so where s 1(1) of the Contracts (Rights of Third Parties) Act 1999 applies	Third parties cannot enforce the statutory contract, and the statutory contract is not subject to s 1 of the Contracts (Rights of Third Parties) Act 1999
Action for breach of contract	If any term of a standard contract is breached, it can give rise to an action for breach of contract	Only those terms of the constitution that relate to membership rights can form the basis for an action for breach of the statutory contract
Rectification of contract	The courts may be willing to rectify a standard contract if it fails to give effect to the parties' intentions, or if it contains a mistake	The courts will not rectify the statutory contract if it fails to give effect to the parties' intentions, or if it contains a mistake[104]
Defeasible on certain grounds	Standard contracts can be defeated on the grounds of mistake, misrepresentation, duress or undue influence	The statutory contract cannot be defeated on the grounds of mistake, misrepresentation, duress or undue influence[105]

Hickman v Kent or Romney Marsh Sheepbreeders' Association [1915] 1 Ch 881 (Ch)

FACTS: The company's articles provided that any dispute between it and a member should be referred to arbitration before any legal proceedings were initiated. The company purported to expel one of its members (Hickman) from its organization but, instead of referring the dispute to arbitration, Hickman petitioned the High Court for an injunction restraining his expulsion.

HELD: The articles formed a contract between the company and its members. The company was therefore permitted to enforce the term of the articles and require disputes to be referred to arbitration. The High Court therefore **stayed** Hickman's legal proceedings, and he was subsequently expelled.

➡ **stay:**
the temporary or permanent suspension of legal proceedings.

---

[103]   Unfair Contract Terms Act 1977, Sch 1, para 1(d)(ii).

[104]   *Scott v Frank F Scott (London) Ltd* [1940] Ch 794 (CA).

[105]   *Bratton Seymour Service Co Ltd v Oxborough* [1992] BCC 471 (CA).

Wood v Odessa Waterworks Co (1889) 42 ChD 636 (Ch)

FACTS: The company's articles provided that the directors may, with the sanction of the company in general meeting, declare a dividend to be paid to the members. The board proposed that a dividend would not be issued, but instead the members would be issued with debenture bonds, and an ordinary resolution was passed confirming this. However, one of the members (Wood) sought an injunction restraining the company from issuing the bonds on the ground that it was a breach of the articles.

HELD: Wood's action succeeded and the injunction was granted. Stirling J stated that the articles provide that:

> the directors may, with the sanction of a general meeting, declare a dividend to be paid to the shareholders. *Prima facie* that means to be paid in cash. The debenture-bonds proposed to be issued are not payments in cash; they are merely agreements or promises to pay: and if the contention of the company prevails a shareholder will be compelled to accept in lieu of cash a debt of the company payable at some uncertain future period. In my opinion that contention ought not to prevail . . . .[106]

5.3.4.3 A contract between the members

Just as the constitution forms a contract between the company and its members, so too does it form a contract amongst the members themselves. Accordingly, a breach of the constitution by a member can be enforced by another member.

Rayfield v Hands [1960] Ch 1 (Ch)

FACTS: Article 11 of a company's articles provided that, if a member wished to sell his shares, he should inform the directors, who would then purchase the shares between them. Rayfield wished to sell his shares and so notified the directors, but the directors refused to purchase his shares. The directors were all members of the company, and so Rayfield sought an order requiring the directors to purchase his shares.

HELD: The High Court ordered that the directors should purchase Rayfield's shares. The articles formed a contract amongst the members themselves, which Rayfield was entitled to enforce.

COMMENT: One might argue that Rayfield should not have been permitted to enforce art 11, as it did not relate to a right amongst members, but concerned a right between the members and the directors. Vaisey J disagreed and stated that the relationship here was between Rayfield and the directors acting in their capacity as members. He came to this conclusion on the basis that the company 'is one of that class of companies which bears a close analogy to a partnership'[107] and, in such companies, the distinction between members and directors is blurred. As a result of this, he stated that '[t]he conclusion to which I have come may not be of so general an application as to extend to the articles of association of every company'.[108]

See LCB Gower, 'Rayfield v Hands—a Postscript and a Drop of Scotch' (1958) 21 MLR 657.

---

[106] (1889) 42 ChD 636 (Ch) 642.

[107] [1960] Ch 1 (Ch) 9. Vaisey J was clearly referring to what we would, today, call a quasi-partnership (discussed at 15.4.1.2).

[108] ibid.

It is, however, important to note that the courts have imposed some notable limitations on the ability to enforce the constitution, to which we now turn. The issue that arises is that the courts have not been consistent as regards the enforcement of these limitations. As a result, it has been stated that cases involving enforcement of the contract have been 'the subject of considerable controversy in the past, and it may very well be that there will be considerable controversy about it in the future'.[109]

5.3.4.4 Outsiders, and outsider rights

One cardinal rule of contract law that applies to both standard contracts and the statutory contract is privity of contract. The statutory contract is formed between a company and its members—persons not party to the statutory contract (known as 'outsiders') are therefore not permitted to enforce the constitution.

Eley v Positive Government Security Life Assurance Co (1876) LR 1 Ex D 88 (CA)

FACTS: Eley, a solicitor, drafted a company's incorporation documents, including its articles which provided that Eley would act as the company's solicitor and could not be removed unless he engaged in some form of misconduct. Soon thereafter, the company ceased to employ Eley and engaged another firm of solicitors. Eley alleged that the company had breached the terms of the articles.

HELD: Eley's action failed. The company might very well have breached the articles, but as Eley was not party to the statutory contract, he could not sue for such a breach.

COMMENT: A few months after the company was incorporated, Eley did become a member of company. However, the judges did not discuss this at all. It is submitted that it would have made no difference, as Eley was attempting to enforce an outsider right (discussed below), but one might have expected the judges to have discussed this.

Section 1(1) of the Contracts (Rights of Third Parties) Act 1999 provides that a third party can enforce a term of a contract if it purports to confer a benefit on him. One might have assumed that a claimant in a similar position to Eley could therefore argue that the term of the articles confers a benefit on him, and so can be enforced by him. However, the 1999 Act provides that s 1 will not apply to the statutory contract created by s 33 of the CA 2006.[110]

Not only can the constitution not be enforced by outsiders, but it has also said that it cannot be used to enforce outsider rights (i.e. rights granted to a member in his capacity other than a member). As Buckley LJ stated, '[t]he purpose of the [constitution] is to define the position of the shareholder as shareholder, and not to bind him in his capacity as an individual'.[111] It follows that '[a]n outsider to whom rights purport to be given by the articles in his capacity as such outsider, whether he is or subsequently becomes a member, cannot sue on those articles treating them as contracts between himself and the company to enforce those rights'.[112] In other words, members can only enforce those

---

[109] *Beattie v E and F Beattie Ltd* [1938] Ch 708 (CA) 721 (Greene MR).
[110] Contracts (Rights of Third Parties) Act 1999, s 6(2).
[111] *Bisgood v Henderson's Transvaal Estates* [1908] 1 Ch 743 (CA) 759.
[112] *Hickman v Kent or Romney Marsh Sheepbreeders Association* [1915] 1 Ch 881 (Ch) 897 (Astbury J).

terms of the constitution that relate to membership rights and members must bring their claim in their capacity as members (case law often uses the phrase 'member *qua* member' with *qua* meaning 'in the capacity of'). For example, as the following case demonstrates, if a person is a member and a director, he will not be allowed to enforce the constitution if he is bringing his clam in his capacity as a director (although, as discussed later, the courts have not been consistent).

Beattie v E and F Beattie Ltd [1938] Ch 708 (CA)

FACTS: Article 133 of the company's articles provided that, in the event of a dispute between the company and its members or a dispute between members, the members shall not commence legal proceedings, but must instead refer the dispute to arbitration. Ernest Beattie ('EB', a director and member) was alleged to have improperly drawn a director's salary without the authorization of the company or its members. Margaret Beattie ('MB', another member) therefore initiated legal proceedings to recover this payment. EB alleged that, because he was a member, art 133 applied and the dispute should be referred to arbitration. He therefore sought to enforce art 133.

HELD: Greene MR stated that 'the contractual force given to the articles of association . . . is limited to such provisions of the articles as apply to the relationship of the members in their capacity as members'.[113] EB was seeking to enforce art 133 in his capacity as a director, not in his capacity as a member. Accordingly, EB could not enforce art 133 and the legal proceedings were permitted to go ahead.

Accordingly, it is important for a member to know whether the constitutional right they are seeking to enforce is a membership right or not. Common membership rights contained in the constitution include:

- the right to attend, speak, and vote at general meetings;
- the method of counting votes at general meetings;
- rights relating to the transfer and transmission of shares;
- the right to a dividend, once it has been validly declared.

Unfortunately, as the Law Commission noted, case law in this area has 'not been uniformly applied by the courts, particularly in cases involving shareholder directors',[114] referring to cases where a member has been apparently permitted to enforce the constitution in his capacity as a director.[115] Indeed, given the number of such cases, it has been argued that 'the proposition that "outsider" rights in the articles are beyond the scope of section 20 is wrong, since it is flatly contrary to all those cases where such rights have actually been enforced'.[116] The enforcement of such rights may be justified in a quasi-partnership, as the dividing line between a member and director is blurred and the members will usually expect to be involved in management, so certain rights conferred upon directors may legitimately be regarded as membership rights.[117] Any

Quasi-partnerships are discussed at 15.4.1.2.

---

113 [1938] Ch 708 (CA) 721.

114 Law Commission, *Shareholder Remedies* (Law Com CP No 142, 1996) para 2.17.

115 See e.g. *Pulbrook v Richmond Consolidated Mining Co* (1878) 9 ChD 610 (Ch); *Salmon v Quin & Axtens Ltd* [1909] 1 Ch 311 (CA) (discussed at 9.2.1.1).

116 Roger Gregory, 'The Section 20 Contract' (1981) 44 MLR 526, 539. Section 20 refers to s 20 of the Companies Act 1948, a predecessor of s 33.

117 See e.g. *Rayfield v Hands* [1960] 1 Ch 1 (Ch) (discussed at 5.3.2).

inconsistencies in this area might be reduced if the CA 2006 expressly stated which rights are to be regarded as membership rights. Such an approach was considered by the Law Commission and the CLRSG, but was ultimately rejected on the ground that such a list could not state every breach that could give rise to a personal action, and that such a list might encourage litigation in trivial cases.[118]

Whilst outsiders may not generally be able to enforce the constitution under s 33, there are alternative ways for an outsider to enforce the constitution. An outsider can enforce a constitutional right, or an outsider right can be enforced, if a separate agreement outside of the constitution provides for such enforcement.[119] This agreement can be express or, as demonstrated in the following example, it can be implied.

 Eg **Enforcing outsider rights through an implied agreement**

Article 24 of the articles of Dragon plc provides that all of the directors, except Jane Dragon, shall be paid £30,000 per year. Jane Dragon uses her majority shareholding to amend art 24 so that the other directors will be paid £25,000 per year. The other directors object and commence proceedings against the company. In such a case, the court may conclude that art 24 forms a separate contract between the directors and the company, which the directors can enforce.[120]

In practice, directors tend not to want their remuneration to be provided for in the articles, as it can be changed without their consent. Accordingly, the remuneration of directors is usually set out in a separate contract of service.

5.3.4.5 Internal irregularities

Even if a constitutional membership right is breached, a member might still be prevented from enforcing the constitution if the breach is regarded by the court as an 'internal irregularity'. An internal irregularity occurs where the 'alleged wrong is a transaction which might be made binding on the corporation and on all its members by a simple majority of the members'.[121] The following case demonstrates this in practice.

 ***MacDougall v Gardiner* (1875) 1 ChD 13 (CA)[122]**

FACTS: The company's articles empowered the chair of a general meeting, with the consent of the meeting, to adjourn the meeting, and to provide for the taking of a vote on a poll if demanded to do so by five shareholders. At a general meeting, it was proposed that the meeting should be adjourned and, following a vote by show of hands, the chair, Gardiner, declared the vote carried. When a group of shareholders demanded that the proposed adjournment be put to a poll, Gardner refused on the ground that the issue of adjournment could not be put to a poll. One of the shareholders, MacDougall, sought, on behalf of the other shareholders (excluding

---

[118] Law Commission, *Shareholder Remedies* (Law Com No 246, 1997) paras 7.10–7.12; CLRSG, 'Modern Company Law for a Competitive Economy: Developing the Framework' (2000) paras 4.91–4.94.

[119] *Re New British Iron Co* [1898] 1 Ch 324 (Ch).

[120] See *Swabey v Port Darwin Gold Mining Co* (1889) 1 Meg 385.

[121] *Prudential Assurance Co Ltd v Newman Industries Ltd (No 2)* [1982] Ch 204 (CA) 210.

[122] See also *Irvine v Union Bank of Australia* (1877) 2 App Cas 366 (PC); *Grant v UK Switchback Railways Co* (1888) 40 ChD 135 (CA).

the directors) (i) a declaration from the court that Gardiner's actions were improper; and (ii) an injunction restraining the directors from carrying out further action without the shareholders' approval.

HELD: Mellish LJ stated:

> if the thing complained of is a thing which in substance the majority of the company are entitled to do, or if something has been done irregularly which the majority of the company are entitled to do regularly, or if something has been done illegally which the majority of the company are entitled to do legally, there can be no use in having a litigation about it, the ultimate end of which is only that a meeting has to be called, and then ultimately the majority gets its wishes.[123]

On this basis, the Court held that the breach committed by the Gardiner was an internal irregularity and so MacDougall's action failed.

This internal irregularity principle is clearly the result of the principle of majority rule, which requires that '[t]he rights of the individual are . . . subordinated to the wishes of the majority'.[124] The issue that has arisen is that, as with cases concerning outsider rights, the court has not applied the 'internal irregularity' principle consistently and has, in a number of cases, allowed actions to succeed concerning constitutional breaches involving internal irregularities, such as the wrongful exclusion of proxy votes,[125] the provision of defective notice of meetings,[126] and inadequate notice of a special resolution.[127] The Law Commission considered identifying in statute which membership rights concerned internal irregularities, but decided against this course of action.[128]

5.4 Resolutions and agreements

Section 17(b) provides that the constitution will include 'any resolutions and agreements to which Chapter 3 applies . . .'. These are listed in s 29(1) and are referred to as 'resolutions and agreements affecting a company's constitution'. However, it is clear that the s 29(1) list goes beyond agreements and resolutions that affect the company's constitution. For example, s 29(1)(a) provides that any special resolution will form part of the company's constitution, even though many special resolutions will involve decisions that have no bearing on the company's constitution. Copies of resolutions and agreements listed under s 29(1) must be forwarded to Companies House within 15 days of them being passed or made,[129] and failure to do so is a criminal offence.[130]

---

[123] (1875) 1 ChD 13 (CA) 25.

[124] RR Drury, 'The Relative Nature of a Shareholder's Right to Enforce the Company Contract' (1986) 45 CLJ 219, 237.

[125] *Oliver v Dalgleish* [1963] 1 WLR 1274 (Ch).

[126] *Alexander v Simpson* (1889) 43 ChD 139 (CA).

[127] *Tiessen v Henderson* [1899] 1 Ch 861 (Ch).

[128] Law Commission, *Shareholder Remedies* (Law Com No 246, 1997) para 7.7.

[129] CA 2006, s 30(1).   [130] ibid s 30(2).

5.5 Other constitutional documents

Section 32 provides the members with the right to be provided with certain 'constitutional documents', thereby indicating that other documents also form part of the company's constitution. These constitutional documents include certain documents discussed above (e.g. the articles, and resolutions and agreements listed in s 29(1)), but also includes past and current certificates of incorporation, the statement of capital, and the statement of guarantee.[131] Failure to provide these documents to a member when requested to do so is a criminal offence.[132]

5.6 Shareholders' agreements

As noted, the company and its members have, through drafting and amending the articles, considerable discretion when determining the internal rules by which the company is governed. An alternative, or additional, method of providing the members with the ability to draft their own rules is through the use of a shareholders' agreement. A shareholders' agreement is simply a separate contract entered into by two or more members (the company itself may also be a party to the agreement),[133] which establishes rules regarding the relationship between the members, and/or the company. A shareholders' agreement can be entered into when the company is first registered or anytime post-incorporation.

It is important to note that shareholders' agreements are not generally considered to be part of the company's constitution, but instead they supplement the constitution. However, the effects of shareholders' agreements are so similar to constitutional provisions that it is appropriate to discuss them alongside the other constitutional documents. It is also worth noting that, whilst other countries have statutorily recognized shareholders' agreements, the CA 2006 does not overtly regulate shareholders' agreements (save for a few provisions which make reference to such agreements).[134]

The question that arises is why a shareholders' agreement is used rather than simply amending the articles. The following example demonstrates how shareholders' agreements can be more advantageous than simply amending the articles, and also demonstrates the type of clauses that may be found in such an agreement.

 Eg   Shareholders' agreements

Jane Dragon is keen to ensure that she retains control of Dragon plc, and to that end, she and the other members of Dragon plc enter into a shareholders' agreement (Dragon plc itself is also a party to this agreement), which provides:

- in the event of a resolution being tabled to remove Jane Dragon as director, her voting power will be trebled;

---

[131] ibid s 32(1).   [132] ibid s 32(3).

[133] In which case, the shareholders' agreement will bear some similarity to the statutory contract created under s 33, as it will bind the company to its members, and the members *inter se*.

[134] See e.g. s 40(3) of the CA 2006, which states that references to limitations upon the directors' powers in s 40 include limitations deriving 'from any agreement between the members of the company or of any class of shareholders'.

- the parties to the agreement will not exercise their power to amend the articles, and;
- no shares can be issued, nor any new directors appointed, without the approval of Jane Dragon.

There are several advantages to placing these clauses in a shareholders' agreement, and not in the articles. First, all the parties to the agreement are bound by all the terms of the agreement, whereas, as discussed at 5.3.4.4, not all the terms of the articles form part of the statutory contract. Second, the agreement can only be altered with the consent of all the parties to it (unless the agreement provides otherwise), so Jane knows that the agreement cannot be altered without her consent. Conversely, the articles can be amended by the majority against the wishes of the minority. Third, as a shareholders' agreement is a private contract, it is not subject to the limitations of the statutory contract (e.g. the restrictions relating to membership rights). Fourth, shareholders' agreements do not have to be made public through registration with Companies House.

However, shareholders' agreements do suffer from a notable disadvantage, namely that, being subject to privity of contract, they only bind the parties to it and not subsequent members (unlike the articles, which automatically bind new members), unless the new member assents to being bound by the agreement. However, it is possible to circumvent this limitation by providing in the agreement that the parties to the agreement will ensure that new members are made party to the agreement through a Deed of Adherence.[135]

Shareholders' agreements are not typically encountered in larger companies, but tend to be more common among smaller companies, such as quasi-partnerships.

> Quasi-partnerships are discussed at 15.4.2.1.

5.6.1 Enforcing a shareholders' agreement

A shareholders' agreement can be enforced by any person who is party to it (subject to the usual contractual rules regarding remoteness, etc.), and remedies for breach can include damages, injunctions, and specific performance. Breach of shareholders' agreement might also provide evidence of unfair prejudice[136] or provide a justification for a compulsory winding-up order. Enforcement of a shareholders' agreement can be more problematic where the company is also party to the agreement, especially where the agreement seeks to restrict the company's statutory powers, as the following case demonstrates.

> The unfair prejudice remedy is discussed at 15.3, and compulsory winding-up orders are discussed at 15.4.

Russell v Northern Bank Development Corp Ltd [1992] 1 WLR 588 (HL)

FACTS: Tyrone Brick Ltd ('TB') had five shareholders—Northern Bank Development Corp Ltd (NBD') held 120 shares, and 80 shares were divided equally between TB's four directors. A shareholders' agreement was entered into between the five shareholders and TB, clause 3 of which provided that no further share capital would be created or issued without the consent

> See LS Sealy, 'Shareholders' Agreements— An Endorsement and a Warning from the House of Lords' (1992) 51 CLJ 437.

---

[135] For an example of this, see *Re Coroin Ltd* [2011] EWHC 3466 (Ch) [42]. However, it should be noted that if a new member is made to enter into the agreement via duress, then the agreement may be set aside (*Antonio v Antonio* [2010] EWHC 1199 (QB)).

[136] Although breach of a shareholders' agreement will not per se constitute unfair prejudice (*Sikorski v Sikorski* [2012] EWHC 1613 (Ch)).

of each of the parties to the agreement. The board of TB called a general meeting and tabled a resolution that would increase TB's share capital from £1,000 to £4 million. Russell (one of TB's shareholders) sought an injunction restraining the other members from voting on the resolution.

HELD: Lord Jauncey stated that the key issue was 'whether [clause] 3 of the agreement constituted an unlawful and invalid fetter on the statutory power of [TB] to increase its share capital or whether it was no more than an agreement between the shareholders as to their manner of voting in a given situation'.[137] The House drew a distinction between the undertaking by TB, and the undertaking by TB's shareholders. The agreement amongst the shareholders simply stated that they would exercise their voting rights in a particular way, which was a perfectly valid agreement. Conversely, the undertaking by TB (i.e. not to increase its share capital) represented an unlawful fetter on the company's statutory powers, and so was void. Accordingly, the House severed the part of the agreement seeking to bind TB, and declared[138] binding the parts of the agreement that operated amongst the five shareholders. In other words, clause 3 bound the shareholders, but did not bind TB.

COMMENT: The reaction to *Russell* has been mixed. Academics do generally agree that *Russell* helped clarify the law.[139] However, it has also been argued that *Russell* was 'a triumph of formalism over substance. This is not necessarily a criticism—formalism plays an important part in the law. But practically it means that those with ingenuity and enough money to pay for costly drafting can step outside the general mandatory regime'.[140] What commentators do agree on is that caution should be exhibited before making the company party to a shareholders' agreement.

CHAPTER SUMMARY

- A company's constitution includes its articles, all resolutions and agreements affecting the company's constitution, and other constitutional documents.

- All companies must have a memorandum of association, but its importance is now much reduced.

- The articles of association form the principal constitutional document and set out the internal rules by which the company is to be run.

- Legislation provides several sets of model articles that can be used by promoters who do not wish to draft their own articles.

- The articles can be amended by passing a special resolution, but both statute and the common law impose limits on a company's ability to amend its articles.

- Section 33 of the CA 2006 provides that the company's constitution forms a contract between the company and its members, and between the members themselves.

---

[137] [1992] 1 WLR 588 (HL) 592.

[138] It is worth noting that the House did not grant the injunction that Russell sought. This was because Russell had no objection to the resolution per se—he was simply concerned that his position would be weakened given that he lacked the necessary funds to take advantage of the rights issue. Given this, the House felt that an injunction was inappropriate, and instead simply declared clause 3 as valid amongst the shareholders, and remitted the case back to the Court of Appeal to make the appropriate order.

[139] See e.g. LS Sealy, 'Shareholders' Agreements—An Endorsement and a Warning from the House of Lords' (1992) 51 CLJ 437, 438.

[140] Giora Shapira, 'Voting Agreements and Corporate Statutory Powers' (1993) 109 LQR 210, 214.

- Outsiders and persons seeking to enforce outsider rights cannot generally enforce the company's constitution.
- Two or more of a company's shareholders may enter into a contract (known as a shareholders' agreement), which sets out terms regarding the relationship between the members and/or the company.

FURTHER READING

Rita Cheung, 'Shareholders' Agreements—Shareholders' Contractual Freedom in Company Law' (2012) 6 JBL 504.
- Discusses the extent to which shareholders' agreements can be used to contract out of company law provisions.

RR Drury, 'The Relative Nature of a Shareholder's Right to Enforce the Company Contract' (1986) 45 CLJ 219.
- Reviews a number of academic viewpoints regarding the members' ability to enforce the constitution.

FG Rixon, 'Competing Interests and Conflicting Principles: An Examination of the Power of Alteration of Articles of Association' (1986) 49 MLR 446.
- Provides an in-depth examination of the members' power to later the articles, and discusses the limitations upon this power.

SELF-TEST QUESTIONS

1. Define the following terms:
- model articles;
- entrenched article provisions;
- statutory contract;
- outsider;
- outsider rights;
- shareholders' agreement.

2. State whether each of the following statements is true or false and, if false, explain why:
- A company's constitution consists of its memorandum and its articles.
- If a company drafts its own set of articles, then the model articles will not apply.
- A company cannot make its articles unalterable.
- The constitution forms a contract between the directors and the members.
- A member can enforce any term in the constitution.

3. 'The contract created by the company's constitution is a highly unusual one, but the ability to enforce the constitution provides the members with a powerful source of protection.' Discuss.

4. Dragon Tools Ltd ('DT') has adopted the model articles for private companies, but has added several new provisions, namely:
- Article 18A provides that 'a director will be required to vacate office if the other directors so require'.
- Article 18B provides that 'any director removed under art 18A who holds shares in DT will be required to sell those shares to the directors of DT at a fair price'.
- Article 18C provides that 'any director removed under art 18A will be entitled to a loss of office payment of £10,000'.

Yvonne, a director and shareholder of DT, has argued repeatedly in board meetings that the company should appoint a qualified company secretary, but the other directors disagree and are growing tired of Yvonne's criticism of the company's management. Accordingly, the other directors use the power granted to them by art 18A and remove Yvonne from office. The directors also state that Yvonne must sell to them all her shares in DT. Yvonne seeks your advice regarding the following:

(a) Are arts 18A and 18B valid and can they be enforced against her?

(b) The directors are offering her the £10,000 loss of office payment provided for under art 18C, but Yvonne's service contract states that, if she is removed from office, she will be paid £20,000. Yvonne wishes to know if she can claim this £20,000.

 ONLINE RESOURCES

This book is accompanied by online resources to better support you in your studies. Visit www.oup.com/uk/roach-company/ for:

- answers to the self-test questions;
- further reading lists;
- multiple-choice questions;
- glossary.

Updates to the law can be found on the author's Twitter account (@UKCompanyLaw) and further resources can be found on the author's blog (www.companylawandgovernance.com).

6 Corporate capacity and liability

- Company contracts
- Corporate capacity
- The agents of a company
- The protection of third parties
- Personal and vicarious liability, and attribution

INTRODUCTION

A company, as a legal person, cannot act of its own volition. It requires natural persons to act on its behalf. However, as Lord Hoffmann noted:

> there would be little sense in deeming such a **persona ficta** to exist unless there were also rules to tell one what acts were to count as acts of the company. It is therefore a necessary part of corporate personality that there should be rules by which acts are attributed to the company. These may be called 'the rules of attribution'.[1]

➡ *persona ficta:* fictional person

This chapter focuses on these rules of attribution, namely those rules that determine the extent to which certain persons can legally commit the company to certain acts, and the extent to which the company can be liable for the actions of those who act on its behalf. In order to understand such rules, it is also important to discuss the contractual capacity of the company itself. The chapter begins by looking at the core rules regarding a company's ability to enter into contracts.

6.1 Company contracts

This section is concerned with how a company can execute certain documents, with the focus on how a company enters into contracts. The basic rules are found in ss 43–44 of the Companies Act 2006 (CA 2006), but they lack consistency. Section 43(1) of the CA 2006 provides that a contract can be (i) made by a company, by writing under is common seal; or (ii) on behalf of a company, by a person acting under its authority, express or implied. However, s 44(1) states that a document is executed by a company by affixing

---

[1] *Meridian Global Funds Management Asia Ltd v Securities Commission* [1995] 2 AC 500 (PC) 506.

its common seal to that document, or by complying with the provisions in s 44(2)–(8). As Palmer correctly notes,[2] this means that (despite what s 43(1) might say), there are in fact three ways by which a company can enter into a contract:

1. by affixing its common seal to the contract;
2. by complying with the rules found in s 44(2)–(8) of the CA 2006; or
3. by a person acting under the company's express or implied authority.

The first two methods are discussed in this section. The third method is considerably broader and more complex and is discussed at 6.3.

6.1.1 Common seal

The first method by which a company can execute a document is by affixing its common seal to that contract. A common seal is essentially the signature of a company and consists of an embossed stamp which is used to leave an impression or indent on the contract being entered into. A company is not required to have a common seal, but it may do so if it wishes.[3] Most companies do not have a common seal, but multinational companies will often retain a seal in case they need to conduct business in a country that still requires use of a seal.[4] Companies may also use a seal to seal securities issued by the company[5] (e.g. on share certificates). If a company does choose to have a seal, then its name must be engraved in legible characters on the seal,[6] and failure to state the name legibly is a criminal offence[7] (although whether this also invalidates the contract is unclear, but would appear unlikely).[8]

How the seal is to be used is a matter for the company's constitution and the constitution is free to impose additional requirements regarding the use of the seal. The model articles provide that the common seal may only be used by the authority of the directors, and the directors may decide by what means and in what form the seal is to be used.[9] The model articles go on to provide that if the seal is affixed to a document, then the document must also be signed by at least one authorized person in the presence of a witness who attests the signature.[10] For this purpose, an authorized person is any director of the company, the company secretary, or any persons authorized by the directors to sign documents to which the common seal is applied.[11]

6.1.2 Execution of documents

With the abolition of the requirement to hold a common seal, an alternative method was required for companies to execute documents. Section 44(2) provides that a document is validly executed if it is signed on behalf of the company by two authorized signatories,

---

[2] Geoffrey Morse, *Palmer's Company Law* (Sweet & Maxwell 2018) para 3.103.   [3] CA 2006, s 45(1).

[4] Section 49(1) provides that a company that has a common seal may also have a seal for use outside the UK.

[5] Section 50(1) provides that a company may have an official seal for sealing securities.

[6] CA 2006, s 45(2). It is common for companies to provide additional information such as the year the business was established or the words 'common seal'.

[7] ibid s 45(3)–(5).

[8] See e.g. *OTV Berwelco Ltd v Technical & General Guarantee Co Ltd* [2002] EWHC 2240 (TCC), [2002] 4 All ER 668, where a contract was held to be validly sealed even though the name on the seal was the company's trading name and not its registered name.

[9] Model articles for private companies, art 49(1) and (2); model articles for public companies, art 81(1) and (2).

[10] Model articles for private companies, art 49(3); model articles for public companies, art 81(3).

[11] Model articles for private companies, art 49(4); model articles for public companies, art 81(4).

or by a director of the company in the presence of a witness who attests the signature. For the purposes of s 44(2), an authorized signatory is:

- every director of the company, and;
- the company secretary (or joint secretary) of that company (if it has one).[12]

In addition to the above procedural rules, two further issues are of crucial importance, namely:

1. whether the company has the capacity to enter into the contract (discussed at 6.2), and;
2. whether the directors have authority to commit the company to entering into such a contract (discussed at 6.3 and 6.4).

6.2 Corporate capacity

A company, as a person, has capacity to enter into contracts. However, the contractual capacity of a company may be limited (e.g. through a provision in the company's articles) and where a company acts outside its capacity, it is said to be acting **ultra vires**. Historically, the *ultra vires* doctrine was a complex and extremely important area of company law, but legal developments over the past 30 years have seen the doctrine rendered irrelevant for many companies. However, despite what some sources might state, the doctrine has not been abolished, and so is still of relevance.

 ultra vires: 'beyond one's powers'

6.2.1 **The *ultra vires* doctrine**

Prior to the CA 2006, all companies had to include, within their memorandum, an objects clause which set out the purposes or objects for which the company was set up. This objects clause had several functions: (i) it served to limit the contractual capacity of the company and the directors' authority; (ii) it informed outside persons as to the purposes of the company; (iii) it protected members and creditors by ensuring that the company only entered into contracts in relation to its legitimate areas of expertise[13] and did not embark on risky frolics; and; (iv) it reinforced the notion that the directors' duty was to act within the company's powers. If the company entered into a contract that was outside its objects clause, then that contract would be *ultra vires* and void.

Ashbury Railway Carriage and Iron Co Ltd v Riche (1874-75) LR 7 HL 653 (HL)

FACTS: The objects of Ashbury Railway Carriage and Iron Co ('Ashbury') were 'to make, and sell, or lend on hire, railway carriages and waggons, and all kinds of railway plant, fittings, machinery, and rolling stock . . .'. Ashbury purchased the right to build a railway line in Belgium, and subcontracted construction work to Riche. A group of Ashbury's members objected to the transaction, and Ashbury later repudiated the contract with Riche. Riche sued, seeking damages for breach of contract, and Ashbury argued that the contract was void as it was *ultra vires*.

---

[12] CA 2006, s 44(3).
[13] See e.g. *Re Introductions Ltd (No 2)* [1969] 1 WLR 1359 (Ch), where a company whose objects stated that it would provide information to overseas visitors and businessmen was held to be acting *ultra vires* when it operated a pig-farming business.

> **HELD:** Ashbury's objects allowed it to construct railway carriages and wagons, and rolling stock—the objects did not allow the company to construct railway lines. Accordingly, the contract with Riche was *ultra vires* and void, and so Riche was unable to claim damages for breach.
>
> **COMMENT:** The decision in *Ashbury* is subject to two principal criticisms. First, it prevented companies from expanding into new areas of business (at the time of *Ashbury*, it was impossible to amend the memorandum). Second, it disadvantaged third parties, who would find transactions entered into with the company rendered void when the company acted *ultra vires*.

➡ *intra vires*:
'within one's powers'

Companies sought to mitigate both criticisms by drafting long and complex objects clauses, but third parties still needed to consult a company's objects to be sure it was acting **intra vires**. As time progressed, the harshness of the *ultra vires* doctrine on third parties was acknowledged and a series of statutory amendments and judicial decisions emasculated the doctrine and provided increased protection to third parties, with two reforms contained in successive Companies Acts rendering the *ultra vires* doctrine irrelevant in many cases.

6.2.2 The Companies Acts reforms

The first major reform is contained in s 31 of the CA 2006, which provides that '[u]nless a company's articles specifically restrict the objects of a company, its objects are unrestricted'.[14] Accordingly, companies incorporated under the CA 2006 do not need an objects clause and such companies will have unrestricted contractual capacity (subject to any other restrictions in the articles). A company incorporated under the CA 2006 that chooses to have an objects clause, or a company incorporated under a prior Companies Act that retains its objects clause, will still be bound by its objects, although the objects clause will form part of the articles and not the memorandum.[15] From this, it follows that such companies can choose to remove their objects clause by passing a special resolution,[16] and so will acquire unrestricted capacity (and, indeed, many larger companies incorporated under prior Companies Acts have removed their objects clause).

The second reform was originally introduced into s 35 of the CA 1985 by the CA 1989, and is now found in s 39 of the CA 2006. Section 39(1) provides that '[t]he validity of an act done by a company shall not be called into question on the ground of lack of capacity by reason of anything in the company's constitution'. Accordingly, a contract entered into by a company cannot be invalidated on the ground that the contract is outside the scope of the company's contractual capacity. Under s 35(2) of the CA 1985, a member could restrain a company from engaging in an *ultra vires* act providing that no legal obligation had yet arisen, but such a provision is not included in the CA 2006. Instead a member of the company (via a derivative claim) or the company itself could seek a remedy from the directors on the ground that they have breached their duty to act in accordance with the company's constitution.[17] Accordingly, determining whether an act is within the company's contractual capacity is still of importance.

---

[14] CA 2006, s 31(1). [15] ibid s 28(1). [16] ibid s 21(1).

[17] ibid s 171(a). Indeed, para 123 of the Explanatory Notes to the 2006 Act states that the removal of the requirement for an objects clause and the existence of the s 171 duty render a s 35(2)-style provision unnecessary.

6.3 The agents of a company

A company may have capacity to enter into a particular contract, but that does not mean that persons who act on the company's behalf are automatically imbued with authority to enter into such a contract on the company's behalf. As noted, s 43(1) of the CA 2006 provides that a contract can be made on behalf of the company by any person acting under its express or implied authority. In practice, most contracts entered into by the company will not actually be executed via the two methods stated in s 44(1), but will be entered into by a director or other person authorized to contract on behalf of the company. Accordingly, determining the authority granted to such persons is vital, with the key issue being their authority as agents. It is therefore vital to understand the distinction between a company's capacity and the authority of agents to contract on its behalf. Consider the following example.

 Section 44 is discussed at 6.1.

> **Eg** **Can a director bind the company?**
>
> Dragon plc adopted the model articles for public companies, but inserted a new art 3A, which states that 'directors are not permitted to enter into any contract that contractually binds Dragon for a period of longer than two years, without the approval of the members'. A supply contract between Dragon and GigaTech Ltd is due to expire soon. Angus, one of Dragon's directors, purports to enter into a contract on behalf of Dragon, renewing the supply contract with GigaTech for a further three years. In fact, the other directors of Dragon were not planning on renewing the contract at all, as they had found a cheaper supplier elsewhere. Accordingly, the board of Dragon refuses to honour the contract. GigaTech commences proceedings for breach of contract, and seeks an order for specific performance.[18]

Dragon generally has contractual capacity to enter into contracts of indefinite duration. Article 3A is not concerned with Dragon's contractual capacity, but instead focuses on the authority of its directors to contract on Dragon's behalf. Whether Dragon is bound will likely depend on whether Angus has authority to enter into the contract with GigaTech. Dragon will try to disown the contract by arguing that Angus did not have authority to enter into it on its behalf. GigaTech will seek to enforce the contract by arguing that Angus did have authority to enter into the contract on behalf of Dragon, but GigaTech will not be able to rely on a clause such as art 3 of the model articles, as such clauses grant power to the directors collectively, and not to individual directors. Further, it is unclear whether GigaTech could rely on s 40 of the CA 2006 as that applies to the powers of 'the directors' and, as discussed at 6.4.1.3, it is unclear whether s 40 applies to the actions of a single director.

 Article 3 is discussed at 9.1, whereas s 40 is discussed at 6.4.1.

Absent any specific article provisions that would empower Angus to enter into the contract (and the model articles do not contain any such provisions), the issue would likely be determined by reference to the law of agency.[19] The law of agency generally provides that a principal is liable for the acts of his agent. As the directors are agents of the company, it follows that generally the company is liable for the authorized acts of its directors. Accordingly, the different types of authority need to be discussed, with the two principal types of authority being actual authority and apparent authority.

---

[18] In a case such as this, GigaTech will likely value performance of the contract over an award of damages. If damages were its preferred remedy, it might consider suing Angus for breach of warranty of authority, especially if its claim for breach against Dragon failed.

[19] Note that the law of agency is a distinct legal topic in its own right, and students may wish to consult a specific text on agency such as Peter G Watts, *Bowstead & Reynolds on Agency* (21st edn, Sweet & Maxwell 2018) or Roderick Munday, *Agency: Law and Principles* (3rd edn, OUP 2016).

6.3.1 **Actual authority**

The classic definition of actual authority was provided by Diplock LJ, who stated that:

> actual authority is a legal relationship between the principal and agent created by a consensual agreement to which they alone are parties. Its scope is to be ascertained by applying ordinary principles of construction of contracts, including any proper implications from the express words used, the usages of the trade, or the course of business between the parties.[20]

This definition indicates that there are two types of actual authority that need to be discussed:

1. express actual authority, which refers to the authority that the company has expressly bestowed upon a person, either orally or in writing; and

2. implied actual authority, which refers to authority that the law deems to have been bestowed by the company upon a person as a result of their dealings, circumstances, or relationship.

6.3.1.1 **Express actual authority**

Lord Denning MR defined express actual authority as 'authority given by express words, such as when a board of directors pass a resolution which authorises two of their number to sign cheques'.[21] Express actual authority is the most straightforward form of authority and refers to that authority that has been expressly conferred upon a person by the company. The most obvious source of express actual authority is the company's constitution, with article provisions such as art 3 of the model articles imbuing the directors with considerable express actual authority.

Article 3 is discussed at 9.1.

The constitution may also limit the directors' express authority. For example, the articles may limit the amount of money that the directors can cause the company to borrow, or they may require member approval for certain transactions. It is worth noting that, generally, the provisions in the articles (such as art 3 of the model articles) confer powers on the directors collectively and not upon individual directors. The articles may expressly authorize individual directors to engage in certain acts, but such authorization usually derives from the board itself through board resolutions delegating[22] or conferring powers upon individual directors. The directors' actual authority is also limited by their having to comply with other rules of law (e.g. the general duties found in ss 171–7 of the CA 2006).

The general duties are discussed in Chapters 10 and 11.

6.3.1.2 **Implied actual authority**

The actual authority of a person can also be implied based on the relationship between the company and that person, or based on their conduct, as seen in the following example.

Eg | **Implied actual authority**

Dragon plc is looking to purchase a piece of machinery. OmniTech Ltd produces the machinery in question and enters into negotiations with Greg, one of Dragon's directors. Greg tells the board of

---

[20] *Freeman & Lockyer v Buckhurst Park Properties (Mangal) Ltd* [1964] 2 QB 480 (CA) 503.

[21] *Hely-Hutchinson v Brayhead Ltd* [1968] 1 QB 549 (CA) 583.

[22] Article 5 of the model articles expressly authorizes the directors to delegate (and sub-delegate) any powers conferred upon them by the articles (delegation is discussed at 9.2.3).

OmniTech that he acts as Dragon's purchasing director and has full authority to enter into contracts of sale on behalf of Dragon. In fact, Greg has never been formally appointed as Dragon's purchasing director, although he has undertaken this role on several occasions with the consent of Dragon's board. A price is agreed for the purchase of the machinery and Greg signs the contract on behalf of Dragon. However, the board of Dragon believes that the purchase price is too high and refuses to honour the sale, contending that Greg lacked authority to enter into the contract on Dragon's behalf.

Does Greg have actual authority to enter into the contract of sale with OmniTech? He almost certainly does not have express actual authority, but he will likely have implied actual authority. Implied actual authority arises in a number of situations.

- An agent has implied authority 'to do whatever is necessary for, or ordinarily incidental to, the effective execution of his express [actual] authority in the usual way'.[23] For example, a director expressly authorized to sell goods on behalf of the company will also have implied authority to negotiate with third parties regarding the sale price of those goods.

- Certain markets, trades, or locations may have their own customs, and the courts may give effect to such customs by holding that an agent has implied authority to act in accordance with the custom in question.[24]

- A director may be appointed to a particular role within the company (e.g. chair, chief executive officer (CEO)), or engaged within a particular aspect of the company's trade or business, but his authority will not be specified in detail. In such cases, a director may have implied authority to do such things that a person in that director's position usually has. Indeed, as the following case demonstrates, this form of implied authority can arise even if the director has not been formally appointed to the role in question (which is why Greg would likely have authority in the example box above).

Hely-Hutchinson v Brayhead Ltd [1968] 1 QB 549 (CA)

FACTS: Richards (the agent) was chair of Brayhead Ltd (the principal) and, although he was not appointed formally as the managing director of the company, he acted as such with the board's acquiescence. Richards, purporting to act on behalf of Brayhead, agreed to indemnify Hely-Hutchinson[25] for any loss in relation to a company named Perdio Electronics Ltd. When Perdio went into liquidation, Hely-Hutchinson sought to enforce the indemnity against Brayhead but, unsurprisingly, the board of Brayhead refused to honour the indemnity, contending that Richards had no authority to enter into the indemnity agreement with Hely-Hutchinson. Hely-Hutchinson commenced proceedings against Brayhead.

HELD: Lord Denning MR stated:

> It is plain that . . . Richards had no express authority to enter into these . . . contracts on behalf of the company: nor had he any such authority implied from the nature of his office. He had been duly appointed chair of the company but that office in itself did not carry with it authority to enter into these contracts without the sanction of the board. But I think he had authority implied from the conduct of the parties and the circumstances of the case.[26]

See RS Nock, 'When is a Director, Not a Director?' (1967) 30 MLR 705.

---

[23] Peter G Watts, *Bowstead & Reynolds on Agency* (21st edn, Sweet & Maxwell 2018) para 3–021.

[24] *Cropper v Cook* (1867–68) LR 3 CP 194.

[25] In the case itself, Hely-Hutchinson is referred to by his commonly known title, Viscount Suirdale.

[26] [1968] 1 QB 549 (CA) 584.

The conduct Lord Denning MR referred to was the fact that 'the board by their conduct over many months had acquiesced in [Richards] acting as their chief executive and committing Brayhead Ltd to contracts without the necessity of sanction from the board'.[27] Accordingly, the indemnity was valid and Hely-Hutchinson's claim succeeded.

The task of the court is to determine whether or not the activities of the agent are usually incidental to the role, occupation, or trade being undertaken. This will be a question of fact in each case. Certainly, the CEO, as head of the company, will have, by virtue of his position, a significant amount of implied authority to bind the company. The chair's implied authority is likely to be substantially less, as the chair's role is to lead the board, not the company. Directors appointed to specific roles will have usually considerable implied authority in relation to the offices they occupy.

The courts will not find implied actual authority to be conferred on a person where it would conflict with an express limitation or prohibition by the company. It is also the case that implied actual authority (indeed actual authority in general) will not exist where the director 'acts in a manner which is contrary to the interests of his company . . .'.[28] In such a case, the director's 'actions will be without authority, and the agreement which he purports to make will not bind the company unless the third party can rely upon the doctrine of apparent authority'.[29] Accordingly, apparent authority will now be discussed.

6.3.2 Apparent authority

Consider the following example.

> **Eg** | **Apparent authority**
>
> Dragon plc is being sued for negligence by MultiTech Ltd. The directors of Dragon pass a board resolution empowering Nancy, Dragon's Legal Director, to contact MultiTech and negotiate the terms of a settlement agreement, but she should not enter into the agreement on behalf of Dragon until the terms of the settlement have been approved by Dragon's board. Nancy arranges a meeting with MultiTech's solicitor and, during the meeting, Nancy proposes a settlement agreement which is accepted by MultiTech's solicitor (MultiTech's solicitor is expressly authorized to accept any suitable offers of settlement). Nancy signs the agreement on behalf of Dragon. Dragon contends that it is not bound by the terms of the settlement, as Nancy had no authority to enter into it on Dragon's behalf.

Nancy clearly does not have express actual authority to settle on Dragon's behalf, as she was instructed only to negotiate with MultiTech. She does not have implied actual authority as she was expressly prohibited from settling without the board's approval. However, it would be unfair if companies were only bound to transactions entered into by directors who act within their actual authority, as third parties who deal with

---

[27] ibid.   [28] *Re Capitol Films Ltd* [2010] EWHC 2240 (Ch) [53] (Snowden QC).   [29] ibid.

directors are unlikely to know what they are actually authorized to do (in the above case, it is highly unlikely that MultiTech's solicitor knew that Nancy was prohibited from settling). Accordingly, 'a principal is bound, not only by such acts of the agent as are within the scope of the agent's actual authority, but by such acts are as within the larger margin of an apparent or ostensible authority . . .'.[30]

Apparent authority (also known as ostensible authority in older case law) is based on the authority that, from the third party's point of view, the director appears to have. Thus, in the above example, Nancy does not have actual authority to bind Dragon to a settlement but, from the point of view of MultiTech's solicitor, what matters is the authority that she appears to have, and she likely appears to have authority to bind Dragon to the settlement as she is the Legal Director. Accordingly, Dragon would likely be bound. From this, it can be seen that '[a]pparent authority is really equivalent to the phrase "appearance of authority". There may be an appearance of authority whether in fact or not there is authority',[31] or, to put it more simply, 'apparent authority is the authority of an agent as it appears to others'.[32] The more authoritative definition of apparent authority was provided by Diplock LJ, who stated that apparent authority refers to:

> a legal relationship between the principal and the contractor [i.e. a third party] created by a representation, made by the principal to the contractor, intended to be and in fact acted upon by the contractor, that the agent has authority to enter on behalf of the principal into a contract of a kind within the scope of the 'apparent' authority, so as to render the principal liable to perform any obligations imposed upon him by such contract. . . . It is irrelevant whether the agent had actual authority to enter into the contract.[33]

From the above quote (and the fact that apparent authority is based in estoppel), it is clear that apparent authority requires three ingredients to be present, namely '(i) a representation; (ii) a reliance on the representation; and (iii) an alteration of your position resulting from such reliance'.[34] Each will now be discussed.

6.3.2.1 Representation

There must be a representation indicating that 'the agent has authority to enter on behalf of the principal into a contract of a kind within the scope of the "apparent" authority, so as to render the principal liable to perform any obligations imposed upon him by such contract'.[35] The representation must come from someone who has actual authority to make the representation in question, which usually means either the company or an agent clothed with actual authority to make the statement.[36] Accordingly, apparent authority will not generally arise where the representation comes from the director

---

[30] *Totterdell v Fareham Blue Brick and Tile Co Ltd* (1866) LR 1 CP 674, 677–8 (Byles J). The phrase 'larger margin' indicates that, in many cases, apparent authority serves to extend the powers of directors in areas where some form of actual authority already exists. However, it is possible for apparent authority to arise where no actual authority already exists.

[31] James L Montrose, 'The Basis of the Power of the Agent in Cases of Actual and Apparent Authority' (1932) 16 Can Bar Rev 756, 764.

[32] *Hely-Hutchinson v Brayhead Ltd* [1968] 1 QB 549 (CA) 583 (Lord Denning MR).

[33] *Freeman & Lockyer v Buckhurst Park (Mangal) Properties Ltd* [1964] 2 QB 480 (CA) 503.

[34] *Rama Corporation Ltd v Proved Tin and General Investments Ltd* [1952] 2 QB 147 (QB) 150 (Slade J).

[35] *Freeman & Lockyer v Buckhurst Park (Mangal) Properties Ltd* [1964] 2 QB 480 (CA) 503 (Diplock LJ).

[36] *Armagas Ltd v Mundogas SA (The Ocean Frost)* [1986] AC 717 (HL).

himself, as to allow otherwise would be to permit a director to self-authorize or, as Lord Donaldson MR stated, 'to pull himself up by his own shoe laces'.[37]

The representation can be made orally or in writing, but the most common form of representation is by conduct, and typically occurs where 'the principal has placed the agent in a position in which the outside world is generally regarded as carrying authority to enter into transactions of the kind in question'.[38] The following case provides an example.

See JL Montrose, 'The Apparent Authority of an Agent of a Company' (1965) 7 Malaya L Rev 253.

Freeman & Lockyer v Buckhurst Park (Mangal) Properties Ltd [1964] 2 QB 480 (CA)

FACTS: Kapoor (the agent) and another person formed Buckhurst Park (Mangal) Properties Ltd ('Buckhurst', the principal), the purpose of which was to purchase and resell a large estate. Kapoor was a director of Buckhurst, along with a number of other persons. Kapoor acted as managing director with the board's acquiescence, although he had never been formally appointed to the role. He engaged a firm of architects (Freeman & Lockyer) on Buckhurst's behalf. The architects completed the work required of them and sought payment of their fees from Buckhurst. Buckhurst refused to pay, alleging that Kapoor lacked authority to engage the architects. The architects sued for payment.

HELD: The claim succeeded and Buckhurst was liable to pay the architects for the work they completed. Diplock LJ stated:

> The representation which creates 'apparent' authority may take a variety of forms of which the commonest is representation by conduct, that is, by permitting the agent to act in some way in the conduct of the principal's business with other persons. By so doing the principal represents to anyone who becomes aware that the agent is so acting that the agent has authority to enter on behalf of the principal into contracts with other persons of the kind which an agent so acting in the conduct of his principal's business has usually 'actual' authority to enter into.[39]

By acquiescing to Kapoor acting as managing director, Buckhurst had represented to the architects that Kapoor had the authority to engage in activities that a managing director would usually be authorized to undertake, including entering into contracts on behalf of the company.

The representation will normally be made prior to the director engaging in the act in question, but apparent authority can also arise based on a subsequent representation.[40]

6.3.2.2 Reliance

Apparent authority will only arise if the third party relied on the representation. From this, it follows that apparent authority will not exist where the third party did not know of the principal's existence,[41] or did not know of the representation. Apparent authority will also not arise where the third party knew, or ought to have known, that the director

---

[37] *United Bank of Kuwait v Hammoud* [1988] 1 WLR 1051 (CA) 1066.
[38] *Armagas Ltd v Mundogas SA (The Ocean Frost)* [1986] AC 717 (HL) 777 (Lord Keith).
[39] [1964] 2 QB 480 (CA) 503–4.
[40] *Spiro v Lintern* [1973] 1 WLR 1002 (CA).
[41] *AL Underwood Ltd v Bank of Liverpool* [1924] 1 KB 775 (CA).

lacked authority[42] (e.g. where the third party knows that the contract is outside the scope of the company's objects).[43] This is not always easy to determine in practice, and so the courts have provided some presumptive indicators:

- Where a transaction is clearly not in the commercial interests of the company, the third party will be put on notice that the director is unlikely to have the requisite authority. In such a case, it will be 'very difficult for the [third party] to assert with any credibility that he believed the agent did have actual authority. Lack of such a belief would be fatal to a claim that the agent had apparent authority.'[44]

- Where a director is engaged in a manner of business that a director of that type would not normally engage in, then the third party will be put on notice that the director may lack authority and the third party should ascertain whether or not the director is authorized to conduct that business.[45]

6.3.2.3 Alteration of position

The third requirement is that the third party must have altered his position as a result of relying on the representation. In estoppel cases not involving agency, it must also be established that the third party acted to his detriment, but it appears that, in agency cases, this is not required and that all the third party need establish is that he altered his position as a result of the representation.[46] Further, this alteration of position need only amount to the third party entering into a contract with the company,[47] which has resulted in several commentators questioning 'whether alteration of position in fact constitutes a separate requirement from reliance.'[48]

6.3.3 Ratification

Even if a director does lack authority as an agent, the company can generally validate the director's actions by ratifying them (usually by the members passing an ordinary resolution).[49] Where ratification occurs, the law will regard ratification as being 'equivalent to antecedent authority'.[50] In other words, the law will regard the director's actions as being authorized when they were undertaken, with the result that the contract between the company and the third party will be enforceable by both parties. Note, however, that ratification will not automatically exonerate the director of any liability he might have for breaching his authority[51] (e.g. for breaching the duty to act within powers found in s 171 of the CA 2006).

---

[42] *Overbrooke Estates Ltd v Glencombe Properties Ltd* [1974] 1 WLR 1335 (Ch). It should be noted that generally the law no longer expects third parties to inquire as to the limitations on the directors' authority to bind the company (see e.g. CA 2006, s 40(2)(b)(i)).

[43] *Rolled Steel Products (Holdings) Ltd v British Steel Corp* [1986] Ch 246 (CA).

[44] *Criterion Properties plc v Stratford UK Properties LLC* [2004] UKHL 28, [2004] 1 WLR 1846 [31] (Lord Scott).

[45] *Midland Bank Ltd v Reckitt* [1933] AC 1 (HL).

[46] See e.g. *Pickard v Sears* (1837) 6 A&E 469; *Freeman v Cooke* (1848) 2 Exch 654; *Rama Corporation Ltd v Proved Tin and General Investments Ltd* [1952] 2 QB 147 (QB); *Freeman & Lockyer v Buckhurst Park (Mangal) Properties Ltd* [1964] 2 QB 480 (CA).

[47] See e.g. *Freeman & Lockyer v Buckhurst Park (Mangal) Properties Ltd* [1964] 2 QB 480 (CA); *Polish Steamship Co v AJ Williams Fuels (Overseas Sales) (The Suwalki)* [1989] 1 Lloyd's Rep 511 (QB); *Arctic Shipping Co Ltd v Mobilia AB (The Tatra)* [1990] 2 Lloyd's Rep 51 (QB).

[48] Roderick Munday, *Agency: Law and Principles* (3rd edn, OUP 2016) 99.

[49] *Grant v United Kingdom Switchback Railway Co* (1888) 40 ChD 135 (CA).

[50] *Koenigsblatt v Sweet* [1923] 2 Ch 314 (CA) 325 (Lord Sterndale MR).

[51] *Suncorp Insurance and Finance v Milano Assicurazioni SpA* [1993] 2 Lloyd's Rep 225 (QB).

6.4 The protection of third parties

There is no doubt that if the company's articles confer general managerial power upon the directors (as art 3 of the model articles does), then the directors collectively will be authorized under s 43 to contract on behalf of the company. However, this power to contractually bind the company can also be limited by law or the company's constitution, as the following example demonstrates.

Eg **Can a director bind the company?**

Dragon plc adopted the model articles for public companies, but inserted a new art 3A, which states that 'the board is not permitted to commit Dragon Ltd to borrowing more than £50,000 unless member approval is obtained'. Despite this, the board causes Dragon to enter into a loan agreement with Welsh Bank plc, under which Dragon will borrow £75,000. Member approval is not obtained and Katy, one of Dragon's members, commences proceedings in order to have the contract between Dragon and Welsh Bank set aside.

If the contract was not executed via s 44(1) (and there is no indication that it was), then it might be argued that the contract is not valid as the directors had no authority to enter into this contract on behalf of the company. However, this would operate harshly on innocent third parties like Welsh Bank, and so the law does put in place measures to protect third parties, of which the most notable is s 40 of the CA 2006.

6.4.1 Section 40 of the CA 2006

English law used to take the view that, as the company's constitution was a publicly available document, third parties that dealt with directors should be aware of the constitutional limitations upon directors' authority[52] (this is known as 'constructive notice'). Accordingly, third parties that dealt with directors who lacked authority received no protection from the law. The law today is very different, largely as a result of the First Company Law Directive,[53] of which Recital 9 of the Preamble states '[t]he protection of third parties must be ensured by provisions which restrict to the greatest possible extent the grounds on which obligations entered into in the name of the company are not valid'.

 Today, the relevant provisions of the First Company Law Directive relating to directors' authority are primarily implemented by ss 40–42 of the CA 2006, with s 40(1) providing that '[i]n favour of a person dealing with a company in good faith, the power of the directors to bind the company, or authorise others to do so, is deemed to be free of any limitation under the company's constitution'. As a result of s 40, 'a third party dealing with a company in good faith need not concern itself about whether a company is acting within its constitution'.[54]

---

[52] *Ernest v Nichols* (1857) 6 HL Cas 401.

[53] Council Directive 2009/101/EC of 16 September 2009 on coordination of safeguards which, for the protection of the interests of members and third parties, are required by Member States of companies within the meaning of the second paragraph of Article 48 of the Treaty, with a view to making such safeguards equivalent [2009] OJ L258/11. Note that the Directive was originally passed in 1968 (Directive 68/151/EEC), but was codified into the 2009 Directive '[i]n the interests of clarity and rationality'.

[54] Explanatory Notes to the CA 2006, para 125.

It is important to note at the outset that s 40 does not grant authority to directors—it merely ensures that constitutional limitations upon directors' authority cannot be used to invalidate contracts entered into with third parties. The director will still need to demonstrate that, absent the constitutional limitation in question, he was authorized to engage in the act in question. To use the example at 6.4, s 40 would not empower the board to enter into contracts on Dragon's behalf. It would simply ensure that, if the board was empowered to contract on Dragon's behalf, then the fact that it exercised that power in breach of art 3A would not invalidate the contract between Dragon and Welsh Bank. It should also be noted that s 40 protects the transaction itself—it does not protect the directors who purported to enter into the transaction. Indeed, s 40(5) provides that s 40 will not affect the liability incurred by the directors as a result of exceeding their powers. Such an action will likely amount to a breach of the duty found in s 171(a) of the CA 2006.

> Section 171(a) is discussed at 10.2.1.

As is discussed in the following sections, s 40 is subject to several limitations. If a third party is not within the scope of s 40, then the transaction will be void,[55] unless it can be established that the director was authorized by some other means (e.g. through authority as an agent).

6.4.1.1 A person dealing with the company

Section 40 operates '[i]n favour of a person dealing with the company', so it follows that the company itself (Dragon plc in the example at 6.4) cannot rely upon s 40 in order to escape a transaction that is unauthorized under the constitution. Section 40(2)(a) provides that a person 'deals' with a company if 'he is a party to any transaction or other act to which the company is a party'. The principal issue that has arisen here is the extent to which s 40 can be relied upon by a director or member of the company.

As regards directors, the issue is relatively simple. The common law position is that the director who purported to enter into the transaction is usually unable to rely on s 40.[56] The position regarding directors is now provided for under s 41 and applies to transactions whose validity depends on s 40.[57] In relation to such transactions, s 41(2) provides that the transaction will be voidable at the company's instance where the company enters into a transaction and the parties to that transaction include (i) a director of the company or of its holding company; or (ii) a person connected with any such director.[58] However, s 41(4) does provide for several instances where the transaction will cease to be voidable (e.g. where the transaction is affirmed by the company). Irrespective of whether or not the company avoids the transaction, any party mentioned in (i) or (ii) or any director who authorized the transaction is liable to account to the company for any gain he has made directly or indirectly by the transaction, and to indemnify the company for any loss or damage resulting from the transaction.[59] However, a person (other than a director of the company) can avoid liability if he can show that, at the time the transaction was entered into, he did not know that the directors had exceeded their powers.[60]

The position regarding members is slightly more complex. Members of the company are able to rely on s 40, but it is important to distinguish between (i) internal dealings

---

[55] See e.g. *Guinness plc v Saunders* [1990] BCLC 402 (HL) (award of remuneration invalid).
[56] *Smith v Henniker-Major & Co* [2002] EWCA Civ 762, [2003] Ch 182.   [57] CA 2006, s 49(1).
[58] A list of persons regarded as being connected with a director can be found in s 252 of the CA 2006 (discussed at 11.4).
[59] CA 2006, s 41(3).   [60] ibid s 41(5).

between the company and its members (e.g. an issue of shares); and (ii) external dealings between the company and a third party who just happens to be a member, but is not acting in such a capacity. The following example demonstrates the distinction.

> ## Eg Members dealing with the company
>
> Dragon plc adopts the model articles for public companies, but adds two new clauses:
>
> (a) Article 3A provides that the directors may, following an ordinary resolution of the company, issue bonus shares.
> (b) Article 3B provides that a director cannot, on behalf of the company, enter into a supply contract for over £5,000 without the approval of the members.
>
> The directors of Dragon decide to issue 5,000 bonus shares to various members, but no ordinary resolution is passed. One thousand of these shares are issued to Sadiq, a sole proprietor who supplies goods to Dragon. Shortly before the shares are issued, Ruby, one of Dragon's directors, purports to enter into a contract with Sadiq, under which Sadiq will supply Dragon with goods, in return for £7,000. Member approval for this transaction is not obtained. Dragon has since decided not to issue the bonus shares, and does not want to honour the supply contract with Sadiq, as it can get the goods cheaper elsewhere.

There is no doubt that, as regards the contract for the supply of goods, Sadiq would be a person dealing with the company and could therefore utilize s 40. However, as the following case demonstrates, as regards the issue of bonus shares, it is unlikely that Sadiq could rely on s 40.

📖 See Christian Twigg-Flesner, 'Sections 35A and 322: Who is a Person "Dealing with the Company"?' (2005) 26 Co Law 195.

> ## EIC Services Ltd v Phipps [2004] EWCA Civ 1069
>
> **FACTS:** The articles of EIC Services Ltd provided that an ordinary resolution was required in order for the directors to issue bonus shares. An issue of bonus shares was made, but no ordinary resolution was passed. One of the members, Barber, sought a declaration from the court that the issue was invalid. Another member, Phipps, sought to rely on s 35A of the CA 1985 (the predecessor to s 40 of the CA 2006), in order to validate the issue of shares.
>
> **HELD:** Phipps could not rely on s 35A. Peter Gibson LJ stated that s 35A 'contemplates a bilateral transaction between the company and the person dealing with the company or an act to which both are parties'[61] and a share issue was not such a transaction. Further, he noted that the First Company Law Directive intended to protect 'third parties' and that 'it is tolerably clear from the Directive itself that third parties do not include members of the company (see, for example, the sixth preamble). In the context of a company, the term "third parties" naturally refers to persons other than the company and its members.'[62]
>
> **COMMENT:** It should be noted that Peter Gibson LJ's comments here were *obiter* only and, therefore, this case only provides persuasive authority for the notion that s 40 will not aid a member of a company in relation to an issue of bonus shares.

---

[61] [2004] EWCA Civ 1069, [2005] 1 WLR 1337 [35].

[62] ibid [37]. Note that what was Recital 6 is now found in Recital 10 of the 2009 Codified Directive—it provides that '[i]t is necesary, in order to ensure certainty in the law as regards relations between the company and third parties, and also between members, to limit the cases in which nullity can arise . . .'.

6.4.1.2 **Good faith**

Section 40 can only be relied upon by persons dealing with the company 'in good faith'. As Hannigan has correctly noted, s 40 'goes to great lengths to ensure that it is difficult for a person dealing with the company to be in bad faith . . .'.[63] This is achieved in three ways. First, s 40(2)(b)(i) provides that a person dealing with the company 'is not bound to enquire as to any limitation on the powers of the directors to bind the company or authorise others to do so'. Accordingly, as regards s 40, the doctrine of constructive notice does not apply and a failure to check whether the director was constitutionally authorized to bind the company will not provide evidence of bad faith. However, s 40(2)(b)(i) only applies in relation to 'any limitation on the powers of the directors to bind the company or authorise others to do so'—it will not absolve the third party from making enquiries in relation to other issues that put him on inquiry.[64]

Second, s 40(2)(b)(ii) provides that a person dealing with the company 'is presumed to have acted in good faith unless the contrary is proved'. Accordingly, the burden of proof is placed upon the person (usually the company) seeking to deny the third party protection under s 40.

Third, s 40(2)(b)(iii) reinforces s 40(2)(b)(i) by providing that a person dealing with the company 'is not to be regarded as acting in bad faith by reason only of his knowing that an act is beyond the powers of the directors under the company's constitution'. This section has been branded as remarkable,[65] on the ground that one would assume that a person (X) who contracts with another person (Y), in full knowledge that Y did not have authority to contract, would be acting in bad faith. However, this is not so and knowledge of the director's lack of constitutional authority will not in itself provide evidence of bad faith.

6.4.1.3 **The power of the directors**

Section 40 refers to the power of the 'directors' to bind the company, leading to the question as to whether it applies only to acts of the entire board, or whether it can also apply to acts of multiple directors or even a single director. The move from the use of the phrase 'board of directors' in s 35A of the CA 1985 to 'the directors' in the CA 2006 indicates that Parliament intended that s 40 should not solely apply to acts of the entire board. Pre-2006 case law makes clear that s 40 can indeed apply to the acts of multiple directors.[66] There is also limited case law authority for the application of s 40 to a single director.[67] Indeed, the Interpretation Act 1978 provides that, unless a contrary intention appears, 'words in the plural shall include the singular'.[68] However, it has been argued that to interpret s 40 as applying to a single director 'is perhaps an ambitious construction of the section, but arguably not entirely outlandish'.[69] A definitive ruling is desirable.

6.4.1.4 **Proceedings to restrain an act to which s 40 applies**

Section 40(4) provides that the principles within s 40 do not affect any right of a member of the company to bring proceedings to restrain the doing of an action that is is beyond

---

[63] Brenda Hannigan, *Company Law* (5th edn, OUP 2018) 198.

[64] *Wrexham Association Football Club Ltd v Crucialmove Ltd* [2006] EWCA Civ 237, [2007] BCC 139 [47].

[65] Geoffrey Morse, *Palmer's Company Law* (Sweet & Maxwell 2018) para 3.313.

[66] *Criterion Properties plc v Stratford UK Properties LLC* [2004] UKHL 28, [2004] 1 WLR 1846.

[67] *International Sales & Agencies Ltd v Marcus* [1982] 2 CMLR 46 (QB) 58–9 (Lawson J).

[68] Interpretation Act 1978, s 6(c).

[69] Geoffrey Morse, *Palmer's Company Law* (Sweet & Maxwell 2018) para 3.310.

the powers of the directors. Accordingly, a member can obtain an injunction to stop the doing of an act that is beyond the power of the directors. However, in practice, this is not an especially useful power as s 40(4) goes on to state that 'no such proceedings lie in respect of an act to be done in fulfilment of a legal obligation arising from a previous act of the company'. Given that the members will likely not know of a transaction until after a legal obligation has arisen, the power granted to the members under s 40(4) is largely useless in practice. Members seeking a remedy in such a case will have to look elsewhere (e.g. by bringing a derivative claim for breach of the duty in s 171(a)).

6.4.2 **The 'indoor management rule'**

The 'indoor management rule' (or 'the rule in *Turquand's* case') was established in the following case.

 Royal British Bank v Turquand (1856) 6 El & Bl 327

FACTS: A company's deed of settlement (effectively its articles) provided that the directors could borrow such sums of money as might be authorized by general meeting of the company. The board purported on behalf of the company to borrow £2,000 from Royal British Bank, but authorization from the general meeting was not obtained. The money was not paid back and so the Bank commenced proceedings against the company (which was now in liquidation). Turquand (the company's liquidator) alleged that the directors had no authority to borrow the money and, by failing to inform itself of the deed of settlement, the Bank should bear the loss.

HELD: Jervis CJ held that the Bank's action should succeed and that the company was bound to pay back the money. He stated that '[f]inding that the authority might be made complete by a resolution, he would have a right to infer the fact of a resolution authorizing that which on the face of the document appeared to be legitimately done'.[70]

COMMENT: Basically, the indoor management rule provides that parties dealing with the company can assume that any internal management preliminaries or rules have been complied with. This is an entirely practical rule—transacting with companies would be unduly burdensome if third parties had to check that every internal procedure had been complied with.

The indoor management rule exists alongside s 40 of the CA 2006 but, in most cases, a third party will find it easier to rely on s 40 than the indoor management rule as s 40 is wider (indeed, today, the Bank's claim would be easily established using s 40). For example, the indoor management rule only applies to internal management rules, whereas s 40 applies to any constitutional limitation upon the directors' powers to bind the company. However, there are cases where s 40 will not apply (e.g. in the case of a company that is a charity)[71] and, in such cases, the internal management rule may be of use. Note, however, that the courts are not willing to allow the internal management rule to outflank s 40. For example, the indoor management rule cannot be used to validate a transaction that would be voidable under s 41,[72] nor can it be used where the third party has been put on notice that the company's internal rules have not been complied with.[73]

---

[70] (1856) 6 El & Bl 327, 332.   [71] CA 2006, s 42(1).   [72] *Morris v Kanssen* [1946] AC 459 (HL).
[73] *Wrexham Association Football Club Ltd v CrucialMove Ltd* [2006] EWCA Civ 237, [2008] 1 BCLC 508.

6.5 Personal and vicarious liability, and attribution

As a person, a company can be liable for civil wrongs and can be convicted for committing criminal offences. A company, however, has 'no soul to be saved and no body to be kicked',[74] nor does the company have a mind. From a liability perspective, this creates a problem as a company, by itself, is incapable of doing anything and requires others to act on its behalf. This leads us to ask who is liable when breaches of the law occur—the company and/or those who act on its behalf. The law has devised four mechanisms to determine upon whom liability should be placed (although overlaps do exist between them):

1. personal liability;
2. strict liability;
3. vicarious liability, and;
4. liability imposed via attribution.

Each of these will now be discussed.

6.5.1 Personal liability

In many cases, establishing who is liable will not be a problem as the law will state who is to be personally liable for a legal breach. In relation to statutory obligations/duties, the relevant provision will usually expressly state upon whom the obligation/duty is placed and who can be held personally liable if the obligation/duty is not complied with. One issue that repeatedly arises is whether personal liability should be imposed upon a company and/or upon those who caused the company to engage in the unlawful act in question. The answer to this depends upon the type of liability.

6.5.1.1 Contractual liability

As discussed at 4.3.3, a company has contractual capacity and so can enter into contracts, on which it is personally liable. However, being an artificial person, a company cannot enter into contracts on its own, and requires others to enter into contracts on its behalf. Bearing this in mind, consider the following example.

 Eg   **The contractual liability of persons acting on behalf of the company**

Dragon plc wishes to purchase a piece of machinery for use in one of its factories in order to fulfil a number of lucrative customer orders, but it has difficulty locating the machine in question. Becky approaches the board of Dragon and informs them that she is a director of MachineCorp Ltd and that MachineCorp would be willing to sell Dragon the relevant machine. She also informs the board that she has authority to negotiate contracts of sale on MachineCorp's behalf. A contract is drawn up between Dragon and MachineCorp for the sale of the machine. However, it transpires that whilst Becky is director of MachineCorp, she does not have authority to contract on MachineCorp's behalf. Further, MachineCorp has recently entered insolvent liquidation and the liquidator has sold the machine to pay off the company's debts. Dragon cannot locate a replacement machine, and so it cannot fulfil the customer orders.

---

[74] *Stepney Corporation v Osofsky* [1937] 3 All ER 289 (CA) 291 (Greer LJ).

In a typical agency relationship, the agent effects a contract between his principal and third party and then drops out of the transaction. It follows that directors and other agents of the company are generally not liable for contracts they enter into on behalf of the company—it is the company that is liable. Indeed, this is even the case where the agent in question does not have authority to commit the company to the contract[75] (and, as discussed at 6.4.1, s 40 of the CA 2006 means that in most cases the company remains liable on the contract). Accordingly, Dragon cannot enforce the contract against Becky, but it can enforce it against MachineCorp. However, suing MachineCorp would be pointless as it no longer has the machine (so specific performance would not be granted) and likely has no funds anyway (so damages for breach would not be paid). However, as Becky has represented that she has authority that she does not have, Dragon could sue her for damages for breach of warranty of authority.[76] MachineCorp's liquidator could also cause MachineCorp to commence proceedings against Becky for breach of her duty to act within powers.[77]

It is important to note that the principle that an agent cannot be held liable on the contract is not absolute and, in certain cases, a third party can enforce the contract against the agent, including the following scenarios:

- Where, based on the construction of the contract, the objective intention of the parties is that the agent should be liable.[78]

- Where the principal is undisclosed, a contract will exist between the agent and the third party, which both can enforce.[79] Thus, if Becky did not disclose that she was acting on behalf of MachineCorp, Dragon could sue her on the contract.

- Where an agent purports to act on behalf of another, but is in fact acting for himself, he will be liable on the contract.[80]

- Where an agent acts on behalf of a non-existent principal, then he will be liable on the contract. This typically occurs where a promoter acts on behalf of a company that has not yet been registered, with s 51 of the CA 2006 providing that a binding contract is created between the promoter and the third party, which either can enforce.

Section 51 is discussed at 3.2.7.

- If the directors are also members of an unlimited company, then they will be personally liable for the company's debts and liabilities.

6.5.1.2 Tortious liability

A company, as a person, can be held personally liable in tort, but there may be no need to make the company personally liable because, as is discussed at 6.5.3, a company is normally vicariously liable for the tortious acts of its employees and agents. However, there are instances where vicarious liability will not be imposed, or where commencing proceedings against the company will be of little aid (e.g. where the company is insolvent). The question that arises is can the claimant sue the person who caused the company to engage in the tortious conduct in question (e.g. a director or employee).

The starting point is that 'a director of a company is not automatically to be identified with his company for the purpose of the law of tort, however small the company may be and however powerful his control over its affairs'.[81] Accordingly, the starting point is that a director who, in acting on behalf of the company, causes it to commit a tort will not be

---

[75] *Ferguson v Wilson* (1866–67) LR 2 Ch App 77.   [76] *Collen v Wright* (1857) 8 E&B 647.
[77] CA 2006, s 171.   [78] *Bridges & Salmon Ltd v Owner of The Swan (The Swan)* [1968] 1 Lloyd's Rep 5.
[79] *Sims v Bond* (1835) 5 B&E 389.   [80] *Railton v Hodgson* (1804) 4 Taunt 576n.
[81] *C Evans & Sons Ltd v Spritebrand Ltd* [1985] 1 WLR 317 (CA) 329 (Slade LJ).

liable for that tort. The advantage of this approach is that it respects the corporate veil and the principles affirmed in *Salomon* and, especially in the case of one-person companies, it preserves the principle of limited liability. The disadvantage of this approach is that it ignores the principle that 'everyone should be responsible for his tortious acts'.[82]

Accordingly, the courts have gone on to provide that '[i]n every case where it is sought to make [a director] liable for his company's torts, it is necessary to examine with care what part he played personally in regard to the act or acts complained of'.[83] Where the director has done no more than 'carry out his constitutional role in the governance of the company [or] carrying out the functions entrusted to him by the company under is constitution',[84] then he will likely not be held liable. However, where the director has engaged in tortious conduct in some personal capacity, then he can be held liable. Of course, determining whether a director has acted on behalf of the company or in a personal capacity is not always easy. The following case provides an example of a situation where the court held that a director was acting in a personal capacity, and so imposed liability on the director.

Standard Chartered Bank v Pakistan National Shipping Corp n [2002] UKHL 43

FACTS: Mehra was the managing director of Oakprime Ltd. Oakprime was the beneficiary of a letter of credit issued by Incombank and confirmed by Standard Chartered Bank ('SCB'). The letter of credit was issued in relation to a cargo of goods being sold by Oakprime, and it was a condition of the letter of credit that the goods had to be shipped no later than 25 October 1993. Loading of the goods was delayed and so Oakprime was not able to ship the goods until November. However, the shipping agents shipping the goods (Pakistan National Shipping Corp, 'PNSC') agreed with Mehra to falsely backdate the goods' shipping documents so they stated the shipping date was 25 October.

Oakprime presented these fraudulent shipping documents to SCB and SCB provided payment under the letter of credit. SCB then sought reimbursement from Incombank, but Incombank rejected SCB's request due to discrepancies in the shipping documents (albeit not the false backdating). The false shipment date was discovered and SCB sued PNSC, Oakprime, and Mehra under the tort of deceit. At first instance, all three parties were held liable as joint tortfeasors.[85] Mehra appealed and the Court of Appeal[86] allowed his appeal, with Lord Rodger in the House of Lords stating that the appeal was allowed 'because Mr Mehra was a director of Oakprime and acted as such when cheating Standard Chartered, his acts must be regarded solely as the acts of Oakprime and he should have no personal civil liability for them'.[87] SCB appealed.

HELD: The House of Lords allowed SCB's appeal and held that Mehra was personally liable. Lord Hoffmann stated that Mehra made a fraudulent misrepresentation intending SCB to rely on it, which it did. He went on to state that, '[t]he fact that by virtue of the law of agency his representation and the knowledge with which he made it would also be attributed to Oakprime would be of interest in

See Chris Noonan and Susan Watson, 'Directors' Tortious Liability—Standard Chartered Bank and the Restoration of Sanity' [2004] JBL 539.

---

82 *Mentmore Manufacturing Co Ltd v National Merchandising Manufacturing Co Inc* (1978) 89 DLR (3d) 195, 202 (Le Dain J), cited with approval in *MCA Records Inc v Charly Records Ltd (No 5)* [2001] EWCA Civ 1441, [2002] BCC 650 [47] (Chadwick LJ).

83 *C Evans & Sons Ltd v Spritebrand Ltd* [1985] 1 WLR 317 (CA) 329 (Slade LJ).

84 *MCA Records Inc v Charly Records Ltd (No 5)* [2001] EWCA Civ 1441, [2002] BCC 650 [49] (Chadwick LJ).

85 *Standard Chartered Bank v Pakistan National Shipping Corp (No 2)* [1998] 1 Lloyd's Rep 684 (QB).

86 *Standard Chartered Bank v Pakistan National Shipping Corp (No 2)* [1998] 1 Lloyd's Rep 218 (CA).

87 [2002] UKHL 43, [2003] 1 AC 959 [39].

an action against Oakprime',[88] but it was irrelevant in this case because '[n]o one can escape liability for his fraud by saying "I wish to make it clear that I am committing this fraud on behalf of someone else and I am not to be personally liable."'[89] Here, 'Mehra was not being sued for the company's tort. He was being sued for his own tort and all the elements of that tort were proved against him.'[90] Accordingly, '[h]is status as a director when he executed the fraud cannot invest him with immunity'.[91]

Lord Rodger, who delivered the other substantive judgment, stated '[w]here someone commits a tortious act, he at least will be liable for the consequences; whether others are liable also depends on the circumstances'.[92] Here, Mehra was held personally liable whilst Oakprime was held to be vicariously liable.

Standard Chartered concerned an intentional tort that did not require the establishment of a duty of care. Where the tort in question does require establishing the existence of a duty, then imposing personal liability on the director appears to be more difficult.

See Jennifer Payne, 'Negligent Misstatement—A Healthier Decision for Company Directors' (1998) 57 CLJ 456.

Williams v Natural Life Health Foods Ltd [1998] 1 WLR 830 (HL)

FACTS: Mistlin was the sole director and principal shareholder in Natural Life Health Foods Ltd ('NLHF'), which was set up to franchise retail health food shops. Williams and Reid (the claimants) wished to acquire a franchise and so NLHF sent them favourable details regarding the franchise's projected financial performance, along with a brochure advertising Mistlin's expertise in the health food trade. The claimants entered into a franchise agreement with NLHF (the claimants dealt with an employee of NHLF and had no direct dealings with Mistlin) but their franchise's turnover was significantly less than what was projected and it soon ceased trading after incurring substantial losses. The claimants sued NHLF, arguing that the financial projections were negligently produced (which was the case). However, NHLF was liquidated shortly thereafter, so the claimants made Mistlin a defendant to the action, claiming negligent misstatement. At first instance[93] and in the Court of Appeal,[94] Mistlin was held liable. Mistlin appealed.

HELD: Mistlin's appeal was allowed and he was held not liable. Lord Steyn stated that the fact that Mistlin was a one-man company did not, in itself, mean that Mistlin was personally answerable to NLHF's customers.[95] In claims for negligent misstatement, the claimant needs to establish that the defendant assumed a responsibility towards the claimant when making the statement in question. On the facts, the House held that such an assumption was not present, stating that, as the claimants had no personal dealings with Mistlin, then '[t]here were no exchanges or conduct crossing the line which could have conveyed to the plaintiffs that Mr Mistlin was willing to assume personal responsibility to them'.[96]

COMMENT: The decision in *Williams* is entirely consistent with the decision in *Standard Chartered*. The question is whether the requirements of the tort in question can be established against the director in question. In *Standard Chartered* they were, whereas in *Williams*, they were not (had Mistlin dealt directly with the claimants, then he might have been held to have assumed a responsibility for the negligent misstatement).[97]

---

[88] ibid [20].   [89] ibid [22].   [90] ibid.   [91] ibid [40] (Lord Rodger).   [92] ibid.

[93] *Williams v Natural Life Health Foods Ltd* [1996] BCC 376 (QB).

[94] *Williams v Natural Life Health Foods Ltd* [1997] BCC 605 (CA).

[95] [1998] 1 WLR 830 (HL) 838.   [96] ibid.

[97] As occurred in *Fairline Shipping Corp v Adamson* [1975] QB 180 (QB).

The consensus is that cases such as *Williams* and *Standard Chartered* have clarified the law in this area and established that whilst the primary method of establishing tortious liability is to place vicarious liability on the company, personal liability can also be placed on the director if the requirements of the tort in question can be established against the director.[98]

6.5.1.3 Criminal liability

It is long established that a company is capable of being found guilty of a criminal offence.[99] However, as the company has no physical existence, two notable limitations exist upon a company's criminal liability (with a third that has now been abolished):

1. being an artificial person, a company is incapable of committing certain offences (e.g. perjury, bigamy, certain driving offences[100]);

2. as a company cannot be imprisoned, it cannot be convicted of an offence for which the only punishment is imprisonment[101] (e.g. murder);

3. it used to be the case that a company could not be convicted of any offence that had a **mens rea** requirement[102] but, as is discussed later, this limitation has been abolished.

➡ **mens rea:** 'guilty mind'. The mental element of a criminal offence.

Where a statute does not expressly state that a company can be found guilty of a particular offence, then the courts will determine whether a company can be found guilty of that offence.[103] In practice, however, most criminal offences are established by statute and the statute will often expressly provide who can be liable. The CA 2006 establishes numerous criminal offences and expressly identifies who can be found guilty of committing those offences (often liability will be placed on the company and/or its officers, but some provisions place liability on a wider group of persons).[104] It is common for company law legislation to provide that the company can be found guilty of an offence, and to also impose criminal liability on the natural persons who caused the company to commit the offence. A wide-ranging example of this can be found in s 432 of the Insolvency Act 1986 (IA 1986), which applies to all criminal offences under the Act, except those excluded by s 432(4).[105] Section 432(2) provides that where a body corporate has been convicted of an offence under the Act and the offence was committed with the consent or connivance of, or to be attributable to any neglect on the part of, any director, manager, secretary, or other similar officer of the body corporate or any person who was purporting to act in any such capacity he, as well as the body corporate, is guilty of the offence and liable to be proceeded against and punished accordingly.

The commission of certain criminal offences by companies has proven problematic and, in a handful of cases, Parliament's response has been to create a version of that offence specific to companies, with the most noteworthy example being the offence of corporate manslaughter under the Corporate Manslaughter and Corporate Homicide Act 2007 ('CMCHA 2007').

---

[98] Neil Campbell and John Armour, 'Demystifying the Civil Liability of Corporate Agents' (2003) 62 CLJ 290, argue that this approach should apply to all civil wrongs, and not just torts.

[99] *R v Birmingham and Gloucester Railway* Co (1842) 3 QB 223.

[100] *Richmond upon Thames LBC v Pinn & Wheeler* [1989] RTR 354 (DC). Note, however, that a company can be convicted of a motoring offence involving the 'use' of a vehicle (*Brown v Grange Tours* [1969] Crim LR 95 (DC)).

[101] *R v ICR Haulage Ltd* [1944] KB 551.   [102] *Pearks, Gunston & Tee Ltd v Ward* [1902] 2 KB 1 (KB).

[103] *R v P&O European Ferries (Dover) Ltd* [1991] 93 Cr App R 72, 84 (Turner J).

[104] See e.g. s 993 of the CA 2006 (discussed at 23.3.3.2) which imposes liability on any person who was knowingly a party to fraudulent trading.   [105] IA 1986, s 432(1).

Corporate manslaughter

The 2007 Act was enacted as a response to public disquiet following a spate of high-profile accidents:

- In 1987, the *Herald of Free Enterprise* sank with the loss of 193 lives. A coroner's inquest returned verdicts of unlawful killing in 187 cases, but the company was acquitted of manslaughter.[106]
- In 1987, a fire broke out at King's Cross Station, killing 31 people. A government report strongly criticized the management of London Underground,[107] but no manslaughter charges were brought.
- In 1988, two trains crashed into each other near Clapham Junction, killing 35 people. British Rail was later fined £250,000 for health-and-safety breaches, but no manslaughter charges were brought.
- In 1988, the Piper Alpha oil platform exploded, killing 167 people. Despite a public inquiry directing severe criticism towards Occidental Petroleum Ltd[108] (the platform's operator), no criminal charges were brought.
- In 1997, seven people were killed when a passenger train collided with a freight train at Southall. Great Western Trains was fined £1.5 million for health-and-safety violations, but no manslaughter charges were brought.
- In 1999, 31 people died when a train crashed at Ladbroke Grove. Thames Trains was fined £2 million for breaches of health-and-safety legislation, but no manslaughter charges were brought.
- In 2000, four people were killed following a train crash at Hatfield. For health and safety violations, Network Rail was fined £3.5 million and Balfour Beatty was fined £10 million, but the directors charged with manslaughter were all acquitted.
- In 2003, a family of four were killed following a gas explosion at their home in Larkhill. Transco plc was fined £15 million for breaching health-and-safety legislation, but was acquitted of manslaughter.

Even though a company could be convicted of manslaughter,[109] such convictions were extremely rare as the company would only be convicted if it could be established that the deaths were the result of the actions and gross negligence of an identifiable member of the directing mind and will within the company,[110] which proved to be almost impossible to establish in larger companies (the few prosecutions that had been secured occurred in relation to small companies).

Parliament's response was to enact the CMCHA 2007 under which an organization[111] would be guilty of corporate manslaughter if the way in which its activities are managed or organized causes a person's death, and amounts to a gross breach of a relevant duty of care owed by the organization to the deceased.[112] A gross breach of duty occurs where the breach of duty 'falls far below what can reasonably be expected of the organisation

---

[106] *R v P&O European Ferries (Dover) Ltd* [1991] 93 Cr App R 72.

[107] *Department of Transport, Investigation into the King's Cross Underground Fire* (Cm 499, 1988).

[108] Lord Cullen, 'The Public Inquiry into the Piper Alpha Disaster' (HMSO 1990).

[109] *R v P&O European Ferries (Dover) Ltd* [1991] 93 Cr App R 72.

[110] *Attorney General's Reference (No 2 of 1999)* [2000] QB 796 (CA).

[111] Section 1(2) of the 2007 Act provides that an 'organisation' includes a corporation and a partnership.

[112] CMCHA 2007, s 1(1).

in the circumstances'.[113] However, an organization will only be guilty if the way in which it is managed or organized by its senior management is a substantial element in that breach.[114]

Organizations found guilty of the offence are liable to pay a fine,[115] and the court can make a remedial order requiring the organization to remedy the breach and any health-and-safety deficiency in the company's policies, systems, or practices.[116] Finally, the court can make a publicity order requiring the organization to publicize details of the offence.[117]

Even though the 2007 Act has, in theory, made it easier to prosecute companies for manslaughter, the first conviction under the 2007 Act was only secured in February 2011.[118] Since then, the number of successful prosecutions has been low (although the number of prosecutions is increasing year on year), they have all been against small and medium-sized companies (not the larger companies that the Act was designed to make it easier to prosecute), and the fines ordered have been lower than that suggested by the Sentencing Council.[119]

6.5.2 Strict liability

Strict liability is a concept that can apply to both civil wrongs and criminal offences, but it tends to arise most notably in relation to criminal offences. A general principle of criminal law is that a person is not guilty of a crime unless he has a 'guilty mind' (the *mens rea*), which requires the prosecution to establish the requisite mental element (e.g. the defendant intended to commit the crime). However, strict liability offences have no *mens rea* requirement, and so no mental element need be established. Such offences facilitate corporate liability as the prosecution will not need to resort to the tricky issue of attribution.

Attribution is discussed at 6.5.4.

The statutory provision that establishes a criminal offence will usually indicate whether it requires *mens rea* or is of strict liability. Unsurprisingly, many of the criminal offences established under the CA 2006 impose strict liability and are often committed simply by the failure to perform an obligated act (e.g. if the articles are amended, then the company will commit an offence if it does not send a copy of the amended articles to the registrar within 15 days).[120] Where statute does not clearly indicate whether an offence is one of strict liability, then the courts will determine this.

6.5.3 Vicarious liability

There is a clear overlap between the personal liability of an employee or agent and the **vicarious liability** of a company, in the sense that an employee/agent who commits an unlawful act may be found personally liable, whilst the company that employs him may be found vicariously liable.

vicarious liability: where a person is liable for the unlawful acts or omissions of another person

---

[113] ibid s 1(4)(b).   [114] ibid s 1(3).   [115] ibid s 1(6).   [116] ibid s 9.   [117] ibid s 10.

[118] *R v Cotswold Geotechnical Holdings Ltd* (17 February 2011). The company was fined £385,000, which had the effect of putting the company out of business. An appeal against the conviction and the amount of the fine was dismissed (*R v Cotswold Geotechnical Holdings Ltd* [2011] EWCA Civ 1337, [2012] 1 Cr App R (S) 26).

[119] See Sarah Field, 'Criminal Liability under the Corporate Manslaughter and Corporate Homicide Act 2007: A Changing Landscape' (2016) 27 ICCLR 229.   [120] CA 2006, s 26.

6.5.3.1 **Civil liability**

See 6.5.1.1 for more on the personal liability of the company and its agents under contract law.

A company may be vicariously liable for civil wrongs committed by other persons. In relation to liability under contract law, vicarious liability is rarely relevant as, under agency rules, personal liability usually attaches to the principal (i.e. the company) and, in those rare instances where an agent is held liable (e.g. for breach of warranty of authority), his liability is also personal.

Conversely, vicarious liability is much more relevant in relation to the tortious acts of persons acting on behalf of the company.[121] It is well established that a company can be vicariously liable for the tortious acts of its employees if three conditions are satisfied:

1. there must be an employer/employee relationship;
2. the employee must have committed a tort; and
3. the tort must have been committed in the course of the employee's employment.

It is the third requirement that has proven difficult to apply in practice, but it is now settled that the courts will apply a 'close-connection' test under which '[t]he question is whether the [employee's] torts were so closely connected with his employment that it would be fair and just to hold the employers vicariously liable'.[122] There is no doubt that the 'close-connection' test provides a broad and claimant-friendly approach (certainly when compared to previous approaches adopted by the court), as the following case demonstrates.

See Sunny SH Chan, 'Hidden Departure from the Lister Close Connection Test' (2016) 3 LMCLQ 352.

Mohamud v WM Morrison Supermarkets plc [2016] UKSC 11

FACTS: Khan was employed by Morrisons as a petrol pump attendant at one of its supermarkets. He was required to ensure that the pumps were kept in good working order and to serve customers. Mohamud, a customer, approached Khan with an enquiry, but Khan subjected Mohamud to a racist tirade and told him to leave. Mohamud returned to his car, but Khan followed him, told him not to come back, and subjected him to a serious, unprovoked, and violent assault. Mohamud commenced proceedings against Morrisons, alleging that it was vicariously liable for Khan's tortious acts. At first instance and in the Court of Appeal,[123] it was held that there was not a sufficiently close connection between Khan's tortious acts and his employment. Mohamud appealed.

HELD: Mohamud's appeal was allowed and Morrisons was held to be vicariously liable for Khan's assault. The Court stated that Khan's racist tirade was 'inexcusable but within the "field of activities" assigned to him'.[124] The assault by Khan that followed was 'an order to keep away from his employer's premises, which he reinforced by violence'.[125] This was:

> a gross abuse of his position, but it was in connection with the business in which he was employed to serve customers. His employers entrusted him with that position and it is just that as between them and the claimant, they should be held responsible for their employee's abuse of it.[126]

---

[121] Many of the principles discussed here are general tortious principles, and so referral to a textbook on the law of torts will be of aid.

[122] *Lister v Hesley Hall Ltd* [2001] UKHL 22, [2002] 1 AC 215 [28] (Lord Steyn).

[123] *Mohamud v WM Morrison Supermarkets plc* [2014] EWCA Civ 116, [2014] 2 All ER 990.

[124] [2016] UKSC 11, [2016] AC 677 [47] (Lord Toulson).

[125] ibid.   [126] ibid.

Corporate vicariously liability also operates in relation to a relationship of agency, so a principal (e.g. the company) can be vicariously liable for the tortious acts of its agents (e.g. a director). Generally, a principal will only be vicariously liable if the agent acts within the scope of his agency but, as the following leading case demonstrates,[127] the breadth of the close-connection test means that a principal can be (although not necessarily will be) liable for the unauthorized acts of his agents.

Dubai Aluminium Co Ltd v Salaam [2002] UKHL 48

See Charles Mitchell, 'Partners in Wrongdoing?' (2003) 119 LQR 364.

FACTS: Amhurst was a senior partner in two successive firms of solicitors (collectively referred to as 'the Amhurst firm'). He assisted two other individuals (Salaam and Tajir) in defrauding Dubai Aluminium out of almost $50 million by drafting certain agreements. However, Amhurst himself did not benefit personally from the fraud. It was accepted that Amhurst's co-partners were entirely innocent. The Amhurst firm settled with Dubai Aluminium and paid it US$10 million. The Amhurst firm then sought a contribution from Salaam and Tajir, but it could only obtain this contribution if it could show that it was responsible for the wrongs committed by Amhurst. Therefore, the Amhurst firm argued that it was vicariously liable.

HELD: The House of Lords held the Amhurst firm to be vicariously liable for Amhurst's actions. Lord Nicholls acknowledged that 'Amhurst had no authority from his partners to conduct himself in this manner.'[128] However, this did not mean that the Amhurst firm was exempt from liability. He stated that the underlying policy behind vicarious liability:

> is based on the recognition that carrying on a business enterprise necessarily involves risks to others. It involves the risk that others will be harmed by wrongful acts committed by the agents through whom the business is carried on. When those risks ripen into loss, it is just that the business should be responsible for compensating the person who has been wronged.[129]

As a result, the imposition of vicarious liability should not be confined to those acting within the employer's authority. Lord Nicholls went on:

> Drafting these particular agreements is to be regarded as an act done within the ordinary course of the firm's business even though they were drafted for a dishonest purpose. Those acts were so closely connected with the acts Mr Amhurst was authorised to do that for the purpose of the liability of the … firm they may fairly and properly be regarded as done by him while acting in the ordinary course of the firm's business.[130]

Accordingly, Salaam was ordered to contribute US$7.5 million and Tajir US$2.5 million.

COMMENT: *Dubai Aluminium* is an unusual case in that the Amhurst firm was arguing that it was vicariously liable for Amhurst's actions. The unusual nature of the case is a major contributory factor to the outcome, as were the policy considerations of the case. Had the Amhurst firm not been deemed vicariously liable, it could not have sought a contribution from Salaam and Tajir, who would have been permitted to keep any monies resulting from their fraudulent activities.

Two final points must be noted. First, in cases involving vicarious liability, the company is not personally liable, but is merely held liable for the acts of others. From this, it follows that it is irrelevant whether the company had capacity to engage in the tortious act

---

[127] Note that this case involved a partnership (with s 5 of the PA 1890 providing that each partner is an agent of the firm and his other partners), but the principles espoused in the case remain relevant to companies.
[128] [2002] UKHL 48, [2003] 2 AC 366 [20].   [129] ibid [21].   [130] ibid [36].

in question.[131] Second, the doctrine of vicarious liability provides the claimant with an alternative defendant, not a substitute.[132] Accordingly, the company and its employee/agent are joint tortfeasors and the claimant is free to proceed against either party for the entire loss, or may sue both.[133]

6.5.3.2 Criminal liability

Vicarious liability has a strong role to play in relation to corporate civil liability (especially tortious liability). Conversely, vicarious liability has played a much more limited role in relation to breaches of criminal law due to the courts' reluctance to hold that a company is criminally liable for the acts of its employees or agents (as such acts do not often fall within the scope of the employment or agency).

Vicarious liability can be imposed if statute expressly states that the company can be found guilty for the criminal acts of others. For example, the Bribery Act 2010 provides that a commercial organization will be guilty of an offence if a person associated with that commercial organization bribes another person (i) to obtain or retain business for the organization; or (ii) to obtain or retain an advantage for the organization.[134] Where statute does not expressly provide for the imposition of vicarious liability, then the courts will determine whether the offence is one of vicarious liability, and the courts are more willing to establish vicarious liability in cases involving strict liability.[135]

In cases not involving strict liability (namely cases that can only be successfully prosecuted if the required mental element (the *mens rea*) is present (e.g. the accused acted with intent or with malice)), the courts have taken a strict stance. The House of Lords has stated that a company cannot be vicariously liable for an offence requiring proof of *mens rea* unless (i) statute provides for such liability; or (ii) the employer delegated his proprietary or managerial functions to the employee who committed the criminal act.[136] This is a sensible position—to hold otherwise would mean that the company could be vicariously liable for the criminal acts of anyone associated with it. However, companies cannot be given total immunity from offences that require proof of *mens rea*, and so the courts established principles under which the *mens rea* of certain persons could be attributed to the company. This doctrine of attribution is discussed next.

6.5.4 Liability imposed via attribution

Certain civil wrongs and criminal offences require a certain mental element to be present for liability to be established (e.g. intent to commit, or knowledge of particular facts). In the corporate context, this poses a difficulty as whilst the company is a person, it does not have a mind of its own and is therefore incapable of having mental states. One solution to this problem is to attribute to the company the knowledge and mental states of certain persons, via what is known as 'identification theory'.

---

[131] *Citizens Life Assurance Co Ltd v Brown* [1904] AC 423 (PC).

[132] Which is confusing given that the Latin word *'vicarius'* means 'substitute'.

[133] See e.g. *Hawley v Luminar Leisure Ltd* [2005] EWHC 5 (QB), [2005] Lloyd's Rep IR 275, where the claimant successfully claimed against the company and the employee who assaulted him. See also *Standard Chartered Bank v Pakistan National Shipping Corp (No 2)* [2002] UKHL 43 (discussed at 6.5.1.2).

[134] Bribery Act 2010, s 7(1).

[135] See e.g. *National Rivers Authority v Alfred McAlpine Homes East Ltd* [1994] 4 All ER 286 (QB).

[136] *Vane v Yiannopoullos* [1965] AC 486 (HL).

6.5.4.1 Identification theory

Identification theory basically provides that the mental state of certain persons is attributed to the company (e.g. the knowledge of such persons is regarded as the knowledge of the company). The following case provides an early example of a situation where, using identification theory, liability was imposed upon a company.

Lennard's Carrying Co Ltd v Asiatic Petroleum Co Ltd [1915] AC 705 (HL)

FACTS: Section 502 of the Merchant Shipping Act 1894 provided that the owner of a seagoing ship was not liable for 'any loss or damage happening without his actual fault or privity' in relation to goods on board the ship that were lost or damaged by fire. Lennard's Carrying Co Ltd ('LC') owned a ship, the cargo hold of which contained a cargo of benzine belonging to Asiatic Petroleum Co Ltd ('Asiatic'). The ship's boilers were in a poor state of disrepair and failed en route, grounding the ship upon a reef, thereby damaging the cargo hold. The benzine escaped, came into contact with the boiler's combustion chambers, and exploded, completely destroying the ship and its cargo. Asiatic sued. It transpired that Lennard, one of LC's directors, knew the ship was unseaworthy. LC argued it had no knowledge of the ship's unseaworthiness and so was not at fault.

HELD: Lennard knew that the ship was unseaworthy and this knowledge was attributed to LC. Accordingly, LC was at fault and so was held liable. Viscount Haldane LC stated that:

> a corporation is an abstraction. It has no mind of its own any more than it has a body of its own; its active and directing will must consequently be sought in the person of somebody who . . . is really the directing mind and will of the corporation, the very ego and centre of the personality of the corporation . . . . [I]f [the director] was the directing mind of the company, then his action must, unless a corporation is not to be liable at all, have been an action which was the action of the company itself within the meaning of s. 502.[137]

Under *Lennard*, a person's mental state would only be attributed to the company if that person represented the 'directing mind and will' of the company, but *Lennard* provided little guidance on who such persons were. A company's constitution will provide the obvious source of guidance and if the company's articles vest general managerial power in the board (as Art 3 of the model articles does), then the board will represent the directing mind and will. The question is can sub-board level employees also fall within the scope of the directing mind and will of the company.

Tesco Supermarkets Ltd v Nattrass [1972] AC 153 (HL)

FACTS: In a Tesco store, a special-offer poster was displayed, which incorrectly stated the price of a packet of washing powder. A customer purchased the product, noticed the price discrepancy and complained to the relevant authority, resulting in Tesco being charged under s 11 of the Trade Descriptions Act 1968, which made it an offence to give a false or misleading indication of the price of goods. However, the Act also provided that no offence would be committed if the defendant could show that the offence was due to 'the act or default of another person'.[138]

---

[137] [1915] AC 705 (HL) 713, 714.   [138] Trade Descriptions Act 1968, s 24(1).

Tesco argued that the incorrectly stated price occurred because the store manager failed to properly supervise his staff, and therefore the act was caused by another person. Tesco went on to state that acts of the store manager could not be attributed to it as he was not part of the directing mind and will of the company.

HELD: Lord Reid stated:

Normally the board of directors, the managing director and perhaps other superior officers of a company carry out the functions of management and speak and act as the company. Their subordinates do not. They carry out orders from above and it can make no difference that they are given some measure of discretion. But the board of directors may delegate some part of their functions of management giving to their delegate full discretion to act independently of instructions from them. I see no difficulty in holding that they have thereby put such a delegate in their place so that within the scope of the delegation he can act as the company. It may not always be easy to draw the line but there are cases in which the line must be drawn.[139]

Applying this, the House held that the store manager was another person and, being one of several hundred store managers, he could not be identified as part of Tesco's directing mind and will. He occupied a 'relatively subordinate post'[140] and there were several layers of management between him and the board. Accordingly, the offence was caused by the default of another person and Tesco was acquitted.

However, the correct approach to attribution, at least in relation to civil wrongs, must be reassessed in light of the following landmark case, which reduced the emphasis placed upon the 'directing-mind-and-will' test and introduced a more contextual and purposive approach.

See Ross Grantham, 'Corporate Knowledge: Identification or Attribution?' (1996) 59 MLR 732.

Meridian Global Funds Management Asia Ltd v Securities Commission [1995] 2 AC 500 (PC)

FACTS: New Zealand legislation provided that a person had to provide notice to various other persons once he knew, or ought to have known, that he had become a 'substantial security holder' in a listed company.[141] Koo (the chief investment officer of Meridian) and Ng (a senior portfolio manager of Meridian) used Meridian's funds to acquire 49 per cent of the shares in another listed company. Koo and Ng were authorized to do this (but were acting for improper purposes), but Meridian's board did not know of the acquisition. Accordingly, Meridian did not disclose that it was a substantial security holder. Meridian argued that it had not breached the legislation as it did not know it had become a substantial security holder. The Securities Commission stated that Meridian did know, as the knowledge of Koo and Ng was attributable to Meridian.

HELD: Lord Hoffmann stated that a company's primary rules of attribution (which are usually found in its constitution), along with general principles of agency and vicarious liability, will usually be enough to determine the company's rights and obligations. However, in some cases, these will not be enough and so the courts may need to determine how a particular rule is to apply to a company. The answer might be that a law was not intended to apply to a company at

---

[139] [1972] AC 153 (HL) 171.   [140] ibid 193 (Lord Pearson).
[141] Securities Amendment Act 1988, s 20(3). Here, 'substantial' meant holding 5 per cent or more of the company's shares.

all,[142] or that a law could only apply if the act giving rise to liability is one that was authorized by the company's constitution. But there will be instances where these solutions are unsatisfactory and so the court will need to 'fashion a special rule of attribution for the particular substantive rule'.[143] Such a rule will need to bear in mind certain questions, such as whether the law in question was meant to apply to a company, and whose acts or knowledge were for this purpose intended to count as the act or knowledge of the company. To answer these questions, the court must apply 'the usual canons of interpretation, taking into account the language of the rule (if it is a statute) and its content and policy'.[144] In some cases, the 'directing-mind-and-will' approach might be appropriate,[145] but in other cases, it might not be. It will be a 'question of construction in each case as to whether the particular rule requires that the knowledge that an act has been done, or the state of mind with which it was done, should be attributed to the company'.[146]

Applying this, the Privy Council held that the policy behind s 20 of the 1988 Act was to compel the immediate disclosure of the identity of persons who become substantial security holders. In terms of whose knowledge was to count as the knowledge of the company, Lord Hoffmann did not feel that this was a case where a special rule of attribution needed to be fashioned, as the case could be determined on agency principles. Accordingly, the person whose knowledge would be attributed to the company is 'the person who, with the authority of the company, acquired the relevant interest',[147] namely Koo. To rule otherwise would allow the policy of s 20 to be defeated as it would encourage board members to pay little attention to what their investment managers were doing. On this basis, Koo's knowledge was attributed to Meridian and it was held liable.

Under Lord Hoffmann's approach, there is no single principle to determining attribution. Instead, the court should look at the rule of law involved in the case and determine the appropriate principle of attribution based on the purpose and context of the rule involved. The following case provides an example of this.

Morris v Bank of India [2005] EWCA Civ 693

FACTS: BCCI collapsed in 1991 after being found to have engaged in large-scale fraud. BCCI's liquidator alleged that the Bank of India ('BoI') knew that, by entering into certain transactions with BCCI, it was defrauding BCCI's creditors, and it had therefore engaged in fraudulent trading under s 213 of the IA 1986. Liability under s 213 can only be established if it can be shown that the defendant 'knowingly' was a party to fraudulent trading. BoI argued that Samant (the employee who was responsible for entering into the transactions on its behalf) was not a board member and so was not part of its directing mind and will. Accordingly, Samant's knowledge could not be attributed to BoI and so BoI was not a knowing party to the fraud.

HELD: Applying the purposive approach established in *Meridian*, the Court stated that the paramount purpose of s 213 is to provide compensation to those who have suffered loss as a result of fraudulent trading.[148] The key issue was whose knowledge would be attributed to the company. In most companies, there is a chain of command and delegation of authority and so it

See Adam Cloherty, 'Knowledge, Attribution and Fraudulent Trading' (2006) 122 LQR 25.

Section 213 is discussed at 23.3.3.1.

---

142 See e.g. *Deutsche Genossenschaftsbank v Burnhope* [1995] 1 WLR 1580 (HL).
143 [1995] 2 AC 500 (PC) 507.   144 ibid.
145 As in *R v St Regis Paper Co Ltd* [2011] EWCA Crim 2527, [2012] PTSR 871.
146 [1995] 2 AC 500 (PC) 511.   147 ibid.
148 [2005] EWCA Civ 693, [2005] BCC 793 [111] (Mummery LJ).

is likely that a fraudulent transaction will be dealt with by someone below board level. It would therefore be 'inappropriate, in the case of a company, to limit attribution for its purposes to the board, or those specifically authorised by a resolution of the board. To limit it in such a way would be to ignore reality, and risk emasculating the effect of the provision.'[149] The question was who had authority in BoI to deal with BCCI in relation to the relevant transactions. Here, that person was Samant. He had a senior position in BoI, had brought the transactions to BoI, was given a free hand to negotiate them, and did not question the transactions, despite their suspiciousness.[150] Accordingly, it was proper that BoI should take responsibility for the consequences and so it was found liable under s 213.

6.5.4.2 Civil and criminal liability

In relation to civil liability, there is no doubt that the approach established in *Meridian* is now the generally accepted approach and it has been applied to a wide range of civil wrongs. However, in relation to criminal liability, the approach in *Meridian* has not gained the same foothold (despite the fact that *Meridian* involved criminal liability) and the directing-mind-and-will test still appears to be highly relevant. Ferran has argued that the effect of *Meridian* on the criminal law has been to establish that 'the narrow directing mind and will test is not determinative in all cases, because there are circumstances in which an additional special rule of attribution will apply.'[151] Hannigan[152] has argued that this has resulted in a two-stage approach:

1. the court will determine whether the defendant falls within the scope of the company's directing mind and will;

2. if the directing mind and will test does not establish guilt then, based upon the purpose and policy of the law in question, the courts will decide whether to fashion a special rule of attribution (i.e. the approach in *Meridian* will apply).

The different approaches evidenced in civil and criminal cases should not be viewed as problematic. In fact, the differences in approach have been welcomed, with Brooke LJ stating:

I would be anxious if the natural development of the civil law in accordance with the thinking of leading judges in this specialist field on the way in which responsibility should be attributed to corporate bodies today had to be cribbed, cabined and confined by decisions of the House of Lords in the criminal law arena.[153]

6.5.4.3 Attribution as a defence

The above discussion relates to the wrongdoing of certain persons being attributed to the company for the purposes of establishing the company's liability. One interesting issue that has arisen from this is whether the actions of certain persons can be attributed to the company for the purposes of establishing a defence to a claim brought by the company. Cases in this area typically involve the defence of *ex turpi causa non oritur actio* (or the 'illegality defence' as it is usually known), which provides that 'you cannot

---

[149] ibid [129].   [150] ibid [131].

[151] Eilis Ferran, 'Corporate Attribution and the Directing Mind and Will' (2011) 127 LQR 239, 245.

[152] Brenda Hannigan, *Company Law* (5th edn, OUP 2018) 89.

[153] *Odyssey Re (London) Ltd v OIC Run Off Ltd* [2001] Lloyd's Rep IR 1 (CA) 64.

recover compensation for loss which you have suffered in consequence of your own criminal act'.[154] So, for example, if a company brought a claim against its directors, could the directors attribute their own wrongdoing to the company and then raise the illegality defence to defeat the company's claim? The Supreme Court has stated that three different situations need to be considered.[155]

The first situation is where a third party is suing the company based on the misconduct of the company's director, employee, or agent. In such a case, the illegality defence will not arise, as the company is not commencing proceedings, but is being proceeded against.[156] Here, the wrongdoing of the director, employee, or agent will either be attributed to the company, or the company will be vicariously liable for such wrongdoing.[157]

The second situation is where the company is pursuing a claim against its director or employee. In such a case, the courts regard the company as the victim of the wrongdoing (and not as the perpetrator), and so the director's/employee's wrongdoing will not be attributed to the company,[158] meaning that the illegality defence will fail. To hold otherwise would undermine many areas of company law. For example, directors owe their general duties to the company. If a director's breach of duty could be attributed to the company, this would prevent a company from ever claiming against a director for breach of duty.[159] Despite this, it was stated in *Stone & Rolls Ltd v Moore Stephens* that director wrongdoing could be attributed to the company where the directors were 'one or more individuals who for fraudulent purposes run a one-man company'.[160] In such a case, the company would become the fraudster and so the illegality defence could succeed. The following case limited the application of this principle, and stated that, in most cases, the director's wrongdoing would not be attributed to the company.

Bilta (UK) Ltd v Nazir (No 2) [2015] UKSC 23

William Day, 'Attributing Illegalities' (2015) 74 CLJ 409.

FACTS: Chopra and Nazir were the only directors of Bilta (UK) Ltd, with Chopra being the sole shareholder. Bilta was wound up in November 2009, whilst owing HMRC around £38 million in unpaid VAT. It was alleged that Chopra and Nazir entered into a 'carousel fraud' with several other parties, the effect of which was to leave Bilta insolvent and unable to pay its VAT liability. Bilta, through its liquidator, commenced proceedings against, *inter alia*, Chopra and Nazir. The defendants sought to strike out the claims on the ground that Chopra's and Nazir's wrongdoing should be attributed to Bilta itself, and therefore Bilta should not be able to bring a claim based on its own illegal acts.

HELD: The strike-out application was dismissed. Lords Toulson and Hodge stated that:

> where the company pursues a claim against a director or employee for breach of duty, it would defeat the company's claim and negate the director's or employee's duty to the company if the act or the state of mind of the latter were to be attributed to the company and the company were thereby to be estopped from founding on the wrong.[161]

---

[154] *Gray v Thames Trains Ltd* [2009] UKHL 33, [2009] 1 AC 1339 [29] (Lord Hoffmann).
[155] *Bilta (UK) Ltd v Nazir (No 2)* [2015] UKSC 23, [2016] AC 1 [87] (Lord Sumption) and [204] (Lords Toulson and Hodge).   [156] ibid [87] (Lord Sumption).
[157] ibid.   [158] *Belmont Finance Corp Ltd v Williams Furniture Ltd* [1979] Ch 250 (CA).
[159] A point acknowledged by Lord Sumption in *Bilta (UK) Ltd v Nazir (No 2)* [2015] UKSC 23, [2016] AC 1 [89].
[160] *Stone & Rolls Ltd v Moore Stephens* [2009] UKHL 39, [2009] 1 AC 1391 [174] (Lord Walker). This is often referred to as the 'sole actor' exception.   [161] [2015] UKSC 23, [2016] AC 1 [206].

Accordingly, Lord Neuberger stated that:

Where a company has been the victim of wrong-doing by its directors, or of which its directors had notice, then the wrong-doing, or knowledge, of the directors cannot be attributed to the company as a defence to a claim brought against the directors by the company's liquidator . . . .[162]

COMMENT: As regards *Stone & Rolls*, the Court could not fully agree on how that case should be regarded, but the general consensus is that the case 'now retains little precedent value'.[163] Lords Toulson and Hodge stated that, 'Stone & Rolls should be regarded as a case which has no majority ratio decidendi. It stands as authority for the point which it decided, namely that on the facts of that case no claim lay against the auditors, but nothing more.'[164] Lord Neuberger stated that *Stone & Rolls* should be 'put on one side and marked "not to be looked at again"'.[165]

The third situation is where the company is pursuing a claim against a third party, but where the wrongdoing of an agent or employee of the company is somehow relevant. Unfortunately, there appears to be significant disagreement here. In *Bilta*, Lords Toulson and Hodge stated that where a company claims against a third party, whether the director's/employee's wrongdoing is attributed to the company 'depends on the nature of the claim'.[166] However, Lord Sumption disagreed with this flexible, policy-based approach and preferred a rule-based approach.[167] This disagreement led Lord Neuberger to state that the law proper approach to illegality needed to be addressed by the Supreme Court, but *Bilta* was not the case to do that.[168] Such an opportunity arose in *Patel v Mirza*,[169] where the Court confirmed (by a majority of six to three) that a policy-based approach should be adopted under which the courts should take into account a range of factors.[170] However, *Patel* did not focus on companies explicitly and unanswered questions still exist. Consider the following example.

 Attribution and the auditor

The accounts of Dragon plc have been audited by Vanguard LLP. Through its negligence, Vanguard fails to notice that several of Dragon's directors have engaged in fraud. Dragon commences proceedings against Vanguard, but Vanguard argues that the directors' fraud should be attributed to Dragon, and therefore Dragon's claim should fail as it has acted unlawfully.

The question is whether Vanguard can successfully raise the illegality defence. In relation to a one-man company, the House of Lords in *Stone & Rolls* stated that the illegality defence could be raised by the auditor[171] and, on the facts, certain Justices in

---

162 ibid [7].   163 William Day, 'Attributing Illegalities' (2015) 74 CLJ 409, 411.

164 [2015] UKSC 23, [2016] AC 1 [154].   165 ibid [30].

166 ibid [207].   167 ibid [98]–[100].   168 ibid [15].

169 [2016] UKSC 42, [2016] 3 WLR 399. See James Goudkamp, 'The End of an Era? Illegality in Private Law in the Supreme Court?' (2017) 133 LQR 14.   170 ibid [82]–[94].

171 *Stone & Rolls Ltd v Moore Stephens* [2009] UKHL 39, [2009] 1 AC 1391.

Bilta agreed[172] (although, as discussed, there was significant disagreement on the issue). However, as noted above, *Stone & Rolls* is a much-criticized case and, unfortunately, the issue was not relevant in *Patel*. Accordingly, significant uncertainties remain in relation to the application of the illegality defence in relation to companies. Fortunately, the application of the defence in the corporate context is rare, but clarification is still desirable.

A final point to note is that attributing the acts or omissions of others to the company for the purposes of raising a defence will be heavily based on the context of the case. For example, in *Singularis Holdings Ltd v Daiwa Capital Markets Europe Ltd*,[173] Sir Geoffrey Vos C noted that one reason why attribution was appropriate in *Stone & Rolls* was because the company was set up purely to perpetrate a fraud, whereas in *Singularis*, one reason why attribution was not appropriate was because the company was set up to carry out legitimate activities.[174]

CHAPTER SUMMARY

- A company can enter into a contract by (i) affixing its common seal to the contract; (ii) complying with the rules in ss 44(2)–(8) of the CA 2006; or (iii) by a person acting under the company's express or implied authority.
- Companies are no longer required to have an objects clause.
- Section 39 of the CA 2006 provides that a contract cannot be invalidated on the ground that the contract is outside the scope of the company's capacity.
- An agent can bind the company if he has the requisite authority. Authority can be actual (express or implied) or apparent.
- Section 40 of the CA 2006 provides that the power of the directors to bind the company, or authorize others to do so, is free of any limitation under the company's constitution.
- When determining upon whom liability should be placed, four methods of liability are used, namely (i) personal liability; (ii) strict liability; (iii) vicarious liability; and (iv) liability imposed via attribution.

FURTHER READING

CMV Clarkson, 'Kicking Corporate Bodies and Damning Their Souls' (1996) 59 MLR 557.
- Examines the law relating to corporate criminal liability and argues that the law should impose direct liability on companies, rather than attribute criminal acts to the company.

Eilis Ferran, 'Corporate Attribution and the Directing Mind and Will' (2011) 127 LQR 239.
- Discusses the impact that *Meridian Global Funds* has had on the law relating to corporate attribution.

Ernest Lim, 'Attribution and the Illegality Defence' (2016) 79 MLR 476.
- Discusses the Supreme Court decision in *Bilta (UK) Ltd v Nazir*.

---

[172] *Bilta (UK) Ltd v Nazir (No 2)* [2015] UKSC 23, [2016] AC 1 [91] (Lord Sumption).
[173] [2018] EWCA Civ 84, [2018] 1 WLR 2777.   [174] ibid [56].

Roderick Munday, *Agency: Law and Principles* (3rd edn, OUP 2016).
- An excellent text on the law of agency.

Sarah Worthington, 'Corporate Attribution and Agency: Back to Basics' (2017) 133 LQR 118.
- Discusses the relevant case law and identifies several problems relating to corporate attribution and agency.

SELF-TEST QUESTIONS

1. Define the following terms:
- common seal;
- *ultra vires*;
- objects clause;
- agency;
- indoor management rule;
- strict liability;
- vicarious liability;
- identification theory.

2. State whether each of the following statements is true or false and, if false, explain why:
- All companies are required to have a common seal.
- If a company enters into a contract that is outside of its objects clause, the contract will be void.
- Actual authority can be express or implied.
- Section 40 of the CA 2006 provides directors with authority to engage in acts that are outside the scope of their authority.
- The company can be liable for the acts of its employees and agents.
- Where a company is suing a director, the director cannot attribute his own wrongdoing to the company for the purposes of raising a defence.

3. 'Despite the decision in *Meridian Global Funds Funds Management Asia Ltd v Securities Commission*, the "directing-mind-and-will" test remains of substantial importance.' Discuss the validity of this quote.

4. Dragon plc has adopted the model articles for public companies, but added a new art 1A, which provides that 'the company shall not enter into any supply contract of over three years in length without the approval of the members'. Dragon is keen to extend a contract with one of its suppliers, Tumble Ltd. At a board meeting, Jane (the CEO of Dragon) stated that it was important that the company does all it can to extend the contract with Tumble, but that the company cannot afford to pay more than what it is currently paying. Steve (a director of Tumble) meets up with Jude (the chair of Dragon) to discuss the contract, although the other directors of Dragon do not know of the meeting, nor do they know that Katie (Dragon's company secretary) arranges for Steve to stay in a five-star hotel. The next day, Jude and Steve agree terms and a five-year extension of the contract is agreed. The extended contract is signed on behalf of Dragon by Jude and Katie.

Jude reports to the other directors of Dragon that a five-year extension of the contract has been agreed, but the other directors are extremely concerned as the price agreed by Jude is double the current price. The directors are also not happy about the prospect of Dragon paying for Steve's hotel stay. Jane seeks your advice regarding whether:
- Dragon is legally bound to pay for Steve's stay in the five-star hotel; and
- Dragon is bound to the supply contract with Tumble.

ONLINE RESOURCES

This book is accompanied by online resources to better support you in your studies. Visit www.oup. com/uk/roach-company/ for:

- answers to the self-test questions;
- further reading lists;
- multiple-choice questions;
- glossary.

Updates to the law can be found on the author's Twitter account (@UKCompanyLaw) and further resources can be found on the author's blog (www.companylawandgovernance.com).

PART III
The board of directors

Part III of this text focuses on the board of directors. The board's role differs depending upon the type of company, but it is a fundamental organ of the company and so a huge amount of law and best practice recommendations exist that aim to ensure the board operates efficiently and does not abuse the considerable powers vested in it. As a result, Part III is the largest part in this text, consisting of six chapters, namely:

CHAPTER 7 CLASSIFICATION OF DIRECTORS
In order to understand how the law regulates directors, you need to understand what a director is and the different types of director that exist. Different types of directors can function in vastly different ways and so it is vital that you understand the differences between the various types of directors.

CHAPTER 8 BOARD APPOINTMENT, STRUCTURE, AND COMPOSITION
The composition and structure of the board can have a significant effect on the company's operation and, in recent years, board composition has become a dominant governance topic. This chapter looks at the process by which directors are appointed and remunerated, the various board structures, the role of the company secretary, and the importance of board diversity.

CHAPTER 9 THE ROLE AND POWERS OF THE BOARD
The board's role will differ considerably depending upon the type of company. This chapter discusses the board's role, including the powers of the board, the division of power between the board and the members, and how the directors exercise their powers (notably through board meetings).

CHAPTER 10 DIRECTORS' DUTIES I: DUTIES OF PERFORMANCE
This first of two chapters on directors' duties looks at the codification of the duties, how breach of duty can be avoided, and the duties in ss 171–4.

CHAPTER 11 DIRECTORS' DUTIES II: CONFLICTS OF INTEREST

The second chapter on directors' duties focuses on those duties relating to conflicts of interests, before moving on to look at transactions involving directors that require member approval.

CHAPTER 12 VACATION OF OFFICE AND DISQUALIFICATION

The final chapter in Part III looks at the various ways in which a director can cease to be a director.

7

Classifications of director

- Who is a director?
- Classifications of director

INTRODUCTION

As a company is a legal entity, it can only act through human intermediaries, with the top level of intermediaries usually being labelled as 'directors'. All companies must have directors, with the Companies Act 2006 (CA 2006) providing that a private company must have at least one director, and a public company must have at least two directors.[1] Legislation, case law, and the constitution of a company all grant powers to directors, subject them to duties and obligations, and impose liability upon them for breaches of the law. It is therefore vital that we know exactly whether a person is a director or not and, if so, what type of director they are.

This chapter begins by discussing how the law determines whether a person is a director. It then moves on to look at the various different types of director and directorial roles that exist, and how they contribute to the UK's company law and governance system.

7.1 Who is a director?

The CA 2006 does not define what a director is, but s 250 provides that '[i]n the Companies Acts "director" includes any person occupying the position of director, by whatever name called'.[2] Two initial points should be noted regarding this formulation.

The first point to note is that as s 250 refers to 'any person', it follows that, at the time of writing, both natural persons and bodies corporate (such as a company or limited liability partnership) can act as a director, although s 155(1) of the CA 2006 does require that a company have at least one director who is a natural person.[3] In practice,

---

[1] CA 2006, s 154. The CA 2006 does not provide for a maximum number of directors, but the articles may specify a limit (the model articles impose no such limit).

[2] Identical wording is found in s 251 of the Insolvency Act 1986 (IA 1986), s 22(4) of the Company Directors Disqualification Act 1986, and s 417(1) of the Financial Services and Markets Act 2000.

[3] Note that once s 156A (discussed below) comes into force, s 155 will be repealed.

corporate directors are rare, with the government estimating that, in 2013, there were around 13,000 corporate directors (around 0.4 per cent of the total number of directors).[4] Concerns had long been expressed that corporate directorships could be misused and could make it difficult to impose liability on those who owned or controlled the subject companies, as the following case demonstrates.

Revenue and Customs Commissioners v Holland [2010] UKSC 51

FACTS: Mr Holland and his wife were the only directors of Pay0 (Directors Services) Ltd ('Pay0'). In order to minimize corporation tax, Holland created a complex corporate structure involving 42 other companies, with Pay0 acting as the sole director for all 42 companies.[5] The tax avoidance scheme failed and all 42 companies went into liquidation, collectively owing around £3.5 million in unpaid tax to Her Majesty's Revenue and Customs (HMRC). Given that Pay0 had minimal funds, HMRC commenced proceedings against Holland for breach of the summary remedy found in s 212 of the Insolvency Act 1986 (IA 1986). In order to establish liability under s 212, HMRC contended that Holland was a *de facto* director of the 42 liquidated companies.

HELD: The Supreme Court rejected HMRC's claim and held that Holland was not a *de facto* director. The justification for this need not be discussed here,[6] but it should be noted that if the law prohibited corporate directors, then Holland would not have been able to implement this scheme using a corporate director—he would have to have acted as director himself for the 42 companies and liability would have more easily established.

See Peter Watts, 'De Facto Directors' (2011) 127 LQR 162.

Section 212 is discussed at 23.3.2, and *de facto* directors are discussed at 7.2.1.

Given the potential misuse of corporate directors, many countries provide that only natural persons can act as directors.[7] With the passing of the Small Business, Enterprise and Employment Act 2015, UK company law also plans to adopt such a stance. The newly inserted s 156A(1) of the CA 2006 provides that '[a] person may not be appointed as a director of a company unless the person is a natural person', although the Secretary of State may pass regulations providing for exceptions to this.[8] Breach of s 156 renders the appointment void and results in a criminal offence being committed by the company purporting to make the appointment, and every officer in default.[9] However, at the time of writing, s 156A is not yet in force and proposals for regulations providing exceptions to s 156A have not been published (although the government has consulted on the issue).[10] On the date that s 156A does come into force, corporate directors appointed before this date will cease to be directors 12 months after s 156A comes into force.[11]

The second point to note is that the phrase 'by whatever name called' makes it clear that a person's job title is not a conclusive factor. Accordingly, a person may be found

---

[4] Department for Business, Innovation, and Skills (BIS), 'Transparency and Trust: Enhancing the Transparency of UK Company Ownership and Increasing Trust in UK Business: Discussion Paper' (BIS 2013) para 5.2.

[5] It should be noted that the events of this case occurred before s 155(1) was in force. Under the CA 1985, a company could have a sole director that was a corporate director.

[6] For an account of the case and the reasoning employed by the Court, see Peter Watts, 'De Facto Directors' (2011) 127 LQR 162.

[7] Examples of such countries include Australia, the Czech Republic, Jersey, and Switzerland, as well as some American states (e.g. Delaware).

[8] CA 2006, s 156B(1).   [9] ibid s 156A(3) and (6).

[10] BIS, 'Corporate Directors: Scope to Exceptions to the Prohibition of Corporate Directors' (BIS 2014).

[11] CA 2006, s 156C(1) and (2).

to be a director even if they are not labelled as such (e.g. board members of companies limited by guarantee are often known as 'governors'). Conversely, a person who is titled as a director may not be regarded as a director under s 250, which is useful give the increasingly common practice of bestowing the title 'director' upon employees below board level (e.g. titling employees engaged in sales or marketing as 'sales directors' or 'marketing directors').

7.2 Classifications of director

The CA 2006 only formally recognizes two types of director, namely 'directors'[12] (discussed at 7.1) and 'shadow directors'[13] (discussed at 7.2.2). In practice, however, there are numerous types of directors and directorial roles, and it is important to identify the type of director for several reasons:

- not all types of director are relevant to all companies (e.g. small private companies will almost certainly not have any non-executive directors);

- statute may provide that only certain types of director can be liable for certain legal breaches (e.g. shadow directors are usually only liable for breaches of the CA 2006 if the relevant provision expressly states so);

- the type of director may be relevant in determining a director's duty of skill and care.

> The duty of skill and care is discussed at 10.5.

Accordingly, this section discusses the various different types of directors and their roles.

7.2.1 *De facto* and *de jure* directors

Section 250 refers to a person 'occupying the position of director', and makes no reference to whether a person has been validly appointed as director. It therefore follows that s 250 is wide enough to cover persons who have been validly appointed as director (***de jure*** directors), and persons who have not been validly appointed, but who nevertheless act as director (***de facto*** directors). It is important to distinguish between the two, as the meaning of the term 'director' will have different meanings in different contexts.[14] For example, even though the CA 2006 does not expressly distinguish between *de jure* and *de facto* directors, it is clear that many provisions will apply to both types of director (e.g. the directors' general duties), but some provisions may, based on their construction, only apply to *de jure* directors.

> *de jure:* in law

> *de facto:* in fact

Identifying whether a person is a *de jure* director is straightforward, but determining whether a person is a *de facto* director is more complex. Historically, the term referred to persons who acted as director, but whose appointment was defective, or had been terminated, but it is now clear that the term also covers persons who have never been appointed.[15] Over the years, a number of cases have discussed the identification of *de facto* directors and the following principles have emerged:

- The person in question must have exercised 'real influence (otherwise than as a professional adviser) in the corporate governance of a company. . .'[16]

---

[12] ibid s 250.   [13] ibid s 251.

[14] *Revenue and Customs Commissioners v Holland* [2010] UKSC 51, [2010] 1 WLR 2793 [93] (Lord Collins).

[15] *Re Lo-Line Electric Motors Ltd* [1988] Ch 477 (Ch).

[16] *Re Kaytech International plc* [1999] BCC 390 (CA) 402 (Robert Walker LJ).

- The person in question must have undertaken 'functions in relation to the company which could properly be discharged only by a director'.[17]
- The person in question must 'participate in directing the affairs of the company . . . [and must act] . . . "on an equal footing" with any de jure directors'.[18]
- It need not be shown that the person in question was held out as a director by the company,[19] nor need it be shown that the person held himself out as a director.[20] However, such holding out will be relevant in determining whether the person is a *de facto* director.[21]

7.2.2 Shadow directors[22]

Consider the following example:

> **Eg** **Shadow directors**
>
> Dragon Supplies Ltd ('DS'), a subsidiary of Dragon plc, is experiencing severe financial difficulties and decides to appoint a consultant from a local firm of accountants to provide advice on how to rescue the business. The consultant provides a series of instructions which, for the last six months, DS's directors have been following. The instructions are poorly thought out and eventually result in DS being liquidated and dissolved. Several of its directors were subsequently disqualified on the ground of unfitness.

The question that arises is whether the consultant should face liability given that it was his instructions that contributed to DS's dissolution. The problem that arises is that the consultant was not appointed as a director of DS, nor has he acted as a director of DS (i.e. he is not a *de jure* or *de facto* director). Despite this, liability could be imposed upon him if it was held that he was a 'shadow director' of DS, with s 251(1) of the CA 2006 defining a shadow director as 'a person in accordance with whose directions or instructions the directors of the company are accustomed to act'.[23] A few points should be noted regarding this definition:

- As s 251 refers to the directors *acting* on the directions/instructions, it follows that the mere *giving* of instructions/directions will not make a person a shadow director.[24]
- In order for a person to be a shadow director, it must be shown that a 'governing majority of the board' was accustomed to acting on his instructions.[25]

---

[17] *Re Hydrodam (Corby) Ltd* [1994] BCC 161 (Ch) 163 (Millett J).

[18] *Secretary of State for Trade and Industry v Hollier* [2006] EWHC 1804 (Ch), [2007] Bus LR 352 [68] (Etherton J).

[19] ibid [66].

[20] *Secretary of State for Trade and Industry v Aviss* [2006] EWHC 1846 (Ch), [2007] BCC 288.

[21] *Secretary of State for Business, Innovation & Skills v Chohan* [2013] EWHC 680 (Ch), [2013] Lloyd's Rep FC 351 [41] (Hildyard J).

[22] This section will consider the definition of a shadow director. The duties owed by a shadow director are discussed at 10.1.2.1, alongside the directors' duties.

[23] Identical definitions are found in s 251 of the IA 1986 and s 22(5) of the Company Directors Disqualification Act 1986. Section 417(1) of the Financial Services and Markets Act 2000 does not define what a shadow director is, but does include the s 251(1) wording within its definition of 'director'.

[24] *Ultraframe (UK) Ltd v Fielding* [2005] EWHC 1638 (Ch), [2006] FSR 17 [1278] (Lewison J).

[25] ibid [1272].

- The directors must be 'accustomed' to acting on the instructions/directions. Therefore, a person will not be a shadow director the first time such instructions/directions are acted upon—the directors must act on the instructions/directions 'over a period of time and as a regular course of conduct'.[26]

- Section 251(2) provides three instances where a person will not be a shadow director, namely where the person is (i) giving advice in a professional capacity (meaning that the consultant in the example above may not be a shadow director); (ii) giving instructions, directions, guidance or advice in the exercise of a function conferred under an enactment, or; (iii) giving guidance or advice in his capacity as a Minister of the Crown.

- The upcoming prohibition on corporate directors does not apply to shadow directors, so a body corporate can be a shadow director.[27]

The rationale behind holding shadow directors liable is that 'a person who effectively controls the activities of a company is to be subject to the same statutory liabilities and disabilities as a person who is a *de jure* director'.[28] However, this does not mean that a shadow director is always treated as a *de jure* director as, in relation to many provisions of the CA 2006, liability will only be imposed if the Act or accompanying regulations expressly provide that the provision applies to shadow directors.

Whether or not a person is a shadow director is highly dependent on the facts, resulting in a measure of uncertainty. Parties such as parent companies[29] controlling shareholders,[30] and consultants[31] have all been held capable of falling within the s 251 definition. In theory, creditors should also be capable of being shadow directors but the courts have been extremely reluctant to hold this (e.g. to date, the courts have refused to classify a bank as a shadow director).[32] In the following case, the Court of Appeal established some general principles regarding shadow directors.

Secretary of State for Trade and Industry v Deverell [2001] Ch 340 (CA)

FACTS: Deverell and Hopkins were appointed on a consultancy basis to provide advice to Euro Express Ltd ('Euro'). Both consultants were afforded extremely broad powers, with Deverell's influence being especially noteworthy. Euro's directors followed his instructions always, he was a signatory to the company's bank account, and, in many areas of company business, his authority was equivalent to that of the directors. Euro went into liquidation, owing its creditors £4.46 million. Euro's three directors were disqualified on the ground of unfitness, but disqualification

See Jennifer Payne, 'Casting Light into the Shadows: Secretary of State for Trade and Industry v Deverell' (2001) 22 Co Law 22.

---

[26] *Re Unisoft Group Ltd (No 3)* [1994] BCC 766 (Ch) 775 (Harman J).

[27] CA 2006, s 156A(4) (not in force at the time of writing).

[28] *Ultraframe (UK) Ltd v Fielding* [2005] EWHC 1638 (Ch), [2006] FSR 17 [1272] (Lewison J).

[29] *Re Hydrodam (Corby) Ltd* [1994] BCC 161 (Ch). Note, however, that s 251(3) of the CA 2006 provides that, for the purposes of certain parts of the CA 2006, a parent company will not be regarded as a shadow director in relation to any of its subsidiaries.

[30] *Secretary of State for Trade and Industry v Aviss* [2006] EWHC 1846 (Ch), [2007] BCC 288.

[31] *Secretary of State for Trade and Industry v Deverell* [2001] Ch 340; *Vivendi SA v Richards* [2013] EWHC 3006 (Ch), [2013] BCC 771.

[32] See e.g. *Re a Company (No 005009 of 1987)* [1988] 4 BCC 424 (Ch); *Ultraframe (UK) Ltd v Fielding* [2005] EWHC 1638 (Ch), [2006] FSR 17. This has led Evripides Hadjinestoros, 'Fear of the Dark: Banks as Shadow Directors' (2013) 34 Co Law 169, 171 to argue that '[a] judicially made exception . . . concerning banks has therefore been formed'.

proceedings were also brought against Deverell and Hopkins, on the ground that they were shadow directors.

HELD: Given the level of power and influence Deverell and Hopkins had, the Court easily found them to be shadow directors. More importantly, Morritt LJ put forward a number of propositions:

- The s 251 definition should be construed in the normal way to give effect to the parliamentary intention ascertainable from the mischief to be dealt with and the words used.
- The purpose of s 251 is to identify those, other than professional advisers, with real influence in the corporate affairs of the company. But it is not necessary that such influence should be exercised over the whole field of its corporate activities.
- Whether any particular communication from the alleged shadow director, whether by words or conduct, is to be classified as a direction or instruction must be objectively ascertained by the court in the light of all the evidence.
- Non-professional advice may come within the s 251 definition.
- It is not necessary to show that the *de jure* directors or some of them cast themselves in a subservient role or surrendered their respective discretions, nor is it necessary to show that the alleged shadow director 'lurked in the shadows'—a person can openly be a shadow director.

Deverell, whilst helpful, has also been criticized on the ground that it effectively merged the concepts of *de facto* director and shadow director. It has been argued that, given the level of influence they exerted, Deverell and Hopkins were actually *de facto* and not shadow directors.[33] The courts' approach to the distinction between *de facto* directors and shadow directors has changed in recent years. Historically, the courts held that the two concepts were mutually exclusive and it is clear that, in many cases, there is a distinction between the two, as explained by Millett J:

> A *de facto* director is a person who assumes to act as a director. He is held out as a director by the company, and claims and purports to be a director, although never actually or validly appointed as such. . . . A shadow director, by contrast, does not claim or purport to act as a director. On the contrary, he claims not to be a director. He lurks in the shadows, sheltering behind others who, he claims, are the only directors of the company to the exclusion of himself. He is not held out as a director by the company.[34]

Despite these differences, the courts came to acknowledge that an overlap did exist between a *de facto* director and shadow director,[35] and that a complete distinction between *de facto* directors and shadow directors was 'impossible to maintain'.[36] In the following case, the court held that the defendant was both a *de facto* director and a shadow director.

---

[33] Chris Noonan and Susan Watson, 'The Nature of Shadow Directorship: Ad Hoc Statutory Intervention or Company Law Principle?' [2006] JBL 763, 773.

[34] *Re Hydrodam (Corby) Ltd* [1994] BCC 161 (Ch) 163. It should be noted that, following *Deverell*, Millett J's assertion that a shadow director 'lurks in the shadows' is not a necessary ingredient. Further, as discussed above, a person need not be held out as a director in order to be a *de facto* director.

[35] *Smithton Ltd v Naggar* [2014] EWCA Civ 939, [2015] 1 WLR 189.

[36] *Revenue and Customs Commissioners v Holland* [2010] UKSC 51, [2010] 1 WLR 2793 [91] (Lord Collins).

Secretary of State for Business, Innovation and Skills v Chohan [2013] EWHC 680 (Ch)

FACTS: UKLI Ltd went into liquidation with debts of over £70 million,[37] after the Financial Services Authority (FSA) held that the business was an unlawful collective investment scheme.[38] It was also contended that Mr Chohan, a former *de jure* director who had resigned from UKLI, used his influence to cause UKLI to improperly advance loans and declare dividends. Disqualification proceedings were issued against six individuals, including Chohan. Five of these individuals accepted disqualification undertakings, but Chohan refused on the ground that he was not a director at the relevant time. Evidence indicated that, despite his resignation, he exerted a strong influence over the directors, through both direct means (authorizing loans and dividend payments) and indirect means (indirect involvement in management decisions).

HELD: Hildyard J stated that 'Mr Chohan's influence was sometimes express and direct, sometimes indirect or implicit; but it was, in my judgment, pervasive, and in terms of having the final say, probably substantially unaffected by his formal resignation.'[39] Given the direct and indirect nature of Chohan's influence, Hildyard J held that he was a *de facto* director and a shadow director and disqualified him for 12 years.

See David Johnson and Brian Cain, 'De Facto and Shadow Directorships' [2013] 37 CSR 9.

7.2.3 Executive and non-executive directors

The CA 2006 never refers to executive and non-executive directors (NEDs), nor does s 250 distinguish between them (although it is clear that both types of director are covered by s 250).[40] Despite this, it is clear that there are significant differences between executive directors and NEDs, as Table 7.1 indicates.

TABLE 7.1 Executive and non-executive directors

	Executive directors	Non-executive directors
Role	Engages in the day-to-day management of the company	Involved in management, but also monitor the executives
Employment Status	Usually appointed under a contract of service, so will be employees	Usually appointed via a letter of appointment and are therefore not employees
Full-time or part-time	Usually full-time	Part-time (usually around 1–2 days per month)
Remuneration	NEDs are paid much less than executive directors. FTSE 100 directors earn, on average, around £2.4 million per year;[41] FTSE 100 NEDs are paid, on average, £70,000 per year.[42]	

---

[37] Also known as *Re UKLI Ltd*. See also *Secretary of State for Trade and Industry v Aviss* [2006] EWHC 1846 (Ch), [2007] BCC 288.

[38] Under s 19(1) of the Financial Services and Markets Act 2000, such schemes required FSA approval, which UKLI had not obtained.

[39] [2013] EWHC 680 (Ch), [2013] Lloyd's Rep FC 351 [50].

[40] Paragraph 278 of the Explanatory Notes to the CA 2006 states that the term 'director' includes both executive and non-executive directors.

[41] Income Data Services, 'FTSE 100 Directors' Total Earnings Jump by 21 per cent in a Year', www.incomesdata.co.uk/wp-content/uploads/2014/10/IDS-FTSE-100-directors-pay-20141.pdf accessed 10 January 2019.

[42] PwC, 'FTSE 100: Non-Executive Director Fees in 2017' PwC 2018) 2.

Over the past 20–30 years, the UK corporate governance system has come to place great emphasis on the importance of NEDs. Indeed, Provision 11 of the UK Corporate Governance Code places such importance on their role that it recommends that at least half the board (excluding the chair) should consist of NEDs, whom the board considers to be independent. Grant Thornton's annual Corporate Governance Review[43] reveals that only 16 FTSE 350 companies did not comply with this recommendation. It should be noted at the outset that NEDs are only found in larger companies, as smaller companies will have no use for them.

7.2.3.1 **The governance role of NEDs**

The importance of NEDs lies in relation to their governance role, with one report branding them as the 'custodians of the governance process'.[44] The UK Corporate Governance Code provides that NEDs' overall role is to 'provide constructive challenge, strategic guidance, offer specialist advice and hold management to account'.[45] More specific roles envisaged by the Code include:

- appraising the chair's position;[46]
- appointing and removing executive directors;[47]
- scrutinising and holding to account the performance of the management and individual executive directors against performance objectives;[48]
- sitting on various board committees (e.g. remuneration, nomination, and audit committees).

The Code therefore envisages that the NEDs will be involved in management of the company, but will also be expected to monitor the company's management. However, it is unclear which role, if either, is to be afforded prominence. The Cadbury Report stated that the focus on the monitoring role 'should not in any way detract from the primary and positive contribution which they are expected to make, as equal board members, to the leadership of the company'.[49] The Hampel Report agreed, stating that the focus on NEDs has resulted in the 'unintended side effect' of overemphasizing their monitoring role.[50] It has also been argued that the NEDs' monitoring function segregates them from the executives and imposes an implicit two-tier board philosophy onto a unitary board structure.[51] Consequently, some commentators are of the opinion that the two roles cannot sit alongside one another,[52] but others argue that likely conflicts are not as significant as believed.[53]

The most significant concerns relate to NED independence. NEDs cannot effectively monitor their executive counterparts, nor can they bring a neutral, third-party perspective to management, if they are not independent of the executives. The danger of a lack of independence can be seen in the following infamous example.

---

[43] Grant Thornton LLP, 'Corporate Governance Review 2018' (Grant Thornton 2018) 34.

[44] Derek Higgs, 'Review of the Role and Effectiveness of Non-Executive Directors' (DTI 2003) para 1.6.

[45] Financial Reporting Council (FRC), 'The UK Corporate Governance Code' (FRC 2018) Principle H.

[46] ibid Provision 12.   [47] ibid Provision 13.   [48] ibid.

[49] 'Report of the Committee on the Financial Aspects of Corporate Governance' (Gee 1992) para 4.10.

[50] The Committee on Corporate Governance, 'Final Report' (Gee 1998) para 3.7.

[51] Sir Owen Green, 'Why Cadbury Leaves a Bitter Taste', *Financial Times* (London, 9 June 1992).

[52] Mahmoud Ezzamel and Robert Watson, 'Wearing Two Hats: The Conflicting Control and Management Roles of Non-Executive Directors' in Kevin Keasey, Steve Thompson, and Mark Wright (eds), *Corporate Governance: Economic, Management and Financial Issues* (OUP 1997).

[53] Laura F Spira and Ruth Bender, 'Compare and Contrast: Perspectives on Board Committees' (2004) 12 CG 489, 498.

Enron and 'independent' directors

From a corporate governance standpoint, Enron's board appeared to be a model of good practice, with 13 of the 15 directors being branded as independent NEDs. However, a report issued following the company's collapse[54] revealed that many of Enron's so-called 'independent' directors had financial ties with the company that cast serious doubts on their independence:

- Between 1996 and 2001, Enron had paid a monthly $6,000 retainer to Lord John Wakeham for consultancy services, in addition to his board remuneration. Another director, John A Urquhart, was also paid $493,914 for consultancy services in 2000 alone.
- Enron director Herbert Winokur also served on the board of the National Tank Company. The National Tank Company generated significant revenues through selling oilfield equipment to Enron subsidiaries.
- Enron made substantial donations to the MD Andersen Cancer Center in Texas. Two of Enron's board members had served as President of the Cancer Center.
- The remuneration received by the independent directors (around $350,000, much of it in the form of share options and therefore risk-free) was described as 'significantly above the norm'.[55]

These financial ties contributed to 'the Enron Board's lack of independence and reluctance to challenge Enron management'.[56] This lack of independence also contributed to a lack of auditor independence, with the report concluding that 'the Enron Audit Committee went through the motions of asking Andersen about its independence, relied on what it was told, and did little more to evaluate the relationship between the auditor and the company'.[57]

Provision 10 of the UK Corporate Governance Code provides that the board should identify in the annual report each NED that it considers to be independent. It then provides a non-exhaustive list of circumstances which are likely to impair, or could appear to impair a NED's independence, namely:

- the NED is or has been an employee of the company or group within the past five years;
- the NED has, or has had within the past three years, a material business relationship with the company, either directly or as a partner, shareholder, director, or senior employee of a body that has such a relationship with the company;
- the NED has received or receives additional remuneration from the company apart from a director's fee, participates in the company's share option or a performance-related pay scheme, or is a member of the company's pension scheme;
- the NED has close family ties with any of the company's advisers, directors, or senior employees;
- the NED holds cross-directorships or has significant links with other directors through involvement in other companies or bodies;
- the NED represents a significant shareholder; or
- the NED has served on the board for more than nine years from the date of their first appointment.

---

[54] Permanent Committee on Investigations of the Committee on Governmental Affairs United States Senate, 'The Role of the Board of Directors in Enron's Collapse' (2002).
[55] ibid 53.   [56] ibid 52.   [57] ibid 58.

The proposed 2018 update to the Code provided that the existence of any of these circumstances would result in the NED not being independent. However, when the 2018 update was published, this was removed and the Code adopted the position in prior Codes, namely that where any of these circumstances apply, and the board nonetheless considers the NED to be independent, it should provide a clear explanation as to why it considers that NED to be independent. In 2018, 68 FTSE 350 companies had NEDs on their board they did not consider to be independent, with the most common reason for the lack of independence being that the NED represented a significant shareholder.[58]

Even where such relationships do not exist, there still exist concerns regarding NED independence. NEDs are often executive directors of other companies, a position which produces a heavy workload: indeed, it has been suggested that persons who have not experienced the responsibilities of executive directorship would be unsuitable for positions as non-executive directors.[59] This means that they will have minimal time to monitor effectively the companies in question and may come to rely on the executives to draw their attention to what is important, and the executives may be tempted to carefully select which information they pass onto the NEDs. Further, given that executive directors and NEDs are often drawn from similar backgrounds, they may socialize with, or serve on other boards as fellow non-executives with the executives they are supposed to monitor. Accordingly, it has been noted that 'most outside directors share management's ideological disposition toward the single issue most central to their monitoring responsibilities: how intensely outside directors should monitor management'.[60] There is also the possibility that non-executives may 'pull their punches . . . out of an innate fear of encouraging non-execs on their own boards to rock the boat too often'.[61]

Historically, the appointment of NEDs was also a cause for concern as most NEDs were selected by the chair of the board (in many cases because the potential NEDs have a personal acquaintance with the chair), with 'the shareholders providing only the official rubber stamp'.[62] This practice has diminished in recent years due to the prevalence of nomination committees but, as is discussed at 8.1.2.1, doubts have been expressed at the effectiveness of nomination committees.

Nomination committees are discussed at 8.1.2.1.

7.2.3.2 Senior Independent Director (SID)

Provision 12 of the UK Corporate Governance Code recommends that '[t]he board should appoint one of the independent non-executive directors to be the senior independent director' (SID), whose roles include:

- acting as 'a sounding board for the chair and to serve as an intermediary for the other directors and shareholders';[63]
- leading the process for appraising the chair.[64]

[58] Grant Thornton LLP, 'Corporate Governance Review 2018' (Grant Thornton 2018) 37.

[59] Ian Stratton, 'Non-Executive Directors: Are They Superfluous?' (1996) 17 Co Law 162, 164.

[60] Ronald J Gilson and Reinier Kraakman, 'Reinventing the Outside Director: An Agenda for Institutional Investors' (1991) 43 Stan L Rev 863, 875.

[61] See 'Knives are Out in the Boardroom', *Financial Times* (London, 1 May 1992) 11.

[62] Lilian Miles and Giles Proctor, 'Re-Designing the Office of Non-Executive Director: Has the Consultation Document Gone Far Enough?' (2000) 21 BLR 143, 144.

[63] FRC, 'The UK Corporate Governance Code' (FRC 2018) Provision 12.   [64] ibid.

In addition, the FRC's 'Guidance on Board Effectiveness' states the following:

- the SID might take responsibility for an orderly succession process for the chair, working closely with the nomination committee;[65]
- the SID should be available to shareholders if they have concerns that contact through the normal channels has failed to resolve or where such contact is inappropriate;[66]
- when the board or company is undergoing a period of stress (e.g. a dispute between the CEO and chair), then the role of the SID becomes critically important and he should work with the relevant parties to resolve significant issues.[67]

7.2.4 Alternate directors

Under certain conditions, a director may be unable to act as a director (e.g. incapacity, or absence from a board meeting). Such a director might wish to appoint someone else to act in his place and this person is called an alternate director. As acting as a director is a personal responsibility, a director cannot appoint someone to act on his behalf unless the articles so permit.

Neither the CA 2006 nor the model articles for private companies provide for the appointment of alternate directors. Article 25(1) of the model articles for public companies does provide that a director (known as 'the appointer') may appoint another director, or any other person approved by a resolution of the directors, to exercise the appointer's powers and carry out the appointer's responsibilities. The articles will specify the authority of the alternate director, with art 26 of the model articles for public companies providing alternates with essentially the same authority as the appointer. One difference is remuneration—the alternate is not entitled to be remunerated for acting as an alternate unless the articles so provide. The model articles also state that the alternate is not an agent of the appointer.

The articles will also set out the circumstances that will terminate the alternate's appointment. Terminating events in the model articles include the appointer revoking the appointment and the death of the appointer.[68]

7.2.5 Nominee directors

Someone with a significant interest in the company (e.g. a major shareholder or creditor) might wish to seek to safeguard their interest by having a say on the make-up of the board. The following example demonstrates how this often works in practice.

> **Eg** **Nominee directors**
>
> Paragon Investments plc owns 5 per cent of shares in Dragon plc and wishes to purchase more shares. However, a condition of the purchase is that Paragon acquires the ability to appoint two directors to Dragon's board. Accordingly, a new class of share is created, and shares of this new class are issued to Paragon. The articles are then altered to provide that the holder of this new class of share shall have the ability to appoint two directors to the board, which Paragon then does.

---

[65] FRC, 'Guidance on Board Effectiveness' (FRC 2018) para 66.   [66] ibid para 67.
[67] ibid para 68.   [68] Model articles for public companies, art 27.

Two notable issues arise regarding nominee directors. The first issue is that the nominee may be put in a position where his loyalty to the company (Dragon) and his appointer (Paragon) conflict. As the following case demonstrates, the nominee's primary duty is to the company.

Scottish Co-Operative Wholesale Society Ltd v Meyer [1959] AC 324 (HL)

FACTS: Scottish Co-Operative Wholesale Society Ltd ('SCW') was the parent of Scottish Textile and Manufacturing Co Ltd ('STM'), and held 4,000 of its 7,900 shares. Meyer and Lucas were STM's joint managing directors and, between them, held the remaining 3,900 shares in STM. The other three directors on STM's board were nominees of SCW. SCW offered to purchase these 3,900 shares, but its offer was refused. Accordingly, SCW sought to force Meyer and Lucas to sell by transferring business away from STM and into a department within SCW, thereby reducing the value of STM's shares and almost bringing STM's business to a standstill. The three nominees knew of, and supported, SCW's plan, but kept this hidden from Meyer and Lucas. Meyer and Lucas sought an order that their shares should be bought out at a price based on their value before SCW's plan was put into effect.

HELD: Meyer and Lucas were entitled to the order they sought. Lord Denning stated that the nominees 'put their duty to the co-operative society above their duty to the textile company. . . . They probably thought that "as nominees" of the co-operative society their first duty was to the co-operative society. In this they were wrong.'[69]

The second issue is that the use of nominee directors reduces transparency, which in turn can facilitate unlawful activities such as tax evasion and money-laundering, as well as lawful, but morally questionable activities, such as tax avoidance. A stark demonstration of this can be in relation to what became known as the 'Sark Lark'.

The 'Sark Lark'

Increases in UK income tax in the 1960s led to a number of UK companies looking to base themselves in countries with more favourable tax arrangements, with one popular location being the Channel Islands.[70] Companies based in Guernsey or Jersey were liable to pay corporation tax, unless directors' meetings were held outside Guernsey or Jersey. Accordingly, such companies held their directors' meetings on the island of Sark,[71] using residents of Sark as nominee directors. These nominees knew nothing of the companies they were directors of—they simply rented their names to these companies and agreed to obey the instructions of the non-nominee directors.

---

[69] [1959] AC 324 (HL) 367.

[70] The Channel Islands consist of the Bailiwicks of Guernsey and Jersey, and several smaller islands (of which Sark is one). They are not part of the UK, but are classed as Crown Dependencies, meaning that the UK Government is responsible for the defence and international relations of the islands.

[71] Sark is a royal fief of Guernsey, but has its own set of laws, and Guernsey cannot generally legislate on Sark's behalf.

The result was that the 575 residents of Sark held between them over 15,000 directorships,[72] with one individual famously holding 3,378 directorships[73] (with each company paying £50–£400 for the privilege).

A Home Office report[74] criticized the tax arrangements of the Channel Islands and Sark and, as a result, reforms were put in place in 1998–99, which effectively curtailed the 'Sark Lark'. However, a number of the nominee directors resident in Sark simply moved to other tax havens and continued acting as nominee directors.[75]

In the UK, recent reforms have sought to improve transparency in this area, notably the introduction of the People with Significant Control (PSC) register, which could improve transparency as it defines a person with significant control as, *inter alia*, a person who 'holds the right, directly or indirectly, to appoint or remove a majority of the board of directors . . .'.[76] However, the large-scale tax evasion/avoidance and money laundering that, according to the leaked 'Panama Papers', occurred principally in UK Overseas Territories and Crown Dependencies, has led to calls for the UK Parliament to legislatively compel such places to improve regulation relating to corporate transparency. The result was that a number of UK Overseas Territories and Crown Dependencies have agreed to share information regarding corporate beneficial ownership with the UK government.[77]

> The PSC register is discussed at 13.3.2.

7.2.6 Specific board roles

In many companies (especially larger companies), it is common for directors to be appointed to undertake specific roles, with the ability to make such appointments usually provided for in the articles. For example, the model articles provide that directors may 'undertake any services for the company that the directors decide',[78] with this commonly resulting in certain directors being appointed to the roles of chief executive officer (CEO) and/or chair.

7.2.6.1 Chief executive officer/managing director

A director cannot be appointed to the role of CEO[79] unless the articles empower the directors to make such an appointment.[80] Unlike Table A, the current model articles

---

[72] Home Office, *Review of Financial Regulation in Crown Dependencies* (CM 4109-i, 1998) para 11.2.3.

[73] The director was later convicted of a number of criminal offences and disqualified from acting as a director.

[74] Home Office, *Review of Financial Regulation in Crown Dependencies* (CM 4109, 1998).

[75] David Leigh, Harold Frayman, and James Ball, 'The "Sark Lark" Britons Scattered Around the World' *The Guardian* (London, 25 November 2012).

[76] CA 2006, Sch 1A, para 4.

[77] See https://www.gov.uk/government/collections/beneficial-ownership-uk-overseas-territories-and-crown-dependencies accessed 10 January 2019.

[78] Model articles for private companies, art 19(1); model articles for public companies, art 23(1). The model articles go on to provide that the directors are entitled to be remunerated for such services as the directors may determine.

[79] Historically, the term 'managing director' was used in the UK, whereas the term 'chief executive officer' (CEO) was used in the US. In recent years, however, it has become more popular to refer to the head of a UK company (especially larger companies) as the CEO.

[80] *Boschoek Proprietary Co Ltd v Fuke* [1906] 1 Ch 148 (Ch) 159 (Swinfen Eady J).

do not expressly provide for the appointment of a CEO. However, the provisions noted above that allow directors to 'undertake any services for the company that the directors decide' would empower the directors to appoint one of their own as CEO.

The role and powers of a CEO are not statutorily defined, and a CEO does not acquire additional powers simply by virtue of being appointed to that role.[81] As the following case demonstrates, the powers of a CEO will depend upon the terms of his appointment (e.g. as stated in the contract appointing him as CEO) and upon the extent to which powers have been delegated to him by the board (e.g. under the articles).

 See Keith Gompertz, 'Company Law—Powers of a Managing Director' [2013] 18 Cov LJ 62.

Smith v Butler [2012] EWCA Civ 314[82]

FACTS: Smith was the company's chair and its majority shareholder. Butler was the managing director. Butler suspected that Smith was defrauding the company and engaged a firm of solicitors to investigate Smith's conduct. Smith was dissatisfied with Butler's running of the company and indicated an intention to use his majority shareholding to appoint another managing director. At a board meeting, Butler accused Smith of defrauding the company, and purported to suspend him from the company. Smith commenced proceedings against Butler and the company, claiming that Butler had no authority to suspend him. Butler contended that he had authority by virtue of his position as managing director. At first instance, Smith's action succeeded.[83] Butler appealed.

HELD: Arden LJ noted that the powers of a managing director are not statutorily defined, but derive from an express delegation from the board (either via the articles or via the managing director's terms of appointment). Here, there was no express delegation of any power to Butler, but Arden LJ stated that it was clearly the intention that some powers would be impliedly delegated to Butler, but what powers? On this, Arden LJ stated that a managing director's implied powers:

> extend to carrying out those functions on which he did not need to obtain the specific directions of the board. This is simply the default position. It is, therefore, subject to the company's articles and anything that the parties have expressly agreed.[84]

Applying this, the court held that Smith's suspension 'was clearly a matter for the whole board, and not for Mr Butler acting alone'.[85] Accordingly, Butler's appeal was dismissed.

COMMENT: *Smith* confirms that if the articles and the managing director's terms of employment are of no aid, then the principles of agency law should be invoked to determine whether the managing director had authority to engage in the act in question. Unfortunately, the law relating to an agent's authority is notoriously complex and fact-dependent and there is scant case law relating to managing directors, thereby leaving the law in a rather uncertain state.

One might imagine that the UK Corporate Governance Code would provide guidance on the role and powers of the CEO but, unfortunately, the Code provides no guidance at all, other than stating that the responsibilities of the CEO should be clear, set out in writing, agreed by the board, and made publicly available.[86] The Code does, however, provide substantial guidance on the role of the chair, to which we now turn.

---

[81] *Mitchell & Hobbs (UK) Ltd v Mill* [1996] 2 BCLC 102 (QB) 107–08 (Anthony Machin QC).

[82] See also *Harold Holdsworth & Co (Wakefield) Ltd v Caddies* [1955] 1 WLR 352 (HL).

[83] *Smith v Butler* [2011] EWHC 2301 (Ch), [2012] 1 BCLC 444.

[84] [2012] EWCA Civ 314, [2012] Bus LR 1836 [28].   [85] ibid [31].

[86] FRC, 'The UK Corporate Governance Code' (FRC 2018) Provision 14. This recommendation also applies to the chair, SID, the board, and board committees.

7.2.6.2 **Chair**

In recent years, following a number of corporate governance scandals, increased importance has been attached to the role of the chair.[87] Companies are not required by law to appoint a chair but, in practice, the vast majority of companies do so. The process for appointing a chair of board meetings is a matter for the articles, with the model articles providing that '[t]he directors may appoint a director to chair their meetings'[88] and may also terminate the chair's appointment at any time.[89] The model articles go on to provide that if the directors have appointed a chair, then he shall also chair general meetings providing that he is present and willing to do so.[90]

The increasing focus on the chair is reflected in the breadth and substance of the role as envisaged under the UK Corporate Governance Code, with Principle F providing that the chair 'leads the board and is responsible for its overall effectiveness in directing the company'. The Code then goes on to state numerous more specific responsibilities of the chair, including:

- seeking regular engagement with major shareholders in order to understand their views on governance and performance, and then ensuring that the board has a clear understanding of the shareholders' views;[91]
- facilitating constructive board relations and the contribution of all NEDS, and ensuring that all directors receive accurate, timely, and clear information;[92]
- holding meetings with the NEDs to scrutinize executive director performance;[93]
- acting on the results of any board evaluation.[94]

Additional guidance on the role of the chair is set out in para 61 of the FRC's 'Guidance on Board Effectiveness', with other notable roles including:

- setting a board agenda, and ensuring that adequate time is available for discussion of all agenda items—this may involve resolving any deadlocks that might arise and it is therefore common for the articles to provide the chair of the board with a casting vote;[95]
- shaping the culture in the boardroom;
- providing guidance and mentoring new directors;
- ensuring that there is a timely flow of accurate, high-quality, and clear information;
- ensuring that all directors are able to discharge their statutory duties;
- ensuring that the board listens to the views of shareholders, the workforce, customers, and other key stakeholders;
- ensuring that the board continually updates its skills, knowledge, and familiarity with the company.

---

[87] The model articles provide that the chair will be known as the 'chairman', but it should be stressed that the word is being used in its gender-neutral dictionary sense. The UK Corporate Governance Code instead uses the word 'chair', and this word will be used in this text.

[88] Model articles for private companies, art 12(1); model articles for public companies, art 12(1). Where the power to appoint a chair is vested in the directors, then the members cannot appoint a chair (*Clark v Workman* [1920] 1 IR 107 (Ch) 114–5 (Ross J)).

[89] Model articles for private companies, art 12(3); model articles for public companies, art 12(4).

[90] Model articles for private companies, art 39(1); model articles for public companies, art 31(1). The model articles go on to provide that if no chair is appointed, or if the chair is unwilling to chair the general meeting, then the directors or the general meeting must appoint a director or member to act as chair of the meeting.

[91] FRC, 'The UK Corporate Governance Code' (FRC 2018) Provision 3.

[92] ibid Principle F.   [93] ibid Provision 13.   [94] ibid Provision 22.

[95] Model articles for private companies, art 13(1); model articles for public companies, art 14(1).

It is clear that, in order to fulfil some of these functions, the chair should maintain a measure of independence. To that end, the Code also recommends that the chair should, on appointment, meet the independence criteria set out in Provision 10,[96] and that the chair should not remain in post beyond nine years from the date of their first appointment to the board.[97]

🔗 Provision 10 is discussed at 7.2.3.1.

7.2.6.3 Other board roles

In larger companies especially, it is common to appoint certain executive directors to other roles. Increasingly, the two most important roles are the finance director and the chief operating officer (COO),[98] although other roles are gaining prominence:

- The finance director (also known as 'chief financial officer' or 'CFO') is usually tasked with managing the financial risks of the company. This involves developing processes and policies to ensure sound financial management of the company, and providing financial guidance on how to meet the company's objectives. Most finance directors have accounting qualifications, or have worked in the financial sector.

- The COO is responsible for ensuring that the organizational operation of the company is geared towards meeting the company's objectives, and complying with legal requirements and best practice.

- The Walker Review recommended that banks and other financial institutions should appoint a chief risk officer ('CRO') whose role would be to 'participate in the risk management and oversight process at the highest level on an enterprise-wide basis. . .'.[99]

- Given the increased risk of cyber-attack and the consequent increase in the importance of cyber-security, it is becoming more common for larger companies to appoint a 'chief security officer' (CSO), whose role is to devise and implement policies that reduce the risk of a successful cyber-attack and to ensure that company data is not compromised.

- Companies may also appoint a director to the role of chief marketing officer (CMO), whose role is to coordinate the marketing activities of the company.

CHAPTER SUMMARY

- Section 250 of the CA 2006 provides that a director 'includes any person occupying the position of director, by whatever name called'.

- A person validly appointed as a director is known as a *de jure* director, whereas a person who has not been validly appointed, but who acts as a director, is known as a *de facto* director.

- A shadow director is 'a person in accordance with whose directions or instructions the directors of a company are accustomed to act'.

- Executive directors are involved in the company's day-to-day management, whereas NEDs are part-time and are involved in management and monitoring the executives.

- An alternate director is someone appointed to act on behalf of another director (e.g. because that director cannot attend a board meeting).

---

[96] FRC, 'The UK Corporate Governance Code' (FRC 2018) Provision 9.
[97] ibid Provision 19.
[98] The CEO, CFO, and COO are often collectively referred to as the C-suite (as they all have 'chief' in their title).
[99] 'A Review of Corporate Governance in UK Banks and Other Financial Industry Entities' (2009) Recommendation 24 and [6.21]–[6.25].

- Certain persons (e.g. major shareholders or creditors) may have the power to nominate a person to the board, and this nominated person is known as a nominee director.
- Many companies (especially larger companies) will appoint some of its directors to specific board roles (e.g. CEO, chair).

FURTHER READING

Chris Noonan and Susan Watson, 'The Nature of Shadow Directorship: Ad Hoc Statutory Intervention or Company Law Principle?' [2006] JBL 763.
- Discusses the concept of the shadow director and argues that it is fundamentally different from *de facto* and *de jure* directorships.

BIS, 'Transparency and Trust: Enhancing the Transparency of UK Company Ownership and Increasing Trust in UK Business: Discussion Paper' (BIS 2013) paras 5.1–5.10.
- Discusses the government's rationale behind the decision to largely prohibit the use of corporate directors.

Derek Higgs, 'Review of the Role and Effectiveness of Non-Executive Directors' (DTI 2003).
- Discusses the role of NEDs and makes a number of recommendations, many of which have since been incorporated into the UK Corporate Governance Code.

FRC, 'Guidance on Board Effectiveness' (FRC 2018) ch 2.
- Provides guidance on the roles of the chair, SID, executive directors, and NEDs.

John de Lacy, 'The Concept of a Company Director: Time for a New Expanded and Unified Statutory Concept?' [2006] JBL 267.
- Argues that statute should provide a unified definition of director that covers *de jure* directors, *de facto* directors, and shadow directors.

Revenue and Customs Commissioners v Holland [2010] UKSC 51, [2010] 1 WLR 2793 [58]–[93].
- Lord Collins provides a useful and detailed discussion of the history and evolution of the law relating to *de facto* directors.

SELF-TEST QUESTIONS

1. Define the following terms:
- *de jure* director;
- *de facto* director;
- shadow director;
- executive director;
- non-executive director;
- alternate director;
- nominee director.

2. State whether each of the following statements is true or false and, if false, explain why:
- A person who is not called a 'director' will not be a director.
- The chairman is the head of the company.
- A *de jure* director is a director who has been validly appointed.
- A person cannot be a *de facto* director and a shadow director.
- A NED who has close family ties with an executive director will not be regarded as independent.
- Every company has the right to appoint one of its directors as CEO.

3. 'The law relating to shadow directors is unclear, and the courts have not drawn a clear distinction between shadow directors and *de facto* directors.' Discuss this quote.

4. In 2015, Dron plc listed its shares on the Main Market of the London Stock Exchange. Its board consists of five executive directors (namely Jane (the CEO), Jude (the chair), Ruby, Ivan, and Anna) and five NEDs (namely Angus, Greg, Sajid, Kate, and Nancy). Note the following:

- Angus, Greg, and Sajid have ben NEDs ever since Dragon re-registered as a public company in 2008;
- Kate has only been a NED for one year: before this, she was a senior manager of Dragon;
- Nancy is married to Ivan.

The board regularly meets with representatives of Welsh Bank plc. Welsh Bank has lent Dragon a considerable amount of money and is keen to ensure that it is paid back. Accordingly, these representatives of Welsh Bank provide the board of Dragon with advice on how the business should be run and this advice is usually followed, although some of the NEDs are uncomfortable with the extent of the representatives' role. One of these representatives advises Dragon to end its supply contract with TechCorp Ltd and instead to enter into a supply agreement with OmniTool Ltd on the ground that OmniTool will provide higher-quality supplies. Dragon does this and the supplies are indeed of a higher quality. What the board of Dragon does not realize is that the representative is married to a director of OmniTool.

Discuss whether there has been any breaches of the law or any best practice recommendations.

 ONLINE RESOURCES

This book is accompanied by online resources to better support you in your studies. Visit www.oup.com/uk/roach-company/ for:

- answers to the self-test questions;
- further reading lists;
- multiple-choice questions;
- glossary.

Updates to the law can be found on the author's Twitter account (@UKCompanyLaw) and further resources can be found on the author's blog (www.companylawandgovernance.com).

8 Board appointment, structure, and composition

- The appointment of directors
- Board structure
- Board diversity

INTRODUCTION

Having examined what a director is and the different types of director that exist, this chapter moves on to look at how those types of director fit into the overall board structure and composition. Board composition has a tremendous effect upon company performance and direction, with the Higgs Review stating that '[t]he composition of the board sends important signals about the values of the company'.[1] Accordingly, the composition of the board is one of the most important company law and corporate governance topics and increased attention has fallen on board composition and structure following the financial crisis and the corporate governance scandals of the past 20–30 years.

This chapter begins by looking at the process by which directors are appointed and remunerated, before moving on to discuss the structure of the board. Finally, the chapter examines the governance topic of the moment, namely board diversity.

8.1 The appointment of directors

All companies are required to appoint a director, with the Companies Act 2006 (CA 2006) providing that a private company must have at least one director, and a public company at least two directors.[2] The process by which directors are appointed is central to good governance, but the appointments process has been the subject of criticism over the past 25 years. A lack of transparency, independence, and diversity in the appointments process led to the boards of larger companies being perceived as 'comfortable clubs of like-minded people, well known to each other, who shared similar interests and

---

[1] Derek Higgs, 'Review of the Role and Effectiveness of Non-Executive Directors' (DTI 2003) para 10.16.

[2] CA 2006, s 154. The CA 2006 does not provide for a maximum number of directors, but the articles may specify a limit (the model articles impose no such limit).

often came from similar backgrounds. . . . [and who] appointed similar people to join their ranks.'[3] Before the appointments process can be discussed, it is important to first note that the law does render some persons ineligible to act as director.

8.1.1 Eligibility

As a general rule, the law does not seek to limit the scope of persons who can be appointed as directors. However, there are instances where the law prohibits or limits certain persons from acting as director:

- As noted, s 156A of the CA 2006 prohibits corporate directors, unless regulations passed by the Secretary of State permit otherwise.[4] At the time of writing, s 156A is not yet in force.
- A company's statutory auditor is not permitted to act as its director.[5]
- The appointment of a person under the age of 16 will be void,[6] unless the appointment is not to take effect until his sixteenth birthday,[7] or the appointment is within an exception specified by the Secretary of State.[8]
- A person who is subject to a disqualification order/undertaking will commit a criminal offence if he acts as director,[9] unless he obtains leave to act from the court.
- An undischarged bankrupt cannot act as a director, nor can they directly or indirectly take part in the promotion, formation, or management of a company, without the leave of the court.[10]
- The company can, via it articles, limit who can be appointed as a director.

 Disqualification orders and undertakings are discussed at 12.6.2.1.

> **Eligibility and the articles**
>
> Examples of companies with article provisons restricting who can be appointed as a director include:
>
> - Article 111(a)(ii) of the articles of Rolls Royce Holdings plc provides that no person can be appointed as chief executive officer (CEO) or chair, unless he is a British citizen, a US citizen, or an EU citizen.
> - Article 108 of Prudential plc's articles provides that a director cannot be appointed if his appointment would exceed the maximum number of directors permitted under the articles (which is 20 according to art 102).
> - Article 91 of Unilever plc's articles provides that a person is not eligible to be appointed as director unless he is recommended by the board, or he is proposed as a director by a resolution requisitioned in accordance with the Companies Acts.

8.1.2 The appointment process

An application to register a company must include a statement of the company's proposed officers, which will identify who will be the company's first directors.[11] Upon the company's incorporation, those persons will be deemed to have been appointed as directors.[12] Thereafter, the process of appointing a director is generally a matter for companies themselves to determine via their articles—the CA 2006 has very little to say on

---

[3] Bob Tricker, *Corporate Governance: Principles, Policies, and Practices* (3rd edn, OUP 2015) 181.

[4] CA 2006, s 156A(1). At the time of writing, no such regulations have been passed.

[5] ibid s 1214(1) and (2). Section 1215(2) provides that breach of s 1214 is a criminal offence.

[6] ibid s 157(1) and (4).   [7] ibid s 157(2).

[8] ibid s 158. At the time of writing, no such exceptions have been specified.

[9] Company Directors Disqualification Act 1986, ss 1 and 13.

[10] ibid s 11(1). Breach of s 11 is a criminal offence.   [11] CA 2006, s 12(1)(a).   [12] ibid s 16(6)(a).

the matter. If the articles are silent on the issue, then the provisions of the model articles will apply and provide that a person can be appointed as director by an ordinary resolution,[13] or by a decision of the directors.[14] If, however, the articles are silent on the issue of appointment, but have excluded the model articles, then the power to appoint directors is vested in the members[15] and is exercisable by passing an ordinary resolution.[16] If the articles confer the power to appoint exclusively upon some other person or group (e.g. the board, or a third party, such as a named member), then the general meeting will have no power of appointment,[17] although it can amend the articles. In all cases, a director's appointment will not take effect until he consents to the appointment.[18]

The power of the members to appoint a director must 'be exercised for the benefit of the company as a whole and not to secure some ulterior advantage',[19] whilst the directors' power of appointment must be exercised in accordance with their general duties (especially the duty to act within powers). Empowering the directors to appoint other directors is problematic and runs the risk that the board will appoint friends and associates, rather than those persons who are best suited to the job. Two methods have evolved to combat this issue, namely the use of nomination committees and the practice of retirement by rotation. Retirement by rotation is discussed in more detail at 12.3, so only the nomination committee is discussed here.

> The duty to act within powers is discussed at 10.2.

8.1.2.1 Nomination committee

In larger companies, the members usually *elect* the directors (albeit after they have been appointed), but it is important to note that members do not *select* the directors. Rather, a list of candidates will be put forward for consideration by the board, who will then choose their preferred candidate. Historically, the list of candidates would be compiled by the CEO and would often consist of associates of the CEO/executives, leading to accusations of an 'old boys network' operating amongst larger companies. This lack of independence and openness in the appointment process can constitute a major governance problem, especially given the increased importance attached to independent non-executive directors (NEDs) under the UK Corporate Governance Code. Indeed, it has been argued that '[t]he greatest barrier to meaningful independence in the boardroom is insider control of the nomination process'.[20]

To combat this, the UK Corporate Governance Code provides that '[a]ppointments to the board should be subject to a formal, rigorous and transparent procedure',[21] with the procedure recommended being the establishment of 'a nomination committee to lead the process for appointments, ensure plans are in place for orderly succession of both the board and senior management positions, and oversee the development of a diverse pipeline for succession'.[22] To ensure independence, a majority of the nomination committee should consist of independent NEDs.[23] Virtually all FTSE 350 companies

---

[13] Section 160(1) of the CA 2006 provides that the general meeting of a public company cannot appoint two or more persons as directors via a single resolution, unless the meeting unanimously agrees beforehand to such a resolution being made.

[14] Model articles for private companies, art 17(1); model articles for public companies, art 20.

[15] *Woolf v East Nigel Gold Mining Co Ltd* (1905) 21 TLR 660 (KB).

[16] *Worcester Corsetry Ltd v Witting* [1936] Ch 640 (CA).

[17] *Blair Open Hearth Furnace Co v Reigart* (1913) 108 LT 665.

[18] *Re British Empire Match Co Ltd* (1888) 59 LT 291.

[19] *Re HR Harmer Ltd* [1959] 1 WLR 62 (CA) 82 (Jenkins LJ).

[20] Robert AG Monks and Nell Minow, *Corporate Governance* (5th edn, Wiley 2011) 309.

[21] Financial Reporting Council (FRC), 'The UK Corporate Governance Code' (FRC 2018) Principle J.

[22] ibid Provision 17.   [23] ibid.

now have a nomination committee, with over 97 per cent of FTSE 350 companies complying fully with the Code's nomination committee membership criteria.[24]

Despite this, nomination committees are often regarded as the 'poor relation'[25] when compared to the other board committees, with Grant Thornton LLP describing them as 'adrift in the doldrums'.[26] Not only do nomination committees meet less than the other committees, but doubts have also been raised regarding the independence of the NEDs on the committee, with Tricker arguing that '[i]f the committee's members have themselves been selected by the chairman, and have worked with him or her for years, they are likely to feel an allegiance towards him or her and support his or her candidates'.[27] Given the widespread dissatisfaction with the nomination committee, many commentators now expect increased attention to focus on its work over the coming years, and there are already indications that the role of the nomination committee is being taken more seriously in companies.[28]

8.1.3 The register of directors

Upon appointment, a director's details should be entered into the register of directors, with s 162(1) providing that every company must keep such a register (although, as is discussed at 8.1.3.1, there is an exception for private companies). The register must be kept available for public inspection, and is usually kept at the company's registered office.[29] Any member of the company can view the register without charge, and any other person can view it upon paying a fee.[30] The registrar must be notified of any changes to the register (or to the register of residential addresses discussed below) within 14 days.[31]

Section 163(1) provides that the particulars that must be registered are the director's name and any former name, a service address (which can be the company's registered office),[32] the country or state (or part of the UK) in which the director is usually resident, his nationality, his business occupation (if any), and his date of birth. Prior to the CA 2006, directors were required to provide their residential address, so that interested parties (e.g. the police, regulators, creditors) could contact them or serve proceedings against them. However, incidents, such as the following, convinced Parliament that the public disclosure of residential addresses was no longer appropriate.

Huntingdon Life Sciences LTD

Huntingdon Life Sciences ('HLS') was a medical research company that provided research services (including testing products on animals) to the pharmaceutical sector. An undercover documentary televised in 1997 showed employees of HLS torturing animals. The employees in question were sacked and later convicted of animal cruelty offences. A campaign called 'Stop

---

[24] Grant Thornton LLP, 'Corporate Governance Review 2018' (Grant Thornton 2018) 35.

[25] Grant Thornton LLP, Corporate Governance Review 2017' (Grant Thornton 2017) 33.

[26] Grant Thornton, 'Corporate Governance Review 2014: Plotting a New Course to Improved Governance' (Grant Thornton 2014) 4.

[27] Bob Tricker, *Corporate Governance: Principles, Policies, and Practices* (3rd edn, OUP 2015) 319.

[28] Institute of Chartered Secretaries and Administrators (ICSA) and Ernst and Young, 'The Nomination Committee—Coming Out of the Shadows' (ICSA 2016) 4.   [29] CA 2006, s 162(3).

[30] ibid s 162(5). Failure to comply is a criminal offence (s 162(6) and (7)).

[31] ibid s 167. Failure to comply is a criminal offence (s 167(4)).   [32] ibid s 163(5).

Huntingdon Animal Cruelty' ('SHAC') was set up to try and close down HLS. SHAC intimidated, harassed, and attacked HLS directors, employees, shareholders, and suppliers. Three men armed with pickaxe handles attacked the managing director of HLS outside his home. Leaflets were sent to hundreds of people living near HLS's directors, falsely claiming that the directors were paedophiles. The vast majority of SHAC's leaders were subsequently jailed for their actions. SHAC disbanded in August 2014. In September 2015, HLS was rebranded as Envigo CRS Ltd.

In order to protect directors from this type of harassment and violence, the CA 2006 removed the residential address requirement and substituted it with the requirement to provide a service address. The company must keep a separate register of the directors' residential addresses[33] and it is, unsurprisingly, under no obligation to make this register available for public inspection (although this information must be provided to the registrar). In fact, a director's service address is categorized as 'protected information',[34] meaning that neither the company nor the registrar can use or disclose the information, except when permitted to do so by the CA 2006.[35]

8.1.3.1 Option to keep information on the public register

Private companies can, instead of keeping their own register of directors, elect to keep the above information on the register maintained by Companies House.[36] If this election is made, then they no longer need to keep their own register of directors—all they need do is notify the registrar of any changes that would be required under s 167 discussed above.[37]

 A private company's ability to elect to keep information on the Companies House register is discussed more at 19.2.1.

8.1.4 Defective appointments

Consider the following example.

Eg **Third parties and defective director appointments**

Ivan, a director of Dragon plc, enters into a contract with Gears Ltd on behalf of Dragon. It subsequently transpires that Ivan's appointment as a director was not in accordance with Dragon's articles. Dragon's other directors, who had reservations about dealing with Gears, state that the contract with Gears will not be honoured because Ivan was not validly appointed as a director, and therefore could not act on behalf of Dragon.

It would be extremely harsh on Gears Ltd if the contract were set aside due to the defect in Ivan's appointment. Accordingly, s 161(1) of the CA 2006 provides that '[t]he acts of a person acting as a director are valid notwithstanding that it is afterwards discovered—

(a) that there was a defect in his appointment;

(b) that he was disqualified from holding office;

---

[33] ibid s 165(1). Failure to comply is a criminal offence (s 165(4)).   [34] ibid s 240(1)(a).
[35] ibid ss 241–2. The limited instances when protected information can be used and disclosed can be found in ss 241–5.   [36] ibid ss 167A(1) and 167C(1).
[37] ibid s 167D(1) and (2). Failure to notify the registrar of these changes is a criminal offence (s 167D(4)).

(c) that he had ceased to hold office;

(d) that he was not entitled to vote on the matter in question.'

The courts have, however, established three important limitations on the principle found in s 161. First, a person can only rely on s 161 if he was acting in good faith.[38] Second, s 161 cannot be relied upon by a person who, at the time of the appointment, knew of the defect in the appointment and knew of the legal effect of the defect.[39] So, to use the example above, Gears could rely on s 161 even if it knew of the defect, providing that it did not know that the defect rendered Ivan's appointment invalid. Third, as s 161(a) applies to defective appointments, it follows that there must have been a purported appointment in the first place. To quote Lord Simonds:

> There is, as it appears to me, a vital distinction between (a) an appointment in which there is a defect or, in other words, a defective appointment, and (b) no appointment at all. . . . The section does not say that the acts of a person acting as director shall be valid notwithstanding that it is afterwards discovered that he was not appointed a director. Even if it did, it might well be contended that at least a purported appointment was postulated. But it does not do so, and it would, I think, be doing violence to plain language to construe the section as covering a case in which there has been no genuine attempt to appoint at all.[40]

8.1.5 Remuneration

Before a person is appointed as a director, that person and the company will usually negotiate to determine the new director's remuneration package. Remuneration practices tend to differ markedly depending on company size. In smaller private companies, remuneration is a relatively uncontroversial topic. The directors, who are usually also major shareholders, are usually paid in the manner that is most tax advantageous. Normally, this will involve the director receiving a small salary for his services as a director, with the bulk of his payment coming in the form of dividends paid on the basis of shares held. The advantages of this approach (as of the tax year 2019/20) include the following:

- drawing a salary of up to £8,632 will not attract income tax or national insurance contributions;
- dividends do not attract national insurance contributions;
- no income tax is paid on the first £2,000 earned in dividend income (this is known as the 'dividend allowance');
- the tax rates paid on dividend income are lower than tax rates paid on a salary.

Conversely, in larger companies, directors' remuneration is an extremely important and controversial governance topic that will crop up several times throughout this text. What is important to note here is that, in an era marked by substantial wealth inequality, there is increasing public and investor dissatisfaction with the levels of board remuneration and the methods by which directors' remuneration is determined. The Investment Association's Executive Remuneration Working Group has

---

[38] *Channel Collieries Trust Ltd v Dover, St Margaret's and Martin Mill Light Railway Co* [1914] 2 Ch 506 (CA) 512 (Lord Cozens-Hardy MR).

[39] *British Asbestos Co Ltd v Boyd* [1903] 2 Ch 439 (Ch) 444–5 (Farwell J).

[40] *Morris v Kanssen and Others* [1946] AC 459 (HL) 471.

stated that 'the current approach to executive pay in listed companies is not fit for purpose'.[41] Increasingly, there is a perception that directors are being excessively rewarded, even when company performance is poor or unmeritorious conduct has occurred. This has led to accusations that some directors are being rewarded for failure, as in the following example.

Carillion plc and rewards for failure

In July 2017, the directors of Carillion plc announced that the company's profits would be £845 million lower than expected. As a result, the company's CEO, Richard Howson, resigned and it was announced that no dividends would be paid. In the following two days, the value of the company's shares dropped by 70 per cent. In January 2018, a compulsory winding-up order was made against Carillion and the liquidation process is still ongoing. Although a large number of Carillion employees were transferred to other suppliers, nearly 2,800 employees have lost their jobs at the time of writing and thousands of suppliers have been adversely affected. A House of Commons report[42] into the company's collapse revealed that:

- between 2012 and 2017, Carillion paid out £333 million more in dividends that it generated in revenue;
- between 2009 and 2018, the amount of money owed by the company increased from £242 million to £1.3 billion;
- the company's pension deficit, which was around £800–900 million, was one of the largest in the FTSE 350.

Allegations were made that some of Carillion's directors were being rewarded for their failure. Howson, who remained as a director following his resignation as CEO, continued to receive his CEO rate of pay (£660,000). The new CEO, Keith Cochrane, was paid even more (£750,000). Other directors received hundreds of thousands in bonuses and share options. It was also revealed that, in 2016, the company's claw-back provisions were weakened to such a degree that none of these sums could be clawed back by the company. These details led Rachel Reeves MP, chair of the BEIS Select Committee, to state that 'Carillion bosses were focused on their own pay packets rather than their obligation to address the company's deteriorating balance sheets. While these directors could still walk off with bonuses intact, workers were left fearing for their jobs and suppliers faced ruin.'[43]

8.1.5.1 **Entitlement to remuneration**

A director can only obtain such remuneration as he is entitled to. *Prima facie* directors, as office holders, have no entitlement to be remunerated. As Bowen LJ stated, '[a] director is not a servant; he is a person doing business for the company, but not upon ordinary terms. It is not implied from the mere fact that he is a director that he is to be paid for it.'[44] This rule derives from the long-established common law principle that directors are not entitled to make a profit from their office, unless such profit has been

---

[41] Executive Remuneration Working Group, 'Interim Report' (2016) 3.

[42] House of Commons Library, 'The Collapse of Carillion' (2018) available from https://researchbriefings. parliament.uk/ResearchBriefing/Summary/CBP-8206 accessed 10 January 2019.

[43] See https://www.parliament.uk/business/committees/committees-a-z/commons-select/work-and-pensions-committee/news-parliament-2017/carillion-board-greed-17-19/ accessed 10 January 2019.

[44] *Hutton v West Cork Railway Co* (1883) 23 ChD 654 (CA) 671.

expressly authorized.[45] From this, it follows that a director will be entitled to remuneration if he is so authorized, with three methods of authorization sufficing, namely:

1. A director will be entitled to remuneration if the company's members approve such remuneration.[46]

2. A director will be entitled to remuneration if he has entered into a contract with the company (e.g. an employment contract) which entitles him to be remunerated.

3. A director will be entitled to remuneration if the articles so provide, with such provisions being commonplace in many companies (the model articles entitle the directors to remuneration for their services as directors, and for any other service they undertake for the company).[47]

Absent these three instances, directors have no authority to pay the company's money to themselves and such payments will be declared void.[48] Having established that a director is entitled to remuneration, the next step is to discuss how that remuneration is determined.

8.1.5.2 Determination of remuneration

The determination of directors' remuneration is a matter for the company's articles, and, if the articles are silent on this, the company can authorize remuneration in general meeting.[49] Historically, the articles normally stated that remuneration was to be decided by the company in general meeting.[50] The current model articles differ and provide that the directors are 'entitled to such remuneration as the directors determine—(a) for their services to the company as directors, and (b) for any other service which they undertake to the company'.[51]

There is a clear conflict of interest in allowing directors to set their own pay, and a real danger that directors will pay themselves more than they deserve, or will award themselves more than the market rate. Indeed, the past two decades are replete with examples of directors who have received handsome remuneration packages, despite weak performance. To combat this, the UK Corporate Governance Code states that '[n]o director should be involved in deciding their own remuneration outcome'.[52] To that end, the board should establish a remuneration committee of at least three independent NEDs,[53] which will then have delegated authority from the board to determine the policy of executive director remuneration, and to set remuneration for the chair, executive directors, and senior management.[54] The remuneration committee should also review workforce remuneration and take this into account when determining director pay. It is worth noting here that the effectiveness of remuneration committees has been doubted, as directors are still being paid significant sums even where the company sustains heavy losses due to poor performance or unlawful conduct.

---

[45] ibid.   [46] *Dunstan v Imperial Gas Light and Coke Co* (1832) 3 B & Ad 125.

[47] Model articles for private companies, art 19(2); model articles for public companies, art 23(2).

[48] *Re George Newman & Co* [1895] 1 Ch 674 (CA); *Guinness plc v Saunders* [1990] 2 AC 663 (HL).

[49] In such a case, remuneration will be regarded as a gratuity (*Re George Newman & Co* [1895] 1 Ch 674 (CA)).

[50] Indeed, art 82 of Table A provided that '[t]he directors shall be entitled to such remuneration as the company may by ordinary resolution determine . . .'.

[51] Model articles for private companies, art 19(2); model articles for public companies, art 23(2).

[52] FRC, The UK Corporate Governance Code (FRC 2018) Principle Q.

[53] ibid Provision 32. For companies below the FTSE 350, the Code recommends that the remuneration committee consist of at least two independent non-executive directors.

[54] The UK Corporate Governance Code (FRC 2018) Provision 33.

8.1.5.3 **Disclosure**

As noted, the law does not seek to regulate the determination of directors' pay, preferring to leave that to the companies themselves via the articles. The law's stance appears to be that it is up to the members through the general meeting to decide whether they agree with the company's remuneration policy. However, the members can only do this if they are fully informed of the company's remuneration policy and have access to the details of each director's pay. To that end, companies are required to disclose certain information regarding directors' remuneration, with three tiers of obligations being in operation.

The first tier of obligations applies to all companies, but such obligations are few in number (recognizing the fact that, in smaller companies, directors' remuneration is not normally a contentious issue). In fact, the only disclosure obligation in the CA 2006 that applies to all companies is the requirement to keep copies of the service contract of each director and shadow director,[55] which can be inspected by any member free of charge.[56] The copies must be kept available for inspection for at least one year following the expiration or termination of the contract.[57] Failure to comply with these rules constitutes a criminal offence by every officer in default.[58]

The second tier of obligations apply only to large and medium-sized companies and derive from the Large and Medium-Sized Companies and Groups (Accounts and Reports) Regulations 2008.[59] Schedule 5, para 1 provides that all large and medium-sized companies must disclose:

What constitutes a large and medium-sized company is discussed at 19.3.1.3.

- the aggregate amount of remuneration paid to the directors;
- the aggregate amount of gains made by directors on the exercise of share options;
- the aggregate amount of money paid or assets received under a long-term incentive scheme; and
- the aggregate value of company contributions paid into directors' pensions schemes.

Unquoted large and medium-sized companies must disclose additional information, namely:

- details regarding the pay of its highest paid director;[60]
- details regarding retirement benefits paid to directors and past directors;[61]
- details regarding payments made to directors for loss of office;[62] and
- details regarding sums paid to third parties in respect of directors' services.[63]

The third tier of obligations apply only to quoted companies, namely the requirement to prepare a remuneration report,[64] which then has to be approved by an ordinary resolution of the members.[65] The remuneration report forms part of the company's annual report, so it, along with the effectiveness of the members' 'say on pay', is discussed in more detail at 19.3.2.4.

---

[55] CA 2006, ss 228(1) and 230. If the contract is not in writing, then a written memorandum setting out the terms must be kept.

[56] ibid s 229(1).   [57] ibid s 228(3).

[58] ibid s 228(5) and (6). Unlike under previous Companies Acts, the company itself is not liable.

[59] SI 2008/410. These regulations were created under s 412 of the CA 2006, which allows the Secretary of State to pass regulations stating what remuneration information must be disclosed in the company's annual accounts.

[60] Large and Medium-Sized Companies and Groups (Accounts and Reports) Regulations 2008, Sch 5, para 2. This information is not required if the amount is less than £200,000.   [61] ibid Sch 5, para 3.

[62] ibid Sch 5, para 4.   [63] ibid Sch 5, para 5.   [64] CA 2006, s 420.   [65] ibid ss 439 and 439A.

8.2 Board structure

Other than mandating the statutory minimum number of directors,[66] the CA 2006 has nothing to say regarding the company's management structure, which casts doubt on whether the directors actually need to form a board. This is backed up by the fact that references to the board in statute are surprisingly sparse—the CA 2006 has over 1,300 sections, yet only fifteen of them refer to the board (and the majority of those refer to board approval of certain reports). The lack of legal prescription continues with regards to the composition of the board. For example, appointment of a chair or CEO, although desirable in certain companies, is not compulsory under statute, nor are companies legally obliged to appoint NEDs.

Accordingly, it could be argued that, under UK law, board structure is not a legal issue, but is instead a commercial and governance issue. Board structure is nevertheless an extremely important topic as the structure of the board has a notable impact upon how it operates. Smaller companies should adopt a structure that allows them to retain control of the business whilst avoiding unnecessary regulatory and financial burdens. Larger companies should adopt a board structure that allows them to effectively fulfil their strategic goals whilst ensuring that governance standards are complied with.

This section begins by examining the two most common board structures in the world, namely the unitary board and the two-tier board.

8.2.1 Unitary and two-tier boards

Boards around the world typically adopt either a unitary or two-tier board structure.

- A unitary board structure is predominant in countries such as the UK, the US, and most EU Member States. Under a unitary board structure, all of the directors (executive or NED) operate on a single board, although board committees will exist that may segregate the directors. A unitary board will undertake all the functions of a board, be they managerial, strategic, or supervisory.

- A two-tier board structure is predominant in countries such as Austria, Denmark, Germany, and the Netherlands. Under a two-tier system, the executive directors are usually segregated from the NEDs, with the latter exercising a supervisory function over the former. It is common for countries with two-tier board systems to provide the employees with a supervisory role too. The classic example of a two-tier board system is that found in Germany.

The German two-tier board structure

The *Aktiengesetz* (German Stock Corporation Act) requires that all *Aktiengesellschaften* ('AG', the German equivalent of a UK plc) have a management board (known as the *Vorstand*) and supervisory board (known as the *Aufsichstrat*):[67]

- The *Vorstand* shall have 'direct responsibility for the management of the company'[68] and all persons on the *Vorstand* manage the company jointly, unless the articles provide otherwise.

---

[66] One for a private company, and two for a public company (CA 2006, s 154). The articles can set a higher minimum.

[67] *Aktiengesetz*, § 30.   [68] ibid § 76(1).

- The *Aufsichstrat* shall comprise of three members (although companies may specify a higher number based on its share capital),[69] with membership usually comprising of shareholders and company employees.[70] The *Aufsichstrat* 'shall supervise the management of the company', but it cannot undertake any management responsibilities.[71] The *Aufsichstrat* is responsible for appointing and, if necessary, removing members of the *Vorstand*.[72] The *Aufsichstrat* also determines the remuneration of members of the *Vorstand*.[73] Members of the *Aufsichstrat* are appointed by the shareholders meeting, and can be removed by the court, or via a power conferred by the articles.[74] A person who is on the *Aufsichstrat* is not permitted to also be a member of the *Vorstand*.[75]

The question that arises is whether it is possible for a UK company to adopt a two-tier board structure. There is nothing in the CA 2006 that prohibits a UK company from adopting a two-tier board structure. Indeed, it could be argued that, as a matter of practice, larger companies do operate something akin to a two-tier management structure, as the board will determine the company's overall strategic direction, whilst the role of day-to-day management will be carried out by executive managers operating below board level. In effect, the board operates as a supervisory board, and the executive managers fulfil the functions of a management board. However, such a system is not traditionally regarded as two-tier, but as a unitary board structure.

The distinction between the board and executive management is discussed at 9.1.

Formal UK recognition of a two-tier board structure does, however, exist. The EU Regulation on the Statute for a European Company,[76] which was passed in 2001 after more than thirty years of negotiation, provides for the creation of a company known as the *Societas Europaea* (SE). Article 38(b) of the Regulation provides that a SE can have either a unitary or a two-tier board structure but, as discussed, SEs have not proven popular in the UK (or amongst other EU Member States).

SEs are discussed more at 3.3.4.3.

8.2.2 Board size

Section 154 of the CA 2006 establishes a minimum size that a board can be (i.e. one for a private company, and two for a public company), but the CA 2006 does not limit the maximum number of directors a board can have. Companies are completely free to mandate board size in their articles, and it is common for the articles of larger companies to mandate a minimum[77] and maximum board size. For example, art 65 of AstraZeneca plc's articles provides that '[u]nless otherwise determined by ordinary resolution, the number of directors (other than alternate directors) shall not be less than 5 nor more than 14'. The board of a small private company is likely to have only a few directors. Larger companies, especially listed companies, are likely to have larger boards due to the presence of

---

[69] ibid § 95.

[70] ibid § 96. The *Mitbestimmungsgesetz* (Co-Determination Act) provides that companies with over 2,000 employees must have at least half of their *Aufsichstrat* comprising of worker representatives.

[71] *Aktiengesetz* § 111(1) and (4).   [72] ibid § 30, 84(1), and 84(3).   [73] ibid § 87(1).

[74] ibid §§ 101(1) and 103.   [75] ibid § 105(1).

[76] Council Regulation 2157/2001/EC of 8 October 2001 on the Statute for a European Company [2001] OJ L294/1.

[77] Of course, a company's articles cannot provide for a lower minimum than that set out in s 154 of the CA 2006.

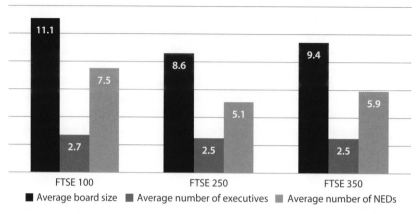

FIGURE 8.1 Average board size in FTSE companies

executive directors and NEDs. The 2016 version of the UK Corporate Governance Code stated that a board 'should be of sufficient size that the requirements of the business can be met and that changes to the board's composition and that of its committees can be managed without undue disruption, and should not be so large as to be unwieldy'.[78] In practice, this has resulted in the boards of listed companies typically being around 8–12 members in size. Figure 8.1 sets out the average board sizes of FTSE companies.[79]

That NEDs outnumber executive directors is no surprise. As discussed at 7.2.3, the UK Corporate Governance Code recommends that at least half the board should be independent NEDs.

8.2.3 Board leadership

Just as the CA 2006 says little about board structure, so too does it say little about board leadership. Whilst the appointment of a CEO or chair might be desirable, it is not compulsory under statute. Indeed, the CA 2006 makes no mention of the managing director or CEO, and the chair of the board is only referred to once.[80] A lone director of a private company may therefore see no need in appointing himself as a managing director or chair. In smaller companies with multiple directors, it is likely that one director will be appointed as managing director.

In listed companies, the position is slightly more complex as the UK Corporate Governance Code provides that '[t]here should be a clear division of responsibilities between the leadership of the board and the executive leadership of the company's business'.[81] In larger companies, this division is achieved by appointing a chair (who heads the board) and a CEO (who heads the company). Historically, it was common for the same person to act as chair and CEO[82] but, following a series of scandals involving

---

[78] FRC, 'The UK Corporate Governance Code' (FRC 2016) B.1 Supporting Principles. The 2018 Code does not contain a similar recommendation.

[79] Statistics derived from Grant Thornton LLP, 'Corporate Governance Review 2015: Trust and Integrity–Loud and Clear' (Grant Thornton 2015) 29.

[80] See s 249(1) of the CA 2006.

[81] FRC, 'The UK Corporate Governance Code' (FRC 2018) Principle G.

[82] In 1988, 328 of the UK's top 500 companies combined the role—see Jay Dayha, John J McConnell, and Nickolaos G Travlos, 'The Cadbury Committee, Corporate Performance, and Top Management Turnover' (2002) 57 J Fin 461, 462.

dominant characters who held both roles (e.g. Robert Maxwell of Mirror Group Newspapers plc, Asil Nadir of Polly Peck International plc), the growing consensus was that, in larger companies, this represented an undesirable concentration of power.

The Cadbury Report stated that the role of chair 'should in principle be separate from that of the chief executive',[83] but the original Combined Code took a less prescriptive view and stated that the roles could be combined as long as it was publicly justified.[84] The Higgs Review stated that '[s]eparation of the roles of chair and chief executive is one of the strengths of the UK corporate governance regime. It avoids concentration of authority and power in one individual and differentiates leadership of the board from running of the business'.[85] Accordingly, the UK Corporate Governance Code provides that '[t]he roles of chair and chief executive should not be exercised by the same individual'.[86] The recommendation has now become a core feature of our corporate governance system, with only four FTSE 350 companies having a combined CEO and chair in 2018.[87] Given this widespread acceptance, it is unsurprising that shareholders often react negatively towards a combined role, even when the person undertaking both roles commands widespread admiration.

Marks & Spencer plc

In May 2004, Sir Stuart Rose was appointed as CEO of Marks & Spencer plc and, over the next few years, his leadership rejuvenated the company's flagging performance. He helped fend off a hostile takeover bid, repositioned the company to attract a broader customer base, and saw the company's yearly profit exceed £1 billion (which had not occurred since 1997). He was universally credited for transforming and re-energizing the company and, in 2006, the World Leadership Forum named him as its '2006 Business Leader of the Year'.

In 2008, the company's chair, Lord Burns, retired and Sir Stuart Rose assumed the role of chair, in addition to staying on as CEO. Shareholder condemnation of this followed and major institutional investors signalled their disapproval. In the 2008 AGM, 22 per cent of investors voted against Rose's appointment as chair. The following year, 38 per cent supported a resolution to appoint an independent chair. Rose continued to be the subject of substantial shareholder unrest until he left the company in 2011.

A related point is whether a retiring or resigning CEO should go on to become the company's chair. The Higgs Review was firmly opposed to this on the ground that 'such a chair can sometimes find it difficult in practice to make room for a new chief executive. In addition, a chair who was formerly the chief executive of the same company may simply take for granted their inside knowledge and fail as an informational bridge to the non-executive directors'.[88] The Code is less prescriptive—although it states that '[a] chief executive should not become chair of the same company',[89] it does then go on to

[83] 'The Report of the Committee on the Financial Aspects of Corporate Governance' (Gee 1992) para 4.09.

[84] 'The Combined Code on Corporate Governance' (1998) Code Provision A.2.1.

[85] Derek Higgs, 'Review of the Role and Effectiveness of Non-Executive Directors' (DTI 2003) para 5.3.

[86] FRC, 'The UK Corporate Governance Code' (FRC 2018) Provision 9.

[87] Grant Thornton LLP, 'Corporate Governance Review 2018' (Grant Thornton 2018) 37.

[88] Derek Higgs, 'Review of the Role and Effectiveness of Non-Executive Directors' (DTI 2003) [5.6].

[89] FRC, 'The UK Corporate Governance Code' (FRC 2018) Provision 9.

provide that if, exceptionally, this is proposed by the board, major shareholders should be consulted ahead of the appointment and the board should set out its reasons to all shareholders and on the company's website.[90]

8.2.4 Board committees

As is discussed at 9.2.3, it is common for a company to include a provision in its articles empowering the directors to delegate their powers to others. The model articles allow the directors to delegate their powers 'to such person or committee . . . as they think fit'.[91] Concerns regarding the concentration of power placed in the board and the lack of board accountability and independence have resulted in the board delegating important powers to board committees.

The UK Corporate Governance Code recommends that three board committees be created, (namely the nomination committee, the audit committee, and the remuneration committee)[92] and almost all listed companies have established these three committees. Each of these committees are discussed in more detail in the relevant sections of this text.

Other board committees, whilst not recommendations of the Code, are nonetheless becoming more prominent, with a notable example being the risk committee. In many listed companies, the oversight of risk management is often delegated to the audit committee.[93] Following the global financial crisis, an increased awareness of risk management resulted in many companies either rebranding their audit committee as an audit and risk committee, or creating a separate risk committee, whose role is to oversee the risk management systems put in place by the board. Indeed, the Walker Review recommended that the boards of FTSE 100 banks and life insurance companies should establish a board risk committee that is separate from the audit committee,[94] and 85 companies in the FTSE 350 now have a separate risk committee.[95] Empirical studies to date appear to indicate that the presence of a risk management committee can result in increased board diligence and improved transparency.[96]

The above committees were created to improve board independence, and increase transparency and accountability. A board committee may also be set up to focus on an aspect of the company's business, thereby lessening the burden upon the board (although the board still bears overall responsibility). For example, finance or strategy committees may be set up to focus on financial and strategic goals. Companies may also set up ad hoc committees to focus on specific issues, such as the launch of major projects, succession planning, or troubleshooting business concerns.

🔗 Nomination, audit, and remuneration committees are discussed at 8.1.2.1, 19.4.4, and 8.1.5.2, respectively.

---

[90] ibid.   [91] Model articles for private companies, art 5(1); model articles for public companies, art 5(1).

[92] FRC, 'The UK Corporate Governance Code' (FRC 2018) Provisions 17, 24, and 32.

[93] Indeed, Provision 25 of the UK Corporate Governance Code provides that, unless the company has a separate risk committee, it will be the role of the audit committee to review internal control and risk management systems.

[94] 'A Review of Corporate Governance in UK Banks and Other Financial Industry Entities: Final Recommendations' (2009) paras 6.11–6.20.

[95] Grant Thornton LLP, 'Corporate Governance Review 2018 (Grant Thornton 2018) 46.

[96] See e.g. Puan Yatim, 'Board Structures and the Establishment of a Risk Management Committee by Malaysian Listed Firms' (2010) 14 JMG 17; Ahmed Al-Hadi, Mostafa Monzur Hasan, and Ahsan Habib, 'Risk Committee, Firm Life Cycle, and Market Risk Disclosure' (2015) 24 CG 145.

The Disclosure Guidance and Transparency Rules (DTRs) provide that the annual report's corporate governance statement must contain a description of the composition and operation of the company's board committees.[97]

The corporate governance statement is discussed at 19.3.2.3.

8.2.5 Company secretary

Whilst company secretaries are officers of the company,[98] they are not per se directors (although it is perfectly permissible for a director to also act as company secretary) and do not form part of the board, although they do attend board meetings. However, their role in relation to the board is so important that it is appropriate to discuss them here—indeed, a leading report on the role of the company secretary described the CEO, chair, and company secretary as 'the triumvirate at the top'.[99]

8.2.5.1 Appointment

Every public company must appoint a company secretary,[100] and may have more than one secretary (who will be known as 'joint secretaries'). The directors of a public company are under a duty to take all reasonable steps to ensure that the secretary has the requisite knowledge, experience, and qualifications.[101] A private company may appoint a company secretary, but is not required to do so,[102] unless the articles provide that a secretary must be appointed. It is expected that larger private companies will retain a secretary.

A company must keep a register of its secretaries,[103] although a private company can elect to instead keep details of its secretaries on the public register at Companies House.[104] Where the secretary is an individual, the register of secretaries must contain the name and address of the company's secretaries.[105] Where the secretary is a body corporate, additional details must be provided.[106]

8.2.5.2 Role

The role of the secretary is not statutorily defined, nor does the CA 2006 actually provide for any tasks that must be undertaken by the secretary. Traditionally, the role of the secretary has been primarily administrative and included tasks such as ensuring the filing of documents at Companies House, maintaining the statutory registers, preparing the agenda and minutes of board/general meetings, and ensuring that general meetings are conducted in accordance with the procedures established in the CA 2006. This is reflected in the secretary's authority as an agent, which also focuses on administrative matters.

---

[97] DTR 7.2.7.   [98] CA 2006, s 1121(2).

[99] Andrew Kakabadse, Nada Korac-Kakabadse, and Nadeem Khan, 'The Company Secretary: Building Trust Through Governance' (ICSA 2014) 7.

[100] CA 2006, s 271. Section 272 provides that breach of s 271 is a criminal offence.

[101] ibid s 273(2) and (3). The Act specifies what qualifications are appropriate, namely (i) acting as a secretary of a public company for at least three of the previous five years; (ii) being a member of a specific body (e.g. the Institute of Chartered Accountants of England and Wales, the Institute of Chartered Secretaries and Administrators); (iii) being a barrister, advocate, or solicitor; or (iv) being a person who, by virtue of his holding or having held any other position or his being a member of any other body, appears to the directors to be capable of discharging the functions of company secretary.

[102] ibid s 270(1).   [103] ibid s 275(1).   [104] ibid ss 274A, 279A–79E.

[105] ibid s 277.   [106] ibid s 278.

> ### Panorama Developments (Guildford) Ltd v Fidelis Furnishing Fabrics Ltd [1971] 2 QB 711 (CA)
>
> **FACTS:** Fidelis employed a company secretary named Bayne. Using Fidelis's notepaper, Bayne hired a number of cars from Panorama, stating that they would be used to transport Fidelis's customers. In fact, Bayne used the cars for personal purposes and not on company business. The hire charges were not paid and so Panorama commenced proceedings against Fidelis for the monies owed. Fidelis, unsurprisingly, refused to pay, stating that Bayne did not have authority to hire the cars.
>
> **HELD:** Bayne did have the requisite authority and therefore Fidelis was liable to pay the hire charges. Lord Denning MR stated that the company secretary:
>
> > is an officer of the company with extensive duties and responsibilities . . . . He is no longer a mere clerk. He regularly makes representations on behalf of the company and enters into contracts on its behalf which come within the day-to-day running of the company's business. So much so that he may be regarded as held out as having authority to do such things on behalf of the company. He is certainly entitled to sign contracts connected with the administrative side of a company's affairs, such as employing staff, and ordering cars, and so forth. All such matters now come within the ostensible authority of a company's secretary.[107]
>
> **COMMENT:** Lord Denning MR noted that the role of the company secretary had increased notably in the decades leading up to the case, meaning that previous case law that regarded the secretary as a 'mere servant'[108] was no longer relevant. It could be argued that the secretary's role has further developed since *Panorama*, to such an extent that Lord Denning's statement could now be regarded as out of date, for reasons discussed below.

It should be noted that *Panorama* relates only to the apparent (ostensible) authority of an agent. It may be the case that an agent will have actual authority to enter into tasks that fall outside the usual administrative remit. Indeed, there is an increasing acceptance that the role of the secretary has expanded beyond the merely administrative, and that secretaries (especially in larger companies) can also have an important commercial and strategic role. A 2012 survey found that only 25 per cent of secretaries questioned characterized their job as administrative, with 33 per cent characterizing it as strategic and the remaining 42 per cent viewing it as a combination of the two.[109] In particular, the secretary is increasingly being viewed as a trusted advisor to the board, and this has been recognized in the UK Corporate Governance Code, which provides that '[a]ll directors should have access to the advice of the company secretary, who is responsible for advising the board on all governance matters'.[110]

8.3 Board diversity

Board diversity is the governance topic of the moment, but recognition of a lack of board diversity has existed for some time. In 2003, the Higgs Review stated that '[i]t is the range of skills and attributes acquired through a diversity of experiences and backgrounds that

---

[107] [1971] 2 QB 711 (CA) 716–17.

[108] *Barnett, Hoares & Co v South London Tramways Co* (1887) 18 QBD 815 (CA) 817 (Lord Esher MR).

[109] The All Parliamentary Corporate Governance Group, 'Elevating the Role of the Company Secretary' (Lintstock 2012) 20.

[110] FRC, 'The UK Corporate Governance Code' (FRC 2018) Provision 16.

combine to create a cohesive and effective board',[111] and went on to recommend that a group be set up to look at how companies could broaden the talent pool from which they draw directors. This group, chaired by Laura Tyson,[112] produced a report that set out the case for, and made recommendations towards, increasing board diversity by appointing NEDs from broader backgrounds.[113]

Unfortunately, the Tyson Report was never acted upon and the issue of board diversity was largely forgotten until 2010, when the government appointed Lord Davies[114] to conduct a review. Unlike the Tyson Report, which examined board diversity in general, Lord Davies's review focused exclusively on gender diversity. Since then, the diversity debate has largely focused on how to increase the number of women on boards and so the bulk of this discussion will focus on gender diversity.

8.3.1 Gender diversity

Lord Davies reported in 2011 and his report made for grim reading. It stated that in 2010, women accounted for only 12.5 per cent of FTSE 100 directors and, at the then rate of increase, it would take over 70 years to achieve gender-balanced boards,[115] leading Lord Davies to state that '[t]his pace of change is not good enough'.[116] Clearly, the lack of women in the boardroom was a social and equality issue, but it is also very much a commercial issue. Lord Davies was of the opinion that '[t]he business case for increasing the number of women on corporate boards is clear',[117] and went on to identify a number of advantages:

1. The appointment of female directors can improve company performance,[118] reduce the risk of insolvency,[119] and improve board decision-making by reducing the likelihood of 'group-think'.[120]

2. As women represent the majority of qualified graduates, companies that tap into this under-utilized pool of talent will gain a competitive advantage over those that do not.[121]

3. Having a more diverse board will allow companies to better understand their customers' needs, thereby becoming more responsive to their markets.[122]

4. Gender-diverse boards tend to have more effective corporate governance practices in place, and are more likely to quickly implement, and adhere to, best practice

---

[111] Derek Higgs, 'Review of the Role and Effectiveness of Non-Executive Directors' (DTI 2003) para 10.1.

[112] Laura Tyson was then Dean of the London Business School, and a former economic advisor to President Bill Clinton.

[113] The Tyson Taskforce on the Recruitment and Development of Non-Executive Directors, 'The Tyson Report on the Recruitment and Development of Non-Executive Directors' (London Business School 2003).

[114] Lord Davies was Minister for Trade, Investment and Small Business from 2009–10. He was also chair and CEO of Standard Chartered plc and held non-executive directorships in Tesco and Diageo plc.

[115] Lord Davies, 'Women on Boards' (2011) 3.   [116] ibid.   [117] ibid.

[118] McKinsey & Co, 'Women Matter: Gender Diversity, a Corporate Performance Driver' (McKinsey 2007) 10–14; Credit Suisse, 'Gender Diversity and Corporate Performance' (Credit Suisse 2012) 12–15.

[119] Nick Wilson and Ali Altanlar, 'Director Characteristics, Gender Balance and Insolvency Risk: An Empirical Study' (30 May 2009), http://papers.ssrn.com/sol3/papers.cfm?abstract_id=1932107 accessed 10 January 2019.

[120] Martha L Maznevski, 'Understanding Our Differences: Performance in Decision-Making Groups with Diverse Members' (1994) 47 Human Relations 531; Deborah D Zelechowski and Diana Bilimoria, 'Characteristics of Women and Men Corporate inside Directors in the US' (2004) 12 CG 337.

[121] Lord Davies, 'Women on Boards' (2011) 9.   [122] ibid 9–10.

recommendations and codes of conduct.[123] For example, UK gender-diverse boards implemented the recommendations of the Higgs Review more quickly than male-dominated boards.[124]

The above benefits are not universally acknowledged and studies do exist that seek to refute the above findings.[125] However, the bulk of the available research indicates that gender-diverse boards have advantages over boards dominated by a single gender. Indeed, Lord Davies was so convinced of this that he stated, 'we are now moving to a place where the business case is no longer in question and it is unacceptable for the voice of women to be absent from the boardroom'.[126] Once the argument for greater diversity is accepted, the next question is how best to achieve it. Two principal approaches can be identified, namely (i) a voluntary/business-led approach; and (ii) a legislative approach. It should, however, be noted that the two approaches are not mutually exclusive and some countries have adopted a legislative quota in relation to certain companies, and a business-led approach for other companies.[127] Unfortunately, there are still a number of countries that adopt neither approach and have no measures in place to encourage greater diversity.[128]

8.3.1.1 A voluntary/business-led approach

The Davies Review rejected the idea of a mandatory quota on the basis that 'board appointments should be made on the basis of business needs, skills and ability'.[129] The review therefore recommended a 'business-led approach' under which businesses would voluntarily strive to comply with a series of recommendations, with the principal recommendation being that FTSE 100 boards should aim for a minimum of 25 per cent female representation by the end of 2015.[130] Additional recommendations included:

- Quoted companies should be required to disclose each year the proportion of women on the board, women in senior management positions, and female employees in the whole organization. In 2013, the CA 2006 was amended to require quoted companies to disclose this information in their strategic report.[131]

> The strategic report is discussed at 19.3.2.1.

- Lord Davies stated that shareholder engagement with the issue of gender diversity could be a key driver in encouraging boards to appoint more women. Whilst some investor groups have toughened their voting policies to encourage gender diversity (e.g. Aviva and Legal & General pledged to vote against the re-election of any nomination committee chair of a FTSE 350 company with no female board members), investor engagement with gender diversity has yet to gain momentum in the way it has for other issues (e.g. executive remuneration). However, as the following example demonstrates, shareholder pressure can have an effect, albeit to date a limited one.

---

[123] Vanessa Anastasopoulos, David AH Brown, and Debra L Brown, 'Women on Boards: Not Just the Right Thing . . . But the Bright Thing' (Conference Board of Canada 2002).

[124] Lord Davies, 'Women on Boards' (2011) 10.

[125] See e.g. Renée B Adams and Daniel Ferreira, 'Women in the Boardroom and their Impact on Governance and Performance' (2009) 94 J Fin Econ 291, who argue (at 291) that 'the average effect of gender diversity on firm performance is negative'.

[126] Lord Davies, 'Women on Boards: Davies Review Annual Report 2014' (2014) 4.

[127] EU Member States that combine legislative measures and a voluntary business-led approach include Austria, Belgium, France, Germany, Greece, the Netherlands, and Spain.

[128] EU Member States that have no national measures (voluntary or mandatory) in place include Bulgaria, Croatia, Cyprus, the Czech Republic, Estonia, Lithuania, Malta, and Slovakia.

[129] Lord Davies, 'Women on Boards' (2011) 18.   [130] ibid.   [131] CA 2006, s 414C(8)(c).

Shareholder activism and gender diversity

At its 2014 AGM, the board of Glencore Xstrata plc (now Glencore plc) faced significant shareholder pressure over the fact that Glencore was the only FTSE 100 company with an all-male board. Several large fund managers indicated they would vote against the re-election of Tony Hayward, the company's chair and chair of the nomination committee. The pressure worked and, whilst Hayward was reappointed, he pledged to appoint a female director before the end of the year. In June 2014, Patrice Merrin was appointed as a NED. However, many shareholders were not placated, with the Pensions Investment Research Consultants stating that the appointment of Merrin still left Glencore as 'the laggard of the FTSE 100'. In response, the company appointed another female NED, namely Gill Marcus in 2017.

The question to ask is how successful this business-led approach has been. There can be no doubt that gender diversity has notably improved since the publication of Lord Davies's 2011 report, with Lord Davies's 25 per cent goal being successfully reached.

However, two notable issues remain. The first is what Lord Davies has termed 'the executive pipeline challenge'. The vast majority of female appointments have been to non-executive roles, with very few appointments to more influential executive positions. Women only occupy 10.2 per cent of executive directorships in FTSE 100 companies[132] and the increase in the number of female executives has been slight. In 2011, there were 18 female executives on FTSE 100 boards—as of October 2018 that figure has only risen to 26.[133] Further, as of October 2018, the FTSE 100 has only six female CEOs and only seven female chairmen.[134]

The second issue is that the progress seen at FTSE 100 level has not been replicated to the same degree in the FTSE 250. For example, in 2011, there were only 27 female executives in the FTSE 250—by October 2018, this had only risen to 29.[135] Since 2015, there have been no all-male boards in the FTSE 100, whereas at the time of writing, five FTSE 250 companies have no female directors.

As a result, Lord Davies stated that 'further work and a renewed focus is required'[136] and he recommended that an independent steering body be re-convened to support business in achieving the above goals and to report on progress. This body, namely the Hampton-Alexander Review, was set up in February 2016 and published its first report in November 2016,[137] in which it established several noteworthy recommendations aimed at addressing the above two issues:

- FTSE 350 boards should aim for a minimum of 33 per cent female board representation by the end of 2020. As of October 2018, women accounted for 26.7 per cent of FTSE 350 directors, with the FTSE 250 (24.9 per cent) still lagging behind the FTSE 100 (30.2 per cent).[138] As a result, FTSE 100 companies are on track to meet the 33 per cent goal, but FTSE 250 companies are not.[139]

---

132 Hampton-Alexander Review, 'FTSE Women Leaders: Improving Gender Balance in FTSE Leadership' (2018) Appendix A.

133 ibid.   134 ibid.   135 ibid.

136 Women on Boards Davies Review, 'Improving the Gender Balance on British Boards: Five-Year Summary' (2015) 28.

137 Hampton-Alexander Review, 'FTSE Women Leaders: Improving Gender Balance in FTSE Leadership' (2016). Like the Davies Review, annual reports followed.

138 Hampton-Alexander Review, 'FTSE Women Leaders: Improving Gender Balance in FTSE Leadership (2018) 9.

139 Cranfield University, 'The Female FTSE Board Report 2018' (Cranfield 2018) 7.

- Stakeholders should work together to ensure more women are appointed to the roles of chair, Senior Independent Director, and executive director positions on FTSE 350 companies.

- FTSE 350 companies should act to improve the under-representation of women on the Executive Committee, and FTSE 100 companies should aim for a minimum of 33 per cent female representation on their Executive Committee by 2020. FTSE 100 companies are currently not on track to meet this goal, with women only accounting for 21.1 per cent of executive committee members[140] (16.3 per cent in the FTSE 250).[141]

- The FRC should amend the UK Corporate Governance Code so that all FTSE 350 companies disclose in their annual report the gender balance on the Executive Committee. This was done with Provision 23 of the 2018 Code stating that the annual report should set out the gender balance of those in 'senior management' (defined as the executive committee and the first layer of management below board level, including the company secretary).

Figure 8.2 sets out the key statistics regarding boardroom gender diversity since 2011.

8.3.1.2 A legislative approach

In contrast with the UK, some countries have introduced legislative quotas that require a certain percentage of female directors by a certain date, with sanctions being imposed on non-compliant companies. 2003 saw the introduction of the first quota system, when Norway amended its Public Limited Liability Companies Act[142] and introduced a quota based on board size.

When the quota was introduced in 2003, women only accounted for 7 per cent of listed company directors. Public companies had until 2008 to comply with the quota, by which time, women accounted for 36 per cent of board members.[143] The most recent statistics state that women account for 41 per cent of listed company directors,[144] which is the highest in the world. It is worth noting that one reason for the success of the Norwegian quota is that a failure to meet the quota could result in the dissolution of the company.

Since then, a number of other countries have followed Norway's example and introduced boardroom quotas, but in the EU, quotas remain a minority solution, with only eight[145] of the 28 EU Member States adopting some form of mandatory quota. However, there exists a proposed EU Directive which would, if passed, require all Member States to implement a quota.

8.3.1.3 The proposed EU Directive

A lack of boardroom diversity is a problem across many EU Member States. A European Commission Working Paper published a few weeks after Lord Davies's original 2011 report revealed that, whilst women made up 45.4 per cent of the EU's workforce and 60

---

[140] Hampton-Alexander Review, 'FTSE Women Leaders: Improving Gender Balance in FTSE Leadership' (2018) 11.

[141] ibid 15.   [142] Norwegian Public Limited Liability Companies Act, § 6–11a(1).

[143] Aagoth Storvik and Mari Teigan, 'Women on Board: The Norwegian Experience (2011), http://library. fes.de/pdf-files/id/ipa/07309.pdf accessed 10 January 2019.

[144] Statistics derived from the European Institute for Gender Equality's Women and Men in Decision-Making Database, https://eige.europa.eu/gender-statistics/dgs/browse/wmidm accessed 10 January 2019.

[145] Namely Austria, Belgium, France, Germany, Greece, Italy, the Netherlands, and Spain.

FTSE 350 Women on Boards - 8 Year Analysis

FTSE 100	Feb 2011	Mar 2012	Mar 2013	Mar 2014	Mar 2015	Oct 2015	Oct 2016	Oct 2017	Oct 2018[15]
Representation of Women	12.5%	15%	17.3%	20.7%	23.5%	26.1%	26.6%	27.7%	30.2%
Number of companies with 33% +	-	-	-	7	16	20	23	28	38
Number of Women on boards	135	163	194	231	263	286	283	294	317
Number of Women NEDs	117 (15.6%)	143 (22.4%)	176 (21.8%)	211 (25.5%)	239 (28.5%)	260 (31.4%)	254 (31.6%)	269 (33.3%)	291 (36.5%)
Number of Women Exec Directors	18 (5.5%)	20 (6.6%)	18 (5.8%)	20 (6.9%)	24 (8.6%)	26 (9.6%)	29(11.2%)	25 (9.8%)	26(10.2%)
Number of Women Chairs	2	1	1	1	3	3	4	6	7
Number of Women CEOs	5	4	3	4	5	5	6	6	6
Number of Women SIDs	-	-	-	-	-	-	-	14	18
Total Directorships	1076	1086	1112	1117	1117	1097	1065	1063	1051
Number of All-Male boards	21	11	7	2	0	0	0	0	0
FTSE 250	Feb 2011	Mar 2012	Mar 2013	Mar 2014	Mar 2015	Oct 2015	Oct 2016	Oct 2017	Oct 2018[15]
Representation of Women	7.8%	9.6%	13.2%	15.6%	18%	19.6%	21.1%	22.8%	24.9%
Number of companies with 33% +	-	-	-	24	26	33	44	54	65
Number of Women on boards	154	189	267	310	365	396	421	453	495
Number of Women NEDs	127 (9.6%)	168 (11.4%)	235 (16.6%)	281 (19.6%)	340 (23%)	368 (24.8%)	388 (26.2%)	415 (27.8%)	466 (30.5%)
Number of Women Exec Directors	27 (4.2%)	28 (4.5%)	32 (5.4%)	29 (5.3%)	25 (4.6%)	28 (5.2%)	33 (6%)	38 (7.7%)	29 (6.3%)
Number of Women Chairs	-	-	-	-	8	10	10	11	15
Number of Women CEOs	10	-	-	-	9	11	12	9	6
Number of Women SIDs	-	-	-	-	-	-	-	43	53
Total Directorships	1974	1969	2023	1987	2028	2019	1993	1983	1990
Number of All-Male boards	131	115	67	48	23	15	13	8	5[16]
FTSE 350 (FTSE 100 + FTSE 250)	Feb 2011	Mar 2012	Mar 2013	Mar 2014	Mar 2015	Oct 2015	Oct 2016	Oct 2017	Oct 2018[15]
Representation of Women	9.5%	11.5%	14.7%	17.4%	20%	21.9%	23%	24.5%	26.7%
Number of companies with 33% +	-	-	-	31	42	53	67	82	103
Number of Women on boards	289	352	461	541	628	682	704	747	812
Number of Women NEDs	244	311	411	492	579	628	642	684	757
Number of Women Exec Directors	45	48	50	49	49	54	62	63	55 (7.7%)
Number of Women Chairs	-	-	-	-	11	13	14	17	22
Number of Women CEOs	15	-	-	-	14	16	18	15	12
Number of Women SIDs	-	-	-	-	-	-	-	57	71
Total Directorships	3050	3055	3135	3104	3145	3116	3058	3046	3041
Number of All-Male boards	152	126	74	50	23	15	13	8	5[16]

Source: BoardEx October 2018
15. All 2018 data as at 1st October unless otherwise stated
16. Includes one additional board which became an All-Male board on the 1st November 2018

FIGURE 8.2 Female directorships in the FTSE 100, 250, and 350

Source: Hampton-Alexander Review, 'FTSE Women Leaders: Improving Gender Balance in FTSE Leadership' (2018) Appendix A.

per cent of university graduates, they accounted for less than 12 per cent of directors in large listed EU companies.[146] Whilst progress has been made since, recent figures (26.2 per cent as of December 2018)[147] are still well below the EU's 'gender balance zone' of 40–60 per cent.

It therefore came as no surprise when, in October 2012, the European Commission proposed a Directive[148] aimed at the boards of large listed companies.[149] The principal provisions of the Directive are found in Art 4 and provide the following:

- Member States shall ensure that the under-represented gender does not hold less than 40 per cent of the non-executive director positions on the board. Companies not meeting this requirement will need to make appointments to those positions in order to attain not less than 40 per cent by 1 January 2020.

- In order to meet this quota, priority shall be given to candidates of the under-represented gender, providing that such candidates are equally qualified in terms of suitability, competence, and professional performance.

In November 2013, the European Parliament by a large majority approved the Directive. The final step (which is currently ongoing) is for the Directive to be approved by the Council of the European Union and, given that the majority of EU Member States support the Directive (the UK, given its focus on the business-led approach discussed earlier, is unsurprisingly opposed), the imposition of an EU-wide boardroom quota seems possible. However, as the process for the UK's exit of the EU is coming to an end, the UK will not be required to implement the Directive should it pass into law.

8.3.2 Ethnic diversity

As noted, the diversity debate to date has focused almost exclusively on gender diversity. Fortunately, in October 2017, the Parker Review published its recommendations in relation to ethnic diversity in the boardroom.[150] The report noted that of the 1,050 directors in the FTSE 100, only 85 (around 8 per cent) were persons of colour, and 51 FTSE 100 companies did not have any directors of colour at all. Accordingly, the report recommended that each FTSE 100 board should have at least one director of colour by 2021, and each FTSE 250 board should have at least one director of colour by 2024. In April 2017, a report by a House of Commons committee recommended that the FRC should embed the promotion of ethnic diversity in the UK Corporate Governance Code.[151] Accordingly, the 2018 update to the Code provides that board appointments should 'promote diversity of gender, social and ethnic backgrounds'.[152]

---

[146] European Commission, 'The Gender Balance in Business Leadership' COM (2011) 246 final, 3–4.

[147] Statistics derived from the European Institute for Gender Equality's Women and Men in Decision-Making Database, https://eige.europa.eu/gender-statistics/dgs/browse/wmidm accessed 10 January 2019.

[148] European Commission, 'Proposal for a Directive of the European Parliament and of the Council on Improving the Gender Balance amongst Non-Executive Directors of Companies Listed on Stock Exchanges and Related Measures' COM (2012) 614 final.

[149] Non-listed companies will not be subject to the Directive, nor will listed companies which (i) employ less than 250 employees; and (ii) have an annual turnover not exceeding €50 million or an annual balance sheet total not exceeding €43 million (see arts 2 and 3).

[150] Parker Review Committee, 'A Report into the Ethnic Diversity of UK Boards' (2017).

[151] Business, Energy and Industrial Strategy Committee, 'Corporate Governance' (2016–17, HC 702) para 132.

[152] FRC, 'The UK Corporate Governance Code' (FRC 2018) Principle J.

CHAPTER SUMMARY

- A private company must appoint at least one director, and a public company must appoint at least two directors.

- The process for appointing a director is a matter for the company's articles, which usually provide that a director can be appointed by an ordinary resolution or by a decision of the directors.

- The determination of a director's remuneration is a matter for the company's articles, which commonly provide that the directors can determine their own remuneration, although larger companies delegate this function to a remuneration committee.

- Every public company must appoint a company secretary. A private company may appoint a company secretary, but it is not required to do so (unless the articles so provide).

- In recent years, board diversity has become a major governance topic. The focus to date has been on increasing gender diversity in the boardroom, but recent attention has also focused on ethnic diversity.

FURTHER READING

Sir Adrian Cadbury, *Corporate Governance and Chairmanship: A Personal View* (OUP 2002) ch 7.
- Looks at the relationship between the chair and CEO, and provides an excellent discussion of whether the role should be combined or split.

Andrew Kakabadse, Nada Korac-Kakabadse, and Nadeem Khan, 'The Company Secretary: Building Trust through Governance' (Institute of Chartered Secretaries and Administrators 2014).
- Sets out the finding of a study that examined—based on interviews with relevant persons— the role of the company secretary.

Christine A Mallin, *Corporate Governance* (6th edn, OUP 2018) ch 8.
- Chapter 8 provides an informative discussion of the principal issues relating to directors and board structure.

Cranfield School of Management Female FTSE Index, www.cranfield.ac.uk/som/research-centres/ global-centre-for-gender-and-leadership/female-ftse-index accessed 10 January 2019.
- Provides access to the Female FTSE Board Reports, the most comprehensive statistics relating to boardroom gender diversity.

Lord Davies, 'Women on Boards' (2011) and annual updates, www.gov.uk/government/collections/ women-on-boards-reports accessed 10 January 2019.
- Provides background information, criticism, and recommendations relating to the current business-led approach to improving gender diversity in UK boardrooms.

ICSA and Ernst and Young, 'The Nomination Committee—Coming Out of the Shadows' (ICSA 2016).
- Discusses the role of the nomination committee and how it operates in practice.

Website of The High Pay Centre http://highpaycentre.org accessed 10 January 2019.
- Provides a wealth of material relating to all facets of the directors' remuneration debate.

SELF-TEST QUESTIONS

1. Define the following terms:
  - unitary board structure;

- two-tier board structure;
- quota.

2. State whether each of the following statements is true or false and, if false, explain why:

- All companies must appoint at least two directors.
- The company appoints a director by passing an ordinary resolution.
- All companies must keep a register of directors.
- Directors are not entitled to be remunerated unless the articles so provide.
- Two-tier boards are not permissible in the UK.
- Only public companies are required to appoint a company secretary.

3. 'Whilst the Davies Review into board diversity has improved gender diversity in FTSE boardrooms, it cannot be regarded as a success.' Discuss this quote.

4. Dragon Technologies plc's ('DT') board consists of seven directors. Mrs Merigold (the CEO), Mr Keyes, Dr Halsey, and Mr Grant are executive directors, and the NEDs are Mr Brute (the chair), Mr Grunt, and Mr Flood. In January, Mr Brute, who has been a NED for 13 years (although he was only appointed as chair two years ago), states that he plans to retire in April. At a March board meeting, the entire board discussed Mr Brute's retirement and drew up a description of the qualities required by the new chair. At the same board meeting, it was also decided that Mrs Merigold would act as chair on a temporary basis until a new chair was appointed.

Mr Brute retired and DT advertised for his replacement. At a board meeting in May, the board discussed the applications received and came up with a shortlist. Mrs Merigold and Mr Keyes stated that they were well acquainted with one applicant, Mr Hook, as he acted as a senior manager for Ghost two years ago and his performance was outstanding. The board interviewed the shortlisted applicants, and decided to offer the job to Mr Hook. Mr Hook accepted and was officially appointed as a NED at a board meeting in June. At this meeting, it was decided that Mrs Merigold would continue to act as chair for two months to allow Mr Hook to complete his induction and to familiarize himself with the company. In August, he took over as chair. At a September board meeting, the board decided to make a further directorial appointment, but has yet to decide the type of director who should be appointed.

After reviewing the above facts, Mr Hook is concerned that DT's board appointments processes are not robust enough. He seeks your advice on whether the company and its board have complied with the law and best practice recommendations. He also seeks your advice on the type of director that should be appointed next.

 ONLINE RESOURCES

This book is accompanied by online resources to better support you in your studies. Visit www.oup.com/uk/roach-company/ for:

- answers to the self-test questions;
- further reading lists;
- multiple-choice questions;
- glossary.

Updates to the law can be found on the author's Twitter account (@UKCompanyLaw) and further resources can be found on the author's blog (www.companylawandgovernance.com).

9 The role and powers of the board

- The role of the board
- The powers of the board

INTRODUCTION

The bulk of corporate scandals that have taken place over the past few decades has ensured that the role played by the directors has remained a (if not, the) fundamental governance issue. Despite this, determining the role and powers of the directors is not always easy. Part of this is due to the fact that the CA 2006 has little to say regarding what the directors actually do, and the powers granted to them to undertake their role. This chapter clarifies and discusses the role of the directors, and the powers granted to them to enable them to perform their role effectively.

9.1 The role of the board

Whilst the Companies Act 2006 (CA 2006) provides that certain obligations must be carried out by the directors,[1] it has little to say regarding the directors' general role. The UK Corporate Governance Code, although aimed primarily at companies with a premium listing, provides that '[a] successful company is led by an effective and entrepreneurial board, whose role is to promote the long-term sustainable success of the company, generating value for shareholders and contributing to wider society',[2] and this is certainly generic enough to be applicable to small and large companies alike.

Limited guidance on the role of the board may be found in the articles, with art 3 of the model articles providing that 'the directors are responsible for the management of the company's business . . .'. This is certainly true in smaller companies, where the scope of the business may be such that the directors can effectively manage it. Indeed, in such companies, the directors will often wish to retain control of the business and so delegation may be minimal or even non-existent. As the company grows, however, the ability of the board to manage

---

[1] For instance, the duty to prepare annual accounts and reports is placed upon the directors (CA 2006, ss 394, 414A, 415, and 420).

[2] Financial Reporting Council (FRC), 'The UK Corporate Governance Code' (FRC 2018) Principle A.

alone becomes more difficult and, in larger companies (especially large listed companies), it is unrealistic to expect a typically-sized board of 8–12 persons to effectively manage the totality of the company's business. Instead, the board will often delegate much of its managerial power to persons operating below board level (and who are largely ignored by the CA 2006), leaving the board to focus on the company's overall strategic direction and governance. This is recognized by the UK Corporate Governance Code, which states that the board should:

- establish the company's purpose, values and strategy, and satisfy itself that these and its culture are aligned;[3]
- ensure that the necessary resources are in place for the company to meet its objectives;[4] and
- establish a framework of prudent and effective controls, which enable risk to be assessed and managed.[5]

Accordingly, in larger companies, the board does not manage the company on a day-to-day basis. Instead, it delegates its managerial powers to executive managers, who report to the executive directors. The board then sets the overall strategic goals of the company, puts in place governance and risk management systems, and reviews the performance of the managers to determine whether these goals are being met and the governance systems are working. As Tricker stated '[m]anagement runs the business; the board ensures that it is being well run and run in the right direction'.[6] Figure 9.1, which is adapted from Tricker's diagram on boards and management,[7] sets out how this works.

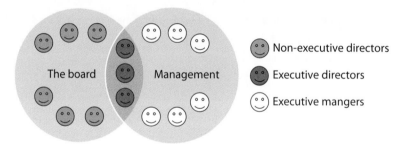

Non-executive directors

Executive directors

Executive mangers

FIGURE 9.1 The relationship between the board and management

It may be thought that the directors' delegation of managerial power is not consistent with the responsibility to manage placed upon them by art 3 of the model articles. In reality, this is not an issue, as art 3 does not actually provide that the directors will manage the company themselves—it merely states that they are 'responsible for the management of the company's business'. The wording used implies that delegation of managerial functions is envisaged and, to that end, the model articles provide the directors with wide powers of delegation. As Davies and Worthington correctly state, the reality is that the articles only provide the 'starting point in determining the role of the board which may be modified substantially . . . through board decisions to delegate authority to management . . .'.[8]

In order to fulfil its role, the board of directors is granted considerable power. These powers, and the limitations placed upon them, are discussed next.

The ability of the directors to delegate is discussed at 9.2.3.

[3] ibid Principle B.   [4] ibid Principle C.   [5] ibid.
[6] Bob Tricker, *Corporate Governance: Principles, Policies, and Practices* (3rd edn, OUP 2015) 45.
[7] ibid 44–5.
[8] Paul L Davies and Sarah Worthington, *Gower's Principles of Modern Company Law* (10th edn, Sweet & Maxwell 2016) 358.

9.2 The powers of the board

Just as the CA 2006 has little to say regarding the role of the directors, so too does it say little about the general managerial powers of the directors. Instead, the issue is largely a matter for the company's articles. In particular, three notable questions arise that will be discussed in the remainder of this chapter, namely:

1. What is the balance of power between the directors and the members?
2. How do directors exercise the powers granted to them?
3. To what extent can directors delegate their powers to others?

It should be noted that the law relating to the powers of the board does not operate in a vacuum, and many areas of the law impact upon the board's exercising of its powers (e.g. the directors must exercise their powers in accordance with their general duties). This section begins by looking at what powers of management are vested in the directors, and how power is divided between the board and the members.

 The general duties are discussed in Chapters 10 and 11.

9.2.1 The division of power between the board and the members

As the company is a legal person, it can only operate with the help of human intermediaries, thereby raising the issue of who has the power to control the company. The power to manage a company is initially vested in the members but, in all but the smallest companies, it is not practical for the members to exercise day-to-day control over the company, and so their powers of management are usually delegated to the directors. This leads us to ask who has the right to manage the company–the directors or the members?

In small, private companies, this question is largely redundant as the directors and members are often the same persons, and so the issue of who can exercise managerial power does not arise (although the capacity in which such persons are acting might be relevant in other areas, such as establishing whether a breach of directors' duties has occurred). In other cases, the division of power between the board and the members is an important issue. The answer is found in the company's articles, as the directors have only such managerial power as is delegated to them by the members via the articles. Most companies have in their articles a provision vesting day-to-day control of the company in the directors as a body, with art 3 of the model articles providing that, '[s]ubject to the articles, the directors are responsible for the management of the company's business, for which purpose they may exercise all the powers of the company'.

As the articles normally vest managerial power in the board, as opposed to individual directors, it follows that the directors must exercise their powers collectively, unless authority is delegated to an individual director or other person.

 Mitchell & Hobbs (UK) Ltd v Mill [1996] 2 BCLC 102 (QB)

FACTS: Mitchell & Hobbs (UK) Ltd ('Mitchell') had two directors, one of whom (Radford) was the managing director. Mitchell experienced financial difficulties and so the company secretary (Mill) withdrew £3,900 from Mitchell's bank account in order to satisfy the creditors' claims. Radford objected to this and instructed Mitchell's solicitors to commence proceedings by Mitchell against Mill for repayment of the money.

> **HELD:** The power of management was bestowed upon the entire board and so Radford required the sanction of the board in order to instruct a solicitor on Mitchell's behalf. There was no evidence that a board meeting had been convened to authorize commencing action against Mill. Accordingly, Radford did not have authority to commence proceedings against Mill, and so Radford's action was struck out.

The members' delegation of power to the directors under the articles appears to differ to other forms of delegation (such as the directors delegating their powers to others). Normally, if A delegates a power to B, then A is still free to exercise that power (as is the case with directors' delegating powers to others). This is not the case here and, where managerial power has been vested in the directors, the members have no right to interfere in management, unless such a power has been reserved to the members in the articles or by statute.

Automatic Self-Cleansing Filter Syndicate Co Ltd v Cuninghame **[1906] 2 Ch 34 (CA)**

FACTS: The articles of the company conferred general powers of management on the directors and provided that they could sell any property of the company on such terms as they deemed fit. The company's members passed an ordinary resolution resolving to sell the assets and undertakings of the company, but the directors did not believe such a sale to be in the interests of the company and so refused to proceed with the sale.

HELD: The right to manage the company and the right to determine which property to sell was vested in the directors. Accordingly, the directors were not compelled to comply with the members' resolution unless the articles so provided.

Clearly, provisions such as art 3 of the model articles tilt the balance of power strongly in favour of the directors and it has been argued that they therefore provide a clear example of Berle & Means' 'separation of ownership and control' in practice. However, it is not so clear. By permitting the powers of the directors to be delineated by the articles (and remember that art 3 is 'subject to the articles', as discussed below), it could be argued that provisions such as art 3 reinforce the idea that managerial power flows from the members in general meeting, as it is the members who ultimately decide what provisions remain in the articles.

The separation of ownership and control is discussed at 14.5.

What is clear is that the CA 2006, more so than previous Companies Acts, does tilt the balance of power in favour of the directors, principally by authorizing them to engage in activities that, under previous Companies Acts, would require member approval or authorization in the articles. For example, s 80 of the CA 1985 provided that the directors could only authorize an allotment of shares if they were authorized to do so by the articles or the company in general meeting. Section 550 of the CA 2006 now allows the directors of a private company with only one class of shares to authorize an allotment of shares of the same class, unless the articles prohibit them from doing so. Whilst this is a worthwhile reform from a practical point of view, it does demonstrate how the Act further empowers the directors.

Section 550 is discussed at 16.4.1.

However, the powers granted to directors under the articles are not limitless and, in several important ways, the members are still able (at least in theory) to exercise a significant amount of power and control, as is discussed at 9.2.1.1–9.2.1.4.

9.2.1.1 'Subject to the articles'

It will be noted that the power of management conferred upon the directors by art 3 is 'subject to the articles'. From this, it follows that the articles can be amended to alter the balance of power between the directors and members, as the following case demonstrates.

Salmon v Quin & Axtens Ltd [1909] 1 Ch 311 (CA)

FACTS: The articles of Quin & Axtens Ltd ('Quin') conferred general powers of management upon the directors, but such powers were subject to the articles. Article 80 provided that resolutions of the directors relating to the acquisition or letting of certain premises would not be valid if either of Quin's two managing directors (who were also members) were to dissent. The directors passed a board resolution resolving to acquire certain property, but one of the managing directors (Salmon) vetoed the resolution. An extraordinary meeting was called and the members passed an ordinary resolution similar to the one the directors attempted to pass. Salmon commenced proceedings, seeking an injunction to restrain the property acquisitions.

HELD: Whilst the directors had a general power of management, it was subject to the articles. Accordingly, Salmon's veto was valid and members could not override it by passing an ordinary resolution.

In both *Automatic Self-Cleansing* and *Salmon*, ordinary resolutions passed by the members could not affect the powers conferred in the articles, because this would permit the members to alter the articles indirectly by ordinary resolution (and alteration requires a special resolution). The members could, if they so wished, amend the articles in order to alter the balance of power, but it is likely that, in all but the smallest companies, the members will want the directors to retain their general power of management.

> Alteration of the articles is discussed at 5.3.3.

The solution to this is usually to provide the members with the ability to direct the directors, usually via the passing of a resolution. Article 4(1) of the model articles provides what is termed a 'reserve power' and provides that the members may 'by special resolution, direct the directors to take, or refrain from taking, specified action'. It should be noted, however, that the courts do tend to pay close scrutiny to such clauses, and are reluctant to let them interfere too much with clauses that provide the directors with general managerial powers. In particular, the courts will not interpret such clauses as providing the members with a general supervisory power over the directors. As Greer LJ stated:

> If powers of management are vested in the directors, they and they alone can exercise these powers. The only way in which the general body of the shareholders can control the exercise of the powers vested by the articles in the directors is by altering their articles, or, if opportunity arises under the articles, by refusing to re-elect the directors of whose actions they disapprove. They cannot themselves usurp the powers which by the articles are vested in the directors any more than the directors can usurp the powers vested by the articles in the general body of shareholders.[9]

---

[9] *John Shaw and Sons (Salford) Ltd v Shaw* [1935] 2 KB 113 (CA) 134.

In practice, reserve powers such as those found in art 4 are rarely used on the ground that there is little need to pass a special resolution compelling the directors to act a certain way, when it is easier to pass an ordinary resolution removing them from office.

The removal of a director is discussed at 12.4.

9.2.1.2 **The power to litigate**

As noted at 4.3.7, one of the consequences of corporate personality is that the company is able to commence legal proceedings in its own right. This leads us to ask who has the right to exercise this power on behalf of the company. The ability to commence proceedings on behalf of the company falls within the general power of management conferred upon the directors by clauses such as art 3 of the model articles.[10] Accordingly, the members will not generally be able to bring claims in the name of the company. However, a notable exception is provided for in the CA 2006, which allows for members to commence a derivative claim in respect of an action vested in the company.

The derivative claim is discussed at 15.2.

9.2.1.3 **Powers vested in the members**

Whilst the articles tend to vest considerable power in the directors, statute tends to place considerable power in the hands of the members, with many powers being exclusively vested in the members (e.g. the ability to approve a substantial property transaction involving a director). Some powers are not exclusive to the members, but nor can they be taken away from the members (e.g. the ability to remove a director under s 168 of the CA 2006). However, as is discussed at 14.5, the ability of the members to exercise these powers in practice is not without difficulty. Despite this, the powers placed into the hands of the members are substantial and continue to grow (as demonstrated by the rules that provide the members of quoted companies with a 'say on pay').

Substantial property transactions are discussed at 11.4.2.

'Say on pay' is discussed at 19.3.2.4.

9.2.1.4 **Reversion of powers**

The powers of management delegated by the members to the directors will revert back to the members if the directors are unwilling or unable to exercise the powers conferred upon them by the articles. This could occur where the directors refuse to attend board meetings,[11] where a board cannot achieve quoracy,[12] or where there is no board of directors at all.[13] However, this reversion will only occur where the board is completely incapable of making decisions and not when a minority of directors use any power conferred upon them by the articles to block the implementation of a decision by the majority of the board (as in *Salmon v Quin & Axtens Ltd*, discussed at 9.2.1.1). In the latter case, the board is precluded from acting by the operation of the articles, not by any incapacity to act.

9.2.2 **Directors' meetings**

The principal mechanism by which the board exercises its managerial function is the directors' meeting (or board meeting).[14] The obvious exception to this is a company that has only one director—in such a case, board meetings serve no purpose at all. Indeed, art 7(2) of the model articles for private companies provides that many of the rules relating to board meetings will not apply to a single-director company.

---

[10] ibid.   [11] *Barron v Potter* [1914] 1 Ch 895 (Ch).   [12] *Foster v Foster* [1916] 1 Ch 532 (Ch).
[13] *Alexander Ward & Co Ltd v Samyang Navigation Co Ltd* [1975] 1 WLR 673 (HL).
[14] Not to be confused with general meetings of the company.

The frequency of board meetings is entirely a matter for the company. In small companies, meetings may be rarely held and only when there is sufficient cause. The Financial Reporting Council's (FRC's) 'Guidance on Board Effectiveness' provides that '[m]eeting regularly is essential for the board to discharge its duties effectively and to allow adequate time for consideration of all the issues falling within its remit'.[15] As a result, larger companies meet at regular, fixed intervals (in 2015, FTSE 350 boards met, on average, 8.4 times per year).[16]

The model articles empower any director to call a board meeting[17] but, in practice, board meetings are usually called by the chair, who will instruct the company secretary to convene a meeting. Generally, the rules relating to board meetings are a matter for the company's articles, so companies have considerable flexibility in determining board meeting procedures.

9.2.2.1 **Notice**

The rules relating to notice of board meetings are a matter for the company's articles, and it is usual for the articles to require some form of notice and, if due notice is not provided, then the meeting may be invalidated.[18] The model articles provide that any director can call a meeting by giving notice of the meeting to the directors, or by authorizing the company secretary (if the company has one) to give such notice.[19] There is debate as to whether notice must be provided to a director who would not have the right to vote at the meeting,[20] but where the articles specify that each director is entitled to notice (as the model articles do), then it is contended that such a director would have right to notice. Notice of a board meeting can be oral, unless the articles specify that it must be in writing—the model articles expressly state that notice need not be in writing,[21] and companies will often expressly state that notice can be in writing or 'by word of mouth'. The model articles require that notice of a meeting must indicate:

(a) its proposed date and time;

(b) where it is to take place, and;

(c) if it is expected that directors participating in the meeting will not be in the same place, how it is proposed that they should communicate with each other during the meeting.[22]

Note that the model articles (and indeed the articles of most companies) do not stipulate how much notice must be provided and, depending upon the facts, notice periods can be very short. For example, in *Browne v La Trinidad*,[23] notice of ten minutes was held to be valid. If a director does feel that notice provided is insufficient, then he should object immediately, or his objection will fail.[24]

Older cases state the directors who are abroad or out of reach of notices need not be given notice,[25] but it has been argued that such cases are unlikely to carry weight today given advances in telecommunications.[26]

---

[15] FRC, 'Guidance on Board Effectiveness' (FRC 2018) para 28.

[16] Grant Thornton LLP, 'Corporate Governance Review 2015: Trust and Integrity—Loud and Clear?' (Grant Thornton 2015) 23.

[17] Model articles for private companies, art 9(1); model articles for public companies, art 8(1)–(3).

[18] *Young v Ladies Imperial Cub Ltd* [1920] 2 KB 523 (CA).

[19] Model articles for private companies, art 9(1); model articles for public companies, art 8(1)–(3).

[20] See the differing opinions of Greer and Slesser LJJ in *John Shaw and Sons (Salford) Ltd v Shaw* [1935] 2 KB 113 (CA).

[21] Model articles for private companies, art 9(3); model articles for public companies, art 8(5).

[22] Model articles for private companies, art 9(2); model articles for public companies, art 8(4).

[23] (1887) 37 ChD 1 (CA).   [24] ibid.   [25] *Halifax Sugar Refining Co Ltd v Franklyn* (1890) 59 LJ Ch 591.

[26] Geoffrey Morse, *Palmer's Company Law* (Sweet & Maxwell 2018) para 8.2112.

9.2.2.2 **Quorum**

➡ **quorum:**
the minimum number of qualifying persons required to be present in order to transact business

In order to validly transact business, a **quorum** will normally be required, with the rules relating to quorums being a matter for the articles. Where the articles do not stipulate a quorum, then a majority of directors will be required to attend the meeting,[27] unless practice of the board over time establishes what constitutes a quorum.[28]

The model articles provide that a quorum for a directors' meeting may be fixed by the directors, but it must not be less than two, and it will be two if the directors have not decided otherwise.[29] However, this will not apply where a private company only has one director.[30] As the following case demonstrates, only directors entitled to vote on a matter will count towards the quorum.

> ### Re Greymouth Point Elizabeth Railway and Coal Co Ltd [1904] 1 Ch 32 (Ch)
>
> **FACTS:** The company's articles set the quorum at two. The articles also permitted directors to enter into contracts with the company, or be interested in any business with the company, but that such directors could not vote on such matters at board meetings. At a board meeting, the three directors present decided that the company should issue debentures to two of the directors present.
>
> **HELD:** The two directors who were granted the debentures clearly had an interest in the matter, and so were not permitted to vote. Accordingly, as only one director was permitted to vote, there was no quorum and so the granting of the debentures was invalid.
>
> **COMMENT:** The model articles state that if a director is interested in a proposed transaction or arrangement with the company, then he will not count towards the quorum.[31] Note that the board cannot avoid such a rule by temporarily reducing its quorum.[32]

Obtaining a quorum may be difficult where directors are abroad or otherwise unavailable. Several options exist. First, a meeting could be postponed until a quorum can be formed. Second, the meeting could be held electronically under which the directors communicate via Skype, teleconference, etc.[33] Third, an absent director could appoint an alternate director to attend the meeting on his behalf.

🔗 Alternate directors are discussed at 7.2.4.

The general rule is that an inquorate meeting cannot transact business.[34] However, this rule can be excluded by the articles, which can specify which business can be conducted by an inquorate meeting.[35] For example, the model articles provide that an inquorate meeting may:

- propose a date for another meeting;

---

[27] *York Tramways Co Ltd v Willow* (1882) 2 QBD 685 (CA).
[28] *Re Tavistock Ironworks Co* (1867) LR 4 Eq 233.
[29] Model articles for private companies, art 11(2); model articles for public companies, art 10(2).
[30] Model articles for private companies, art 7(2).
[31] Model articles for private companies, art 14(1); model articles for public companies, art 16(1).
[32] *Re North Eastern Insurance Co Ltd* [1919] 1 Ch 198 (Ch).
[33] Article 10(2) of the model articles for private companies and art 9(2) of the model articles for public companies provide that it is irrelevant where directors are or how they communicate.
[34] *Faure Electric Accumulator Co Ltd v Phillipart* (1888) 58 LT 525 (QB).
[35] *Re Scottish Petroleum Co (No 2)* (1883) 23 ChD 413 (CA).

- appoint further directors or;
- call a general meeting so that the members can appoint further directors.[36]

Decisions at an inquorate board meeting may be saved if the *Duomatic* principle applies,[37] or if the articles provide for unanimous decision-making, which is discussed next.

The *Duomatic* principle is discussed at 14.2.

9.2.2.3 Board decision-making

The rules regarding director decision-making are a matter for the company's articles. The model articles provide that decisions at meetings can be made via resolutions, with a simple majority of the participating directors being required.[38] The default rule is that, where the votes for and against are equal, the resolution is lost.[39] However, this rule is usually excluded by providing for a casting vote (the model articles grant this to the chair).[40] Of course, if a private company only has one director, then the normal rules for decision-making will not normally apply and that director can simply make decisions himself.[41]

The model articles also provide for additional decision-making procedures, and these differ for public and private companies:

- Directors of private companies can make decisions without a meeting if all the eligible directors (i.e. those entitled to vote on the matter if it had been tabled at a meeting) indicate to each other by any means that they share a common view on a matter.[42] The existence of this procedure acknowledges that, in many private companies, formal board meetings may not occur very often and so some other efficient mechanism for decision-making is useful. Note that the eligible directors must still meet the quorum requirements.[43]

- Directors of public companies may make decisions without a meeting, via a written resolution. Any director may propose a written resolution by giving written notice of the proposed resolution to each director, which must state the proposed resolution and the time by which it must be adopted.[44] The resolution is passed once all the directors entitled to vote on it at a directors' meeting sign a copy of the resolution, providing that they would have formed a quorum at such a meeting.[45]

9.2.2.4 Minutes

Every company must record all minutes of proceedings at directors' meetings, and must keep these records for at least ten years from the date of the meeting.[46] Failure to keep such minutes is a criminal offence, although decisions taken at the relevant meeting will be unaffected.[47] Minutes that have been authenticated by the chair will provide evidence of the proceedings of that meeting.[48]

The model articles also require records to be kept of every unanimous decisions or majority decision (in the case of private companies), and directors' written resolutions (in the case of public companies) for a period of ten years.[49]

---

[36] Model articles for private companies, art 14(1); model articles for public companies, art 16(1).

[37] *Eurobrokers Holdings Ltd v Monecor (London) Ltd* [2003] EWCA Civ 105; [2003] BCC 573.

[38] Model articles for private companies, art 7(1); model articles for public companies, art 13(1).

[39] *Moodie v W&J Shepherd (Bookbinders) Ltd* [1949] 2 All ER 1044 (HL).

[40] Model articles for private companies, art 13(1); model articles for public companies, art 14(1).

[41] Model articles for private companies, art 7(2).   [42] ibid art 8(1).

[43] ibid art 8(4).   [44] Model articles for public companies, art 17(1), (3), (4), and (5).

[45] ibid art 18(1).   [46] CA 2006, s 248(1) and (2).

[47] *Re North Hallenbeagle Mining Co* (1866–67) LR 2 Ch App 321.   [48] CA 2006, s 249(1).

[49] Model articles for private companies, art 15; model articles for public companies, art 18(4).

9.2.3 **Delegation of powers**

As noted at 9.1, in larger companies, the board delegates much of its managerial power to executive managers. However, the default position is that the board does not have authority to delegate powers granted to it, unless the articles so provide.[50] In practice, the ability to delegate powers to others (e.g. to persons who have expertise in an area that the board lacks) is extremely useful, and so it is common for a company's articles to provide for delegation. Article 5(1) of the model articles confers a wide power of delegation, stating that the directors may delegate any powers conferred upon them by the articles to any person or committee as they think fit. Further, art 5(2) provides that the directors can permit such a person or committee to sub-delegate delegated powers to others.

As discussed at 8.2.4, the UK Corporate Governance Code recommends that boards delegate powers to three committees, namely a nomination committee, an audit committee, and a remuneration committee.[51] Specific types of company may establish other committees. For example, the Walker Review recommended that FTSE-100 listed banks or insurance companies should establish a board risk committee.[52] Article 6(1) of the model articles provide that committees that have had directorial power delegated to them should, as far as they are applicable, follow procedures set out in the articles governing decision-making by the directors. Where this is not possible, the board may make rules of procedure which will then prevail over the relevant rules found in the articles.

Delegation of a power does not deprive the board of the ability to exercise that power.[53] The board can, at any time, revoke any delegation of its powers, either expressly, or impliedly by exercising the powers that were delegated. Whether the revocation is temporary or permanent will depend upon the board's intention.

CHAPTER SUMMARY

- In smaller companies, directors will manage the company and will delegate little, if any, of their powers. In larger companies, the directors will set the strategic direction of the company and will delegate much of their managerial powers to sub-board level managers.

- The powers of the board are a matter for the company's articles, with most articles providing that the board is responsible for managing the company and may exercise all the company's powers.

- A company's articles usually provide the directors with the ability to delegate their powers to others.

- The principal method by which the board exercises its managerial powers is via board meetings. The rules relating to board meetings are largely a matter for the company's articles.

---

[50] *Re Leeds Banking Co* (1865–66) LR 1 Ch App 561.
[51] FRC, 'The UK Corporate Governance Code' (FRC 2018) Provisions 17, 24, and 32.
[52] 'A Review of Corporate Governance in UK Banks and Other Financial Industry Entities: Final Recommendations' (2009) paras 6.11–6.20.
[53] *Huth v Clarke* (1890) 25 QBD 391 (QB).

FURTHER READING

Andrew Kakabadse, Nada Korac-Kakabadse, and Nadeem Khan, 'The Company Secretary: Building Trust through Governance' (Institute of Chartered Secretaries and Administrators (ICSA) 2014).
* Discusses the role of the company secretary and argues that the role is often misunderstood or improperly utilized by the company.

Bob Tricker, *Corporate Governance: Principles, Policies, and Practices* (3rd edn, OUP 2015) ch 7.
* Provides an excellent and practical discussion of the functions of the board.

GD Goldberg, 'Article 80 of Table A of the Companies Act 1980' (1970) 33 MLR 177.
* Despite its age, this article provides a highly relevant and interesting discussion on article provisions that confer general powers of management upon the directors.

ICSA, 'Boardroom Behaviours' (ICSA 2009).
* An interesting report that looks at how boards behave, and argues that guidance on appropriate behaviour should be incorporated into the UK Corporate Governance Code.

FRC, 'Guidance on Board Effectiveness' (FRC 2018).
* Provides guidance on the role of the board and fleshes out the relevant recommendations found in the UK Corporate Governance Code.

SELF-TEST QUESTIONS

1. Define the following terms:
* quorum;
* minutes;
* reserve power;
* casting vote.

2. State whether each of the following statements is true or false and, if false, explain why:
* The model articles provide that the directors may exercise all the powers of the company, and so the members cannot interfere in management.
* The directors' powers of management will revert back to the members if the directors refuse to attend board meetings.
* The articles of most companies do not specify how much notice must be provided for a board meeting.
* If the articles do not state what constitutes a quorum, then two directors will constitute a quorum.
* The directors may only delegate their powers if the articles so allow.

3. 'In most companies, the division of power between the directors and the members is excessively unbalanced in favour of the directors.' Do you agree with this quote? Provide reasons for your answer.

4. Dragon Tools Ltd ('DT') has adopted the model articles for private companies, but has added an additional article, namely 3A, which provides that 'any decision of the directors that involves expenditure of over £10,000 requires the approval of Dragon plc' (DT's parent company). DT's directors decide to acquire a piece of land on which to build a new factory. Belinda, the chief executive officer (CEO) of DT, is authorized to conclude an agreement for the purchase of the land and, on behalf of DT, she enters into negotiations with LandCorp Ltd to purchase a piece of land.

A board meeting is convened to discuss the possible purchase of the land. However, two directors attend, namely Belinda and Walter. Ahmed could not attend as he was away on company business, and Yvonne did not attend as she claimed she was not informed of the meeting. At the meeting, Belinda tells Walter that the £50,000 price is a bargain and DT should purchase the land and immediately, as a delay could risk the land being sold to someone else. Walter agrees and they pass a board resolution agreeing to purchase the land, and another resolution authorizing Belinda to enter into the sale agreement on behalf of DT. A contract is entered into between DT and LandCorp. Dragon's approval was not obtained.

The board of Dragon plc hears of the purchase of the land and also discovers that Walter is a majority shareholder of LandCorp. Dragon seeks your advice on whether the contract between DT and LandCorp can be avoided.

ONLINE RESOURCES

This book is accompanied by online resources to better support you in your studies. Visit www.oup. com/uk/roach-company/ for:

- answers to the self-test questions;
- further reading lists;
- multiple-choice questions;
- glossary.

Updates to the law can be found on the author's Twitter account (@UKCompanyLaw) and further resources can be found on the author's blog (www.companylawandgovernance.com).

10 Directors' duties I: duties of performance

- Directors' duties: the basics
- Duty to act within powers
- Duty to promote the success of the company
- Duty to exercise independent judgment
- Duty to exercise reasonable care, skill, and diligence

INTRODUCTION

As discussed at 9.2.1, it is usual for the articles of a company to place managerial power in the hands of the directors, and the members are generally precluded from interfering in the exercise of this power. However, such a concentration of power is open to abuse; for example, the directors may act in a way that benefits themselves and not the company. UK company law employs several methods to discourage such abuse, with perhaps the most important method being the imposition of a number of duties upon directors.

Directors are subject to a range of duties from differing sources. Statutes such as the Insolvency Act 1986 (IA 1986), Financial Services and Markets Act 2000 (FSMA 2000), and the Companies Act 2006 (CA 2006) impose a range of obligations upon directors, as does the common law. Directors will owe duties as agents of the company and, if they have a contract of service (as most executives do), they will also owe duties as employees. However, there has long been a set of duties that have occupied a special place in company law: a set of duties that exists in order to ensure that the directors act in the company's interests, and not for their own benefit. Historically, these duties were simply known as 'directors' duties', but following their codification, they are now referred to in the CA 2006 as the 'general duties'. In some cases, compliance with the general duties will be insufficient and certain transactions or arrangements will require member approval. Figure 10.1 sets out the general duties and those transactions involving directors that require member approval.

The law relating to directors' duties is a vast and extremely important topic that impacts upon many other areas of company law. To simplify the discussion, it will be discussed over two chapters. This chapter covers some basic introductory issues relating to directors' duties before discussing the duties found in ss 171–4 of the CA 2006 (here, labelled as the duties of performance). Chapter 11 discusses the conflict of interest duties found in ss 175–7, and 182 of the CA 2006, as well as looking at transactions involving directors that require member approval.

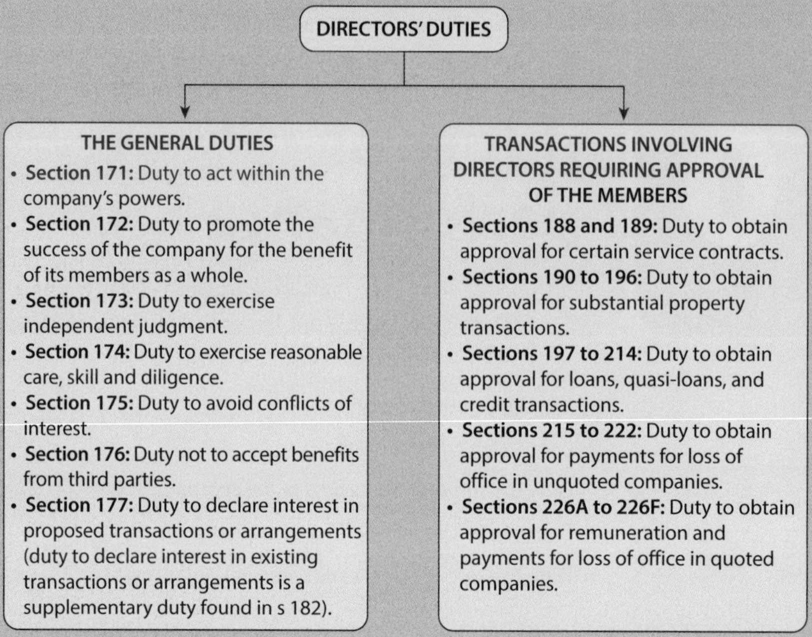

FIGURE 10.1 Directors' duties

Source: Roach, *Concentrate Company Law* (5th edn, OUP 2018).

10.1 Directors' duties: the basics

Before the general duties themselves can be discussed, it is important to establish the basic foundational rules and principles upon which the general duties are based, beginning with their codification.

10.1.1 Codification

Historically, the duties of directors were derived from a mass of case law based on the common law of negligence and equitable duties similar to those imposed on trustees. The result was that the law was unclear, inaccessible, and out of date. Accordingly, as far back as 1895[1] it had been suggested that directors' duties should be **codified** in some manner, but it was only following a 1999 Law Commission report[2] and a review of company law[3] that it was finally decided to enact a statutory statement of directors'

codification: the process whereby law is restated in statute

---

[1] Davey Committee, *Report of the Departmental Committee to Inquire What Amendments are Necessary in the Acts Relating to Joint Stock Companies Incorporated with Limited Liability* (C 7779, HMSO 1895).

[2] Law Commission, *Company Directors: Regulating Conflicts of Interest and Formulating a Statement of Duties* (Law Com No 261, 1999).

duties. The Company Law Review Steering Group outlined three principal reasons for codification:

1. it will 'provide greater clarity on what is expected of directors and make the law more accessible';

2. it will 'enable defects in the present law to be corrected in important areas where it no longer corresponds to accepted norms of modern business practice'; and

3. it will address the question of 'scope' (i.e. in whose interests should companies be run) 'in a way which reflects modern business needs and wider expectations of responsible business behaviour'.[4]

The result can be found in ss 170–87 of the Companies Act 2006, which codify the common law and equitable duties, and sets these 'general duties' out in a more accessible and up-to-date manner.

10.1.2 **The general duties**

The restated duties are referred to in the Act as the 'general duties' and are 'based on certain common law rules and equitable principles as they apply in relation to directors and have effect in place of those rules and principles as regards the duties owed to a company by a director'.[5] It is clear therefore that, whilst the general duties have replaced the common law duties, they have not radically altered them, but have rather restated them in a more appropriate manner (although, as is discussed, several notable reforms have been made). Doubtless, this is to ensure that the authoritative and extremely useful body of case law that has developed should remain relevant—an assertion that is backed up by s 170(4), which provides that 'regard shall be had to the corresponding common law rules and equitable principles in interpreting and applying the general duties'. In this sense, codification will be of limited benefit only, as a director who wishes to completely understand the operation of a duty will need to consult the relevant case law or obtain legal advice.

It is important to note that the general duties do not exist in isolation and are not mutually exclusive—a point emphasized by s 179, which provides that '[e]xcept as otherwise provided, more than one of the general duties may apply in any given case'. The following example provides a situation in which multiple duties might be relevant.

Eg **Multiple general duties**

Dragon plc is negotiating to purchase goods from TechSupply plc. Anna, one of Dragon's directors, is a majority shareholder and non-executive director (NED) in TechSupply, but the other directors of Dragon do not know this. If Anna does not disclose her interest in the transaction prior to it being entered into, she could be in breach of the duty found in s 177. If she still has not disclosed her interest once the transaction is entered into, she could also be in breach of the supplementary duty found in s 182. If she knew she was in breach, her failure to disclose the breach could also amount to a breach of the duty found in s 172. Any directors who knew Anna was acting in breach of duty may also be in breach of the s 172 duty if they fail to disclose her breach.

---

[3] Company Law Review Steering Group, 'Modern Company Law for a Competitive Economy: Final Report, Vol 1' (DTI 2001).

[4] ibid para 3.7.   [5] CA 2006, s 170(3).

10.1.2.1 **To whom do the duties apply?**

Even though s 170(1) states that the general duties are 'owed by a director', it is too simplistic to say that the duties are owed by all directors for two reasons:

1. The duties may in fact be owed by persons who are not directors, as s 170(2) makes it clear that the duties in ss 175 and 176 can continue to apply to persons who cease to be directors.

2. There appears to be some confusion as to which types of director owe duties in some cases. There is no doubt that *de jure* directors become subject to the general duties upon appointment.[6] The position of *de facto* directors is slightly less clear. It has been argued that, as *de facto* directors fall within the 'definition' of director found in s 250 of the CA 2006, then the general duties apply to them fully.[7] However, the Supreme Court has stated that '[i]t does not follow that "de facto director" must be given the same meaning in all of the different contexts in which a "director" may be liable'[8] and that 'the crucial question is whether the person [was] part of the corporate governance structure [and that he] assumed a role in the company sufficient to impose on him a fiduciary duty to the company'. Whilst this would appear to be the authoritative view, it should, however, be noted that this case concerned events that occurred prior to the general duties coming into force, so whether Lord Hope's statement applies to the general duties is not entirely clear.

The application of the general duties to shadow directors is currently developing. Until the passing of the Small Business, Enterprise and Employment Act 2015 (SBEEA 2015), s 170(5) of the CA 2006 stated that the general duties 'apply to shadow directors where, and to the extent that, the corresponding common law rules or equitable principles so apply', thereby leaving the issue to the courts. Unfortunately, the courts struggled to clearly and consistently articulate what duties shadow directors are subject to. Historically, the courts adopted a restrictive approach stating that shadow directors would not normally be subject to fiduciary duties.[9] More recent cases, however, take a more open view, stating that shadow directors will typically owe duties in relation to the directions or instructions they give to the *de jure* directors.[10] This more open approach is now reflected in the amended s 170(5), which now provides that the general duties apply to a shadow director 'where and to the extent that they are capable of so applying',[11] meaning that the general duties will apply to shadow directors, unless they are not capable of so applying.[12] Further, the Secretary of State is now empowered to make regulations setting out how the general duties are to apply to shadow directors.[13] At the time of writing, no such regulations have been made and the Department for Business, Energy and Industrial Strategy (BEIS) has not indicated whether it intends to legislate in this area.

10.1.2.2 **To whom are the duties owed?**

It is important to understand to which persons the general duties are owed, because, generally, only such persons can sue the director(s) for breach of duty. The common law has long established that the directors owe their duties to the company only.

---

[6] Prior to appointment, directors-elect are not subject to the general duties (*Lindgren v L&P Estates Co Ltd* [1968] Ch 572 (CA)).

[7] Geoffrey Morse, *Palmer's Company Law* (Sweet & Maxwell 2018) para 8.2412; Paul L Davies and Sarah Worthington, *Gower & Davies's Principles of Modern Company Law* (9th edn, Sweet & Maxwell 2012) 510.

[8] *Commissioners for HM Revenue and Customs v Holland* [2010] UKSC 51, [2010] 1 WLR 2793 [93] (Lord Hope).

[9] *Ultraframe (UK) Ltd v Fielding* [2005] EWHC 1638 (Ch), [2006] FSR 17 [1279]–[1295] (Lewison J).

[10] *Vivendi SA v Richards* [2013] EWHC 3006 (Ch), [2013] BCC 771 [143] (Newey J).

[11] CA 2006, s 170(5).   [12] SBEEA 2015, Explanatory Note, para 603.   [13] ibid s 89(2).

Percival v Wright [1902] Ch 421 (Ch)

FACTS: The claimants were joint holders of shares in Nixon's Navigation Co Ltd ('Nixon's'). The claimants wished to sell their shares, so Nixon's chair and two other directors agreed to purchase them. However, after the sale was completed, the claimants discovered that, during the negotiations for the sale of the shares, the board knew that a third party wished to purchase the shares in Nixon's for considerably more than was paid to the claimants. The claimants commenced proceedings on the basis that the directors were under a duty to disclose this information.

HELD: Swinfey Eady J held that the directors owed no duties (including a duty to disclose information of the type) to the members, and so the claimants' claim to have the share purchase set aside failed.

Statute preserves the common law position by providing that the general duties 'are owed by a director of a company to the company'.[14] Accordingly, directors do not owe their duties to members,[15] creditors,[16] employees, fellow directors,[17] nominees,[18] or anyone else, and the only persons who can sue for breach of duty are the company itself, or someone who is empowered to act on behalf of the company. This would obviously include the board but can also include members who commence a derivative claim.

The derivative claim is discussed at 15.2.

Whilst the general duties are owed exclusively to the company, outside of the scope of the general duties, the directors may owe specific duties to persons other than the company, depending upon the circumstances. For example, in limited circumstances, the directors may owe a duty directly to the members, including:

1. where a director undertakes to act as agent for one or more members, he will owe a duty directly to those members,[19] but such a duty derives from his position as an agent and not by virtue of him being a director;

2. where the company is the target of a takeover bid, the directors may owe a direct duty to the members to provide honest advice regarding the bid and not to prevent the members from obtaining the best price for their shares.[20]

10.1.2.3 Remedies and limitation periods

Although the general duties are set out in statute, the specific remedies for their breach are not. Instead, s 178(1) provides that the consequences of breaching the general duties are the same as those that would apply if the corresponding common law or equitable principle were to have been breached (which means that recourse to the relevant case law will still be required). In this text, these remedies are discussed alongside the corresponding general duty. It should also be noted that a breach of duty may result in other forms of action being taken against the director (e.g. disqualification).

---

[14] CA 2006, s 170(1).

[15] *Multinational Gas and Petrochemical Co v Multinational Gas and Petrochemical Services Ltd* [1983] Ch 258 (CA).

[16] ibid.   [17] *Kohn v Meehan* (Ch, 31 Jan 2003).

[18] *Hawkes v Cuddy* [2009] EWCA Civ 291, [2010] BCC 597.

[19] *Allen v Hyatt* (1914) 30 TLR 444 (PC).

[20] *Heron International Ltd v Lord Grade* [1983] BCLC 244 (CA).

Parties seeking a remedy will also need to bear in mind the relevant limitation periods. An action alleging breach of duty must normally be brought within six years of the date on which the action accrued.[21] However, in two cases, there will be no limitation period and an action can be brought at any time. These instances apply to directors, who are regarded as trustees for the purposes of s 21 because they 'are entrusted with the stewardship of the company's property and owe fiduciary duties to the company in respect of that stewardship'.[22] The two instances are:

1. where a director was party to a fraud or fraudulent breach of trust;[23] or
2. where the director is in possession of the company's property or proceeds of the company, or where the director has received company property and converted it to his use.[24]

10.1.3 Avoiding liability

A director who could be held liable for breaching the duties discussed in this chapter and Chapter 11 may be able to obtain relief from such liability in several ways.

10.1.3.1 Consent, approval, or authorization by the members

Section 180(4)(a) of the CA 2006 provides that the general duties have effect subject to any rule of law enabling the company to give authority for anything to be done (or omitted) by the directors (or any of them) that would otherwise be a breach of duty. The following example demonstrates this.

 Authorization of the members

The articles of Dragon plc provide that the board is empowered to authorize transactions involving directors that could conflict with the company's interests. Dragon is considering whether to enter into a supply agreement with MegaTech plc. Greg, one of Dragon's directors, is a major shareholder in MegaTech and so has a conflict of interest. Normally, the other directors of Dragon could authorize this conflict, as the articles permit them to do so.[25] However, the other directors of Dragon are also directors of MegaTech, and so are not permitted to authorize Greg's conflict.[26] In this case, the members of Dragon could authorize Greg's conflict as the law has long provided for member approval in such cases, and s 180(4) serves to preserve this rule.

In addition, s 180(1) provides for specific rules relating to consent in cases involving the duties found in ss 175 and 177 of the CA 2006. These are discussed alongside their corresponding duties.

---

[21] Limitation Act 1980, s 21(3).

[22] *Burnden Holdings (UK) Ltd v Fielding* [2018] UKSC 14, [2018] 2 WLR 885 [11] (Lord Briggs).

[23] Limitation Act 1980, s 21(1)(a). This will include a fraudulent breach of duty (*First Subsea Ltd v Balltec Ltd* [2017] EWCA Civ 186, [2018] Ch 25 (permission to appeal to the Supreme Court has been granted)).

[24] Limitation Act 1980, s 21(1)(b). Section 21(1)(b) will continue to apply where the property in question remained legally and beneficially owned by the company (*Burnden Holdings (UK) Ltd v Fielding* [2018] UKSC 14, [2018] 2 WLR 885).

[25] As discussed at 11.1.4, s 175(5)(b) allows the directors of a public company to authorize a conflict if the articles so permit.

[26] CA 2006, s 175(6)(a).

10.1.3.2 **Exclusion and indemnity clauses**

A director may attempt to avoid liability for negligence, default, breach of duty, or breach of trust via a provision (e.g. in the articles or in his service contract) excluding such liability.[27] Section 232(1) of the CA 2006 provides that such a provision is void. The director may also try to obtain relief via a provision requiring the company to indemnify the director for any loss or liability sustained by him due to his breach of duty. Again, such a provision will be void,[28] except:

- where the company purchases and maintains insurance for a director in relation to liability for breach of duty;[29]
- where the company indemnifies directors in respect of proceedings brought by third parties;[30] or
- where the company, which is a trustee of an occupational pension scheme, indemnifies the director for liability incurred in connection with the company's activities as a trustee for an occupational pension scheme.[31]

10.1.3.3 **Ratification**

Section 239 of the CA 2006 puts in place a statutory scheme concerning the ratification of acts and omissions of directors (including former directors and shadow directors)[32] that amount to negligence, default, breach of duty, or breach of trust. Ratification requires a resolution of the company's members,[33] although s 239(6)(a) does state that the unanimous assent rule can apply. Where the director is also a member of the company, his votes (and those of members connected to him) will be disregarded,[34] although if the vote takes place at a company meeting, he may attend and will be counted towards the quorum.[35] Section 239(7) provides that s 239 does not affect any other enactment or rule of law imposing additional requirements for valid ratification, and so additional requirements imposed by the courts will remain valid, including:

 The unanimous assent rule is discussed at 14.2.

- The directors must have fully disclosed their interest in the transaction in breach.[36]
- The ratification by the members must be informed,[37] and the decision to ratify must be 'honest, bona fide and in the best interest of the company'.[38]
- The ratification 'must not be brought about by unfair or improper means, and is not illegal or oppressive towards the shareholders who oppose it'.[39]

Where effective ratification occurs, any cause of action that the company had in respect of the breach is extinguished, but this new scheme does not affect any previous rules of

---

[27] For an example of such a provision, which did permit the director to avoid liability, see *Re City Equitable Fire Insurance Co Ltd* [1925] Ch 407 (CA). This case led to the enactment of s 78 of the Companies Act 1928, which was the forerunner to s 232 of the CA 2006.

[28] CA 2006, s 232(2).   [29] ibid s 233.   [30] ibid s 234.   [31] ibid s 235.

[32] ibid s 239(5).   [33] ibid s 239(2).   [34] ibid s 239(3) and (4).

[35] ibid s 239(4). This is in contrast to the pre-CA 2006 position, which permitted an interested director's vote to count, provided that it was made in good faith (*North-West Transportation Co Ltd v Beatty* (1887) 12 App Cas 589 (PC)).

[36] *Kaye v Croydon Tramways Co* [1898] 1 Ch 358 (CA).   [37] *Knight v Frost* [1999] 1 BCLC 364 (Ch).

[38] *Madoff Securities International Ltd v Raven* [2011] EWHC 3102 (Comm), [2012] 2 All ER (Comm) 634 [123] (Flaux J).

[39] *North-West Transportation Co Ltd v Beatty* (1887) 12 App Cas 589 (PC) 593–4 (Sir Richard Baggallay), affirmed by *Franbar Holdings Ltd v Patel* [2008] EWHC 1534 (Ch), [2008] BCC 885.

law denying the ability to ratify.[40] Accordingly, acts that could not be ratified under pre-CA 2006 law (such as illegal acts,[41] acts not bona fide or honest,[42] and acts that involved a 'fraud on the minority'[43]) cannot be ratified under s 239.

10.1.3.4 **Relief from the court**

A director who is unable to obtain authorization or ratification from the directors or the members has one last option for avoiding liability—namely, the ability of the court to grant relief. Section 1157(1) allows a court that has found an officer (including a director, manager, or secretary)[44] or auditor of the company liable for negligence, default, breach of duty, or breach of trust, to grant that officer/auditor, either wholly or partly, relief from liability on such terms as it sees fit. Section 1157(2) allows an officer/auditor to petition the court for such relief where he has reason to believe that such a claim for negligence, etc. will be made against him.

The courts have imposed a number of limitations upon the availability of relief under s 1157. First, relief is not available in cases where a director has been completely inactive.[45] Second, Knox J in *Re Produce Marketing Consortium Ltd*[46] stated that relief from liability is not available in cases involving directors found liable for wrongful trading. Third, s 1157 only applies in cases involving claims by or on behalf of a company involving personal breaches of an officer/auditor.[47] Accordingly, relief under s 1157 is not available in cases where a third party is claiming against an officer/auditor for the company's default, or is seeking to recover a debt owed by an officer/auditor.[48] Finally, relief will only be granted where the court is of the opinion that the officer/auditor has established, on the balance of probabilities, that he has:

- acted honestly—a test that is subjective, meaning that the crucial factor is whether the officer actually believed that he acted honestly;[49]
- acted reasonably, which, unlike honesty, must be assessed objectively;[50]
- given all of the circumstances of the case, ought fairly to be excused. Given that *all* of the circumstances of the case need to be examined, it is very rare that a case involving the granting of relief under s 1157 will be struck out and, usually, a full trial should occur.[51]

The following case provides a classic example of the courts' discretion to grant relief from liability.

---

[40] CA 2007, s 239(7).   [41] *Re Exchange Banking Co (Flitcroft's Case)* (1882) 21 ChD 519 (CA).

[42] *Bowthorpe Holdings Ltd v Hills* [2002] EWHC 2331 (Ch), [2003] 1 BCLC 226.

[43] *Burland v Earle* [1902] AC 83 (PC).   [44] CA 2006, s 1173(1).

[45] *Lexi Holdings plc v Luqman* [2007] EWHC 2652 (Ch) (discussed at 10.5.1.2). This is a corollary of the requirement that the director must act reasonably (discussed below) and, by definition, an inactive director has not acted reasonably.

[46] [1989] 1 WLR 745 (Ch). This limitation has been criticized. See Derek French, *Mayson, French & Ryan on Company Law* (35th edn, OUP 2018) 506.

[47] *Custom and Excise Commissioners v Hedon Alpha Ltd* [1981] 2 QB 818 (CA).

[48] See e.g. *First Independent Factors and Finance Ltd v Mountford* [2008] EWHC 835 (Ch), [2008] BCC] 598; *Commissioners of Inland Revenue v McEntaggart* [2004] EWHC 3431 (Ch), [2007] BCC 260.

[49] *Coleman Taymar Ltd v Oakes* [2001] 2 BCLC 749 (Ch).

[50] *Re MDA Investment Management Ltd* [2004] EWHC 42 (Ch), [2005] BCC 783.

[51] *Equitable Life Assurance Society v Bowley* [2003] EWHC 2263 (Comm), [2004] 1 BCLC 180.

Re Duomatic Ltd [1969] 2 Ch 365 (Ch)

FACTS: Duomatic Ltd had three directors (Elvins, Hanly, and East), who owned all of Duomatic's ordinary shares. Elvins and East were critical of Hanly's performance and wished to remove him. Hanly threatened to sue if they tried to dismiss him so, instead, Elvins and East caused the company to pay Hanly £4,000 to leave. Hanly did so and transferred his shares to Elvins. Duomatic's articles provided that the directors' remuneration had to be authorized by the members, but no such resolution was ever passed. Instead, the directors drew sums from Duomatic as needed and, at the end of the year, the sums drawn were totalled and entered into Duomatic's accounts as 'directors' salaries'. These sums were drawn with the knowledge and approval of all of the members who were entitled to vote at general meetings. This practice continued until the year prior to Duomatic's liquidation, when Elvins, who by now was the majority shareholder, drew £9,000 before the company's final accounts had been prepared. Duomatic entered voluntary liquidation and the liquidator sought to claim (i) sums drawn by Elvins as salary; (ii) the £9,000 drawn by Elvins in the final year; and (iii) the £4,000 loss-of-office payment paid to Hanly.

HELD: Buckley J held that there was little doubt that all three payments were paid in breach of duty; the question arising was whether relief could be obtained. Regarding (i), the court held that relief should be granted and so the payment remained valid. Buckley J stated that:

> where it can be shown that all shareholders who have a right to attend and vote at a general meeting of the company assent to some matter which a general meeting of the company could carry into effect, that assent is as binding as a resolution in general meeting would be.[52]

The court also granted relief for (ii), stating that Elvins was merely following a practice that had been followed in preceding years. However, Buckley J refused to grant relief for (iii) and held that Elvins and Hanly were jointly liable to pay back the £4,000. There was no disclosure or authorization under what, today, would be s 217 of the CA 2006, and it was therefore a misapplication of Duomatic's funds.

Section 217 is discussed at 11.4.4.1.

Having covered the basic issues surrounding the general duties, we will now look at the general duties themselves, beginning with the duty to act within powers.

10.2 Duty to act within powers

The first general duty is contained in s 171 and is an amalgam of two prior common law duties, namely:

(a) the duty to act in accordance with the company's constitution; and

(b) the duty to exercise powers only for the purposes for which they are conferred.

10.2.1 Duty to act in accordance with the constitution

As discussed at 9.2.1, a company's articles typically confer exclusive managerial power upon the directors. However, it is common for companies to impose some form of limitation on the power of the directors via the constitution and, if a director acts in a manner that is not in accordance with the company's constitution, then he may find himself

---

[52] [1969] 2 Ch 365 (Ch) 373.

in breach of the duty in s 171(a), which provides that a director 'must act in accordance with the company's constitution'.

A director who breaches the s 171(a) duty will be required to account for any gains made and to indemnify the company for any losses resulting from the relevant act. However, as discussed at 6.2.2, any transactions or contracts that result from an *ultra vires* act will still bind the company.[53] At common law, liability for breach of s 171(a) can be avoided if the members ratify the breach by passing an ordinary resolution,[54] and ratification will now be conducted via the s 239 procedure. It should be noted that a resolution relieving a director of liability for breaching the articles will not effect a change in the articles—the usual procedure must still be followed to amend the articles.

> The s 239 ratification procedure is discussed at 10.1.3.3.

10.2.2 Duty to exercise powers for purposes for which they are conferred

Of the two duties in s 171, it is generally regarded that the duty is s 171(b) is the more important. The duty in s 171(b) is based on the common law 'proper purpose' doctrine[55] and provides that directors 'only exercise powers for the purposes for which they are conferred'. A purpose outside this scope is usually known as an 'improper purpose', and the burden of proof for establishing that a purpose is improper is placed upon the claimant.[56] The purpose of this duty was set out by Lord Sumption, who stated:

> The rule that the fiduciary powers of directors may be exercised only for the purposes for which they were conferred is one of the main means by which equity enforces the proper conduct of directors. It is also fundamental to the constitutional distinction between the respective domains of the board and the shareholders. These considerations are particularly important when the company is in play between competing groups seeking to control or influence its affairs.[57]

10.2.2.1 The four-part test

In *Howard Smith Ltd v Ampol Petroleum Ltd*,[58] Lord Wilberforce set out the test used by the courts in order to determine whether the exercise of a duty was proper, namely that:

> it is necessary to start with a consideration of the power whose exercise is in question. . . . Having ascertained, on a fair view, the nature of this power, and having defined as can best be done in the light of modern conditions the, or some, limits within which it may be exercised, it is then necessary for the court, if a particular exercise of it is challenged, to examine the substantial purpose for which it was exercised, and to reach a conclusion whether that purpose was proper or not.[59]

---

[53] CA 2006, ss 39 and 40.

[54] *Grant v United Kingdom Switchback Railways Co* (1888) 40 ChD 135 (CA).

[55] The classic exposition of this comes from Lord Greene MR in *Re Smith & Fawcett Ltd* [1942] Ch 304 (CA) 306, who stated that the directors must act 'not for any collateral purpose'.

[56] *Re Coalport China Co* [1895] 2 Ch 404 (CA).

[57] *Eclairs Group Ltd v JKX Oil & Gas plc* [2015] UKSC 71, [2016] 3 All ER 641 [37].

[58] [1974] AC 821 (PC).   [59] ibid 835.

It has been argued that Lord Wilberforce's test involves four parts.[60] First, the court will determine what power is being exercised. The duty is extremely broad as it can apply to any power exercised by a director, including the power to enter into contracts on the company's behalf,[61] to make calls on shares[62] or to order shares be forfeited,[63] to refuse to register a share transfer,[64] to expel a member,[65] to call general meetings,[66] and to borrow and provide security.[67] Despite the breadth of the duty, in practice, cases have tended to congregate around certain powers, most notably the power to allot shares (e.g. *Howard Smith* itself discussed below). The breadth of the duty means that a breach of the other general duties might also constitute a breach of s 171(b)—for example, a director who improperly acts so as to benefit himself financially might find, in addition to a breach of the s 171(b) duty, that the duty in s 172 or one of the conflict of interest duties might also be breached.

Second, the court will then determine 'the proper purpose for which that power was delegated to the directors'.[68] This will involve determining 'the nature of the power [and] in light of modern conditions the, or some, limits within which it may be exercised . . .'.[69] The rationale behind this focus on the limits of the power was explained by Turner LJ, who stated '[p]owers given to [the directors] for one purpose cannot, in my opinion, be used by them for another and different purpose. To permit such proceedings on the part of the directors of companies would be to sanction not the use but the abuse of their powers'.[70] The most obvious way in which the limits of a power are exceeded is where the directors act outside the scope of the constitution (thereby demonstrating a notable overlap between the duties in s 171(a) and (b)). However, constitutional limits are not the only factor. Indeed, as Lord Sumption has noted, '[t]he purpose of a power conferred by a company's articles is rarely expressed in the instrument itself'.[71] The purpose of a power cannot be determined in advance and will need to be determined by a range of factors, including the power's 'context and effect'.[72] This breadth and flexibility is essential as 'the variety of situations facing directors of different types of company in different situations cannot be anticipated'.[73]

Third, the court will determine 'the substantial purpose for which the power was in fact exercised'.[74] The existence of this part of the test acknowledges that directors will often exercise powers for a range of purposes, and it may be the case that both proper and improper purposes are present. *Howard Smith* itself demonstrates that, in such a case, it is the propriety of the substantial purpose that will determine whether a breach of s 171(b) has occurred.

---

[60] *Extrasure Travel Insurances Ltd v Scattergood* [2003] 1 BCLC 598 (Ch) [92] (Jonathan Crow); *Madoff Securities International Ltd v Raven* [2013] EWHC 3147 (Comm), [2014] Lloyd's Rep FC 95 [196] (Popplewell J).

[61] *Lee Panavision Ltd v Lee Lighting Ltd* [1991] BCC 620 (CA).

[62] *Galloway v Hallé Concerts Society* [1915] 2 Ch 233 (Ch).

[63] *Re Agriculturalist Cattle Insurance Co* (1866) LR 1 Ch App 161.

[64] *Re Smith & Fawcett Ltd* [1942] Ch 304 (CA).

[65] *Gaiman v National Association for Mental Health* [1971] Ch 317 (Ch).

[66] *Pergamon Press Ltd v Maxwell* [1970] 1 WLR 1167 (Ch).

[67] *Rolled Steel Products (Holdings) Ltd v British Steel Corp* [1986] Ch 246 (CA).

[68] *Extrasure Travel Insurances Ltd v Scattergood* [2003] 1 BCLC 598 (Ch) [92] (Jonathan Crow).

[69] *Howard Smith Ltd v Ampol Petroleum Ltd* [1974] AC 821 (PC) 835.

[70] *Re Cameron's Coalbrook Steam Coal, and Swansea and Lougher Railway Co* (1854) 5 De GM&G 284, 298.

[71] *Eclairs Group Ltd v JKX Oil & Gas plc* [2015] UKSC 71, [2015] Bus LR 1395 [31].

[72] ibid.   [73] *Howard Smith Ltd v Ampol Petroleum Ltd* [1974] AC 821 (PC) 835 (Lord Wilberforce).

[74] *Extrasure Travel Insurances Ltd v Scattergood* [2003] 1 BCLC 598 (Ch) [92] (Jonathan Crow).

See JH Farrar, 'Abuse of Power by Directors' (1974) 33 CLJ 221.

Howard Smith Ltd v Ampol Petroleum Ltd [1974] AC 821 (PC)

FACTS: Ampol Petroleum Ltd ('Ampol') controlled 55 per cent of the shares in RW Miller (Holdings) Ltd ('Miller') and wished to take it over. A rival bid was made by Howard Smith Ltd ('HS') but was rejected by Miller's majority shareholder—namely, Ampol. Miller favoured HS's bid because it was higher than Ampol's bid but, given that Ampol was Miller's majority shareholder, HS's bid could never succeed. Miller's directors therefore caused Miller to issue $10 million worth of new shares to HS, the purpose of which was twofold: first, it would allow Miller to raise much-needed finance for the building of two oil tankers; and second, it would relegate Ampol's holdings to 37 per cent, thereby making it a minority shareholder. Ampol alleged that the issuing of the shares was for an improper purpose.

HELD: The substantial purpose was to 'dilute the majority voting power held by Ampol . . . so as to enable a then minority of shareholders to sell their shares more advantageously'.[75] Lord Wilberforce went on to state that 'an issue of shares purely for the purpose of creating voting power has repeatedly been condemned',[76] so it was held that the directors of HS had acted for an improper purpose and the allotment of shares was set aside.

COMMENT: As noted, many cases relating to the s 171(b) duty relate to the directors' power to issue shares and the courts have repeatedly stated that the directors may not use their power to allot shares 'merely for the purpose of maintaining their control or the control of themselves and their friends over the affairs of the company, or merely for the purpose of defeating the wishes of the existing majority of shareholders'.[77] Similarly, it will be a breach of s 171(b) if the substantial purpose of an allotment of shares is to financially benefit the directors themselves.[78]

Fourth and finally, after determining the substantial purpose, the court will 'decide whether that purpose was proper'.[79] The traditional viewpoint, as evidenced in *Howard Smith*, is that if the substantial purpose is improper, a breach will occur irrespective of the fact that other subservient proper purposes exist. Conversely, if the substantial purpose is proper, no breach will occur, even if subservient improper purposes exist. However, this view was challenged by Lord Sumption in the following case.

See Richard Nolan, 'Proper Purposes in the Supreme Court' (2016) 132 LQR 369.

Section 793 is discussed at 13.3.1.1.

Eclairs Group Ltd v JKX Oil & Gas plc [2015] UKSC 71

FACTS: The board of JKX Oil & Gas plc ('JKX') believed that JKX was the target of a 'corporate raid' under which two minority shareholders, Eclairs Group Ltd ('Eclairs') and Glengary Overseas Ltd ('Glengary'), would seek to obtain control of JKX. Section 793 of the CA 2006 allows a company to issue a notice to a person, requiring that person to disclose certain information regarding their shares. Article 42 of JKX's articles provided that, if a s 793 notice was not complied with, JKX could place restrictions upon the non-complying party, including disenfranchising that party's shares. JKX issued a s 793 notice to Eclairs and Glengary, but was not satisfied with the information received. Accordingly, JKX's directors exercised the power under art 42, thereby preventing Eclairs and Glengary from voting at the upcoming AGM (Eclairs and Glengary planned to vote against a

---

[75] [1974] AC 821 (PC) 837 (Lord Wilberforce).   [76] ibid.
[77] *Piercy v S Mills & Co Ltd* [1920] 1 Ch 77 (Ch) 84 (Peterson J).
[78] *Ngurli Ltd v McCann* (1953) 90 CLR 425.
[79] *Extrasure Travel Insurances Ltd v Scattergood* [2003] 1 BCLC 598 (Ch) [92] (Jonathan Crow).

number of resolutions tabled by the board of JKX). Eclairs and Glengary contended that the board of JKX had exercised the art 42 power for an improper purpose.

HELD: The s 171(b) duty was breached. Lord Sumption stated that 'a battle for control of the company is probably the one in which the proper purpose rule has the most valuable part to play'.[80] He went on to distinguish between 'protecting the company and its shareholders against the consequences of non-provision of the information, and seeking to manipulate the fate of particular shareholders' resolutions or to alter the balance of forces at the company's general meetings'.[81] The Court held unanimously that the board of JKX had exercised the power in art 42 for the latter purpose and, unsurprisingly, held this to be an improper purpose. Accordingly, the disenfranchisement of Eclairs and Glengary was invalid and the votes of these companies would count, resulting in the retrospective invalidation of two resolutions at JKX's AGM.

COMMENT: Lord Sumption, who gave the leading judgment, appeared to move away from *Howard Smith* somewhat by stating *obiter* that the s 171(b) duty provides that directors should exercise their powers 'only' for the purposes for which they are conferred and, therefore, '[t]hat duty is broken if they allow themselves to be influenced by any improper purpose'.[82] In adopting this position, Lord Sumption was advocating the application of the 'but for' test adopted in Australia,[83] under which the courts will ask but for the improper purpose, would the power have been exercised. Whilst Lord Hodge agreed with Lord Sumption, Lord Mance did not,[84] and the other two Justices declined to express a view on this point, meaning that, for the time being, the traditional view of *Howard Smith* remains good law.

One question that has arisen is whether liability under s 171(b) is strict, or whether it requires some level of knowledge or fault on the part of the directors. Whilst there is authority for the imposition of strict liability,[85] and most of the comments on this issue are *obiter*, the more popular view tends to be that a director cannot be found in breach of s 171(b) 'unless he knows that it is an improper purpose or of the facts which make the purpose improper'.[86] Accordingly, 'the state of mind of those who acted, and the motive on which they acted, are all important . . .'.[87] However, whilst the courts will take the subjective intentions of the directors into account, the courts' determination of the propriety of the purpose will be conducted objectively. As Lord Wilberforce stated:

> when a dispute arises whether directors of a company made a particular decision for one purpose or for another, or whether, there being more than one purpose, one or another purpose was the substantial or primary purpose, the court . . . is entitled to look at the situation objectively. . . .[88]

Accordingly, 'statements by the directors about their subjective intention, whilst relevant, are not conclusive'.[89] For example, the court can find that a breach of s 171(b) has

---

[80] [2015] UKSC 71, [2016] 3 All ER 641 [42].   [81] ibid [33].   [82] ibid [21].

[83] *Whitehouse v Carlton House Pty* (1987) 162 CLR 258 (High Court of Australia).

[84] [2015] UKSC 71, [2016] 3 All ER 641 [53].

[85] See e.g. the judgment of Lord Hope in *Revenue and Customs Commissioners v Holland* [2010] UKSC 51, [2010] 1 WLR 2793.

[86] *Madoff Securities International Ltd v Raven* [2013] EWHC 3147 (Comm), [2014] Lloyd's Rep FC 95 [200] (Popplewell J).

[87] *Hindle v John Cotton Ltd* (1919) 56 SLR 625, 630 (Viscount Finlay).

[88] *Howard Smith Ltd v Ampol Petroleum Ltd* [1974] AC 821 (PC) 832.

[89] *Advance Bank of Australia Ltd v FAI Insurances Australia Ltd* (1987) 9 NSWLR 464, 485 (Kirby P).

occurred even where a director honestly believed that his actions were bona fide in the company's interests.[90] The courts have stated that their role should not be overly interventionist. For example, Lord Wilberforce stated '[t]here is no appeal on merits from management decisions to courts of law: nor will courts of law assume to act as a kind of supervisory board over decisions within the powers of management honestly arrived at'.[91] Despite this, it has been argued that the increased prominence that the courts have attached to the proper purpose duty 'involves to a large extent the court substituting its own judgment for that of the directors'[92] and that 'there can be no question but that the courts are themselves becoming involved and playing an interventionist role'.[93]

10.2.2.2 Remedies

Where a director acts for an improper purpose, he may be required to account for any gains made or compensate the company for any loss sustained,[94] unless the members ratify the breach of duty.[95] In addition, any agreement entered into by a director in breach of s 171(b) is voidable at the company's instance,[96] unless the agreement is ratified.[97] However, a third party to such an agreement will be able to enforce it against the company if the director had authority to enter into it, as the following case demonstrates.

See Peter Watts, 'Authority and Mismotivation' (2005) 121 LQR 4.

Criterion Properties plc v Stratford UK Properties LLC [2004] UKHL 28

FACTS: Criterion Properties plc ('Criterion') entered into a joint venture with Stratford UK Properties LLC (referred to here and in the case as 'Oaktree'). Glaser, the managing director of Criterion, caused Criterion to enter into a contract, clause 7A of which contained a 'poison pill' provision. The provision provided that, if any person gained control of Criterion, or if Glaser or the chair of Criterion were to cease to be a director or employee of Criterion, then Criterion had to buy Oaktree out of the joint venture on terms that were extremely favourable to Oaktree. The purpose of clause 7A was to deter a takeover of Criterion by ensuring that Criterion's value would be much reduced following a takeover. Glaser was dismissed by Criterion and Oaktree sought to exercise clause 7A. Criterion refused to honour clause 7A (largely on the ground that the rest of Criterion's board had not authorized Glaser to enter into the agreement that contained clause 7A) and commenced proceedings, alleging that in entering into the poison pill agreement, Glaser had acted for an improper purpose, and so it could set aside the agreement.

HELD: The House of Lords stated that, in determining whether Oaktree could enforce clause 7A, the issue was not whether Glaser had acted for an improper purpose. The key issue was whether, based on agency law principles, Glaser had actual or apparent authority to enter into the poison pill agreement on behalf of Criterion. If he did, then Oaktree could enforce the agreement against Criterion. If not, it could not be enforced. As the issue of Glaser's authority was not addressed at

---

90 *Hogg v Cramphorn Ltd* [1967] Ch 254 (Ch).   91 ibid 832.
92 Len Sealy, 'Directors' Duties Revisited' (2001) 22 Co Law 79, 82.   93 ibid.
94 *Extrasure Travel Insurances Ltd v Scattergood* [2003] 1 BCLC 598 (Ch).
95 *Hogg v Cramphorn Ltd* [1967] Ch 254 (Ch).
96 *Howard Smith Ltd v Ampol Petroleum Ltd* [1974] AC 821 (PC).
97 *Bamford v Bamford* [1970] 2 Ch 212 (CA).

first instance nor in the Court of Appeal, it was not open for the House to determine the issue, and had to be resolved at trial.

COMMENT: A third party may be able to hold the company to an agreement if the third party can take advantage of s 40 of the CA 2006. It should be noted that utilizing s 40 to bind the company to the act of a director will not absolve that director of liability for breach of duty.[98]

Section 40 is discussed at 6.4.1.

A breach of s 171(b) might also result in separate proceedings under which the director could be disqualified, usually on the ground of unfitness.[99]

10.3 Duty to promote the success of the company

The duty contained in s 172 has been labelled as 'one of the more important and controversial provisions in the Companies Act 2006'[100] and was undoubtedly the duty that received most Parliamentary discussion during the passage of the Companies Bill. Section 172 contains a reformulation of the common law duty to act bona fide in the interests of the company.[101] Section 172(1) requires the director to 'act in the way he considers, in good faith, would be most likely to promote the success of the company for the benefit of its members as a whole'. The burden of establishing a breach of s 172 is placed upon the person alleging breach of duty.[102]

Before the key phrases found in s 172 are discussed, it is important to note that the s 172 duty is a broad one and often impacts upon other duties. For example, in *Item Software (UK) Ltd v Fassihi*,[103] the Court held that a director who breaches a fiduciary duty will be required to disclose that breach of duty to the company if the duty to act in the interests of the company requires such disclosure. The court in *British Midland Tool Ltd v Midland International Tooling Ltd*[104] held that this obligation extends to disclosing the breaches of fellow directors. In keeping with the subjective nature of this duty, the key factor is whether the director honestly considers that it is in the company's interest to know about the breach.[105] Clearly, disclosure of a breach of duty will usually be in the company's interests and a failure to do so might result in a breach of s 172, in addition to a breach of the original duty. A failure to disclose can result in a loss of employment benefits (e.g. share options, or certain employment rights) and may provide a justification for summary dismissal.[106] In *GHLM Trading Ltd v Maroo*,[107] Newey J went further and stated,

---

[98] CA 2006, s 40(5).   [99] See e.g. *Re Looe Fish Ltd* [1993] BCC 348 (Ch).

[100] Geoffrey Morse, *Palmer's Company Law* (Sweet & Maxwell 2018) para 8.2601.

[101] *Re Smith and Fawcett Ltd* [1942] Ch 304 (CA) 306 (Lord Greene MR): the directors must act 'bona fide in what they consider—not what a court may consider—is in the interest of the company . . .'.

[102] *Charles Forte Investments v Amanda* [1964] Ch 240 (CA).

[103] [2004] EWCA Civ 1244, [2004] BCC 994.

[104] [2003] EWHC 466 (Ch), [2003] 2 BCLC 523.

[105] *Fulham Football Club (1987) Ltd v Tigana* [2004] EWHC 2585 (QB).

[106] *Tesco Stores Ltd v Pook* [2003] EWHC 823 (Ch), [2004] IRLR 618.

[107] [2012] EWHC 61 (Ch), [2012] 2 BCLC 369.

obiter, that this duty of disclosure could extend to disclosing matters other than wrongdoing and that disclosure might be justified to a person other than a board member.

10.3.1 'Act in the way he considers'

A director is required to 'act in the way he considers' promotes the success of the company, thereby indicating that the duty is subjective. The significance of this was set out by Jonathan Parker J, who stated:

> The question is not whether, viewed objectively by the court, the particular act or omission which is challenged was in fact in the interests of the company; still less is the question whether the court, had it been in the position of the director at the relevant time, might have acted differently. Rather, the question is whether the director honestly believed that his act or omission was in the interests of the company. The issue is as to the director's state of mind.[108]

The rationale behind this approach is straightforward—it is not the court's place to substitute its beliefs for those of the directors. As Lord Wilberforce stated '[t]here is no appeal on merits from management decisions to courts of law: nor will courts of law assume to act as a kind of supervisory board over decisions within the powers of management honestly arrived at'.[109] It follows that, provided that the decision of the directors was honest, it does not matter that it was unreasonable.[110] The subjectivity of the duty can be seen in the following case.

Regentcrest plc v Cohen [2001] BCC 494 (Ch)

FACTS: In 1988, Regentcrest plc agreed to purchase all the shares in Greenground Ltd, so that it could acquire and develop a piece of land that Greenground owned. Greenground's shares were owned by Scott and Farley (two directors of Regentcrest) and Cohen (a former director of Regentcrest). The contract for the sale of the shares contained a clawback provision which provided that if the asset value of Greenground (namely the value of the piece of land) decreased up to the date of the completion of the land's development, then Scott, Farley, and Cohen would be liable to pay Regentcrest the shortfall in cash. By 1990, Regentcrest was in serious financial difficulty and the value of the land had fallen by £1.5 million. Despite this, the board of Regentcrest decided to waive all claims under the clawback provision, providing that Scott and Farley worked for Regentcrest for no remuneration for the next three years.[111] A few weeks later, Regentcrest went into liquidation and the liquidator alleged that the directors of Regentcrest had, in waiving the clawback provision, not acted in the interests of the company and were more concerned with protecting Scott and Farley from liability.

HELD: Jonathan Parker J was convinced that the directors of Regentcrest had decided to waive the clawback claim due to a desire to 'maintain a united board, and not to create a situation in which two of the directors were being sued by Regentcrest and were contesting the claim'.[112] As the directors honestly believed such action to be in Regentcrest's interests, there was no breach of duty.

---

[108] *Regentcrest plc v Cohen* [2001] BCC 494 (Ch) 513.

[109] *Howard Smith Ltd v Ampol Petroleum Ltd* [1974] AC 821 (PC) 832.

[110] *Extrasure Travel Insurance Ltd v Scattergood* [2003] 1 BCLC 598 (Ch).

[111] It should be noted that Scott and Farley took no part in this board decision due to the obvious conflict of interest.

[112] [2001] BCC 494 (Ch) 519.

There are, however, two problems with a subjective test. First, in *Hutton v West Cork Rly Co*,[113] Bowen LJ stated that if the duty were entirely subjective then 'you might have a lunatic conducting the affairs of the company, and paying away its money with both hands in a manner perfectly bona fide yet perfectly irrational'.[114] Accordingly, the courts will closely examine the evidence and try to determine whether or not the directors honestly believed that their actions were designed to promote the success of the company for the benefit of its members. It should be noted that the test still remains primarily subjective—the court is simply objectively determining, based on the evidence, whether the directors had the subjective motives they claimed to have.[115] So, for example, where a director's act or omission causes the company harm, the court will not be easily persuaded that the director honestly believed his actions to be in the company's interest.[116]

Second, a subjective text will, for obvious reasons, be of no aid where the directors did not consider at all whether their actions promoted the success of the company. In such a case, the test to be applied is an objective one, as the following case established.

Charterbridge Corporation Ltd v Lloyds Bank Ltd [1970] Ch 62 (Ch)

FACTS: Pomeroy Developments (Castleford) Ltd ('Castleford') was one of a group of companies, which was headed by Pomeroy Developments Ltd ('PD'). The shares in all the companies in the group were either owned or controlled by Mr and Mrs Pomeroy. The board of Castleford caused it to enter into an agreement with Lloyds Bank, which provided that Castleford would guarantee the indebtedness of PD and other companies in the group. This guarantee was secured by way of a charge. A dispute arose regarding the enforcement of the charge and was contended that the agreement between Castleford and Lloyds Bank was void, *inter alia*, because the directors of Castleford did not believe it to be bona fide in the interests of the company.

HELD: Pennycuick J noted that 'the directors of Castleford looked to the benefit of the group as a whole and did not give separate consideration to the benefit of Castleford'.[117] Accordingly, a subjective test was of no use. In such a case, the test would be 'whether an intelligent and honest man in the position of a director of the company concerned, could, in the whole of the existing circumstances, have reasonably believed that the transactions were for the benefit of the company'.[118] Applying this test, Pennycuick J held that the agreement was valid.

COMMENT: The approach taken in *Charterbridge* has been criticized and it has been argued that directors who fail to consider the company's interests should be found to have breached the s 172 duty.[119] Pennycuick J thought such an approach to be 'unduly stringent',[120] noting that such an approach could lead to a director being found in breach of duty even where his actions actually do benefit the company.

---

[113] (1883) LR 23 ChD 654 (CA).   [114] ibid 671.   [115] *Regentcrest plc v Cohen* [2001] BCC 494 (Ch).
[116] ibid.   [117] [1970] Ch 62 (Ch) 74.   [118] ibid.
[119] See e.g. Rosemary Teele Langford and Ian M Ramsay, 'Directors' Duty to Act in the Interests of the Company—Subjective or Objective?' [2015] JBL 173, 181.
[120] [1970] Ch 62 (Ch) 74.

10.3.2 'Success of the company'

The common law bona fide duty defined 'the company' to effectively mean the members. It is clear that, under the s 172 duty, the phrase 'the company' refers to the entity itself. The rationale behind phrasing the duty to refer to the company and the members was set out by the Company Law Review Steering Group as follows:

> We believe there is value in inserting a reference to the success of the company, since what is in view is not the individual interests of members, but their interests as members of an association with the purposes and the mutual arrangements embodied in the constitution; the objective is to be achieved by the directors successfully managing the complex of relationships and resources which comprise the company's undertaking.[121]

The key question to ask is how success is to be determined and the Act provides no guidance on this. The word 'success' is a broad one that could include a range of performance measures, both financial and non-financial (as is appropriate, given the broad range of purposes that companies are set up for). In most commercial companies, success is normally measured financially, but the company itself is free to define its success in other terms. As Lord Goldsmith noted during debate on the Company Law Reform Bill 'for a commercial company, success will normally mean long-term increase in value, but the company's constitution and decisions made under it may also lay down the appropriate success model for the company'.[122] Accordingly, companies are free to determine what they regard as a success by inserting provisions into their articles that indicate how success is to be determined, although very few companies do.

10.3.3 'For the benefit of its members as a whole'

The duty does not focus on the company's success as an end in itself. Instead, the directors must promote the success of the company for the benefit of its members as a whole. The Company Law Review Steering Group did consider removing reference to the members and defining success simply by reference to the company, but rejected this approach on the ground that 'it would allow directors a discretionary power to set any interest above that of shareholders whenever their view of what constitutes "the company's success" required it'.[123]

Accordingly, the question to ask is how the members' benefit is to be assessed. For most members, the principal motive behind purchasing shares will be to acquire a financial return, so it might be assumed that what is of benefit to the members would be determined financially. A financial benefit can, however, take numerous forms (e.g. increases in share value, higher dividend payments, etc.). It could also be argued that Lord Goldsmith's statement that success normally means a 'long term increase in value' could be interpreted to mean that benefitting members means increasing share value

---

[121] Company Law Review Steering Group (CLRSG), 'Modern Company Law for a Competitive Economy: Developing the Framework' (DTI 2000) para 3.51.
[122] HL Deb 6 Feb 2006, vol 678, col GC258.
[123] CLRSG, 'Modern Company Law for a Competitive Economy: Developing the Framework' (DTI 2000) [3.52].

over the long term (although, rather worryingly, the Kay Review found that some directors thought s 172 required them to maximize the current share price).[124] Fortunately, the courts have not sought to place strict parameters on what a benefit is, and have even acknowledged that shares are often purchased for non-financial motives, meaning that directors may be acting in the company's interests even if their actions cause the share price to decrease, as occurred in the following case.

CAS (Nominees) Ltd v Nottingham Forest plc [2002] BCC 145 (Ch)

FACTS: In 1997, Nottingham Forest plc ('NF plc') was set up by a consortium of investors to allow them to purchase all the shares in Nottingham Forest FC Ltd ('NF Ltd'), the company that owned Nottingham Forest Football Club. In 1999, it was proposed that, in order to raise much-needed finance, NF plc would cause NF Ltd to issue new shares that would be acquired by an outside investor. The effect of this was that NF plc would become a minority shareholder of NF Ltd. A number of NF plc's minority shareholders petitioned the court, stating that, as the effect of the share issue was to relegate NF plc to the status of minority shareholder, it was not in the interests of the company.

HELD: The petition was dismissed. Hart J stated that:

> conventional value drivers, and valuation methods, are inappropriate to most football club shares. The primary driver of value of a controlling interest in a football club is the desire of individuals (or a group of individuals) to control or have significant influence over the club. That desire would not arise from any expectation on the part of the investor that he would see a financial return. It was simply the desire to own or control a football club for its own sake.[125]

The formulation of the s 172 duty leads us to ask whether the interests of the company or its members should take priority. In many cases, the interests of the company and its members will align, so no problem arises, but there will be cases where their interests conflict. Whilst a number of academics contend that the interests of the company should be given priority,[126] the case law does not seem to establish this categorically. What the case law appears to say is that where the interests of the company and part of its membership conflict preference should be given to the interests of the company. As Arden J stated, '[t]he law does not require the interests of the company to be sacrificed in the particular interests of *a group of shareholders*'.[127]

Mutual Life Insurance Co of New York v Rank Organisation Ltd [1985] BCLC 11 (Ch)

FACTS: Rank Organisation Ltd issued twenty million shares, half of which were made available, on preferential terms, to existing shareholders. However, existing shareholders in the US and Canada were excluded from this offer on the ground that to include them would require the company to comply with complex legislation in those countries which would prove costly and therefore

---

[124] Department for Business, Innovation and Skills (BIS), 'The Kay Review of UK Equity Markets and Long-Term Decision Making: Final Report' (BIS 2012) 17.

[125] [2002] BCC 145 (Ch) 171.

[126] See e.g. Geoffrey Morse, *Palmer's Company Law* (Sweet & Maxwell 2018) para 8.2605.

[127] *Re BSB Holdings Ltd (No 2)* [1996] 1 BCLC 155 (Ch) 251 (italics added).

> would not be in the company's interests. Mutual Life Insurance Co of New York (an organization acting on behalf of a number of Rank's American shareholders) objected to the exclusion.
>
> **HELD:** Rank's directors had exercised their powers in the interest of the company, and the directors, in favouring the company over some part of the members, had not therefore breached their duty.
>
> **COMMENT:** *Mutual Life* shows that the directors can favour the company over part of its membership. Whether the directors can favour the company over the members as a whole is unclear.

It should be noted that the directors are required to promote the success of the company to benefit the members *as a whole*. From this, it follows that decisions that benefit one group of members over another could amount to a breach of s 172.[128] This is backed up by s 172(1)(f), which requires the directors to have regard to 'the need to act fairly between members of the company'.

Finally, s 172(2) provides that '[w]here or to the extent that the purposes of the company consist of or include purposes other than the benefit of its members, [s 172(1)] has effect as if the reference to promoting the success of the company for the benefit of its members were to achieving those purposes'. So, for example, a company set up to promote environmental protection could insert a provision in its articles providing that all profits are to be invested into environmental protection programmes. The existence of s 172(2) recognizes that there are companies that do not exist primarily in order to benefit their members, and s 172(2) allows such companies to prioritize other concerns (e.g. social, charitable, or environmental goals) over the benefit of the members. Whilst most companies are unlikely to utilize s 172(2), it will be of use to non-profit companies or Community Interest Companies.

🔗 Community interest companies are discussed at 3.3.4.1.

10.3.4 **Relevant factors**

A common criticism levelled at the common law bona fide duty was that it overly prioritized the interests of the members and failed to acknowledge the effects that directors' actions can have on other stakeholders (e.g. creditors, employees, the environment, etc.). Mindful of this, the Company Law Review Steering Group explored two options aimed at ensuring that the directors took a more stakeholder-inclusive approach:

1. The 'enlightened shareholder value approach' argues that 'the ultimate objective of companies as currently enshrined in law (i.e. to generate maximum value for shareholders) is in principle the best means also of securing overall prosperity and welfare'.[129] However, it then goes on to note that 'exclusive focus on the short-term financial bottom line, in the erroneous belief that this equates to shareholder value, will often be incompatible with the cultivation of co-operative relationships, which are likely to involve short-term costs but to bring greater benefits in the longer term'.[130]

2. The 'pluralist approach' argues that 'the ultimate objective of maximising shareholder value will not achieve maximum prosperity and welfare'[131] and therefore 'company law

---

[128] *Mills v Mills* (1938) 60 CLR 150 (High Court of Australia).

[129] CLRSG, 'Modern Company Law for a Competitive Economy: The Strategic Framework' (DTI 1999) para 5.1.12.

[130] ibid.   [131] ibid para 5.1.13.

should be modified to include other objectives so that a company is required to serve a wider range of interests, not subordinate to, or as a means of achieving, shareholder value (as envisaged in the enlightened shareholder value view), but as valid in their own right.[132]

The Review Group rejected the pluralist approach on several grounds, namely that (i) it would confer an overly broad discretion upon directors; (ii) it might not achieve its objectives, given the largely unpoliced nature of managerial discretion; and (iii) it would allow directors to frustrate a takeover bid against the wishes of the shareholders where a wider public interest would require it.[133] It was also noted that a suitably drafted enlightened shareholder value approach would render a pluralist approach redundant. Accordingly, the task was to draft a formulation that gave priority to the members, but also required directors to take into account the interests of other stakeholders. The result can be found in s 172(1), which provides that the directors must 'have regard (amongst other matters) to:

(a) the likely consequences of any decision in the long term,

(b) the interests of the company's employees,

(c) the need to foster the company's business relationships with suppliers, customers and others,

(d) the impact of the company's operations on the community and the environment,

(e) the desirability of the company maintaining a reputation for high standards of business conduct, and

(f) the need to act fairly as between members of the company'.

A large company is required to include a 'section 172(1) statement' in its strategic report, which sets out how it has had regard to the matters contained in s 172(1). It should be noted that the phrase 'amongst other matters' indicates that the factors listed are not exhaustive. For example, as Lord Goldsmith noted, the listed factors make no reference to the profitability of a transaction, nor do they refer to the short-term consequences of the directors' actions.[134] Rather than attempt to exhaustively state all the factors (which would likely be impossible) the government preferred to identify key factors, and then allow directors to have regard to other factors deemed relevant.

🔗 The section 172(1) statement is discussed at 19.3.2.1.

It is important to note that, even though the directors must have regard to the interests of certain persons under s 172(1), none of those persons have standing to bring a claim against the directors for breach of duty (except the members who can bring a derivative claim on behalf of the company). This is because, as was discussed at 10.1.2.2, the duty in s 172 (like all general duties) is owed to the company, and it is therefore the company that has the right to commence proceedings for breach. It has been argued that the inability of stakeholders to sue for breach renders s 172 'toothless'.[135]

The directors must 'have regard' to the factors in s 172(1)(a)–(f), leading us to ask what 'have regard' means. It is clear that 'have regard' does not permit the directors to use the factors in s 172(1)(a)–(f) to override the principal duty to promote the success

---

[132] ibid.

[133] For a more detailed discussion of the reasons for rejecting a pluralist approach, see CLRSG, 'Modern Company Law for a Competitive Economy: Developing the Framework' (DTI 2000) paras 3.24–3.31.

[134] HL Deb 9 May 2006, vol 681, col 846.

[135] Ji Lian Yap, 'Considering the Enlightened Shareholder Value Principle' (2010) 31 Co Law 35, 36.

of the company. Lord Goldsmith stated that 'while a director must have regard to the various factors, that is subordinate to the overriding duty to act in the way the director, "considers, in good faith, would be most likely to promote the success of the company"'.[136] Accordingly, the directors can only have regard to the s 172(1) factors to the extent that they also promote the success of the company for the benefit if its members and 'if a director puts one of those factors ahead of his overarching duty to promote the success of the company, he acts in breach of that duty to the company'.[137]

As to what degree of consideration the directors must give to the s 172(1) factors, Lord Goldsmith stated:

> We want the director to give such consideration to the factors identified as is necessary for the decision that he has to take, and no more than that. We do not intend a director to be required to do more than good faith and the duty of skill and care would require, nor do we want it to be possible for a director acting in good faith to be held liable for a process failure where it could not have affected the outcome.[138]

Where having regard to the factors listed in s 172(1) produces several (possibly conflicting) courses of action, then the course of action to be taken is a matter for the directors' 'good faith business judgment'.[139] Several of the factors listed in s 172(1) deserve further discussion.

10.3.4.1 'Consequences of any decision in the long term'

Directors must have regard to 'the likely consequences of any decision in the long term'.[140] The Company Law Reform Bill (which, in time, became the CA 2006) originally stated that the directors must take into account 'the likely consequences of any decision in both the long term and the short term'.[141] That Parliament ultimately chose to remove reference to short-term consequences indicates that it considers the long-term well-being of the company to be more important. That does not mean that short-term consequences are irrelevant, but that directors will need to balance short-term and long-term consequences and, if there is a conflict between the short- and long-term consequences of an act, the long-term consequences should be prioritized. This is also reflected in Principle A of the UK Corporate Governance Code, which provides that the role of the board is to 'promote the long-term sustainable success of the company . . .'.

The danger of focusing on short-term goals has been a focus of recent governance reports. Sir David Walker's review of the role of banks in the financial crisis noted that the crisis was caused, in part, by 'the weight that has increasingly been given by many shareholders and boards to short-term horizons and objectives'.[142] Sir John Kay, in his report on equity markets and long-term decision-making, 'identified many cases in which poor decision making had damaged the long-term success of the company'.[143] These include General Electric Company plc (GEC) and Imperial Chemical Industries

---

[136] HL Deb 9 May 2006, vol 681, col 845.

[137] HC Comm D 11 July 2006, col 591 (Margaret Hodge MP).

[138] HL Deb 9 May 2006, vol 681, col 846.   [139] ibid.   [140] CA 2006, s 172(1)(a).

[141] Department of Trade and Industry (DTI), *Company Law Reform* (Cm 6426, 2005) 90.

[142] 'A Review of Corporate Governance in UK Banks and Other Financial Industry Entities' (2009) para 1.26.

[143] 'The Kay Review of UK Equity Markets and Long-Term Decision Making: Final Report' (BIS 2012) 18.

plc (ICI)—two major UK industrial companies that, due to a focus on short-term gains, made a number of disastrous business decisions that resulted in ICI disposing of much of its business and eventually being acquired, whilst GEC ended up being broken up.

10.3.4.2 'Interests of the company's employees'

Although the general view is that s 172 of the CA 2006 first implemented the enlightened shareholder value approach, it is actually the case that 'a statutory declaration of an enlightened shareholder value duty'[144] was implemented by s 46 of the Companies Act 1980 (CA 1980), later replaced by s 309 of the Companies Act 1985 (CA 1985). Section 309(1) provided that '[t]he matters to which the directors of a company are to have regard in the performance of their functions include the interests of the company's employees in general, as well as the interests of its members'. Unfortunately, it proved to be ineffective, with Sealy describing it as 'either one of the most incompetent or one of the most cynical pieces of drafting on record'.[145] Accordingly, the Company Law Review Steering Group concluded that retaining s 309 was 'neither desirable nor politically sustainable'[146] and it was instead recommended that the interests of the employees be one of the factors listed (which it is in s 172(1)(b)).

10.3.4.3 'The community and the environment'

The interests of employees, creditors, and groups of members had been recognized as worthy of protection prior to the CA 2006. The Company Law Review, however, recognized that a company's responsibilities go beyond 'the need to ensure effective business relationships [and that] corporate citizens should behave ethically and should have regard to a range of public interests'.[147] Accordingly, s 172(1)(d) expressly requires directors to have regard to 'the impact of the company's operations on the community and the environment.'

There is no doubt that increasingly companies are being judged not just on their financial performance, but also upon their social and environmental impact, and so it is absolutely correct that directors should have regard to such factors. The recognition of these wider factors is evidenced in a company's disclosure obligations, which increasingly include information relating to wider environmental and social factors:

- The strategic report of a quoted company must include information about environmental matters (including the impact of the company's business on the environment), and social, community and human rights issues.[148]

  The strategic report is discussed at 19.3.2.1.

- The directors' report of a quoted company must provide details of the annual tonnage of greenhouse gas emissions that result from the company's activities.[149]

  The directors' report is discussed at 19.3.2.2.

---

[144] CLRSG, 'Modern Company Law for a Competitive Economy: The Strategic Framework' (DTI 1999) [5.1.21].

[145] LS Sealy, 'Directors' "Wider" Responsibilities—Problems Conceptual, Practical and Procedural' (1987–8) 13 Mon LR 164, 177.

[146] CLRSG, 'Modern Company Law for a Competitive Economy: Completing the Structure' (DTI 2000) [3.22].

[147] CLRSG, 'Modern Company Law for a Competitive Economy: The Strategic Framework' (DTI 1999) para 5.1.40.

[148] CA 2006, s 414C(7).

[149] ibid s 416 and Large and Medium-Sized Companies and Groups (Accounts and Reports) Regulations 2008, SI 2008/410, Sch 7, Pt 7.

The slavery and human trafficking statement is discussed at 19.5.4.

- Certain commercial organizations[150] are required to prepare and publish a slavery and human trafficking statement that sets out the steps the organization has taken to ensure that slavery and human trafficking have not taken place in any part of its business and its supply chains.[151]

10.3.4.4 'Need to act fairly as between members'

Section 172(1)(f) provides that the directors must have regard to 'the need to act fairly as between members of the company'. This is merely a codification of a principle that had long been established,[152] and is a corollary of the need to promote the success of the company for the benefit of its members as a whole. The following case provides an example of a situation where a breach of duty was established on the ground that the directors had not acted fairly as between members.

> ### Re McCarthy Surfacing Ltd [2008] EWHC 2279 (Ch)
>
> **FACTS**: The three McCarthy brothers each owned 20 per cent of the shares in McCarthy Surfacing Ltd ('the company') and were its directors. The remaining 40 per cent of the company's shares were split equally between Hequet and Hoare. The company acquired a lucrative contract with Thames Water, and the company and the McCarthy Brothers entered into a series of 'bonus agreements' under which 100 per cent of the profits from the contract would go to the McCarthy brothers and certain non-shareholder employees (with the result that Hequet and Hoare would receive nothing). Further, the company had, for a number of years, not declared any dividends. Hequet and Hoare petitioned the court under s 994 of the CA 2006, alleging that their interests as members had been unfairly prejudiced on the ground that, *inter alia*, the McCarthy brothers had not acted fairly as between members.
>
> **HELD**: The petition was granted. The Court stated that the bonus agreements were 'a calculated scheme . . . to ensure that no part of the profits of the Thames Water contract became available for distribution to shareholders'[153] and therefore 'the bonus agreements contravened the directors' duty to act fairly between shareholders . . .'.[154] On the issue of the non-declaration of dividends, it was held that '[t]his is not a case where the board has bona fide decided not to declare dividends in the best interests of the Company. It is a case where the board has consistently failed to consider whether or not to declare dividends, and that must be a breach of duty.'[155]

10.3.4.5 Creditors

This list of factors in s 172(1) contains a notable omission—namely, the company's creditors (although, of course, suppliers, customers, and employees may be creditors). Instead, s 172(3) provides that s 172 'has effect subject to any enactment or rule of law requiring directors, in certain circumstances, to consider or act in the interests of creditors of the company'. Accordingly, we need to discuss those rules of law that, in some way, require directors to consider the interests of creditors.

---

[150] Namely those that supply goods and services and have an annual turnover of not less than £36 million. See s 54(2) of the Modern Slavery Act 2015 and reg 2 of the Modern Slavery Act 2015 (Transparency in Supply Chains) Regulations 2015, SI 2015/1833.

[151] Modern Slavery Act 2015, s 54.

[152] *Mutual Life Assurance Co of New York v Rank Organisation Ltd* [1985] BCLC 11 (Ch) 21 (Goulding J).

[153] [2008] EWHC 2279 (Ch), [2009] BCC 464 [74] (Michael Furness QC).

[154] ibid [80].   [155] ibid [83].

In terms of statute, there are a number of statutory provisions that relate to the directors' conduct towards creditors and, as a result of s 172(3), a breach of these provisions could potentially (although not necessarily) also amount to a breach of s 172. Examples would include the provisions relating to the summary remedy,[156] fraudulent trading,[157] wrongful trading,[158] transactions and an undervalue,[159] and preferences.[160] The potential advantage of proceedings under s 172(3) over the relevant statutory provision in the IA 1986 is that the former proceedings will not be subject to the conditions found in the latter. So, for example, in *Re HLC Environmental Projects Ltd*,[161] certain actions of the directors did not amount to a preference because they fell outside the two-year time limit imposed by s 240(1) of the IA 1986. Those actions did, however, constitute a breach of s 172 as that section is not subject to the two-year time limit.

As regards the common law, there exists a well-established string of authority that states that the directors should take into account the interests of the company's creditors. Impetus for this line of authority came from a number of Australian cases, with the most notable case being *Kinsela v Russell Kinsela Pty*,[162] where Street CJ stated that:

> In a solvent company the proprietary interests of the shareholders entitle them as a general body to be regarded as the company when questions of the duty of directors arise. . . . But where a company is insolvent the interests of the creditors intrude. They become prospectively entitled . . . to displace the power of the shareholders and directors to deal with the company's assets.[163]

In the UK, principles of this kind first permeated English law in the case of *Lonrho Ltd v Shell Petroleum Ltd*,[164] when Lord Diplock stated that the interests of the company 'are not exclusively those of shareholders but may also include those of creditors'.[165] More notably, in *Brady v Brady*,[166] Nourse LJ stated that where the company 'is both going and solvent, first and foremost come the shareholders . . . Conversely, where the company is insolvent, or even doubtfully solvent, the interests of the company are in reality the interests of the existing creditors alone'.[167]

Although there are judicial statements to the contrary,[168] it is clear that the directors do not owe a duty to the creditors directly—the duty is owed to the company.[169] What is less clear is exactly when the duty to consider creditors' interests actually arises. Over the years, various points in time have been advocated, including when the company was actually insolvent,[170] 'doubtfully solvent',[171] and when liquidation was a 'real

---

156 IA 1986, s 212 (discussed at 23.3.2).   157 ibid ss 213 and 246ZA (discussed at 23.3.3.1).
158 ibid ss 214 and 246ZB (discussed at 23.3.4).   159 ibid s 238 (discussed at 23.4.1).
160 ibid s 239 (discussed at 23.4.2).   161 [2013] EWHC 2876 (Ch), [2014] BCC 337.
162 (1986) 4 NSWLR 722 (New South Wales Court of Appeal).
163 ibid 730.   164 (1980) 1 WLR 627 (HL).   165 ibid 634.
166 [1987] 3 BCC 535 (CA). See also *Winkworth v Edward Baron Development Co Ltd* [1987] 1 All ER 114 (HL) and *West Mercia Safetywear Ltd v Dodd* [1988] BCLC 250 (CA) (in the latter case, *Kinsela* was approved).
167 *Brady v Brady* [1987] 3 BCC 535 (CA) 552.
168 See e.g. *Winkworth v Edward Baron Development Co Ltd* [1987] 1 All ER 114 (HL) 118 (Lord Templeman).
169 *Kuwait v Asia Bank EC v National Mutual Life Nominees Ltd* [1991] 1 AC 187 (PC).
170 *Re Pantone 485 Ltd* [2002] 1 BCLC 266 (Ch).
171 *Re Horsley & Weight Ltd* [1982] 1 Ch 442 (CA) 455 (Templeman LJ).
172 *Grove v Flavel* (1986) 11 ACLR 161.

possibility'.[172] However, in the case of *Re HLC Environmental Projects Ltd*,[173] the court moved away from seeking to establish a definite point in time when the duty arises, and instead stated that:

> It is clear that established, definite insolvency before the transaction or dealing in question is not a pre-requisite for a duty to consider the interests of creditors to arise. The underlying principle is that directors are not free to take action which puts at real (as opposed to remote) risk the creditors' prospects of being paid, without first having considered their interests rather than those of the company and its shareholders. If, on the other hand, a company is going to be able to pay its creditors in any event, *ex hypothesi* there need be no such constraint on the directors. Exactly when the risk to creditors' interests becomes real for these purposes will ultimately have to be judged on a case by case basis.[174]

In the more recent case of *BTI 2014 LLC v Sequana SA*,[175] Rose J stated that '[t]he essence of the test is that the directors ought in their conduct of the company's business to be anticipating the insolvency of the company because when that occurs, the creditors have a greater claim to the assets of the company than the shareholders'.[176]

It is contended that the approach in *HLC Environmental Projects* is preferable to that evidenced in *BTI* and the other cases that attempt to determine the trigger point of the duty by reference to closeness of insolvency. The principal disadvantage of this approach, other than its lack of clarity, is that it usually resulted in the duty coming into effect too late to be of any aid to creditors—once a company is close to insolvency, the creditors' chances of being paid may be minimal or non-existent. The *HLC* approach, by focusing on the effect on creditors' chances of payment, avoids this criticism (although one could question how significant the risk of non-payment must be for the duty to trigger). However, in practice, the issue may not be significant in the majority of cases. Cases involving a possible breach of the failure to consider creditors' interests (which are rare) tend to arise in relation to insolvent companies that were then liquidated. Accordingly, in most cases, it will be clear that the duty to consider creditors' interests has indeed been triggered.

Once the duty is triggered, the question is to what extent the creditors' interests should intrude into those of the members. Where the company is insolvent, then the bulk of English authority states that the interests of the creditors become 'paramount'[177] and effectively displace those of the members.[178] In cases where the company is not insolvent, the approach is less clear. There is a strong line of authority which states that if the company is of doubtful solvency or close to insolvency, then the creditors' interests become paramount.[179] However, there also exists authority for the view that, where the company is not insolvent, but is experiencing difficulties which place its creditors at risk, then 'the duties which the directors owe to the company are extended so as to

---

[173] [2013] EWHC 2876 (Ch), [2014] BCC 337.

[174] ibid [89] (John Randall QC).   [175] [2016] EWHC 1686 (Ch).   [176] ibid [478].

[177] *Re HLC Environmental Projects Ltd* [2013] EWHC 2876 (Ch), [2014] BCC 337 [92] (John Randall QC).

[178] See e.g. *Re Pantone 485 Ltd* [2002] 1 BCLC 266 (Ch); *Wilson v Masters International Ltd* [2009] EWHC 1753 (Ch), [2010] BCC 834; *Re Capitol Films Ltd* [2010] EWHC 2240 (Ch).

[179] See e.g. *Colin Gwyer & Associates Ltd v London Wharf (Limehouse) Ltd* [2002] EWHC 2748 (Ch), [2003] BCC 885; *GHLM Trading Ltd v Maroo* [2012] EWHC 61 (Ch), [2012] BCLC 369; *Re HLC Environmental Projects Ltd* [2013] EWHC 2876 (Ch), [2014] BCC 337.

encompass the interests of the company's creditors as a whole, as well as those of the shareholders',[180] thereby indicating that the directors must balance the interests of members and creditors.

A definitive higher court ruling is needed that sets out (i) when the duty to consider creditors' interests comes into effect; and (ii) the extent to which the creditors' interests displace those of the members.

10.3.5 Remedies

An act that breaches the duty imposed by s 172 is voidable at the company's instance. Where the act also causes loss to the company, any directors in breach may be required to compensate the company for such loss.[181] Breach of the common law bona fide duty was unratifiable by the members. Section 180(4)(a) preserves any common law rules enabling ratification, but it is unclear whether this section also preserves rules prohibiting ratification. In any event, the breach can be ratified by the s 239 procedure.

10.4 Duty to exercise independent judgment

Section 173(1) provides that '[a] director of a company must exercise independent judgment'. This duty is broadly a reformulation and encapsulation of the common law duty placed upon directors not to fetter their discretion when exercising their powers.[182] Lord Denning MR highlighted the rationale behind that duty when he stated that 'no one, who has duties of a fiduciary nature to discharge, can be allowed to enter into an engagement by which he binds himself to disregard those duties or to act inconsistently with them'.[183]

It should be noted that s 173 does not require a director to be independent. As the Solicitor-General stated during the passage of the Companies Bill '[a]lthough [a director] is exercising an independent judgment, that does not mean that he must be independent himself'.[184] From this, it follows that a director who is not independent (e.g. because he has an interest that conflicts with the company's interests) will not be in breach of s 173 per se, although he may be in breach of the conflict-of-interest duties in ss 175–7.

The s 173 duty is not absolute and three principal exceptions can be identified. First, although not stated in s 173, it is clear that the duty will not be breached simply because a director relies upon the advice of another person. However, reliance upon advice does not exclude the operation of s 173. As Lord Goldsmith stated:

> The duty does not prevent a director from relying on the advice or work of others, but the final judgment must be his responsibility. . . . Indeed, in certain circumstances directors may be in breach of duty if they fail to take appropriate

The conflict of interest duties are discussed in Ch 11.

---

[180] *Ultraframe (UK) Ltd v Fielding* [2005] EWHC 1638 (Ch), [2006] FSR 17 [1304] (Lewison J). See also *Re MDA Investment Management Ltd (No 1)* [2003] EWHC 2277 (Ch), [2005] BCC 783; *Re Kudos Business Solutions Ltd* [2011] EWHC 1436 (Ch), [2012] 2 BCLC 65.

[181] *Extrasure Travel Insurances Ltd v Scattergood* [2003] 1 BCLC 598 (Ch).

[182] *Re Englefield Colliery Co* (1878) LR 8 ChD 388 (CA).

[183] *Boulting v Association of Cinematograph, Television and Allied Technicians* [1963] 2 QB 606 (CA) 626.

[184] HC SC Deb (D) 11 July 2006, col 600.

advice—for example, legal advice. As with all advice, slavish reliance is not acceptable, and the obtaining of outside advice does not absolve directors from exercising their judgment on the basis of such advice.[185]

Second, under the common law, the courts recognized that directors could fetter their discretion and bind themselves to act in a certain way if they bona fide believed such action to be in the interests of the company.

 See Andrew Griffiths, 'The Best Interests of Fulham FC: Directors' Fiduciary Duties in Giving Contractual Undertakings' [1993] JBL 576.

Fulham Football Club Ltd v Cabra Estates plc [1992] BCC 863 (CA)

FACTS: Vicenza Developments Ltd (a subsidiary of Cabra Estates plc) owned the freehold to Craven Cottage, the home ground of Fulham FC. Vicenza wished to redevelop the ground, which would require Fulham FC to move, but planning permission was not granted because the local council wished the club to remain at the ground. Undeterred, Vicenza entered into an agreement with Fulham FC whereby, in return for substantial payments, Fulham FC would support the scheme. Later, Fulham FC changed its mind and wished to remain at the football ground, and therefore sought a declaration that the agreement was invalid, because it was based on its directors fettering their own discretion.

HELD: The Court of Appeal refused to make such a declaration and held the agreement valid. Neill LJ stated that:

> directors are under a duty to act bona fide in the interests of their company. However, it does not follow from that proposition that directors can never make a contract by which they bind themselves to the future exercise of their powers in a particular manner, even though the contract taken as a whole is manifestly for the benefit of the company. Such a rule could well prevent companies from entering into contracts which were commercially beneficial to them.[186]

As the agreement conferred substantial benefits on Fulham FC and as its directors honestly believed it to be in the interests of the company when they entered into it, the agreement was not an improper fettering of the directors' discretion.

The *ratio* of *Fulham Football Club* has not been preserved exactly in s 173. Instead, s 173(2)(a) provides that the duty will not be infringed where the directors act 'in accordance with an agreement duly entered into by the company that restricts the future exercise of discretion by its directors'. There is no reference here to the agreement being in the interests of the company, although it has been argued that this is implied through the presence of the word 'duly'.[187] It has also been stated that the presence of the s 172 duty means that any fettering of discretion would not be valid unless it promoted the success of the company.[188]

Third, s 173(2)(b) provides that the duty is not infringed where the director acts in a way that is authorized by the company's constitution. The utility of s 173(2)(b) can best be seen in cases involving nominee directors. Nominee directors can rely on advice from the person who nominated them, but they cannot generally blindly follow the instructions of

Nominee directors are discussed at 7.2.5.

---

[185] HL Deb 6 Feb 2006, col 282.   [186] [1992] BCC 863 (CA) 875.

[187] Paul L Davies and Sarah Worthington, *Gower's Principles of Modern Company Law* (10th edn, Sweet & Maxwell 2016) 500.

[188] Andrew Keay, 'The Duty of Directors to Exercise Independent Judgment' (2008) 29 Co Law 290, 295.

such a person.[189] However, the exception in s 173(2)(b) means that a company can place a provision in its articles providing that a nominee director must follow the instructions of his nominator, thereby absolving the director of the duty to exercise independent judgment.[190] However, such a director will still be subject to the other general duties, meaning that a nominee director would have to disobey the instructions of his nominator if, for example, such instructions did not promote the success of the company.

10.4.1 Remedies

Any agreement entered into that contravenes the duty to exercise independent judgment will be voidable at the company's instance. Any directors in breach will be required to account for any gains made and to indemnify the company for any loss sustained as a result of the agreement.

10.5 Duty to exercise reasonable care, skill, and diligence

Section 174(1) of the CA 2006 provides that '[a] director of a company must exercise reasonable care, skill and diligence'. The common law predecessor to this was established in the case of *Re City Equitable Fire Insurance Co Ltd*,[191] where Romer J stated that '[a] director need not exhibit in the performance of his duties a greater degree of skill than may reasonably be expected from a person of his knowledge and experience'.[192] From this, it is clear that the common law duty was a subjective one, based on the skills and experience that the director actually had. Accordingly, a director with little or no skills or experience would be subject to an extremely low standard of care, as the following case demonstrates.

Re Brazilian Rubber Plantations and Estates Ltd [1911] 1 Ch 425 (Ch)

FACTS: Brazilian Rubber Plantations and Estates Ltd ('the company') was set up in order to purchase land in Brazil and use that land to cultivate rubber and other produce. The company had four directors, three of whom had no experience in the rubber business[193] (Indeed, two of them had no business experience at all.) A prospectus was issued and members of the public were invited to purchase shares in the company. The prospectus contained a number of statements that were untrue, and parts of the prospectus were fabricated. The truth was subsequently discovered and, shortly thereafter, the company went into liquidation. The liquidator sought damages from the directors on the ground that, in signing off on the prospectus, they had not acted with skill and care.

---

[189] *Scottish Cooperative Wholesale Society Ltd v Meyer* [1959] AC 324 (HL).
[190] HC SC Deb (D) 11 July 2006, col 600.   [191] [1925] Ch 407 (CA).   [192] ibid 427.
[193] The other director was a rubber broker, but he was told that his involvement was simply to value the rubber when it arrived in England, which it never did.
[194] [1911] 1 Ch 425 (Ch) 437.

> **HELD:** Neville J stated that a director is not 'bound to bring any special qualifications to his office. He may undertake the management of a rubber company in complete ignorance of everything connected with rubber, without incurring responsibility for the mistakes which may result from such ignorance.'[194] Accordingly, he held that the directors had not acted in breach of duty.

The effect of a subjective duty was to allow unqualified, disinterested, or inexperienced directors to use such deficiencies as a shield against liability. Realizing that this was too low a standard, the courts introduced an objective element into the standard of care[195] and this dual objective–subjective test has been codified into s 174(2).

10.5.1 **The standard of care**

Section 174(2) provides that the standard of care, skill, and diligence expected from a director is based on that of a reasonably diligent person with:

- (a) the general knowledge, skill, and experience that may reasonably be expected of a person carrying out the functions carried out by the director in relation to the company; and
- (b) the general knowledge, skill, and experience that the director has.

The test contained in s 174(2)(a) imposes an objective minimum standard of care, skill, and diligence that will apply to all directors, irrespective of their individual capabilities. It will, however, take into account the functions of the director, so the standard is likely to alter depending on, for example, whether the director is executive or non-executive, or whether the director sits on the board of a small private company or a large quoted company. Section 174(2)(b) imposes a subjective standard that will apply where the director in question has some special skill or ability (e.g. he is a lawyer, or accountant, etc.), and will serve to raise the standard of care expected (accordingly, the directors' subjective skills can no longer reduce the standard expected). The rationale behind imposing a higher standard of care upon such directors is that, because they were appointed to bring such skills to bear (and are likely to be paid more for having such skills), a higher standard will require them to use such skills. The counter-argument is that the higher standard could deter qualified persons from undertaking directorial office.

Section 174 does not provide any guidance on how the test is to be applied, and it is clear that '[t]he extent of the duty, and the question whether it has been discharged, must depend on the facts of each particular case . . .'[196] It is accordingly difficult to lay down any absolute rules, but prior case law does establish some guiding principles, with perhaps the most useful guidance coming from one notable case that resulted from the collapse of Barings Bank plc. This case also demonstrates the disastrous consequences that can arise if directors do not act with sufficient care and skill.

---

[195] *Norman v Theodore Goddard* [1992] BCC 14 (Ch). This objective element was taken from the test to determine the presence of wrongful trading found in s 214 of the IA 1986 (discussed at 23.3.4).
[196] *Re Barings plc (No 5)* [1999] 1 BCLC 433 (Ch) 489 (Jonathan Parker J).

The collapse of Barings Bank plc

Barings Bank plc was one of the UK's most well-established banks. In 1992, it appointed Nick Leeson as the general manager of Barings Futures (Singapore) Pte Ltd, and he began to trade on the Singapore International Monetary Exchange. Leeson, without proper authorization, engaged in increasingly speculative trades that, initially, made substantial profits, but which soon started to result in heavy losses. By the end of 1992, the losses were £2 million; by 1993, they had risen to £23 million, and by 1994, the losses were £208 million. All this time, Leeson had been utilizing a hidden account to hide these losses, and was actually fraudulently reporting a profit (and claiming bonuses based on these non-existent profits). He also falsified documentation in order to move money from client accounts to better hide his losses. In February 1995, his activities were uncovered and Leeson fled Singapore, by which time Barings' losses stood at £827 million. Barings could not sustain these losses and it collapsed a few days later. It was subsequently sold for £1 to ING, the Dutch financial services group. Leeson was subsequently arrested and sentenced to 6.5 years in prison for various breaches of Singapore securities law.

A mass of litigation arose from the collapse of Barings, but, for our purposes, the key case related to the disqualification proceedings brought against three of its directors. It was alleged that these directors, in failing to adequately supervise Leeson, had breached the duty of care and skill to such a degree that disqualification was warranted. At first instance,[197] Jonathan Parker J imposed disqualification orders of between four and six years. More importantly, he laid down several principles regarding the duty of care and skill:

- 'Directors have, both collectively and individually, a continuing duty to acquire and maintain a sufficient knowledge and understanding of the company's business to enable them properly to discharge their duties as directors.'[198]
- 'Whilst directors are entitled (subject to the articles of association of the company) to delegate particular functions to those below them in the management chain, and to trust their competence and integrity to a reasonable extent, the exercise of the power of delegation does not absolve a director from the duty to supervise the discharge of the delegated functions.'[199]

One of the directors appealed, but his appeal was dismissed and the Court of Appeal affirmed the principles laid down by Jonathan Parker J.[200]

These two principles laid down by Jonathan Parker J deserve further consideration, as well as the issue of director inactivity.

10.5.1.1 Duty to acquire and maintain knowledge

In *Re Brazilian Rubber Plantations* (discussed at 10.5), the directors avoided a breach of duty as they had no knowledge of the rubber business. This is no longer the case and directors who lack sufficient knowledge of the company's business may find themselves in breach of duty. For example, in *Re Barings plc (No 5)*, Jonathan Parker J stated that the level of knowledge of one of the directors regarding Leeson's activities was 'woefully inadequate to enable him to discharge his management responsibilities',[201] with similar criticisms being levelled at the other directors. Directors must also ensure that

---

[197] ibid.   [198] ibid 489.   [199] ibid.   [200] *Re Barings Bank plc (No 5)* [2001] BCC 273 (CA).
[201] [1999] 1 BCLC 433 (Ch) 515.

they keep themselves informed of developments regarding the company's business, with the Financial Reporting Council's (FRC's) 'Guidance on Board Effectiveness' stating that one role of the chair is to ensure that 'all directors continually update their skills, knowledge and familiarity with the company to fulfil their role both on the board and committees.'[202]

The fact that a director takes no part in the company's business will not absolve him of the duty to acquire sufficient knowledge of the company's business. This typically occurs in small family-run companies, such as in the following case.

Re Park House Properties Ltd [1998] BCC 847 (Ch)

FACTS: Park House Properties Ltd had four directors, namely Mr Carter, Mrs Carter, and their two children. Mrs Carter took no part in the company's business and the two children, despite having employment contracts with the company, took no part in management either. The company experienced financial difficulties, stopped paying tax, and was not filing its accounts at Companies House. Eventually it was liquidated. The Secretary of State applied for disqualification orders against all four directors, but the liquidator did not believe that Mrs Carter or the children should be disqualified.

HELD: Mr Carter was disqualified for four years on the ground of unfitness. The other three directors were also disqualified for two years each. Neuberger J stated that:

A person who knowingly is a director of a company and takes no part whatever in the management of the company, no steps whatever to keep himself or herself informed of the affairs of the company and leaves everything to another director who makes the sort of errors Mr Carter made is, in my judgment, unfit in the absence of special circumstances.[203]

10.5.1.2 Delegation and reliance on others

Consider the following example.

Delegation and the s 174 duty

Dragon plc acquires a lucrative new supply contract to provide goods to Ranger plc. The board of Dragon authorizes James, a sub-board-level manager, to project manage the new supply contract and ensure that its terms are complied with. James's management of the project is poor—goods are not supplied on time and are not in a satisfactory state. Ranger sues Dragon for breach of contract and is awarded damages. The publicity from this litigation causes the share price of Dragon to drop, and several members commence derivative claims against the directors.

The question that arises is whether the directors can face liability for James's poor project management under s 174. The starting point must be to recognize that, in all but the smallest companies, directors cannot undertake every task themselves, and will therefore delegate managerial functions to others (as the model articles so permit). As the Earl of Halsbury LC stated '[t]he business of life could not go on if people could not

Delegation of managerial functions is discussed at 9.2.3.

---

[202] FRC, 'Guidance on Board Effectiveness' (FRC 2018) para 61.   [203] [1988] BCC 847 (Ch) 869.

trust those who are put into a position of trust for the express purpose of attending to details of management'.[204] Accordingly, directors are entitled to rely on the competence of those they rely on or delegate functions to, as the following case demonstrates.

Dovey v Cory [1901] AC 477 (HL)

FACTS: Cory was a director of the National Bank of Wales Ltd. A series of unlawful acts (such as fraudulent balance-sheet statements, improper advances of money to customers, and payment of dividends out of capital) led to the Bank sustaining significant losses. These unlawful acts were engaged in by the Bank's manager and chair, and it was accepted that Cory had no knowledge of these acts and took no part in them. Despite this, it was alleged that Cory had breached the duty of care and skill on the ground that he should have been more questioning and should have discovered the existence of the unlawful conduct.

HELD: Cory had not breached the duty of care and skill. Lord Davey stated that Cory was 'entitled to rely upon the judgment, information, and advice of the chair and general manager, as to whose integrity, skill, and competence he had no reason for suspicion'.[205]

However, the ability to delegate and rely on others cannot be absolute and it is subject to two notable exceptions. First, the directors must exercise reasonable skill and care when choosing who to rely on or delegate their functions to. Accordingly, based on the example box above, if there was reason to doubt James's competence (e.g. prior poor management of projects), then the directors may be in breach of s 174 for delegating functions to him.

Second, 'the power of delegation does not absolve a director from the duty to supervise the discharge of the delegated functions'.[206] In *Re Barings plc (No 5)*, it was clear that the three directors exercised virtually no supervision over Leeson at all. Directors are not only expected to supervise those they delegate powers to—the duty may also require directors to monitor their fellow directors, as occurred in the following case.

Re Landhurst Leasing plc [1999] 1 BCLC 286 (Ch)

FACTS: Ball and Ashworth were directors of Landhurst Leasing plc ('Landhurst'). Dyer, Thom and Illidge were originally employees of Landhurst, but were later appointed to the board (although, in practice, they occupied 'junior' roles compared to Ball and Ashworth). Ball and Ashworth engaged in a series of unlawful activities, including receiving bribes, which resulted in them being convicted and imprisoned for a series of offences. Disqualification proceedings were brought against Dyer, Thom, and Illidge on the ground that they had 'buried their heads in the sand in relation to various matters during their respective periods of office which greater directorial alertness would or might have prevented'.[207]

HELD: Hart J stated that 'a director may rely on his co-directors to the extent that (a) the matter in question lies with their sphere of responsibility given the way in which the particular business is

---

204 *Dovey v Cory* [1901] AC 477 (HL) 486.   205 ibid 492.
206 *Re Barings plc (No 5)* [1999] 1 BCLC 433 (Ch) 489.   207 [1999] 1 BCLC 286 (Ch) 297 (Hart J).

organised and (b) that there exist no grounds for suspicion that that reliance may be misplaced'.[208] He went on to state that even if reliance is justified, 'a director may still be in breach of duty if he leaves to others matters for which the board as a whole must take responsibility'.[209] Applying this, he disqualified Dyer and Illidge and found them in breach of duty as they (i) failed to see that the company's business was properly controlled; (ii) did not ensure that company procedures were not overridden; and (iii) failed to prevent the company from entering into sham agreements. After looking at Thom's role in the company, Hart J held that his lapses did not deserve disqualification.

COMMENT: An example of this monitoring is provided in the UK Corporate Governance Code, which states that the non-executives directors should 'scrutinize and hold to account the performance of the management and individual executive directors . . .'.[210] However, *Landhurst* demonstrates that all directors (not just the NEDs) may be required to act as whistleblowers and bring to light the misdeeds of fellow directors—indeed, as noted at 10.3, a failure to disclose such misdeeds might also amount to a breach of the s 172 duty.

The identity or characteristics of a person may also be of relevance in determining whether supervision of that person was sufficient, especially if such factors put the directors on suspicion, as occurred in the following case.

See Ji Lian Yap, 'Hear No Evil, See No Evil, Speak No Evil: The Total Inactivity of Non-Executive Directors' (2009) 20 ICCLR 412.

Lexi Holdings plc v Luqman [2009] EWCA Civ 117

FACTS: Luqman was the managing director of Lexi Holdings plc ('Lexi'), and his two sisters were NEDs, although they were largely inactive. Luqman unlawfully misappropriated £59.6 million of Lexi's money via several bank accounts, and forwarded some of this money to his sisters. Shortly thereafter, Lexi went into administration. Lexi commenced proceedings against the sisters, seeking to recover the misappropriated monies. At first instance, it was held that, whilst the sisters had acted in breach of duty, Lexi could only recover part of the monies that had been paid to the sisters on the ground that Luqman was a 'persuasive, sophisticated, charming and highly intelligent liar'[211] and if the sisters had sought to challenge his actions, he would have 'fobbed them off'. Lexi appealed.

HELD: The appeal was allowed and the sisters were, along with Luqman, liable for the money that was stolen from Lexi. The Court held, *inter alia*, that the sisters knew that Luqman had been convicted and imprisoned on several occasions for obtaining property by deception. As a result of this, the sisters should have been 'on guard in relation to explanations from [Luqman]'[212] and had they done so, they would have discovered their brother's unlawful actions. They could then have informed the auditors, which would have curtailed Luqman's ability to misappropriate further funds.

Section 1157 is discussed at 10.1.3.4.

COMMENT: One other point worth noting is that the sisters sought to rely on s 727 of the CA 1985 (now s 1157 of the CA 2006) to obtain relief from liability. This was rejected on the ground that '[c]omplete inactivity as a director is by definition unreasonable'.[213]

---

[208] ibid 346.   [209] ibid.

[210] FRC, 'The UK Corporate Governance Code' (FRC 2018) Provision 13.

[211] [2008] EWHC 1639 (Ch), [2008] 2 BCLC 725 [69] (Briggs J).

[212] [2009] EWCA Civ 117, [2009] BCC 716 [45] (Sir Andrew Morritt C).

[213] [2007] EWHC 2652 (Ch) [226] (Briggs J).

There is an overlap between the two principles established by Jonathan Parker J, in that, in order to maintain sufficient knowledge of the company's business, a director will likely have to rely on knowledge acquired from others. Directors can rely on others to provide them with information, but such reliance will not absolve the director from liability for the inaccuracy of such information if the director knew or ought to have known of its inaccuracy.

Re Queens Moat Houses plc [2004] EWHC 1730 (Ch)

FACTS: Bairstow was an executive director and chair of Queens Moat Houses plc from 1969 to 1993. The company's accounts were prepared by the company's Finance Department. Inspectors appointed by the Secretary of State found that the company's financial statements were 'false and misleading' and that dividends were declared based on profits that did not exist. Bairstow was not a qualified accountant, but he did have 'very considerable experience as a business man'.[214] The Secretary of State commenced disqualification proceedings against Bairstow.

HELD: Sir Donald Rattee stated that Bairstow was not 'under a duty to query the draft financial statements produced to the Board by the Finance Department, save to the extent that they included matters which should . . . have been apparent to a man of Mr Bairstow's business experience and knowledge of this particular company's affairs as being of at least doubtful accuracy or propriety'.[215] Applying this, he held that in relation to certain technical aspects of the accounts, Bairstow would not be expected to know of the errors, and would be entitled to rely on the figures as prepared by the Finance Department. However, there were misleading figures in the accounts (notably in relation to the company's turnover and profits) that should have been apparent to someone with Bairstow's experience. Accordingly, he had breached the duty to exercise skill and care and was disqualified for six years.

10.5.1.3 Inactivity and abdication of responsibility

Delegation of managerial functions is permissible, but abdication is not, and a director who takes little or no part in the company's management, or who abrogates his responsibilities, will likely be found in breach of duty. As Lord Woolf MR stated, '[i]t is of the greatest importance that any individual who undertakes the statutory and fiduciary obligations of being a company director should realise that these are inescapable personal responsibilities'.[216] The following case provides an example of how inactivity can result in breach of duty.[217]

Dorchester Finance Co Ltd v Stebbing [1989] BCLC 498 (Ch)

FACTS: Dorchester Finance Co Ltd ('Dorchester') was a money-lending company. Its three directors were Stebbing, Parsons, and Hamilton, but only Stebbing worked full-time—the other two (who were NEDs) left the management to Stebbing and visited the company's premises infrequently.

---

[214] [2004] EWHC 1730 (Ch), [2005] 1 BCLC 136 [7] (Sir Donal Rattee).   [215] ibid [35].

[216] *Re Westmid Packing Services Ltd (No 3)* [1998] BCC 836 (CA) 843.

[217] The cases of *Lexi Holdings plc v Luqman* (discussed at 10.5.1.2) and *Re Park House Properties Ltd* (discussed at 10.5.1.1) are also examples of this point.

Parsons and Hamilton signed blank cheques for Stebbing to use on company business. However, Stebbing used these cheques to misapply nearly £400,000 of Dorchester's assets. Stebbing had clearly breached the duty of care and skill, but it was also alleged that Parsons and Hamilton were also in breach.

HELD: Parsons and Hamilton were also in breach of duty and, along with Stebbing, were required to compensate the company for its losses. Foster J stated:

> The signing of blank cheques by Hamilton and Parsons was in my judgment negligent, as it allowed Stebbing to do as he pleased. Apart from that they not only failed to exhibit the necessary skill and care in the performance of their duties as directors, but also failed to perform any duty at all as directors of Dorchester.[218]

The issue of abdication of responsibility often arises in relation to professional advisers. Directors are, of course, free to rely on professional advisers, such as lawyers, accountants, etc. (indeed, a failure to take advice from such persons would be most unwise). However, in the following case, the director in question relied on advisers to such an extent as to constitute an abdication of his responsibilities.

Re Bradcrown Ltd [2002] BCC 428 (Ch)

FACTS: Sonn was one of three directors of TL Ireland & Co (Holdings) Ltd ('TLI'). TLI took assignment of a lease which eventually became onerous. After taking advice from accountants and solicitors, the directors of TLI decided to implement a demerger scheme, the effect of which was transfer all of TLI's assets (apart from the lease) to other companies for no consideration. Shortly thereafter, TLI was wound up for non-payment of rent. The liquidator alleged that, in transferring away the assets for no consideration, the directors had not acted with care and skill. Two of the directors summarily accepted disqualification orders. Sonn refused on the ground that he was entitled to rely on the professional advice he was given.

HELD: Lawrence Collins J looked at the extent to which Sonn had relied on professional advice and stated that Sonn 'asked no questions and sought no advice. He simply did what he was told, and abdicated all responsibility. In these circumstances he cannot seek refuge in the fact that professional advisers were involved in the transactions.'[219] Accordingly, Sonn 'appears to have abrogated his responsibility at every stage'[220] and was therefore in breach of duty. He was disqualified for two years.

10.5.2 **Remedies**

A director who causes his company to sustain loss due to his failure to exercise reasonable skill, care, and diligence will be liable to compensate the company for such loss. It should be noted, however, that obtaining compensation for a breach of s 174 is not easy, as the claimant will need to prove that the acts of the director(s) in question were the

---

[218] [1989] BCLC 498 (Ch) 505. [219] [2002] BCC 428 (Ch) 439. [220] ibid 438.

cause of the company's loss. The problem has been set out as follows by looking at the typical facts in these types of cases:

> a rogue, reasonably trusted by all, at the centre of the action, his frauds deceiving even the auditors; and a board of directors, many of them non-executive, meeting only at intervals and justifiably delegating many functions to committees or subordinate officers. On such facts, it is virtually impossible to hold that the acts (or, more likely, the omissions) of those directors who were not directly involved in the wrongdoing were the *cause* of the company's loss.[221]

Morse goes on to note that this difficulty explains why most of the cases involving directors' negligence are not brought under s 174, but are brought under the Company Directors Disqualification Act 1986.[222]

CHAPTER SUMMARY

- The general duties of directors are now found in the CA 2006, although the courts will still have regard to pre-CA 2006 case law when interpreting and applying the duties. These duties are owed to the company.
- A breach of duty may be avoided if the breach is approved or authorized, ratified under s 239, or if the court relieves the director of liability under s 1157.
- Section 171 provides that a director is under a duty to act in accordance with the company's constitution and to exercise powers only for the purposes for which they are conferred.
- Section 172 provides that a director is under a duty to act in the way he considers, in good faith, would be most likely to promote the success of the company for the benefit of its members as a whole.
- Section 172(1) contains a list of factors the directors must 'have regard' to, including the likely consequences of any decision in the long term, the interests of the company's employees, and the impact of the company's operations on the community and the environment.
- Section 173 provides that a director must exercise independent judgment.
- Section 174 provides that a director must exercise reasonable skill, care, and diligence.
- The standard expected under s 174 is that of a reasonably diligent person with (i) the general knowledge, skill, and experience that may reasonably be expected of a person carrying out the functions carried out by the director in relation to the company; and (ii) the general knowledge, skill, and experience that the director has.

FURTHER READING

Alistair Alcock, 'An Accidental Change to Directors' Duties?' (2009) 30 Co Law 362.
- Discusses the extent to which ss 171 and 172 differ to their corresponding prior common law duties.

---

[221] Geoffrey Morse, *Palmer's Company Law* (Sweet & Maxwell 2018) para 8.2820.   [222] ibid para 8.2821.

Rod Edmunds and John Lowry, 'The Continuing Value of Relief for Directors' Breach of Duty' (2003) 66 MLR 195.

- Discusses the courts' ability to grant relief for breach of duty and argues that a more radical approach is required than that found in s 1157.

Deryn Fisher, 'The Enlightened Shareholder: Leaving Stakeholders in the Dark' (2009) 20 ICCLR 10.

- Discusses the likely impact of the s 172 duty and argues that, in practice, it will not make directors consider more the interests of stakeholders.

Andrew Keay, 'The Duty of Directors to Exercise Independent Judgment' (2008) 29 Co Law 290.

- Discusses the common law background to the s 173 duty and discusses how the common law differs to the s 173 duty.

Law Commission, *Company Directors: Regulating Conflicts of Interest and Formulating a Statement of Duties* (Law Com No 261, Cm 4436, HMSO 1999) 32–55.

- Part 4 explores the different options for codification of directors' duties. Part 5 looks at the standard of a director's duty of care and skill.

SELF-TEST QUESTIONS

1. Define the following terms:

- general duties;
- enlightened shareholder value approach;
- pluralist approach.

2. State whether each of the following statements is true or false and, if false, explain why:

- The CA 2006 has codified all the law relating to directors' duties.
- The general duties only apply to persons who are current directors.
- The members can ratify a director's breach of duty.
- A director will be in breach of the s 171 duty if they exercise their powers for any improper purpose.
- The s 172 duty requires the directors to balance equally the interests of the company, its members, and its stakeholders (e.g. employees).
- The s 174 standard of care adopts an objective and a subjective test.

3. 'In adopting the enlightened shareholder value approach, it is clear that the duty imposed by s 172 of the CA 2006 will do little to improve the position of a company's stakeholders. The correct approach would have been to adopt a formulation that embodied the pluralist approach.' Do you agree with this statement?

4. Belinda, Walter, Ahmed and Yvonne are the directors of Dragon Tools Ltd ('ST'). Sixty per cent of ST's shares are held by Dragon plc, with the four directors each holding 10 per cent of ST's shares.

For some time, a lucrative contract of sale has existed between ST and UK Electricals Ltd, under which ST provides tools to UK Electricals Ltd. Belinda and Ahmed meet with an agent of UK Electricals in order to discuss renewing this supply contract. Belinda stated that the board had agreed that, based on an increase in manufacturing costs, ST would need to increase its prices by 15 per cent. Ahmed was not aware of this increase and, based on his knowledge, it had never been discussed at a board meeting. Despite this, he said nothing. The agent of UK Electricals stated that he would inform the board of the increase. A few days later, Belinda contacts the agent and states that the tools can be obtained more cheaply from Toolbox Ltd (Belinda is a director and majority shareholder of Toolbox). As a result, UK Electricals does not renew its contract with ST and instead enters into a supply contract with Toolbox.

At a board meeting, Walter tells the board that he has heard rumours the Dragon plc is considering selling its shares in ST to Partridge plc. The board of ST are concerned about the effect that this change in control might have, and so they cause ST to issue a batch of new shares that they purchase. As a result of this, Dragon plc's holding in ST is reduced to 25 per cent.

The board of Dragon plc has become aware of the above issues and seeks your advice on (i) whether any breaches of the law have taken place; and (ii) if any breaches have taken place, how can a remedy be obtained.

ONLINE RESOURCES

This book is accompanied by online resources to better support you in your studies. Visit www.oup. com/uk/roach-company/ for:

- answers to the self-test questions;
- further reading lists;
- multiple-choice questions;
- glossary.

Updates to the law can be found on the author's Twitter account (@UKCompanyLaw) and further resources can be found on the author's blog (www.companylawandgovernance.com).

11

Directors' duties II: conflicts of interest

- Duty to avoid conflicts of interest
- Duty not to accept benefits from third parties
- Duty to declare interest in transactions or arrangements
- Transactions requiring member approval

INTRODUCTION

Fiduciaries (such as directors) are generally prohibited from putting themselves in a position where their interests and duties conflict.[1] As directors owe their duties to the company (and are agents of the company), equity has long provided that directors should not allow their interests to conflict with those of the company. This was effected via two rules:

- the 'no-conflict rule', which provides that 'no one having duties to discharge shall be allowed to enter into engagements in which he has or can have a personal interest conflicting or which possibly may conflict with the interests of those whom he is bound to protect';[2]

- the 'no-profit rule', which provides that 'a person in a fiduciary position . . . is not, unless otherwise expressly provided, entitled to make a profit'.[3]

These two rules[4] have now been codified across three general duties (ss 175–7) and one supplementary duty (s 182), but pre-Companies Act 2006 (CA 2006) case law remains very relevant. It is not the most elegant approach—there is notable potential for overlap between some of the duties, and there are notable, but technical, differences between the duties in terms of scope. The conflict duties are discussed in detail at 11.1–11.3, and a brief overview is provided in Table 11.1.

In addition to the conflict duties, the CA 2006 also provides that certain transactions and agreements (which can be regarded as producing very specific forms of conflict of interest) must be approved by the members. These transactions and arrangements are at 11.4. The chapter begins by looking at what is perhaps the principal and most wide-ranging duty relating to conflicts of interest, namely the duty found in s 175.

---

[1] *Bray v Ford* [1896] AC 44 (HL).
[2] *Aberdeen Rly Co v Blaikie Bros* (1854) 1 Macq 461 (HL) 471 (Lord Cranworth).
[3] *Bray v Ford* [1896] AC 44 (HL) 51 (Lord Herschell).
[4] It is worth noting that some judges (e.g. Lord Upjohn in *Boardman v Phipps* [1967] 2 AC 46 (HL) 123) regard the no-profit rule as merely part of the no-conflict rule, and not as a separate rule.

TABLE 11.1 The conflict-of-interest duties

Duty	Disclosure required?	When is disclosure required?	Is authorization required?
Section 175—To avoid conflicts of interest	Sections 175–176 do not expressly require the director to disclose the conflict/benefit (although pre-CA 2006 case law does). However, as authorization is required, the director will, in practice, need to disclose the existence of the conflict/benefit prior to obtaining authorization. Further, the courts have made clear that a director should disclose the existence of a conflict/benefit in order to comply with the duty to act in the interests of the company* and it is likely that this will continue to apply in relation to the duty imposed by s 172		Yes. In private companies, the directors can authorize the conflict, providing that the constitution does not preclude such authorization. In public companies, the directors can authorize the conflict only if the constitution so provides
Section 176—Not to accept benefits from third parties			Yes. The benefit must be authorized by the members in general meeting
Section 177—To declare interest in proposed transactions or arrangements with the company	Yes. The director must disclose the nature and extent of the interest to the other directors	Disclosure must be made prior to the company entering into the transaction or arrangement	No, but if the directors do not approve of the transaction/arrangement, they are likely to prevent the company from entering into it
Section 182—To declare interest in existing transactions or arrangements entered into by the company	Yes. The director must disclose the nature and extent of the interest to the other directors	Disclosure must be made as soon as is reasonably practicable	No

Industrial Developments Consultants Ltd v Cooley [1972] 1 WLR 443.

11.1 Duty to avoid conflicts of interest

Section 175 imposes the first of three general duties relating to conflicts of interest, and is a reformulation of the no-conflict rule.[5] Section 175(1) provides that '[a] director of a company must avoid a situation in which he has, or can have, a direct or indirect interest that conflicts, or possibly may conflict, with the interests of the company'. Common examples of the sorts of circumstances that could (though not necessarily will) constitute a breach of the s 175 duty include:

- a director helps a competing company (e.g. by sitting on its board, or by providing it with consultancy services);
- a director learns of a business opportunity, or acquires information, whilst director of a company, and then exploits that opportunity/information to benefit himself personally;
- a director uses the company's property to benefit himself financially;
- a director of a company is also a major shareholder, customer, supplier, or creditor of that company;

---

[5] Explanatory Notes to the CA 2006, para 338.

● a director of a company owns personal assets, the value of which could be affected by the company's activities.

Two phrases within s 175(1) deserve further explanation. First, the phrase 'direct or indirect interest' indicates that the director need not be party to the transaction or arrangement that gives rise to the conflict in order for a breach to arise. An example of this would be 'where a director represents a major shareholder in the company whose interests conflict with those of the company'.[6] Second, the phrase 'possibly may conflict' indicates that an actual conflict need not exist in order for s 175 to be breached—potential conflicts are also covered. This renders the s 175 duty potentially very wide. However, the scope of potential conflicts was reduced by Lord Upjohn when he stated:

> The phrase 'possibly may conflict' requires consideration. In my view it means that the reasonable man looking at the relevant facts and circumstances of the particular case would think that there was a real sensible possibility of conflict; not that you could imagine some situation arising which might, in some conceivable possibility in events not contemplated as real sensible possibilities by any reasonable person, result in a conflict.[7]

This is backed up by s 175(4)(a),[8] which provides that the s 175 duty will not be infringed 'if the situation cannot reasonably be regarded as likely to give rise to a conflict of interest'. Indeed, cl 175(4)(a) of the Company Law Reform Bill originally stated that the duty would not be infringed where there was 'no real possibility of a conflict of interest'. An example of a situation where s 175(4)(a) might apply is where a director exploits an opportunity that falls outside the scope of his company's business. As Warren J stated, 'a director of a company selling fashion clothing for women could hardly be in breach of the "no conflict" rule if he took a stake in a company distributing farm machinery'.[9]

Other sections help set out the scope of s 175. Section 175(7) provides that '[a]ny reference in this section to a conflict of interest includes a conflict of interest and duty and a conflict of duties'. The following example demonstrates the relevance of this.

 Conflict of interest and duty, and conflict of duty

Sajid is an executive director of Dragon plc, and is also a non-executive director (NED) of Halo plc. Dragon and Halo do not currently engage in competing business. Sajid sells a plot of land that he owns to Dragon for about twice its market value. Dragon plans to use the land to build a factory, which will produce exactly the same type of components that Halo's factories produce. The directors of Dragon believe that this factory can be extremely profitable.

Sajid's interest (i.e. to secure as high a price for the land as possible) is clearly in conflict with his duty to promote the success of Dragon. The fact that the land will be used by Dragon to engage in competition with Halo places Sajid in a position where his duties to Dragon and his duties to Halo will also probably conflict.

---

[6] GC100, 'Companies Act 2006—Directors' Conflict of Interest' (GC100, 2008) para 2.2.

[7] *Boardman v Phipps* [1967] 2 AC 46 (HL) 124.

[8] For a detailed discussion of s 175(4)(a), see Ernest Lim, 'Directors' Fiduciary Duties: A New Analytical Framework' (2013) 129 LQR 242.

[9] *Wilson v West Coast Capital* [2005] EWHC 3009 (Ch), [2007] BCC 717 [253].

The CA 2006 provides that there are two notable instances where the s 175 duty will not apply. First, the duty 'does not apply to a conflict of interest arising in relation to a transaction or arrangement with the company'.[10] It is therefore clear that s 175 is concerned with transactions/arrangements with third parties. Where the transaction/arrangement is with the company, then the relevant duties are found in ss 177 and 182 (discussed at 11.3). Second, the duty will not apply in relation to the transactions covered by Ch 10, Pts 4 and 4A (discussed at 11.4) and, under those provisions, approval has been obtained or is not needed.[11]

Section 175(2) provides that the s 175 duty 'applies in particular to the exploitation of any property, information or opportunity . . .'. Focusing on these specific forms of conflict indicates that the statutory duty is strongly (although not exclusively) based on what is known as the 'corporate opportunity' doctrine.

11.1.1 The corporate opportunity doctrine

The corporate opportunity doctrine is based upon the premise that the director breaches his duty if he takes advantage of property, information, or an opportunity and, in doing so, his interests conflict with those of the company. Note that s 175(2) does not, contrary to earlier case law,[12] require the property, information, or opportunity to be one that 'belongs' to the company, nor does it require the director to come across the property, information, or opportunity whilst acting as director. As the following case demonstrates, all that is required is that the director, by exploiting the property, information, or opportunity, puts himself in a position where his interests conflict with those of the company.

Bhullar v Bhullar [2003] EWCA Civ 424

FACTS: For over 50 years, the families of two brothers (Mohan and Sohan) had run Bhullar Bros Ltd, a company that, *inter alia*, let commercial property. The families fell out and it was decided that they would go their separate ways. The directors from Mohan's family decided that the company should not acquire any further properties and the directors from Sohan's family agreed. One of Sohan's directors discovered, by chance and not whilst acting in the course of the company's business, a piece of property adjacent to property owned by the company. Through another company that he owned, Sohan acquired this property without informing Mohan. Mohan discovered the acquisition and alleged that Sohan had breached his fiduciary duties.

HELD: Sohan had breached his fiduciary duties. Despite the fact that Sohan had acquired knowledge of the property in a 'private' capacity, Jonathan Parker LJ stated that:

> the relevant question . . . is not whether the party to whom the duty is owed . . . had some kind of beneficial interest in the opportunity: in my judgment that would be too formalistic and restrictive an approach. Rather, the question is simply whether the fiduciary's exploitation of the opportunity is such as to attract the application of the rule.[13]

The Court found that Sohan's acquisition of the property was a conflict, and he had a duty to inform the company of the opportunity. Whether or not the company could, or would, have acquired the property was irrelevant.

COMMENT: Understandably, this case has been criticized—notably, because the company agreed (at Mohan's behest) not to acquire any more properties. The Court, in effect, allowed Mohan to

See Dan D Prentice and Jennifer Payne, 'The Corporate Opportunity Doctrine' (2004) 120 LQR 198.

---

[10] CA 2006, s 175(3).   [11] ibid s 180(2).   [12] See e.g. *Cook v Deeks* [1916] 1 AC 554 (PC).
[13] [2003] EWCA Civ 424, [2003] BCC 711 [28].

change his mind opportunistically at the moment an attractive commercial opportunity arose. Further, under *Bhullar*, the definition of a corporate opportunity is very wide indeed and would include 'not only what the company is interested in, but what it could be interested in. It would be in keeping with the approach in *Bhullar* to treat anything of economic value to the company as potentially within the company's line of business, and therefore a corporate opportunity'.[14]

In *Bhullar*, a breach arose even though company chose not to acquire any further properties. Would the situation be different if a company was unable to enter into the transaction in question that ultimately caused the conflict? The answer is no, as s 175(2) states that 'it is immaterial whether the company could take advantage of the property, information or opportunity'. This is demonstrated in the following controversial case.

 Regal (Hastings) Ltd v Gulliver [1967] 2 AC 134 (HL)

FACTS: Regal (Hastings) Ltd ('Regal') owned a cinema. With a view to expanding or selling the business, it was decided that Regal would acquire the leases to two cinemas. A subsidiary, Amalgamated Cinemas Ltd ('Amalgamated'), which was managed by the same directors as Regal, was set up to acquire the leases. However, the landlord of the two cinemas was not willing to lease the cinemas unless Amalgamated had a paid-up share capital of £5,000 (which it did not) or the directors were willing to give personal guarantees to the landlord (which they were not). Regal could not afford to purchase £5,000 worth of shares in Amalgamated, so it was decided that Regal would purchase £2,000 worth of shares and six other persons (including the directors of Regal and Amalgamated) would purchase £3,000 of shares between them. Several weeks later, the business was sold via a takeover and the directors made a substantial profit on the sale of the shares. Regal, now under the control of new directors, commenced proceedings against the former directors for breach of duty.

HELD: The House accepted that 'in taking up these shares in Amalgamated, [the former directors] acted with bona fides, intending to act in the interest of Regal'.[15] However, Lord Russell went on to state:

> The rule of equity which insists on those, who by use of a fiduciary position make a profit, being liable to account for that profit, in no way depends on fraud, or absence of bona fides; or upon such questions or considerations as whether the profit would or should otherwise have gone to the plaintiff, or whether the profiteer was under a duty to obtain the source of the profit for the plaintiff, or whether he took a risk or acted as he did for the benefit of the plaintiff, or whether the plaintiff has in fact been damaged or benefited by his action. The liability arises from the mere fact of a profit having, in the stated circumstances, been made. The profiteer, however honest and well- intentioned, cannot escape the risk of being called upon to account.[16]

Accordingly, the defendants had breached the no-conflict duty and were required to account to Regal for the profit they made on the sale of the shares.

COMMENT: This case demonstrates the strictness of the duty. The defendants acted bona fide, in the interests of Regal, they used their own money, and they did not deprive Regal of an advantage—in fact, without the defendants' help, Regal could not have profited of

---

[14] Dan D Prentice and Jennifer Payne, 'The Corporate Opportunity Doctrine' (2004) 120 LQR 198, 201–2.
[15] [1967] 2 AC 134 (HL) 143 (Viscount Sankey).   [16] ibid 144–5.

the opportunity. The House refused to allow this to act as a defence on the ground that, in most cases, courts cannot investigate companies to determine their financial ability to enter into a transaction.[17] Lord Porter acknowledged that, as a result of the decision, Regal received 'an unexpected windfall'[18] but stated that 'the principle that a person occupying a fiduciary relationship shall not make a profit by reason thereof is of such vital importance that the possible consequence in the present case is in fact as it is in law an immaterial consideration'.[19]

The defendants could have avoided a breach of duty if they obtained member approval for the conflict,[20] so why did they not do so? The answer is that the defendants did not feel the need to do so because they controlled the shares in Regal and such a resolution would have been a formality. The House did not accept this as a defence.

The strictness of the approach in the above cases reinforces the notion that the duty is meant to act as a deterrent. The duty is preventative—directors must *avoid* conflicts of interest. However, the strictness has been criticized and it has been contrasted with the more relaxed approach found in other Commonwealth countries, such as the following Canadian case.

Peso Silver Mines v Cropper (1966) SCR 673[21]

FACTS: Cropper was the managing director of Peso Silver Mines Ltd ('Peso'). A prospector offered to sell to Peso three mining claims. Peso's board decided to reject the offer, largely on the ground that the clams were unproven and of speculative value. A few months later, 'after the matter had passed out of [Cropper's] mind',[22] a group formed with a view to acquiring the prospector's claims, and Cropper was asked if he wanted to contribute to purchasing the claims, which he did. Two companies, Cross Bow Mines Ltd and Mayo Silver Mines Ltd, were incorporated to purchase the claims and develop them, with Cropper being a director and shareholder of both.

Peso was subsequently taken over by Charter Oil Co Ltd and new directors were appointed to Peso's board. Peso's new chair, Berliz, instructed all directors to disclose their interests in other mining companies, so Cropper disclosed his interest in Cross Bow and Mayo. After Cropper refused to turn over to Peso his interest in these companies at cost, he was asked to vacate office but he refused. Peso commenced proceedings against Cropper, claiming that the shares he held in Cross Bow and Mayo were obtained as result of his position as a director of Peso and amounted to a conflict of interest.

HELD: The Supreme Court of Canada rejected Peso's claim and held that Cropper had not breached any duties. Cartwright J stated that 'I find it impossible to say that [Cropper] obtained the interests he holds in Cross Bow and Mayo by reason of the fact he was director of [Peso] . . .'.[23] The board of Peso, when rejecting the prospector's offer, did so for bona fide reasons. When the prospector later approached Cropper, 'it was not in his capacity as a director of [Peso], but as an individual member of the public whom [the prospector] was seeking to interest as a co-adventurer'.[24]

See Jie Li, 'The Peso Silver Case: An Opportunity to Soften the Rigid Approach of the English Courts on the Problem of Corporate Opportunity' (2011) 32 Co Law 68.

---

[17] ibid 154 (Lord Wright).   [18] ibid 157.   [19] ibid.   [20] ibid 150 (Lord Russell).
[21] See also *Canadian Aero Service v O'Malley* (1971) 23 DLR (3d) 632 (Court of Appeal (Ontario)).
[22] (1966) SCR 673, 677.   [23] ibid 682.   [24] ibid.

> **COMMENT:** It has been argued that *Peso* is an example of a case that should fall within s 175(4)(a), namely that no breach would occur because 'the situation cannot reasonably be regarded as likely to give rise to a conflict of interest'.[25] The strictness of the current law could be reduced, whilst maintaining the deterrent effect, by imposing on directors the burden of proving that s 175(4)(a) applied. Such an approach was tentatively advanced by Arden LJ.[26]

Where the conflict relates to information acquired by the director, then the courts distinguish between different types of information. General 'know how' (even if confidential) acquired whilst working for the company can be used by a director in subsequent companies and no breach will occur. The rationale behind this is that directors 'acquire a general fund of knowledge and expertise in the course of their work, and it is plainly in the public interest that they should be free to exploit it in a new position'.[27] However, a director is not permitted to utilize 'trade-secrets' in a subsequent employment.[28] What amounts to a trade secret will depend upon the facts of the case. For example, in *Item Software (UK) Ltd v Fassihi*,[29] the director's employment contract stipulated that trade secrets would include '[c]ompany databases, customer lists, business strategy, sales strategy, sales agreements, agency agreements, suppliers agreements, technical "know how" and investigations not within the public domain, employee records and financial records'.

A number of the leading cases concerning conflicts of interest relate to situations where a director occupies multiple directorships.

11.1.2 Multiple directorships

A conflict of interest can clearly arise where a director holds multiple directorships. Unless the articles provide otherwise, a director is free to sit on the boards of multiple companies (indeed, such arrangements are reasonably common). Whilst multiple directorships are not generally prohibited, companies subject to the UK Corporate Governance Code should bear in mind the following recommendations found in Provision 15:

- when making new appointments, the board should take into account other demands on directors' time;
- additional external appointments should not be undertaken without the prior approval of the board, with the reasons for permitting significant appointments explained in the annual report;
- full-time executive directors should not take on more than one non-executive directorship or other significant appointment.

If a director sits on the board of multiple companies that are not in competition with one another, then no issue of conflict typically arises. An example of this would be where an executive of company A acts as a non-executive of company B, and company A and company B operate in completely different sectors. However, consider the following example.

---

[25] Ernest Lim, 'Directors' Fiduciary Duties: A New Analytical Framework' (2013) 129 LQR 242, 249.

[26] *Murad v Al-Saraj* [2005] EWCA Civ 959, [2005] WTLR 1573 [82].

[27] *Island Export Finance Ltd v Umunna* [1986] BCLC 460 (QB) 482 (Hutchinson J).

[28] *FSS Travel & Leisure Systems Ltd v Johnson* [1998] IRLR 382 (CA).

[29] [2002] EWHC 3116 (Ch). [2003] BCC 858.

Eg **Competing directorships**

Angus is a part-time executive director of Dragon plc, working for the company for three days every week. The other two days per week he spends as a director of Salamander plc. Salamander is one of Dragon's main competitors.

Clearly, in this case, Angus has a notable conflict of interest under s 175. One would assume that a director cannot sit on the boards of competing companies. After all, it is a well-established rule of equity that a director 'is not allowed to put himself in a position where his interest and duty conflict'[30] and there are numerous examples of instances where fiduciaries are prohibited from competing.[31] Such a rule is justified, for, as Justice Brandeis stated:

> The practice of interlocking directorates is the root of many evils. . . . Applied to rival corporations, it tends to the suppression of competition . . . Applied to corporations which deal with each other, it tends to disloyalty and to violation of the fundamental law that no man can serve two masters. In either event, it tends to inefficiency; for it removes incentive and destroys soundness of judgment.[32]

However, in *London and Mashonaland Exploration Co Ltd v New Mashonaland Exploration Co Ltd*,[33] Chitty J stated that, generally, a director was permitted to act as director for a rival company (unless the articles or his service contract prohibited this), and this principle has been judicially upheld at the highest level.[34] Unsurprisingly, however, *Mashonaland* has been criticized, with Christie stating that it was simply 'wrongly decided'[35] and that the courts should 'unhesitatingly acknowledge that these judgments are inconsistent with long established principles of Equity regulating directors'.[36] Such an acknowledgement impliedly came from Sedley LJ in the following case.

In Plus Group Ltd v Pyke [2002] EWCA Civ 370

FACTS: Pyke and Plank were the directors of In Plus Group Ltd ('IPG'). Pyke suffered a stroke and was unable to involve himself in IPG's management, and so Plank solely managed IPG. Pyke recovered and sought to once again become involved in IPG's management, but Plank excluded Pyke from management and eventually removed Pyke as a director in March 1998. However, in June 1997, Pyke set up a rival company and obtained a number of contracts from IPG's main customer. IPG commenced proceedings, alleging that Pyke had acted in breach of duty by competing with IPG.

HELD: The Court unanimously held that Pyke had not acted in breach of duty, but the reasoning of the judges was not unanimous. Brooke LJ stated that '[t]here is no completely rigid rule that a director may not be involved in the business of a company which is in competition with

See Ross Grantham, 'Can Directors Compete With the Company?' (2003) 66 MLR 109.

---

[30] *Bray v Ford* [1896] AC 44 (HL) 51 (Lord Herschell).

[31] See e.g. s 30 of the Partnership Act 1890, which generally prohibits partners from engaging in business that competes with the firm.

[32] Louis Brandeis, 'Breaking the Money Trusts' (1913) *Harper's Weekly*, 6 December, 13.

[33] [1891] WN 165.   [34] See e.g. *Bell v Lever Bros* [1932] AC 161 (HL).

[35] Michael Christie, 'The Director's Fiduciary Duty Not to Compete' (1992) 55 MLR 506, 506.

[36] ibid 520.

another company of which he was a director'.[37] He went on to state that there was no need to resolve the 'controversy' that *Mashonaland* created, as the facts of the present case were so unusual.[38] Brooke LJ stated that no duty was breached as Pyke had been excluded from management, was not permitted to withdraw his money and was not being remunerated, and was not making use of any confidential information he acquired whilst acting as a director of IPG.[39]

Sedley LJ took a different approach that was critical of *Mashonaland*. He stated that these types of cases are 'fact-specific'[40] and that there 'has never been any warrant for treating [Chitty J's] decision . . . as a licence for directors or other fiduciaries to put themselves or to stay put in situations where their duties and/or interests can come into conflict'.[41] He stated that Pyke had not acted in breach of duty, but that the space for absolving Pyke was 'very narrow indeed'.[42] Sedley LJ held that the duty had not been breached as Pyke had been excluded from the management of IPG.

COMMENT: Where does this case leave *Mashonaland*? Two of the three judges refused to comment on its validity, whilst Sedley LJ was clearly of the opinion that *Mashonaland* did not establish a general principle. Several academics have argued that *Mashonaland* was a product of its time and that subsequent developments mean that 'the proposition that a director may compete with his company is inconsistent with the now well-established fiduciary character of the office of director'.[43] Accordingly, one could argue that the general position is that directors, as fiduciaries, should not compete with the company, but the facts of the case (as in *Mashonaland* and *In Group Plus*) may justify competing directorships in certain cases. A definitive ruling is desirable.

In practice, directors with competing directorships are extremely rare as most directors who wish to compete with their company tend to resign first and then set up a new competing company or join an existing competitor. However, as 11.1.3 discusses, resigning does not necessarily exclude the operation of the s 175 duty.

11.1.3 Former directors

Consider the example about resigning in order to acquire a corporate opportunity.

Eg | **Resigning in order to acquire a corporate opportunity**

MegaFlight plc wishes to purchase engines for use in its new fleet of aircraft. Greg, an experienced engineer and director of Dragon plc, was tasked with negotiating with MegaFlight's board in order to acquire the contract. For some time, Greg has been considering resigning from Dragon and setting up his own engine-manufacturing company, as he has concerns with the way Dragon has been managed. He is confident that, if he did so, he could acquire the contract from MegaFlight. Accordingly, he resigns and sets up a new company, EngineTech Ltd. Shortly thereafter, MegaFlight agrees to purchase the engines from EngineTech.

---

[37] [2002] EWCA Civ 370, [2003] BCC 332 [72].　　[38] ibid [75].　　[39] ibid [76].
[40] ibid [90].　　[41] ibid [88].　　[42] ibid [89].
[43] Ross Grantham, 'Can Directors Compete With the Company?' (2003) 66 MLR 109, 111.

Clearly, in this example, Greg's interests (i.e. to set up a new company and acquire the contract) conflict with those of Dragon. The first question is whether Greg can avoid a breach of s 175 by resigning from Dragon. Generally, resignation brings to an end the director's duty under s 175, except where s 170(2)(a) applies. This provision states that a person who ceases to be a director continues to be subject to s 175 as regards the exploitation of any property, information, or opportunity of which he became aware at a time when he was a director. Clearly, Greg would fall within this.

Section 170(2)(a) merely establishes that Greg is subject to the s 175 duty. The second question is whether Greg breached the duty in s 175. Answering this involves balancing differing interests. Directors are free to resign from a company and set up another company, even one in direct competition with their former company.[44] To rule otherwise would serve to stifle competition and innovation, and illegitimately restrain trade,[45] as well as being against the public interest. However, companies must also be able to protect their business opportunities and information from directors who would seek to misappropriate them. The balancing of these objectives is evident from Hart J's statement that:

> By resigning his directorship [a director] will put an end to his fiduciary obligations to the company so far as concerns any future activity by himself (provided that it does not involve the exploitation of confidential information or business opportunities available to him by virtue of his directorship). A director who wishes to engage in a competing business and not to disclose his intentions to the company ought, in my judgment, to resign his office as soon as his intention has been irrevocably formed and he has launched himself in the actual taking of preparatory steps.[46]

The following case provides a clear example of a situation where a resigning director exploited an opportunity belonging to the company for his own personal gain.

Industrial Development Consultants Ltd v Cooley [1972] 1 WLR 443[47]

FACTS: Cooley, an architect, was appointed as managing director of Industrial Development Consultants Ltd ('IDC'). Cooley corresponded with the Eastern Gas Board about the possibility of IDC designing and constructing a series of depots for the Gas Board, but the Gas Board rejected this as they wished to deal with a private architect, as opposed to a consultancy firm (which is what IDC was). Around a year later, the deputy chair of the Gas Board met with Cooley, and was told that the Gas Board was once again looking for someone to build the depots. Cooley did not pass this information onto IDC. Instead, he realized that if he could be released from IDC quickly, he might be able to secure the depot contract for himself. Cooley was able to secure a quick release from his employment at IDC by falsely representing that he was seriously ill. A few weeks later, Cooley acquired the depot contract from the Gas Board. IDC learned of this and commenced proceedings against Cooley.

---

[44] *Balston Ltd v Headline Filters Ltd* [1990] FSR 385 (Ch).

[45] *Berryland Books Ltd v BK Books Ltd* [2009] EWHC 1877 (Ch), [2009] 2 BCLC 709 [25] (Hodge J).

[46] *British Midland Tool Ltd v Midland International Tooling Ltd* [2003] EWHC 466 (Ch), [2003] 2 BCLC 523 [89]. It should be noted that the point in time in which the director should resign will depend on the facts of the case.

[47] See also *Canadian Aero Service v O'Malley* (1973) 40 DLR (3d) 371 (Supreme Court of Canada).

HELD: Roskill J stated that Cooley was obliged to pass on to IDC the information he received (namely that the Gas Board was once again looking to build the depots) because he occupied a fiduciary position in relation to the company. In failing to do so, and in acquiring the contract, he had 'embarked upon a deliberate policy and course of conduct which put his personal interest as a potential contracting party with the Eastern Gas Board in direct conflict with his pre-existing and continuing duty as managing director of [IDC]'.[48] Accordingly, Cooley had acted in breach of duty and was ordered to account for the profits made from the contract.

It is important to note that resigning and setting up a competing business is not a breach of s 175 per se. As Falconer J stated:

> an intention by a director of a company to set up business in competition with the company after his directorship has ceased is not to be regarded as a conflict in interest within the context of the principle, having regard to the rules of public policy as to restraint of trade, nor is the taking of any preliminary steps to investigate or forward that intention so long as there is no actual competitive activity, such as, for instance, competitive tendering or actual trading, while he remains a director.[49]

What is required is the exploitation of property, information, or opportunity of which the former director became aware at a time when he was a director, and such exploitation amounted to a conflict of interest. Cooley clearly exploited an opportunity that he became aware of when he was a director of IDC, and his actions clearly placed him in a position where his own interests and those of IDC conflicted. However, in other cases, the issue is not so straightforward, and other factors might persuade the court that no conflict exists. The length of time between the director resigning and exploiting an opportunity might lead the court to conclude that no conflict existed. As the following case indicates, the circumstances behind the director's resignation can also have a significant impact.

Island Export Finance Ltd v Umunna [1986] BCLC 460 (QB)

FACTS: Umunna was the managing director of Island Export Finance Ltd ('IEF'). In 1976, Umunna secured a contract for IEF to provide postal boxes to the Cameroon postal authorities. In 1977, Umunna resigned from IEF following a falling out with the other directors, largely related to his remuneration. Shortly thereafter, Umunna secured similar business for his own company (Benosi International Ltd) from the Cameroon Postal authority. IEF commenced proceedings, alleging that Umunna had acted in breach of duty.

HELD: Hutchinson J stated that:

> When Mr Umunna resigned . . . his motive was not a desire to appropriate the postal caller box business to his own company, but rather his own deep sense of dissatisfaction with his role as managing director of [IEF] and his desire to branch out on his own by seeking, through Benosi, to open up West African business for himself.[50]

---

48 [1972] 1 WLR 443, 451.   49 *Balston Ltd v Headline Filters Ltd* [1990] FSR 385 (Ch) 412.
50 [1986] BCLC 460 (QB) 477.

He also noted that '[a]t the date [Umunna] resigned, [IEF] was not actively engaged in seeking further or repeat orders, nor did it take any steps to that end prior to a date in the latter part of 1978'.[51] Accordingly, Umunna had not breached his duty and IEF's claim failed.

Where the director's principal motive for resignation is not a desire to compete, then it seems that the courts will be less willing to find a breach. A number of cases where no breach was established concern situations where the resigning director resigned primarily due to poor treatment or disagreement with fellow directors, with a number of cases concerning directors who resigned after being excluded from management by their fellow directors.

Foster Bryant Surveying Ltd v Bryant [2007] EWCA Civ 200

FACTS: Foster Surveying Consultancy Ltd ('FCS') was set up by Foster, who was the majority shareholder. FCS entered into an agreement with Alliance Leisure Services Ltd ('Alliance') under which FCS would exclusively undertake work for Alliance. Foster proposed that Bryant join FCS. Bryant obtained 40 per cent of FCS's shares, became a director, and the company's name was changed to Foster Bryant Surveying Ltd ('FBS'). Bryant's wife also became an employee of FBS.

Two years later, Foster had lost confidence in Bryant's abilities. Foster informed Bryant that Mrs Bryant was to be made redundant. Bryant resigned immediately. However, before Bryant's resignation took effect, Alliance requested that Bryant undertake work for it on a retainer basis, which he accepted. Although still a director of FBS, Bryant was excluded from management until his agreed departure date some three months later. Alliance offered to share its work between FBS and Bryant, but Foster refused this offer. FBS commenced proceedings against Bryant, alleging that he had breached the no-conflict duty.

HELD: Bryant had not acted in breach of duty. Rix LJ stated '[t]here must be some relevant connection or link between the resignation and the obtaining of the business'.[52] Here, there was no such link as Bryant's 'resignation was not planned with an ulterior motive. He did not seek employment, or a retainer, or any business from Alliance. It was offered to him . . .'.[53] Accordingly, 'the resignation was innocent of any disloyalty or conflict of interest; the acceptance of an offer of future employment was likewise innocent; and there is no finding of any property or maturing business opportunity taken or exploited by Mr Bryant'.[54]

COMMENT: Rix LJ expressly recognized the balancing act that needs to be undertaken in cases of this kind. He stated:

It is possibly above all when a director is leaving that a company needs the protection which the law relating to directors' fiduciary duties provides. But it is also when a director is forced out of his own company that he needs the protection that the law allows to someone who has thereafter to earn his living.[55]

See John Lowry and Jen Sloszar, 'Judicial Pragmatism: Directors' Duties and Post-Resignation Conflicts of Duty' [2008] JBL 83.

---

[51] ibid.   [52] [2007] EWCA Civ 200, [2007] Bus LR 1565 [68].

[53] ibid [87].   [54] ibid [89].   [55] ibid [48].

11.1.4 **Authorization and ratification**

Under the common law, a conflict of interest would not constitute a breach of duty, and the director could keep any profit arising from such a conflict, if the conflict was authorized. Authorization would occur where the director disclosed the conflict and obtained consent from the company in general meeting,[56] but companies were able to (and usually did) state in their articles that disclosure to the board was sufficient.[57] In effect, authorization excluded the operation of the no-conflict and no-profit rules.

The Company Law Review acknowledged that allowing directors to authorize conflicts could create problems (such as collusion), and it also stated that requiring member authorization is 'impractical and onerous, is inconsistent with the principle that it is for the board to make business assessments, and stifles entrepreneurial activity'.[58] It therefore stated that board authorization of conflicts would 'strike the right balance between . . . encouraging efficient business operations and the take-up of new business opportunities . . . and . . . providing effective protection against abuse'.[59] This recommendation was accepted by Parliament and s 175(4)(b) provides that the s 175 duty will not be breached 'if the matter has been authorized by the directors'. However, the ability of the directors to authorize a conflict is limited in several ways:

- The directors of a private company can authorize a conflict as long as that there is nothing to the contrary in the company's constitution[60] (e.g. if the articles require member approval, then authorization from the directors will not suffice).

- The directors of a public company can only provide authorization if the articles so provide[61] and, if the articles do not provide for this, member approval will be required.

- Authorization cannot be retrospective.

- The directors cannot authorize a conflict that, under statute, requires member approval. The obvious examples of this are the transactions found in Part 10, Chs 4 and 4A of the CA 2006 (discussed at 11.4).

- The vote of the director in conflict (and any other 'interested' directors) will not count towards the authorizing vote or the quorum whilst the vote is held.[62] A situation may accordingly arise where the company cannot establish a quorum (e.g. because all the directors are conflicted or interested in the conflict),[63] in which case board authorization will not be possible, and the directors will have to fall back on the common law requirement of member authorization.

- The directors' power to authorize a conflict must, like all other powers, be exercised in accordance with the general duties, notably the duties in ss 171, 172, and 174. It is important to note that authorization will ensure that the s 175 duty is not breached, but it will not absolve a director if the conflict also amounts to a breach of any other general duties (e.g. the s 172 duty).

---

[56] *Aberdeen Rly Co v Blaikie Bros* (1854) 1 Macq 461 (HL).

[57] Companies (Tables A to F) Regulations 1985, Table A, art 85.

[58] Company Law Review Steering Group (CLRSG), 'Modern Company Law for a Competitive Economy: Final Report, vol 1' (DTI 2001) para 3.23.

[59] ibid para 3.27.

[60] CA 2006, s 175(4)(b) and (5)(a). The model articles for private companies contain no contrary provisions.

[61] ibid s 175(4)(b) and (5)(b). The model articles for public companies contain no such provision.

[62] ibid s 175(6).   [63] See e.g. *Lee Panavision Ltd v Lee Lighting Ltd* [1991] BCC 620 (CA).

As s 180(4) preserves the common law rules relating to authorization, the members in general meeting can also authorize the conflict. Authorization is usually by ordinary resolution but, as the following case indicates, a resolution is not required.

Sharma v Sharma [2013] EWCA Civ 1287

FACTS: The Sharma family (consisting of Kesh, Jagdish, Sunny, and Raj) ran a series of successful businesses, although Kesh took all the major business decisions. Anushka, a dentist, married Sunny. Anushka acquired two dental practices, and was offered the opportunity to acquire a third. Anushka and the Sharma family agreed to set up a company, Aspire Dental Care Ltd ('Aspire'), to acquire the third dental practice. The shares in Aspire were equally split between Anushka, Kesh, Sunny, and Raj, with Anushka as Aspire's only director. At a meeting, Anushka raised the possibility of acquiring other dental practices in her own name, and Kesh, Sunny, and Raj stated that she could acquire other dental practices if she wished. Aspire subsequently acquired four other dental practices, and Anushka acquired five practices in her own name. Anushka and Sunny's marriage broke down. During divorce proceedings, it became necessary to determine who was the legal owner of the five practices acquired by Anushka. The Sharma family contended that Anushka, in acquiring the five practices in her own name, had breached s 175.

HELD: Jackson LJ stated that '[i]f the shareholders with full knowledge of the relevant facts consent to the director exploiting those opportunities for his own personal gain, then that conduct is not a breach of the fiduciary or statutory duty'.[64] He also stated that '[i]f the shareholders with full knowledge of the relevant facts acquiesce in the director's proposed conduct, then that may constitute consent'.[65] Applying this, he held that Anushka had fully disclosed to the other members of Aspire her plan for acquiring further practices in her own name and they all acquiesced, and this was sufficient to amount to agreement under the *Re Duomatic* principle. Accordingly, Anushka had not breached the s 175 duty.

> The *Re Duomatic* principle is discussed at 14.2.

If, for whatever reason, authorization cannot be obtained, the consequences of breach of duty can be avoided by obtaining ratification under s 239. If the conflicted director is a member, then his votes (and those of any members connected to him) will not count towards the ratifying resolution.[66]

> Section 239 is discussed at 10.1.3.3.

A director who is in a position of conflict will not be in breach of s 175 if the articles contain provisions for dealing with conflicts of interest, and the director acts in accordance with those provisions.[67]

11.1.5 Remedies

Where a director breaches s 175, any resulting contract is voidable at the company's instance, provided that the third party involved has notice of the director's breach.[68] In addition, the company can require the director to account for any profit made as a result of the conflict.[69] As noted above, these consequences will be avoided if the members ratify the breach of duty under s 239.

---

[64] 2013 EWCA Civ 1287, [2014] BCC 73 [52].   [65] ibid.
[66] CA 2006, s 239(3) and (4).   [67] ibid s 180(4)(b).
[68] *Hely-Hutchinson & Co Ltd v Brayhead Ltd* [1968] 1 QB 549 (CA).
[69] *Aberdeen Rly Co v Blaikie Bros* (1854) 1 Macq 461 (HL).

11.2 Duty not to accept benefits from third parties

The duty found in s 176 is a reformulation of the common law rule that provides that those who occupy a fiduciary position cannot accept a bribe or make a secret commission.[70] Section 176(1) provides that a director must not accept from a third party a benefit conferred by reason of his being a director, or by doing (or not doing) anything as a director. It should also be noted that directors, as agents of the company, are subject to an independent common-law duty not to accept bribes.[71] As with the s 175 duty, *mala fides* is not a requirement and it will therefore be no defence for the director to argue that he accepted the benefit in good faith. The duty extends to a former director in relation to acts or omissions prior to his ceasing to be a director.[72]

➡ *mala fides*: 'bad faith'

11.2.1 'Benefit'

The CA 2006 does not define what a 'benefit' is for the purposes of s 176, but the Solicitor-General stated that 'benefit' is defined in accordance 'with the ordinary dictionary meaning of the word'[73] and will therefore include 'benefits of any description, including non-financial benefits'.[74] Certain benefits are expressly excluded from the scope of the s 176 duty:

- As s 176 applies to benefits received from third parties, s 176(2) provides that the duty will not apply to benefits received from the company itself, an associated body corporate,[75] or a person acting on behalf of the company or an associated body corporate.

- A benefit received by a director from a person by whom his services (as a director or otherwise) are provided to the company are excluded from the s 176 duty.[76] This would include benefits received as a result of the director's service contract (e.g. remuneration).

- The duty does not apply to a benefit that 'cannot reasonably be regarded as likely to give rise to a conflict of interest'.[77] The presence of this exclusion might lead us to wonder why s 176 exists at all, as benefits that amount to a conflict of interest would appear to be covered by the s 175 duty to avoid conflicts. Indeed, there is a notable overlap between the duties in ss 175 and 176,[78] but there is a crucial difference, and it relates to the way that conflicts and benefits are authorized.

11.2.2 Authorization

As noted at 11.1.4, a conflict of interest that arises solely under s 175 can be authorized by the board.[79] A benefit that falls within s 176 cannot be authorized by the board, and must instead be authorized by the members[80] (or, if a breach has occurred, the members can also ratify the breach under s 239). This clearly indicates that the receipt of

---

[70] *Attorney General of Hong Kong v Reid* [1994] 1 AC 324 (PC).

[71] Discussion of this duty is outside the scope of this text, but for more, see Eric Baskind, Greg Osborne, and Lee Roach, *Commercial Law* (3rd edn, OUP 2019) 127.

[72] CA 2006, s 170(2)(b).   [73] HC Comm D 11 July 2006, col 622.   [74] ibid.

[75] Section 256 of the CA 2006 provides that bodies corporate are associated if one is the subsidiary of the other or both are subsidiaries of the same body corporate.

[76] CA 2006, s 176(3).   [77] ibid s 176(4).

[78] Explanatory Notes to the CA 2006, para 344.   [79] CA 2006, s 175(4) and (5).

[80] Authorization by the members is not expressly stated, but is a consequence of s 180(4)(a).

third-party benefits constitutes a much greater danger to board impartiality than the conflicts covered by s 175 alone (indeed, under the rules of agency, such benefits would be classed as 'bribes'). It has been argued that the requirement of member authorization amounts to a 'near-ban on the receipt of third-party benefits'.[81]

A director who has received a third-party benefit will not be in breach of s 176 if the articles contain provisions for dealing with conflicts of interest, and the director acts in accordance with those provisions.[82]

11.2.3 Remedies and offences

Where a director accepts an unauthorized third-party benefit, the company can rescind the contract[83] and the benefit can be recovered. Instead of recovering the benefit, the company may claim damages in fraud from either the director in breach or the third party.[84] In addition, the company can summarily terminate the director's service contract and dismiss him.[85] Under agency law, if the benefit amounts to a bribe, then other consequences can also follow (e.g. the director might lose any right to remuneration).[86]

If a director requests, agrees to receive, or receives a bribe, then he will commit an either-way offence,[87] punishable by a fine or imprisonment.[88]

11.3 Duty to declare interest in transactions or arrangements

Section 177 imposes a duty upon directors in relation to *proposed* transactions or arrangements, whereas s 182 imposes a duty in relation to *existing* transactions or arrangements. Section 177 is clearly a general duty, but the exact status of s 182 is unclear, although its location in Chapter 3 of Pt 10 would indicate that it is a supplementary duty and not a general duty in its own right. Each duty will be examined separately.

11.3.1 Proposed transactions or arrangements

An equitable rule has long existed which provides that directors cannot have an interest in a transaction with the company, unless the interest is authorized by the members.[89] The inconvenience of obtaining member approval can be avoided by inserting a provision in the articles stating that directors have merely to disclose the interest and, as most companies had such an article provision,[90] the Company Law Review recommended that disclosure should suffice.[91] Accordingly, s 177(1) provides that '[i]f a director of a company is in any way, directly or indirectly, interested in a proposed transaction or

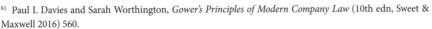

---

[81] Paul L Davies and Sarah Worthington, *Gower's Principles of Modern Company Law* (10th edn, Sweet & Maxwell 2016) 560.

[82] CA 2006, s 180(4)(b).   [83] *Shipway v Broadwood* [1899] 1 QB 369 (CA).

[84] *Mahesan v Malaysia Government Officers' Co-operative Housing Society Ltd* [1979] AC 374 (PC).

[85] *Boston Deep Sea Fishing Co v Ansell* (1888) 39 ChD 39 (CA).

[86] *Andrews v Ramsay & Co* [1903] 2 KB 635 (KB).   [87] Bribery Act 2010, s 2.   [88] ibid s 11(1).

[89] *Aberdeen Rly Co v Blaikie Bros* (1854) 1 Macq 461 (HL).

[90] Indeed, art 85 of Table A contained such a provision.

[91] CLRSG, 'Modern Company Law for a Competitive Economy: Developing the Framework' (DTI 2000) para 3.62.

arrangement with the company, he must declare the nature and extent of that interest to the other directors'.

The s 177 duty applies only to directors who have an interest in transactions or arrangements with the company. Where the interest arises due to a transaction or arrangement with a third party, then s 177 will not apply and instead ss 175–6 will apply. However, as the duty covers direct and indirect interests, a director need not be party to the transaction or arrangement in order for the duty to arise. The following provides an example of this.

> **Eg** **An indirect interest under s 177**
>
> Dragon plc is considering entering into a contract with Hayden Ltd. Joanne is Hayden Ltd's only director, and she is married to Nancy, who is a director of Dragon. In this case, Nancy has an indirect interest in the proposed transaction between Dragon and Hayden and so must comply with s 177.

As to what amounts to an 'interest' in a transaction or arrangement, the Act is silent. Examples include (i) a director entering into a contract with his company;[92] (ii) company A and company B propose to contract, but a director of company A is a director or shareholder of company B;[93] or (iii) a director of company A executes a personal guarantee in favour of company B for the debts of company A.[94]

11.3.1.1 Declaration of interest

In order to avoid a breach of s 177, a director must declare his interest to the other directors—he need not obtain their approval, although if the other directors do not approve, then they will likely ensure that the company does not enter into the transaction or arrangement. The requirement of declaration to the other directors constitutes the minimum requirement. A company, if it so chooses, can impose more exacting requirements in its constitution,[95] for example, by inserting a provision in the articles requiring authorization by the board or general meeting.

The Act does not specify how the declaration should be made, although it does state that the declaration may (but need not) be made at a meeting of the directors, by notice in writing, or by general notice.[96] However, in order for the declaration to be valid, the director must comply with the following requirements:

- the declaration must be made before the company enters into the transaction or arrangement;[97]
- it is not enough for a director merely to state that he has an interest in a proposed transaction or arrangement—he must also declare the nature and extent of the interest;[98]
- if a declaration proves to be, or becomes, inaccurate or incomplete, then if the company has not yet entered into the transaction or arrangement, the director must make a further declaration correcting the previous one before the company enters into the transaction or arrangement.[99]

---

[92] *Movitex Ltd v Bulfield* [1988] BCLC 104 (Ch) (directors leased land they owned the company they worked for).

[93] *Gwembe Valley Development Co Ltd v Koshy* [2003] EWCA Civ 1048, [2004] 1 BCLC 131 (company A purchased currency from company B, which was controlled by the managing director of company A).

[94] *Rolled Steel Products (Holdings) Ltd v British Steel Corp* [1986] Ch 246 (CA).

[95] CA 2006, s 180(1).   [96] ibid s 177(2).   [97] ibid s 177(4).

[98] ibid s 177(1).   [99] ibid s 177(3).

There are a number of instances where a declaration is not required, namely (i) where the interest cannot reasonably be regarded as likely to give rise to a conflict of interest;[100] (ii) where the director in question is not aware of the interest, or of the transaction or arrangement;[101] (iii) where the other directors are aware of the interest;[102] or (iv) where a company only has one director.[103]

Following the declaration, the other directors will resolve on whether the company should proceed with the transaction or arrangement. The director with the interest cannot, under the model articles, participate in the board resolution,[104] nor will he count towards the quorum during that resolution.[105]

11.3.2 Existing transactions or arrangements

Section 182(1) provides that '[w]here a director of a company is in any way, directly or indirectly, interested in a transaction or arrangement that has been entered into by the company, he must declare the nature and extent of the interest to the other directors'.

11.3.2.1 Declaration of interest

As with s 177, a breach of s 182 can be avoided if the director declares his interest. Note that if a declaration under s 177 takes place, a subsequent declaration under s 182 is not required once the transaction or arrangement is entered into.[106] The rules relating to s 182 declarations are largely the same as for s 177 declarations (including those instances where a declaration is not required), but there are some key differences:

- A declaration under s 182 must be made 'as soon as is reasonably practicable',[107] whereas, under s 177, a declaration need only occur at a time prior to the transaction or arrangement being entered into.[108]
- The declaration must be made at a meeting of the directors, by notice in writing, or by general notice.[109] Where the director is a shadow director, then the declaration must be made by notice in writing.[110]

11.3.3 Remedies and offences

Where the director contravenes s 177, the transaction or arrangement is voidable at the company's instance.[111] That this is the only consequence for breach of s 177 can be criticized on several grounds. First, it appears that a director who has breached s 177 can keep any profit acquired if the transaction or arrangement proceeds. Second, if rescission is not available (e.g. because a third party's rights would be affected), then there will be no consequences for the director's breach of duty. Third, Sealy has argued that 'the

---

[100] ibid s 177(6)(a).   [101] ibid s 177(5).

[102] ibid s 177(6)(b). In this context, the directors are treated as being aware of anything of which they ought reasonably to be aware.

[103] Explanatory Notes to the CA 2006, para 352.

[104] Model articles for private companies, art 14(1); model articles for public companies, arts 13(3) and 16(1).

[105] Model articles for private companies, art 14(1); model articles for public companies, art 16(1).

[106] CA 2006, s 182(1).

[107] ibid s 182(4). If the declaration is not made as soon as is reasonably practicable, the director remains obliged to make the declaration.

[108] ibid s 177(4).   [109] ibid s 182(2).   [110] ibid s 187.

[111] *Hely-Hutchinson v Brayhead Ltd* [1968] 1 QB 549 (CA).

law should not allow directors who are guilty of undisclosed self-dealing to go unpunished . . .'.[112] Section 317 of the CA 1985 (the predecessor to ss 177 and 182) imposed criminal liability upon a director who failed to disclose an interest in a proposed transaction or arrangement, but a breach of s 177 carries no such liability. For these reasons, it has been stated that s 177 is 'not a provision designed to impose liability on directors, but a provision designed to afford protection to those who comply with it'.[113]

Criminal liability is, however, imposed for a breach of the duty in s 182.[114] The reasoning behind the imposition of differing forms of liability in ss 177 and 182 was set out by Lord Goldsmith, who stated, 'because one is here concerned with an existing transaction or arrangement, the failure to declare cannot affect the validity of the transaction or give rise to any other civil consequences. . . . That is why a criminal offence is created.'[115]

A director can be liable under both ss 177 and 182 if he does not disclose his interest in a proposed transaction, and then does not disclose once the same transaction has been entered into by the company.

11.4 Transactions requiring member approval

As regards the conflict of interest general duties discussed thus far, it is clear that the law has moved away from requiring member approval, and will now permit most conflicts to be authorized by mere board disclosure or approval. However, certain transactions and arrangements involving directors and the company are deemed to constitute particularly risky forms of conflicts of interest and so are subject to special rules found in Pt 10, Chs 4 and 4A of the CA 2006 . In relation to these transactions or arrangements, the directors[116] must comply with the general duties (of which s 177 will likely be the most relevant) and obtain prior approval from the members.[117] Approval requires 'a resolution of the members',[118] which will generally be an ordinary resolution, unless the articles specify a higher majority or unanimity.[119]

Before the relevant transactions and arrangements are discussed, it is worth noting that the provisions in Pt 10, Chs 4 and 4A repeatedly refer to persons who are 'connected' to a director. Section 252(2) provides that the following (and only the following) are connected persons:

(a) members of the director's family;[120]

(b) a body corporate with whom the director is connected;[121]

---

[112] Len Sealy, 'The Statutory Statement of Directors' Duties: Devil in the Detail' (2008) 228 (Co LN 1, 3.

[113] Geoffrey Morse, *Palmer's Company Law* (Sweet & Maxwell 2018) para 8.3122.

[114] CA 2006, s 183.   [115] HL Comm 9 February 2006, col GC338.

[116] Section 223(1) of the CA 2006 also provides that, for the purposes of ss 188–222, a shadow director is treated as a director.

[117] ibid s 180(3). Note though that s 180(2) provides that if member approval is obtained under Chs 4 or 4A, then the director need not comply with ss 175 or 176.

[118] ibid ss 188(2)(a), 190(1), 197(1), 198(2), 201(2), 217(1), 226B(1)(b), and 226C(1)(b).   [119] ibid s 281(3).

[120] Section 253 provides that this includes the director's spouse or civil partner, his cohabiting partner, his parents, or his children or step-children.

[121] Section 254 provides that a director is connected to a body corporate if he and persons connected to him together (i) are interested in shares with a nominal value equal to at least 20 per cent of the share capital; or (ii) are entitled to exercise or control more than 20 per cent of the voting power at a general meeting.

(c) trustees of a trust, the beneficiaries of which include the director or members of his family or a connected body corporate, or the terms of which confer a power on the trustees that may be exercised for the benefit of any such person;

(d) any partner of the director or the partner of a person connected to the director by virtue of (a), (b), or (c) above;

(e) a firm that is a legal person under the law (e.g. a limited liability partnership (LLP)) and (i) in which the director is a partner; or (ii) one of the partners is connected to a director by virtue of (a), (b), or (c) above.

11.4.1 Service contracts

Historically, directors would attempt to negotiate lengthy service contracts in order to entrench their position, as the example demonstrates.

Eg Entrenchment through lengthy service contracts

Angela is appointed as a director of Dragon plc. She has negotiated a ten-year service contract and is to be paid £1 million per year. After one year, it is apparent that she is incompetent. The members wish to remove her from office, but as s 168(5) preserves the director's right to compensation for breach of contract; removing her might allow her to recover £9 million in damages (£1 million × the number of years left on her contract). Angela's position is entrenched by making it prohibitively expensive to remove her. If the entire board colluded to have similar contracts, the board of Dragon could become virtually irremovable. This would severely emasculate the power to remove a director found in s 168.

The s 168 power of removal is discussed at 12.4.1.

In order to avoid such a situation, s 188(1) provides that a director cannot have a guaranteed term of employment[122] with the company or, if it is a holding company, with any of its subsidiaries, that is or may be longer than two years[123] in length unless it has been approved in advance[124] by a resolution of the company's members. However, approval is not required if the company is not a UK-registered company or if it is a wholly owned subsidiary of another body corporate.[125]

As regards companies with a premium listing, Provision 39 of the UK Corporate Governance Code goes further by recommending that '[n]otice or contract periods should be one year or less'. Service contracts of a year or less are now generally standard in listed companies, but the directors of larger companies often have rolling contracts which, after a specified period,[126] are replaced (automatically or by agreement) with a new fixed-term contract. The Law Commission was critical of rolling contracts on the ground that they allow directors 'to enjoy a long term service contract without breaking

---

[122] Section 188(7) defines employment as any employment under a service contract.

[123] Section 319 of the CA 1985 (the predecessor to s 188) set this period at five years.

[124] Section 188 does not expressly state that approval must be provided before the contract is made, but it is a consequence in s 188(5) and prior approval was deemed necessary in *Wright v Atlas Wright (Europe) Ltd* [1999] BCC 163 (CA).

[125] CA 2006, s 188(6).

[126] An extreme example of this is where the contract is novated daily, so that a new contract (with a refreshed notice period) comes into effect each day.

the statutory limit',[127] but its recommendations relating to regulating rolling contracts were not implemented. Ultimately, the use of rolling contracts may not be problematic in Financial Times Stock Exchange 350 (FTSE 350) companies due to the fact that the vast majority of such companies[128] comply with the Code's recommendation that directors are subject to annual re-election by the members.[129]

In order for the members to vote on an informed basis, s 188(5) provides that a memorandum setting out the proposed contract must be made available to the members. Where the resolution is a written one, the memorandum must be sent at or before the time when the proposed written resolution is sent. Where the resolution takes place at a meeting, the memorandum must be made available for inspection at the company's registered office at least 15 days before the date of the meeting, and at the meeting itself.

A provision in a service contract that provides a director with guaranteed employment for over two years is void if member approval has not been obtained.[130] Note that the contract itself is not void, merely the contravening term. Further, the contract will also be deemed to contain a term allowing the company to terminate it at any time by giving reasonable notice.[131]

11.4.2 Substantial property transactions

Where a director has an interest in a proposed transaction or arrangement, s 177 generally requires him to declare that interest to the other directors. Where, however, a transaction or arrangement[132] amounts to a 'substantial property transaction', disclosure to the directors is insufficient and a company may not enter into such an arrangement unless it has been approved by a resolution of the members or is conditional on such approval being obtained.[133] Two types of arrangement require member approval:

1. where a director of the company or of its holding company, or a person connected with such a director, acquires, or is to acquire, from the company (directly or indirectly) a substantial non-cash asset;

2. where the company acquires, or is to acquire, a substantial non-cash asset (directly or indirectly) from such a director or a person so connected.

A 'non-cash asset' is 'any property or interest in property, other than cash'[134] and a non-cash asset is substantial if its value (i) is over £100,000; or (ii) exceeds 10 per cent of the company's asset value and is more than £5,000.[135] The following case provides an example of the above rules in action.

---

[127] Law Commission, *Company Directors: Regulating Conflicts of Interest and Formulating a Statement of Duties* (Law Com No 261, 1999) para 9.2.

[128] Grant Thornton, 'Trust and Integrity—Loud and Clear?' (Grant Thornton 2015) 52 shows that 98.4 per cent of FTSE 350 companies subject their directors to annual election by the members.

[129] Financial Reporting Council (FRC), 'The UK Corporate Governance Code' (FRC 2018) Provision 18.

[130] CA 2006, s 189(a).   [131] ibid s 189(b).

[132] The use of the word 'arrangement' in s 190 includes an agreement or understanding that does not have contractual effect (*Re Duckwari plc* [1999] Ch 253 (CA)).

[133] CA 2006, s 190(1). Section 190(2) provides that where the director or a connected person is a director of the company's holding company (or is connected to such a director), then the arrangement must also be approved by a resolution of the members of the holding company.

[134] ibid s 1163(1).   [135] ibid s 191(2).

Re Duckwari plc [1995] BCC 89 (Ch and CA)

FACTS: Cooper was a director of Duckwari plc and was a director and major shareholder of Offerventure Ltd. Offerventure agreed to purchase a piece of property for £495,000 and paid a 10 per cent deposit of £49,500 to the sellers. Before the contract of sale was concluded, Cooper, on behalf of Offerventure, contacted Duckwari's board and proposed that Offerventure would pass the property to Duckwari, in return for which Duckwari would pay the balance price and would reimburse Offerventure the £49,500 it paid as a deposit. The board of Duckwari agreed (but member approval was not sought) and the deal went ahead. Subsequently, the property market collapsed and the value of the property decreased substantially (Duckwari eventually sold it for £177,970). Duckwari sought to avoid the transaction by commencing proceedings against Cooper and Offerventure on the ground that the deal was a substantial property transaction, and member approval should have been obtained.

HELD: The first issue to determine was whether Duckwari had acquired a 'non-cash asset'. Duckwari was acquiring either 'the benefit of the purchase contract or (what comes to the same thing) Offerventure's beneficial interest in the property'.[136] Both of these clearly constituted an interest in property and so Duckwari had acquired a non-cash asset. The Court held that the non-cash asset was 'substantial' as it was worth at least £49,500, and 10 per cent of Duckwari's asset value was £44,399.

Taking the above all together, Duckwari had acquired a substantial non-cash asset from a person (Offerventure) who was connected to one of Duckari's directors, namely Cooper. Accordingly, the agreement was one that required the approval of Duckwari's members and, as such approval had not been obtained, the Court held that Cooper, the other directors of Duckwari, and Offerventure were liable to indemnify Duckwari for the whole of its loss.

See Tim Pryce-Brown, 'Directors in Company Asset Transactions' (1995) 16 Co Law 212.

Section 190 does not require the approval of every single detail of the transaction, but the 'central aspects' must be approved.[137] For example, in the case of a sale of an asset, the members would need to approve 'the price, or possibly a minimum price, or at least a yardstick by reference to which the price is to be fixed'.[138] Approval can be obtained via the *Re Duomatic* rule.[139]

11.4.2.1 Exceptions

There are a number of instances where a substantial property transaction will not require member approval, including:

- where the company is not a UK-registered company, or is the wholly owned subsidiary of another body corporate;[140]
- where the transaction relates to anything that a director is entitled to under his service contract, or to a payment for loss of office;[141]
- where the transaction is between a company and a person in his character as a member of that company;[142]
- where a transaction is (i) between a holding company and its wholly owned subsidiary; or (ii) between two wholly owned subsidiaries of the same holding company;[143]

---

[136] [1995] BCC 89 (CA) 98 (Millet LJ).
[137] *Demite Ltd v Protec Health Ltd* [1998] BCC 638 (Ch) 649 (Park J).
[138] ibid.   [139] *NBH Ltd v Hoare* [2006] EWHC 73 (Ch), [2006] 2 BCLC 649.
[140] CA 2006, s 190(4).   [141] ibid s 190(6).   [142] ibid s 192(a).   [143] ibid s 192(b).

- where a company is in administration, or is being compulsorily wound up or wound up via a creditors' voluntary winding up;[144]

- where a transaction takes place on a recognized investment exchange effected by a director (or a person connected with him) through the agency of an independent broker.[145]

11.4.2.2 Remedies

No liability is placed upon the company if member approval is not obtained.[146] A substantial property transaction entered into without member approval is voidable at the company's instance, unless restitution is impossible, the company has been indemnified, or avoidance would affect the rights of a person who had acquired those rights bona fide for value and without actual notice of the contravention.[147] The transaction also cannot be avoided if the members subsequently pass, within a reasonable period, a resolution affirming the transaction.[148]

Irrespective of whether the arrangement was avoided, any director or connected person who was involved in the arrangement (including any directors who authorized the arrangement) will be liable to account for any direct or indirect gains made, and are also required to indemnify the company for any losses sustained as a result of the arrangement.[149] However, a connected person or director who authorized the arrangement can escape liability if he shows that, at the time that the arrangement was entered into, he was unaware of the relevant circumstances constituting the contravention.[150]

11.4.3 Loans, quasi-loans, and credit transactions

There are many rules regarding a director's ability to dispose of assets belonging to the company. Directors may try and avoid those rules and seek to benefit themselves financially through the misuse of loans, as the following example demonstrates.

 Directors and loans

At a board meeting, the directors of Dragon plc agree that the company will loan Ruby, one of Dragon's directors, the sum of £50,000. The loan agreement does not provide for Ruby to pay any interest on the loan, no security is provided by Ruby, and no date is stipulated for the loan's repayment. Several other directors of Dragon have received similar loans over the years. At no point has the company sought to recover the amounts loaned.

In this example, the directors have essentially caused Dragon to gift money to the directors. It has long been a cause of concern that loans and other transactions could be abused in this way, so successive Companies Acts have placed limits upon the company's ability to make loans to its directors. Under previous Companies Acts, a company was prohibited from making any form of loan to one of its directors (subject to several

---

[144] ibid s 193.   [145] ibid s 194.   [146] ibid s 190(3).   [147] ibid s 195(2).   [148] ibid s 196.
[149] ibid s 195(3).   [150] ibid s 195(7).

exceptions) and breach of this prohibition constituted a criminal offence. The rationale behind this was stated by the Cohen Committee:

> We consider it undesirable that directors should borrow from their companies. If the director can offer good security, it is no hardship for him to borrow from other sources. If he cannot offer good security, it is undesirable that he should obtain from the company credit which he would not be able to obtain elsewhere.[151]

The Law Commission rejected the proposal that loans, etc. to directors could be made if member approval was required, on the ground that it 'would involve adding further complexities to existing legislation which would be contrary to our remit to simplify and modernise the provisions . . .'[152] However, the Company Law Review disagreed and recommended that loans, etc. should be permitted if member approval was obtained,[153] and this has been implemented in the CA 2006, albeit subject to some notable exceptions.

11.4.3.1 Loans

Section 197(1) provides that a company may not make a loan to a director of the company or of its holding company, or give a guarantee or provide security in connection with a loan made by any person to such a director, unless the transaction has been approved by a resolution of the members. If the director is a director of the company's holding company, then the loan must also be approved by a resolution of the holding company's members.[154]

11.4.3.2 Quasi-loans

A quasi-loan occurs where the company agrees to pay a sum on behalf of the director, or where the company reimburses expenses incurred by another party due to actions of the director, on the understanding that the director (or someone acting on his behalf) will later reimburse the company.[155]

Eg **Quasi-loans**

Kate, a director of Dragon plc, owes £12,000 to Welsh Bank plc. Dragon pays £12,000 to Welsh Bank in fulfilment of Kate's debt, and it is agreed that Kate will reimburse Dragon the £12,000 within six months. The £12,000 payment made by Dragon is a quasi-loan and would require member approval.

A public company (or a company associated[156] with a public company) cannot make a quasi-loan to a director, or give a guarantee or provide security in connection with a

---

[151] *Report of the Committee on Company Law Amendment* (Cmnd 6659, 1945) para 94.

[152] Law Commission, *Company Directors: Regulating Conflicts of Interest and Formulating a Statement of Duties* (Law Com No 261, 1999) para 12.40.

[153] CLRSG, 'Modern Company Law for a Competitive Economy: Completing the Structure' (CLRSG, 2000) para 4.21.

[154] CA 2006, s 197(2).   [155] ibid s 199(1).

[156] Section 256 of the CA 2006 provides that bodies corporate are associated if one is the subsidiary of the other or both are subsidiaries of the same body corporate.

quasi-loan made by any person to such a director, unless it has been approved by a resolution of the members.[157] From this, it follows that a private company is free to provide a director with a quasi-loan.

11.4.3.3 Credit transactions

A 'credit transaction' is one under which the company (i) supplies any goods or sells any land under a hire-purchase agreement or a conditional sale agreement; (ii) leases or hires any land or goods in return for periodical payments; or (iii) otherwise disposes of land or supplies goods or services on the understanding that payment is to be deferred.[158]

Eg Credit transactions

Dragon plc is looking to sell off some of its older stock of company cars. Sajid, a director of Dragon, asks if he can purchase one of the cars on hire purchase terms, with 12 monthly payments of £1,000 and a final payment of £5,000 coming out of his salary. Dragon agrees. This is a credit transaction and would require member approval.

A public company (or a company associated with a public company) cannot enter into a credit transaction with a director, or give a guarantee or provide security in connection with a credit transaction entered into by any person for the benefit of such a director, unless it has been approved by a resolution of the members.[159] From this, it follows that a private company is free to enter into a credit transaction with a director.

11.4.3.4 Exceptions

The above requirements for member approval do not apply in a number of situations, namely:

- where the company is not a UK-registered company, or is a wholly owned subsidiary of another body corporate;[160]
- where a loan, quasi-loan, or credit transaction does not exceed £50,000 or is provided to meet the director's expenditure on company business;[161]
- where a company provides a director with funds to meet expenditure incurred by the director in defending any criminal or civil proceedings in connection with (i) any alleged negligence, default, breach of duty, or breach of trust by him in relation to the company or an associated company; or (ii) an application for relief (e.g. under s 1157 of the CA 2006);[162]
- where a company provides a director with funds to meet expenditure incurred by the director in defending himself in an investigation or action taken by a regulatory authority in connection with any alleged negligence, default, breach of duty, or breach of trust by him in relation to the company or an associated company;[163]
- where the loan or quasi-loan does not exceed £10,000,[164] or a credit transaction that (i) does not exceed £15,000;[165] or (ii) is entered into by a company in the ordinary course of

---

[157] CA 2006, s 198(1) and (2).   [158] ibid s 202(1).   [159] ibid s 201(1) and (2).
[160] ibid ss 197(5), 198(6), and 201(6).   [161] ibid s 204.   [162] ibid s 205.
[163] ibid s 206.   [164] ibid s 207(1).   [165] ibid s 207(2).

its business and the director is not treated differently than a person of the same financial standing who is not connected with the company;[166]

- where the loan, quasi-loan, or credit transaction is made to an associated body corporate;[167]
- where a money-lending company makes a loan or quasi-loan to a director in the ordinary course of the company's business, and the director is not treated differently than a person of the same financial standing who is not connected with the company.[168]

11.4.3.5 Remedies

Where member approval is required, a failure to obtain such approval renders the loan, quasi-loan, or credit transaction voidable at the company's instance, unless restitution is impossible, the company has been indemnified, or avoidance would affect the rights of a person who had acquired those rights bona fide for value and without actual notice of the contravention.[169] The transaction also cannot be avoided if the members subsequently pass, within a reasonable period, a resolution affirming the transaction.[170]

Irrespective of whether the transaction or arrangement is avoided, the director who entered into the transaction, any persons connected to such a director, or any other directors who authorized the transaction, is liable to account to the company for any gains made and is also liable to indemnify the company for any losses sustained as a result of the transaction or arrangement.[171]

11.4.4 Remuneration and payments for loss of office

In recent years, payments made by companies (especially quoted companies) to departing directors (such payments are often referred to as 'golden goodbyes' or 'golden parachutes') have become extremely controversial, especially where the payment is being made to a director who has not been effective. Sections 215–22 and 226A–226F put in place rules relating to remuneration and member approval, but the rules differ depending on whether the company is quoted or unquoted.

11.4.4.1 Payments for loss of office in unquoted companies

Sections 215–22 put in place rules relating to loss-of-office payments in unquoted companies.[172] Section 217(1) provides that a company may not make a payment for loss of office to a director unless the payment has been approved by a resolution of the members.[173] Similar provisions require member approval for loss-of-office payments made by any person in connection with the transfer of the whole or part of the undertaking or property of the company,[174] and any person in connection with a transfer of any shares in the company or any of its subsidiaries, resulting from a takeover bid.[175] Section 215 defines what a 'payment for loss of office' is, and it includes a payment made to a director or past director:

- by way of compensation for loss of office as a director of the company;

---

[166] ibid s 207(3).   [167] ibid s 208.   [168] ibid s 209.   [169] ibid s 213(1) and (2).

[170] ibid s 214.   [171] ibid s 213(3) and (4).

[172] Section 215(5) states that the rules in ss 215–22 do not generally apply to quoted companies.

[173] Where a company makes a payment to a director of its holding company, then the approval of the holding company's members is also required (CA 2006, s 217(2)).

[174] CA 2006, s 218.   [175] ibid s 219.

- by way of compensation for loss, while a director, of any other office or employment in connection with the management affairs of the company (or of a subsidiary undertaking of the company);

- as consideration for, or in connection with, his retirement as director or an officer;

- as consideration for or employee involved in the management of the affairs of the company (or of a subsidiary undertaking of the company).

However, the requirement of member approval does not apply to:

- a company that is not a registered UK company, or a company that is a wholly owned subsidiary of another body corporate;[176]

- a payment made in good faith in discharge of an existing legal obligation, or by way of damages for breach of such an obligation.[177] An existing legal obligation is defined as 'an obligation of the company, or any body corporate associated with it, that was not entered into in connection with, or in consequence of, the event giving rise to the payment for loss of office'.[178] The obvious example of this would be a loss-of-office payment provision in a service contract. This is a noteworthy exception as most golden parachutes are provided for in a director's service contract, meaning that most loss-of-office payments will not require member approval;

- a payment made in good faith by way of settlement or compromise of any claim arising in connection with the termination of a person's office or employment, or by way of pension in respect of past services;[179]

- a payment that does not exceed £200.[180]

Where member approval is not obtained, the recipient of the payment will hold the payment on trust for the company, and any director who authorized the payment is jointly and severally liable to indemnify the company for any loss resulting from the payment.[181]

11.4.4.2 Remuneration and payments for loss of office in quoted companies

The above rules in ss 215–22 do not apply to quoted companies. Instead, quoted companies are subject to the rules in ss 226A–226F (which were inserted into the CA 2006 by the Enterprise and Regulatory Reform Act 2013 (ERRA 2013)) and lay down rules relating to remuneration and loss-of-office payments. As regards remuneration, s 226B(1) provides that a quoted company may not make a remuneration payment to a person who is, or is to be or has been, a director of the company unless:

The remuneration policy is discussed at 19.3.2.4.

(a) the payment is consistent with the approved directors' remuneration policy; or

(b) the payment is approved by resolution of the members of the company.

As regards loss-of-office payments, such payments have become extremely controversial. In the US, massive golden parachutes are common amongst larger companies, with the largest payment being granted to Jack Welch, the former chief executive officer (CEO) of General Electric who, upon his retirement received over $417.3 million. Also noteworthy was the golden parachute of Bill Johnson, who was appointed as CEO of Duke Energy, but resigned a few hours later—for this, he was awarded a golden parachute of $44.4 million. In the UK, golden parachutes have not reached such heights, but they are extremely controversial, especially where the departing director has not been

---

[176] ibid s 217(4). [177] ibid s 220(1)(a) and (b).
[178] ibid s 220(2). [179] ibid s 220(1)(c) and (d), [180] ibid s 221(1). [181] ibid s 222(1).

perceived as successful. There is an increasing perception that such payments represent a 'reward for failure'.

 Golden parachutes as 'rewards for failure'

Examples of departing directors being perceived as being rewarded for failure include the following:

- Bob Diamond was the CEO of Barclays when a number of employees were convicted of manipulating the London interbank offered rate (LIBOR), with UK and US regulators fining Barclays £290 million. Upon resigning in 2012, he was due to receive £2 million in compensation and £20 million in share options, but, following intense pressure, he chose not to exercise his options.
- Tony Hayward was CEO of BP when it sustained record losses following the Deepwater Horizon oil spill in the Gulf of Mexico. Upon resigning in 2010, he was awarded a severance payment of £1 million and a pension valued at £11 million.
- Fred Goodwin, former CEO of the Royal Bank of Scotland (RBS), oversaw a policy of overly aggressive expansion which resulted in RBS sustaining losses of £28 billion. The bank only survived after it was bailed out by the government. Upon leaving in 2008, he had a pension valued at £16.6 million (but it was later reduced by one-third). Other directors of RBS were also revealed to have sizeable golden parachutes.

In a 2012 consultation document, the Department for Business, Innovation and Skills (BIS) stated that 'the Government sees no clear case for [directors] to receive exit payments that represent an extremely generous package in comparison to other employees' termination packages'.[182] Accordingly, the government recommended that all loss-of-office payments that exceeded one year's base salary should be subject to a binding shareholder vote.[183] However, following consultation, the requirement for mandatory shareholder approval of loss-of-office payments was dropped. Instead, quoted companies are required to state in their remuneration report policy how loss-of-office payments are calculated.[184] This policy is then subject to a binding vote.[185] Section 226C(1) then goes on to provide that no payment for loss of office may be made by any person to a person who is, or has been, a director of a quoted company, unless:

This binding vote is discussed more at 19.3.2.4.

(a) the payment is consistent with the approved directors' remuneration policy; or

(b) the payment is approved by resolution of the members of the company.

A payment made in contravention of the above rules will be held by the recipient on trust for the company, and any director who authorized the payment is jointly and severally liable to indemnify the company for any loss resulting from the payment.[186]

---

[182] BIS, 'Executive Pay: Shareholder Voting Rights Consultation' (BIS 2012) para 109.

[183] ibid para 122.

[184] Large and Medium-Sized Companies and Groups (Accounts and Reports) Regulations 2008, SI 2008/410, Sch 8, para 37.

[185] CA 2006, s 439A.

[186] ibid s 226E(1).

CHAPTER SUMMARY

- Section 175 provides that a director must avoid a situation in which he has, or can have, an interest that conflicts with that of the company.

- The s 175 duty will not be breached if the conflict in question was authorized. In a private company, the directors can authorize the conflict unless the articles state otherwise. In a public company, the directors can only authorize the conflict if the articles so provide.

- Section 176 provides that a director must not accept, from a third party, a benefit conferred by reason of his being a director, or by doing (or not doing) anything as a director. A breach of s 176 will not occur if the benefit is authorized by the members.

- Section 177 provides that a director who is interested in a proposed transaction or arrangement with the company must disclose the nature and extent of that interest to the other directors.

- Section 182 provides that a director who is interested in a transaction or arrangement that has been entered into by the company must disclose the nature and extent of that interest to the other directors.

- A director cannot have a guaranteed term of employment with the company, unless it has been approved by the members in advance.

- Member approval is required if a director is interested in a 'substantial property transaction' involving the company.

- Member approval is required if a director is to enter into a loan, quasi-loan, or credit transaction with the company.

- Certain loss-of-office payments made to a departing director require member approval.

FURTHER READING

Bryan Clark, 'UK Company Law Reform and the Directors' Exploitation of "Corporate Opportunities"' (2006) 17 ICCLR 231.
- Discusses the corporate opportunity doctrine and argues that the retention by the CA 2006 of a strict approach is correct.

David Kershaw, *Company Law in Context: Text and Materials* (2nd edn, OUP 2012) chs 13 and 14.
- Discusses in detail the rationale behind, and operation of, the duties discussed in this chapter.

Ernest Lim, 'Directors' Fiduciary Duties: A New Analytical Framework' (2013) 129 LQR 242.
- Provides a detailed discussion of s 175(4)(a) and proposes a framework that might improve the application of s 175(4)(a).

Law Commission, *Company Directors: Regulating Conflicts of Interest and Formulating a Statement of Duties* (Law Com No 261, Cm 4436, HMSO 1999) 32–55.
- Parts 6–12 of this report look at those transactions involving directors that require member approval.

SELF-TEST QUESTIONS

1. Define the following terms:
- corporate opportunity doctrine;
- substantial property transaction;

- non-cash asset;
- quasi-loan.

2. State whether each of the following statements is true or false and, if false, explain why:

   - The s 175 duty applies only in relation to transactions or arrangements between a director and the company.
   - A director of a company cannot also act as director for a competing company.
   - A s 175 conflict can only be authorized by the members.
   - A s 176 third-party benefit can only be authorized by the members.
   - Section 177 provides that a director who has an interest in a proposed transaction/arrangement with the company must obtain the authorization of the other directors.
   - A breach of s 182 is a criminal offence.
   - If a director fails to obtain member approval for a service contract over two years in length, then the contract is void.
   - A loss-of-office payment made to a director of a quoted company will only be valid if it is approved by a resolution of the members.

3. 'The treatment of conflict of interest duties in the CA 2006 is inelegant and serves to render the law more complex and confusing that was the case under the common law. The no-conflict and no-profit rules were much easier to understand.' Do you agree with this statement? Provide reasons for your answer.

4. At a recent board meeting, the directors of Dragon plc discussed several potential transactions and other matters:

   - Jude, who chairs the remuneration committee, recommended that all directors of Dragon be provided with a £5,000 payment when they leave office. This term would be added to the directors' service contracts as they were renewed. Jude notes that his contract is due for renewal in a few months' time and, to demonstrate his long-term commitment to Dragon, he states that he would be willing to sign a five-year contract.
   - The board discussed the need to build a new factory and Ivan stated that he found a suitable piece of land upon which the factory could be built and that the asking price was £130,000. Ivan did not disclose that the land was owed by his wife and, if the sale went ahead, Ivan would be paid £13,000 commission.
   - The board has authorized Sajid to negotiate and conclude a supply agreement with TechGoods Ltd. However, unbeknownst to Dragon's board, Sajid is a major shareholder in TechGoods. Sajid informed the board of TechGoods that, if they followed his instructions, he could secure a contract with Dragon.

   Discuss the lawfulness of the above transactions and, if any duties or laws would be breached by entering into the transactions, what steps could be taken to avoid breaching the law?

ONLINE RESOURCES

This book is accompanied by online resources to better support you in your studies. Visit www.oup.com/uk/roach-company/ for:

- answers to the self-test questions;
- further reading lists;
- multiple-choice questions;
- glossary.

Updates to the law can be found on the author's Twitter account (@UKCompanyLaw) and further resources can be found on the author's blog (www.companylawandgovernance.com).

12 Vacation of office and disqualification

- Resignation
- Vacation of office in accordance with the articles
- Retirement by rotation
- Removal
- Succession planning
- Disqualification

INTRODUCTION

This final chapter on the board of directors focuses on how the directors can cease to be directors. Directors value their jobs and the possibility of losing office can act as a powerful incentive to act in a particular manner. Conversely, directors who feel that their position is unassailably secure may be tempted to act in a self-serving manner. Accordingly, the law relating to the vacation of office is an important governance safeguard.

Five broad methods of vacation of office can be identified: (i) resignation; (ii) vacation of office in accordance with the articles; (iii) retirement by rotation; (iv) removal; and (v) disqualification. It should be noted that there is some overlap between these methods and they do not operate in isolation; for example, it is common for the articles to provide that a director will vacate office if he is disqualified. Each of these five methods of vacation will now be discussed, beginning with resignation.

12.1 Resignation

A director may, at any time, resign from office by giving notice to the company, and the company must accept his resignation. The precise rules regarding resignation are a matter for the company's articles[1] and the director's contract of service (if he has one).

---

[1] Article 18(f) of the model articles for private companies and art 22(f) of the model articles for public companies simply provide that a person ceases to be a director as soon as notification is received by the company from the director that the director is resigning from office as director, and such resignation has taken effect in accordance with its terms.

The general rule is that resignation is effective as soon as it is given[2] but, where the director operates under a contract of service (as is usually the case for executive directors), the contract will usually require the director to provide a period of notice. The following case demonstrates, *inter alia*, that where the contract provides for no notice period, a requirement to provide reasonable notice will be implied in the contract.

CMS Dolphin Ltd v Simonet [2002] BCC 600 (Ch)

FACTS: Simonet was the managing director of CMS Dolphin Ltd ('CMS'). He resigned with immediate effect from the company and set up a rival company, Blue (GB) Ltd ('Blue'). Shortly after, all the staff of CMS left and joined Blue, and many of CMS's clients transferred their business to Blue. CMS argued that Simonet was in breach of his fiduciary duty and should be liable to account for any profit gained due to the business he diverted from CMS to Blue.

HELD: Lawrence Collins J stated that, absent an express term requiring notice, a term requiring reasonable notice will be implied into the contract (on the facts of the case, three months' notice was held to be reasonable). By failing to provide reasonable notice, Simonet had acted in breach of contract, thereby entitling CMS to damages.

COMMENT: Lawrence Collins J stated that a director's power to resign from office is not a fiduciary one, and a director is free to resign even if the consequences for the company are disastrous. Furthermore, a director is not precluded from using his skill, knowledge, or connections to compete with his former company. However, the circumstances surrounding a resignation can still result in liability. Here, it was clear that Simonet had exploited his resignation to obtain business opportunities from CMS, and this was regarded as a misappropriation of CMS's property, for which Simonet was required to pay equitable compensation or an account of profits.

See Archana Sinha, 'Directors' Duties—Breach of Fiduciary Duties' (2002) 13 ICCLR 266.

A resignation involves a director voluntarily removing himself from office. However, in some cases, a resignation may be more akin to a removal, namely where the members (notably the institutional investors) place pressure upon a director to resign, as occurred in relation to Sir Philip Watts, the former chairman of the Royal Dutch/Shell Group plc.

Resignation following member pressure

In the late 1990s, Watts was head of Shell's exploration and production unit and was responsible for evaluating how much oil Shell had in reserve. In 1997, Watts put in place a new system for calculating Shell's 'proven reserves', namely the amount of oil that, with reasonable certainty, would be recoverable in future years. On 9 January 2004, Shell disclosed that, under this system, it had overstated the amount of oil it had in reserve by 3.9 billion barrels—subsequent restatements would quantify the overstatement at 4.47 billion barrels. Over £2.9 billion was wiped off Shell's market valuation upon the announcement, and Shell would later admit that the overstatement led to exaggerated profit forecasts.

Understandably, Shell's shareholders were unhappy and called for Watts's resignation (by now, Watts was Shell's chairman). Initially, he refused to step down, but institutional investor pressure mounted and a group of US investors indicated that they were going to initiate a class action lawsuit. The pressure exerted by Shell's shareholders was such that less than a month later Watts resigned.

---

[2] *OBC Caspian Ltd v Thorp* (1998) SLT 653. Once given, a notice of resignation cannot be retracted without the consent of the company (*Glossop v Glossop* [1907] 2 Ch 370 (Ch)).

12.2 Vacation of office in accordance with the articles

A company's articles may lay down circumstances that will cause a director to cease to hold office. For example, the model articles[3] state that a person will cease to be a director in several circumstances, including:

- if he is prohibited from being a director by virtue of the Companies Act 2006 (CA 2006), or is prohibited from being a director by law (e.g. because he has been disqualified);
- if a bankruptcy order is made against him;[4]
- if a registered medical practitioner who is treating that person gives a written opinion to the company stating that that person has become physically or mentally incapable of acting as a director and may remain so for more than three months.

Vacation of office via the articles

Companies will often add into their articles additional circumstances that will result in vacation of office, with examples being:

- articles 72 and 84.1.7 of Barclays plc's articles provide that a person will vacate office if, within two months of being appointed, he does not hold an interest in ordinary shares with a nominal value of at least £500;
- article 83(iii) of Marks and Spencer Group plc's articles provides that a director will stop being a director if 'not less than three quarters of the directors pass a resolution or sign a written notice removing the director from office';
- article 125(k) of Pearson plc's articles provides that a director shall vacate office if, without the approval of the board, he becomes a director, auditor, or other officer of any company carrying on similar business to Pearson, and the board resolves that his office should be vacated.

A director may be reappointed as a director once the relevant circumstance has passed (e.g. if a mentally incapacitated director reacquires mental capacity), but whilst the event is current, he cannot hold office as a director and the other directors cannot waive the effects of any article provision causing a director to cease to hold office.[5]

12.3 Retirement by rotation

Retirement by rotation refers to a system under which the directors are required to periodically step down from office and, if they so wish, can then seek re-election. The CA 2006 does not require retirement by rotation—it is entirely a matter for the company's articles. In private companies, the directors will wish to retain as much control as possible, and such companies will therefore generally not require retirement by rotation.[6]

---

[3] Model articles for private companies limited by shares, art 18; model articles for public companies, art 22.
[4] This is backed up by s 11(1) of the Company Directors Disqualification Act 1986, which provides that it is a criminal offence for an undischarged bankrupt to act as a director, except with leave of the court (discussed at 12.6.1.10).
[5] *Re Bodega Co Ltd* [1904] 1 Ch 276 (Ch).
[6] The model articles for private companies do not require retirement by rotation.

Conversely, retirement by rotation is common in public companies, with art 21(1) of the model articles for public companies providing that all the directors of a public company must retire at its first annual general meeting (AGM) and, if they so wish, may seek re-election. Article 21(2) then goes on to state that, at every subsequent AGM, any directors appointed by the directors since the last AGM, or any directors who were not appointed or re-appointed at one of the preceding two AGMs, must retire from office and may offer themselves for reappointment by the members. In practice, this means that:

- directors who were appointed by the board must step down at the very next AGM and can, if they so wish, seek re-election;
- in all other cases, the directors must stand down at least every three years and may seek re-election.

Provision 18 of the UK Corporate Governance Code goes further than art 21 by recommending that all directors of companies with a premium listing should be subject to annual re-election by the members. Initially, this recommendation was extremely controversial, with many directors fearing that annual elections would see an increase in director turnover, and would encourage directors to favour a short-termist view. In the event, these fears were not borne out and annual re-election amongst Financial Times Stock Exchange 350 (FTSE 350) companies is now almost universally practised, with 98.4 per cent of FTSE 350 companies re-electing their directors annually.[7]

In theory, retirement by rotation should act as a useful governance mechanism. Directors, being aware that they will need to seek periodic re-election, have a strong incentive to perform well. If the members are not satisfied with a director's performance, they can choose not to re-appoint the director or to appoint someone who is standing against the director. In practice, retirement by rotation is not especially effective, largely because directors in public companies normally run unopposed. In large public companies, members overwhelmingly tend to vote for the person nominated by the nomination committee. As this is almost always an incumbent director, it has been argued that '[t]he key for a director's re-election is remaining on the firm's slate'.[8]

12.4 Removal

The directors of a company may be formally removed from office in two principal ways, namely (i) under a power granted by statute; and (ii) under a power granted by the articles. In practice, it is very rare for a director to be removed—the usual course of action is for a director to resign or to not seek re-election once their period of office expires.

12.4.1 **Removal under statute**

Statute may provide certain persons with the power to remove a director (or directors) from office. For example, a director of a company in administration can be removed by the administrator.[9] The most noteworthy power of removal is found in s 168(1) of

---

[7] Grant Thornton LLP, 'Corporate Governance Review 2015: Trust and Integrity—Loud and Clear' (Grant Thornton 2015) 52.

[8] Lucian Arye Bebchuk, 'The Case for Shareholder Access to the Ballot' in John Armour and Joseph A McCahery (eds), *After Enron: Improving Corporate Law and Modernising Securities Regulation in Europe and the US* (Hart 2006) 239.

[9] Insolvency Act 1986 (IA 1986), Sch B1, para 61(a).

the CA 2006, which provides that '[a] company may by ordinary resolution at a meeting remove a director[10] before the expiration of his period of office, notwithstanding anything in any agreement between it and him'. The power contained in s 168 is important as UK company law vests significant managerial power in the board, and does not generally seek to encourage the members to interfere with that power. Allowing the members to remove the directors reinforces the default position of ultimate power being placed in the hands of the company in general meeting.

The division of power between the board and the members is discussed at 9.2.1.

For a removal under s 168 to be valid, several procedural rules must be complied with:

The members' ability to call a meeting is discussed at 14.3.1.1.

- As the resolution must be passed 'at a meeting', the written resolution procedure cannot be used.[11] Accordingly, the members will either need to table a resolution at an upcoming general meeting or call for a meeting to be held.

- Special notice (namely clear 28 days)[12] is required for the resolution[13] and the company must send a copy of the resolution to the director(s) concerned.[14]

- The director(s) whose removal is sought may, understandably, wish to protest against the resolution. Accordingly, such directors have a right to be heard at the meeting where the resolution is tabled,[15] and to make written representations to the company.[16] If these representations are received in time, the company must send them to every member to whom notice of the meeting has been sent.[17]

Initially, the power granted to members under s 168 appears extremely substantial, but, in practice, its effectiveness is emasculated, leading Keay to argue that 'while shareholders might have more legal power in technical terms to control boards, compared with their American counterparts, it is exceedingly difficult for UK shareholders to discipline directors as a matter of practice'.[18] Four reasons can be advanced for the practical ineffectiveness of s 168.

First, removal under s 168 does not deprive the director of any compensation payable as a result of the removal,[19] nor will it deprive him of any rights he might have if he is an employee (e.g. the right to claim for wrongful or unfair dismissal). Members seeking the removal of a director are advised to inspect the service contract[20] beforehand because, if the director's remuneration is high and/or the period remaining on his service contract is lengthy, removing him may be extremely costly. In recent years, this fear is less pronounced due to s 188 of the CA 2006 (which requires member approval for service contracts over two years) and Provision 39 of the UK Corporate Governance Code (which recommends that notice or contract periods should be set at one year or less).

Section 188 is discussed at 11.4.1.

Second, the power afforded to the members under s 168 exists notwithstanding anything in the agreement between the company and the directors—this essentially means that s 168 is a mandatory rule and the power it grants to the members cannot be taken away by anything in the company's articles or the director's service contract. However, s 168 does not prohibit the company from including in its articles provisions that may

---

[10] Although the phrase 'remove a director' is used, a single s 168 resolution can be used to dismiss multiple directors, or even the entire board (*National Roads and Motorists' Association Ltd v Scandrett* [2002] NSWSC 1123 (New South Wales Supreme Court)).

[11] CA 2006, s 288(2)(a).   [12] ibid s 312(1).   [13] ibid s 168(2).

[14] ibid s169(1).   [15] ibid s 169(2).   [16] ibid s 169(3).

[17] ibid. If the representations are sent too late, the director(s) can require that the representations be read out at the meeting (s 169(4)).

[18] Andrew Keay, 'Company Directors Behaving Poorly: Disciplinary Options for Shareholders' [2007] JBL 656, 682.

[19] CA 2006, s 168(5)(a).

[20] Section 229(1) of the CA 2006 (discussed at 8.1.5.3) provides the members with the right to inspect the directors' service contracts free of charge.

affect the operation of s 168, notably a weighted voting clause. Such a clause usually provides that, upon the occurrence of a specified event (e.g. a vote to remove a director from office), the voting power of specified persons shall be increased (usually to such an extent as to enable such persons to defeat the resolution). The following case demonstrates how a weighted voting clause operates in practice and how it can impact upon the power granted to the members by s 168.

 Bushell v Faith [1970] AC 1099 (HL)

FACTS: A company had 300 shares, equally divided between three siblings, namely Bushell, Faith, and Bayne. Bushell and Faith were the company's only directors. Article 9 of the company's articles provided that, in relation to resolutions to remove a director, the shares of the director involved would carry three votes per share, instead of the usual one. Bushell and Bayne sought a resolution to remove Faith from office, but art 9 meant that Faith's shares were worth 300 votes, whereas Bushell and Bayne could only muster 200 votes between them. Accordingly, Faith argued that the resolution was defeated. Bushell contended that the resolution was passed by 200 votes, compared to Faith's 100 votes, and she sought an injunction preventing Faith from acting as a director.

HELD: The claim failed. Article 9 was effective and the resolution was therefore validly defeated. The Companies Act 1948 did not expressly state that such clauses were invalid and there was therefore no reason to imply such an intention.

COMMENT: Unsurprisingly, the decision in *Bushell* has proved controversial on the ground that a weighted voting clause could serve to entrench a director and make him irremovable. To uphold clauses such as art 9 would, according to Lord Morris (dissenting), make a 'mockery of the law'.[21] In practice, the effect of *Bushell* is more limited. First, it has been argued that the decision was justified on the ground that the company in question was a quasi-partnership,[22] in which all of the members will expect to be involved in management. It may therefore be the case that such clauses are effective only in relation to such companies (although there are no *obiter dicta* or *rationes* to this effect). Second, it has been argued that such clauses would be 'inappropriate in public companies'[23] and are impossible in companies with a premium listing, as shares in such companies must 'carry an equal number of votes on any shareholder vote'.[24] Third, a weighted voting clause could be removed by passing a special resolution (although admittedly, members with not less than 75 per cent of the company's votes could probably defeat even a director with weighted voting rights).

See Dan Prentice, 'Removal of Directors from Office' (1969) 32 MLR 693.

Third, s 168 removals are rarities in large public companies (but see the Petropavlovsk example at 14.3.4.1) because gaining enough support to pass an ordinary resolution can be extremely difficult. Dissatisfied shareholders are unlikely to have sufficient votes by themselves so need to obtain other shareholders' support, which can be problematic due to difficulties in forming shareholder coalitions. Consequently, it has been argued that the ability of the members to remove the directors is 'largely a myth. Attempts to replace directors are extremely rare, even in firms that systematically underperform over a long period of time.'[25]

The difficulties of forming coalitions are discussed at 14.5.1.

---

[21] [1970] AC 1099 (HL) 1106.

[22] See CM Schmitthoff, 'How the English Discovered the Private Company' in Pieter Zonderland (ed), *Quo Vadis Ius Societatum?* (Kluwer 1972).

[23] Geoffrey Morse, *Palmer's Company Law* (Sweet & Maxwell 2018) para 8.1321.

[24] Listing Rules, r 7.2.1A, Premium Listing Principle 3.

[25] Lucian Arye Bebchuk, 'The Case for Shareholder Access to the Ballot' in John Armour and Joseph A McCahery (eds), *After Enron: Improving Corporate Law and Modernising Securities Regulation in Europe and the US* (Hart 2006) 239.

On the very rare occasions that it appears that a s 168 removal might succeed, the director in question will often resign or will be removed by the directors in an attempt to avoid the negative publicity associated with a s 168 removal, as occurred in the following example.

Patientline UK Ltd and the removal of a director

In 2006, major institutional investors in Patientline UK Ltd called an extraordinary general meeting and tabled a resolution calling for the removal of the company's chairman, Derek Lewis. During Lewis's tenure as chief executive officer (CEO) and chairman, the company's shares had fallen in value by over 80 per cent. Initially, the board stated that it would support Lewis and Patientline would bear the costs of the extraordinary general meeting (EGM).[26] However, the day before the EGM was due to take place, the board announced that Lewis had stood down from his role.[27] It is not entirely clear whether Lewis voluntarily resigned or whether he was removed by the board.

Fourth, s 168(5)(b) provides that s 168 should not be construed as derogating from any power to remove a director that exists outside s 168. The significance of this is discussed next.

12.4.2 **Removal under the articles**

Many companies tend to provide for the power of removal via a clause in the articles. Usually, the clause empowers the board to remove a director (these were historically known as 'Cecil King'[28] clauses) and, like all powers granted to a director, it must be exercised in accordance with the general duties.[29]

Article clauses providing for director removal

Common examples of article clauses providing for board removal of a director include:

- article 83(iii) of Marks and Spencer Group plc's articles provides that a director will vacate office if 'not less than three-quarters of the directors pass a resolution or sign a written notice requiring the director to resign';
- article 93(iv) of BP plc's articles provides that a director will vacate office if he is absent, without permission, from any board meetings for a continuous period of six months or more, and notice in writing is served upon him, signed by all the other directors, stating that he is to vacate office.

---

[26] See Richard Irving, 'Rebel Shareholder Trues to Disconnect Patientlines Chief' *The Times* (London, 22 March 2006).

[27] See Peter Klinger, 'Patientline Oust Lewis before Fight at EGM' *The Times* (London, 4 April 2006).

[28] So called after Cecil King, the chairman of International Publishing Corporation—the largest publishing empire in the world in the 1960s. In 1968, its flagship paper, *The Daily Mirror*, published a front-page story calling for Prime Minister Harold Wilson to resign. The story was published at King's insistence, against the wishes of the board. The board therefore unanimously voted to remove King from office.

[29] However, where a power is exercised for an ulterior motive, then it would appear to be the case that the removal will remain valid (*Lee v Chou Wen Hsein* [1984] 1 WLR 1202 (PC)).

At 12.4.1, it was noted that member pressure can cause a director to resign. Member pressure can also be placed upon the board to exercise their power of removal under the articles. Such cases are, unsurprisingly, exceptionally rare, as a director faced with the prospect of being removed by the board will usually resign to avoid negative publicity and the tarnishing of his reputation.

The articles may also provide the members with a power to remove a director, although this is rare. The question that arises is what the relationship is between the members' power of removal under the articles and their power of removal under s 168. Section 168(5)(b) provides that s 168 should not be construed as derogating from any power to remove a director that exists outside s 168. Accordingly, the power to remove a director under s 168 exists alongside any other power, such as a power in the articles. The potential difficulty that arises is demonstrated in the following example.

> **Eg** **Removal of a director under the articles**
>
> Article 18(g) of Dragon Goods Ltd's (DG') articles provides that a director ceases to be a director 'once an ordinary resolution of the members is passed'. A written resolution is sent to all the members which proposes that Sophie, one of DG's directors, is to be removed from office under art 18(g). The resolution is passed. Sophie claims that the resolution was invalid as she was not provided with special notice, nor was she given the opportunity to make representations at a meeting (which are requirements for removal under s 168).

The question that arises is whether Sophie's removal is invalid as the resolution did not comply with the requirements set out in s 168 of the CA 2006. The answer is no, as Sophie was not removed under s 168—she was removed under art 18(g) of DG's articles. The fact that art 18(g) does not provide for the safeguards found in s 168 will not affect its validity.[30]

12.5 Succession planning

Irrespective of how a director leaves office, a key goal for the company will be the appointment of the departing director's successor. Succession planning is now recognized as a key governance issue, with the Financial Reporting Council (FRC) stating that sound succession planning contributes to the long-term success of a company, principally because it 'ensures a continuous supply of suitable people (or a process to identify them), who are ready to take over when directors, senior staff and other key employees leave the company in a range of situations'.[31] Accordingly, the UK Corporate Governance Code recommends that 'an effective succession plan should be maintained for the board and senior management'.[32] In terms of how far ahead the company should plan, the FRC identifies three types of planning:

1. contingency planning for sudden and unforeseen departures;

---

[30] *Browne v Panga Pty Ltd* (1995) 120 FLR 34 (Federal Court of Australia).
[31] FRC, 'UK Board Succession Planning' (FRC 2015) 1.
[32] FRC, 'The UK Corporate Governance Code' (FRC 2018) Principle J.

2. medium-term planning which relates to the orderly replacement of current board members and senior executives (e.g. due to retirement), and;

3. long-term planning, which relates to the relationship between the delivery of the company's strategy and objectives to the skills needed on the board now and in the future.[33]

Although succession planning is relevant to the entire board, increased focus is often placed on planning the succession of the CEO or chairman. Ensuring smooth succession for these top posts is a 'perpetual responsibility that begins right after the party celebrating a new hire for the top position'.[34] A CEO or chairman may take another job, or may become ill, in which case it is vital that companies have in place a procedure to ensure a smooth succession. Sometimes, a well-planned succession procedure may be put in effect years before the CEO leaves office, as was the case with Apple.

Apple and succession planning

Steve Jobs was the founder and CEO of Apple Inc, and was credited with turning the company into the success it is today. Two months before he died, in August 2011, Jobs resigned as CEO and Tim Cook was appointed as his successor. The departure of a charismatic and popular CEO can often have a detrimental effect upon the company's outlook and finances, but Apple's succession plan had been in place for years and helped ensure a smooth transition.

In October 2003, Jobs was diagnosed with cancer, leading to immediate speculation regarding his ability to continue as CEO. In 2005, Cook was promoted to Chief Operations Officer, thereby ensuring that he was working closely alongside Jobs. Cook appeared in more public corporate events, thereby ensuring that, when he took over, he was well known to the public, stakeholders, and investors. Between 2004 and 2011, Jobs would take three medical leaves of absence and, on each occasion, Cook either acted as interim CEO or *de facto* head of the company in Jobs's absence, so he had experience of undertaking the top job. Accordingly, by the time Cook took over, he had been positioned as the obvious choice to succeed Jobs. Jobs's resignation letter stated that he strongly recommended that the board implement its succession plan and appoint Cook as CEO, which it did almost immediately. As a result, the transition proceeded smoothly with minimal disruption to the business (the fact that Jobs stayed on as chairman probably helped, even though it is generally regarded that CEOs should not stay on as chairmen, for fear of undermining the new CEO).

Unfortunately, there exists concern regarding the effectiveness of succession planning in large UK companies. In 2018, 84.3 per cent of FTSE 350 companies only provided basic or general descriptions of their succession planning procedures (only 13.7 per cent provided good or detailed descriptions),[35] leading the FRC to state that 'companies are not spending enough time considering board and senior management succession'.[36] As a result of this, succession planning was made more prominent in the 2018 update to the UK Corporate Governance Code.

---

[33] FRC, 'Guidance on Board Effectiveness' (FRC 2018) para 100.
[34] Robert AG Monks and Nell Minow, *Corporate Governance* (5th edn, Wiley 2011) 308.
[35] Grant Thornton LLP, 'Corporate Governance Review 2018' (Grant Thornton 2018) 41.
[36] FRC, 'Developments in Corporate Governance and Stewardship 2017' (FRC 2017) 7.

12.6 Disqualification

Historically, the power to disqualify a director was provided for in the Companies Acts, but the regime was basic and lacking compared to today's disqualification regime. The Cork Committee was of the opinion that the law should 'severely [penalise] those who abuse the privilege of limited liability',[37] and therefore recommended that the disqualification regime be expanded, which ultimately led to the passing of the Company Directors' Disqualification Act 1986 ('CDDA 1986'). Since then, the regime has been strengthened by the Insolvency Act 2000, the Enterprise Act 2002 and, most recently, the Small Business, Enterprise and Employment Act 2015 ('SBEEA 2015'). The disqualification regime will continue to evolve in the future. For example, currently the rules in the CDDA 1986 do not apply to directors of dissolved companies. Accordingly, the government has announced that it will amend the CDDA 1986 so that directors of dissolved companies can be investigated and, if necessary, disqualified, without the need to restore the company.[38]

As the CDDA 1986 can result in a person being disqualified as a director of a company or member of a limited liability partnership (LLP), it accords with the above recommendation of the Cork Committee by depriving disqualified persons of the ability to conduct business with limited liability. Such persons, if they wish to conduct business, will have to do so via an unlimited structure, such as a sole proprietorship or partnership. Of course, businesses may not want to do business with such persons, and so it is important that information regarding disqualified persons is publicly available. To that end, s 18 of the CDDA 1986 empowers the Secretary of State to make regulations[39] that require officers of the court to provide disqualification-related information, which will then be included within a register of disqualified persons. Although the CDDA 1986 states that the register can be inspected upon payment of a fee,[40] details of disqualified directors can be obtained free of charge by using the Companies House Service.[41] A separate, more detailed register of disqualifications that occurred in the previous three months can be found on the Insolvency Service's website.[42]

Clearly, the most important facet of the disqualification regime that a director should understand is what sort of activity can (or, in some cases, will) result in disqualification. Accordingly, the grounds for disqualification are discussed next.

12.6.1 The grounds for disqualification

Disqualification is only available on specified grounds found in ss 2–11 of the CDDA 1986. The grounds for disqualification have expanded since the CDDA 1986 was passed, and will continue to do so in the future. For example, the government has stated that it plans to introduce a measure to allow for the disqualification of a director of a holding company who does not give due consideration to the interests of the stakeholders of a financially distressed subsidiary when it is sold.[43]

---

[37] *Report of the Review Committee on Insolvency Law and Practice* (Cmnd 8558, 1982) para 1815.

[38] Department for Business, Energy and Industrial Strategy (BEIS), 'Insolvency and Corporate Governance: Government Response' (BEIS 2018) paras 4.4–4.8.

[39] Namely the Companies (Disqualification Orders) Regulations 2009, SI 2009/2471.

[40] CDDA 1986, s 18(4).

[41] See https://beta.companieshouse.gov.uk/search/disqualified-officers accessed 10 January 2019.

[42] See www.insolvencydirect.bis.gov.uk/IESdatabase/viewdirectorsummary-new.asp accessed 10 January 2019.

[43] BEIS, 'Insolvency and Corporate Governance: Government Response' (BEIS 2018) para 2.8.

TABLE 12.1 The grounds for disqualification

Section	Ground	Mandatory disqualification	Disqualification period	Disqualification undertaking available
2	Conviction of an indictable offence	No	15 years maximum	No
3	Persistent breaches of companies legislation	No	5 years maximum	No
4	Fraud or breach of duty during winding up	No	15 years maximum	No
5	Summary convictions relating to companies legislation	No	5 years maximum	No
5A	Conviction of certain offences abroad	No	15 years maximum	Yes
6	Unfitness in an insolvent company	Yes	2–15 years	Yes (via s 7(2A))
8	Expedient in the public interest	No	15 years maximum	Yes
8ZA	Person instructing unfit director of insolvent company	No	2–15 years	Yes
8ZD	Person instructing unfit director	No	15 years maximum	Yes
9A	Breach of competition law	Yes	15 years maximum	Yes
10	Participation in fraudulent or wrongful trading under the Insolvency Act 1986	No	15 years maximum	No
11	Undischarged bankrupts	Yes, as disqualification is automatic	Whilst order or undertaking remains in force	No

When determining whether to disqualify, the courts and Secretary of State (as applicable) must take into account the list of factors found in Sch 1 of the CDDA 1986,[44] although factors not listed can also be taken into account.[45]

Table 12.1 sets out the grounds of disqualification and other useful information regarding each ground. Each ground will then be discussed in more detail.

12.6.1.1 Conviction of an indictable offence

Section 2 provides that a disqualification order[46] may be made against a person where he is convicted of an indictable offence in connection with the promotion, formation, management, liquidation, or striking off of a company, or with the receivership of a company's property, or with his being an administrative receiver of a company.[47] Where the disqualification order is made by a court of summary jurisdiction (i.e. a magistrates'

---

[44] CDDA 1986, s 12C (note that s 12C does not apply to disqualifications under s 2(2)(b) or (c)). The factors found in Sch 1, paras (1)–(4) must be taken into account in all cases, whereas the factors found in Sch 1, paras (5)–(7) are additional factors to be taken into account where the person is or has been a director.
[45] *Re Bath Glass Ltd* [1988] BCLC 329 (Ch) 332.
[46] A disqualification undertaking is not available.   [47] CDDA 1986, s 2(1).

court), then the maximum period of disqualification is five years—in all other cases, the maximum period is 15 years.[48]

12.6.1.2 Persistent breaches of companies legislation

Section 3 provides that a disqualification order[49] of up to five years may be made against a person where it appears that he has been persistently in default in relation to provisions of the companies legislation requiring any return, account, or other document to be filed with, delivered or sent, or notice of any matter to be given, to the registrar of companies.[50] Persistent default is conclusively established where, within a five-year period ending on the date of the disqualification application, the person was found guilty of three or more defaults.[51]

12.6.1.3 Fraud or breach of duty during winding up

Section 4 provides that a disqualification order[52] of up to 15 years may be made against a person if, in the course of a winding up, it appears that he:

(a) has been found guilty of the offence found in s 993 of the CA 2006 (namely, fraudulent trading),[53] or;

Section 993 is discussed at 23.3.3.2.

(b) has been found guilty of any fraud in relation to the company, whilst an officer, liquidator, receiver, or administrative receiver of the company; or

(c) has engaged in any breach of duty as an officer, liquidator, receiver, or administrative receiver.[54]

12.6.1.4 Summary convictions relating to companies legislation

Section 5 provides that a disqualification order[55] of up to five years may be made against a person where the following two conditions are satisfied:

(a) the person is summarily convicted of an offence in consequence of a contravention of, or failure to comply with, any provision of the companies legislation requiring a return, account or other document to be filed with, delivered or sent, or notice of any matter to be given, to the registrar of companies,[56] and;

(b) during the 5 years prior to the date of the conviction, the person has had made against him, or been convicted of, at least three defaults in relation to the provisions specified in (a) above.[57]

12.6.1.5 Conviction of certain offences abroad

Prior to the passing of the SBEEA 2015, persons who were disqualified from being directors overseas, or who were convicted overseas of an offence in relation to the management of a company, were freely able to become directors of UK companies. The government was concerned that, in an increasingly globalized economy, this was a weakness of the UK's disqualification regime.[58] Accordingly, the 2015 Act inserted a new s 5A into the

---

[48] ibid s 2(3).   [49] A disqualification undertaking is not available.   [50] CDDA 1986, s 3(1).
[51] ibid s 3(2).   [52] A disqualification undertaking is not available.
[53] Not to be confused with fraudulent trading under s 213 of IA 1986, which is subject to disqualification under s 10 of the CDDA 1986 (see 12.6.1.9).
[54] CDDA 1986, s 4(1).   [55] A disqualification undertaking is not available.
[56] CDDA 1986, s 5(1).   [57] ibid s 5(3).
[58] Department for Business Innovation and Skills (BIS), 'Trust and Transparency: Enhancing the Transparency of UK Company Ownership and Increasing Trust in UK Business: Government Response' (BIS 2014) para 226.

CDDA 1986, which provides that the Secretary of State can seek a disqualification order or undertaking of up to 15 years against a person who has been convicted of a relevant foreign offence. A relevant foreign offence is an offence committed outside Great Britain:

- in connection with (i) the promotion, formation, management, liquidation, or striking off of a company, or (ii) the receivership of a company's property, or (iii) a person being an administrative receiver of the company, and
- which corresponds to an indictable offence.[59]

In addition, the 2015 Act amended Sch 1 of the CDDA 1986 so that overseas misconduct must be taken into account when determining whether to disqualify in all cases under the CDDA 1986.

12.6.1.6 Unfitness in an insolvent company

The vast majority of disqualifications occur under s 6—in 2017/18, of the 1,231 disqualifications reported by the Insolvency Service, 1,104 (89.7 per cent) were made under s 6.[60] Section 6 provides that the court shall make a disqualification order against a person where it is satisfied that:

- (a) he is or has been a director or shadow director of a company which has at any time become insolvent (whether while he was a director or subsequently), and
- (b) his conduct of a director of that company (either taken alone or taken together with his conduct as a director/shadow director of other companies) makes him unfit to be concerned in the management of a company.[61]

As the court 'shall' make a disqualification order, it follows that a disqualification order under s 6 is mandatory if the above two conditions are satisfied, although a disqualification undertaking can be accepted in place of a disqualification order.[62] However, disqualification under s 6 can only occur if an application to the court for disqualification is made, and an application can only be brought by the Secretary of State or, if the Secretary of State so directs, an official receiver.[63] It is worth noting here that, in practice, the majority of the powers granted to the Secretary of State under the CDDA 1986 are usually delegated to the Insolvency Service,[64] an executive agency of the Department of Business, Energy and Industrial Strategy.

The key question to ask is what sort of conduct can constitute unfitness under s 6. The starting point is to determine the purpose behind disqualification and, on this, the courts have been extremely clear. In *Re Sevenoaks Stationers (Retail) Ltd*,[65] Dillon LJ stated that:

> It is beyond dispute that the purpose of . . . s 6 is to protect the public, and in particular potential creditors of companies, from losing money through companies becoming insolvent when the directors of those companies are people unfit to be concerned in the management of a company.[66]

---

[59] CDDA 1986, s 5A(3).

[60] Insolvency Service, 'Insolvency Service Enforcement Outcomes: 2018/19 Monthly Data Tables' (Insolvency Service 2018) Table 1a

[61] CDDA 1986, s 6(1) and (3C).   [62] ibid s 7(2A).

[63] ibid s 7(1). Note that the official receiver can only bring an application in relation to companies that were compulsorily liquidated (discussed at 23.1.2).

[64] See www.gov.uk/government/organisations/insolvency-service accessed 10 January 2019.

[65] [1991] Ch 164 (CA). See also *Re Lo-Line Electric Motors Ltd* [1988] Ch 477 (Ch) 486.   [66] ibid 176.

It has also been stated that the existence of the disqualification regime can deter directors from engaging in unmeritorious conduct, thereby 'improving the standard of conduct observed by directors'.[67] Unfortunately, the deterrent effect of the disqualification regime can be doubted, largely because of the lack of awareness of its existence. Numerous surveys conducted over the previous 20 years have shown low levels of awareness,[68] with the Insolvency Service's 2012 Stakeholder Confidence Survey finding that only 43 per cent of directors questioned were aware of the disqualification regime.[69] More worryingly, only 37 per cent of those directors were of the opinion that disqualification was an effective deterrent.[70]

From the case law, it is clear that disqualifications under s 6 are highly dependent upon the facts of the case. As such, existing cases are only of limited help and one should be cautious when relying on them. Bearing this in mind, examples of conduct that could warrant disqualification under s 6 include the following:

- Taking 'unwarranted risks with creditors' money',[71] such as (i) obtaining goods on credit when the directors knew the company was in danger of liquidation;[72] (ii) continuing to trade at a time when the directors knew there was no prospect of meeting the creditors' claims or of avoiding liquidation;[73] (iii) non-payment of creditors, or only paying creditors whose services are essential for the company's continued survival;[74] or (iv) providing a preference to a creditor.[75]

- Displaying 'a lack of commercial probity'.[76] This broad term can include conduct such as (i) making misrepresentations in relation to the company's products or financial standing;[77] (ii) operating a company for personal benefit, and achieving nothing for the shareholders;[78] or (iii) receiving excessive remuneration when a company was trading at a loss.[79] It should be noted that taking unwarranted risks with the creditors' money is often regarded as indicating a lack of commercial probity.

- Note that mismanagement, incompetence, or negligence will not normally result in disqualification, but they can do in cases involving 'gross negligence or total incompetence',[80] or where the negligence or incompetence are 'of a high degree'.[81] It has been argued that refusing to disqualify for mere incompetence does not fit in with the protective purpose behind disqualification.[82]

---

[67] *Re Barings plc* [1998] BCC 583 (Ch) 590 (Sir Richard Scott VC).

[68] See e.g. National Audit Office, 'Insolvency Service Executive Agency, Company Director Disqualification—A Follow-Up Report' (House of Commons Papers 1998); Robert Baldwin, 'The New Punitive Regulation' (2004) 67 MLR 351.

[69] Insolvency Service, 'Stakeholder Confidence Survey 2012' (SPA Future Thinking 2012) 28.

[70] ibid 30.   [71] *Re Living Images Ltd* [1996] BCC 112 (Ch) 126 (Laddie J).

[72] *Re Keypak Homecare Ltd (No 2)* [1990] BCC 117 (Ch).

[73] *Secretary of State for Trade and Industry v Creggan* [2002] 1 BCLC 99.

[74] *Re Sevenoaks Stationers (Retail) Ltd* [1991] Ch 164 (Ch).

[75] *Re Sykes (Butchers) Ltd* [1998] BCC 484 (Ch). This is even the case where the preference is not a statutory preference contravening s 239 of the IA 1986 (discussed at 23.4.2).

[76] *Re Lo-Line Electric Motors Ltd* [1988] Ch 477 (Ch) 486 (Browne-Wilkinson VC).

[77] *Secretary of State for Business, Enterprise and Regulatory Reform v Sullman* [2008] EWHC 3179 (Ch), [2010] BCC 500.

[78] *Secretary of State for Business, Innovation and Skills v Pawson* [2015] EWHC 2626 (Ch). Note that this case was brought under s 8, but the Court relied heavily on s 6 case law in reaching its decision.

[79] *Re Synthetic Technology Ltd* [1993] BCC 549 (Ch).

[80] *Re Lo-Line Electric Motors Ltd* [1988] Ch 477 (Ch) 486 (Browne-Wilkinson VC).

[81] *Re Barings plc (No 5)* [1999] 1 BCLC 433 (Ch) 484 (Jonathan Parker J).

[82] See e.g. Vanessa Finch, 'Disqualification of Directors: A Plea for Competence' (1990) 53 MLR 385.

- Breaches of duty can result in disqualification (usually as displaying a lack of probity). However, a breach of duty may not be sufficient per se to warrant disqualification,[83] and disqualification can arise in cases where no breach of duty exists.[84]

- Conduct need not be unlawful or dishonest to be unfit,[85] but such conduct will clearly provide powerful evidence for disqualification. Examples include (i) failing to pay workers the National Minimum Wage;[86] (ii) failure to file accounts and annual returns;[87] (iii) employing illegal immigrants;[88] or (iv) using the company to evade immigration laws.[89]

A director disqualified under s 6 can be disqualified for a maximum of 15 years. Unlike most other grounds for disqualification, s 6 is subject to a minimum disqualification period—namely, two years. In *Re Sevenoaks Stationers (Retail) Ltd*,[90] Dillon LJ divided s 6[91] cases into three brackets:

1. disqualification periods of two to five years should apply where disqualification is mandatory, but the case is, relatively, not very serious;

2. disqualification periods of between 6 and 10 years should be reserved for serious cases that do not fall into (a) above;

3. disqualification periods of 10 years or more should be reserved for particularly serious cases. This may include a case in which a director already has one period of disqualification imposed upon him and is disqualified a second time.[92]

Since 2009, the average disqualification period has hovered between 4.7 and 6.3 years, with the 2017/18 average being 5.7 years.[93] Disqualifications of over 10 years are rare—of the 1,231 disqualifications in 2017/18, only 93 were over 10 years in length.[94] Disqualifications of 15 years are extremely rare, but the following high-profile case provides an example of the sort of heinous activity that warranted a maximum 15-year disqualification order.

Secretary of State for Business, Innovation & Skills v Whyte [2014] CSOH 148

FACTS: Rangers Football Club plc owed significant sums of money to the Lloyds Banking Group. In May 2011, the controlling interest in Rangers was acquired by Wavetower Ltd, and the debt owed to Lloyds was assigned to Wavetower. Wavetower was owned by Liberty Capital

---

[83] *Re Deaduck Ltd* [2000] 1 BCLC 148 (Ch).

[84] *Secretary of State for Business, Enterprise and Regulatory Reform v Sullman* [2008] EWHC 3179 (Ch), [2010] BCC 500.

[85] *Re Deaduck Ltd* [2000] 1 BCLC 148 (Ch).

[86] See www.gov.uk/government/news/security-company-director-given-9-year-ban-for-exploiting-workers accessed 10 January 2019.

[87] *Re Cladrose Ltd* [1990] BCC 11 (Ch).

[88] See www.gov.uk/government/news/bosham-restaurant-owner-gets-6-year-ban-for-hiring-illegal-workers accessed 10 January 2019.

[89] *R v Kashyap* [2008] EWCA Crim 775, [2008] 2 Cr App R (S) 109.   [90] [1991] Ch 164 (CA).

[91] In *Re Samuel Sherman plc* [1991] 1 WLR 1070 (Ch), the Court held that the same principles also apply to s 8 cases.

[92] [1991] Ch 164 (CA) 174.

[93] Insolvency Service, 'Insolvency Service Enforcement Outcomes: 2018/19 Monthly Data Tables' (Insolvency Service 2018) Table 1b.

[94] ibid.

Ltd, which was owned and controlled by Whyte. Upon becoming chairman of Rangers in 2011, Whyte caused Rangers to enter into an agreement with Ticketus LLP, under which Rangers sold to Ticketus for £24 million the right to sell season tickets for the next three years (essentially, Rangers sold to Ticketus its principal method of generating revenue). Whyte did not inform the other board members that he was going to enter into this agreement, nor did he inform them that Ticketus had been acquired by Wavetower. Rangers loaned the £24 million to Liberty, which used the money to pay off Rangers' debt to Lloyds. Therefore, the principal purpose of the Ticketus agreement was not to benefit Rangers, but to facilitate Whyte's acquisition of Rangers, and clearing the debt Wavetower owed to Lloyds.[95] Other failings were also noted, notably that Whyte, to the exclusion of the other directors, caused Rangers to stop paying tax that was due. Rangers was placed into administration in February 2012 (by which time, it owed HMRC £10.5 million in unpaid tax) and was wound up in October 2012.

HELD: Lord Tyre, in disqualifying Whyte for 15 years, stated that Whyte's conduct consisted of:

a combination of dishonesty, disregard for the interests of the companies to which he owed duties and of the creditors of those companies, use of Crown debts to finance trade, misappropriation of company funds . . . for private purposes, and wilful breach of a director's administrative duties, the effect of all of which is that the case can be regarded as quite out of the ordinary. . . . I am of the opinion that the appropriate course of action is to impose as long a period of disqualification as I am statutorily empowered to do.[96]

COMMENT: This was, unsurprisingly, not the end of Whyte's troubles. As part of the Ticketus agreement, Whyte had represented that he had never been disqualified as a director. In fact, he had been disqualified in 2000 for a period of seven years. Ticketus successfully sued Whyte in misrepresentation for the £17.7 million it had spent in pre-purchasing season tickets.[97] Whyte could not pay and was declared bankrupt in October 2015. Whyte was charged with several offences relating to his acquisition of Rangers in 2011, but was acquitted in 2017.

Finally, it should be noted that s 6 only applies to persons who are, or were, directors or shadow directors. Accordingly, other persons whose instructions or influence resulted in a director being disqualified under s 6 were, until recently, not subject to disqualification. To combat this, the SBEEA 2015 added a new s 8ZA into the CDDA 1986, which provides that the Secretary of State can apply for a disqualification order of between 2 and 15 years against a person ('P') if the court is satisfied that:

(a) a disqualification order under s 6 has been made against a person (the 'main transgressor') who is or has been a director (but not a shadow director) of a company; and

(b) P exercised the requisite amount of influence over the main transgressor,[98] which will occur where the conduct that led to the main transgressor's disqualification was the result of the main transgressor acting in accordance with P's directions of instructions.[99]

The Secretary of State may accept a disqualification undertaking from P instead of seeking a disqualification order.[100]

---

[95] Lord Tyre believed this constituted unlawful financial assistance under s 658 of the CA 2006 (discussed at 17.2).
[96] [2014] CSOH 148 [13].
[97] See *Ticketus LLP v Whyte* [2013] EWHC 4069 (Ch).   [98] CDDA 1986, s 8ZA(1).
[99] ibid s 8ZA(3). Note that merely acting upon P's advice if given in a professional capacity, will not be enough to establish the requisite amount of influence (s 8ZA(3)).
[100] ibid s 8ZC.

12.6.1.7 Expedient in the public interest

Section 8 provides that a disqualification order or undertaking of up to 15 years can be obtained if it appears to the Secretary of State that it is expedient in the public interest that a person who is, or has been, a director or shadow director should be disqualified.[101] The court will only grant a disqualification order if it is satisfied that the person's conduct in relation to the company makes him unfit to be a director,[102] so there is a clear overlap between s 6 and s 8 cases. Cases under s 6 are limited to insolvent companies, whereas s 8 is not so limited. This would lead us to conclude that s 8 cases would be more numerous, but the opposite is true and, in practice, disqualifications are usually made under s 6, as opposed to s 8—in 2017/18, there were 1,104 disqualifications under s 6, compared to only 76 under s 8.[103] This is because disqualification proceedings normally result from the liquidation of a company, and so s 6 is the preferred ground. However, where the company is not insolvent, then no application under s 6 can lie, and so s 8 will acquire increased importance.

Section 8 only applies to persons who are current and former directors or shadow directors. However, just as s 8ZA allows for the disqualification of persons whose influence results in others being disqualified under s 6, so too do ss 8ZD and 8ZE allow for the disqualification of those whose influence results in another person being disqualified under s 8. The main difference to note between s 8ZA and s 8ZD is that the latter is not subject to the two-year minimum disqualification period.[104]

12.6.1.8 Breach of competition law

The Enterprise Act 2002 inserted ss 9A–9E into the CDDA 1986 to provide for the imposition of competition disqualification orders and competition undertakings for a period of up to 15 years (although, as noted below, this power was only first used in December 2016). These are imposed where a director commits a breach of competition law, and the court considers that his conduct as a director makes him unfit to be concerned in the management of a company.[105] If these two conditions are satisfied, then a disqualification order must be imposed, unless the Competition and Markets Authority or other specified regulator accepts a competition undertaking in place of an order.[106]

Disqualification and the operation of a cartel

In December 2016, the Competition and Markets Authority secured its first disqualification under the competition provisions. Trod Ltd agreed with a competitor, GB eye Ltd, that they would not undercut each other's prices for posters and frames sold on Amazon's website. GB eye Ltd reported the existence of this cartel agreement to the Competition and Markets Authority (and, as a result, it avoided being punished) and, following an investigation, Trod Ltd admitted to implementing an illegal cartel. Trod Ltd was fined £163,371 and Daniel Aston, manging director of Trod Ltd, gave a disqualification undertaking that he would not act as a director for five years.

---

[101] ibid s 8(1).   [102] ibid s 8(2).

[103] Insolvency Service, 'Insolvency Service Enforcement Outcomes: 2018/19 Monthly Data Tables' (Insolvency Service 2018) Table 1a.

[104] CDDA 1986, s 8ZD(5).   [105] ibid ss 9A(1)–(3).   [106] ibid s 9B.

12.6.1.9 **Participation in fraudulent or wrongful trading under the IA 1986**

Sections 213 and 214 of the IA 1986, which relate to fraudulent[107] and wrongful trading,[108] respectively, allow the court to order a person to contribute to a company's assets. Section 10 of the CDDA 1986 provides that where the court so orders, it can also disqualify the person for up to 15 years. No application for disqualification is needed—the court can impose a disqualification order on its own initiative.

Disqualification under s 10 is conditional upon a person being found liable for fraudulent or wrongful trading. Where no such liability is sought or established, but the person has engaged in conduct that could fall within those sections, then this may justify disqualification on the ground of unfitness in s 6.[109] This is useful as litigation under ss 213 and 214 is relatively rare.

Fraudulent and wrongful trading are discussed at 23.3.3 and 23.3.4 respectively.

12.6.1.10 **Bankruptcy**

Section 11 of the CDDA 1986 provides that it is a criminal offence for a person to act as a director or to directly or indirectly take part or be concerned in the promotion, formation, or management of a company, without the leave of the court, at any time when that person is an undischarged bankrupt.[110] The disqualification can even extend beyond bankruptcy, as it also covers persons subject to a bankruptcy restriction order or undertaking[111]—these are similar to disqualification orders and undertakings and simply restrict the activities of formerly bankrupt persons.

The key feature of s 11 is that disqualification is automatic—a disqualification order or undertaking is not required. The rationale behind this strict approach is that if the person concerned cannot responsibly manage their own financial affairs, they should not be in a position to manage the assets of others.

12.6.2 **Enforcement**

Responsibility for enforcement of the disqualification regime is dependent upon the ground of disqualification in question. In relation to the grounds of disqualification in ss 2–4 of the CDDA 1986, then an application for a disqualification order can be sought by the Secretary of State, the official receiver, the liquidator, or any past or present member or creditor of the company.[112] As regards competition disqualification orders under s 9A, responsibility for enforcement rests with the Competition and Markets Authority (CMA), and other specified regulators.[113] Most disqualifications take place under s 6 and, under this ground, only the Secretary of State may apply for a disqualification order or accept a disqualification undertaking.[114] As noted, in practice, the Secretary of State's powers are delegated to the Insolvency Service, which often works closely with other bodies (such as Companies House, the Serious Fraud Office, and the Financial Conduct Authority) when investigating potential subjects of a disqualification order or undertaking.

---

[107] Note that s 10 only applies to fraudulent trading under the IA 1986. Fraudulent trading under s 993 of the CA 2006 (discussed at 23.3.3.2) is covered under the s 4 ground for disqualification.

[108] Note that whilst s 10 applies to s 214 (wrongful trading in relation to a company in insolvent liquidation), it does not appear to apply to s 246ZB (wrongful trading in a company in insolvent administration).

[109] See e.g. *Secretary of State for Trade and Industry v Lubriani (No 2)* [1998] BCC 264 (Ch) (disqualification under s 6, where the directors carried on trading past insolvency to the detriment of the company's creditors).

[110] CDDA 1986, s 11(1) and (2)(a).   [111] ibid s 11(2)(b).

[112] ibid s 16(2).   [113] ibid ss 9A(10) and 9E(2).

[114] ibid s 7(1). The same is true as regards the related grounds for disqualification found in ss 8ZA and 8ZD.

12.6.2.1 **Disqualification orders and undertakings**

A director can be disqualified via a disqualification order or a disqualification undertaking. The effects of a disqualification order and undertaking are the same, namely that, for a period specified in the order or undertaking, the person in question:

(a) shall not be a director of a company, act as receiver of a company's property or in any way, whether directly or indirectly, be concerned or take part in the promotion, formation or management of a company unless (in each case) he has the leave of the court, and

(b) he shall not act as an insolvency practitioner.[115]

A disqualification order or undertaking must cover all of the activities in (a) and (b) so, for example, it is not possible for an order or undertaking to disqualify a person from promoting or forming a company, but to permit him to manage a company,[116] nor is it possible to disqualify a person from acting as director of a specific type of company.[117] The inclusion of the phrase 'concerned or take part in' in s 1(1)(a) means that a wide range of persons can be subject to a disqualification order or undertaking. For example, in *R v Campbell*,[118] a person who acted as a management consultant for a company was disqualified for five years.

A disqualification order is an order of the court providing that a person is to be disqualified.[119] Given that disqualification is designed primarily to protect the public, it is desirable that disqualifications are put into effect quickly. However, court delays mean that disqualification orders may not be granted quickly, and there will be the associated expense of litigation. A number of judges had judicially proposed that an out-of-court procedure be introduced,[120] and this was finally introduced by the Insolvency Act 2000, which amended the CDDA 1986 to allow for disqualification through a disqualification undertaking, which allows the Secretary of State[121] to accept from a person an undertaking that, for a specified period, they will not engage in the activity stated above.[122] In practice, it is not the Secretary of State personally who accepts the undertaking, but the Insolvency Service acting on behalf of the Secretary of State. A disqualification undertaking, once accepted, has the same legal force as a disqualification order.

The Secretary of State need not accept an undertaking, and the CDDA 1986 limits his ability to accept an undertaking in two ways:

---

[115] ibid ss 1(1) and 1A(1). As most of the provisions of the CDDA 1986 also apply to LLPs, a disqualification order or undertaking can also disqualify a person from acting as a member of an LLP (Limited Liability Partnerships Regulations 2001, SI 2001/1090, reg 4(2)).

[116] *Re Gower Enterprises Ltd (No 2)* [1995] BCC 1081 (Ch). Of course, a person may obtain leave from the court to engage in the promotion, formation, or management of a company (see 12.6.2.2), so this situation is possible in practice.

[117] *R v Ward* [2001] EWCA Crim 1648, [2002] BCC 953 (refusal to allow a disqualification order to apply to public companies only).

[118] (1984) 78 Cr App R 95 (CA). This was a criminal case as it concerned Campbell's unsuccessful appeal against his conviction for breaching the disqualification order.

[119] CDDA 1986, s 1(1).

[120] See e.g. *Practice Direction (No 1 of 1995)* [1996] 1 All ER 442 (Ch); *Secretary of State for Trade and Industry v Rogers* [1996] 1 WLR 1569 (CA) 1574; *Official Receiver v Cooper* [1999] BCC 115 (Ch) 119.

[121] In relation to s 9A (disqualification for breaches of competition law), the Competition and Markets Authority may accept the undertaking (CDDA 1986, s 9B).

[122] CDDA 1986, s 1A(1).

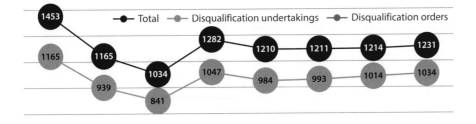

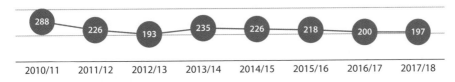

FIGURE 12.1 Disqualification orders and undertakings, 2010–2018

Source: Statistics derived from the Insolvency Service's Enforcement Outcomes Statistics, available from www.gov.uk/government/collections/insolvency-service-enforcement-outcomes accessed 10 January 2019.

1. Disqualification undertakings are only available where the disqualification application is brought under ss 5A, 7, 8, 8ZC, 8ZE, or 9A[123] and the Secretary of State[124] is of the opinion that the person has engaged in the disqualifying conduct found in those sections.[125] It has been argued that there is 'no logical reason' why undertakings should not be available in cases concerning other grounds for disqualification.[126]

2. The Secretary of State can only accept the undertaking if it appears to him that an undertaking is 'expedient in the public interest'.[127]

Despite these limitations, disqualification undertakings have become widely used and, as Figure 12.1 demonstrates, disqualification undertakings outnumber disqualification orders by a significant margin (which is unsurprising given their expedience and low cost when compared to disqualification orders). However, several concerns exist.

First, in the case of a disqualification order, the court will determine whether the conduct complained of merits disqualification. As it takes place in court, it will come with the safeguards for due process, and the publicity of a decision in open court. Conversely, an undertaking, being an out-of-court procedure, is a much less open procedure (although the Insolvency Service does post details of undertakings accepted on its website). Second, directors may feel pressurized into an undertaking, rather than going through the process of contesting a disqualification order, especially given the rules relating to costs. If a director offers an undertaking after court proceedings have been commenced then, if the undertaking is accepted, this will halt the proceedings, but the director will be liable for the costs of the proceedings to date.[128] Conversely, if

---

[123] ibid. Section 9B provides that competition undertakings are available for breaches of s 9A.

[124] In the case of competition undertakings, it will be the Competition and Markets Authority that makes this determination.

[125] CDDA 1986, ss 5A(4)(a), 7(2A), 8(2A)(a), 8ZC(1), 8ZE(1), and 9B.

[126] Adrian Walters, 'Directors' Disqualification after the Insolvency Act 2000: The New Regime' (2001) 3 Insolv L 86, 90.

[127] CDDA 1986, ss 5A(4)(b), 7(2A), 8(2A)(b), 8ZC(1), and 8ZE(1).

[128] *Practice Direction: Directors Disqualification Proceedings* [2015] BCC 224,

a director offers an undertaking prior to proceedings commencing, then he will not be required to pay any costs if the undertaking is accepted. If the period of disqualification specified in an undertaking is slightly less than might be expected under a disqualification order, then the person might feel even more pressure to accept an undertaking.

Breach of a disqualification order or undertaking, or the commission of the s 11 offence, can result in several consequences:

- an either way offence will be committed;[129]
- the person in breach will become personally liable for the relevant debts of the company if he is involved in the management of the company.[130] Such liability will also be imposed upon a person who is involved in the management of a company, and acts upon instructions of a person who he knows is either (i) subject to a disqualification order or undertaking; or (ii) is an undischarged bankrupt.[131]

The CDDA 1986 contains no express provision for appealing against the imposition of a disqualification order. However, the Court of Appeal has confirmed that both the High Court and the Court of Appeal have jurisdiction to stay or suspend a disqualification order.[132] However, the Court also stated that an appeal would only lie in exceptional circumstances and, in most cases, the normal course of action would be for the disqualified person to seek leave to act,[133] which is discussed next.

12.6.2.2 Applying for leave to act

A person subject to a disqualification order or undertaking may apply to the court for leave to act (i.e. to engage in any acts that are prohibited by the disqualification order or undertaking).[134] The CDDA 1986 provides no guidance, nor imposes any limitations upon the courts' discretion in determining whether to grant leave to act—it is a discretion 'unfettered by any statutory condition or criterion'.[135] In the absence of statutory guidance, the courts have established a number of guiding principles.[136] When s 6 was discussed, it was noted that the law needs to balance the need to protect the public with the rights of the individual concerned. This has resulted in the 'need-and-protection' approach which provides that, in order for leave to act to be granted, 'the court must be satisfied that there is a need to make the order and, more importantly, that if the order is made the public will remain adequately protected'.[137] In this context, 'need' refers not to the need of the disqualified person to act, but to whether the company has need of the disqualified person's services as a director.[138] However, where the company is small, separating the needs of the director and the company may not be easy.[139]

---

[129] CDDA 1986, s 13.   [130] ibid s 15(1)(a).   [131] ibid s 15(1)(b).

[132] *Secretary of State for Trade and Industry v Bannister* [1996] 1 WLR 118 (CA). The issue of whether the County Court has jurisdiction of stay or to suspend a disqualification order was left for further argument in a later case (no such case has yet occurred).

[133] ibid 124 (Morritt LJ).

[134] CDDA 1986, s 17. Note that a disqualified person cannot apply for leave to act as an insolvency practitioner (ss 17(1) and (3)).

[135] *Re Dawes and Henderson (Agencies) Ltd* [2000] BCC 204 (Ch) 211 (Sir Richard Scott VC).

[136] For a discussion of these principles, see Sandra Bristoll, 'Permission to Act Whilst Disqualified—A Balancing Act' (2014) 27 Insolv Int 49.

[137] *Re Gibson Davies Ltd* [1995] BCC 11 (Ch) 14 (Sir Mervyn Davies). See also *Re Cargo Agency Ltd* [1992] BCLC 686 (Ch).

[138] ibid 15.

[139] *Re Tech Textiles Ltd* [1998] 1 BCLC 259 (Ch); *Secretary of State for Trade and Industry v Barnett* [1998] 2 BCLC 64 (Ch).

What is clear is that for disqualification to adequately protect the public, leave to act under s 17 must be granted rarely.[140] Arden J stated that leave to act 'is not to be too freely given. Legislative policy requires the disqualification of unfit directors to minimise the risk of harm to the public, and the Courts must not by granting leave prevent the achievement of this policy.'[141] Where leave to act is granted, it is usually subject to conditions, with the following case providing an example of the breadth of conditions that can be imposed to protect the public and to minimize the chances of the director repeating the conduct that resulted in his disqualification.

Harris v Secretary of State for Business, Innovation and Skills [2013] EWHC 2514 (Ch)

FACTS: Harris incorporated Digital Docs Ltd ('DDL') in 2003, and was a director of the company from 2009 until its liquidation in 2011. During his directorship, DDL failed to submit VAT returns and, at the date of its liquidation, it had accrued VAT liabilities of £211,000, despite the fact that it had paid out £152,000 to its directors. Harris gave an undertaking to the Secretary of State that he would not act as a director for four years. He was also the director of other companies, and he sought leave to act in relation to three of these companies (namely CSL, TVIG, and CLL). Harris proposed conditions that could be attached to his leave to act, including the full payment of tax, and a promise not to borrow money from any of these companies.

HELD: The Court granted Harris leave to act in relation to one of the three companies, on the ground that Harris's involvement in it was vital. However, the Court stated that the proposed conditions put forward by Harris were not enough and several additional conditions were imposed, including:

- prohibiting a dividend being paid out on CSL's share capital if it would reduce CSL's distributable profits to less than £50,000;
- requiring CSL to appoint an experienced accountant to undertake a stock valuation;
- requiring the board of CSL to undergo monthly monitoring, and an annual review by an independent firm of auditors.

If a person is granted leave to act subject to conditions, then, if those conditions are not complied with, that person will be contravening the CDDA 1986, and so will be subject to the same criminal penalties and personal liability as if they had breached the disqualification order or undertaking.[142]

12.6.2.3 Compensation orders and undertakings

As noted, the principal purpose of disqualification is protection of the public. However, disqualification does not directly benefit those who have suffered loss due to the actions of the disqualified person (e.g. the company's creditors).[143] Accordingly, in July 2013, the

---

[140] See Alice Belcher, 'What Makes a Director Fit? An Analysis of the Workings of Section 17 of the Company Directors Disqualification Act 1986' (2012) 16 Edin LR 386, whose study showed that between 2001 and 2010, only 159 persons were granted leave to act.

[141] *Re Tech Textiles Ltd* [1998] 1 BCLC 259 (Ch).

[142] *Re Brian Sheridan Cars Ltd* [1995] BCC 1035 (Ch). These are discussed at 12.6.2.1.

[143] For more, see Nicole Kar, Robert Walker, and Glen Davis, 'Competition Disqualification Orders and the Lessons which Can Be Learned from the Insolvency Context' (2011) 10 Comp LJ 306.

government proposed empowering the courts to make a compensatory award alongside the making of a disqualification order.[144] With the passing of the SBEEA 2015, the CDDA 1986 was amended to allow for the courts to make compensation orders, and for the Secretary of State to accept compensation undertakings. A compensation order or undertaking can only be made if two conditions are met, namely:

(a) the person is subject to a disqualification order or undertaking; and

(b) the conduct to which the order or undertaking relates has caused loss to one or more creditors of an insolvent company of which the person has at any time been a director.[145]

A compensation order or undertaking will require the disqualified person to pay a specified amount to either (i) the Secretary of State for the benefit of the creditor(s) or class of creditor(s) specified; or (ii) as a contribution to the assets of the company.[146] The court has the power to reduce the amount payable under a compensation undertaking, or to provide that the undertaking is not to have effect.[147] At the time of writing, the power to make a compensation order or accept a compensation undertaking has not yet been exercised.

CHAPTER SUMMARY

- There are five broad ways in which a director can be removed from office, namely (i) resignation; (ii) vacation of office in accordance with the articles; (iii) retirement by rotation; (iv) removal; and (v) disqualification.

- A director can resign at any time by giving notice to the company, which must accept his resignation.

- A company's articles can specify what circumstances will cause a director to vacate office.

- A company's articles can require its directors to periodically vacate office and, if they so wish, seek re-election.

- Section 168 of the CA 2006 provides that a director can be removed from office by a company passing an ordinary resolution at a meeting.

- A director can be removed by a power provided for under the articles.

- Under the Company Directors Disqualification Act 1986, a director can be disqualified from acting as a director, either (i) by the court imposing a disqualification order; or (ii) by the Secretary of State accepting a disqualification undertaking from the director in question.

FURTHER READING

Alice Belcher, 'What Makes a Director Fit? An Analysis of the Workings of Section 17 of the Company Directors Disqualification Act 1986' (2012) 16 Edin LR 386.
- Examines the law and practice relating to disqualified directors being given leave to act.

---

[144] BIS, 'Transparency and Trust: Enhancing the Transparency of UK Company Ownership and Increasing Trust in UK Business: Discussion Paper' (BIS 2013) 72.

[145] CDDA 1986, s 15A(3). Procedural rules relating to compensation orders can be found in the Compensation Orders (Disqualified Directors) Proceedings (England and Wales) Rules 2016, SI 2016/890.

[146] CDDA 1986, s 15B(1) and (2).   [147] ibid s 15C(1).

Andrew Keay, 'Company Directors Behaving Poorly: Disciplinary Options for Shareholders' [2007] JBL 656.

- An excellent article that discusses the various options that members have for disciplining or removing a director.

BIS, 'Transparency & Trust: Enhancing the Transparency of UK Company Ownership and Increasing Trust in UK Business: Discussion Paper' (BIS 2013) Part B.

- Discusses the UK director regulatory system, with a focus on the disqualification regime. Discusses reform suggestions, some of which were introduced by the SBEEA 2015.

Kenneth Simmonds, 'Corporate Governance: Real Power, Cecil King and Machiavelli' (1999) 7 CG 3.

- Despite its age, this article provides an interesting discussion of article provisions empowering boards to remove directors.

Richard Williams, 'Disqualifying Directors: A Remedy Worse than the Disease?' (2007) 7 JCLS 213.

- Discusses whether the disqualification regime has protected the public from abuses of limited liability, and whether it has acted as a deterrent.

SELF-TEST QUESTIONS

1. Define the following terms:

- retirement by rotation;
- special notice;
- weighted voting clause;
- succession planning;
- disqualification undertaking.

2. State whether each of the following statements is true or false and, if false, explain why:

- A company must accept a director's resignation.
- A s 168 resolution can be passed at a meeting or, if the company is private, via a written resolution.
- The CA 2006 requires that a director of a public companies must retire at least every three years, and may then seek re-election.
- A director disqualified under s 6 of the CDDA 1986 must be disqualified for at least two years.
- A director can only be disqualified for committing certain offences, but only if those offences were committed in the UK.
- A director can only be disqualified by court order.
- A disqualified director can be required to pay compensation to a creditor who has suffered loss due to the director's conduct.

3. 'The reforms made to the Company Directors Disqualification Act 1986 by the Small Business, Enterprise and Employment Act 2015 are largely superficial, and will do little to substantively improve the effectiveness of the disqualification regime.' Do you agree with this quote? Provide reasons for your answers.

4. You are the company secretary for Dragon Tools Ltd ('DT'). The company has three directors (Walter, Yvonne, and Ahmed), each of whom owns 10 per cent of the company's shares. Upon incorporation, DT adopted the model articles subject to a supplementary article (art 3(2)) which states that each director is entitled to be a director for life and is to receive £20,000 remuneration per year. The directors also have service contracts for five years under which they each receive remuneration of £50,000 per year. These contracts came into effect, without the knowledge of the other shareholders, when the directors were re-appointed in 2016.

A number of the non-director shareholders have become dissatisfied with the way that the company is being run. They are particularly unhappy with Walter's continued employment with the company and membership of the board of directors, as he rarely attends board meetings and appears to have no interest at all in being involved in the company's management. Six of these shareholders want Walter to be removed from office.

These members seek your advice as to whether they can remove Walter from the board and terminate his service contract. They also wish to know if they can remove art 3(2) from the articles.

 ONLINE RESOURCES

This book is accompanied by online resources to better support you in your studies. Visit www.oup.com/uk/roach-company/ for:

- answers to the self-test questions;
- further reading lists;
- multiple-choice questions;
- glossary.

Updates to the law can be found on the author's Twitter account (@UKCompanyLaw) and further resources can be found on the author's blog (www.companylawandgovernance.com).

PART IV
Membership of the company

Having discussed the board of directors in Part III, Part IV moves on to look at the other major organ of the company, namely the members. Members occupy several vital roles, including providing capital to the company and engaging in key decisions regarding the running and governance of the company. Part IV consists of the following chapters:

CHAPTER 13 MEMBERSHIP
Chapter 13 looks at the concept of membership. What makes a person a member and how does a member differ to a shareholder? In recent years, concerns have arisen regarding the transparency of a company's membership and so this chapter looks at how the law seeks to make company 'ownership' more transparent.

CHAPTER 14 MEETINGS AND INVESTOR ENGAGEMENT
This chapter looks at the role and importance of general meetings, the significant body of procedural rules by which general meetings are run, and the extent to which a company's members actually engage with general meetings.

CHAPTER 15 MEMBERS' REMEDIES
This final chapter looks at three remedies that aim to protect a company's members (especially its minority shareholders), namely (i) the derivative claim; (ii) the unfair prejudice petition; and (iii) the petition to wind up the company.

13

Membership

- What is membership?
- The register of members
- Transparency and the register of members
- Termination of membership

INTRODUCTION

Every company must have at least one member,[1] although the majority of companies have more. Most companies are small private companies with a small number of members (as reflected in the fact that the average number of members per company is two),[2] but larger listed companies may have hundreds of thousands of members.

This chapter explores the concept of membership, looking at who can and cannot become a member of a company, how information relating to members is kept and maintained, how the law has sought to make the relationship between companies and their members more transparent, and how membership can be terminated. Before these issues can be discussed, it is first important to discuss what 'membership' is. It will be seen that, whilst a member is often a shareholder and vice versa, this is not always the case. Even if a person is a member and a shareholder, their rights as members may differ to their rights as shareholders. Whilst this chapter focuses on membership, the law relating to shares and share capital is discussed in Chapter 16.

13.1 What is membership?

Company law legislation typically does not use the word 'shareholder' all that often and instead the word 'member' tends to be used. One obvious reason for this is that company law needs to cater for companies without a share capital—such companies have

---

[1] Section 1(1) of the Companies Act 1985 (CA 1985) required all companies to have at least two members. In 1992, in order to comply with the Twelfth Company Law Directive, a new s 1(3A) was inserted into the 1985 Act to allow for the creation of single-member private companies. Section 7(1) of the CA 2006 provides that a company is formed 'by one or more persons . . .', meaning that any type of company can now be created with a single member.
[2] Companies House, 'Companies Register Activities in the United Kingdom 2017–18' (Companies House 2018) Table A7.

members, but no shareholders. Many rights and obligations within company law legislation are imposed on members and so it is extremely important to be able to determine whether a person is a member (see e.g. the cases of *Enviroco* and *Re Nuneaton*, discussed at 13.1.2 and 13.1.1 respectively, whose results turned on whether a person was a member).

The key provision is s 112 of the Companies Act 2006 (CA 2006), which provides for two ways in which a person can become a member:

1. the subscribers of a company's memorandum are deemed to have agreed to become members of the company and, upon the company's registration, they become members and their names must be entered as such in the register of members;

2. every other person who agrees to become a member of the company and whose name is entered in its register of members is a member of the company.

Section 112 makes no mention of shares or shareholdings, so being a shareholder will not automatically make a person a member (although in a company with a share capital, the shareholders will almost always become members). Accordingly, a clear distinction between a shareholder and a member can arise in certain instances:

- As noted, a company without a share capital will have members, but no shareholders.
- In a company with a share capital, there may be a good reason why a shareholder's name should not be entered into the register of members (several reasons are discussed in this section). Such a person will be a shareholder, but not a member[3] (although that shareholder can apply for a rectification order placing his name of the register).

Rectification of the register is discussed at 13.2.3.

- It may be the case that a person will be a member of a company with a share capital, even if he holds no shares, as occurred in *Re Nuneaton* (discussed below).

13.1.1 Agreement

Looking at s 112, it is clear that a person cannot become a member unless he agrees to become a member. In relation to a newly registered company, the subscribers to the memorandum are deemed to agree to become members. In all other cases, the member must agree to become a member, or must have authorized another to agree on his behalf. All that is required is for the prospective member to indicate assent—there is no need for a contract of agreement to exist between the company and prospective member, as the following case demonstrates.

Re Nuneaton Borough Association Football Club Ltd [1989] 5 BCC 377 (CA)

FACTS: Nuneaton Borough Association Football Club Ltd ('Nuneaton') owned a football club that was experiencing financial difficulties. Mr Shooter offered to inject capital into the club by purchasing shares in Nuneaton and, in order to effect this, general meetings were held to approve an increase of Nuneaton's **authorized share capital**. Nuneaton then purported to allot 10,000 shares to Shooter, for which he paid £10,000, and his name was entered into the register of members. However, due to procedural errors, the general meetings were invalid, meaning that the shares purportedly allotted to Shooter were never validly created and so Shooter was not a shareholder. A dispute arose and Shooter petitioned the court under the unfair prejudice remedy. Nuneaton correctly stated that only members can bring an unfair prejudice petition and argued

authorized share capital: the total nominal value of shares that may be allotted by a company (see 16.2.3)

---

[3] Similarly, prior to the abolition of bearer shares (discussed at 16.4.3), the holders of such shares were shareholders, but were not members as their names were not entered into the register of members.

that Shooter was not a member because agreement required the existence of a contract between the company and the prospective member, and no such contract was present here.

HELD: Shooter had standing to bring the petition. He had clearly agreed to become a member and his name had been entered into the register of members. Fox LJ stated that s 112:

merely requires the agreement of the person to become a member. . . . As a matter of English the word 'agrees' is, I think, satisfied by mere assent. Thus the Shorter Oxford English Dictionary includes among the meanings of 'agree', the meaning 'to accept favourably . . . To accede, consent to.' The result seems to me to be workable and reasonable in practical terms and I see no need for a requirement of a contract.[4]

The requirement for agreement means that, if a person has not agreed to become a member, then that person will not be a member. This will be the case even if his name has been entered into the register of members[5] (in which case, he may apply to the court for an order rectifying the register).

13.1.2 Entry into the register of members

In relation to a newly created company, the subscribers to the company's memorandum will become members, even if their names are not entered into the register of members[6] (i.e. all that is required is agreement, which is deemed). In all other cases, mere agreement to be a member is not enough and s 112(2) states that a person will only become a member if his name[7] is also entered into the register of members. In many companies, it will be for the directors to determine whether a person's name is entered into the register (although this will usually be undertaken by the company secretary if the company has one). In large listed companies, the membership changes so rapidly that professional share registrars are often engaged to maintain the register of members.

The courts take an extremely strict approach regarding those listed in the register of members and s 112 'reflects a fundamental principle of United Kingdom company law, namely that, except where express provision is made to the contrary, the person on the register of the members is the member to the exclusion of any other person, unless and until the register is rectified'.[8] The following complex Scottish case demonstrates this.

Enviroco Ltd v Farstad Supply A/S [2011] UKSC 16

FACTS: Farstad owned a vessel, which it chartered to Asco UK Ltd. Farstad engaged Enviroco to clean the vessel's oil tanks, but during cleaning, a fire broke out, killing one of Enviroco's employees and causing substantial damage to the vessel. Farstad commenced proceedings against Enviroco, seeking £2.7 million in damages. What made the case complex was that Asco UK Ltd and Enviroco were both subsidiaries of ASCO plc, and the charterparty between Farstad and Asco UK Ltd contained a provision stating that Farstad would indemnify 'affiliates' of Asco UK Ltd, with 'affiliate' being defined by reference to the meaning of 'subsidiary' under the Companies

See Luh Luh Lan, 'The Curious Case of a Subsidiary' (2012) 128 LQR 351.

---

[4] [1989] 5 BCC 377 (CA) 380.

[5] *Re Nuneaton Borough Association Football Club Ltd (No 1)* [1989] BCLC 454 (Ch).

[6] CA 2006, s 112(1); CA 2006, Explanatory Notes, para 239.

[7] The courts have stated that a person will still be a member, even if a false or fictitious name is entered onto the register (*Re Hercules Insurance Co* (1872) LR 13 Eq 566).

[8] *Enviroco Ltd v Farstad Supply A/S* [2011] UKSC 16, [2011] 1 WLR 921 [37] (Lord Collins).

Act 1985 (CA 1985).[9] Enviroco sought to rely on this clause, arguing that it was an affiliate of Asco UK Ltd because it and Asco UK Ltd were both subsidiaries of ASCO plc. To make matters more complex, prior to the fire, ASCO plc had charged the shares it owned in Enviroco to secure obligations it had made to the Bank of Scotland and, in accordance with Scottish law, the Bank's nominee was registered in the register of members in relation to those shares. The issue therefore was whether, at the time of the fire, ASCO plc was a member of Enviroco (and therefore its parent). In order to rely on the indemnity clause, the answer would need to be yes.

HELD: Lord Collins stated that membership was 'determined by entry on the register of members'.[10] It was the name of the Bank's nominee who appeared on the register of members, and not ASCO plc. Accordingly, it followed that ASCO plc was not a member of Enviroco and so Enviroco was not its subsidiary. As a result, Enviroco could not rely on the indemnity clause as it was not an affiliate of Asco UK Ltd.

As is discussed at 13.2, private companies may choose not to keep their own register of members and may instead choose the keep member information on the public register of Companies House. In such a case:

- there is no obligation on a company to enter the names of subscribers to the memorandum in the register of members;
- when a person agrees to become a member post-incorporation, the company must provide Companies House with the details of the prospective member.[11]

13.1.3 **Restrictions and limitations**

The general rule is that anyone can be a member of a company. However, exceptions and restrictions to this general rule do exist.

13.1.3.1 **Minors**

The company is free to accept a minor[12] as a member,[13] except where the articles prohibit minors from becoming members.[14] Even where no such article provision exists, a company is still free to refuse to register a minor as a member or to register a transfer of shares to a minor.[15] One reason why such a power could be useful is because contracting with a minor carries risks. If a company enters into a contract with a minor, then the minor may enforce the contract against the company, but the company cannot enforce the contract against the minor as the contract is normally voidable at the minor's instance whilst he remains a minor, or within a reasonable time following attainment of the age of majority. However, it is important to bear in mind that if a minor enters into a contract with a company to purchase shares in that company and then seeks to

---

[9] The events of this case occurred between 1994 and 2002, so the CA 1985 was the governing legislation.

[10] [2011] UKSC 16, [2011] 1 WLR 921 [38].   [11] CA 2006, s 112(3).

[12] In England and Wales, a minor is anyone under the age of 18 (Family Law Reform Act 1969, s 1(1)). In Scotland, a minor is also anyone under the age of 18 (Age of Majority (Scotland) Act 1969, s 1(1)), but s 1(1) of the Age of Legal Capacity (Scotland) Act 1991 provides that persons of 16 or over acquire legal capacity to enter into any transaction.

[13] *Re Laxon & Co (No 2)* [1892] 3 Ch 555 (Ch) (a minor may subscribe to a company's memorandum); *Re Blakely Ordnance Co* (1868–69) LR 4 Ch App 31 (shares may be transferred to a minor).

[14] *Re Royal Navy School* [1910] 1 Ch 806 (Ch). The model articles contain no such prohibition.

[15] *Re Asiatic Banking Corporation, Symon's Case* (1869–70) LR 5 Ch App 298.

repudiate that contract, he cannot reclaim the purchase price of the shares, unless there has been a total failure of consideration.[16] If, however, the shares were partly paid, then the minor will not be liable for the outstanding amount following repudiation.

13.1.3.2 Unincorporated associations

Unincorporated associations have no legal personality and therefore should not be accepted as members,[17] and companies are free to reject a transfer of shares to a partnership.[18] In the case of an ordinary partnership, then the name(s) of the relevant partners (usually the ones who purchased shares in the company) should instead be entered into the register of members. However, the name of an ordinary partnership may be entered into the register if all the partners agree and, in such a case, the partners will be held liable as members.[19]

13.1.3.3 Companies as members

Companies are generally free to hold shares in, and become members of, other companies. However, this general rule is subject to several exceptions. A company cannot be a member of itself[20] and, as a corollary, is generally prohibited from acquiring its own shares.[21] Parent/holding companies sought to circumvent this prohibition by instead having their subsidiaries become members of, or hold shares in, their parent. This circumvention has now been curtailed as the CA 2006 provides that an incorporated subsidiary is generally prohibited from being a member of its holding company, and any allotment or transfer of shares by a holding company to its subsidiary will be void.[22] However, there are three instances where a subsidiary is permitted to be a member of, or hold shares in, its holding company, namely:

The prohibition on a company acquiring its own shares is discussed at 17.2.

1. where the subsidiary is not a body corporate;

2. where the subsidiary is concerned only as a personal representative or trustee;[23] or

3. where the subsidiary is holding shares in its holding company in the ordinary course of its business as an intermediary.[24] This typically occurs where the subsidiary is a dealer in shares.

Where a large or medium-sized company has shares in it held by, or on behalf of, a subsidiary undertaking, then it must disclose this in its annual accounts.[25]

13.2 The register of members

As discussed at 13.1, a likely determination of whether a person is a member is whether their name is entered into the register of members. The general rule is that every company must keep a register of its members[26] at its registered office or its single alternative

---

[16] *Steinberg v Scala (Leeds) Ltd* [1923] 2 Ch 452 (CA).

[17] Scottish partnerships are an exception to this, as they have legal personality (PA 1890, s 4(2)).

[18] *Re Vagliano Anthracite Collieries* [1910] WN 187.

[19] *Re Land Credit Co of Ireland, Weikersheim's Case* (1972–73) LR 8 Ch App 841.

[20] *Trevor v Whitworth* (1887) 12 App Cas 409 (HL).   [21] CA 2006, s 658 (discussed at 17.2).

[22] ibid s 136(1). The prohibition also applies to a nominee acting on behalf of a subsidiary (s 144).

[23] ibid s 138.   [24] ibid s 141.

[25] Large and Medium-Sized Companies and Groups (Accounts and Reports) Regulations 2008, Sch 4, para 3.

[26] CA 2006, s 113(1).

inspection location ('SAIL').[27] Failure to keep a register of members constitutes a criminal offence.[28] However, an exception to this exists in relation to private companies, who can elect to either:

- keep their own register of members; or
- keep the relevant information on the central register maintained by Companies House.[29]

The register of members and the membership information on the central register do not provide conclusive evidence of membership matters.[30] Instead, where a company maintains its own register of members, then that register will provide *prima facie* evidence of any matters which are by the CA 2006 directed or authorized to be inserted into it.[31] Where a private company keeps its information on the central register, then the central register will provide *prima facie* evidence of any matters which are by the CA 2006 directed or authorized to be inserted into it.[32]

13.2.1 **Content**

Section 113 of the CA 2006 sets out what information must be stated in the register of members, including:

- the names and addresses[33] of each member.[34] Where shares are jointly held, then the names of each joint holder must be stated. Where shares are registered in the name of a nominee, then the name of the nominee (and not the beneficial owner) must be the name registered;
- the date on which each person was registered as a member;
- the date on which any person ceased to be a member;
- if the company has a share capital, a statement of the shares of each member, setting out the number of shares the member holds (and, if applicable, the class of shares) and the amount paid or agreed to be considered as paid on the shares;
- if the company does not have a share capital, but it does have more than one class of member, the register must identify to which class each member belongs.

Note that s 113 does not apply to companies with uncertificated shares.[35] Instead, such companies are required to maintain a register of members as specified by the Uncertificated Securities Regulations 2001. In effect, these Regulations require the company to maintain an 'issuer register of members',[36] which is broadly similar to the register of members under s 113 of the CA 2006.[37] In addition, an 'Operator register of members' is also required,[38] and will be maintained by Euroclear.

The role of Euroclear is discussed at 16.7.3.1.

13.2.2 **Right of inspection**

If a company maintains its own register of members, then that register must be open for inspection at the company's registered office or SAIL. Any member may inspect the

---

[27] ibid ss 114(1) and 136; Companies (Company Records) Regulations 2008, SI 2008/3006, reg 3.
[28] CA 2006, s 13(7) and (8).   [29] ibid s 128A.
[30] *Re Reese River Silver Mining Co* (1869–70) LR 4 HL 64 (HL).   [31] CA 2006, s 127.
[32] ibid s 128H(1). Note, however, that s 128H(1) does not apply to the information to be included under ss 128B(5)(b) or 128B(6).
[33] The address need not be a residential address.
[34] If a limited company only has a single member, then, along with the name and address of the member, the register must state that the company only has one member (CA 2006, s 123(1)).
[35] Uncertificated Securities Regulations 2001, SI 2001/3755, Sch 4, para 2(4).   [36] ibid reg 20(1)(a).
[37] ibid Sch 4, para 2.   [38] ibid reg 20(1)(b).

register free of charge, and any other person may inspect the register upon payment of a fee.[39] Any person may obtain a copy of the register upon payment of a fee.[40]

There are, however, limitations upon the right of inspection. A person wishing to inspect the register must make a request to the company to that effect, and this request must provide specified information, such as his name and address, the purpose for which the information will be used, and whether the information will be disclosed to others.[41] Within five working days of the receipt of the request, the company must either comply with the request or apply to the court for an order (known as a 'no-access order') that the request was not made for a proper purpose.[42] If such an order is made, the court will direct that the company not comply with the request, and can also direct that it need not comply with requests for a similar purpose.[43]

When determining whether a request is being made for a proper purpose, the courts should use a two-stage process, namely (i) the purpose of the inspection request must be established; and (ii) the court must determine if that purpose was proper.[44] The exercise of the courts' ability to issue a no-access order under the CA 2006 was first examined in the following case.

Re Burry & Knight Ltd [2014] EWCA Civ 604

FACTS: Knight was a member of Burry & Knight Ltd ('B&K'). He had concerns regarding B&K's management and had requested that an independent investigation into the company take place, but this request was refused. Some years later, he revived his allegations and requested a copy of B&K's register of members. His request stated that he wished to (i) study B&K's shareholding; (ii) tell the other members his concerns regarding B&K's directors; and (iii) advise the other members to obtain professional advice regarding share valuation in the future. B&K's registrar sought a no-access order on the ground that Knight's request was for an improper purpose.

HELD: During her leading judgment, Arden LJ established useful guidance points regarding the granting of no-access orders:

- The words 'proper purpose' should be given their 'ordinary natural meaning'[45] and a proper purpose ought generally to 'relate to the member's interest in that capacity and to the exercise of shareholder rights'.[46]
- It is not possible to provide an exhaustive definition of what a proper purpose is. A guidance note published by the Institute of Chartered Secretaries and Administrators (ICSA)[47] does exist and the courts may have regard to this note, but this guidance is non-binding and non-exhaustive.[48]
- Where there are multiple purposes—some proper and some not—then a proper purpose will not necessarily be tainted by being coupled to an improper purpose.[49]
- The purpose of the request will normally be stated in the request itself, but the court is not restricted to the purpose as stated in the request document.[50]
- The onus is on the company to show that the member's purpose is improper.[51]

---

[39] CA 2006, s 116(1).   [40] ibid s 116(2).   [41] ibid s 116(3) and (4).   [42] ibid s 117(1) and (3).

[43] ibid s 117(3) and (4).

[44] *Burberry Group plc v Fox-Davies* [2017] EWCA Civ 1129, [2018] Bus LR 332 [34] (David Richards LJ).

[45] [2014] EWCA Civ 604, [2014] 1 WLR 4046 [18].   [46] ibid.

[47] ICSA, 'ICSA Guidance on the Access to the Register of Members: Proper Purpose Test' (ICSA 2018).

[48] [2014] EWCA Civ 604, [2014] 1 WLR 4046 [19].   [49] ibid [20].   [50] ibid [21].   [51] ibid [22].

- A strong presumption exists in favour of shareholder democracy and corporate transparency, and so no-access orders should be granted 'sparingly and with circumspection'.[52]
- The only ground for a no-access order is that the member's request is for an improper purpose.[53]

Applying this, the court held that Knight's request was for an improper purpose. Arden LJ stated that the information that Knight sought to convey to his fellow members was not going to confer any benefit upon them, and that he was pursuing matters that were 'very stale'.[54] The registrar inferred that Knight wished to obtain the information not for the stated purposes, but in order to conduct a vendetta against certain persons who controlled B&K. Arden LJ stated that the registrar was entitled to draw this inference and so the granting of a no-access order was justified.

In the subsequent case of *Burberry Group plc v Fox-Davies*,[55] further guidance was provided:

- Determining whether an inspection was for a proper purpose will depend on the precise facts and circumstances of the case.[56]
- To be a proper purpose, it may be, but need not be, in the interest of the company or its members.[57]
- The propriety of the purpose is to be assessed objectively and does not depend on the company's subjective view.[58]
- Aside from the requirement to pay a fee, the law does not distinguish requests from members and non-members.[59]

13.2.3 **Rectification**

It may be the case that the register of members contains an error. In such a case, the law does not empower the company to rectify the error itself.[60] Instead an application must be made to the court under s 125(1) of the CA 2006,[61] which provides that a rectification order may be sought if:

(a) the name of any person is, without sufficient cause, entered in or omitted from a company's register of members; or

(b) default occurs or unnecessary delay takes place in entering on the register the fact of any person having ceased to be a member.

An application can be made by the person aggrieved, any member of the company, or the company itself. Upon receipt of an application, the court may refuse the application, or it may order rectification of the register and payment of damages by the company to the party aggrieved.[62] Accordingly, rectification is discretionary, and the exercise of the courts' discretion is demonstrated in the following case.

---

[52] ibid [24].   [53] ibid [26].   [54] ibid [73].   [55] [2017] EWCA Civ 1129, [2018] Bus LR 332.
[56] ibid [35].   [57] ibid [45].   [58] ibid [45].   [59] ibid [50].
[60] *Gardiner v Victoria Estates Co Ltd* (1885) 12 R 1356.
[61] Where a private company elects to keep member information on the central register of Companies House, the relevant provision is s 128G, which operates in almost the same way as s 125, except the court order sought will compel the company to deliver to Companies House the information necessary to rectify the error.
[62] CA 2006, s 125(2). Note, however, that damages will not normally be awarded (*RAC Holdings Ltd* (8 December 2000)).

Re Piccadilly Radio plc [1989] 5 BCC 692 (Ch)

FACTS: Piccadilly Radio plc ('PR') was licensed by the Independent Broadcasting Authority ('IBA'). PR's articles prohibited the transfer of PR's shares without the approval of the IBA. PR proposed a merger with another radio station, but shortly after, a rival bidder ('Miss World') announced an intention to make an offer for PR's shares. A meeting was convened to vote on the rival bids, but before this meeting took place, two companies which held shares in PR (one of which was a subsidiary of Miss World) applied to the court for a rectification order on the ground that a share transfer had taken place without the IBA's approval (the transfer in question was from Virgin Vision Ltd ('Virgin') to two other companies, namely 'Allied' and 'Albion'). The two applicants stated that Allied and Albion's names should be removed from the register (and consequently their votes (which, notably, would not have been in favour of Miss World's bid) should not count at the meeting) and that Virgin should have its name restored to the register.

HELD: The court held that the shares were validly transferred to Allied, but the share transfer to Albion was in breach of PR's articles. Despite this, a rectification order was refused for several reasons. First, the applicants had no interest in the shares held by Albion, nor were they seeking to have their own names restored to the register. They were seeking to restore Virgin's name to the register, but Virgin itself did not seek restoration (indeed, Millett J stated that Virgin was 'embarrassed by the application').[63] Second, Millett J stated that, when deciding whether to grant a rectification order, '[t]he court must consider the circumstances in which and the purpose for which the relief is sought'.[64] In this case:

> the applicants were not aggrieved by the fact that the Shares had been transferred without the consent of the IBA, but by the fact that they had been transferred to a company which was unwilling to support the Miss World offer. They were searching for a means to disenfranchise the expected opposition to their offer. . . . A less meritorious claim was difficult to imagine.[65]

Examples of situations where a rectification order was granted include:

- where the applicant had not agreed to become a member, but his name was nevertheless placed on the register of members;[66]
- where the applicant agreed to become a member, but his name was, due to an administrative oversight, not entered onto the register of members;[67]
- where a company removed the shareholder's name from the register based on a forged share transfer document;[68]
- where the applicant was induced to purchase shares by a misrepresentation;[69]
- where the directors wrongfully allotted shares to themselves;[70]
- where the register of members was thrown into a skip and physically lost.[71]

Where the court makes a rectification order, it will also order that notice of the rectification be given to Companies House.[72]

---

[63] [1989] 5 BCC 692 (Ch) 704.   [64] ibid.   [65] ibid 705.

[66] *Re R Bolton & Co Ltd (No 1)* [1894] 3 Ch 356 (CA).

[67] *Greenwich Millennium Exhibition Ltd v New Millennium Experience Co Ltd* [2003] EWHC 1823 (Ch), [2004] 1 All ER 687.

[68] *Re Bahia and San Francisco Railway Co Ltd* (1867–68) LR 3 QB 584.

[69] *Re Russian (Vyksounsky) Ironworks Co* (1865–66) LR 1 Ch App 574.

[70] *Re Thundercrest Ltd* [1994] BCC 857 (Ch).   [71] *Re Data Express Ltd* The Times, 27 April 1987 (Ch).

[72] CA 2006, s 125(4).

13.3 Transparency and the register of members

It is important to distinguish between the legal ownership and beneficial ownership of shares as this has a notable impact upon the transparency of the register of members. The legal owner of shares is the person whose name is entered in the register of members, whereas the beneficial owner is 'the person who ultimately owns or controls the shares'.[73] Historically, the majority of UK quoted shares were held by individuals whose names would appear on the register of members, and so legal and beneficial ownership would reside in the same person. However, it is possible for the beneficial owner of shares to have those shares registered in the name of an intermediary (this person is known as the 'nominee'), in which case the legal owner of the shares will be the nominee. Further, with the increase in institutional investment, it is now common for quoted shares to be held by an intermediary on behalf of others, resulting in the past 50 years witnessing a significant decline in individual ownership and 'an explosion of intermediation'.[74]

Where shares are registered in the name of a nominee, then the name of the nominee must be stated in the register of members, and not the name of the beneficial owner. Indeed, generally, company law focuses largely on the legal owner and not the beneficial owner[75] and it is only the legal owner who can generally exercise membership rights.[76] The result of this is that, especially in larger companies, the register of members may not provide an accurate indicator of who ultimately controls a company, as the following example indicates.

 Eg **Disguising the extent of a shareholding**

Wraith plc's share capital consists of 10,000 ordinary shares. The register of members states that the three largest shareholdings in Wraith are:

- 1,000 shares held by Empire Accountants Ltd;
- 500 shares held by Mrs Earley; and
- 1,500 shares held by Dragon plc.

Unknown to Wraith, Mrs Earley and Empire Accountants are nominees of Dragon plc. Therefore, according to the register of members, Dragon plc holds a 15 per cent shareholding but, in reality, it controls 30 per cent of Wraith's shares. Dragon is utilizing these nominees so that it can amass enough shares for a takeover bid of Wraith without alerting the board of Wraith to its activities.

In the above example, Dragon plc is using nominees for a legitimate commercial justification, and so absolutely prohibiting the use of nominees would not be desirable. However, it is also the case that nominees can also be used for nefarious purposes. As

---

[73] Department for Business, Innovation and Skills (BIS), 'Transparency and Trust: Enhancing the Transparency of Company Ownership and Increasing Trust in UK Business: Discussion Paper' (BIS 2013) 23.
[74] 'The Kay Review of UK Equity Markets and Long-Term Decision Making: Final Report' (2012) para 3.7.
[75] CA 2006, s 126.
[76] Note, however, that s 145 of the CA 2006 does state that a company may provide in its articles that a member can nominate another person to enjoy or exercise all or any specified rights of the member in relation to the company. Few companies, however, have such article provisions.

the government stated in 2013, the use of nominees and other intermediaries means that '[i]ndividuals can use a company to conceal their identity and facilitate a range of criminal activity, from money laundering and terrorist financing to sanctions and tax evasion'.[77] Irrespective of the reasons why nominees are used, their existence results in a reduction in transparency and so several measures have been put into place to try and make company ownership and control more transparent.

13.3.1 Disclosure of interests in shares

As the example box at the start of 13.3 demonstrates, companies (and their boards) have a legitimate interest in knowing who has an interest in their shares. The directors of a private company usually can seek information regarding a new shareholder's identity and characteristics prior to registering that shareholder's details in the register of members. If any concerns arise, private companies are then generally free to refuse to register a transfer of shares. In public companies, this is not the case, and such companies must usually register any transfer of shares made. Clearly, a company such as Wraith plc would want to know if any of its registered members were acting as nominees, or if other persons have an interest in the company's shares. Such companies can turn to Pt 22 of the CA 2006 for aid.

Part 22 applies to persons who have an interest in the shares of a public company. The phrase 'interest in shares' is defined very broadly and includes 'an interest of any kind whatsoever in the shares'.[78] Despite the breadth of this, the CA 2006 does provide more specific detail on what constitutes an interest in shares in ss 820–25. Of special relevance to the example box above is s 824, which relates to agreements between two or more persons to acquire interests in a particular company (the 'target company').

13.3.1.1 Notice requiring information about interests in shares

If a public company knows or has reasonable cause to believe that a person is interested in its shares, or if a person has been so interested in the previous three years, then it may issue a notice to that person.[79] This notice may require that person to confirm whether they have an interest in the company's shares and, if they do have such an interest, to provide further information regarding that interest, including the identity of persons interested in the shares, whether a s 824 agreements exists, and whether interested persons are or were parties to arrangements or agreements relating to the exercise of rights conferred by those shares.[80] If the company chooses not to exercise the power to issue a s 793 notice, then members holding at least 10 per cent of the company's paid-up capital can require the company to issue a s 793 notice.[81]

Accordingly, in the example box at the start of 13.3, Wraith could issue a notice to Dragon plc, Mrs Earley, or Empire Accountants, and the recipient of the notice would need to disclose the identities of the other persons, the existence of any agreements to acquire an interest in Wraith, or other agreements as to the exercise of their shares in Wraith. Note that if any of these parties refused to comply with the s 793 notice (which would include not providing full and truthful knowledge),[82] then Wraith could apply

---

[77] BIS, 'Transparency and Trust: Enhancing the Transparency of Company Ownership and Increasing Trust in UK Business: Discussion Paper' (BIS 2013) 22.
[78] CA 2006, s 820(2)(a).   [79] ibid s 793(1).
[80] ibid s 793(5). Failure to comply with a s 793 notice is a criminal offence (s 795).
[81] ibid s 803.   [82] *Re TR Technology Investment Trust plc* [1988] BCLC 256 (Ch).

to the court for an order directing that the shares of the relevant persons be subject to restrictions,[83] with such restrictions including rendering void a transfer of shares, removing the voting rights attached to the shares, preventing further shares from being issued to that person, or providing that no payments will be made by the company in respect of those shares.[84]

13.3.1.2 Register of interests disclosed

A company must keep a register of any information it has received as a result of a s 793 notice,[85] and this is known as the 'register of interests disclosed'. Information received under a 793 notice must be entered into this register within three days of receipt,[86] and must be kept in the register for at least six years.[87] The register must be made available for inspection at the company's registered office or SAIL[88] and any person can inspect the register free of charge[89] and obtain a copy of the register upon paying a fee.[90]

13.3.2 The PSC register

A s 793 notice is useful, but it requires a company to know or have reasonable cause to believe that a person has an interest in its shares, and the company must then go through the s 793 procedure. In the absence of this, a company will not generally know who its beneficial owners are. In addition, prior to 2016, companies were not required to identify who their beneficial owners were and this allowed companies (especially complex webs of companies) to engage in unlawful or morally questionable activities, whilst shrouding the identities of those who ultimately controlled such companies. Concerns regarding beneficial ownership were heightened following the leaking of the Panama Papers.

The 'Panama Papers' and corporate transparency

In early 2015, 11.5 million confidential documents were leaked to *Süddeutsche Zeitung*, a German newspaper. These documents came from the internal database of Mossack Fonseca, a Panamanian law firm, and were published in April 2016.[91] It was alleged that Mossack Fonseca had provided services to wealthy persons, including prominent public officials, celebrities, companies, and corporate leaders that allowed them to use offshore companies and other investment vehicles to engage in criminal activities (such as tax evasion, money laundering, and evading sanctions), as well as lawful, but morally questionable, activities (such as tax avoidance). Many of the tax havens in which these offshore companies were based had laws in place that made it almost impossible to discover who actually owned and controlled companies incorporated there, making it extremely difficult to identify who had engaged in the alleged nefarious activities.

---

[83] CA 2006, s 794(1). [84] ibid s 797(1).

[85] ibid s 808(1). Failure to keep this register is a criminal offence (s 808(5)). [86] ibid s 808(2).

[87] ibid ss 815(1) and 816. Information can be removed prior to this if it is incorrect (s 817).

[88] ibid s 809(1). Failure to comply with this section is a criminal offence (s 809(4)). [89] ibid s 811(1).

[90] ibid s 811(2).

[91] The papers and commentary on them can be obtained from https://www.icij.org/investigations/panama-papers accessed 10 January 2019.

Repercussions were immediate. Within days of papers being published, the Prime Minister of Iceland resigned following public anger over his failure to disclose the existence of an offshore company owned by him and his wife held that held bonds in banks that collapsed during the 2008 financial crisis. Since then, significant sums has been recovered by governments, 79 countries have announced responses to the leaked information, and over 6,500 individuals and companies have been investigated.[92] In March 2018, Mossack Fonseca announced that, as a result of the reputational and economic damage it suffered following the leak, it was shutting down.

An international problem demanded an international solution and, in relation to transparency and beneficial ownership, four developments are noteworthy:

- In 2013, whilst under the UK's Presidency, the G8 decided that action needed to be taken to make beneficial ownership of companies more transparent, and so the G8's Action Plan committed the G8 to implementing rules requiring companies 'to obtain and hold their beneficial ownership and basic information, and ensure documentation of this information is accurate'.[93] In 2014, a similar commitment was made by the G20.[94]

- In 2015, the EU's Fourth Anti-Money Laundering Directive[95] ('4AMLD') was passed. Article 30 of the Directive requires Member States to ensure that companies hold adequate, accurate, and current information on their beneficial ownership, and that this information is held on a central register in each Member State.

- In April 2018, the European Parliament adopted the Fifth Anti-Money Laundering Directive[96] (5AMLD), which came into force in July 2018. 5AMLD does not replace 4AMLD, but merely amends it. EU Member States have until January 2020 in which to implement 5AMLD and, even though the UK will have likely left EU by then, the UK government has stated that it will implement 5AMLD.

- In October 2018, the EU adopted the Sixth Anti-Money Laundering Directive (6AMLD), which extends the scope of criminal liability for money-laundering-related offences. The UK will not be bound by this directive, but it will affect UK companies with subsidiaries in the EU, so it will be interesting to see how the UK government responds to the 6AMLD.

The Small Business, Enterprise and Employment Act 2015 (SBEEA 2015) introduced a new Pt 21A into the CA 2006 which, along with the Register of People with Significant Control Regulations 2016,[97] requires companies to maintain a register of people with significant control ('the PSC register'). The information on this register will also be stored on the central register of Companies House. As a result of these rules being introduced, the UK is only one of three countries amongst the G20 that is currently regarded as having a 'very strong framework' for the identification of beneficial owners of companies.[98]

---

[92] Will Fitzgibbon and Emilia Diaz-Struck, 'By the Numbers: Eight Months of Panama Papers Global Impact' (International Consortium of Investigative Journalists, 1 December 2016) https://panamapapers.icij.org/blog/20161201-impact-graphic.html accessed 10 January 2019.

[93] 'G8 Action Plan Principles to Prevent the Misuse of Companies and Legal Arrangements' (G8 2013).

[94] 'G20 High-Level Principles on Beneficial Ownership Transparency' (G20 2014).

[95] European Parliament and Council Directive (EU) 2015/849 on the prevention of the use of the financial system for the purposes of money laundering or terrorist financing [2015] OJ L141/73.

[96] European Parliament and Council Directive (EU) 2018/843 amending Directive (EU) 2015/849 on the prevention of the use of the financial system for the purposes of money laundering or terrorist financing, and amending Directives 2009/138/EC and 2013/36/EU [2018] OJ L156/43.

[97] SI 2016/339.

[98] Transparency International, 'G20 Leaders or Laggards? Reviewing G20 Promises on Ending Anonymous Companies' (2018) 11. The other two are Italy and France. Spain also has a very strong framework, but it is not part of the G20 (although it is a permanently invited guest to G20 meetings).

Originally, it was only UK companies that were required to keep a register of beneficial ownership and UK Crown Dependencies (i.e. Jersey, Guernsey, and the Isle of Man) and British Overseas Territories (e.g. Bermuda, the Cayman Islands, Gibraltar) were not, which was problematic as such areas are often used for money laundering and tax evasion purposes. These gaps are now being filled, as follows:

- Crown Dependencies are being pushed to comply with 5AMLD and introduce public registers of beneficial owners.
- By the end of 2020, the Secretary of State must prepare a draft Order in Council requiring the government of any British Overseas Territory to introduce a publicly accessible register of beneficial ownership (if it has not done so already).[99]

13.3.2.1 The legal requirements

All companies, apart from those excluded from the operation of Pt 21A,[100] must keep a PSC register,[101] although private companies may instead elect to have PSC information kept on the central register of Companies House.[102] Companies are under a duty to take reasonable steps to find out if there is a registrable person/legal entity in relation to the company and, if so, to identify them.[103] The company must then give notice to such registrable persons/entities requiring them to state whether or not they are registrable and, if so, to confirm or correct any matters in the notice.[104] Where the company does not send out such a notice, any such registrable persons are still under a duty to notify the company that they are registrable.[105]

The 'required particulars' that must be kept in the PSC register can be found in s 790K and include the person's name, address, country of residence, nationality, the date the person became a registrable PSC, and the nature of his control over the company. Further details are also required under the 2016 Regulations, such as particulars as to the nature of the person's control.[106] Companies are required to keep their PSC register up to date,[107] and information relating to PSCs also now forms part of the confirmation statement.[108]

As activities such as tax evasion and money laundering often occur cross-border, art 30(5) of the 4AMLD (as originally enacted) required that the information on the PSC register is made available to competent law enforcement authorities and financial intelligence units across the European Union (EU), but it did not require that the register be made available to members or the public. UK law went further than the 4AMLD by providing that any person can inspect, at the company's registered office or SAIL, the PSC register free of charge.[109] Each company's PSC register is also freely available

Confirmation statements are discussed at 19.5.1.

---

[99] Sanctions and Anti-Money Laundering Act 2018, s 51(2).

[100] The list of excluded companies is found in s 790B and the 2016 Regulations and covers (i) companies subject to Chapter 5 of the DTRs; (ii) companies whose shares are trading on a regulated market in a European Economic Area (EEA) State other than the UK; and (iii) companies with shares traded on a market listed in Sch 1 of the 2016 Regulations.

[101] CA 2006, s 790M(1). Failure to keep a PSC register is a criminal offence (s 790M(12) and (13)).

[102] ibid ss 790W–790ZD.

[103] ibid s 790D(1). Companies and officers that breach this duty commit a criminal offence (s 790F).

[104] ibid s 790D(2)–(4).   [105] ibid s 790G.

[106] Register of People with Significant Control Regulations 2016, reg 7 and Sch 2. See regs 9–17 for additional information required.

[107] CA 2006, ss 790E. PSCs are also required to provide the company with updated information (s 790H).

[108] ibid ss 853H and 853I.

[109] ibid ss 790N(1) and 790O(1). A copy of the register can be taken upon the payment of a fee (s 790O(2)).

online via the Companies House Service. At the time of writing, the UK is the only G20 country that requires PSC registers to be made publicly available. However, the 5AMLD amends art 30(5) of the 4AMLD to require that the register be accessible in all cases to, *inter alia*, 'any member of the general public.'

13.3.2.2 What is a PSC?

The PSC register must contain particulars of registrable people with significant control, so the central issue is when a person has significant control over the company. The answer is found in Sch 1A, Pt 1 of the CA 2006, which specifies five conditions, at least one of which needs to be met to render a person a PSC:

(a) a person holds, directly or indirectly, more than 25 per cent of the company's shares;

(b) a person holds, directly or indirectly, more than 25 per cent of the company's voting rights;

(c) a person holds the right, directly or indirectly, to appoint or remove a majority of the company's directors;

(d) a person has the right to exercise, or actually exercises, significant influence or control over the company, or;

(e) the trustees of a trust or the members of the firm that is not a legal person (i) meet any of the conditions in (a)–(d) above in relation to the company or would do so if they were individuals; and (ii) have the right to exercise, or actually exercise significant influence or control over the activities of that trust or firm.

The following example demonstrates these conditions in practice.

Eg **What is a PSC?**

The share capital of Dragon Goods Ltd ('DG') consists of 100 ordinary shares divided up as follows:

- 25 shares are owned by Dragon plc, and the articles of DG provide that Dragon plc has the right to appoint or remove directors as it sees fit;
- 26 shares are owned by Jane, the chief executive officer (CEO) of Dragon plc;
- 19 shares are owned by Welsh Bank plc, and the articles of DG provide that the company can only borrow money with Welsh Bank's consent;
- 20 shares are owned by Carstein Ltd. Carstein's two directors, Mrs Vlad and Mr Templehof, also own six shares and four shares, respectively in DG. Carstein Ltd, Mrs Vlad, and Mr Templehof have agreed to coordinate their voting activities.

Based on the above:

- Dragon plc does not have enough shares/voting rights to constitute a PSC under (a) or (b), but it does constitute a PSC under (c);
- Jane is a PSC under (a) and (b);
- Welsh Bank's veto over borrowing would constitute significant influence or control[110] of DG, so it meets condition (d);

---

[110] Holding absolute veto rights over borrowing decisions is identified as a form of significant influence or control in the Secretary of State's accompanying guidance: see BIS, 'Statutory Guidance on the Meaning of "Significant Influence or Control" Over Companies in the Context of the Register of People with Significant Control' (BIS 2016) para 2.7.

- Initially, neither Carstein, Mrs Vlad, nor Mr Templehof would seem to constitute PSCs. However, if two or more shareholders are subject to a joint arrangement as to how they will exercise their shares (as is the case here), then each of them is treated as holding the combined shares/voting rights of all of them.[111] Accordingly, Carstein, Mrs Vlad, and Mr Templehof are each treated as PSCs under (a) and (b) by virtue of holding 30 per cent of DG's shares/voting rights.

13.4 Termination of membership

A person ceases to be a member of a company when his name is removed from the register of members. This can occur in numerous ways including:

- where a member transfers, transmits, bequeaths, or gifts his shares to another person, and that person's name is entered into the register of members in respect of the shares;
- where a member's shares are forfeited[112] or surrendered;[113]
- where the contract to sell shares to the member is subsequently rescinded (e.g. due to misrepresentation) or declared void (e.g. due to mistake);
- where an event occurs that, under the articles, will cause a member to cease being a member;[114]
- where a member is declared bankrupt and (i) his shares are registered in the name of his trustee in bankruptcy; or (ii) the trustee in bankruptcy disclaims the member's shares.[115]

Note that the death of a member (or dissolution if the member if a body corporate) will not in itself terminate the membership.[116] Instead, the benefits and liabilities of membership will continue to accrue to the estate of the deceased/dissolved member until another person's name is entered into the register in respect to that member's interest.

CHAPTER SUMMARY

- Section 112 of the CA 2006 provides that a person is a member if they have agreed to become a member and their name is entered into the register of members.

- Every company must keep a register of its members, although private companies can elect to keep the required information on the central register maintained by Companies House.

- In order to help improve the transparency of company ownership, certain companies are required to keep a register of interests disclosed and a register of persons with significant control.

- A person's membership is terminated when his name is removed from the register of members.

---

[111] CA 2006, Sch 1A, para 12.
[112] *Re China Steam Ship Co* (1868) LR 6 Eq 232.   [113] *Trevor v Whitworth* (1887) 12 App Cas 409 (HL).
[114] *Sidebottom v Kershaw Leese & Co Ltd* [1920] 1 Ch 154 (CA) (articles allowed for compulsory purchase of shares of members who competed with the company).
[115] See e.g. s 315 of the Insolvency Act 1986 (IA 1986).
[116] *Re BW Estates Ltd* [2017] EWCA Civ 1201, [2018] Ch 511 [71] (Sir Geoffrey Vos C).

FURTHER READING

BIS, 'Statutory Guidance on the Meaning of "Significant Influence or Control" over Companies in the Context of the Register of People with Significant Control' (BIS 2016).

* Discusses in detail what amounts to 'significant influence or control' in relation to the PSC register.

BIS, 'Transparency and Trust: Enhancing the Transparency of UK Company Ownership and Increasing Trust in UK Business' (BIS 2014) Part A.

* A discussion paper examining the rationale behind the introduction of the PSC register.

Transparency International, 'G20 Leaders or Laggards? Reviewing G20 Promises on Ending Anonymous Companies' (Transparency International 2018).

* Examines and assess the law relating to beneficial company ownership in G20 countries and ranks their effectiveness.

www.globalwitness.org accessed 10 January 2019.

* Amongst other things, this site provides periodic updates and commentary on the data that is coming out of the PSC register.

SELF-TEST QUESTIONS

1. Define the following terms:

* member;
* no-access order;
* beneficial ownership;
* people with significant control.

2. State whether each of the following statements is true or false and, if false, explain why:

* A member will also be a shareholder.
* In order to become a member of a company, a person must expressly agree to become a member.
* A minor cannot become a member of a company.
* Anyone can inspect the register of members free of charge.
* A person who holds 25 per cent of a company's shares will be a PSC.
* A person's membership of a company will be terminated if he is declared bankrupt.

3. 'The introduction of the PSC register will go a long way towards making company ownership more transparent.' Do you agree with this statement?

4. Dragon Tools Ltd ('DT'), a subsidiary of Dragon plc, has recently issues a batch of 1,500 shares, as follows:

* Sutton & Co., a local firm of solicitors that is in the process of transferring its business to a LLP, purchases 100 shares;
* Doogie, a teenager who made millions after creating a UK-based social media site called MyFace, purchases 1,000 shares;
* DT could not find buyers for the remaining 400 shares and so DT itself purchased them.

Including the 1,500 shares, DT has issued 3,500 shares. Doogie requests to see a copy of DT's register of members, as he intends to use this information to (i) determine whether he should attempt to take over DT; and (ii) he wishes to use the information to market MyFace to DT's members. The board agree to Doogie's request and he obtains a copy of the register of members. However, he notices that his name has not been entered into the register.

Discuss the above, paying particular attention to (i) whether Sutton & Co. and Doogie are members of the company; (ii) what rules should have been followed following the issue of shares; and (iii) whether any laws have been breached.

 ONLINE RESOURCES

This book is accompanied by online resources to better support you in your studies. Visit www.oup.com/uk/roach-company/ for:

- answers to the self-test questions;
- further reading lists;
- multiple-choice questions;
- glossary.

Updates to the law can be found on the author's Twitter account (@UKCompanyLaw) and further resources can be found on the author's blog (www.companylawandgovernance.com).

14 Meetings and investor engagement

- Resolutions
- Unanimous assent
- General meetings
- Class meetings
- Investor engagement

INTRODUCTION

As is discussed at 9.2.1, the general power to manage the company is usually vested in the directors by the company's articles. Despite this, there are still numerous extremely important powers that may be exercised by the members, including:

- amending the company's articles;[1]
- approving the change of status of a company (e.g. converting from a private company to a public company,[2] or vice versa);[3]
- removing a director (or directors) from office;[4]
- approving numerous transactions involving directors;
- ratifying conduct of the directors that amounts to negligence, default, breach of duty, or breach of trust;[5]
- resolving to have the company wound up.[6]

This chapter examines how members exercise their decision-making powers, and the extent to which they engage with such powers. As Figure 14.1 indicates, members make decisions in one of two ways, namely (i) via a resolution; or (ii) by unanimous assent. The method used depends largely on the type of company:

- Private companies can make decisions via either of these two methods.[7] As noted, however, private companies tend to have a small number of members, and it is common for the directors to hold all or most the shares. In keeping with the 'think small first' philosophy

---

[1] Companies Act 2006 (CA 2006), s 21(1).   [2] ibid s 90(1).   [3] ibid s 97(1).   [4] ibid s 168(1).
[5] ibid s 239.   [6] Insolvency Act 1986 (IA 1986), s 122(1)(a).   [7] CA 2006, s 281(1) and (4).

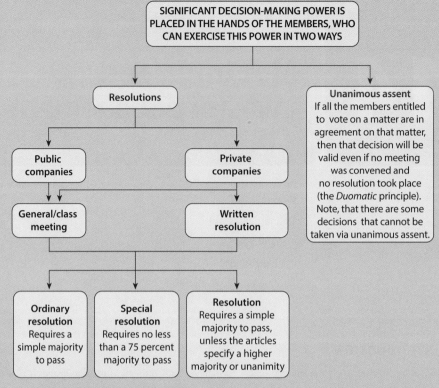

FIGURE 14.1 Decision-making powers of the members

Source: Roach, *Concentrate Company Law* (5th edn, OUP 2018).

of the CA 2006, private companies are not generally required to hold meetings,[8] which is advantageous as convening and running meetings does involve compliance with a notable body of rules which could be burdensome for private companies to adhere to. Therefore, the members of private companies usually make decisions via the written resolution procedure or via the unanimous assent rule.

- In public companies, decisions of the company must be made via resolutions at a meeting[9] (usually the annual general meeting), unless the unanimous assent rule is used (which is very rare because public companies often have many members and so obtaining unanimous assent is often unrealistic).

These two methods of decision-making are now discussed, beginning with resolutions.

---

[8] There are exceptions to this. A private company will need to hold a meeting if its articles so require (the model articles contain no such requirements). Further, a resolution to remove a director (CA 2006, s 168) or an auditor (CA 2006, s 510) can only be taken at a meeting.

[9] CA 2006, s 281(2).

14.1 Resolutions

The members of all types of company can make decisions via the passing of resolutions (so called because the decision resolves the members, company, directors, etc. to a particular course of action). A resolution is simply a vote that requires a specified majority vote in its favour in order to be passed. Resolutions must be passed either at a meeting of the company or via the written resolution procedure,[10] and it is important to distinguish between these two methods as they differ in terms of how the majority is calculated:

- where the resolution is tabled at a meeting, the requisite majority is calculated based on the votes cast by those eligible to vote[11] (i.e. votes are calculated based only on those who actually vote);

- where a written resolution is used, the requisite majority is calculated based on the voting rights of the total number of members eligible to vote,[12] not just those who actually do vote.

The following example demonstrates the distinction.

 Calculating a majority

Dragon Tools Ltd has ten members (of which only four take any interest in the company's affairs), with each member holding ten ordinary shares. The board wants to amend the company's articles (which requires a special resolution to be passed, which requires a majority of not less than 75 per cent) and decides to utilize the written resolution procedure. Only the four active members vote, with three voting in favour and one against. Accordingly, the resolution fails as the members voting for it only represent 30 per cent of the total voting rights of members eligible to vote.

The directors call a general meeting and table the resolution, with the vote being conducted on a show of hands. Only the four active members attend the meeting and, again, three vote in favour of the resolution and one votes against (no proxies are appointed). This time, the resolution is passed as it has secured the support of 75 per cent of the votes cast by members eligible to vote.

Majorities are determined based on those members who are eligible to vote. The general rule is that anyone present on the register of members is eligible to vote,[13] but there are exceptions to this:

- Companies may, if their articles so permit, issue non-voting shares and the holders of such shares will not be eligible to vote. It should be noted that institutional investors and regulators have been critical of the use of such shares, and it has even been recommended that non-voting shares should be prohibited.[14]

- The articles can restrict who is eligible to vote. For example, the articles might provide that only members with fully paid-up shares may exercise the voting rights on those shares.[15] It is quite common for a company's articles to provide that preference shareholders are not entitled to attend or vote at general meetings, except in limited circumstances.

---

[10] Although, as discussed at 14.1.2, only private companies may use the written resolution procedure.

[11] CA 2006, ss 282(3) and (4), and 283(4) and (5).   [12] ibid ss 282(2) and 283(2).

[13] *Pender v Lushington* (1877) 6 ChD 70 (Ch).

[14] See the Note of Dissent in Board of Trade, *Report of the Company Law Committee* (Cmnd 1749, 1962) 207–10.

[15] Indeed, this is stated in art 41 of the model articles for public companies.

- During state of war, an enemy alien is not permitted to exercise voting rights in respect of shares he holds in a UK company.[16]

- Non-members may have the right to vote if the articles so provide (e.g. the articles may give debenture holders the right to vote), although this is very rare in practice.

14.1.1 Ordinary and special resolutions

The majority required depends upon whether the resolution is an ordinary or a special resolution. Statute or the articles will normally specify which type of resolution is required. However, statute or the articles may sometimes simply state that a 'resolution' is required, without specifying its type. In such cases, the resolution required will be an ordinary resolution, but the company is free to require a higher majority (or unanimity) by inserting a provision in its articles to that effect.[17] Where statute specifies that an ordinary or special resolution is required, the articles cannot alter the majority required.

14.1.1.1 Ordinary resolutions

An ordinary resolution has been referred to as the 'default resolution',[18] meaning that an ordinary resolution will be sufficient unless statute or the articles state otherwise. Most decision-making powers granted to the members are exercised via passing an ordinary resolution. An ordinary resolution is one passed by a simple majority of the members or a class of members[19] (that is, over 50 per cent). How this is calculated depends on the type of vote:

- at a meeting on a show of hands, an ordinary resolution will be passed if it is voted for by a simple majority of the votes cast by those entitled to vote;[20]

- at a meeting on a poll, an ordinary resolution will be passed if it is voted for by members representing a simple majority of the total voting rights of members who are entitled to vote in person or by **proxy**;[21]

- a written resolution will be passed if it is voted for by members representing a simple majority of the total voting rights of eligible members.[22]

As an ordinary resolution requires a simple majority, it follows that an exact 50 per cent split will mean that the resolution does not pass. Prior to the CA 2006, it was common for the articles to give the chair of the meeting a casting vote,[23] but the general belief is that s 282 does not allow for this. The draft model articles to the CA 2006 did provide the chair with a casting vote, but this was removed from the final model articles. Instead, subordinate legislation now provides that if, before 1 October 2007, a company's articles provided the chair with a casting vote, then that provision will continue to have effect.[24] However, this will not apply to traded companies and so the chairmen of such companies cannot have a casting vote.[25]

Ordinary resolutions are not generally subject to any specific notice requirements. However, several ordinary resolutions[26] do require special notice (i.e. notice of the resolution must be provided at least 28 days prior to the meeting).[27]

Voting on a show of hands and by poll is discussed at 14.3.5.1.

→ **proxy:**
a person appointed to attend, speak or vote at general meetings on behalf of a member (discussed at 14.3.5.2)

---

[16] *Robson v Premier Oil and Pipe Line Co Ltd* [1915] 2 Ch 124 (CA).
[17] CA 2006, s 281(3). [18] Geoffrey Morse, *Palmer's Company Law* (Sweet & Maxwell 2018) para 7.408.
[19] CA 2006, s 282(1). [20] ibid s 282(3). [21] ibid s 282(4). [22] ibid s 282(2).
[23] Indeed, art 50 of Table A did just that (Companies (Tables A to F) Regulations 1985, Sch 1, para 50).
[24] Companies Act 2006 (Commencement No 3, Consequential Amendments, Transitional Provisions and Savings) Order 2007, SI 2007/2194, Sch 3, para 23A.
[25] ibid Sch 3, para 23A(4).
[26] Such as a resolution to remove a director (CA 2006, s 168(2)) or an auditor (CA 2006, s 511(1)) from office.
[27] CA 2006, s 312(1).

14.1.1.2 Special resolutions

Special resolutions tend to be reserved for more important decisions such as amending the articles,[28] re-registering a company,[29] and winding up a company.[30] A special resolution is one passed by a majority of not less than 75 per cent[31] and again, how this is calculated depends on the type of vote:

- at a meeting on a show of hands, a special resolution will be passed if it is voted for by a majority of not less than 75 per cent of the votes cast by those entitled to vote;[32]
- at a meeting on a poll, a special resolution will be passed if it is voted for by members representing not less than 75 per cent of the total voting rights of members who are entitled to vote in person or by proxy;[33]
- a written resolution will be passed if it is voted for by members representing not less than 75 per cent of the total voting rights of eligible members.[34]

A resolution passed at a meeting will not be a special resolution unless the notice of the meeting included a text of the resolution and specified the intention to propose the resolution as a special resolution.[35]

14.1.2 Written resolutions

As discussed at 14.3, convening and running a meeting involves compliance with a substantial body of procedures that can prove onerous and potentially costly, especially for smaller companies. Further, where the number of members is small or where the directors and members are the same persons, convening a meeting to pass resolutions seems a somewhat redundant exercise. Accordingly, Ch 2 of Pt 13 of the CA 2006 allows private companies to pass a written resolution in substitution for a resolution passed at a meeting. This is the only written resolution procedure that can be used (e.g. companies cannot devise their own procedure under their articles), and a private company's ability to make a decision via a written resolution cannot be excluded by the articles.[36] The written resolution procedure can be used for any resolution, except a resolution to remove a director or auditor before the expiry of his term of office.[37]

A written resolution can be proposed by the directors;[38] or the members holding 5 per cent of the total voting rights in the company or some other lower percentage specified in the articles.[39] In both cases, a copy of the resolution must be sent to every member eligible to vote[40] and it can be sent by hard copy, in electronic form, or by means of a website.[41] Eligible members must also be provided, with guidance on how to signify agreement and the date by which the resolution must be passed if it is not to lapse.[42] Where the resolution is proposed by the members, then the members may also require the company to circulate a statement of not more than 1,000 words on the subject matter of the resolution.[43] Failure to comply with these requirements constitutes an either-way offence,[44] but the validity of the resolution, if passed, will not be affected.[45]

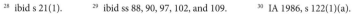

[28] ibid s 21(1).   [29] ibid ss 88, 90, 97, 102, and 109.   [30] IA 1986, s 122(1)(a).
[31] CA 2006, s 283(1).   [32] ibid s 283(4).   [33] ibid s 283(5).   [34] ibid s 283(2).
[35] ibid s 283(6).   [36] ibid s 300.   [37] ibid s 288(2).   [38] ibid s 288(3)(a).
[39] ibid ss 288(3)(b) and 292(1) and (5).   [40] ibid ss 291(2) and 293(1)(a).
[41] ibid ss 291(3)(a) and 293(2)(a).   [42] ibid ss 291(4) and 293(4).   [43] ibid s 292(3).
[44] ibid ss 291(5) and 293(5).   [45] ibid ss 291(7) and 293(7).

Written resolutions require the same majorities, and have the same force, as resolutions passed at meetings,[46] namely:

- an ordinary resolution will be passed if it is voted for by members representing a simple majority of the total voting rights of eligible members;[47]
- a special resolution will be passed if it is voted for by members representing not less than 75 per cent of the total voting rights of eligible members.[48]

Where the company has a share capital, each member has one vote per share, whereas in all other cases each member has one vote.[49] A member's agreement to the resolution cannot be revoked once it is given.[50] Once the required majority of eligible members has been reached, the resolution is passed.[51] However, if this majority is not reached before the end of a certain period, the resolution will lapse. This period can be specified in the company's articles, but if it is not, the resolution will lapse 28 days after the copy of the resolution was first circulated to the company's members.[52]

14.2 Unanimous assent

Complying with the numerous procedural requirements relating to meetings and resolutions could be regarded as needlessly stringent and burdensome where it is apparent that a course of action commands overwhelming support of the members, especially in the case of smaller companies. In such a case, it could be thought 'idle to insist upon formality as a precondition to the validity of an act which all those competent to effect it had agreed should be effected'.[53] Accordingly, the common law has long provided that if all the members entitled to vote on a matter agree on the matter, then that agreement is valid, even if no meeting was convened and no resolution took place.[54] This rule is often known as the *Duomatic* principle, named after the following case.

Re Duomatic Ltd [1969] 2 Ch 365 (Ch)

FACTS: The articles of Duomatic Ltd required that the directors' remuneration would be determined by the general meeting. Elvins and Hanly were Duomatic's only directors and they held all the ordinary shares (non-voting preference shares were held by another company). Elvins and Hanly drew a salary, but this was never authorized by the general meeting. When Duomatic subsequently went into liquidation, the liquidator sought repayment of the sums paid as salaries on the ground that approval of the general meeting had not been obtained.

HELD: Buckley J stated:

where it can be shown that all shareholders who have a right to attend and vote at a general meeting[55] of the company assent to some matter which a general meeting of the company could

---

[46] ibid s 288(5). Under the CA 1985, all written resolutions required unanimity, thereby hampering their utility.

[47] CA 2006, s 282(2). [48] ibid s 283(2). [49] ibid s 284(1). [50] ibid s 296(3). [51] ibid s 296(4).

[52] ibid s 297(1). [53] *Re New Cedos Engineering Co Ltd* [1994] 1 BCLC 797 (Ch) 814 (Oliver J).

[54] *Baroness Wenlock v The River Dee Co* (1883) 36 ChD 675 (CA); *Re Express Engineering Works Ltd* [1920] 1 Ch 466 (CA).

[55] It has since been held that the *Duomatic* principle also applies to class meetings (*Re Torvale Group Ltd* [2000] BCC 626 (Ch)).

carry into effect, that assent is as binding as a resolution in general meeting would be.[56]As Elvins and Hanly held all the voting shares, their unanimous assent was regarded as valid authorization of their remuneration, and so they were not required to repay the salaries they drew.

The *Duomatic* principle is now regarded as 'established law'[57] and it has been relied on successfully numerous times in UK courts. Indeed, the Company Law Review Steering Group (CLRSG) recommended that the principle be codified in order to provide certainty in terms of when it could be used.[58] The government disagreed, stating that 'the benefits of codification (clarity and certainty) would be outweighed by the disadvantages that would result from loss of flexibility'[59] and so the principle is unaffected by the CA 2006.[60]

14.2.1 Scope

The *Duomatic* principle is broad in scope and has been applied to numerous decisions. It can be used in place of resolutions at general meetings or class meetings.[61] A decision by unanimous assent can be used in place of almost any resolution. In one case, it was held that a decision could not be taken by unanimous assent if statute required a special resolution,[62] but the weight of authority indicates that unanimous assent can replace a special resolution.[63] The courts have questioned whether the *Duomatic* principle can apply where statute states that a resolution is required. This will depend upon the provision in question. For example, where statute expressly or impliedly excludes the *Duomatic* principle (e.g. by requiring that member approval is obtained at a meeting),[64] then the *Duomatic* principle will not apply. In other cases, however, unanimous assent will suffice so, for example, the *Duomatic* principle can apply to a decision to approve a long-term service contract[65] or a substantial property transaction.[66]

One issue that remains unclear is whether the *Duomatic* principle only applies to registered members or whether the assent of beneficial owners also counts.[67] The quote above from Buckley J in *Re Duomatic Ltd* refers to 'shareholders who have a right to attend and vote at a general meeting', which would indicate that the *Duomatic* principle only applies to registered members and not to beneficial owners.[68] However, in more recent cases, the courts have favoured the view that the *Duomatic* principle does apply to beneficial owners.[69] Unfortunately, in these cases, the opinions expressed were *dicta* only and the issue was left open. Definitive clarification is desirable.

⌒⌐ Beneficial ownership is discussed at 13.3.

---

[56] [1969] 2 Ch 365 (Ch) 373.   [57] *Re Bailey, Hay & Co Ltd* [1971] 1 WLR 1357 (Ch) 1366 (Brightman J).

[58] CLRSG, 'Modern Company Law for a Competitive Economy: Final Report' (DTI 2001) para 7.20.

[59] Department of Trade and Industry (DTI), *Modernising Company Law* (Cm 5553, 2002) para 2.34.

[60] CA 2006, s 281(4)(a).   [61] *Re Torvale Group Ltd* [2000] BCC 626 (Ch).

[62] *Re Barry Artist Ltd* [1985] 1 WLR 1305 (Ch).

[63] In *Cane v Jones* [1980] 1 WLR 1451 (Ch) and *Re Sherlock Holmes International Society Ltd* [2016] EWHC 1076 (Ch), unanimous assent was sufficient to amend the articles.

[64] *Re Oceanrose Investments Ltd* [2008] EWHC 3475 (Ch), [2009] Bus LR 947.

[65] *Wright v Atlas Wright (Europe) Ltd* [1999] BCC 163 (CA).

[66] *NBH Ltd v Hoare* [2006] EWHC 73 (Ch), [2006] 2 BCLC 649.

[67] For more, see Peter Watts, 'Informal Unanimous Assent of Beneficial Shareholders' (2006) 122 LQR 15.

[68] A point made by Lindsay J in *Domoney v Godinho* [2004] EWHC 328 (Ch), [2004] 2 BCLC 15 [44].

[69] *Shahar v Tsitsekkos* [2004] EWHC 2659 (Ch) [67] (Mann J); *Re Tulsesense Ltd* [2010] EWHC 244 (Ch), [2010] 2 BCLC 525 [42] (Newey J).

14.2.2 **Methods of assent**

Numerous methods of assent have been deemed valid and the courts have imposed few restrictions on how the members must assent. As Neuberger J stated '[w]hether the approval is given in advance or after the event, whether it is characterised as an agreement, ratification, waiver, or estoppel, and whether the members of the group give their consent in different ways at different times, does not matter'.[70] Assent can be express or implied. Assent can be in writing, oral, or can occur via conduct (either a one-off act or a consistent course of conduct).[71] Assent can occur at a meeting, or informally without a meeting taking place.

One issue that has arisen is whether assent can be inferred through silence. This will depend on the facts of the case. A simple internal decision by a member with no manifestation of assent or acquiescence will not suffice.[72] The following case provides an example of where members' silence amounted to assent via acquiescence.

 Re Bailey, Hay & Co [1971] 1 WLR 1357 (Ch)

FACTS: Bailey, Hay & Co Ltd ('BH') had five shareholders. A general meeting was convened and a resolution tabled to voluntarily wind up BH. Despite being provided with insufficient notice of the meeting,[73] all five shareholders attended and the resolution was passed (two of the shareholders voted for the resolution, and three shareholders abstained). Three-and-a-half years later, the liquidator alleged that payments made by BH to Bailey Fertilizers Ltd ('BF', one of the abstaining shareholders) constituted a fraudulent preference. BF and the other two abstaining shareholders (who were directors of BF) challenged the accusation by stating that BH was not actually in liquidation, as they were provided with insufficient notice of the meeting, and so the resolution to wind up BH was invalid.

HELD: Brightman J held that abstaining shareholders' acquiescence amounted to assent and so there was unanimous assent. He stated that the abstaining shareholders:

> outwardly accepted the resolution to wind up as decisively as if they had positively voted in favour of it. If corporators attend a meeting without protest, stand by without protest while their fellow-members purport to pass a resolution, permit all persons concerned to act for years on the basis that that resolution was duly passed and rule their own conduct on the basis that the resolution is an established fact, think it is idle for them to contend that they did not assent to the purported resolution.[74]

14.2.3 **Conditions, limitations, and restrictions**

As the procedural rules relating to meetings and resolutions are designed to protect the members as a whole, it is unsurprising that the ability of the members to make a decision through unanimous assent without a meeting is subject to several conditions:

- Nothing less than unanimity will suffice. Thus, a member who held 99 per cent of a company's shares could not take advantage of the *Duomatic* principle by himself.[75] However,

---

[70] *EIC Services Ltd v Phipps* [2003] EWHC 1507 (Ch), [2003] 1 WLR 2360 [122].

[71] *Re BW Estates Ltd* [2016] EWHC 2156 (Ch), [2016] BCC 814.

[72] *Re Tulsesense Ltd* [2010] EWHC 244 (Ch), [2010] 2 BCLC 525.

[73] The shareholders were provided with 14 days' notice, instead of 14 clear days' notice, resulting in the meeting taking place one day short of the required notice period (clear days are discussed at 14.3.3.2).

[74] [1971] 1 WLR 1357 (Ch) 1367. [75] *Re D'Jan of London* [1994] 1 BCLC 561 (Ch).

the *Duomatic* principle was applied to bind four shareholders (who held themselves out as the sole shareholders) to a transaction they assented, even though it later transpired that, unbeknownst to the four shareholders, a fifth shareholder existed.[76]

- Unanimous assent will only suffice if the members who assented had 'appropriate or "full" knowledge'[77] of the matter in question.

- Actual assent must be obtained. If a member's assent has not been sought, then the *Duomatic* principle will not apply, even if that member would probably have given it if asked.[78] The courts will take an objective approach to determining whether assent has taken place, and will require 'material from which an observer could discern (or in the case of acquiescence) infer assent'.[79]

In addition, a number of restrictions and limitations have been placed upon the *Duomatic* principle:

- Unanimous assent will not suffice where the decision in question could not have been taken at a meeting (e.g. because the assenting members could not form a quorum).[80]

- The *Duomatic* principle 'does not permit shareholders to do informally what they could not have done formally by way of written resolution or at a meeting'.[81] Accordingly, it cannot be used to authorize or ratify an *ultra vires* act[82] or an unlawful payment of dividends.[83]

- As the *Duomatic* principle requires the consent of all the members, it follows that it cannot apply where a member is incapable of consenting (e.g. where a member is a company that no longer exists).[84]

- Making a decision via unanimous assent involves the members effectively waiving statutory safeguards aimed at protecting their interests, which is perfectly justifiable. What is not justifiable is for the members to override safeguards designed to protect others.[85] For example, the *Duomatic* principle will likely not apply to the members' ability to remove a director or auditor, as the relevant provisions[86] serve to protect the interests of the director or auditor concerned,[87] and it would defeat the purpose of those provisions if the members could override them.

- It has been stated *obiter* that the *Duomatic* principle cannot be used to approve or authorize a transaction that is not bona fide or honest,[88] or authorize a transaction that is likely to jeopardize a company's solvency or cause loss to its creditors.[89]

---

[76] *Pena v Dale* [2003] EWHC 1065 (Ch), [2004] 2 BCLC 508.

[77] *EIC Services Ltd v Phipps* [2003] EWHC 1507 (Ch), [2003] 1 WLR 2360 [135] (Neuberger J). The decision in this case was successfully appealed, but not in relation to the *Duomatic* principle.

[78] ibid [146].   [79] *Re Tulsesense Ltd* [2010] EWHC 244 (Ch), [2010] 2 BCLC 525 [41] (Newey J).

[80] *Re New Cedos Engineering Co Ltd* [1994] 1 BCLC 797 (Ch).

[81] *Madoff Securities International Ltd v Raven* [2013] EWHC 3147 (Ch), [2014] Lloyd's Rep FC 95 [269] (Popplewell J).

[82] *Rolled Steel Products (Holdings) Ltd v British Steel Corp* [1986] Ch 246 (CA).

[83] *Secretary of State for Business, Innovation and Skills v Doffman* [2010] EWHC 3175 (Ch), [2011] 2 BCLC 541.

[84] *Re BW Estates Ltd* [2017 EWCA Civ 1201, [2018] Ch 511 [83] (Sir Geoffrey Vos C).

[85] *Kinlan v Crimmin* [2006] EWHC 779 (Ch), [2007] BCC 106 [44] (Sales J); *Dashfield v Davidson* [2008] BCC 222 (Ch) [72] (McCahill J).

[86] Namely ss 168–9 and ss 510–11 of the CA 2006. It will be remembered that these decisions also cannot be made by written resolution.

[87] *Bonham-Carter v Situ Ventures Ltd* [2012] EWHC 230 (Ch), [2012] BCC 717 [36] (Richard Sheldon QC) (*Duomatic* principle did not apply to the removal of a director under s 168).

[88] *Bowthorpe Holdings Ltd v Hills* [2002] EWHC 2331 (Ch), [2003] 1 BCLC 226 [50] (Sir Andrew Morritt VC).

[89] ibid; *Re Horsley & Weight Ltd* [1982] Ch 442 (CA).

14.3 General meetings

As noted, the resolutions of public companies must be passed at meetings, whereas resolutions of private companies can be passed at meetings or via a written resolution.[90] Because of this, it is only public companies and larger private companies that tend to hold general meetings, and even then they only tend to hold one general meeting per year, namely the annual general meeting (AGM).

Under prior Companies Acts, two forms of general meeting existed, namely the annual general meeting and the extraordinary general meeting (EGM, namely any general meeting that was not an AGM). Private companies under the CA 2006 do not need to hold AGMs, so any meetings they do hold will likely just be general meetings, so describing them as 'extraordinary' would be inaccurate. Accordingly, the CA 2006 no longer uses the term EGM. Instead the AGM is simply regarded as a special form of general meeting, and subject to certain unique rules that do not apply to other general meetings.

Our discussion of general meetings begins by looking at the process by which general meetings are called.

14.3.1 The calling of meetings

The directors of a company may call a general meeting of the company.[91] This power, like all others granted to directors, must be exercised in accordance with the directors' general duties. The usual procedure for calling a general meeting is that the board will pass a resolution at a board meeting proposing that a general meeting take place. However, there are instances where the board will be compelled to call a meeting (e.g. where the net assets of a public company are half or less of its called-up share capital).[92]

The vast majority of general meetings will be called by the directors, but other persons can order a general meeting be called. For example, an auditor can require the directors to call a general meeting if notice of his resignation is accompanied by a statement setting out his reasons for resigning.[93] However, of more importance here is the ability of the members or the court to order that a meeting be called.

14.3.1.1 Member-requisitioned meetings

Section 303 of the CA 2006 provides that the members can require the directors to call a general meeting[94] of the company, providing that the members requiring the meeting represent:

- 5 per cent of the paid-up share capital of the company that carries the right to vote at general meetings, or;
- if the company does not have a share capital, 5 per cent of the voting rights of all the members having the right to vote at general meetings.[95]

The members' request, which can be made in hard copy or in electronic form,[96] must state the general nature of the business to be dealt with at the meeting and may (not

---

[90] CA 2006, s 281(1) and (2).   [91] ibid s 302.   [92] ibid s 656(1).

[93] ibid s 518(2) (this statement is discussed at 19.4.6.1).

[94] Section 303 cannot be used to require the directors to call a class meeting (s 334(2)(a)).

[95] CA 2006, s 303(1) and (2).   [96] ibid s 303(6)(a).

must) also include the text of any resolutions proposed to be voted on at the meeting.[97] Note only the directors and the members making the request have the right to place business on the meeting's agenda.[98]

Once a valid request has been received, the directors must, within 21 days, call a general meeting, which must be held within 28 days of the date of the notice convening the meeting.[99] If the request proposes a resolution intended to be voted on at the meeting, the notice of the meeting must also include notice of the resolution.[100] If the directors fail to comply with a valid request from the members to call a meeting, then the members who requested the meeting, or any of them representing over half of the total voting rights of the company, may call a meeting themselves at the company's expense, provided that such expenses are reasonable.[101] This meeting must take place within three months of the date on which the directors became subject to the requirement to call a meeting.[102]

14.3.1.2 **Court-ordered meetings**

The court is empowered to order the calling of a meeting if, for any reason, it is impracticable to call a meeting or conduct a meeting in the manner prescribed by the company's articles or the CA 2006.[103] The following case provides an example of a situation where it was impracticable to conduct a meeting in accordance with the company's articles.

Re British Union for the Abolition of Vivisection [1995] BCLC 1 (Ch)

FACTS: The company's articles stated that proxy votes were not permitted and meetings had to be attended in person. This made holding meetings difficult, and so a meeting was called to amend the articles to allow proxy voting. The meeting became disorderly and, before any business was conducted, it was closed down by the police for fear it could have descended into a riot. The company's board applied to the court for an order convening a meeting at which only the board members should be allowed to personally attend, with other members being able to vote by way of a postal ballot.

HELD: Rimer J stated that a member should 'feel free to attend and vote at general meetings and is not to be deterred from doing so by the fear that the extremism of a radical minority of members will or may cause the meetings to degenerate into violent and potentially dangerous demonstrations'.[104] Based on the 'special and unusual circumstances of the case',[105] he therefore held that it was impracticable to call a meeting in accordance with the company's articles and so granted the order sought by the company's directors.

COMMENT: A year before *Re British Union* was decided, the Court of Appeal in *Harman v BML Group Ltd* refused a s 306 application, *inter alia*, because 'section [306] should not be pressed into use to rewrite the shareholders' agreement'.[106] Despite this, the High Court in *Re British*

See Clare MS McGlynn, 'Re-Writing the Corporate Constitution' [1995] JBL 585.

Harman is discussed at later in 14.3.1.2.

---

[97] ibid s 303(4). [98] *Ball v Metal Industries Ltd* 1957 SC 315 (Court of Session).
[99] CA 2006, s 304(1).
[100] ibid s 304(2). If any special resolutions are tabled, then the general requirements relating to special resolutions in s 283 must also be complied with.
[101] ibid s 305(1) and (6). [102] ibid s 305(3). [103] ibid s 306(1) and (2).
[104] [1995] BCLC 1 (Ch) 14. [105] ibid 15.
[106] *Harman v BML Group Ltd* [1994] 1 WLR 893 (CA) 899 (Henry LJ).

Union ordered a meeting be held under s 306, even though this would constitute a 'fundamental change'[107] to the company's constitution. *Harman* was not cited in *Re British Union* and it has been argued that this constitutes a 'serious error',[108] and it could even be argued that *Re British Union* should be regarded as *per incuriam*.

The courts' power to call a meeting can be exercised by the court on its own volition, or following an application from a director or member entitled to vote at the meeting.[109] It has been stated that the purpose of s 306 is to allow a company 'to get on with managing its affairs without being frustrated by the impracticability of calling or conducting a general meeting in the manner prescribed by the articles and the Act'.[110] To facilitate this, when ordering a meeting, the court has full discretion as to how the meeting should be called, held, and conducted, including the ability to overrule other rules relating to general meetings. Examples include:

- the courts can vary or override a provision in a shareholders' agreement;[111]
- the court can limit the number of members who may attend the meeting;[112]
- the court can reduce the quorum requirement, and can even order that a single member constitutes a quorum.[113] This is useful where attaining a quorum is difficult due to the members being geographically spread out,[114] or where members die, leaving behind insufficient members to achieve a quorum.[115] As the following case demonstrates, it is also useful where certain members seek to frustrate a meeting by refusing to attend, thereby preventing the meeting from being quorate.

Re El Sombrero Ltd [1958] Ch 900 (Ch)

FACTS: Laubscher held 900 shares in El Sombrero Ltd ('Sombrero'). The other two members held 50 shares each and were Sombrero's only directors. Sombrero's articles provided that a quorum consisted of two members. Laubscher wished to remove the directors from office under s 184 of the Companies Act 1948 (CA 1948, a predecessor to s 168 of the CA 2006), which required passing an ordinary resolution at a meeting. However, the two directors refused to call an AGM and refused to attend any meeting, thereby rendering it inquorate. Laubscher petitioned the court for an order calling a general meeting.

HELD: Wynn-Parry J stated that it was 'quite obvious that the only reason why the [directors] refuse to call an annual general meeting is because the inevitable result of convening and

---

107 [1995] BCLC 1 (Ch) 16 (Rimer J).

108 Clare MS McGlynn, 'Re-Writing the Corporate Constitution' [1995] JBL 585, 588.

109 CA 2006, s 306(2).

110 *Vectone Entertainment Holding Ltd v South Entertainment Ltd* [2004] EWHC 744 (Ch), [2005] BCC 123 [32] (Richard Sheldon QC).

111 *Union Music Ltd v Watson* [2003] EWCA Civ 180, [2004] BCC 37.

112 *Re British Union for the Abolition of Vivisection* [1995] BCLC 1 (Ch).

113 CA 2006, s 306(4).

114 *Edinburgh Workmen's Houses Improvement Co Ltd* 1935 SC 56 (Court of Session) (articles required a quorum of thirteen—this was not practicable as many members were not based in Edinburgh, and so the court reduced the quorum to five).

115 *Re Beckers Pty Ltd* (1942) 59 WN (NSW) 206.

holding that meeting would be that they would find that they had ceased to be directors'.[116] If the court did not order a meeting, then it would deprive Laubscher of a statutory right, namely the right to remove directors under s 184. Accordingly, the court ordered a meeting be held and that one member would constitute a quorum.

Despite the breadth of s 306, the courts have placed two notable limits upon their ability to order meetings. First, the courts have stated that s 306 cannot be used to affect the balance of power between members, as the following case demonstrates.

Ross v Telford [1998] 1 BCLC 82 (CA)

FACTS: Ross and Telford, a husband and wife, were directors and equal shareholders of a company ('PLB'), as well as being the directors of another company ('Linkside'). The shares in Linkside were equally split between Ross and PLB. The articles of both PLB and Linkside provided that the quorum for board meetings and general meetings was two. This meant that board meetings and general meetings were potentially deadlocked if Ross and Telford disagreed. Ross and Telford divorced. Ross later caused Linkside to commence proceeding against a bank, but was advised that as the proceedings were brought without the authority of Linkside's board (i.e. without Telford's authorization), the action would be struck out. As Linkside was deadlocked, Ross applied to the court for an order that a meeting of Linkside be called and that one member present constitute a quorum.

HELD: Ross's application was rejected. Nourse LJ stated that s 306:

 is a procedural section not designed to affect substantive voting rights or to shift the balance of power between shareholders in a case where they have agreed that power shall be shared equally and where the potential deadlock is something which must be taken to have been agreed on with the consent and for the protection of each of them.[117]

COMMENT: This case demonstrates that if two members wish to have equal shareholdings, then, to avoid deadlock, it is important to have some form of deadlock-resolution mechanism in the articles or in a shareholders' agreement.

See Richard Barham, 'Company Law—Equal Shareholdings' (1997) 8 ICCLR 167.

Second, the courts will not order a meeting where to do so would override the class rights of members, as the following case demonstrates.

Harman v BML Group Ltd [1994] 1 WLR 893 (CA)

FACTS: The company ('BML') had two classes of shares, namely A shares that were held by Harman, Mills, Lees, and Boyle, and B shares that were held by Blumenthal. A shareholders' agreement provided that a shareholders' meeting would not be quorate unless a B shareholder (or his proxy) was present. Blumenthal alleged that two of BML's directors, namely Harman and Mills, had paid themselves too much. Realizing that Blumenthal could frustrate BML's business by not attending meetings, Harman and Mills applied to the court for an order calling a meeting at which any two shareholders would constitute a quorum.

See Clare MS McGlynn, 'Re-Writing the Corporate Constitution' [1995] JBL 585.

---

[116] [1958] Ch 900 (Ch) 907.   [117] [1998] 1 BCLC 82 (CA) 87.

> **HELD**: Dillon LJ stated that the provision in the shareholders' agreement had the same effect as if it had been set out as a class right in the articles, and that it was not right to invoke s 306 'to override class rights attached to a class of shares which have been deliberately—in this case by the shareholders' agreement—imposed for the protection of the holders of those shares . . .'.[118] The provision in the shareholders' agreement was designed to provide protection to Blumenthal, and s 306 could not be used to override that. Accordingly, the application of Harman and Mills was rejected.

Section 996 is discussed at 15.3.7.

It has been argued that s 306 is not the only provision that allows the courts to call a meeting, and that the broad remedial powers granted to the court under s 996 would also allow the court to call a meeting.[119]

14.3.2 **Physical and electronic meetings**

In *Byng v London Life Association Ltd*,[120] Browne-Wilkinson VC stated that '[t]he rationale behind the requirement for meetings . . . is that the members shall be able to attend in person so as to debate and vote on matters affecting the company'.[121] This, however, does not mean that members need to be physically present in the same room, as Browne-Wilkinson VC went on to state that 'without being physically in the same room [the members] can be electronically in each other's presence so as to hear and be heard and to see and be seen'.[122] The Shareholder Rights Directive requires Member States to permit companies 'to offer to their shareholders any form of participation in the general meeting by electronic means . . .'.[123] This was implemented by inserting a new s 360A into the CA 2006, which provides that nothing in Pt 13 is to be taken to preclude the holding and conducting of a meeting in such a way that persons who are not present together at the same place may by electronic means attend and speak and vote at it.[124] The model articles also provide that, in determining attendance at a general meeting, it is immaterial whether any two or more members attending it are in the same place as each other.[125]

Accordingly, meetings can be held physically or electronically, or a combination of the two, and the decision as to which will usually be a matter for the company's articles.[126] Currently, the overwhelming majority of meetings are held physically, with everyone present in the same room or building. In fact, to date, only one UK listed company has held a fully electronic meeting.

---

[118] [1994] 1 WLR 893 (CA) 898.

[119] Geoffrey Morse, *Palmer's Company Law* (Sweet & Maxwell 2018) para 7.521.

[120] [1970] Ch 170 (CA).   [121] ibid 183.   [122] ibid.

[123] Directive 2007/36/EC of the European Parliament and of the Council of 11 July 2007 on the exercise of certain rights of shareholders in listed companies [2007] OJ L184/17, art 8.

[124] CA 2006, s 360A(1).

[125] Model articles for private companies, art 37(4); model articles for public companies, art 29(4).

[126] If a company is considering holding an electronic meeting, it will usually amend its articles to empower the directors to determine what type of meeting will be held. For example, art 57 of Jimmy Choo plc's articles provided that '[t]he board shall determine whether a general meeting is to be held as a physical general meeting or an electronic general meeting'.

The UK's first electronic annual general meeting[127]

In 2014, it was announced that shares in Jimmy Choo Ltd would be listed on the London Stock Exchange and so Jimmy Choo plc was incorporated. It held its first AGM in 2015 as a physical meeting, but decided that its 2016 AGM would be conducted electronically. Accordingly, in 2015, the company sought permission from its shareholders by proposing the adoption of new articles[128] that catered for an electronic AGM (these new articles were supported by 100 per cent of the shareholders who voted). The company engaged Equiniti to manage the AGM.

Given the prevalence of smartphones, it was decided that the meeting would be conducted using an app (Lumi, a company that specialized in real-time audience engagement technology, was engaged to design the app).[129] Shareholders could download the app onto their phone/tablet, or access it via an internet browser, and then securely log in using credentials provided in the notice of the meeting.[130] Shareholders could use the app to listen to presentations, vote on resolutions, and participate in the Q&A with the board. The meeting took place on the 15 June 2016 and appeared to go smoothly. Indeed, the company stated that the 2016 AGM was much better 'attended' than the 2015 physical AGM. Accordingly, the 2017 AGM was also conducted electronically. In November 2017, Jimmy Choo plc was acquired by Michael Kors Holdings Ltd and re-registered as Jimmy Choo Group Ltd (and so no longer needs to hold an AGM).

The advantages of an electronic meeting are clear. They are likely to cost less than physical meetings and will also have a much smaller carbon footprint compared to a physical meeting. Electronic meetings can provide all the members with the opportunity to participate, regardless of their location (this is especially useful if significant numbers of shareholders are based outside the UK), which could result in an increase in shareholder engagement. A 2016 survey found that 23 per cent of retail investors questioned would like to attend an AGM, but only 6 per cent actually do so.[131] Forty-three per cent of those questioned said that they would be more likely to attend an electronic AGM.[132] However, at the time of writing, Jimmy Choo remains the only UK company to have held a fully electronic AGM.

14.3.3 **Notice of meetings**

For meetings to be effective, it is desirable that those attending have sufficient knowledge of the matters to be covered at the meeting (especially those matters subject to resolutions), which may involve those attending engaging in research or coordinating their activities. This will require time and so the law provides that resolutions passed at general

---

[127] For more, see https://equiniti.com/focus/jimmychoo-case-study/index.html accessed 10 January 2019.

[128] Although the model articles are broad enough to cater for electronic meetings, it is wise to provide more detailed bespoke provisions, to reassure members of the practicality and security of the arrangements.

[129] See www.lumiglobal.com/about/press-releases/2016/jimmy-choo-finds-the-perfect-fit-for-first-uk-elec accessed 10 January 2019.

[130] Despite the meeting being held electronically, notice was sent out via the usual manner and not electronically.

[131] Equiniti, 'Retail Investors: Technology Led Change and the Opportunity (Need) for Increased Engagement' (Equiniti 2016) 6.

[132] ibid.

meetings are only valid if adequate notice of the meeting and of the resolution is provided to those entitled to such notice.[133] Notice cannot be conditional (i.e. the meeting will only take place upon a specified condition being fulfilled),[134] and once a meeting has been validly convened, it cannot be postponed or cancelled, unless the articles so provide.[135]

Complying with the rules relating to notice is vital as the general rule is that failure to provide notice, or failure to provide sufficient notice, invalidates the meeting[136] and any resolutions passed at it.[137] However, there are some definite and possible exceptions to this:

- Where the failure to provide notice to one or more persons is accidental, then this will not invalidate the meeting.[138]

- It has been argued that a member who did not receive notice of a meeting, but who nevertheless attended and voted at the meeting, would likely not be permitted to raise an objection to the meeting due to his lack of notice.[139]

- It has been stated *obiter* that a meeting will be properly convened even though a member was not provided with notice, if the conveners knew that the member could not attend the meeting.[140]

14.3.3.1 Who is entitled to notice?

The general rule is that notice of a general meeting must be provided to every member[141] of the company (irrespective of whether they are entitled to vote or not) and every director.[142] However, this is subject to the articles,[143] so the articles may provide that certain members or directors are not entitled to notice. For example, in larger companies, it is common for the articles to provide that preference shareholders are not entitled to notice except in limited circumstances. The auditor is also entitled to notice of a general meeting,[144] and this cannot be excluded by the articles.

14.3.3.2 Length of notice

The amount of notice that must be provided depends on the type of company and the type of meeting. The notice periods in the CA 2006 are measured in 'clear days', which basically means that the day on which the notice is given and the day on which the meeting takes place are excluded.[145] The notice periods are as follows:

(a) The default rule is that at least 14 clear days' notice must be given.[146]

(b) In the case of the AGM of a public company, at least 21 clear days' notice must be given.[147] If the company has a premium listing, then the Financial Reporting Council (FRC) recommends that 20 working days' notice should be given.[148]

---

[133] CA 2006, s 301.   [134] *Alexander v Simpson* (1889) 43 ChD 139 (CA).

[135] *Smith v Paringa Mines Ltd* [1906] 2 Ch 193 (Ch). The model articles do not provide for this.

[136] *Smythe v Darley* (1849) HL Cas 789 (HL). This is the case even if the member asks not to be given notice (*Re Portuguese Consolidated Copper Mines Ltd* (1889) 42 ChD 160 (CA)).

[137] CA 2006, s 301.   [138] ibid s 313(1).

[139] Derek French *Mayson, French & Ryan on Company Law* (35th edn, OUP 2018) 369.

[140] *Young v Ladies' Imperial Club Ltd* [1920] 2 KB 523 (CA) 528 (Lord Sterndale MR).

[141] This includes any person entitled to a share in consequence of the death or bankruptcy of a member (s 310(2)).

[142] CA 2006, s 310(1).   [143] ibid s 310(4)(b).   [144] ibid s 502(2)(a).   [145] ibid s 360.

[146] ibid s 307(1) and (2)(b).   [147] ibid s 307(2)(a).

[148] FRC, 'Guidance on Board Effectiveness' (FRC 2018) para 36.

(c) Where the company is a traded company, then at least 21 clear days' notice must be provided.[149] However, this can be reduced to at least 14 clear days if the meeting is not an AGM, the company offers the members the ability to vote by electronic means, and a special resolution is passed reducing the notice period to not less than 14 clear days.[150] As a result of this, it has now become common practice for traded companies to table a special resolution at an AGM authorizing the company to provide 14 clear days' notice for general meetings.

(d) As is discussed later, notice does not need to be given for an adjourned meeting, unless the articles so provide.

Adjourned meetings are discussed at 14.3.4.4.

The Act establishes minimum notice periods, but the company's articles are free to specify longer notice periods.[151] The articles cannot specify a shorter notice period, but a procedure exists that allows companies (other than traded companies) to provide shorter notice than that required under the CA 2006 or the articles, where the members with a right to attend and vote at the meeting agree to shorter notice.[152] The majorities required are:

- at least 90 per cent of the members of a private company must agree to shorter notice;[153]
- at least 95 per cent of the members of a public company must agree to shorter notice;[154]
- unanimous assent is required to provide shorter notice of the AGM of a public company.[155]

If shorter notice has been agreed, then the notice provided is a matter for the members' choosing and can be extremely brief.

Though this section of the book focuses on the notice required for a meeting, it is worth noting that certain resolutions have their own notice requirements. A resolution to dismiss a director under s 168 or remove an auditor under s 511 requires 'special notice'.[156] Special notice must be provided at least 28 clear days prior to the meeting where the resolution will be voted on.[157] Where practicable, the company must provide its member with notice of the resolution in the same manner and at the same time as it gives notice of the meeting.[158]

14.3.3.3 Manner in which notice is to be given

Notice of a general meeting must be given in hard copy form, in electronic form, or by means of a website (or partly by one such means and partly by another).[159] Where notice is provided by means of a website, then the company must notify the member that the notice is on the website and this notification must state (i) that it concerns notice of a company meeting; (ii) the place, date, and time of the meeting; and (iii) in the case of a public company, whether the meeting will be an AGM.[160] The notice must stay on the website up until the conclusion of the meeting.[161]

14.3.3.4 Content of notice and circulars

Notice of a general meeting must state the following:

- the time, date, and place of the meeting;[162]

---

[149] CA 2006, s 307A(1)(b).   [150] ibid s 307A(1)(a) and (2)–(4).
[151] ibid ss 307(3) and 307A(6).   [152] ibid s 307(4) and (5).
[153] ibid s 307(6)(a). The articles can specify a higher percentage up to 95 per cent.
[154] ibid s 307(6)(b).   [155] ibid ss 307(7) and 337(2).   [156] ibid ss 168(2) and 511(1).
[157] ibid s 312(1).   [158] ibid s 312(2).   [159] ibid s 308.
[160] ibid s 309(2). Failure to comply with the rules in s 309 will render the notice ineffective (s 309(1)).
[161] ibid s 309(3).   [162] ibid s 311(1).

- the general nature of the business to be dealt with at the meeting,[163] but in companies other than traded companies, this requirement can be modified by the articles;[164]

- if a special resolution is tabled at a meeting, the text of the resolution should be included and the intention to propose the resolution as a special resolution should be stated;[165]

- the notice must contain, with reasonable prominence, a statement informing the member of his rights in relation to appointing a proxy;[166]

- the notice of an AGM of a public company must state that the meeting is an AGM.[167]

Traded companies are subject to additional requirements. The notice must contain a statement giving the address of a website which will contain specified information that the company must publish in advance of the meeting.[168] The notice must also set out additional information specified in s 311(3), such as the procedures that the member will need to comply with to be able to attend and vote at the meeting. The notice of an AGM of a private company that is a traded company must also state that the meeting is an AGM.[169]

Certain resolutions will require additional information be sent alongside the notice of the meeting. For example, if a resolution is proposed to disapply pre-emption rights, the notice of the meeting must be accompanied by a written statement of the directors setting out why they recommend the resolution be passed, the amount to be paid for the shares in question, and the directors' justification for that amount.[170] Outside these statutory requirements, it is usual for the notice to be accompanied by a circular, which will provide additional information on the business to be covered and resolutions tabled at the meeting. Indeed, the failure to provide such information might invalidate the notice and the meeting, as the courts have held that the members need to be provided with sufficient information to enable them to decide whether to attend the meeting.[171] Some judges have gone further and stated that the directors are under a duty to provide the members with sufficient information to enable them to decide whether to vote for or against the resolutions tabled at the meeting.[172] A recurring feature among cases in this area is that the directors have an interest in a resolution, but fail to disclose this in the notice or circular. As the following case indicates, this can result in the resolution being invalidated.

Kaye v Croydon Tramways Co [1898] 1 Ch 358 (CA)

FACTS: An agreement was reached under which British Electric Traction Co Ltd ('BET') would purchase Croydon Tramways Co ('CT'), after which the directors of CT would vacate office. A term of the agreement was that, in addition to the purchase price, BET would also pay a sum of money to the directors of CT for loss of office. The agreement was conditional upon it being adopted by the members of CT and so a meeting was convened to seek the members' approval. The notice of

---

[163] ibid s 311(2).   [164] ibid.

[165] ibid s 283(6)(a). Failure to provide this information will invalidate the resolution.

[166] ibid s 325(1).   [167] ibid s 337(1).

[168] ibid s 311(3)(a). The information required is specified in s 311A.   [169] ibid s 337(1).

[170] ibid s 571(7). Other provisions in the CA 2006 that require information to accompany the notice include ss 169(3), 314(1), and 511(4).

[171] *Tiessen v Henderson* [1899] 1 Ch 861 (Ch).

[172] *Rackham v Peek Foods Ltd* [1990] BCLC 895, 899 (Templeman J).

the meeting and circular stated that the meeting was being convened to obtain agreement for the sale of CT, but no mention was made of the payment to CT's directors. The meeting took place and member approval was secured. Kaye, a member of CT, then discovered the payment to CT's directors and issued proceedings.

HELD: Legislation at the time required the notice to 'specify the purpose for which the meeting is called'.[173] Lindley MR stated that the notice did indeed do this, but that it was:

> most artfully framed to mislead the shareholders. It is a tricky notice, and it is to my mind playing with words to tell shareholders that they are convened for the purpose of considering a contract for the sale of their undertaking, and to conceal from them that a large portion of that purchase-money is not to be paid to the vendors who sell that undertaking . . . [The notice] must be stated fairly: it must not be stated so as to mislead; and one of the main purposes of this agreement, so far as the directors care about it, is that they shall get a large sum of money without disclosing the fact to their shareholders.[174]

Accordingly, the Court held the resolution to be ineffective and imposed an injunction preventing the agreement from being put into effect until it was duly sanctioned by the members of CT.

14.3.3.5 Members' statements

As discussed, the members may, subject to certain conditions being met, call a meeting and/or table resolutions at a meeting. Such members will likely wish to inform the other members why they called the meeting or tabled a resolution. Accordingly, the CA 2006 allows the members to require the company to circulate a statement to all members entitled to receive notice of a general meeting.[175] The statement, which can be up to 1,000 words, must relate to a matter referred to in a proposed resolution, or some other business, to be dealt with at the meeting.[176] However, the company is only required to circulate the statement once it receives requests to do so from:

- members representing at least 5 per cent of the total voting rights of all the members who have a relevant right to vote (excluding voting rights attached to treasury shares); or
- at least 100 members who have a relevant right to vote and hold shares in the company on which there has been paid up an average sum, per member, of at least £100.[177]

In addition, the request must be in hard copy form, it must identify the statement to be circulated, it must be authenticated by the persons making it, and it must be received by the company at least one week before the meeting to which it relates.[178] If all these conditions are satisfied, then the company must send out the statement in the same manner as the notice of the meeting and, at the same time as, or as soon as is reasonably practicable after, it gives notice of the meeting.[179] The cost of circulating this statement cannot be placed upon the members who requested the statement's circulation if the meeting to which the request is made is the AGM of a public company, or if the request is received before the end of the financial year pending the meeting.[180] In other cases, the members who requested the statement must pay the costs of circulation, unless the company resolves otherwise.[181]

---

[173] Companies Clauses Consolidation Act 1845, s 71.   [174] [1898] 1 Ch 358 (CA) 369–70.
[175] CA 2006, s 314(1).   [176] ibid.   [177] ibid s 314(2).   [178] ibid s 314(4).
[179] ibid s 315(1). Failure to send out the statement constitutes a criminal offence (ss 315(3) and (4)).
[180] ibid s 316(1).   [181] ibid s 316(2)(a).

A company (or another person who feels aggrieved) can negate a s 314 request by applying to the court, who can order that the company need not circulate the statement if the court is satisfied that the rights conferred by s 314 are being abused.[182]

14.3.4 Procedure at meetings

In addition to the procedures relating to the calling of general meetings and the provision of notice, the actual meeting itself is also subject to a raft of procedural requirements. Adherence with these procedures is vital, as failure to do so can invalidate the entire meeting. Before these requirements are examined, the role of the agenda must be discussed.

14.3.4.1 The agenda

What is covered at a general meeting is a matter for the meeting's agenda. It is not compulsory to have an agenda, but most meetings do so as it provides the meeting with direction and allows those attending to conduct research on the agenda items prior to the meeting. Typically, only those matters on the agenda will be covered at the meeting, although meetings of larger companies will usually have an 'any other business' section. The law does not stipulate what items of business must be discussed at a general meeting. Instead, this is usually a matter for the board (especially the chair) in consultation with the company secretary.

It is important, however, that the members are able to add items of business to the agenda. If they could not, certain resolutions (e.g. a resolution to remove a director under s 168) would likely never be tabled. Accordingly, the CA 2006 states that the members of a public company[183] may require the company to give notice of a resolution to be moved at the next AGM.[184] However, the company is only required to give such notice if three conditions are satisfied:

1. the resolution cannot be moved at the AGM if (i) it would, if passed, be ineffective; (ii) it is defamatory; or (iii) it is frivolous or vexatious;[185]

2. the company is only required to give notice of the resolution if it has received requests from members representing (i) at least 5 per cent of the total voting rights of all the members who have the right to vote on the resolution; or (ii) there are at least 100 members who have the right to vote on the resolution and hold shares in the company on which there has been paid up an average sum, per member, of at least £100;[186]

3. the members' request must be in hard copy or electronic form, identify the resolution, be authenticated by the persons making it, and be received by the company not later than six weeks before the AGM or, if later, the time at which notice is given of that meeting.[187]

It should be noted that member-proposed resolutions are rare and, in most cases, the board will not support the resolution tabled by the members and will usually include a statement in the notice of the meeting as to why they oppose it, along with a recommendation to vote against it. The 2018 AGM of Petropavlovsk plc provides a rare and dramatic example of successful member-proposed resolutions.

---

[182] ibid s 317(1).

[183] The members of private companies are not granted this power, probably because (i) in most private companies, the members and directors are the same persons; and (ii) private companies tend to make decisions via the written resolution procedure or the unanimous assent rule, and not via meetings.

[184] CA 2006, s 338(1).   [185] ibid s 338(2).   [186] ibid s 338(3).   [187] ibid s 338(4).

The 2018 AGM of Petropavlovsk plc

Petropavlovsk plc is a London-based gold-mining company (although its operations primarily take place in Russia) whose shares are listed on the London Stock Exchange's Main Market. Two of Petropavlovsk's major shareholders successfully tabled 11 resolutions at the 2018 AGM. In the statement accompanying these resolutions, the two shareholders stated that Petropavlovsk's board had not gained the confidence of the market or the company's key management, and this had resulted in the company's share price performing poorly.[188] The board of Petropavlovsk recommended that the company's shareholders vote against all 11 resolutions.

Of the 11 resolutions proposed by the two shareholders, 10 successfully passed, including three resolutions appointing new directors, five resolutions removing existing directors, and one resolution removing all directors appointed since May 2018.[189] Further examples of shareholder anger were seen in the 71.54 per cent of shareholders voting against the company's remuneration report, and five resolutions to re-elect five directors were defeated.

In the case of the AGM of a traded company, the members can also request the company to include in the business to be dealt with at the AGM any matter which may be properly included in the business.[190] This is subject to similar conditions as the right to require the company to give notice of a resolution.[191]

The costs of giving notice of the members' resolution or circulating the members' request for business to be dealt with must be borne by the company if the request is received before the end of the financial year preceding the meeting.[192] In all other cases, the members making the request must bear the cost, unless the company resolves otherwise.[193] As discussed, the members can also require the company to provide a statement from the members, which will likely set out why the resolution was tabled and recommend how to vote, or why the matter was included in the business to be dealt with.

> The members' statement is discussed at 14.3.3.5.

14.3.4.2 **Quorum**

A general meeting (and any decisions made at it) will only be valid if a quorum is present. In relation to general meetings, a quorum is the minimum number of 'qualifying persons' required to be present at the meeting. A qualifying person is:

- an individual who is a member of the company;
- a representative of a corporate member; or
- a proxy of the member.[194]

> Proxies are discussed at 14.3.5.2.

The general rule is that two qualifying persons constitute a quorum, unless the articles provide otherwise.[195] However, the meeting will not be quorate if the only qualifying persons present are two corporate representatives or two proxies of the same member.[196] The general rule is that a single qualifying member cannot form a quorum as 'a meeting

> Corporate representatives are discussed at 14.3.5.3.

---

[188] Petropavlovsk plc, 'Notice of Annual General Meeting' (2018) 3, www.petropavlovsk.net/wp-content/uploads/2018/06/PETRO_NoM_29.06.2018-1.pdf accessed 10 January 2019.

[189] As a result, all of Petropavlovsk's existing directors, except one, were removed.

[190] ibid s 338A(1).   [191] ibid s 338A(2)-(5).   [192] ibid ss 340(1) and 340B(1).

[193] ibid ss 340(2)(a) and 340B(2)(a).

[194] ibid s 318(3). In all cases, the member in question must be entitled to vote (*Henderson v James Loutitt and Co Ltd* (1894) 21 R 674).

[195] ibid s 318(2). The model articles do not specify what constitutes a quorum.   [196] ibid.

is not properly constituted if only one individual is present, for there is no one for him to meet'.[197] However, a single qualifying person can form a quorum if:

- the company is a limited company and it only has one member; or[198]
- the court convenes a meeting, then it can direct that one member of the company present at the meeting constitutes a quorum.[199]

A meeting that lacks a quorum is said to be 'inquorate'. If a quorum is not present when the meeting commences, then it may not proceed.[200] A meeting that starts quorate, but subsequently becomes inquorate (e.g. because a sufficient number of qualifying persons leave) can continue if the articles so provide.[201]

14.3.4.3 **Chair**

It is usual for a person to be appointed as chair of a general meeting,[202] with the chair's role being 'to preserve order, and to take care that the proceedings are conducted in a proper manner, and that the sense of the meeting is properly ascertained with regard to any question which is properly before the meeting'.[203] The CA 2006 provides that a member may be elected to be chair of the general meeting by a resolution of the company passed at the meeting.[204] This power is subject to the articles, so the articles may specify who may and may not be chair and the method of appointment.[205] For example, the model articles provide that the directors may appoint a chair and, if a chair has not been appointed, then the directors present at the meeting may appoint a chair.[206] In practice, the chair is usually a director, with the articles often providing that the chair of the board will chair general meetings.

14.3.4.4 **Adjournment**

A meeting may, for various reasons, end prematurely before its business has been completed, with a view to reconvening at some point in the future (this reconvened meeting is known as the 'adjourned meeting'). The common law provides the chair with the power to adjourn a meeting where disorder occurs,[207] or where a poll has been validly demanded, but the poll cannot be taken forthwith.[208] Outside of these instances, the rules relating to adjournment are a matter for the company's articles, with the model articles providing that:

- if a meeting is not quorate within half an hour of the time it was due to start, or if it starts quorate but then becomes inquorate, then the chair must adjourn the meeting;

---

[197] *Neil McLeod & Sons Ltd* 1967 SC 16 (Court of Session) 21 (Lord President Clyde).
[198] CA 2006, s 318(1).   [199] ibid s 306(4).
[200] *Re Cambrian Peat, Fuel and Charcoal Co Ltd* (1875) 31 LT 773. The model articles provide that if there is no quorum within half an hour of the time the meeting started, then the chair must adjourn the meeting (model articles for private companies, art 41(1); model articles for public companies, art 33(1)).
[201] *Re Hartley Baird Ltd* [1955] Ch 143 (Ch). The model articles provide that if a quorate general meeting becomes inquorate, then the chair must adjourn it (model articles for private companies, art 41(1); model articles for public companies, art 33(1)).
[202] Larger companies might also appoint a deputy chair or deputy chairs.
[203] *National Dwellings Society v Sykes* [1894] Ch 159 (Ch) 162 (Chitty J).
[204] CA 2006, s 319(1).   [205] ibid s 319(2).
[206] Model articles for private companies, art 39(1) and (2); model articles for public companies, art 31(1) and (2). If no directors are present, then the meeting may appoint the chair.
[207] Depending on the level of disorder, the chair may be under a duty to adjourn (*John v Rees* [1970] Ch 345 (Ch)).
[208] *Jackson v Hamlyn* [1953] Ch 577 (Ch) (meeting was adjourned where the poll would take two hours to organize, but the meeting venue was only booked for a further 45 minutes).

- the chair may adjourn the meeting if the meeting consents to an adjournment;

- the chair may adjourn the meeting if it appears to him that an adjournment is necessary to protect the safety of any person attending the meeting or ensure that the business of the meeting is conducted in an orderly manner;

- the chair must adjourn a general meeting if directed to do so by the general meeting.[209]

Once a meeting is validly adjourned, the members cannot then continue with the meeting.[210] If, however, the chair improperly adjourns the meeting, then the members may appoint another chair and continue the meeting.[211] It is usual for the articles to provide that the chair must set the time and date of the adjourned meeting when adjourning the original meeting.[212] The adjourned meeting is not regarded as a new meeting, but as a continuation of the original meeting. This means that notice of the adjourned meeting need not be given, unless the articles so provide.[213] However, any resolutions passed at the adjourned meeting cannot be regarded as being passed prior to that meeting[214] (e.g. at the original meeting).

14.3.5 **Voting at a meeting**

The passing of resolutions constitutes perhaps the most important activity at a meeting, so the rules relating to voting are of the utmost importance. The ability to vote is regarded as a key membership right and the law generally provides members with freedom as to how they can exercise their votes. As Lord Maugham stated, 'the shareholder's vote is a right of property, and prima facie may be exercised by a shareholder as he thinks fit in his own interest'.[215] This is even the case where the member is also a director—for example, a director, when exercising his right to vote as a member, may vote purely in his own interests, even if such interests are adverse to the interests of the company.[216] However, there are some important limitations on the ability to vote:

- The articles may place restrictions upon a member's ability to vote (e.g. by allowing the company to issue shares with restricted or no voting rights).

- Statute may limit a member's ability to vote. For example, if a resolution has been tabled to ratify a director's negligence, default, breach of duty, or breach of trust, then the director (or any member connected to him) in question will not be permitted to vote on the matter.[217]

- The courts have, in limited circumstances, placed limits upon the majority's power to bind the minority. Examples include (i) when altering the articles, the amendment must be bona fide for the benefit of the company;[218] (ii) when voting at a class meeting, the power to bind a minority 'must be exercised for the purpose of benefiting the class as a whole, and not merely individual members only';[219] and (iii) when voting on the appointment of

---

[209] Model articles for private companies, art 41(2) and (3); model articles for public companies, art 33(2) and (3)

[210] *R v Gaborian* (1809) 11 East 77. [211] *National Dwellings Society v Sykes* [1894] Ch 159 (Ch).

[212] The model articles provide for this (model articles for private companies, art 41(4)(a); model articles for public companies, art 33(4)(a)).

[213] The model articles require seven days' notice if the adjourned meeting is to take place more than 14 days after the original meeting (model articles for private companies, art 41(5); model articles for public companies, art 33(5)).

[214] CA 2006, s 332. [215] *Carruth v Imperial Chemical Industries Ltd* [1937] AC 707 (HL) 765.

[216] *Pender v Lushington* (1877) ChD 70 (Ch). [217] CA 2006, s 239(3) and (4).

[218] *Allen v Gold Reefs of West Africa Ltd* [1900] 1 Ch 656 (CA) (discussed at 5.3.3.2).

[219] *British America Nickel Corp Ltd v MJ O'Brien Ltd* [1927] AC 369 (PC) 371 (Viscount Haldane).

a director, the majority's power 'must within broad limits be exercised for the benefit of the company as a whole and not to secure some ulterior advantage'.[220]

The rules relating to voting are now discussed, beginning with the two methods of voting.

14.3.5.1 Methods of voting

Regarding the passing of resolutions at a meeting, there are two methods of voting, namely (i) on a show of hands; or (ii) by poll. The general rule is that, unless the articles provide otherwise,[221] resolutions are taken on a show of hands. In such a case, unless the articles provide otherwise, each member will have one vote.[222] The votes will be counted and the chair will declare whether the resolution has passed or not. In the absence of proof to the contrary, this declaration will provide conclusive evidence of the number of votes cast for and against the resolution.[223] The model articles for both private and public companies provide that a resolution at a meeting will be decided on a show of hands unless a poll is demanded in accordance with the articles,[224] and most companies tend to adopt a similar rule. In practice, most larger companies conduct votes by poll for three reasons: (i) larger shareholders want voting power commensurate with their shareholdings; (ii) a show of hands is an imprecise method of counting;[225] and (iii) counting hands can be complex in larger meetings, especially as proxy voting is extensive.

Unless the articles provide otherwise, where a vote is taken on a poll, each member will have one vote per share, unless the company has no share capital, in which case, each member has one vote.[226] A member with multiple votes need not cast all his votes the same way.[227]

The members have the right to demand that a vote be taken on a poll and any provision in the articles that purports to exclude this right is void, unless it relates to the election of a chair or the adjournment of the meeting.[228] Companies can, however, place restrictions upon the right to demand a poll, but this ability is limited, with the CA 2006 providing that a provision in the articles is void if it would make ineffective a demand for a poll by:

- not less than five members having the right to vote on the resolution, or;
- a member or members representing not less than 10 per cent of the total voting rights of all the members having the right to vote on the resolution; or
- a member or members holding shares in the company conferring a right to vote on the resolution, being shares on which an aggregate sum has been paid up equal to not less than 10 per cent of the total sum paid up on all the shares conferring that right.[229]

The model articles are less restrictive than this and provide that a poll may be demanded by the chair, the directors, two or more persons having the right to vote on the resolution,

Proxies are discussed at 14.3.5.2.

---

[220] *Re HR Harmer Ltd* [1959] 1 WLR 62 (CA) 82 (Jenkins LJ).

[221] *Speechley v Allott* [2014] EWCA Civ 230, [2014] LLR 817 (articles precluded voting by a show of hands).

[222] CA 2006, s 284(2) and (4).   [223] ibid s 320(1).

[224] Model articles for private companies limited by shares, art 42; model articles for public companies, art 34.

[225] Sir William Scott in *Anthony v Seger* (1789) 1 Hag Con 9, 13 described voting on a show of hands as 'a rude and imperfect declaration of the sentiments of the electors'.

[226] CA 2006, s 284(3) and (4).   [227] ibid s 322.   [228] ibid s 321(1).

[229] ibid s 321(2). In practice, many larger companies impose the maximum limitations permissible under s 321(2).

or a person or persons representing not less than one-tenth of the total voting rights of all the shareholders having the right to vote on the resolution.[230] The model articles also provide that a poll can be demanded before the meeting takes place or at the meeting, either before a vote on a show of hands takes place or after.[231] Where both forms of vote take place, the vote by a show of hands will be nullified and replaced by the result of the vote by poll.[232]

Where a poll is taken at a general meeting of a quoted company or traded company, then specified information must be published on the company's website, including the date of the meeting, the text of the resolution, and the number of votes cast for and against the resolution.[233] Subject to certain limitations and conditions, the members of a quoted company can also require the directors to obtain an independent report on any poll taken, or to be taken, at a general meeting.[234]

14.3.5.2 Proxies

Members need not personally attend a meeting as the CA 2006 grants a member the right to appoint another person[235] (who may or may not be a member) to exercise his right to attend, speak, and vote at meetings of the company,[236] and this person is known as a 'proxy'. The ability to appoint a proxy cannot be restricted by a company's articles, but the articles may confer upon a member greater powers to appoint a proxy than those found under the CA 2006.[237] In large public companies, the appointment of proxies is especially important, because only a small minority of the company's members will attend the meeting. Most members will therefore vote by proxy and will usually accept the company's nominated proxy, thereby giving the company a notable advantage.

When a company sends out notice of a meeting, that notice must include, with reasonable prominence, a statement informing the member of his right to appoint a proxy.[238] In larger companies, this notice will often nominate a person (usually the chair of the board) to act as proxy, but the member is free to change this and choose his own proxy. The appointment of a proxy must be made in writing where the meeting is of a traded company.[239] In practice, most appointments will be in writing, as a company's articles will normally require a document (often known as a 'proxy form' or 'proxy notice') to be filed with the company within a certain time prior to the meeting.[240] However, such a provision will be void if it requires the document to be filed more than 48 hours before the meeting.[241] If a proxy form is not filed within the specified period, it cannot be used.[242]

---

[230] Model articles for private companies, art 44(2); model articles for public companies, art 36(2).

[231] Model articles for private companies, art 44(1); model articles for public companies, art 36(1).

[232] *Anthony v Seger* (1789) 1 Hag Con 9.   [233] CA 2006, s 341(1) and (1A).

[234] ibid s 342(1).

[235] Where the member holds multiple shares, he may appoint multiple proxies to exercise the rights found in different shares, (CA 2006, s 324(2)).

[236] CA 2006, s 324(1).

[237] ibid s 331. See e.g. art 45(4) of the model articles for private companies, which provides that a proxy appointed for a meeting will also be appointed for the adjourned meeting.

[238] ibid s 325(1). Failure to comply with this constitutes a criminal offence, but will not affect the validity of, or anything done at, the meeting (s 325(2)–(4)).

[239] ibid s 327(A1).

[240] The model articles require a proxy notice to be filed with the company identifying the appointing member and the person being appointed as proxy. Article 45 of the model articles for private companies does not impose a time limit, whereas art 39 of the model articles for public companies does.

[241] CA 2006, s 327(2)(a).   [242] *Shaw v Tati Concessions Ltd* [1913] 1 Ch 292 (Ch).

A validly appointed proxy is entitled to vote at a meeting (either on a show of hands or by poll) and can demand a poll if his appointing member (on his own or along with others) satisfies the conditions to demand a poll.[243] If the appointing member provides the proxy with no instructions, then the proxy may vote as he wishes. If instructions are given, then the proxy must vote in accordance with them.[244] The proxy form appointing the proxy will either be 'two-way' (which enables the member to instruct the proxy to vote for or against each resolution) or 'three-way' (i.e. which enables the member to instruct the proxy to vote for, against, or abstain for each resolution).[245]

Being a form of agency, a proxy's appointment can be revoked by the appointing member (the model articles provide expressly for this),[246] unless the agency is irrevocable. In the case of a traded company, the termination of a proxy's authority must be notified to the company in writing.[247]

14.3.5.3 Corporate representatives

A member can appoint a proxy irrespective of whether that member is a natural or legal person. In addition, where a company (A) holds shares in another company (B), then A can, following a resolution of its directors or governing body, authorize a person or persons to act as its representative at any meeting of B.[248] That corporate representative is entitled to exercise, on behalf of A, the same powers as A could exercise if it were an individual member of B.[249]

An obvious question to ask is whether it is preferable for a corporate member to appoint a proxy or a corporate representative. Historically, the rules relating to proxies and corporate members differed considerably, meaning that one method might be preferable based on the circumstances. Today, the rules are more similar and so the issue is less important. However, corporate representatives have one notable advantage over proxies. As noted, a proxy will only be validly appointed if specified documentation is filed with the company by a specified deadline. Conversely, a corporate representative need generally file no documentation and can simply turn up at the meeting.

14.3.6 The annual general meeting

Under the CA 1985, both public and private companies were required to hold an AGM.[250] Parliament recognized that, for many smaller companies (especially those where the members and directors were the same people), AGMs served little purpose, and so the CA 1985 was amended in 1989 to allow private companies to opt out of the requirement to hold an AGM if all the members so agreed.[251] The CLRSG acknowledged that AGMs were of little use for smaller companies and so recommended that, instead of having to opt out of the AGM requirement, private companies should be automatically

---

[243] CA 2006, s 329(1).   [244] ibid s 324A.

[245] The proxy forms of listed companies must be three-way (Listing Rules, LR 9.3.6(2)). The Jenkins Committee (Board of Trade, *Report of the Company Law Committee* (Cmnd 1749, 1962) para 464) recommended that three way forms should be a statutory requirement, but this recommendation was never acted upon.

[246] Model articles for private companies, art 46(2); model articles for public companies, art 39(6).

[247] CA 2006, s 330(A1).   [248] ibid s 323(1).   [249] ibid s 323(2).

[250] Companies Act 1985 (CA 1985), s 366 (now repealed).   [251] ibid s 366A (now repealed).

opted out and could opt in to having an AGM if they so wish.[252] Accordingly, the CA 2006 does not generally require private companies to hold an AGM, but they can do so if they wish. However, a private company will be required to hold an AGM if it is a traded company[253] or if the company's articles require that an AGM be held.[254] In practice, only larger private companies hold AGMs.

Public companies must hold an AGM every year within a six-month period beginning with the day following its accounting reference date.[255] Failure to hold an AGM within this period constitutes a criminal offence.[256] Generally, the AGM is subject to the same rules as general meetings, albeit subject to some modifications as discussed in previous sections.

The accounting reference date is discussed at 19.3.1.2.

As with other general meetings, the law does not prescribe what business must be dealt with at the AGM, but it is customary that certain matters be dealt with:

- the annual accounts and reports are laid before the meeting;[257]
- a resolution relating to the accounts and reports will usually take place (usually where the members agree to receive the accounts and reports);
- the remuneration report is put to the members for approval (if the company is quoted);[258]
- the appointment of directors and re-electing directors that have retired by rotation is put to the members for approval;
- appointing/re-appointing an auditor and approving the auditor's remuneration is usually carried out (typically, a resolution will be tabled authorizing the board or the audit committee to approve the auditor's remuneration);
- a final dividend is recommended for declaration;
- directors or the company are provided with authorization to engage in certain acts (e.g. allot shares, disapply pre-emption rights, authorize the company to purchase its own shares etc);
- approval of short notice of a general meeting is sought.[259]

14.3.7 Records of resolutions and meetings

Every company must keep records consisting of (i) copies of all resolutions of members passed otherwise than at general meetings (e.g. written resolutions); (ii) minutes of all proceedings of general meetings; and (iii) details of decisions taken by a sole member.[260] These records must be kept for at least 10 years, beginning on the date of the resolution, meeting, or decision.[261] Any member of the company has the right to inspect these records free of charge and, upon payment of a fee, may take a copy of the records.[262] These rules also apply to resolutions and meetings of holders of a class of shares.[263]

---

[252] CLRSG, 'Modern Company Law for a Competitive Economy: Developing the Framework' (2000) paras 7.87–7.88.

[253] CA 2006, s 336(1A). Such a company must hold an AGM in each period of nine months beginning with the day following its accounting reference date. Very few private companies are traded companies.

[254] Companies Act 2006 (Commencement No 3, Consequential Amendments, Transitional Provisions and Savings) Order, Sch 3, para 32.

[255] CA 2006, s 336(1). This period is increased to nine months in the case of a traded company (s 336(1A)).

[256] ibid s 336(3).   [257] ibid s 437(1).   [258] ibid ss 439 and 439A (discussed at 19.3.2.4).

[259] ibid s 337(2).   [260] ibid s 355(1). The details relating to decisions of sole members are found in s 357.

[261] ibid s 355(2).   [262] ibid s 358.   [263] ibid s 359.

14.4 Class meetings

General meetings are so called because, usually, all the members are entitled to attend. In some cases, however, companies are required to hold a class meeting in which only one class of member is entitled to attend. The obvious example is where a company has several classes of share and seeks to vary the rights of one of those classes of shareholder. Generally, class meetings are conducted via the same rules as apply to general meetings,[264] but there are some differences:

🔗 The variation of class rights is discussed at 16.6.1.

- In a class meeting, only the members of the class in question are entitled to attend. However, if others (including other classes of shareholder) do attend and no objection is raised to their presence, then the members of the class in question will be deemed to have waived any objection to their presence.[265]

- Whereas the members have the power to require the directors to call a general meeting, the members of a particular class do not have the right to call a class meeting.[266]

- Whilst the court has the power to call a general meeting, it does not have the power to call a class meeting.[267]

- Where a class meeting is called to determine whether class rights should be varied, then the rules relating to quorums and votes by poll differ to those in a general meeting.[268]

- Certain additional obligations placed upon traded companies when holding general meetings will not apply to class meetings of a traded company.[269]

14.5 Investor engagement

The European Commission, in its Green Paper on corporate governance, stated that 'the corporate governance framework is built on the assumption that shareholders engage with companies and hold the management to account for its performance'.[270] From a governance perspective, investor engagement and general meetings are of little importance to many private companies for two reasons:

1. As the CLRSG noted, general meetings can only be an effective governance mechanism if 'most of the votes are held by members other than the directors or those under their influence'.[271] In many private companies, the members are the directors, and 'a formal general meeting of members serves little purpose where the directors and the members are largely the same people'.[272] Accordingly, in such companies, general meetings and investor engagement tend not to be a central governance issue.

2. As private companies do not need to hold an AGM and as almost all resolutions can be passed without holding a meeting, many private companies conduct their business without ever holding a general meeting.

---

[264] ibid ss 334(1) and 335(1).

[265] *Carruth v Imperial Chemical Industries Ltd* [1937] AC 707 (HL) 767–8 (Lord Maugham).

[266] CA 2006, ss 334(2)(a) and 335(2)(a).   [267] ibid ss 334(2)(b) and 335(2)(b).

[268] ibid ss 334(3) and 335(3). These differences are discussed at 16.6.1.2.   [269] ibid s 334(2)(c).

[270] European Commission, 'Green Paper: The EU Corporate Governance Framework' COM (2011) 164 final, 3.

[271] CLRSG, 'Modern Company Law for a Competitive Economy: Company General Meetings and Shareholder Communications' (1999) para 18.

[272] ibid.

Accordingly, our discussion here focuses on investor engagement in larger companies, especially quoted companies. The question to ask is what investor engagement is. To quote the EU Green Paper again, investor engagement refers to 'actively monitoring companies, engaging in a dialogue with the company's board, and using shareholder rights, including voting and cooperation with other shareholders, if need be to improve the governance of the investee company in the interests of long-term value creation'.[273]

From this, it can be seen that the principal mechanism through which investors can engage with the company is through the general meeting. Unfortunately, the widespread consensus is that general meetings are not as effective as they should be, with Sir Adrian Cadbury stating that '[i]f too many Annual General Meetings are at present an opportunity missed, this is because shareholders do not make the most of them and, in some cases, boards do not encourage them to do so'.[274] The reasons for this are several, but a key reason is that, historically, the shareholdings in quoted companies were widely dispersed, both in terms of number (such companies may have hundreds of thousands, or even millions, of members) and geography (a quoted company's members may be spread throughout the world). This made it difficult for shareholders to actively engage with the company and so investor engagement decreased, leading to what has become known as 'the separation of ownership and control'[275] (i.e. those who controlled companies—the directors—had effectively been able to escape effective scrutiny of those who owned the company—the members).

The law has sought to encourage greater investor engagement (e.g. through provisions designed to encourage electronic meetings and decision-making), but engagement remains a problem. Indeed, the CLRSG recommended that public companies should be able to dispense with the holding of an AGM on the basis that 'the AGM is in many cases ineffective in fulfilling the functions assigned to it by theory . . . and companies should have the option of replacing it with something less cumbersome to achieve the indispensable governance functions of the institution'.[276] However, under the CLRSG's proposals, the AGM could only be dispensed with if all the members agreed, and the government was of the opinion that, in public companies, securing unanimous agreement would be exceptionally rare and so the CLRSG's recommendation was rejected.[277]

Electronic meetings are discussed at 14.3.2.

It was hoped that changes in ownership patterns over the past 40 years would result in a unification of ownership and control. In particular, it was hoped that the increasing concentration of share ownership in the hands of institutional investors would lead to greater investor engagement.

14.5.1 Institutional investors

Often, we will transfer money to others so that they can look after it for us, or return it to us should certain contingencies occur. We open bank accounts and trust banks to look after our money. We pay money into pension funds, so that we will have a source of

[273] European Commission, 'Green Paper: The EU Corporate Governance Framework' COM (2011) 164 final, para 2.1.

[274] 'Report of the Committee on the Financial Aspects of Corporate Governance' (Gee & Co Ltd 1992) para 6.7.

[275] AA Berle and GC Means, *The Modern Corporation and Private Property* (Harcourt Brace 1932).

[276] CLRSG, 'Modern Company Law for a Competitive Economy: Company General Meetings and Shareholder Communications' (1999) para 24.

[277] DTI, *Company Law Reform* (Cm 6456, 2005) 31.

income upon retirement. We take out insurance policies so that, if certain unfortunate events occur, we will be compensated for any loss suffered. When we transfer our money to banks, insurance companies, or pension funds holders, they do not simply hold the money, but instead use it to make a profit for themselves, often by investing in the share market. And because they usually have access to much greater funds than individuals, they can invest much more heavily in the share market. The increasing share ownership of pension funds, insurance companies, unit trusts, and banks (or 'institutional investors', as they have come to be known) has transformed the UK corporate governance landscape, as Figure 14.2 indicates.

As Figure 14.2 indicates, until the late 1970s, individual shareholders were the largest single group of shareholders. Soon thereafter, however, the holdings of individual shareholders fell significantly and institutional investor shareholdings increased notably. By the 1980s and1990s, well over half the shares in quoted companies were controlled by institutional investors. It was hoped that this concentration of share ownership could result in a reversal of the separation of ownership and control and that investors could once again effectively hold management to account. The Wilson Committee, which was set up to examine the operation of UK financial institutions, reported in 1980:

> there now exists a body of shareholders which collectively owns a significant proportion of the equity of many companies and which has the ability to mobilise the support of other shareholders. . . . If a company gets into obvious difficulties, institutions with substantial holdings can seldom dispose of them without realising a considerable financial loss . . . and this gives them a strong incentive to take action about weak or inadequate management. Even when difficulties are less evident, it may well be in the interests of large institutional shareholders to commit time and effort to trying to improve company's management, rather than simply disposing of their holdings.[278]

Commentators had high hopes for the ability of institutional investors to exercise more control and improve standards of corporate governance, with one commentator

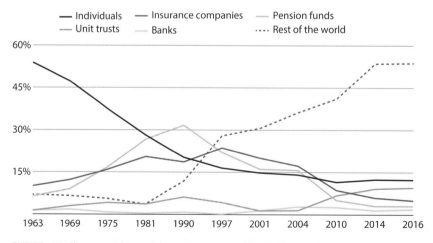

FIGURE 14.2 Share ownership statistics

---

[278] *Committee to Review Functioning of Financial Institutions* (Cmnd 7937, 1980) para 250.

stating, 'the holdings of these institutions are now so large that a manageable number of funds could feasibly join hands to supervise managers in a new system of control'.[279] Unfortunately, in practice, this new system of control never materialized and institutional investors have not become the corporate stewards that many hoped they would be. Several reasons have been advanced for this, but it should be noted that determining the exact level of institutional investor activism is difficult because institutional investors tend to engage in 'behind-the-scenes' negotiation. The reason for this is that, if a large institutional investor were to publicly display dissatisfaction with the way that a company is run, other members could panic, which could trigger a 'race to exit'. Certainly, experience has demonstrated that, in many cases, if a dispute between the company and its institutional investor becomes public, then everyone ultimately loses as the company's share price usually slumps. However, even taking into account the institutions' reputation for behind-the-scenes activism, there is still a widespread belief that institutional investors have not yet had the impact that many believed they would and several reasons have been advanced for this.

First, in order to diversify their risk, a single institutional investor will typically only hold a small percentage of a company's shares. Accordingly, a single institutional investor will normally need to try and form a coalition with other investors. However, forming and maintaining a coalition of institutional investors can be a difficult task. Shareholder activism involves expense in terms of time, effort, and cost. As the benefits of shareholder activism usually go to all the members (not just the active ones), it follows that passive members have no real incentive to expend resources in aiding the active members. This is known as the 'free rider' problem as the passive members can free-ride off the active members' efforts, and can therefore prevent effective coalitions from forming.

Second, institutional investors can only act as effective stewards if they have sufficient information on the companies in which they hold shares. Acquiring such information can be costly. For smaller members, the costs of acquiring such information will usually outweigh the benefits of activism. Institutional investors may be able to bear the cost of acquiring information, but they will also need to disseminate that information to the other members. The combined costs of acquiring and disseminating the information may outweigh the benefits that would be gained should their efforts succeed. This may encourage the investors to engage in 'rational apathy'[280] (i.e. doing nothing).

Third, institutional investor activism may be affected by conflicts of interest that discourage them from activism. For example, a pension fund manager holds shares in company X, but also wants to manage the pension fund of company X. The danger is that the pension fund manager might be wary of engaging in stewardship of company X if he feels that this might adversely affect his ability to secure the right to manage company X's pension fund.

Fourth, as Figure 14.2 demonstrates, domestic institutional investment has declined notably over the past 20 years and the single largest group of shareholders are now overseas investors (principally overseas institutional investors). For such investors, geographical and logistical reasons may impact upon their ability to engage with the companies they hold shares in. Indeed, as is discussed below, engagement from overseas investors has been low.

[279] AF Conrad, 'Beyond Managerialism: Investor Capitalism?' (1988) 2 U Mich JL Reform 117, 119.
[280] JN Gordon, 'The Mandatory Structure of Corporation Law' (1989) 89 Colum L Rev 1549, 1576.

This is not to say that institutional investors had had no impact and, in certain areas, there have been several high-profile examples of institutional investor activism. For example, institutional investors have had an impact in relation to directors' remuneration.

The shareholders' 'say on pay' is discussed at 19.3.2.4.

Institutional activism and directors' pay

Since 2002, shareholders of quoted companies have had the right to vote on the directors' remuneration report. In the vast majority of cases, the shareholders approve the report. However, there have been a number of notable instances where, as a result of institutional investor activism, remuneration reports have been rejected:

- The first remuneration report to be rejected by the shareholders was that of GlaxoSmithKline in 2003 (discussed at 19.3.2.4).
- In 2009, the remuneration report of the Royal Bank of Scotland (RBS) was opposed by over 90 per cent of shareholders (the largest ever shareholder rebellion on directors' pay) following the news that disgraced former CEO Fred Goodwin would receive a £703,000-a-year pension.
- 2012 saw a series of remuneration report rebellions that have now been dubbed as a 'shareholder spring'. Companies whose reports were rejected or faced substantial levels of shareholder opposition included AstraZeneca, Aviva, Barclays, Trinity Mirror, and WPP.
- In 2016, nearly 60 per cent of the shareholders voted against BP's remuneration report, following the revelation that the board would receive the maximum bonus despite the company reporting an annual loss.

It should, however, be noted that these examples are noteworthy precisely because they are rare (indeed, even during the so-called shareholder spring, average voting levels in favour of remuneration reports were over 90 per cent). The level of institutional investor activism remains a matter of concern. These concerns were amplified following the financial crisis. Lord Myners, the former Financial Services Secretary to the Treasury, described institutional investors as 'absentee landlords'[281] and stated that institutional investor inactivity had contributed to what he termed the 'ownerless corporation'.[282] In 2009, a review was set up to look at corporate governance in banks following the financial crisis. The Walker Review identified a number of factors that led to the crisis, one of which was a lack of institutional investor engagement. The Review stated that 'board and director shortcomings . . . would have been tackled more effectively had there been more vigorous scrutiny and engagement by major investors acting as owners'.[283] The Review noted that the Combined Code did contain recommendations regarding

---

[281] Lord Myners, 'Association of Investment Companies' (April 2009) https://webarchive.nationalarchives. gov.uk/20091204223814/http://www.hm-treasury.gov.uk/speech_fsst_210409.htm accessed 10 January 2019.

[282] BBC, 'Leading Questions: Paul Myners' (1 August 2009) http://news.bbc.co.uk/1/hi/business/8179024.stm accessed 10 January 2019.

[283] 'A Review of Corporate Governance in UK Banks and Other Financial Industry Entities: Final Recommendations' (HM Treasury, 2009) para 5.11.

institutional investor engagement, but these should be separated from the Combined Code, expanded upon, and placed into a new 'Stewardship Code'.[284]

14.5.2 The UK Stewardship Code

The first UK Stewardship Code was published in July 2010 and based heavily on an existing set of principles established by the now-defunct Institutional Shareholders' Committee (ISC).[285] The Code was updated in 2012 but has not been updated since (though the FRC has stated that it intends to consult on updating the Code in January 2019, aiming to publish an updated Code mid-year). The Code is based around seven key Principles, namely:

1. Institutional investors should publicly disclose their policy on how they will discharge their stewardship responsibilities.

2. Institutional investors should have a robust policy on managing conflicts of interest in relation to stewardship, which should be publicly disclosed.

3. Institutional investors should monitor their investee companies.

4. Institutional investors should establish clear guidelines on when and how they will escalate their stewardship activities.

5. Institutional investors should be willing to act collectively with other investors where appropriate.

6. Institutional investors should have a clear policy on voting and disclosure of voting activity.

7. Institutional investors should report periodically on their stewardship and voting activities.

Baroness Hogg, Chair of the FRC when the Code was first published, stated that the Code would hopefully 'be a catalyst for better engagement between shareholders and companies and create a stronger link between governance and the investment process'.[286] Unfortunately, the general opinion amongst commentators is that the impact of the Code is likely to be modest at best,[287] and the FRC admits that there is still an 'engagement deficit'.[288]

The first problem relates to the Code's scope. The Code is 'directed in the first instance to institutional investors, by which is meant asset owners and asset managers with equity holdings in UK listed companies'.[289] As Figure 14.2 indicates, the most recent statistics reveal that the majority of shares (53.8 per cent)[290] in UK quoted companies are held by overseas investors. The FRC 'hope[s] that investors based outside the UK will commit to the Code',[291] but this has not happened and an examination of the list of signatories to the Code reveals very few overseas investors. This problem is exacerbated by the decline in domestic institutional investment. For example, in 1990, pension funds held 31.7 per

---

[284] ibid para 5.40.

[285] ISC, 'Code on the Responsibilities of Institutional Investors' (ISC 2009). For a more detailed discussion of the origins of the UK Stewardship Code, see Lee Roach, 'The UK Stewardship Code' (2011) 11 JCLS 463.

[286] FRC, 'FRC Press Notice 306' (FRC 2010).

[287] See e.g. Lee Roach, 'The UK Stewardship Code' (2011) 11 JCLS 463; Brian R Cheffins, 'The Stewardship Code's Achilles' Heel' (2010) 73 MLR 1004; Arad Reisberg, 'The UK Stewardship Code: On the Road to Nowhere?' (2015) 15 JCLS 217.

[288] FRC, 'Developments in Corporate Governance 2013' (FRC 2013) 4.

[289] FRC, 'The UK Stewardship Code' (FRC 2012) 2.

[290] Office for National Statistics (ONS), 'Ownership of UK Quoted Shares: 2014' (ONS 2015) Table 1.

[291] FRC, 'Implementation of the UK Stewardship Code (FRC 2010) para 25.

cent of shares in UK quoted companies—by 2014, this figure had fallen to 3 per cent.[292] As Cheffins notes, '[i]f the Stewardship Code had been introduced twenty years ago, its "reach" would have been extensive'.[293] Today, the Code's reach is much less impressive and it has been argued that the Code is 'oblivious to the fact that shareholders who are not the [Code's] main targets now collectively dominate UK share registers'.[294]

The second problem relates to enforcement and transparency. The UK Stewardship Code, like the UK Corporate Governance Code, operates on a comply-or-explain basis. However, while the UK Corporate Governance Code has a measure of legal backing in the form of the Listing Rules (which require that listed companies comply or explain against the Code), the UK Stewardship Code has no such backing. Instead, institutional investors voluntarily sign up to the Stewardship Code and signatories who choose not to comply with its Principles 'should deliver meaningful explanations that enable the reader to understand their approach to stewardship'.[295] The problem is that the explanations provided by signatories vary considerably in quality. To try and improve the quality of explanations, in 2016, the FRC decided to assign signatories to one of three tiers based on the quality of their Code statements:

1. Tier 1 signatories provide a good-quality and transparent description of their approach to stewardship and explanations of an alternative approach where necessary.

2. Tier 2 signatories meet many of the reporting expectations but report less transparently on their approach to stewardship or do not provide explanations where they depart from provisions of the Code.

3. Tier 3 signatories require significant reporting improvements to be made to ensure the approach is more transparent. Signatories have not engaged with the process of improving their statements and their statements continue to be generic and provide little or no explanations where they depart from provisions of the Code.

Since the tier system was introduced, the number of Tier 1 and 2 signatories has slowly increased, but the FRC is still concerned at the number of Tier 3 signatories. Accordingly, in 2017, it decided to remove the Tier 3 category of signatory.[296]

The third problem relates to content. The Walker Review recommended that the ISC Code could form the basis of the Stewardship Code,[297] but the FRC's consultation revealed widespread dissatisfaction with the ISC Code, with many respondents stating that the ISC Code would need substantial strengthening. Suggestions for reform were received from a wide array of respondents, but these reform suggestions were ignored and the 2010 Stewardship Code was an almost verbatim reproduction of the ISC Code. Some reforms were introduced in 2012, but the Stewardship Code is still mostly based on the ISC Code that was largely regarded as weak in 2010. To make matters worse, the Stewardship Code has been updated infrequently. An update to the 2012 Code was only announced in January 2019, and is due to come into effect in July 2019. The result of these flaws is that the Code is 'travelling along the road to nowhere'.[298]

The 2019 update to the Code is discussed in the 'Latest news' section at xviii.

---

292 ONS, 'Ownership of UK Quoted Shares: 2014' (ONS 2015) Table 1.

293 Brian R Cheffins, 'The Stewardship Code's Achilles' Heel' (2010) 73 MLR 1004, 1017.

294 Arad Reisberg, 'The UK Stewardship Code: On the Road to Nowhere?' (2015) 15 JCLS 217, 236.

295 FRC, 'The UK Stewardship Code' (FRC 2012) 4.

296 See FRC, 'Developments in Corporate Governance and Stewardship 2016' (FRC 2017) 26.

297 'A Review of Corporate Governance in UK Banks and Other Financial Industry Entities: Final Recommendations' (HM Treasury, 2009) para 5.40.

298 Arad Reisberg, 'The UK Stewardship Code: On the Road to Nowhere?' (2015) 15 JCLS 217, 217.

CHAPTER SUMMARY

- Members make decisions by passing resolutions or by using the unanimous assent rule.

- An ordinary resolution requires a simple majority to pass, whereas a special resolution requires a majority of not less than 75 per cent.

- Private companies can pass resolutions using the written resolution procedure.

- A decision can be taken by the members, without a resolution, if all the members entitled to vote on the matter agree.

- Private companies do not need to hold an AGM, whereas public companies do. General meetings are subject to a range of procedural rules that must be complied with (e.g. members are entitled to notice of meetings).

- It is generally regarded that investor engagement could be much improved. It was hoped that the growth of institutional investment would result in increased engagement, but the increase has not been as significant as hoped.

- To encourage institutional investors to engage more, the FRC has published the UK Stewardship Code.

FURTHER READING

Arad Reisberg, 'The UK Stewardship Code: On the Road to Nowhere?' (2015) 15 JCLS 217.
- Argues that the UK Stewardship Code has not succeeded in improving shareholder engagement.

Brian R Cheffins, *Corporate Ownership and Control: British Business Transformed* (OUP 2008).
- An excellent discussion of how the ownership of UK companies has affected UK corporate governance. Provides a detailed examination of institutional investor engagement.

Deirdre Ahern and Karen Maher, 'The Continuing Evolution of Proxy Representation' (2011) 2 JBL 125.
- Discusses the history, legal regulation, and future role of proxy voting.

Richard C Nolan, 'The Continuing Evolution of Shareholder Governance' (2006) 65 CLJ 92.
- Examines the evolution of the law that governs shareholder decision-making and argues that the law can serve to unduly restrict shareholder governance.

Ross Grantham, 'The Unanimous Consent Rule in Company Law' (1993) 52 CLJ 245.
- Discusses the *Duomatic* principle and argues that the scope of the principle needs to be reconsidered.

SELF-TEST QUESTIONS

1. Define the following terms:
- ordinary resolution;
- special resolution;
- written resolution;
- general meeting;
- class meeting;
- a poll vote;
- proxy;

- corporate representative;
- institutional investor.

2. State whether each of the following statements is true or false and, if false, explain why:

- Public companies must make decisions via resolutions at a meeting.
- An ordinary resolution is passed if 50 per cent or more of the members vote in favour of it.
- Only private companies can use the written resolution procedure.
- A company can make a decision without a resolution being passed if all the members agree on the matter.
- Only the directors may call a general meeting of the company.
- Members must be provided with 21 days' notice of the AGM of a private company.
- Two qualifying persons attending a general meeting will usually constitute a quorum.
- Where a vote is taken by poll, each member will have one vote per share.
- A member can only appoint a proxy if the articles so provide.

3. Discuss the extent to which the UK Stewardship Code has been effective in improving institutional investor engagement.

4. Katie is a director of Spartan plc and Wraith Ltd. Hades Investments Ltd is a fund manager that holds a significant number of shares in both Spartan and Wraith. Hades has, for some time, had significant doubts regarding Katie's abilities as a director. After discussing the issue with several other dissatisfied shareholders, Hades Investments decides that Katie should be removed from the boards of Spartan and Wraith. Hades therefore seeks your advice regarding the following:

- Explain the various ways that Katie's removal from office could be secured.
- Will a meeting need to be called? If so, explain the procedures that would need to be followed.
- Explain to Hades the practical issues it might face in getting any resolutions passed.

ONLINE RESOURCES

This book is accompanied by online resources to better support you in your studies. Visit www.oup.com/uk/roach-company/ for:

- answers to the self-test questions;
- further reading lists;
- multiple-choice questions;
- glossary.

Updates to the law can be found on the author's Twitter account (@UKCompanyLaw) and further resources can be found on the author's blog (www.companylawandgovernance.com).

15 Members' remedies

- Personal, corporate, and representative actions
- The statutory derivative claim
- The unfair prejudice petition
- The petition for winding up

INTRODUCTION

Where the company, its directors, or members have engaged in some form of act or omission that has caused loss to a member or members, how can redress be obtained? The problem that arises is that, often, the parties who have caused the loss are the ones who have the ability to seek redress (usually through the company). Members, especially minority shareholders, who sustain loss due to the wrongdoer's acts or omissions could, without the law's aid, be left without a remedy. Where the wrongdoers have breached the company's constitution, the member may be able to sue for breach of contract, as was discussed at 5.3.4. Here, the focus is on three remedies[1] provided under statute, namely:

1. the statutory derivative claim;
2. the unfair prejudice petition; and
3. the petition to wind up the company.

Figure 15.1 provides an overview of the key member remedies. However, before these statutory member remedies are discussed, it is important to note that a member may have a personal right to seek a remedy that is independent of these three statutory remedies (although overlaps may exist).

---

[1] These remedies are traditionally known as 'shareholder remedies' (indeed, virtually all current texts use this term). However, given that they are available to members and not just shareholders (indeed, the relevant legislative provisions use the word 'member'), they will be referred to here as members' or member remedies.

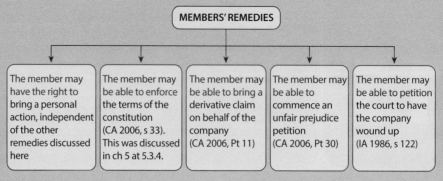

FIGURE 15.1 Members' remedies

15.1 Personal, corporate, and representative actions

A member may be able to obtain redress for a wrong done to him by commencing a personal action in his own name:

● The constitution forms a contract between the company and its members, and between the members themselves.[2] From this, it follows that a member can commence a personal action for breach of contract if certain provisions of the constitution are breached by the company or a fellow member.

● If a shareholders' agreement exists, then a member has a personal right to commence a claim for breach of contract if that agreement is breached.

● Statute may provide a member with a personal remedy where specific rights have been breached. For example, a person can apply to the court for an order rectifying the register of members if their name is, without sufficient cause, entered or omitted from the register of members.[3]

● Two of the statutory member remedies discussed in this chapter are examples of personal actions, namely the unfair prejudice petition and the petition to wind up the company.

● A director owes his duties to the company,[4] and so a member cannot normally commence a personal claim for breach of duty (although as discussed at 15.2, he may have the right to bring a derivative claim on behalf of the company). However, there are highly limited instances where a director will owe a duty directly to a member and, in such a case, a member may commence a personal action against the director.

In many cases, a member will bring a personal action in order to obtain a remedy for himself. Where multiple members have suffered a loss, then each member can bring a separate personal action, or they can engage in a collective action.

Shareholders' agreements are discussed at 5.6.

When a director owes a duty directly to the members is discussed at 10.1.2.2.

15.1.1 Personal actions and corporate actions

A person may engage in an unlawful act or omission that causes loss to both the company and its members. In such a case, the company will have the right to bring an action against the wrongdoer, and the members will also likely have a personal right to sue the wrongdoer. The general rule is that, in such a case, both actions can proceed.

---

[2] Companies Act 2006 (CA 2006), s 33.   [3] ibid s 125(1) (discussed at 13.2.3).   [4] ibid s 170(1).

Pender v Lushington (1877) 6 ChD 70 (Ch)

FACTS: The articles of Direct United States Co Ltd ('DUS') provided that its members would have one vote for every 10 shares, up to a maximum of 100 votes. Consequently, members with over 1,000 shares would not have voting power commensurate to their shares. To avoid this, members with over 1,000 shares (of which Pender was one) transferred some of their excess shares to several nominees, thereby unlocking the votes within them. DUS's chair (Lushington) refused to accept the nominees' votes, resulting in a resolution tabled by Pender being defeated. Pender alleged that his votes were improperly rejected and brought a representative action on behalf of himself and the other members whose votes were rejected, and commenced a derivative action on behalf of DUS.

HELD: Jessel MR stated that the shares were properly transferred and registered to the nominees, so refusing to accept that their votes constituted a breach of the articles. He went on to state that Pender had a right to sue on this breach himself and on behalf of DUS. An injunction was granted restraining the rejection of the nominees' votes.

However, there is a major exception to this principle in the form of the 'no reflective loss' principle, which can serve to prevent the member's claim from proceeding.

15.1.1.1 The no reflective loss principle

Consider the following (fictitious) example.

The 'no reflective loss' principle

The directors of Dragon plc commit an act of negligence that causes the company financial loss. As a result, Dragon issues a profit warning, stating that it does not expect to make a profit this financial year and abandons its plans to pay a dividend. Following the announcement, the value of the company's shares decreases significantly. Marc, a member of Dragon, wishes to commence a personal claim against the directors involved for the losses he has sustained.

In this example, the directors' negligence has caused loss to both Dragon and its members, with both having a personal cause of action against the directors. However, it is likely that the members will not be able to recover their losses from Dragon due to what is known as the no reflective loss principle, which provides that the members cannot sue a person for losses sustained if those losses are merely reflective of losses sustained by the company and which could be recovered by the company. In the example above, the loss sustained by Marc (and the other members) is merely reflective of the loss sustained by Dragon, and Dragon could recover this loss by suing the directors. In such a case, the company is the proper claimant (which, as discussed later, is the first principle of the rule in *Foss v Harbottle*) and its claim will generally 'trump that of the shareholder',[5] as the following case demonstrates.

The rule in *Foss v Harbottle* is discussed at 15.2.1.

---

[5] *Day v Cook* [2001] EWCA Civ 592, [2003] BCC 256 [38] (Arden LJ). Note that Arden LJ stated that the company's claim will 'always' trump that of the shareholder, but as discussed below, this is no longer the case and an exception to the 'no reflective loss' principle has been created in the case of *Giles v Rhind*.

📖 See LS Sealy, 'A Setback for the Minority Shareholder' (1982) 41 CLJ 247.

Prudential Assurance Co Ltd v Newman Industries Ltd (No 2) [1982] Ch 204 (CA)

FACTS: Bartlett and Laughton were directors of two companies, namely Newman Industries Ltd ('Newman') and Thomas Poole & Gladstone China Ltd ('TPG'). TPG was experiencing financial difficulties and so Bartlett and Laughton devised a scheme to sell TPG's assets to Newman. The valuation of the assets was based on misleading information provided by Bartlett and Laughton, with the result that Newman paid £445,000 more for the assets than it need have paid. The Listing Rules required that the shareholders of Newman approve the sale, and such approval was obtained, again based on misleading information provided by Bartlett and Laughton. Upon discovering the deception, Prudential Assurance Co Ltd ('Prudential'), which held 3.2 per cent of shares in Newman, commenced proceedings against Bartlett, Laughton, and TPG via three different claims:

(i) a derivative claim on behalf of Newman for the losses sustained by Newman;

(ii) a personal action against the defendants for the losses it sustained; and

(iii) a representative action on behalf of all the other members of Newman.

At first instance,[6] it was held that the defendants had indeed perpetrated a fraud and that the derivative and personal claims could be joined in one action. Bartlett and Laughton appealed.

HELD: The appeal was allowed in part. The Court of Appeal stated that the personal claim brought by Prudential was 'misconceived'[7] and that a member cannot:

> recover damages merely because the company in which he is interested has suffered damage. He cannot recover a sum equal to the diminution in the market value of his shares, or equal to the likely diminution in dividend, because such a 'loss' is merely a reflection of the loss suffered by the company. The shareholder does not suffer any personal loss. His only 'loss' is through the company, in the diminution in the value of the net assets of the company, in which he has (say) a 3 per cent shareholding. The plaintiff's shares are merely a right of participation in the company on the terms of the articles of association. The shares themselves, his right of participation, are not directly affected by the wrongdoing.[8]

Whether Prudential had the right to bring a derivative action did not form a ground of appeal and so the Court did not rule on this.

Prudential was regarded as a controversial decision at the time and was criticized strongly, with Sealy stating that 'to describe the judgment as disappointing would be a major understatement'[9] before stating that 'the court washed its hands of all concern and responsibility for the control of corporate fraud, airily passing the buck to the City and the legislature with a disdain reminiscent of Pilate himself'.[10] Despite the criticism, the rule is now well established, with its rationale being set out by Lord Millett:

> If the shareholder is allowed to recover in respect of such loss, then either there will be double recovery at the expense of the defendant or the shareholder will recover at the expense of the company and its creditors and other shareholders. Neither course can be permitted . . . Justice to the defendant requires the

---

[6] *Prudential Assurance Co Ltd v Newman Industries Ltd (No 2)* [1981] Ch 257 (Ch).

[7] [1982] Ch 204 (CA) 222.   [8] ibid 222–3.

[9] LS Sealy, 'A Setback for Minority Shareholders' (1982) 41 CLJ 247, 247.   [10] ibid.

exclusion of one claim or the other; protection of the interests of the company's creditors requires that it is the company which is allowed to recover to the exclusion of the shareholders.[11]

The no reflective loss principle tries to strike a balance between two potentially competing aims, as identified by Lord Bingham:

> On the one hand the court must respect the principle of company autonomy, ensure that the company's creditors are not prejudiced by the action of individual shareholders and ensure that a party does not recover compensation for a loss which another party has suffered. On the other, the court must be astute to ensure that the party who has in fact suffered loss is not arbitrarily denied fair compensation.[12]

The following case demonstrates this balancing act in practice and provides useful clarification on the scope of the no reflective loss principle.

 Johnson v Gore Wood & Co (No 1) [2002] 2 AC 1 (HL)

FACTS: Johnson was managing director and majority shareholder in Westway Homes Ltd ('Westway'). On Westway's behalf, he instructed Gore Wood & Co ('GW') to act as solicitors for Westway in relation to a purchase of land. Westway alleged that GW acted negligently and so commenced proceedings against GW for professional negligence, with Johnson stating that he also intended to personally sue GW for the losses he sustained. The case between Westway and GW was eventually settled, but Johnson's personal claim against GW proceeded. GW applied to have Johnson's claim struck out, *inter alia*, on the ground that his losses were reflective of those sustained by Westway.

HELD: The Court reiterated the validity of the no reflective loss principle, with Lord Bingham stating, '[n]o action lies at the suit of a shareholder suing in that capacity and no other to make good a diminution in the value of the shareholder's shareholding where that merely reflects the loss suffered by the company'.[13] On this basis, one head of damage sought by Johnson (namely the diminution in the value of his pension and shareholding) was struck out as it was reflective of Westway's loss. Lord Bingham did, however, state that a member could sue for a diminution in value of his shareholding if he had a cause of action, and the company suffered loss but had no cause of action to sue to recover that loss,[14] but this was not applicable here. In relation to the other heads of damage sought by Johnson, Lord Bingham stated:

> Where a company suffers loss caused by a breach of duty to it, and a shareholder suffers a loss separate and distinct from that suffered by the company caused by breach of a duty independently owed to the shareholder, each may sue to recover the loss caused to it by breach of the duty owed to it but neither may recover loss caused to the other by breach of the duty owed to that other.[15]

See Eilis Ferran, 'Litigation by Shareholders and Reflective Loss' (2001) 60 CLJ 245.

---

[11] *Johnson v Gore Wood & Co (No 1)* [2002] AC 1 (HL) 62.   [12] ibid 36.

[13] ibid 35. Lord Millett (at 66) stated that reflective loss does not just include the diminution of the value of shares, but also includes 'the loss of dividends . . . and all other payments which the shareholder might have obtained from the company if it had not been deprived of its funds'.

[14] ibid. For an example of such a situation, see *George Fischer (Great Britain) Ltd v Multi Construction Ltd* [1995] BCC 310 (CA).

[15] [2002] AC 1 (HL) 35–6.

> Applying this, the Court held that most of the heads of damage sought by Johnson would not be struck out as they were separate and distinct losses to those sustained by the company (e.g. additional tax liabilities sustained by Johnson due to GW's negligence). Such losses were not reflective of Westway's loss.

The no reflective loss principle applies to any situation where the company and members have a cause of action deriving from the same facts (even if their causes of action are different),[16] and will generally prevent the member's personal claim from proceeding 'even if the company has failed or declined to make good that loss'.[17] However, if the principal rationale behind the no reflective loss rule is to prevent double recovery, then there should be no objection to a member bringing a claim in cases where the company has declined to commence proceedings.[18] The no reflective loss principle also applies where the member brings a personal claim in a non-member capacity (e.g. where he claims in his capacity as a creditor or an employee).[19] This has been rightly criticized on the ground that it places members who are employees or creditors in a worse position than if they were not members.[20]

The no reflective loss principle is not absolute and the courts have crafted one exception, namely that where the defendant's conduct leaves the company unable to commence proceedings, then a member may commence a personal claim, even if his loss is reflective of that of the company.

📖 See Andrew Bowen, 'Giles v Rhind' (2003) 65 Bus LB 1.

Giles v Rhind [2002] EWCA Civ 1428[21]

FACTS: Giles and Rhind were directors and shareholders of Surrey Hill Foods Ltd ('SHF'). A dispute arose and the board of SHF decided that Rhind should leave the company. Terms were agreed for Rhind's resignation, with one term being that the provisions of the shareholders' agreement that existed between them would continue. Rhind set up a new company and, in breach of the shareholders' agreement, he diverted a lucrative contract from SHF to his new company. SHF commenced proceedings against Rhind but, due to Rhind's actions, SHF became insolvent and lacked the funds to continue the claim. Accordingly, Giles commenced a personal claim against Rhind for the reduction in the value of his shares caused by Rhind's conduct. At first instance, Giles's claim failed because his losses were merely reflective of SHF's losses.[22] Giles appealed.

HELD: The appeal was allowed and Giles was permitted to pursue his personal claim against Rhind. Waller LJ noted that in *Johnson*, Lord Bignham stated that if a company had no cause of action, then the shareholder could bring a claim, even if the loss was reflective. Waller LJ stated

---

[16] *Day v Cook* [2001] EWCA Civ 592, [2003] BCC 256 [79] (Arden LJ).

[17] *Johnson v Gore Wood & Co (No 1)* [2002] AC 1 (HL) 35 (Lord Bingham).

[18] Charles Mitchell, 'Shareholders' Claims for Reflective Loss' (2004) 120 LQR 457, 464.

[19] *Gardner v Parker* [2004] EWCA Civ 781, [2005] BCC 46.

[20] Paul L Davies and Sarah Worthington, *Gower & Davies Principles of Modern Company Law* (10th edn, Sweet & Maxwell 2016) 611.

[21] See also *Perry v Day* [2004] EWHC 3372 (Ch), [2005] 2 BCLC 405.

[22] *Giles v Rhind* [2001] 2 BCLC 582 (Ch).

> that 'the same should be true of a situation in which the wrongdoer has disabled the company from pursuing that cause of action'.[23] He justified this by stating that:
>
> > It seems hardly right that the wrongdoer who is in breach of contract to a shareholder can answer the shareholder by saying 'the company had a cause of action which it is true I prevented it from bringing, but that fact alone means that I the wrongdoer do not have to pay anybody'.[24]

15.1.2 Representative actions and Group Litigation Orders

It may be the case that the actions of the company or its directors cause loss to multiple members. In such a case, the possibility of collective action exists. The UK does not have an American-style 'class action' system but, in relation to company law issues, Part 19 of the Civil Procedure Rules provides for two collective action mechanisms, namely the representative action and the Group Litigation Order (GLO). It should be noted that both of these actions are opt-in, so if the action is successful, only those claimants who opted in to the action will generally be entitled to a remedy.[25]

Where more than one person has the same interest in a claim, a representative action may be commenced by or against one or more of the persons who have the same interest as representatives of any other persons who have that interest.[26] From this, it follows that where more than one member is wronged, a wronged member can (alone, or with other wronged members) commence proceedings on behalf of himself and other wronged members. Any judgment resulting from the claim is binding on all persons represented in the claim, and can be enforced against those not party to the claim with the court's permission.[27]

Representative actions can be useful, but they cannot be used where the claimants seek differing remedies or where each claimant's claim is based on materially different facts. For this reason, in recent years, there has been an increase in GLOs, although they still remain relatively rare.[28] A GLO is a tool to facilitate the management of cases where multiple claims arise from common or related issues of fact or law.[29] The claimants who opt in to the GLO will be entered onto a 'group register' and the claims will be heard by the court that made the GLO (thereby avoiding the need for multiple proceedings and the possibility of inconsistent outcomes). If the claim is successful, the judgment will be binding on all claimants on the group register, unless the court orders otherwise.[30] The key difference between a representative action and a GLO is that, in the latter, each claimant on the group register brings an individual claim, whereas in the former, the claim is brought on behalf of others. The following provides an example of a successful GLO (albeit one brought by the employees of a company, and not its members):

---

[23] [2002] EWCA Civ 1428, [2003] Ch 618 [35].   [24] ibid [34].

[25] In relation to competition law, an opt-out form of action does exist, namely the Collective Proceedings Order, but that is outside the scope of this text.

[26] Civil Procedure Rules 1998 (CPR 1998), r 19.6(1).   [27] ibid r 19.6(4)(a).

[28] At the time of writing, 105 GLOs have been made since 2000—see www.gov.uk/guidance/group-litigation-orders accessed 10 January 2019.

[29] CPR 1998, r 19.10.   [30] ibid r 19.12(1)(a).

Morrisons Supermarket and data protection

In January 2014, Mr Skelton, an employee of WM Morrison Supermarkets plc ('Morrisons'), uploaded a file to a file-sharing website that contained the personal details (e.g. names, addresses, phone numbers, bank details) of nearly 100,000 Morrisons' employees. Upon learning of the data breach, Morrisons took steps to have the website taken down and it identified Skelton as the source of the leaked information (he was subsequently sentenced to eight years' imprisonment for various offences).

The 5,518 employees of Morrisons whose data had been disclosed sought and obtained a GLO. They commenced proceedings against Morrisons alleging that Morrisons was personally liable for its own acts or omissions, and vicariously liable for the acts of Skelton. The High Court held that Morrisons was not personally liable, but it was vicariously liable for Skelton's wrongdoing.[31] Morrisons' appeal to the Court of Appeal was dismissed,[32] but it has stated it plans to appeal to the Supreme Court. Should this appeal be dismissed, Morrisons will be liable to pay the employees party to the GLO signification amounts in damages (the amount of compensation will not be determined until the appeal is resolved).

15.2 The statutory derivative claim

Consider the following example.

The rationale behind derivative proceedings

Stanley, the chief executive officer (CEO) of Dragon Goods Ltd ('DG') owns 75 per cent of its shares. He has personally appointed the other two directors to the board, with each owning 5 per cent of the company's shares. The remaining shares are held by Katja, who runs a business that supplies goods to DG. Katja discovers that Stanley is also a director of a company that competes with DG, but DG's other directors are unaware of this. Katja informs the other directors of Stanley's conflict of interest and demands that action be taken.

Stanley has likely acted in breach of duty (namely, the s 175 duty to avoid conflicts of interest), but a director owes his duties to the company[33] and only the company can generally commence proceedings for breach. Who can commence proceedings on behalf of the company is a matter for its articles, with the decision to commence proceedings on behalf of the company usually being vested in the board of directors.[34] Accordingly, the other directors of DG could commence proceedings in DG's name against Stanley, even if Stanley objected in his guise as majority shareholder.[35] However, the other directors of

---

[31] *Various Claimants v Wm Morrison Supermarkets plc* [2017] EWHC 3113, [2018] 3 WLR 691.

[32] *Wm Morrison Supermarkets plc v Various Claimants* [2018] EWCA Civ 2339.

[33] CA 2006, s 170(1).

[34] Article 3 of the model articles provides that the directors may 'exercise all the powers of the company', which would include the right to litigate on behalf of the company. Where a company is in liquidation or administration, then the liquidator or administrator (as applicable) also has the right to commence or defend proceedings on the company's behalf.

[35] *John Shaw & Sons (Salford) Ltd* [1935] 2 KB 113 (CA).

DG may be reluctant to commence proceedings against Stanley as they owe him their jobs and he could use his majority holding to dismiss them if he so wished (although it could be argued that a failure to commence proceedings would not be in accordance with their s 172 duty).

The issue that concerns us here is whether a member (such as Katja) can commence litigation on the company's behalf where the directors are unwilling to do so. If the articles expressly empower Katja to commence proceedings on behalf of the company, then the answer will be yes, but such provisions are extremely rare. The articles might empower the members collectively to commence proceedings, but this would be of no aid as Stanley is the majority shareholder. It has even been stated that the members have a power to commence proceedings on behalf of the company by passing an ordinary resolution, irrespective of what the articles state,[36] but it is unlikely that this rule has survived the CA 2006 reforms in relation to derivative claims. Absent empowering article provisions, members generally have no right to litigate in the company's name due to what is known as 'the rule in *Foss v Harbottle*' but, as is discussed at 15.2.2, an important exception does exist to this general rule, namely the derivative claim.

15.2.1 The rule in *Foss v Harbottle*

The rule in *Foss v Harbottle* is derived from the following case.

Foss v Harbottle (1843) 2 Hare 461

FACTS: Foss and Turton were shareholders of the Victoria Park Company ('VPC'). They claimed that the directors of VPC (one of whom was Harbottle) had, in breach of duty, caused VPC to enter into a series of fraudulent transactions. Accordingly, Foss and Turton commenced proceedings 'on behalf of themselves and all the other members of the corporation, except those who committed the injuries complained of'.[37]

HELD: Wigram VC stated that VPC 'is an incorporated body, and the conduct with which the Defendants are charged in this suit is an injury not to the Plaintiffs exclusively; it is an injury to the whole corporation . . .'.[38] He went on to state that Foss and Turton had assumed the right to sue on behalf of VPC, but '[i]t was not, nor could it successfully be, argued that it was a matter of course for any individual members of a corporation thus to assume to themselves the right of suing in the name of the corporation'.[39] In the circumstances, there was nothing to prevent VPC itself from obtaining redress, so the claim failed.

It has been stated that the rule in *Foss v Harbottle* consists of two principles.[40] The most significant principle to derive from *Foss* is that where a wrong is done to a company, the company is the proper claimant to seek redress. This 'proper claimant principle' was

---

[36] *Marshall's Valve Gear Co Ltd v Manning, Wardle & Co Ltd* [1909] 1 Ch 267 (Ch); *Alexander Ward & Co Ltd v Samyang Navigation Co Ltd* [1975] 1 WLR 673 (HL). Again, this would be of no aid as Marcus is the majority shareholder.

[37] (1843) 2 Hare 461, 490 (Wigram VC).   [38] ibid.   [39] ibid.

[40] See e.g. *Prudential Assurance Co Ltd v Newman Industries Ltd (No 2)* [1982] Ch 204 (CA) 210; Law Commission, *Shareholder Remedies* (Law Com CP No 142, 1996) para 1.06.

explained clearly by the Court of Appeal stating, 'A cannot, as a general rule, bring an action against B to recover damages or secure other relief on behalf of C for an injury done by B to C. C is the proper plaintiff because C is the party injured, and, therefore, the person in whom the cause of action is vested.'[41] The proper claimant principle is clearly a corollary of a company's separate personality and has the advantage of preventing a multiplicity of claims. As Mellish LJ stated:

> Looking to the nature of these companies, looking at the way in which their articles are formed, and that they are not all lawyers who attend these meetings, nothing can be more likely than that there should be something more or less irregular done at them—some directors may have been irregularly appointed, some directors as irregularly turned out, or something or other may have been done which ought not to have been done according to the proper construction of the articles. Now, if that gives a right to every member of the company to file a bill to have the question decided, then if there happens to be one cantankerous member, or one member who loves litigation, everything of this kind will be litigated; whereas, if the bill must be filed in the name of the company, then, unless there is a majority who really wish for litigation, the litigation will not go on. Therefore, holding that such suits must be brought in the name of the company does certainly greatly tend to stop litigation.[42]

If third parties were permitted to bring actions on behalf of the company, this could lead to multiple actions being brought against one person for the same wrong. As the Law Commission stated, '[a]s the company is, in law, a separate legal entity, it is the proper plaintiff where it has suffered injury, otherwise a defendant could face as many actions as there are shareholders'.[43]

The second principle is known as the 'irregularity principle' and provides that where some irregularity is committed, an aggrieved member cannot commence proceedings where the irregularity is one that can be ratified by a simple majority of the members. Again, quoting Mellish LJ:

> if the thing complained of is a thing which in substance the majority of the company are entitled to do, or if something has been done irregularly which the majority of the company are entitled to do regularly, or if something has been done illegally which the majority of the company are entitled to do legally, there can be no use in having a litigation about it, the ultimate end of which is only that a meeting has to be called, and then ultimately the majority gets its wishes.[44]

The irregularity principle has several justifications. First, it upholds the principle of majority rule. Second, it upholds the general principle that the courts will not generally interfere in the internal matters of a company. As Wedderburn noted, '[t]he law had long recognised majority rule as a fundamental principle concerning corporations, so that there was no difficulty in expressing majority rule as the justification for the refusal to interfere in internal management'.[45]

---

[41] *Prudential Assurance Co Ltd v Newman Industries Ltd (No 2)* [1982] Ch 204 (CA) 210.
[42] *Macdougall v Gardiner* (1875) 1 ChD 13 (CA) 25.
[43] Law Commission, *Shareholder Remedies* (Law Com CP No 142, 1996) para 4.3.
[44] *Macdougall v Gardiner* (1875) 1 ChD 13 (CA) 25.
[45] KW Wedderburn, 'Shareholders' Rights and the Rule in *Foss v Harbottle*' [1957] CLJ 194, 198.

The rule in *Foss v Harbottle* cannot be absolute, for reasons best explained by Lord Denning MR, who stated that if a company is:

> defrauded by a wrongdoer, the company itself is the one person to sue for the damage . . .. But suppose it is defrauded by insiders who control its affairs—by directors who hold a majority of the shares—who then can sue for damages? Those directors are themselves the wrongdoers. If a board meeting is held, they will not authorise the proceedings to be taken by the company against themselves. If a general meeting is called, they will vote down any suggestion that the company should sue them themselves. Yet the company is the one person who is damnified. It is the one person who should sue. In one way or another some means must be found for the company to sue. Otherwise the law would fail in its purpose. Injustice would be done without redress.[46]

The judiciary's response to allow for redress of this injustice was the creation of the derivative action.

15.2.1.1 The common law derivative action

A derivative action allowed a member to commence proceedings for a wrong done to the company. It was so called because the member was bringing an action based on rights derived from the company. This derivation is reinforced by the fact that, if the derivative action succeeded, the remedy was granted to the company, not to the member who brought the action. Historically, it has been stated that there were four instances where a derivative action could be brought:[47]

1. where the act complained of was illegal[48] or *ultra vires*;[49]

2. where the act complained of infringed the personal rights of a member (e.g. the failure to provide sufficient notice of meetings,[50] the failure to provide dividends in the manner provided for by the articles,[51] or the improper rejection of votes);[52]

3. where the act complained of could only be done or sanctioned by the passing of a special resolution;[53] and

4. where the act complained of constituted a 'fraud on the minority'.

It was generally acknowledged that the only 'true' exception to *Foss* (and so the only 'true' derivative action) was the fraud on the minority exception. The reason for this is that the first three so-called exceptions did not concern rights vested in the company, but concerned personal rights belonging to the member. Accordingly, they were not 'exceptions' to *Foss*, but rather areas in which *Foss* had no application.

The fraud on the minority exception was created specifically for those instances in which those who control the company (including those having the right to commence litigation on the company's behalf) have committed some form of fraud. 'Fraud' is

---

[46] *Wallersteiner v Moir (No 2)* [1975] 2 WLR 389 (CA) 390 (Lord Denning MR).

[47] See the judgment of Jenkins LJ in *Edwards v Halliwell* [1950] 2 All ER 1064 (CA).

[48] See e.g. *Taylor v National Union of Mineworkers (Derbyshire Area)* [1985] BCLC 237 (unlawful strike action).

[49] See e.g. *Simpson v Westminster Palace Hotel Co* (1860) 8 HL Cas 712 (HL).

[50] *Baillie v Oriental Telephone and Electric Co Ltd* [1915] 1 Ch 503 (CA).

[51] *Wood v Odessa Waterworks Co* (1889) 42 ChD 636 (Ch).

[52] *Pender v Lushington* (1877) 6 Ch D 70 (Ch).   [53] *Edwards v Halliwell* [1950] 2 All ER 1064 (CA).

defined widely to include actual fraud (e.g. a breach of the Theft Act 1968, or the Fraud Act 2006) and equitable fraud (e.g. conduct tainted with impropriety), although the courts have maintained that negligence, however gross, is not a fraud on the minority.[54] Where an act of negligence benefits those who control the company, thereby tainting it with impropriety, this can constitute a fraud on the minority.[55]

A court would, however, deny a member a right to sue on behalf of the company, even if there was fraud on the minority, if it did not serve the interests of justice. Examples of cases in which a member has been denied the chance to bring a derivative action include where the conduct of the member seeking to sue is itself tainted by impropriety,[56] or where the independent members (i.e. not the wrongdoer or the applicant) have already indicated that they do not wish there to be litigation on behalf of the company.[57]

Whilst the Law Commission agreed with the underlying approach of the rule in *Foss v Harbottle* (i.e. that members should rarely be able to commence actions for wrongs done to the company), it was also of the opinion that the rules relating to derivative actions had become 'complicated and unwieldy'.[58] As a result of the Law Commission's recommendations (which were largely adopted by the Company Law Review Steering Group (CLRSG)), Pt 11 of the CA 2006 now allows for the making of a statutory derivative claim.

It is important to note that the provisions contained in Pt 11 do not have a marked effect on the rule in *Foss v Harbottle* itself; the proper claimant principle remains intact, but the irregularity principle is modified slightly. Under the common law, an act that could be ratified by the members could not found a derivative action. Under Pt 11, actual ratification/authorization will result in a derivative claim being refused permission to continue,[59] while potential ratification/authorization is a factor the court will take into account when determining whether to grant permission for the claim to continue.[60]

The provisions of Pt 11 now broadly replace the common law rules relating to when a derivative action may be brought. However, it should be noted that the CA 2006 does not expressly abolish the common law derivative action, and not all derivative actions fall within the scope of Pt 11. Notably, two forms of derivative action fall outside Pt 11 (namely multiple derivative actions and actions involving foreign companies) and so will continue to be subject to the common law rules. Both of these will be briefly discussed.

15.2.1.2 Multiple derivative actions

The statutory derivative claim is often referred to as the 'ordinary derivative claim' and applies where the derivative claimant is a member of the company that was wronged and is seeking redress on behalf of that company. Bearing this in mind, consider the following example.

---

[54] *Pavlides v Jensen* [1956] Ch 565 (Ch).   [55] *Daniels v Daniels* [1978] Ch 406 (Ch).

[56] *Nurcombe v Nurcombe* [1985] 1 WLR 370 (CA).   [57] *Smith v Croft (No 2)* [1988] Ch 114 (Ch).

[58] Law Commission, *Shareholder Remedies* (Law Com No 246, 1997) para 6.4. See also Geoffrey Morse, *Palmer's Company Law* (Sweet & Maxwell 2016) para 8.3704.1, who describes the common law rules as 'complex, unclear and highly restrictive'.

[59] CA 2006, s 263(2)(b) and (c).   [60] ibid s 263(3)(c) and (d).

Eg **The multiple derivative action**

Belinda and Ahmed are directors and the majority shareholders of Dragon Tools Ltd ('DT'). They are also the directors of Mechanical Ltd ('Mechanical'), a wholly-owned subsidiary of DT. Belinda and Ahmed act in breach of duty whilst acting as directors of Mechanical. Sally, a member of DT, wishes to obtain redress on behalf of Mechanical.

Here, the proper claimant is Mechanical, but Belinda and Ahmed are its directors, so it is unlikely to sue. DT, as the only member of Mechanical, could commence a derivative claim against Belinda and Ahmed, but this is unlikely as Belinda and Ahmed are also directors of DT. The issue is can Sally, a member of DT, commence derivative proceedings on behalf of Mechanical, even though she is not a member of Mechanical. Under the common law, the courts permitted derivative actions to be brought by non-members in limited cases,[61] with such actions being known as 'multiple' or 'double' derivative actions. However, such actions do not appear to fall within the scope of the ordinary derivative claim under the CA 2006, and debate arose regarding whether multiple derivative claims were permissible under the CA 2006, with the following case providing the answer.

Re Fort Gilkicker Ltd **[2013] EWHC 348 (Ch)**

FACTS: Universal Project Management Services Ltd ('UPMS') and Pearce were the only two members of Askett Hawk Properties LLP ('the LLP'). Fort Gilkicker Ltd ('FG') was set up by the LLP to engage in a property development, and the shares in FG were owned by the LLP. Pearce acted as a director of FG. UPMS alleged that, whilst Pearce was a director of FG, he misappropriated a business opportunity that belonged to FG and caused it to be diverted to another company that he controlled. UPMS sought to commence a derivative claim on behalf of FG (which would be a multiple claim as UPMS was not a member of FG), and the court had to determine whether to grant permission for the claim to continue. As part of this, the court had to determine whether multiple derivative actions survived the CA 2006 coming into force.

HELD: Briggs J stated that whilst the ordinary derivative action (i.e. where a member brought an action on behalf of a company he was a member of) was abolished by the CA 2006, 'the 2006 Act did not do away with the multiple derivative action'.[62] Accordingly, multiple derivative actions are not subject to the provisions of Pt 11 of the CA 2006, but continue to be subject to the common law rules. Applying this, Briggs J held that a fraud on the minority had been committed by Pearce and so permission to continue the action was granted.

COMMENT: Whilst the decision has undoubtedly brought clarity to this area of the law, it does mean that the common law rules and statutory rules are still both in place. Briggs J acknowledged the inadequacy of this, stating that:

See Tan Cheng-Han, 'Multiple Derivative Actions' (2013) 129 LQR 337.

---

[61] See e.g. *Wallersteiner v Moir (No 2)* [1975] 1 QB 373 (CA); *Airey v Cordell* [2006] EWHC 2728 (Ch), [2007] Bus LR 391.
[62] [2013] EWHC 348 (Ch), [2013] Ch 551 [44]. See also *Abouraya v Sigmund* [2014] EWHC 277 (Ch), [2015] BCC 503, where the approach of Briggs J was followed.

> A conclusion that what Parliament in fact achieved in 2006 was to place a statutory code for derivative claims by members of the wronged company alongside a continued obscure, complicated and unwieldy common law regime for derivative claims by others does not commend itself as an exercise in commonsense.[63]
>
> It has therefore been argued that clarity should be restored by extending the scope of Pt 11 to cover multiple derivative actions.[64]

15.2.1.3 Claims involving foreign companies

The provisions relating to the statutory derivative claim apply 'to proceedings in England and Wales or Northern Ireland by a member of the company'.[65] The courts have interpreted this to mean that the provisions of Pt 11 only apply to companies registered under the CA 2006, and therefore the common law rules relating to derivative actions will continue to apply to claims involving foreign companies.[66]

15.2.2 Scope of the statutory derivative claim

Section 260(1) defines a derivative claim as one brought by a member in respect of a cause of action vested in the company, seeking relief on behalf of the company. From this definition, several consequences follow:

- The claim must be brought by a member. However, for the purposes of Pt 11, this will include a person who is not a member, but to whom shares in the company have been transferred or transmitted by operation of law[67] (e.g. where shares are inherited). If a person ceases to be a member, he will lose the right to commence derivative proceedings, even if the cause of action arose whilst he was a member.

- The cause of action must be vested in the company. Where the cause of action is vested personally in the member only, then derivative proceedings cannot be brought. However, a director's act or omission may result in an action being vested in the company and a personal action belonging to the member. In such a case, derivative proceedings can proceed (and may eclipse the member's personal action due to the no reflective loss principle).

The no reflective loss principle is discussed at 15.1.1.1.

- As the member is seeking relief on behalf of the company, any benefits obtained because of the claim accrue to the company and not to the derivative claimant. To ensure that the company can enforce the judgment, the Civil Procedure Rules provide that the company must be made a defendant to the claim.[68]

- As the cause of action vests in the company, it is immaterial whether the cause of action occurred before or after the derivative claimant became a member.[69]

The actions of a member could found a common law derivative action,[70] but a statutory derivative claim can only be based on the act or omission of a director[71] (which includes shadow directors and former directors).[72] Despite this, a derivative claim

---

[63] ibid [34].

[64] Tan Cheng-Han, 'Multiple Derivative Actions' (2013) 129 LQR 337, 339. [65] CA 2006, s 260(1).

[66] *Novatrust Ltd v Kea Investments Ltd* [2014] EWHC 4061 (Ch).

[67] CA 2006, s 260(5)(c).   [68] CPR 1998, r 19.9(3).   [69] CA 2006, s 260(4).

[70] See e.g. *Estmanco (Kilner House) Ltd v Greater London Council* [1982] 1 WLR (QB).

[71] CA 2006, s 260(3).   [72] ibid s 260(5)(a) and (b).

may be brought against a director or another person (or both).[73] However, a claim could only be brought against a person other than the director 'in very narrow circumstances, where the damage suffered by the company arose from an act involving a breach of duty etc on the part of the director (e.g. for knowing receipt of money or property transferred in breach of trust or for knowing assistance in a breach of trust)'.[74] In other words, a claim can only be brought against a third party who is in some way connected to the director's act or omission, as the following example demonstrates.

> **Eg** **Derivative claims and third parties**
>
> Walter is a director of Dragon Tools Ltd ('DT'). Whist acting for DT, he informs one of DT's customers that the goods sold by ST can be obtained more cheaply from Ember Ltd. The client stops buying goods from DT and instead obtains the goods from Ember. Ankur, a member of DT, discovers this and also discovers that Walter is the sole director and shareholder of Ember.

Walter will likely be in breach of the duty to avoid conflicts of interest contained in s 175 of the CA 2006. Ankur could commence a derivative claim against Walter, and he could also commence a derivative claim against Ember on the ground that it 'dishonestly assisted in a breach of fiduciary duty'.[75]

15.2.2.1 Grounds for a derivative claim

A derivative claim can only be brought under Pt 11 of the Act, or in pursuance of a court order under s 994.[76] Not all causes of action vested in the company are subject to derivative proceedings, with s 260(3) providing that a claim can only arise from an actual or proposed act or omission by a director involving:

- **Negligence**: Negligence could not found a common law derivative action unless the wrongdoer gained some form of benefit from the negligent act. This limitation is not preserved by the Act, leading to a concern from directors that the number of derivative claims will substantially increase. The Law Commission branded this concern as 'overstated',[77] and it has been proven correct as the number of derivative claims has been low.

- **Default**: 'Default' is a general term used in many pieces of legislation that refers to a failure to perform a legally obligated act (e.g. obtain member approval for transactions under Pt 10, Ch 4 of the CA 2006). Accordingly, this is a rather broad term that will cover a breach of many statutory obligations.

- **Breach of duty**: Accordingly, a member will have standing to commence a derivative claim for breach of the general duties discussed in Chapters 10 and 11.

- **Breach of trust**: A 'breach of trust' occurs where a trustee engages in some form of improper act in relation to trust property, or breaches a duty placed upon him in relation to his position as a trustee. Directors can be trustees and so will be subject to duties in relation to trust property (e.g. property of the company).

---

[73] ibid s 260(3).   [74] CA 2006, Explanatory Notes, para 494.
[75] *Iesini v Westrip Holdings Ltd* [2009] EWHC 2526 (Ch), [2010] BCC 420 [75] (Lewison J).
[76] CA 2006, s 260(2).
[77] Law Commission, *Shareholder Remedies* (Law Com No 246, 1997) para 6.41.

15.2.3 **The derivative claim process**

A derivative claim starts when the derivative claimant issues a claim form.[78] Section 261(1) of the CA 2006 provides that a member who brings a derivative claim must apply to the court for permission to continue it. Accordingly, at the same time that the claim form is issued, the claimant must also file an application notice for permission to continue the claim along with the written evidence in support of his permission application.[79] The claimant must notify the company of the claim, unless notifying the company would be likely to frustrate some part of the remedy sought, in which case the court can order that the company need not be notified for a specified period.[80]

The principal hurdle for a derivative claimant is obtaining permission from the court to continue the claim, with ss 261–4 establishing a two-stage process for determining whether permission should be granted. Figure 15.2 sets out this two-stage process.

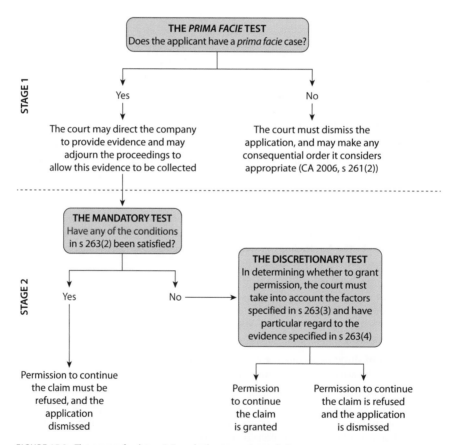

FIGURE 15.2: The process for determining whether to grant permission

Source: Roach, *Concentrate Company Law* (5th edn, OUP 2018).

---

[78] CPR 1998, r 19.9(2).   [79] ibid r 19.9A(2).   [80] ibid r 19.9A(4) and (7).

15.2.3.1 **Stage 1: establishing a *prima facie* case**

Under the first stage, the member must establish that there is a *prima facie* case for the granting of permission to continue the claim.[81] This stage occurs without the company's involvement and the claimant must not make the company a respondent to the application at this stage.[82] The court will consider the claimant's application for permission to continue the claim and, if a *prima facie* case is not established, the court must dismiss the claim and can make any consequential order that it considers appropriate.[83] The purpose of the *prima facie* test is to save time and expense by screening out unmeritorious or weak claims before the company and defendant become involved. Lewison J stated that establishing a *prima facie* case 'necessarily entails a decision that there is a *prima facie* case both that the company has a good cause of action and that the cause of action arises out of a directors' default, breach of duty (etc)'.[84] The majority of cases to date have successfully established a *prima facie* case, so it appears that establishing a *prima facie* case is not an especially difficult hurdle to overcome.

If the member establishes that he has a *prima facie* case, then the court may give directions to the company as to the evidence that it must produce and may adjourn the proceedings to allow such evidence to be obtained.[85] The claim will then move onto the second stage, in which the court will decide whether to grant permission to proceed. This second stage can itself be sub-divided into two parts (which this text labels 2A and 2B), with the first part being referred to as the 'mandatory test'.

15.2.3.2 **Stage 2A: the mandatory test**

The first part of the stage 2 test can be found in s 263(2), which provides that permission to continue the claim must[86] be refused in three circumstances. The first is where the court is satisfied that a person acting in accordance with s 172 (duty to promote the success of the company) would not seek to continue the claim.[87] Guidance as to what factors might be relevant in determining this include:

The s 172 duty is discussed at 10.3.

> such matters as the prospects of success of the claim, the ability of the company to make a recovery on any award of damages, the disruption which would be caused to the development of the company's business by having to concentrate on the proceedings, the costs of the proceedings and any damage to the company's reputation and business if the proceedings were to fail.[88]

Further factors that might be relevant include:

> the size of the claim; the strength of the claim; the cost of the proceedings; the company's ability to fund the proceedings; the ability of the potential defendants to satisfy a judgment; the impact on the company if it lost the claim and had to pay not only its own costs but the defendant's as well; any disruption to the company's activities while the claim is pursued; whether the prosecution of the claim would damage the company in other ways (e.g.

---

[81] CA 2006, s 261(2).   [82] CPR 1998, r 19.9A(3).   [83] CA 2006, s 261(2).
[84] *Iesini v Westrip Holdings Ltd* [2009] EWHC 2526 (Ch), [2010] BCC 420 [78].
[85] CA 2006, s 261(3).   [86] Which is why it is known as the 'mandatory test'.
[87] CA 2006, s 263(2)(a).
[88] *Franbar Holdings Ltd v Patel* [2008] EWHC 1534 (Ch), [2008] BCC 885 [36] (William Trower QC).

by losing the services of a valuable employee or alienating a key supplier or customer) and so on.[89]

In practice, refusal of permission to continue on this ground is likely to be rare, as the court has stated that the weighing of the above considerations 'is essentially a commercial decision, which the court is ill-equipped to take, except in a clear case'[90] and therefore s 263(2)(a) 'will apply only where the court is satisfied that *no* director acting in accordance with section 172 would seek to continue the claim'.[91]

The second circumstance where permission to continue must be refused is where the cause of action arises from an act or omission that is yet to occur, and the act or omission has been authorized by the company.[92] Where statute provides no rules on authorization, then authorization will be governed by the common law rules,[93] which typically involve obtaining the consent of the members in general meeting. Where specific rules on authorization apply, then these must be complied with, as the following example demonstrates.

> ### Eg · Refusal of permission due to authorization
>
> Nancy is a director of Dragon plc. She has been offered a role as a non-executive director (NED) of Sterling plc, a company that supplies goods to Dragon. Nancy informs the board of Dragon of the job offer, and the board agrees that she can have two days off per month to act as NED for Sterling (the articles of Dragon provide that the board can authorize conflicts of interest). Sally, a member of Dragon, discovers this and commences a derivative claim on behalf of Dragon in which she seeks an injunction preventing Nancy from taking the job.
>
> Nancy acting as a director for Sterling might place her in a conflict-of-interest situation, as Sterling does business with Dragon. However, the s 175 duty to avoid a conflict of interest will not be breached if the director obtains authorization which, in a public company, can be given by the directors if the constitution so provides.[94] Accordingly, the relevant act has been authorized and so permission to continue the claim would be refused (given that authorization was granted, it is also probably the case that no breach of duty has occurred, and so the case may not even make it past the *prima facie* stage).

The final circumstance where permission to continue must be refused is where the cause of action arises from an act or omission that has already occurred, and the act or omission was authorized by the company before it occurred or has been ratified by the company since it occurred.[95] What amounts to authorization here is the same as under s 263(2)(b) discussed above. The law relating to ratification can be found in s 239 of the CA 2006, which essentially requires an ordinary resolution to be passed. Prior to the passing of the CA 2006, the director whose behaviour was being ratified could vote on the ratification resolution (providing that he was a member and was acting in good faith).[96] Under the CA 2006, where the director is also a member, then his votes (and

🔗 Ratification under s 239 is discussed in more detail at 10.1.3.3.

---

[89] *Iesini v Westrip Holdings Ltd* [2009] EWHC 2526 (Ch), [2010] BCC 420 [85] (Lewison J).

[90] ibid.

[91] ibid [86]. For an example of a case that did fall foul of s 263(2)(a), see *Bridge v Daley* [2015] EWHC 2121 (Ch).

[92] CA 2006, s 263(2)(b).   [93] ibid s 180(4).   [94] ibid s 175(4)(b) and (5)(b).

[95] ibid s 263(2)(c).   [96] *North-West Transportation Co Ltd v Beatty* (1887) 12 App Cas 589 (PC).

those of members connected to him) will be disregarded,[97] although if the vote takes place at a company meeting, he may attend and will be counted towards the quorum.[98]

15.2.3.3 Stage 2B: the discretionary test

If the claim does not fall foul of the mandatory test, it can progress onto the second part of stage 2, which can be termed the 'discretionary test'. Here, the courts will determine whether permission should be granted for the claim to continue, but the standard that the claim must meet is not clear. Lewison J stated that 'I do not consider that at the second stage this is simply a matter of establishing a *prima facie* case . . . because that forms the first stage of the procedure.'[99] However, it has been argued that the *prima facie* test might still be relevant at stage 2 as 'the court might revise its view as to a *prima facie* case once it has received evidence and argument from the other side . . .'.[100] In the absence of such a revision, then it is clear that '[a]t the second stage, something more must be needed'[101] than simply establishing a *prima facie* case, but it is not clear what this extra element is. It has been said that, at stage 2, it would be 'quite wrong . . . to embark on anything like a mini-trial of the action'.[102] However, Hannigan has argued that '[p]ractice appears to be veering towards the type of mini-trial at the permission stage which was so criticised when claims were governed by the common law and which was meant to be addressed by the statutory reforms'.[103] It would appear that, at this stage, there is no threshold test on the merits of the case and the court will simply 'do the best it can on the material before it'.[104]

Limited guidance on the application of the discretionary test derives from s 263(3) and (4), which provides a non-exhaustive list of seven factors that the court must[105] take into account when determining whether or not to grant permission. The first is 'whether the member is acting in good faith in seeking to continue the claim'.[106] In the majority of cases to date, this has been deemed a relevant factor, but establishing a lack of good faith has proven extremely difficult as the court has stated that 'as long as there is a real purpose in bringing the proceedings',[107] then arguments based on a lack of good faith will not be maintained. Examples of situations where permission could be refused due a lack of good faith include where the claimant participated in the wrongdoing on which his claim is based,[108] or where the claimant is pursuing an 'ulterior motive unrelated to the subject matter of the litigation'.[109] Examples of ulterior motives include where the claim

---

[97] CA 2006, s 239(3) and (4).   [98] ibid s 239(4).

[99] *Iesini v Westrip Holdings Ltd* [2009] EWHC 2526 (Ch), [2010] BCC 420 [79].

[100] *Stainer v Lee* [2010] EWHC 1539 (Ch), [2011] BCC 134 [29] (Roth J).

[101] *Iesini v Westrip Holdings Ltd* [2009] EWHC 2526 (Ch), [2010] BCC 420 [79].

[102] *Fanmailuk.com Ltd v Cooper* [2008] EWHC 2198 (Ch), [2009] BCC 877 [2] (Robert Englehart QC).

[103] Brenda Hannigan, *Company Law* (5th edn, OUP 2018) 562.

[104] *Iesini v Westrip Holdings Ltd* [2009] EWHC 2526 (Ch), [2010] BCC 420 [79] (Lewison J).

[105] This means that the factors that are relevant to the case must be taken into account, and the court has a discretion to take other factors into account if it so wishes (*Franbar Holdings Ltd v Patel* [2008] EWHC 1534 (Ch), [2008] BCC 885 [31] (William Trower QC)).

[106] CA 2006, s 263(3)(a).

[107] *Mission Capital plc v Sinclair* [2008] EWHC 1339 (Ch), [2008] BCC 866 [42] (Floyd J).

[108] *Iesini v Westrip Holdings Ltd* [2009] EWHC 2526 (Ch), [2010] BCC 420.

[109] *Goldsmith v Sperrings* [1977] 1 WLR 478 (CA) 503 (Bridge LJ). Note that this is a not a derivative claim case, but it was cited with approval in *Iesini v Westrip Holdings Ltd* [2009] EWHC 2526 (Ch), [2010] BCC 420 [119].

was brought to further a familial dispute,[110] or where a claim was brought to further the claimant's interests as a creditor of the company.[111] Note, however, that an ulterior motive for bringing a claim will not cause the claim to fail where the claim would benefit the company.[112]

The second factor is 'the importance that a person acting in accordance with section 172 (duty to promote the success of the company) would attach to it'.[113] It was noted at 15.2.3.2 that permission must be refused where a person acting in accordance with s 172 (duty to promote the success of the company) would not seek to continue the claim,[114] and many of the factors relevant to s 263(2)(a) will also be applicable here in determining the importance attached to the claim. The following case provides a good example of a situation where little importance was attached to a claim.

Mission Capital plc v Sinclair [2008] EWHC 1339 (Ch)

FACTS: Mission Capital plc ('MC') had five directors, of which Emma and Ronald Sinclair ('the Sinclairs') were two. Their service contracts provided that their employment could be immediately terminated if they engaged in unacceptable conduct. MC terminated the Sinclairs' employment on the grounds that they failed to submit financial information and failed to meet financial forecasts. The Sinclairs disputed this. MC obtained an injunction that excluded the Sinclairs from MC's premises. The Sinclairs, *inter alia*, brought a derivative claim and sought permission to continue it.

COMMENT: Permission to continue the claim was refused. Floyd J stated:

> Although I could not be satisfied that the notional section 172 director would not continue the claim, I do not believe that he would attach that much importance to it. Would a company which had wrongfully dismissed a director normally take action against those responsible for the damage that it has suffered? It would depend, but I suspect that the action it would take in preference would be to replace the directors.[115]

The third factor is where the cause of action results from an act or omission that is yet to occur, whether the act or omission could be, and in the circumstances would be, likely to be authorized or ratified,[116] and the fourth factor is 'where the cause of action arises from an act or omission that has already occurred, whether the act or omission could be, and in the circumstances would be likely to be, ratified by the company'.[117] Section 263(2)(c) states that the court must refuse permission if actual authorization or ratification has taken place,[118] but s 263(3)(c) and (d) indicate that potential authorization or ratification is a factor to be taken into account.

The fifth factor is 'whether the company has decided not to pursue the claim'.[119] The decision to litigate on the company's behalf is usually taken by the directors, so the court

---

[110] *Barrett v Duckett* [1995] BCC 362 (CA).

[111] *Abouraya v Sigmund* [2014] EWHC 277 (Ch), [2015] BCC 503.

[112] *Mission Capital plc v Sinclair* [2008] EWHC 1339 (Ch), [2008] BCC 866; *Iesini v Westrip Holdings Ltd* [2009] EWHC 2526 (Ch), [2010] BCC 420.

[113] CA 2006, s 263(3)(b).   [114] ibid s 263(2)(a).

[115] *Mission Capital plc v Sinclair* [2008] EWHC 1339 (Ch), [2008] BCC 866 [43].

[116] CA 2006, s 263(3)(c).   [117] ibid s 263(3)(d).   [118] ibid s 263(2)(b) and (c).

[119] ibid s 263(3)(e).

here is assessing the directors' decision to commence proceedings against one of their own. From this, it follows that a decision by the company not to commence a claim will carry 'very little weight'[120] where the defendant directors constitute the majority of the board. However, where the decision is independently taken and valid reasons exist not to commence proceedings, then this can result in permission being refused, as demonstrated in the following case.

Kleanthous v Paphitis [2011] EWHC 2287 (Ch)

FACTS: Paphitis was a director of Ryman Group Ltd ('Ryman'). Paphitis discussed with Ryman's other directors the possibility of Ryman acquiring La Senza, but the directors decided not to do so. Paphitis decided to acquire La Senza himself and he asked Ryman's board if Ryman would lend funds to Xunely Ltd (a company controlled by Paphitis and which had two Ryman directors on its board), which would be used to acquire La Senza. Ryman's board agreed and Xunely acquired La Senza. Kleanthous, a member of Ryman, claimed that Paphitis had committed a breach of duty by diverting a business opportunity away from Ryman and towards Xunely. Kleanthous commenced derivative proceedings on Ryman's behalf against Paphitis and several other directors. Shortly after the claim was issued, Ryman set up a board committee, consisting of the two directors who were not defendants, to seek professional advice and make recommendations regarding the litigation. This committee concluded that 'the negative effect on the Company's businesses of the Company bringing or continuing a claim against the Defendant Directors greatly outweighs any benefit to the Company by pursuing the claim'. Negative effects included the likelihood of losing several experienced directors, as well as damaging the reputation of Paphitis, which would, in turn, damage the reputation of Ryman.[121] Kleanthous sought permission to continue his derivative claim.

HELD: Permission to continue the claim was refused. Newey J attached 'considerable weight'[122] to the conclusion reached by the independent committee which 'strongly opposed, on a reasoned basis'[123] the claim from going ahead.

See Baljit Chohan, 'Diggers and Dragons: Two Contrasting Cases on Directors' Duties' [2011] Corp Brief 7.

The sixth factor is 'whether the act or omission in respect of which the claim is brought gives rise to a cause of action that the member could pursue in his own right rather than on behalf of the company'.[124] A director's act or omission might form the basis of a derivative claim, but it might also grant the member a personal action (e.g. unfair prejudice under s 994, or a breach of the s 33 contract). The key consideration is not whether an alternative remedy is available, but whether that alternative remedy is more appropriate—'[t]he adequacy of the remedy available to the member in his own right is . . . a matter which will go into the balance when assessing the weight of this consideration on the facts of the case'.[125]

---

[120] *Cullen Investments Ltd v Brown* [2015] EWHC 473 (Ch), [2015] BCC 539 [57] (Mark Anderson QC).

[121] Paphitis is one of the 'Dragons' on Dragon's Den and his increased profile meant that any damage to his reputation would likely impact on that of Ryman's.

[122] [2011] EWHC 2287 (Ch), [2012] BCC 676 [75].   [123] ibid [85].

[124] CA 2006, s 263(3)(e).

[125] *Franbar Holdings Ltd v Patel* [2008] EWHC 1534 (Ch), [2008] BCC 885 [50] (William Trower QC).

Franbar Holdings Ltd v Patel [2008] EWHC 1534 (Ch)

FACTS: Medicentres (UK) Ltd ('Medicentres') was a wholly owned subsidiary of Franbar Holdings Ltd ('Franbar'). Franbar sold 75 per cent of its shares in Medicentres to Casualty Plus Ltd ('CP'). Franbar and CP entered into a shareholders' agreement, under which Franbar appointed one director to Medicentres' board and CP appointed two (namely Patel and du Plessis). Franbar commenced a derivative claim against CP, Patel, and du Plessis, alleging that the directors had breached their duties to Medicentres, and they had driven down Medicentres' share price by driving business away from it. Based on the same facts, Franbar also claimed against CP for breach of the shareholders' agreement and commenced an unfair prejudice petition against CP, Patel, and du Plessis.

HELD: Franbar was denied permission to continue the derivative claim. William Trower QC stated that 'there is no aspect of the derivative claim for which Franbar cannot be compensated by relief granted in the section 994 petition or the shareholders' action . . .'[126] He went on to state:

> I can see no reason why Franbar should not be granted such relief on the unfair prejudice petition as may be necessary to ensure that the interest which it seeks to realise is valued on a basis which takes full account of the value of the complaints it wishes to pursue on behalf of Medicentres in the derivative claim.[127]

Accordingly, 'the availability (and indeed use) of both the section 994 petition and the shareholders' action weigh in the balance against the grant of permission to continue the derivative action'.[128]

COMMENT: From this and other cases,[129] it appears that if the remedy sought by the claimant under the derivative claim could also be obtained via an unfair prejudice petition, then the court will likely refuse permission to continue the derivative claim. However, refusal of permission to continue the claim under s 263(3)(f) is less likely to occur if the claimant has some appropriate reason for not seeking the alternative remedy (e.g. he wishes to remain a member of the company and so does not wish to bring an unfair prejudice petition, as the remedy afforded would likely be his shares being bought out).

The seventh and final factor is granted its own sub-section and provides that 'the court shall have particular regard to any evidence before it as to the views of members of the company who have no personal interest, direct or indirect, in the matter'.[130] The rationale behind this factor was stated by Knox J:

> I remain unconvinced that a just result is achieved by a single minority shareholder having the right to involve a company in an action for recovery of compensation for the company if all the other minority shareholders are for disinterested reasons satisfied that the proceedings will be productive of more harm than good.[131]

However, the need for s 263(4) can be doubted on the ground that if the other members do not wish for the claim to proceed, they can simply ratify the director's act, in which case permission to continue must be refused.[132] The problem with this viewpoint is that it does not take into account how difficult authorization or ratification is to secure in

---

[126] ibid [49].   [127] ibid [51].   [128] ibid [53].

[129] See e.g. _Kleanthous v Paphitis_ [2011] EWHC 2287 (Ch), [2012] BCC 676, where the derivative claimant was seeking a share purchase order, which is the usual remedy in unfair prejudice cases.

[130] CA 2006, s 263(4).   [131] _Smith v Croft (No 2)_ [1988] Ch 114 (Ch) 185.

[132] CA 2006, s 263(2)(c).

larger companies. As Lord Hodgson stated when the Company Law Reform Bill was being debated, the inclusion of s 263(4) 'will help to address concerns that it is not practicable or desirable for major quoted companies to ask shareholders formally to approve directors' commercial decisions'.[133]

15.2.3.4 **Costs**

A member considering commencing a derivative claim will need to consider the issue of costs. The CA 2006 provides no guidance on who pays the costs of a derivative claim, but the general rule in UK civil litigation is that the losing party pays his costs and the costs of the successful party.[134] However, as regards derivative claims, this rule is problematic as the benefits of a successful claim go to the company and not the derivative claimant. Accordingly, if the claimant succeeds, the company benefits, but if he loses, he may be required to pay his costs and those of the other party. This would likely act as a significant disincentive to the bringing of derivative claims, and so the Court of Appeal stated that:

> where a shareholder has in good faith and on reasonable grounds sued as plaintiff in a minority shareholder's action, the benefit of which, if successful, will accrue to the company and only indirectly to the plaintiff as a member of the company, and which it would have been reasonable for an independent board of directors to bring in the company's name, it would . . . clearly be a proper exercise of judicial discretion to order the company to pay the plaintiff's costs.[135]

From this, it follows that the court has the discretion to order the company to pay the costs of a derivative claim, and this is reflected in the Civil Procedure Rules which state that '[t]he court may order the company, body corporate or trade union for the benefit of which a derivative claim is brought to indemnify the claimant against liability for costs incurred in the permission application or in the derivative claim or both'.[136]

Where a derivative claim is brought against a director, then the company may agree to pay the director's costs. This could be regarded as a loan or a quasi-loan to the director and, as discussed, such transactions will normally require prior member approval. However, member approval is not required if, in the event of the director losing the case, the director repays the costs incurred by the company.[137] In larger companies, directors may have their costs covered by professional indemnity insurance.

 Loans and quasi-loans are discussed at 11.4.3.

15.3 **The unfair prejudice petition**

Part 30 of the CA 2006 consists of a mere six sections, yet it provides what is perhaps the most important member remedy. It is worth noting at the outset that, for reasons discussed at 15.3.6.2, the unfair prejudice remedy is of increased importance to members of private companies (indeed, almost all the key cases involve private companies). Section 994(1) allows a member to petition the court for a remedy on the ground:

(a) that the company's affairs are being or have been conducted in a manner that is unfairly prejudicial to the interests of members generally, or of some part of its members (including at least himself); or

---

[133] HL Deb 9 May 2006, vol 681, col 884.   [134] CPR 1998, r 44.2(2)(a).

[135] *Wallersteiner v Moir (No 2)* [1975] 2 WLR 389 (CA) 404 (Buckley LJ).   [136] CPR 1998, r 19.9E.

[137] CA 2006, s 205(1) and (2).

(b) that an actual or proposed act or omission of the company (including an act or omission on its behalf) is or would be so prejudicial.

Before discussing the unfair prejudice remedy, it is worth briefly looking at why the remedy was created and how it has evolved.

15.3.1 **The oppressive conduct remedy**

Prior to 1948, the only statutory remedy available to an aggrieved member was to petition the court for an order winding up the company. In many cases, such a drastic remedy would be inappropriate and so s 210 of the CA 1948 provided an 'alternative remedy to winding up in cases of oppression'. The oppressive conduct remedy has been described as 'a remarkable statutory innovation'[138] but, in practice, only a few cases succeeded as the remedy was restrictively interpreted by the courts and a successful petition required the petitioner to show that the facts of the case would justify winding up the company.[139] Accordingly, the Jenkins Committee recommended that the oppressive conduct remedy be replaced with a remedy based on unfairly prejudicial conduct, and a petitioner need not show that a winding up was justified[140] Such a remedy was (eventually) introduced by s 75 of the CA 1980. Section 75 was largely re-enacted as s 459 of the CA 1985, and s 459 was largely re-enacted by s 994 of the CA 2006. Accordingly, case law decided under ss 75 and 459 remains relevant today.

15.3.2 **The petitioner and respondent**

It is important to understand who has legal standing to commence an unfair prejudice petition (the 'petitioner'), and against whom an unfair prejudice petition may be commenced (the 'respondent').

15.3.2.1 **Who may petition the court?**

The following have standing to commence an unfair prejudice petition:

Section 112 is discussed at 13.1.

- Any member has standing to commence an unfair prejudice petition.[141] This would include nominee members,[142] as such persons fall within the definition of 'member' in s 112. Although s 994 was primarily designed for minority shareholders (and most petitions are brought by minority shareholders), a majority shareholder has standing to commence a petition,[143] although, the court may refuse to grant a remedy if the majority shareholder could use his majority shareholding to remedy the conduct himself[144] (e.g. by removing the directors).

- A person who is not a member may commence a petition if shares in the company have been transferred or transmitted to him by operation of law[145] (e.g. a trustee in bankruptcy).

---

138 Geoffrey Morse, *Palmer's Company Law* (Sweet & Maxwell 2018) para 8.3801.
139 CA 1948, s 210(2)(b) (now repealed).
140 Board of Trade, *Report of the Company Law Committee* (Cmnd 1749, 1962) para 212.
141 CA 2006, s 994(1). Former members do not have standing (*Re a Company* [1986] 2 All ER 253 (Ch)).
142 *Atlasview Ltd v Brightview Ltd* [2004] EWHC 1056 (Ch), [2004] 2 BCLC 191.
143 *Re Legal Negotiators Ltd* [1999] BCC 547 (CA).
144 *Re Baltic Real Estate Ltd* [1992] BCC 629 (Ch).   145 CA 2006, s 994(2).

- In several circumstances (such as where he has received a report under s 437 of the CA 1985), the Secretary of State is empowered to commence an unfair prejudice petition.[146] Such petitions are extremely rare and reported cases only appear to refer to one instance where such a petition was successful.[147]

- As ss 994–6 of the CA 2006 apply to limited liability partnerships (LLPs),[148] a member of an LLP can also commence an unfair prejudice petition. However, the members of an LLP may by unanimous agreement exclude a member's right to commence an unfair prejudice petition (in practice, the LLP agreements of most larger LLPs contain such an exclusion).

15.3.2.2 Against whom may a petition be brought?

As noted, s 994 allows a member to petition the court for a remedy on the ground:

(a) that the company's affairs are being or have been conducted in a manner that is unfairly prejudicial to the interests of members generally, or of some part of its members (including at least himself); or

(b) that an actual or proposed act or omission of the company (including an act or omission on its behalf) is or would be so prejudicial.

There are, accordingly, two grounds on which to base a claim, and the two grounds are aimed at differing respondents. In *Graham v Every*,[149] Arden LJ stated that (b) requires an act or omission of the company and therefore 'the petitioner must identify something which the company does or fails to do'.[150] Ground (a), however, is not subject to this limitation and so a claim on that ground can be based on the actions of other persons (notably directors or members). This means that, between the two grounds, claims can be brought against a range of persons including the company (or an LLP), directors, members,[151] and even third parties (e.g. third parties who have 'improperly assisted'[152] in the act complained of). Most cases are either brought against a director (or directors) and/or a controlling member (or members).

Arden LJ noted that, irrespective of who the respondent is, the petitioner will need to demonstrate that the respondent's conduct amounts to conduct of the company's affairs.[153] This is the first of several key phrases within s 994 that requires further discussion.

15.3.3 'The company's affairs'

Section 994 applies where 'the company's affairs' are being conducted in an unfairly prejudicial manner. From this, it follows that an s 994 petition will fail if it is brought against a member or director who is acting in a private capacity (i.e. in relation to his own affairs, and not those of the company).

---

[146] ibid s 995.   [147] *Re Scitec Group Ltd* [2012] EWHC 661 (Ch).

[148] Limited Liability Partnerships (Application of Companies Act 2006) Regulations 2009, SI 2009/1804, reg 48.

[149] [2014] EWCA Civ 191, [2014] BCC 376.   [150] ibid [37].

[151] A claim can also, in appropriate cases, be made against former members (*Re Little Olympian Each Ways Ltd (No 3)* [1995] 1 BCLC 636 (Ch)). This prevents members from avoiding a petition by selling their shares.

[152] *Re Fahey Developments Ltd* [1996] BCC 320 (Ch) 325 (Charles Aldous QC).

[153] *Graham v Every* [2014] EWCA Civ 191, [2014] BCC 376 [37].

See Robert Goddard, 'An Oppressed Majority?' (1999) 20 Co Law 241.

 Quasi-partnerships are discussed at 15.4.1.2.

Re Legal Costs Negotiators Ltd [1999] BCC 547 (CA) [154]

FACTS: The four directors of Legal Costs Negotiators Ltd ('LCN') each held 25 per cent of LCN's shares and were employees of LCN. Due to alleged mismanagement, one of the directors (Hateley) was dismissed as an employee and later resigned as a director. The other three directors offered to purchase Hateley's shares at fair value, but Hateley refused. The three directors commenced an unfair prejudice petition against Hateley. They argued that LCN was a quasi-partnership and so there was a legitimate expectation that 'each would contribute and continue to contribute to the company and be engaged full time on its business'.[155] As Hateley was no longer a director or employee, he was in breach of this expectation and relief should therefore be granted (namely an order requiring Hateley to sell his shares). Hateley sought to have the petition struck out.

HELD: Peter Gibson LJ stated that Hateley's 'retention of those shares is not conduct of the company's affairs ...'.[156] The alleged mismanagement of Hateley did concern the company's affairs, but 'that conduct had been terminated by his removal as employee and director'.[157] Accordingly, the claim against Hateley was struck out.

However, it is important to note that what amounts to 'the company's affairs' is highly fact-specific and an act or omission that might not normally be regarded as the company's affairs might become so on the facts of the case, as the following case demonstrates.

 See Andrew Bowen, 'Unfairly Prejudicial Conduct, Pre-Emption Clauses and Good Faith' (2014) 132 Bus LB 1.

Graham v Every [2014] EWCA Civ 191

FACTS: Graham and several other individuals were directors and members of Below Zero London Ltd ('BZL'). The directors were not paid a salary, but were remunerated by way of dividend. A share pre-emption agreement existed between the members which provided that if a member wished to sell his shares, he was to first offer them to the existing shareholders pro rata. The relationship between Graham and the other directors soured and he was removed as a director. He commenced a s 994 petition stating that two of the respondents (one of which was Every) had not complied with the pre-emption agreement and had sold their shares to an outsider without first offering them to the existing shareholders. As he would have bought these shares if offered them,[158] he argued that this amounted to unfairly prejudicial conduct. At first instance, Graham's claim was struck out because breach of the pre-emption agreement did not amount to conduct of the affairs of the company. Graham appealed.

HELD: Graham's appeal was allowed. Arden LJ noted that 'a mere breach of a pre-emption agreement would not in itself constitute the conduct of the affairs of a company or an act of omission of the company within section 994'.[159] However, as the directors were remunerated by way of dividend:

the size of a director's shareholding would dictate his reward for his work on the Company's business. How directors were to be remunerated and the Company's distributions policy are

[154] See also *Re Unisoft Group Ltd (No 3)* [1994] BCC 766 (Ch); *Re Leeds United Holdings plc* [1997] BCC 131 (Ch).

[155] [1999] BCC 547 (CA) 549.   [156] ibid 552.   [157] ibid.

[158] An important point was that, if Graham had been able to acquire these shares, his shareholding would have increased to 27 per cent, which would have allowed him to defeat a special resolution.

[159] [2014] EWCA Civ 191, [2014] BCC 376 [30].

within the conduct of the company's affairs. So, by denying Mr Graham's pre-emption right at a time when Mr Graham was still a director, Mr Every was arguably interfering with the way in which the parties had agreed that the Company would remunerate its directors.[160]

In some cases, the courts have adopted a rather broad interpretation of what constitutes 'the company's affairs', as the following case starkly demonstrates.

Re Home & Office Fire Extinguishers Ltd [2012] EWHC 917 (Ch)

FACTS: Two brothers, Simon and Guy, were the only directors and members of Home and Office Fire Extinguishers Ltd ('HOFE'). Simon asked Guy for an advance on his salary, but Guy refused as HOFE was struggling financially. A dispute resulted in a physical altercation between the brothers, with each alleging that the other attacked him with a hammer. Simon was charged with intent to cause grievous bodily harm and was prohibited from going near HOFE's offices. Guy purported to terminate Simon's employment. Simon was subsequently acquitted. Each commenced a s 994 petition against the other, seeking an order compelling the other to sell his shares.

HELD: Nicholas Strauss QC held that, based on the evidence, Simon had initiated the attack. He went on to state that Simon's conduct related to the affairs of HOFE because his conduct 'was a breach of the implied understanding that he and Guy, would act properly and in good faith towards each other, and it was also a single event which made it impossible for them to continue their association as directors of, and shareholders in, the Company'[161] and it was 'essentially a reaction to a decision taken by Guy concerning the Company's finances'.[162] Accordingly, Simon was ordered to sell his shares to Guy.

The final issue to be discussed is whether 'the company's affairs' must refer to the company that the petitioner is a member of. The following case demonstrates that a member in a parent company may be able to bring a claim in relation to the activities of a subsidiary.[163]

Re Citybranch Group Ltd [2004] EWCA Civ 815

FACTS: Gross and Rackind each held 50 per cent of the shares in Citybranch Ltd ('Citybranch') and were its only directors. The business of Citybranch was conducted entirely by three wholly owned subsidiaries (of which Gross and Rackind were also directors). A dispute arose and Rackind sought to wind up Citybranch. Gross responded by alleging that Rackind had breached his duties in relation to two of the subsidiaries and this unfairly prejudiced Gross's interests as a member. Rackind argued that the petition should be struck out as the conduct complained of related to Citybranch's subsidiaries and not Citybranch itself, and Gross was not a member of any of the subsidiaries.

See Robert Goddard and Hans C Hirt, 'Section 459 and Corporate Groups' [2005] JBL 247.

---

[160] ibid [40].   [161] [2012] EWHC 917 (Ch) [72].   [162] ibid.

[163] The opposite is also true, so a member of a subsidiary may be able to bring a claim based on the activities of the parent (*Scottish Co-operative Wholesale Society Ltd v Meyer* [1959] AC 324 (HL)).

HELD: Sir Martin Nourse stated that 'the expression "the affairs of the company" is one of the widest import which can include the affairs of a subsidiary'.[164] He went on to state, 'I would hold that the affairs of a subsidiary can also be the affairs of its holding company, especially where, as here, the directors of the holding company, which necessarily controls the affairs of the subsidiary, also represent a majority of the directors of the subsidiary'.[165] Accordingly, the court refused to strike out Gross's petition.

COMMENT: Unsurprisingly, the decision has been criticized and it has been argued that the approach adopted in *Citybranch* 'continues a judicial trend favouring rights and expectations of shareholders and disregarding the separate legal personality of companies'.[166] The case also leaves many questions unanswered. For example, it was accepted that the four companies in *Citybranch* effectively operated a quasi-partnership, but it is not clear whether the *ratio* of *Citybranch* only applies to such companies.

15.3.4 'Actual or proposed acts or omissions'

Most s 994 petitions are based on actual acts or omissions (i.e. those that have already occurred). In such case, the CA 2006 does not require that the petitioner was a member at the time the conduct in question occurred (e.g. a petition can be based on conduct that occurred before the petitioner became a member).[167] However, in such a case, no petition can lie if the members consented to the conduct at the time it occurred.[168]

The oppressive conduct remedy under the CA 1948 did not allow a member to commence proceedings to prevent proposed oppressive conduct. Instead, he had to 'sit idly by and wait for it to materialise before petitioning the court'.[169] The problem with limiting the remedy to past acts was that if the act resulted in the company's liquidation, then it would be too late for the situation to be rectified. This flaw has been remedied as s 994(1)(b) refers to a 'proposed act', clearly indicating that s 994 is not limited to acts that have already occurred. However, the courts have stated that 'mere fears as to the future'[170] cannot found the basis of an unfair prejudice claim.

The oppression remedy under the CA 1948 did not expressly cover omissions, but the House of Lords remedied this lacuna by stating that 'the affairs of a company can . . . be conducted oppressively by the directors doing nothing to defend its interests when they ought to do something'.[171] Section 994(1)(b) expressly states that omissions can constitute unfairly prejudicial conduct.

15.3.5 'Unfairly prejudicial'

For the petition to succeed, the conduct complained of must be 'unfairly prejudicial'. The CA 2006 does not provide any guidance on what amounts to unfair prejudice apart from stating that a removal of a company's auditor shall be regarded as unfair

---

[164] [2004] EWCA Civ 815, [2005] 1 WLR 3505 [26].   [165] ibid.

[166] Robert Goddard and Hans C Hirt, 'Section 459 and Corporate Groups' [2005] JBL 247, 252.

[167] *Lloyd v Casey* [2002] 1 BCLC 454 (Ch).

[168] *Re Batesons Hotels (1958)* [2013] EWHC 2530 (Ch), [2014] 1 BCLC 507.

[169] David Milman, 'Anticipated Unfair Prejudice' (1987) 8 Co Law 272, 272.

[170] *Re Astec (BSR) plc* [1999] BCC 59 (Ch) 81 (Jonathan Parker J).

[171] *Scottish Co-operative Wholesale Society Ltd v Meyer* [1959] AC 324 (HL) 367 (Lord Denning).

prejudice if the removal is on the grounds of divergence of opinions on accounting treatment or audit procedures, or any other improper grounds.[172] Accordingly, what constitutes unfairly prejudicial conduct has been left to the courts to determine.

When determining whether conduct is unfairly prejudicial, the courts adopt an objective approach.[173] As a result:

> it is not necessary for the petitioner to show that the persons who have de facto control of the company have acted as they did in the conscious knowledge that this was unfair to the petitioner or that they were acting in bad faith; the test, I think, is whether a reasonable bystander observing the consequences of their conduct, would regard it as having unfairly prejudiced the petitioner's interests.[174]

The courts have not sought to apply a technical or limited interpretation of the words 'unfairly prejudicial', and have stated that '[t]he words "unfairly prejudicial" are general words and they should be applied flexibly to meet the circumstances of the particular case . . .'.[175] As the words 'unfairly prejudicial' are general words, the courts have not sought to impose a general standard or test, but it has been emphasized that the courts' discretion must be judiciously exercised. In *O'Neill v Phillips*,[176] Lord Hoffmann (who was involved in many of the major unfair prejudice cases) stated that Parliament chose the concept of fairness to:

> free the court from technical considerations of legal right and to confer a wide power to do what appeared just and equitable. But this does not mean that the court can do whatever the individual judge happens to think fair. The concept of fairness must be applied judicially and the content which it is given by the courts must be based upon rational principles . . ..[177]

The conduct complained of 'must be both prejudicial (in the sense of causing prejudice or harm to the relevant interest) and also unfairly so: conduct may be unfair without being prejudicial or prejudicial without being unfair, and it is not sufficient if the conduct only satisfies one of these tests'.[178] In the following case, the petition failed because the conduct complained of was unfair, but not prejudicial.

Rock (Nominees) Ltd v RCO (Holdings) plc [2004] EWCA Civ 118

FACTS: Rock (Nominees) Ltd ('Rock') held 2.48 per cent of the shares in RCO (Holdings) plc ('RCO'). As a result of a takeover, ISS Brentwood plc ('Brentwood') acquired 96.4 per cent of the shares in RCO. The purpose of the takeover was to acquire control of a wholly-owned subsidiary of RCO.

[172] CA 2006, s 994(1A).   [173] *Re Guidezone Ltd* [2000] 2 BCLC 321 (Ch).
[174] *Re Bovey Hotel Ventures Ltd* (Ch, 31 July 1981 (Slade J), quoted with approval in *Re RA Noble & Sons (Clothing) Ltd* [1983] BCLC 273 (Ch) 290–91 (Nourse J). It should be noted that in *Re Saul D Harrison and Sons plc* [1995] 1 BCLC 14 (CA), Hoffmann LJ expressed some doubts as to whether a 'reasonable bystander' test was appropriate.
[175] *Re Saul D Harrison and Sons plc* [1995] 1 BCLC 14 (CA) 30 (Neill LJ).
[176] [1999] 1 WLR 1092 (HL).   [177] ibid 1098.
[178] *Re Saul D Harrison and Sons plc* [1995] 1 BCLC 14 (CA) 31 (Neill LJ).

Accordingly, it was agreed that the shares in the subsidiary would be sold to ISS (UK) Ltd (a member of the same corporate group as Brentwood). Four directors of RCO were also directors of ISS (UK) Ltd. Rock commenced an unfair prejudice petition, alleging that the shares in the subsidiary were sold at an undervalue and that the four directors were conflicted and so were in breach of their fiduciary duties.

HELD: The Court agreed with the first-instance judge, who stated that the four directors were 'in a position of hopeless conflict'[179] and so had breached their fiduciary duties. Accordingly, the directors had acted unfairly. However, looking at all the evidence, the Court was satisfied that the price paid for the subsidiary's shares was 'the best price reasonably obtainable'.[180] Accordingly, 'no harm was in fact done and no damage or prejudice caused'[181] and so Rock's petition was dismissed.

Conversely, in the following case, the conduct complained of was prejudicial, but not unfair.

Re Metropolis Motorcycles Ltd [2006] EWHC 364 (Ch)

FACTS: Hale and Waldock went into partnership. In 1994, they incorporated Metropolis Motorcycles Ltd ('MM'), and it was decided to transfer the assets of the partnership to MM. In 1997, Hale moved away, leaving Waldock to largely manage the business by himself. Hale wished to return and, in 2000, it was agreed that Hale could draw £6,000 per month from the business's profits, but Waldock would continue to manage the business. Prior to the partnership's assets being transferred to MM in 2001, Waldock realized that the business's finances had deteriorated. Hale only discovered the deterioration after he signed the agreement transferring the partnership's assets to MM. Following the transfer, Waldock stopped Hale drawing from the company's profits, and ran MM without any reference to Hale. Hale argued that, in failing to inform him of the deterioration of the business's finances, Waldock misled him into signing the transfer agreement and this, along with stopping Hale's drawings of profits, amounted to unfair prejudice.

HELD: Hale's petition was dismissed. Mann J stated that 'there are elements of prejudice to Mr Hale in the manner in which the company's affairs have been conducted . . .'[182] However, he held that there was not the requisite level of unfairness, largely due to Hale's 'own decision to withdraw from active participation and to leave himself in essentially as an investor'.[183]

It has been stated that '[t]he requirement of prejudice means that the conduct must be shown to have done the members harm and I believe harm in a commercial sense, not in a merely emotional sense'.[184] This does not mean that the harm sustained must be financial. For example, '[i]t may be enough to show that the rights of the petitioning member have been infringed without showing that that led to any financial loss'.[185] Similarly,

---

[179] [2003] EWHC 936 (Ch), [2003] BCLC 493 [101] (Peter Smith J).

[180] [2004] EWCA Civ 118, [2004] BCC 466 [76] (Jonathan Parker LJ).   [181] ibid [79].

[182] [2006] EWHC 364 (Ch), [2007] 1 BCLC 520 [89].   [183] ibid [91].

[184] *Re Unisoft Group Ltd (No 3)* [1994] BCC 766 (Ch) 767 (Harman J).

[185] *Re Coroin Ltd* [2013] EWCA Civ 781, [2014] BCC 14 [16] (Arden LJ).

it has been held that, in a quasi-partnership, a breakdown in the partnership relation-ship can amount to unfair prejudice, even if no tangible harm has occurred.[186] However, '[w]here the acts complained of have no adverse financial consequence, it may be more difficult to establish relevant prejudice'.[187]

It is clear from the above that determining whether unfair prejudice is present is strongly based on the facts of the case. As Lord Hoffmann stated, '[al]though fairness is a notion which can be applied to all kinds of activities, its content will depend upon the context in which it is being used. Conduct which is perfectly fair between competing businessmen may not be fair between members of a family'.[188] Examples of the type of conduct that could constitute unfair prejudice will now be discussed, but note that these categories are by no means exhaustive (and can overlap).

15.3.5.1 Serious mismanagement

In *Re Elgindata Ltd*,[189] Warner J stated that 'the court would ordinarily be very reluc-tant to accept that managerial decisions could amount to unfairly prejudicial conduct'.[190] Accordingly, mismanagement will normally not amount to unfair prejudice. However, he went on to say, 'I do not doubt that in appropriate cases it is open to the court to find that serious mismanagement of a company's business constitutes conduct that is unfairly prejudi-cial to the interests of minority shareholders'.[191] The following case provides such an example.

Re Macro (Ipswich) Ltd [1994] 2 BCLC 354 (Ch)

FACTS: The case concerned two companies involved in the business of letting residential properties and garages. Thompson was a director and shareholder in both companies. The petitioners were members of both companies and alleged that Thompson had engaged in serious mismanagement over a prolonged period.

HELD: Arden J listed the various forms of mismanagement that had occurred:

I am satisfied that the companies suffered prejudice in consequence of failure to have a planned maintenance programme, the failure to supervise repairs, the failure to inspect properties regularly, the failure to let on protected shorthold tenancies, the taking of commissions from builders doing work for the companies by employees of Thompson's, the charging of excessive management charges and secretarial salary and the mismanagement of litigation.[192]

She went on to note that 'several of the acts of mismanagement which the plaintiffs have identified were repeated over many years'[193] and therefore held that 'those acts (and Mr Thompson's failures to prevent or rectify them) are sufficiently significant and serious to justify intervention by the court under [s 996]'.[194]

COMMENT: Thompson's mismanagement would likely constitute a breach of duty. Accordingly, it has been argued that mismanagement will only amount to unfairly prejudicial conduct where the director in question breached the duties found in ss 172 or 174.[195] However, the courts have repeatedly referred to serious mismanagement as a separate ground of unfair prejudice.

See John Lowry, 'The Elasticity of Unfair Prejudice: Stretching the Ambit of the Companies Act 1985, s 459' (1995) 3 LMCLQ 337.

---

[186] *Gerrard v Koby* [2004] EWCA Civ 1763 (Ch), [2005] BCC 181.
[187] *Re Coroin Ltd* [2012] EWHC 2343 (Ch) [631] (David Richards J).
[188] *O'Neill v Phillips* [1999] 1 WLR 1092 (HL) 1098.   [189] [1991] BCLC 959 (Ch).
[190] ibid 993.   [191] ibid.   [192] [1994] 2 BCLC 354 (Ch) 404.   [193] ibid 406.
[194] ibid.
[195] David Kershaw, *Company Law in Context: Text and Materials* (2nd edn, OUP 2012) 695.

15.3.5.2 **Abuse of a controlling position**

Many successful unfair prejudice petitions involve the directors or controlling share-holders abusing their position in some way. Very often, this will result in them improp-erly obtaining for themselves some form of advantage, usually at the expense of the minority shareholders. Examples include:

- where the directors of a company sell that company's assets at an undervalue to another company they control;[196]
- where the directors of company A and company B transfer business from company A to company B in order to reduce the profits distributed to shareholders in company A;[197]
- where the directors urge the members to accept a takeover bid from a company in which they have a favourable interest, whilst misleading the members into rejecting a more favourable rival bid;[198]
- where the directors pay themselves excessive remuneration,[199] or remuneration paid in breach of the company's articles[200] (such cases are often accompanied by the directors rec-ommending low or no dividend payments);[201]
- where the directors and majority shareholders decide not to pay out a declared dividend and instead distribute the profits to themselves as management fees;[202]
- a failure to consider paying dividends,[203] or a refusal to pay higher dividends for a pro-longed period despite profits being available.[204]

15.3.5.3 **Breach of directors' duties**

Several of the above cases concerning abuse of a controlling position involved directors acting in breach of their duties. For example, several cases involve directors who divert company assets or business to another company they control, which would likely be a breach of the duty to avoid conflicts of interest. Accordingly, it is clear that a breach of the general duties can amount to unfairly prejudicial conduct. However, it is important to note that most cases concerning breach of duty involve private companies and the courts appear more reluctant to hold that a breach of duty in a public company amounts to unfairly prejudicial conduct.[205]

15.3.5.4 **Breach of statutory rights or the constitution**

Breach of certain statutory rights or constitutional provisions may amount to unfairly prejudicial conduct, as the following case demonstrates.

---

[196] *Re Little Olympian Each Ways Ltd (No 3)* [1995] 1 BCLC 636 (Ch).
[197] *Re London School of Electronics Ltd* [1986] Ch 211 (Ch).
[198] *Re a Company (No 008699 of 1985)* [1986] BCLC 382 (Ch).
[199] *Re a Company (No 002612 of 1984)* [1986] 2 BCC 99,453 (CA).
[200] *Irvine v Irvine (No 1)* [2006] EWHC 406 (Ch), [2007] 1 BCLC 349.
[201] *Re a Company (No 004415 of 1996)* [1997] 1 BCLC 479 (Ch).
[202] *Grace v Biagioli* [2005] EWCA Civ 1222, [2006] BCC 85.
[203] *Re McCarthy Surfacing Ltd* [2008] EWHC 2279 (Ch), [2009] 1 BCLC 622.
[204] *Re Sam Weller & Sons Ltd* [1990] Ch 682 (Ch) (same dividend paid for 37 years, despite profits being available to pay higher dividends).
[205] See e.g. *Re Carrington Viyella plc* (1983) 1 BCC 98951 (Ch) (failure to obtain member approval for director's service contract over two years did not amount to unfair prejudice).

> ### Re a Company (No 00789 of 1987) [1990] BCLC 384 (Ch)
>
> **FACTS:** Kelly was the controlling shareholder and chair of a company that ran a football club. Due to Kelly's managerial failings, the company did not prepare proper financial accounts each year, and it failed to hold the required annual general meetings. Further, when extraordinary meetings were called, inadequate notice was provided and the statutory procedures for short notice were not complied with. A member commenced an unfair prejudice petition.
>
> **HELD:** Harman J stated that the company's affairs were 'managed under Mr Kelly's control with a very large near total disregard of the requirements of the Companies Act and of the articles . . .'.[206] Consequently, the members 'were wholly deprived of any opportunity to consider the affairs of the company, to vote on the election or re-election of directors, or in any other way to know what was going on'.[207] This amounted to unfairly prejudicial conduct and so the court ordered that Kelly should sell his shares to the petitioner.

However, it is important to note that 'trivial and technical infringements' are not intended to give rise to an unfair prejudice petition.[208] The rationale behind this was stated by Purle J:

> isolated trivial complaints, even when in breach of some legal requirement, having no impact on the value of the petitioner's shares, or upon any realistic objective assessment of the integrity and competence of the board, will not be visited by the threat of an unfair prejudice petition, but should be left to be dealt with by the regime of sanctions and other remedies the law provides.[209]

However, he did go on to state that where statute or the constitution lay down absolute standards, then the court should respect those 'and not be too ready to dismiss anything other than minor, inadvertent departures as "trivial"'.[210]

15.3.5.5 Criminal conduct

Generally, the civil law cannot be used to enforce a breach of criminal law. This is because '[t]he criminal law is best enforced directly by courts of criminal jurisdiction, who have to try criminal cases in accordance with criminal procedure and in recognition of the protections afforded to a citizen by our system of criminal justice'.[211] However, the courts have held that this general rule does not apply to unfair prejudice petitions,[212] and so criminal conduct can amount to unfairly prejudicial conduct.

15.3.5.6 Exclusion from management

In some cases, excluding a member from participating in the management of a company can amount to unfair prejudice. The issue that arises here is whether a right to participate in management is regarded as a membership interest. This will be discussed next.

---

206 [1990] BCLC 384 (Ch) 388.   207 ibid 393.
208 *Re Saul D Harrison & Sons plc* [1994] BCC 475 (CA) 489 (Hoffmann LJ).
209 *Re Sunrise Radio Ltd* [2009] EWHC 2983 (Ch), [2010] 1 BCLC 367 [7].   210 ibid [8].
211 *Bermuda Cablevision Ltd v Colica Trust Co Ltd* [1998] AC 198 (PC) 209 (Lord Steyn).   212 ibid.

15.3.6 'Interests of members'

The conduct must unfairly prejudice the 'the interests of members generally or some part of its members (including at least [the petitioner])'. Defining the extent of the members' interests has proven to be a complex issue that has generated a substantial body of case law. What is clear is that a member's interests are wider than a member's rights. The rights of a member are found in the relevant legislation and the company's constitution, but a member's interests go beyond this,[213] as the following case demonstrates.

Re Sam Weller & Sons Ltd [1990] Ch 682 (Ch)

FACTS: Sam Weller & Sons Ltd ('SW'), a small family-run company, had significant cash reserves, including over £464,000 in undistributed profits, but it had paid the same low dividend (14 pence per share) for the previous 37 years.[214] SW had one director, Sam, who was paid a salary (his two sons were also employees of the company). The petitioners, who were members of the company, commenced an unfair prejudice petition alleging that, *inter alia*, the low dividend payments constituted unfairly prejudicial conduct. SW and Sam sought to strike out the petition on the ground that the dividend policy affected all the members equally, and so did not prejudice the petitioners.

HELD: The strike-out application was dismissed. Whilst a policy of low dividend payments did not breach the members' rights, '[t]he word "interests" is wider than a term such as "rights"... Parliament recognised that members may have different interests, even if their rights as members are the same'.[215] Peter Gibson J stated that it may be in the interests of Sam to retain the major part of the profits in order to enhance the value of his own shareholding, but his interests are not the same as those of other members and that:

> It may well be in the interests of the other shareholders, including the petitioners, that a more immediate benefit should accrue to them in the form of larger dividends. As their only income from the company is by way of dividend, their interests may be not only prejudiced by the policy of low dividend payments, but unfairly prejudiced.[216]

COMMENT: This case is not authority for the proposition that the payment of low dividends will amount to unfairly prejudicial conduct. Peter Gibson J stated:

> I do not intend to suggest that a shareholder who does not receive an income from the company except by way of dividend is always entitled to complain whenever the company is controlled by persons who do derive an income from the company and when profits are not fully distributed by way of dividend.... I have no doubt the court will view with great caution allegations of unfair prejudice on this ground.[217]

However, here the facts of the case were 'striking because of the absence of any increase in the dividend for so many years and because of the amount of accumulated profits and the amount of cash in hand'.[218]

---

[213] *Re a Company (No 00477 of 1986)* [1986] BCLC 376 (Ch).

[214] In the year in which the petition was brought, SW's profits were £36,330 and the dividend paid amounted to £2,520 (representing one-fourteenth of the company's profits).

[215] [1990] Ch 682 (Ch) 690 (Peter Gibson J).   [216] ibid 693.

[217] ibid.   [218] ibid.

It is important to note, however, that despite the breadth of the word 'interests', it must be the petitioner's interests as a member that have been unfairly prejudiced. However, as 15.3.6.1–15.3.6.3 demonstrates, the courts have interpreted this requirement broadly.

15.3.6.1 Member *qua* member

An oppressive conduct petition would only be successful if the member brought the claim in his capacity as a member (this is often referred to as member *qua* member), and this requirement was enforced strictly. Whilst this requirement still exists in relation to the unfair prejudice remedy, the courts take a much more flexible and broad approach as to when a member is acting *qua* member. As Lord Hoffmann stated, 'the requirement that prejudice must be suffered as a member should not be too narrow or technically construed'.[219] For example, the courts have held that in quasi-partnership companies, the interests of a member might extend to holding office as a director.[220] The following case provides a notable example of how flexibly the member *qua* member requirement has been applied.

➡ *qua*: 'in the capacity of'

 Gamlestaden Fastigheter AB v Baltic Partners Ltd [2007] UKPC 26[221]

📖 See Tony Singla, 'Unfair Prejudice in the Privy Council' (2007) 123 LQR 542.

FACTS: Gamlestaden Fastigheter AB ('GF') entered into a joint venture with a man named Karlsten. The venture operated through Baltic Partners Ltd ('Baltic'). GF held 22 per cent of the shares in Baltic and, in order to finance the joint venture, it had also made substantial loans to Baltic over a two-year period. GF alleged that Karlsten and others had withdrawn substantial funds from the venture with the approval of Baltic's directors, but that no consideration had been provided for the withdrawals. GF alleged that this constituted unfairly prejudicial conduct and argued that Baltic's directors should compensate Baltic for the withdrawals that they authorized. At the time of the hearing, Baltic was insolvent and its directors therefore argued that the payment of compensation to Baltic would benefit GF in its capacity as a creditor, but would not benefit it in its capacity as a member and, as such, the conduct did not affect its interests as a member. At first instance, this was accepted and GF's petition was struck out. GF appealed.

HELD: The Privy Council allowed GF's appeal, with Lord Scott stating:

[I]n a case where an investor in a joint venture company has, in pursuance of the joint venture agreement, invested not only in subscribing for shares but also in advancing loan capital, the investor ought not . . . to be precluded from the grant of relief . . . on the ground that the relief would benefit the investor only as loan creditor and not as member.[222]

COMMENT: This case clearly demonstrates how flexibly the courts are prepared to apply the member *qua* member requirement, but it does not abolish it. Lord Scott stated that, in many cases, a failure to bring a claim *qua* member 'might justifiably lead to a refusal of relief'.[223] Another important point to note is that GF did not seek compensation for itself, but on behalf of Baltic. GF therefore enforced a right on behalf of Baltic, which would normally be prohibited by the rule in *Foss v Harbottle*. A prior derivative action had failed on the ground that the case did not come within any of the common law exceptions to *Foss*. To allow GF to use the unfair prejudice remedy to obtain relief for Baltic confirms that a principal reason for the remedy's creation was to outflank the rule in *Foss v Harbottle* where fairness requires.

---

[219] *O'Neill v Phillips* [1999] 1 WLR 1092 (HL) 1105.
[220] *Re a Company (No 00477 of 1986)* [1986] 2 BCC 99171 (Ch).
[221] See also *R&H Electrical Ltd v Haden Bill Electrical Ltd* [1995] BCC 959 (Ch).
[222] [2007] UKPC 26, [2007] BCC 272 [37].   [223] ibid [36].

The courts have, however, only been prepared to relax the member *qua* member rule so far and the courts will still require the petitioner's interest to be sufficiently related to his membership. Thus, the courts have rejected claims where the petitioner has brought a claim in his capacity as an employee of the company,[224] or where a claim is brought in the capacity of a freeholder of land upon which a business was run, as opposed to a member of the company that runs the business.[225]

15.3.6.2 Equitable considerations

The members may agree that the company is to be run in a certain way, but that agreement may never be formalized or inserted into the constitution (and so may not constitute a membership 'right'). Hoffmann LJ referred to:

> a fundamental understanding between the shareholders which formed the basis of their association but was not put into contractual form, such as an assumption that each of the parties who has ventured his capital will also participate in the management of the company and receive the return on his investment in the form of salary rather than dividend.[226]

The issue here is whether breach of such an informal agreement or understanding constitutes a membership interest. Hoffmann LJ stated that adherence to such agreements or understandings can constitute a 'legitimate expectation'[227] of the members that can form the basis of an unfair prejudice petition. Lord Hoffmann has since stated that use of the phrase 'legitimate expectations' was a mistake and instead the court is recognizing 'equitable principles' or 'equitable considerations'.[228] The only unfair prejudice petition to ever reach the House of Lords[229] demonstrates the courts' approach.

See Dan D Prentice and Jennifer Payne, 'Section 459 and the Companies Act 1985: The House of Lords' View' (1999) 115 LQR 587.

O'Neill v Phillips [1999] 1 WLR 1092 (HL)

FACTS: Phillips was director of Pectel Ltd and owned all 100 of its shares. In 1985, he gave twenty-five shares to O'Neill (who was an employee) and made him a director. Phillips also retired from the board, leaving O'Neill as *de facto* managing director. Pectel's profits were split between Phillips (75 per cent) and O'Neill (25 per cent), but Phillips voluntarily gave up 25 per cent of his profits, so that their share of the profits was equal. The possibility of increasing O'Neill's shareholding to 50 per cent was also discussed, but never acted upon. In 1991, the business experienced difficulties and Phillips returned to oversee management. He offered O'Neill the opportunity to manage, under Phillips's direction, either the English or German branch of the business—O'Neill chose the German branch. Later in the year, Phillips claimed to be entitled once again to receive 75 per cent of the profits and O'Neill left the company, claiming unfair prejudice. The Court of Appeal held that O'Neill had a legitimate expectation that he would receive 50 per cent of the profits and would receive 50 per cent of the shares. Phillips appealed.

---

[224] *Re John Reid & Sons (Strucsteel) Ltd* [2003] EWHC 2329 (Ch), [2003] 2 BCLC 319.

[225] *Re JE Cade & Son Ltd* [1992] BCLC 213 (Ch).

[226] *Re Saul D Harrison and Sons plc* [1995] 1 BCLC 14 (CA) 19–20.   [227] ibid 19.

[228] *O'Neill v Phillips* [1990] 1 WLR 1092 (HL) 1099, 1102.

[229] No unfair prejudice case has yet to reach the Supreme Court.

> **HELD:** The House of Lords allowed Phillips's appeal. Lord Hoffmann stressed that:
>
> a member of a company will not ordinarily be entitled to complain of unfairness unless there has been some breach of the terms on which he agreed that the affairs of the company should be conducted. But ... there will be cases in which equitable considerations make it unfair for those conducting the affairs of the company to rely upon their strict legal powers. Thus unfairness may consist in a breach of the rules or in using the rules in a manner which equity would regard as contrary to good faith.[230]
>
> On the facts, the House held that O'Neill had not been excluded from management, nor had Phillips promised to transfer any shares to O'Neill (even if O'Neill had hopes of such a transfer). Further, Phillips had not promised that O'Neill would always receive 50 per cent of the profits. Rather, O'Neill had, at most, been promised 50 per cent of the profits whilst he remained *de facto* managing director. Phillips had not breached the articles or memorandum, nor was there anything giving rise to the equitable considerations of which Lord Hoffmann spoke.

O'Neill shows that the petitioner must demonstrate that the facts give rise to the equitable considerations of which Lord Hoffmann spoke. This will be largely determined by the type of company in question. In larger companies (especially public companies), it is highly unlikely that the members will have informal agreements or understandings in place, and even if they do, they are unlikely to be enforced. As Jonathan Parker J noted:

> the concept of 'legitimate expectation' ... can have no place in the context of public listed companies .... If the market in a company's shares is to have any credibility, members of the public dealing in that market must it seems to me be entitled to proceed on the footing that the constitution of the company is as it appears in the company's public documents, unaffected by any extraneous equitable considerations and constraints.[231]

It is likely that this rule will also apply to most small companies too.[232] Equitable considerations are more likely to arise in quasi-partnerships, with the most common equitable consideration being a member's right to be involved in the company's management.

15.3.6.3 Exclusion from management

Although the category of equitable considerations is open-ended, the majority of unfair prejudice cases have involved members being excluded from management of a quasi-partnership. The exclusion from management is an excellent example of when equitable considerations will be relevant. In public companies and larger private companies, the members will have no expectations beyond those found in the company's constitution[233] and they will certainly not expect to participate in management (which is why most unfair prejudice cases involve private companies). Conversely, in quasi-partnerships, the members are likely to have an expectation that they will participate in management and so exclusion can amount to unfairly prejudice conduct.

---

[230] [1990] 1 WLR 1092 (HL) 1098–9.   [231] *Re Astec (BSR) plc* [1999] BCC 59 (Ch) 87.
[232] ibid 86.   [233] *Re Blue Arrow plc* [1987] BCLC 585 (Ch).

Re Ghyll Beck Driving Range Ltd [1993] BCLC 1126 (Ch)

FACTS: Betts agreed with three other persons to build a golf driving range, with each person agreeing to put £25,000 into the venture. A company, Ghyll Beck Driving Range Ltd ('GB'), was incorporated with all four becoming directors and each holding one share. Two of the directors (including Betts) put in the £25,000 agreed, but the other two directors (the Padleys) did not and failed to contribute sufficiently to GB's management due to business commitments elsewhere. This culminated in Betts and one of the Padleys having a physical altercation at the driving range. Thereafter, Betts was excluded from the management of GB and so he commenced an unfair prejudice petition against the other three directors.

HELD: Vinelott J stated that the Padleys had engaged in a dishonest attempt to escape making their full contribution and that one of the Padley's manufactured evidence during the trial. Accordingly, he held that, following the altercation, Betts 'could no longer trust his co-participants to deal fairly with him'[234] and had been unfairly excluded from management. Accordingly, Betts' petition succeeded and the respondents were ordered to purchase his shares.

The expectation to manage must be legitimate: a mere hope that the company's affairs will be run in a certain way will be insufficient and the court will only seek to enforce what was actually agreed. As Lord Hoffmann stated, the unfair prejudice remedy 'enables the court to give full effect to the terms and understandings on which the members of the company become associated but not to rewrite them'.[235] Even if the petitioner does have an expectation to manage, the facts of the case may lead the court to conclude that his exclusion was not unfairly prejudicial, especially if his own actions contributed to his exclusion.

Woolwich v Milne [2003] EWHC 414 (Ch)[236]

FACTS: Woolwich and three other persons formed a television production company called Twenty Twenty Productions Ltd ('TT'). Woolwich had a reputation as a harsh taskmaster and had, on several occasions, engaged in bullying conduct towards TT's employees. He was warned about his conduct by the other directors, and told that his conduct placed TT's survival in jeopardy as it exposed TT to potential litigation. Despite this, he continued to engage in aggressive and intimidatory conduct towards the employees. A disciplinary hearing was called, but Woolwich did not attend. The other three directors used their shareholdings to remove Woolwich from office, and later decided to sell their shares in TT to a new company in which they would retain a majority holding. They did not offer to buy Woolwich's shares as he stated he would only accept an offer in excess of 10 times the valuation obtained by the other members. Woolwich alleged that his exclusion from management and the failure of the respondents to make a reasonable offer for his shares amounted to unfairly prejudicial conduct.

---

[234] [1993] BCLC 1126 (Ch) 1134.

[235] *Re Postgate and Denby (Agencies) Ltd* [1987] BCLC 8 (Ch) 14.

[236] See also *Grace v Biagioli* [2005] EWCA Civ 1222, [2006] BCC 85 (excluded director put himself in a position of conflict); *Hawkes v Cuddy* [2007] EWCA Civ 1072, [2008] BCC 125 (excluded director was precluded by law from participating in management).

HELD: Woolwich's petition was dismissed. As regards Woolwich's exclusion from management, Sir Donald Rattee stated that:

> If it had not been for his own conduct, which led to his removal, I think that removal would probably have been unfair, but the fact is that he was not removed for no reason. He was removed because his fellow shareholders and directors concluded . . . that Mr. Woolwich's continued involvement in the management of the company's business, whether as director or employee, placed the efficient conduct of that business in serious jeopardy, in that he was treating staff in the production management department in a wholly inappropriate way . . . .

Unsurprisingly, given that Woolwich was seeking an outrageous sum for his shares, the failure of the respondents to offer to purchase Woolwich's shares was not deemed to constitute unfairly prejudicial conduct.

Given that exclusion from management cases in quasi-partnerships form most unfair prejudice petitions, the Law Commission recommended that, in certain circumstances, a shareholder's exclusion from the management of a private company would be presumed to constitute unfairly prejudicial conduct.[237] This recommendation was not acted upon.

15.3.7 Remedies

Where an unfair prejudice petition is successful, then s 996 provides the court with significant remedial flexibility, being able to make 'such order as it thinks fit for giving relief in respect of the matters complained of'.[238] From this, it is clear that 'the greatest possible flexibility was intended by the legislature to be given to the courts'.[239] Section 996(2) provides a non-exhaustive list of examples of orders that the court may make:

- an order regulating the conduct of the company's affairs in the future (e.g. in *Re HR Harmer Ltd*,[240] the Court of Appeal allowed an elderly director, who snooped on staff, ignored board decisions, and insulted customers, to remain as chair of the company, but deprived him of any executive role);

- an order requiring the company to refrain from doing an act complained of, or to perform an act that it has failed to perform (e.g. in *McGuinness v Bremner plc*,[241] a company that failed to hold a requisitioned meeting of the members was ordered to do so);

- an order authorizing civil proceedings to be brought in the name and on behalf of the company by such persons and on such terms as the court may direct;

- an order requiring the company not to make any, or any specified, alterations in its articles without the leave of the court;

- an order providing for the purchase of the shares of any members of the company by other members or by the company itself and, in the case of a purchase by the company itself, a reduction of the company's capital accordingly. This is by far the most common remedy sought and ordered under s 996.

> Share purchase orders are discussed in more detail at 15.3.7.1.

---

[237] Law Commission, *Shareholder Remedies* (Law Com No 246, 1997) paras 3.26–3.62.

[238] CA 2006, s 996(1).

[239] *Supreme Travels Ltd v Little Olympian Each-Ways Ltd* [1994] BCC 947 (Ch) 950 (Lindsay J).

[240] [1959] 1 WLR 62 (CA).   [241] (1988) 4 BCC 161 (Court of Session).

The petitioner must specify the relief that he seeks[242] and that relief must be 'appropriate to the unfairly prejudicial conduct of which the petitioner complains'.[243] Note, however, that if unfair prejudice is founded, the court is not bound to grant the petitioner the relief he sought.[244] Indeed, the court must consider the full range of remedies available and 'the relief need not be directed solely towards remedying the particular things that have happened',[245] although preventing future reoccurrences of the conduct complained of is clearly important. As Patten J stated, the court is 'entitled to look at the realities and practicalities of the overall situation, past, present and future'.[246] This breadth means that the court can take into account not just the effects that the conduct has had on the petitioning member, but the effects on third parties (such as creditors).[247] As Burnton LJ stated, 'I do not see why the court should close its eyes to the interests of others, and the effect of any order made under section 996 on them, although of course the weight to be given to their interests will depend on the circumstances.'[248]

Although a s 994 petition is a personal remedy, it is possible for a member to seek relief on behalf of the company, but only where the only purpose of the application is to obtain payment of a sum of money to the company, and there is some real financial benefit to be derived therefrom by the petitioning member.[249] The courts are wary of petitioners effectively trying to use the unfair prejudice remedy to avoid the procedural limitations of a derivative claim.

The unfair prejudice petition is not an equitable remedy. Accordingly, there is no requirement for the petitioner to 'come with clean hands',[250] but unmeritorious behaviour on the part of the petitioner might lead the court to conclude that the conduct complained of was not unfair, or that the remedy granted should be reduced.[251]

A s 994 petition is not subject to a limitation period, but because the granting of relief is discretionary, the court may refuse to grant a remedy where a substantial period has elapsed between the unfairly prejudicial conduct and the petition being brought.[252] The lack of a limitation period is likely due to the fact that '[u]nfair prejudice proceedings generally raise numerous factual issues entailing examination of events over a considerable period of time'.[253] The result of this is that 'trials of s 994 petitions can be long and complex'.[254] For example, in one case concerning shares worth around £24,600, the legal costs amounted to £320,000.[255] The case of *Re Freudiana Music Co Ltd*[256] took over

---

[242] Companies (Unfair Prejudice Applications) Proceedings Rules 2009, SI 2009/2469, art 3(2). The relief sought need not be specified if the petitioner is willing to accept what order the court thinks fit.

[243] *Re JE Cade & Son Ltd* [1991] BCC 360 (Ch) 368 (Warner J).

[244] *Re Full Cup International Trading Ltd* [1995] BCC 682 (Ch); *Hawkes v Cuddy* [2009] EWCA Civ 291, [2010] BCC 597.

[245] *Re a Company (No 008126 of 1989)* [1992] BCC 542 (Ch) 554 (Richard Sykes QC).

[246] *Grace v Biagioli* [2005] EWCA Civ 1222, [2006] BCC 85 [73].

[247] In *Hawkes v Cuddy* [2009] EWCA Civ 291, [2010] BCC 597 [84], Burnton LJ stated that the interests of creditors may, depending on the facts, 'be decisive in deciding what order should be made'.

[248] *Hawkes v Cuddy* [2009] EWCA Civ 291, [2010] BCC 597 [84].

[249] *Gamlestaden Fastigheter AB v Baltic Partners Ltd* [2007] UKPC 26, [2007] 4 All ER 164 [36]. This case is discussed at 15.3.6.1.

[250] *Re London School of Electronics Ltd* [1986] Ch 211 (Ch).   [251] ibid.

[252] *Re Grandactual Ltd* [2005] EWHC 1415 (Ch), [2006] BCC 73 (nine-year delay between conduct and petition).

[253] *Re Tobian Properties Ltd* [2012] EWCA Civ 998, [2013] Bus LR 753 [27] (Arden LJ).   [254] ibid.

[255] *Re Elgindata Ltd* [1991] 1 BCLC 959 (Ch).   [256] *The Times* (London, 4 December 1995) (CA).

165 days of court time, with the successful respondent awarded costs of £2 million. The courts are aware of this, with Arden LJ stating that, '[c]ourts must, where possible, find ways and means of reducing the hearing times for these cases'.[257]

15.3.7.1 Share purchase orders

As noted, the most common remedy sought and awarded is a share purchase order, of which there are three types:

1. The court may order the respondent (usually the majority shareholder) to buy the shares of the petitioner (usually a minority shareholder). This is the most common remedy sought and ordered.

2. The court may order the respondent to sell his shares to the petitioner. This relief is rarely sought, but it has been granted in several cases[258] (including in some cases where the majority shareholder was ordered to sell his shares to the petitioner).[259]

3. The court may order the company concerned to purchase the shares of the petitioner.

The rationale behind the popularity of a share purchase order was stated by Patten J:

> In most cases, the usual order to make will be the one requiring the Respondents to buy out the petitioning shareholder at a price to be fixed by the court . . . .. The reasons for making such an order are in most cases obvious. It will free the petitioner from the company and enable him to extract his share of the value of its business and assets in return for foregoing any future right to dividends. The company and its business will be preserved for the benefit of the Respondent shareholders, free from his claims and the possibility of future difficulties between shareholders will be removed. In cases of serious prejudice and conflict between shareholders, it is unlikely that any regime or safeguards which the court can impose, will be as effective to preserve the peace and to safeguard the rights of the minority.[260]

Unfortunately, the CA 2006 provides no guidance on what principles should be adhered to when determining the price of the shares. Two questions are of importance. The first is how the shares should be valued. The overriding principle is that 'the price fixed by the court must be fair'[261] and, accordingly, an array of factors can have an impact upon the valuation process. For example, the unfairly prejudicial conduct that has taken place is clearly of importance, especially if it adversely affected the share price. Often, this means that 'the court is actually valuing shares, not as they are, but as they would have been if events had followed a different course'[262] (i.e. had the unfairly prejudicial conduct not taken place).

Most s 994 petitioners are minority shareholders and so the 'issue of central concern is whether the price should be discounted to reflect a minority shareholder's lack of control, something which would undoubtedly occur in a voluntary sale of a minority

---

257 *Re Coroin Ltd* [2013] EWCA Civ 781, [2014] BCC 14 [14].
258 *Re Hedgehog Golf Co Ltd* [2010] EWHC 390 (Ch); *Oak Investment Partners XII Ltd Parnership v Boughtwood* [2010] EWCA Civ 23, [2010] 2 BCLC 459; *Goodchild v Taylor* [2018] EWHC 2946 (Ch).
259 *Re Brenfield Squash Racquets Club Ltd* [1996] 2 BCLC 184 (Ch).
260 *Grace v Biagioli* [2005] EWCA Civ 1222, [2006] BCC 85 [75].
261 *Re Bird Precision Bellows Ltd* [1984] Ch 149 (Ch) 429 (Nourse J).
262 *Profinance Trust SA v Gladstone* [2001] EWCA Civ 1031, [2002] 1 WLR 1024 [31] (Robert Walker LJ).

interest in a company'.[263] On this, Nourse J stated that 'there is in my judgment no rule of universal application',[264] but the courts have developed general principles based on the company involved:

- Where the company is a quasi-partnership, the shares will usually be valued on a pro-rata basis, without applying any discount. As noted, many s 994 cases are brought by members of a quasi-partnership who have been excluded from management. Accordingly, the sale of the shares is essentially being forced on the petitioner due to the unfairly prejudicial conduct of the respondent, so it would be 'most unfair that he should be bought out on the fictional basis applicable to a free election to sell his shares . . .'.[265] However, this is a general principle only and a discount may be applied if the facts merit it; for example, where petitioner purchased the shares purely as an investment,[266] or where the member left of his own volition.[267]

- Where the company is not a quasi-partnership, then the share price will usually be discounted to reflect the fact that it is a minority holding and the fact that the shares were likely bought as an investment only.[268] Again, this is a general principle only and the courts may decide not to apply a discount based on the facts.[269]

The second question is what date the shares should be valued at. There appears to be no general rule regarding when the valuation should be made,[270] but Nourse J stated that '[p]rima facie an interest in a going concern ought to be valued at the date on which it is ordered to be purchased'[271] and the Court of Appeal has stated that this is to be the starting point.[272] However, the Court then went on to state that 'there are many cases in which fairness (to one side or the other) requires the court to take another date'.[273] For example, in *Re OC Transport Services Ltd*,[274] the court held that the date of valuation should be before the conduct complained of took place, as the conduct had adversely affected the share price. Accordingly, the valuation date was set at two-and-a-half years before the date of the petition.

15.3.7.2 **The availability of winding up**

One question that has arisen is whether the court has the power under s 996 to wind up a company. Nothing in s 996 indicates that winding up is not available, but the Law Commission opined that winding up is not available[275] based on the first-instance judgment of Ferris J in *Re Full Cup International Trading Ltd*.[276] However, a measure of uncertainty exists as, in the more recent case of *Apex Global Management Ltd v FI Call Ltd*,[277] Hildyard J stated that 'the court should not ordinarily make a winding-up order pursuant to section 996, given the specific provisions for such a remedy . . .'.[278] In practice, this uncertainty is not a major issue as very few petitioners would seek a winding-up order in an unfair prejudice petition (such petitioners would usually seek a winding up order under s 122 of the Insolvency Act 1986 (IA 1986)). However, judicial or

The relationship between s 994 and s 122 is discussed at 15.4.2.1.

---

[263] DD Prentice, 'Minority Shareholder Oppression: Valuation of Shares' (1986) 102 LQR 179, 181.

[264] *Re Bird Precision Bellows Ltd* [1984] Ch 149 (Ch) 431.   [265] ibid 430.   [266] ibid 431.

[267] *Re Phoenix Office Supplies Ltd* [2002] EWCA Civ 1740, [2003] BCC 11.

[268] *Re Elgindata Ltd (No 1)* [1991] BCLC 959.

[269] See e.g. *Re Sunrise Radio Ltd* [2009] EWHC 2893 (Ch), [2010] 1 BCLC 367.

[270] *Re London School of Electronics Ltd* [1986] Ch 211 (Ch) 224 (Nourse J).   [271] ibid.

[272] *Profinance Trust SA v Gladstone* [2001] EWCA Civ 1031, [2002] 1 WLR 1024 [60] (Robert Walker LJ).

[273] ibid [61].   [274] (1984) 1 BCC 99068 (Ch).

[275] Law Commission, *Shareholder Remedies* (Law Com CP No 142, 1996) para 8.18.

[276] [1995] BCC 682 (Ch) 694.   [277] [2015] EWHC 3269 (Ch).   [278] ibid [51].

statutory clarification is desirable. The Law Commission recommended that winding up should be added to the list of example remedies now found in s 996(2),[279] but this recommendation was rejected by the CLRSG[280] and did not make it into the CA 2006.

15.3.7.3 Relationship with other remedies

A member may have several remedies available to him, and this might impact upon a member's ability to bring an unfair prejudice petition in several ways:

- The availability of an alternative remedy might result in an unfair prejudice petition being dismissed. For example, in *Re Legal Costs Negotiators Ltd*,[281] an unfair prejudice petition was dismissed, *inter alia*, because the petitioner, as a majority shareholder, could pass a resolution that would have terminated the prejudicial state of affairs.

- Unfairly prejudicial conduct may also justify winding up the company. The relationship between the unfair prejudice remedy and the winding-up petition is discussed at 15.4.2.1.

- Certain conduct (e.g. a director breaching a general duty) may amount to unfairly prejudicial conduct and it may also allow a member to commence a derivative claim. The courts will not strike out an unfair prejudice petition merely because the conduct complained of could also form the basis of a derivative claim.[282] Instead, if both claims are brought based largely on the same conduct, the court will, based on the complaint, examine both remedies and determine which is more appropriate. For example, if a successful unfair prejudice petition can obtain the relief sought, then permission to continue the derivative claim will likely be refused.[283]

15.4 The petition for winding up

Perhaps the most extreme remedy available to an aggrieved member is to petition the court for an order winding up the company. Despite the remedial flexibility afforded to the court in cases involving unfairly prejudicial conduct, winding up is likely not available under s 996 of the CA 2006 (although, as noted, this issue is not clear). A member desiring the winding up of the company will need to petition the court under s 122(1) of the IA 1986 for a compulsory winding-up order.

 Compulsory winding up orders are discussed at 23.1.2.

Section 122(1) provides seven grounds for a compulsory winding-up order, of which two are relevant here. A company may be wound up where the company passes a special resolution resolving that the company should be wound up.[284] This will, however, likely be of no use to an aggrieved minority shareholder, for whom the key provision is s 122(1)(g), which is discussed next.

15.4.1 Just and equitable winding up

Section 122(1)(g) empowers the court to wind up a company if it is 'of the opinion that it is just and equitable that the company should be wound up'. The words 'just and equitable'

---

[279] Law Commission, *Shareholder Remedies* (Law Com No 246, 1997) para 4.35.

[280] CLRSG, 'Modern Company Law for a Competitive Economy: Developing the Framework' (2000) para 4.105.

[281] [1999] BCC 547 (CA) (discussed at 15.3.3). See also *Re Baltic Real Estate Ltd (No 2)* [1992] BCC 629 (Ch).

[282] *Re Fahey Development Ltd* [1996] BCC 320 (Ch).

[283] See e.g. *Mission Capital plc v Sinclair* [2008] EWHC 1339 (Ch), [2008] BCC 866 (discussed at 15.2.3.3).

[284] IA 1986, s 122(1)(a).

are clearly extremely broad, but the courts have not sought to establish any limits on their interpretation. As Neville J stated, '[t]he words "just and equitable" are words of the widest significance, and do not limit the jurisdiction of the court to any case. It is a question of fact, and each case must depend upon its own circumstances.'[285] Accordingly, a wide range of activities have justified winding up, including:

- Where a company is fraudulently promoted, a winding-up order may be appropriate. For example, in *Re London and County Coal Co*,[286] a company was set up and sold shares, but the promoters had no intention that the company would carry on any business. The court had no hesitation in winding up the 'wretched concern'.[287]

- A company may be wound up if it was set up for an unlawful purpose,[288] or for a fraudulent purpose.[289]

- A company may be wound up if it is deadlocked, but quite what amounts to a 'deadlock' is not entirely clear. An inability to make company decisions will certainly amount to a deadlock. Thus, in *Re Yenidje Tobacco Co Ltd*,[290] a company was wound up when its two directors (who each held 50 per cent of the company's shares) refused to talk to one another.

- Where a company's objects clause indicates that it has been formed for a particular purpose (known as the company's 'substratum'), a winding-up order will be made if that purpose can no longer fulfilled.[291] Cases involving a loss of substratum are likely to disappear over time, because companies created under the CA 2006 have unrestricted objects by default.[292]

- A winding-up order may be made if the petitioner can demonstrate that there is a 'justifiable lack of confidence in the management of the company's affairs'.[293] Such instances tend to be classified as cases involving a 'lack of probity', and clearly this is a broad and vague ground for winding up. Examples of conduct that have merited winding up here include (i) a failure to submit accounts or hold general meetings when required;[294] (ii) stealing money from the company;[295] (iii) a director selling corporate assets to a rival company he controls;[296] (iv) where a controller of the company regards the company as his property;[297] and (v) where the controller acted in an oppressive manner.[298] Note, however, that mere inefficiency, carelessness, or negligence will not be enough to justify a winding up.[299]

Whilst the courts may not seek to limit the type of case subject to s 122(1)(g), the law does impose limitations in terms of who may petition the court for a winding-up order.

---

[285] *Re Blériot Manufacturing Aircraft Co Ltd* (1916) 32 TLR 253, 255.

[286] (1866–67) LR 3 Eq 355.   [287] ibid 361 (Sir W Page-Wood VC).

[288] *Re International Securities Corp* (1908) 99 LT 581 (unlawful dealing in lottery bonds).

[289] *Re Thomas Edward Brinsmead & Sons* [1897] 1 Ch 406 (CA) (company formed to make pianos which would be passed off as being made by a more established firm).

[290] [1916] 2 Ch 426 (CA).

[291] *Re German Date Coffee Co* (1882) 20 ChD 169 (CA) (company formed to take advantage of a patent that was never granted).

[292] CA 2006, s 31(1).

[293] *Loch v John Blackwood Ltd* [1924] AC 783 (PC) 788 (Lord Shaw).   [294] ibid.

[295] *Re Worldhams Park Golf Course Ltd* [1988] 1 BCLC 554 (Ch).

[296] *Re Concrete Column Clamps Ltd* [1953] 4 DLR 60.   [297] *Thomson v Drysdale* 1925 SC 311.

[298] *Re HR Harmer Ltd* [1959] 1 WLR 62 (CA). Note that the petitioner did not seek a winding-up order, so one was not granted. However, the Court did state that winding up would be justified.

[299] *Re Five Minute Car Wash Service Ltd* [1966] 1 WLR 745 (Ch).

15.4.1.1 **Standing to petition the court**

Both statute and the courts have established rules regarding who has standing to seek a winding-up petition. The starting point in s 124(1) of the IA 1986, which sets out who can apply to the court for a compulsory winding-up order. For our purposes, it should be noted that members or shareholders are not expressly listed. Instead, s 124(1) provides that a winding-up application can be made by a 'contributory or contributories', with a contributory being a 'person liable to contribute to the assets of a company in the event of its being wound up . . .'.[300] This would obviously include a shareholder whose shares were partly paid up but it would arguably not include a shareholder whose shares were fully paid. Given that, in most companies, shares are fully paid up, this would be a significant limitation upon the scope of s 122, so it is not surprising that the courts will permit fully paid-up members to petition the court under s 122. However, such a member will need to demonstrate that he has a 'tangible interest'[301] that entitles him to ask for a winding up. This will generally require the member to show that there is a 'prima facie probability that there will be assets available for distribution amongst the shareholders'.[302] From this, it would appear that a fully paid-up member of an insolvent company would not have standing to petition the court under s 122 as he has no tangible interest in the company. However, Oliver J has stated that surplus assets are not the only type of tangible interest and that a fully paid-up member will have standing to apply for winding up if he can show that the winding up would 'achieve some advantage, or avoid or minimise some disadvantage, which would accrue to him by virtue of his membership of the company'.[303] Oliver J gives the example of a member who wishes to wind up a company because he is engaged in litigation with that company, although he goes on to acknowledge that this is not the type of interest that Jessel MR had in mind when he devised the 'tangible interest' test.

Section 124(1) is discussed in more detail at 23.1.2.1.

As s 122(1)(g) is an equitable remedy, it follows that the petitioner's own conduct may be relevant in determining whether a winding-up petition can proceed. The maxim 'he who comes to Equity must do so with clean hands' applies to the winding-up remedy,[304] and so a petition will not be successful if, for example, it is the petitioner's own misconduct that causes a breakdown in confidence between him and other parties,[305] or if the petitioner is not seeking the relief sought but is instead using a winding-up petition to put pressure on the company.[306]

15.4.1.2 **Quasi-partnerships**

Section 122(1)(g), along with other member remedies (especially the unfair prejudice remedy), acquires an increased importance where the company in question is a 'quasi-partnership'. What constitutes a quasi-partnership and the importance of s 122(1)(g) to such companies was the subject of the following landmark case.

---

[300] IA 1986, s 79(1).
[301] *Re Rica Gold Washing Co* (1879) 11 ChD 36 (CA) 43 (Jessel MR).
[302] *Re Othery Construction Ltd* [1966] 1 WLR 69 (Ch) 72 (Buckley J).
[303] *Re Chesterfield Catering Co Ltd* [1977] Ch 373 (Ch) 380.
[304] *Ebrahimi v Westbourne Galleries Ltd* [1973] AC 360 (HL) 387 (Lord Cross). [305] ibid.
[306] *Re a Company (No 0089 of 1894)* [1894] 2 Ch 349 (Ch).

See Dan D Prentice, 'Winding Up on the Just and Equitable Ground: The Partnership Analogy' (1973) 89 LQR 107.

Ebrahimi v Westbourne Galleries Ltd [1973] AC 360 (HL)

FACTS: In 1945, Ebrahimi and Nazar formed a partnership that sold rugs and carpets, and it was understood that both parties would be involved in managing the firm. In 1958, they incorporated the business (Westbourne Galleries Ltd), and Ebrahimi and Nazar became the company's first directors, with each holding 500 shares. Shortly thereafter, George (Nazar's son) also became a director and Ebrahimi and Nazar each transferred 100 shares to him. In 1969, a dispute arose, and Nazar and George used their majority shareholding to vote Ebrahimi out of office. As Westbourne distributed its profits as directors' fees and not as dividends, Ebrahimi's removal from office meant that he was entitled to no share in the profits (unless a dividend was declared, which the company had never done). Ebrahimi petitioned the court for a winding-up order.

HELD: The House held that Nazar and George had, in removing Ebrahimi as a director, acted in accordance with the Companies Act 1948 and Westbourne's articles. However, Lord Wilberforce stated that the words 'just and equitable' are:

> a recognition of the fact that a limited company is more than a mere legal entity, with a personality in law of its own: that there is room in company law for recognition of the fact that behind it, or amongst it, there are individuals, with rights, expectations and obligations inter se which are not necessarily submerged in the company structure. That structure is defined by the Companies Act and by the articles of association by which shareholders agree to be bound. In most companies and in most contexts, this definition is sufficient and exhaustive, equally so whether the company is large or small. The 'just and equitable' provision does not . . . entitle one party to disregard the obligation he assumes by entering a company, nor the court to dispense him from it. It does, as equity always does, enable the court to subject the exercise of legal rights to equitable considerations; considerations, that is, of a personal character arising between one individual and another, which may make it unjust, or inequitable, to insist on legal rights, or to exercise them in a particular way.[307]

The question that arose is when such 'equitable considerations' would arise. On this, Lord Wilberforce stated:

> It would be impossible, and wholly undesirable, to define the circumstances in which these considerations may arise. Certainly, the fact that a company is a small one, or a private company, is not enough. There are very many of these where the association is a purely commercial one, of which it can safely be said that the basis of association is adequately and exhaustively laid down in the articles. The superimposition of equitable considerations requires something more, which typically may include one, or probably more, of the following elements: (i) an association formed or continued on the basis of a personal relationship, involving mutual confidence—this element will often be found where a pre-existing partnership has been converted into a limited company; (ii) an agreement, or understanding, that all, or some (for there may be 'sleeping' members), of the shareholders shall participate in the conduct of the business; (iii) restriction upon the transfer of the members' interest in the company—so that if confidence is lost, or one member is removed from management, he cannot take out his stake and go elsewhere.[308]

Lord Wilberforce noted that companies that exhibited these characteristics were referred to as 'quasi-partnerships' and that Westbourne was clearly such a company. Accordingly, equitable considerations would be relevant here. The relevant consideration here was the fact that when Nazar and Ebrahimi set up the partnership, it was understood that both parties would be involved in managing the firm and, when the business was incorporated, there was an indisputable

---

[307] [1973] AC 360 (HL) 379.   [308] ibid.

inference that 'the character of the association would, as a matter of personal relation and good faith, remain the same'.[309] By removing Ebrahimi from office, the Nazars had inequitably breached this understanding, and so the winding up of Westbourne was ordered.

Ebrahimi basically establishes that where a company is a quasi-partnership, the conduct of the controllers should not be judged purely based on the rights of the parties (as usually provided for in statute or the articles), but also by the legitimate expectations of the parties and any informal agreements that exist between them. The courts have confirmed on multiple occasions that, in quasi-partnerships, there will often be an expectation that the members will participate in management and that exclusion of a member from management will likely justify the winding up of the company even if the right of exclusion is lawfully exercised[310] (as it was in *Ebrahimi*).

15.4.2 The relationship between winding up and the other remedies

Prior to the Companies Act 1948, the courts would not make a winding-up order if the petitioner had an alternative remedy available. The rationale behind this was to prevent the dissolution of companies that were still commercially viable. Today, the law acknowledges that, even where multiple remedies are available, winding up may still be appropriate. Section 125(2) of the IA 1986 provides that, where a petition is made by a contributory, the court must refuse to grant a winding-up order if some other remedy is available and the petitioner is acting unreasonably in seeking to have the company wound up instead of pursuing that other remedy. Note that this other remedy need not be one of the statutory remedies discussed in this chapter. For example, if an offer is made to purchase the petitioner's shares, his winding-up petition may be rejected if the court thinks that he acted unreasonably in refusing the offer.[311] It is important, however, to understand the relationship between the winding-up petition and the other statutory remedies discussed in this chapter, with the principal overlap being between a winding-up petition and an unfair prejudice petition.

15.4.2.1 Winding up and the unfair prejudice remedy

Given that the unfair prejudice remedy was introduced to allow for a remedy other than winding up, it is unsurprising that the number of s 122(1)(g) petitions has decreased since the unfair prejudice remedy was introduced. Historically, it was common for a petitioner to seek a remedy under the unfair prejudice provisions and apply for a winding-up order. The inclusion of the winding-up petition placed significant pressure on the defendant because a compulsory winding up generally commences when the winding-up petition is presented to the court.[312] From that point onward, the company is

---

[309] ibid 380 (Lord Wilberforce).

[310] See e.g. *Re Davis and Collett Ltd* [1935] Ch 693 (Ch); *Tay Bok Choon v Tahansan Sdn Bhd* [1987] 1 WLR 413 (PC).

[311] *Re a Company (No 002567 of 1982)* [1983] 1 WLR 927 (Ch). Note, however, that this is not a blanket rule and a petitioner may be acting reasonably if he refuses to sell his shares, such as where the mechanism for valuing the shares results in a risk that the shares would be sold at a discount (*Virdi v Abbey Leisure Ltd* [1990] BCC 60 (CA)).

[312] IA 1986, s 129(2).

effectively paralysed as any disposition of the company's property, any transfer of shares, or any alteration of the status of the company's members is void, unless the court otherwise orders.[313]

Whilst it is the case that an unfairly prejudicial act may also justify winding up the company, the two remedies do have differing scopes. For example, in most cases involving a deadlock,[314] the petitioners are not treated unfairly, and so whilst a winding-up order might be appropriate, a remedy under s 994 would not be granted. It is also true that the two remedies 'ask the court to consider different questions: on a winding-up petition, the question is whether the company's existence should be ended; on an unfair prejudice petition, the question is how the company's existence should be continued'.[315]

Given these differences, and the courts' concern that the addition of a winding-up petition was being used to place undue pressure on the defendant, a Practice Direction was issued which states that a winding-up petition should only accompany an unfair prejudice petition if winding up 'is the relief which the petitioner prefers or if it is considered that it may be the only relief to which he is entitled'.[316]

CHAPTER SUMMARY

- A member who is wronged may be able to commence a personal action against the person(s) who wronged him.

- Collective forms of action exist in the form of representative actions and GLOs.

- Where both a member and the company have a cause of action arising out of the same set of facts, both actions will be permitted to go ahead, unless the member's loss is reflective of that of the company.

- Where a company has sustained a loss, a member may be able to bring a derivative claim on behalf of the company (CA 2006, Pt 11).

- In order to continue a derivative claim, the member must obtain permission from the court to continue the claim.

- A member can petition the court for a remedy where the company's affairs have been conducted in a manner that is unfairly prejudicial to that member's interests as a member (CA 2006, Pt 30).

- In unfair prejudice cases, the most common remedy is a share purchase order (usually where the company is ordered to purchase the claimant's shares).

- A member can petition the court for a winding-up order, with the relevant ground here being winding up where the court thinks it is just an equitable to do so (IA 1986, s 122(1)(g)).

---

[313] ibid s 127(1) (discussed at 23.1.2.4).
[314] See e.g. *Hawkes v Cuddy* [2009] EWCA Civ 291, [2010] BCC 597.
[315] Derek French, *Mayson, French & Ryan on Company Law* (35th edn, OUP 2018) 587.
[316] *Practice Direction (Companies Court: Contributory's Petition)* [1990] 1 WLR 490 (Ch).

FURTHER READING

MR Chesterman, 'The "Just and Equitable" Winding Up of Small Private Companies' (1973) 36 MLR 129.
* Discusses the winding-up remedy found in the IA 1986, s 122(1)(g), focusing on its use in relation to quasi-partnerships.

Paul L Davies and Sarah Worthington, *Gower's Principles of Modern Company Law* (10th edn, Sweet & Maxwell 2016) ch 20.
* A detailed, yet lucid, account of the unfair prejudice remedy and the ability to petition the court for a winding-up order on just and equitable grounds.

Law Commission, *Shareholder Remedies: Consultation Paper* (Law Com CP No 142, 1996).
* A consultation paper that discusses the rule in *Foss v Harbottle*, the unfair prejudicial remedy, and the winding-up petition.

Charles Mitchell, 'Shareholders' Claims for Reflective Loss' (2004) 120 LQR 457.
* Provides a readable and analytical account of the no reflective loss principle.

Jill Poole and Pauline Roberts, 'Shareholder Remedies: Efficient Litigation and the Unfair Prejudice Remedy' [1999] JBL 38.
* Discusses the Law Commission's proposed reforms of the unfair prejudice remedy, focusing on those measures designed to make s 994 cases less lengthy and costly.

Paul von Nessen, SH Goo, and Chee Keong Low, 'The Statutory Derivative Action: Now Showing Near You' (2008) 7 JBL 627.
* Discusses the worldwide proliferation of the statutory derivative claim and examines how such derivative claims operate in the UK, Commonwealth countries, the US, and Hong Kong.

KW Wedderburn, 'Shareholders' Rights and the Rule in *Foss v Harbottle*' [1957] CLJ 194.
* Despite its age, this remains a seminal article on the ability of a member to enforce the constitution and how this ability relates to the rule in *Foss v Harbottle*.

SELF-TEST QUESTIONS

1. Define the following terms:
* no reflective loss principle;
* representative action;
* group litigation order;
* derivative claim;
* proper claimant principle;
* irregularity principle;
* quasi-partnership.

2. State whether each of the following statements is true or false and, if false, explain why:
* Where an unlawful act causes loss to both the company and a member, the general rule is that both may commence actions against the perpetrator of the act.
* Where the company has been wronged, the members can usually bring a claim on behalf of the company.
* The common law derivative action has been abolished.
* A derivative claim can be brought in relation to a cause of action that occurred before the derivative claimant became a member.
* The court will refuse permission to continue a derivative claim where the act or omission in respect of which the claim is brought gives rise to a cause of action that the member could pursue in his own right rather than on behalf of the company.

- Section 994 allows a person to bring a claim where the company's affairs have been conducted in a manner that is unfair or prejudicial to his interest as a member.
- Criminal conduct can amount to unfairly prejudicial conduct.
- The most common remedy awarded under s 996 is a share purchase order.
- A member cannot bring both a s 994 petition and a winding-up petition.

3. 'The statutory derivative claim provides a much more useful remedy than the common law derivative action.' Discuss the validity of this quote.

4. Stanley, Sophie, and Kim are the directors of Dragon Goods Ltd ('DG'), a company that manufactures tools that are then sold by Dragon Tools Ltd (another company in the Dragon Group). The company has issued 1,000 shares as follows:

- 500 shares are held by Dragon plc (DG's parent company);
- each of the three directors holds 100 shares;
- 200 shares are held by Dominic, a local businessman whose firm is one of DG's principal suppliers.

DG has adopted the model articles, but has added a provision stating that each director is to receive a salary of £150,000 per year. The articles also provide that 'the business of Dragon Goods Ltd is the manufacture of tools'. For the past few years, DG has not paid a dividend as the profits made by the company are used to pay the directors' salaries. This has angered Dominic, but DG's directors assure him that, if profits increase, a dividend will be paid.

For a few months, Sophie and Kim have been trying to persuade Stanley that DG should diversify its business into providing electrical components for consumer products. Stanley disagrees, stating that 'the company should stick to what is it good at'. At a board meeting, an argument ensued in relation to DG's future direction, which led to Stanley falling out with Sophie and Kim. Since then, Sophie and Kim have outvoted Stanley at all directors' meetings and have sought to make all the business decisions themselves. As a result, DG began manufacturing electrical components. Since this meeting, Stanley has stopped attending board meetings.

At the most recent board meeting, in Stanley's absence, Sophie and Kim voted to remove Stanley as a director and he was subsequently informed of this. This meeting also noted that, as a result of DG diversifying into electrical components, DG's profits had improved in recent months and so Sophie and Kim proposed that their salaries should be increased to £200,000. The directors of Dragon plc agreed and so the articles of DG were amended to provide that Sophie and Kim would receive an annual salary of £200,000.

Dominic and Stanley are angry at the way events have unfolded, and seek your advice as to whether Sophie, Kim, or DG have engaged in any breaches of the law and, if so, what remedies (if any) are available.

 ## ONLINE RESOURCES

This book is accompanied by online resources to better support you in your studies. Visit www.oup.com/uk/roach-company/ for:

- answers to the self-test questions;
- further reading lists;
- multiple-choice questions;
- glossary.

Updates to the law can be found on the author's Twitter account (@UKCompanyLaw) and further resources can be found on the author's blog (www.companylawandgovernance.com).

PART V
Finance and transparency

Part V of this text focuses on corporate finance and transparency. The vast majority of companies can function only if they can obtain enough finance (or 'capital' as it is usually termed). The *Oxford English Dictionary* defines 'capital' as 'of or pertaining to the original funds of a trader, company or corporation', but company lawyers tends to use the word 'capital' to principally refer to capital received by the company in payment for shares. However, it is important to note that share capital is only one form of capital and, in some companies, it may not even be the most important source of capital. Depending on the company's financial position, debt capital (i.e. capital raised through borrowing) may be a more important source of capital (especially if the company is struggling financially and cannot find any purchasers for its shares). Accordingly, Part V focuses on how companies raise and maintain capital and the different types of capital that exist. Companies are also required to disclose significant amounts of information relating to their finances, but are also required to disclose increasing amounts of non-financial information too.

All of the above issues are discussed in Part V, which consists of the following chapters:

CHAPTER 16 SHARE CAPITAL
This chapter examines what share capital is and the different types of share capital that exist. It looks at the rules for issuing shares, the different types of shares that can be issued, and the rights attached to different shares, and how shares can be transferred and transmitted.

CHAPTER 17 THE MAINTENANCE OF CAPITAL
This chapter examines what is known as the capital maintenance doctrine—a series of rules designed to protect the company's creditors by ensuring that capital is maintained and not returned to the company's members.

CHAPTER 18 PUBLIC OFFERS OF SHARES
This chapter looks at the sources of securities regulation, the rules relating to offering shares to the public, the various UK stock exchanges, and the process by which securities are listed.

CHAPTER 19 **CORPORATE TRANSPARENCY**

This chapter examines the UK's corporate transparency regime, including the statutory registers, the annual accounts and reports, the role of the auditor, and other notable disclosure obligations.

CHAPTER 20 **DEBT CAPITAL AND SECURITY**

This chapter discusses why companies borrow money, the various sources of debt capital, and the rules relating to secured and unsecured borrowing.

16

Share capital

- What is a share?
- Terminology relating to capital
- Minimum share capital
- Allotment and issuing of shares
- Payment for shares
- Class rights
- Transfer of shares
- Transmission of shares

INTRODUCTION

The vast majority of companies in the UK have a share capital, and with good reason. The share is one of the defining characteristics of a company and the ability to allot shares is one of the most important benefits of incorporation. This chapter starts by discussing what a share actually is, and the terminology relating to share capital. It then moves on to discuss the various rules relating to the allotment of shares, including the process of allotment and the types of shares that can be allotted. One of the most important benefits of a share is its transferability, so the final topic discussed in this chapter is the rules relating to the transfer and transmission of shares.

16.1 What is a share?

Section 540(1) of the Companies Act 2006 (CA 2006) defines a 'share' as a 'share in the company's share capital', but this rather unhelpful definition grossly undervalues the full nature of a share. A share is an item of property[1] (known as a 'thing in action')[2] that confers upon it holder 'rights and obligations which are defined by the Companies Act and by the memorandum and articles of association of the company'.[3] A 'thing' (formerly

---

[1] CA 2006, s 541. [2] *Colonial Bank v Whinney* (1886) 11 App Cas 426.
[3] *Commissioners of Inland Revenue v Crossman* [1937] AC 26 (HL) 66 (Lord Russell).

known as a 'chose') is simply an asset other than land, with a 'thing in action' being an intangible thing.[4] Several points should be noted:

- A share does not give a shareholder a proprietary right over the assets of the company.[5] A shareholder may own 50 per cent of the shares in a company, but he is not entitled to 50 per cent of the assets, nor can he demand 50 per cent of the profits.
- Shares that have been allotted and issued do not belong to the company,[6] but to the holder of the shares.
- As shares are items of property, they can be transferred from person to person, with the process of transfer subject to the rules specified in the company's articles,[7] which may, in the case of a private company, restrict transferability.[8]
- As a share is intangible, it can only be claimed or enforced by legal action, as opposed to by taking possession of it.[9]

The transfer of shares is discussed at 16.7.

Shares in quoted companies are used principally as an investment: the investor is looking for income or capital growth, and may not expect to exercise any significant control over the actions of the directors (although the increase in institutional investment has challenged this notion). Shareholders in private companies, many of which are small and/or family-run, may well be involved in management or may otherwise work for the company. In such companies, shares represent a measure of the degree of control that a person has over the company.

Institutional investors are discussed at 14.5.1.

16.2 Terminology relating to capital

The law relating to share capital is heavy in terminology, which can render the subject complex. Before the rules relating to share capital can be discussed, it is essential to first explain a number of terms that will crop up throughout this chapter (and this text).

16.2.1 Nominal value

All shares in a limited company with a share capital are required to have a fixed 'nominal' value[10] (also known as 'par' value), and failure to attach a nominal value to an allotment of shares will render the allotment void.[11] The nominal value represents a notional value of a share's worth, but, in reality, the nominal value may bear no resemblance whatsoever to the share's actual value. The nominal value of a share represents the minimum price for which the share can be allotted and also sets the level of liability of a shareholder if the company is wound up. In other words, upon liquidation, if the shareholder has paid the nominal value, he cannot usually be required to contribute more.

The prohibition on allotting shares at a discount is discussed at 16.5.2.

---

[4] Tangible things are known as 'things in possession'.

[5] *Borland's Trustee v Steel Bros & Co Ltd* [1901] 1 Ch 279 (Ch).

[6] *Pilmer v Duke Group Ltd* [2001] 2 BCLC 773. An exception to this is where a public company holds treasury shares.

[7] CA 2006, s 544(1).

[8] For instance, art 26(5) of the model articles for private companies limited by shares allows the directors to refuse to register a share transfer.

[9] *Torkington v Magee* [1902] 2 KB 427 (KB) 430 (Channell J).

[10] CA 2006, s 542(1). It follows that unlimited companies can issue shares with no nominal value.

[11] ibid s 542(2).

16.2.2 **Share premium**

Whilst shares cannot be allotted for less than their nominal value, it is common for shares to be sold for more than their nominal value and the excess is known as the 'share premium'. Where a company issues shares at a premium, then a sum equivalent to the aggregate value of the premiums must be transferred to an account called the 'share premium account'.[12] Where the company in question is a public company, the premium must be fully paid at the time of allotment.[13]

16.2.3 **Authorized share capital**

Prior to the CA 2006, companies were required to state in their memoranda the total nominal value of shares that may be allotted by the company and this value would represent the company's authorized share capital.

 Eg **Authorized share capital**

Dragon plc has an authorized share capital of £10 million. Thus, the maximum number of shares that it could allot could not have a combined nominal value of over £10 million. So, for example, it could allot:

- twenty million shares with a nominal value of 50 pence; or
- ten million shares with a nominal value of £1; or
- five million shares with a nominal value of £2, etc.

In practice, the requirement to state the authorized share capital was largely pointless. Companies would choose an arbitrary and inflated figure, confident that it would never be reached. Even if it were reached, passing an ordinary resolution could increase the authorized share capital. Accordingly, companies incorporated under the CA 2006 are not required to state the authorized share capital. However, companies that were incorporated under prior Companies Acts that have retained their authorized share capital provisions, and companies incorporated under the CA 2006 that have chosen to include an authorized share capital clause in their constitution, will be bound by the amount stated.

16.2.4 **Allotted, issued, and unissued share capital**

Authorized share capital represents the maximum nominal value of shares that can be allotted. The total nominal value of the shares that actually have been allotted is known as the 'allotted share capital'.[14]

 Eg **Allotted share capital**

Dragon plc has allotted 3 million shares with a nominal value of £3 each. Accordingly, its allotted share capital is £9 million. A company's allotted share capital cannot exceed its authorized share capital.

---

[12] ibid s 610(1).
[13] ibid s 586(1). One quarter of the nominal value of the shares must also be paid at the time of allotment.
[14] ibid s 546(1)(b).

Once allotted shares have been registered to a member in the register of members, those shares are said to be issued,[15] with the 'issued share capital' representing the total nominal value of shares that have been issued.[16] 'Unissued' share capital represents the difference between the authorized share capital and the issued share capital (i.e. the nominal value of shares that could still be issued). Obviously, companies that have no authorized share capital limitation will not have an unissued share capital.

16.2.5 Paid-up, called-up, and uncalled share capital

Shareholders may not be required to pay fully for their shares upon allotment. The company may allow for shares may be partly paid for at allotment (i.e. the payment made is less than the nominal value), with the remainder to be paid at a later date or in instalments. The combined total of the nominal share capital that has actually been paid is known as the 'paid-up share capital'.

 Eg **Paid-up share capital**

Dragon Goods Ltd has allotted and issued 1,000 shares with a nominal value of £1 each (its allotted/issued share capital is therefore £1,000). The company allows allottees to pay 50 pence on allotment and the remainder (or part of the remainder) is to be paid at a later date to be specified by the company. All 1,000 shares are allotted and purchased, and every shareholder pays the required 50 pence per share only. No shareholder pays more than 50 pence at allotment. The paid-up capital is therefore £500.

If shares are not fully paid for, the company may call for any outstanding amounts to be paid, or the company may require payment in instalments and an instalment may have become due. The paid-up share capital plus the amount called for or the instalment due is known as the 'called-up share capital'.

 Eg **Called-up share capital**

Following on from the Dragon Goods example above, the company then calls for an additional 25 pence per share to be paid. The called-up share capital is determined via the following formula:
Paid-up share capital + (number of shares allotted × amount called for).
Calling for 25 pence on 1,000 shares would result in £250 being called for. Adding this to the paid-up share capital (£500) results in a called-up share capital of £750. Note that the amount called for forms part of the called-up capital irrespective of whether it is paid or not.

The difference between the company's allotted capital and its called-up capital (i.e. the amount that the company can still call on) is known as the 'uncalled share capital'.

16.3 Minimum share capital

Private companies with a share capital are not subject to a minimum share capital requirement and can accordingly be set up by issuing a single one penny share to a single member. Conversely, a public company cannot conduct business until it has been issued

---

[15] *National Westminster Bank plc v Inland Revenue Commissioners* [1995] 1 AC 119 (HL).
[16] CA 2006, s 546(1)(a).

with a trading certificate,[17] and the registrar of companies will not issue a trading certificate unless he is satisfied that the nominal value of the company's allotted share capital is not less than the authorized minimum,[18] which is currently £50,000[19] or €57,100.[20]

The rationale behind the imposition of minimum capital requirements upon public companies is to attempt to ensure that there is always a minimum level of capital available to satisfy the company's debts. However, it is widely acknowledged that, in practice, the minimum capital requirement does little to aid creditors for three reasons:

1. The authorized minimum is simply too low to offer creditors any real security, and has been described as 'derisory'[21] and 'miniscule compared to the size of the debts of most public companies'.[22]

2. The shares do not even need to be fully paid up. Only one-quarter of the nominal value and the whole of the premium need be paid up at the time of allotment.[23]

3. The authorized minimum is measured at the time that the company wishes to commence trading, but little account is taken of the possibility that it will be reduced once trading commences. Once the company has commenced trading, the only safeguard imposed is that should the company's assets fall to half or less than its called-up share capital, then the directors must call a general meeting to consider what steps, if any, should be taken.[24] By the time that the assets reach this level, it is highly likely that some form of insolvency procedure is already in place, thereby rendering the general meeting largely useless.

16.4 Allotment and issuing of shares

There are two principal methods by which a person can become a shareholder in a company. First, as shares are freely transferable (subject to any limitations contained in the articles),[25] a person can become a shareholder by obtaining shares from an existing shareholder. Second, a person can become a shareholder by obtaining from the company new shares that it has allotted to him. The first method is discussed at 16.7, whereas the allotment and issue of new shares is discussed here. The terms 'allotment' and 'issue' are often used interchangeably, but there is a distinction:

● Shares are allotted 'when a person acquires the unconditional right to be included in the company's register of members in respect of the shares'.[26] For example, if a company stipulates that shares will only be allotted once a certain condition is met (e.g. the shares are fully paid for), then those shares will only be allotted once the condition is satisfied.

● Shares are issued when the person's name is actually entered into the register of members.[27] From this, it follows that the issuing of shares takes place after they have been allotted.

There are numerous reasons why a company may decide to allot new shares:

● The principal reason why a company allots shares is to raise money. This money may be desired or needed for a range of reasons (e.g. to finance expansion and growth of the business, to pay off debt, to fund a new business opportunity, to fund a takeover bid, etc.).

● Companies may allot shares to existing shareholders instead of paying out a cash dividend, or pay out a bonus issue of shares.

The trading certificate is discussed at 3.2.5.1.

---

[17] ibid s 761(1).   [18] ibid s 761(2).   [19] ibid s 763(1).
[20] Companies (Authorised) Minimum) Regulations 2009, SI 2009/2425, reg 2.
[21] Paul L Davies and Sarah Worthington, *Gower's Principles of Modern Company Law* (10th edn, Sweet & Maxwell 2016) 263.
[22] Louise Gullifer and Jennifer Payne, *Corporate Finance Law: Principles and Policy* (Hart Publishing 2011) 127.
[23] CA 2006, s 586(1).   [24] ibid s 656.   [25] ibid s 544(1).   [26] ibid s 558.
[27] *National Westminster Bank v Inland Revenue Commissioners* [1995] 1 AC 119 (HL).

- Shares may be allotted to a person (usually an employee) to comply with a share options scheme.
- Shares can be allotted to affect who controls the company. This is especially important in smaller companies where the founders will wish to retain control over the company.
- Shares may be issued to a person as payment for services rendered, goods sold, etc.

16.4.1 The power to allot shares

A company with a share capital is able to create and allot new shares. The decision to allot shares is usually taken by the directors acting on the company's behalf. However, the directors can only allot shares on the company's behalf if they are empowered to do so under ss 550 or 551 of the CA 2006.[28] Any director who knowingly contravenes, or permits, or authorizes a contravention of the rules in ss 550 or 551 commits a criminal offence, although the allotment itself will remain valid.[29]

TABLE 16.1 The power to allot shares

Type of company	Power to issue shares	Provisions in the articles
A private company with only one class of share that wishes to allot shares of the same class.	The directors may allot shares of the same class, except to the extent that they are prohibited from doing so by the company's articles.	A provision in the articles empowering the directors to allot shares is not required, but the articles may limit the directors' power to allot shares (the model articles contain no such limitations).
Any other type of company, namely: • a private company with multiple classes of share; • a private company with only one class of share that wishes to issue a different class of share; • a public company.	The directors will only have the power to allot shares if: • they are authorized to do so by the company's articles, or; • the members pass a resolution authorizing the directors to allot shares.	The model articles provide that 'the company may issue shares with such rights or restrictions as may be determined by ordinary resolution'. Accordingly, under the model articles, the directors are not authorized to allot shares without the passing of a resolution.

Sections 550–1 are summarized in Table 16.1 and provide that:

- where a private company has only one class of share and it wishes to allot more shares of the same class, the directors can exercise the power to allot shares, subject to any limitations contained in the company's articles;[30]
- in all other cases, the directors may only exercise the power to allot shares if they are authorized to do so by the company's articles (which will be the case in many companies that do not adopt the model articles) or by a resolution of the company.[31] This authority can be general or limited to a particular allotment, and can be conditional or unconditional.[32] All forms of authority are, however, subject to the following rules:

    (a) The authorization must state the maximum number of shares that can be allotted under it.[33]

---

[28] CA 2006, s 549(1).   [29] ibid s 549(4)–(6).

[30] ibid s 550. The model articles contain no such limitations.

[31] ibid s 551(1).   [32] ibid s 551(2).   [33] ibid s 551(3)(a).

(b) The authorization must specify a date on which it is to expire and this date cannot be longer than five years after authorization is granted.[34] Authorization can be renewed, but the renewal is also subject to a five-year maximum.[35]

(c) The authorization can be revoked or varied at any time by passing a resolution of the company.[36]

If the directors do have the authority to allot shares, then, like all powers granted to the directors, it must be exercised in accordance with their general duties. Many of the cases involving the s 171(b) proper purpose duty involve the directors' power to allot shares.

> The s 171(b) proper purpose duty is discussed at 10.2.2.

16.4.2 **The allotment price**

When a company allots shares, it needs to determine the price at which the shares are allotted. This price may be the nominal value of the shares, but it is more common for the price to be greater than the nominal value (the excess is known as the 'share premium'). The decision to allot shares at nominal value or at a premium is a commercial one and so the company is under no obligation to allot shares at a premium.[37] However, the directors should give careful consideration to the allotment price because, as the following case demonstrates, a failure to give proper consideration can have adverse legal consequences.

Re Sunrise Radio Ltd [2009] EWHC 2893 (Ch)

FACTS: Kohli, Jain, Walshe, and Lit were the directors and shareholders of Sunrise Radio Ltd ('Sunrise'). In 1999, Kohli resigned as a director, but remained a shareholder (holding around 15 per cent of Sunrise's shares). In 2005, Sunrise allotted shares to a company that was controlled by Lit. These shares were allotted at nominal value, even though they were worth much more. The allotment also had the effect of diluting Kohli's shareholding in Sunrise to 8.3 per cent. Kohli commenced proceedings.

HELD: Whilst the court accepted that the allotment of shares was made because Sunrise genuinely needed the cash, it noted that, in allotting the shares at nominal value, they were allotted at significantly less than what they were worth.[38] The directors, in failing to consider whether to allot the shares at a premium, had breached their fiduciary duty and had acted in a manner that was unfairly prejudicial to Kohli's interests as a member.[39] The directors of Sunrise were ordered to buy out Kohli's shares.

Whilst a company is free to issue shares at nominal value or at a premium, it is prohibited from allotting shares at a discount (i.e. for less than their nominal value). This is discussed in more detail at 16.5.2, when payment for shares is discussed.

16.4.3 **Limitations and prohibitions**

The law imposes a number of general limitations and prohibitions on a company's ability to allot shares, including:

---

[34] ibid s 551(3)(b). Where authorization is contained in the articles upon incorporation, authorization cannot exceed five years following the company's incorporation.
[35] ibid s 551(3)(b) and (4)(a).   [36] ibid s 551(4)(b).   [37] *Hilder v Dexter* [1902] AC 474 (HL).
[38] [2009] EWHC 2893 (Ch) [105] (Purle QC).   [39] ibid [95] and [113].

- if a company's memorandum states its authorized share capital, then the company cannot allot shares beyond the amount stated;

- the directors' ability to exercise the power to allot shares is subject the general duties, and many cases involving directors' duties (especially the s 171 duty to act within powers) concern the directors' power to allot shares.

The s 171 duty is discussed at 10.2.

A further limitation lies in relation to share warrants. As discussed at 13.2, the register of members is used to determine conclusive evidence of title to shares, with the share certificate also providing *prima facie* evidence of title. Prior to 26 May 2015, a third method of evidencing title also existed, namely the share warrant to bearer (also known as 'bearer shares').[40] A share warrant is simply a document stating that the holder of the document is entitled to the shares specified in the document. No person's name is printed on the warrant, nor is the name of the warrant holder registered in the register of members[41] (the register will simply note that the warrant exists, the date it was issued, and state what shares are included in the warrant).[42] As a share warrant was a negotiable instrument, the shares subject to the warrant could be transferred simply by handing over the warrant to the person acquiring the shares.[43]

The above rules meant that it was largely impossible for companies to know who held their bearer shares. The government noted that this opacity led to several issues:

> A number of international standards have highlighted the misuse of bearer shares as a way to facilitate tax evasion and money laundering. Bearer shares also permit a level of opacity which is incompatible with the principles of our ambition to know who really owns and controls UK companies.[44]

Accordingly, the CA 2006 and the Small Business, Enterprise and Employment Act 2015 (SBEEA 2015) now provide the following:

- No share warrant can be issued by a company from 26 May 2015 onwards.[45]

- Share warrant holders had up until 26 February 2016 in which they could voluntarily surrender their share warrants, which would then be converted into registered shares and the warrant holder's name would be entered into the register of members.[46] Within two months of the date of surrender, the company must have ready for delivery a share certificate for the shares specified in the warrant.[47] Any warrants not surrendered by 26 February would, along with the shares it covered, be cancelled,[48] although the nominal value of the shares and any share premium would be paid into court and could be claimed by the warrant holder for up to three years afterwards.[49] Any money not claimed after this period must be paid into the Consolidated Fund.[50]

Whilst the prohibition of share warrants is a welcome reform, its impact will be limited. Whilst share warrants are more popular in Continental European systems, they were never popular in the UK, with only around 900 active companies using them prior to their abolition (representing around 0.05 per cent of the total number of companies).[51]

---

[40] Companies could only issue share warrants if their articles so permitted (CA 2006, s 779(1)).
[41] Accordingly, the holder of a share warrant was not a member, although the articles could specify that a warrant holder was a member (CA 2006, s 122(3)).
[42] CA 2006, s 122(1).   [43] ibid s 779(2).
[44] Department for Business, Innovation and Skills (BIS), 'Transparency and Trust: Enhancing the Transparency of UK Company Ownership and Increasing Trust in Business: Discussion Paper (BIS 2013) para 28.
[45] CA 2006, s 779(4).   [46] SBEEA 2015, Sch 4, para 1(2) and (3).   [47] ibid Sch 4, para 1(4).
[48] ibid Sch 4, paras 5 and 6.   [49] ibid Sch 4, paras 9 and 10.   [50] ibid Sch 4, para 12.
[51] BIS, 'Transparency and Trust: Enhancing the Transparency of UK Company Ownership and Increasing Trust in Business: Discussion Paper (BIS 2013) para 3.4.

16.4.4 **Pre-emption rights**

An inevitable consequence of a new allotment of shares is the dilution of the share-holdings of existing shareholders, and possibly even a change in control. Accordingly, to 'provide a company's shareholders with protection from wealth transfer and erosion of control',[52] existing shareholders of a company are given a right of pre-emption. This basically provides that a company must not allot equity securities to a person unless it has made an offer to each person who holds ordinary shares in the company to allot to him, on the same or more favourable terms, a proportion of those securities that is as nearly as practicable equal to the proportion in nominal value held by him of the ordinary share capital of the company.[53] Basically, this means that a new allotment of shares must be offered first to the existing shareholders to allow them to maintain their existing holding, as the following example demonstrates.

Eg **Pre-emption rights**

Dragon Goods Ltd ('DG') has issued 1,000 shares, divided between Jayne (100 shares), Ian (300 shares), and Katja (600 shares). DG decides to issue another 5,000 shares. In order to comply with the three shareholders' pre-emption rights, it will need to offer them the opportunity to purchase the following:

- to maintain her 10 per cent holding, DG will need to offer Jayne 500 shares for purchase;
- to maintain his 30 per cent holding, DG will need to offer Ian 1,500 shares for purchase;
- to maintain her 60 per cent holding, DG will need to offer Katja 3,000 shares for purchase.

An allotment that contravenes the pre-emption rights of existing shareholders is still valid, but the company and every officer who knowingly authorized or permitted the contravention are jointly and severally liable to compensate the shareholders who would have benefited from the pre-emptive offer.[54]

There are a number of instances where the members' right of pre-emption will not apply.

16.4.4.1 **Non-application of pre-emption rights**

There are four situations where pre-emption rights will not apply, namely:

1. Pre-emption rights only apply to an allotment of 'equity securities' which are defined as (i) ordinary shares in the company; or (ii) rights to subscribe for, or to convert securities into, ordinary shares in the company.[55] Accordingly, if the shares allotted are not equity securities, no right of pre-emption will exist.

2. Pre-emption rights do not apply where the shares to be allotted are **bonus shares**.[56]

3. Pre-emption rights do not apply to an allotment of shares that are, or are to be, wholly or partly paid up otherwise than in cash.[57]

4. Pre-emption rights do not apply where the shares are allotted or transferred pursuant to an employee share scheme.[58]

➡ **bonus shares:** shares allotted to existing shareholders and paid for out of the company's distributable profits

---

[52] Paul Myners, 'Pre-emption Rights: Final Report' (DTI 2005) 9–10.
[53] CA 2006, s 561(1).   [54] ibid s 563(2).   [55] ibid s 560(1).
[56] ibid s 564.   [57] ibid s 565.   [58] ibid s 566.

16.4.4.2 Exclusion/disapplication of pre-emption rights

In addition to those instances where pre-emption rights do not apply, there also a number of instances where pre-emption rights can be excluded or disapplied, namely:

- A private company can exclude pre-emption rights by placing a provision in its articles to that effect.[59] The exclusion can be general or it can apply to a specified allotment of shares.[60]
- The pre-emption right provided for under the CA 2006 is excluded where a company's articles provide for a right of pre-emption in relation to ordinary shares of a particular class, and that right is complied with.[61]
- Pre-emption rights will not apply to an allotment of equity securities where the directors of a private company with only one class of shares have been authorized, either via the articles or by the passing of a special resolution, to ignore the right of pre-emption.[62]
- Where the directors are authorized to allot shares under s 551, then they may be given the power to allot shares, ignoring any pre-emption rights if such a power is given to them by a provision in the articles or by the passing of a special resolution.[63]
- Where the directors are authorized to allot shares under s 551, then the company may, by passing a special resolution, resolve that pre-emption rights will not apply to a specified allotment,[64] providing that the directors make a written statement setting out specified information (e.g. their reasons for disapplying pre-emption rights).[65]

16.4.5 Contracts of allotment

When a company allots shares, persons interested in acquiring the shares can apply to the company for those shares. From this application, a contract of allotment may be created (i.e. a contract under which the company agrees to allot a certain number of shares to the applicant).

16.4.5.1 Offer and acceptance

A contract for the allotment of shares, like any other contract, requires offer and acceptance (consideration (i.e. payment for shares) is discussed at 16.5). The principal issue that arises here is identifying who the offeror and offeree are, and when acceptance occurs (i.e. when a binding contract comes into existence).

Usual practice is that the application is made in writing, but an oral application is also valid[66] (unless the company has specified that the application must be in writing). From this, it follows that the general position is that the applicant (i.e. the potential shareholder) makes the offer, which the company is then free to accept or reject. This is even the case where the company has issued a prospectus—the prospectus will be regarded as an invitation to treat and not an offer. Standard contractual rules apply to the contract for allotment, namely:

- The application for shares (i.e. the offer) can be revoked by the applicant any time before it has been accepted by the company.[67]
- The offer will lapse if it is not accepted within a reasonable time.[68]

---

[59] ibid s 567(1).   [60] ibid s 567(2).   [61] ibid s 568.   [62] ibid s 569(1).
[63] ibid s 570(1).   [64] ibid s 571(1).   [65] ibid s 571(6).
[66] *The New Theatre Company Ltd (Bloxham's Case)* (1864) 33 Beav 474.
[67] *Ramsgate Victoria Hotel Co v Montefiore* (1866) LR 1 Exch 109.
[68] ibid. This will not be the case where the offer specifies a time limit for acceptance—in this case, the specified limit will apply.

- Acceptance occurs not when the shares are allotted to the applicant, but when the company notifies the applicant that his offer has been accepted.[69] This notification is usually in writing, but it need not be[70] (e.g. acceptance can be oral or by conduct).[71] If acceptance is made via post, then the postal rule will apply and acceptance will take place once the acceptance is posted.[72]

- Acceptance must match the terms of the offer (i.e. it must be unconditional). If the purported acceptance seeks to amend the offer or introduce new terms, then it will amount to a counter-offer[73] (so the company will become the offeror, and the applicant can choose to accept or reject the counter-offer).

16.4.5.2 Remedies for breach

If the applicant breaches the contract of allotment and refuses to take the shares allotted to him, the court can decree specific performance and order the applicant to take the shares. Similarly, if the company refuses to allot shares under a contract of allotment, it can be ordered to allot the shares.[74] However, the court is unlikely to order specific performance if damages would be an adequate remedy (e.g. where a company refuses to allot shares, but 'it would be perfectly simple to take the [damages] and go out and buy the shares in the market').[75]

16.4.6 Share certificates

The general rule is that a company must, within two months of the allotment of any shares, complete and have ready for delivery share certificates for the shares allotted.[76] However, this rule will not apply where (i) the conditions of the issue of the shares provide that no certificate will be issued;[77] (ii) the shares are allotted to a financial institution;[78] or (iii) the shares issued are uncertificated.[79] These rules may also be found in a company's articles,[80] or the articles may extend the rights relating to a share certificate.

What information is stated on a share certificate is largely a matter for the company's articles, with the model articles providing that each certificate must specify:

- in respect of how many shares, and of what class, the certificate is issued;
- the nominal value of the shares;
- the amount paid up on the shares, and;
- any distinguishing numbers assigned to them.[81] Note that the CA 2006 provides that shares need to be numbered, subject to certain exceptions.[82]

---

[69] *Re Scottish Petroleum Co (No 2)* (1883) 23 ChD 413 (CA).

[70] Unless, of course, the offer specifies that acceptance must be in writing.

[71] *Forget v Cement Products Co of Canada* [1961] WN 259 (a letter demanding payment for the shares was deemed to amount to acceptance by conduct).

[72] *Household Fire & Carriage Accident Insurance Co Ltd v Grant* (1879) 4 Ex D 216 (CA).

[73] *Re Leeds Banking Co* (1865–66) LR 1 Eq 225.   [74] *Sri Lanka Omnibus Co v Perera* [1952] AC 76 (PC).

[75] *Re BTR plc* (1988) 4 BCC 45 (Ch) 49 (Harman J).

[76] CA 2006, s 769(1). Failure to comply is a criminal offence (s 769(3) and (4)).   [77] ibid s 769(2)(a).

[78] ibid ss 769(2)(b) and 778(1).   [79] Uncertificated Securities Regulations 2001, SI 2001/3755, reg 38(2).

[80] Article 24 of the model articles for private companies provides shareholders with the right to a share certificate. Article 46 of the model articles for public companies provides shareholders with the right to a share certificate, but repeats several of the exceptions noted above.

[81] Model articles for private companies, art 24(2); model articles for public companies, art 47(1).

[82] CA 2006, s 543.

In addition, the model articles provide that share certificates must have affixed to them the company's common seal, or should be otherwise executed in accordance with the Companies Acts.[83]

The seal and the execution of documents are discussed at 6.1.

16.4.6.1 Evidence of title and estoppel

Should a shareholder ever have to prove that he holds title to shares (e.g. because he wishes to transfer them), the share certificate provides a convenient way to do this. In this sense, the share certificate is:

> a declaration by the company to all the world that the person in whose name the certificate is made out, and to whom it is given, is a shareholder in the company, and it is given by the company with the intention that it shall be so used by the person to whom it is given and acted upon in the sale and transfer of shares.[84]

However, it is important to note that a share certificate only provides *prima facie* evidence of title to shares,[85] and can therefore be rebutted if another person can prove that the title is defective. Despite this, it has long been held that a company may be **estopped** from denying the validity of information stated by a share certificate, as the following case demonstrates.

estop:
to deny the exercise of a right

Bloomenthal v Ford [1897] AC 156 (HL)

FACTS: Bloomenthal lent £1,000 to a company, and the company agreed to provide Bloomenthal with fully paid shares as security for the loan. The company provided Bloomenthal with certificates for 10,000 shares, which stated that Bloomenthal was the registered holder of the shares and that all 10,000 shares were fully paid up. In fact, unbeknown to Bloomenthal, the shares were not fully paid up and no money had been paid on them. Accordingly, when the company went into liquidation, Bloomenthal's name was placed on the list of contributories.

HELD: By virtue of the share certificate, the company represented to Bloomenthal that the shares were fully paid up. By lending the money to the company, Bloomenthal relied upon that representation. Accordingly, the requirements for estoppel were established, and so the company was estopped from denying the validity of the information on the share certificate. The House therefore ordered that Bloomenthal's name should be removed from the list of contributories.

It is, however, important to note that where the person issuing or authorizing the share certificate did so without proper authority, then estoppel will not arise and the company can validly challenge the information on the share certificate. Examples of this include:

- where the company secretary fraudulently and without authority affixed the company's common seal to the share certificate and forged the signature of two directors;[86] and
- where the articles required a board resolution to affix the common seal to documents, but the common seal was affixed to a share certificate without any such resolution taking place.[87]

---

[83] Model articles for private companies, art 24(5); model articles for public companies, art 47(2).

[84] *Re Bahia and San Francisco Railway Co Ltd* (1867–68) LR 3 QB 584, 595 (Cockburn CJ).

[85] CA 2006, s 768(1). Conclusive evidence can be found in the register of members.

[86] *Ruben v Great Fingall Consolidated* [1906] AC 439 (HL). Compare this to *Dixon v Kennaway & Co* [1900] 1 Ch 833 (Ch), where the secretary fraudulently obtained the board's approval to issue a share certificate. Estoppel was allowed as the issuing of the certificate was authorized.

[87] *South London Greyhound Racecourses Ltd v Wake* [1931] 1 Ch 496 (Ch).

16.5 Payment for shares

Having discussed the allotment of shares, the chapter moves on to look at the rules relating to the payment for shares.

16.5.1 Nil, partly paid, and fully paid shares

As discussed at 16.5.2, shares cannot be allotted at a discount (i.e. for less than their nominal value). However, this does not mean that shares must be paid for fully on allotment. Depending on the terms of the allotment, shares may be allotted:

- fully paid, where the full nominal value is payable on allotment; or
- partly paid, where less than the nominal value is payable on allotment, with the remainder due later; or
- nil-paid, where no payment is due on allotment, and the full price is payable at some point in the future.

Whether shares are allotted fully, partly, or nil-paid is a matter for the company's articles or the terms of the allotment. In practice, private companies will almost always require allottees to fully pay for their shares on allotment (indeed, art 21 of the model articles for private companies provides that all shares must be fully paid up). Public companies are more likely to allot partly paid shares, but it should be noted that, if a public company does decide to allot partly paid shares, then at least one-quarter of the nominal value and all of the premium must be paid on allotment.[88]

16.5.1.1 Instalments and calls for payment

Where shares are allotted nil- or partly paid, the allottee will be required to pay either the full or remaining value of the shares (as applicable) at some point in the future, usually via one of two methods:

1. The most common method of payment involves the allottee paying for the shares in a series of fixed instalments on specified dates.

2. The company can make a call for payment (known as a 'call notice'), which will require the allottee to pay a specified amount (this amount may be the full remaining amount or part of the remaining amount) by a specified date. The rules relating to issuing a call notice are a matter for the company's articles, which usually vest in the directors the power to make a call notice.[89] However, this power is subject to two notable limitations:

   - Like all powers granted to the directors, the power to make a call notice must be exercised in compliance with their general duties. Absent a breach of duty, the courts are very reluctant to interfere with the directors' judgement in making call notices.[90] However, if a shareholder can establish that a call notice has been improperly made, the court can issue an injunction preventing the call notice from being enforced.[91]

   - The general rule is that shareholders must be treated equally and so the company cannot require different calls on different shares[92] (e.g. allowing different shareholders to pay by different deadlines). However, the CA 2006 provides that companies may make different calls on different shares if the articles so authorize.[93]

---

[88] CA 2006, s 586(1). This will not apply if the allotment was in pursuance of an employees' share scheme (s 586(2)).
[89] See e.g. art 54(1) of the model articles for public companies.
[90] See e.g. *Odessa Tramways Co v Mendel* (1878) 8 ChD 235 (CA).
[91] *Lamb v Sambas Rubber and Gutta Percha Co Ltd* [1908] 1 Ch 845 (Ch).
[92] *Preston v The Grand Collier Dock Co* (1840) 11 Sim 327.
[93] CA 2006, s 581. Article 53 of the model articles for public companies provides such authorization.

16.5.1.2 Remedies for non-payment

Although payment in instalments and payment following a call are legally distinct,[94] it is common for a failure to pay either to be treated the same (indeed, art 56 of the model articles for public companies provides that failure to pay an instalment is to be regarded the same as a failure to pay following a call for payment). If a shareholder fails to pay an instalment or call for payment then, as a result of s 172, a duty is placed on the directors to take all reasonable steps to enforce payment.[95] There are three principal methods of enforcing payment. First, the company can commence proceedings against the shareholder to recover the sum owed. The remaining two methods are dependent upon the articles providing for them.

➡ **lien:**
the right to hold the property of another person until that person satisfies an obligation

Second, the articles may provide that the company has a **lien** over any partly paid shares.[96] For example, the model articles for public companies provide that the company has a lien over partly paid shares.[97] If a shareholder fails to pay an instalment or call for payment by the due date, the company can issue a lien enforcement notice in respect of the affected shares, which will require payment within 14 days of the notice.[98] If this notice is not complied with, the company can sell those shares.[99]

Third, the articles may provide for the forfeiture of the shares in question.[100] For example, the model articles for public companies provides that if a shareholder has not paid an instalment or complied with a call notice, then the company can send the shareholder a notice of intended forfeiture, which will require payment within 14 days.[101] If this notice is not complied with, the directors may decide that the affected shares are forfeited.[102] This power, like all powers granted to directors, must be exercised in accordance with their general duties. Further, the power of forfeiture is construed strictly and must be exercised in accordance with the articles—any irregularity, no matter how slight, will render the forfeiture ineffective.[103] Article 60 of the model articles for public companies provides that forfeiture has several effects:

- the forfeited shares become the property of the company[104] and may be sold, re-allotted, or otherwise disposed of as the directors see fit;
- the shareholder ceases to be a member in respect of those shares, and must surrender the share certificates relating to the forfeited shares;
- all interests the shareholder has in the forfeited shares, and any claims or demands against the company in respect of it, are extinguished; and
- the shareholder remains liable to the company for the unpaid amount on the shares (absent this provision, the shareholder would be relieved of the obligation to pay the unpaid amount on the shares).

---

[94] *Croskey v The Bank of Wales* (1863) 4 Giff 314 (an instalment payment due is not a call for payment).

[95] *Spackman v Evans* (1868) LR 3 HL 171 (HL).

[96] Note that a public company is normally not permitted to have a lien over its own shares, but this prohibition does not apply to liens over partly-paid shares (CA 2006, s 670(2)).

[97] Model articles for public companies, art 52(1).   [98] ibid art 53(1) and (2).   [99] ibid art 53(1).

[100] Note that if the articles do not provide such a power, then no inherent right of forfeiture exists (*Clarke v Hart* (1858) 6 HL Cas 633 (PC)).

[101] Model articles for public companies, art 58.   [102] ibid art 59.

[103] *Johnson v Lyttle's Iron Agency* (1877) 5 ChD 687 (CA) (incorrect date stated on the notice of intended forfeiture rendered the forfeiture ineffective).

[104] Note, however, that the company may not exercise any voting rights in respect of forfeited shares (CA 2006, s 662(1)(a) and (5)).

Note that the directors may accept the shareholder surrendering his shares in lieu of forfeiture, but only if the articles so provide.[105] The effect of surrendering the shares is the same as forfeiture.

16.5.2 **Allotment of shares at a discount**

Whilst the allottee may not need to pay the full value for the share on allotment (unless full payment is required), the full value will need to be paid eventually. A company is not permitted to allot shares at a discount (i.e. for less than their nominal value), with the rationale behind this prohibition being set out in the following case.

 Ooregum Gold Mining Co of India Ltd v Roper [1892] AC 125 (HL)

FACTS: A company needed money and so, to attract investment, it allotted 120,000 £1 preference shares with 75 pence credited as already paid (although this 75 pence was not actually paid), meaning that subscribers were only liable to pay 25 pence. A member of the company commenced proceedings to determine whether the share allotment was valid.

HELD: The House held that the company had no power to allot shares at a discount. Accordingly, the share allotment was *ultra vires* and the allottees of the shares were liable to pay the full £1 per share. Lord Halsbury LC stated that an agreement to purchase shares in a limited company is 'an agreement to become liable to pay the company the amount for which the share has been created. That agreement is one which the company itself has no authority to alter or qualify . . '.[106] The rationale behind this prohibition is that, in a limited company, a member's liability continues so long as anything remains unpaid on his shares and '[n]othing but payment, and payment in full, can put an end to the liability'.[107]

The prohibition is now found in s 580(1) of the CA 2006, which provides that '[a] com-pany's shares must not be allotted at a discount'. If shares are allotted at a discount, the allottee is liable to pay to the company an amount equal to the discount, including interest.[108] In addition, the company and every officer in default commit an offence.[109] Two points regarding this prohibition should be noted. First, a limited exception to the s 580 prohibition exists in relation to certain commission payments. To understand how this works, consider the following example.

Eg **Permitted commission payments**

Dragon plc allots 10,000 £1 shares and invites interested persons to make offers to purchase the shares. Dragon also enters into an agreement with Red Bank plc, under which Red Bank agrees to purchase any shares that have not been sold within a six-month period (this is known as an underwriting agreement). In return for underwriting the shares, Dragon will pay Red Bank a commission payment of £1,000. Six months later, only 8,000 shares have been allotted, and so Red Bank purchases the remaining 2,000 shares for £2,000.

---

[105] ibid s 659(2)(c). Article 62 of the model articles for public companies provides for the surrendering of shares.
[106] [1892] AC 125 (HL) 134.   [107] ibid 145 (Lord Macnaghten).   [108] CA 2006, s 580(2).

Red Bank obtained £2,000 of shares, but because of the £1,000 commission payment it received, it effectively obtained those shares for £1,000. This could be viewed as an allotment at a discount and so such commission payments are generally prohibited.[110] However, s 553(1) provides that a company may pay a commission to a person in consideration for that person (i) subscribing or agreeing to subscribe for shares (as occurred in the example above); or (ii) procuring or agreeing to procure subscriptions for shares in the company. In order for s 553(1) to apply, two conditions must be satisfied:

1. the payment of the commission must be authorized by the company's articles;[111] and
2. the commission paid (or agreed to be paid) must not exceed 10 per cent of the price at which the shares are issued, or the amount or rate authorized by the articles, whichever is less.[112]

Second, the effectiveness of the prohibition can, at least in relation to private companies, be reduced by the fact that shares can be purchased in 'money or money's worth', which is discussed next.

16.5.3 'Money or money's worth'

The CA 2006 provides that shares allotted by a company, or any premium on them, may be paid up in money or money's worth (including goodwill and know-how).[113] Accordingly, shares can be paid for in cash or via non-cash consideration (e.g. with goods, property, services, or even by transferring an existing business to a company in return for shares (as Mr Salomon did)). Where payment is in cash, then problems rarely arise, although s 553 does provide a definition of what 'cash consideration' is and includes cash received by the company, payment by cheque, and an undertaking to pay cash to the company at a future date.[114]

Salomon is discussed at 4.2.2.

It is where payment for shares is made is money's worth that matters can become more complex and the potential for abuse is increased. The relevant legal rules differ for private and public companies.

16.5.3.1 Private companies

Consider the following example.

Eg | Private companies and non-cash consideration

Roman Consultants Ltd (Roman') agrees to provide Dragon Tools Ltd ('DT') with certain consultancy services. DT agrees to pay for these services by allotting shares to Roman. The services provided by Roman were worth around £600, but DT overvalues the services and states they were worth £1,000. Accordingly, it issues 1,000 £1 shares to Roman.

By overvaluing the consultancy services provided, the shares allotted to Roman were effectively allotted at a discount (Roman received £1,000 worth of shares in return for £600 of

---

[109] ibid s 590.   [110] ibid s 552(1).
[111] Article 44(1) of the model articles for public companies provides such authorization.
[112] CA 2006, s 553(2). The model articles for public companies do not specify an amount or rate.
[113] ibid, s 582(1).   [114] ibid s 583(3).

non-cash consideration). This demonstrates that, in private companies, paying for shares with non-cash consideration can be used to circumvent the prohibition on allotting shares at a discount. This has long been recognized, with Lord Watson stating that the:

> state of the law is certainly calculated to induce companies who are in want of money, and whose shares are unsaleable except at a discount, to pay extravagant prices for goods or work to persons who are willing to take payment in shares. The rule is capable of being abused, and I have little doubt that it has been liberally construed in practice.[115]

Unlike public companies, private companies are not subject to specific statutory rules regarding non-cash consideration. Accordingly, regulation has been left to the courts, who have stated that they would refuse to give effect to 'a colourable transaction, entered into for the purpose or with the obvious result of enabling the company to issue its shares at a discount'.[116] However, it is also the case that 'so long as the company honestly regards the consideration given as fairly representing the nominal value of the shares in cash, its estimate ought not to be critically examined'.[117] The result of this is that the courts will only review the adequacy of non-cash consideration where it is clearly colourable or illusory.[118] As a result, it is likely to be rather easy in practice for the directors of a private company to issue shares at a discount if they so choose.

16.5.3.2 **Public companies**

Regarding public companies, the rules are more stringent. These rules were introduced principally in order to implement the Second European Community (EC) Company Law Directive,[119] and impose a number of limitations on using non-cash consideration to pay for the shares in a public company.

First, a public company must not accept from a person an undertaking that, as payment for shares or any premium, that person or another will do work or perform services for the company or any other person.[120] If this prohibition is breached, then the undertaking is still enforceable[121] but:

- the holder of the shares will be required to pay to the company an amount equal to their nominal value, together with the whole of any premium, or if relevant the proportion of that amount that is treated as paid up;[122] and
- the company and every officer in default will have committed an offence.[123]

Second, a public company must not allot shares as fully or partly paid up for non-cash consideration if the consideration is or includes an undertaking which is to be performed more than five years after the date of the allotment.[124] If this prohibition is breached, then the undertaking is still enforceable[125] but:

- the allottee is liable to pay the company an amount equal to aggregate of the shares' nominal value, together with the whole of any premium, or if relevant the proportion of the aggregate amount that is treated as paid up by the undertaking;[126] and
- the company and every officer in default will have committed an offence.[127]

---

[115] *Ooregum Gold Mining Co of India Ltd v Roper* [1892] AC 125 (HL) 137.   [116] ibid.   [117] ibid.
[118] *Re Wragg Ltd* [1897] 1 Ch 796 (CA) 836 (Smith LJ).
[119] Now replaced by Directive 12/30/EU [2012] OJ L315/74, art 10.   [120] CA 2006, s 585(1).
[121] ibid s 591(1).   [122] ibid s 585(2). A subsequent holder may face liability too (s 588).
[123] ibid s 590.   [124] ibid s 587(1).   [125] ibid s 591(1).
[126] ibid s 587(2). A subsequent holder may face liability too (s 588).   [127] ibid s 590.

Third, and perhaps most importantly, s 593(1) provides that a public company must not allot shares as fully or partly paid up otherwise than in cash unless three conditions are satisfied, namely:

1. the non-cash consideration has been independently valued;
2. the valuer's report has been made available to the company during the six months immediately preceding the allotment of the shares; and
3. a copy of the report has been sent to the proposed allottee.

 The eligibility and independence of a statutory auditor are discussed at 19.4.2.2.

In order to ensure the valuation is fair and independent, the CA 2006 provides that the valuation and report must be made by a person who is eligible for appointment as a statutory auditor,[128] and meets the independence requirements set out in s 1151.[129] The valuer's report must state:

- the nominal value of the shares to be paid for by the consideration in question;
- the amount of any premium payable on the shares;
- the description of the consideration, the method used to value it, and the date of the valuation; and
- the extent to which the nominal value of the shares and any premium are to be treated as paid up by the consideration or in cash.[130]

In addition, the report must contain or be accompanied by a note by the valuer that provides certain information, notably that, on the basis of his valuation, the value of the consideration is not less than the aggregate of the nominal value of the shares and the whole of any premium.[131] A copy of the report must be delivered to Companies House at the same time as the company files the return on the allotment of the shares.[132]

If the company allots shares in contravention of s 593(1) and the allottee has not received a copy of the valuer's report or there has been some contravention of ss 593 or 596 that the allottee knew or ought to have known amounted to a contravention, then the allottee is liable to pay to the company an amount equal to the nominal value of the shares and the whole of any premium, with interest.[133] However, a person found liable can apply to the court to be exempted, in whole or in part, from the liability, and the court can grant such relief where it appears to the court just and equitable to do so.[134] The following case demonstrates these rules in action.

> ### Re Ossory Estates plc (1988) 4 BCC 460 (Ch)
>
> **FACTS:** Impco Properties GB Ltd ('Impco') agreed to sell a number of properties to Ossory Estates plc ('Ossory'). Ossory would pay £1.49 million in cash, with the remaining £1.76 million coming in the form of 8 million shares allotted to Impco. An independent valuation was therefore required, but the valuer's report was never sent to Impco. Accordingly, Impco would be liable to pay to Ossory an amount equal to the nominal value of the shares (namely £1.76 million). Impco applied for relief exempting it from liability.
>
> **HELD:** Harman J noted that, if relief was not granted, the 'somewhat startling conclusion'[135] would be that Impco, having transferred the properties to Ossory, would become liable to pay a further

---

[128] ibid s 1150(1)(a). [129] ibid s 1150(1)(b).
[130] ibid s 596(2). [131] ibid s 596(3). [132] ibid s 597(1) and (2).
[133] ibid s 593(3). [134] ibid s 606(1) and (2).

£1.76 million to Ossory. When considering whether to grant relief, the overriding principle the court must have regard to is whether the company that allotted the shares has received money or money's worth at least equal to the aggregate of the nominal value of the shares and any premium.[136] Here, Ossory had already sold a number of the properties it purchased from Impco for a substantial profit. Harman J held that the amount Ossory had received had therefore likely exceeded the aggregate of the nominal value of the shares. He therefore ordered that Impco be granted relief, so it was not liable to pay the £1.76 million to Ossory.

In addition to the above civil consequences, a breach of s 593 results in the commission of an offence by the company and every officer in default.[137]

16.6 Class rights

Most companies with a share capital will only have one class of share (and so only one class of shareholder), which are usually known as 'ordinary shares' (discussed below). Most companies without a share capital will only have one class of member. However, provided that the articles so authorize,[138] companies are free to have multiple classes of member or multiple classes of share conferring different rights (these are known as 'class rights'). Examples of class rights include:

- differing nominal values for different classes of share;[139]
- different classes of shareholder/member may have different voting rights (e.g. increased, decreased, or no voting rights);
- shares that provide that the holder will only receive a dividend once the ordinary shareholders have received a certain amount (these are known as 'deferred shares').

As most class rights involve different classes of share, this section will focus on class rights found in shares. The utility of issuing shares with differing class rights is demonstrated in the following example.

Eg **The utility of class rights**

Dragon Tools Ltd ('DT') is experiencing financial difficulties. Isaac, a local businessman who runs a company that supplies goods to DT, states that he is prepared to offer financial aid to DT, but on the following conditions:

- in return for his aid, he wishes to receive 5,000 shares in DT;
- these shares should entitle him to a fixed 5 per cent dividend on whatever profits DT makes;
- he wishes to have the right to appoint a director to the board of DT.

---

[135] (1988) 4 BCC 460 (Ch) 462.   [136] CA 2006, s 606(4).   [137] ibid s 607.

[138] *Andrews v Gas Meter Co* [1897] 1 Ch 361 (CA). Both the model articles for private companies (art 22) and public companies (art 43) permit companies to 'issue shares with such rights or restrictions as may be determined by ordinary resolution'.

[139] *Re Scandinavian Bank Group plc* [1988] Ch 87 (Ch).

> The board of DT is happy to agree to the above, but is concerned that the number of shares Isaac will receive will give him the ability to defeat special resolutions. A solution could be to issue to Isaac a new class of non-voting ordinary share, and amend the articles to provide that holders of this class of share are entitled to a fixed 5 per cent dividend on DT's profits and have the right to appoint a director to the board.

There is no limit to the type of rights that can be attached to shares of different classes, so class rights are a very versatile tool in establishing different rights between shareholders. More common types of share class, include:

- **Ordinary shares**: the CA 2006 defines 'ordinary shares' as shares other than shares that, as respect dividends and capital, carry a right to participate only up to a specified amount in a distribution.[140] If a company only has one class of shares, then they will almost always be ordinary shares. Unless the articles provide otherwise, ordinary shareholders will typically have (i) the right to vote at general meetings (usually one vote per share);[141] (ii) the right to a dividend once validly declared; and (iii) the right to surplus capital once the creditors have been paid in the event of a company's winding up. It is possible for a company to have multiple classes of ordinary shares (e.g. ordinary shares with voting rights and non-voting ordinary shares).

- **Preference shares**: the precise rights granted to preference shareholders will depend upon the articles or terms of the share issue, but preference shares normally provide the holder with preferential claims on any surplus assets on winding up and/or entitle the holder to a predetermined fixed percentage dividend before anything is payable to the ordinary shareholders. As the dividend is usually expressed as a fixed percentage of the nominal value, this might mean that the preference shareholders actually receive less of a dividend than the ordinary shareholders (whose dividend rights are normally unlimited). Unless stated otherwise, dividend rights attached to preference shares are cumulative,[142] so if a dividend is not paid in one year, the entitlement is carried forward to the next year and, if the profits so allow, the preference shareholder will receive a double payment.

- **Deferred shares**: deferred shares (or 'founders' shares') typically provide that their holders are not entitled to a dividend or surplus assets upon liquidation unless the ordinary shareholders have first been paid. Deferred shares were once common, but are rare today.

- **Redeemable shares**: these shares offer their holder temporary membership, and can be bought back by the company, usually upon the company or holder's insistence.

Redeemable shares are discussed at 17.2.1.

- **Golden shares**: a golden share will usually give its holder the ability to outvote all other shares. Historically, golden shares were held by governments in newly privatized companies to ensure they retained control and to protect national interests. Over time, golden shares have become rare, largely due to many of them being held in breach of EU law.[143]

16.6.1 Variation of class rights

Consider the following example.

---

[140] CA 2006, s 560(1).   [141] ibid s 284(3).   [142] *Webb v Earle* (1875) LR 20 Eq 556.
[143] See e.g. Case C-98/01 *Commission v United Kingdom* [2003] ECR I-4641, where the European Court of Justice held that the UK government's golden share in the British Airports Authority was deemed in breach of European Union (EU) law.

Variation of class rights

Dragon plc has two classes of share, namely (i) ordinary shares; and (ii) preference shares that entitle their holders to increased dividends and increased voting rights. As a result of the rights attached to the preference shares, the holders of the ordinary shares have received very low dividends and have found it almost impossible to oppose any resolutions tabled by the preference shareholders. Accordingly, the ordinary shareholders table a resolution at the upcoming AGM in which they seek to remove the enhanced rights provided to the preference shareholders.

Here, we are concerned with the process by which class rights can be varied and, as in the example above, the extent to which class rights can be varied against the wishes of the holders of shares of the affected class. However, before looking at the procedures for varying class rights, it is important to define what constitutes a 'variation'.

16.6.1.1 What is a 'variation'?

One might assume that any alteration of class rights would constitute a variation, but this is not the case. The CA 2006 provides only limited guidance on what constitutes a variation, stating:

- abrogation (i.e. repeal or abolition) of a right will constitute a variation;[144]
- any amendment of a provision contained in a company's articles for the variation of the rights attached to a class of shares, or the insertion of any such provision into the articles, is itself to be treated as a variation of those rights.[145]

Outside of these instances, whether an alteration constitutes a variation has largely been left to the courts and it is clear that the courts have adopted a restrictive approach. The courts distinguish between an alteration that affects a class right (which may amount to a variation) and an alteration that merely affects the enjoyment of a class right (which will not amount to a variation). This approach was established in the following case.

 White v Bristol Aeroplane Co Ltd [1953] Ch 65 (CA)

FACTS: The articles of Bristol Aeroplane Co Ltd ('Bristol') provided that 'the rights or privileges attached to any class of shares . . . may be affected, modified, varied, dealt with, or abrogated in any manner with the sanction of an extraordinary resolution passed at a separate meeting of the members of that class'.[146] Bristol sought to issue new ordinary shares and preference shares to the company's existing ordinary shareholders, and so a general meeting was convened to approve the share issue. White, an existing preference shareholder, argued that the effect of the share issue was to dilute the preference shareholders' voting power and so the rights attached to his shares were 'affected', meaning that a separate meeting of the preference shareholders would need to be convened to approve the share issue.

HELD: Evershed MR stated that there was no doubt that the share issue would affect the enjoyment of, and the capacity to make effective use of, the rights attached to White's preference

---

[144] CA 2006, ss 630(6) and 631(6).   [145] ibid ss 630(5) and 631(5).
[146] See also _Greenhalgh v Arderne Cinemas Ltd_ [1946] 1 All ER 512 (CA).

shares. However, he went on to say that 'there is to my mind a distinction, and a sensible distinction, between an affecting of the rights and an affecting of the enjoyment of the rights, or of the stockholders' capacity to turn them to account'.[147] The issuing of the preference shares affected the preference shareholders' enjoyment of their rights, but it did not affect the rights themselves, which remained the same. Accordingly, there was no variation of class rights and so a separate meeting of the preference shareholders was not required.

The following case starkly demonstrates the distinction between variation of class rights and alteration of the enjoyment of those rights. Providing that the right remains the same, an alteration will not be classified as a variation if its effect is to render the right less valuable or even to render the right worthless.[148]

Re Mackenzie and Co Ltd [1916] 2 Ch 450 (Ch)

FACTS: The company had issued preference shares, each with a nominal value of £20. The preference shareholders were entitled to a 4 per cent dividend on the amount paid up and, because the preference shares were fully paid up, this entitled them to 80 pence per share. The articles were amended to reduce the nominal value of the preference shares to £12, thereby reducing the dividend to 48 pence per share.

HELD: The alteration of the articles did not constitute a variation of the class right, because the right had remained the same (that is, 4 per cent of the amount paid up). The alteration had simply rendered the right less valuable.

The result of this approach is that the protection afforded by ss 630 and 631 is limited and shareholders have, without their consent, lost the benefits associated with a class right. Shareholders who have sufficient power to amend the articles can protect their class rights by specifying in the articles exactly what alterations to class rights will require a separate class meeting. As the following case demonstrates, where article provisions are designed to protect class rights from a particular variation, the courts will give effect to such a purpose.

Re Northern Engineering Industries plc [1994] BCC 618 (CA)

FACTS: Article 6 of Northern Engineering Industries plc ('NEI') provided that preference shareholders' class rights could only be varied by passing an extraordinary resolution at a separate class meeting. Article 7(B) went on to provide that a reduction in capital paid up on such shares was deemed to be a variation. A resolution was passed at a general meeting resolving to pay off the preference shares and cancel them. The preference shareholders argued that this was clearly a reduction in capital and so a separate class meeting should have been called. NEI argued that the word 'reduction' implied a reduction from a larger number to a smaller number, and did not therefore include reducing the capital to zero (which is what the resolution proposed to do to the preference shares).

---

[147] [1953] Ch 65 (CA) 74.   [148] *Dimbula Valley (Ceylon) Tea Co Ltd v Laurie* [1961] Ch 353 (Ch).

HELD: Millett LJ agreed with NEI that 'the word "reduction" connotes diminution and not extinction',[149] but he went on to state that 'words take their meaning and effect from their surroundings'. What matters was not the dictionary definition of 'reduction', but its meaning in the context of art 7(b). Article 7(b) was clearly included in order to protect the preference shareholders from 'without their consent, a premature repayment of their investment'.[150] Accordingly, to hold that art 7(b) did not apply in this case would make 'a nonsense of the protection which has been afforded them'.[151] The Court held that a separate class meeting was therefore required and, as no meeting had been held, the lower court was correct to refuse to confirm the reduction in capital.

16.6.1.2 Methods of variation

To ensure that a class of shareholders cannot have their rights unduly varied, the CA 2006 establishes a procedure regarding the variation of class rights. Section 630(2)[152] provides that there are only two ways in which class rights can be varied:

1. Where the company's articles contain a class rights variation clause (i.e. a clause specifying how class rights are to be varied), a variation is valid if it complies with that clause.[153] The model articles do not contain a class rights variation clause, but most companies with multiple classes of share will include a class rights variation clause in their articles.

2. Where the articles contain no variation clause, a variation will be valid if the class rights holders in question consent to the variation.[154] The required consent is as follows:

   - To vary class rights attached to a class of shares, the consent required is either (i) consent in writing from the holders of at least three-quarters in nominal value of the shares of that class; or (ii) a special resolution passed at a class meeting of holders of the class of shares in question.[155]

   - To vary the class rights of a class of member in a company without a share capital, the consent required is either (i) consent in writing from at least three-quarters of the members of that class; or (ii) a special resolution passed at a class meeting of the members of the class in question.[156]

Where a separate class meeting is held to vote on a variation of class rights, the general rules relating to meetings will apply,[157] subject to a number of exceptions.[158] Two rules are modified in relation to class meetings voting on a variation of class rights, namely:

1. The quorum for such a meeting is two persons present holding at least one-third in nominal value of the issued share capital of the class in question.[159] In the case of an adjourned meeting, the quorum is one person present holding shares of the class in question.[160]

2. Any member may demand a poll.[161]

When voting on a variation to class rights, the shareholders must exercise their vote for the dominant purpose of benefitting the class as a whole, as the following case demonstrates.

---

[149] [1994] BCC 618 (CA) 621.   [150] ibid 622.   [151] ibid.

[152] This section applies to companies with a share capital. Section 631 imposes similar rules on companies without a share capital.

[153] CA 2006, s 630(2)(a).   [154] ibid ss 630(2)(b) and 631(2)(b).

[155] ibid s 630(4).   [156] ibid s 631(4).   [157] ibid s 334(1).

[158] The provisions that do not apply are specified in s 334(2).   [159] CA 2006, s 334(4)(a).

[160] ibid s 334(4)(b).   [161] ibid s 334(6).

British America Nickel Corp Ltd v MJ O'Brien Ltd [1927] AC 369 (PC)

FACTS: British America Nickel Corp Ltd ('BANC') issued bonds secured by a trust deed. This deed stated that the rights of the bondholders could be modified if bondholders, consisting of at least three-quarters in value, agreed to the modification. A modification of the bondholders' rights was proposed and the requisite majority was obtained. However, it transpired that Booth, one of the bondholders who approved of the modification (and without whose support the modification would not have been approved), was promised $2 million worth of ordinary shares in return for supporting the modification. This arrangement was not disclosed to the other bondholders. A bondholder who did not support the modification commenced proceedings against BANC.

HELD: Viscount Haldane stated that the power to vote on the variation of a class right 'must be exercised for the purpose of benefitting the class as a whole, and not merely individual members only'.[162] Here, Booth had subordinated the interests of the class as a whole to his own interest. Accordingly, the court held that the resolution was invalid and the modification was therefore *ultra vires*.

COMMENT: It would appear that the problem here was not the fact that Booth was induced to support the modification, but that the inducement was not disclosed or offered to other bondholders. In *Azevedo v Imcopa Importação*,[163] payments were offered by the company to every noteholder who supported the resolution varying their class rights. In finding that these 'consent payments' were lawful, Lloyd LJ stated:

> I see nothing wrong in principle with the idea that a company, which has taken the view that a particular course of action is in its best interests and in those of its creditors and shareholders, but which requires favourable votes from one or more classes, should take part in the process which leads to the relevant resolution being put to the necessary vote. It seems to me that it would be extraordinary to suggest that the company cannot take part in the process. Indeed, in practical terms, it must do so. The only issue is whether it is allowed to strengthen its urging and encouragement in favour of a vote by offering an incentive. For my part I find no objection to that in principle under English law, so long as all is open and above board.[164]

16.6.1.3 Right to object a variation

Where a class right is varied, the holders of not less than 15 per cent of the issued shares of the class of shares in question (in the case of a company with a share capital) or members amounting to not less than 15 per cent of the class of member in question (in the case of a company without a share capital) may apply to the court to have the variation cancelled, provided that they did not consent in writing to the variation or vote in favour of the resolution approving the variation.[165] If such an application is made, the variation will have no effect until it has been confirmed by the court.[166] The court will either confirm the variation or refuse to confirm the variation if the variation would unfairly prejudice the shareholders/members of the relevant class.[167] The court's decision is final.[168]

---

[162] [1927] AC 369 (PC) 371.   [163] [2013] EWCA Civ 364, [2015] QB 1.   [164] ibid [69].

[165] CA 2006, ss 633(2) and 634(2). The application must be made within 21 days of the consent or resolution (s 633(4)).

[166] ibid ss 633(3) and 634(3).   [167] ibid ss 633(5) and 634(5).   [168] ibid.

16.6.1.4 **Notice of the variation**

Where the rights attached to any shares of a company are varied, the company must, within one month of the variation, provide Companies House with the particulars of the variation.[169] Failure to do so constitutes an offence.[170]

16.7 Transfer of shares

Shares are items of personal property[171] and so may be transferred from one person to another. Here, the word 'transfer' is being used to refer to the passing of shares from one person to another, other than via the operation of law.[172] This can occur in numerous ways, but it typically occurs (i) where a shareholder contractually agrees to sell his shares to another person; or (ii) where a shareholder agrees to gift the shares to another person.

A transfer of shares may have a significant effect upon the company—it can affect the balance of power within a company, and can even result in a complete change of control (notably in a takeover situation). Accordingly, before looking at the process for transferring shares, it is important to first consider the extent to which a shareholder is free to transfer his shares and whether limitations can be placed upon this freedom.

16.7.1 **Freedom to transfer shares**

Statute provides that shares are transferable,[173] and so a shareholder has a general right to transfer his shares to someone else. The directors have no inherent power to refuse to register a transfer of shares[174] but, as discussed next, such a power may be bestowed upon them.

16.7.1.1 **Restrictions on the right to transfer**

A shareholders' freedom to transfer shares is *prima facie* only. In practice, two significant categories of restriction exist that can restrict the transferability of shares. The first category is restrictions imposed by the law, which would include:

- if the agreement to transfer shares was tainted in its creation by illegality;[175]
- if the transferee does not have the capacity to hold shares.

The second category is restrictions imposed by the articles. The CA 2006 provides that shares are transferable in accordance with the company's articles.[176] From this, it follows that companies can include, within their articles, restrictions on the transferability of their shares. Before looking at examples of such restrictions, three points should be noted:

1. In practice, only private companies tend to restrict the transferability of their shares (largely due to the directors, who are usually also the majority shareholders, wishing to retain control, especially if the business is family-run). Indeed, listed companies are

---

[169] ibid s 637(1).   [170] ibid s 637(2).   [171] ibid s 541.

[172] Shares passing from one person to another via the operation of law is known as 'transmission' and is discussed at 16.8.

[173] CA 2006, s 544(1). From this, it follows that there is no need to provide the shareholders with authority to transfer their shares (e.g. via the articles) (*Re Smith, Knight & Co* (1868–69) LR 4 Ch App 20).

[174] *Re Smith, Knight & Co* (1868–69) LR 4 Ch App 20.

[175] *Chase Manhattan Equities Ltd v Goodman* [1991] BCC 308 (Ch).   [176] CA 2006, s 554(1).

prohibited from using such restrictions as the Listing Rules provide that, in order to be listed, securities must be 'freely transferable' and 'free from all liens and from any restriction on the right to transfer'.[177]

2. A power to refuse a transfer will usually not be implied by the courts,[178] and so should be expressly provided for. The right to refuse a transfer must be expressed clearly—as Greene MR stated '[t]he right [to transfer shares], if it is to be cut down, must be cut down with satisfactory clarity'.[179] Accordingly, if the power to refuse a transfer is ambiguous, the court will give it its narrow interpretation.[180]

3. Prior to the CA 2006, companies were able to include a provision in their articles which provided that no reasons would be given for a refusal to register a transfer of shares. This made it extremely difficult for a transferee to challenge a refusal. Accordingly, the Company Law Review (CLR) recommended that companies should have to provide their reasons for refusing to register a transfer.[181] The CA 2006 now provides that if a company refuses to register a transfer of shares, then it must inform the transferee of the refusal, and provide reasons for the refusal, as soon as practicable and, at the latest, within two months after the date on which the transfer is lodged with it.[182] Failure to comply constitutes a criminal offence.[183]

In practice, there are two common forms of restriction found in a company's articles. The first form of restriction is a power given to the directors to refuse to register a transfer of shares. This power may be general and broad—art 26(5) of the model articles for private companies simply provides that '[t]he directors may refuse to register the transfer of a share . . .'. Alternatively, the power to refuse may be more specific or limited—art 63(5) of the model articles for public companies provides specified instances where the directors can refuse to register the transfer of a share (e.g. where the share is not fully paid up, or where the transfer is in favour of more than four transferees). Irrespective of the nature of the power of refusal, it must be exercised in accordance with the directors' general duties (notably the duties in ss 171 and 172). The following case demonstrates that the courts do give considerable leeway to the directors when exercising the power to refuse to register a transfer of shares.

Re Smith and Fawcett Ltd [1942] Ch 304 (CA)

FACTS: Smith and Fawcett were the only directors and shareholders of Smith and Fawcett Ltd ('SF'), with each holding 4,001 shares. Article 10 of SF's articles provided that the directors may 'at any time in their absolute and uncontrolled discretion refuse to register any transfer of shares . . .'. Fawcett died and his son, acting in his capacity as Fawcett's executor, applied to have Fawcett's shares registered in his name. Smith refused to register the 4,001 shares in the son's name, but instead offered to register 2,001 shares in the son's name. Smith offered to buy the remaining 2,000 shares himself at a fixed price set by himself. Fawcett's son commenced proceedings seeking to obtain an order to rectify the register to provide that he held the 4,001 shares.

HELD: Regarding the breadth of art 10, Greene MR stated '[t]here is nothing . . . in principle or in authority to make it impossible to draft such a wide and comprehensive power to directors to refuse

---

177 Listing Rules, LR 2.2.4. The Listing Rules do provide some very limited exceptions to this.
178 *Greenhalgh v Mallard* [1943] 2 All ER 234 (CA).
179 *Re Smith and Fawcett Ltd* [1942] Ch 304 (CA) 306.
180 See e.g. *Moodie v W&J Shepherd (Bookbinders)* [1949] 2 All ER 1044 (HL).
181 CLR, 'Modern Company Law for a Competitive Economy: Final Report: Vol I' (2001) paras 7.42–7.45.
182 CA 2006, s 771(1).   183 ibid s 771(3).

to transfer as to enable them to take into account any matter which they conceive to be in the interests of the company. . .'[184] The key issue is 'whether on the true construction of the particular article the directors are limited by anything except their bona fide view as to the interests of the company'.[185] Fawcett's son contended that Smith was not acting in the interests of the company, but acted in his own interests (i.e. to acquire the shares for himself at an undervalue in order to obtain majority control). Greene MR was of the opinion that Fawcett's son had not provided sufficient evidence for this contention, and so Smith's refusal to register the shares was valid.

The second form of restriction concerns pre-emption rights. These have already been discussed in relation to the allotment of new shares, but they can also apply to a transfer of shares if the articles so provide (it is common for the articles of private companies in particular to provide for pre-emption rights, although the model articles do not). Such an article provision will aim to 'prevent sales of shares to strangers so long as other members of the company are willing to buy them'[186] and will therefore typically provide that if a member wishes to transfer his shares, he must first offer them to the other shareholders or to specified persons (e.g. those shareholders who are directors) at a price to be determined by an independent person or by a formulation set out in the articles. The articles may give those shareholders the option to purchase the shares, or they may provide that specified persons must purchase the shares (e.g. the directors may be obliged to purchase the shares of a shareholder who dies).[187] If the transferor breaches the pre-emption right and transfers his shares to an outside party before offering them to existing members, then the directors must not register the transfer of the shares.[188]

Pre-emption rights are discussed at 16.4.4.

The discussion now moves on to look at the process for transferring shares. The process differs depending on whether the shares are certificated or uncertificated.

16.7.2 Transfer of certificated shares

In relation to certificated shares (i.e. shares in relation to which a share certificate has been issued), then the CA 2006 requires that the transfer is effected via an 'instrument of transfer'.

16.7.2.1 Instrument of transfer

Section 770(1) of the CA 2006 provides that a company may not register a transfer of its shares unless a proper instrument of transfer has been delivered to it. As is discussed at 16.7.3, this requirement does not apply to a transfer of uncertificated shares, so the instrument of transfer is only required for a transfer of certificated shares. The purpose behind the requirement for an instrument of transfer is to ensure that **stamp duty** is paid on the transfer. Accordingly, any instrument that is capable of attracting stamp duty will be regarded as a proper instrument of transfer.[189]

A company may specify in its articles what is to amount to a proper instrument of transfer, with the model articles providing that shares may be transferred 'by means of an instrument of transfer in any usual form or any other form approved by the

stamp duty: a tax payable on documents that effect transfers of certain assets or property (e.g. shares)

---

[184] [1942] Ch 304 (CA) 308.   [185] ibid.

[186] *Lyle & Scott Ltd v Scott's Trustees* [1959] AC 763 (HL) 777 (Lord Reid).

[187] See e.g. *Dean v Prince* [1954] Ch 409 (CA).

[188] *Tett v Phoenix Property and Investment Co Ltd* (1986) 2 BCC 99140 (CA).

[189] *Re Paradise Motor Co Ltd* [1968] 1 WLR 1125 (CA).

directors'.[190] The 'usual form' referred to here is the 'stock transfer form', which is found in Sch 1 of the Stock Transfer Act 1963. This Act provides that fully paid-up shares may be transferred by the transferor executing this form and specifying the name and address of the transferee.[191] In fact, this stock transfer form will be regarded as a proper instrument of transfer, even if the company's articles specify additional requirements or require the use of some other form.

16.7.2.2 The transfer procedure

Assuming that the stock transfer form is used, the process for transfer is set out in Figure 16.1.

The articles may specify that the transferor remains the holder of the shares until a specified time or event. For example, the model articles provide that the transferor will remain the holder of certificated shares until the transferee's name is entered in the register of members as the holder of those shares.[192]

16.7.2.3 Forged transfers

Where a company registers a transfer of shares based on a forged transfer, the share transfer is a 'pure nullity',[193] even if the purported transferor's name is removed from the register and a share certificate issued to the purported transferee.[194] Consequently, the true owner of the shares has the right to have his name restored to the register of members,[195] and the company may also be liable to compensate the transferee who relied on the forged transfer.

> ### Re Bahia and San Francisco Railway Co Ltd (1867-68) LR 3 QB 584 (QB)
>
> **FACTS:** Trittin held five shares in Bahia and San Francisco Railway Co. Ltd ('Bahia'). A transfer of the shares, purportedly by Trittin, was made to Stocken and Goldner. Bahia's company secretary registered the transfer, removed Trittin's name from the register of members, and placed Stocken and Goldner's names into the register and issued them with share certificates. Stocken and Goldner subsequently transferred four shares to Burton and one to Goodburn. It was then discovered that the original transfer, purportedly from Trittin, was a forgery. Bahia was ordered to restore Trittin's name to the register of members in respect of the five shares. Burton and Goodburn sued Bahia.
>
> **HELD:** In issuing a share certificate to Stocken and Goldner, Bahia had stated that Stocken and Goldner were entitled to those shares. Burton and Godburn had relied upon that statement and so Bahia was estopped from denying that statement's truth. Accordingly, Bahia was ordered to pay damages to Burton and Goodburn for the loss of the shares.

---

[190] Model articles for private companies, art 26(1); model articles for public companies, art 63(1).

[191] Stock Transfer Act 1963, s 1(1) and (4). It has been argued that this form cannot be used in relation to partly-paid shares, but it has been argued by Geoffrey Morse, *Palmer's Company Law* (Sweet & Maxwell 2018) para 6.430 that it can be used in relation to partly-paid shares providing that the transfer is also executed by the transferee (see *Dempsey v Celtic Football and Athletic Co Ltd* [1993] BCC 514).

[192] Model articles for private companies, art 26(4); model articles for public companies, art 63(4).

[193] *Ruben v Great Fingall Consolidated* [1906] AC 439 (HL) 443 (Lord Loreburn LC).

[194] *Simm v Anglo-American Telegraph Co* (1879) 5 QBD 188 (CA).

[195] *Davis v Bank of England* (1824) 2 Bing 393.

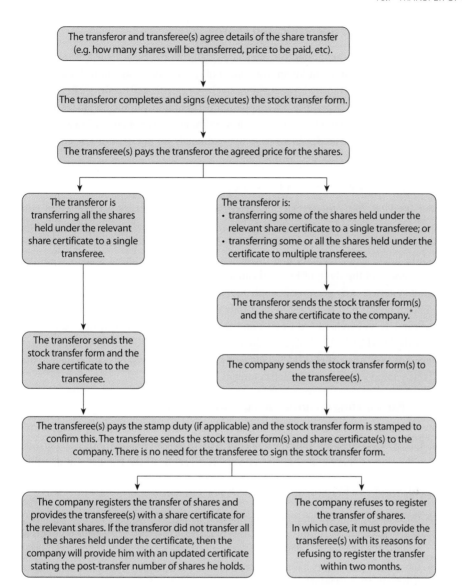

FIGURE 16.1 Transfer of certificated shares

*The form and share certificate are first sent to the company so that it can verify that the transferor has the shares in question and the certificate covers those shares. Where the transferor is keeping some of the shares held under the certificate, then the share certificate is not sent to the transferee(s) as this might enable the transferee to falsely argue that the transferor intends to transfer all of the shares under the certificate.

The person seeking to effect the forged transfer cannot claim on the basis of estoppel. In fact, where the company sustains loss due to the forged transfer, then it can claim an indemnity from the person seeking to effect the forged transfer, even if that person is innocent and was not involved in the forgery.[196]

---

[196] *Sheffield Corporation v Barclay* [1905] AC 392 (HL).

16.7.3 **Transfer of uncertificated shares**

Where shares are uncertificated (i.e. no share certificate has been issued in relation to them), then the requirement for an instrument of transfer does not apply.[197] Instead, an alternative system of transfer is provided for by the Uncertificated Securities Regulations 2001 ('USR 2001').[198] In practice, this happens most commonly in relation to listed companies, whose shares tend to be uncertificated (although it is not compulsory for listed shares to be uncertificated). As a result, approximately 88 per cent of UK equities in value are held in uncertificated form.[199]

16.7.3.1 **A 'relevant system' and 'operator'**

Under the USR 2001, the transfer of uncertificated shares occurs via a 'relevant system',[200] which is defined as 'a computer-based system, and procedures, which enable title to units of a security to be evidenced and transferred without a written instrument, and which facilitate supplementary and incidental matters'.[201] A relevant system is run by an 'operator' and the Bank of England can approve a person to act as an operator of a relevant system.[202] Any person can apply to the Bank of England to seek its approval to become an operator.[203] However, to date, only one operator has been approved, namely Euroclear UK and Ireland Ltd ('EUI') and the relevant system that it operates in the UK is called CREST.[204] The USR 2001 do not apply solely to CREST, but to any relevant system; however, given that CREST is currently the only approved relevant system in the UK, this section will focus on transfers under CREST.

16.7.3.2 **Participating securities and participating issuers**

Shares can only be transferred via CREST if they are deemed to be 'participating securities'. A class of a company's shares will only be a participating security if (i) EUI permits title to the class of share to be transferred via CREST; and (ii) the company in question permits the class of share to be held in uncertificated form and permits it to be transferred via CREST.[205] In addition:

- the company's articles must be consistent with (i) the class of shares in question being held in uncertificated form; (ii) the transfer of shares of that class being made by means of CREST; and (iii) the USR 2001;[206] or
- the company's directors have passed a resolution stating that title to the class of shares may be transferred using CREST.[207]

EUI will not permit shares to be transferred via CREST unless they comply with its own set of rules, known as the CREST Rules.[208] In particular, Rule 7 imposes a lengthy list of conditions that must be met by the company and the shares it wishes to become participating securities.

---

[197] This is because the requirement for an instrument of transfer does not apply to transfers that come within the scope of regulations passed under Pt 21, Ch 2 of the CA 2006 (CA 2006, s 770(1)(b)(ii)), which would include the Uncertificated Securities Regulations 2001.

[198] SI 2001/3755.

[199] Euroclear, 'Streamlined Real-time Settlement: Euroclear UK and Ireland's CREST System' (Euroclear 2012).

[200] The relevant EU legislation (namely EU Regulation 909/2014) uses the phrase 'central securities depository'.

[201] USR 2001, reg 2(1).   [202] ibid reg 3(1).   [203] ibid reg 4(1).

[204] CREST is an acronym of 'Certificateless Registry for Electronic Share Transfer'. When CREST was first created, EUI was known as CRESTCo Ltd.

[205] USR 201, reg 14.   [206] ibid reg 15.   [207] ibid reg 16.

[208] Euroclear, 'CREST Rules' (Euroclear 2018).

The transferor (seller) of the shares and the transferee (buyer) will agree the terms of the transfer (e.g. how many shares will be transferred, the price to be paid, when the transfer will take place, etc.).

↓

The transferor and transferee will send their instructions for the share transfer to CREST. CREST will then check:

- whether the instructions of the transferor and transferee match up; and
- whether the transferor holds the shares he is purporting to transfer.

↓

On the specified transfer date, CREST will transfer the transferor's shares to the transferee, which will involve:

- amending the transferor's stock account by removing the transferred shares;
- transferring the shares into the stock account of the transferee;
- transferring the agreed purchase price from the transferee's settlement bank to the transferor's settlement bank (CREST operates on a 'delivery versus payment' basis, so the transfer of the shares and payment for this shares will occur simultaneously — this will also be the point where title in the shares passes from the transferor to transferee);
- EUI's operator register of members will be updated to reflect the transfer; and
- any participating issuers involved will be sent a message requiring them to update their issue register of members.

FIGURE 16.2 Transfer of uncertificated shares

Any company that has issued participating securities is known as a 'participating issuer'[209] and each participating issuer is required to maintain a register (known as the 'issue register of members'),[210] which must contain specified information (e.g. names and addresses of its members, details of certificated shares held by each member, etc.).[211] EUI is also obliged to maintain a register (known as 'the operator register of members') in respect of every company which is a participating issuer.[212] This register must contain specified information in relation to each class of securities, such as the names and addresses of members who hold uncertificated shares in the company, and details of the uncertificated shares held.[213]

16.7.3.3 The transfer procedure

The procedure for transferring uncertificated shares is set out in Figure 16.2.

Where a valid transfer takes place in accordance with the USR 2001, then EUI must register the transfer. It can only refuse to register a transfer if it falls within reg 27(2) or (4). Regulation 27(2) provides that EUI can refuse to register a transfer if it has actual notice that the transfer is:

- prohibited by an order of a UK court;
- prohibited or avoided by or under an enactment; or
- a transfer to a deceased person.

Regulation 27(4) allows EUI to refuse to register a transfer where the instruction requires a transfer of shares:

- to an entity which is not a natural or legal person;
- to a minor;

---

209 USR 2001, reg 3(1). 210 ibid reg 20(1)(a). 211 ibid Sch 4, para 2.
212 ibid reg 20(1)(b) and (3). 213 ibid Sch 4, para 4.

- to be held jointly in the names of more persons than is permitted under the terms of the issue of the shares; or
- where EUI has actual notice of any of the matters contained in reg 35(5)(a) (e.g. that the information contained in the transfer is not correct).

It should also be noted that the USR 2001 allow for the conversion of shares when being transferred, so a person who holds certificated shares can transfer them to a person who will then hold those shares in uncertificated form,[214] or vice versa.[215]

16.8 Transmission of shares

The 'transmission' of shares occurs where shares pass from one person (the transmittor) to another person (the transmittee) due to the operation of law, and not via the transfer procedures discussed above. The transmission of shares principally occurs in three situations:

1. Death: when a shareholder dies, his shares will be transmitted to his personal representative, who can then deal with them accordingly (e.g. by transferring them to the deceased's beneficiaries).[216] The company must accept, as sufficient evidence of the representative's entitlement to the shares, any document that provides sufficient evidence of (i) a grant of probate; (ii) letters of administration of the deceased's estate; or (iii) confirmation as executor of the deceased person.[217]

2. Bankruptcy: where a shareholder is declared bankrupt, then his shares (as part of his estate) will be transmitted to his trustee in bankruptcy,[218] who will then deal with them accordingly (e.g. by selling them to satisfy the bankrupt's debts, or transferring them directly to the bankrupt's creditors). Unless the articles provide otherwise, the bankrupt will remain a member of the company and can exercise the voting rights attached to the shares,[219] but the trustee can direct the bankrupt as to how to exercise those voting rights.[220]

3. Mental Health Act 1983 patients: where a shareholder becomes a patient under the Mental Health Act 1983, then his shares (as part of his estate) will be transmitted to a receiver appointed by the Court of Protection.

Where shares are transmitted, no instrument of transfer is required because the shares are not being transferred.[221] Upon transmission, the rights and status of the transmittee is usually a matter for the articles. For example, the model articles provide the following:

- If title to a share passes to a transmittee, the company may only recognize the transmittee as having any title to that share.[222]
- A transmittee who produces such evidence of entitlement to shares as the directors so require may (i) subject to the articles, choose to become the holder of those shares or to have them transferred to another person; and (ii) subject to the articles, and pending any transfer of shares to another person, has the same rights as the holder had.[223]

---

[214] ibid reg 33. This is often known as 'dematerialization'.
[215] ibid reg 32. This is often known as 'materialization'.
[216] Section 773 of the CA 2006 provides that the personal representative may transfer the shares to another, even though the personal representative is not a member.
[217] CA 2006, s 774.   [218] IA 1986, ss 283(1) and 306.
[219] *Morgan v Gray* [1953] Ch 83 (Ch).   [220] ibid.   [221] CA 2006, s 770(2).
[222] Model articles for private companies, art 27(1); model articles for public companies, art 65(1).
[223] Model articles for private companies, art 27(2); model articles for public companies, art 66(1).

However, where the transmission occurs due to the death or bankruptcy of a shareholder, then the transmittee does not have the right to attend or vote at a general meeting, unless he becomes the holder of those shares.[224]

The transmission of shares does not automatically make the transmittee a member of the company[225] because a person only becomes a member if he agrees to become a member.[226] If the transmittee does agree to become a member, then he can be registered as a member (unless the articles provide otherwise).[227] Once registered, the transmittee will become personally liable on the shares.[228]

CHAPTER SUMMARY

- A share is an item of property that confers upon its holder rights as set out in the CA 2006 and the constitution.

- A public company must have an allotted share capital of at least £50,000. Private companies are not subject to a minimum share capital requirement.

- Who has the power to allot shares depends upon the type of company, the class of share being allotted, and how many other classes of shares the company has.

- Shareholders generally have a right of pre-emption meaning that, when a company issues new shares, they have to first be offered to the existing shareholders.

- A company is not permitted to allot shares for less than their nominal value.

- Companies are free to issue shares of different classes if they are authorized to do so by their articles.

- Class rights can only be varied if (i) the variation complies with a class rights variation clause in the articles; or (ii) the variation complies with the applicable rules in the CA 2006.

- A transfer of shares usually occurs where a shareholder sells or gifts his shares to another.

- A transmission of shares occurs where shares pass from one person to another due to the operation of law.

FURTHER READING

Alexander Daehnert, 'The Minimum Capital Requirement—An Anachronism under Conservation: Parts 1 and 2' (2009) 34 Co Law 3 and 34.
- Provides a detailed criticism of the minimum capital requirement placed upon public companies. Argues that the requirement is burdensome and anachronistic.

Paul Myners, 'Pre-Emption Rights: Final Report' (DTI 2005).
- Analyses the law relating to pre-emption rights and discusses why such rights are needed.

Robert R Pennington, 'Can Shares in Companies Be Defined?' (1989) 10 Co Law 140.
- Discusses the nature of the share since the first chartered companies up to the proliferation of the registered company.

---

[224] Model articles for private companies, art 27(3); model articles for public companies, art 66(2).
[225] *Stewart v James Keiller & Sons* (1902) 4 F 657 (OH).
[226] CA 2006, s 112(2) (discussed at 13.1).
[227] *Scott v Frank F Scott (London) Ltd* [1940] Ch 794 (CA).
[228] *Re Cheshire Banking Co* (1886) 32 ChD 301 (CA).

Sarah Worthington, 'Shares and Shareholders: Property, Power and Entitlement' (2001) 22 Co Law 258 and 307.

- This two-part article examines the legal nature of the share, and how this has affected corporate governance reform.

www.euroclear.com accessed 30 October 2018.

- The website of Euroclear UK and Ireland Ltd Provides a wealth of information relating to Euroclear and CREST, including the CREST Rules and the CREST Reference Manual (some documents require registration to access).

SELF-TEST QUESTIONS

1. Define the following terms:

- nominal value;
- share premium;
- authorized share capital;
- allotted share capital;
- paid-up share capital;
- called-up share capital;
- pre-emption right;
- transmission of shares.

2. State whether each of the following statements is true or false and, if false, explain why:

- The allotment of shares occurs before the issuing of shares.
- The directors of a private company have the authority to allot shares only if the articles so provide.
- A private company can exclude pre-emption rights via its articles.
- A member to whom shares have been allotted must be provided with a share certificate in relation to those shares.
- A share certificate provides conclusive proof of share ownership.
- Shares cannot be allotted for less than their nominal value.
- Shares must be paid for in cash.
- Class rights may only be varied via the procedure set out in the CA 2006.

3. The memorandum of Dragon plc provides that its authorized share capital is £2 million. Since the company's incorporation, it has allotted 1.2 million shares, all with a nominal value of £1.50. The terms of all allotments to date have provided that shares can be partly paid for with a minimum of 90 pence payable at allotment and the remainder due when called for. Of the 1.2 million shares, 500,000 have 90 pence paid up, 400,000 have £1.20 paid up, and the remainder are fully paid up. The company calls for 10 pence per share on all unpaid shares, but not all the members pay the called-for amount. Based on the information provided, calculate Dragon's:

- issued share capital;
- unissued share capital;
- paid-up capital;
- called-up capital; and
- uncalled capital.

4. Dragon Goods Ltd ('DG') has issued 7,000 £1 shares, with the company's three directors (Sophie, Stanley, and Kim) each holding 1,000 shares. 2,000 shares are held by Sanjeet, a local businessman, and the remaining 2,000 shares are held by a number of smaller investors.

Since it was incorporated, DG has run at a loss and Sanjeet believes this is down to the directors' poor management of the company. He believes that, with new management, the company could be extremely profitable. Accordingly, Sanjeet starts buying the shares of the smaller investors in the hope that he can acquire enough shares to dismiss the directors.

The directors of DG discover Sanjeet's plan. Accordingly, they cause DG to allot 3,000 new shares (with a nominal value of £1.50) and they are offered to Gabrielle, who is Sophie's partner. However, Gabrielle cannot currently afford to purchase the shares, so she offers to sell her car to DG in exchange for the shares. The car is worth £4,000, but the directors of DG accept the car as full payment, on the condition that Gabrielle use her shares to defeat any resolution that seeks to remove the directors from office.

Stanley decides he wants rid of Sanjeet for good. Accordingly, he forges a stock transfer form, which provides that Sanjeet agrees to sell all his shares to Stanley for £1 each. The form is registered by the company and Sanjeet's name is removed from the register of members.

Sanjeet approaches you, seeking your advice as to the legality of the actions of DG and its directors.

ONLINE RESOURCES

This book is accompanied by online resources to better support you in your studies. Visit www.oup.com/uk/roach-company/ for:

- answers to the self-test questions;
- further reading lists;
- multiple-choice questions;
- glossary.

Updates to the law can be found on the author's Twitter account (@UKCompanyLaw) and further resources can be found on the author's blog (www.companylawandgovernance.com).

17 | The maintenance of capital

- Alteration of share capital
- Acquisition of own shares
- Financial assistance to acquire shares
- Distributions

INTRODUCTION

Chapter 16 discussed shares and share capital. This chapter moves on to discuss a series of rules designed to prevent capital from being unduly reduced, which can adversely affect the creditors' chances to being repaid. Before looking at the operation of these rules, it is important to discuss the overarching aims behind these rules. The following case, out of which some of the principal capital maintenance rules grew, demonstrates the overarching principle behind these rules.

 ***Trevor v Whitworth* (1887) 12 App Cas 409 (HL)**

FACTS: The articles of James Schofield & Sons Ltd ('Schofield') provided that it could purchase its own shares. Whitworth sold his shares in Schofield to Schofield, but before Schofield had fully paid Whitworth for the shares, it went into liquidation. Whitworth commenced proceedings[1] against Schofield for the sum outstanding.

HELD: The House noted that certain rules in the Companies Act 1862 (CA 1862) were designed to restrict the ability of a company to reduce its share capital, as it is the share capital that the creditors look to for payment. Lord Watson stated that:

the effect of these statutory restrictions is to prohibit every transaction between a company and a shareholder, by means of which the money already paid to the company in respect of his shares is returned to him, unless the Court has sanctioned the transaction. Paid-up capital may be diminished or lost in the course of the company's trading . . . but persons who deal with, and give credit to a limited company, naturally rely upon the fact that the company is trading with a certain amount of capital already paid, as well as upon the responsibility of its members for the capital remaining at call; and they are entitled to assume that no part of the capital which has been paid into the coffers of the company has been subsequently paid out, except in the legitimate course of its business.[2]

---

[1] To be precise, it was Whitworth's executors who commenced proceedings, as Whitworth had died prior to the case being heard.

[2] (1887) 12 App Cas 409 (HL) 423–24.

As the effect of the share purchase was to return capital to Whitworth, the House held that Schofield had no power to purchase its own shares and so Whitworth's claim failed.

As discussed at 17.2, a company can, in limited circumstances, purchase its own shares.

Trevor v Whitworth established the overarching principle behind the capital maintenance rules, which is that a company may not return capital to its members unless statute so provides. This is essentially a creditor protection measure—the creditors look to a company's share capital for payment, and so the company should not be permitted to reduce that capital (and thereby reduce the creditors' chances of being repaid) by returning it to its members. As Cotton LJ stated, a company's share capital is 'liable to be spent or lost in carrying on the business of the company, but no part of it can be returned to a member so as to take away from the fund to which the creditors have a right to look as that out of which they are to be paid'.[3] The courts have since extended the rules to also cover capital being given away to non-members.[4]

The approach in *Trevor v Whitworth* was a response to the members of companies being granted limited liability.[5] As discussed at 3.3.3.1, limited liability can adversely affect the position of a company's creditors as, if the shares are fully paid up, they cannot look to the shareholders for payment. To counterbalance this, the capital maintenance doctrine was developed, which consists of a series of rules that aim to protect creditors by ensuring that capital is maintained and is not returned to the members, unless so authorized by statute. Initially, these rules were developed by the courts in the mid-to-late nineteenth century, but were soon incorporated into statute and are today found in the Companies Act 2006 (CA 2006). Mention should also be made of the Second Company Law Directive,[6] which introduced significant changes to the law in relation to capital maintenance and public companies.

Some of the capital maintenance rules have already been discussed (e.g. the requirement for a public company to have an authorized minimum amount of capital, and the prohibition on a company issuing its shares at a discount), and all the rules are set out in Figure 17.1. This chapter discusses the remaining rules, beginning with the rules relating to the alteration of capital.

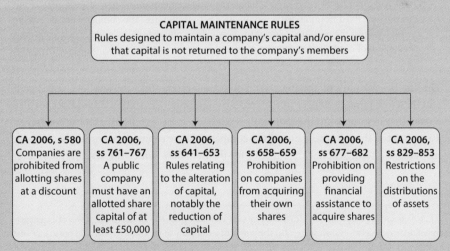

FIGURE 17.1 The capital maintenance rules

---

[3] *Guinness v Land Corporation of Ireland* (1882) 22 ChD 349 (CA) 375.

[4] *Ridge Securities Ltd v IRC* [1964] 1 WLR 479 (Ch).

[5] *Ooregum Gold Mining Co of India Ltd v Roper* [1892] AC 125 (HL) 133 (Lord Halsbury LC).

[6] Note that the original Second Company Law Directive (Council Directive 77/91/EEC) that was passed in 1976 was consolidated in 2012 as Directive 2012/30/EU.

17.1 Alteration of share capital

A company may only alter its share capital in accordance with the CA 2006, with s 617 providing an exhaustive list[7] of seven ways in which a limited company with a share capital can alter its share capital. Six of these are as follows:

1. A company may increase its share capital by allotting new shares.[8]

2. A company may sub-divide all or any of its share capital.[9] Sub-division involves a company converting a number of shares into a larger number of shares with a lower nominal value[10] (e.g. converting 100 £10 shares into 200 £5 shares or 1,000 £1 shares). A company may sub-divide its shares by passing an ordinary resolution,[11] although the articles may provide for a more stringent procedure.[12] The advantage of sub-division is that it lowers the nominal value of the shares, thereby making them a more attractive proposition for those who felt the original value was too high.

3. A company may consolidate all or any of its share capital.[13] Consolidation is the opposite of sub-division and involves the conversion of a number of shares into a smaller number of shares with a higher nominal value[14] (e.g. converting 100 £1 shares into 50 £2 shares or 10 £10 shares, etc.). A company may consolidate its shares by passing an ordinary resolution,[15] although the articles can provide for a more stringent procedure.[16] Consolidation can be useful where the company feels that the number of shares it has is excessive and unwieldy, but the process is rarely used.

4. A company may reconvert stock into shares.[17] Companies used to be able to convert shares into stock,[18] but this fell out of popularity due to reforms contained in the Companies Act 1948 (CA 1948). Nevertheless, some older companies may still have stock and the CA 2006 allows limited companies to convert stock back into shares by passing an ordinary resolution.[19]

5. A limited company may redenominate its share capital or any class of its share capital,[20] which involves converting shares having a fixed nominal value in one currency to having a fixed nominal value in another currency.[21] A resolution is required to redenominate share capital.[22]

6. Given the nature of currency exchanges, a redenomination of share capital may result in the new fixed nominal value not being a round number. The company may therefore wish to adjust the nominal value of the newly denominated shares, and it can do this via a reduction of capital.[23] A reduction of capital in connection with redenomination requires a special resolution to be passed.[24]

The first five methods of altering capital do not adversely affect the level of share capital and therefore pose no danger to the creditors' interests. The sixth method does involve a reduction in capital, but the reduction is not likely to be significant as it cannot exceed 10 per cent of the nominal value of the company's share capital.[25] Accordingly, these six methods of altering capital are a matter for the members alone. The seventh method of

---

[7] CA 2006, s 617(1). However, s 617(5) does provide that nothing in s 617 affects (i) the power of a company to purchase or redeem its own shares; (ii) the power of a company to purchase its shares in pursuance of a court order; (iii) the forfeiture of shares, or shares surrendered in lieu of forfeiture; (iv) the cancellation of shares; and (v) the power of a company to enter into a compromise or arrangement under Pt 26 of the Act.
[8] CA 2006, s 617(1)(a).   [9] ibid s 617(3)(a).   [10] ibid s 618(1)(a).   [11] ibid s 618(3).
[12] ibid s 618(5).   [13] ibid s 617(3)(a).   [14] ibid s 618(1)(b).   [15] ibid s 618(3).
[16] ibid s 618(5).   [17] ibid s 617(3)(b).   [18] This is now prohibited by s 540(2) of the CA 2006.
[19] CA 2006, s 620(1) and (2).   [20] ibid s 617(4).   [21] ibid s 622(1).   [22] ibid.
[23] ibid ss 617(4) and 626(1).   [24] ibid s 626(2).   [25] ibid s 626(4).

altering share capital, namely a reduction of capital, does have the potential to adversely affect the creditors' interests and it is therefore subject to stringent regulation and so is discussed separately.

17.1.1 **Reduction of share capital**

It is a long-held principle that a company may only reduce its share capital 'in the manner permitted by the statutes'[26] with the first such procedure being introduced by the Companies Act 1867 (CA 1867). Under the CA 1985, a company could only reduce its share capital if (i) the articles permitted a reduction; (ii) a special resolution was obtained authorizing the reduction; and (iii) the court approved the reduction.[27] The Company Law Review Steering Group (CLRSG) was of the opinion that 'reduction of capital should become a simpler and more efficient process'[28] and so it recommended that all companies should be able to reduce their capital by passing a special resolution supported by a solvency statement.[29] However, the majority of respondents stated that the court procedure should be retained[30] and so ss 641–53 provide for two methods to reduce capital, namely:

1. any limited company may reduce its share capital by passing a special resolution followed by confirmation from the court;

2. a private company may reduce its share capital by passing a special resolution supported by a solvency statement.[31]

Before these two methods are discussed, some general points must be noted. The Act indicates that the only way to reduce capital is via the two methods set out in ss 641–53,[32] but this is not actually the case. There are several provisions in the CA 2006 that can result in a reduction of capital (e.g. the rules relating to the redemption or cancelling of shares). In those instances, the provisions in question establish safeguards to protect the interests of the company's creditors. Here, we are concerned with the more wide-ranging power found in ss 641–53.

The fact that the Act allows companies to reduce their capital demonstrates that a reduction can be beneficial to the company. The following example demonstrates why a reduction can be beneficial to the company and other persons.

 Eg **Dividends and a reduction of capital**

Dragon Goods Ltd ('DG') was incorporated in 2017 with an allotted share capital of £100,000. Its first year of trading was not successful and it made a loss of £10,000. The board therefore decided to reduce DG's share capital by £30,000, and this was done in accordance with the CA 2006 through the solvency statement procedure. The results of this reduction are that the

---

[26] *Trevor v Whitworth* (1887) 12 App Cas 409 (HL) 423 (Lord Watson).

[27] Companies Act 1985 (CA 1985), s 135 (now repealed).

[28] CLRSG, 'Modern Company Law for a Competitive Economy: The Strategic Framework' (1999) para 5.4.7.

[29] ibid.

[30] CLRSG, 'Modern Company Law for a Competitive Economy: Completing the Structure' (2000) para 7.9.

[31] CA 2006, s 641(1).   [32] ibid s 617(2)(b).

£10,000 loss would be wiped out and DG would acquire a distributable reserve of £20,000.[33] DG may decide to keep this reserve (e.g. to offset future losses) or it could spend the reserve (e.g. by paying a dividend to the members, or by using the money to fund a share buy-back or redemption of shares).

Providing that the relevant provisions are followed correctly, the company's motive for reducing its share capital is irrelevant.[34] However, the courts have stated that a reduction will not be approved if it 'was not for any discernible purpose at all but simply an act in a vacuum . . .'.[35]

The Act provides companies with considerable discretion as to how they may reduce share capital by stating that 'a company may reduce its share capital . . . in any way'.[36] This is, however, subject to two limitations. First, a company that seeks to reduce its capital by special resolution supported by solvency statement cannot do so if the result of the reduction is that there would be no members of the company holding shares other than redeemable shares.[37] Second, a company may not reduce its share capital by either method if the reduction is part of a scheme under which a person is to acquire all the shares in the company or all the shares in one or more classes, other than those he already holds.[38]

🔗 The rationale behind this second limitation is discussed at 2.1.1.4.

Although companies may reduce capital in any way, the Act does provide three examples of ways to reduce capital and these tend to be the most common:

1. The company may extinguish or reduce the liability on any of its shares in respect of share capital not paid up.[39]

2. The company may, either with or without extinguishing or reducing liability on any of its shares, cancel any paid-up share capital that is lost or unrepresented by available assets.[40]

3. The company may, either with or without extinguishing or reducing liability on any of its shares, repay any paid-up share capital in excess of the company's wants.[41]

🔗 Class rights and their variation are discussed at 16.6.

The company may, if it so wishes, include a provision in its articles excluding or restricting its ability to reduce its share capital.[42] If a reduction of capital constitutes a variation of a class right, then the procedure for the variation of class rights will also need to be followed.

Having discussed these general points, the two methods of reducing capital will now be examined.

17.1.1.1 Special resolution and court confirmation

The first method of effecting a reduction of capital is available to all types of limited company, and involves the company passing a special resolution and then applying to the court for an order confirming the reduction.[43] In deciding whether to confirm the

---

[33] Section 654(1) of the CA 2006 provides that a reserve arising from a reduction of capital is not distributable. However, this is subject to the Companies (Reduction of Share Capital) Order 2008, SI 2008/1915, art 3(2), which provides that a private company that reduces its capital via the solvency statement procedure is not subject to s 654(1) and the reserve arising from the reduction is treated as a realized profit.

[34] *Westburn Sugar Refineries Ltd, Petitioners* [1951] AC 625 (HL).

[35] *Re Ratners Group plc* (1988) 4 BCC 293 (Ch) 296 (Harman J).   [36] CA 2006, s 641(3).

[37] ibid s 641(2).   [38] ibid s 641(2A).   [39] ibid s 641(4)(a).   [40] ibid s 641(4)(b)(i).

[41] ibid s 641(4)(b)(ii).   [42] ibid s 641(6).   [43] ibid s 641(1)(b).

reduction, the court's discretion is not subject to any limitation[44] (e.g. the courts have confirmed a reduction that breaches the rights of shareholders)[45] and it may confirm the reduction on such terms as it thinks fit.[46] When determining whether to approve the reduction, the courts have established a number of principles:

- A reduction will only be confirmed if 'creditors of the company are safeguarded so that money cannot be applied in any way that would be detrimental to creditors'.[47] The interests of the creditors will be the primary concern of the courts.

- The reduction will only be confirmed if 'the proposed reduction affects all shareholders of equal standing in a similar manner, or that those treated in a different manner from their equals have consented to that different treatment'.[48]

- A reduction will only be confirmed if 'the cause of the reduction . . . was properly put to shareholders so that they could exercise an informed choice, and that the cause is proved by the evidence before the court'.[49] The explanatory materials relating to the reduction should be in a circular accompanying the notice summoning the meeting.[50]

- The court will examine whether the procedure by which the reduction is carried out is formally correct.[51]

- The court will take into account the public interest, which can include 'the interest of those members of the public who may be induced to take shares in the company'.[52]

In practice, it is very rare for the court to not confirm a reduction. This is because the reduction is usually designed in such a way as to elicit the support of the members and creditors. Members who do object to the reduction can do little (unless the reduction constitutes a variation of a class right), but s 646 does provide an important right to creditors who object to the reduction. If the proposed reduction of capital involves a diminution of liability in respect of unpaid share capital or the payment to a shareholder of any paid-up share capital, then s 646 will apply unless the court directs otherwise.[53] Section 646 provides that a creditor is entitled to object to a reduction of capital if:

- at a date fixed by the court, the creditor is entitled to a debt or claim that, if that date were the commencement of the winding up of the company, would be admissible in proof against the company; and

- the creditor can show that there is a real likelihood that the reduction will result in the company being unable to discharge his debt or claim when it fell due.[54]

The court will establish a list of creditors entitled to object and will ascertain the nature and amounts of their debt or claims.[55] The court can, if it thinks fit, dispense with the consent of a creditor on the list if the company pays the creditor's debt or satisfies his claim.[56] The significance of this is that a court must not confirm a reduction unless it is satisfied that every creditor entitled to object to the reduction has either consented to the reduction, or his debt or claim has been discharged, or has determined, or has been secured.[57] In practice, few creditors object to a reduction because companies, wisely,

---

[44] *British and American Trustee and Finance Corp Ltd v Couper* [1894] AC 399 (HL).

[45] *Banknock Coal Co Ltd* (1897) 24 R 476 (Court of Session).   [46] CA 2006, s 648(1).

[47] *Re Ratners Group plc* (1988) 4 BCC 293 (Ch) 295 (Harman J).

[48] *Re Jupiter House Investments (Cambridge) Ltd* [1985] 1 WLR 975 (Ch) 978 (Harman J).   [49] ibid.

[50] *Re Thorn EMI plc* (1988) 4 BCC 698 (Ch) 701.

[51] *Scottish Insurance Corp Ltd v Wilsons & Clyde Coal Co Ltd* [1949] AC 462 (HL) 486 (Lord Simonds).

[52] *Poole v National Bank of China Ltd* [1907] AC 229 (HL) 239 (Lord Macnaghten).

[53] CA 2006, s 645(2). The court can also apply s 646 even if the s 645(2) criteria are not met (s 645(4)).

[54] ibid s 646(1).   [55] ibid s 646(2) and (3).   [56] ibid s 646(4).   [57] ibid s 648(2).

seek to obtain the creditors' consent prior to beginning the reduction process, or will seek to prevent the creditor from objecting (e.g. by repaying the creditor and so discharging the debt).

Upon obtaining court confirmation, the company should deliver a copy of the court order and a statement of capital (approved by the court) to Companies House, where it will be registered.[58] However, if the reduction reduces the share capital of a public company below the authorized minimum, then Companies House must not register the reduction unless the court so directs or the company re-registers as private.[59] In these circumstances, the Act does provide an expedited procedure that allows a public company to re-register as private without having to pass the usual special resolution.[60] Upon registration of the court order and statement of capital, the reduction in capital takes effect.[61]

A public company's authorized minimum capital is discussed at 16.3.

17.1.1.2 Special resolution and solvency statement

Prior to 1 October 2008,[62] a reduction of capital could only be effected if court approval was obtained. To make the reduction process more efficient, the CLRSG recommended that the requirement of court approval be removed,[63] but the government decided to retain it in relation to public companies.[64] Accordingly, the second method of reducing capital is only available to private companies and involves the company passing a special resolution that is supported by a solvency statement from the directors.[65]

A solvency statement is a statement stating that each of the directors has formed the opinion that:

- as regards the company's situation at the date of the statement, there is no ground on which the company could then be found to be unable to pay (or otherwise discharge) its debts; and

- the company will be able to pay (or otherwise discharge) its debts as they fall due during the year immediately following the date of the statement. Alternatively, if it is intended to commence the winding up of the company within 12 months of the date of the statement, each director must be of the opinion that the company will be able to pay (or otherwise discharge) its debts in full within 12 months of the commencement of the winding up.[66]

The phrase 'each of the directors' means that the reduction will only be effective if all the directors make the solvency statement. If a director refuses to make the statement, then the reduction can only proceed if that director resigns or is removed.

In forming the above opinions, the directors must take into account all the company's liabilities (including any contingent or prospective liabilities).[67] If the directors make a solvency statement without having reasonable grounds for the opinions expressed in it, and the statement is delivered to the registrar, then an offence is committed by each director in default.[68] The Act provides for no civil consequences, but case law provides that the reduction would be void,[69] and the shareholders may have to pay back any capital they received as a result of the reduction.[70]

---

[58] ibid s 649(1).   [59] ibid s 650(1) and (2).   [60] ibid s 651.   [61] ibid s 649(3).

[62] This being the date that s 641 of the CA 2006 came into effect.

[63] CLRSG, 'Modern Company Law for a Competitive Economy: Company Formation and Capital Maintenance' (1999) para 3.27.

[64] Department of Trade and Industry, *Company Law Reform* (Cm 6456, 2005) 42.

[65] CA 2006, s 641(1)(a).   [66] ibid s 643(1).   [67] ibid s 643(2).   [68] ibid s 643(4).

[69] *Macpherson v European Strategic Bureau Ltd* [2002] BCC 39 (CA).

[70] *Re Halt Garage (1964) Ltd* [1982] 3 All ER 1016 (Ch).

This statement must be made not more than 15 days before the special resolution is passed.[71] Where the resolution is proposed as a written resolution, then a copy of the solvency statement must be sent to every eligible member at or before the time when the proposed resolution is sent.[72] Where the resolution is proposed at a meeting, a copy of the solvency statement must be made available for inspection by the members throughout that meeting.[73] A failure to comply with these provisions will not invalidate the resolution,[74] but each officer in default will commit a criminal offence.[75] It is also likely that the members will vote against the special resolution if the solvency statement is not made available.

Within 15 days of the resolution being passed, a copy of the statement, along with a statement of capital (which will indicate the share capital of the company following the reduction) and a copy of the resolution, must be delivered to Companies House.[76] The resolution will not take effect until Companies House registers these documents.[77]

17.1.2 Duty of directors upon a serious loss of capital

Section 656 of the CA 2006 is located within the provisions relating to a reduction of capital, but its application is much wider. It provides that where the net assets of a public company fall to half or less of its called-up share capital, then the directors must call a general meeting of the company to consider whether any steps, and if so what, should be taken to deal with the situation.[78] This meeting must be called by the directors no later than 28 days after the directors became aware of the serious loss of capital,[79] and the meeting must take place no later than 56 days after they first became aware.[80]

These rules were first introduced in the CA 1980[81] in order to implement the Second European Community (EC) Company Law Directive. The problem with s 656 is that it is very vague and places little emphasis on the directors to actually act. Article 17(1) of the Directive was more specific and required the directors to 'consider whether the company should be wound up or any other measures taken'. One might argue whether or not s 656 effectively implements art 17.

17.2 Acquisition of own shares

As discussed in the Introduction to this chapter, the courts have long held that a company cannot purchase its own shares on the ground that this would return capital to the shareholders.[82] Further reasons for the prohibition were that a company could purchase its own shares in an attempt to manipulate its own share price and it would allow companies to reduce capital whilst avoiding the procedures for reducing capital laid down in statute. The prohibition became statutory under the CA 1980,[83] with s 658(1) of the CA 2006 now generally prohibiting limited companies from acquiring their own shares. If a

---

[71] CA 2006, s 642(1)(a).   [72] ibid s 642(2).   [73] ibid s 642(3).   [74] ibid s 642(4)

[75] ibid s 644(7).   [76] ibid s 644(1).   [77] ibid s 644(4).   [78] ibid s 656(1).

[79] ibid s 656(2). It follows from this that the s 656 obligation only arises where a director knows of the serious loss of capital.

[80] ibid s 656(3).   [81] Companies Act 1980 (CA 1980), s 34 (now repealed).

[82] *Trevor v Whitworth* (1887) 12 App Cas 409 (HL).   [83] CA 1980, s 35 (now repealed).

company does contravene s 658, then a criminal offence is committed by the company and every officer who is in default, and the purported acquisition will be void.[84]

Keen to encourage investment in smaller companies, the CA 1980 introduced several exceptions to the general prohibition that have been expanded on since. Today, the CA 2006 provides that:

- a limited company may acquire any of its own fully paid shares otherwise than for valuable consideration;[85]

- as discussed at 17.1.1, a company may acquire its own shares as part of a valid reduction of capital;[86]

- as discussed at 15.3.7.1, the court may order that a company purchase its own shares from a member if the member's interests have been unfairly prejudiced under s 994 of the CA 2006.[87]

Two other exceptions are more complex and are deserving of more discussion, namely redeemable shares and the purchase of own shares.

17.2.1 Redeemable shares

Consider the following example.

Eg **The rationale behind redeemable shares**

Kate holds 500 shares in Dragon Tools Ltd ('DT'). She wishes to sell these shares, but cannot find anyone willing to buy them. Karl owns 26 per cent of DT's shares, and has used his holding to defeat every special resolution proposed by the directors. He is doing this as a protest at the level of dividends paid out over the past few years, which he sees as being too low. The directors believe that Karl's actions are hindering the company's business.

The above situation demonstrates a problem that can arise in private companies that may hinder investment. As shares in private companies are not easily marketable (due to such shares not being tradable on a stock exchange), potential investors may be reluctant to purchase shares for fear that they will be locked in (as has happened to Kate). The owners of private companies may be reluctant to issue shares to outsiders for fear that an outsider will gain too much control (an especially acute concern if the company is family-owned), which has occurred in relation to Karl. Keen to encourage investment in private companies, the newly-elected Conservative government of 1979 proposed that companies should be able to issue redeemable shares, and this was implemented via the CA 1981.[88]

Redeemable shares are shares issued by the company on the condition that they will be bought back (i.e. redeemed) by the company at some point in the future. The terms

---

[84] CA 2006, s 658(2).   [85] ibid s 659(1).   [86] ibid s 659(2)(a).

[87] ibid s 659(2)(b)(iv). Other courts orders not subject to the s 658 prohibition can be found in ss 98, 721, and 759.

[88] Companies Act 1981 (CA 1981), s 45 (now repealed). Prior to the 1981 Act, companies could issue redeemable preference shares (Companies Act 1929 (CA 1929), s 46), but the 1981 Act allowed companies to issue any shares as redeemable.

of the issue will set out how the power of redemption is exercised (e.g. the terms might provide that the company or shareholder has the power to insist upon redemption, or that redemption will occur on a specified date). Using the example above, if the shares issued to Kate were redeemable shares, then she would be able to insist upon DT purchasing them from her. If the shares issued to Karl were redeemable shares, then DT would be able to insist that he sell them back to DT. It should be noted that redeemable shares can be useful for larger companies too (although such companies rarely issue redeemable shares). For example, if a company feels that its debt-to-equity ratio is too low, it can redeem shares to increase its **gearing**.

➡ **gearing:** the ratio of a company's debt capital to its share capital (discussed at 20.1.1.1)

17.2.1.1 The power to issue redeemable shares

The CA 2006 provides that a public company may issue redeemable shares if it is authorized to do so by its articles.[89] Authorization in the articles is not required in order for a private company to issue redeemable shares,[90] but the articles may exclude or restrict redeemable shares being issued.[91] One limitation that all companies are subject to is that redeemable shares cannot be issued at a time when there are no issued shares of a company that are not redeemable.[92]

The terms of redemption (i.e. when redemption will occur) is a matter for the company's articles and must be stated in the articles,[93] unless the directors are authorized to determine the terms of redemption by the articles or a resolution of the company.[94] If the directors are so authorized, then they must determine the terms of redemption before the shares are allotted.[95]

17.2.1.2 Payment and financing

Only fully paid-up shares can be redeemed[96] on the basis that, if partly paid shares could be redeemed, then the company (and its creditors) would lose the uncalled capital. The general rule is that the company must pay for the redeemable shares upon redemption.[97] However, payment can be made at a later date if the company and the holder of the shares agree to this.[98]

Of crucial importance is the source of the payment. In order to prevent capital being returned to the shareholders (and the adverse effect this would have on the company's creditors), the general rule is that redeemable shares must be paid for out of distributable profits of the company or out of the proceeds of a fresh issue of shares made for the purpose of the redemption.[99] If a premium is paid on the shares, this must be paid for out of distributable profits,[100] unless the redeemable shares were issued at a premium, in which case the premium payable on redemption can be paid for out of a fresh issue of shares.[101]

---

[89] CA 2006, s 684(1) and (3). Article 43(2) of the model articles for public companies provides authorization.

[90] CA 2006, ss 684(1) and (2). Despite this, art 22(2) of the model articles for private companies provides such authorization.

[91] The model articles for private companies contain no exclusions or limitations.

[92] CA 2006, s 684(4).   [93] ibid s 685(4).

[94] ibid s 685(1). Article 22(2) of the model articles for private companies and art 43(2) of the model articles for public companies authorizes the directors to determine the terms of redemption.

[95] CA 2006, s 685(3)(a).   [96] ibid s 686(1).   [97] ibid s 686(3).

[98] ibid s 686(2). Under prior Companies Acts, this was not permitted and deferred payment rendered the redemption void (*Kinlan v Crimmin* [2006] EWHC 779 (Ch), [2007] BCC 106).

[99] CA 2006, s 687(2).   [100] ibid s 687(3).   [101] ibid s 687(4).

A private company can pay for redeemable shares out of capital. This is discussed at 17.2.3.

17.2.1.3 Consequences of redemption

Upon redemption, redeemable shares are cancelled and the company's share capital must be reduced by the nominal value of the shares redeemed.[102] If the shares were purchased wholly out of the company's profits, the amount by which the company's issued share capital was diminished must be transferred to the capital redemption reserve.[103] Within one month of the redemption, the company must notify Companies House of the redemption, specify the shares redeemed, and provide a statement of capital.[104]

17.2.2 Purchase of own shares

Redeemable shares are useful, but they do suffer from a notable flaw. Only redeemable shares can be redeemed, so they must be issued as redeemable shares, which requires a measure of foresight on behalf of the directors. The CA 1981 introduced a procedure that enabled a company to purchase any of its shares (not just redeemable shares), and this is often referred to as a 'share buyback'. The question that arises is why a company would wish to purchase its own shares. Buybacks tend to be used by companies that have a capital surplus and can be used as an alternative to, or in conjunction with, a payment of dividends. The following example indicates the potential advantages that can arise from a buyback, but it should be noted that there is disagreement regarding the likelihood of these advantages arising and much will depend upon the specific circumstances of the company in question.

> **Eg** **The advantages of a share buyback**
>
> Over the past few years, Dragon plc has made a profit of £20 million per year and currently has cash reserves in the bank of £40 million. Of the £20 million profit it makes each year, £1 million of this derives from interest earned from its cash reserves. It currently has 50 million shares issued. Accordingly, Dragon's earnings per share ('EPS') is 40 pence. The board believes that Dragon's current share price of £2 per share is undervaluing the company, so it decides to use all its cash reserves to fund a share buyback. Accordingly, Dragon buys 20 million of its shares, and then cancels them. The effects (actual and potential) of this are:
>
> - The number of shares issued will fall to 30 million.
> - Dragon's profit will fall by £1 million as it is no longer deriving £1 million in interest from its cash reserves (which were wiped out to fund the buyback).
> - Dragon's EPS will increase to 63 pence. This will benefit Dragon's shareholders if Dragon later decides to pay out a dividend, as each shareholder will potentially receive more per share. Depending on the circumstances, a buyback could be more tax efficient from the shareholders' point of view than receiving a dividend.
> - The directors may see their remuneration increase if it is tied to EPS. Of course, the concern is that directors will propose buybacks simply to increase their own remuneration.

---

[102] ibid s 688.   [103] ibid s 733(1) and (2)(a).   [104] ibid s 689.

- Dragon's share price could increase. This could be caused by simple supply and demand (less shares are in circulation, so supply is decreased), or because Dragon's **price–earnings ratio** has increased. Before the buyback, Dragon's price–earnings ratio was 5 (200 pence divided by 40 pence). Following the buyback, if investors still value Dragon's price–earnings ratio at 5, they may be willing to pay up to £3.15 per share. Conventional wisdom states that a company's share price will increase following a buyback, but this is dependent on several factors (e.g. the timing of the buyback). If Dragon's shares are undervalued, a buyback could be used to correct this. The company could then later issue more shares at the higher share price. Alternatively, instead of cancelling the repurchased shares, it could retain them as treasury shares and then sell them if the share price increases.

➡ **price–earnings ratio:** a method of valuing a company, calculated by dividing the company's share price by its earnings per share

🔗 Treasury shares are discussed at 17.2.2.6.

In recent years, buybacks have become much more common and much larger in scope, especially in the US. For example, in September 2016, Microsoft announced that its board had authorized up to $40 billion to be used to fund a buyback.[105] In the UK, the rules regarding buybacks have been relaxed over the years (especially for private companies) and so they are becoming more popular in the UK.

17.2.2.1 The power to purchase shares

Section 690(1) of the CA 2006 provides that a limited company may purchase its own shares (including redeemable shares), subject to any restriction or prohibition in the company's articles.[106] However, this ability is subject to three restrictions:

1. A company cannot purchase its own shares if, as a result of the purchase, there would no longer be any shares other than redeemable shares or shares held as treasury shares.[107]

2. A limited company can only purchase fully paid shares.[108]

3. A company can only purchase its own shares if it follows the procedure set out in Ch 4 of Pt 18 of the CA 2006. The procedure that must be adopted depends on whether the purchase is a market purchase or an off-market purchase.

17.2.2.2 Market purchases

A market purchase is one that takes place on a recognized investment exchange and is subject to a marketing arrangement on the exchange[109] (e.g. the shares are officially listed).[110] The procedure for a market purchase is less onerous that for an off-market purchase because the investment exchange and the United Kingdom Listing Authority (UKLA, currently the FCA) will impose its own rules. A company may only make a market purchase of its own shares if the purchase has first been authorized by a resolution of the company.[111] This authority may be general or it may limit the purchase to a particular class or description of shares (e.g. the company can only purchase preference shares), and the authority may be unconditional or subject to conditions.[112] The

---

[105] See https://news.microsoft.com/2016/09/20/microsoft-announces-quarterly-dividend-increase-and-share-repurchase-program-2/#sm.00bk46x5112dflc11lp1wyn7d83cv accessed 10 January 2019.

[106] The model articles contain no such prohibitions or restrictions.   [107] CA 2006, s 690(2).

[108] ibid s 691(1).   [109] ibid s 693(4).   [110] ibid s 693(3)(a).

[111] ibid s 701(1).   [112] ibid s 701(2).

authority must specify the maximum number of shares that the company may acquire, and it must determine the maximum and minimum prices that may be paid for the shares.[113] The authority must specify a date on which it is to expire, and this date cannot be more than five years after the resolution is passed.[114] The authority can be renewed, or varied or revoked, by a resolution of the company.[115] A resolution conferring, renewing, varying, or revoking authorization for a market purchase must be forwarded to Companies House within 15 days after it is passed.[116]

17.2.2.3 **Off-market purchases**

A purchase is off-market if the shares are (i) not purchased on a recognized investment exchange; or (ii) are purchased on a recognized investment exchange, but are not subject to a marketing arrangement on the exchange.[117] A company may only make an off-market purchase of its own shares in pursuance of a contract that has been approved prior to the purchase. Approval must take one of two forms, namely:

- the terms of the contract must be authorized by a resolution of the company before the contract is entered into; or
- the contract must provide that no shares may be purchased until its terms have been authorized by a resolution of the company.[118]

The authority conferred may be varied, revoked, or renewed by a resolution of the company.[119] In the case of a public company, a resolution conferring, varying, or renewing authority must specify a date on which it is to expire, and this date cannot be more than five years after the resolution is passed.[120]

The rules relating to disclosure and voting rights differ depending on whether a resolution is proposed as a written resolution or at a meeting:

- Where a resolution conferring, varying, revoking, or renewing authority is proposed as a written resolution, then a copy of the contract (if it is in writing) or a memorandum of its terms (if it is not in writing) must be sent to every eligible member at or before the time when the proposed resolution is sent to him.[121] A member who holds shares to which the resolution relates will not be an eligible member[122] and so cannot vote on the resolution.

- Where a resolution conferring, varying, revoking, or renewing authority is proposed at a meeting, then a copy of the contract (if it is in writing) or a memorandum of its terms (if it is not in writing) must be made available for inspection by members at the company's registered office (for not less than 15 days ending on the date of the meeting) and at the meeting itself.[123] The resolution will be ineffective if (i) any member holding shares to which the resolution relates exercises voting rights in relation to the resolution; and (ii) the resolution would not have been passed if he had not done so.[124]

17.2.2.4 **Payment and financing**

Where a limited company purchases its own shares, then the shares must be paid for on purchase,[125] unless a private limited company is purchasing the shares for the purposes of an employee share scheme.[126] This differs to redeemable shares, where the company and the shareholders in question can agree to payment at a later date.

---

[113] ibid s 701(3). [114] ibid s 701(5). [115] ibid s 701(4). [116] ibid ss 701(8) and 30.
[117] ibid s 693(2). [118] ibid s 694(2). [119] ibid s 694(4). [120] ibid s 694(5).
[121] ibid s 696(2)(a). [122] ibid s 695(2). [123] ibid s 696(2)(b). [124] ibid s 695(3).
[125] ibid s 691(2). [126] ibid s 691(3).

The general rule is that a purchase of shares must be paid for out of distributable profits of the company or out of the proceeds of a fresh issue of shares made for the purpose of financing the purchase.[127] If a premium is paid on the shares, this must be paid for out of distributable profits,[128] unless the shares were issued at a premium, in which case the premium payable on purchase can be paid for out of a fresh issue of shares.[129] However, a private company can pay for its shares out of capital by following the complex process in ss 709–23 of the CA 2006.[130] However, a simpler process exists that allows private companies to purchase their own shares out of capital, providing that:

- the purchase is authorized by the company's articles; and
- the total price paid for the shares in the financial year does not exceed £15,000 or the nominal value of 5 per cent of its fully paid-up share capital at the beginning of the financial year (whichever is the lower).[131]

This process for purchasing shares out of capital is discussed at 17.2.3.

17.2.2.5 Consequences of purchase

Upon purchase, the purchased shares are cancelled and the company's share capital must be reduced by the nominal value of the shares cancelled.[132] If the shares were purchased wholly out of the company's profits, the amount by which the company's issued share capital was diminished must be transferred to the capital redemption reserve.[133]

Within 28 days of the purchase, the company must deliver a return to Companies House, which must state the number and nominal value of the shares purchased and the date on which they were delivered to the company.[134] Public companies must also provide details regarding the price paid for the shares.[135]

17.2.2.6 Treasury shares

As noted, when a limited company purchases its own shares, those shares are treated as cancelled.[136] However, an exception exists whereby the shares need not be cancelled and the company can instead choose to hold the shares as 'treasury shares',[137] but the company can only do this if the purchase of the shares was made out of distributable profits.[138]

Treasury shares are simply shares that the company holds 'in treasury'. Where such shares are held by the company, then the company's name must be entered in the register of members as the member holding the shares.[139] A company with treasury shares may:

- hold onto the shares;[140]
- sell the shares for cash consideration;[141]
- transfer the shares for the purposes of or pursuant to an employees' share scheme;[142] or
- cancel the shares at any time.[143]

---

[127] ibid s 692(2)(a).   [128] ibid s 692(2)(b).   [129] ibid s 692(3).   [130] ibid s 692(1).
[131] ibid s 692(1ZA).   [132] ibid s 706(b).   [133] ibid s 733(1) and (2)(b).
[134] ibid s 707(1) and (3).   [135] ibid s 707(4).   [136] ibid ss 688 and 706(b).
[137] ibid s 706(a).   [138] ibid s 724(1)(b).   [139] ibid s 724(4)   [140] ibid s 724(3)(a).
[141] ibid ss 724(3)(b) and 727(1)(a).   [142] ibid ss 724(3)(b) and 727(1) (b).
[143] ibid ss 724(3)(b) and 729(1). This will involve a reduction of capital, but s 729(5) provides that the company will not need to comply with the reduction of capital rules found in ss 641–53.

If the company does sell, transfer, or cancel the shares, then it must notify Companies House no later than 28 days following the sale, transfer, or cancellation.[144] The company is subject to certain limitations regarding its usage of treasury shares:

- the company must not exercise any right in respect of the treasury shares (in particular, the right to attend and vote at meetings) and any purported exercise of such a right is void;[145] and
- no dividend may be paid and no other distribution of the company's assets may be made to the company, in respect of the treasury shares.[146]

A breach of any of the rules relating to treasury shares constitutes a criminal offence committed by the company and every officer in default.[147]

17.2.3 Redeeming or purchasing shares out of capital

As discussed at 17.2.2, in those instances where a company can purchase its own shares, the shares must be paid for out of the company's distributable profits or via the proceeds of a fresh issue of shares. However, this may prove impossible for private companies, who may lack sufficient profits or who cannot find sufficient purchasers for their shares. Accordingly, the CA 1981 first permitted private companies to redeem or purchase shares out of capital, providing the articles so authorized.[148] Today, authorization from the articles is not required, although the articles may exclude or restrict a private company's ability to redeem or purchase shares out of capital.[149]

Parliament was clearly aware of the dangers of allowing shares to be redeemed or purchased out of capital (especially the dangers to the creditors), and so ss 709–23 contain two notable safeguards designed to protect the company's members and creditors. First, to minimize the effect upon the company's capital, s 710 provides that before resorting to using capital as payment for the shares, the company must first use any available profits and the proceeds of any fresh issue of shares made for the purpose of redemption or purchase.[150] Once this has been used, any capital that is required for the redemption or purchase of the shares is known as the 'permissible capital payment'.[151]

Second, the Act puts in place a strict procedure that must be followed, and this procedure contains numerous safeguards designed to ensure that the members and creditors are fully informed and their interests are protected. This procedure will now be discussed.

17.2.3.1 The procedure

A payment out of capital by a private company for the redemption or purchase of its own shares will only be lawful if the procedure established by ss 714–20 is followed.[152] Figure 17.2 sets out this five-stage procedure.

Any member (other than one who voted for the resolution) or creditor of the company may, within five weeks of the resolution, apply to the court for an order cancelling the resolution.[153] Upon such an application, the court may adjourn the proceedings in order that an arrangement may be made to the satisfaction of the court for the purchase

---

[144] ibid ss 728(1) and 730(1).   [145] ibid s 726(2).   [146] ibid s 726(3).   [147] ibid s 732(1).
[148] CA 1981, s 54(1) (now repealed).
[149] CA 2006, s 709(1). No exclusion or limitations are found in the model articles for private companies.
[150] CA 2006, s 710(1).   [151] ibid s 710(2).   [152] ibid s 713(1).   [153] ibid s 721(1) and (2).

I. Directors' statement (ss 714(1)–(5) and 715)

- The directors must make a statement specifying the permissible capital payment. The statement must also state, having made full inquiry into the affairs and prospects of the company, the directors have formed the opinion that (i) immediately after the payment out of capital is made, there will be no grounds on which the company could be found unable to pay its debts; and (ii) as regards the year following the payment, the company will be able to carry on business as a going concern throughout that year.
- If the directors make this statement without having reasonable grounds for the opinions expressed in it, an offence is committed by every director in default.
- Section 76 of the IA 1986 provides that if the company is wound up within one year of the date of the payment and the company's assets are not sufficient to meet the company's debts and liabilities, then the person from whom the shares were redeemed or purchased will be liable to contribute to the company's assets an amount not exceeding the payment that was made in respect of his shares. The directors who signed the statement are also jointly and severally liable with this person to contribute that amount.

↓

II. Auditor's report (s 714(6))

The directors' statement must be accompanied by a report by the company's auditor which states that (i) he has inquired into the company's affairs; (ii) the amount specified as the permissible capital payment is properly determined; and (iii) he is not aware of anything to indicate that the opinion expressed by the directors in their statement is unreasonable in all the circumstances.

↓

III. Special resolution (ss 716–18)

- Within one week of the directors' statement, the payment out of capital must be approved by a special resolution of the company.
- Where the resolution is proposed as a written resolution, then a copy of the directors' statement and the auditor's report must be sent to every eligible member at or before the time when the proposed resolution is sent to him. Failure to comply with this requirement will render the resolution ineffective. A member who holds shares to which the resolution relates is not an eligible member and cannot vote on the resolution.
- Where the resolution is proposed at a meeting, it will not be effective if a copy of the directors' statement and auditor's report is not made available for inspection by the members at the meeting. The resolution will also be ineffective if (i) any member holding shares to which the resolution relates exercises voting rights on the resolution; and (ii) the resolution would not have been passed if he had not done so.

↓

IV. Public notice (s 719)

- Within one week following the special resolution being passed, the company must publish a notice in *The Gazette* stating that the company has approved a payment out of capital for the purpose of acquiring its own shares by redemption or purchase (or both). The notice must also state (i) the amount of the permissible capital payment; (ii) the date of the resolution; (iii) where the directors' statement and auditor's report are available for inspection; (iv) stating that any creditor may, at any time within five weeks following the resolution, apply for an order preventing the payment.
- The company must also either publish the above information in an appropriate national newspaper, or give notice in writing to that effect to each of its creditors.

↓

V. Payment (s 723)

The payment out of capital must be made no earlier than five weeks after the resolution, and no later than seven weeks after the resolution. However, the seven-week period can be extended by the court if an application is made to the court for an order cancelling the resolution.

FIGURE 17.2 Redeeming or purchasing shares out of capital

of the interests of the dissenting members or for the protection of the dissenting creditors, and may give such directions and make such orders as it thinks expedient for facilitating or carrying into effect any such arrangement.[154] If no such adjournment is made, then the court must make an order either cancelling or confirming the resolution, and it may do so on such terms and conditions as it thinks fit.[155] This court order may provide for the purchase by the company of the shares of any of its members and, if necessary, amend the company's articles.[156] The court can also require the company not to make any, or any specified, amendments to its articles without leave of the court.[157]

17.2.3.2 **Employee share schemes**

Where a private company wishes to purchase its own shares out of capital for the purposes of an employee share scheme, then a less strict procedure can be used.[158] Here, payment out of capital can be made if the company passes a special resolution supported by a solvency statement[159] (the solvency statement is the same as for a reduction of capital).

The solvency statement is discussed at 17.1.1.2.

17.3 Financial assistance to acquire shares

As is discussed later in this section, the general rule is that a public company is prohibited from providing financial assistance to another person to acquire its shares. Unlike many other statutory capital maintenance rules which evolved out of nineteenth-century case law, the prohibition of financial assistance was implemented following the recommendations of the Greene Report in 1926.[160] The following example gives an indication of the type of activity the Greene Committee wished to prevent.

> **Eg** **Financial assistance to acquire shares**
>
> Dragon plc wishes to acquire Lotus Ltd, but lacks sufficient funds to acquire a majority of Lotus's shares. The directors of Lotus wish the takeover to proceed, so they cause Lotus to loan £100,000 to Dragon. Dragon then uses this money to purchase enough shares in Lotus to take it over.

In this example, Lotus has effectively provided the money for Dragon's acquisition of Lotus's shares. The Greene Committee was of the opinion that this was 'highly improper . . . [and] . . . [s]uch an arrangement appears to us to offend against the spirit if not the letter of the law which prohibits a company from trafficking in its own shares and the practice is open to the gravest abuses'.[161] Accordingly, the Committee recommended that companies should be prohibited from providing any financial assistance in connection with a purchase of their own shares by another person, and this was implemented by s 45 of the CA 1929, which later became s 54 of the CA 1948.

---

[154] CA 2006, s 721(3).   [155] ibid s 721(4).   [156] ibid s 721(6).   [157] ibid s 721(7).
[158] ibid s 720A(1).   [159] ibid s 720A(1) and (2).
[160] Board of Trade, *Report of the Company Law Amendment Committee* (Cmnd 2657, 1926).
[161] ibid para 30.

The problem with the prohibition, as noted by the Jenkins Committee, was that it was drafted 'in terms so wide and general that it appears to penalise a number of innocent transactions'.[162] The Jenkins Committee did suggest several reforms, but they were not acted upon. The passing of the Second Company Law Directive[163] limited the ability of Parliament to relax the prohibition in relation to public companies, but following two heavily criticized cases,[164] it was decided that the rules relating to private companies needed to be relaxed. As a result, the CA 1981 introduced a 'whitewash' procedure that allowed private companies to provide financial assistance if certain conditions were satisfied.[165] The whitewash provisions were carried through to the CA 1985,[166] but the CLRSG heavily criticized these provisions, stating:

> These provisions are among the most difficult of the Act, and in many cases it is all but impossible for a company to assess whether a proposed course of action is lawful or not. The provisions are arbitrary in their effect on private companies, and innocuous transactions may be rendered unlawful by criminal law requirements that are often unenforceable and by civil sanctions of wide and damaging effect.[167]

This uncertainty resulted in companies spending significant sums each year on costly legal advice. The CLRSG noted that, for smaller companies, 'the costs involved in complying with the legislation are disproportionate'[168] and that other areas of the law can more effectively combat the mischief that the prohibition on financial assistance was designed to combat. Accordingly, the CLRSG recommended that the prohibition on financial assistance should not apply to private companies, and this recommendation was implemented by ss 677–83 of the CA 2006. The prohibition on financial assistance will continue to apply to public companies though, and Parliament's ability to affect this is (currently) limited by its obligations to enforce the Second Company Law Directive.[169]

Before we discuss the current rules, is important to discuss exactly what sort of activity constitutes 'financial assistance'.

17.3.1 Financial assistance

Of crucial importance is what type of activity constitutes financial assistance. Section 677(1) of the CA 2006 provides that 'financial assistance' means financial assistance given by way of gift, guarantee, security, indemnity, release or waiver, or loan, and any other financial assistance given by a company where (i) the net assets of the company are reduced to a material extent by the giving of the assistance; or (ii) the company has

---

[162] Board of Trade, *Report of the Company Law Committee* (Cmnd 1749, 1962) para 171.

[163] Council Directive 77/91/EEC [1977] OJ L26/1.

[164] Namely *Belmont Finance Corp v Williams Furniture Ltd (No 2)* [1980] 1 All ER 393 (CA) and *Armour Hick Northern Ltd v Whitehouse* [1980] 1 WLR 1520 (Ch).

[165] CA 1981, s 43 (now repealed).   [166] CA 1985, ss 155–8 (now repealed).

[167] CLRSG, 'Modern Company Law for a Competitive Economy: Final Report (Volume One)' (2001) para 2.30.

[168] CLRSG, 'Modern Company Law for a Competitive Economy: Developing the Framework (2000) para 7.19.

[169] For a criticism of the rationale behind the prohibition, even in relation to public companies, see Eilis Ferran, 'Corporate Transactions and Financial Assistance: Shifting Policy Perceptions but Static Law' (2004) 63 CLJ 225.

no assets. This will cover a broad range of transactions, but several limitations must be borne in mind. First, the words used in s 677(1) (e.g. 'guarantee', 'indemnity', etc.) will be interpreted based upon their 'recognised legal meaning',[170] and not based upon the dictionary definition of these terms. Second, the court has stated (rather unsurprisingly) that only financial assistance falls within the legislative prohibition.[171] Third, when determining whether a company has provided financial assistance, the court will:

> examine the commercial realities of the transaction and decide whether it can properly be described as the giving of financial assistance by the company, bearing in mind that the section is a penal one and should not be strained to cover transactions which are not fairly within it.[172]

The following case provides an example of a transaction that appeared to amount to financial assistance, but was held not to be once the court examined the 'commercial substance and reality'[173] of the transaction.

See Hand C Hirt, 'The Scope of Prohibited Financial Assistance after MT Realisations Ltd (in Liquidation) v Digital Equipment Co Ltd' (2004) 25 Co Law 9.

MT Realisations Ltd v Digital Equipment Co Ltd [2003] EWCA Civ 494

FACTS: MT Realisations Ltd ('MTR') was a subsidiary in the Digital group of companies. MTR was loss-making and, to help MRT survive, Digital Equipment Co Ltd ('DE', the holding company of the Digital group) had loaned MTR around £8 million, secured by dentures. MTI Holdings (UK) Ltd ('MTI') wished to acquire MTR and so it entered into two agreements with DE, under which:

1. MTI would purchase DE's shares in MTR for £1 and;

2. the £8 million that MTR owed to DE was assigned to MTI for £6.5 million (so MTR would now owe £8 million to MTI). MTI would pay DE the £6.5 million in instalments.

MTI struggled to pay the instalments, and so the agreement was amended to provide that any amounts owed by the Digital companies to MTR would, instead of being paid to MTR, be used to offset the amount MTI owed DE. MTR went into liquidation and the liquidator alleged that the amended agreement involved MTR providing financial assistance (i.e. MTR's funds were being used to finance MTI's acquisition of MTR's shares).

HELD: The Court held that MTR had not provided MTI with financial assistance. Mummery LJ stated that 'in order to appreciate the "commercial realities," it is necessary to more closely examine MTI's legal right against MTR . . .'[174] MTI was a secured creditor of MTR and so could take steps to enforce its rights against MTR in respect of sums that MTR received from DE and other companies in the Digital Group. Accordingly, MTI was not the recipient of financial assistance, but was simply enforcing its security rights against MTR. In other words, 'nothing was given by MTR to MTI, which it had not already acquired as its own resource by assignment from Digital UK in order to secure performance of the obligation to re-pay the inter-company loans due on demand from MTR to Digital UK'.[175]

---

[170] *British and Commonwealth Holdings plc v Barclays Bank plc* [1996] 1 WLR 1 (CA) 14 (Aldous LJ).

[171] ibid 15.

[172] *Charterhouse Investment Trust v Tempest Diesels Ltd* [1986] BCLC 1 (Ch) 10 (Hoffmann J).

[173] *Chaston v SWP Group plc* [2002] EWCA Civ 1999, [2003] BCC 140 [38] (Arden LJ).

[174] [2003] EWCA Civ 494, [2003] BCC 415 [29].   [175] ibid.

It will be noted that, generally, s 677(1) makes no mention of detriment.[176] Accordingly, to qualify as financial assistance, there is no need to establish that the person providing the financial assistance suffered any form of detriment.[177] Indeed, if a company provided financial assistance in the form of a loan, the assistance might be beneficial to that company, but the fact that the assistance benefits the company providing it will not in itself render the assistance lawful.[178]

17.3.2 **When financial assistance is prohibited**

Not all financial assistance is prohibited. Financial assistance to purchase shares will only be prohibited if it falls within the circumstances set out in ss 678–9, which provides for three broad types of prohibited financial assistance. As noted at 17.3, the prohibition today largely applies only to public companies.

17.3.2.1 **Assistance for acquisition of shares in a public company**

Where a person is acquiring, or proposing to acquire, shares in a public company, then that company, or a subsidiary of that company (if it is registered in the UK),[179] is prohibited from giving financial assistance directly or indirectly for the purpose of the acquisition before or at the same time as the acquisition took place.[180]

 Eg | **Assistance for acquisition of shares in a public company**

> Hades Investment Ltd wishes to purchase shares in Dragon plc, but lacks sufficient funds. Dragon plc and Dragon Goods Ltd (a subsidiary of Spartan) each lend Hades £50,000, which it then uses to purchase shares in Dragon. Both Dragon and Dragon Goods have engaged in prohibited financial assistance.

The above prohibition will not apply where a company is giving financial assistance for the acquisition of shares in it or its holding company and:

- the assistance is given in good faith in the interests of the company; and
- the company's principal purpose in giving the assistance is not for the purpose of acquiring the shares, or the giving of assistance for the purpose of acquiring shares but is only an incidental part of some larger purpose of the company.[181]

An example of this can be seen in *Re Uniq plc*,[182] where the court held that financial assistance was lawful because it was part of a scheme of arrangement designed to restructure a corporate group (so the assistance was part of a larger purpose) and the restructuring was necessary to prevent the parent and its principal subsidiary becoming insolvent (so the assistance was in the interests of the company).

---

[176] An exception to this lies in relation to s 677(1)(d), which applies where the net assets of the company have been reduced to a material extent by the giving of the assistance.
[177] *Chaston v SWP Group plc* [2002] EWCA Civ 1999, [2003] BCC 140 [41] (Arden LJ).   [178] ibid [46].
[179] A foreign subsidiary of an English parent company may provide financial assistance in the purchasing of its parent's shares (*Arab Bank plc v Mercantile Holdings Ltd* [1994] Ch 71 (Ch)).
[180] CA 2006, s 678(1).   [181] ibid s 678(2).   [182] [2011] EWHC 749 (Ch), [2012] 1 BCLC 783.

17.3.2.2 Assistance by a public company for acquisition of shares

Where a person is acquiring or proposing to acquire shares in a private company, it is not lawful for a public company that is a subsidiary of that company to give financial assistance directly or indirectly for the purpose of the acquisition before or at the same time as the acquisition took place.[183]

Eg   Assistance by public company for acquisition of shares

Hades Investment Ltd wishes to purchase shares in Dragon Tools Ltd, but lacks sufficient funds. Dragon Components plc (a subsidiary of Dragon Tools) lends Hades £20,000, which it then uses to purchase shares in Dragon Tools. Dragon Components has engaged in prohibited financial assistance.

The above prohibition will not apply where a company is giving financial assistance for the acquisition of shares in it or its holding company and:

- the assistance is given in good faith in the interests of the company; and
- the company's principal purpose in giving the assistance is not for the purpose of acquiring the shares, or the giving of assistance is for the purpose of acquiring shares but this is only an incidental part of some larger purpose of the company.[184]

17.3.2.3 Assistance to reduce or discharge liability

The above two forms of prohibited financial assistance occur where the financial assistance is provided before or at the time of the acquisition. There are two forms of prohibited financial assistance that occur after the acquisition has taken place, namely:

1. Where a person has acquired shares in a company and a liability has been incurred (by that person or another) for the purpose of the acquisition, then that company, or a subsidiary of that company, many not give financial assistance directly or indirectly for the purpose of reducing or discharging the liability if, at the time the assistance is given, the company in which the shares were acquired is a public company.[185]

2. Where a person has acquired shares in a private company and a liability has been incurred (by that person or another) for the purpose of the acquisition, then a public company that is a subsidiary of that company may not give financial assistance directly or indirectly for the purpose of reducing or discharging the liability.[186]

Eg   Assistance to reduce or discharge liability

Hades Investment Ltd wishes to acquire shares in Dragon plc, but is concerned about expending funds on the purchase. Hades and Dragon enter into an agreement under which Hades agrees to purchase £20,000 worth of Dragon's shares, with payment due in one week's time. Hades acquires the shares and, two days later, Dragon lends Hades £20,000. Hades uses this money to pay for the shares. Dragon plc has engaged in prohibited financial assistance.

---

[183] CA 2006, s 679(1).   [184] ibid s 679(2).   [185] ibid s 678(3).   [186] ibid s 679(3).

In both cases, the prohibition will not apply where a company is giving financial assistance and:

- the assistance is given in good faith in the interests of the company; and
- the company's principal purpose in giving the assistance is not to reduce or discharge any liability incurred by the person for the purpose of the acquisition of shares, or the reduction or discharge of such liability is only an incidental part of some larger purpose of the company.[187]

17.3.2.4 Distinguishing between 'purpose' and 'reason'

It will be noted that each of the above three forms of prohibited financial assistance is subject to an exception based on whether (i) the company's principal purpose in giving the assistance is not for the purpose of acquiring the shares/reducing or discharging liability; or (ii) the giving of assistance is only an incidental part of some larger purpose of the company. The following case has notably limited the scope of this exception.

Brady v Brady [1989] AC 755 (HL)

See DL Morgan, 'Brady v Brady—A Family Feud' [1988] JBL 412.

FACTS: A family business was conducted through a group of companies, of which two brothers were the only directors and majority shareholders. A dispute arose between them, and the companies became deadlocked. To avoid the adverse consequences that would follow a deadlock, it was decided that the business would be divided between the brothers. A complex scheme was put into place, part of which involved one company in the group providing financial assistance to another company to acquire its shares. It was argued that the financial assistance was lawful because it was part of a larger purpose (i.e. the division of the business) and was incidental to that purpose.

HELD: Lord Oliver, who gave the leading judgment, stated that 'it is important to distinguish between a purpose and the reason why a purpose is formed'.[188] He went on to state that a 'larger' purpose is not the same as a 'more important' purpose. Applying this, the House held that whilst the reason behind the financial assistance was to help divide up the business, the purpose behind the assistance was to assist a company to purchase the shares in another. The assistance was 'not a mere incident of the scheme devised to break the deadlock. It was the essence of the scheme itself and the object which the scheme set out to achieve.'[189] Accordingly, the financial assistance was not an incidental part of a larger purpose and so it was unlawful.

COMMENT: Lord Oliver believed that the restrictive approach he advocated was necessary to ensure that the 'larger purpose' exception 'does not in effect provide a blank cheque for avoiding the effective application of [the prohibition on financial assistance] in every case'.[190] The reaction has been mixed. Some commentators agree with Lord Oliver and argue that a restricted approach is necessary so that the prohibition itself 'has some bite'.[191] Others have argued that the approach in *Brady* is too restrictive and given that the consequence of not permitting the assistance was the collapse of the whole scheme, 'it is difficult to envisage a situation where the "larger purpose" exception will be applicable'.[192]

---

[187] ibid ss 678(4) and 679(4).

[188] [1989] AC 755 (HL) 779. It is worth noting that Lord Oliver's analysis was *obiter*, but it has been followed in subsequent cases (see e.g. *Plaut v Steiner* (1989) 5 BCC 352 (Ch)).

[189] *Brady v Brady* [1989] AC 780 (Lord Oliver).   [190] ibid 779.

[191] Kenneth Polack, 'Companies Act 1985—Scope of Section 153' (1988) 47 CLJ, 359, 362.

[192] Brenda Hannigan and Rosa Greaves, 'Gratuitous Transfers and Financial Assistance after Brady' (1989) 10 Co Law 135, 139.

17.3.3 Exceptions

Sections 681–2 provide for numerous exceptions to the general prohibition discussed at 17.3.2, and classifies these exceptions as either unconditional or conditional.

17.3.3.1 Unconditional exceptions

Section 681 sets out eight transactions that will not constitute prohibited financial assistance. In all cases, these transactions are regulated by the CA 2006 or the IA 1986 and have their own safeguards in place to protect members and creditors. The transactions are:

1. a distribution of a company's assets by way of dividend lawfully made;
2. a distribution of a company's assets made in the course of its winding up;
3. an allotment of bonus shares;
4. a reduction of capital made in accordance with statute;
5. a redemption or purchase of shares made in accordance with statute;
6. anything done in pursuance of a court order under a Pt 26 arrangement or reconstruction;
7. anything done under an arrangement made in pursuance of s 110 of the IA 1986; or
8. anything done under an arrangement made between a company and its creditors that is binding on the creditors by virtue of Pt 1 of the IA 1986 1986.

17.3.3.2 Conditional exceptions

Section 682 provides that certain transactions will not constitute prohibited financial conduct, but only if one of two conditions are satisfied, namely:

1. the company giving the assistance is a private company; or
2. the company giving the assistance is a public company, and (i) the company has net assets that are not reduced by the giving of the assistance; or (ii) to the extent that the assets are so reduced, the assistance is provided out of distributable profits.

The transactions listed in s 682 include:

- where the lending of money is part of the ordinary business of the company, the lending of money in the ordinary course of the company's business;
- the provision by the company, in good faith and in the interests of the company or its holding company, of financial assistance for the purposes of an employee share scheme;
- the making by the company of loans to persons (other than directors) employed in good faith by the company with a view to enabling those persons to acquire fully paid shares in the company or its holding company to be held by them by way of beneficial ownership.

17.3.4 Consequences of engaging in prohibited financial assistance

If a company engages in prohibited financial assistance, then an offence is committed by the company and every officer of the company who is in default.[193] The CA 2006 provides for no other consequences, but pre-2006 case law (which still applies) provides for several civil consequences:

- An agreement to provide unlawful financial assistance is unenforceable,[194] unless the unlawful element can be severed, in which case the remaining agreement can be enforced.[195]

---

[193] CA 2006, s 680(1).   [194] *Heald v O'Connor* [1971] 1 WLR 497 (QB).
[195] *Carney v Herbert* [1985] AC 301 (PC).

- A director who is party to a transaction that amounts to prohibited financial assistance may be held in breach of duty,[196] likely the s 171 duty to act within powers. This means that a member may commence a derivative claim on behalf of the company to recover the sums spent in prohibited financial assistance.[197]

- Directors who cause a company to provide prohibited financial assistance may be disqualified.[198]

- A recipient of prohibited financial assistance will be liable to account for the sum received if he knew or ought to have known of the impropriety of the transaction.[199]

- A person who knowingly assists the directors to cause the company to provide prohibited financial assistance can be personally liable to the company.[200]

17.4 Distributions

Part 23 of the CA 2006 establishes rules regarding when a company can make a distribution to its members. Easily the most popular form of distribution is a dividend, which is simply a distribution of the company's profits to its members, usually determined at x pence per share. The following example demonstrates the operation of a dividend payment in practice.

Eg   A dividend payment

Dragon plc has issued 10,000 shares and decides to issue a dividend of 20 pence per share. Dragon's articles provide that each member's entitlement to a dividend is based on the proportion of the amount paid up on his shares.[201] Dragon's shares are issued as follows:

- 5,000 shares were issued to Jesse, and they are fully paid up. Accordingly, Jesse's dividend payment will be £1,000 (5,000 × £0.20 = £1,000).

- 3,000 shares were issued to Cassidy, of which 50 per cent of the purchase price was paid on allotment, with the remainder due in six months' time. Accordingly, Cassidy's dividend payment will be £300 (3,000 × £0.20 = £600. 50 per cent of £600 is £300).

- 2,000 shares were issued to Eugene, of which 20 per cent of the purchase price was paid on allotment, with the remainder due in six months' time. Accordingly, Eugene's dividend payment will be £80 (2,000 × £0.20 = £400. 20 per cent of £400 is £80).

Although a dividend is the most common form of distribution, the definition of 'distribution' for the purposes of Pt 23 is much wider and means 'every description of distribution of a company's assets to its members, whether in cash or otherwise . . .'.[202] However, the following will not constitute a distribution under Pt 23:

- an issue of shares as fully- or partly-paid bonus shares;

---

[196] *Re In a Flap Envelope Co Ltd* [2003] EWHC 3047 (Ch), [2003] BCC 487.
[197] *Smith v Croft (No 2)* [1988] Ch 114 (Ch).
[198] *Re Continental Assurance Co of London plc (No 1)* [1996] BCC 888 (Ch).
[199] *Belmont Finance Corp v Williams Furniture Ltd (No 2)* [1980] 1 All ER 393 (CA).   [200] ibid.
[201] This is a common provision and can be found in art 71(1) of the model articles for public companies.
[202] CA 2006, s 829(1).

- the reduction of share capital (i) by extinguishing or reducing the liability of any of the members on any of the company's shares in respect of capital not paid up; or (ii) by repaying paid-up share capital;
- the redemption or purchase of the company's own shares; or
- a distribution of assets to members of the company on its winding up.[203]

This breadth of this definition is important as companies may try to disguise a distribution to avoid the rules in the CA 2006, as occurred in the following case.

See Antony Mair, 'Ultra Vires and Aveling Barford Plus Ca Change' (1991) 2 ICCLR 37.

Aveling Barford Ltd v Perion Ltd (1989) 5 BCC 677 (Ch)

FACTS: Dr Lee was the sole beneficial owner of two companies, Aveling Barford Ltd ('AB') and Perion Ltd ('Perion'). AB was solvent, but it was experiencing financial difficulties and had no distributable profits. In February 1987, AB sold to Perion a piece of land for £350,000, even though it had been valued at £650,000 a few months before. In August 1987, Perion sold the land to a third party for £1.56 million. AB commenced proceedings against Perion, contending that it was liable to account for the profit it had made on the sale.

HELD: The sale of the land from AB to Perion was a 'dressed-up distribution'[204] and, as AB had no distributable profits at the time of the sale, the sale was *ultra vires* and void.

COMMENT: AB was not Perion's parent company. AB had not made a distribution to one of its members, but to another company that just happened to be controlled by the same person who controlled AB. Despite this, Hoffmann J stated that it was irrelevant that the distribution was made to Perion and not to Dr Lee. This significantly increases the scope of what might amount to a distribution.

17.4.1 Why pay a dividend?

It is important to understand why companies may wish, or feel pressured, to pay out a dividend. There are numerous important advantages to paying out a dividend:

- Investors are, for obvious reasons, attracted to companies that provide stable dividends, which encourages shareholder loyalty. The payment of dividends can signify a company's financial stability and well-being, and provide an indicator that the directors have positive expectations regarding future performance. This can result in the company's shares being more sought after, which can increase the share price.
- The payment of dividends allows shareholders to financially gain from holding shares, without having to sell those shares.
- If a company has significant cash reserves, but no obvious use for that cash, it may be preferable to pay a dividend, then the members can reinvest the money received by purchasing more shares in the company, which can also help increase the share price.
- If dividends are paid in the form of shares, this can allow a member to increase his shareholding without expending any additional capital.

---

[203] ibid s 829(2).   [204] (1989) 5 BCC 677 (Ch) 683 (Hoffmann J).

However, the decision to pay out a dividend should be taken carefully, as there are also disadvantages to paying a dividend:

- Once a company starts paying a dividend, the members will likely expect a dividend to be paid regularly. If a company reduces or stops paying dividends, this will likely not be viewed favourably by the members, who may sell their shares (thus potentially reducing the share price), and attracting new investors may prove difficult.

- A dividend reduces the company's financial reserves, thereby reducing the amount of money that can be re-invested in the company, or used to pay off unexpected liabilities that might arise. The payment of excessive dividends can accordingly hinder the company's growth or cause it to be unable to pay unexpected debts or liabilities.

- Companies that pay a dividend need to have robust systems in place to ensure that the dividend is lawfully paid and that each member so entitled receives the correct amount. This may be administratively burdensome.

- The pressure to pay a dividend each year may result in the company adopting an overly short-term approach.

There are two principal types of dividend, namely an interim dividend and a final dividend. Table 17.1 sets out the differences between the two.

In recent years, there has been a growing trend for companies to only pay interim dividends, with the result that dividend approval is never subject to shareholder

TABLE 17.1 Interim and final dividends

	Interim dividend	Final dividend
Definition	A dividend paid out before the company's final accounts have been prepared (i.e. paid during a company's financial year).	A dividend paid out once the final accounts have been prepared (i.e. paid following the end of the company's financial year).
Relevant accounts	An interim dividend can be paid out if the annual accounts for the previous year justify it.[205] If they do not, then interim accounts must be used.[206]	A final dividend is usually based on the company's last annual accounts.[207]
Member authorization	The articles will usually empower the directors to pay an interim dividend without member approval.[208]	The articles usually provide that a final dividend must be 'declared' by the members passing an ordinary resolution.[209]
Debt due	An interim dividend is not regarded as a debt of the company owed to the members.	A final dividend, once validly declared, is a debt of the company owed to the members.
Rescission or variation	The directors may rescind an interim dividend, or vary its amount.[210]	Neither the directors nor members can rescind the payment of a final dividend and, once declared, the amount cannot be varied.

[205] CA 2006, ss 836(2) and 840.   [206] ibid ss 836(2)(a) and 838.   [207] ibid s 836(2).
[208] Model articles for private companies, art 30(1); model articles for public companies, art 70(1).
[209] Model articles for private companies, art 30(1); model articles for private companies, art 70(1).
[210] *Lagunas Nitrate Co v Lagunas Syndicate* [1899] 2 Ch 392 (CA).

scrutiny.[211] This has led to the suggestion that at least one shareholder vote should be required per year, irrespective of whether the dividend if interim or final.

The type of company is a relevant factor to consider when determining whether to pay a dividend and what type of dividend. In private companies, where the directors and members are often the same persons, dividends are often used alongside remuneration to provide a tax-efficient method of returning the profit to the director shareholders. Normally, this will involve the director receiving a small salary for his services as a director, with the bulk of his payment coming in the form of dividends (usually interim dividends, as they can be paid out by the directors without the need for an ordinary resolution). The advantages of returning profit via dividends as opposed to remuneration are:

- dividends do not attract National Insurance Contributions;
- no income tax is paid on the first £2,000 earned in dividend income (this is known as the 'dividend allowance'); [212]
- the tax rates paid on dividend income are slightly lower than tax rates paid on a salary.

Public companies with distributable profits have several options available to them:

- The company could simply keep the money in its reserves in case it was needed (e.g. to fund an unexpected business opportunity, or pay off an unexpected liability).
- The company could re-invest the profit back into itself to stimulate growth and generate larger profits in the future.
- The company could buy back its shares.
- The company could pay a dividend. In larger public companies (especially quoted companies), there will be an expectation that a portion of the distributable profits will be distributed as a dividend. In fact, it is common for listed companies to pay out a quarterly or half-yearly interim dividend followed by a final dividend at the end of its financial year.

17.4.2 The legal framework

Before looking at the rules relating to dividends, it is important to note that the government has stated that the UK's dividend regime is 'complex and potentially too backwards looking with insufficient weight placed on current profitability and future prospects and hence providing only limited protection for creditors'.[213] Accordingly, the government has stated that it intends to consult with relevant bodies to consider whether to undertake a comprehensive review of the UK's dividend regime.[214]

It is a long-established principle of company law that every company has an implied power to distribute its profits in the form of a dividend, but this does not mean that the company must distribute its profits (or part of them) as a dividend each year.[215] The members may have an expectation of a dividend (especially in larger companies), but they generally have no automatic right to a dividend. An exception to this is where the company has profits available for distribution and its articles mandate a distribution

---

[211] Department for Business, Energy and Industrial Strategy (BEIS), 'Insolvency and Corporate Governance: Government Response' (BEIS 2018) para 1.41.

[212] Prior to April 2018, the Dividend Allowance was £5,000. This reduction has meant that the financial advantages of taking dividends as opposed to a salary have been reduced notably.

[213] BEIS, 'Insolvency and Corporate Governance: Government Response' (BEIS 2018) para 1.46.

[214] ibid paras 1.47–1.48.   [215] *Burland v Earle* [1902] AC 83 (PC).

(e.g. by stating that a certain percentage of the distributable profits must be distributed by way of dividend). Conversely, the articles of some companies (e.g. charitable companies) may mandate that the company cannot distribute its profits to members. Outside of these mandated instances, the articles usually provide the directors with a discretion as to whether to pay a dividend or not, and it is the articles that set out the procedure for the payment of a dividend.

 The procedure for paying a dividend is discussed at 17.4.5.

Whereas statute has little to say regarding the procedure for paying a dividend, it imposes notable limitations regarding the source of the dividend payment. Originally, these limitations were imposed by the common law,[216] the most notable of which was the rule that dividends could not be paid out of capital.[217] Unfortunately, from the creditors' point of view, the application of this rule became less strict and effective over time—for example, the courts did not require companies to make up lost capital before paying out a dividend.[218]

This changed following the passing of the Second EC Company Law Directive, which was implemented by the CA 1980. The 1980 Act introduced new, strict rules relating to how dividends are to be paid, the principal one being that dividends could only be distributed out of 'profits available for the purpose'.[219] This rule survives today in the CA 2006.

17.4.3 Profits available for distribution

The statutory rules relating to distributions of assets can be found in Pt 23 of the CA 2006, of which the principal provision is s 830(1), which provides that '[a] company may only make a distribution out of profits available for the purpose'. 'Profits available for the purpose', are defined as the company's 'accumulated, realised profits, so far as not previously utilised by distribution or capitalisation, less its accumulated, realised losses, so far as not previously written off in a reduction or reorganisation of capital duly made'.[220] Put simply, the company must calculate its accumulated, realized profits and then deduct from this its accumulated, realized losses. If the final figure is a positive one, then this represents the amount that can be distributed to the members. Key to this calculation are the words 'accumulated' and 'realized'.

17.4.3.1 Accumulated profits and losses

Consider the following example.

> ### Eg   Accumulated profits
>
> In the 2016/17 financial year, Dragon plc's accounts showed that it made a profit of £1 million, but it decided to issue no dividend. Due to increased competition and the loss of several lucrative contracts, in 2017/18, the company made a loss of £3 million, and again no dividend was issued. In 2018/19, Dragon managed to re-acquire some of these contracts and it made a profit of £500,000. Worried that its members would sell their shares due to the lack of dividend payments, the directors of Dragon decided to issue a dividend of £400,000 to its members.

---

[216] For a discussion of the common law origins and development of the distribution rules, see Basil S Yamey, 'Aspects of the Law Relating to Company Dividends' (1941) 4 MLR 273.

[217] *Re Exchange Banking Co, Flitcroft's Case* (1882) 21 ChD 519 (CA).

[218] *Lee v Neuchatel Asphalte Co* (1889) 41 ChD 1 (CA).   [219] CA 1980, s 39(1) (now repealed).

[220] CA 2006, s 830(2).

Under pre-CA 1980 rules, Dragon would be able to pay a dividend in 2018/19, even though it has not made up the loss suffered the previous year. However, since 1980, dividends can only be paid based on 'accumulated' profits and losses, which basically means that companies need to take into account performance in previous years when determining whether a dividend is payable in the current year. In the above example, Dragon could only pay a dividend in 2018/19 if the profit it made in that year was enough to replace any losses that it suffered in previous years (which does not appear to be the case).

17.4.3.2 **Realized profits and losses**

Consider the following example.

 Eg   Realized profits and losses

In May 2018, Dragon plc estimates that its profits for the 2018/19 financial year will be £10 million. Accordingly, in June 2018, it decides to pay out a dividend of £8 million to its members. However, come April 2019, it is clear that Dragon's estimation of its profits was incorrect and the company only made a profit of £5 million. As a result, the £3 million shortfall will have to come out of Dragon's capital.

To ensure that this does not occur, companies cannot base dividends on estimated profits, and distributions must be made based on 'realized' profits and losses, which are defined as 'such profits or losses of the company as fall to be treated as realised in accordance with principles generally accepted at the time when the accounts are prepared, with respect to the determination for accounting purposes of realised profits or losses'.[221] From this, it follows that the concept of realized profit and loss is to be determined based on generally accepted accounting practices at the time, meaning that the concept of realized profit and loss will change over time.

The current accounting practices can be found in Financial Reporting Standard 18, which provides that profits are treated as realized 'only when realised in the form either of cash or of other assets the ultimate cash realisation of which can be assessed with reasonable certainty'.[222] Realised losses are defined as:

- any amount written off by way of providing for depreciation or diminution in the value of assets; or

- any amount retained as reasonably necessary for the purpose of providing for any liability the nature of which is clearly defined and which is either likely to be incurred, or certain to be incurred but uncertain as to amount or as to the date on which it will arise.[223]

More detailed guidance on realized profits and losses is provided by the Institute of Chartered Accountants of England and Wales (ICAEW) and the Institute of Chartered Accountants of Scotland (ICAS) in Technical Release Tech 02/17BL.[224]

---

[221] ibid s 853(4).

[222] Accounting Standards Board, 'Financial Reporting Standard 18' (ASB, 2000) para 28.

[223] CA 2006, s 841(2); Small Companies and Groups (Accounts and Directors' Report) Regulations 2008, Sch 7, paras 1, 2, and 6; Large and Medium-sized Companies and Groups (Accounts and Reports) Regulations 2008, Sch 9, paras 1, 2, and 8.

[224] ICAEW and ICAS, 'Guidance on Realised and Distributable Profits under the Companies Act 2006' (2017) paras 3.1–3.75.

17.4.3.3 **Net asset rules relating to public companies**

Public companies are subject to an additional limitation, namely that a public company may only make a distribution:

- if the amount of its net assets is not less than the aggregate of its called-up share capital and undistributable reserves; and
- if, and to the extent that, the distribution does not reduce the amount of those assets to less than that aggregate.[225]

A company's net assets are defined as 'the aggregate of the company's assets less the aggregate of its liabilities'.[226] A company's undistributable reserves are:

- its share premium account;
- its capital redemption reserve;
- the amount by which its accumulated, realized profits (so far as not previously utilized by capitalization) exceed its accumulated, realized losses (so far as not previously written off in a reduction or reorganization of capital duly made);
- any other reserve which the company is forbidden from distributing by any enactment or by its articles.[227]

17.4.4 **Justification of distribution by reference to accounts**

Historically, it was extremely difficult (if not impossible) to tell whether a distribution was paid out of profit or capital.[228] To a significant degree, this difficulty has been avoided by the imposition of detailed rules regarding the setting out and publication of the company's accounts. Accordingly, when a company determines if it has distributable profits, it is vital that it does so in accordance with the relevant accounting rules. Accordingly, when a company determines whether it can make a distribution in accordance with the above rules, it must do so by reference to 'relevant accounts',[229] which normally means the company's last annual accounts[230] that were circulated to the members in accordance with the CA 2006's requirements.[231] This requirement is essential to protect the company's creditors and, therefore, this requirement cannot be waived by the members.[232]

The circulation of accounts is discussed at 19.3.3.1.

In order to be relied on, the last annual accounts must be prepared in accordance with the CA 2006,[233] and they must have been audited (unless the company is exempt from audit and the directors took advantage of that exception).[234] If any of the above requirements are not satisfied, then the accounts may not be relied on and the distribution will be treated as contravening the CA 2006.[235] These rules are applied strictly—for

---

[225] CA 2006, s 831(1).   [226] ibid s 831(2).   [227] ibid s 831(4).

[228] *Dovey v Cory* [1901] AC 477 (HL) 487 (Earl of Halsbury LC).   [229] CA 2006, s 836(1).

[230] ibid s 836(2). There are exceptions to this in s 836(2). For example, where a distribution is proposed to be declared during the company's first accounting reference period, it will obviously have no prior annual accounts. In this case, the company can justify the distribution by reference to its initial accounts (ibid s 836(2)(b)).

[231] ibid s 837(1).   [232] *Precision Drippings Ltd v Precision Drippings Marketing Ltd* [1986] Ch 447 CA).

[233] CA 2006, s 837(2).

[234] ibid s 837(3). If the auditor's report was qualified, s 837(4) imposes additional requirements (e.g. the auditor must provide a statement indicating whether matters that caused his report to be qualified are relevant in determining whether a distribution would breach Pt 23 of the CA 2006).

[235] ibid s 836(4).

example where a company's accounts were prepared incorrectly, the distribution was declared invalid, even though the company may have had sufficient profits to make the distribution in question.[236]

17.4.5 **Procedure for paying a dividend**

Once it has been determined that a company has distributable profits that it wishes to distribute by way of a dividend the next step is to follow the company's procedures for the payment of dividends. The CA 2006 has little to say regarding this process—it is a matter for the company's articles, and most companies adopt a three-stage procedure like that found in the model articles,[237] and set out in Figure 17.3.

As Figure 17.3 demonstrates, this typical procedure provides that the payment of a dividend is largely a matter for the directors' discretion. Like all others powers conferred upon directors, the power to recommend or make a dividend must be exercised in accordance with the general duties, especially the duties in s 171 (duty to act within powers) and s 172 (duty to promote the success of the company).

17.4.5.1 **Payment**

The standard method of paying a dividend is to send the member a dividend warrant, which is essentially a cheque authorizing the company's bank to pay the member's bank the dividend amount. However, the articles may provide for other payment methods

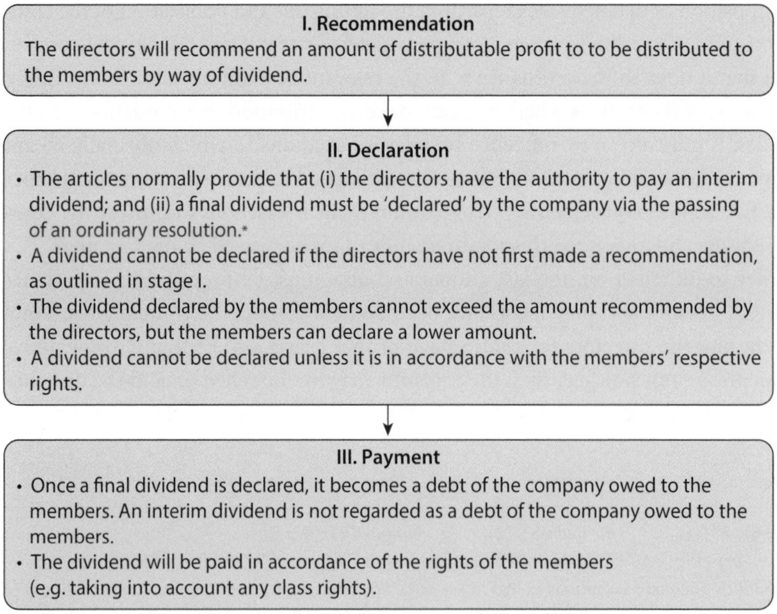

I. Recommendation
The directors will recommend an amount of distributable profit to to be distributed to the members by way of dividend.

↓

II. Declaration
- The articles normally provide that (i) the directors have the authority to pay an interim dividend; and (ii) a final dividend must be 'declared' by the company via the passing of an ordinary resolution.*
- A dividend cannot be declared if the directors have not first made a recommendation, as outlined in stage I.
- The dividend declared by the members cannot exceed the amount recommended by the directors, but the members can declare a lower amount.
- A dividend cannot be declared unless it is in accordance with the members' respective rights.

↓

III. Payment
- Once a final dividend is declared, it becomes a debt of the company owed to the members. An interim dividend is not regarded as a debt of the company owed to the members.
- The dividend will be paid in accordance of the rights of the members (e.g. taking into account any class rights).

*Model articles for private companies, art 30(1); model articles for public companies, art 70(1).

FIGURE 17.3 Procedure for paying a dividend

---

[236] *Bairstow v Queens Moat Houses plc* [2001] EWCA Civ 712, [2002] BCC 91 (discussed at 17.4.6.2).

[237] Model articles for private companies, art 30; model articles for public companies, art 70.

(e.g. the model articles allow members to write to the company requesting their dividend be paid directly into their bank account).[238] Companies with a large number of members instead tend to send their members a dividend mandate form to complete, which instructs the company to pay the dividend into a bank account of the member's choosing. The advantage of this from the company's perspective is that (i) it results in less unclaimed dividends; and (ii) instead of sending individual cheques to each member, it simply sends larger cheques to the relevant banks (e.g. if 5,000 members banked with the Royal Bank of Scotland (RBS), then the company sends one cheque to RBS covering the dividend payments of all 5,000 members, along with a list of how much should be paid to each member).

The general rule is that a company must pay dividends in cash.[239] However, this rule is subject to the articles, which may provide for some other form of payment (e.g. the model articles allow a company to pay all or part of a dividend by transferring non-cash assets of equivalent value to its members).[240] In recent years, scrip dividends are becoming more popular—a scrip dividend is where a company allows its members to choose between receiving a cash dividend or a dividend in the form of newly issued and fully paid-up shares. Scrip dividends have several advantages over cash dividends, including:

- the members increase their shareholdings for free, and without having to pay brokerage expenses or stamp duty;
- the company retains the profit that it would otherwise pay as a dividend, which can then be used by the company (e.g. to re-invest or expand its business);
- payment in shares may be preferable if the company's cash reserves are low;
- the company's share base is increased, which could reduce its gearing and make it easier to secure borrowing.

> Gearing is discussed at 20.1.1.1.

To obtain the above benefits, companies may wish to encourage members to take a scrip dividend. This can be done by offering an enhanced scrip dividend, under which the shares issued will be of a greater value than the cash dividend.

17.4.6 **Consequences of unlawful distributions**

An unlawful distribution can result in liability being placed on the members, the directors, and, if the dividend is paid based on incorrect accounts, the auditor.

17.4.6.1 **Liability of the members**

Where a distribution (or part of a distribution) is made by a company to a member in contravention of the provisions in Pt 23 then if, at the time of the distribution, the member knew or had reasonable grounds to believe that the distribution contravened Pt 23, then:

- he is liable to repay the distribution (or part of it, as the case may be) to the company; or
- if the distribution was not made in cash, the member is liable to pay the company a sum equal to the value of the distribution (or part) at the time.[241]

---

[238] Model articles for private companies, art 31(1)(a); model articles for public companies, art 72(1)(a).
[239] *Wood v Odessa Waterworks Co* (1889) 42 ChD 636 (Ch).
[240] Model articles for private companies, art 34(1); model articles for public companies, art 76(1).
[241] CA 2006, s 847(1) and (2).

The question that arises is how to determine whether the member knew or had reasonable grounds to believe that the distribution breached Pt 23, and this was discussed in the following case.

See Jennifer Payne, 'Recipient Liability for Unlawful Dividends' (2007) 1 LMCLQ 7.

It's a Wrap (UK) Ltd v Gula [2006] EWCA Civ 544

FACTS: Mr and Mrs Gula ('the Gulas') were the only directors and members of It's a Wrap Ltd ('Wrap'). An accountant advised the Gulas to take their remuneration in the form of dividends and so, between 2000 and 2002, the Gulas each received a dividend of £14,000 per year, even though the company made no profit in those years. When Wrap went into liquidation, the liquidator sought to recover from the Gulas the £56,000 paid in unlawful dividend payments. At first instance, the liquidator's action failed on the ground that the Gulas were not aware of the relevant statutory provisions and had no grounds for believing that they were contravening statute.[242] The liquidator appealed.

HELD: The liquidator's appeal was allowed and the Court held that the Gulas had to repay the dividends they received. Chadwick LJ stated:

> it is enough that the member has the relevant knowledge of facts which, if they exist, lead to the conclusion that the distribution does contravene the statutory provisions; it is not necessary that the member has the relevant knowledge of the legal rules and the consequences of those rules when properly applied to the facts.[243]

Applying this, the Gulas knew that the dividends were not being paid out of profits as there were no profits. This knowledge was enough to satisfy the condition that they knew the dividend was paid in contravention of the statutory requirements.

17.4.6.2 Liability of the directors

Historically, liability for an unlawful dividend payment primarily fell upon the directors, but this changed under the CA 1980. Today, the CA 2006 says nothing about the liability of a director for recommending, authorizing, or paying out an unlawful dividend, but the common law does place significant liability upon directors.

Directors who authorize the payment of an unlawful dividend are jointly and severally liable to repay the amount of the dividend to the company, irrespective of whether the dividend was authorized by the general meeting.[244] As the following case demonstrates, this can result in significant liability being imposed on the directors.

Bairstow v Queens Moat Houses plc [2001] EWCA Civ 712

FACTS: Queens Moat Houses plc ('QMH') dismissed four of its directors for, *inter alia*, authorizing the payment of an unlawful dividend (because there were no distributable reserves, and the dividend was based on misleading accounts). The former directors sued for wrongful dismissal, and QMH counterclaimed for the value of the unlawful dividend paid out. At first instance,[245] the directors' wrongful dismissal action was dismissed as the directors, in paying out an unlawful dividend, had breached their duties of skill and care. QMH's counterclaim succeeded and the directors were ordered to pay back just under £42 million. The directors appealed.

---

[242] [2005] EWHC 2015 (Ch), [2006] BCC 52.   [243] [2006] EWCA Civ 544, [2006] BCC 626 [50].

[244] *Re Exchange Banking Co, Flitcroft's Case* (1882) 21 ChD 519 (CA). This case further held that, even if the shareholders knew the true facts, they could not ratify the dividend payment.

[245] [2000] BCC 1025 (QB).

HELD: The appeal was dismissed and, having corrected some errors regarding the quantum of damages, the directors were ordered to repay QMH over £78.5 million. Robert Walker LJ (who gave the only substantive judgment) provided guidance regarding director liability:

- The directors contended that QMH had wholly-owned subsidiaries which could have legitimately paid out dividends to QMH, which in turn, would have given QMH sufficient distributable profits to have paid out the dividend in question. Robert Walker LJ stated that even if this were correct, it would not affect the directors' liability (although it may be relevant in determining whether to grant relief).[246]
- The directors are liable to repay an unlawful dividend payment irrespective of whether the company is solvent or insolvent.[247]
- Where an unlawful dividend is paid based on improperly prepared accounts, then the directors will be liable to repay the full amount of the unlawful dividend. This is the case even if the company could pay out a dividend had the accounts been prepared properly.[248]
- The directors sought relief from liability under s 727 of the CA 1985 (today, s 1157 of the CA 2006). Robert Walker LJ stated that such relief would only be granted where the directors had acted honestly and reasonably in paying out the unlawful dividend.[249] Here, the former directors had prepared false accounts and so relief was not granted.

Section 1157 is discussed at 10.1.3.4.

Where, based on properly prepared accounts, a company has distributable profits, then the directors will not be liable for the full amount of the unlawful dividend, but merely the amount that is unlawful[250] (i.e. that amount in excess of the company's distributable profits).

A director that is ordered to repay dividends to the company can seek recovery of that amount from those members who were aware of the illegality, but the amount that the director can recover from such a member is limited to the amount that the member received.[251]

17.4.6.3 Liability of the auditor

Where an unlawful dividend has been paid out based on audited accounts, the company may commence proceedings against the auditor if the audit was not conducted properly.

Re Thomas Gerrard & Son Ltd [1968] Ch 455 (Ch)

FACTS: Croston, the managing director of Thomas Gerrard & Son Ltd ('TG'), falsified its accounts to give an inflated impression of the profits being made. TG's auditor certified the accounts without making proper inquiries. Based on the accounts, tax was paid and a dividend declared. Croston's fraud was discovered and, instead of being profitable, TG was 'hopelessly insolvent'.[252] TG went into liquidation and its liquidator commenced proceedings against the auditor, alleging it was negligent in respect of its audit of the accounts.

HELD: The auditor had failed to use reasonable skill and care. The payment of the dividend was 'the natural and probable result of the false picture which [the auditor] allowed the accounts to present'.[253] The amount of tax that was payable was also a natural consequence. Accordingly, the auditor was liable to compensate TG for the dividend paid out and the excessive tax TG had paid.

---

[246] [2001] EWCA Civ 712, [2002] BCC 91 [36].   [247] ibid [44].   [248] ibid [54].   [249] ibid [63].
[250] *Re Marini Ltd* [2003] EWHC 334 (Ch), [2004] BCC 172.
[251] *Moxham v Grant* [1900] 1 QB 88 (CA).   [252] [1968] Ch 455 (Ch) 458 (Pennycuick J).
[253] ibid 478 (Pennycuick J).

CHAPTER SUMMARY

- The principal aim of the capital maintenance rules is to prevent capital being returned to shareholders.
- Any limited company can reduce its share capital by passing a special resolution followed by court confirmation. A private company can reduce its share capital by passing a special resolution supported by a solvency statement.
- Companies are generally prohibited from acquiring their own shares, but there are exceptions to this (e.g. redeemable shares).
- Public companies are generally prohibited from providing financial assistance to others to acquire their shares.
- A company can generally only pay a dividend out of distributable profits.
- The typical three-stage process for paying dividends is (i) the directors recommend an amount to be distributed by way of dividend; (ii) the company declares the dividend by passing an ordinary resolution; and (iii) the dividend is paid out.

FURTHER READING

Charles Proctor, 'Financial Assistance: New Proposals and New Perspectives?' (2007) 28 Co Law 3.
- Compares the rules relating to financial assistance to acquire shares in the CA 1985 and CA 2006.

Eilis Ferran, 'Corporate Transactions and Financial Assistance: Shifting Policy Perceptions but Static Law' (2004) 63 CLJ 225.
- Argues that justifications for the prohibition on providing financial assistance to acquire shares are unsatisfactory, and provides recommendations regarding how the prohibition should be limited.

Federico Clementelli, '(Under)valuing the Rules on Capital Maintenance' (2012) 23 ICCLR 191.
- Discusses the capital maintenance rules and advances suggestions for reform.

John H Armour, 'Share Capital and Creditor Protection: Efficient Rules for a Modern Company Law' (2000) 63 MLR 355.
- Discusses the effectiveness of the capital maintenance rules from an economic viewpoint and argues that certain restrictions are haphazard and not justified.

SELF-TEST QUESTIONS

1. Define the following terms:
- solvency statement;
- redeemable shares;
- treasury shares;
- dividend;
- interim dividend;
- final dividend;
- accumulated profits;
- realized profits.

2. State whether each of the following statements is true or false and, if false, explain why:

   - The principal aim behind the capital maintenance rules is to protect creditors by preventing capital from being returned to the shareholders.
   - A company requires court approval in order to reduce its share capital.
   - Companies are generally prohibited from acquiring their own shares.
   - Companies are prohibited from providing financial assistance to others to acquire their shares.
   - If a company has made a profit, then the company's members have the right to be paid a dividend.
   - The CA 2006 provides that if the directors recommend an unlawful dividend, then they will be liable to repay the amount of that dividend to the company, irrespective of whether the recommendation was approved by the members.

3. 'The reforms to the capital maintenance rules introduced by the CA 2006 have improved matters little, and the rules are still excessively strict, complex, and unnecessary.' Discuss this quote.

4. Dragon Goods Ltd ('DG') has issued 5,000 shares, all with a nominal value of £1 each. Stanley and Sophie (two of DG's three directors) each own 1,000 shares. Theo, a local businessman, owns 2,000 shares and the remaining 1,000 shares are owned by a number of local investors.

   Since it was incorporated, DG has run at a loss and has never made a profit. Theo believes that this is due to the directors' poor management of the company. He also believes that, with new management, the company could be extremely profitable. He therefore starts buying from the local investors the shares that they hold in DG with a view to voting DG's directors out of office.

   DG's directors discover Theo's plan. Accordingly, they cause DG to issue 3,000 new shares and offer to sell them to their friend, Gabrielle. However, Gabrielle cannot afford to buy these shares, but she does offer to sell her car to DG as part-payment for the shares. The car is only worth £1,500 but DG's directors accept the car as part-payment providing that Gabrielle uses the voting rights attached to her shares to defeat any resolution that aims to remove the directors from office. The remaining payment comes in the form of £500, which Gabrielle loans from DG.

   Theo, realizing that his scheme to oust the directors has failed, wishes to sell his shares, but he cannot find a buyer. Stanley tells Theo the DG will purchase the shares. By now, Theo has 2,500 shares and he agrees to sell them to DG. DG purchases the shares and they are duly cancelled. Having rid themselves of the troublesome Theo, the directors of DG recommend that a dividend be paid at a rate of 10 pence per share. Gabrielle agrees and between them, the dividend is declared and paid out.

   Discuss the validity of the actions undertaken by DG and its directors.

ONLINE RESOURCES

This book is accompanied by online resources to better support you in your studies. Visit www.oup.com/uk/roach-company/ for:

- answers to the self-test questions;
- further reading lists;
- multiple-choice questions;
- glossary.

Updates to the law can be found on the author's Twitter account (@UKCompanyLaw) and further resources can be found on the author's blog (www.companylawandgovernance.com).

18 Public offers of shares

- Sources of securities regulation
- Offering shares to the public
- UK stock exchanges
- The listing of securities
- The prospectus
- Continuing obligations
- Sanctions

INTRODUCTION

A public company may reach a point where its existing inflow of capital is not enough to fund its expansion plans, or it may wish to undertake a project and need additional capital to finance it. Such a company will likely consider offering its shares to the public in order to raise the required capital; this chapter discusses how public companies can raise capital by offering their shares to the public, and how public offers of shares are regulated. Many students often assume that all public companies offer their shares to the public by trading them on a stock market, but this is not the case. A public company need never offer its shares to the public at all. As regards those public companies that do, they can do so without trading their shares on a stock market or admitting them for listing.

Legislation regulating public offers of shares tends not to use the word 'shares', but instead used the word 'securities', which encompasses more than shares. Unfortunately, different Acts define this term differently. The Financial Services and Markets Act 2000 defines securities as 'anything which has been, or may be, admitted to the official list',[1] whereas the Companies Act 2006 (CA 2006) defines securities as 'shares or debentures'.[2]

Before looking at the rules relating to the public offer of shares, it is important to understand the legal framework within which such rules operate.

> ⧉ The official list is discussed at 18.4.

18.1 Sources of securities regulation

The UK framework of securities regulation comprises of a mixture of different legal sources. A significant portion of UK securities law is derived from European Union (EU) law.

---

[1] Financial Services and Markets Act 2000, s 102A(2).   [2] CA 2006, s 755(5).

18.1.1 **EU law**

The free movement of capital is one of the four pillars of the EU, but it could not be effectively achieved when each EU Member State had its own set of different laws regulating financial markets. Following several failed attempts to create an EU-wide financial market, a breakthrough was achieved in 2001 with the publication of the Lamfalussy Report.[3] This report stated that '[a]n integrated European financial market will enable, subject to proper prudential safeguards and investor protection, capital and financial services to flow freely throughout the European Union'.[4] To that end, the report recommended that the framework for an integrated financial market be established via EU legislation, which led to the passing of the following directives:

- the Consolidated Admission and Reporting Directive (CARD),[5] which aims to coordinate the rules and regulations amongst Member States regarding the admission of securities for listing without necessarily making them uniform;[6]

- the Prospectus Directive,[7] which aims to 'harmonise requirements for the drawing up, approval and distribution of the prospectus to be published when securities are offered to the public or admitted to trading on a regulated market situated or operating within a Member State'[8]—as discussed at 18.5, the Prospectus Directive is in the process of being replaced by the 2017 Prospectus Regulation;[9]

- the Transparency Obligations Directive,[10] which 'establishes requirements in relation to the disclosure of periodic and ongoing information about issuers whose securities are already admitted to trading on a regulated market situated or operating within a Member State'.[11]

All of these directives have been implemented into domestic law, and it is to domestic law that we now turn.

18.1.2 **Financial Services and Markets Act 2000**

The principal piece of UK securities legislation is the Financial Services and Markets Act 2000 (FSMA 2000), which replaced the Financial Services Act 1986. One of the key aims of the Act is to ensure that financial services are properly regulated and supervised and carried out by suitably authorized persons. Accordingly, a key provision of the Act is s 19, which provides that a person may not carry out a regulated activity in the UK, unless he is an authorized person or an exempt person (this is known as 'the general prohibition'). Three terms require elaboration:

- **Regulated activity**: a regulated activity is an activity which is carried on by way of a business and relates to an investment of a specified kind.[12] Schedule 2 of the Act provides a

---

[3] 'Final Report of the Committee of Wise Men on the Regulation of European Securities Markets' (2001).

[4] ibid 9.

[5] Directive 2001/34/EC of 28 May 2001 on the admission of securities to official stock exchange listing and on information to be published on those securities [2001] OJ L184/1.

[6] ibid Recital, para 11.

[7] Directive 2003/71/EC of 4 November 2003 on the prospectus to be published when securities are offered to the public or admitted to trading and amending Directive 2001/34/EC [2003] OJ L345/64.

[8] ibid Art 1.

[9] Regulation 2017/1129/EU of 14 June 2017 on the prospectus to be published when securities are offered to the public or admitted to trading and repealing Directive 2001/34/EC [2017] OJ L168/12.

[10] Directive 2004/109/EC of 15 December 2004 on the harmonisation of transparency requirements in relation to information about issuers whose securities are admitted to trading on a regulated market and amending Directive 2001/34/EC [2004] OJ L390/38.

[11] ibid Art 1.   [12] FSMA 2000, s 22(1).

list of regulated activities including dealing in investments either as principal or agent, arranging deals in investments, managing investments, or providing investment advice.

- **Authorized person**: section 31 lists when persons will be authorized, with the principal method of authorization being where the Financial Conduct Authority (FCA) authorizes a person to carry on a regulated activity.[13]
- **Exempt person**: an exempt person is a person who is exempted from the s 19 general prohibition.[14] For example, certain professionals (e.g. solicitors, accountants) are exempt persons when providing certain professional services.[15]

For our purposes, the key parts of the FSMA 2000 are Pts IA (which establishes the various regulators, notably the FCA) and VI (which establishes rules relating to official listing).

18.1.2.1 The Financial Conduct Authority

Article 105 of CARD provides that EU Member States shall appoint one or more 'competent authorities' for the purposes of the Directive. When FSMA 2000 was enacted, it provided that the UK's competent authority was the Financial Services Authority[16] (FSA), a body created by the FSMA 2000[17] that replaced the various bodies that regulated financial services at the time. Following the financial crisis, the government acknowledged that 'regulators failed in recognising and responding to the problems that were emerging in the financial system'.[18] As a result, Parliament passed the Financial Services Act 2012, which significantly amended the FSMA 2000, notably by inserting a new Pt IA that split the FSA into two new bodies, namely the FCA and the Prudential Regulation Authority.[19] For the purposes of securities regulation, the FCA is the competent authority acting in its capacity as the 'UK Listing Authority' (although the FCA has decide to phase out the use of this term).

The FCA's overarching function (which is known as its 'strategic objective') is to ensure that the financial markets and markets for financial services function well.[20] The FCA must, so far as is reasonably practicable, act in a way which is compatible with this strategic objective, but it must also act in a way that advances one or more of these operational objectives:[21]

- to secure an appropriate degree of protection for consumers;[22]
- to protect and enhance the integrity of the UK financial system;[23] and
- to promote effective competition in the interests of consumers for regulated financial services or services provided by a recognized investment exchange in carrying on regulated activities.[24]

The FCA's strategic objective and its operational objectives are broad and high-level. In relation to securities regulation, the FCA has three key specific objectives:

1. The FCA maintains the official list,[25] which is a list of securities that the FCA has admitted to listing.
2. The FCA determines which securities are admitted to the official list.[26]
3. The FCA is empowered to make rules under the FSMA 2000,[27] with s 137A(1) stating that the FCA may make such rules as appear necessary or expedient for the purposes of advancing one or more of its operational objectives. These rules are discussed next.

---

[13] ibid s 31(1)(1) and Pt IV.   [14] ibid s 38(1).   [15] ibid s 327.
[16] ibid s 72 (now repealed).   [17] ibid s 1 (now repealed).
[18] HM Treasury, *A New Approach to Financial Regulation: Judgement, Focus and Stability* (Cm 7874, 2010) para 1.3.
[19] Financial Services Act 2012, s 6.   [20] FSMA 2000, ss 1B(2) and 1F.
[21] ibid s 1B(1).   [22] ibid s 1C.   [23] ibid s 1D.
[24] ibid s 1E.   [25] ibid s 74(1).   [26] ibid s 74(2).   [27] ibid s 1B(6)(a).

18.1.3 **The FCA Handbook**

The rules that the FCA creates under the FSMA 2000 are found in the FCA Handbook.[28] The Handbook consists of nine sections known as 'blocks', with each block consisting of a series of modules.[29] Each module contains a series of rules (which are binding), guidance (which is not binding), and directions (which are binding on persons to whom they are addressed).

18.1.3.1 **Listing, Prospectus, and Disclosure**

For the purposes of securities regulation, block 7 is the key block as it deals with listing, prospectuses, and disclosure. Block 7 is divided into three modules:

1. **Listing Rules**: these implement CARD and set out the conditions that must be met in order for shares to be listed on the official list, the process for listing shares, and the obligations that listed companies must continue to meet.

2. **Prospectus Rules**: the Prospectus Rules implement in part the Prospectus Directive and set out rules regarding the preparation, approval, and publication of a prospectus.

3. **Disclosure Guidance and Transparency Rules**: the Disclosure Guidance and Transparency Rules (DTRs) implement in part three directives. First, they implement the Transparency Obligations Directive and make other rules 'to ensure there is adequate transparency of and access to information in the UK financial markets'.[30] Second, the DTRs implement parts of the Audit Directive and set out rules regarding the establishment of an audit committee. Third, they implement parts of the Accounting Directive, which requires companies to publish a corporate governance statement. The DTRs also set out rules to ensure that relevant information is disclosed to the market in a fair and prompt manner.

All of these rules are discussed in more detail in this chapter, and in other parts of this text.

18.1.4 **Stock exchange rules**

The stock exchange upon which a company's shares are traded may also have its own rules that must be complied with. For example, a company that wishes to list its shares on the Main Market of the London Stock Exchange must not only comply with the relevant rules in the FCA Handbook, but it must also comply with the London Stock Exchange's own Admission and Disclosure Standards.[31] All member firms of the exchange must comply with the Rules of the London Stock Exchange.[32]

∞ The Main Market is discussed at 18.3.1.

18.2 Offering shares to the public

Public companies are under no obligation to offer[33] to sell their shares to the public. However, a public offer of shares may be necessary in order to fund the company's expansion plans or to fund a particular project. In the following example, the company's entire purpose necessitated several public offers of shares to raise the necessary finance.

---

[28] See www.handbook.fca.org.uk accessed 10 January 2019.

[29] For more on the structure of the Handbook, see FCA, 'Reader's Guide: An Introduction to the Handbook' (FCA 2017).

[30] DTR 1A.1.3. [31] London Stock Exchange, 'Admission and Disclosure Standards' (October 2018).

[32] London Stock Exchange, 'Rules of the London Stock Exchange: Rule Book' (January 2018).

[33] Technically, the company does not offer the shares at all. Instead, it makes an invitation to treat, with the potential purchasers making the offer (*Re Metropolitan Fire Insurance Co* [1900] 2 Ch 671 (Ch)).

Financing the Channel Tunnel

In 1986, the UK and French governments accepted a proposal from Eurotunnel to build a tunnel between the UK and France. The 1986 Treaty of Canterbury provided the legal framework for the construction and operation of the tunnel, but Art 1 stated that the tunnel 'shall be financed without recourse to government funds or to government guarantees of a financial or commercial nature'. Accordingly, in order for the tunnel to be viable, a significant amount of private capital would need to be raised. It was decided that the finance would be raised via a combination of selling shares and borrowing, but obtaining the requisite loan capital was conditional upon obtaining sufficient equity capital.[34] Accordingly, the viability of the project largely rested on whether sufficient shares could be sold. In 1986, Eurotunnel plc and Eurotunnel SA raised £258 million through a placing of shares, with a general public offer raising a further £770 million in 1987. As a result, the funding arrangements for the tunnel were finalized in late 1987. However, the projected costs for the tunnel increased dramatically and further loans and offers of shares were made in the 1990s in order to help raise the finance needed to complete the project. The Channel Tunnel officially opened in 1994.

The placing of shares are discussed at 18.2.3.2.

This section looks at the rules relating to public offers of shares. Public companies who offer their shares to the public will often do so by admitting their shares to a market on a stock exchange. However, this is not required, and a public company is free to sell its shares to the public without placing those shares on a formal market (this is known as 'over-the-counter' trading). For example, a public company could simply enter into a private agreement with the purchaser to purchase a specified number of shares. Over-the-counter trading can be especially useful for public companies that cannot meet the eligibility requirements imposed by a market, or who simply do not wish to expend the time and money needed to meet such requirements. One eligibility requirement that must be satisfied before shares can be offered to the public is that the company must be a public company.

18.2.1 Prohibition on private companies offering shares

Section 755(1) of the CA 2006 provides that a private limited company must not offer, allot, or agree to allot any securities[35] to the public. The question that arises is what constitutes an offer to the public. The Act provides that an offer to any section of the public will amount to an offer to the public.[36] However, an offer will not be regarded as an offer to the public if it:

- is not being calculated to result, directly or indirectly, in securities of the company becoming available to persons other than those receiving the offer;[37] or

- otherwise being a private concern of the person receiving it and the person making it.[38] An offer is (unless the contrary is proved) regarded as being of a private concern if it is made to persons connected to the company or as part of an employees' share scheme, and is renounceable only by persons within those groups.[39]

---

[34] The European Investment Bank, a significant financier of the tunnel, would only provide a loan if it could be demonstrated that the project was funded to completion.

[35] Section 755(5) defines 'securities' to mean 'shares or debentures'.   [36] CA 2006, s 756(2).

[37] ibid s 756(3)(a).   [38] ibid s 756(3)(b).   [39] ibid s 756(4).

A company will not contravene the s 755(1) prohibition if (i) it acts in good faith in pursuance of arrangements under which it is to re-register as a public company before the securities are allotted; or (ii) as part of the terms of the offer it undertakes to re-register as a public company within six months after the date the offer is made, and that undertaking is complied with.[40]

18.2.1.1 Contravention of s 755

Under the Companies Act 1985 (CA 1985), a company that offered its shares to the public committed a criminal offence.[41] The CA 2006 does not impose criminal liability and an allotment of shares in contravention of s 755 will remain valid.[42] The potential consequences of a breach of 755 are as follows:

- if a company is proposing to act in contravention of s 755, the court can make an order restraining the company from contravening s 755;[43]
- if a company has contravened s 755, the court can make an order requiring the company to re-register as a public company, although no such order will be made if the company does not meet the requirements for a public company or it is impractical or undesirable for the company to take the steps to meet such requirements;[44]
- if the court does not order re-registration, then it may make a remedial order[45] and/or an order for the company to be wound up;[46]
- a contravention of s 755 may also result in other related rules being breached (e.g. the rules requiring the publication of a prospectus).

The requirement to publish a prospectus is discussed at 18.5.1.

18.2.2 Advantages and disadvantages

Before deciding whether to offer its shares to the public or not, the company will need to consider carefully the advantages of making such an offer and whether they outweigh the disadvantages. Table 18.1 sets out the potential advantages and disadvantages of offering shares to the public (note that the advantages and disadvantages of listing those shares are discussed at 18.4.1.1).

TABLE 18.1 The advantages and disadvantages of offering shares to the public

Advantages	Disadvantages
• Allows the company to expand its shareholder base • Facilitates the raising of finance, which can be used to benefit the company (e.g. by expanding the company's business) • It may allow existing shareholders to more easily exit the company	• Public companies are subject to much more regulation than private companies • Offering shares to the public comes with its own set of rules (especially if the shares are traded on a market or listed), which can be burdensome • The company may be more likely to be taken over

---

[40] ibid s 755(3) and (4).   [41] CA 1985, s 81 (now repealed).   [42] CA 2006, s 760.
[43] ibid s 757(1) and (2).   [44] ibid s 758(1) and (2).
[45] A remedial order is an order the effect of which is to put a person affected by a contravention of s 755 in a position he would have been in had the contravention not occurred (s 759(1)).
[46] CA 2006, s 758(3)(b).

18.2.3 **Types of public offer**

A company that does decide to offer its shares to the public will need to decide which method of public offer is most beneficial, with several different forms of offer being available. When a company offers its shares to the public for the first time, this is often known as an 'initial public offering' (IPO). An IPO can raise massive amounts of capital, especially if its IPO takes place on a major stock market. To date, the largest IPO took place in 2014 when Alibaba Holdings Group went public on the New York Stock Exchange, raising around $25 billion. Following its initial offering, a company may subsequently seek to raise more capital via subsequent public offerings.

18.2.3.1 **Offers for subscription and offers for sale**

For larger companies that wish to raise substantial amounts of capital by offering their shares to the public at large, an offer for sale or offer for subscription may be the most appropriate form of public offer. The offer for subscription used to be the more popular method (especially for initial offerings) and involves the company offering its shares to the general public, although the company will often appoint an investment bank to make the offer on its behalf. Persons can then subscribe for the shares, which are then allotted to them directly by the company. The CA 2006 provides that, under an offer for subscription, the shares cannot be allotted unless the issue is subscribed for in full or the terms of the offer provide that the shares may be allotted in any event.[47] To ensure that the offer is subscribed in full, the company offering the shares will typically enter into an underwriting agreement under which the underwriter undertakes to take up any shares that the public have not subscribed for.

Today, large-scale initial offerings are usually conducted via an offer for sale. The key difference between an offer for subscription and an offer for sale is that, under the latter, the company will allot all the shares in question to an investment bank (or a syndicate of banks if the offer is large enough) and the bank will then offer the shares to the general public. Accordingly, the risk of the offer is placed upon the bank and not the company, which avoids the need for the company to enter into an underwriting agreement because the bank will hold any shares that are not sold (although the bank may enter into an underwriting agreement with another bank).

Offers for subscription and sale can be used for initial offerings and subsequent offerings but, given their scale, they are the most expensive and time-consuming forms of public offer. For companies that wish to avoid this time and expense, or who do not wish to offer shares to the public at large, a placing may be preferable.

18.2.3.2 **Placings**

A placing can be used for an initial or subsequent offering, and usually involves the company allotting shares to an investment bank. The bank will then offer the shares to a person or limited group of persons (usually institutional investor clients of the bank). A number of placings are increasingly carried out via a process known as 'bookbuilding', under which the bank will discuss with institutional investors how many shares they are interested in purchasing at various theoretical price levels. This information will then be used to determine the actual price of the placed shares.

---

[47] ibid s 578(1).

As a placing is made to a limited group of persons and not to the public at large, advertising and administrative costs can be reduced and a prospectus may not be required. However, a placing can have negative consequences for existing shareholders, as the following example demonstrates.

Placings and pre-emption rights

At Glencore plc's 2015 AGM, shareholders approved plans to place shares worth up to 10 per cent of the company's existing share capital. At this AGM, the board stated that it would not disapply existing shareholders' pre-emption rights, even though the members had empowered them to do so. On 15 September 2015, Glencore announced that it was placing 1.3 million shares, but the board had reconsidered the pre-emption issue and decided to disapply existing shareholders' pre-emption rights on the ground that Glencore needed to raise capital quickly. The placing, worth around £1.6 billion, was completed on 16 September 2015.

By disapplying pre-emption rights, the placing had diluted the holdings of existing shareholders (consequently reducing their voting power and future dividend payments). Glencore's board was widely criticized, with the Institute of Directors stating:

> Glencore's conduct falls short of what we would expect of a major global company. Their decision appears to be in direct contravention of the rights of shareholders and goes against a pledge they made at their AGM . . .. What is particularly worrying is the fact that Glencore failed to consult all of their shareholders,[48] in particular minority shareholders, during this whole process. It is vitally important, especially when firms are intent on contradicting previous commitments to shareholders, that they open a dialogue with all investors at the earliest opportunity . . .. This whole episode sets a worrying precedent.[49]

Pre-emption rights are discussed at 16.4.4.

18.2.3.3 Rights issues

It may be the case that a company that has raised capital by offering its shares to the public will want to raise further capital. This could be done via one of the above methods, but the most popular method is to make a rights issue. A rights issue is an offer to sell shares to the company's existing shareholders and, in order to respect their pre-emption rights, each shareholder is offered shares in proportion to the size of their existing holdings. Indeed, the existence of pre-emption rights means that a rights issue is the default form of subsequent offering, although such rights can be disapplied. From the company's perspective, the advantage of a rights offer is that, by only making the offer to existing shareholders, the costs of advertising the offer are reduced.

From the perspective of the existing shareholders, rights issues are attractive for two reasons. First, companies will often discount the price of the shares offered in order to induce existing shareholders to take up the offer. It is also the case that, following a rights issue, it is normal for the company's share price to drop, and so the shares should normally be discounted to reflect this. Second, existing shareholders who choose not to take up the offer are usually able to sell the right to buy the discounted shares to another person.[50]

---

[48] The Pre-Emption Group's Statement of Principles on Disapplying Pre-emption Rights states that, before disapplying pre-emption rights, a company should engage in a dialogue with its shareholders.

[49] See www.iod.com/news/enterprising-women/article/glencore-share-deal-flies-in-the-face-of-shareholder-rights accessed 10 January 2019.

[50] A rights issue that does not provide an existing shareholder with the ability to sell the right to buy the shares is known as an 'open offer'.

Indeed, in the case of a listed company, the Listing Rules provide that where an existing shareholder does not take up his right to subscribe to a rights issue, the listed company must sell the shares and provide the shareholder with any premium obtained.[51]

18.3 UK stock exchanges

A company that wishes to offer its shares to the public may wish to facilitate that aim by trading its shares on a market within a stock exchange, although it does not have to do so. There is a widespread belief that the London Stock Exchange is the only stock exchange in the UK, but this is not the case and any person can offer stock exchange services providing they have obtained permission to do so from the FCA (usually be applying for and being granted a recognition order stating that the applicant is a 'recognized investment exchange' (RIE)).[52] There are currently two RIEs that offer share-trading services, namely the London Stock Exchange[53] and NEX Exchange,[54] with several overseas stock exchanges (e.g. Nasdaq) having recognized overseas investment exchange status.[55] These exchanges offer a range of markets designed for differing types of company which usually provide primary markets (where companies sell new shares) and secondary markets (where shares that are not new are traded).

→ **cross-listing:** where a single company lists its shares on multiple markets

A UK company need not trade its shares on a UK market—it may trade its shares on a market elsewhere (similarly, overseas companies may trade on a UK market). Larger quoted companies will often **cross-list** their shares on multiple markets in different countries (e.g. a notable number of Financial Times Stock Exchange 100 (FTSE 100) companies have their primary listing on the London Stock Exchange's Main Market with a secondary listing on the New York Stock Exchange). The focus here is on UK securities markets, with the dominant stock exchange in the UK being the London Stock Exchange.

18.3.1 The London Stock Exchange

The London Stock Exchange (LSE) was established in 1801, although its origins can be traced to the Royal Exchange created in 1571. The LSE is owned and operated by London Stock Exchange Group plc, which is itself a FTSE 100 company. The LSE is currently the third largest stock exchange in the world[56] and is the largest in Europe. As of January 2019, over 2,150 companies from around 35 countries trade their shares on one of the LSE's markets,[57] of which the two most important are:

- **The Main Market**: the LSE describes the Main Market as 'London's flagship market for larger, more established companies'[58] and as such many of the world's largest and best-known companies trade their shares on the Main Market. Over 2,600 companies from

---

[51] Listing Rules, LR 9.5.4. [52] FSMA 2000, s 290.

[53] See www.londonstockexchange.com accessed 10 January 2019.

[54] See www.nexexchange.com accessed 10 January 2019.

[55] The Financial Services Register (https://register.fca.org.uk accessed 10 January 2019) provides a list of all recognized exchanges, along with all persons regulated by the FCA.

[56] Behind the New York Stock Exchange and Nasdaq.

[57] A full list can be found at www.londonstockexchange.com/statistics/companies-and-issuers/companies-and-issuers.htm accessed 10 January 2019.

[58] See www.londonstockexchange.com/companies-and-advisors/main-market/main-market/home.htm accessed 10 January 2019.

over 60 countries have securities traded on the main market. Only listed securities can be traded on the Main Market and a listing on the Main Market 'demonstrates a commitment to high standards'[59] (especially if a premium listing is sought). Consequently, the Main Market is the LSE's most heavily regulated market.

Premium listing is discussed at 18.4.1.2.

- **AIM**: AIM (formerly an abbreviation for the 'Alternative Investment Market') was launched in 1995 with the aim of providing 'a dedicated growth market for small and medium-sized companies'.[60] Consequently, the 930 or so companies that trade their securities on AIM tend to be smaller and less well known than companies with securities listed on the Main Market. AIM is less strictly regulated than the Main Market. Securities traded on AIM are not listed[61] and so the companies trading on AIM need not comply with the Listing Rules—instead, AIM has its own set of rules known as the AIM Rules for Companies.[62] It is reasonably common for companies to admit their securities to AIM as a stepping stone with a view to listing them on the Main Market in the future.

18.4 The listing of securities

The word 'listing' is often used to refer to a company offering its securities to the public on a market, but this is incorrect. Admitting securities to a market and seeking a listing for those securities are two separate issues and a company can trade its shares on a market without obtaining a listing. For example, as noted above, AIM is a public market for securities, but securities admitted to AIM are unlisted. The glossary to the FCA Handbook states that a listed security is 'any security that is admitted to an official list'. Accordingly, this section focuses on the process by which a company's securities may be admitted by the FCA onto the official list.

18.4.1 Pre-application considerations

The listing of securities involves applying to the FCA for the securities to be admitted to the official list. However, before such an application is made, the potential applicant will need to consider certain issues, namely whether a listing a desirable and, if so, what type of listing to apply for.

18.4.1.1 The advantages and disadvantages of listing

The potential applicant will need to decide whether it is in its interests to actually list its shares. There is no doubt that listing securities comes with some significant advantages:

- listed companies have access to deep pools of capital, so can raise significant amounts of capital by offering to sell their securities;
- listed securities are traded on a regulated market run by an FCA-approved, recognized investment exchange, which helps provide buyers with confidence;
- companies that become listed will gain access to markets that unlisted companies do not have access to (e.g. the LSE's Main Market);
- listed companies tend to have a high public profile and there is a certain prestige attached to being a listed company;
- becoming a listed company allows access to certain benchmarking tools (e.g. only listed companies can form part of certain FTSE indices, such as the FTSE 100, 250, and 350).

---

[59] LSE, 'Main Market: A Guide to Listing on the London Stock Exchange' (LSE 2010) 7.
[60] LSE, 'A Guide to AIM' (LSE 2015) 6.   [61] The predecessor to AIM was called the Unlisted Securities Market.
[62] LSE, 'AIM Rules for Companies' (March 2018).

However, the fact that the majority of public companies choose not to list their shares indicates that there are significant disadvantages to listing, including:

- the eligibility requirements for listing are notable and many public companies will be unable to satisfy them;
- the process of applying for a listing is complex and can involve considerable expense;
- once a company's securities are listed, there will be ongoing costs (e.g. listing fees, compliance costs);
- listed companies are subject to considerably more regulation than unlisted companies, notably in the form of the Listing Rules. Companies with a premium listing must also comply or explain against the UK Corporate Governance Code.

18.4.1.2 Standard and premium listing

A company that decides to list its shares may decide between a standard listing or a premium listing, with there being two principal differences between the two:

1. A premium listing is only available for equity shares of commercial companies, close-ended investment companies, and open-ended investment companies. Any other listing will be a standard listing.[63]

2. A standard listing only requires compliance with the minimum EU directive standards. A premium listing requires compliance with rules that go beyond the EU requirements,[64] namely a range of additional obligations found in the Listing Rules which impose additional requirements regarding the listing of shares[65] and compliance with additional continuing obligations once shares are listed.[66] In addition, the Introduction to the UK Corporate Governance Code provides that it applies to all companies with a premium listing, and such companies must comply or explain against the Code.[67]

Comply or explain is discussed at 2.2.2.1.

The question is why would a company choose a listing that imposes more onerous requirements. The LSE states that a premium listing shows that the company is 'expected to meet the UK's highest standards of regulation and corporate governance—and as a consequence may enjoy a lower cost of capital through greater transparency and through building investor confidence'.[68] It is also the case that only companies with a premium listing are eligible to be included within the FTSE 350 indices. However, it has been argued that the existence of the premium listing:

> reflects a continued nervousness about the efficacy of the listing rules . . .. [The] premium listing requirements constitute a form of 'gold-plating' . . . which is intended to cement the place of London as a principal venue for the issue of securities because those stringent premium listing requirements are expected to reassure investors as to diligence with which those securities have been brought to listing by the issuer, its professional advisors, its sponsor, and the UKLA.[69]

It is a breach of the Listing Rules for a company that does not have a premium listing to describe itself or hold itself out as having a premium listing.[70] A company with a premium listing can change to a standard listing and vice versa, providing that it complies with the transfer rules in LR 5.4A of the Listing Rules.

---

[63] Listing Rules, LR 1.5.1(3).   [64] ibid LR 1.5.1(2).   [65] ibid LR 6.
[66] See e.g. Listing Rules, LR 7.2.1A, LR 9–13, and LR 15–16.   [67] ibid LR 9.8.6(6).
[68] See www.londonstockexchange.com/companies-and-advisors/main-market/companies/primary-and-secondary-listing/listing-categories.htm accessed 10 January 2019.
[69] Geoffrey Morse, *Palmer's Company Law* (Sweet & Maxwell 2018) para 5.529.
[70] Listing Rules, LR 1.5.2.

18.4.2 Eligibility for listing

EU Member States must not admit securities to an official listing unless the conditions laid down in CARD are satisfied.[71] CARD establishes the minimum conditions that must be satisfied for an official listing, but Member States are generally free to impose additional or more stringent conditions.[72] In the UK, CARD's minimum conditions have been implemented by the Listing Rules, which also impose their own additional and more stringent eligibility requirements. Other eligibility requirements are found in the FSMA 2000, and the FCA can also establish its own eligibility requirements. If all these conditions are not complied with, the FCA cannot grant an application for listing.[73]

The FSMA 2000 imposes two conditions that apply to all applications for listing. First, the FCA will not entertain an application unless it is made by, or with the consent of, the issuer of the relevant securities.[74] Second, the FCA will not entertain an application in respect of securities that are issued by specified bodies,[75] namely private companies and old public companies.[76]

The eligibility requirements differ depending on whether a standard or premium listing is sought. All applicants for listing must meet the conditions for a standard listing, with additional requirements being imposed for those applicants seeking a premium listing.[77] Table 18.2 sets out the principal eligibility requirements for a standard listing and premium listing.

In addition to the relevant requirements, the applicant will need to meet the LSE's own requirements as set out in its Admission and Disclosure Standards. Many of these requirements mirror, or are similar to, those found in the Listing Rules, but some additional requirements are imposed (e.g. the securities admitted to trading must be eligible for electronic settlement).[78]

18.4.3 Applying for securities to be listed

The process for applying for securities to be listed is set out in LR 3 of the Listing Rules. Basically, it requires the applicant to submit specified documentation and to pay the relevant fee. The applicant will book a date with the FCA on which its application documentation will be reviewed (known as the 'listing hearing'). Where the securities take the form of shares, then two days before the date of the listing hearing, the applicant must submit to the FCA specified documentation including:

- a completed Application for Admission of Securities to the Official List;
- a copy of the prospectus or listing particulars, as approved by the FCA;
- any circular that was published in connection with the application; and
- written confirmation of the number of shares to be allotted.[79]

The applicant will need to provide additional documentation on the day of the listing hearing, namely a Shareholder Statement (which provides details of all the applicant's shares) and a Pricing Statement (which provides details of the price the shares will be

---

[71] CARD, Art 5.   [72] ibid Art 8.   [73] FSMA 2000, s 75(4).

[74] ibid s 75(2).   [75] ibid s 75(3).

[76] Financial Services and Markets Act 2000 (Official Listing of Securities) Regulations 2001, SI 2001/2956, reg 3.

[77] Listing Rules, LR 6.1.2.   [78] LSE, 'Admission and Disclosure Standards' (October 2018) rule 2.7.

[79] Listing Rules, LR 3.3.2. LR 4 imposes similar rules in relation to other forms of securities.

TABLE 18.2 Eligibility requirements for standard and premium listing

Requirements for a standard listing	Additional requirements for a premium listing
The applicant must be duly incorporated and must be operating in conformity with its constitution (LR 2.2.1)	If a company does not have an existing premium listing or is not applying for admission of equity shares that already have a premium listing, then the following conditions must be met:
The securities to be listed must (i) comply with the law of the applicant's place of incorporation; (ii) be authorized in accordance with the applicant's constitution; and (iii) have any necessary statutory or other consents (LR 2.2.2)	• the applicant must have published or filed historical financial information as set out in LR 6.2.1, and this historical data must have been audited (LR 6.2.1 and 6.2.4)—this information must demonstrate that the applicant has a revenue-earning track record (LR 6.3.1);
The shares must be admitted to trading on a regulated market operated by a RIE (LR 2.2.3)	• the applicant must demonstrate that it carries on an independent business as its main activity (LR 6.4.1) and that it exercises operational control over that business (LR 6.6.1);
The securities to be listed must be freely transferable, fully paid,* and free from all liens and any restrictions on the right of transfer (LR 2.2.4)	• an applicant with a controlling shareholder must demonstrate that it is able to carry on an independent business (LR 6.5.1);
The expected aggregate value of the securities to be listed must be at least £700,000 for shares, and £200,000 for debt securities (LR 2.2.7(1))**	• the applicant must demonstrate that it and its subsidiaries have sufficient working capital available for at least the 12 months following the publication of the prospectus (LR 6.7.1), and; • the applicant's constitution must allow it to comply with the Listing Rules (LR 6.9.1)
All of the securities of a class in question must be admitted to listing (LR 2.2.9)	A company with, or applying for, a premium listing of its equity shares, must appoint an FCA-approved sponsor (LR 8). The role of the sponsor is (i) to assure the FCA that the responsibilities of the company under the Listing Rules have been met; (ii) to explain or confirm to the FCA that the Listing Rules are being complied with; and (iii) to guide the company in understanding and meeting its responsibilities under the Listing Rules and the DTRs (LR 8.3.1)
A prospectus must have been approved by the FCA and published (LR 2.2.10)	
If an application is made for a class of shares, at least 25 per cent of that class must, no later than at the time of admission, be distributed to the public (LR 14.2.2)	

*The FCA may allow partly-paid shares to be listed if it is satisfied that their transferability is not restricted and investors have been provided with appropriate information to enable dealings in the securities to take place on an open and proper basis (LR 2.2.5).

**The FCA may allow securities with a lower aggregate value to be admitted if it is satisfied there will be an adequate market for the securities concerned (LR 2.2.8).

offered for).[80] The applicant must pay a fee to the FCA for reviewing the application documentation.[81]

18.4.4 **The FCA's decision**

Upon receipt of the application, the FCA will decide whether to admit the applicant's securities for listing. In deciding this, the FCA is not limited to the information provided by the applicant, and it may take into account any information that it considers

---

[80] ibid LR 3.3.3.

[81] Details of the fees payable are found in Annex 12 of FEES 3, which forms part of the Fees Manual in block 1 (High Level Standards) of the FCA Handbook.

appropriate.[82] It may also request additional information from the applicant or other exchanges or regulators.[83] The listing must be refused if the application does not comply with the requirements in the Listing Rules or with any additional requirements imposed by the FCA.[84] The FCA may refuse an application in two additional circumstances:

- if, for a reason related to the issuer, the FCA considers that granting the listing would be detrimental to the interests of investors;[85] or
- if the application relates to securities already officially listed in another European Economic Area (EEA) State, and the issuer has failed to comply with obligations in relation to that listing.[86]

The FCA must notify the applicant of its decision within six months of the application being received or, if the applicant was required to provide the FCA with further information relating to the application, within six months of the date on which that information was provided.[87] If a decision to admit the securities is not made within that period, the application is deemed to be refused.[88] The FCA will either admit the securities to listing, or it will refuse:.

- If the FCA decides to admit the securities, it must provide the applicant with written notice of this.[89] The admission will only become effective when it has been announced by a regulatory information service (RIS).[90] Once securities are admitted to the official list, their admission cannot be called into question on the ground that any admission requirement or condition was not complied with.[91]
- If the FCA refuses the application, it must provide the applicant with a decision notice to that effect.[92] The applicant may appeal the decision to the Upper Tribunal.[93]

18.5 The prospectus

The Prospectus Directive states that:

> The provision of full information concerning securities and issuers of those securities promotes, together with rules on the conduct of business, the protection of investors. Moreover, such information provides an effective means of increasing confidence in securities and thus of contributing to the proper functioning and development of securities markets. The appropriate way to make this information available is to publish a prospectus.[94]

The Directive was implemented in the UK by the Prospectus Regulations 2005,[95] which amended the FSMA 2000. The Prospectus Directive was amended several times, resulting in subsequent further changes to the 2000 Act. A 2015 consultation document[96] identified a number of shortcomings of the Prospectus Directive and so, in 2017, a new EU Prospectus Regulation[97] was passed which will fully replace the rules found in the Prospectus Directive by July 2019. Some changes to the FSMA 2000 have already

[82] Listing Rules, LR 3.2.6(3). [83] ibid LR 3.2.6(1), (2) and (4). [84] FSMA 2000, s 75(2) and (4).
[85] ibid s 75(6). [86] ibid s 75(7). [87] ibid s 76(1). [88] ibid s 76(2). [89] ibid s 76(3).
[90] Listing Rules, LR 3.2.7. [91] FSMA 2000, s 76(7). [92] ibid s 76(5).
[93] ibid ss 76(6) and 417(1). [94] Prospectus Directive, Recital 18. [95] SI 2005/1433.
[96] European Commission, 'Consultation Document: Review of the Prospectus Directive' (February 2015).
[97] Regulation 2017/1129/EU of 14 June 2017 on the prospectus to be published when securities are offered to the public or admitted to trading and repealing Directive 2001/34/EC [2017] OJ L168/12.

been made to implement certain Regulation requirements and it is expected that the UK will implement the Regulation even though it will have likely left the EU by July 2019 (although, at the time of writing, this has not been confirmed). Currently, the relevant domestic rules can be found in Pt VI of the FSMA 2000 (notably ss 84–87I) and the Prospectus Rules found in the FCA Handbook, but some of these rules will change once the Prospectus Regulation comes fully into force.

18.5.1 The prospectus requirement

The core requirement to publish a prospectus is found in s 85 of the FSMA 2000, which provides that a company must make an approved prospectus available to the public if:

- it offers transferable securities to the public in the UK;[98] or
- it requests the admission of transferable securities onto a UK regulated market.[99]

The prospectus must be made available to the public before the offer or request for admission is made. A person who fails to comply with these requirements commits a criminal offence[100] and is liable to be sued for breach of statutory duty by anyone who suffers loss due to the contravention.[101]

It may be the case that after the prospectus has been approved, a fact in it may change or a mistake may be spotted. Accordingly, if, during the relevant period, there arises a significant new factor, material mistake, or inaccuracy relating to the information included in an approved prospectus, the company must submit to the FCA a supplementary prospectus containing details of the new factor, mistake, or inaccuracy.[102] The 'relevant period' begins when the prospectus is approved and ends with the closure of the offer or when trading in those securities on a regulated market begins.[103] Any persons who agreed to buy or subscribe for the shares the original prospectus relates to may withdraw their acceptance of the offer up to the end of the second working day following the publication of the supplementary prospectus, providing that the securities have not been delivered.[104]

18.5.1.1 Exemptions

The FSMA 2000 and the Prospectus Rules set out a number of exemptions to the s 85 requirement (i.e. instances where a prospectus will not be required). It should be noted that some of these exemptions apply only to specified offers of shares, whereas others only apply to specified requests to admit shares to a regulated market. From this, it follows that an offer for shares may be exempt, but an approved prospectus may still be required if the shares are to be admitted to a UK regulated market (or vice versa).

The exemptions fall into three categories. First, the offer to the public of certain types of transferable security will not require a prospectus[105] (e.g. where the total consideration for the securities being offered is less than ∈ 1 million).[106] Second, the admission to trading on a regulated market of certain types of transferable security (e.g. non-equity securities issued by the government of an EEA State) will not require a prospectus.[107] Third, s 86(1) provides that, in a number of instances, a prospectus will not be required, including:

---

[98] FSMA 2000, s 85(1).   [99] ibid s 85(2).   [100] ibid s 85(3).   [101] ibid s 85(4).
[102] ibid s 87G(1) and (2).   [103] ibid s 87G(3).   [104] ibid s 87Q(4)–(6).
[105] ibid s 85(5) and Sch 11A.   [106] ibid Sch 11A, para 9.   [107] ibid s 85(6) and Sch 11A, Pt 1.

- where the offer is made or directed to qualified investors only;

- where the offer is made or directed at fewer than 150 persons (other than qualified investors) per EEA State;

- where the minimum consideration payable by each person under the offer is at least € 100,000 (or equivalent amount);

- where the total consideration for the transferable securities being offered cannot exceed € 8 million (or equivalent amount);

- where the transferable securities are being sold or placed through a financial intermediary.

18.5.2 **Content**

The structure and content of a prospectus is principally set out in PR2 of the Prospectus Rules and, in order for prospectuses to be passported around the EEA, PR2 implements the relevant EU rules. The overarching aim of the prospectus is to provide, in a form that is comprehensible and easy to analyse, information necessary to enable investors to make an informed assessment of (i) the assets and liabilities, financial position, profits and losses, and prospects of the issuer of the transferable securities and of any guarantor; and (ii) the rights attaching to the transferable securities.[108]

Passporting is discussed at 18.5.3.1.

In terms of structure, the prospectus can be drawn up as a single document, or it can be divided up into three separate documents,[109] namely:

1. the registration document, which contains information relating to the issuer;[110]

2. the securities note, which contains information on the securities to be offered or admitted to trading on a regulated market;[111] and

3. the summary,[112] which must convey concisely, in non-technical language, the key information relevant to the securities and, when read with the rest of the prospectus, must be an aid to investors considering whether to invest in the securities.[113]

The advantage of dividing up a prospectus into three separate documents is that, once it is approved, if the issuer wishes to offer more securities or admit more securities to a regulated market, it does not need to draw up a new prospectus—it need only draw up a new securities note and summary.[114]

The exact information that must be included within the prospectus depends on the nature of the securities and their issuer,[115] and a detailed examination is well beyond the scope of this text. What should be noted here is that there is certain information that must be included in all prospectuses (this information forms what is called the 'base prospectus'),[116] and additional information (often known as 'building blocks') may then need to be added depending on the nature of the securities and their issuer.

18.5.3 **Approval and publication**

The Prospectus Directive and the Prospectus Regulation provide that a prospectus cannot be published until it has been approved by a competent authority of the home Member State.[117] Accordingly, the prospectus of a UK-registered company must be

---

[108] ibid s 87A(2). [109] Prospectus Rules, PR 2.2.1. [110] ibid PR 2.2.2(2). [111] ibid.
[112] FSMA 2000, s 87A(5). [113] ibid s 87A(6). [114] Prospectus Rules, PR 2.2.4.
[115] FSMA 2000, s 87A(4). [116] Prospectus Rules, PR 2.2.7 and 2.3.
[117] Prospectus Directive, Art 13(1); Prospectus Regulation, Art 20(1).

approved by the FCA before it can be published.[118] The FCA will not approve a prospectus unless three conditions are satisfied:

1. The UK is the issuer's home state.[119]

2. The prospectus contains the necessary information[120] and this information is presented in a form which is comprehensible and easy to analyse.[121] Note, however, that the FCA can authorize the omission of required information in certain instances (e.g. where disclosure would be contrary to the public interest or would be seriously detrimental to the issuer).[122]

3. All the other relevant requirements found in Pt VI of the FSMA 2000 or the Prospectus Directive have been complied with.[123]

The FCA must provide the issuer with a decision in writing within 10 working days in the case of a new issuer, and within 20 working days in all other cases.[124] If approval is not granted, then the FCA must state its reasons for not granting approval.[125] The applicant may appeal the FCA's decision to the Upper Tribunal.[126] If approval is granted, then the prospectus should be made available to the public as soon as practicable and, in any case, at a reasonable time in advance of the securities being offered.[127] A prospectus is deemed to be made available to the public if it is published:

- in one or more newspapers;
- in printed form freely available from the relevant regulated market or the issuer's registered office; or
- in electronic form on the websites of the issuer or the relevant regulated market.[128]

18.5.3.1 **Passporting**

A listed company registered in one country may wish to offer its shares to the public in another country or countries. However, this would become burdensome if the company had to publish a separate prospectus in each country in which it wished to offer its shares. Accordingly, the Prospectus Directive introduced the concept of 'passporting', which provides that a prospectus approved by a competent authority in an EEA Member State (the 'home' state) will also be regarded as approved in any other EEA Member State (the 'host' state).[129] Accordingly, a prospectus approved by a non-UK EEA State must be accepted by the FCA, although the FCA will require from the issuer of the prospectus a certificate of approval from the issuer's home competent authority, a copy of the approved prospectus and, if requested by the FCA, a translation of the prospectus's summary.[130]

The UK's withdrawal from the EU (and the EEA) will mean that the passporting rights of UK-registered companies will be lost (unless any post-Brexit trade deal entered into between the EU and the UK preserves passporting rights in some form). UK-registered companies that wish to offer their shares in another EEA state will need to have their prospectuses approved by the competent authority of that state.

---

[118] FSMA 2000, s 85(7); Prospectus Rules, PR 3.1.10.   [119] FSMA 2000, s 87A(1)(a).
[120] ibid s 87A(1)(b) and (2).   [121] ibid s 87A(3).   [122] ibid s 87B(1).
[123] ibid s 87A(1)(c).   [124] ibid ss 87C(1)–(3) and 87D(1) and (2).
[125] ibid s 87D(4) and (5).   [126] ibid s 87D(6).   [127] Prospectus Rules, PR 3.2.2.
[128] ibid PR 3.2.4.   [129] Prospectus Directive, Art 17; Prospectus Regulation, Art 24.
[130] FSMA 2000, s 87H(1).

18.5.4 **Liability for untrue or misleading statements, or omissions**

Section 90(1) of the FSMA 2000 provides that a person responsible for a prospectus is liable to pay compensation to a person who has acquired securities to which the prospectus applies, and has suffered loss in respect of those securities as a result of any untrue or misleading statement in the prospectus or the omission of any information required to be in the prospectus. A few points should be made regarding s 90(1):

- Section 90(1) imposes three distinct heads of liability, namely where the prospectus contains material which is (i) untrue; or (ii) misleading; or (iii) if it omits information which it is required to include.

- Liability is imposed on 'any person responsible' for the prospectus, with detailed rules identifying such persons being found in PR 5.5 of the Prospectus Rules. For example, where the prospectus relates to equity shares, persons responsible include the issuer of the securities, each director,[131] and persons who accept responsibility for or authorize the contents of the prospectus.[132]

- A person can obtain compensation if they have 'acquired securities' based on the prospectus, which includes a person who has contracted to acquire securities or has an interest in them.[133] Accordingly, a person need not actually have purchased the securities in order to claim compensation.

- The House of Lords held that damages for breach of a predecessor provision to s 90 are assessed in the same way as damages for the tort of deceit[134] and so it is likely that compensation under s 90 will be assessed in the same way.

- The imposition of liability under s 90 does not affect any other liability that might arise elsewhere.[135] So, for example, a person who is responsible for an untrue or misleading statement in a prospectus may also be liable for negligent misstatement or misrepresentation.

18.5.4.1 **Exemptions**

Schedule 10 of the FSMA 2000 contains a list of instances where liability under s 90 will not be imposed,[136] including:

- where the person responsible for the prospectus reasonably believed that the statement was true and not misleading, or that the information that was omitted was properly omitted;[137]

- where, before the securities were acquired, a correction was published in a manner calculated to bring it to the attention of persons likely to acquire the securities, or that the person responsible took all such reasonable steps to secure such publication and reasonably believed it had taken place;[138]

- where the information in the prospectus that causes loss was a statement made by an official person or contained in a public official document;[139]

- where the person who suffered the loss acquired the securities knowing that the information in the prospectus was false or misleading, or knew that it contained omitted material.[140]

---

[131] Liability will not be imposed on a director in the unlikely event that a prospectus was published without his knowledge or consent (Prospectus Rules, PR 5.5.6).

[132] Prospectus Rules, PR 5.5.3(2).   [133] FSMA 2000, s 90(7).

[134] *Clark v Urquhart* [1930] AC 28 (HL).   [135] FSMA 2000, s 90(6).

[136] These are often referred to as defences, but technically they are not defences to s 90, but are instances where s 90 will have no application.

[137] FSMA 2000, Sch 10, para 1.   [138] ibid Sch 10, para 3.

[139] ibid Sch 10, para 5.   [140] ibid Sch 10, para 6.

18.6 Continuing obligations

The admission of a company's securities onto the official list does not mark the end of the listing process. For as long as the securities remain listed, a listed company must comply with a range of obligations derived from numerous sources, and these are referred to as 'continuing obligations'. These continuing obligations are extensive and discussion of them is beyond the scope of this text, but Table 18.3 provides an overview of the principal continuing obligations imposed upon listed companies.

TABLE 18.3 Continuing obligations

Obligation	Standard listing	Premium listing
Listing Principles/Premium Listing Principles	Must comply with the Listing Principles (LR 7.2.1)	Must comply with the Listing Principles and the Premium Listing Principles (LR 7.2.1 and 7.2.1A)
Sponsor	N/a	Must have a sponsor for certain transactions (LR 8)
Continuing obligations in LR 9	N/a	Must comply with the obligations found in LR 9
Significant transactions	N/a	Must comply with the rules relating to significant transactions (LR 10)
Related party transactions	N/a	Must comply with the rules relating to related party transactions (LR 11)
Dealing in own securities	Must comply with ss 690–708 of the CA 2006	Must comply with ss 690–708 of the CA 2006 and LR 12
Disclosure and control of inside information	All listed companies must comply with the rules on inside information found in DTR 2 and Arts 17 and 18 of the EU Market Abuse Regulation	
Persons discharging managerial responsibilities	All listed companies must disclose details of certain transactions involving persons discharging managerial responsibility (DTR 3 and Art 19 of the EU Market Abuse Regulation)	
Periodic financial reporting	All listed companies must provide annual and half-yearly financial reports (DTR 4)	
Vote holder and issuer notification	All listed companies must provide details of the acquisition/disposal of major shareholdings/voting rights and other specified transactions (DTR 5)	
Continuing obligations in DTR 6	All listed companies must comply with the continuing obligations in DTR 6	
Corporate governance	All listed companies must have an audit committee and must include a corporate governance statement in their annual report (DTR 7). Companies with a premium listing must comply with additional rules in LR 9.8.6	
Suspension, cancellation, and restoring of listing	Companies that wish to suspend, cancel or restore their listing must comply with the rules in LR 5. LR 5 also establishes rules for changing from a standard to a premium listing and vice versa	

TABLE 18.4 The Premium Listing Principles

Premium Listing Principle 1	A listed company must take reasonable steps to enable its directors to understand their responsibilities and obligations as directors
Premium Listing Principle 2	A listed company must act with integrity towards the holders and potential holders of its premium listed shares
Premium Listing Principle 3	All equity shares in a class that has been admitted to premium listing must carry an equal number of votes on any shareholder vote
Premium Listing Principle 4	Where a listed company has more than one class of equity shares admitted to premium listing, the aggregate voting rights of the shares in each class should be broadly proportionate to the relative interests of those classes in the equity of the listed company
Premium Listing Principle 5	A listed company must ensure that it treats all holders of the same class of its listed equity shares that are in the same position equally in respect of the rights attaching to those listed equity shares
Premium Listing Principle 6	A listed company must communicate information to holders and potential holders of its listed equity shares in such a way as to avoid the creation of a false market in those listed equity shares

18.6.1 **The Listing and Premium Listing Principles**

Special mention should be made of two sets of rules found in LR 7, namely the Listing Principles and the Premium Listing Principles. The aim behind these Principles is 'to ensure that listed companies pay due regard to the fundamental role they play in maintaining market confidence and ensuring fair and orderly markets'[141] and to assist companies in identifying their obligations and responsibilities under the Listing Rules, the DTRs, and the corporate governance rules.[142]

The Listing Principles, which apply to every listed company,[143] contain two Principles. Listing Principle 1 states that a listed company must take reasonable steps to establish and maintain adequate procedures, systems, and controls to enable it to comply with its obligations, whereas Listing Principle 2 provides that a listed company must deal with the FCA in an open and co-operative manner.[144]

The Premium Listing Principles[145] apply to every listed company with a premium listing of equity shares[146] and are set out in Table 18.4.

18.7 Sanctions

Companies that offer their shares to the public are subject to a range of rules that other companies are not subject to. If such companies breach these rules, sanctions can be imposed upon them by the FCA. In order to determine whether a contravention has occurred, the FCA may appoint one or more persons to conduct an investigation.[147] If a breach has occurred, the FCA has available to it several sanctions, which will now be discussed.

---

[141] Listing Rules, LR 7.1.2.   [142] ibid LR 7.1.3.   [143] ibid LR 7.1.1(1).
[144] ibid LR 7.2.1.   [145] ibid LR 7.2.1A.   [146] ibid LR 7.1.1(2).   [147] FSMA 2000, s 97.

18.7.1 **Financial penalty or censure**

The FCA can impose a financial penalty of such amount as it considers appropriate upon specified persons if it considers that:

- a provision of the Listing Rules has been contravened;[148]
- a provision of Pt VI of FSMA 2000 or the Prospectus Rules have been contravened;[149]
- a provision of the DTRs or corporate governance rules have been contravened;[150] or
- a person whose securities have been suspended or prohibited from trading under s 89L of the FSMA 2000 contravenes the suspension or prohibition.[151]

The following example, which involves the largest penalty imposed upon a company to date for a breach of the DTRs, demonstrates the above in practice.

Penalty for breach of the DTRs[152]

In 2011, Rio Tinto plc ('RT') acquired a company that held mining interests in Mozambique (this company was renamed Rio Tinto Coal Mozambique ('RTCM')). RT's valuation of RTCM was based on how much coal RTCM would be able to transport from the mines to the coast for export. However, in early 2012, RT realized that RTCM would be unable to transport as much coal as projected and higher-cost transport methods would have to be used.

International Accounting Standard ('IAS') 34 provides that a company's interim financial report must include details of any events that impair the valuation of its assets, with the extent of the impairment to be assessed via an impairment test. The inability to transport as much coal as projected constituted an impairment of the value of RTCM and so RT should have conducted an impairment test and then reported on this impairment in its 2012 interim report. RT failed to carry out such a test and the impairment was not reported until 2013, when RT reported an 80 per cent reduction in RTCM's value.

The FCA determined that RT's actions contravened DTR 4.2.4, which requires a company's interim accounts to be prepared in accordance with International Accounting Standard 34. The FCA imposed a penalty on RT, which it first calculated at £39.1 million. However, as RT agreed to settle at an early stage in the investigation, the penalty was reduced by 30 per cent to £27.38 million.

If the FCA is entitled to impose a penalty upon a person, it may, instead of imposing the penalty, publish a statement censuring him.[153] Guidance on when public censure may be more appropriate than a penalty can be found in Decision Procedure and Penalty 6.4 (DEPP 6.4) of the Decision Procedure and Penalties Manual in the FCA Handbook.

18.7.2 **Suspension or discontinuance of listing**

The FCA may, in accordance with the Listing Rules, suspend the listing of any securities.[154] The Listing Rules provide that the FCA can suspend a listing of any securities if the smooth operation of the market is, or may be, temporarily jeopardized or

[148] ibid s 91(1).   [149] ibid s 91(1A).   [150] ibid s 91(1B)(a).   [151] ibid s 91(1B)(b).
[152] Full details of this example can be found at www.fca.org.uk/publication/final-notices/rio-tinto-plc-2017.pdf accessed 10 January 2019.
[153] FSMA 2000, s 91(3).   [154] ibid s 77(2).

if it necessary to protect investors.[155] Examples of when suspension may occur include where the issuer:

- has failed to meet its continuing obligations for listing;
- has failed to publish financial information in accordance with the Listing Rules;
- is unable to assess accurately its financial position and inform the market accordingly; or
- where the issuer's securities have been suspended elsewhere.[156]

Carillion and the suspension of securities

On 15 January 2018, Carillion plc, announced to the LSE that it had entered into compulsory liquidation with immediate effect. Later that same day, the FCA announced that it was temporarily suspending Carillion's shares from the official list, meaning that it shares could not be traded on the Main Market of LSE whilst the suspension remained in effect (the suspension is still in effect).

The collapse of Carillion is discussed more at 8.1.5.

The FCA may, in accordance with the Listing Rules, discontinue a listing of securities if it is satisfied that there are special circumstances that preclude normal regular dealings in those securities.[157] The FCA can discontinue a listing on its own initiative or following an application from the issuer of those securities.[158] Examples of situations where a listing may be cancelled include:

- where the Listing Rules require that shares no longer be listed;
- where the issuer no longer satisfied the continuing obligations for listing; or
- where the securities' listing has been suspended for more than six months.[159]

This power to suspend or discontinue a listing can be exercised by the FCA on its own initiative or following an application from the issuer of those securities.[160] An issuer whose securities are suspended is still required to comply with the continuing obligations found in the Listing Rules.[161] An issuer can appeal the FCA's decision to suspend or discontinue a listing to the Upper Tribunal.[162] This right of appeal extends only to the company issuer itself, and so the shareholders affected by the suspension or discontinuation cannot appeal the FCA's decision.[163]

CHAPTER SUMMARY

- Public companies do not need to offer their shares to the public, nor are they required to trade them on a stock market or admit them to the official list.

- The principal domestic rules relating to public offers of shares are found in the Financial Services and Markets Act 2000, the Listing Rules, the Prospectus Rules, and the Disclosure and Transparency Rules.

---

[155] Listing Rules, LR 5.1.1(1).   [156] ibid LR 5.1.2.
[157] FSMA 2000, s 77(1); Listing Rules, LR 5.2.1.   [158] FSMA 2000, s 77(2).
[159] Listing Rules, LR 5.2.2.   [160] FSMA 2000, s 77(2).   [161] ibid s 77(3).
[162] ibid s 77(5).   [163] *R v International Stock Exchange of the UK ex p Else* [1993] QB 534 (CA).

- The Financial Conduct Authority is the competent authority under the FSMA 2000 and is responsible for regulating the listing of securities.
- Private companies cannot offer their shares to the public.
- There are several types of public offer including offers for subscription, offers for sale, placings, and rights issues.
- The London Stock Exchange is the principal UK stock exchange, and its two principal markets are the Main Market and AIM.
- Companies that offer securities to the public or seek to admit securities to a UK regulated market must first publish a prospectus.
- Listed companies must comply with a range of continuing obligations for as long as their securities remain listed.
- Contravention of various rules relating to securities can result in the imposition of a financial penalty, publication of a censure, or the securities listing could be suspended or discontinued.

FURTHER READING

Alistair Hudson, *The Law of Finance* (2nd edn, Sweet & Maxwell 2013) chs 8 and 35–9.
- Provides an excellent discussion of the UK's financial services regulatory system and structure.

Louise Gullifer and Jennifer Payne, *Corporate Finance Law: Principles and Policy* (Hart 2011) ch 35.
- Provides a practical discussion of the law and practice relating to the public offer of shares.

Gill North, 'Listed Company Disclosure and Financial Market Transparency: Is This a Battle Worth Fighting or Merely Public and Regulatory Mantra?' (2014) 6 JBL 484.
- Discusses the disclosure obligations placed upon listed companies in light of the Kay Review.

Charlotte Villiers, 'Implementing the Transparency Directive: A Further Step Towards Consolidating the FSAP' (2007) 28 Co Law 257.
- Discusses the UK implementation of the 2004 Transparency Directive.

www.fca.org.uk accessed 10 January 2019.
- The website of the Financial Conduct Authority. Provides details of the FCA's role as a competent authority and guidance on the listing process. The FCA Handbook can be found at www.handbook.fca.org.uk accessed 30 October 2018.

www.londonstockexchange.com accessed 10 January 2019.
- The website of the London Stock Exchange. Provides details on the LSE's various markets and provides guidance on admission and the different types of listing.

SELF-TEST QUESTIONS

1. Define the following terms:

- securities;
- placing;
- rights issue;
- listing;
- premium listing;
- prospectus;
- passporting.

2. State whether each of the following statements is true or false and, if false, explain why:

- The FCA acts as the UK Listing Authority.
- A private company that offers its shares to the public commits a criminal offence.
- An offer for subscription occurs where a company allots shares to an investment bank, and the bank then offers them to the public.
- Any public company can apply to have its securities listed.
- A company only needs to publish a prospectus if it is to offer its shares on the Main Market of the London Stock Exchange.
- A prospectus must be approved by the FCA before it is published.

3. 'The EU has had a major impact upon the law relating to the public offers of shares and, as a result, the UK's withdrawal from the EU will have serious repercussions for UK securities regulation.' Discuss.

4. The directors of Spartan Tools Ltd wish to expand their business and require a significant amount of capital to do so. The company does not wish to take on any more debt and so is considering whether this capital can be raised by re-registering the company and public and by selling shares. Accordingly, the directors seek your advice on the following:

- What are the advantages and disadvantages of offering shares to the public as a means of raising capital?
- If the company did decide to offer its shares to the public, should it trade those shares on a stock exchange?
- Should the company consider applying for its shares to be included on the official list?

 ONLINE RESOURCES

This book is accompanied by online resources to better support you in your studies. Visit www.oup.com/uk/roach-company/ for:

- answers to the self-test questions;
- further reading lists;
- multiple-choice questions;
- glossary.

Updates to the law can be found on the author's Twitter account (@UKCompanyLaw) and further resources can be found on the author's blog (www.companylawandgovernance.com).

19 Corporate transparency

- The UK's corporate transparency regime
- Statutory registers
- Annual accounts and reports
- Auditors
- Other disclosure obligations

INTRODUCTION

Conducting a business through a company brings many positive advantages, notably corporate personality and limited liability. It has long been recognized that these benefits come with a price, and that price is disclosure. Requiring companies to act in a transparent manner and to disclose specified information are key features of the UK company law and corporate governance system. Disclosure requirements manifest themselves in numerous ways, including:

- companies are required to keep a range of statutory registers (e.g. the register of members);
- companies are required to prepare and publish annual accounts and reports;
- companies are required to disclose significant amounts of information to Companies House, and to ensure this information is updated in a timely manner;
- listed companies are required to disclose specified information to the market;
- listed companies are required to disclose how they comply with the UK Corporate Governance Code and explain any areas of non-compliance.

Some of these forms of disclosure have been discussed in other chapters. This chapter focuses on some key disclosure requirements that have not yet been discussed, notably the requirement to prepare annual accounts and reports. Before the chapter looks at the disclosure requirements, it is first important to discuss why corporate disclosure is so important.

19.1 The UK's corporate transparency regime

The UK's corporate transparency regime is predominantly statutory, with the vast majority of disclosure requirements being found in the Companies Act 2006 (CA 2006) and accompanying subordinate legislation. For quoted companies, additional disclosure obligations are found in the Listing Rules and the Disclosure Guidance and Transparency Rules (DTRs). For companies with a premium listing, the UK Corporate Governance Code also contains a number of recommendations regarding corporate disclosure. In addition to company-law disclosure requirements, a number of non-company-law statutes also impose disclosure obligations on companies (e.g. the slavery and human trafficking statement, discussed at 19.5.4).

It is important to understand why disclosure is so central to the UK company law system. There has been significant debate regarding the purported benefits of requiring companies to disclose certain information. A detailed discussion is outside the scope of this text, but it has been argued that disclosure can result in the following benefits:

- Transparency demonstrates respect for stakeholders and provides them with information to decide whether to deal with the company. For example, the ability to access a company's accounts is extremely valuable as it benefits investors considering investing in the company (to see how profitable the company is), or creditors considering lending to the company (to assess the risk of non-payment).

- The guidance to Principle 7 of the UK Stewardship Code provides that '[t]ransparency is an important feature of effective stewardship' as access to company information allows the members to more effectively undertake their stewardship role. A significant informational asymmetry exists between the company and its members, and disclosure rules help rebalance this asymmetry.

- Transparency enables markets to operate more efficiently and, importantly, it allows shares to be more accurately priced. Effective disclosure rules help reduce the risk that false or misleading information is placed into the public arena.

- A transparent company may be viewed as having nothing to hide and so may find that its reputation is enhanced. A company that knows it must operate in an open manner will be discouraged from engaging in unlawful or unmeritorious conduct that could harm its reputation.

In the absence of disclosure rules, companies might be tempted to disclose only positive news or disclose information in a manner that presents their position in an overly favourable light. The existence of disclosure rules ensures that companies are required to disclose specified information, be it positive or negative. However, the existence of disclosure rules per se is not enough. In order to secure the above benefits of transparency, corporate disclosure should exhibit three characteristics:

1. Corporate information should be easy to obtain. The benefits of transparency will be greatly reduced if the information is difficult to obtain, or if it can only be obtained by specialists. Fortunately, in the UK, corporate information is easily obtainable. For example, quoted companies are required to publish significant amounts of information on their websites and, with the launch of the Companies House Service, accessing company information online is free and straightforward.

   The Companies House Service is discussed at 19.1.1.2.

2. Corporate information should be understandable. Stakeholders cannot act (or cannot act effectively) based on information they cannot understand and the Financial Reporting Council (FRC) has emphasized the need for reports to be clear, with the avoidance of

jargon and boiler-plate text.[1] Given the complexity of some reporting issues, it is unrealistic to expect all stakeholders to fully understand the information disclosed, but a significant proportion should. For example, it has been estimated that, in order for the market to work properly, at least one-third of shareholders should be able to understand information disclosed.[2] Unfortunately, concerns still exist that certain forms of corporate disclosure (e.g. remuneration reports) are too long and overly complex.[3]

3. Corporate information should be concise. Two issues arise here. The first is that excessive levels of corporate information (or 'information overload' as it has been referred to) may discourage stakeholders from engaging with the various sources of corporate information. The second issue is that, even if stakeholders do engage, they may be unable to digest the mass of information provided, leading to the market not responding properly to the information disclosed.[4] Unfortunately, it would appear that this is an issue in the UK, especially in relation to the annual accounts and reports which, for a Financial Times Stock Exchange 350 (FTSE 350) company, average 190 pages in length.[5] The FRC has expressed concerns regarding the length and accessibility of annual accounts and reports[6] and, as the following example shows, companies are trying to respond.

The annual report and accounts of HSBC Holdings plc[7]

HSBC's 2015 annual report and accounts were 502 pages in length. For the following year's report and accounts, each contributing department was tasked with a 20 per cent page-count reduction. This, in addition, to the use of cross-referencing, a reduction in repetition, and robust editing, meant that the 2016 annual reports and accounts were 286 pages in length. The 2017 report and accounts were 270 pages in length.

It could be argued that HSBC's 2017 report and accounts are still worryingly lengthy, but quoted companies are subject to increasing disclosure requirements and the length of reports must be borne in mind when increasing the disclosure burden.

19.1.1 **Companies House**

A key component of the UK's corporate transparency regime is Companies House, whose 2016/17 annual report states that it 'registers the information companies supply under statute, and makes that information available to the public'.[8] From this, it can be seen that Companies House has two key roles relating to corporate transparency:

1. it collects the information that companies disclose to it under statute and stores it in a central register; and

2. it provides access to this register in a number of different ways.

---

[1] FRC, 'Annual Review of Corporate Reporting 2017/18' (FRC 2018) 40.

[2] Anthony Ogus, *Regulation: Legal Form and Economic Theory* (Hart 2004) 123.

[3] FRC, 'Annual Review of Corporate Reporting 2017/18' (FRC 2018) 38.

[4] Karsten Engsig Sorensen, 'Disclosure in EU Corporate Governance—A Remedy in Need of Adjustment?' (2009) 10 EBOR 255, 274.

[5] Ernst & Young, 'Annual Reporting in 2017/18: Demonstrating Purpose, Creating Value' (EY 2018) 4.

[6] FRC, 'Annual Review of Corporate Reporting 2015/16' (FRC 2016) 4.

[7] More details on this example can be found at Ernst & Young, 'Annual Reporting in 2016/17: Broad Perspective, Clear Focus' (EY 2017) 20.

[8] Companies House, 'Annual Report and Accounts 2016/17' (Companies House 2017) 6.

19.1.1.1 **The register**

Throughout this text, discussion has focused on the significant amount of information that companies are required under statute to deliver to Companies House. The registrar of Companies House is under an obligation to keep records of all this information, and these records are known as 'the register'.[9] To facilitate this record-keeping, the registrar can impose requirements as to the form, authentication, and manner of delivery of documents delivered to Companies House[10] (these are known as the 'registrar's rules').[11] Different sets of registrar's rules exist for different forms of delivery and authentication (e.g. the registrar's (electronic) rules 2009). Notably, the registrar cannot currently compel companies to submit information by electronic means,[12] so companies can still submit information in hard copy or electronically. However, the Secretary of State can make regulations requiring documents to be delivered by electronic means,[13] and as Companies House is committed to becoming a 100 per cent digital organization,[14] this power is likely to be exercised by the Secretary of State in the foreseeable future. Companies House already strongly encourages electronic submission (by charging significantly more for paper submission) and, in 2018, over 85 per cent of all Companies House transactions were completed digitally.[15]

Any document that does not meet the registrar's requirements for form or delivery, or which does not contain the required content, will not be regarded as being properly delivered[16] and will likely be rejected (although the registrar can choose to accept and register such a document).[17] Note, however, that even if the registrar accepts an improperly delivered document, this does not mean that the original requirement to properly deliver the document will have been satisfied, and any liability that flows from a failure to deliver the document can still be imposed.[18]

Once a document has been validly delivered, it will be registered and will become part of the register. The legal date of registration is when Companies House registered the document,[19] not when it was delivered to Companies House.

19.1.1.2 **Access to the register**

The register contains a huge amount of information relating to UK companies and this can be an extremely useful source of information for those who deal with companies. Potential investors may use this information when deciding whether to buy shares. Creditors may use this information when deciding to loan money. Suppliers may use this information before deciding whether to supply goods. As Lord Henley, the Parliamentary Under-Secretary for BEIS, stated:

> The register of companies is more than a list of corporate entities and their directors, it's an important national asset. It is a vast source of information that supports the

---

[9] CA 2006, s 1080(1) and (2).   [10] ibid s 1068(1).

[11] ibid s 1117. The registrar's rules can be found at www.gov.uk/guidance/registrars-rules accessed 30 October 2018.

[12] CA 2006, s 1068(6).

[13] To date, this has only been done once, namely in regs 14 and 15 of the Reports on Payments to Governments Regulations 2014, SI 2014/3209.

[14] Companies House, 'Our Strategy 2017 to 2020' (Companies House 2017) 13.

[15] Companies House, 'Business Plan 2018 to 2019' (Companies House 2018) 14.

[16] CA 2006, s 1072(1).   [17] ibid s 1073(1).

[18] Companies House, 'Registrar's Rules and Powers' (Companies House 2016) 8.

[19] *Re Globespan Airways Ltd* [2012] EWCA Civ 1159, [2013] 1 WLR 1122.

limited liability regime by giving vital information on companies, trading history of directors and the people that control those companies. This helps those wanting to do business with those companies find information to assist in business decisions.[20]

Accordingly, it is important that persons have access to the information contained in the register. Any person may inspect the register,[21] but s 1087 specifies that certain material is not to be made available for inspection (e.g. directors' residential addresses).[22] In addition, any person may require a copy of any material on the register.[23] Companies House may (and indeed does) charge a fee for inspecting the register and taking copies of information on it.[24]

Companies House offers a number of different ways to access information on the register. Anyone can visit a Companies House information centre[25] and access documentation on the register for a fee. However, this is a rather cumbersome way to access the register and, thankfully, Companies House is committed to providing free, online access to company information via its Companies House Service (CHS).[26] CHS allows anyone to access online (either through the internet or Companies House's mobile app) all of the public information held by Companies House free of charge. A supplementary service called 'Follow' allows persons to register an account, choose which companies to follow, and the user will be provided with alerts of any filings or changes to the register information of the followed companies. CHS has, unsurprisingly, proved to be extremely popular and is accessed, on average, 15 million times a day.[27]

In addition to CHS, Companies House offer a number of other (arguably more outdated) ways to access company information:

- WebCheck allows users to obtain basic company information free of charge and to download company documentation for a fee;
- Companies House's contact centre can take orders for company information, which it will then send out by post or email;
- company information can be purchased on DVD;
- Companies House offers a number of different data products (e.g. the 'company data product', which provides free monthly snapshots of company data).

19.1.1.3 Accuracy of information on the register

Companies House has stated that '[f]or the register to be a valuable source of information for searchers, they need to be able to have confidence that the data is current, complete and correct'.[28] Whilst the vast majority of information on the register is accurate, Companies House has indicated that it does wish to improve the quality of data integrity on the register,[29] meaning that there is incorrect data on the register.

There are three principal reasons why information on the register may be inaccurate. The first reason is that a company may not have supplied Companies House with the required information. The various statutory disclosure provisions usually specify the consequences of a failure to supply Companies House with required information, with criminal liability usually being imposed. In addition, the CA 2006 also provides that if a company has failed

---

[20] Companies House, 'Annual Report and Accounts 2017/18' (Companies House 2018) 2.

[21] CA 2006, s 1085(1).   [22] ibid s 1087(1)(b).   [23] ibid s 1086(1).

[24] ibid s 1063(2)(c). The fees can be found in Sch 2.

[25] Located in Cardiff, Belfast, Edinburgh, and London.

[26] See https://beta.companieshouse.gov.uk accessed 10 January 2019.

[27] Companies House, 'Our Strategy 2017 to 2020' (Companies House 2017) 8.   [28] ibid 18.

[29] Companies House, 'Annual Report and Accounts 2016/17' (Companies House 2017) 4.

to file a required document with Companies House, then the registrar or any member or creditor may notify the company of the obligation to file the specified document.[30] If, after 14 days, the company has not complied, the registrar or any member or creditor may apply to the court for an order directing the company to file the required document within a specified time.[31] A repeated failure to file information may lead the registrar to conclude that the company is defunct, which could lead to the company being struck off the register.[32]

The second reason is that a company has supplied Companies House with inaccurate information. Again, the statutory provision in question may specify the consequences of providing false or inaccurate information. In addition, the CA 2006 makes it an offence for a person to knowingly or recklessly deliver to the registrar a document that is misleading, false, or deceptive.[33] This indicates that the onus on filing accurate information is placed on the person providing the information, not Companies House, and so it follows that Companies House is not liable to third parties who rely on inaccurate information that is provided to, and then registered by, Companies House.

The third reason is that the company provided Companies House with accurate information, but it was incorrectly entered into the register by Companies House. In such a case, Companies House can be liable, as the following unfortunate case demonstrates.

The striking off of a defunct company is discussed at 23.5.

Sebry v Companies House [2015] EWHC 115 (QB)

FACTS: Taylor & Sons Ltd was a successful Cardiff-based company, whereas Taylor & Son Ltd was a Manchester-based company that was experiencing financial difficulties and was wound up in January 2009. Companies House received the winding-up order in February 2009 but it was negligently recorded on the register against Taylor & Sons. The results of the error were catastrophic—news of Taylor & Sons' apparent liquidation spread very quickly. Suppliers cancelled their contracts, creditors refused to provide any more credit, and key customers cancelled their orders. In April 2009, Taylor & Sons entered administration and over 250 employees lost their jobs. Sebry, Taylor & Sons' managing director, commenced proceedings against Companies House and the Registrar of Companies for negligence and breach of statutory duty. Companies House denied owing Taylor & Sons a duty of care.

HELD: In finding Companies House liable, Edis J stated:

> It appears to me that where the Registrar undertakes to alter the status of a company on the Register which it is his duty to keep, in particular by recording a winding up order against it, he does assume a responsibility to that company (but not to anyone else) to take reasonable care to ensure that the winding up order is not registered against the wrong company.[34]

Accordingly, Companies House had assumed a responsibility towards Taylor & Sons, but not to third parties who might rely on the information on the register in relation to that company. In other words, Companies House owes a duty to register accurately the information that is provided to it, but is not under a duty to verify the accuracy of the information it is provided with.

See the author's blog post at https://companylawandgovernance.com/2016/06/30/companies-house-and-the-9-million-typo accessed 10 January 2019.

In an attempt to improve the accuracy of information on the register, in July 2017, Companies House added the 'report it now' feature to its Companies House Service. This feature allows users to report inaccurate information to Companies House and has resulted in over 58,000 reports being made.[35]

---

[30] CA 2006, s 1113(1) and (2).   [31] ibid s 1113(3).   [32] ibid s 1000.   [33] ibid s 1112.
[34] [2015] EWHC 115 (QB), [2015] BCC 236 [111].
[35] Companies House, 'Annual Report and Accounts 2017/18' (Companies House 2018) 4.

19.1.1.4 Removal of unnecessary or inaccurate information

To discourage companies from providing unnecessary information (i.e. information that is not necessary to comply with a statutory obligation, or is not authorized to be delivered to the registrar),[36] the CA 2006 provides that, if the unnecessary material cannot be separated from the rest of the document, the document is treated as not being properly delivered.[37] If the unnecessary material can be separated, then the registrar may register the document either (i) without the unnecessary material; or (ii) as delivered.[38]

As regards inaccurate information, several provisions exist to remedy the presence of inaccurate information on the register:

- Where information in a document delivered to the registrar is inconsistent with information on the register, the registrar may notify the company of the inconsistency and require the company to take steps to resolve the inconsistency.[39]

- An application can be made requiring the registrar to remove from the register material that (i) derives from anything invalid or ineffective or that was done without the authority of the company or overseas company to which the material relates; or (ii) is factually inaccurate, or is derived from something that is factually inaccurate or forged.[40]

19.1.2 Financial Reporting Council

Note that the government plans to replace the FRC, as discussed at xviii in the 'Latest news' section.

Brief mention should also be made of the Financial Reporting Council ('FRC'), which currently undertakes a number of important functions in relation to corporate transparency including:

- providing public oversight of statutory auditors, including setting standards by which auditors operate, applying eligibility criteria, monitoring the work engaged in by auditors, and investigating statutory auditors;

- issuing accounting standards, monitoring their compliance, and investigating and disciplining breaches of those standards;

- monitoring companies' corporate reporting and ensuring that it complies with statutory requirements; and

- monitoring and maintaining the UK Corporate Governance Code and the UK Stewardship Code.[41]

In October 2018, the FRC announced that it was launching a project to 'challenge existing thinking about corporate reporting and consider how companies should better meet the information needs of shareholders and other stakeholders'.[42] This project will review financial and non-financial disclosures and produce a paper in the second half of 2019 that will result in calls for action and changes to regulation and practice.

19.2 Statutory registers

The CA 2006 provides that companies must keep certain registers, and provides that these registers must be made available for inspection. The registers that must be kept (subject to some exceptions) are:

- the register of members (discussed at 13.2);

---

[36] CA 2006, s 1074(2).   [37] ibid s 1074(4).   [38] ibid s 1074(5).   [39] ibid s 1093(1).
[40] Registrar of Companies and Applications for Striking Off Regulations 2009, SI 2009/1803, regs 4–5.
[41] FRC, 'FRC Roles and Responsibilities: Schedule of Functions and Powers' (FRC 2017).
[42] See www.frc.org.uk/news/october-2018/frc-to-examine-the-future-of-corporate-reporting accessed 9 November 2018.

- the register of directors (discussed at 8.1.3);
- the register of directors' residential addresses (discussed at 8.1.3);
- the register of secretaries (discussed at 8.2.5.1);
- the register of interests disclosed (discussed at 13.3.1.2); and
- the register of people with significant control (PSC) (discussed at 13.3.2).

In addition, others registers (namely the register of debentures, and the register of charges) are not required, but may be kept if the company so chooses. All of the above registers have been discussed elsewhere in this text, so they will not be discussed again. However, for convenience, Table 19.1 sets out some basic information about each register.

It should be noted that the government has recently consulted on the introduction of a new register, namely the register of overseas entities.[43] This register, which would be kept by the registrar of companies, would require overseas entities (namely any legal entity governed by the law of a country or territory outside the UK)[44] that wish to own land in the UK to disclose information regarding their beneficial owners and to register them. At the time of writing, the government has not yet responded to the consultation.

19.2.1 Election to keep information on the public register

Consider the following example:

 The register of directors

Dragon Goods Ltd keeps its own register of directors at its registered office. The information contained in the register of directors is filed with Companies House and forms part of Companies House's public register,[45] the contents of which are available to the public.

It could be argued that it is pointless to require Dragon Goods to keep its own register, given that the information is replicated in Companies House's public register. Accordingly, the Small Business, Enterprise and Employment Act 2015 (SBEEA 2015) amended the CA 2006 to provide private companies[46] with the right to make an election regarding each of the registers noted above, except the register of interests disclosed. Private companies can either:

- comply with the traditional rules and keep and file their own registers; or
- elect to keep the information on the relevant register on the public register maintained by Companies House. If this election is made, then the company no longer needs to keep its

---

[43] See www.gov.uk/government/consultations/draft-registration-of-overseas-entities-bill accessed 10 January 2019.

[44] Draft Registration of Overseas Entities Bill, cl 2(1).

[45] Section 1080 of the CA 2006 provides that any documents delivered to Companies House under any enactment are collectively known as 'the register'. This register is discussed at 19.1.1.1.

[46] The CA 2006 provides the Secretary of State with the power to extend the relevant provisions to cover public companies. At the time of writing, this power has not been exercised.

TABLE 19.1 Statutory registers

	Register of members	Register of directors	Register of directors' residential addresses	Register of secretaries	Register of people with significant control	Register of debentures	Register of charges
Must be kept by	Each of these registers must be kept by all companies				Every company, except those subject to DTR 5 requirements, and companies who trade on a regulated market in an EEA State other than the UK	These registers are not required, but companies may choose to keep either of these registers if they so wish	
Right of inspection	Can be inspected by anyone	Can be inspected by anyone	Cannot be inspected	Can be inspected by anyone	Can be inspected by anyone	Can be inspected by anyone (if it exists)	No right to inspect the register, but any person may inspect the charge instrument
Free to inspect	Free for members; other persons must pay a fee	Free for members; other persons must pay a fee	Cannot be inspected	Free for members; other persons must pay a fee	Free to inspect	Free for debenture holders and shareholders; other persons must pay a fee	Free for members and creditors; other persons must pay a fee
Can elect to keep on public register	Private companies may elect to keep the information on any of these registers on the public register maintained by Companies House				No	No	No

own register(s)—all it needs do is inform Companies House of any changes to the information contained in the relevant register(s). A company that elects to keep its information on the public register may change its mind and keep its own register, or vice versa.

There is one important consideration for a private company to bear in mind when deciding whether to maintain a register or elect to keep the information on the public register. Certain information (e.g. members' addresses) is protected (i.e. should not normally be disclosed) when on a register maintained by the company. If a private company elects to keep its register information on the public register, this protected information will become public.

19.3 Annual accounts and reports

The preparation and publication of a company's annual accounts and reports constitutes a company's most important and single largest act of disclosure. What constitutes a company's 'annual accounts and reports' is set out in s 471 and depends on whether the company is quoted or unquoted, as Figure 19.1 indicates.

The content of the annual accounts and reports is largely a matter for the CA 2006, with each successive Companies Act adding to the amount of material that must be disclosed, especially for larger companies. The benefit of this is that the annual accounts and reports provide more information than ever and the scope of information is broader and more contextual (and therefore of interest to a wider group of stakeholders). However, two notable disadvantages result from this:

1. Annual accounts and reports are longer than they have ever been. Between 2012 and 2018, the average length of a FTSE 350 company's annual accounts and reports increased by over 25 per cent from 148 pages to 190 pages,[47] with some reports being much larger (e.g. HSBC Holdings plc's 2015 Annual Report and Accounts was 502 pages long). This length imposes cost burdens upon the company and may also discourage stakeholders from engaging with the accounts and reports.

2. The continually increasing disclosure burden has resulted in some companies struggling, or being unwilling, to engage fully with the disclosure requirements. The standard of corporate reporting in the UK is generally good, but there are notable areas of concern. In

FIGURE 19.1 Annual accounts and reports

---

[47] Ernst & Young, 'Annual Reporting in 2016/17: Broad Perspective, Clear Focus' (EY 2017) 9; Ernst & Young, 'Annual Reporting in 2017/18: Demonstrating Purpose, Creating Value' (EY 2018) 4.

2017/18, the FRC reviewed 220 annual and interim reports and accounts and wrote to 101 companies identifying substantive issues with those reports.[48]

This section begins by looking at a company's annual accounts.

19.3.1 Annual accounts

The company's annual accounts provide the single most important source of financial information relating to a company. A company's annual accounts consist of any individual accounts prepared by the company in relation to a financial year and any group accounts prepared by the company for that year.[49] Before looking at the distinction between individual and group accounts, it is important to discuss the records on which the accounts are based and the period that the accounts cover.

19.3.1.1 Accounting records

A company's accounts will only be accurate if the company keeps adequate accounting records. Accordingly, the CA 2006 provides that every company must keep adequate accounting records,[50] which means records that are sufficient:

- to show and explain the company's transactions;
- to disclose with reasonable accuracy, at any time, the financial position of the company at that time; and
- to enable the directors to ensure that any accounts required to be prepared comply with the CA 2006 and, where applicable, Art 4 of the International Accounting Standards Regulation.[51]

These records must be kept for three years in the case of a private company, and six years in the case of a public company.[52] A failure to keep adequate accounting records is a criminal offence,[53] as is a failure to keep the records for the requisite period.[54] Breach of these requirements can also result in a director being disqualified.[55]

19.3.1.2 Financial years and accounting reference dates/periods

The annual accounts of a company must cover a period known as its 'financial year'. In order to calculate a company's financial year, we first need to know its 'accounting reference date' and its 'accounting reference period':

- A company's accounting reference date is normally the last day of the month on which the anniversary of its incorporation falls.[56]
- A company's first accounting reference period begins on the date of its incorporation and ends on its accounting reference date.[57] Subsequent accounting reference periods are periods of twelve months beginning the day after the company's accounting reference date.[58]

---

[48] FRC, 'Annual Review of Corporate Governance and Reporting 2017/2018' (FRC 2018) 58.
[49] CA 2006, s 471(1).   [50] ibid s 386(1).   [51] ibid s 386(2).
[52] ibid s 388(4). Company officers must be allowed to inspect these records at any time (s 388(1)).
[53] ibid s 387(1).   [54] ibid s 389(1).
[55] See e.g. *Re Galeforce Pleating Co Ltd* [1999] 2 BCLC 704 (Ch).
[56] CA 2006, s 391(4). For companies incorporated before 1 April 1996, slightly different rules may apply (s 391(2)).
[57] ibid s 391(5).   [58] ibid s 391(6).

A company's first financial year begins on the day of its first accounting reference period and ends with the last day of that period, or some other date not more than seven days before or after that period, as the directors may determine.[59] Subsequent financial years begin on the day following the end of the previous financial year, and end on the last day of its next accounting reference period, or some other date not more than seven days before or after that period, as the directors may determine.[60] The following example demonstrates this.

 Eg **A company's financial year**

Dragon Products Ltd was incorporated on the 11 May 2018. Accordingly, its accounting reference date will be 31 May 2019, and its first accounting reference period and first financial year will start on 11 May 2018 and will end on 31 May 2019 (the directors did not exercise their power to choose a different end-date for the financial year). Subsequent accounting reference periods and financial years will run from 1 July to 31 May.

Note that companies can change their accounting reference date[61] (which will also change its accounting reference period and financial year). In a corporate group, the directors of a parent company should ensure that the financial years of its subsidiaries coincide with that of the parent, unless there are good reasons against this.[62]

19.3.1.3 Individual accounts

The directors of a company (except a dormant subsidiary)[63] must prepare accounts for each of that company's financial years and these are known as 'individual accounts'.[64] These accounts must be prepared in accordance with s 396 or international accounting standards.[65] Section 396 provides that the accounts must provide specified basic information (e.g. the company's registered number, whether it is public or private, etc.),[66] along with:

- a balance sheet as to the last day of the financial year, which must give a fair and true view of the state of affairs of the company as at the end of the financial year; and

- a profit-and-loss account that provides a fair and true view of the profit or loss of the company for the financial year.[67]

In addition, the Act provides that the notes to a company's accounts must contain information about employee numbers and costs,[68] and regulations may be passed which require the notes to contain information relating to related undertakings, directors' remuneration, and directors' benefits[69] (these regulations have now been passed).[70] The Act goes on to provide that the accounts must comply with regulations passed by the Secretary of State, and these regulations place different obligations regarding the form and content of the accounts upon companies based on their size (the basic effect is that smaller companies are subject to simpler and fewer disclosure obligations). A detailed

---

[59] ibid s 390(2).   [60] ibid s 390(3).   [61] ibid s 392.   [62] ibid s 390(5).
[63] ibid ss 394A–394C.   [64] ibid s 394.   [65] ibid s 395(1).   [66] ibid s 396(1).
[67] ibid s 396(1) and (2).   [68] ibid s 411.   [69] ibid ss 409, 412, and 413.
[70] Small Companies and Groups (Accounts and Directors' Report) Regulations 2008; Large and Medium-Sized Companies and Groups (Accounts and Reports) Regulations 2008.

examination of the accounts requirements for each type of company is beyond the scope of this text, but the basic accounts for each type of company are as follows:

- **Micro-entities**: micro-entities are not required to comply in full with the requirements in s 396. Micro-entities can file simpler accounts (known as 'abridged accounts') that contain less information, notably a simpler, abridged balance sheet.[71] Micro-entities are also entitled to all the exemptions afforded to small companies.

- **Small companies**: small companies must generally comply with the requirements set out in s 396, but are permitted to prepare abridged accounts if all the members so consent[72] (if so, the directors must deliver to the registrar a statement that all the members have consented to the abridgement).[73] Small companies must deliver copies of the annual accounts to Companies House, but may choose to omit the profit-and-loss account[74] (i.e. only the balance sheet must be delivered).[75] If the profit-and-loss account is omitted, the balance sheet must disclose this fact.[76] Small companies are exempt from certain disclosures regarding the average number of employees.[77]

- **Medium-sized companies**: medium-sized companies are generally required to prepare and file full accounts, with subordinate legislation providing only very limited exclusions (e.g. medium-sized companies do not need to disclose whether the accounts have been prepared in accordance with applicable accounting standards).[78]

- **Large companies**: large companies must prepare and file full annual accounts and are not entitled to any exemptions available to other companies.

Under the CA 2006, a company's size is based on three criteria, namely its turnover, balance sheet total, and the number of employees that it has, as set out in Table 19.2. Not all three criteria need be satisfied. In a company's first financial year, it need only satisfy at least two criteria out of three. A company that is classified as a certain size in its first year will continue to be classified as such unless it fails to satisfy at least two criteria in two consecutive financial years.

TABLE 19.2 Company size

	Micro-entity (s 384A)	Small (s 382(3))	Medium (s 465(3))	Large
Turnover	Not more than £623,000	Not more than £10.2 million	Not more than £36 million	Any company that is not a micro-entity, small, or medium-sized
Balance sheet total	Not more than £316,000	Not more than £5.1 million	Not more than £18 million	
Number of employees	Not more than 10	Not more than 50	Not more than 250	
	Public companies and traded companies cannot be classified as micro-entitles, small, or medium-sized (ss 384(2) and 467(2)).			

[71] Small Companies and Groups (Accounts and Directors' Report) Regulations 2008, Sch 1, para 1A.
[72] ibid.　[73] CA 2006, s 444(2A).　[74] ibid s 444(1)(b)(i)　[75] ibid s 444(1)(a).
[76] ibid s 444(5A).　[77] ibid s 411(1A).
[78] Large and Medium-Sized Companies and Groups (Accounts and Reports) Regulations 2008, reg 4(2A).

19.3.1.4 **Group accounts**

Where, at the end of a financial year, a company is a parent company, then its directors, in addition to preparing individual accounts for the parent, must also prepare group accounts for that financial year.[79] However, certain parent companies (e.g. those subject to the small companies regime) are not required to prepare group accounts.[80]

Group accounts must be prepared in accordance with s 404 or in accordance with international accounting standards.[81] Section 404 provides that the group accounts must provide certain basic information (e.g. the company's registered number, whether it is public or private, etc.).[82] They must also provide:

- a consolidated balance sheet dealing with the state of affairs of the parent company and its subsidiaries; and
- a consolidated profit-and-loss account dealing with the profit and loss of the parent company and its subsidiaries.[83]

In addition, there are specific requirements, in terms of form and content, placed upon small parent companies,[84] and large and medium-sized parent companies.[85] The group accounts must give a true and fair view of the state of affairs as at the end of the financial year, and the profit or loss for the financial year, of the undertakings included in the consolidation as a whole.[86] All the parent company's subsidiaries must be included within the consolidation, although the Act does provide that, in certain cases, a subsidiary can be excluded (e.g. where its inclusion is not material for the purpose of giving a true and fair view).[87]

19.3.2 **Annual reports**

The annual accounts are accompanied by the 'annual reports', which consist of:

- the strategic report;
- the directors' report;
- the auditor's report; and
- the directors' remuneration report (only applies to quoted companies).[88]

Each of these reports is discussed in more detail at 19.3.2.1–19.3.2.4 (including the corporate governance statement, which may form part of the directors' report), but first it is important to note that, in recent years, there has been a notable move towards increased 'narrative reporting', which has been defined as 'non-financial information that is included in company reports in order to provide a broad and meaningful picture of a company's business, its market position, strategy, performance and future prospects'.[89] Historically, a company's annual reports contained little non-financial information and

---

[79] CA 2006, s 399(2).   [80] ibid ss 399(2A), (2B), and (3), 400, 401, and 402.

[81] ibid s 403(2). Note that some parent companies must prepare their accounts in accordance with international accounting standards (s 403(1)).

[82] ibid s 404(A1).   [83] ibid s 404(1).

[84] Small Companies and Groups (Accounts and Directors' Report) Regulations 2008, reg 8 and Sch 6.

[85] Large and Medium-Sized Companies and Groups (Accounts and Reports) Regulations 2008, reg 9 and Sch 6.

[86] CA 2006, s 404(2).   [87] ibid s 405(2). Other exceptions are found in s 405(3).

[88] ibid s 471(2) and (3).

[89] Department for Business, Innovation and Skills (BIS), 'The Future of Narrative Reporting—A Consultation' (BIS 2010) para 20.

was only of real interest to a company's members, but this is no longer the case and it has been argued that increased narrative reporting brings several benefits:

- it provides investors, stakeholders, and consumers with easy access to information on the impact of businesses on society;[90]
- greater transparency makes companies perform better, both in financial and non-financial terms, which will lead to more growth, employment, and trust among stakeholders;[91] and
- appropriate non-financial disclosure is an essential element to enable sustainable finance.[92]

The drive towards increased narrative reporting has come from the European Union (EU) via two directives, namely:

- Directive 2013/34/EU[93] (the EU Accounting Directive), which was implemented in the UK by the Companies Act 2006 (Strategic Report and Directors' Report) Regulations 2013,[94] and requires companies to include specified non-financial information in their strategic report and directors' report;
- Directive 2014/95/EU[95] (the Non-Financial Reporting Directive), which was implemented in the UK by the Companies, Partnerships and Groups (Accounts and Non-Financial Reporting) Regulations 2016,[96] and requires certain companies to provide a non-financial information statement as part of their strategic report.

The non-financial information statement is discussed at 19.3.2.1.

Accordingly, a company's annual reports now provide a more balanced mixture of financial and non-financial information. However, this has come at the cost of length—annual reports are now longer than ever and narrative reporting has had a notable effect on their length. In 2012/13 (the year before the strategic report was introduced), a FTSE 350 company's annual report averaged 148 pages in length.[97] By 2017/18, this had increased by over 25 per cent to 190 pages in length.[98]

The auditor's report is discussed at 19.4.3.

Each report will now be discussed, except the auditor's report, which will be discussed alongside the role of the auditor.

19.3.2.1 Strategic report

The directors of a company (except a small company)[99] must prepare a strategic report for each financial year of the company.[100] Where the company is a parent company and the directors prepare group accounts, then the report must be a group strategic report that covers all the companies in the corporate group.[101] The strategic report must be approved by the board of directors and signed on behalf of the board by a director or secretary of the company.[102] Failure to prepare a strategic report is a criminal offence.[103]

The CA 2006 itself sets out the purpose of the strategic report, namely to 'inform members of the company and help them assess how the directors have performed their

---

[90] BIS, 'The Non-Financial Reporting Directive: A Call for Views on Effective Reporting Alongside Proposals to Implement EU Requirements' (BIS 2016) para 20.

[91] European Commission, 'Guidelines on Non-Financial Reporting' [2017] OJ C215/01, 2.   [92] ibid.

[93] Council Directive 2013/34/EU of 26 June 2013 on the annual financial statements consolidated financial statements and related reports of certain types of undertakings, amending Directive 2006/43/EC of the European Parliament and of the Council and repealing Council Directives 78/660/EEC and 83/349/EEC [2013] OJ L182/19.

[94] SI 2013/1970.

[95] Council Directive 2014/95/EU of 22 October 2014 amending Directive 2013/34/EU as regards disclosure of non-financial and diversity information by certain large undertakings and groups [2014] OJ L330/1.

[96] SI 2016/1245.

[97] Ernst & Young, 'Annual Reporting in 2016/17: Broad Perspective, Clear Focus' (EY 2017) 9.

[98] Ernst & Young, 'Annual Reporting in 2017/18: Demonstrating Purpose, Creating Value' (EY 2018) 4.

[99] CA 2006, ss 414A(2) and 414B.   [100] ibid s 414A(1).   [101] ibid s 414A(3).

[102] ibid s 414D(1).   [103] ibid s 414A(5).

duty under section 172 (duty to promote the success of the company)'.[104] To this end, companies classified as large under the CA 2006 are required to include within the strategic report a 'section 172(1) statement', which describes how the directors have had regard to the matters set out in s 172(1)(a)–(f) when performing their duty under s 172.[105] In addition, the strategic report must contain a fair review of the company's business and a description of the principal risks and uncertainties facing the company[106] (e.g. for many larger companies, the risks and uncertainties surrounding Brexit have figured prominently in the strategic review). This review must provide a comprehensive analysis of the development and performance of the company's business during the financial year, and the position of the company's business at the end of that year.[107] The strategic report of a quoted company must include:

Section 172 is discussed at 10.3.

- a description of a company's strategy and business model; and
- a breakdown showing at the end of each financial year the number of persons of each sex who were directors, senior managers, and employees of the company.[108]

The strategic report of a quoted company must, to the extent necessary for an understanding of the company's business, also include:

- details of the main trends and factors likely to affect the future development, performance, and position of the company's business; and
- information about (i) environmental matters; (ii) the company's employees; and (iii) social, community, and human rights issues.[109]

A traded company, banking company, or insurance company must also include a non-financial information statement as part of its strategic report.[110] However, this requirement will not apply if the company was small or medium-sized in that financial year[111] or if it had no more than 500 employees.[112] The statement must contain information on:

- environmental matters (including the impact of the company's business on the environment);
- the company's employees;
- social matters;
- respect for human rights; and
- anti-corruption and anti-bribery matters.[113]

Detailed guidance on the strategic report has been published by the FRC,[114] but despite this, the FRC has found that the strategic report is an area of corporate reporting that is

---

[104] ibid s 414C(1).

[105] ibid s 414CZA(1) and (2). Unquoted companies must place a copy of the s 172(1) statement on their website (s 426B((1) and (2)).

[106] ibid s 414C(2). Further details on this review are set out in s 414C(3)–(6).   [107] ibid s 414C(3).

[108] ibid s 414C(8). FRC, 'Annual Review of Corporate Reporting 2017/18' (FRC 2018) 28 revealed that only 55 FTSE 100 companies fully complied with this requirement. In response, the FRC published guidance on diversity reporting (FRC, 'Board Diversity Reporting' (FRC 2018)).

[109] ibid s 414C(7).

[110] ibid s 414CA(1). Other companies may include such a statement if they so wish (s 414CA(10)).

[111] ibid s 414CA(3).   [112] ibid s 414CA(4).

[113] ibid s 414CB(1). A report by PwC found that many companies had not engaged fully with the new reporting requirement for a non-financial information statement (see PwC, 'Responding to the New Non-Financial Reporting Regulations: More for Companies to Do in Year Two' (PwC, 2018)).

[114] FRC, 'Guidance on the Strategic Report' (FRC 2018).

'most frequently the subject of challenges'.[115] The FRC has noted a number of areas where strategic reports contain little or none of the information specified[116] and, as the following example demonstrates, the FRC will take public action to address these concerns.

The strategic report of Sports Direct plc

The FRC's Conduct Committee opened an investigation into Sports Direct's 2015 annual report and accounts on the ground, *inter alia*, that it was not complying with the CA 2006's provisions regarding the strategic report. The investigation concluded that, as the report and accounts contained no discussion of the company's international stores, it had not provided a balanced and comprehensive analysis of the company's business (as required under s 414C(3)). The FRC discussed this with Sports Direct's directors and they agreed to include specific commentary regarding the company's international stores in its strategic report. This information was included in the company's 2017 annual report and accounts. As a result, the FRC concluded its investigation and announced this to the market.[117]

19.3.2.2 Directors' report

The directors of a company (except a company that qualifies as a micro-entity)[118] must prepare a directors' report for each financial year.[119] The directors of a small company must prepare a directors' report, but they are not required to file it with Companies House (although they may if they so wish).[120] Failure to prepare a directors' report if so required is a criminal offence.[121]

The directors' report must include:

- the names of the persons who were, at any time during the financial year, directors of the company;[122]
- the amount that the directors recommend should be paid by way of dividend;[123]
- a statement providing that (i) so far as each director is aware, there is no relevant audit information of which the company's auditor is unaware; and (ii) each director has taken all the steps that he ought to have taken as a director to make himself aware of any relevant audit information and to establish that the company's auditor is aware of that information;[124]
- details of any indemnity provisions that benefit one or more directors.[125]

If the company is large or medium-sized, the directors' report must also include:

- specified details of political donations exceeding £2,000 made by the company;[126]
- specified information relating to the use of financial instruments by the company;[127]
- miscellaneous information, including particulars of important events affecting the company, and an indication of likely future developments in the company's business;[128]

---

[115] FRC, 'Annual Review of Corporate Reporting 2016/17' (FRC 2017) 22.   [116] ibid 22–9.

[117] See https://frc.org.uk/news/december-2016/findings-of-the-financial-reporting-review-panel-i accessed 10 January 2019.

[118] CA 2006, s 415(1A).   [119] ibid s 415(1).   [120] ibid ss 415A and 444A(1)(b).

[121] ibid s 415(4) and (5).   [122] ibid s 416(1)(a).

[123] ibid s 416(3). Note that a small company need not include this information.

[124] ibid s 418(2). Companies that are exempt from audit need to provide this statement (s 418(1)).

[125] ibid s 236.

[126] Large and Medium-Sized Companies and Groups (Accounts and Reports) Regulations 2008, Sch 7, paras 3 and 4.

[127] ibid Sch 7, para 6.   [128] ibid Sch 7, para 7.

- specified details regarding the company's acquisition of its own shares;[129]

- a description of the company's policy regarding the employment of disabled persons;[130]

- a description of the action that has been taken in the financial year to (i) provide employees with information on matters of concern to them; (ii) consult employees, so that their views can be taken into account; (iii) encourage the involvement of employees in the company's performance through an employees' share scheme or some other means, and; (iv) achieve a common awareness on the part of all employees of the financial and economic factors affecting the company's performance;[131]

- a statement summarizing how the directors have had regard to the need to foster the company's business relationships with suppliers, customers, and others, and the effect of that regard, including on the principal decisions taken by the company during the financial year;

- if a company has securities carrying voting rights that are traded on a regulated market, then the report must contain specified information including the structure of the company's capital, restrictions on the transfer of securities, and details of persons with significant holdings in the company;[132]

- if the company is a quoted company, the report must include specified details concerning the company's greenhouse gas emissions.[133]

The Companies (Miscellaneous Reporting) Regulations 2018 inserted new provisions into the Large and Medium-Sized Companies and Groups (Accounts and Reports) Regulations 2008 that will apply to any company that is not subject to DTR 7.2 (discussed at 19.3.2.3) and (i) has more than 2,000 employees; and/or (ii) has a turnover of more than £200 million and a balance sheet total of more than £2 billion.[134] Such companies will be required to include in their directors' report a 'statement of corporate governance arrangements'[135] that states:

- which corporate governance code, if any, the company applied in that financial year;

- how the company applied the code; and

- if the company departed from the code, its reasons for doing so.[136]

The directors' report must be approved by the board and signed off by a director or secretary of the company.[137]

19.3.2.3 Corporate governance statement

As discussed at 2.2.2.1, the UK's corporate governance system is based around the concept of 'comply or explain'. The legal manifestation of this is found in the DTR 7.2, which provides that a company whose shares are traded on a regulated market must provide a corporate governance statement as (i) part of its directors' report;[138] or (ii) in a separate report published with and in the same manner as its annual report or, on the company's website and referred to in the directors' report.[139] Most larger companies will place the corporate governance statement in its own section within the annual report.

---

[129] ibid Sch 7, paras 8 and 9.

[130] ibid Sch 7, para 10 (note that this requirement only applies to companies whose weekly average number of employees exceeds 250).

[131] ibid Sch 7, para 11.   [132] ibid Sch 7, paras 13 and 14.   [133] ibid Sch 7, paras 15–20.

[134] ibid Sch 7, para 23(3).

[135] This should not be confused with the 'corporate governance statement' discussed at 19.3.2.3.

[136] Large and Medium-Sized Companies and Groups (Accounts and Reports) Regulations 2008, Sch 7, para 26(1).

[137] CA 2006, s 419(1).   [138] DTR 7.2.1R and 7.2.9R.   [139] ibid 7.2.9R.

The corporate governance statement must state:

- the corporate governance code to which the company is subject or which the company has voluntarily decided to apply[140] (e.g. the UK Corporate Governance Code);
- if the company has departed from the relevant corporate governance code, it must explain which parts it has departed from and the reasons for doing so;[141]
- a description of the main feature of the company's internal control and risk management systems;[142]
- specified information relating to the company's share capital;[143]
- a description of the composition and operation of the company's administrative, management and supervisory bodies and their committees,[144] and a description of the diversity policy that applies to these bodies and how that policy is implemented.[145]

Perhaps the most important part of the statement is the explanations provided for non-compliance with the UK Corporate Governance Code. Following studies showing weak explanations among some companies, the FRC published guidance on what constitutes a good explanation.[146] Despite a general improvement in the quality of explanations, there is still much scope for improvement, with Grant Thornton's most recent Corporate Governance Review noting numerous areas where explanations lack detail and even situations where non-compliance is not explained at all.[147]

19.3.2.4 Directors' remuneration report

In addition to the remuneration information that must be disclosed as part of the annual accounts, the directors of a quoted company must also prepare a directors' remuneration report for each financial year.[148] The content of the remuneration report is set out in Sch 8 of the Large and Medium-Sized Companies and Groups (Accounts and Reports) Regulations 2008 and includes:

- a single total figure of remuneration for each director;
- details of each director's pension entitlements;
- details of payments to past directors;
- details of payments for loss of office;
- details of directors' shareholdings and share interests;
- a performance graph and table providing details of company performance over the past five years;
- the percentage change in remuneration of the chief executive officer (CEO);
- information setting out the pay ratio of the CEO compared to other employees;
- a statement on how the company intends to implement the previous year's remuneration policy;
- a separate section of the report providing specified details on the directors' remuneration policy of the company.

---

[140] ibid 7.2.2R.

[141] ibid 7.2.3R. Note that companies that comply with the Listing Rules provisions relating to comply or explain (namely LR 9.8.6R(6)) will satisfy the requirements of DTR 7.2.2R and 7.2.3R (7.2.4R).

[142] ibid 7.2.5R and 7.2.10R.   [143] ibid 7.2.6R.   [144] ibid 7.2.7R.

[145] ibid 7.2.8A(1)R. For more information on diversity reporting, see FRC, 'Board Diversity Reporting' (FRC 2018).

[146] FRC, 'What Constitutes an Explanation Under "Comply or Explain"?' (FRC 2012).

[147] Grant Thornton LLP, 'Corporate Governance Review 2018' (Grant Thornton 2018).

[148] CA 2006, s 420(1). Failure to prepare this report is a criminal offence (s 420(2)).

Certain parts of the remuneration report are subject to audit.[149] The remuneration report must be approved by the board and signed off by a director or secretary.[150] More importantly, from a governance point of view, the remuneration report is subject to member approval in the form of an advisory and a binding vote.

A quoted company must table an ordinary resolution at the accounts meeting (usually the annual general meeting (AGM)) to decide whether to approve the remuneration report.[151] Two important points should be noted:

1. the remuneration policy section of the report is not subject to this vote[152] (as it is subject to the binding vote discussed later in this section); and

2. this vote is not binding on the company. It is advisory only and so the directors' entitlement to remuneration is not dependent upon the resolution being passed.[153] However, if the members do reject the remuneration report, the directors tend to take this seriously, as the members who voted against the report would also likely have the votes to vote the directors out of office. The first instance of a remuneration report being rejected provides an example of this.

The advisory vote on the directors' remuneration report

In 2002 (the year in which the advisory vote was first introduced),[154] it was revealed that Jean-Pierre Garnier, CEO of GlaxoSmithKline plc, was due to receive an £11 million remuneration package, along with a golden parachute of up to £22 million. The company's institutional investors started mobilizing to vote against approving the remuneration report, as did certain investor trade bodies (notably the Association of British Insurers (ABI) and Pensions and Investment Research Consultants (PIRC)). The board, realizing that the report might be rejected, offered a series of last-minute concessions (notably the replacement of several non-executive directors (NEDs)). Despite this, in May 2003 at the company's AGM, the shareholders rejected the remuneration report by 50.72 percent to 49.28 per cent.

Although the vote was advisory only, the board took significant action. The board removed two key members of the remuneration committee (including its chair). Mr Garnier's remuneration was halved, as was his golden parachute and the length of his service contract.

Not all companies acted as Glaxo did. Between 2003 and 2013, 22 companies had their remuneration reports rejected, but nine companies took no action following the rejection.[155] This inaction led the government to conclude that:

> [w]hilst it is clear that in some cases, having a large proportion of shareholders withhold support for remuneration proposals has triggered a substantial re-thinking of policy, historical voting records, feedback from shareholders and anecdotal evidence suggest that not all companies are responding adequately to shareholder concerns.[156]

---

[149] Large and Medium-Sized Companies and Groups (Accounts and Reports) Regulations 2008, Sch 8, paras 42–43.

[150] CA 2006, s 422(1).   [151] ibid s 439(1).   [152] ibid.   [153] ibid s 439(5).

[154] Namely by the Directors' Remuneration Report Regulations 2002, SI 2002/1986 (now repealed).

[155] Ernestine Ndzi, 'UK Shareholder Voting on Directors' Remuneration: Has the Binding Vote Made any Difference?' (2017) 38 Co Law 139, 140.

[156] BIS, 'Shareholder Pay: Shareholder Voting Rights Consultation' (BIS 2012) para 4.

The government therefore decided to strengthen the members' say on pay, which led to a new s 439A being introduced into the CA 2006, which provides that a quoted company must table an ordinary resolution at the accounts meeting (usually the AGM) to decide whether to approve the remuneration policy section of the remuneration report.[157] This resolution need not take place every year, but must take place at least every three years.[158] The key feature of this resolution is that it is binding and a quoted company cannot make a remuneration payment to a director unless it is consistent with the approved remuneration policy or it has been approved by a resolution of the members.[159] Any payments that contravene this will be of no effect.[160] The following example demonstrates the weaknesses of the advisory vote and how the presence of the binding vote can have a stronger effect on director pay.

The advisory vote and the binding vote

At its 2014 AGM, the remuneration report of BP plc was approved, as was its remuneration policy. In 2015, as a result of the Deepwater Horizon incident and falling oil prices, BP posted its largest ever operating loss (£4.5 billion) and announced it was axing 7,000 jobs. Despite this, the company awarded its CEO, Bob Dudley, a 20 per cent pay increase, taking his pay up to £14 million. Institutional investors were angered by this and, at the 2016 AGM, 59.29 per cent of shareholders voted to reject the company's remuneration report.[161] This was one of the largest ever votes against a remuneration report,[162] but the vote was advisory only and, as the money had already been paid to Dudley, it had little immediate effect.

Conscious that the remuneration policy would be subject to a binding vote in 2017, BP's chair ordered a review of its remuneration policy and entered into talks with major shareholders. The result was that Dudley's pay for 2017 was cut by 40 per cent to £9.3 million, the bonus scheme was amended to make it more difficult to earn bonuses, and the size of bonus payments was reduced.[163] As a result of these changes, both the remuneration report and remuneration policy were approved by over 97 per cent of shareholders at the 2017 AGM.[164]

Although the past few years have seen several high-profile remuneration defeats (e.g. Weir Group plc, Smith & Nephew plc, Shire plc, Pearson plc, Royal Mail plc) and significant levels of opposition (e.g. Morrison Supermarkets plc, Thomas Cook Group plc, WPP plc, Persimmon plc), it is rare for a remuneration report or policy to be rejected. The vast majority of FTSE 350 remuneration reports are approved by over 90 per cent of those voting and, in 2018, only five FTSE All-Share companies[165] had their remuneration reports rejected, and only one FTSE All-Share company had its remuneration policy rejected.[166] However, it is increasingly common for reports and policies to face significant opposition (defined in practice as over 20 per cent). The Investment Association maintains a public register[167] of FTSE All-Share companies that have received significant shareholder opposition to proposed resolutions and it shows that, in 2018, 47 such

---

[157] CA 2006, s 439A(1).   [158] ibid s 439A(1)(b).   [159] ibid s 226B(1).   [160] ibid s 226E(1).

[161] BP, 'AGM 2016 Poll Results' (BP 2016) 1.

[162] The largest to date appears to be the 90.42 per cent of shareholders who voted against the remuneration report of the Royal Bank of Scotland Group plc in 2009.

[163] BP, 'Annual Report and Form 20-F 2016' (BP 2017) 80–1.

[164] BP, 'AGM 2017 Poll Results' (BP 2017) 1.

[165] Namely Inmarsat plc (58.59 per cent), Northgate plc (57.97 per cent), Playtech plc (59.38 per cent), Royal Mail plc (70.17 per cent), and Petropavlovsk plc (71.54 per cent).

[166] Namely Centamin plc (52.01 per cent).

[167] See www.theinvestmentassociation.org/publicregister.html accessed 10 January 2019.

companies faced significant levels of shareholder opposition to their remuneration reports and 15 faced significant opposition to their remuneration policies.

Even where a remuneration report is not rejected, significant levels of opposition coupled with the reputational damage that results from coverage of significant remuneration packages can result in companies taking action, as the following example demonstrates. Indeed, it could be argued that the reputational damage caused by public coverage of directors' pay places much greater pressure on directors than the rules relating to say on pay.

Jeff Fairburn and Persimmon Homes

Jeff Fairburn was appointed CEO of Persimmon plc. He was widely perceived as being an effective CEO and, between 2013 and 2018, Persimmon's market cap increased from £3.4 billion to £7.5 billion, largely due to significant increases in Persimmon's share price. In 2012, a long-term incentive plan was set up and, due to the notable increases in the company's share price, Fairburn received a £75 million pay-out in 2017 (which was reduced from £100 million following negative media coverage).

This pay-out was subject to considerable media coverage and criticism (largely due to the fact that it was not capped—something that the company later apologized for) and, at the 2018 AGM, 48.5 per cent of shareholders voted against the company's remuneration report.[168] As a result of continuing media coverage (including a disastrous television interview),[169] in November 2018, Persimmon announced that Fairburn would step down as CEO 'by mutual agreement and at the request of the Company'.[170] This announcement regarding Fairburn stated that 'the Board believes that the distraction around his remuneration from the 2012 LTIP scheme continues to have a negative impact on the reputation of the business and consequently on Jeff's ability to continue in his role'.[171]

19.3.3 Circulation, publication, and filing

Preparation of the annual accounts and reports would be of little use if they were not easily accessible. Accordingly, the CA 2006 provides for a series of rules regarding the circulation, publication, and filing of the accounts and reports.

19.3.3.1 Circulation of accounts and reports

Every company must send a copy of its annual accounts and reports for each financial year to every member, every debenture holder, and every person who is entitled to receive notice of general meetings.[172] This can involve sending a hard copy of the accounts, or they can be sent electronically, as long as the rules relating to electronic communications have been complied with. The time limit for when these must be sent is as follows:

- For a private company, they must be sent not later than the end of the period for filing accounts and reports or, if earlier, the date on which it actually delivers its accounts and reports to the registrar.[173]

---

[168] See www.persimmonhomes.com/corporate/media/350884/agm-poll-results-250418.pdf accessed 10 January 2019.

[169] See https://www.bbc.co.uk/news/business-45915486 accessed 10 January 2019.

[170] See www.persimmonhomes.com/corporate/investors/regulatory-news-(rns)/rns-news/13857614 accessed 10 January 2019.

[171] ibid.

[172] CA 2006, s 423(1). Failure to send the accounts and reports, or a failure to send them within the specified time limit, is a criminal offence (s 425).

[173] ibid s 424(2).

- For a public company, they must be sent at least 21 days before the date of the relevant accounts meeting.[174] If the accounts and reports are sent later than this, they will be deemed to have been duly sent if so agreed by all the members entitled to attend and vote at the relevant accounts meeting.[175]

The option exists to send specified persons a copy of the strategic report and supplementary material, instead of a copy of the full accounts and reports.[176] The persons are a member, a debenture holder, a person entitled to receive notice of general meetings, and a person nominated to enjoy information rights under s 146 of the CA 2006.[177] However, before sending such persons a copy of the strategic report and supplementary material, the company must first ascertain that the person does not want to receive a copy of the full accounts and reports.[178]

19.3.3.2 Website publication of accounts and reports

A quoted company must ensure that its annual accounts and reports are made available on its website[179] as soon as is reasonably practicable.[180] These accounts and reports must remain available on the company's website until the accounts and reports for the next financial year are made available on its website.[181] Failure to comply with these requirements is a criminal offence.[182]

19.3.3.3 Right to demand copies of the accounts and reports

A member or debenture holder is entitled to be provided with, and demand without charge, a single copy of the company's most recent annual accounts and reports.[183] This is in addition to the right to be sent a copy of the accounts and reports, discussed at 19.3.3.1.[184] If the demand is not complied with within seven days of its receipt by the company, then a criminal offence will have been committed.[185]

19.3.3.4 Laying of accounts and reports before the general meeting

Providing the members with copies of the accounts and reports is useful, but does little to allow them to express their views on the information provided in those accounts and reports. Accordingly, the law has long held that companies should lay their accounts and reports before the general meeting. Now that private companies are no longer required to have general meetings, the obligation to lay the annual accounts and reports before the general meeting applies only to the directors of public companies,[186] and this must be done no later than the end of the period for the filing of accounts and reports[187] (discussed at 19.3.3.5). In practice, this usually takes place at the company's AGM. Failure to comply with these rules constitutes a criminal offence,[188] but it will be a defence if the defendant can show that he took all reasonable steps to secure compliance with the above rules.[189]

---

[174] ibid s 424(3).   [175] ibid s 424(4).

[176] ibid s 426(1). The specified supplementary material is set out in s 426A.

[177] Companies (Receipt of Accounts and Reports) Regulations 2013, SI 2013/1973, reg 4(1). Regulation 5 sets out those instances where sending the strategic report and supplementary material is prohibited.

[178] ibid reg 6(1).

[179] CA 2006, s 430(1)(a). Companies subject to the DTRs must publish their annual financial report at the latest four months after the end of the financial year (DTR, 4.1.3R).

[180] CA 2006, s 430(4)(a).   [181] ibid s 430(1)(b).   [182] ibid s 430(6).

[183] ibid ss 431(1) and 432(1).   [184] ibid ss 431(2) and 432(2).   [185] ibid ss 431(3) and 432(3).

[186] ibid s 437(1). This meeting will be known as an 'accounts meeting' (s 437(3)).

[187] ibid s 437(2).   [188] ibid s 438(1).   [189] ibid s 438(2).

The key question is what 'laying the accounts before the general meeting' involves. The CA 2006 provides no guidance, so it will largely be a matter for each public company to determine. In practice, this will usually involve the company tabling a resolution at its AGM 'to receive the reports and accounts'. Note that as the resolution is normally to 'receive' the reports and accounts, and not to 'approve' them;[190] the resolution's defeat would not have an effect upon the validity of the reports and accounts. However, it would signify that the members disagree with the auditor's report and the information as presented by the board (which would indicate a massive loss of confidence in the directors). For this reason, it is almost unheard of for such resolutions to be lost.

19.3.3.5 Filing of accounts and reports

The directors must deliver to Companies House a copy of the annual accounts and reports,[191] and this must be done before the end of the period allowed for filing accounts.[192] This period is:

- for a private company, nine months after the end of the relevant accounting reference period; and
- for a public company, six months after the end of that period.[193]

Not all companies are required to file a full copy of the annual accounts and reports. Small companies are exempt from filing certain information (e.g. the directors' report).[194] Unlimited companies do not need file accounts and reports at all if certain conditions are met.[195] Dormant subsidiaries are generally not required to file their annual accounts.[196]

A failure to file accounts and reports within the stipulated time limit when required to do so can result in any or all of the following:

- a criminal offence will be committed,[197] but it will be a defence if the defendant can show that he took all reasonable steps to secure compliance with the relevant rules;[198]
- the court may, following an application from any member or creditor of the company, make an order compelling the company to file the accounts and reports within such time as the order specifies;[199]
- the company is liable to a civil penalty, with the amount of the penalty based on how late the filing was, namely (i) £500 if not more than 3 months late; (ii) £1,000 if more than 3 months late, but not more than 6 months late; and (iii) £2,000 if more than 6 months late.[200]

19.4 Auditors

The auditor's report is a key part of a company's annual accounts and reports, so it is important to not only discuss this report, but also the role of the auditor in general. It is important at the outset to distinguish between a 'statutory audit' and an 'internal audit'. The audit of annual accounts that a company is legally required to undertake is known as a 'statutory audit' and the auditor conducting it is known as a 'statutory auditor'.[201]

---

[190] Although, as discussed at 19.3.2.4, the members of a quoted company do have approval rights in relation to the directors' remuneration report.

[191] CA 2006, s 441(1).   [192] ibid s 442(1).   [193] ibid s 442(2).

[194] ibid ss 444(1)(b)(ii) and 444A(1)(b).   [195] ibid s 448(1) and (2).   [196] ibid s 448A.

[197] ibid s 451(1).   [198] ibid s 451(2).   [199] ibid s 452(1).

[200] Companies (Late Filing Penalties) and Limited Liability Partnerships (Filing Periods and Late Filing Penalties) Regulations 2008, SI 2008/497, reg 2(2).

[201] CA 2006, s 1210(1).

Conversely, an internal audit is not a legal requirement, but Provision 26 of the UK Corporate Governance Code does provide that if a company has no internal audit function, then its annual report should explain why not and how internal audit assurance is to be achieved. According to the Chartered Institute of Internal Auditors, the purpose of an internal audit is to 'provide independent assurance that an organisation's risk management, governance and internal control processes are operating effectively'.[202] To that end, the internal auditor will undertake numerous assessments, including:

- how effectively the company manages risk;
- how effective are the company's internal controls; and
- to what extent the company is complying with the relevant laws, regulations, codes of conduct, and best practice recommendations.

Here, we are focusing on the role of the statutory auditor, whose principal role is to report on the company's accounts, notably whether they represent a fair and true view of the company's finances. The advantages of auditing accounts are obvious. A company's accounts are generally publicly available and are used by a wide variety of stakeholders (e.g. investors when deciding to purchase shares, creditors when deciding whether to loan the company money, etc.). Such persons will only act based on accurate information and having audited accounts will therefore allow such stakeholders to confidently rely on the information contained in the accounts.

However, a statutory audit can only carry out his function if he is independent of the company he is auditing. The demise of Arthur Andersen LLP following the Enron scandal is a dramatic example of the dire consequences that can result from an auditor that lacks independence. Throughout 19.4, several measures are discussed that aim to promote auditor independence (namely audit committees, rules relating to non-audit services, and auditor rotation). The CA 2006 does contain some general safeguards, notably in Sch 10, para 9, which provides that the auditors' supervisory bodies must have adequate rules and practices designed to ensure that:

- statutory audit work is conducted properly and with integrity;
- statutory auditors do not have any interests that conflict with the proper conduct of the audit; and
- statutory auditors take steps to safeguard their independence.

Before looking at the rules relating to the appointment of auditors, it is worth briefly discussing the audit market among larger companies, as this has been a cause of concern in recent years.

19.4.1 **Market concentration**

Amongst accountancy firms, there has long been a group of firms that are so much larger than the rest that they have occupied their own group (this group is known 'the Big X', with 'X' referring to the number of firms in that group). Originally, eight firms occupied this group, but due to the collapse of Arthur Andersen and a series of mergers, today this group is known as 'the Big Four' and consists of:

1. PricewaterhouseCoopers International Ltd (usually known as 'PwC');
2. Ernst & Young Global Ltd (usually known as 'EY');

---

[202] See www.iia.org.uk/about-us accessed 30 October 2018.

3. Deloitte Touche Tohmatsu Ltd (usually known as 'Deloitte');

4. KPMG International Cooperative (usually known as 'KPMG').[203]

Concerns exist regarding the extent to which the Big Four dominate the audit market for FTSE companies. Indeed, the market for statutory audit services for large companies was referred to the Competition Commission in 2011. Despite issuing a package of remedies, little has changed. All but one FTSE 100 companies are audited by a Big Four firm, and 241 FTSE 250 companies are audited by a Big Four firm.[204] It is unsurprising that the Big Four are keen to retain such audits—in 2016, the average audit fee for a FTSE 100 company was £6.7 million,[205] with some being much larger (HSBC's 2016 audit fee was £67.3 million).[206] Some have hoped that the rules relating to mandatory rotation introduced by the EU Audit Regulation would help increase competition but, although a notable number of FTSE companies have changed auditor, they have simply changed from one Big Four firm to another, resulting in the FRC concluding that there has been no diversification in the UK audit market and, in fact, the Big Four have increased their market share of FTSE 350 audits.[207]

Following the collapse of Carillion plc and a number of poor reviews regarding audit quality, in October 2018, the Competition and Markets Authority announced that it was undertaking a market study into the effectiveness of the statutory audit market, which would include an examination of the concentration of the audit market with a view to reducing barriers to non-Big Four firms auditing large companies.[208]

Auditor rotation is discussed at 19.4.6.4.

The CMA's update paper on reform is discussed at xviii in the 'Latest news' section.

19.4.2 Appointment

An auditor can only undertake his function effectively if he is suitably qualified and independent of the company being audited. This can only be achieved if a robust appointments process is in place, and it is therefore no surprise that the appointment of an auditor is subject to a considerable body of rules and best practice recommendations.

19.4.2.1 The requirement to appoint an auditor

The general rule is that every company must appoint an auditor or auditors for each financial year, unless the directors reasonably resolve otherwise on the ground that audited accounts are unlikely to be required.[209] Section 475(1) of the CA 2006 provides that a company's annual accounts for a financial year must be audited, subject to four exceptions:

Note the CMA's proposals relating to joint audits, discussed at xviii in the 'Latest news' section.

1. A company that qualifies as a small company is not required to have its accounts audited.[210] Note, however, that certain companies (e.g. public companies) are excluded from this exemption and will need to have their accounts audited.[211]

Small companies are discussed at 19.3.1.3.

2. Subsidiary companies are not required to have their accounts audited if they meet certain conditions set out in s 479A.

---

[203] It is worth noting that the Big Four are not single firms, but each one is a series of firms that collectively form a professional services network. The entities listed here coordinate the activities of the firms in the network.
[204] FRC, 'Key Facts and Trends in the Accountancy Profession' (FRC 2018) 50.
[205] Grant Thornton LLP, 'Corporate Governance Review 2017 (Grant Thornton 2017) 48.
[206] HSBC Holdings plc, 'Annual Report and Accounts 2016' (HSBC 2017) 212.
[207] FRC, 'Developments in Audit' (FRC 2018) 21.
[208] See www.gov.uk/cma-cases/statutory-audit-market-study accessed 10 January 2019.
[209] CA 2006, ss 485(1) and 489(1).   [210] ibid s 477(1).   [211] ibid s 478.

3. Dormant companies are not required to have their accounts audited.[212]

4. Certain non-profit-making companies do not need to appoint an auditor as they are subject to a public-sector audit.[213]

For those companies that must appoint an auditor, the rules of appointment differ slightly for private and public companies. As regards private companies, the appointment of an auditor in a company's first financial year can be made by the directors any time before the company's first period for appointing auditors.[214] For all subsequent years, the appointment should be made before the end of the period for appointing auditors[215] and will usually be made by the members passing an ordinary resolution[216] (although the directors are empowered to make appointments in specified circumstances).[217] However, if no such appointment has been made by this time, then the auditor in office will be deemed to be reappointed, unless:

- he was appointed by the directors;
- the company's articles require actual reappointment;
- the deemed reappointment is prevented under s 488 (i.e. members representing at least 5 per cent of the company's voting rights notify the company that they do not want the auditor to be reappointed);
- the members have resolved that the auditor should not be reappointed;
- the directors have resolved that no auditor should be appointed for the financial year in question; or

> 🔗 The maximum engagement period is discussed more at 19.4.6.4.

- the company is a public interest entity and the auditor's appointment breaches the maximum engagement period.[218]

As regards public companies, the appointment of an auditor in a company's first financial year can be made by the directors any time before the company's first accounts meeting.[219] For all subsequent years, the appointment must be made before the end of the accounts meeting at which the company's annual accounts and reports for the previous financial year have been laid[220] and will usually be made by the members passing an ordinary resolution[221] (although the directors are empowered to make appointments in specified circumstances).[222] There is no automatic process for reappointment. As regards larger public companies, the audit committee plays a significant role in the appointment of the auditor (indeed, the EU Audit Regulation provides that the audit committee essentially runs the process of appointing an auditor).[223]

> 🔗 The audit committee is discussed at 19.4.4.

If a company fails to appoint an auditor when it is required to do so, the Secretary of State can appoint an auditor to fill the vacancy.[224]

19.4.2.2 Eligibility

Only persons eligible to be appointed as a statutory auditor may undertake a statutory audit of a company. The CA 2006 provides that an individual or firm is only eligible for appointment as a statutory auditor if two conditions are met:

1. The individual or firm is a member of a recognized supervisory body,[225] although a person who is subject to the rules of a supervisory body in seeking appointment as an auditor

---

[212] ibid s 480. A 'dormant company' is defined in s 1169.   [213] ibid s 482.

[214] The 'period for appointing auditors' is a 28-day period beginning with the end of the time allowed for sending out copies of the company's annual accounts and reports for the previous financial year or, if earlier, the day on which copies of the annual accounts and reports were actually sent out (s 485(2)).

[215] CA 2006, s 485(2).   [216] ibid s 485(4).   [217] ibid s 485(3).   [218] ibid s 487(2).

[219] ibid s 489(3)(a).   [220] ibid s 489(2).   [221] ibid s 489(4).   [222] ibid s 489(3).

[223] EU Audit Regulation, Art 16.   [224] CA 2006, 486 and 490.   [225] ibid s 1212(1)(a).

is to be regarded as a member, irrespective of whether or not that person is a member.[226] Organizations can apply to the Secretary of State for recognition as a supervisory body,[227] with recognized bodies including the Institute of Chartered Accountants in England and Wales (ICAEW), and the Association of Chartered Certified Accountants.

2. The individual or firm is eligible for appointment under the rules of the supervisory body that it is a member of.[228]

A person may not act as a statutory auditor if he is ineligible to do so.[229] If a person, at any time during his term of office, becomes ineligible for appointment, then he must immediately resign and notify the company that he has resigned by reason of his becoming ineligible.[230] Acting as an auditor while ineligible or failing to notify the company of ineligibility is a criminal offence.[231] In addition, EU Member States must keep a register of persons eligible to act as statutory auditor[232] and it is a criminal offence for any person whose name does not appear on this auditor to describe or hold himself out as being a registered auditor.[233]

In addition, s 1214 of the CA 2006 imposes an independence requirement by prohibiting certain persons from acting as auditor, including:

(a) an officer or employee of the company or associated undertaking;[234] or

(b) a partner or employee of a person within (a), or a partnership to which a person within (a) is a partner.[235]

If a person, at any time during his term of office, falls within (a) or (b) above, then he must immediately resign and notify the company that he has resigned by reason of his lack of independence.[236] Acting as an auditor while in breach of s 1214 of failing to notify the company of a lack of independence is a criminal offence.[237]

Where an audit is conducted by an ineligible person or by a person prohibited to do so due to a lack of independence, then the Secretary of State may direct the company to retain an appropriate person to conduct a second audit of the company.[238]

19.4.2.3 Remuneration

The general rule is that the remuneration of the auditor is fixed by the person(s) who appointed him, so:

- the remuneration of an auditor appointed by the members must be fixed by the members by ordinary resolution, or by some manner as the members may by ordinary resolution determine;
- the remuneration of an auditor appointed by the directors must be fixed by the directors; and
- the remuneration of an auditor appointed by the Secretary of State must be fixed by the Secretary of State.[239]

---

[226] ibid s 1217(2).
[227] ibid Sch 10. Applications are actually made to the FRC, to whom the Secretary of State has delegated recognition powers (Statutory Auditors (Amendment of Companies Act 2006 and Delegation of Functions etc) Order 2012, SI 2012/1741, art 7).
[228] CA 2006, s 1212(1)(b). [229] ibid s 1213(1). [230] ibid s 1213(2). [231] ibid s 1213(3).
[232] ibid s 1239(1). See www.auditregister.org.uk accessed 10 January 2019.
[233] ibid s 1250(2).
[234] An 'associated undertaking' of a company is (i) a parent or subsidiary of the company; or (ii) a subsidiary of a parent of the company (CA 2006, s 1214(6)).
[235] CA 2006, s 1214(1)–(3). [236] ibid s 1215(1). [237] ibid s 1215(2). [238] ibid s 1248.
[239] ibid s 492(1)–(3).

Large and medium-sized companies must, in a note to the annual accounts, disclose the remuneration that the company paid to the auditor for auditing its accounts.[240]

There are two instances where the remuneration of an auditor can have an adverse effect upon his independence. First, the fee income received from undertaking an audit may constitute a significant portion of an auditor's total fee income, creating a situation whereby the auditor is dependent on that fee income in order to survive. This clearly could affect an auditor's independence and so Art 4(3) of the EU Audit Regulation provides that where the total fees that an auditor received from a public interest entity (PIE) in each of the previous three consecutive financial years exceed 15 per cent of the auditor's total fee income, then this must be disclosed to the audit committee by the statutory auditor, who will discuss with the audit committee whether this constitutes a threat to his independence and what safeguards should be applied. Where the fees continue to exceed 15 per cent, the audit committee shall decide whether the statutory auditor may continue to carry on the statutory audit for an additional period which shall not exceed two years.

PIEs are discussed at 19.4.6.4.

Second, it is common for an auditor (especially in the case of the Big Four) to also provide other services (known as 'non-audit services'), including internal audit services, tax planning advice, IT provision, recruitment advice, or general business consultancy services. Indeed, the provision of such services was often more lucrative than the provision of audit services. The concern is that, where an auditor provides non-audit services to an audit client, its desire to keep the non-audit work might result in it compromising the quality and rigour of its audit, which would therefore compromise the auditor's independence (indeed, some reports have noted that Arthur Andersen is a prime example of an auditor whose independence was compromised in order to retain non-audit services).[241] Several measures have been introduced to regulate the provision of non-audit services:

- Large companies must disclose, in a note to their annual accounts, any remuneration paid to the auditor in relation to the period that the accounts relate to.[242]

- Section 5 of Part B of the FRC's Revised Ethical Standard 2016 establishes detailed rules regarding the provision of non-audit services to a PIE by its statutory auditor.

- Article 5 of the EU Audit Regulation provides that an auditor conducting a statutory audit of a PIE cannot provide specified non-audit services to that PIE, including specified tax services, bookkeeping and preparation of financial accounts, legal services, and internal audit services. This rule has been expanded upon in the UK by 5.167R of the FRC's Revised Ethical Standard 2016.

- In relation to non-audit services not prohibited by Art 5, Art 4 of the EU Audit Regulation provides that where a statutory auditor of a PIE provides non-audit services to that PIE, the total fees for such services cannot exceed 70 per cent of the audit fee (averaged over the previous three years). This rule has been expanded upon in the UK by 4.34R of the FRC's Revised Ethical Standard 2016. As a result, the fee income received by the Big Four for providing non-audit services to their audit clients fell by 8.9 per cent in 2016/17.[243]

The reforms proposed by the CMA are noted at xviii in the 'Latest news' section.

The Competition and Market Authority has stated that, as part of its market study into the statutory audit market, it would examine the possibility of separating audit and

---

[240] CA 2006, s 494; Companies (Disclosure of Auditor Remuneration and Liability Limitation Agreements) Regulations, regs 4 and 5.

[241] See e.g. Oxera, 'Ownership Rules of Audit Firms and their Consequences for Audit Market Concentration' (Oxera 2007) para 1.2.3.

[242] Companies (Disclosure of Auditor Remuneration and Liability Limitation Agreements) Regulations, reg 5(1)(b).

[243] FRC, 'Developments in Audit' (FRC 2018) 28.

non-audit services, thereby creating audit-only firms.[244] It has been reported that, in their responses to this study, Deloitte and KPMG have both backed a ban on UK auditors providing non-audit services to their audit clients.[245]

The CMA's proposals are discussed at xviii in the 'Latest news' section.

19.4.3 The auditor's report

As discussed at 19.4.2.1, the general rule is that a company must have its accounts audited, subject to several exceptions.[246] This requirement is satisfied by the auditor making a report to the company's members on the annual accounts of the company[247] and, as discussed at 19.3, this auditor's report forms part of the company's annual reports. The rationale behind requiring a company to have its accounts audited was set out by Lord Oliver in the seminal case of *Caparo Industries plc v Dickman*,[248] who stated:

> It is the auditors' function to ensure, so far as possible, that the financial information as to the company's affairs prepared by the directors accurately reflects the company's position in order, first, to protect the company itself from the consequences of undetected errors or, possibly, wrongdoing (by, for instance, declaring dividends out of capital) and, secondly, to provide shareholders with reliable intelligence for the purpose of enabling them to scrutinise the conduct of the company's affairs and to exercise their collective powers to reward or control or remove those to whom that conduct has been confided.[249]

It is not only the shareholders who rely on the annual accounts, and a wide group of stakeholders will rely on the accounts being accurate. Knowing this, the directors may be tempted to paint the company's financial position in an overly favourable light or, as has occurred in a number of cases, to fraudulently represent the company's financial position (e.g. state that a company is profitable when it is not). The auditor's report therefore should act as an independent third-party verification of the information contained in the accounts.

19.4.3.1 Contents of the auditor's report

The content of the auditor's report is set out in the CA 2006, with highly detailed guidance on the report's content and form being set out in the International Standard on Auditing 700, which has been adapted to the UK market by the FRC.[250] The auditor's report must include (and typically starts with) the name of the company whose accounts are being audited, the period covered by the accounts, and the financial framework that has been applied to the accounts.[251] Beyond that, the auditor's report must state:

- whether, in the auditor's opinion, the annual accounts (i) give a fair and true view of the company's finances; (ii) have been prepared in accordance with the relevant financial reporting framework; and (iii) have been prepared in accordance with the requirements of the CA 2006;[252]

---

[244] See https://assets.publishing.service.gov.uk/government/uploads/system/uploads/attachment_data/file/746890/letter_from_andrew_tyrie.pdf accessed 10 January 2019.

[245] See www.cityam.com/268807/deloitte-calls-audit-market-cap-and-ban-selling-extra accessed 10 January 2019.

[246] CA 2006, s 475(1).   [247] ibid s 495(1).   [248] [1990] 2 AC 605 (HL).   [249] ibid 630.

[250] FRC, 'International Standard on Auditing (UK) 700' (FRC 2016).

[251] CA 2006, s 495(2).   [252] ibid s 495(3).

- whether the report is qualified or unqualified and must include a reference to any matters which the auditor wishes to draw attention to without qualifying the report;[253]

- a statement on any material uncertainty relating to events or conditions that may cast significant doubt upon the company's ability to continue to adopt the going concern basic of accounting;[254]

- the auditor's place of establishment;[255]

- whether, in the auditor's opinion, the information given in the strategic report and the directors' report is consistent with the accounts, and whether those reports are prepared in accordance with applicable legal requirements;[256]

- whether the auditor has identified material misstatements in the strategic report and the directors' report and, if so, indicate the nature of those misstatements;[257]

- in the case of a quoted company, whether the auditable part of the directors' remuneration report (i) has been properly prepared in accordance with the CA 2006;[258]

- where the company prepares a separate corporate governance statement, whether, in the auditor's opinion, the statement complies with specified requirements found in the DTR, and whether this information is consistent with the accounts, complies with the applicable legal requirements, and contains and material misstatements;[259]

- where a company is required to prepare a corporate governance statement and no such statement is included in the directors' report, the auditor should ascertain whether the statement has been prepared and, if not, state this in the report;[260]

- whether the auditor is of the opinion that (i) adequate accounting records have not been kept; (ii) the company's individual accounts are not in agreement with the accounting records and returns; or (iii) in the case of a quoted company, that the auditable part of the directors' remuneration report is not in agreement with the accounting records and returns;[261]

- if the auditor has not been able to obtain all the information and explanations which are necessary for the purposes of his audit;[262]

- if specified required information regarding the disclosure of directors' benefits and remuneration is not disclosed, then, as far as the auditor is reasonably able to do so, the required particulars;[263]

- whether the directors have prepared the accounts using the small companies exemption or if they have taken advantage of the small companies exemption in relation to the strategic report or the directors' report and, in the auditor's opinion, they were not entitled to do so.[264]

The report must state the name of the auditor and, where the auditor is an individual, must be signed and dated by him.[265] Where the auditor is a firm, the report must be signed by the senior statutory auditor in his own name, for and on behalf of the auditor.[266]

19.4.3.2 **Duties and rights**

A company's auditor, in preparing the auditor's report, must carry out such investigations as will enable him to form an opinion as to whether adequate accounting records have been kept and whether the company's accounts and remuneration report (if the company is quoted) are in agreement with those accounts.[267] To facilitate this

---

[253] ibid s 495(4)(a) and (b).   [254] ibid s 495(4)(c).   [255] ibid s 495(4)(d).
[256] ibid s 496(1)(a).   [257] ibid s 496(1)(b) and (c).   [258] ibid s 497(1).
[259] ibid s 497A(1).   [260] ibid s 498A.   [261] ibid s 498(2).   [262] ibid s 498(3).
[263] ibid s 498(4).   [264] ibid s 498(5).   [265] ibid s 503(1) and (2).
[266] ibid ss 503(3) and 504.   [267] ibid s 498(2).

investigation, the CA 2006 provides auditors with significant information rights. An auditor has a right of access, at all times, to the company's books, accounts, and vouchers.[268] An auditor can require specified persons to provide such information or explanations as he thinks necessary for the performance of his duties, including:

(a) any officer or employee of the company;

(b) any person holding or accountable for any of the company's books, accounts. or vouchers;

(c) any subsidiary of the company which is a body corporate incorporated in the United Kingdom;

(d) any officer, employee, or auditor of any such subsidiary undertaking or any person holding or accountable for any books, accounts, or vouchers of any such subsidiary undertaking;

(e) any person who fell within (a) to (d) at a time to which the information or explanations required by the auditor relates or relate.[269]

Any such person who fails to provide the required information or explanation commits a criminal offence.[270] It is also an offence for such persons to provide information that is misleading, false, or deceptive in a material particular.[271]

If the auditor is of the opinion that adequate accounting records have not been kept, the company's individual accounts are not in agreement with the accounting records and returns, or, the directors' remuneration report is not in agreement with the accounting records or returns, then he must state this in the auditor's report.[272]

19.4.4 **The audit committee**

The value of the audit committee has been long recognized. Since 1978, the New York Stock Exchange has required listed companies to have an audit committee. In the UK, the Cadbury Committee was the first major report to recommend listed companies having an audit committee, but by then, audit committees were already commonplace amongst larger companies, with two-thirds of FTSE 250 companies having set up an audit committee.[273] Today, the audit committee is a standard feature of the boards of larger companies (and is arguably the most important board committee), with the FRC stating that audit committees are 'fundamental to ensuring that investors and other stakeholders can have confidence in the quality and independence of the audit work being carried out'.[274] The importance of the audit committee's role is reflected in the fact that certain companies are now required to have an audit committee.

The rules and recommendations relating to audit committees are found in Regulation 537/2014[275] ('the EU Audit Regulation'), Directive 2006/43[276] ('the EU Audit Directive'), the DTR (which largely recreated the Directive's provisions on audit committees), and the

The CMA's reforms relating to audit committees are noted at xxiii.

---

[268] ibid s 499(1)(a).   [269] ibid s 499(1)(b) and (2).   [270] ibid s 501(3)–(5).

[271] ibid s 501(1) and (2).   [272] ibid s 498(2).

[273] 'Report of the Committee on the Financial Aspects of Corporate Governance' (Gee & Co 1992) para 4.33.

[274] FRC, 'Developments in Auditing 2016/17' (FRC 2017) 41.

[275] Council Regulation No 537/2014/EU of 16 April 2014 on specific requirements regarding statutory audit of public-interest entities and repealing Commission Decision 2005/909/EC [2014] OJ L158/77.

[276] Council Directive 2006/43/EC of 17 May 2006 on statutory audits of annual accounts and consolidated accounts, amending Council Directives 78/660/EEC and 83/349/EEC and repealing Council Directive 84/253/EEC [2006] OJ L157/87.

🔗 Public-interest
entities are discussed at
19.4.6.4.

UK Corporate Governance Code. In addition, the FRC has provided more detailed guidance for audit committees on their composition and function.[277] Each PIE is required to have a body that fulfils the functions of an audit committee[278] (i.e. an audit committee is not required if some other body is performing an equivalent functions),[279] and the Code recommends that companies with a premium listing establish an audit committee.[280]

19.4.4.1 Composition

Given the important role undertaken by the audit committee, it is vital that it is comprised of suitably qualified persons who are sufficiently independent. The EU Audit Directive and the DTR provide that the majority of the members of a PIE's audit committee must be independent and at least one member must have competence in accounting and/or auditing.[281] The committee members as a whole must have competence relevant to the sector in which the PIE is operating.[282] The UK Corporate Governance Code recommends that the audit committee should consist of at least three independent NEDs, and the chair should not be a member of the committee.[283] Ninety-eight per cent of FTSE 350 companies comply with the Code's recommendations regarding audit committee composition.[284]

19.4.4.2 Role

Elsewhere in this text, some specific functions of the audit committee are discussed. Here, the broad functions of the committee will be discussed, with Provision 25 of the UK Corporate Governance Code[285] stating that the main roles and responsibilities of the audit committee should include:

- monitoring the integrity of the financial statements of the company and any formal announcements relating to the company's financial performance, and reviewing significant financial reporting judgements contained in them;

- reviewing the company's internal financial controls and, unless expressly addressed by a separate board risk committee composed of independent directors, or by the board itself, reviewing the company's internal control and risk management systems;

- monitoring and reviewing the effectiveness of the company's internal audit function, or where there is not one, considering annually whether there is a need for one and making a recommendation to the board;

- conducting the tender process and making recommendations to the board, in relation to the appointment, reappointment, and removal of the external auditor, and approving the remuneration and terms of engagement of the external auditor;

- reviewing and monitoring the external auditor's independence and objectivity, and the effectiveness of the audit process, taking into consideration relevant UK professional and regulatory requirements;

---

[277] FRC, 'Guidance on Audit Committees' (FRC 2016).
[278] EU Audit Directive, Art 39(1); DTR, 7.1.1R.
[279] EU Audit Directive, Art 39(4).
[280] FRC, 'UK Corporate Governance Code' (FRC 2018) Provision 24.
[281] EU Audit Directive, Art 39(1); DTR, 7.1.1A R.
[282] EU Audit Directive, Art 39(1).
[283] FRC, 'UK Corporate Governance Code' (FRC 2018) Provision 24.
[284] FRC, 'Annual Review of Corporate Governance and Reporting 2017/18' (FRC 2018) 32.
[285] A similar exposition of the committee's role can be found in the EU Audit Directive, Art 39(6) and DTR, 7.1.3R.

- developing and implementing policy on the engagement of the external auditor to supply non-audit services, taking into account the regulations and ethical guidance in this regard, and reporting to the board on any improvement or action required; and

- reporting to the board on how it has discharged its responsibilities (Provision 26 states that the company's annual report should describe the work of the audit committee).

There is little doubt that the functions performed by the audit committee have increased notably over the past twenty years. Indeed, in the past few years alone, the EU Audit Regulation and Directive have expanded the role of the audit committee (although not in a notable way, and most of the specific audit committee tasks sets out in the Regulation and Directive fall broadly within the general functions set out in the Code).

19.4.5 **Auditor liability**

This section of the text discusses the different forms of liability that can be imposed upon an auditor, and how that liability can be limited. Over the past twenty years, the size and number of claims being brought against auditors (especially larger firms) has increased notably and Arthur Andersen's role in the Enron scandal has placed auditor liability firmly in the spotlight.

Although this section does look at criminal liability, the bulk of discussion in this area concerns civil liability, with the rules relating to civil liability being largely case-law based. However, there are some relevant statutory provisions that impose liability upon auditors (e.g. the summary remedy in s 212 of the Insolvency Act 1986 (IA 1986)). Regarding an auditor's civil liability, the starting point is to note that an auditor owes his clients a duty to act with reasonable care and skill, and this duty arises in contract[286] and tort.[287] The following statement of Lopes LJ is often regarded as a statement of what this duty entails:

Section 212 is discussed at 23.3.2.

> It is the duty of an auditor to bring to bear on the work he has to perform that skill, care, and caution which a reasonably competent, careful, and cautious auditor would use. What is reasonable skill, care, and caution must depend on the particular circumstances of each case. An auditor is not bound to be a detective, or, as was said, to approach his work with suspicion or with a foregone conclusion that there is something wrong. He is a watch-dog, but not a bloodhound. He is justified in believing tried servants of the company in whom confidence is placed by the company. He is entitled to assume that they are honest, and to rely upon their representations, provided he takes reasonable care. If there is anything calculated to excite suspicion he should probe it to the bottom; but in the absence of anything of that kind he is only bound to be reasonably cautious and careful.[288]

However, it is likely that this rather ageing exposition of an auditor's duty of care is no longer fully accepted, especially those sections about relying on information provided by the directors. Indeed, the courts have already acknowledged this, with Lord Denning stating:

> An auditor is not to be confined to the mechanics of checking vouchers and making arithmetical computations. He is not to be written off as a professional 'adder-upper and subtractor'. His vital task is to take care to see that errors are

---

[286] *Berg Sons & Co Ltd v Adams* [1992] BCC 6661 (QB).
[287] *Henderson v Merrett Syndicates Ltd (No 1)* [1995] 2 AC 145 (HL).
[288] *Re Kingston Cotton Mill Co (No 2)* [1896] 2 Ch 279 (CA) 288–9.

not made, be they errors of computation, or errors of omission or commission, or downright untruths. To perform this task properly he must come to it with an inquiring mind—not suspicious of dishonesty, I agree—but suspecting that someone may have made a mistake somewhere and that a check must be made to ensure that there has been none.[289]

This is backed up by the International Standard on Auditing (ISA) (UK) 200, which provides that '[t]he auditor shall plan and perform an audit with professional skepticism recognizing that circumstances may exist that cause the financial statements to be materially misstated'.[290] The courts have stated that such professional standards constitute 'very strong evidence as to what is the proper standard which should be adopted'.[291] In relation to this, the FRC has stated that '[w]e continue to identify problems with insufficient challenge of management and professional scepticism exercised by auditors when auditing key judgement areas (for example, goodwill impairment or long-term contracts)'.[292]

The scope of an auditor's liability will differ depending on whether liability arises in contract or tort.

19.4.5.1 Contractual liability

The agreement to audit a company will be contractual and so, if an auditor breaches a term of this contract, the company may sue the auditor for breach of contract. As noted at 19.4.5, the auditor is also subject to a common-law duty to act with reasonable skill and care, but it is common for this to be expressly provided for in the audit contract itself. Further, statute provides that, in a contract for the supply of a service, the supplier (i.e. the auditor) is subject to an implied term that he will carry out the service with reasonable care and skill.[293]

19.4.5.2 Tortious liability

Where an auditor has made statements in the auditor's report that he knows to be false, he can be liable under the tort of deceit. However, such cases are extremely rare and tortious liability more frequently arises under the tort of negligence. The following example indicates how this might work.

 Eg The scope of tortious auditor liability

Dragon plc's accounts indicate that, in 2018/19, it made a profit of £20 million. Dragon's auditor, Shelley & Smith LLP, signed off on the accounts and its report stated that the accounts provided a fair and true view of Dragon's financial position. Relying on the information in the accounts:

- Finn, a local wealthy businessman, purchases 10,000 shares in Dragon;
- Welsh Bank plc loans Dragon £100,000, with repayment to be made in a series of instalments.

It subsequently comes to light that Dragon's directors used some creative accounting practices in order to hide certain losses and, in fact, the company is not operating at a profit at all. Shelley & Smith was negligent in not discovering this. As a result, the value of Dragon's shares drops and no dividend is paid. Dragon also misses its first instalment payment to Welsh Bank.

---

[289] *Fomento (Sterling Area) Ltd v Selsdon Fountain Pen Co Ltd* [1958] 1 WLR 45 (HL) 61.

[290] FRC, 'International Standard on Auditing (UK) 200' (FRC 2016) para 15.

[291] *Lloyd Cheyham & Co Ltd v Littlejohn & Co Ltd* [1987] BCLC 303 (QB) 313 (Woolf J).

[292] FRC, 'Developments in Audit 2018 (FRC 2018) 8.   [293] Supply of Goods and Services Act 1982, s 13.

There is no doubt that Shelley & Smith is liable to Dragon. The trickier issue that arises is whether Shelley & Smith is liable to third parties such as Finn and Welsh Bank plc. The problem that arises is that, as accounts and reports are often freely available, an extremely wide range of persons may rely on them, resulting in the imposition of 'liability in an indeterminate amount for an indeterminate time to an indeterminate class'.[294] To prevent such indiscriminate liability, the courts have long sought to place certain limits upon the extent of auditor liability. Historically, the tort of negligence only covered negligent acts, not negligent statements and, when liability for negligent statements (known as 'negligent misstatement') was introduced, it was limited to situations in which a contractual or fiduciary relationship existed (neither of which would likely apply in Finn or Welsh Bank's case as they had no contractual or fiduciary relationship with Shelley & Smith). This changed following the case of *Hedley Byrne & Co Ltd v Heller & Partners Ltd*,[295] where the House of Lords accepted, albeit tentatively, that third parties could obtain a remedy from the auditor providing that a special relationship existed between the auditor and the third party. Difficulty regarding determining when such a relationship existed led to a re-examination of the law in the following seminal case.

Caparo Industries plc v Dickman [1990] 2 AC 605 (HL)

FACTS: Caparo Industries plc ('Caparo') was considering initiating a takeover bid of Fidelity plc ('Fidelity'). Before making the bid, Caparo scrutinized Fidelity's annual accounts, which had been signed off by Fidelity's auditor, Touche Ross ('TR'). The accounts stated that Fidelity's pre-tax profits were £1.2 million and, relying on this, Caparo purchased shares in Fidelity and took it over. Caparo subsequently discovered that the accounts were inaccurate and that Fidelity was actually running at a loss of £400,000, and that a number of Fidelity's directors were apparently engaged in fraudulent activities. Caparo sued TR and Dickman (one of TR's directors), alleging that the audit of Fidelity was negligent and that they owed it a duty of care.

HELD: In order for a duty of care to arise, there must be, *inter alia*, a relationship of sufficient proximity between the person making the statement (the adviser) and the person alleging that the duty exists (the advisee). This relationship will typically exist where:

1. the advice is required for a purpose, whether particularly specified or generally described, which is made known, either actually or inferentially, to the adviser at the time when the advice is given;

2. the adviser knows, either actually or inferentially, that his advice will be communicated to the advisee, either specifically or as a member of an ascertainable class, in order that it should be used by the advisee for that purpose;

3. it is known either actually or inferentially, that the advice so communicated is likely to be acted upon by the advisee for that purpose without independent inquiry; and

4. it is so acted upon by the advisee to his detriment.[296]

Applying this, the House held that TR did not owe a duty to Caparo. The purposes of the statutory audit are to protect the company and allow its members to exercise informed control over it.[297]

See Robyn Martin, 'Categories of Negligence and Duties of Care: Caparo in the House of Lords' (1990) 53 MLR 824.

[294] *Ultramares Corp v Touche* (1932) 174 NE 441 (New York Court of Appeals) 441 (Cardozo CJ).
[295] [1964] AC 465 (HL).   [296] [1990] 2 AC 605 (HL) 638.   [297] ibid 632.

> The statutory purpose of an audit is not to protect the interests of those who may invest in the company[298] or to facilitate the making of informed investment decisions.[299] Accordingly, an auditor does not generally owe a duty to members of the public at large or individual investors who use the accounts to decide whether to buy shares[300] or engage in a takeover bid.[301] If liability to such persons is be established, the existence of a special relationship must be established.

Caparo focused on whether a duty is owed to existing or future members, but subsequent cases have applied the rule in *Caparo* to provide that generally no duty will be owed to existing or future creditors.[302] To ensure that a duty is not owed to third parties, the ICAEW recommends that the auditor's report states that '[t]o the fullest extent permitted by law, we do not accept or assume responsibility to anyone other than the company and the company's members as a body, for our audit work, for this report, or for the opinions we have formed'.[303]

It is clear that the House in *Caparo* interpreted the purpose of the auditor's report in a narrow manner and, as a result, an auditor will not owe a duty to a third party in most cases. However, liability can be imposed where a special relationship exists, although this test now seems to be based on the auditor assuming a responsibility towards a third party. Examples of situations where an auditor might assume a responsibility towards a third person, and so could be liable in negligence, include:

- where an auditor is asked to value the shares of a private company and he knew that the valuation would be used to determine the price for which the shares would be sold, the auditor can be liable to those who relied on the valuation;[304]
- where an auditor is aware that his work will be used by third parties for a specific purpose, he can be liable to those third parties for negligence related to that work.[305]

Even if a third party can establish that a duty of care is owed, it will still need to establish that the duty was breached, causation was present, and the loss sustained was not too remote. In more recent cases, however, the requirements of causation and remoteness have been absorbed into the issue of whether a duty of care exists. As Arden LJ stated:

> Starting with Caparo v Dickman, the courts have moved away from characterising questions as to the measure of damages for the tort of negligence as questions of causation and remoteness. The path that once led in that direction now leads in a new direction. The courts now analyse such questions by enquiring whether the duty which the tortfeasor owed was a duty in respect of the kind of loss of which the victim complains. Duty is no longer determined in abstraction from the consequences or vice-versa.[306]

A defence for negligence is for the defendant to show that the claimant is seeking a remedy for the consequences of his own illegal act. So, for example, if a director of a

---

[298] ibid 649–50. [299] ibid 631. [300] ibid 623 and 662. [301] ibid 662.

[302] *Al-Saudi Banque v Clark Pixley* [1990] Ch 313 (Ch).

[303] Institute of Chartered Accountants in England and Wales (ICAEW), 'Technical Release Audit 01/03: The Auditor's Report and Auditors' Duty of Care to Third Parties' (ICAEW 2003) para 4.

[304] *Arenson v Casson Beckman Rutley & Co* [1977] AC 405 (HL).

[305] *Morgan Crucible Co plc v Hill Samuel & Co Ltd* [1991] Ch 295 (CA).

[306] *Johnson v Gore Wood & Co (No 2)* [2003] EWCA Civ 1728, [2003] NPC 147 [91].

company engaged in fraud and the auditor negligently failed to spot this, if the company then sued the auditor, could the auditor claim that the director's fraud would be attributed to the company, thereby allowing the auditor to raise the company's own illegal act as a defence? Where the company is a one-man company, then the courts have stated that the director's wrongdoing will not be attributed to the company,[307] and so the auditor cannot rely on the illegality defence.

19.4.5.3 Exemption and limitation of civil liability

An auditor may seek to exclude or limit his liability for negligence, breach of duty, etc., but the law strictly limits an auditor's ability to do this. The starting point is s 532, which applies to any provision:

- that exempts an auditor from any liability that would attach to him in connection with any negligence, default, breach of duty, or breach of trust occurring in the course of auditing a company's accounts; or
- by which a company provides an indemnity for an auditor against any liability attaching to him in connection with any negligence, default, breach of duty, or breach of trust occurring in the course of auditing a company's accounts.[308]

Any such provision is rendered void, subject to two exceptions.[309] The first exception provides that a company can indemnify an auditor against any liability incurred by him (i) in defending proceedings (civil or criminal) in which he is acquitted or judgment given in his favour; or (ii) in connection with an application under s 1157 in which relief is granted to him.[310]

The relief of liability under s 1157 is discussed at 10.1.3.4.

The second exception is more complex and applies to liability limitation agreements ('LLAs'). Historically, accountancy firms' business structure of choice was the partnership (although many larger firms have now converted to limited liability partnerships (LLPs)). The issue that arose was that the partners are jointly and severally liable for the debts and liabilities of the partnership.[311] So, if a company collapses due to the directors' fraud, and the auditors were negligent in failing to uncover that fraud (or as in the case of Enron's auditor, Arthur Andersen, were complicit in the fraud), the auditors could find themselves liable to pay 100 per cent of the damages in any resulting legal proceedings. Indeed, in such a case, the auditor will have 'deeper pockets' than the company or its directors, so it is often the preferred defendant. Larger accountancy firms (especially the Big Four) argued that this placed them in an unfairly vulnerable position, especially because claims against auditors had notably increased in size and amount. Accordingly, auditors began lobbying for some sort of system of proportionate liability (i.e. the auditor would only be liable for the proportion of the loss it caused). Following a lengthy lobbying effort and consultation process, the Companies Bill was amended at a late stage to allow auditors to protect themselves via LLAs.[312]

An LLA is an agreement between the auditor and the company that purports to limit the amount of liability owed to a company by an auditor in respect of any negligence, default, breach of duty, or breach of trust occurring in the course of auditing a

---

[307] *Bilta (UK) Ltd v Nazir* [2015] UKSC 23, [2015] 2 WLR 1168 (discussed at 6.5.4.3).
[308] CA 2006, s 532(1).   [309] ibid s 532(2).   [310] ibid s 533.
[311] Partnership Act 1890, ss 9 and 12.
[312] For a detailed discussion of the auditors' case and why LLAs were introduced, see Lee Roach, 'Auditor Liability: The Case for Limitation: Part 1' (2010) 31 Co Law 136.

company's accounts of which the auditor may be guilty in relation to the company.[313] If a company enters into a LLA with its auditor, then it must disclose in a note to its annual accounts the principal terms of the LLA and the date it was approved by the members.[314] In order for a LLA to be valid, it must comply with the conditions set out in ss 535 and 536,[315] namely:

- an LLA cannot apply for more than one financial year, and it must specify the financial year to which it applies;[316] and

- an LLA must be authorized by a resolution of the company's members (this resolution can occur before or after the LLA is entered into).[317]

An LLA can only limit an auditor's liability to such amount that is fair and reasonable in all the circumstances.[318] This is striking for two reasons. First, the word 'amount' indicates that the limitation need not be based on proportionate liability and can be a simple liability cap. Indeed, the Act itself provides that it is immaterial how an LLA is framed, and the limitation need not be a sum of money or a formula.[319] This affords auditors a level of freedom they did not lobby for (indeed, auditors did not lobby for a liability cap as they never thought they would get it). However, shortly after LLAs were introduced, major institutional investors and their trade bodies stated that fixed liability caps are not appropriate and that they would vote against such a cap.[320]

Second, under other pieces of legislation regulating exclusion and limitation clauses (notably the Unfair Contract Terms Act 1977), an unfair or unreasonable clause will be rendered void. However, an LLA that limits liability to an amount that is unfair or unreasonable will not be rendered void—the limitation will simply be amended to an amount that is fair and reasonable.[321] This is even more notable given that LLAs are excluded from several key safeguards in the Unfair Contract Terms Act 1977.[322]

The result is that LLAs appear to be a gift to auditors—indeed, it has been described by an in-house lawyer at KPMG as 'a Holy Grail that the auditors never thought they would get'.[323] It is therefore notable that LLAs have hardly been adopted and no listed company has adopted an LLA. The principal reason for this is that the Securities and Exchange Commission ('SEC', the US's equivalent to the FCA) states that a company's auditor must be independent,[324] but the SEC stated that the presence of an LLA would compromise an auditor's independence and so the SEC would not accept a financial report audited by an auditor who entered into an LLA with the company. As a result, many UK companies (especially those who also have shares listed on the New York Stock Exchange) did not even bother proposing LLAs to their shareholders. Consequently, LLAs amongst larger companies have been described as a 'dead duck'.[325]

---

[313] CA 2006, s 534(1). For a detailed discussion of LLAs, see Lee Roach, 'Auditor Liability: Liability Limitation Agreements: Part 2' (2010) 31 Co Law 167.

[314] CA 2006, s 538; Companies (Disclosure of Auditor Remuneration and Liability Limitation Agreements) Regulations 2008, SI 2008/489, reg 8(1).

[315] CA 2006, 534(2).   [316] ibid s 535(1).   [317] ibid s 536.

[318] ibid s 537(2).   [319] ibid s 535(4).

[320] See e.g. National Association of Pension Funds (NAPF), 'Corporate Governance Policy and Voting Guidelines' (NAPF 2007).

[321] CA 2006, s 537(2).   [322] ibid s 534(3)(b).   [323] —'On the Audit Trail' (2005) The Lawyer 11.

[324] SEC Rules and Regulations, §210.2–01.

[325] R Bruce, 'Limited Liability: Ignominious End for a Great Idea' *Financial Times* (London, 4 February 2009), quoting the then managing director of Deloitte.

19.4.5.4 **Criminal liability**

Section 507 creates two criminal offences in connection with the auditor's report, both of which are punishable by a fine:[326]

1. where a person knowingly or recklessly causes an auditor's report to include any matter that is misleading, false, or deceptive in a material particular;[327]

2. where a person knowingly or recklessly causes an auditor's report to omit certain specified statements.[328]

Only certain persons can be found guilty of the s 507 offences, namely:

- where the auditor is an individual, that individual and any employee or agent of his who is eligible for appointment as auditor of the company;

- where the auditor is a firm, any director, member, employee, or agent of the firm who is eligible for appointment as auditor of the company.[329]

The Theft Act 1968 also provides for the offence of false accounting, which is committed where a person dishonestly, with a view to gain for himself or another or with intent to cause loss to another (i) destroys, defaces, conceals, or falsifies any account or any record or document made or required for any accounting purpose; or (ii) in furnishing information for any purpose produces or makes use of any account, or any such record or document as aforesaid, which to his knowledge is or may be misleading, false, or deceptive in a material particular.[330] A person convicted of this offence can be imprisoned for up to seven years.[331]

19.4.5.5 **The Accountancy Scheme**

The FRC is empowered to act as the disciplinary body for accountants and accountancy firms. To that end, the FRC is empowered to investigate and impose sanctions on accountants and accountancy firms that engage in misconduct. The relevant rules are found in the Accountancy Scheme,[332] which defines 'misconduct' as:

> an act or omission or a series of acts or omissions, by a Member or Member Firm in the course of his or its professional activities (including as a partner, member, director, consultant, agent, or employee in or of any organisation or as an individual) or otherwise, which falls significantly short of the standards reasonably to be expected of a Member or Member Firm or has brought, or is likely to bring, discredit to the Member or the Member Firm or to the accountancy profession.[333]

The following provides an example of the type of activity that constitutes misconduct and the sanctions available to the FRC.

 The audits of Nichols plc and the University of Salford

In 2009, Mr Healey retired as a partner of Grant Thornton UK LLP, but continued to provide the firm with consultancy services.[334] In 2010, he was appointed to the audit committee of the University of Salford and, in 2011, he was also appointed as chair of the audit committee of

---

[326] CA 2006, s 507(4).   [327] ibid s 507(1).   [328] ibid s 507(2).   [329] ibid s 507(3).
[330] Theft Act 1968, s 17(1).   [331] ibid s 17(2).   [332] FRC, 'The Accountancy Scheme' (FRC 2014).
[333] ibid para 2(1).
[334] A detailed account of the facts and findings of the FRC can be found at www.frc.org.uk/news/august-2018/sanctions-against-grant-thornton---audits-of-nicho accessed 10 January 2019.

Nichols plc. The issue that arose was that the financial statements of both bodies were audited by Grant Thornton. Accordingly, Healey was sat on the audit committees of bodies that were audited by Grant Thornton at a time when he was providing consultancy services to Grant Thornton.

Unsurprisingly, the FRC concluded that this conflict meant that Grant Thornton could not be considered independent in relation to eight audits carried out between 2010 and 2013. The FRC concluded that Grant Thornton, Healey, and several partners of Grant Thornton had engaged in misconduct and issued the following sanctions:

- Grant Thornton was issued with a severe reprimand and fined £3 million;
- Healey was excluded from the ICAEW for a recommended period of five years and fined £150,000;
- three partners of Grant Thornton who were involved in the audits were reprimanded and fined.

19.4.6 **Vacation of office**

An auditor can vacate office in one of three ways, namely (i) he can be removed; (ii) he can resign; or (iii) he can be replaced. In addition, the important issue of auditor rotation is also discussed.

19.4.6.1 **Removal**

The members of a company may be concerned that an auditor lacks independence (e.g. because he is too close to the directors) or competence (e.g. because he conducts a negligent audit). Accordingly, the CA 2006 provides that the members of a company may, at any time, remove an auditor by passing an ordinary resolution.[335] Special notice of the resolution is required and the resolution must be passed at a meeting[336] (i.e. the written resolution procedure cannot be used).

There is a danger that the members may seek to remove an auditor for improper reasons, and so the Act imposes several safeguards. Similar safeguards exist to those given to a director who is being removed (e.g. the right to make a representation at the meeting seeking the auditor's removal).[337] A notable safeguard is found in s 519, which provides that an auditor who is ceasing to hold office must send to the company a statement of his reasons for doing so,[338] unless he satisfies either of the following two conditions:

1. the auditor of a private company is ceasing to hold office at the end of the period for appointing auditors, or the auditor of a public company is ceasing to hold office at the end of an accounts meeting; or

2. the auditor's reasons for ceasing to hold office are all exempt reasons[339] or there are no matters connected with his ceasing to hold office that he considers need to be brought to the attention of the members or creditors.[340]

---

[335] CA 2006, s 510(1) and (2)(a). This resolution is the only way that an auditor can be removed prior to his expiration of office (s 510(4)).

[336] ibid ss 510(2) and 511.   [337] These safeguards are set out in s 511.

[338] CA 2006, s 519(2). The statement must also be sent to the appropriate audit authority (s 522(1)), namely the FRC.

[339] As set out in s 519A(3).

[340] CA 2006, s 519(2A) and (2B). These exceptions will not apply where the company is a public interest company (s 519(1)) and, as regards such companies, the s 519 statement must be sent.

The statement must provide basic information (e.g. the auditor's name and address), but where there are matters connected with the auditor's ceasing to hold office that the auditor considers need to be brought to the attention of the members or creditors, he must state those reasons.[341]

Although the members have the right to remove the auditor, legal consequences may still result from the removal:

- removing an auditor will not deprive that auditor of compensation or damages payable as a result of his removal;[342]
- the removal of the company's auditor on grounds of divergence of opinions on accounting treatments or audit procedures or on any other improper grounds shall be treated as being unfairly prejudicial to the interests of some part of the company's members.[343]

The unfair prejudice remedy is discussed at 15.3.

19.4.6.2 Resignation

An auditor can resign his office at any time by sending a notice to that company to that effect.[344] Where the company is a public interest company, the notice will be ineffective unless it is accompanied by a s 519 statement[345] (discussed at 19.4.6.1). An effective notification of resignation ends the auditor's term of office on the date it is received by the company, or on such later date as may be stated in the notice.[346]

19.4.6.3 Replacement

Replacement of an auditor could occur where:

- the company's auditor has been removed or has resigned, and a new auditor must be appointed; or
- the company's auditor reaches the end of his term of office and, instead of reappointing him, the company decides to appoint a new auditor.

Two different procedures exist for replacing an auditor. The first applies only where the term of office of the auditor of a private company is to expire (i.e. it does not apply where an auditor has been removed or has resigned).[347] In such a case, the auditor can be replaced with another auditor by passing a written resolution.[348]

The second procedure can apply where an auditor has been removed, has resigned, or his term of office is to expire.[349] In such cases, the auditor can be replaced with another auditor by passing a resolution at a general meeting. Special notice of the resolution is required, unless the auditor was removed or resigned.[350]

The replacement of an auditor may be a cause of suspicion. For example, the directors may seek to rid themselves of an auditor who has proved adept at uncovering their misdeeds. However, increasingly, the replacement of an auditor is not viewed as contentious, especially as companies are encouraged (and, in some cases, required) to rotate their auditors at certain intervals, which is discussed next.

19.4.6.4 Rotation

Auditor rotation is technically a form of replacement, but it is such a long-standing and controversial issue that it deserves to be discussed separately. As discussed, in

---

[341] ibid s 519(3) and (3A).   [342] ibid s 510(3).   [343] ibid s 994(1A).
[344] ibid s 516(1).   [345] ibid s 516(2).   [346] ibid s 516(3).   [347] ibid s 514(1).   [348] ibid.
[349] ibid s 515(1) and (1A).   [350] ibid.

order for an auditor to undertake his function effectively, he must be independent. The problem that arises is that the longer an auditor audits a company, the more familiar he is likely to become with the directors, which can adversely affect his independence. As a 2010 EU Green Paper stated '[s]ituations where a company has appointed the same audit firm for decades seem incompatible with desirable standards of independence'.[351] Unfortunately, this was common practice, especially among larger companies. A 2011 study by the Office of Fair Trading (OFT) found that, on average, FTSE 100 companies only changed their auditor every 43 years, with FTSE 250 companies changing every 24 years.[352] An extreme example of this is Barclays Bank plc, whose accounts were audited by the same firm (namely PwC) for over 120 years (between 1896 and 2017).

The issue was how to address this, and one method that has been repeatedly suggested is auditor rotation (i.e. to require companies to change their auditor after a specified period). Audit firms (especially the Big Four) strongly opposed mandatory rotation and so less stringent reforms were originally introduced, namely requiring listed companies to change their audit partner (but not their audit firm) every seven years,[353] and mandatory tendering at least every 10 years for auditors of FTSE 350 companies[354] (both rules are still in effect). Following the financial crisis, the EU stated that auditor independence needed to be strengthened and so it decided to introduce a system of mandatory auditor rotation. This was introduced by the EU Audit Regulation, which was adopted in 2014, with the Preamble stating that '[i]n order to address the familiarity threat and therefore reinforce the independence of statutory auditors and audit firms, it is important to establish a maximum duration of the audit engagement of a statutory auditor or an audit firm in a particular audited entity'.[355]

The key provisions relating to auditor rotation apply only to PIEs, which are (i) entities whose transferable securities are admitted to trading on a regulated market within an EU Member State (e.g. a UK listed company); (ii) credit institutions; and (iii) insurance undertakings.[356] Although the EU Audit Regulation is directly applicable, it has been implemented into the CA 2006:

- The default rule is that the auditor of a PIE has a 'maximum engagement period' (i.e. the maximum period an auditor can audit a company before having to be replaced) of 10 years.[357]

- The EU Audit Regulation gives Member States the option of extending the maximum engagement period to 20 years, providing that the audit is subject to a qualifying selection procedure (e.g. a competitive public tender) within years.[358] The UK has chosen to adopt this option.[359] As noted above, FTSE 350 companies are required to put their statutory audit out to tender at least every 10 years.

---

[351] European Commission, 'Audit Policy: Lessons from the Crisis' COM (2010) 561 final, 11.

[352] OFT, 'Statutory Audit: Market Investigation Reference to the Competition Commission of the Supply of Statutory Audit Services to Large Companies in the UK' (OFT 2011) para 5.18.

[353] Auditing Practices Board, 'APB Ethical Standard 3 (Revised)' (APB 2009) para 19.

[354] The Statutory Audit Services for Large Companies Market Investigation (Mandatory Use of Competitive Tender Processes and Audit Committee Responsibilities) Order 2014, para 4(a).

[355] ibid Preamble, para 21.   [356] EU Audit Directive, Art 2(13); CA 2006, s 494A.

[357] CA 2006, s 494ZA(1).   [358] EU Audit Regulation, art 17(4).

[359] CA 2006, s494ZA(1). What amounts to a qualifying selection procedure is set out in ss 485A, 485B, 489A, and 489B.

- A PIE can apply to the FRC for an extension of the maximum engagement period, and the FRC can, if exceptional circumstances exist, extend this period by up to two years[360] (i.e. 12 years if no tender has taken place, and 22 years if a tender has taken place).

- Where an auditor (A) has reached the maximum engagement period and is replaced by the PIE with another auditor, the PIE cannot once again appoint A as its auditor within a four-year period following the expiration of the maximum engagement period.[361]

- Transitional arrangements are in place which apply until June 2023.[362]

The reforms have had an immediate effect, with an unprecedented number of FTSE companies changing their auditors and putting audits out to tender between 2014 and 2017. For example, in 2015, 23 FTSE 100 companies put their audit out to tender, resulting in 21 companies appointing a new auditor[363] (a level of change unheard of prior to the above reforms being introduced). This activity continued into 2016 and 2017. As a result, 47 per cent of auditors of FTSE 350 companies in 2017 had been in place for five years or fewer, compared to only 22 per cent in 2012.[364]

19.5 Other disclosure obligations

In addition to the disclosure obligations discussed thus far, companies are subject to a broad range of other disclosure obligations, some of which are discussed below.

19.5.1 Confirmation statement

Companies had long been required to submit each year to Companies House an annual return,[365] which provided basic company information (e.g its registered address, details concerning the directors, information regarding share capital, etc.).[366] The benefits of this were:

- it provided a snapshot of the company at a given time;
- it brought together basic information regarding the company in a single place; and
- it acted as a safety net for those companies who had not updated their filings during the year.[367]

The problem that arose was that the vast majority of companies update this information as it occurs (indeed, in many cases, companies are legally obliged to inform Companies House of such changes). As a result, for many companies, the annual return merely served to provide Companies House with information it already had, resulting in 'unnecessary duplication and burdens on businesses'.[368] Accordingly, the SBEEA 2015 abolished the annual return and has replaced it with a confirmation statement.

---

[360] ibid s 494ZA(2) and (3). For more, see FRC, 'Process for Applications to Extend the Maximum Duration of the Audit Engagement' (FRC 2016).

[361] CA 2006, ss 485C(1) and 489C(1).   [362] ibid s 494ZA(1).

[363] FRC, 'Developments in Audit 2016/17' (FRC 2017) 17.

[364] FRC, 'Developments in Audit 2018' (FRC 2018) 23.

[365] CA 2006, s 854 (now repealed).   [366] ibid ss 855–7 (now repealed).

[367] BIS, 'Company Filing Requirements: Red Tape Challenge' (BIS 2013) para 25.

[368] BIS, 'Trust and Transparency: Enhancing the Transparency of UK Company Ownership and Increasing Trust in UK Business: Discussion Paper' (BIS 2013) 34.

Every company is required to deliver to Companies House a confirmation statement,[369] which is a statement confirming that all the information required to be delivered to Companies House in the relevant confirmation period[370] has been delivered, or is being delivered alongside the confirmation statement. The statement must be delivered to Companies House within a 14-day period following the review period,[371] which is:

- the period of 12 months beginning on the day of the company's incorporation;
- each period of 12 months beginning on the day after the end of the previous review period.[372]

The information required to be delivered to Companies House is specified in ss 853B–853H, and includes:

- information regarding 'relevant events' (e.g. change of registered address);
- changes in the company's principal business activities;
- information regarding the company's share capital; and
- specified information regarding the company's shares and shareholders.

The advantage of the confirmation statement over the annual return is that, if Companies House already has the specified information, then the company need not provide it again—the confirmation statement can simply confirm that the company has already delivered the required information to Companies House. In practice, however, the confirmation statement is unlikely to be of major benefit for most companies as 99 per cent of companies submitted their annual returns online[373] and the online return could be pre-populated with the previous return's information. This meant that the company need only expend effort on updating any information that had changed (which is largely the case under the confirmation statement). The confirmation statement will, therefore, only be of real benefit to the very small minority of companies that submitted their returns in hard copy, and such companies would have to submit online eventually as Companies House intends to go paperless.

19.5.2 Periodic financial reporting

The DTRs require that a company whose securities are traded on a regulated market provide periodic reports on its financial affairs, namely in the form of (i) an annual financial report; and (ii) half-yearly financial reports.

19.5.2.1 Annual financial report

A company whose transferable securities are admitted to trading on a regulated market must, within a four-month period following the end of the company's financial year, publish an annual financial report.[374] This report must include:

- the audited financial statements;

---

[369] CA 2006, s 853A(1).

[370] As regards the company's first confirmation statement, the 'confirmation period' begins on the date of incorporation and ends on a date specified in the statement (the 'confirmation date'). For subsequent confirmation statements, the confirmation period begins on the day after the last statement's confirmation date and ends with the confirmation date of the statement concerned (s 853A(3)).

[371] Failure to do so is a criminal offence (s 853L). Note that only 70 per cent of companies filed their confirmation statements on time (Companies House, 'Annual Report and Accounts 2017/18' (Companies House 2018) 11).

[372] CA 2006, s 853A(5).

[373] Companies House, 'Annual Report and Accounts 2015/16' (Companies House 2016) 3.

- a management report, which contains a fair review of the company's business and a description of the principal risks and uncertainties facing the company; and

- responsibility statements, which state that the above documents provide a true and fair view.[375]

The annual financial report must remain publicly available for at least 10 years.[376]

19.5.2.2 **Half-yearly financial reports**

A company whose shares or debt securities are admitted to trading on a UK regulated market must make public a half-yearly financial report covering the first six months of the financial year.[377] The report must contain:

- a condensed set of financial statements (namely a condensed balance sheet, condensed profit-and-loss account, and explanatory notes);

- an interim management report, which provides details of important events that affected the company, and principal risks and uncertainties; and

- responsibility statements, stating that the above documents provide a fair and true view.[378]

This report must be made public as soon as possible, but no later than three months after the end of the period to which the report relates,[379] and it must remain available to the public for at least 10 years.[380]

19.5.3 **Gender and ethnic pay gap reporting**

A 2015 government consultation revealed a gender pay gap of 19.1 per cent between the average earnings of men and women[381] (i.e. a woman earns around 81p for every £1 a man earns). The government's response to this was to increase transparency surrounding gender-pay differences as this will 'enable the impact of those workplace policies and practices promoting gender equality to be monitored and remedial action to be prioritised'.[382] Accordingly, the government exercised the power granted to it under s 78(1) of the Equality Act 2010, which empowers a Minister to make regulations that require employers to publish information relating to the pay of employees for the purpose of showing whether there are differences in the pay of male and female employees. The Equality Act 2010 (Gender Pay Gap Information) Regulations 2017[383] (EA(GPGI)R 2017) came into force on 6 April 2017.

The Regulations apply to any 'relevant employer', which is defined as an employer who has 250 or more employees.[384] A relevant employer must make public each year specified information relating to the different rates of pay between men and women[385] (e.g. different hourly rates of pay, different levels of bonus pay, etc.). This information must be accompanied by a statement confirming that the information is accurate, and the statement must be signed by a director (or equivalent).[386] The required information and statement must be published on the employer's website and must remain there for at least three years,[387] and it must also be reported to the government's gender

---

[374] DTR, 4.1.1R and 4.1.3R.   [375] ibid 4.1.5R—4.1.12R.   [376] ibid 4.1.4R.

[377] ibid 4.2.1R and 4.2.2R(1).   [378] ibid 4.2.3R.   [379] ibid 4.2.2R(2).   [380] ibid 4.2.2R(3).

[381] Government Equalities Office, 'Closing the Gender Pay Gap: Government Consultation' (2015) para 1.1.

[382] Government Equalities Office, 'Closing the Gender Pay Gap: Government Response to the Consultation' (2016) 5.

[383] SI 2017/172.   [384] EA(GPGI)R 2017, reg 1(2).   [385] ibid reg 2(1).

[386] ibid reg 14(1) and (2)(a).   [387] ibid reg 15(1).

pay service.[388] Unfortunately, early indicators show that around 5 per cent of relevant employers are submitting inaccurate data.[389]

The EA(GPGI)R 2017 do not provide for any sanction for relevant employers who do not publish the required information. However, a failure to comply with the 2017 Regulations will constitute an unlawful act under s 34 of the Equality Act 2006, which will allow the Equality and Human Rights Commission to take enforcement action. Such employers may also face reputational damage.

The McGregor-Smith Review,[390] which looked at race in the workplace, noted that gender pay reporting had resulted in employers taking action in order to address the gender pay gap. The Review therefore recommended that companies should also be required to disclose details regarding disparities in pay among ethnic employees in order to address disparities in ethnic pay.[391] The government responded by saying that it believed that whilst ethnicity pay reporting was desirable, it should not be mandatory and should be voluntary.[392] However, very few companies chose to report ethnic pay data and so, in October 2018, the government published a consultation document[393] in which it stated that it would introduce mandatory ethnicity pay reporting. At the time of writing, the consultation has recently closed, and the government is considering how to proceed.

19.5.4 Slavery and human trafficking statement

A 2013 report[394] highlighted the extent to which modern slavery[395] constituted a major problem in the UK. The government's response was the enactment of the Modern Slavery Act 2015, of which s 54 is the key provision for our purposes. Section 54 requires a commercial organization (defined as a body corporate or partnership)[396] to prepare, for each financial year, a slavery and human trafficking statement.[397] This obligation only applies to commercial organizations that supply goods or services and have a turnover of not less than £36 million.[398] A slavery and human trafficking statement is:

- a statement of the steps the organization has taken during the financial year to ensure that slavery and human trafficking is not taking place in any of its supply chains and in any part of its business; or
- a statement that the organization has taken no such steps.[399]

---

[388] ibid reg 15(2). Information reported can be viewed at https://gender-pay-gap.service.gov.uk accessed 10 January 2019.

[389] Billy Ehrenberg-Shannon, Aleksandra Wisniewska, and Sarah Gordon, 'Cluster of UK Companies Reports Highly Improbably Gender Pay Gap Data' *Financial Times* (London 7 December 2017).

[390] McGregor-Smith Review, 'Race in the Workplace' (2017) available at www.gov.uk/government/publications/race-in-the-workplace-the-mcgregor-smith-review accessed 10 January 2019.

[391] ibid 15.

[392] See https://assets.publishing.service.gov.uk/government/uploads/system/uploads/attachment_data/file/594365/race-in-workplace-mcgregor-smith-review-response.pdf accessed 10 January 2019.

[393] BEIS, 'Ethnicity Pay Reporting: Government Consultation' (BEIS 2018).

[394] Centre for Social Justice, 'It Happens Here: Equipping the United Kingdom to Fight Modern Slavery' (Centre for Social Justice 2013).

[395] The term 'modern slavery' is used in the report to refer collectively to human trafficking, slavery, servitude, and forced labour.

[396] Modern Slavery Act 2015, s 54(12).   [397] ibid s 54(1).

[398] ibid s 54(2); Modern Slavery Act 2015 (Transparency in Supply Chains) Regulations 2015, SI 2015/1833, reg 2.

[399] Modern Slavery Act 2015, s 54(4).

The statement must be approved by the board of directors and signed by a director[400] and, if the organization has a website, it must be published on that website.[401] Companies may also include the statement within their annual report—many companies publish their statement alongside their annual report.

If an organization is required to prepare a statement and does not, the Secretary of State can obtain an injunction compelling the organization to prepare a statement.[402] There is no sanction if the organization states that it has not taken steps to ensure no slavery or human trafficking has taken place in its supply chains or business, but the company's reputation might suffer and stakeholders may decide to do business elsewhere. The media do track these statements and, whilst the government has not established a central depository for slavery and human trafficking statements, the Business and Human Rights Resource Centre has set up a Modern Slavery Registry[403] that, at the time of writing, contains nearly 7,600 statements.

The government's 2018 Annual Report on Modern Slavery noted that the quality of slavery and human trafficking statements could improve.[404] Accordingly, in October 2018, the Home Office wrote to the CEOs of 17,000 companies, warning them that slavery and trafficking statements needed to improve.[405] The government estimated that only 60 per cent of applicable companies published a slavery and human trafficking statement and, of those statements that were published, some were poor in quality and did not meet the legal requirements.

CHAPTER SUMMARY

- Companies House maintains a register of all information provided to it by companies, which can be inspected by anyone.

- Companies are required to keep a number of statutory registers, but private companies may instead elect to have Companies House keep the relevant information on its central register.

- All companies are generally required to prepare accounts for each financial year and these are known as 'individual accounts'.

- Parent companies, in addition to preparing individual accounts, must also prepare group accounts.

- The annual reports consist of the strategic report, the directors' report, the auditor's report, and (if the company is quoted) the directors' remuneration report.

- In recent years, there has been a move towards increased reporting of non-financial information (this is known as 'narrative reporting').

- Companies must send copies of their annual accounts and reports to specified persons and quoted companies must publish them on their website. Public companies must lay the accounts and reports before the general meeting.

---

[400] ibid s 54(6)(a).   [401] ibid s 54(7).

[402] ibid s 54(11). Failure to comply with this injunction will constitute contempt of court.

[403] See www.modernslaveryregistry.org accessed 10 January 2019.

[404] HM Government, '2018 UK Annual Report on Modern Slavery' (2018) paras 2.80–2.85.

[405] See www.gov.uk/government/news/home-office-tells-business-open-up-on-modern-slavery-or-face-further-action accessed 10 January 2019.

- The role of a statutory auditor is to report on whether the company's accounts represent a fair and true view of the company's finances.

- A statutory auditor must be independent of the company and several reforms have been introduced in recent years to promote auditor independence (e.g. rules relating to non-audit services, mandatory rotation).

- An audit can be liable to the company in contract and tort. Auditors can be liable in tort to third parties, but this will only occur where there is a relationship of sufficient proximity. As a result, auditors will typically not owe a duty of care to current or potential members/creditors.

- An auditor can vacate office by being removed, by resigning, or by being replaced. A system of mandatory auditor rotation has been introduced for PIEs.

FURTHER READING

EY, 'Annual Reporting in 2017/18: Demonstrating Purpose, Creating Value (EY 2018).
- Provides a practical discussion and evaluation of the annual accounts and reports of FTSE companies in 2018.

FRC, 'Annual Review of Corporate Governance and Reporting 2017/18' (FRC 2018).
- Provides an assessment of UK corporate reporting in 2017/18. Highlights areas where reporting is weak and in need of improvement.

Karsten Engsig Sorensen, 'Disclosure in EU Corporate Governance—A Remedy in Need of Adjustment?' (2009) 10 EBOR 255.
- Although focusing on EU corporate reporting, this article contains a lot of discussion that is applicable to corporate transparency in general.

Lee Roach, 'Auditor Liability' (2010) 31 Co Law 136 and 167.
- This two-part article examines the rules relating to auditor liability and discusses liability limitation agreements.

Walter Doralt et al, 'Auditor Independence at the Crossroads—Regulation and Incentives' (2012) 13 EBOR 89.
- Provides an overview of some of the key issues in relation to audit independence, and sets out the cornerstones for an effective regulatory system.

SELF-TEST QUESTIONS

1. Define the following terms:

- accounting reference date;
- accounting reference period;
- financial year;
- group accounts;
- annual reports
- auditor;
- liability limitation agreement;
- maximum engagement period;
- confirmation statement.

2. State whether each of the following statements is true or false and, if false, explain why:

- Companies House does not owe a duty to third parties as regards the accuracy of information on its register.
- Companies can, instead of keeping their own registers, elect to keep the required information on the public register at Companies House.
- All companies must keep adequate accounting records.
- All companies must prepare a strategic report for each financial year.
- Only quoted companies must prepare a directors' remuneration report.
- A public company must table a resolution at its AGM to receive the reports and accounts.
- All companies must appoint an auditor for each financial year.
- A listed company must change its auditor at least every 10 years.

3. Discuss the importance and effectiveness of disclosure as a tool of corporate accountability.

4. Dragon Products Ltd ('DP') was incorporated in January 2018. At the end of 2018, the company had a turnover of £9 million and a balance sheet total of £4.5 million. You are the company secretary of DP, whose directors ask you to explain the following:

- What statutory registers must the company maintain?
- Do the directors of DP need to prepare full annual accounts and what period must these accounts cover?
- What annual reports will DP need to provide?
- Explain DP's obligations regarding circulation and filing of the annual accounts and reports.
- Does DP need to appoint an auditor and have its accounts audited?
- Does DP need to appoint an audit committee?
- Explain to DP its obligations relating to the delivery of a confirmation statement.

 ## ONLINE RESOURCES

This book is accompanied by online resources to better support you in your studies. Visit www.oup.com/uk/roach-company/ for:

- answers to the self-test questions;
- further reading lists;
- multiple-choice questions;
- glossary.

Updates to the law can be found on the author's Twitter account (@UKCompanyLaw) and further resources can be found on the author's blog (www.companylawandgovernance.com).

20 | Debt capital and security

- Corporate borrowing
- Secured and unsecured borrowing
- Fixed and floating charges
- Determining the type of charge
- Registration of charges
- Receivership

INTRODUCTION

Chapter 16 discussed share capital. This chapter moves on to discuss the other form of capital, namely capital obtained through borrowing (known as 'debt capital' or 'loan capital'). For many companies, debt capital is an extremely important source of capital, so the chapter looks at why companies borrow and their borrowing powers. It is important that those who lend money to the company are adequately protected, so the chapter also looks at the various ways that creditors can improve their chances of being repaid, principally by the taking of security.

20.1 Corporate borrowing

This section looks at why companies borrow, their ability to borrow, and the different types of borrowing facility that exist.

20.1.1 Why do companies borrow?

There are several reasons why companies seek to borrow. An obvious reason is that the company is struggling financially so other forms of capital (i.e. share capital and retained profits) are insufficient to meet the company's debts or liabilities. In such a case, debt capital may be the only obtainable form of capital (although lenders may be unwilling to lend to such companies) as the company will likely have no retained profits and share capital will prove insufficient. Indeed, for most companies, share capital is usually an insufficient form of capital—the average UK company has only two shareholders[1] and, as the majority of companies are small private companies, the share capital they contribute will usually be minimal. The company could issue more shares, but it may not wish to as this could adversely affect the current shareholders' level of control.

Even if a company is financially healthy, debt capital is still likely to be an important source of capital. Such a company might have a healthy level of retained profit that could be used to pay off its debts, etc., but it might instead wish to use this profit for another commercially beneficial reason (e.g. to expand the business, or to pay a dividend). Accordingly, for most companies, debt capital represents an important form of capital and can be more important than share capital.

20.1.1.1 **Gearing**

Many companies operate with a mixture of equity capital and debt capital. The ratio of debt capital to equity capital in a company is known as 'gearing' and is usually expressed as a percentage (e.g. if a company has a share capital of £1 million and it has borrowed £200,000, it will have a gearing of 20 per cent). A company that has a high ratio of debt capital to equity capital is said to have high gearing, whereas a company with a low ratio is said to have low gearing. A company would be well advised to consider its gearing, especially as some lenders will take into account a company's gearing when determining whether to lend. Some lenders, upon lending money, may require that a company does not exceed a specified gearing ratio. A detailed discussion of gearing is beyond the scope of this text, but Table 20.1 sets out the principal advantages and disadvantages of low and high gearing.

TABLE 20.1 The advantages and disadvantages of gearing

	Advantages	Disadvantages
Low gearing	• Less risk of defaulting on loans, and so less risk of insolvency • Creditors may be more willing to provide debt capital and on better terms • Increased cost of credit (e.g. increases in interest rates) more easily borne	• Shareholders may expect more regular or higher dividend payments • May be an indication that the company has no ideas for expansion
High gearing	• Debt capital can be used to expand the business or other beneficial projects • May be able to provide an increase dividend • Borrowing may be quicker and easier than allotting shares • The return on debt capital is usually lower than that expected for equity capital	• More likely the company will default on loans; this, in turn, makes the company more likely to become insolvent • Creditors and suppliers may demand increased protection (e.g. higher interest rate) • More susceptible to unexpected economic events • May make it more difficult to obtain debt capital

There is no optimal gearing ratio that applies to all companies[2]—instead, a company's optimal gearing level at a particular point in time will depend on a combination

---

[1] Companies House, 'Company Register Activities in the United Kingdom 2017-18' (Companies House 2018) Table A7.

[2] F Modigliani and MH Miller, 'The Cost of Capital, Corporation Finance and the Theory of Investment' (1958) 48 American Economic Review 433.

of factors. For this reason, a company's gearing will probably fluctuate during its lifespan. For example, during times of expansion, the company will likely be more highly geared and will then revert to a lower gearing when its size becomes more stable.

20.1.2 The power to borrow and grant security

Here, we are concerned with the company's power to borrow and the directors' ability to enter into loan agreements on behalf of the company (including granting security over the company's assets). As regards the company's ability to borrow, two notable limitations should be noted:

1. A public company must not exercise any borrowing powers unless it has first been issued with a trading certificate.[3]

2. The company's constitution may limit its ability to borrow. As a result of changes to the *ultra vires* rules,[4] a company's ability to borrow cannot be called into question on the ground of lack of capacity by reason of anything in the company's constitution.

The trading certificate is discussed at 3.2.5.1.

The principal issue is whether persons acting on behalf of the company (notably, the directors) are empowered to exercise borrowing powers on behalf of the company. This will depend on the articles and whether such persons have actual or apparent authority to enter into loan agreements on the company's behalf. In many cases, such persons will have actual authority as the company's articles will bestow upon them a power to borrow, either expressly or via a general clause providing them with broad powers (e.g. the broad power of management conferred upon the directors by art 3 of the model articles would include authorization to exercise the company's borrowing powers). However, it is not uncommon (especially amongst private companies) to limit the directors' borrowing powers in some way (e.g. the articles may require that loans over a specified amount be first approved by the general meeting). If the directors do breach their borrowing powers, then the loan agreement will likely remain valid (either via the operation of s 40 of the CA 2006 or the rule in *Turquand's* case), but the directors will likely breach the duty to act within powers found in s 171. In addition, the directors may be liable for breach of warranty of authority.

Actual and apparent authority are discussed at 6.3.

Article 3 is discussed at 9.2.1.

Section 40 is discussed at 6.4.1, whereas *Turquand's* case is discussed at 6.4.2.

The power to borrow on behalf of the company also implicitly includes the power to grant security over the company's assets to facilitate such borrowing (unless the articles provide otherwise).

20.1.3 Sources of debt capital

If a company decides to borrow, then a key decision will be to decide what form of borrowing to engage in. Loan agreements are usually contractual in nature and so can take whatever form the parties so wish (as long as the agreement is not unlawful or contrary to public policy). As a result, loan agreements can take many different forms and a detailed discussion of the different forms of credit is beyond the scope of this text,[5] but a brief discussion of the principal sources of debt capital will be helpful.

---

[3] Companies Act 2006 (CA 2006), s 761(1).

[4] Namely s 39 of the CA 2006, which is discussed at 6.2.2.

[5] For a detailed discussion, see Louise Gullifer and Jennifer Payne, *Corporate Finance Law: Principles and Policy* (Hart 2011).

20.1.3.1 **Loans**

The simplest, and most popular, form of credit is a loan. This involves an agreement under which the creditor will loan a sum of money to the company (or to a third party specified by the company). Loans come in two principal forms:

1. **Term loans**: a term loan involves a company simply borrowing a sum of money from a debtor, with repayment of the sum borrowed (this sum is known as the 'principal') plus interest[6] being due by a specified date. Repayment is usually made via single payment or a a series of instalments. The lender is usually an external party (e.g. a bank), but it could also be someone connected to the company (e.g. a director, member, or other company within the corporate group).

2. **Overdraft**: one of the most popular forms of corporate borrowing (especially for smaller companies) is an overdraft facility, which involves the company withdrawing from its current account more money than it has deposited into it. An overdraft facility usually comes into operation via an agreement between the company and the bank, but if the company seeks to draw more funds from a current account than it has, this can impliedly constitute an offer to set up an overdraft facility.[7] Once an overdraft facility exists, the company is free to draw upon it until such time as it reaches the agreed limit (the company and the bank can negotiate to increase this limit). An overdraft is usually repayable on demand, but the parties can agree otherwise.

The type of loan most useful to the company will be determined by several factors. First, if the company desires flexibility, then an overdraft may be more appropriate as it allows the company to determine how much it borrows and when. As the company only borrows when it wants or needs to, this could also help minimize the cost of credit. Second, the type of transaction for which the loan is needed is relevant. If the company needs the money for a one-off transaction or project, then a term loan might be more suitable. Conversely, if the expenditure is recurring, an overdraft might be more useful.

20.1.3.2 **Debt securities**

Debt securities are, in some respects, similar to shares. Like shares, debt securities are tradeable financial instruments that a company can issue in order to raise finance. Once issued, debt securities can then be traded like shares and, to facilitate this, they can be traded on a stock exchange (indeed, the worldwide market for debt securities is substantially larger than that of equity securities). The principal difference is that a holder of debt securities is not usually a member of the company, but is instead a creditor.

A typical debt security provides that the company will promise to pay the holder of the security a specified sum on a specified date (known as the 'maturity date'), along with interest. Before deciding whether to issue debt securities, and before deciding whether to purchase debt securities, the company and potential investors should make themselves aware of the potential advantages and disadvantages of debt securities, as set out in Table 20.2.

20.1.3.3 **Hybrids**

Mention should be made of what have become known as 'hybrid' securities, of which two main types can be identified. The first type combines elements of equity and debt securities into a single security. It has been argued that preference shares are a form of hybrid security as, like a debt security, it provides holders with a fixed return on capital and no right to participate in any surplus profit.[8] The second type of hybrid allows for

---

[6] It should be noted that, unless the loan agreement provides for the payment of interest, no interest will be payable (*London Chatham and Dover Railway Co v South Eastern Railway Co* [1983] AC 429 (HL)).

[7] *Barclays Bank Ltd v WJ Simms Son & Cooke (Southern) Ltd* [1980] QB 677 (QB).

[8] Louise Gullifer and Jennifer Payne, *Corporate Finance Law: Principles and Policy* (Hart 2011) 44.

TABLE 20.2 Debt securities

Advantages	Disadvantages
Usually a cheaper way of raising capital than obtaining a loan	Debt securities must be repaid, whereas dividends need not be paid
Typically provide the holder a higher rate of interest than would be obtained from a current account	Repayment can only be made on the maturity date, so debt securities are less flexible than loans
Provide a more predictable income stream than shares	Issuing debt securities increases a company's gearing
Interest paid is tax deductible	Holders have no claims on profits, so may be viewed as less attractive than shares
The market price of debt securities tends to fluctuate less than the price of shares	Interest payments may inhibit the company's ability to engage in other activities
Issuing debt securities does not dilute the members' control of the company	

conversion from one type of security into another (e.g. conversion from a debt security into an equity security, or vice versa).

20.1.3.4 **Debentures**

At this point, it is important to discuss what is meant by the word 'debenture' because several statutory provisions apply specifically to debentures.[9] The business community generally uses the word 'debenture' to refer to the document that acknowledges a company's indebtedness and provides for security to be taken on the loan. The CA 2006 does not define what a debenture is, but provides that it 'includes debenture stock, bonds and any other securities of a company, whether or not constituting a charge on the company'.[10] It is therefore clear that, in including unsecured credit, the Act's conception of a debenture is wider than the commercial usage. This approach has been followed by the courts, who have described a debenture in similarly broad terms (e.g. 'a document which either creates a debt or acknowledges it').[11]

20.2 Secured and unsecured borrowing

When a creditor lends money to a company, the creditor's principal concern is that the money loaned is repaid. If the company defaults on the loan, the creditor may sue the company for breach, but this cause of action will be of little aid if the company is insolvent and does not have sufficient assets to pay. Accordingly, it is common for creditors to seek extra protection by obtaining some form of right over the company's assets if the company fails to adhere to the terms of the loan agreement. In such a case, the company is said to have 'secured' the loan or it has 'taken out security' on the loan. In *Bristol Airport plc v Powdrill*,[12] Browne-Wilkinson VC accepted that 'security' could be defined as follows:

> Security is created where a person ('the creditor') to whom an obligation is owed by another ('the debtor') by statute or contract, in addition to the personal

---

[9] See e.g. CA 2006, ss 740, 743–4, 752, and 769.
[10] ibid s 738.   [11] *Levy v Abercorris Slate and Slab Co* (1888) LR 37 ChD 260 (Ch) 264 (Chitty J).
[12] [1990] Ch 744 (CA).

promise of the debtor to discharge the obligation, obtains rights exercisable against some property in which the debtor has an interest in order to enforce the discharge of the debtor's obligation to the creditor.[13]

The 'rights exercisable' referred to usually means 'a contractual right enabling the creditor to sell his debtor's goods and apply the proceeds in or towards satisfaction of the debt . . .'[14]

The forms of security discussed in this chapter are consensual and the parties may choose to transact on a secured or unsecured basis. However, from the creditor's point of view, there are three significant advantages to taking out security on a loan:

1. Should the company breach the terms of the security agreement (e.g. by defaulting on the loan), the creditor will be able to enforce the rights contained in the security agreement, which might allow the creditor to recover the entire amount owed.

2. In the event of a company being liquidated, secured debts rank above unsecured debts. Unsecured debts rank behind debts secured by fixed charge, liquidation expenses, preferential debts, and debts secured by floating charge. In many liquidations, once those debts have been paid, there will be little, if any, left over for the unsecured creditors.

> The ranking of debts on insolvency is discussed at 23.2.3.

3. The security agreement might entitle the creditor to rights that other persons do not have (e.g. the right to certain information or managerial input in certain events, the right to nominate a director to the board).

Having discussed what security is, the different types of security will now be discussed.

20.2.1 Types of security

Statute does not exhaustively set out what devices constitute security, but the Insolvency Act 1986 (IA 1986) does provide that the word 'security' means 'any mortgage, charge, lien or other security'.[15] In *Re Cosslett (Contractors) Ltd*,[16] Millett LJ stated that:

> There are only four kinds of consensual security known to English law: (i) pledge; (ii) contractual lien; (iii) equitable charge and (iv) mortgage. A pledge and a contractual lien both depend on the delivery of possession to the creditor. . . . . Neither a mortgage nor a charge depends on the delivery of possession.[17]

From this, it is clear that there are two broad categories of security, namely possessory security (which requires a transfer of possession of the secured assets) and non-possessory security (which does not require a transfer of possession).

20.2.1.1 Possessory security

Possessory security involves the creditor having physical possession of an asset belonging to the borrower, on the condition that the asset is returned once the borrower pays off the debt owed. The two forms of possessory security are:

1. **Pledge**: a pledge involves the creditor taking possession of an asset of the borrower as security. The creditor may hold on to this asset until the borrower's obligations have been fulfilled, and has the right to sell the asset if the borrower defaults on its obligations.

2. **Lien**: a lien is 'a right given to a creditor by contract to detain goods of the debtor to secure payment or performance of some other obligation, the goods having been delivered to the creditor for some purpose other than security, such as storage or repair'.[18]

---

[13] ibid 760. Note that Browne-Wilkinson VC accepted that this did not provide a comprehensive definition.
[14] *Smith v Bridgend CBC* [2001] UKHL 58, [2002] 1 AC 336 [53] (Lord Scott).   [15] IA 1986, s 248.
[16] [1998] Ch 495 (CA).   [17] ibid 508.
[18] Ewan McKendrick, *Goode on Commercial Law* (5th edn, Penguin 2017) 632.

Pledges and liens operate in a very similar manner, but there are two key differences between them. First, 'in the case of a pledge the owner delivers possession to the creditor as security, whereas in the case of a lien the creditor retains possession of goods previously delivered to him for some other purpose'.[19] Second, a pledge contains an implied power to sell the secured asset if the borrower defaults, whereas a lien contains no such implicit power and it will need to be expressly provided for in the loan agreement.

Possessory security provides the creditor with a significant level of protection, but can be extremely disadvantageous to the borrower, who will be unable to use the secured asset. To remedy this, non-possessory forms of security were developed.

20.2.1.2 **Non-possessory security**

Non-possessory security involves the creditor taking security over an asset of the borrower, but the borrower retains possession of the asset and can continue to make use of it (although this usage may be restricted). As there is usually no transfer of possession,[20] non-possessory security can be taken over a wide array of assets and is therefore more flexible than possessory security. There are two forms of non-possessory security:

1. **Mortgage**: a mortgage involves the borrower transferring legal title of the secured asset to the creditor, on the condition that title will be transferred back to the borrower once its obligations have been fulfilled. However, if the borrower defaults on its obligations, the creditor can take possession of the secured asset and, if the loan agreement so provides, will have the right to sell it.

2. **Equitable charge**: an equitable charge does not usually involve the transfer of title or possession of the charged asset. Instead, it provides the creditor with the right to appropriate the charged asset if the borrower defaults on its obligations under the loan agreement. The creditor can then use this appropriation to discharge the borrower's debt (e.g. by selling the charged asset if the charge instrument so provides).

Although the mortgage and equitable charge are distinct forms of security, the CA 2006 provides that the word 'charge' includes a mortgage,[21] and so the word 'charge' will be used to cover both forms of non-possessory security. Charges come in two forms, namely fixed charges and floating charges and these are discussed next.

20.3 Fixed and floating charges

Before discussing the two types of charges, it is worth briefly explaining some simple terminology via the following example.

 Eg **The terminology surrounding charges**

Dragon plc borrows £100,000 from Welsh Bank plc. The loan is secured by a fixed charge taken over Dragon's corporate headquarters. The person who grants the charge (i.e. Dragon) is known as the 'chargor'. The person to whom the charge is granted (i.e. Welsh Bank plc) is known as the 'chargee' or 'chargeholder'.

---

[19] *Re Cosslett (Contractors) Ltd* [1998] Ch 495 (CA) 508.

[20] It should be noted that it is possible for a mortgage and a charge to require transfer of possession of the secured asset. The point to note is that, unlike pledges and liens, these types of security are not dependent on a transfer of possession and, as such, are usually non-possessory.

[21] CA 2006, s 859A(7).

TABLE 20.3 The differences between a fixed charge and a floating charge

	Fixed charge	Floating charge
Can be created by	Incorporated and unincorporated bodies	Incorporated bodies only
Subject matter of charge	Usually taken over a specific, identifiable asset or assets (e.g. a building)	Usually taken over a class of assets, or the entire undertaking
Effect on the charged asset(s)	The ability of the chargor to deal with the charged asset will usually be limited or completely restricted	Prior to crystallization, the chargor will usually be free to deal with the charged assets
Better suited for which assets	Better suited for assets that the company does not need to deal with or dispose	Suitable for all types of assets
Charged assets availability to the liquidator	No	Yes
Priority	Ranks ahead of all other debts	Ranks behind fixed chargeholders, liquidation expenses and preferential creditors
Prescribed part must be set aside for the unsecured creditors	No	Yes
Charge can be set aside by liquidator or administrator	No	Yes
Assets can be disposed of by administrator	Assets subject to a fixed charge can only be disposed of by an administrator if a court order is first obtained	Assets subject to a floating charge can be disposed of by an administrator without first obtaining a court order

A charge can be either fixed or floating. Both types of charges are discussed in more detail below, but Table 20.3 summarizes the principal differences between them.

As will be discussed, each type of charge suffers from its own advantages and disadvantages. To mitigate these, it is common for powerful creditors (such as large banks) to obtain a fixed charge over specific assets, and a floating charge over all the assets and the undertaking itself.

20.3.1 **Fixed charges**

A fixed charge (sometimes known as a 'specific' charge) must be taken over an asset that is sufficiently identifiable[22] and is therefore usually taken over permanent assets (e.g. land, buildings, etc.). From a creditor's point of view, a fixed charge is almost always preferable to a floating charge for several reasons:

● The company cannot dispose of the charged assets, unless it repays the loan or obtains the consent of the chargeholder.[23] This helps ensure that the assets are available to satisfy the

---

[22] *Illingworth v Illingworth* [1904] AC 355 (HL).
[23] *Agnew v Inland Revenue Commissioner* [2001] UKPC 28, [2001] 2 AC 710.

creditor's claim should the company default. If the company does dispose of the charged assets without the authorization of the chargeholder, then the chargeholder will be afforded a remedy for breach of contract, or may obtain an injunction restraining the disposition. If the disposition is not restrained, the person who acquired the charged assets will remain subject to the charge, unless they are a good faith purchaser with no knowledge of the fixed charge.

- A fixed charge will usually provide that no further fixed charges can be created over the same assets. If this is not provided for, and two fixed charges ae taken over the same assets, then they rank in order of time when they were first created (i.e. the first takes priority over the second, etc.). Where a fixed charge and a floating charge are taken over the same assets, then the fixed charge takes priority even if it was created after the floating charge.[24]

- In the event of default, a fixed chargeholder is afforded a wide range of remedies, some of which are extremely useful. The chargeholder will usually have the right to take possession of the charged assets and sell them to satisfy the debt (alternatively the chargeholder can appoint a receiver to take possession of, and then sell, the assets). The chargeholder will also usually have the right to foreclosure, which involves the chargeholder applying to the court for an order stating that the chargeholder becomes the absolute owner of the charged assets. Note, however, that if the charge is equitable (e.g. not a mortgage), then the chargeholder will not have the right to possession[25] or foreclosure.[26]

- In the event of a company's liquidation, property secured by fixed charge is not available to the liquidator. This effectively means that debts secured by fixed charge rank ahead of all other debts (unless the charge instrument allows otherwise), including debts secured by floating charge (which, as discussed at 20.3.2, rank behind several classes of debt). Further, a liquidator can set aside a floating charge in certain cases, whereas he cannot set aside a fixed charge.

From a company's point of view, a fixed charge can be problematic as it restricts the company's ability to deal with the charged asset. Accordingly, it is not suitable for assets that the company will need to use or dispose of (e.g. raw materials used in the production of goods). The result of this is that a fixed charge provides a very powerful form of security, but it is also inflexible. To remedy this, a more flexible form of charge was needed, and this led to the creation of the floating charge.

20.3.2 Floating charges

That the floating charge was created to offset the inflexibility of the fixed charge is evident in the following statement by Lord Millett:

> The floating charge is capable of affording the creditor, by a single instrument, an effective and comprehensive security upon the entire undertaking of the debtor company and its assets from time to time, while at the same time leaving the company free to deal with its assets and pay its trade creditors in the ordinary course of business without reference to the holder of the charge.[27]

Lord Macnaghten has described the floating charge as:

> an equitable charge on the assets for the time being of a going concern. It attaches to the subject charged in the varying condition in which it happens to

---

[24] *Re Castell & Brown Ltd* [1898] 1 Ch 315 (Ch).
[25] *Garfitt v Allen* (1887) 37 ChD 48 (Ch). Though the chargeholder can apply to the court for an order appointing a receiver to take possession of the charged assets.
[26] *Re Lloyd* [1903] 1 Ch 385 (CA).
[27] *Agnew v Inland Revenue Commissioner* [2001] UKPC 28, [2001] 2 AC 710 [8].

be from time to time. It is of the essence of such a charge that it remains dormant until the undertaking charged ceases to be a going concern, or until the person in whose favour the charge is created intervenes.[28]

In *Re Yorkshire Woolcombers Association Ltd*,[29] Romer LJ identified the three key characteristics of a floating charge:

1. the charge is taken over a class of assets present or future[30] (in practice, it is common for a floating charge to be taken over all the assets and business of the company);

2. that class of assets is one which, in the ordinary course of the company's business, would be changing from time to time (e.g. stock in trade); and

3. until some future step is taken by the chargeholder, the company is free to use the charged assets.[31]

It is this third characteristic that provides the floating charge with its flexibility. The charge floats over the charged assets and, whilst it continues to float, the company is free to deal with the charged assets (e.g. it can sell or lease the charged assets). A more complicated issue is whether the company can grant subsequent charges over the assets covered by the original floating charge that rank ahead of the original floating charge. The courts have stated that such a charge can indeed be created,[32] but the following should be noted:

- A company cannot grant a subsequent floating charge over all the same assets as the original floating charge and have the subsequent floating charge rank ahead of the original charge, unless the terms of the original charge allow for this.[33]

- A subsequent floating charge can be created over part of the assets subject to a prior floating charge.[34] To prevent a subsequent charge having priority over the prior charge, it is common for the prior charge to contain a 'negative pledge clause' that provides that the company will not create any subsequent floating charges over the assets of the prior floating charge that will take priority from the prior floating charge.

- Where the original floating charge is taken over all the assets and business of the company, a subsequent floating charge may also be taken over all the company's assets and business, but the original charge will retain priority.[35]

The flexibility of a floating charge is its key advantage over a fixed charge. Other notable advantages include the fact that debts secured by floating charge rank ahead of unsecured debts and deferred debts, and a qualifying floating chargeholder has the right to appoint an administrator.[36] However, in most other respects, floating charges offer an inferior level of security to a creditor when compared to a fixed charge:

- Upon a company's liquidation, debts secured by floating charge rank behind debts secured by fixed charge, liquidation expenses, and preferential debts. These debts may

---

[28] *Governments Stock and Other Securities Co Ltd v Manila Railway Co Ltd* [1897] AC 81 (HL) 86.

[29] [1903] 2 Ch 284 (CA).

[30] The fact that a floating charge can be taken over future assets means that it is possible to take a floating charge over a class of assets that, at the time the charge is created, does not yet exist (*SAW (SW) 2010 Ltd v Wilson* [2017] EWCA Civ 1001, [2018] 2 WLR 636).

[31] [1903] 2 Ch 284 (CA) 295. Note that he did say that it was possible for a floating charge to be created that did not contain these characteristics.

[32] *Wheatley v Silkstone and Haigh Moor Coal Co* (1885) 29 ChD 715 (Ch).

[33] *Re Benjamin Cope & Sons Ltd* [1914] 1 Ch 800 (Ch).

[34] *Re Automatic Bottle Makers Ltd* [1926] Ch 412 (CA).

[35] *Re Benjamin Cope & Sons Ltd* [1914] 1 Ch 800 (Ch).

[36] IA 1986, Sch B1, para 14 (discussed at 21.1.2.2).

be substantial and may result in the floating chargeholder receiving only a portion of the debt owed to him or he may receive nothing at all. This is compounded by the fact that, even if funds remain in order to pay the debt of the floating chargeholder, a portion of this money must be set aside and used to pay the unsecured creditors.

- As the company is free to use the charged assets, it can 'withdraw all or most of the assets of an insolvent company from the scope of a liquidation and leave the liquidator with little more than an empty shell and unable to pay preferential creditors'.[37]

- A liquidator can set aside certain floating charges, whereas he cannot set aside fixed charges.

- Only incorporated bodies can grant a floating charge—unincorporated bodies (e.g. sole proprietorships, partnerships) cannot.

The setting aside of floating charges is discussed at 23.4.4.

20.3.2.1 Crystallization

In *Illingworth v Illingworth*,[38] Lord Macnaghten stated that the floating charge is 'ambulatory and shifting in its nature, hovering over and so to speak floating with the property which it is intended to affect until some event occurs or some act is done which causes it to settle and fasten on the subject of the charge within its reach and grasp'.[39] Upon the occurrence of this event, the charge becomes a fixed charge (this process has become known as 'crystallization') and fixes on the charged assets that exist at the time the charge crystallizes. At this point, the assets become encumbered in the same way as those subject to a fixed charge, so the company may not dispose of them without the chargeholder's consent.[40]

As the charge is created via contract, it is open to the parties to specify in the charge instrument what events will cause the charge to crystallize. However, the courts have stated that it is an implied term of the instrument that a floating charge will crystallize if the company goes into liquidation,[41] if its business ceases,[42] or if a receiver is appointed,[43] although the parties can expressly provide in the charge instrument that these events will not cause the charge to crystallize.[44] Outside of these instances, the parties are usually free to specify which events will cause crystallization. For example, the charge may provide that crystallization occurs if the company defaults on a loan instalment, or cannot repay an overdraft upon demand. It is increasingly common for the charge instrument to contain a term (known as a 'semi-automatic crystallization clause'), which provides that crystallization will occur upon the chargeholder giving notice of crystallization to the company.[45]

Aside from liquidation and the cessation of the company's business, crystallization will only usually occur if the chargeholder intervenes in some way (e.g. by appointing a receiver or giving notice of crystallization). One question that arose is whether a charge instrument could contain an 'automatic crystallization clause'[46] (i.e. a clause that provides that the charge will automatically crystallize upon some event, without the need

---

[37] *Agnew v Inland Revenue Commissioner* [2001] UKPC 28, [2001] 2 AC 710 [9] (Lord Millett).
[38] [1904] AC 355 (HL).   [39] ibid 358.
[40] *Evans v Rival Granite Quarries Ltd* [1910] 2 KB 979 (CA).
[41] *Re Panama New Zealand and Australian Royal Mail Co* (1870) LR 5 Ch App 318 (CA).
[42] *Re Woodroffes (Musical Instruments) Ltd* [1986] Ch 366 (Ch).
[43] *Re Carshalton Park Estate Ltd* [1908] 2 Ch 62 (Ch).   [44] *Re Real Meat Co Ltd* [1996] BCC 254 (Ch).
[45] *Re Brightlife Ltd* [1987] Ch 200 (Ch).
[46] For more, see Andrew Wilkinson, 'Automatic Crystallisation of Floating Charges' (1987) 8 Co Law 75.

for any intervention by the chargeholder). Such clauses were originally controversial, with the principal criticisms being that a complex automatic crystallization clause could result in the charge crystallizing without the parties knowing, or that the charge could crystallize in circumstances where the chargeholder would prefer the charge to remain uncrystallized.[47] This led the Cork Committee to conclude that 'there is no place for [automatic crystallization clauses] in modern insolvency law'[48] and that those situations when a floating charge would crystallize should be specified in statute and limited to those specified instances.[49] This advice was not acted upon and the courts have now confirmed that automatic crystallization clauses are valid.[50]

20.4 Determining the type of charge

Table 20.3 indicates that there are numerous differences between fixed and floating charges, with each type of charge having its own characteristics and advantages and disadvantages. It is therefore important to be able to distinguish between the two types of charge, but it is not always clear whether a charge is fixed or floating and this ambiguity may be used by a party to try and gain the advantages of both types of charge (typically by creating a charge purporting to be a fixed charge, but operating similar to a floating charge). Accordingly, it is important that the courts have a process in place to determine whether a charge is fixed or floating, with the following case establishing the current approach.

Agnew v Inland Revenue Commissioner [2001] UKPC 28

FACTS: Brumark Investments Ltd ('Brumark') had granted its bank security over its **book debts**. This security was expressed as a fixed and floating charge. The purported fixed charge was taken over Brumark's book debts and their proceeds. However, certain proceeds were excluded from the fixed charge and were instead subject to a floating charge, most notably proceeds of the book debts that were collected by the company before the bank required them to be paid into a specified account with itself. The bank could require uncollected proceeds to be paid into the specified account at any time, but it never did. Accordingly, the company was free to collect the proceeds of the book debts, which would remove them from the scope of the fixed charge. Brumark subsequently went into receivership and a dispute arose regarding the status of the purported fixed charge.

HELD: The two-stage approach to determining the status of a charge was set out by Lord Millett:

> At the first stage [the court] must construe the instrument of charge and seek to gather the intentions of the parties from the language they have used. But the object at this stage of the process is not to discover whether the parties intended to create a fixed or a floating charge. It is to ascertain the nature of the rights and obligations which the parties intended to grant each other in respect of the charged assets. Once these have been ascertained, the Court can then embark on the second stage of the process, which is one of categorisation. This is a

See Alan Berg, 'Brumark Investments Ltd and the "Innominate Charge"' [2001] JBL 532.

➡ **book debts:** sums of money due to a creditor, usually for goods or services supplied or work carried out (discussed at 20.4.1)

---

[47] To a degree, this can be remedied by including a clause in the charge that allows the chargeholder to de-crystallize a crystallized charge (*Covacich v Riordan* [1994] 2 NZLR 502 (New Zealand High Court)).
[48] *Report of the Review Committee on Insolvency Law and Practice* (Cmnd 8558, 1982) para 1579.
[49] ibid para 1580.   [50] *Re Brightlife Ltd* [1987] Ch 200 (Ch).

> matter of law. It does not depend on the intention of the parties. If their intention, properly gathered from the language of the instrument, is to grant the company rights in respect of the charged assets which are inconsistent with the nature of a fixed charge, then the charge cannot be a fixed charge however they may have chosen to describe it.[51]
>
> The key issue was whether 'the company should be free to deal with the charged assets and withdraw them from the security without the consent of the holder of the charge; or, to put the question another way, whether the charged assets were intended to be under the control of the company or of the charge holder'.[52] Here, Brumark was able to collect the proceeds of the book debts and thereby remove them from the scope of the fixed charge (i.e. Brumark was in control of the charged assets). The court stated that this was 'inconsistent with the nature of a fixed charge'[53] and so the purported fixed charge was held to be a floating charge.[54]

From this, it follows that the key factor in determining the type of charge is not whether the charge is expressed as fixed or floating,[55] but the rights and obligations which the parties intended to grant one another based on the language used in the instrument. Where the rights and obligations under the instrument do not match the charge type as described in the charge, then the parties' 'ill-chosen language must yield to the substance'.[56] In many cases, determining the type of charge will not prove a challenge, but one area that has cause the courts some difficulty is where a fixed charge is taken over revolving assets, most notably book debts.

20.4.1 Charges over revolving assets

Fixed charges are best taken over assets that the company does not wish to deal with, such as its business premises or plant and machinery. As the courts have repeatedly noted, the concept of the fixed charge 'does not fit so comfortably in the case of assets which come and go in the normal routine of business operations. It was for assets of that sort that the idea of a floating charge evolved.'[57] However, despite this, the creditor will likely wish for the assets to be secured by a fixed charge because:

> a fixed charge confers the best type of security on a creditor. A floating charge is considerably better than no charge at all, but it is not as good as a fixed charge. Any creditor will want to have a fixed charge if it can. There is therefore every incentive for a creditor to whom a debenture is being issued to express it as creating fixed charges rather than floating charges over as many of the debtor's assets as possible. Further, the creditor tends to have the whip hand in this respect. It puts forward the terms of the debenture, and the debtor is likely to accept them. . . . As long as the creditor takes care so to word the debenture that, if it fails to

---

[51] [2001] UKPC 28, [2001] 2 AC 710 [32].   [52] ibid.   [53] ibid [49].

[54] Most cases in this area involve a purported fixed charge being held to be floating. For an example of a case where a purported floating charge was held to be fixed, see *Russell Cooke Trust Co Ltd v Elliot* [2007] EWHC 1443 (Ch), [2007] 2 BCLC 637.

[55] The instrument's classification of the charge is relevant, but not conclusive (*Street v Mountford* [1985] AC 809 (HL)).

[56] *Orion Finance Ltd v Crown Financial Management Ltd* [1996] BCC 621 (CA) 626 (Millett LJ).

[57] *Re ASRS Establishment Ltd* [2000] 1 BCLC 727 (Ch) 732 (Park J).

create a fixed charge over an asset of the debtor, it succeeds in creating a floating charge . . . there is nothing to be lost by stating that a charge is to be a fixed charge.[58]

The result is that a creditor may attempt to take a fixed charge over revolving assets in order to gain priority in the event of the company's liquidation. However, if the company is wound up, the other creditors (notably preferential creditors who rank behind fixed chargeholders, but ahead of floating chargeholders) may commence proceedings contending that, as the charge is taken over revolving assets, it is more likely to be a floating charge only. A number of such cases have occurred and the majority of them involve a creditor purporting to take a fixed charge over a company's book debts. The Insolvency Service defines book debts as 'sums of money owed to a bankrupt, partnership or company . . . usually for goods or services supplied or work carried out'.[59] Book debts provide an income stream for the company and are therefore a corporate asset over which security can be taken.

Initially, the courts adopted a rather lax approach. In *Siebe Gorman & Co Ltd v Barclays Bank Ltd*,[60] a charge expressed to be fixed was taken over a company's book debts, with the proceeds of the book debts being paid into an account with the chargee bank. Despite the fact that the company was free to use the proceeds paid into this account (and so had control of the charged assets), the court held that the charge remained a fixed charge. Subsequent cases (most notably *Re New Bullas Trading Ltd*)[61] affirmed this position. However, beginning with the case of *Agnew v Inland Revenue Commissioner*,[62] the courts have adopted a much stricter approach to fixed charges taken over book debts and, since then, most cases involving purported fixed charges being taken over book debts have resulted in the charges being classified by the courts as floating. The following case, which overruled *Siebe Gorman* and *New Bullas Trading*, now provides the leading authority in this area and, for the time being, appears to have resolved the issue.

> *Agnew* is discussed at 20.4.

Re Spectrum Plus Ltd [2005] UKHL 41

FACTS: Spectrum Plus Ltd ('Spectrum') obtained an overdraft facility from National Westminster Bank ('Natwest'), which was secured by Natwest taking what was expressed as a 'specific charge' (i.e. a fixed charge) over Spectrum's book debts. The charge provided that Spectrum could not sell, charge, or assign the book debts without Natwest's consent, and that the proceeds of the book debts were to be paid into a specified account that Spectrum held with Natwest. However, Spectrum was free to draw on this account (which it did), providing that the overdraft amount was not exceeded. Spectrum was subsequently voluntarily wound up, owing Natwest £165,407. A number of Spectrum's preferential creditors argued that the charge was a floating charge only, and so their debt ranked ahead of Natwest's. Natwest commenced proceedings, seeking a declaration from the court that the charge was a fixed charge.

> See Richard Nolan, 'A Spectrum of Opinion' (2005) 64 CLJ 554.

---

[58] ibid.

[59] Insolvency Service, 'Book Debts' (November 2008) www.insolvencydirect.bis.gov.uk/casehelpmanual/B/BookDebts.htm accessed 10 January 2019.

[60] [1979] 2 Lloyd's Rep 142 (Ch).   [61] [1994] BCC 36 (CA).

[62] [2001] UKPC 28, [2001] 2 AC 710.

HELD: The House held that it was possible to create a fixed charge over a company's book debts. However:

the essential characteristic of a floating charge, the characteristic that distinguishes it from a fixed charge, is that the asset subject to the charge is not finally appropriated as a security for the payment of the debt until the occurrence of some future event. In the meantime the chargor is left free to use the charged asset and to remove it from the security.[63]

By being able to draw from the bank account into which the book debt proceeds were paid, Spectrum was free to use the charged assets and was free to remove them from the security provided by the charge. Accordingly, the House held that the charge held by Natwest was not a fixed charge, but was a floating charge. As a result, the preferential creditors' debts held priority over Natwest's debt.

COMMENT: The decision in *Spectrum* is unsurprising. In most cases involving purported fixed charges being taken over book debts, the courts held that the charge was in fact a floating charge. However, the House did acknowledge that a fixed charge could be taken over book debts, but to ensure that the charge remains fixed, the assets subject to the security must be preserved for the benefit of the chargee. Lord Hope approved of Worthington's[64] suggestion as to how this could occur:

- the charge could prevent all dealings with the book debts, so they are preserved for the benefit of the chargee's security; or
- the charge could prevent all dealings with the book debts other than their collection, and to require the proceeds when collected to be paid (i) to the chargee directly; or (ii) into an account with the chargee bank (this account must be blocked, so the chargor cannot access the proceeds); or (iii) into a separate account with a third-party bank, which the chargee then takes a fixed charge over.[65]

20.5 Registration of charges

To understand why the registration of charges is so important, consider the following example.

Eg **Registration of charges**

Dragon Goods Ltd ('DG') borrows £50,000 from Welsh Bank plc, and this loan is secured by a fixed charge over DG's factory and its contents. A few months later, DG borrows £30,000 from Cardiff Bank plc, and this loan is secured by a floating charge over the manufacturing equipment belonging to DG (most of which is contained within its factory). Cardiff Bank is not aware of the existence of the charge held by Welsh Bank.

In the event of DG's liquidation or it defaulting on its loan obligations, the fixed charge of Welsh Bank would take priority and could serve to render Cardiff Bank's charge worthless (as Welsh Bank might seize and sell all the assets covered by Cardiff Bank's charge). Accordingly, before taking a charge on any assets, creditors will want to know if those assets are already subject to any form of security.

---

[63] [2005] UKHL 41, [2005] 2 AC 680 [111] (Lord Scott).

[64] Sarah Worthington, 'An "Unsatisfactory Areas of the Law"—Fixed and Floating Charges Yet Again' (2004) 1 ICR 175, 182.

[65] [2005] UKHL 41, [2005] 2 AC 680 [54].

Traditionally, the law's answer to the above problem was to require companies to keep a register of charges (which had to be made available for inspection) and to require charges to be registered at Companies House. The advantages of such a scheme are that 'it provides information on the state of the encumbrances on a company's property to those who may be interested'[66] and 'it assists companies in enabling them to give some form of assurance to potential lenders that their property is unencumbered'.[67]

It is important to note that this registration system underwent a fundamental change in 2013. In order to understand how the 2013 reforms have affected the law relating to registration of charges, it is first important to understand how the pre-2013 system of registration operated.

20.5.1 Registration prior to the 2013 reforms

Since 1862, all companies were required to keep, at their registered office, a register of charges affecting the company's property, which could be inspected by any member or creditor of the company.[68] In 1901, a registration system was introduced, which required companies to register charges with Companies House,[69] and a failure to do so amounted to a criminal offence.[70] This system of registration changed little over the decades, despite significant criticism being levelled at it.[71]

The first major impetus for reform came when the Company Law Review Steering Group (CLRSG) proposed that a new system of registration be introduced, under which the charge itself would not need to be registered, but only specified particulars relating to the charge.[72] However, due to having insufficient time to consult on this new system, the CLRSG recommended that the issue be looked at in more detail by the Law Commission.[73] The Law Commission recommended that such a system should be introduced.[74] However, the responses to a subsequent Department of Trade and Industry (DTI) consultation[75] indicated that further work was required and so this new system was not included within the CA 2006 when first enacted. Instead, the Act merely provided that the Secretary of State could pass regulations that modify the registration system in the CA 2006.[76]

In 2010, the Department for Business, Innovation and Skills (BIS) published a consultation document in which it proposed amending the CA 2006 to introduce a new system of charge registration similar to that recommended by the CLRSG and the Law Commission.[77] This resulted in the passing of the Companies Act 2006 (Amendment of Part 25) Regulations 2013,[78] which repealed large parts of the original Pt 25 and replaced it with ss 859A–859Q, which set out the current system of registration.

---

[66] Law Commission, *Registration of Security Interests: Company Charges and Property Other Then Land* (Law Com CP No 164, 2002) para 2.21.

[67] ibid.   [68] Companies Act 1862, s 43 (now repealed).

[69] Companies Act 1900, s 14 (now repealed).   [70] ibid s 18 (now repealed).

[71] On this, see Peter Graham, 'Registration of Company Charges' [2014] JBL 175, 176–78.

[72] CLRSG, 'Company Law for a Competitive Economy: Final Report: Vol 1' (2001) para 12.20.

[73] ibid para 12.8.   [74] Law Commission, *Company Security Interests* (Law Com No 296, 2005) Part 3.

[75] DTI, 'The Registration of Companies' Security Interests (Company Charges)' (DTI 2005).

[76] CA 2006, s 894.

[77] BIS, 'Registration of Charges Created by Companies and Limited Liability Partnerships: Proposals to Amend the Current Scheme and Relating to Specialist Registers' (BIS 2010).   [78] SI 2013/600.

TABLE 20.4 The registration of charges

	Pre-2013 system	Current system
Charges capable of being registered?	Only those charges specified in statute	All charges, subject to limited exceptions
Company required to keep a register of charges?	Yes	No
Charge must be registered with Companies House?	Yes	No
Criminal sanctions for failure to register?	Yes	No
Company required to keep copies of charge instruments?	Yes	Yes
Charge generally void if not registered?	Yes	Yes

20.5.2 The current system of registration

Before looking at the current registration system in more detail, it is worth noting here the principal similarities and differences between the pre-2013 registration system and the current system, as set out in Table 20.4.

The current system provides increased clarity in terms of which charges can be registered. The pre-2013 registration system applied only to specified charges,[79] but it was not always entirely clear whether a charge came within those specified. Conversely, the current system applies to all charges,[80] subject to a limited number of specific exceptions.[81] Under the current system companies are no longer required to keep a register of charges,[82] although they are required to keep copies of any instrument that creates, varies, or amends a charge.[83] Any creditor or member of the company can inspect these instruments for free, and anyone else can inspect them upon paying a fee.[84]

Companies are also no longer required to register charges with Companies House. Instead, the Act provides that the company or any person interested in the charge *may* register the charge with Companies House.[85] Registration involves the company or any interested person delivering to Companies House a statement of particulars and a certified copy of the charge instrument before the end of the period allowed for delivery.[86] The information required in the statement of particulars is specified in s 859D, and the period allowed for delivery generally begins on the day after the date that the charge was created and lasts for 21 days.[87] The potentially adverse consequence of this is that there will be an 'invisibility' period of up to 21 days where a charge will exist, but will not appear on the register. In such cases, prudent creditors would be advised to contact the company directly to discover if any charges exist that have not yet been registered.

Accordingly, neither the company nor any party interested in the charge is required to register it (although Companies House is required to register the charge if a statement of particulars is delivered to it within the specified period).[88] It might be thought

---

[79] Admittedly, the list of charges specified in the now-repealed s 860(7) covered almost every form of charge.
[80] CA 2006, s 859A(1).   [81] ibid s 859A(6).
[82] Except in relation to charges created before the date the 2013 reforms came into force (i.e. 6 April 2013).
[83] CA 2006, s 859P(1).   [84] ibid s 859Q.   [85] ibid s 859A(2).   [86] ibid s 859A(2) and (3).
[87] ibid s 859A(4). Section 859E provides more detail on the date that a charge is created.
[88] ibid s 859A(2).

that this would result in many charges not being registered, but the consequences of non-registration (namely the 'sanction of invalidity')[89] are so significant that, in practice, companies or chargeholders will feel a strong obligation to register the charge. The next section looks at these consequences, but first looks at the effects of registration.

20.5.3 **The effects of registration and non-registration**

Key to an understanding of the new registration system is an appreciation of the effects of registration and, perhaps more importantly, the effects of not registering a charge.

20.5.3.1 **The effects of registration**

There are four principal effects of registering a charge in accordance with Pt 25. First, the registrar must include in the register of companies the information provided by the person registering the charge.[90] This information is freely accessible online (via the Companies House Service) or by visiting Companies House.

Second, a company must keep a copy of (i) every instrument creating a charge that is capable of registration; and (ii) every instrument effecting any variation or amendment of such a charge.[91] These documents must be kept available for inspection at the company's registered office or single alternative inspection location (SAIL).[92] Any creditor or member of the company can inspect these documents for free, and any other person can inspect them upon payment of a fee.[93]

Third, the registrar must provide a certificate of registration to the person who registered the charge.[94] This certificate provides 'conclusive evidence that the documents required . . . were delivered to the registrar before the end of the relevant period allowed for delivery.'[95] This will even be the case if the particulars delivered to Companies House are incorrect,[96] or if the registrar issues a certificate when they should not have.[97] From this, it follows that the information contained in the register cannot be relied on completely, or as McCormack stated '[t]he moral of the story is that the register signifies only the existence of a registrable charge and not the amount secured or the property covered by the charge.'[98]

Fourth, the Act is silent on the notice that is provided by registering a charge, so the common law rules will likely apply. In *Wilson v Kelland*,[99] Eve J stated that registration amounts to 'constructive notice of the charge . . . but not of any special provisions contained in that charge.'[100] In other words, registration provides notice to the world that the charge exists, but does not provide notice as to its terms. However, it has been argued that this is no longer the position and that, as certain particulars need to be registered in order for registration to be effective, registration of the charge will provide constructive notice of those particulars.[101]

---

[89] CLRSG, 'Company Law for a Competitive Economy: Final Report: Vol 1' (2001) para 12.44.

[90] CA 2006, s 859I(2)(b).

[91] ibid s 859P(1). The use of the word 'capable' indicates that this obligation applies irrespective of whether the charge is registered.

[92] ibid s 859Q(2).   [93] ibid s 859Q(4).   [94] ibid s 859I(3).   [95] ibid s 859I(6).

[96] *National Union and Provincial Bank of England v Charnley* [1924] 1 KB 431 (CA).

[97] *Ali v Top Marques Car Rental Ltd* [2006] EWHC 109 (Ch).

[98] Gerard McCormack, 'Conclusiveness in the Registration of Company Charge Procedure' (1989) 10 Co Law 175, 177.

[99] [1910] 2 Ch 306 (Ch).   [100] ibid 313.

[101] Peter Graham, 'Registration of Company Charges' [2014] JBL 175, 192.

20.5.3.2 The effects of non-registration

If a charge has not been registered within the relevant period, then s 859H provides that two effects follow. First, the charge will be void (so far as any security on the company's property or undertaking is conferred by it) against a liquidator, administrator, or creditor of the company.[102] The following example demonstrates the impact of this.

Eg | **The effect of s 859H**

Dragon Goods Ltd ('DG') owes money to the following:

- £50,000 to Black Sheep Bank, which is secured by way of a fixed charge over a factory owned by DG—this charge has not been registered;
- £30,000 to South Downs Bank, which is secured by a fixed charge over DG's headquarters—this charge has not been registered;
- £40,000 to New Forest Bank, which is secured by fixed charge over DG's headquarters—this charge was created after the charge granted to South Downs Bank and it has been registered.

DG enters administration. As the charge held by Black Sheep Bank is not registered, it is void against the administrator and so he sells the charged asset (the factory) to help satisfy some of DG's debts. This allows DG to leave administration, but its financial problems increase and the company is soon placed into liquidation. Normally, South Downs Bank would enforce its charge, appropriate DG's headquarters and sell it. However, as this charge is unregistered, it is void against a creditor, and so South Downs Bank cannot enforce it. Further, this will allow New Forest Bank to ignore South Downs Bank's unregistered charge[103]—New Forest Bank can appropriate DG's headquarters and sell it to satisfy the debt owed.

Section 859H 'makes void a security; not the debt, not the cause of action, but the security . . .'[104] Accordingly, where s 859H applies, the security afforded by the charge will be invalidated, but the obligation to repay the sum owed will remain. For the following two reasons, s 859H has been described as imposing only 'partial voidness'[105] on the charge:

1. The charge is only void against a liquidator, administrator, or creditor. Accordingly, it is not void against other persons (e.g. the company itself (providing that it is not in administration or in the process of being liquidated),[106] or third parties who are not creditors).

2. The courts have held that s 859H 'leaves the security to stand as against the company while it is a going concern'.[107] Accordingly, the charge will only be rendered void if the company is in liquidation or administration.[108] So, if goods subject to an unregistered charge are seized by the chargeholder prior to the company going into liquidation, then the liquidator will have no claim over those goods upon liquidation.[109]

---

[102] CA 2006, s 859H(3).

[103] As discussed at 20.3.1, charges normally rank by date of creation, so if South Downs Bank's charge had been registered, it would have ranked ahead of the charge held by New Forest Bank (indeed, South Downs Bank's charge, if valid, would likely have prevented any other charges being created over the company's headquarters).

[104] *Re Monolithic Building Company* [1915] 1 Ch 643 (CA) 667 (Phillimore LJ).

[105] Sarah Worthington, *Sealy & Worthington's Text, Cases & Materials in Company Law* (11th edn, OUP 2016) 629.

[106] *Re Monolithic Building Company* [1915] 1 Ch 643 (CA).   [107] ibid 667 (Phillimore LJ).

[108] *Smith v Bridgend County Borough Council* [2001] UKHL 58, [2002] 1 AC 336.

[109] *Re Toomer* (1883) 23 ChD 254 (CA).

Second, the loss of secured status will most notably affect the creditor, and so the Act provides that if a charge becomes void under s 859H, then the money secured by the charge becomes immediately payable.[110]

20.5.3.3 The application for an extension

If a charge has not been registered within the period allowed for delivery, then s 859F allows the company or a person interested in the charge to apply to the court for an order extending the period allowed for delivery. The court will only grant such an extension if:

- the failure to deliver the required documents was accidental or due to inadvertence or some other sufficient cause or is not of a nature to prejudice the position of creditors or shareholders of the company; or
- on other grounds, it is just and equitable to grant relief.[111]

The courts' ability to grant an extension is discretionary and need not be exercised even if the above conditions are met,[112] although it usually is. If the court does order an extension, it may do so 'on such terms and conditions as seem to the court just and expedient'.[113] For example, it is usual practice for the court to provide that the order for extension is to be without prejudice to the rights of the parties acquired during the period between the date of the charge's creation and the date of its actual registration.[114]

20.6 Receivership

Receivership is a mechanism by which a secured creditor (e.g. a fixed or floating charge-holder) can recover payment owed. The usual procedure is that the court or the creditor appoints a receiver, who then takes control of the charged assets and uses them to satisfy the debt of the creditor on whose behalf he was appointed. In practice, receiverships are rare—in 2017/18, only 8 receivers were appointed in the UK.[115]

20.6.1 Appointment of a receiver

A receiver can be appointed in one of two ways. First, the court can appoint a receiver upon an application from a creditor or debenture holder.[116] If the application is successful, the Official Receiver attached to the court will act on behalf of the applicant. Second, the instrument creating the security may confer upon the chargeholder the power to appoint a receiver without the need to apply to the court. The majority of receivers are appointed via this second method.

There are two notable restrictions on who can be appointed as a receiver. A body corporate (that is, a company or limited liability partnership (LLP)) cannot act as a receiver, and if one does so, it will commit an either-way offence.[117] Similarly, an undischarged bankrupt commits an offence if he acts as a receiver, unless the court has appointed him.[118]

---

[110] CA 2006, s 859H(4).   [111] ibid s 859F(2).   [112] See e.g. *Re Telomatic Ltd* [1993] BCC 404 (Ch).
[113] CA 2006, s 859F(3).   [114] *Re Joplin Brewery Co Ltd* [1902] 1 Ch 79 (Ch).
[115] Insolvency Service, 'Insolvency Statistics, July to September 2018 (Q3 2018)' (Insolvency Service 2018) Tables 1a, 9, and 12.
[116] IA 1986, s 32.   [117] ibid s 30.   [118] ibid s 31.

20.6.2 **Role of a receiver**

Where a receiver is appointed by a creditor, then the receiver's principal duty is to the creditor who appointed him and he is free to subordinate the interests of the company, or the other creditors, to those of his client. Where the receiver is appointed by the court, then he is accountable to the court and need not obey the instructions of the creditor who applied to the court for his appointment.

The role of the receiver and the obligations that he owes depend upon the nature of his appointment. Where a person is appointed solely to act as a receiver, his principal duty will be to realize the charged assets and to satisfy the debt of the creditor on whose behalf he has been appointed. He will have power only to deal with the charged assets and will have no general powers of management (in turn, the directors will lose the power to deal with the charged assets if they had such a power). However, it is usual for the instrument creating the security to provide that the receiver will be an agent of the company, and he will therefore be able to enter into contracts and engage in other acts on the company's behalf. It is also common for a person to be appointed as both receiver and manager. In such a case, the person will have the normal powers of a receiver, but will also have a general power to manage the company (and this power displaces that of the directors, although the directors still retain office). As the receiver's powers are limited to the charged assets, however, a general power of management over the company arises only in relation to a floating charge taken over the whole of the undertaking.

20.6.3 **Administrative receivership**

A special form of receiver must be mentioned—namely, an administrative receiver. The office of administrative receiver was created by the Insolvency Act 1985 and has been largely abolished by the Enterprise Act 2002. An administrative receiver is a receiver or manager of the whole (or substantially the whole) of a company's property, who is appointed by or on behalf of the holders of any debentures of the company secured by floating charge.[119] An administrative receiver can be appointed by such a floating chargeholder, but only if the charge was registered before 15 September 2003.[120]

The administrative receiver has the sole right to deal with the charged assets. Given that administrative receivers can only be appointed by chargeholders whose charges relate to the whole (or substantially the whole) of the company's business, this means that administrative receivers usually have considerable powers over the company (to the point where the directors usually cease to manage the company, but remain in office). This is reflected in ss 42–3 and Sch 1 of the IA 1986, which confer extremely broad powers upon administrative receivers.

Administrative receivers are agents of the company[121] and so can engage in acts on the company's behalf but, unlike other agents, administrative receivers are personally liable for any contracts entered into by them in the carrying out of their functions (except in so far as the contract of appointment provides otherwise).[122] Like a normal receiver, an

---

[119] ibid s 29(2)(a).

[120] ibid s 72A; Insolvency Act 1986, Section 72A (Appointed Date) Order 2003, SI 2003/2095, art 2.

[121] IA 1986, s 44(1)(a). The agency ends if the company goes into liquidation.

[122] ibid s 44(1)(b). An administrative receiver can obtain an indemnity from the company in respect of such liability (s 44(1)(c)).

administrative receiver is tasked with realizing the charged assets and satisfying the debt of the floating chargeholder who appointed him. However, certain debts rank ahead of those of floating chargeholders (e.g. preferential debts) and these debts must be paid out of the proceeds of the charged assets before the floating chargeholder can be paid.

Once his task is complete (or if he vacates office for some other reason), the administrative receiver's relationship with that company ends and, if the company has survived, the directors regain their powers (although, in practice, the company usually has few assets left to manage and its liquidation is likely).

CHAPTER SUMMARY

- The principal form of security is a charge, which can be either fixed or floating.
- A fixed charge is taken over a fixed identifiable asset and, in the event of default, it allows the chargeholder to take possession of the charged asset and sell it.
- A floating charge floats over the charged assets and so the company can continue to use and dispose of the charged assets.
- Certain events will cause a floating charge to become fixed on the charged assets, and this is known as 'crystallization'.
- When determining whether a charge is fixed or floating, the courts will focus not how the charge is labelled, but on the rights and obligations which the parties intended to grant each other.
- Fixed charges are best taken over permanent assets (e.g. buildings), whereas floating charges can be taken over revolving assets (e.g. book debts, stock in trade).
- Companies are no longer required to register charges, but a failure to register the charge will render the charge void against a liquidator, administrator, or creditor (i.e. the debt will lose its secured status).

FURTHER READING

Alan Berg, 'The Cuckoo in the Nest of Corporate Insolvency: Some Aspects of the Spectrum Case' [2006] JBL 22.
- Provides an extremely detailed discussion of the case of *Re Spectrum Plus Ltd*.

Andrew Wilkinson, 'Automatic Crystallisation of Floating Charges' (1987) 2 Co Law 75.
- Discusses automatic crystallization clauses and looks at the argument against allowing floating charges to automatically crystallize.

Law Commission, *Registration of Security Interests: Company Charges and Property Other Then Land* (Law Com CP No 164, 2002) and Law Commission, *Company Security Interests* (Law Com No 296, 2005).
- The Law Commission consultation paper and report that led to the 2013 reform of the system of registration of charges.

Louis G Doyle, 'The Residual Status of Directors in Receivership' (1996) 17 Co Law 131.
- Discusses the role and duties of the directors in a company in receivership.

Louise Gullifer and Jennifer Payne, *Corporate Finance Law: Principles and Policy* (Hart 2011) chs 2, 3, and 6.
- Chapter 2 provides a detailed account of the sources of debt capital. Chapter 3 discusses the relationship between equity and debt capital. Chapter 6 looks at the various forms of security.

Peter Graham, 'Registration of Company Charges' [2014] JBL 175.
- Compares the pre-2013 system of registration of charges to the current system. Discusses the advantages and disadvantages of the current system.

SELF-TEST QUESTIONS

1. Define the following terms:

- gearing;
- security;
- debt securities;
- debenture;
- fixed charge;
- floating charge;
- crystallization;
- book debts.

2. State whether each of the following statements is true or false and, if false, explain why:

- A company cannot deal in assets subject to a fixed charge, unless the chargeholder agrees.
- A floating charge cannot be taken over the exact same assets as a prior floating charge, unless the terms of the prior floating charge allow for this.
- Only companies and partnerships can grant floating charges.
- If a charge instrument provides that a charge is fixed or floating, then that categorization will be conclusive.
- It is possible to take a floating charge over revolving assets, such as book debts.
- A company must keep a register of charges.

3. 'The current system providing for the registration of charges is a significant improvement over the pre-201 system of registration.' Discuss this statement.

4. Dragon Technologies Ltd ('DT') is in the business of building personal computers using components that it purchases from third parties. DT's articles provide that 'the company may only borrow amounts in excess of £20,000 if the members so agree by passing a resolution'. DT is experiencing significant financial difficulties and quickly needs an injection if capital if it is to survive. Accordingly, the directors of DT (who also own all DT's shares) apply to Bronze Bank for a loan of £30,000. The bank agrees to the loan, which is granted on the following secured basis:

- the bank acquired a fixed charge over DT's corporate headquarters and this charge was registered with Companies House a month later;
- the bank acquired a charge expressed as a fixed charge over 'all the components used to manufacture personal computers' and this charge was registered with Companies House two days later;
- the bank acquired a floating charge over all the assets of DT, and this charge was registered with Companies House two days later.

It is a condition of the above charges that DT periodically updates Bronze Bank as to DT's financial position. DT's financial position has continued to deteriorate and Bronze Bank seeks your advice regarding the following:

(a) Were the directors of DT empowered to borrow the £30,000 from Bronze Bank?

(b) Discuss the validity and status of the three charges held by Bronze Bank.

(c) Could Bronze Bank appoint an administrator and, if so, what effect would this have on the above charges?

(d) Could Bronze Bank have DT liquidated and, if so, what effect would this have on the above charges and would it have priority over the claims of any other creditors?

ONLINE RESOURCES

This book is accompanied by online resources to better support you in your studies. Visit www.oup.com/uk/roach-company/ for:

- answers to the self-test questions;
- further reading lists;
- multiple-choice questions;
- glossary.

Updates to the law can be found on the author's Twitter account (@UKCompanyLaw) and further resources can be found on the author's blog (www.companylawandgovernance.com).

PART VI
Corporate rescue, restructuring, and insolvency

Part VI is the final part of this text and it focuses on corporate rescue, restructuring, and insolvency. During the course of a company's existence, it may wish to takeover another company, or it may need or wish to reconstruct itself in some way. This reconstruction may be undertaken for commercial advantages, or it may be undertaken in order to try and save a struggling company. Struggling companies can also take advantage of several rescue procedures, provided for by the law. Should the rescue procedure not work, then it may be necessary to bring about the end of the company.

The chapters contained in Part VI are:

CHAPTER 21 CORPORATE RESCUE
This chapter discusses the rationale behind the rescue culture and the two principal rescue mechanisms, namely administration and the company voluntary arrangement.

CHAPTER 22 CORPORATE RECONSTRUCTIONS AND TAKEOVERS
This chapter examines the legal framework that regulates takeovers, as well as discussing corporate reconstruction via a scheme of arrangement and a scheme of reconstruction.

CHAPTER 23 LIQUIDATION, DISSOLUTION, AND RESTORATION
This chapter discusses the different types of liquidation, the powers of a liquidator, and the ways in which a company can be dissolved and restored.

21 Corporate rescue

- Administration
- Company voluntary arrangements
- Proposals for reform

INTRODUCTION

The financial collapse of a company and its subsequent liquidation and dissolution can have a substantial effect on a significant number of persons:

- the company's employees will lose their jobs;
- the company's creditors are unlikely to recover in full the debt owed to them;
- the company's members will lose the value of their investment and their shares will become worthless;
- suppliers that relied on the company may be forced into liquidation;
- retailers that sold the company's goods may be adversely affected;
- tax revenue will be lost;
- if the company is a large national or multinational company, its collapse can adversely affect the local, national or, as the following US example demonstrates, even the worldwide economy.

The collapse of Lehman Brothers Holdings Inc.[1]

In early 2008, Lehman Brothers Holdings Inc. ('Lehman'), then the US's fourth largest investment bank, reported record revenues of nearly $60 billion and its shares were trading at $65 per share. By the 12 September 2008, its share price had fallen by 95 per cent to less than $4 per share and three days later, it filed for bankruptcy, with debts of $613 billion. It remains the largest ever corporate insolvency. Lehman's business was broken up and sold to various parties. The process to liquidate Lehman is still ongoing.

---

[1] For a detailed discussion, see the Report of the Examiner in the Chapter 11 Proceedings of Lehman Brothers, available from https://jenner.com/lehman accessed 10 January 2019.

The collapse of Lehman led to extreme volatility in the US financial markets, with the Dow Jones Index dropping 504 points (the worst drop since the reopening of the market following the 9/11 attack). This had significant impacts on other financial firms, with the notable example being AIG, which would have also collapsed had the US government not provided a $182 billion bailout. To strengthen the financial sector, in October 2008, US Congress approved the Troubled Asset Relief Program, a $700 billion rescue package.[2]

Lehman's collapse had global repercussions too. Events at Lehman intensified the global financial crisis considerably, with commentators stating that Lehman's collapse 'almost brought down the world's financial system'[3] and 'triggered a system-wide crisis of confidence in banks across the globe'.[4] Lehman's clients and parties that had dealings with Lehman sustained significant losses, which in turn had adverse effects on businesses with no direct links to Lehman. Banking sectors around the world were in chaos. In October 2008, concerns regarding the stability of UK banks led to the government announcing a £500 billion rescue package. Countries around the world slid into recession.

One would therefore assume that the law would establish mechanisms designed to help companies in a financially precarious position. However, prior to the passing of the Insolvency Act 1985 and its replacement by the Insolvency Act 1986 (IA 1986), the law did little to help struggling companies, who were basically 'left to die'. The problem is one of balancing interests. The pre-1985 law protected creditors by seeking to ensure that the creditors recovered as much of the money owed to them as possible, but the result of this was invariably that companies were liquidated and dissolved, even where they might have been rescued. Alternatively, one could argue that the law should seek to aid financially vulnerable companies by creating a 'rescue culture',[5] whereby such companies are encouraged to attempt to return to profitability. This balancing of interests was recognized by the Cork Report which stated that one of the aims of insolvency law was:

> to relieve and protect where necessary the insolvent . . . from any harassment and undue demands by his creditors, whilst taking into consideration the rights which the insolvent . . . should legitimately continue to enjoy; at the same time, to have regard to the rights of creditors whose own position may be at risk due to the insolvency.[6]

The Cork Report firmly favoured the fostering of a rescue culture, stating that insolvency law should 'provide means for the preservation of viable commercial enterprises capable of making a useful contribution to the economic life of the country'.[7] The view strongly shaped the Insolvency Acts of 1985 and 1986 which provided for two mechanisms designed to help rescue struggling companies, namely administration and the company voluntary arrangement. The financial

---

[2] This was later reduced to $475 billion by the Dodd-Frank Wall Street Reform and Consumer Protection Act.

[3] 'The Origins of the Financial Crisis: Crash Course', *The Economist* (London, 7 September 2013).

[4] Andrew Clark, 'How the Collapse of Lehman Brothers Pushed Capitalism to the Brink', *The Guardian* (London, 4 September 2009).

[5] For a detailed discussion of the advantages and disadvantages of a rescue culture, see Muir Hunter, 'The Nature and Functions of a Rescue Culture' [1999] JBL 491; Vanessa Finch, *Corporate Insolvency Law: Perspectives and Principles* (2nd edn, CUP 2009) ch 6.

[6] *Report of the Review Committee on Insolvency Law and Practice* (Cmnd 8558, HMSO 1982) para 198.

[7] ibid.

crisis brought with it a renewed focus on the importance of a rescue culture and, in 2014, the European Union (EU) Commission passed a Recommendation which encouraged Member States 'to put in place a framework that enables the efficient restructuring of viable enterprises in financial difficulty and give honest entrepreneurs a second chance . . .'.[8] The key word here is 'viable'—it has long been recognized that not all companies should be the subject of rescue and that '[c]orporate rescue mechanisms are not intended to maintain inefficient firms that are not economically viable . . .'.[9]

The various rescue mechanisms are discussed in this chapter, along with the Insolvency Service's proposals for reforms in this area. The principal rescue mechanism, and the mechanism that has proved most popular, is administration and so it is discussed first.

21.1 Administration

In January 2009, the UK officially entered recession for the first time since 1991. The preceding few months were notable for the unprecedented number[10] of prominent high-street companies (e.g. The Pier, Woolworths, Zavvi, USC, Whittard of Chelsea, and MFI) that went into administration. Even once the recession was over, the continuing difficult economic conditions resulted in many more well-known companies entering administration (e.g. HMV, Blockbuster, Comet, JJB Sports, Peacocks). 2018 was notable for the number of high-street retail companies that went into administration including Coast, Poundworld, Henri Lloyd, House of Fraser, Bench, and Toys 'R' Us. A number of these companies still survive today due to being placed into administration.

Administration was introduced following the recommendations of the Cork Report. This report noted that floating chargeholders often had the right to appoint a receiver who could, if the charge instrument empowered him so, take over the company's management which, in some cases, led to an ailing business returning to profitability, upon which time the receiver relinquishes control to the directors. The report regarded this as 'of outstanding benefit to the general public and to society as a whole'[11] and so recommended that, in a wider range of circumstances, provision should be made to enable to person to appoint an administrator who would be empowered to engage in measures designed to rescue the company. This recommendation was implemented by the Insolvency Act 1985 and re-enacted in Pt II and Sch B1 of the IA 1986. As Figure 21.1 demonstrates, administration is the most popular rescue procedure when compared to company voluntary arrangements.

---

[8] Commission Recommendation 2014/135/EU of 12 March 2014 on a new approach to business failure and insolvency [2014] OJ L74.

[9] Insolvency Service, 'A Review of Company Rescue and Business Reconstruction Mechanisms' (HMSO 2000) para 24. This can be contrasted with the US's Chapter 11 procedure, which is generally available to all.

[10] Figure 21.1 demonstrates clearly an increase in administrator appointments being made in 2009 compared to the years that followed.

[11] *Report of the Review Committee on Insolvency Law and Practice* (Cmnd 8558, HMSO 1982) para 495.

FIGURE 21.1 Rescue procedures in the UK

Source: Statistics derived from the Insolvency Service's Insolvency Statistics, available from www.gov.uk/government/collections/insolvency-service-official-statistics.

Administration also offers potential benefits over liquidation:

- the company may be rescued and can continue contributing to society by providing goods and services, paying tax, taking on employees, etc.;
- administration is likely to be cheaper than liquidation;
- placing the company in administration may allow the company's business to be sold as a going concern for a satisfactory price, rather than a 'fire sale' on liquidation, during which the assets are sold off for whatever price the liquidator can get;
- administration allows a company currently trading profitably, but burdened by debt from past unsuccessful enterprises, to trade on with some form of debt moratorium; and
- if administration is successful, creditors will likely have better prospects of being repaid.

Of course, these benefits are conditional on administration being successful, and so it is important to consider what the purpose of administration is.

21.1.1 The purpose of administration

Administration is likely the most pro-rescue procedure found in the IA 1986, as demonstrated by the hierarchy of three objectives (as set out in Figure 21.2) that are collectively referred to as 'the purpose of administration'.[12]

This seemingly strict hierarchy of objectives is not so strict in practice as much is based on the professional judgement of the administrator (e.g. whether objectives (b) or (c) are pursued depends in part on what the administrator 'thinks' is reasonably

---

[12] IA 1986, Sch B1, para 3.

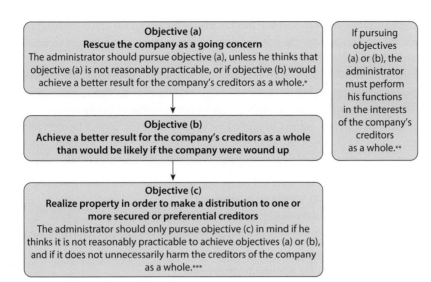

FIGURE 21.2 The purpose of administration

*IA 1986, Sch B1, para 3(3). ** IA 1986, Sch B1, para 3(2). *** IA 1986, Sch B1, para 3(4).

practicable). This allows the administrator to quite easily depart from objective (a) which is rarely pursued in practice (although it should remain the first objective considered). The most common outcome of administration is that the business of the company is sold to a third party and the company is then liquidated and dissolved (this outcome would fall within objective (b)). This demonstrates that administrators distinguish between (i) rescuing the business of the company; and (ii) rescuing the company itself (a distinction that the IA 1986 itself does not make). From this, it follows that, in practice, it is only objective (a) that is concerned with rescuing the company, whereas objectives (b) and (c) focus more on rescuing the business.[13] From this, Frisby has contended that rescuing the corporate entity can be thought of as a 'pure rescue', whereas rescuing the business is more accurately thought of as a form of 'corporate recycling'.[14]

21.1.2 Appointment of an administrator

Upon the appointment of an administrator, the company is said to 'enter administration' and will remain 'in administration' until such time as the administrator's appointment ceases.[15] The IA 1986 provides that an administrator can be appointed in three different ways:[16]

1. by an administration order of the court;
2. by the holder of a qualifying floating charge; or
3. by the company or its directors.

Accordingly, the first method requires a court order, whilst the other two methods are out-of-court procedures. Companies tend to prefer the out-of-court procedures as they

---

[13] John M Wood, 'The Objectives of Administration' (2015) 36 Co Law 1, 6.
[14] Sandra Frisby, 'In Search of a Rescue Regime: The Enterprise Act 2002' (2004) 67 MLR 247, 248–9.
[15] IA 1986, Sch B1, para 1(2).   [16] ibid Sch B1, para 2.

are cheaper, easier, quicker, and will involve less publicity, but the court procedure does have some advantages over the out-of-court procedures that might make it more useful in certain circumstances.

Each of these three methods of appointment is subject to limitations specific to each method of appointment, but there are several general restrictions that apply to all methods of appointment. First, only a qualified insolvency practitioner can be appointed as an administrator.[17] Second, subject to limited exceptions, a person cannot be appointed as administrator of a company that is already in administration.[18] Third, a person cannot be appointed as administrator of a company that is in liquidation, subject to two exceptions:

1. where the company is subject to a compulsory winding-up order, then a qualifying floating chargeholder may appoint an administrator;[19]

2. the liquidator may make an administration application.[20]

Each method of appointment will now be discussed.

21.1.2.1 Appointment by administration order

An administrator can be appointed by the court making an administration order.[21] This will require an administration application to be made to the court, but only certain persons have standing to bring an application, including:

- the company, its directors, or one or more creditors of the company (or any combination of these persons);[22]
- the supervisor of a company voluntary arrangement (CVA);[23]
- the liquidator of the company;[24]
- the Financial Conduct Authority (FCA).[25]

Upon receipt of an application, the court may make an administration order if two conditions are satisfied,[26] namely:

1. The company is or is likely to become unable to pay its debts.[27] The word 'likely' has been interpreted to mean that the applicant must show that it is 'more probable than not'[28] that the company will become unable to pay its debts.

2. The administration order is reasonably likely to achieve the purpose of administration. Here, the word 'likely' requires the applicant to demonstrate that there is a 'real prospect that the administration order will achieve its purpose'.[29]

Note that as the IA 1986 states that the court 'may' make an administration order, it follows that, even if the above two conditions are met, the court may still refuse to make an administration order. Upon hearing an administration application, the court may:

- make the administration order sought;
- dismiss the application;

---

[17] ibid Sch B1, para 6.   [18] ibid Sch B1, para 7.

[19] ibid Sch B1, para 37.   [20] ibid Sch B1, para 38(1).   [21] ibid Sch B1, para 10.

[22] ibid Sch B1, para 12(1).   [23] ibid Sch B1, para 12(1) and s 7(4)(b).   [24] ibid Sch B1, para 38(1).

[25] Financial Services and Markets Act 2000 (FSMA 2000), s 359(1).

[26] IA 1986, Sch B1, para 11.

[27] Ths condition need not be satisfied if the applicant could appoint an administrator by virtue of being a qualifying floating chargeholder (IA 1986, Sch B1, para 35).

[28] *Re AA Mutual International Insurance Co Ltd* [2004] EWHC 2430 (Ch), [2005] 2 BCLC 8 [21] (Lewison J).

[29] ibid.

- adjourn the hearing;
- make an interim order;
- treat the application as a winding-up petition and make any order it could make under s 125; or
- make any other order which the court thinks appropriate.[30]

21.1.2.2 Appointment by qualifying floating chargeholder

Under Sch B1, para 14, the holder of a 'qualifying floating charge' in respect of the company's property may appoint an administrator. A floating charge will be qualifying if (i) it alone, or in combination with any other forms of security, covers the whole or substantially the whole of the company's property;[31] and (ii) the instrument which created the charge:

- states that para 14 applies to the charge; or
- purports to empower the holder to appoint an administrator; or
- purports to empower the holder to appoint an administrative receiver.[32]

This power of appointment is subject to three limitations. First, no appointment can be made unless the floating chargeholder has given at least two business days' written notice to any holder of a prior qualifying floating charge, or the holder of any prior qualifying floating charge has consented to the making of the appointment.[33] Second, a floating chargeholder cannot appoint an administrator while his charge is unenforceable[34] (e.g. because it was avoided under s 245). Third, an administrator cannot be appointed if a provisional liquidator of the company has been appointed, or an administrative receiver of the company is in office.[35]

Section 245 is discussed at 23.4.4.

21.1.2.3 Appointment by the company or directors

Schedule B1, para 22 provides that an administrator may be appointed by the company or its directors. In practice, appointment by the directors[36] is more common as appointment by the company generally requires the members to pass an ordinary resolution (unless the company's articles empower the board to appoint an administrator on behalf of the company). The ability of the company or directors to appoint an administrator is subject to several limitations:

- an administrator cannot be appointed within 12 months of (i) the ending of a previous administration initiated under para 22;[37] or (ii) the ending of a moratorium under Sch A1 which failed to result in a voluntary arrangement being in force;[38]
- an administrator cannot be appointed if (i) a petition to wind up the company has been presented and has not yet been disposed of; (ii) an administrative application has been made and is not yet disposed of; or (iii) an administrative receiver of the company is in office.[39]

The company or directors must give at least five business days' written notice to qualifying floating chargeholders and any person who is or may be entitled to appoint an

---

[30] IA 1986, Sch B1, para 13(1).

[31] ibid Sch B1, para 14(3).   [32] ibid Sch B1, para 14(2).

[33] ibid Sch B1, para 15(1). A floating charge is prior to another if it was created first or is treated as having priority (Sch B1, para 15(2)). The contents of this notice are specified in r 3.16 of the Insolvency (England and Wales) Rules 2016.

[34] IA 1986, Sch B1, para 16.   [35] ibid Sch B1, para 17.

[36] In such a case, a majority of the directors must agree to the appointment (IA 1986, Sch B1, para 105).

[37] IA 1986, Sch B1, para 23(2).   [38] ibid Sch B1, para 24.   [39] ibid Sch B1, para 25.

administrative receiver.[40] This notice must identify the proposed administrator and it must be filed with the court, along with a statutory declaration stating, *inter alia*, that the company is unable or is unlikely to be able to pay its debts, and that the company is not in liquidation.[41] A notice of appointment must also be filed with the court.[42] Once these notices have been filed, the appointment of the administrator takes effect.[43]

21.1.3 Effects of administration

A company entering administration results in several potentially beneficial effects, which are designed to enable the administrator to better pursue the purpose of administration.

21.1.3.1 Dismissal of winding-up petitions and receivers

The purpose of administration could not be achieved if persons were free to wind up a company in administration. Accordingly, if a winding-up petition has been sought against a company, then that petition shall be dismissed if an administration order is made, and shall be suspended if an administrator is appointed by a qualifying floating chargeholder.[44] This means that the appointment of an administrator can be used to fend off the liquidation of a company, as the following example demonstrates.

Portsmouth Football Club and administration

Portsmouth City Football Club Ltd ('Portsmouth FC') first entered administration in 1998 and was rescued following a takeover deal. In 2009, it again experienced severe financial difficulties and was unable to pay tax as it was due, resulting in Her Majesty's Revenue and Customs (HMRC) filing a winding-up petition in December 2009. In February 2010, prior to the winding-up petition being heard, Portpin Ltd (a qualifying floating chargeholder) appointed an administrator. This caused HMRC's winding up petition to be suspended and it was withdrawn in March. The administrator proposed that a CVA be entered into and the administrator be authorized to sell Portsmouth FC's assets. The CVA was approved[45] and, in October 2010, the business and its assets were sold to a new company, Portsmouth Football Club (2010) Ltd. Portsmouth FC left administration in February 2011 and was later dissolved.

In January 2012, HMRC launched a winding-up petition against Portsmouth Football Club (2010) Ltd for unpaid tax, but a qualifying floating chargeholder again appointed an administrator and the company entered administration. HMRC once again withdrew its winding-up petition. In April 2013, Portsmouth Football Club (2010) left administration and its assets were sold to Portsmouth Community Football Club Ltd, which is primarily owned by the Pompey Supporters Trust.[46] In September 2014, the Trust announced that the club was debt-free and had paid off its creditors.

---

[40] ibid Sch B1, para 26. The contents of this notice are specified in r 3.23 of the Insolvency (England and Wales) Rules 2016.

[41] IA 1986, Sch B1, para 27.   [42] ibid Sch B1, para 29.   [43] ibid Sch B1, para 31.

[44] ibid Sch B1, para 40(1). This will not apply to a public interest petition (Sch B1, para 40(2)(a)).

[45] Under the terms of the CVA, HMRC would not have received the full amount owed to it and it sought a court order suspending the CVA, but this was rejected (*HMRC v Portsmouth City Football Club Ltd* [2010] EWHC 2013 (Ch), [2011] BCC 149).

[46] The Pompey Supporters Trust is a trust consisting of fans of Portsmouth FC who contributed money to enable the Trust to purchase the club.

When a company enters administration (irrespective of how he is appointed), then any receiver shall vacate office if the administrator requires him to.[47] When an administration order takes effect, then any administrative receiver shall vacate office.[48]

21.1.3.2 Effects on directors

A company entering administration does not automatically result in the directors ceasing to hold office (although the administrator is empowered to appoint and remove directors).[49] Accordingly, the directors remain subject to any statutory obligations and duties (e.g. the general duties). However, the IA 1986 provides that an officer of a company in administration may not exercise a management power without the consent of the administrator.[50] The result of this is that, for the duration of the administration, the powers of the directors are effectively suspended.

An administrator is also empowered to bring proceedings on behalf of the company,[51] which can include bringing proceedings against the directors (e.g. if the administrator believes that the directors have engaged in fraudulent trading[52] or wrongful trading).[53]

21.1.3.3 The moratorium

Perhaps the most beneficial aspect of administration is the imposition of the statutory moratorium. The purpose of administration (especially objective (a)) would be frustrated if the company's creditors were able to enforce their security during administration, or if creditors could petition for the company's winding up. Accordingly, unless permission has been obtained from the administrator or the court, no creditor may during the period of the administration:

- take steps to enforce security over the company's property;
- take steps to repossess goods in the company's possession under a hire-purchase agreement; or
- institute or continue any legal process (including legal proceedings, execution, and distress) against the company or property of the company.[54]

In addition, during the period of administration, (i) a resolution cannot be made to wind the company up, nor can a compulsory winding up be ordered;[55] and (ii) an administrative receiver cannot be appointed.[56] The rationale behind the moratorium is clear: it grants the company vital breathing space, and allows the administrator to put his proposals into effect and enter into arrangements with the creditors, with the aim of rescuing the company. However, this moratorium only applies to companies in administration and so a financially struggling company is still vulnerable prior to the company formally entering administration. To combat this, the IA 1986 provides for an interim moratorium which applies:

- where an application for an administration order has been made, the interim moratorium commences when the application has not yet been granted or dismissed, or where the application has been granted but the administration has not yet taken effect;[57]

---

[47] IA 1986, Sch B1, para 41(1).   [48] ibid Sch B1, para 41(2).
[49] ibid Sch B1, para 61.   [50] ibid Sch B1, para 64(1).   [51] ibid Sch 1, para 5.
[52] ibid s 246ZA.   [53] ibid s 246ZB.   [54] ibid Sch B1, para 43.
[55] ibid Sch B1, para 42. Note that there are exceptions to this (e.g. a public interest winding-up petition can be brought).
[56] ibid Sch B1, para 43(6A).   [57] ibid Sch B1, para 44(1).

- where a qualifying floating chargeholder files notice of an intention to appoint an administrator, then the interim moratorium commences when the notice is filed and expires upon the appointment of the administrator taking effect, or five business days after the filing of the notice without an administrator being appointed.[58]

21.1.3.4 **Publicity**

It is important that persons who deal with a company in administration are aware of this. Accordingly, while a company is in administration, every business document issued by or on behalf of the company or the administrator, and all the company's websites, must state the name of the administrator and that the affairs, business, and property of the company are being managed by the administrator.[59] Failure to comply with this requirement constitutes a criminal offence.[60]

21.1.4 **The proposals**

Upon appointment, the administrator's principal task is to determine how best to achieve the purpose of administration. Accordingly, within eight weeks following his appointment, the administrator must prepare proposals for achieving the purpose of administration and send them to the registrar of companies, and every member and creditor of whose address he is aware.[61]

Within 10 weeks of the company entering into administration, the administrator must seek a decision from the creditors as to whether they approve the proposals,[62] although Sch B1, para 52(1) provides several instances where a decision of the creditors need not be sought (e.g. where the company has sufficient property to enable each creditor to be paid in full). Historically, decisions by creditors had to be taken at a meeting of the creditors, but the Small Business, Enterprise and Employment Act 2015 (SBEEA 2015) abolished this requirement[63] and the creditors' decision can now be taken by using one of two decision-making methods:

- the qualifying decision procedure, can be used with the details of this procedure (e.g. how the result of the decision is determined) to be decided by the administrator;[64] or
- the 'deemed consent procedure' can be used, under which the proposal will be approved unless 10 per cent of the creditors in value object to the proposal.[65] If such a percentage does object, then the decision will not be deemed to have been made and, if a decision on the same matter is sought again, it must be sought using a qualifying decision procedure.[66]

Two outcomes can follow based on whether approval is obtained or not:

- The creditors approve the proposals without modification, or approve them with modifications (providing the administrator consents to the modifications).[67] Once approved, the administrator must manage the affairs of the company in accordance with the approved proposals.[68] Following approval, if the administrator wishes to revise the proposals, then a creditors' meeting will need to be summoned to approve the revised proposals.[69]

---

[58] ibid Sch B1, para 44(2). [59] ibid Sch B1, para 45(1). [60] ibid Sch B1, para 45(2).
[61] ibid Sch B1, para 49. Under Sch B1, para 107, this eight-week period can be extended by the court following an application by the administrator.
[62] ibid Sch B1, para 51. Under Sch B1, para 107, this 10-week period can be extended by the court following an application by the administrator.
[63] Although s 246ZE of the IA 1986 empowers the creditors to summon a creditors' meeting, providing that those creditors represent at least 10 per cent in value or number of the creditors, or there are 10 of them.
[64] IA 1986, s 246ZE(2). [65] ibid s 246ZF. [66] ibid 246ZF(5). [67] ibid Sch B1, para 53(1).
[68] ibid Sch B1, para 68(1). [69] ibid Sch B1, para 54.

- The creditors do not approve the proposals, in which case the court may (i) terminate the administrator's appointment; (ii) adjourn the hearing conditionally or unconditionally; (iii) make an interim order; (iv) make an order on a petition for winding up; or (iv) make any other order that it thinks appropriate.[70]

21.1.5 **Powers of an administrator**

An administrator is an officer[71] and agent[72] of the company and is granted extensive powers, being able to 'do anything necessary or expedient for the management of the affairs, business and property of the company'.[73] Schedule B1, para 60(1) provides that the administrator also has the powers listed in Sch 1, which provides a list of 23 powers, including the power to:

- take possession of, collect, and get in the property of the company, and, for that purpose, to take such proceedings as may seem to him expedient;
- sell or otherwise dispose of the property of the company by public auction or private contract;
- raise or borrow money and grant security over the company's property;
- bring or defend any action or other legal proceedings in the name and on behalf of the company;
- appoint agents and appoint and dismiss employees;
- make any payment that is necessary or incidental to the performance of his functions;
- carry on the business of the company and establish subsidiaries of the company;
- present or defend a petition for the winding up of the company.

Further powers are listed in Sch B1, including the power to appoint and remove directors, call a meeting of the members, and seek a decision on any matter from the company's creditors.[74] It should be noted that as the administrator can do 'anything necessary or expedient for the management of the affairs, business and property of the company', the powers listed in Schs 1 and B1 should not be regarded as exhaustive.

21.1.5.1 **Pre-packs**

The above powers of an administrator can be exercised as soon as the administrator is appointed, meaning that an administrator can exercise these powers prior to his proposals being approved. The cause for concern that has arisen here is that this allows the administrator to sell the assets of the company without the creditor's consent which may, depending on the terms of the sale, adversely affect the creditors' chances of being repaid. The courts are aware of this concern and have stated that an administrator can sell the company's assets prior to his proposals being approved if he believes the sale to be in the best interests of the creditors.[75] This allows for a pre-packaged administration (or 'pre-packs' as they are known), which has been defined as 'an arrangement under which the sale of all or part of a company's business or assets is negotiated with a purchaser prior to the appointment of an administrator and the administrator effects the sale immediately on, or shortly after, appointment'.[76] The following provides an example of such a pre-pack.

---

[70] ibid Sch B1, para 55(2).   [71] ibid Sch B1, para 5.   [72] ibid Sch B1, para 69.
[73] ibid Sch B1, para 59(1).   [74] ibid Sch B1, paras 61–3.
[75] *Re Transbus International Ltd* [2004] EWHC 932 (Ch), [2004] 1 WLR 2654.
[76] Statement of Insolvency Practice 16, para 1.

The pre-pack of Dreams Ltd

Founded in 1985, Dreams Ltd is the UK's largest specialist bed retailer. In 2013, the company was experiencing severe financial difficulties and was unable to pay its debts. It was placed into administration on the 5 March 2013, but was sold the next day to Sun Capital Partners as part of a pre-pack deal under which Sun Capital paid £35 million for 171 of Dreams' 266 stores (the remaining 95 stores were Dreams' least profitable, and remained open for business whilst the administrator looked for a buyer). As a result of the pre-pack, the company was saved from almost certain liquidation, customer orders were honoured, and nearly 1,700 employees kept their jobs. In addition, Dreams' creditors were paid 75 per cent of the debts owed to them (considerably more than they would have received had the company been liquidated).

The success of the pre-pack is evident in that Dreams was subsequently able to pay off all its debts, its turnover increased significantly, and its profits trebled. Sun Capital is now looking to sell the company for £400 million.

A clear advantage of pre-packs is speed. They allow for the details of the rescue to be negotiated prior to administration, and then put into effect quickly (as evidenced by the one day that Dreams Ltd spent in administration), thereby helping to keep the costs of administration low. Finch argues that this speed is:

> particularly valuable in sectors or businesses where a protracted, public restructuring would dramatically affect corporate value—as, for instance, in a regulated sector (where possibilities of retaining licences, franchises and other valued positions may be affected) or where a business is built on human rather than physical assets (where there are dangers that the best staff will be lost to competitors), or where a brand or portfolio would be damaged by adverse publicity or public uncertainty.[77]

The concern, however, is that this speedy implementation 'will tend to ride roughshod over the procedural and substantive interests of less powerful creditors'[78] and that '[t]he speed and secrecy of the operation often lead to a deal being executed about which the unsecured creditors know nothing, have no say in and which leaves them empty handed'.[79] One notable concern arises where the buyers of the company's assets are its former directors or owners. In such a case, the business may be able to continue with minimal interruption whilst maintaining the goodwill generated by the business, but the fact that the original directors or owners are running the company means that the company is effectively **phoenixed**. The response to such concerns is a strong judicial reaffirmation that a pre-pack should only be effected if it is in the interests of the company's creditors.[80] In addition, the Insolvency Service and the regulatory bodies for insolvency practitioners met to discuss how to best regulate pre-packs. The result was the publication of Statement of Insolvency Practice 16, which provides that the administrator

➡️ **Phoenix company**: a company with the same (or very similar) name to a company that has been liquidated, and which was set up by the directors of the liquidated company (discussed at 23.3.5)

---

[77] Vanessa Finch, 'Pre-Packaged Administrations: Bargains in the Shadow of Insolvency or Shadowy Bargains?' [2006] JBL 568, 571.

[78] ibid 568.

[79] Peter Walton, 'When is Pre-Packaged Administration Appropriate?—A Theoretical Consideration' (2011) 20 Nott LJ 1, 3.

[80] See e.g. *DKLL Solicitors v Revenue and Customs Commissioners* [2007] EWHC 2067 (Ch), [2007] BCC 908; *Re Kaley Vending Ltd* [2009] EWHC 904 (Ch), [2009] BCC 578.

must provide creditors with sufficient information (known as the 'SIP 16 statement') that would enable a reasonable and informed third party to conclude that the pre-pack was appropriate and that the administrator had acted with due regard for the creditors' interests. The administrator will need to justify why the pre-pack was undertaken and what alternatives were considered.

Despite SIP 16, concerns still exist regarding the potential for pre-packs to be abused, which has resulted in two further developments:

- The SBEEA 2015 amended the IA 1986 to empower the Secretary of State to pass regulations enabling him to prohibit pre-packs, or impose requirements or conditions upon pre-packs.[81] To date, no such regulations have been passed.

- The Graham Review recommended the creation of a 'Pre-Pack Pool'[82] and this was established in November 2015.[83] The Pool is an independent body of experienced businesspersons. Parties involved in a proposed pre-pack may apply to the Pool and a member of the Pool will review the proposed pre-pack and offer an opinion on its reasonableness. Note that the scheme is entirely voluntary and the Pool's opinion carries no legal weight.

21.1.6 Termination of administration

An administrator's appointment can be terminated in numerous ways. There is one form of automatic termination, namely that the administrator's appointment automatically terminates one year after he was appointed.[84] However, this period can be extended in two ways:

1. The administrator can apply to the court for an extension.[85] The court can grant as many extensions as it wishes for as long as it wishes, but it cannot grant an extension after the administrator's period in office has expired.[86]

2. The administrator's term of office can be extended by up to one year by consent.[87] Consent is required from each secured creditor, and (if the company has any) from the unsecured creditors.[88] Note that this method of extension can only be used once.[89]

In all other cases, the termination of administration is not automatic and requires some form of action:

- Following an application from the administrator, the court can terminate an administrator's appointment,[90] but only if the administrator thinks that (i) the purpose of administration cannot be achieved; (ii) the company should not have entered administration; or (iii) the company's creditors decide that the administrator should apply for a termination of his appointment.[91]

- Where an administrator is appointed by a qualifying floating chargeholder, the company, or its directors, then if the administrator thinks that the purpose of administration has been fulfilled, he may file a notice with the court and with Companies House, which will terminate his appointment.[92]

- A creditor can apply to the court for an order terminating the administrator's appointment on the ground that the person who appointed him or applied for an administration order did so for an improper motive.[93]

---

[81] IA 1986, Sch B1, para 60A.

[82] Teresa Graham, 'Graham Review into Pre-Pack Administration' (2014) para 9.1, available from www.gov.uk/government/publications/graham-review-into-pre-pack-administration accessed 10 January 2019.

[83] See www.prepackpool.co.uk accessed 10 January 2019.   [84] IA 1986, Sch B1, para 76(1).

[85] ibid Sch B1, para 76(2)(a).   [86] ibid Sch B1, para 77(1).   [87] ibid Sch B1, para 76(2)(b).

[88] ibid Sch B1, para 78(1).   [89] ibid Sch B1, para 78(4)(a).   [90] ibid Sch B1, para 79(1).

[91] ibid Sch B1, para 79(2).   [92] ibid Sch B1, para 80.   [93] ibid Sch B1, para 81.

- If a company in administration is subject to a winding-up petition on public interest grounds, the court will usually order that the administrator's appointment will cease, although it may also provide that the appointment will continue.[94]

- The administrator's appointment will cease if he sends notice to the registrar of Companies House indicating that he intends to place the company into a creditors' voluntary liquidation,[95] or that he intends to dissolve it.[96]

21.2 Company voluntary arrangements

The CVA is an important, but not very popular,[97] rescue procedure that basically allows a company to enter into a binding arrangement with its creditors. As a CVA is an insolvency procedure, it is usually invoked by insolvent companies and can result in turning around a company's fortunes if the underlying business is sound and if the CVA is carefully structured, as the following example demonstrates (this example also demonstrates how, in some cases, a CVA can be preferable to administration).

Travelodge and the CVA

Travelodge Hotels Ltd operates one of the largest hotel chains in the UK. In 2012, the company had debts of £500 million and, despite reasonable financial performance, it was unable to keep up with interest payments on those debts (which amounted to around £100 million per year). Accordingly, in August 2012, the company proposed a CVA which provided that Travelodge would pay reduced rent on 109 of the 500 hotels it leased,[98] and 49 hotels that it leased would be offloaded onto other operators. In conjunction with the CVA, the company and three of its largest creditors agreed to a financial restructuring of the company under which, in return for obtaining control of the company, these creditors would inject £75 million into the company and write off £709 million of the company's debt. KPMG (who supervised the CVA) stated that if the company was put into administration, the unsecured creditors could expect to receive 0.2 per cent of the debt owed to them, but under the CVA, the debt they would recover would be 23.4 per cent.

The CVA was approved by 97 per cent of the company's creditors and 96 per cent of the hotel's landlords, and was put into effect in September 2012. £55 million of the £75 million injection was used to refurbish the company's hotels. Over the course of the next five years, the company's financial performance was turned around, with significant increases in turnover and profits. In 2016, the company announced it was opening 19 new hotels. The creditors who obtained control of the company put the company up for sale in 2015 for £1 billion, but these plans were suspended in 2016.

---

[94] ibid Sch B1, para 82.   [95] ibid Sch B1, para 83.   [96] ibid Sch B1, para 84.

[97] Although, recently, a notable number of well-known high-street retailers have used a CVA in an attempt to rescue their business (e.g. Toys 'R' Us, House of Fraser, Mothercare, Prezzo, Carluccio's, Jamie's Italian, Carpetright).

[98] Travelodge operates a leasehold business model under which the vast majority of the hotels it operates are not owned by Travelodge, but leased from landlords. Catherine KY Wong, 'Will Company Voluntary Arrangements Play a Significant Role in the UK's Rescue Culture?' (2017) 38 Co Law 122, 122–3 argues that CVAs may have more of a role to play in retail businesses, as such businesses are generally reliant on leased properties (as is the case with Travelodge).

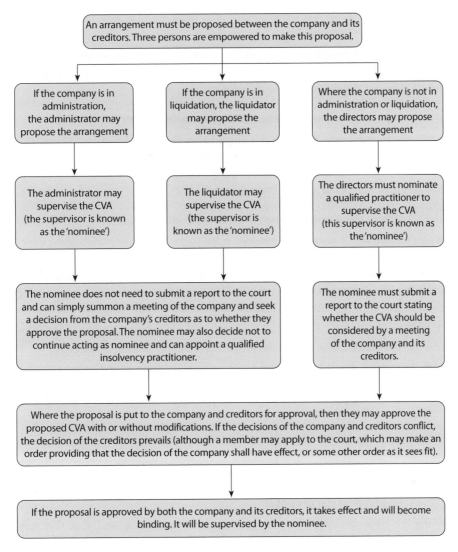

FIGURE 21.3 The CVA process

Although the CVA was technically introduced by the IA 1985, the provisions of that Act relating to CVAs never actually came into force, and the key provisions today are found in Pt I (namely ss 1–7B) and Sch A1 of the IA 1986. The procedures for putting a CVA into place will now be discussed, but Figure 21.3 sets out the process.

21.2.1 Proposal of a CVA

The first step in entering into a CVA is the proposal of an arrangement between the company and its creditors. Three persons are empowered to propose such an arrangement:

1. Where the company is in administration, the administrator may propose the arrangement.[99]
2. Where the company is being wound up, the liquidator may propose the arrangement.[100]

---

[99] IA 1986, s 1(3)(a).   [100] ibid s 1(3)(b).

3. Where the company is not in administration or being wound up, then the directors may propose the arrangement.[101]

The proposal must provide for some person (known as the 'nominee') who will supervise the CVA, and this person must be a qualified insolvency practitioner.[102] The procedure that follows depends upon who the nominee is.

21.2.1.1 Where the nominee is the administrator/liquidator

Where the company is in administration/liquidation, then the administrator/liquidator (as applicable) can act as nominee (although they can choose not to). Here, the nominee shall simply summon a meeting of the company and seek a decision from the company's creditors as to whether to approve the proposal.[103]

21.2.1.2 Where the nominee is not the administrator/liquidator

Where the nominee is not an administrator or liquidator (which occurs where the directors proposed the CVA, or the administrator/liquidator decided not to act as nominee) and the directors are not seeking a moratorium, then a qualified insolvency practitioner will have to be appointed to act as nominee. That nominee must, within 28 days of being given notice of the proposed CVA, submit a report to the court stating whether in his opinion:

- the proposed CVA has a reasonable prospect of being approved and implemented;
- the proposal should be considered by a meeting of the company and by the company's creditors; and
- if it should, the date on which, and time and place at which, he proposes a meeting of the company should be held.[104]

If the nominee reports that the proposal should be considered by a meeting of the company and by the company's creditors, he should summon a meeting of the company and seek a decision from the company's creditors.[105]

21.2.1.3 Approval of the proposal

Where the proposal is put to the company and creditors for approval, then they may approve the proposed CVA with or without modifications.[106] Neither the company nor its creditors can approve a proposal or modification if it (i) affects the right of a secured creditor of the company to enforce his security, except with the concurrence of the creditor concerned;[107] or (ii) affects the priority of any preferential debt, unless the preferential creditor concerned concurs.[108] As a result of (i), most secured creditors do not join CVA plans, meaning that companies usually need to engage in separate negotiations with each secured creditor, which often increases the cost and duration of the rescue process.[109]

Approval is obtained as follows:

- At the meeting of the company, approval is granted if a majority (in value) of the members vote in favour of approving the proposal.[110]

---

[101] ibid s 1(1).   [102] ibid s 1(2).   [103] ibid s 3(2).   [104] ibid s 2(2).
[105] ibid s 3(1).   [106] ibid s 4(1).   [107] ibid s 4(3).   [108] ibid s 4(4).
[109] Insolvency Service, 'A Review of the Corporate Insolvency Framework: A Consultation on Options for Reform' (Insolvency Service 2016) paras 9.3–9.4.
[110] Insolvency (England and Wales) Rules 2016, r 2.36(1).

- The creditors will decide if they approve of the proposal by way of a qualifying decision procedure,[111] with the details of this procedure (e.g. how the result of the decision is determined) to be decided by the nominee.[112] Alternatively, the 'deemed consent procedure' can be used, under which the proposal will be approved unless 10 per cent of the creditors in value object to the proposal.[113]

The decisions of the members and the creditors must be reported to the court.[114] If the decisions of the members and the creditors conflict, then the decision of the creditors prevails,[115] but a member may, within twenty-eight days, apply to the court, which may order that the decision of the meeting of the company shall have effect, or make any other order that it sees fit.[116]

If the proposal is approved by both the members and the creditors, it takes effect as if made by the company at the time the creditors approved it. The nominee will become known as the 'supervisor' and will supervise the CVA.[117] The CVA will bind every person who had notice of, or was entitled to vote, in the qualifying decision procedure by which the creditors' decision to approve the CVA was made.[118] If the company is being wound up or is in administration, then the court may (i) stay the winding up or terminate the administrator's appointment (as applicable); and/or (ii) give such directions with respect to the winding up or administration as it thinks appropriate for facilitating the implementation of the CVA.[119]

Within 28 days of the report of the meeting being given to the court, a nominee, liquidator, or administrator (if the company is in liquidation or administration), or anyone who had a right to vote as a member or creditor, can apply to the court on the ground that:

- the CVA unfairly prejudices the interests of a creditor, member, or contributory of the company; and/or
- there has been some material irregularity at or in relation to the meeting of the company, or in relation to the decision procedure in which the creditors decided to approve the CVA.[120]

If the court agrees with the applicant, it can (i) revoke or suspend any decision approving the CVA; (ii) give directions for a further meeting of the company to be convened to consider a revised proposal; or (iii) direct any person to seek a decision from the creditors as to whether they approve the revised proposal.[121]

21.2.2 Eligible companies and the moratorium

As noted, CVAs are useful, but underused. One reason for this is that it is relatively easy for a dissenting creditor to derail a CVA by appointing an administrator or receiver, or by petitioning the court for a winding-up order. To combat this, a form of CVA was introduced by the Insolvency Act 2000 that provides 'eligible companies' with a moratorium similar to that available to companies in administration.[122] An 'eligible' company is basically a company that is classified as a 'small company' under the CA 2006.[123]

Small companies are discussed at 19.3.1.3.

---

[111] IA 1986, s 3(3). [112] ibid s 246ZE(2). [113] ibid s 246ZF. [114] ibid s 4(6) and (6A).
[115] ibid s 4A(2)(b). [116] ibid s 4A(3) and (6). [117] ibid s 7(2). [118] ibid s 5(2).
[119] ibid s 5(3). [120] ibid s 6(1)–(3). [121] ibid s 6(4). [122] ibid s 1A.
[123] ibid Sch A1, para 3.

However, Sch A1 does provide for a list of companies that, even if classified as small, will not be eligible for a moratorium, including:

- certain insurance companies, banking companies, and financial institutions;[124]
- companies in administration or liquidation, or companies that have a CVA already in effect;[125]
- if a moratorium has been in force at any time during the 12 months ending on the day of the filing and (i) no CVA had effect when the moratorium came to an end; or (ii) a voluntary arrangement which had effect at any time in that period ended prematurely;[126]
- companies in which an administrator appointed by the company or the directors held office in the period of 12 months ending on the day of the filing;[127]
- companies subject to certain agreements under which they incur debts or liabilities of at least £10 million.[128]

If a company is eligible, it can apply for a moratorium by filing specified documents with the court, including the terms of the proposed CVA, a statement of the company's affairs, a statement from the nominee consenting to act, and a statement from the nominee that the proposed CVA has a reasonable prospect of being approved and implemented.[129] The moratorium comes into force once these documents are filed with the court[130] and Sch A1, para 12 provides for the following during the moratorium:

- no petition may be presented to wind up the company, and no resolution pay be passed to wind up the company;
- no meeting of the company can be called, except with the consent of the nominee or leave of the court;
- no administrator can be appointed by the company, its directors, or by a qualifying floating chargeholder, nor can an administrative receiver be appointed;
- no other steps may be taken to enforce any security over the company's property, or to repossess goods in the company's possession under any hire-purchase agreement, except with the leave of the court and subject to such terms as the court may impose.

The moratorium ends on the day on which the meeting of the company is first held or the day on which the company's creditors decide to approve the CVA (whichever is the later).[131] If, however, the meeting of the company has not been held or if the creditors have not decided to approve the CVA within 28 days of the moratorium commencing, then the moratorium will end at the end of the twenty-eighth day, unless an extension to the moratorium is sought.[132] The members or creditors may decide to extend the moratorium by up to two months.[133] Once the moratorium comes to an end, the nominee must advertise this fact, and notify the court, the registrar of companies, the company, and any creditor of the company.[134]

The moratorium is certainly useful and, from the perspective of the board, one advantage the CVA has over administration is that it allows the directors to remain in control of the company. Unfortunately, in practice, very few companies qualify for the moratorium because CVAs tend to be more useful for larger companies with complex

---

[124] ibid Sch A1, para 2.　　[125] ibid Sch A1, para 4(1)(a), (b), and (d).
[126] ibid Sch A1, para 4(1)(f).　　[127] ibid Sch A1, para 4(1)(fa).
[128] ibid Sch A1, paras 4A–4K.　　[129] ibid Sch A1, para 7.　　[130] ibid Sch A1, para 8.
[131] ibid Sch A1, para 8(2).　　[132] ibid Sch A1, para 8(2)–(4).　　[133] ibid Sch A1, para 32.
[134] ibid Sch A1, para 11.

financing and multiple creditors, leading Fletcher to state that 'the restricted terms of access to this procedure greatly diminish its practical value'.[135] As a result, fewer than 10 per cent of small companies that propose a CVA use the moratorium.[136] This has resulted in the government stating that 'the CVA regime in its current form and scope is limited as a tool for company rescue'[137] and so the government has stated that it intends to introduce several reforms to the UK's rescue system, one of which is that the CVA moratorium for small companies will be abolished.[138] These reforms will now be discussed.

21.3 Proposals for reform

The UK's rescue regime has been largely unchanged since 2003, since which time the global financial crisis has led many countries to re-examine whether aspects of their rescue and restructuring procedures are fit for purpose. The government decided to consult on the issue and, in May 2016, the Insolvency Service published a consultation document[139] that set out several proposals for reform. It is worth noting that several of the proposed reforms were first proposed in a 2009 consultation document,[140] but were not acted upon. The government is clearly of the opinion that the time is right to try again as, in its August 2018 response document,[141] it stated that it would proceed with a number of reform proposals.

21.3.1 **A preliminary moratorium**

The World Bank recommends that 'a stay of actions by secured creditors should be imposed . . . in reorganization proceedings where the collateral is needed for the reorganization. . . . Exceptions to the general rule on a stay of enforcement actions should be limited and clearly defined.'[142] Clearly the World Bank believes a moratorium should be much more generally available than is currently the case under UK law, where a moratorium is only generally available to companies in administration, or small companies who enter into a CVA. Therefore, the Insolvency Service proposed that a 'preliminary moratorium' should be available to insolvent companies or companies that are, or imminently will be, in financial difficulty.[143] This moratorium would give the company some

---

[135] Ian F Fletcher, 'UK Corporate Rescue' (2004) 5 European Business Organisation Law Review 119, 130.

[136] Department for Business, Energy and Industrial Strategy (BEIS), 'Insolvency and Corporate Governance: Government Response' (BEIS 2018) para 5.14.

[137] Insolvency Service, 'A Review of the Corporate Insolvency Framework: A Consultation on Options for Reform' (Insolvency Service 2016) para 9.2.

[138] BEIS, 'Insolvency and Corporate Governance: Government Response' (BEIS 2018) para 5.14.

[139] Insolvency Service, 'A Review of the Corporate Insolvency Framework: A Consultation on Options for Reform' (Insolvency Service 2016).

[140] Insolvency Service, 'Encouraging Company Rescue—A Consultation' (Insolvency Service 2009).

[141] BEIS, 'Insolvency and Corporate Governance: Government Response' (BEIS 2018).

[142] The World Bank, 'Principles for Effective Insolvency and Creditor/Debtor Rights System' (2015) Principle C5.3.

[143] Insolvency Service, 'A Review of the Corporate Insolvency Framework: A Consultation on Options for Reform' (Insolvency Service 2016) paras 7.7 and 7.18.

breathing space whilst it considered its options for rescue (e.g. entering administration or entering into a CVA).

The government has accepted the proposal,[144] subject to some modifications. Detailed proposals will follow (which may be subject to consultation and so changes may occur), but the response document provides that the moratorium will operate as follows:

- The moratorium will be available to all companies who have a legitimate reason for seeking protection, and this will be determined based on the company's financial state, namely whether the company will become insolvent if action is not taken.[145] There will be other qualifying criteria that will need to be met (e.g. on the balance of probabilities, rescue is more likely than not).[146]

- Certain companies will be excluded from the moratorium (e.g. companies that are already insolvent).[147]

- The moratorium will be triggered by filing the necessary documents at court.[148]

- The moratorium will be supervised by a person known as a 'monitor',[149] and this person must be an insolvency practitioner.[150] The monitor will also determine whether the qualifying criteria are met.

- The moratorium, which will be modelled on the moratorium available to a company in administration, will last for an initial period of 28 days,[151] but can be extended by a further 28 days.[152] Larger companies with more complex debt structures may require more time, and so it will be possible to extend the moratorium beyond 56 days in certain cases.[153]

- The company's directors will remain in control of the company during the moratorium,[154] but the approval of the monitor will be required for certain transactions (e.g. any sale or disposition of assets outside the normal course of business).[155]

21.3.2 A new, flexible restructuring plan

As noted, CVAs are not popular and the government believes their effectiveness to be limited. One reason for this is that a CVA cannot affect the right of a secured creditor to enforce his security, unless he consents.[156] The Insolvency Service proposed a 'flexible restructuring plan' that is similar to a CVA, but it would bind all creditors, including secured creditors.[157] The Insolvency Service also proposes that this plan will come with a cram-down mechanism, which will allow the plan to be imposed on junior classes of creditor even if they disagree.[158] The consultation paper noted that these features need not be part of a new standalone procedure, and could instead be incorporated into the CVA framework. [159]

The government has decided to proceed with the creation of a new restructuring procedure[160] that will operate alongside existing procedures, and can operate alongside the

---

[144] BEIS, 'Insolvency and Corporate Governance: Government Response' (BEIS 2018) para 5.9.

[145] ibid para 5.29.   [146] ibid para 5.31.   [147] ibid para 5.28.   [148] ibid para 5.19.

[149] ibid para 5.25.   [150] ibid para 5.63.   [151] ibid para 5.49.   [152] ibid para 5.52.

[153] ibid para 5.54.   [154] ibid para 5.65.   [155] ibid para 5.69.

[156] IA 1986, s 4(3), discussed at 21.2.1.3.

[157] Insolvency Service, 'A Review of the Corporate Insolvency Framework: A Consultation on Options for Reform' (Insolvency Service 2016) para 9.10.

[158] ibid para 9.11.   [159] ibid para 9.14.

[160] BEIS, 'Insolvency and Corporate Governance: Government Response' (BEIS 2018) para 5.123.

proposed preliminary moratorium. The proposed rules in the response document are as follows:

- Certain companies will not be able to take advantage of this new restructuring procedure (e.g. companies currently excluded from the CVA small company moratorium).[161]

- The restructuring procedure will be available to solvent and insolvent companies, and no financial conditions will need to be met.[162]

- The process for entering into the new restructuring plan will resemble that of a scheme of arrangement.[163]

- The terms of the restructuring plan will be for the company to determine, as will the length of time in which the plan will operate.[164]

- The plan will need to be approved by 75 per cent in value of each class of creditor affected by the plan.[165] The plan will be able to bind dissenting creditors, subject to safeguards.[166]

Schemes of arrangement are discussed at 22.2.

21.3.3 Rescue finance

The Insolvency Service notes that '[t]he availability of finance is a key aspect of any effective corporate rescue regime'.[167] Unlike some countries that have established rescue finance providers (such as the US), UK lenders are understandably reluctant to lend money to financially struggling companies and where they do, the cost of borrowing is often much higher than normal. The question is how to encourage lenders to provide finance to struggling companies. This is not an easy question to answer which explains why, instead of recommending a reform, the Insolvency Service sought feedback on several possible reforms:

- Creditors who provide rescue finance would be given super-priority status in administration expenses,[168] meaning that such creditors would rank ahead of all others. The issue with this reform is that administrator's expenses are usually paid in full, so this reform would have a modest impact. An alternative is to rank rescue finance providers ahead of administration expenses, but this could deter insolvency practitioners from acting as administrators.

- A creditor providing rescue finance will likely want security. However, the provision of rescue finance is often frustrated because an existing secured creditor utilizes a negative pledge clause to prevent the granting of new security. The Insolvency Service sought views on whether such negative pledge clauses should be overridden where the secured creditor unreasonably refuses to grant consent for the company to grant security.[169]

The rescue finance reforms were first proposed in 2009, but were not acted upon due to a lack of support. Based on the responses to the consultation, little has changed, with 73 per cent of responses disagreeing with the proposals on the grounds that there is a market for rescue finance and changes to the priority of creditors could increase the cost of borrowing.[170] Accordingly, the government has decided not to proceed with this reform at this time, but will keep the matter under review.[171]

---

[161] ibid para 5.129.

[162] ibid para 5.130.   [163] ibid para 5.135.   [164] ibid paras 5.140 and 5.142.

[165] ibid para 5.153.   [166] ibid para 5.148.

[167] Insolvency Service, 'A Review of the Corporate Insolvency Framework: A Consultation on Options for Reform' (Insolvency Service 2016) para 10.1.

[168] ibid para 10.16.   [169] ibid para 10.20.

[170] Insolvency Service, 'Summary of Responses: A Review of the Corporate Insolvency Framework' (Insolvency Service 2016) para 5.2.

[171] BEIS, 'Insolvency and Corporate Governance: Government Response' (BEIS 2018) para 5.186.

CHAPTER SUMMARY

- The UK has sought to adopt a rescue culture, under which the law offers struggling companies access to several rescue mechanisms.

- The principal rescue mechanism is administration, under which an administrator is appointed to try and fulfil the purpose of administration.

- An administrator can be appointed by (i) the court; (ii) the holder of a qualifying floating charge; or (iii) the company or its directors.

- A moratorium is imposed once a company enters administration, which prevents certain actions from proceedings (e.g. creditors cannot take steps to enforce their security).

- A company voluntary arrangement is a rescue procedure that allows a company to enter into a binding agreement with its creditors.

- A CVA begins with a proposal being made, and that proposal must then be approved by the company and creditors.

- A CVA does not normally impose a moratorium, but it can do so if the company in question is a small company.

FURTHER READING

Jennifer Payne, 'A New UK Debt Restructuring Regime? A Critique of the Insolvency Service's Consultation Paper' (2016), 'https://www.law.ox.ac.uk/business-law-blog/blog/2016/06/new-uk-debt-restructuring-regime-critique-insolvency-service's accessed 10 January 2019.
- Discusses the reform proposes put forward by the Insolvency Service in its 2016 consultation paper.

John Tribe, 'Company Voluntary Arrangements and Rescue: A New Hope and a Tudor Orthodoxy' [2009] JBL 454.
- Critically examines the history, usage and effectiveness of CVAs.

John M Wood, 'The Objectives of Administration' (2015) 36 Co Law 1.
- Provides a detailed discussion of the purpose of administration. Argues that the results of administration may not necessarily conform with the hierarchy of objectives.

Muir Hunter, 'The Nature and Functions of a Rescue Culture' [1999] JBL 491.
- Discusses in depth what constitutes a rescue culture and whether such a culture is desirable or justified.

Teresa Graham, 'Graham Review into Pre-Pack Administration' (2014).
- An independent report commissioned by the government which reviewed the law and practice relating to pre-pack administrations, and made several reform recommendations.

Vanessa Finch, 'Corporate Rescue in a World of Debt' [2008] JBL 756.
- Examines how corporate rescue has evolved based on changes in the market for credit.

Report of the Review Committee on Insolvency Law and Practice (Cmnd 8558, HMSO 1982).
- The recommendations of the Cork Report led to the Insolvency Acts of 1985 and 1986. This report recommended, *inter alia*, that UK insolvency law should foster a rescue culture.

SELF-TEST QUESTIONS

1. Define the following terms:

- rescue culture;
- moratorium;
- pre-pack administration;
- company voluntary arrangement.

2. State whether each of the following statements is true or false and, if false, explain why:

- The principal purpose of administration is to rescue the business of the company as a going concern.
- An administrator can only be appointed by the company or by the court.
- When a company enters administration, the directors will vacate office.
- An administrator's appointment will automatically terminate after one year, unless an extension is obtained.
- A CVA does not come with a moratorium.
- A receiver is a person appointed by a secured creditor to recover payment owed to that creditor.

3. To what extent has the UK adopted a rescue culture, and should the law seek to rescue financially struggling companies?

4. Dragon plc borrowed £2 million from Welsh Bank plc to renovate several of its factories and purchase new equipment. This loan was secured by way of a fixed charge over the company's headquarters. The renovations were completed and the equipment purchased, but the company then experienced a significant downturn in performance and it has struggled to pay its debts. Dragon also had an overdraft with Welsh Bank, and the bank agreed to increase Dagon's overdraft limit in return for a floating charge 'over all the assets and business of the company'.

Dragon's financial position continued to decline and it now cannot pay its debts as they fall due. Dragon has fully drawn on its overdraft facility and it owes HMRC £100,000 in unpaid tax. Accordingly, HMRC filed a petition to wind up the company.

Concerned that it will not be repaid in full, a bank manager of Welsh Bank has requested a meeting with the board of Dragon. Prior to the meeting, the bank manager seeks your advice regarding the following:

- If HMRC's winding-up petition is granted, will the bank be repaid in full?
- Could the bank recover the debt owed to it by appointing a receiver?
- Would the bank stand a better chance of being repaid if Dragon was placed in administration? If so, can the bank appoint an administrator, bearing in mind HMRC's winding-up petition? If the bank is able to appoint an administrator, set out the process by which the administrator would be appointed.

ONLINE RESOURCES

This book is accompanied by online resources to better support you in your studies. Visit www.oup.com/uk/roach-company/ for:

- answers to the self-test questions;
- further reading lists;
- multiple-choice questions;
- glossary.

Updates to the law can be found on the author's Twitter account (@UKCompanyLaw) and further resources can be found on the author's blog (www.companylawandgovernance.com).

Corporate reconstructions and takeovers

- Reconstruction under s 110 of the IA 1986
- Schemes of arrangement
- Takeovers

INTRODUCTION

It may become necessary or desirable for a company to reconfigure or restructure itself. This may be done for commercial advantages, to better organize its business, or it may form part of an attempt to rescue the company. This chapter examines two of the principal forms of corporate reconstruction, namely:

- a reconstruction under s 110 of the Insolvency Act (IA 1986) (often referred to as a 'scheme of reconstruction'); and

- a scheme of arrangement under Pt 26 of the Companies Act 2006 (CA 2006).

A company may also look to expand or diversify its business and one way this can be achieved is by taking over other companies. Accordingly, the rules relating to takeovers are also discussed.

22.1 Reconstruction under s 110 of the IA 1986

Section 110 provides a useful mechanism for restructuring a company or group of companies, especially in the case of private or family-run businesses.[1] A s 110 reconstruction involves a company (the 'transferor company') transferring or selling all or part of its business or property to another company (the 'transferee company') or limited liability partnership (LLP), and the transferor company is then voluntarily wound up. This can be useful in several instances, including:

---

[1] Company Law Review Steering Group (CLRSG), 'Modern Company Law for a Competitive Economy: Completing the Structure' (2000) para 11.13.

- where a company wants to sell part of its business, it can transfer that part of the business to a new company and then sell that company;

- where a company engages in multiple lines of business with differing business goals, then each line of business can be transferred to several new companies (often referred to as a 'demerger'), and each company can then pursue its own strategy, which could result in each business being more profitable;

- if the company is engaging in a risky or loss-making form of business, it can transfer this business to a new company, thereby segregating it from any other companies in the group;

- as the transferee can be an LLP, s 110 can effectively be used to convert a company to an LLP.

22.1.1 **The reconstruction process**

The process for reconstruction under s 110 is as follows. The transferor company will convene a general meeting where a resolution to voluntarily wind up the company will be tabled.[2] In addition, the s 110 reconstruction must be sanctioned, with the form of sanction depending on the type of voluntary winding up:

- In the case of a members' voluntary winding up, the reconstruction is sanctioned by passing a special resolution (the 's 110 resolution') conferring authority on the liquidator to proceed with the reconstruction.[3] In this instance, court approval is not required, which is a major advantage of a s 110 reconstruction, especially compared to a scheme of arrangement (which does require court approval).

- In the case of a creditors' voluntary winding up, the reconstruction must be sanctioned by the court or the liquidation committee.[4]

⚭ Schemes of arrangement are discussed at 22.2.

If the resolution is passed and the sanction obtained, then the reconstruction will be put into effect and will bind all members of the transferor company,[5] as well as its creditors.[6] The reconstruction will involve the transferor company being liquidated and all or part of its business or property[7] being transferred or sold to another company or LLP[8] (or multiple companies or LLPs). Two points should be noted:

1. the transferor company must be a company registered under the Companies Acts;

2. a transferee company need not be registered under the Companies Acts,[9] and so can include chartered companies or foreign companies.[10]

In return for the transfer/sale, the members of the transferor company will usually receive shares in the transferee company, but could instead receive policies or some other interest in the transferee company.[11] If the members are to receive shares, then these must be issued to the members in accordance with their rights and interests in the transferor company.[12]

---

[2] If the transferor company is private, then the written resolution procedure may be used.

[3] IA 1986, s 110(3)(a).   [4] ibid s 110(3)(b).   [5] ibid s 110(5).

[6] *Re City & County Investment Co* (1879) 13 ChD 475 (CA).

[7] Where the transferor company is to sell or transfer all of its business or property, it will retain such sums as will be required to pay the liquidator.

[8] IA 1986, s 110(1). Note that the transfer or sale cannot be made to an individual (*Bird v Bird's Patent Deodorizing and Utilizing Sewage Co* (1874) LR 9 Ch App 358).

[9] IA 1986, s 110(1)(a).   [10] *Re Irrigation Co of France, ex p Fox* (1871) LR 6 Ch App 176.

[11] IA 1986, s 110(2)(a).   [12] *Griffith v Paget* (1877) LR 6 ChD 511 (Ch).

22.1.2 **Dissenting members and creditors**

There may be members or creditors who oppose the s 110 reconstruction. As regards dissenting members, a reconstruction under s 110 is binding on all members of the transferor company, irrespective of whether they voted for it or not.[13] However, a member of the transferor company who did not vote in favour of the s 110 resolution can require the liquidator to either (i) abstain from carrying out the reconstruction; or (ii) purchase the dissenting member's shares at a price to be determined by arbitration or agreement.[14] In order for this to arise, the dissenting member must express his dissent, in writing, to the liquidator and this written dissenting statement must be left at the company's registered office within seven days of the s 110 resolution being passed.[15]

As noted, the reconstruction also binds the creditors of the transferor company. Accordingly, the debt owed to such creditors will not automatically be transferred to the transferee company, although it is common for the transferee to agree to indemnify the creditors of the transferor company. In the absence of such an indemnity, the creditors must look to the liquidator of the transferor company for satisfaction of the debt. Such creditors may therefore be opposed to the reconstruction, but neither ss 110 or 111 provide the creditors with a power of dissent. Instead, there are two other forms of action potentially available to the creditors:

- The loan agreement between the transferor company and the creditor may provide the creditor with some form of protection that will apply in the event of a reconstruction.

Compulsory winding up is discussed at 23.1.2.

- The creditor can seek to derail the reconstruction by petitioning the court for a compulsory winding-up order of the transferor company (usually on the ground that the company cannot pay its debts or on just and equitable grounds). If a winding-up order is granted within a year of the passing of the s 110 resolution, then the s 110 resolution will be regarded as invalid unless sanctioned by the court.[16] To avoid the risk of the entire reconstruction being derailed in this manner, the liquidator will often retain enough assets to ensure that the creditors' debts are repaid as fully as possible.

22.2 Schemes of arrangement

Part 26 of the CA 2006 allows companies to enter into a binding arrangement or reconstruction that is known as a scheme of arrangement. A scheme of arrangement is a compromise or arrangement between a company and (i) its creditors, or any class of them; or (ii) its members, or any class of them.[17] A major advantage of such a scheme is its flexibility. Part 26 sets out the procedures for effecting a scheme, but it lays down no rules regarding the scheme's terms. As a result, a scheme of arrangement is extremely versatile and can be used for a wide range of purposes, including:

- **Takeovers**: it is reasonably common to effect a takeover via a scheme of arrangement. Indeed, the CA 2006 itself notes that a scheme can be used where 'the whole or any part of the undertaking or the property of any company concerned in the scheme . . . is to be transferred to another company . . .'.[18] This is typically done via a 'transfer scheme' under

---

[13] IA 1986, s 110(5).

[14] ibid s 111(2). Section 111(3) makes clear that it is the liquidator who chooses which of these two outcomes will occur.

[15] ibid.   [16] ibid s 110(6).   [17] CA 2006, s 895(1).   [18] ibid s 900(1)(b).

which the bidder and the target will agree the terms of the takeover, and the target will then enter into a scheme of arrangement with its shareholders under which the shareholders agree to sell their shares to the bidder.

- **Mergers**: the CA 2006 provides that a scheme can be for the purpose of 'the amalgamation of any two or more companies',[19] although this is not a common usage for a scheme of arrangement.

- **Corporate rescue**: a scheme of arrangement can be used to attempt the rescue of a financially struggling company (e.g. an administrator may cause the company to enter into a scheme with its creditors in order to fulfil the purpose of administration). Unlike other formal rescue procedures (e.g. administration), a scheme of arrangement is not dependent on the company being insolvent, and so it can be put into effect at an earlier stage and so may stand a better chance of preventing insolvency.

- **Rearranging share capital**: a scheme can be used to restructure a company's share capital (e.g. dividing one class of share into multiple classes of share or vice versa).[20]

22.2.1 Scope of Pt 26

The scope of Pt 26 is determined largely by what amounts to a 'compromise or arrangement' and what is a 'company' for the purposes of Pt 26.

22.2.1.1 'Compromise or arrangement'

The CA 2006 does not define what a 'compromise or arrangement' is, although it does state that an arrangement includes 'a reorganisation of the company's share capital by the consolidation of shares of different classes or by the division of shares into shares of different classes, or by both of those methods'.[21] Accordingly, the issue has been left to the courts, with the following case setting out the approach that the courts have adopted.

> ### Re National Farmers Union Development Trust Ltd [1972] 1 WLR 1548 (Ch)
>
> **FACTS:** The objects of NFU Development Trust Ltd ('NFU') provided that it was to assist farmers and encourage farming. NFU had 94,000 members. This large membership imposed notable administration costs, resulting in a significant portion of NFU's income being spent on administration and very little being spent on promoting its objects. Accordingly, in order to reduce administration costs, a scheme was proposed under which the number of members would be reduced to seven—all the other members would cease to be members and would lose all their rights. The scheme was approved by the requisite majority and court sanction was applied for.
>
> **HELD:** Brightman J stated:
>
> > The word 'compromise' implies some element of accommodation on each side. It is not apt to describe total surrender. A claimant who abandons his claim is not compromising it. Similarly, I think that the word 'arrangement' in this section implies some element of give and take. Confiscation is not my idea of an arrangement. A member whose rights are expropriated without any compensating advantage is not, in my view, having his rights rearranged in any legitimate sense of that expression.[22]

---

[19] ibid s 900(1)(a).   [20] ibid s 895(2).   [21] ibid s 895(2).   [22] [1972] 1 WLR 1548 (Ch) 1555.

Here, the vast majority of the members would be giving up all of their rights without receiving any compensation for this. As this amounted to a surrender of rights, it did not constitute a compromise or arrangement and so the court refused to sanction the scheme.

COMMENT: Whilst Brightman J seemed to regard a compromise and arrangement as being similar, most other courts distinguish between the two. The consensus is that an arrangement is wider than a compromise, and an arrangement need not involve an element of compromise.[23]

A compromise or arrangement will usually alter the rights of the affected members or creditors, but an alteration of rights is not a necessary requirement under Pt 26.[24]

22.2.1.2 'Company'

For the purposes of Pt 26, the word 'company' means 'any company liable to be wound up under the Insolvency Act 1986 . . . '.[25] This can encompass not only UK-registered companies, but also foreign companies. However, in *Re Real Estate Development Co*,[26] the court imposed three limitations on the ability to wind up a foreign company, namely:

1. the company must have a sufficiently close connection with England and Wales to justify the court exercising its jurisdiction;
2. the person petitioning for the company's winding up is a person over whom the court could exercise jurisdiction and is someone who is concerned or who has an interest in the proper distribution of the company's assets; and
3. there was a reasonable possibility that if a winding-up order was made, some real benefit would accrue to the petitioner.

22.2.2 The three-stage process

In *Re BTR plc*,[27] Chadwick LJ stated that the formal process for effecting a scheme of arrangement consists of three stages, namely:

1. an application is made to the court to summon meetings of those members and creditors who will be affected by the scheme;
2. the relevant meetings are held to determine whether the scheme is to be approved; and
3. an application is made to the court to sanction the scheme.

Each stage of the scheme is discussed at 22.2.2.1–22.2.2.3, but it is worth noting here that the procedurally onerous nature of this three-stage process is a major disadvantage. As has been noted:

> The procedural requirements of a scheme are onerous. The issue of class meetings is complex and potentially difficult. Extensive and detailed explanatory statements must be produced by the company. There is also the matter of two court hearings, and close oversight of the process by the court.[28]

---

[23] *Re Guardian Assurance Co* [1917] 1 Ch 431 (CA).
[24] *Re T&N Ltd* [2006] EWHC 1447 (Ch), [2007] 1 All ER 851.
[25] CA 2006, s 895(2).   [26] [1991] BCLC 210 (Ch).   [27] [2000] 1 BCLC 740 (CA) 742.
[28] Jennifer Payne, 'Debt Restructuring in English Law: Lessons from the United States and the Need for Reform' (2014) 130 LQR 282, 291–2.

22.2.2.1 Stage 1: application to summon meetings

The first stage is that an application is made to the court to summon meetings of all the members (or any class of them) or creditors (or any class of them).[29] The purpose of this stage is to 'ensure that those who are to be affected by the compromise or arrangement proposed have a proper opportunity of being present (in person or by proxy) at the meeting or meetings at which the proposals are to be considered and voted upon'.[30] This application can be made by:

- the company;
- any creditor of the company;
- the liquidator (if the company is in liquidation); or
- the administrator (if the company is in administration).[31]

The application will need to make clear whether the scheme affects all the members or creditors, or only certain classes of member or creditor. If the scheme only affects certain classes of member or creditor, then the application will need to identify exactly which classes of members or creditors are affected. Separate meetings of each class of affected member and creditor will then be convened in stage 2. It is important to correctly identify the affected classes of members or creditors for two reasons. First, meetings need not be convened for any class of member or creditor not affected by the scheme, as the following case demonstrates.

Re Bluebrook Ltd [2009] EWHC 2114 (Ch)

FACTS: Spirecove Ltd was a subsidiary of Bluebrook Ltd. Bluebrook owed £313 million to a group of senior lenders, and Spirecove owed £119 million to a separate group of creditors (referred to as 'mezzanine lenders'). Both debts were secured over the assets of the Bluebrook group, with the debts of the senior lenders having priority. The group was insolvent and, in order to restructure it, a scheme was proposed between Bluebrook and the senior lenders under which the business and assets of the group would be transferred to a new corporate group. The senior lenders would receive shares in these new companies in return for giving up some of the debt owed to them.[32] The mezzanine lenders were not party to this scheme and so, if the scheme went ahead, there would be no assets left in the Bluebrook group to pay them. The senior lenders overwhelmingly approved the scheme (a meeting of the mezzanine lenders was not summoned) and the court's sanction was sought. The mezzanine lenders challenged the scheme, arguing that they were affected by the scheme and so their approval should have been sought.

HELD: Mann J stated that '[a] company is free to select the creditors with whom it wishes to enter into an arrangement'[33] and 'it is not necessary for the company to consult any class of creditors (or contributories) who are not affected, either because their rights are untouched or because they have no economic interest in the company'.[34] Mann J held that the value of the Bluebrook group was less than the value of the debt owed to the senior lenders. Accordingly, the mezzanine lenders had no prospect of being paid and so had no economic interest in the scheme. The mezzanine lenders' challenge failed and the scheme was sanctioned.

---

[29] CA 2006, s 896(1).

[30] *Re Hawk Insurance Co Ltd* [2001] EWCA Civ 241, [2002] BCC 300 [12] (Chadwick LJ).

[31] CA 2006, s 896(2).

[32] In other words, the debt was being novated from the Bluebrook group to the new corporate group (albeit a reduced amount, so the new group would owe the senior lenders £185 million).

[33] [2009] EWHC 2114 (Ch), [2010] BCC 209 [23].   [34] ibid [25].

Second, if the applicant does not correctly identify the classes of member or creditor affected by the scheme, the court will refuse to sanction the scheme in stage 3. Unfortunately, as the CLRSG noted, 'sometimes it is not easy for those promoting a scheme to identify appropriate classes of creditors or members'.[35] The difficulty lies in determining what amounts to a 'class' of creditor or member. The test to determine this was set out by Bowen LJ, who stated:

> It seems to me that we must give such meaning to the term 'class' as will prevent the section being so worked as to result in confiscation and injustice and that it must be confined to those persons whose rights are not so dissimilar as to make it impossible for them to consult together with a view to their common interest.[36]

Bowen LJ's test essentially asks whether the affected members'/creditors' rights differ to such an extent as to make it impossible for them to consult together and so will require separate meetings (i.e. it focuses on the dissimilarities between rights). The courts have now also confirmed that the test should take into account the similarities between members' rights—Chadwick LJ stated that members 'whose rights are sufficiently similar to the right of others that they can properly consult together should be required to do so; lest by ordering separate meetings the court gives a veto to a minority group'.[37] Both tests were neatly encapsulated by Lord Millett, who stated:

> Persons whose rights are so dissimilar that they cannot sensibly consult together with a view to their common interest must be given separate meetings. Persons whose rights are sufficiently similar that they can consult together with a view to their common interest should be summoned to a single meeting.[38]

It has been stated that this test aims to provide a balancing act, stating that '[a] class with genuinely different rights requires the protection of a separate meeting so that they will not be swamped by the votes of others. But if too many artificial distinctions are taken, the scheme is at the mercy of a veto by any one of the consequent meetings.'[39] This latter point explains why most disputes in this area involve an allegation that the company has identified too few classes—directors realize that the more classes there are, the greater the chance there is that the scheme will not gain the support of all those classes.

Bowen LJ's test focuses on the *rights* of members and creditors. In one case, *Re Hellenic & General Trust*,[40] the court held that separate class meetings of the members were required even though all the members held the same class of shares (and therefore had the same rights). The decision was justified on the basis that the *interests* of various shareholders differed. However, this case has been restricted and subsequent cases have reasserted the traditional focus on the members'/creditors' rights. In *Re BTR plc*,[41] Jonathan Parker J stated 'I find it difficult to understand the concept of an interest arising out of a right as being something separate from the right itself'[42] and, in *Re UDL Holdings Ltd*,[43] Lord Millett stated '[t]he test is based on similarity or dissimilarity of legal rights against the company, not on similarity or dissimilarity of interests not

---

[35] CLRSG, 'Modern Company Law for a Competitive Economy: Completing the Structure' (2000) para 11.9.
[36] *Sovereign Life Assurance Co v Dodd* [1892] 2 QB 573 (CA) 583.
[37] *Re Hawk Insurance Co Ltd* [2001] EWCA Civ 241, [2002] BCC 300 [33].
[38] *Re UDL Holdings Ltd* [2002] 1 HKC 172 (Hong Kong Court of Final Appeal) [27].
[39] Geoffrey Morse, *Palmer's Company Law* (Sweet & Maxwell 2018) para 12.040.
[40] [1976] 1 WLR 123 (Ch).   [41] [1999] 2 BCLC 675 (Ch).   [42] ibid 682.
[43] [2002] 1 HKC 172 (Hong Kong Court of Final Appeal).

derived from such legal rights'.[44] However, this is not to say that the members'/creditors' interests are not relevant as the courts have stated that the effect of the scheme upon the members'/creditors' interests can be considered by the court in stage 3 when deciding whether to sanction the scheme.[45]

In the following case, the court was extremely critical of the procedure under which a company determines the composition of the classes and, if that composition was incorrect, the court would refuse to sanction the scheme at stage 3.

 Re Hawk Insurance Co Ltd [2001] EWCA Civ 241

FACTS: The provisional liquidator of Hawk Insurance Co Ltd ('Hawk') proposed a scheme of arrangement between Hawk and its creditors. The application stated that the creditors affected by the scheme constituted a single class and so a single meeting of these creditors was summoned, where the scheme was unanimously approved. At first instance, Arden J refused to sanction the scheme because she did not believe that the affected creditors constituted a single class.[46] The provisional liquidator appealed.

HELD: The appeal was allowed and the scheme was sanctioned. Chadwick LJ stated that '[t]he question whether or not those were the meetings which the scheme actually required is left to be decided at the third stage; by which time a wrong decision by the applicant at the outset will have led to a considerable waste of time and expense'.[47] He went on to state that 'an applicant is entitled to feel aggrieved if, in the absence of opposition from any creditor, the court holds, at the third stage and on its own motion, that the order which it made at the first stage was pointless'.[48]

COMMENT: The CLRSG expressed dissatisfaction with the decision in *Hawk* on the ground that the scheme was sanctioned even though the creditors affected appeared to have different rights.[49] This led the CLRSG to propose that legislation should define the word 'class',[50] but this recommendation was not acted upon.

In order to avoid the wasted expense and court time referred to by Chadwick LJ in *Re Hawk*, a Practice Statement[51] was issued, the purpose of which is to 'enable issues concerning the composition of classes of creditor and the summoning of meetings to be identified and if appropriate resolved early in the proceedings'. The key practice points include:

- It is the responsibility of the applicant to determine whether more than one meeting of creditors is required by a scheme and if so to ensure that those meetings are properly constituted.

- The applicant should, as soon as possible, draw the court's attention to any issues which may arise as to the constitution of meetings of creditors or which otherwise affect the conduct of those meetings. Where such an issue has been drawn to the court's attention, the court will consider whether to also give directions to resolve that issue (which can include postponement of the meeting until the issue is resolved).

- Any creditor affected by the scheme should be notified of it, the purpose of the scheme, the meetings of creditors that will be required, and the composition of those meetings.

---

[44] ibid [27].

[45] *Primacom Holdings GmbH v Credit Agricole* [2011] EWHC 3746 (Ch), [2013] BCC 201 [49] (Hildyard J).

[46] [2001] BCC 57 (Ch).   [47] [2001] EWCA Civ 241, [2002] BCC 300 [19].   [48] ibid [21].

[49] CLRSG, 'Company Law for a Competitive Economy: Final Report' (DTI 2001) para 13.8.   [50] ibid.

[51] *Practice Statement (Companies: Schemes of Arrangement)* [2002] 1 WLR 1345 (Ch).

- While creditors who feel they have been unfairly treated can raise objections to the scheme at the sanction hearing (stage 3), the court will expect them to show good reasons why they did not raise the issue at an earlier stage.

Although this Practice Statement states that it applies to arrangements between companies and creditors, it has been argued that '[t]here seems little reason why the same principles should not apply in general to classes of shareholders'.[52] The CLRSG proposed more radical solutions to the issue of class composition, recommending that the court should have discretion to determine the composition of the meetings at stage 1, and that the court should be able to sanction a scheme even if the classes were wrongly decided, providing that the court is satisfied that an incorrect composition of classes did not have any substantive effect on the outcome.[53] Neither of these recommended reforms was acted upon.

22.2.2.2 Stage 2: holding of meetings

Once the court has approved the application summoning the relevant meetings, these meetings will need to be summoned to approve the scheme. This involves two steps. The first step is that the company must provide the relevant members or creditors with notice of the relevant meetings and this notice must also contain an explanatory statement[54] that:

- explains the effect of the compromise or arrangement; and
- states any material interests of the directors of the company (whether as directors or as members or as creditors of the company or otherwise), and the effect on those interests of the compromise or arrangement, in so far as it is different from the effect on the like interests of other persons.[55]

It may be the case that the information provided in the explanatory statement changes in the period between the statement being circulated and the meetings being held. In such a case, the company should inform the relevant members or creditors of the change prior to the meeting—a failure to do so could result in the court refusing to sanction the scheme.[56]

The second step involves holding the relevant meetings to determine whether the scheme is approved. Separate meetings must be held of each affected class of member or creditor, and the scheme will only be approved if every meeting approves the scheme. A meeting will approve the scheme if a majority in number representing at least 75 per cent in value of those present and voting (either in person or by proxy) approve the scheme.[57] From this, it follows that two conditions need to be satisfied:

1. a majority in number of the class of persons present and voting must vote in favour of the scheme; and
2. at least 75 per cent in value of the persons present and voting must vote in favour of the scheme.[58]

---

[52] Geoffrey Morse, *Palmer's Company Law* (Sweet & Maxwell 2018) para 12.039.
[53] CLRSG, 'Company Law for a Competitive Economy: Final Report' (DTI 2001) paras 13.6–13.7.
[54] CA 2006, s 897(1)(b).
[55] ibid s 897(2). Failure to provide such a statement or to include the required information is a criminal offence (s 897(5)).
[56] *Re Jessel Trust Ltd* [1985] BCLC 119 (Ch).   [57] CA 2006, s 899(1).
[58] *Re Dee Valley Group plc* [2017] EWHC 184 (Ch), [2018] Ch 55 [1] (Sir Geoffrey Vos).

22.2.2.3 **Stage 3: court sanction**

If the relevant members or creditors approve the scheme, then an application may be made to the court for an order sanctioning the scheme.[59] The court is not bound to follow the decision of the members or creditors in stage 2. In practice, the court is reluctant to refuse to sanction a scheme if the requisite majorities have been obtained, and will be even more reluctant to do so if the majorities in favour go well beyond that required under statute. As Lindley LJ stated:

> we are not to register their decisions, but to see that they have been properly convened and have been properly consulted, and have considered the matter from a proper point of view, that is, with a view to the interests of the class to which they belong and are empowered to bind, the Court ought to be slow to differ from them. It should do so without hesitation if there is anything wrong; but it ought not to do so, in my judgment, unless something is brought to the attention of the Court to shew that there has been some material oversight or miscarriage.[60]

When deciding whether to sanction the scheme, the court will seek to determine a number of issues. First, the court will seek to 'ensure that the meeting or meetings have been summoned and held in accordance with [the court order granted in stage 1]'.[61] From this, it follows that the court will not sanction a scheme if:

- the stage 1 meetings were not correctly constituted (e.g. because the stage 1 application did not correctly identify which classes of member or creditor would be affected by the scheme); or
- the explanatory statement was not sent or did not contain the required information.

Second, the court will seek to 'ensure that the proposals have been approved by the requisite majority of those present at the meeting or meetings'.[62] The court will not sanction a scheme if the required majorities have not been obtained at stage 2, even if the court is of the opinion that the scheme is beneficial and would have been prepared to confirm it.[63] Even if the required majorities have been obtained, the court may refuse to sanction the scheme if the summoning and holding of the meetings were subject to some procedural irregularity, although minor or accidental irregularities will likely not result in the court refusing to sanction the scheme.[64]

Third, the court will seek to 'ensure that the views and interests of those who have not approved the proposals at the meeting or meetings (either because they were not present or, being present, did not vote in favour of the proposals) receive impartial consideration'.[65] The court is not there to rubber-stamp the views of the majority and will consider the views of minority interests and those who did not vote. It may be the case that a member or creditor who did not vote in favour of the scheme may raise an objection that the court believes should result in the scheme being refused sanction, as occurred in the following case.

---

[59] CA 2006, s 899(1).
[60] *Re English, Scottish, and Australian Chartered Bank* [1893] 3 Ch 385 (CA) 409.
[61] *Re Hawk Insurance Co Ltd* [2001] EWCA Civ 241, [2002] BCC 300 [12] (Chadwick LJ).   [62] ibid.
[63] *Re Neath and Brecon Railway Co* [1892] 1 Ch 349 (CA).
[64] See e.g. *Re Halcrow Holdings Ltd* [2011] EWHC 3662 (Ch), [2012] Pens LR 113 (accidental failure to notify 306 out of 1,175 members of a meeting to approve a scheme did not prevent the court sanctioning it).
[65] *Re Hawk Insurance Co Ltd* [2001] EWCA Civ 241, [2002] BCC 300 [12] (Chadwick LJ).

> ### British America Nickel Corp Ltd v MJ O'Brien Ltd [1927] AC 369 (PC)
>
> **FACTS**: British America Nickel Corp Ltd ('BANC') issued mortgage bonds that provided that the rights of the bondholders could be varied if bondholders representing not less than 75 per cent in value sanctioned the variation. A scheme that would modify the rights of the bondholders was proposed and sanctioned by the requisite majority. However, this majority would not have been obtained had BANC not promised to issue a large block of shares to a bondholder, and this promise of shares was not disclosed in the scheme documentation. When details of this promise came to light, MJ O'Brien Ltd (a bondholder that had voted against the scheme) challenged the scheme.
>
> **HELD:** Viscount Haldane stated that BANC's duty was to 'look to the difficulties of the bondholders as a class, and not to give any one of these bondholders a special personal advantage, not forming part of the scheme to be voted for, in order to induce him to assent'.[66] As it had breached this duty, the court refused to sanction the scheme and held that the resolution approving the scheme was invalid.
>
> **COMMENT:** The court refused to sanction the scheme because the inducement to assent was not disclosed and was not offered to other bondholders. It follows that the scheme is more likely to be sanctioned where the inducement is disclosed[67] and it is offered to all affected persons.[68]

Finally, the court will consider whether 'the [proposed scheme] is such that an intelligent and honest man, a member of the class concerned and acting in respect of his interest, might reasonably approve'.[69]

If the court does decide to sanction the scheme, the court order sanctioning the scheme will have no effect until a copy of it has been delivered to Companies House.[70] After the order is made, every copy of the company's articles issued by the company must be accompanied by a copy of the order, unless the effect of the order has been incorporated into the articles.[71]

22.2.3 The effects of the scheme

Once the scheme is sanctioned by the court and a copy of the court order is sent to Companies House, it binds the company and those creditors or members who are parties to the scheme,[72] including those who voted against it. That the majority can bind the minority to the scheme is a major advantage of a scheme of arrangement.

The scheme is only binding on those party to it—creditors and members not party to the scheme are not bound by its terms, nor are third parties. However, third-party rights may be affected by the scheme, as the following case demonstrates.

---

66 [1927] AC 369 (PC) 378–9.

67 *Goodfellow v Nelson Line (Liverpool) Ltd* [1912] 2 Ch 324 (Ch).

68 *Azevedo v Importacao, Exportaacao e Industria de Oleos Ltda* [2013] EWCA Civ 364, [2015] QB 1.

69 *Re Dorman Long & Co Ltd* [1934] Ch 635 (Ch) 657 (Maugham J).

70 CA 2006, s 899(4).   71 ibid s 901(3).

72 ibid s 899(3) and (4). If the company is in the process of being wound up, it also binds the liquidator and any contributories (s 899(3)(b)).

Re La Seda de Barcelona SA [2010] EWHC 1364 (Ch)

FACTS: La Seda de Barcelona SA ('Seda') was the Spanish parent of a group of companies, one of which (Artenius UK Ltd ('Artenius')) was incorporated in the UK. A debt agreement was entered into by Seda, with Artenius acting as guarantor. Owing to a lack of liquidity, Seda defaulted on the agreement. To avoid the group entering into insolvency proceedings, a scheme was proposed between Seda and its creditors, which provided that the affected creditors would release Artenius from its obligations as guarantor, in return for which Artenius would release its claims against Seda. The issue that arose was whether the court had jurisdiction to sanction a scheme that affected the rights of Artenius's creditors, when Artenius itself was not a party to the scheme.

HELD: The court sanctioned the scheme on the ground that it gave rise to 'the requisite element of give and take between the scheme creditors and [Seda]'.[73] Proudman J justified sanctioning the scheme because '[t]he release of Artenius benefits the scheme creditors because Artenius' release of [Seda] and other group companies improves the financial position of [Seda] and the other group companies'.[74]

COMMENT: The scheme in *La Seda* involved releasing an obligation of a third party (Artenius). In the subsequent case of *Re Apcoa Parking Holdings GmbH*,[75] the court stated that a Pt 26 scheme can be used to release or vary third-party rights, but cannot create new obligations:

> the imposition of a new obligation to third parties is very different from the release in whole or in part of an obligation to such third parties. More generally, I am not persuaded that obligations may be imposed under a scheme of arrangement under Part 26: in creditors' schemes, it appears to me likely that the jurisdiction exists for the purpose of varying the rights of creditors in their capacity as such, and not imposing on such creditors new obligations.[76]

As noted, an advantage of a scheme of arrangement is its flexibility, but this flexibility generally ends once the scheme comes into effect. A binding scheme cannot be amended by the acquiescence of the affected members or creditors.[77] However, in *Re Cape plc*,[78] the court stated that it had jurisdiction to sanction a scheme whose terms contained a post-sanction power of amendment[79] (which would be useful where the scheme operates over a lengthy period of time), although the court did go on to state that '[t]here are strong reasons why in most cases the court is unlikely to exercise the jurisdiction to sanction a scheme with provisions for future amendments'.[80]

22.3 Takeovers

There is no authoritative or universally accepted definition of what a 'takeover' is, but a takeover is generally regarded as a transaction under which one company (referred to as the 'bidder' or 'offeror') acquires sufficient shares in another company (referred to as the 'target' or 'offeree') to give it control. This leads us to ask how many shares the offeror must acquire in order to gain control of the offeree. The answer depends upon the type of company:

---

[73] [2010] EWHC 1364 (Ch), [2011] 1 BCLC 555 [19] (Proudman J).   [74] ibid [20].

[75] [2014] EWHC 3849 (Ch), [2015] 4 All ER 572.   [76] ibid [164] (Hildyard J).

[77] *Devi v People's Bank of Northern India Ltd* [1938] 4 All ER 337 (PC).

[78] [2006] EWHC 1315 (Ch), [2006] 3 All ER 1222.   [79] ibid [72].

[80] ibid [73] (David Richards J).

- In many private companies, the directors and shareholders will be the same persons and all the shareholders will play a role in running the company. Accordingly, a bidder would likely need to acquire a majority stake in the company in order to acquire control.

- In a public company (especially quoted companies), many shareholders do not actively participate in the governance of the company (e.g. voting at general meetings). Accordingly, control of such a company can be acquired with a smaller stake. The relevant rules define 'control' as holding an interest in shares carrying 30 per cent or more of the voting rights of a company, irrespective of whether such an interest provides *de facto* control.[81]

In a private company, a takeover can be effected in a straightforward manner by the bidder entering into private agreements with the target's shareholders to purchase their shares. Conversely, in public companies (especially quoted companies), takeovers tend to be much more complex and a substantial body of rules has arisen to regulate such takeovers. Some of these rules are found in the CA 2006 (notably Pt 28), but the bulk of the rules are found in the City Code on Takeovers and Mergers (with the twelfth edition (2016) being the most recent at the time of writing). This Code was created in 1968 and operated on a self-regulatory basis until the implementation of the 2004 Takeover Directive.[82] The purpose of the Directive was to 'create Community-wide clarity and transparency in respect of legal issues to be settled in the event of takeover bids and to prevent patterns of corporate restructuring within the Community from being distorted by arbitrary differences in governance and management cultures'.[83] This Directive requires Member States to 'designate the authority or authorities competent to supervise bids for the purposes of the rules which they make or introduce pursuant to this Directive'.[84] In the UK, this authority is the Panel on Takeovers and Mergers[85] (commonly known as 'the Takeover Panel').

The City Code is discussed more at 22.3.2.

22.3.1 The Panel on Takeovers and Mergers

The Takeover Panel has been regulating takeovers in the UK since 1968, but it did so largely on a self-regulatory basis. Following the passing of the Takeover Directive and its implementation in Pt 28 of the CA 2006, the Panel now operates on a statutory footing.

22.3.1.1 Functions and powers

The CA 2006 provides that the functions of the Panel are set out in Pt 28, Ch 1,[86] which provides that the Panel is to have three broad functions:

1. The Panel must make rules giving effect to specified articles of the Takeover Directive.[87] These rules, namely the City Code on Takeovers and Mergers (or 'Takeover Code' as it is usually known), are discussed at 22.3.2.

2. The Panel may provide rulings on the interpretation, application, or effect of the Takeover Code,[88] and these rulings have binding effect.[89] At first instance, these rulings are provided by the Panel Executive. Decisions of the Panel Executive are subject to review (effectively an appeal) by the Hearings Committee,[90] and the Panel's decision are also

---

[81] Takeover Code, Definitions, C7.
[82] Directive 2004/25/EC of 21 April 2004 on takeover bids [2004] OJ L142/12.
[83] ibid Preamble, para 3.   [84] ibid Art 4(1).
[85] CA 2006, s 942(1). See www.thetakeoverpanel.org.uk accessed 10 January 2019.
[86] ibid, s 942(1).   [87] ibid s 943(1). Namely Arts 3.1, 4.2, 5, 6.1–6.3, 7–9, and 13.
[88] ibid s 945(1).   [89] ibid s 945(2).   [90] ibid s 951(1).

subject to judicial review.[91] Decisions of the Hearings Committee can be appealed to an independent tribunal, known as the Takeover Appeal Board.[92] Decisions of the Takeover Appeal Board cannot be appealed.

3. The Panel can provide directions in order (i) to restrain a person from acting (or continuing to act) in breach of the Takeover Code; (ii) to restrain a person from doing (or continuing to do) a particular thing, pending determination of whether that or any other conduct of his is or would be a breach of the Takeover Code; or (iii) otherwise to secure compliance with the Takeover Code.[93]

The Panel is empowered to 'do anything that it considers necessary or expedient for the purposes of, or in connection with, its functions'[94] and it is therefore granted significant statutory powers. The principal power is that the Panel can, by notice, require a person to provide any documents or information as specified in the notice.[95] Information provided to the Panel in the exercise of its functions cannot be disclosed without the consent of the relevant individual or business,[96] although certain disclosures are permitted[97] (e.g. disclosures made for the purpose of allowing the Panel to carry out any of its functions).

22.3.1.2 Structure and composition

The Takeover Panel consists of up to 36 members, all having expertise in takeovers, securities markets, industry, and commerce. The Panel's Chairman, Deputy Chairman, and up to 20 other members are appointed based on the recommendations of the Panel's nomination committee. In addition, 12 Panel members are appointed from a range of major financial and business organizations, including the Confederation of British Industry, the Institute of Chartered Accountants in England and Wales (ICAEW), and the Investment Association.

The Takeover Panel's day-to-day work is carried out by the Panel Executive, which operates independently of the Takeover Panel. The Panel Executive:

> takes the lead in examining the circumstances of takeover bids and, if thought necessary, referring them to the Panel for consideration and adjudication according to the Rules. Almost daily it is called upon to give advice and rulings, which are mostly accepted . . . The executive and where necessary the Panel monitors, so to speak, take-over bids and mergers as they develop to ensure, as far as possible, that the Code is being observed. It acts as a sort of fire brigade to extinguish quickly the flames of unacceptable and unfair practice.[98]

In addition, the CA 2006 provides that the Takeover Panel may make arrangements for its functions to be discharged by a committee or sub-committee,[99] of which five exist, namely:

- The Hearings Committee reviews rulings of the Panel Executive, and also hears disciplinary proceedings in cases where the Panel Executive thinks there has been a breach of the Takeover Code.[100]

---

[91] *R v Panel on Takeovers and Mergers, ex p Datafin plc* [1987] QB 815 (CA).
[92] CA 2006, s 951(3). See www.thetakeoverappealboard.org.uk accessed 10 January 2019.
[93] ibid, s 946.   [94] ibid s 942(2).   [95] ibid s 947(1).
[96] ibid s 948(1)–(2). Breach of s 948 constitutes a criminal offence (ibid s 949).
[97] ibid s 948(3) and Sch 2.
[98] *R v Panel and Takeovers and Mergers ex p Guinness plc* (1988) 4 BCC 325 (QB) 337–8 (Watkins LJ).
[99] CA 2006, s 942(3)(a).   [100] Takeover Code, Introduction, s 4(c).

- The Code Committee is responsible for keeping the Code under review, and for proposing, consulting on, making, and issuing amendments to the Code.[101] A member of the Code Committee cannot simultaneously or subsequently be a member of the Hearings Committee.

- The Panel also has the corporate governance committees similar to those found in a listed company, namely (i) a finance, audit, and risk committee; (ii) a nomination committee; and (iii) a remuneration committee.

22.3.2 The City Code on Takeovers and Mergers

The City Code on Takeovers and Mergers (usually known as the 'Takeover Code') was first published in 1968. Since then, it has been amended numerous times with the current Code at the time of writing being the twelfth edition, which was published in 2016. The Code was drafted to 'reflect the collective opinion of those professionally involved in the field of takeovers as to appropriate business standards and as to how fairness to offeree company shareholders and an orderly framework for takeovers can be achieved'.[102] The Code provides that its principal purposes are:

> to ensure that shareholders in an offeree company are treated fairly and are not denied an opportunity to decide on the merits of a takeover and that shareholders in the offeree company of the same class are afforded equivalent treatment by an offeror. The Code also provides an orderly framework within which takeovers are conducted. In addition, it is designed to promote, in conjunction with other regulatory regimes, the integrity of the financial markets.[103]

From this, it follows that the Code is not concerned with the commercial or financial merits of a takeover as these are matters for the company and its shareholders to determine. Nor is the Code concerned with the effect that a takeover or merger will have upon competition—that is a matter for the government and the Competition and Markets Authority.

22.3.2.1 Scope

The provisions of the Takeover Directive apply to 'takeover bids for the securities of companies governed by the laws of Member States, where all or some of those securities are admitted to trading on a regulated market'.[104] In other words, the Directive only applies to takeover bids for the securities of listed companies. Conversely, the scope of the Takeover Code is notably wider and applies to three types of company, as follows:

(i) The Code applies to all offers (not falling within (iii) below) for companies which have their registered offices in the UK/Channel Islands/Isle of Man if any of their securities are admitted to trading on a regulated market or multilateral trading facility in the UK or on any stock exchange in the Channel Islands/Isle of Man.

(ii) The Code applies to all offers (not falling within (i) or (iii)) for public and private companies which have their registered offices in the UK/Channel Islands/Isle of Man, and which are considered by the Panel to have their place of central management and control in the UK/Channel Islands/Isle of Man.

(iii) The Code applies to companies with a shared jurisdiction (i.e. those traded companies registered in the UK and another European Economic Area (EEA) State).[105]

---

[101] ibid Introduction, s 4(b).   [102] ibid Introduction, s 2(a).   [103] ibid Introduction, s 2(a).
[104] Takeover Directive, Art 1(1).   [105] Takeover Code, Introduction, s 3(a).

22.3.2.2 The General Principles and rules

The Takeover Code consists of two forms of provisions, namely (i) the General Principles; and (ii) rules (with certain rules being elaborated on via a series of appendices to the Code). Article 3(1) of the Takeover Directive provides that Member States shall ensure that six General Principles are complied with, and these are repeated in the Takeover Code, which describes them as 'statements of standards of commercial behaviour'.[106] The General Principles are:

1. All holders of the securities of an offeree company of the same class must be afforded equivalent treatment; moreover, if a person acquires control of a company, the other holders of securities must be protected.

2. The holders of the securities of an offeree company must have sufficient time and information to enable them to reach a properly informed decision on the bid; where it advises the holders of securities, the board of the offeree company must give its views on the effects of implementation of the bid on employment, conditions of employment, and the locations of the company's places of business.

3. The board of an offeree company must act in the interests of the company as a whole and must not deny the holders of securities the opportunity to decide on the merits of the bid.

4. False markets must not be created in the securities of the offeree company, of the offeror company, or of any other company concerned by the bid in such a way that the rise or fall of the prices of the securities becomes artificial and the normal functioning of the markets is distorted.

5. An offeror must announce a bid only after ensuring that he/she can fulfil in full any cash consideration, if such is offered, and after taking all reasonable measures to secure the implementation of any other type of consideration.

6. An offeree company must not be hindered in the conduct of its affairs for longer than is reasonable by a bid for its securities.

The Takeover Code states that the General Principles are 'expressed in broad general terms and the Code does not define the precise extent of, or the limitations on, their application'.[107] The reasoning behind expressing them in such broad language is so that they can be 'applied in accordance with their spirit in order to achieve their underlying purpose'.[108] From this, it follows that a breach of the Code can occur where no rule has been breached, but a person has failed to act in accordance with a General Principle.[109]

The vast majority of the Code comes in the form of 38 detailed rules and '[a]lthough most of the rules are expressed in less general terms than the General Principles, they are not framed in technical language and, like the General Principles, are to be interpreted to achieve their underlying purpose. Therefore, their spirit must be observed as well as their letter'.[110] The Takeover Code recognizes that a measure of flexibility is required when applying its rules and it may be the case that the application of a rule in a particular situation may be inappropriate or have unexpected adverse consequences. Accordingly, the Code provides that the Panel may derogate or grant a person a waiver from the application of a rule either:

- in the circumstances set out by the rule; or
- in other circumstances where the Panel considers that the particular rule would operate unduly harshly or in an unnecessarily restrictive or burdensome or otherwise inappropriate manner (in which case a reasoned decision will be given).[111]

---

[106] ibid Introduction, s 2(b).   [107] ibid Introduction s 2(b).   [108] ibid.
[109] See e.g. Takeover Panel Statement 1974/03 Mount Charlotte Investments Ltd/Gale Lister & Co Ltd.
[110] Takeover Code, Introduction, s 2(b).   [111] ibid Introduction, s 2(c).

However, a derogation or waiver will only be granted if, in the case of a transaction and rule subject to the Directive, the General Principles have been respected.

23.3.2.3 **Enforcement**

The CA 2006 provides that the Takeover Code may contain rules conferring upon the Panel the power to impose sanctions on those who breach the Code or refuse to comply with a direction of the Panel.[112] The Code therefore provides that the Hearings Committee can commence disciplinary proceedings where it considers that there has been a breach of the Code or a ruling of the Panel Executive.[113] Sanctions that may be imposed include:

- issuing a private or public statement of censure;
- suspending or withdrawing any exemption, approval, or other special status which the Panel has granted to a person, or imposing conditions on the continuing enjoyment of such exemption, approval, or special status;
- reporting the offender's conduct to a UK or overseas regulatory or professional body (notably the Financial Conduct Authority (FCA)) so that body can decide whether to take enforcement action; and/or
- publishing a Panel Statement indicating that the offender is someone who, in the Hearings Committee's opinion, is not likely to comply with the Code[114] (known as 'cold-shouldering'). Cold-shouldering is the most serious disciplinary action available to the Panel as, under FCA rules and the rules of other professional bodies, their members become obliged to not act for the cold-shouldered person. Its seriousness is demonstrated by the fact that the Panel has only exercised its cold-shouldering powers three times, with the most recent example being set out below.[115]

Cold-shouldering

The mandatory offer is discussed at 22.3.3.3.

The Takeover Code requires that a person must make a mandatory offer for all the shares in a company if he acquires an interest in shares which carry 30 per cent or more of the voting rights in a company.[116] Via a series of companies controlled by him and his family, Mr Morton owned 28.3 per cent of shares in Hubco Investments plc. Groundlinks Ltd (another company controlled by Morton's family) acquired a further 3.4 per cent of Hubco's shares, resulting in Morton's family controlling 31.6 per cent of Hubco's shares. Morton did not make a mandatory offer on the ground that Groundlinks had purchased the shares for the benefit of a third party, namely Mr Garner (who was a friend of Morton's son). It transpired that the agreement between Morton and Garner was concocted after the shares had been purchased, meaning Morton's explanation was false. The Panel commenced an investigation.

The Takeover Code provides that any person dealing with the Panel is expected to do so in an open and cooperative way,[117] and both Morton and Garner had failed to do so. The Hearings Committee agreed with the Panel Executive that Morton and Garner had 'systematically provided to the Executive information which they knew to be false' and that both men had 'invented the agreement' in order to avoid the obligation to make a mandatory offer.[118] Accordingly, Morton was cold-shouldered for six years and Garner was cold-shouldered for two years.

---

[112] CA 2006, s 952(1).   [113] Takeover Code, Introduction, s 10(a).   [114] ibid Introduction, s 10(b).

[115] Details of these two of these instances (including the example here) can be found at www.thetakeoverpanel. org.uk/the-code/compliance/cold-shouldering accessed 10 January 2019.

[116] Takeover Code, rule 9.   [117] ibid Introduction, s 9(a).

[118] In a rather ironic twist, the Panel found that Morton's family had acted in concert with other shareholders of Hubco, meaning that Morton and these other parties already controlled more than 50 per cent of Hubco's shares and therefore the mandatory offer rules would not have been triggered.

The Act also provides that the Code may confer upon the Panel the power to order a person to pay compensation as it thinks just and reasonable if that person is in breach of a rule, the effect of which is to require the payment of money.[119] Accordingly, the Takeover Code provides that if certain breaches of the Code occur, the Panel can make a compensation ruling requiring the transgressor to pay to the holders, or former holders, of the offeree company such amount as it thinks just and reasonable so as to ensure that such holders receive what they would have been entitled to receive if the relevant rule had been complied with.[120]

In addition to the sanctions provided for under the Takeover Code, the Takeover Panel can apply to the court and, if the court is satisfied that there is a reasonable likelihood that a person will contravene a rule-based requirement or that a person has contravened a rule-based requirement or a disclosure requirement, then the court may make any order it thinks fit to secure compliance with the requirement.[121] In itself, contravention of a rule-based requirement does not make the transaction void or unenforceable,[122] nor will it give rise to an action for breach of statutory duty.[123]

22.3.3 **The conduct of takeovers**

The Takeover Code stands at 424 pages in length, and so a full examination of the Code's rules is not possible here. Here, the focus will be on providing an overview of the principal rules found within the Code.

22.3.3.1 **The approach and announcements**

General Principle 4 of the Code provides that '[f]alse markets must not be created in the securities of the offeree company, of the offeror company or of any other company concerned by the bid . . .'. Rules 1–2 of the Code are therefore largely concerned with ensuring that appropriate information regarding takeover offers (or possible offers) is announced publicly and in a timely manner. Accordingly, rule 2.2 requires that an announcement of an offer or possible offer is made in certain circumstances, including:

- where the offeror notifies the offeree's board of a firm intention to make an offer;
- where the offeror acquires enough shares to trigger a mandatory offer;
- where, before or following an approach by an offeror, the offeree is subject to rumour and speculation (e.g. rumours that it is to be subject to a takeover offer) or there is untoward movement in its share price.

The announcement of an offer or possible offer commences the 'offer period'. Rule 1 provides that where an offeror intends to make a takeover offer, it must at first instance notify the board of the offeree company that it has a firm intention to make an offer. The offeror must also announce that it has made a firm intention to make an offer.[124] This announcement must include the information specified in rule 2.7 (notably the terms of the offer must be included). An offeror should not make this announcement unless it has every reason to believe that it can and will be able to implement the offer.[125] This is because, once the announcement has been made, the offeror must proceed to make the offer, unless the offer is subject to pre-conditions[126] (i.e. conditions that must be satisfied

---

[119] CA 2006, s 954(1).   [120] Takeover Code, Introduction, s 10(c).   [121] CA 2006, s 955(1).
[122] ibid s 956(2).   [123] ibid s 956(1).   [124] Takeover Code, rules 2.2(a) and 2.3(a).
[125] ibid rule 2.7(a).   [126] ibid rule 2.7(b).

before the offer becomes binding on the offeror). It is standard for takeover offers to be subject to pre-conditions, with many offers containing an acceptance condition which provides that the offeror will only be bound by the terms of the offer if a certain percentage of the offeree's shareholders accept it (it is common for this percentage to be set at a level that will allow the offeror to squeeze out the offeree's shareholders). However, such pre-conditions are closely regulated by rule 13 and the offeror must consult and gain approval from the Panel if pre-conditions are to be included in the offer.[127] Below is an example of a case where the Panel refused to allow a pre-condition to be relied upon.

 Squeeze-out rights are discussed at 22.3.4.2.

Offeror not permitted to invoke a pre-condition

In August 2001, WPP Group plc announced a takeover offer of Tempus Group plc and, on 10 September 2001, WPP published its offer document.[128] The following day, the terrorist attack on the World Trade Centre took place. WPP's offer document contained a material adverse change clause that provided that WPP was only bound by the offer if no material adverse change or deterioration had occurred in the business, assets, or profits of Tempus. The events of 9/11 had indeed caused a deterioration in Tempus's performance and so WPP sought to rely on the clause and withdraw its offer.

The Takeover Panel stated that, in order to rely on the clause, the adverse change would need to be 'of very considerable significance striking at the heart of the purpose of the transaction in question, analogous, as the 1974/2 Panel Statement put it, to something that would justify frustration of a legal contract'.[129] Whilst Tempus's 2001 accounts did show a decline in performance, the Panel was not persuaded that they showed a material long-term decline in Tempus's prospects. Accordingly, the adverse change was not significant enough to allow WPP to rely on the clause and it was required to proceed with the takeover offer.

Historically, an offeror could announce a possible offer, and then a significant amount of time could pass before an offer was made or not, during which time the offeree's board and shareholders, not to mention the markets, would be left in a state of uncertainty. To prevent this, rule 2.6 provides for what has become known as a 'put up or shut up' announcement. Rule 2.6(a) provides that, within 28 days of a potential offer being announced (or later if the Panel grants an extension), that potential offeror must either:

- announce a firm intention to make an offer; or
- announce that it does not intend to make an offer. If it announces that it does not intend to make an offer, then it may not make an offer within a six-month period following the announcement.[130]

23.3.3.2 Restricted dealings

Rules 4–8 establish restrictions on certain type of dealing. Certain types of dealing are expressly prohibited, including:

---

[127] ibid rule 13.3.

[128] Full details of this example can be found in Panel Statement 2001/15, www.thetakeoverpanel.org.uk/wp-content/uploads/2008/12/2001-15.pdf accessed 10 January 2019.

[129] ibid para 16.   [130] Takeover Code, rule 2.8.

- No person, except the offeror, who is privy to confidential price-sensitive information concerning a takeover offer may deal in the securities of the offeree company between the time when there is reason to suppose that an approach or an offer is contemplated and the announcement of the approach or offer or of the termination of the discussions.[131]

- During an offer period, the offeror must not sell any securities in the offeree company, unless the Takeover Panel consents to the sale.[132]

Certain types of dealing are not prohibited, but must be disclosed. For example, upon a takeover offer being made, both the offeror and offeree are required to make a public Opening Position Disclosure, which is an announcement containing details of interests or short positions in, or rights to subscribe for, any relevant securities of a party to the offer if the person concerned has such a position.[133]

22.3.3.3 **The mandatory offer**

Rule 9 contains one of the Code's most important rules, namely the rule on mandatory offers. If a person acquires control of a company, other shareholders may feel powerless and may therefore wish to exit the company. Accordingly, since 1972, the Code has provided shareholders with the ability to exit the company by requiring a person who acquires a controlling interest in a company to make a mandatory offer to purchase the shares of all the other shareholders. Rule 9 applies where:

- a person (on his own or acting in concert with others) acquires an interest in shares that carry at least 30 per cent or more of the company's voting rights; or

- a person (acting on his own or in concert with others) is interested in shares which carry between 30 and 50 per cent of the company's voting rights, and that person (or someone acting in concert with him) acquires an interest in any other shares that increases the percentage of shares carrying voting rights in which he is interested.[134]

In either case, the person in question must make an offer to the holders of any class of equity shares (whether voting or non-voting) and to any holders of transferable securities carrying voting rights.[135] However, there is a danger that the person with the controlling interest may use his strong bargaining position to pressure minority shareholders into selling their shares cheaply. To prevent this, the Takeover Directive provides that the offer to purchase the shares must be at an 'equitable price'[136] and so the Code provides that the price offered for the shares is the highest price at which the offeror (or any person acting in concert with him) paid for the shares in the 12-month period prior to announcing the offer to purchase the shares.[137]

The requirement to make a mandatory offer can be waived by the Takeover Panel in several circumstances:[138]

- Where a new issue of shares would result in a mandatory offer being triggered, the Panel can waive the requirement to make a mandatory offer if there is an independent vote at a shareholders' meeting agreeing to waive the requirement to make a mandatory offer. This so-called 'whitewash' procedure will only be valid if the documents to be sent to the shareholders in advance of the meeting are approved by the Takeover Panel.

- Where an issue of news shares triggers a mandatory offer, the Panel can waive the requirement to make a mandatory offer if the company is in such a serious financial position that the only way it can be saved is by implementing an urgent rescue operation that involves the issuing of new shares.

---

[131] ibid rule 4.1(a).   [132] ibid rule 4.2(a).   [133] ibid rules 8.1–8.2.   [134] ibid rule 9.1.
[135] ibid.   [136] Takeover Directive, Art 5(1).   [137] Takeover Code, rule 9.5(a).
[138] ibid rule 9, Notes on Dispensations from Rule 9.   [139] ibid rule 14.1.

- Where, due to an inadvertent mistake, a person acquires enough shares to trigger a mandatory offer, the Panel will not require an offer to be made if that person disposes to persons unconnected him sufficient shares so that his interest is reduced to below 30 per cent.

22.3.3.4 Rules applicable to all offers

General Principle 1 of the Code provides that '[a]ll holders of the securities of an offeree company of the same class must be afforded equivalent treatment'. Accordingly, the Code establishes several rules that aim to ensure equal treatment:

- where a company has more than one class of equity share capital, a comparable offer must be made for each class;[139]
- except with the consent of the Panel, the offeror may not make arrangements with shareholders of the offeree that provide favourable conditions that are not extended to all shareholders.[140]

22.3.3.5 Conduct during the offer

The Code establishes rules of conduct that must be maintained during the offer. Rules 19 and 20 are concerned with the provision of information. Rule 19 is concerned with the quality of information provided during an offer and states *inter alia* that any document, announcement, or information published, or statement made, during the course of an offer must be prepared with the highest standards of care and accuracy. Rule 20 aims to ensure that the relevant information is provided to shareholders of the offeree company at the same time and in the same manner.

General Principle 3 of the Code provides that the board of the offeree 'must not deny the holders of securities the opportunity to decide on the merits of the bid'. Accordingly, rule 21.1 prohibits directors of the offeree from taking any action which could result in the offer being frustrated or its shareholders being denied an opportunity to vote on its merits, unless the shareholders in general meeting approve of such conduct. Such action could also result in a breach of the duty to exercise powers for the purposes for which they are conferred, although the courts have struggled to provide a consistent approach on this issue. It is clear that, where there are competing bids, the directors are not obliged to recommend the highest bid,[141] but they must not act in such a way as to prevent the shareholders from obtaining the highest price for their shares.[142] In the UK, it is relatively rare for the directors to put in place arrangements that seek to frustrate a bid or render a bid unattractive (such mechanisms, which are more prevalent in the US, are often referred to as 'poison pills'), but the following case provides such an example.

The proper purpose duty is discussed at 10.2.2.

See Peter Watts, 'Authority and Mismotivation' (2005) 121 LQR 4.

Criterion Properties plc v Stratford UK Properties LLC [2004] UKHL 28

FACTS: Criterion Properties plc ('Criterion') and Stratford UK Properties LLC (referred to in the case as 'Oaktree') entered into an agreement to facilitate a joint venture. Glaser, Criterion's managing director, later caused Criterion to enter into a second supplementary agreement (the 'SSA') with Oaktree, the effect of which was to require Criterion to buy out Oaktree at a price well

---

[140] ibid rule 16.1.
[141] *Dawson International plc v Coats Paton (No 1)* (1988) 4 BCC 305 (Court of Session).
[142] *Heron International Ltd v Lord Grade* [1983] BCLC 244 (CA).

above market value in the event of Criterion being taken over. Criterion sought to have the SSA set aside and argued that Glaser acted in breach of duty in causing Criterion to enter into the SSA. At first instance[143] and in the Court of Appeal,[144] Criterion's action was dismissed, although both courts thought the SSA was not in Criterion's commercial interests. Criterion appealed to the House of Lords.

HELD: Criterion's appeal was dismissed. The House held that the validity of the SSA turned solely on whether Glaser had authority to cause Criterion to enter into the SSA. The House stated that, as this issue has not been brought up by the lower courts or counsel, this issue could not be resolved here and would need to be resolved at trial. Accordingly, the SSA itself did not need to be discussed, but Lord Scott did provide some comments. He queried whether it was open to the board to authorize a company to enter into a poison pill which involves, as the SSA did, the company divesting its own assets upon a takeover.[145] He went on to state that, in determining whether Glaser had authority to enter into a SSA, it was necessary to take into account the extent to which the SSA 'went beyond simply including provisions to deter an unwanted predator but would have deterred also the most desirable of predators . . .'[146]

22.3.3.6 Documents from the boards

General Principle 2 provides that '[t]he holders of the securities of an offeree company must have sufficient time and information to enable them to reach a properly informed decision on the bid'. Accordingly, rules 23–7 impose obligations on the offeror and offeree regarding the publication of certain documentation. The starting point is rule 23.1 which states that:

> Shareholders must be given sufficient information and advice to enable them to reach a properly informed decision as to the merits or demerits of an offer. Such information must be available to shareholders early enough to enable them to make a decision in good time. No relevant information should be withheld from them.

Rules 24 and 25 provide for two documents to be provided to shareholders of the offeree, and it is an offence to publish a document which does not comply with rules 24 or 25.[147] The two documents are:

1. Offer document: within 28 days of the announcement of a firm intention to make an offer, the offeror must send an offer document to shareholders of the offeree,[148] and place it on a website.[149] The offer document must provide specified information including (i) the long-term commercial justification for the offer; (ii) financial information regarding the offeror, offeree, and the offer; (iii) details of the offeror's interests and dealings with the offeree; (iv) details of directors' emoluments; and (v) whether any special arrangements exist between the offeror and the offeree's directors or shareholders (including recent directors and shareholders).[150] The offer document must also state the time allowed for acceptance of the offer.[151]

2. Response circular: within 14 days of the publication of the offer document, the board of the offeree must send a circular to its shareholders[152] in which it sets out the board's

---

[143] [2002] EWHC 496 (Ch), [2002] BCLC 151.   [144] [2002] EWCA Civ 1883, [2003] 1 WLR 2108.
[145] [2004] UKHL 28, [2004] 1 WLR 1846 [29].   [146] ibid [29].   [147] CA 2006, s 953.
[148] Takeover Code, rule 24.1(a).   [149] ibid rule 24.1(c).   [150] ibid rules 24.2–24.6.
[151] ibid rule 24.7.   [152] ibid rule 25.1(a).

opinion on the offer and its reasons for that opinion and must include the effects of implementation of the offer and the offeror's strategic plans for the offeree.[153] If the board is opposed to the takeover, the takeover is known as a 'hostile takeover'.

22.3.3.7 The offer timetable

In order to ensure that the offeree's shareholders have sufficient time to consider the information contained in the offer document and to comply with the Takeover Directive's rule that '[t]he time allowed for the acceptance of a bid should be regulated',[154] the Code establishes an offer timetable, which is set out in Figure 22.1.

22.3.4 Squeeze-out and sell-out rights

The above rules are found in the Takeover Code, but an important set of rules are found in the CA 2006, namely those rules relating to squeeze-out and sell-out rights. To understand how squeeze-out and sell-out rights operate, consider the following example.

 Eg Squeeze-out and sell-out rights

Dragon plc makes a takeover offer for Beacon plc. The vast majority of Beacon's shareholders accept the offer, which results in Dragon acquiring 93 per cent of Beacon's shares.

Dragon may wish to acquire all the shares in Beacon, but the remaining shareholders may not wish to sell them. It may alternatively be the case that the remaining shareholders of Beacon no longer wish to be members and so may wish to exit the company. Squeeze-out and sell-out rights aim to cater for these goals:

- Squeeze-out rights allow an offeror who has acquired sufficient shares/voting rights in the offeree to compulsorily purchase the shares of the remaining shareholders. This is especially useful where the offeror wishes to acquire the offeree as a wholly-owned subsidiary as it ensures that this objective is 'not undermined by a small minority or because some shareholders cannot be traced'.[155]

- Sell-out rights allow the shareholders of the offeree to compel the offeror to acquire their shares if certain conditions ae fulfilled. Minority shareholders may feel isolated and powerless where the offeror has acquired the vast majority of the offeree's shares and so will value the ability to exit the company.

It is clear that squeeze-out and sell-out rights aim to 'strike a balance between the interests of a bidder whose takeover offer was sufficient to enable it to obtain acceptances from 90 per cent or more of the shares to which the offer related, and the interests of the minority who refused the offer'.[156]

22.3.4.1 'Takeover offer'

Squeeze-out and sell-out rights only apply where there has been a 'takeover offer' as defined under s 974 of the CA 2006, namely where an offer to acquire shares in a company satisfies the following two conditions:

---

[153] ibid rule 25.2.   [154] Takeover Directive, Preamble, para 14.
[155] *Re Greythorn Ltd* [2002] BCC 559 (Ch) 567 (Robert Hildyard QC).   [156] ibid.

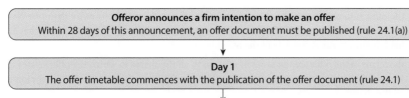

Offeror announces a firm intention to make an offer
Within 28 days of this announcement, an offer document must be published (rule 24.1(a))

↓

Day 1
The offer timetable commences with the publication of the offer document (rule 24.1)

↓

Day 14
Except with the consent of the Panel, the response circular must be sent within 14 days of the offer document being published (rule 25.1(a))

↓

Day 21
The offer must remain open for at least 21 days (rule 31.1), so Day 21 is the earliest first closing date

↓

Day 39
After Day 39, the board of the offeree should not announce any new material information, unless the Panel so consents (rule 31.9)

↓

Day 42
An accepting shareholder can withdraw his acceptance up to 21 days following the first closing date (rule 34.1), so if the first closing date is Day 21, withdrawal of acceptance cannot occur after Day 42

↓

Day 46
An offeror cannot send a revised offer document after Day 46 (rule 32.1(c))

↓

Day 53
A competing offeror cannot announce a firm intention to make an offer after Day 53 (rule 2.6(d) and (e))

↓

Day 60
Unless the Panel so consents, Day 60 is the maximum period up to which an offer (whether revised or not) can be extended (rule 31.6), so Day 60 is usually the latest final closing date possible

↓

Day 74
An offer that has become unconditional as to acceptances must remain open for acceptance for at least another 14 days (rule 31.4), so if an offer became unconditional as to acceptances on Day 60, it must remain open until at least Day 74

↓

Day 81
All conditions must be fulfilled or the offer will lapse within 21 days of the first closing date or the date the offer becomes unconditional as to acceptances, whichever is the later (rule 31.7). Accordingly, if the offer becomes unconditional as to acceptances on Day 60, all other offer conditions must be satisfied by Day 81 or the offer will lapse

↓

Consideration sent to the accepting shareholders
The consideration for the offeree's shares must be sent to accepting shareholders within 14 days of the first closing date, the date the offer became wholly unconditional, or the date of receipt of acceptance (whichever is the later) (rule 31.8).

FIGURE 22.1 The offer timetable

1. the offer is to acquire all the shares in a company or, where there is more than one class of shares in a company, all of the shares of one or more classes (other than shares that are held by the offeror at the date of the offer);[157]

2. the terms of the offer are the same in relation to all the shares to which the offer relates or, where the shares to which the offer relates include shares of different classes, in relation to all the shares of each class.[158]

22.3.4.2 **Squeeze-out rights**

Section 979 of the CA 2006 (which implements Art 15 of the Takeover Directive) provides the offeror with the right to compulsorily acquire the remaining shares in a company (i.e. to squeeze out the remaining shareholders). However, this right only arises if the offeror has acquired or unconditionally contracted to acquire (i) not less than 90 per cent in value of the shares to which the offer relates; and (ii) in a case where the shares to which the offer relates are voting shares, not less than 90 per cent of the voting rights carried by those shares.[159]

Treasury shares are discussed at 17.2.2.6.

When calculating whether the offeror has acquired sufficient shares to trigger squeeze-out rights, certain types of shares are not counted, namely (i) relevant treasury shares;[160] (ii) shares already held by the offeror at the date of the offer;[161] and (iii) shares already held by 'associates' of the offeror at the date of the offer.[162]

If the offeror has acquired the requisite shares/voting rights, then he can exercise his squeeze-out rights by giving notice to the other shareholders that he desires to acquire their shares.[163] An offeror who has not acquired the requisite shares/voting rights may nevertheless be able to provide such notice if the court so orders, but it will only do so if:

(a) the offeror has after reasonable enquiry been unable to trace one or more of the persons holding shares to which the offer relates;

(b) the usual 90 percent requirement would have been met if the person, or all the persons, mentioned in paragraph (a) above had accepted the offer; and

(c) the consideration offered is fair and reasonable.[164]

The notice must be given (i) within three months beginning on the day after the last day on which the offer can be accepted; or (ii) if the offer is not governed by the Takeover Code, within six months beginning on the date of the offer.[165] A shareholder receiving a notice may, within six weeks of receiving the notice, challenge the notice by applying to the court.[166] The court may then either:

● order that the offeror is not entitled and bound to acquire the shares to which the offer relates; or

● amend the terms on which the offeror is entitled and bound to acquire the shares as the court thinks fit.[167]

---

[157] CA 2006, s 974(2).   [158] ibid s 974(3).

[159] ibid s 979(1) and (2). This rule applies to takeover offers that relate to a single class of share. Where the offer relates to different classes of share, s 979(3) and (4) impose a similar threshold to apply to the classes of shares in question.

[160] ibid s 974(4). Relevant treasury shares are (i) shares held by the company on the date of the offer; or (ii) shares that became treasury shares after the date of the offer but before a specified date (ibid s 974(6)).

[161] ibid ss 974(2) and 975.   [162] ibid s 975(4). An 'associate' is defined in s 988.

[163] ibid s 979(2) and (4).   [164] ibid s 986(9).   [165] ibid s 980(2) and (3).   [166] ibid s 986(1) and (2).

[167] ibid s 986(1). Although these remedies are alternatives, the applicant may pursue both (although only one will be granted).

Given the significant majority required to trigger squeeze-out rights, it is unsurprising that few challenges succeed. As Maugham J stated:

> prima facie the court ought to regard the scheme as a fair one inasmuch as it seems to me impossible to suppose that the court, in the absence of very strong grounds, is to be entitled to set up its own view of the fairness of the scheme in opposition to so very large a majority of the shareholders who are concerned.[168]

Such a challenge will only succeed where 'it is affirmatively established that, notwithstanding the views of a very large majority of shareholders, the scheme is unfair'.[169] The onus on establishing unfairness is placed on the applicant[170] and the test of fairness is based on 'whether the offer is fair to the offerees as a body and not whether it is fair to a particular shareholder in the peculiar circumstances of his own case'.[171] The following case provides an example of where unfairness was established.

 Re Bugle Press Ltd [1961] Ch 270 (CA)

FACTS: Re Bugle Press Ltd ('Bugle') had issued 10,000 shares. Jackson and Shaw (Bugle's directors) held 4,500 shares each, with the remaining 1,000 shares being held by Treby. Jackson and Shaw incorporated Jackson and Shaw (Holdings) Ltd ('JSH'), with Jackson and Shaw as its only directors and shareholders. JSH carried on no business. JSH made a takeover offer of Bugle. Unsurprisingly, Jackson and Shaw accepted the offer, but Treby refused on the ground that the offer price was too low. As the offer had been accepted by 90 per cent of Bugle's shareholders, JSH provided Treby with notice that it wished to compulsorily acquire his shares. Treby challenged the notice.

HELD: Treby's challenge succeeded and the court ordered that the JSH could not compulsorily acquire Treby's shares. Buckley J stated that squeeze-out rights apply 'where the offeror is independent of the shareholders in the transferor company or at least independent of that part or fraction of them from which the 90 per cent is to be derived'.[172] Here, the offeror (JSH) and the majority shareholders were effectively the same persons. Harman LJ was more critical, describing Jackson and Shaw's actions as 'a barefaced attempt to evade that fundamental rule of company law which forbids the majority of shareholders, unless the articles so provide, to expropriate a minority'.[173]

If no challenge is made to the court,[174] then the offeror becomes entitled and bound to acquire the shares to which the notice relates on the terms of the offer.[175] At the end of a six-week period beginning on the date of the notice, the offeror must send a copy of the notice to the company and provide payment to the company for the shares which the notice relates to.[176] The company must then register the offeror as the holder of the acquired shares.[177] The payment received by the company is held on trust by the company for the former holders of the shares[178] and the company must make reasonable enquiries to find such persons.[179] If these persons are found, the money is paid to them, but if they are not found within a 12-year period, the money received must be paid into court.[180]

---

168 _Re Hoare & Co Ltd_ [1933] All ER Rep 105 (Ch) 107.   169 ibid.   170 ibid.
171 _Re Grierson, Oldham & Adams Ltd_ [1968] Ch 17 (Ch) 32 (Plowman J).
172 [1961] Ch 270 (CA) 287.   173 ibid 287–8.
174 If a challenge is made, squeeze-out rights cannot be exercised or the notice withdrawn until the challenge has been disposed of (_Re Greythorn Ltd_ [2002] BCC 559 (Ch)).
175 CA 2006, s 981(2).   176 ibid s 981(6).   177 ibid s 981(7).
178 ibid s 981(9).   179 ibid s 982(5)(a).   180 ibid s 982(4).

22.3.4.3 **Sell-out rights**

It may be the case that an offeror decides not to exercise his squeeze-out rights, but the minority shareholders wish to exit the company (which would not be surprising given their relatively powerless position). Section 983 of the CA 2006 (which implements Art 16 of the Takeover Directive) provides a shareholder with sell-out rights (i.e. the right to compel the offeror to purchase his shares) but only if several conditions are satisfied, namely:

- the takeover offer relates to that shareholder's shares and that person has not accepted the takeover offer;
- the offer period has not expired;
- the offeror has by virtue of acceptances of the offer acquired or unconditionally contracted to acquire some (but not all) of the shares to which the offer relates; and
- those shares, with or without any other shares in the company which he has acquired or contracted to acquire amount to not less than 90 per cent in value of all the voting shares in the company and carry not less than 90 per cent of the voting rights in the company.[181]

In order to exercise his sell-out rights, the shareholder must write to the offeror requiring that his shares be acquired.[182] It may be the case that some shareholders are not aware of their sell-out rights and so, within one month of the sell-out rights being acquired, the offeror must write to any shareholder who has not accepted his offer and inform them of their sell-out rights.[183] A shareholder may exercise his sell-out rights up to three months beginning at the end of the offer period or, if later, the date on which the offeror notifies the shareholder of his sell-out rights.[184]

Where a shareholder exercises his sell-out rights, the offeror becomes bound to acquire that shareholder's shares on the terms of the takeover offer or such other terms as may be agreed.[185] A shareholder who wishes to sell his shares can apply to the court, which can order that the offeror is bound to acquire the shares on such terms as the court thinks fit[186]—this can be useful where the shareholder wishes to sell his shares, but is not satisfied with the terms of the takeover offer. However, as is the case with challenges to squeeze-out rights, such challenges rarely succeed.

CHAPTER SUMMARY

- A reconstruction under s 110 of the IA 1986 involves all or part of a company's business or property being transferred or sold to one or more new companies, and the original company is then voluntarily wound up.

- A s 110 reconstruction binds all members and creditors who are affected by it, even those who did not vote for it.

- A scheme of arrangement, under Pt 26 of the CA 2006, is a compromise or arrangement between a company and (i) its creditors, or any class of them; or (ii) its members, or any class of them.

---

[181] ibid s 983(1) and (2). This rule applies to takeover offers that relate to a single class of share. Where the offer relates to different classes of share, s 983(4) imposes a similar threshold to apply to the classes of shares in question.
[182] ibid s 984(1).
[183] ibid s 984(3). The offeror need not comply with this if he has given notice of his desire to exercise his squeeze-out rights (s 984(4)).
[184] ibid s 984(2).   [185] ibid s 985(2).
[186] ibid s 986(3). The offeror may also apply to the court for such an order.

- Implementing a scheme of arrangement is a three-stage process, namely (i) an application is made to the court to summon meetings of those members and creditors who will be affected by the scheme; (ii) the relevant meetings are held to determine whether the scheme is to be approved; and (iii) an application is made to the court to sanction the scheme.

- Takeovers are regulated by the Panel on Takeovers and Mergers, who are responsible for drafting and updating the City Code on Takeovers and Mergers.

- The CA 2006 provides offerors with the ability to squeeze out minority shareholders, and provides minority shareholders with the right to compel the offeror to buy them out.

FURTHER READING

Maurice Dwyer, 'Section 110 Reconstructions in Private Equity Transactions' (2002) 13 ICCLR 295.
- Provides a clear overview, along with examples, of the s 110 procedure and looks at why such a procedure is useful.

Andrew Johnston, 'Takeover Regulation: Historical and Theoretical Perspectives on the City Code' (2007) 66 CLJ 422.
- Discusses the emergence of the hostile takeover and examines the background to the introduction of the Takeover Code.

Jennifer Payne, 'Debt Restructuring in English Law: Lessons from the United States and the Need for Reform' (2014) 130 LQR 282.
- Looks at the various mechanisms (including schemes of arrangement) that can be used to restructure a company' debts.

Charles Zhen Qu, 'Sanctioning Schemes of Arrangement: The Need for Granting a Court a Curative Power' [2016] JBL 13.
- Discusses the court's role in sanctioning schemes of arrangement.

Beate Sjafjell, 'The Core of Corporate Governance: Implications of the Takeover Directive for Corporate Governance in Europe' (2011) 22 EBL Rev 641.
- Discusses how the Takeover Directive affects the governance of companies, focusing on the effects on the offeror and the offeree's board and shareholders.

SELF-TEST QUESTIONS

1. Define the following terms:
- scheme of arrangement;
- takeover;
- mandatory offer;
- squeeze-out rights;
- sell-out rights.

2. State whether each of the following statements is true or false and, if false, explain why:
- A scheme of arrangement is a binding agreement between a company and (i) its members; (ii) its directors; or (iii) its creditors.
- A scheme of arrangement involves two court hearings.
- A scheme of arrangement binds only those persons who voted for it.
- The Takeover Code is not concerned with the financial or commercial merits of a takeover bid, nor is it concerned with the implications on competition.

- If a person acquires at least 30 per cent of a company's shares, he must make an offer to all the remaining shareholders.
- Squeeze-out and sell-out rights come into effect once the bidder has acquired over 50 per cent of a company's shares.

3. Analyse the advantages and disadvantages of the scheme of arrangement.

4. Spartan plc is considering diversifying its business into the manufacture of certain PC components. It has acquired 29.6 per cent of the shares in PC Tech plc, a company that specializes in manufacturing PC components. Spartan is considering taking over PC Tech, but before it makes an offer, it seeks your advice regarding the following:

- What percentage of PC Tech's shares will Spartan need to acquire in order to take it over?
- A shareholder who owns 2 per cent of PC Tech's shares has offered to sell them to Spartan, and Spartan seeks your advice on whether it should accept this offer.
- If Spartan were to make a bid for PC Tech, explain the principal rules that Spartan would need to comply with.
- The directors of Spartan have stated that, ideally, they would like PC Tech to become a wholly owned subsidiary of Spartan and seek your advice as to how to achieve this aim.

ONLINE RESOURCES

This book is accompanied by online resources to better support you in your studies. Visit www.oup.com/uk/roach-company/ for:

- answers to the self-test questions;
- further reading lists;
- multiple-choice questions;
- glossary.

Updates to the law can be found on the author's Twitter account (@UKCompanyLaw) and further resources can be found on the author's blog (www.companylawandgovernance.com).

23 Liquidation, dissolution, and restoration

- Types of liquidation
- Role and powers of the liquidator
- Malpractice before and during liquidation
- Adjustment of prior transactions
- Dissolution
- Restoration

INTRODUCTION

In 2017/18, the existence of 466,347 companies was brought to an end.[1] The reasons for ending a company's existence are numerous. A company's existence may be ended voluntarily by those who control it, or it may be ended against the wishes of such persons. It may end due to poor financial performance, or it may end due to a range of non-financial reasons. The law therefore needs to provide flexible processes that bring a company's existence to an end, and this final chapter of the book discusses the two processes that lead to a company's existence ending, namely:

1. **Liquidation**: this is the procedure where by the assets of the company are collected and realized, its debts and liabilities paid, and the surplus (if any) distributed to persons so entitled. Liquidated companies then go on to be dissolved.

2. **Dissolution**: this is the process whereby the company is removed from the register of companies, thereby ending its existence.

It may be the case that a dissolved company was wrongly dissolved or has unfinished business to take care of, and will therefore need to be resurrected, and so a third process will also be discussed, namely restoration. The chapter begins by looking at the two forms of liquidation.

---

[1] Companies House, 'Companies Register Activities 2017 to 2018' (Companies House 2018) Table A9.

23.1 Types of liquidation

Chapter 21 discussed rescue mechanisms. In many cases, rescue is not possible and a company that is unable to trade its way out of financial difficulty will likely be placed into liquidation (also known as 'winding up'). Liquidation often is the penultimate step in ending a company's existence[2] and is the process whereby the assets of the company are collected and realized, its debts and liabilities paid, and the surplus distributed to persons so entitled. The Insolvency Act 1986 (IA 1986) provides for two types of liquidation, namely:

1. voluntary winding up; and
2. winding up by the court (almost always known in practice as 'compulsory winding up').

Both types of liquidation are available to solvent and insolvent companies, but the significant differences between them means that both must be examined separately.

23.1.1 Voluntary winding up

Of the two types of liquidation, voluntary liquidation is easily the most popular—in 2017/18, there were 3,311 compulsory liquidations in the UK, compared to 22,318 voluntary liquidations.[3] The principal reason for this is that the court is rarely involved in voluntary liquidations—as the Cork Report stated '[t]he purpose of voluntary winding up is to avoid involving the courts and to allow the company and its creditors to settle affairs between themselves with, however, recourse to the Court in the case of difficulty or dispute.'[4] As a result of this, voluntary liquidations can be conducted more speedily and with less cost. The courts will only tend to get involved if some form of malpractice is discovered (e.g. of the kind discussed at 23.3) or if a major dispute arises between the parties involved which the court is called upon to resolve.

There are two types of voluntary winding up, namely (i) a members' voluntary winding up; and (ii) a creditors' voluntary winding up. The differences between them are discussed at 23.1.1.1, but both types of voluntary winding up are commenced in the same manner, namely by the company passing a special resolution resolving that the company be wound up voluntarily.[5] However, a resolution (i.e. an ordinary resolution or some other majority specified in the articles) will suffice where the articles provide that the company is to expire after a fixed duration, or the company is to be dissolved upon a specified event occurring and that event occurs.[6]

A voluntary winding up is deemed to commence at the time the resolution is passed.[7] A copy of the resolution must be forwarded to the registrar of companies within 15 days of it being passed,[8] and an advertisement giving notice of the resolution must be placed in *The Gazette* within 14 days of the resolution being passed.[9] Once the winding up commences:

- the company must cease to carry on its business, except so far as may be required for its beneficial winding up;[10] and
- any transfer of shares (except a transfer made to or with the sanction of the liquidator), and any alteration in the status of the company's members is void.[11]

---

[2] The final step (i.e. dissolution) is discussed at 23.5. It is worth noting that most companies that are dissolved are not liquidated.

[3] Companies House, 'Companies Register Activities 2017 to 2018' (Companies House 2018) Table A10.

[4] *Report of the Review Committee on Insolvency Law and Practice* (Cmnd 8558, HMSO 1982) para 176.

[5] IA 1986, s 84(1)(b).   [6] ibid s 84(1)(a).   [7] ibid s 86.

[8] IA 1986 s 84(3) and CA 2006, s 30(1).   [9] IA 1986, s 85(1).   [10] ibid s 87(1).   [11] ibid s 88.

23.1.1.1 Members' and creditors' voluntary winding up

Only solvent companies can be wound up via a members' voluntary winding up, whereas a creditors' voluntary winding up can be used in relation to solvent and insolvent companies (although most are insolvent). This distinction manifests itself via the making of a declaration of solvency by the directors—if such a declaration is made in the five-week period prior to the date of the resolution, the winding up with be a members' winding up.[12] If no declaration is made, it will be a creditors' voluntary winding up.[13]

A declaration of solvency is a declaration of the directors[14] providing that they have made a full inquiry into the company's affairs and that, having done so, they have formed the opinion that the company will be able to pay its debts in full (including interest) within such a period as specified in the declaration (this period cannot exceed 12 months from the date of the commencement of the winding up).[15] The declaration must be delivered to the registrar of companies within 15 days of the resolution being passed.[16]

A director who makes a declaration of solvency without having reasonable grounds for the opinion in it, will commit a criminal offence.[17] If the liquidator is of the opinion that the company will be unable to pay its debts within the period specified in the declaration, then he must send a statement of affairs it to the company's creditors.[18] The company's creditors may then nominate a person to act as liquidator[19] and, if they do so, the winding up will become a creditors' voluntary winding up.[20]

23.1.1.2 Appointment of the liquidator

In the case of a members' voluntary winding up, the company in general meeting shall appoint a liquidator[21] (usually at the same meeting where the resolution to wind up the company is passed). Upon the liquidator's appointment, the powers of the directors will cease, except in so far as the company in general meeting or the liquidator sanctions their continued use.[22]

In the case of a creditors' voluntary winding up, the company can nominate a person to act as the liquidator.[23] However, the creditors may also nominate a person to act as liquidator[24] and, if no nomination is made by the company, the creditors' nominee will become the liquidator.[25] If the company and the creditors nominate different persons, then any director, member, or creditor of the company may apply to the court for an order directing that (i) the company's nominee shall be liquidator instead of, or jointly with, the creditors' nominee; or (ii) some other person be appointed instead of the person nominated by the creditors.[26] Once a liquidator is appointed, all the powers of the directors cease except those which the liquidation committee (or the creditors if no such committee exists) allows the directors to continue to use.[27]

23.1.1.3 Liquidation committee

The creditors in a creditors' voluntary winding up have the right to appoint no more than five persons to act as a liquidation committee.[28] If no such committee is appointed

---

[12] ibid ss 89(2)(a) and 90.   [13] ibid s 90.

[14] If the company has two directors, both must make the declaration in order for it to be valid. Where the company has more than two directors, a majority must make the declaration for it to be valid (s 89(1)).

[15] IA 1986, s 89(1).   [16] ibid s 89(3).

[17] ibid s 89(4). If the company is wound up within five weeks of the declaration being made, and its debts are not paid in full within the period specified, it will be presumed that the directors did not have reasonable grounds (s 89(5)).

[18] ibid s 95(1)–(4).   [19] ibid s 95(4B).   [20] ibid s 96(1)(a).   [21] ibid s 91(1).

[22] ibid s 91(2).   [23] ibid s 100(1).   [24] ibid s 100(1A).   [25] ibid s 100(2).

[26] ibid s 100(3).   [27] ibid s 103.   [28] ibid s 101(1).

by the creditors, the company may appoint such persons to act as members of the committee.[29] However, the creditors may veto all or some of the company's appointments[30] and, following an application to the court by the creditors, the court may appoint other persons to act in place of the vetoed persons.[31] The liquidation committee is granted various powers under statute, including:

- the power to determine the liquidator's remuneration;[32]
- the power to require the liquidator to deliver a report to them regarding the progress of the winding up indicating any matters to which the committee's attention should be drawn;[33]
- the power to allow the directors to continue to use their powers;[34]
- the power to sanction a scheme under s 110 of the IA 1986.[35]

Section 110 is discussed at 22.1.

23.1.2 **Winding up by the court**

Winding up by the court (or 'compulsory winding up' as it is almost always known in practice) occurs where a person petitions the court for an order to wind up a company, and the court makes such an order. The rules relating to compulsory winding up are found in ss 117–62 of the IA 1986.

23.1.2.1 **Who may petition the court?**

Only specified persons have the right to petition the court for a winding-up order.[36] However, the list of such persons is broad. The principal provision is s 124, which empowers the following to petition the court:

- the company (such petitions are rare, as the company would likely prefer a voluntary winding up);
- the directors of the company;
- any creditor or creditors of the company, including any contingent or prospective creditor or creditors (in practice, the vast majority of winding-up petitions are brought by a creditor or creditors);
- a contributory or contributories[37] (a 'contributory' is a person liable to contribute to the assets of the company upon it being wound up[38] (e.g. a shareholder whose shares are not fully paid up));
- a liquidator within the meaning of Art 3(1) of the EU Regulation on Insolvency proceedings;[39]
- the designated officer in a magistrates' court;
- the Secretary of State;[40]

---

[29] ibid s 101(2).

[30] ibid s 101(3)(1). However, the court can override the creditors' veto and provide that all or some of the company's appointees should continue.

[31] ibid s 103(3)(b).   [32] Insolvency (England and Wales) Rules 2016 (IR 2016), r 18.20.

[33] ibid r 17.23.   [34] IA 1986, s 103.   [35] ibid s 110(3)(b).

[36] This right cannot be taken from such persons by the articles (*Re Peveril Gold Mines Ltd* [1898] 1 Ch 122 (CA)).

[37] Note that a contributory can only present a winding-up petition if (i) the number of members is reduced below two; or (ii) the shares allotted to him were held by him and registered in his name for at least six months during the 18 months before the commencement of the winding up (IA 1986, s 124(2)).

[38] IA 1986, s 79(1).

[39] Council Regulation 1346/2000/EC of 29 May 2000 on insolvency proceedings [2000] OJ L160/1.

[40] The Secretary of State may only petition under specified grounds, namely ss 122(1)(b) or (c), 124A, or 124B (IA 1986, s 122(4)).

- the Financial Conduct Authority (FCA);
- the Regulator of Community Interest Companies;
- an official receiver (providing that the company is in voluntary liquidation).

Other statutory provisions empower other persons (e.g. an administrator)[41] to apply for a winding-up petition.

23.1.2.2 Circumstances where a winding-up order may be made

A winding-up petition may only be brought in circumstances specified in statute, notably s 122 of the IA 1986, which specifies seven circumstances of which only two are of relevance for the purposes of this chapter:

1. the company is unable to pay its debts;
2. the court is of the opinion that it is just and equitable that the company should be wound up.

Just and equitable winding up is discussed at 15.4, so here the inability to pay debts will be discussed. This is the most popular circumstance in which a compulsory winding-up order is made (which explains why creditors are the most popular applicants). The use of the word 'debts' does not mean that the company must be unable to pay all its debts—the inability to pay a single debt[42] will suffice. The question that arises is when a company will be unable to pay its debts. Guidance is provided in s 123 which provides that a company is deemed unable to pay its debts:

(a) if a creditor, who is owed more than £750, leaves at the company's office a statutory demand requiring the company to pay the sum due and, for a three-week period thereafter, the company has not paid the sum due;[43] or

(b) if a judgment has been executed against the company in the UK, and the company fails to satisfy that judgment;[44] or

(c) if it is proved to the satisfaction of the court that the company is unable to pay its debts as they fall due;[45] or

(d) if it is proved to the satisfaction of the court that the value of the company's assets is less than the amount of its liabilities, taking into account its contingent and prospective liabilities.[46]

The tests in s 123(1) (namely (a), (b), and (c) above) are based on debts that are due and so are known as 'cash-flow' tests. The test in s 123(2) (namely (d)) is referred to as the 'balance-sheet' test and can be based on contingent or prospective debts. The balance-sheet test is often used by creditors as a means of establishing that the company cannot pay its debts, and this provision was discussed by the Supreme Court in *BNY Corporate Trustee Services Ltd v Eurosail-UK 2007-3BL plc*.[47] The Court of Appeal had ruled that s 123(2) 'can only be relied on by a future or contingent creditor of a company which has reached "the end of the road . . ."'[48] or the 'point of no return'.[49] This was strongly criticized on the ground that it stretches the wording of s 123(2) and introduces a new requirement that is not mentioned in s 123(2) itself or any prior case law[50] and, therefore, made the balance-sheet test much more difficult to satisfy. Unsurprisingly, the

---

[41] IA 1986, Sch 1, para 21.

[42] The creditor to whom the debt is owed will usually be the petitioner, but this need not be the case.

[43] IA 1986, s 123(1)(a).   [44] ibid s 123(1)(b), (c), and (d).   [45] ibid s 123(1)(e).

[46] ibid s 123(2).   [47] [2013] UKSC 28, [2013] 1 WLR 1408.

[48] [2011] EWCA Civ 227, [2011] 1 WLR 2524 [58] (Lord Neuberger MR).   [49] ibid [52].

[50] Peter Walton, '"Inability to Pay Debts": Beyond the Point of No Return?' (2013) 2 JBL 212, 233.

Supreme Court moved away from this, with Lord Walker stating that the phrase '"point of no return" should not pass into common usage as a paraphrase of the effect of section 123(2)'.[51] He went on to state a number of other points relating to s 123:

- The cash-flow test is not simply concerned with debts that are presently due, but also with debts 'falling from time to time in the reasonably near future'.[52] What is the reasonably near future will depend on all the circumstances of the case.

- Once the debts move beyond the reasonably near future, an application of the cash-flow test become purely speculative and the balance-sheet test 'becomes the only sensible test'.[53] It is, however, 'very far from an exact test'[54] and the burden of proof is placed on the person who is alleging that the company is balance-sheet insolvent.

- Lord Walker agreed[55] with Toulson LJ in the Court of Appeal who stated that s 123(2) requires the court 'to make a judgment whether it has been established that, looking at the company's assets and making proper allowance for its prospective and contingent liabilities, it cannot reasonably be expected to be able to meet those liabilities. If so, it will be deemed insolvent although it is currently able to pay its debts as they fall due. The more distant the liabilities, the harder this will be to establish'.[56]

23.1.2.3 The winding-up order

Section 122 refers to circumstances in which the company *may* be wound up. From this, it follows that the existence of such circumstances will not automatically result in a winding-up order being made. A winding-up order is granted at the court's discretion and the court may decide that compelling reasons exist not to grant the order (e.g. because the petition is an abuse of process).[57]

Where a winding-up order is made, then the winding up will be deemed to commence at the time of the presentation of the winding-up petition,[58] unless before the petition was presented, a resolution was passed to voluntarily wind up the company, in which case the winding up will commence at the time the resolution was passed.[59] The court may appoint a provisional liquidator at any time between the winding-up petition being presented and the winding-up order being made.[60] The purpose behind appointing a provisional liquidator is 'to keep things in status quo and to prevent anybody from getting priority'[61] (i.e. to preserve the company's assets and to prevent certain parties from prioritizing their position upon liquidation). A provisional liquidator does not have the right to wind up the company or distribute its assets—that requires a liquidator (i.e. not provisional) to be appointed.

The making of a winding-up order has the following effects:

- a liquidator will be appointed (discussed below);
- a copy of the winding-up order must be forwarded by the company to the registrar of companies;[62]
- the liquidator (or provisional liquidator) will take into his custody or under his control all the property to which the company is, or appears to be, entitled;[63]
- the directors will cease to hold office;[64]

---

[51] [2013] UKSC 28, [2013] 1 WLR 1408 [42].   [52] ibid [37].   [53] ibid.
[54] ibid.   [55] ibid [42].   [56] [2011] EWCA Civ 227, [2011] 1 WLR 2524 [119].
[57] *Re a Company (No 001573 of 1983)* (1983) 1 BCC 98937 (Ch).   [58] IA 1986, s 129(2).
[59] ibid s 129(1).
[60] ibid s 135(1) and (2). The process for appointing a provisional liquidator can be found in r 7.33 of the IR 2016.
[61] *Re Dry Docks Corporation of London* (1888) 39 ChD 306 (Ch) 309 (Kay J).   [62] IA 1986, s 130(1).
[63] ibid s 144(1).   [64] *Measures Bros Ltd v Measures* [1910] 2 Ch 248 (CA).

- certain dispositions of property will become prohibited (discussed at 23.1.2.4);
- certain legal proceedings will be stayed (discussed at 23.1.2.5).

Upon a winding-up order being made, the official receiver attached to the court becomes the company's liquidator until such time as another person is appointed.[65] Another person may be appointed in several ways:

- The official receiver may seek nominations from the company's creditors and contributories for the purpose for choosing a person to act as liquidator in place of the official receiver.[66] The creditors and contributories may then nominate a person to act as liquidator.[67] The person nominated by the creditors will then become to liquidator, unless they have not nominated anyone, in which case the contributories' nominee will become the liquidator.[68] Where the creditors and contributories nominate different persons, then any creditor or contributory may apply to the court for an order either (i) appointing the contributories' nominee instead of, or jointly with, the creditors' nominee; or (ii) appointing some other person to be liquidator instead of the creditors' nominee.[69]

- The official receiver may apply to the Secretary of State to appoint a person as liquidator in his place.[70]

23.1.2.4 Avoidance of property dispositions

Where the court orders that a company be wound up, the winding up is generally deemed to commence at the time of the presentation of the winding-up petition.[71] There is a danger that, between the petition being presented and the court order being made, the property and assets of the company may be dissipated to the prejudice of the company's creditors. To prevent this, s 127(1) provides that, in a compulsory winding up, any disposition of the company's property, and any transfer of shares, or alteration in the status of the company's members, made after the commencement of the winding up is void, unless the court orders otherwise. It has been argued that s 127 tries to strike a balance between two competing interests, namely:

> On the one hand, the allegedly insolvent company must be allowed to continue trading until the court has had an opportunity to examine the [validity] of the petition; on the other hand, the company's directors must be prevented from dealing with the corporate assets in a way detrimental to the interests of the general creditors.[72]

The key issue in this area, and the issue that the case law has focused strongly on, is what amounts to a 'disposition of the company's property'. A number of cases, of which the following is the most notable, have focused on whether a payment out of the company's bank account constitutes a disposition of property and, if so, who is to be liable.

Hollicourt (Contracts) Ltd v Bank of Ireland [2001] Ch 555 (CA)

FACTS: In February 1996, a petition was presented to the court to wind up Hollicourt (Contracts) Ltd ('Hollicourt'), and this was publicized a few weeks later. Hollicourt had a bank account with the Bank of Ireland, but the Bank was unaware of the winding-up petition until May (at which point it froze the

See Christopher Hare, 'Banker's Liability for Post-Petition Dispositions' (2001) 60 CLJ 468.

---

[65] IA 1986, s 136(1) and (2).   [66] ibid s 136(4).   [67] ibid s 139(2).   [68] ibid s 139(3).
[69] ibid s 139(4).   [70] ibid s 137(1).   [71] ibid s 129(3).
[72] Christopher Hare, 'Banker's Liability for Post-Petition Dispositions' (2001) 60 CLJ 468, 468–9.

account). Accordingly, between February and May, the Bank continued to debit Hollicourt's account with payments to third parties that totalled £156,200. In June, the court ordered that Hollicourt be wound up and Hollicourt's liquidator commenced proceedings against the Bank on the ground that the payments made to third parties were dispositions of the company's property and were therefore void. At first instance,[73] the court held that the payments were a s 127 disposition and the Bank was therefore liable to repay the liquidator the value of the payments made. The Bank appealed.

HELD: The appeal was allowed. There was no doubt that the payments were a disposition under s 127, but the Bank was not liable for them as the dispositions were not made in favour of the Bank. Accordingly, Hollicourt could seek to recover the payments from the third parties to whom they were made, but not from the Bank. Mummery LJ stated that s 127:

> enables the company to recover the amounts disposed of, but only from the payees. It does not enable the company to recover the amounts from the bank, which has only acted in accordance with the instructions as the company's agent to make payments to the payees out of the company's bank account.[74]

A post-winding-up disposition under s 127 is void, but s 127 itself provides no guidance on remedies (e.g. how the disposed assets can be recovered). Accordingly, it has been held that the appropriate remedy will 'be determined by the general law'.[75] In most cases, where the property is tangible or where it amounts to money drawn from a bank account, this will not prove problematic as the transfer will be void, and so the transferee will be required to return the property due to a lack of title. Not all dispositions under s 127 will be void, however, as the court has a discretion to order that a s 127 disposition is not void (it does this by issuing a 'validation order'). A validation order can be granted at the time of the winding-up petition, or it can be made in advance of a winding up.[76]

23.1.2.5 Staying of proceedings

Section 130(2) provides that when a winding-up order has been made, no legal action or proceedings shall be proceeded with or commenced against the company or its property, except by leave of the court and subject to such terms as the court may impose. The rationale behind staying such proceedings was set out by James LJ, who stated that s 130(2) was:

> intended, not for the purpose of harassing, or impeding, or injuring third persons, but for the purpose of preserving the limited assets of the company or bankrupt in the best way for distribution among all the persons who have claims upon them. There being only a small fund or a limited fund to be divided among a great number of persons, it would be monstrous that one or more of them should be harassing the company with actions and incurring costs which would increase the claims against the company and diminish the assets which ought to be divided among all the creditors.[77]

🔗 The *pari passu* principle is discussed at 23.2.3.

Therefore, the purpose of s 130(2) is to 'preserve the pari passu ranking of unsecured creditors in a winding up and to prevent any individual unsecured creditor from

---

[73] *Hollicourt (Contracts) Ltd v Bank of Ireland* [2000] 1 WLR 895 (Ch).   [74] [2001] Ch 555 (CA) 566.

[75] *Re J Leslie Engineers Co Ltd* [1976] 1 WLR 292 (Ch) 298 (Oliver J).

[76] *Re AI Levy (Holdings) Ltd* [1964] Ch 19 (Ch).

[77] *Re David Lloyd & Co* (1877) 6 ChD 339 (CA) 344.

obtaining an illegitimate advantage over other unsecured creditors in the collective process of winding up'.[78] The staying of proceedings is automatic, but the court can lift the stay and allow the proceedings to commence or continue. The courts' discretion is 'broad and unfettered'[79] and it has the 'freedom to do what is right and fair in all the circumstances'.[80] In practice, the most common example of the court lifting a stay is in relation to claims brought by secured creditors. The rationale behind this is that 'a secured creditor is in a position where he can justly claim that he is independent of the liquidation, since he is enforcing a right, not against the company, but to his own property'.[81]

23.1.3 **Notification of liquidation**

Persons considering dealing with a company in liquidation should be made aware of that fact, as they may not wish to deal with such a company. Accordingly, a company in liquidation is required to state that it is being wound up:

- on every invoice, order for goods, business letter, or order form issued by or on behalf of the company or the liquidator; and
- on all the company's websites.[82]

23.2 Role and powers of the liquidator

The IA 1986 provides that the general role of a liquidator is to gather, realize, and distribute the assets of the company to its creditors and, if there is a surplus, to persons so entitled.[83] In fulfilling this role, the liquidator acts as an agent of the company[84] and owes his duties to the company[85] (not to individual creditors). From this, it follows that the liquidator himself can be liable for breach of fiduciary duty or under statute (e.g. for breach of the summary remedy in s 212).

To facilitate the liquidator in fulfilling this role, the liquidator is granted a wide array of powers:

The summary remedy is discussed at 23.3.2.

- Sections 165–67 provides that the liquidator may exercise the powers in Sch 4,[86] which include the power to (i) pay any class of creditors in full; (ii) make any compromise or arrangement with creditors or persons claiming to be creditors; and (iii) compromise all calls, debts and liabilities, and all claims subsisting between the company and a contributory or other debtor or person apprehending liability to the company. Additionally, the liquidator may bring legal proceedings under specified provisions.[87] This is an important

---

[78] *Nordic Trustee ASA v OGX Petroleo e Gas SA* [2016] EWHC 25 (Ch), [2017] 2 All ER 217 [50] (Snowden J).
[79] *Bourne v Charit-Email Technology Partnership LLP* [2009] EWHC 1901 (Ch), [2010] BCLC 210 [2] (Proudman J).
[80] *Re Aro Co Ltd* [1980] Ch 196 (CA) 209 (Brightman LJ).   [81] ibid 204 (Brightman LJ).
[82] IA 1986, s 188(1). Failure to comply is a criminal offence (ibid s 188(2)).
[83] ibid ss 107 (voluntary winding up) and 143(1) (compulsory winding up).
[84] *Knowles v Scott* [1981] 1 Ch 717 (Ch).   [85] ibid.
[86] Note that in the case of a creditors' voluntary winding up, these powers cannot be exercised, except with the sanction of the court, before (i) the company's creditors nominate a person to be liquidator; or (ii) the procedure by which the company's creditors were to have made such a nomination concludes without a nomination having been made (IA 1986, s 166(2)).
[87] Namely , ss 213, 214, 238, 239, 242, 243, and 423 of the IA 1986.

power as these provisions allow the liquidator to augment the company's assets by claiming contributions from certain persons (discussed at 23.3) or to avoid or adjust certain transactions (discussed at 23.4).

- The liquidator can 'disclaim any onerous property',[88] with such property being defined as any unprofitable contract, and other property of the company which is unsaleable or not readily saleable, or is such that it may give rise to a liability to pay money or perform any other onerous act.[89] The act of disclaimer serves to determine (i.e. terminate) the rights, interests, and liabilities of the company in respect of the property disclaimed.[90] However, any person sustaining loss or damage as a result of the disclaimer will be deemed to be a creditor of the company, and may prove such loss or damage in the winding up.[91]

- Where a person has in his possession or control any property, books, papers, or records to which the company appears to be entitled, then the court can require that person to pay, deliver, convey, surrender, or transfer the property, books, papers, or records to the liquidator.[92]

- Certain persons (e.g. former/current employees or officers of the company)[93] are required to give the liquidator such information concerning the promotion, formation, business, dealings, affairs, or property as the liquidator may reasonably require.[94] Such persons may also be required to attend on the liquidator at such times as he requires.[95] Failure to cooperate with the liquidator, without reasonable excuse, is a criminal offence.[96]

23.2.1 The anti-deprivation rule

The liquidator's ability to pay off the company's creditors would be severely impeded or completely frustrated if the company's assets could be removed from the company's estate at the point of insolvency. Accordingly, the courts have long held that '[t]here cannot be a valid contract that a man's property shall remain his until his bankruptcy, and on the happening of that event shall go over to someone else, and be taken away from his creditors'.[97] This rule, which has come to be known as the anti-deprivation rule, provides that 'the parties cannot, on bankruptcy, deprive the bankrupt of property which would otherwise be available for creditors'.[98] The following case demonstrates this rule in action.

See Henry Phillips, 'Folgate London Market Ltd v Chaucer Insurance plc' (2011) 8 ICR 441.

Folgate London Market Ltd v Chaucer Insurance plc [2011] EWCA Civ 328

FACTS: Mayhew was injured in a driving incident due to the negligence of an employee of Milbank Trucks Ltd ('Milbank'). Mayhew sued Milbank, and Milbank sought to claim on its insurance policy with Chaucer Insurance plc ('Chaucer'). However, Chaucer refused to cover Milbank due to an exception in the policy. The insurance policy had been arranged by Folgate London Market Ltd ('Folgate'), who Milbank sued for negligence in arranging the policy. Folgate and Milbank settled, with the settlement agreement providing that Folgate would indemnify Milbank for 85 per cent of the damages it had to pay Mayhew. However, cl 11 of the agreement also provided that Milbank's right to an indemnity would cease if it went into administration. Prior to paying damages to

---

[88] IA 1986, s 178(2).   [89] ibid s 178(3).   [90] ibid s 178(4)(a).   [91] ibid s 178(6).
[92] ibid s 234(1) and (2).   [93] ibid s 235(3).   [94] ibid s 235(2)(a).   [95] ibid s 235(2)(b).
[96] ibid s 235(5).   [97] *Re Harrison, ex p Jay* (1879) 14 ChD 19 (CA) 26 (Cotton LJ).
[98] *Belmont Park Investments Pty Ltd v BNY Corporate Trustee Services Ltd* [2011] UKSC 38, [2012] 1 AC 383 [104] (Lord Collins).

Mayhew, Milbank went into insolvent administration. Chaucer was joined as a defendant to the proceedings brought by Mayhew, and the interest in the settlement agreement was assigned to Chaucer. Chaucer sought to enforce the settlement agreement against Folgate, and argued that cl 11 breached the anti-deprivation rule.

HELD: Clause 11 breached the anti-deprivation rule. Rimer LJ stated that the commercial objective of cl 11 was:

> a naked attempt to provide that, whilst Milbank's right to payment and Folgate's obligation to pay were to survive so long as the payment would accrue exclusively to the benefit of Mr Mayhew, they were to be extinguished if such payment would instead be available for Milbank's creditors generally in the event of its insolvency.[99]

This was 'not a commercial purpose so much as a collateral device to avoid the consequences of the insolvency legislation'.[100] This was contrary to public policy and so clause 11 was held to be void.

Over the centuries, a mass of confusing case law developed regarding the anti-deprivation rule, described by Fletcher as 'a veritable minefield of traps and tripwires into which the unwary venture at their peril'.[101] Some judges even questioned whether the rule needed to exist at all, given the developments in insolvency legislation.[102] Accordingly, the Supreme Court has now provided much-needed guidance on the rule in *Belmont Park Investments Pty Ltd v BNY Corporate Trustee Services Ltd*.[103] Lord Collins, who delivered the majority judgment, stated that the rule 'is too well-established to be discarded despite the detailed provisions set out in modern insolvency legislation, all of which must be taken to have been enacted against the background of the rule'.[104] He proceeded to establish several principles regarding the operation of the rule:

- A deliberate intention to evade the insolvency laws is required,[105] although this intention need not be subjective and may be inferred.[106] Accordingly, 'in borderline cases a commercially sensible transaction entered into in good faith should not be held to infringe the anti-deprivation rule'.[107]

- Despite statutory developments, 'party autonomy is at the heart of English commercial law'.[108] Accordingly, 'it is desirable that, so far as possible, the courts give effect to contractual terms which parties have agreed. And there is a particularly strong case for autonomy in cases of complex financial instruments . . .'.[109] As a result, 'the modern tendency has been to uphold commercially justifiable contractual provisions which have been said to offend the anti-deprivation rule'.[110]

- The anti-deprivation rule will not apply if the deprivation takes place for reasons other than bankruptcy.[111]

- The source of the assets is an important and, in some cases, a decisive factor. For example, 'if the source of the assets is the person to whom they are to go on bankruptcy that may well be

---

[99] [2011] EWCA Civ 28, [2011] Bus LR 1327 [22].   [100] ibid.

[101] Ian Fletcher, 'Supreme Court Decision in Belmont Park Investments Pty Ltd v BNY Corporate Trustee Services Ltd' (2012) 25 Insolv Int 25, 26.

[102] See e.g. Patten LJ in *Belmont Park Investments Pty Ltd v BNY Corporate Trustee Services Ltd* [2009] EWCA Civ 1160, [2010] Ch 347 [171]–[172].

[103] [2011] UKSC 38, [2012] 1 AC 383.   [104] ibid [102].   [105] ibid [78].   [106] ibid [79].

[107] ibid. This led the Supreme Court in *Belmont* to conclude that the anti-deprivation rule was not breached (see [108]–[113]).

[108] ibid [103].   [109] ibid.   [110] ibid [104].   [111] ibid [80].

an important, and sometimes decisive, factor in a conclusion that the transaction was a commercial one entered into in good faith and outside the scope of the anti-deprivation rule'.[112]

Persons who rely on the type of clause found in *Belmont Park* will doubtless be pleased with the Supreme Court's decision and Lord Collins' reasoning. However, it has been argued that the case has weakened the anti-deprivation rule, with Worthington stating that the approach in *Belmont Park* 'suggests that parties may have legitimate business purposes for avoiding the insolvency regime. That seems wrong. Any avoidance, whether intentional or inevitable, is surely a fraud on the statute'.[113]

23.2.2 **Proof of debts**

Rule 14.3(1) of the Insolvency (England and Wales) Rules 2016 (IR 2016) provides that a creditor wishing to recover a debt from a company in liquidation or administration must provide the liquidator or administrator with proof of that debt, unless (i) r 14.3[114] or an order of the court provides otherwise; or (ii) it is a members' voluntary winding up, in which case the creditor is not required to provide proof unless the liquidator so demands. Accordingly, the liquidator is not required to pay all debts of the company, only those that have been proved or that do not require proof.

Rule 14.2 defines what a 'provable debt' is, with r 14.2(1) stating that all claims by creditors (except as provided for under r 14.2) are provable as debts against the company, whether they are present or future, certain or contingent, ascertained or sounding only in damages. However, a debt will only be provable if the company was subject to it (i) at the relevant date; or (ii) after the relevant date by virtue of an obligation incurred before that date.[115] The 'relevant date' is generally the date on which the company went into liquidation.[116]

If a debt is provable, then in order to claim, the creditor must submit a document known as a 'proof'. There is no prescribed form for this proof, but r 14.4 lists what information must be included in the proof (e.g. the creditor's name, the amount of his claim, etc.). Unless the court provides otherwise, the cost of proving the debt is placed on the creditor.[117] The liquidator will examine the proof and can accept or reject it (in whole or in part) as proof of a debt.[118] If it is accepted, the debt will be proved. If it is rejected (in whole or in part), the liquidator must provide reasons for the rejection.[119] If the creditor is dissatisfied with the liquidator's decision, he can apply to the court for the decision to be reversed or varied.[120]

23.2.3 **The order of distribution**

Once the liquidator has gathered the company's assets and, if applicable, augmented them via legal proceedings discussed at 23.3, his task is then to distribute those assets to the creditors and, if any surplus remains, to persons so entitled.[121] Key to the distribution

---

[112] ibid [98].

[113] Sarah Worthington, 'Good Faith, Flawed Assets and the Emasculation of the UK Anti-Deprivation Rule' (2012) 75 MLR 112, 121.

[114] For instance, r 14.3(3)(a) provides that proof is not required where the debt is a 'small debt', which is a debt that does not exceed £1,000 (r 14.1(3)).

[115] IR 2016, rr 14.1(3) and 14.4(1)(d). Indeed, it will not be a 'debt' at all for the purposes of r 14 if the company was not subject to it at the relevant date.

[116] ibid r 14.1(3).   [117] ibid r 14.5.   [118] ibid r 14.7(1).   [119] ibid r 14.7(2).

[120] ibid 4 14.8(1).   [121] IA 1986, s 143(1).

of the company's assets is what is known as the ***pari passu*** rule, which provides that if the assets of the company are insufficient to fully pay off all of the company's creditors, then the creditors will receive an equal percentage of the debt owed to them.[122] However, the *pari passu* rule is subject to several exceptions, notably:

➡ *pari passu*: 'with equal step'

- A creditor can prioritize his claim by obtaining some form of security (e.g. a fixed or floating charge).
- Statute provides that certain debts rank ahead of, or behind, other debts.
- Statute allows for the setting-off of mutual debts. This occurs where, before a company goes into liquidation[123] or administration,[124] and there have been mutual dealings between a company and a creditor of the company, which usually means that each owes a debt to the other.[125] The following example demonstrates how setting-off works and how it can result in certain debts being prioritized.

Eg **Setting-off**

Dragon Tools Ltd ('DT') goes into liquidation, owing £5,000 to Heavy Wrench Ltd and £10,000 to other unsecured creditors. Prior to DT's liquidation, Heavy Wrench purchased a batch of tools from DT for £10,000 and payment has not yet occurred. Before DT's liquidator distributes its assets, he must take into account what DT and Heavy Wrench owe each other and these sums must be set off against one another.[126] Accordingly, the £10,000 Heavy Wrench owes to DT will be set off against the £5,000 DT owes to Heavy Wrench (in effect, the £5,000 owed to Heavy Wrench has been prioritized to the debt owed to the other creditors). The result will be that, on liquidation, Heavy Wrench will need to pay £5,000 to the liquidator and this will then form part of the company's assets for distribution to the other creditors.[127]

The result of these exceptions is that not all debts rank equally, and a hierarchy of debts can exist (as set out in Figure 23.1). The liquidator must pay each class of debt in turn, so higher-ranking debts stand a better chance of being repaid. If a group of debts cannot be paid in full, the general rule is that each creditor within that group will be paid *pari passu*. Of course, lower-ranking debts will then go unpaid. In practice, upon liquidation, creditors rarely recover 100 per cent of the debt owed. For example, preferential creditors typically recover on average 83 per cent of the debt owed to them, whilst unsecured creditors typically only recover 4 per cent of the debt owed.[128]

It will be noted that certain types of creditor are omitted from Figure 23.1. This is because certain types of property are outside the scope of the liquidator's control, notably (i) property subject to a fixed charge; and (ii) property subject to a **retention of title clause**. In both cases, the creditor can take possession of the property in question, and so it will not be available to the liquidator. Effectively, such creditors rank ahead of those in Figure 23.1. Each debt in Figure 23.1 will now be discussed.

➡ **retention of title clause:** a clause in a contract for the sale of goods that provides the seller will retain title to the goods until they are fully paid for

---

[122] ibid s 107 (which applies to voluntary liquidations) and Insolvency (England and Wales) Rules 2016, r 14.12 (which applies to compulsory liquidations).

[123] IR 2016, r 14.25.   [124] ibid r 14.24.   [125] ibid r 14.25(1).

[126] ibid r 14.25(2).

[127] ibid r 14.25(4). Note that if the set-off resulted in a balance being owed to the creditor, then this balance would be payable to the creditor (r 14.25(3)).

[128] HM Treasury, 'Budget 2018: Protecting Your Taxes in Insolvency' (HM Treasury, 2018).

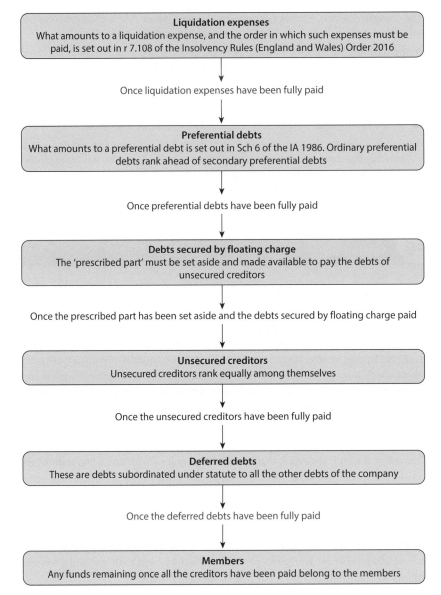

FIGURE 23.1 The order of distribution

Source: Roach, *Concentrate Company Law* (5th edn, OUP 2018).

23.2.3.1 Liquidation expenses

Two provisions in the IA 1986 establish that liquidation expenses have priority over all other claims (except, obviously, debts secured by fixed charge):

- Section 115 provides that, in relation to voluntary winding up, '[a]ll expenses properly incurred in the winding up, including the remuneration of the liquidator, are payable out of the company's assets in priority to all other claims'.

- Section 175(1), which applies to all types of winding up, provides that a company's preferential debts shall be paid in priority to all other debts, but s 175(1A) goes on to provide that ordinary preferential debts rank after winding-up expenses.

Given the 'super priority' status of liquidation expenses, it is important to be able to identify exactly what a liquidation expense is. Rule 7.108(1) of the IR 2016 provides that '[a]ll fees, costs, charges and other expenses incurred in the course of the winding up are to be treated as expenses of the winding up'. Rule 7.108(4) then lists 18 types of expenses that are classified as liquidation expenses. Liquidation expenses do not rank equally amongst themselves, with r 7.108(4) also setting out the order of priority in which the 18 types of liquidation expenses must be paid. However, s 156 provides that if the company's assets are not sufficient to satisfy the liquidation expenses, the court may make an order setting out the order of priority as it thinks just (in practice, this power to modify the order of distribution is rarely used).

In *Buchler v Talbot*,[129] the House of Lords held that property and assets covered by a floating charge could not be used to cover liquidation expenses. However, this has now been reversed by s 176ZA(1) of the IA 1986, which provides that '[t]he expenses of winding up . . . so far as the assets of the company available for payment of general creditors are insufficient to meet them, have priority over any claims to property comprised in or subject to any floating charge created by the company and shall be paid out of any such property accordingly'.

23.2.3.2 **Preferential debts**

Preferential debts rank ahead of all other debts, except liquidation expenses[130] and debts secured by fixed charge. Section 386 provides that the list of preferential debts can be found in Sch 6, which includes contributions to occupational pension schemes and remuneration owed to employees (although preferential status is only given to the last four months' back pay[131] and is limited to £800).[132] In its 2018 Budget, the government stated that it planned to afford preferential debt status to taxes paid by employees and customers of the company that are held by the company (e.g. VAT, income tax, NI contributions).[133] This reform is expected to come into effect in April 2020.

Section 386(1A) and (1B) provides that preferential debts are classified as either 'ordinary preferential debts' or 'secondary preferential debts'. This significance of this is that secondary preferential debts are only paid once the ordinary preferential debts have been paid in full.[134] Ordinary and secondary preferential debts rank equally amongst themselves,[135] so, for example, if there are insufficient assets to pay off fully the ordinary preferential creditors, payment will be made *pari passu* to each ordinary preferential creditor (which means that the secondary preferential creditors would be unpaid).

The Cork Committee noted that, at the time, unsecured creditors often went unpaid due to the existence of preferential debts.[136] It therefore recommended that the class of preferential debts be reduced, with the key recommendation being that Crown debts (principally sums owed by the company to Her Majesty's Revenue and Customs (HMRC)) should lose their preferential status as HMRC had its own far-reaching powers to claim money owed to it.[137] A 2001 governmental report noted that abolishing

---

[129] [2004] UKHL 9, [2004] 2 AC 298.   [130] IA 1986, s 175(1) and (1A).   [131] ibid Sch 6, para 9.

[132] Insolvency Proceedings (Monetary Limits) Order 1986, SI 1986/1996, art 4.

[133] HM Treasury, 'Budget 2018' (HM Treasury, 2018) para 3.87. For more detail, see HM Treasury, 'Budget 2018: Protecting Your Taxes in Insolvency' (HM Treasury, 2018).

[134] IA 1986, s 175(1B).   [135] ibid s 175(1)(A) and (1B).

[136] *Report of the Review Committee on Insolvency Law and Practice* (Cmnd 8558, HMSO 1982) para 1396.

[137] ibid paras 1409–25.

preferential status for Crown debts would free up to £100 million for other creditors.[138] Accordingly, the Enterprise Act 2002 amended Sch 6 to abolish the preferential status of Crown debts, so such debts will now rank as unsecured (although, as noted, employee/customer taxes held by the company will rank as preferential from April 2020).

23.2.3.3 Debts secured by floating charge

Debts secured by floating charge are subject to two notable weaknesses:

1. they come behind debts secured by fixed charge, liquidation expenses,[139] and preferential debts;[140] and

2. the proceeds of certain claims made by a liquidator or administrator[141] are not available to satisfy debts secured by floating charge.[142]

Despite this, a floating charge does provide a creditor with a powerful form of security, especially as the charge can be taken over all the assets and business of the company. The reduction over time in the number of preferential creditors also strengthened the position of floating chargeholders. This led the Cork Committee to conclude that '[i]t is neither inappropriate nor unfair to insist upon some concession in return for the benefit of the general body of creditors, particularly as former preferential creditors will be among them'.[143] This concession was introduced by the Enterprise Act 2002 via the insertion of a new s 176A into the IA 1986. Section 176A applies to floating charges created on or after 15 September 2003[144] which relate to the property of a company which has gone into liquidation or administration, or of which there is a provisional liquidator or receiver.[145] The liquidator, administrator, or receiver is required to set aside a portion of the assets that would normally be used to satisfy the debts of the floating chargeholders.[146] The portion that must be set aside (which is known as the prescribed part') is:

- where the company's net property does not exceed £10,000 in value, 50 per cent of that property;

- where the company's net property does exceed £10,000 in value, 50 per cent of the first £10,000 in value, and 20 per cent of that part of the company's net property that exceeds £10,000.[147]

At the time of writing, the value of the prescribed part shall not exceed £600,000,[148] but the government has stated that it plans to increase this cap.[149] The prescribed part must be set aside and made available to satisfy the unsecured debts of the company.[150] If the prescribed part exceeds the amount required to satisfy the unsecured debts, then the surplus will be returned and made available to satisfy the debts secured by floating charge.[151] If the prescribed part is not enough to cover the unsecured debts, it will be distributed *pari passu*. The following example demonstrates these rules in action.

---

[138] Insolvency Service, *Productive and Enterprise: Insolvency—A Second Chance* (Cm 5234, 2001) para 4.15.
[139] IA 1986, ss 115 and 175(1) and (1A).   [140] ibid s 175(1) and (1A).
[141] Notably proceeds obtained under provisions relating to fraudulent trading, wrongful trading, transactions at an undervalue, and preferences (all of which are discussed at 23.3 and 23.4).
[142] IA 1986, s 176ZB.
[143] *Report of the Review Committee on Insolvency Law and Practice* (Cmnd 8558, HMSO 1982) para 1531.
[144] IA 1986, s 176A(9) and Insolvency Act 1986 (Prescribed Part) Order 2003, SI 2003/2097, art 1(1).
[145] IA 1986, s 176A(1).   [146] ibid s 176A(2)(b).
[147] Insolvency Act 1986 (Prescribed Part) Order 2003, art 3(1).   [148] ibid art 3(2).
[149] Department for Business, Energy and Industrial Strategy (BEIS), 'Insolvency and Corporate Governance: Government Response' (BEIS 2018) para 1.84.
[150] IA 1986, s 176A(2)(a).   [151] ibid s 176A(2)(b).

Eg **The 'prescribed part'**

Dragon Goods Ltd ('DG') owes money to the following:

- £30,000 to various preferential creditors;
- £120,000 to Welsh Bank plc, and this loan has been secured by a floating charge taken over all the assets and business of DG; and
- £46,000 to three unsecured creditors, namely (i) £20,000 owed to Red Ltd; (ii) £14,000 owed to Blue Ltd; and (iii) £12,000 owed to White Ltd.

DG is placed into liquidation, with £150,000 being available to pay off the creditors. £20,000 is used to pay off the liquidation expenses, and £30,000 is then used to pay off the preferential debts, leaving £100,000 to pay off Welsh Bank plc. However, the prescribed part must be first set aside, namely:

- 50 per cent of the first £10,000 = £5,000; and
- 20 per cent of the property that exceeds £10,000 = £18,000 (20 per cent of £90,000).

Accordingly, £23,000 would be set aside to pay off DG's unsecured creditors, leaving £77,000 to be distributed to Welsh Bank plc. The remaining £43,000 owed to Welsh Bank would be on an unsecured basis, but note that a floating (or fixed) chargeholder cannot participate in the prescribed part in respect of any unsecured part of their debt.[152] Accordingly, the £23,000 prescribed part cannot be used to pay off the remaining debt owed to Welsh Bank.

As there is not enough to fully pay off the unsecured creditors, each unsecured creditor would be paid *pari passu*, so Red Ltd would receive £10,000, Blue Ltd would receive £7,000, and White Ltd would receive £6,000 (each creditor receives 50 per cent of the debt owed to them).

In a number of instances, the requirement to set aside the prescribed part will not apply, namely:

- where it has been disapplied by a voluntary arrangement in respect of the company;[153]
- where it has been disapplied by a compromise or arrangement under Pt 26 of the CA 2006;[154] or

Part 26 is discussed at 22.2.

- where the liquidator, administrator, or receiver applies to the court for an order on the ground that the cost of making a distribution to unsecured creditors would be disproportionate to the benefits, and the courts grants such an order.[155]

23.2.3.4 **Unsecured debts**

Any remaining funds (including the prescribed part, if applicable) will then be distributed to the unsecured creditors. Unsecured creditors rank equally amongst themselves[156] so, if there are insufficient assets to pay them all fully, they will be paid *pari*

---

[152] *Re Airbase (UK) Ltd* [2008] EWHC 124 (Ch), [2008] 1 WLR 1516. An exception to this is where the chargeholder surrenders the whole of their security and so becomes an unsecured creditor (*Kelly v Inflexion Fund 2 Ltd* [2010] EWHC 2850 (Ch), [2011] BCC 93).

[153] IA 1986, s 176A(4)(a).   [154] ibid s 176A(4)(b).   [155] ibid s 176A(5).

[156] An exception to this is where an unsecured creditor enters into an agreement with the company, under which his debt is subordinated to that of the other unsecured creditors (*Re Maxwell Communications Corp plc (No 2)* [1993] 1 WLR 1402 (Ch)).

passu. In many liquidations, the unsecured creditors will often go unpaid, or they will recover only part of the debt owed to them.

23.2.3.5 Deferred debts

Certain debts, which are known as 'deferred debts' or 'postponed debts', are subordinated under statute to the other debts of the company. Deferred debts include:

- interest that is payable on any debt proved in the winding up, but this interest is only payable once all the other debts have been paid;[157]
- any sum due to a member by way of dividends, profits, or otherwise;[158]
- where a creditor of the company has engaged in wrongful or fraudulent trading under the IA 1986, then the court may order that any debt owed by the company to that creditor will only be payable once all the other debts of the company have been paid.[159]

23.2.3.6 Members

Any funds remaining once all the company's creditors have been paid (which will only occur if the company was solvent upon liquidation) belong to the company's members. How such funds are to be distributed among the members is a matter for the company's articles (the model articles are silent on this).

23.3 Malpractice before and during liquidation

Sections 212–19 (which apply to companies in liquidation) and 246ZA–ZC (which apply to companies in administration) of the IA 1986 allow a liquidator or administrator to augment the assets of a company by commencing proceedings against certain persons who have engaged in specified forms of malpractice. This benefits the company's creditors by providing additional assets that can be used to pay off the company's debts and liabilities. In addition, ss 206–11 of the IA 1986 and s 993 of the CA 2006 impose criminal liability on persons who have engaged in specified malpractice.

23.3.1 Offences of fraud, deception, etc.

Sections 206–11 impose criminal liability on certain persons (usually past and present officers of the company) who have engaged in certain fraudulent and deceptive conduct, namely:

- fraud in anticipation of the company being wound up[160] (e.g. concealing/removing company property, falsifying book entries);
- transactions in fraud of creditors[161] (e.g. gifting company property);
- misconduct in the course of winding up[162] (e.g. concealing information from the liquidator);
- falsification of company books;[163]
- material omissions from statements relating to the company's affairs;[164] and
- false representations to creditors.[165]

---

[157] IA 1986, s 189(1) and (2).   [158] ibid s 74(2)(f).   [159] ibid ss 215(4) and 246ZC.   [160] ibid s 206.
[161] ibid s 207.   [162] ibid s 208.   [163] ibid s 209.   [164] ibid s 210.   [165] ibid s 211.

23.3.2 Summary remedy

Section 212 of the IA 1986 provides a summary remedy that applies where, in the course of a winding up, it appears that a person misapplies or retains, or becomes accountable for, any money or any other property of the company, or is guilty of any **misfeasance** or breach of any fiduciary or any other duty in relation to the company.[166] A person can only be held liable under s 212 if he:

> **misfeasance:** the improper or unlawful performance of a lawful act

(a) is or has been an officer of the company;

(b) has acted as liquidator or administrative receiver of the company; or

(c) not being within (a) or (b), but is or has been concerned, or has taken part, in the promotion, formation, or management of a company.[167]

This is clearly a wide list of persons, although the majority of s 212 claims are brought against directors. As s 212 does not expressly cover shadow directors, the courts have held that they cannot be held liable under s 212.[168] However, this may require reassessment following recent developments relating to the imposition of duties upon shadow directors.

The utility of s 212 was set out by Chadwick LJ, who stated that it 'provides a summary procedure in a liquidation for obtaining a remedy against delinquent directors without the need for an action in the name of the company'.[169] However, he went on to note that s 212 'does not, in itself, create new rights and obligations'.[170] Section 212 does not create a legal wrong—it merely 'provides a convenient and effective procedure for the recovery of money or property from a person who has committed a wrongful act according to established rules governing the conduct of company affairs'.[171] As such, it is no more than a 'procedural section'[172] that allows certain persons to commence a claim that would normally be vested in the company. The only persons who have standing to commence a s 212 application are an official receiver, a liquidator, or any creditor or contributory.[173] Upon such an application, the court may examine the conduct of the defendant and compel him:

- to repay, restore, or account for the money or property or any part of it, with interest at such rate as the court thinks fit; or

- to contribute such sum to the company's assets by way of compensation in respect of the misfeasance or breach of duty as the court thinks fit.[174]

23.3.3 Fraudulent trading

The concept of fraudulent trading exists under both the CA 2006 and the IA 1986.

23.3.3.1 Fraudulent trading under the IA 1986

Sections 213 and 246ZA of the IA 1986 apply where, in the course of a winding up or while a company is in administration, it appears that any business of the company has

---

[166] ibid s 212(1). [167] ibid.

[168] *Revenue and Customs Commissioners v Holland* [2010] UKSC 51, [2010] 1 WLR 2793 [22] (Lord Hope).

[169] *Cohen v Selby* [2002] BCC 82 (CA) 87. [170] ibid.

[171] Geoffrey Morse, *Palmer's Company Law* (Sweet & Maxwell 2018) para 15.599.14.

[172] *Re B Johnson & Co (Builders) Ltd* [1955] Ch 634 (CA) 648 (Evershed MR).

[173] IA 1986, s 212(3). Note, however, that a contributory can only make an application with the leave of the court (s 212(5)).

[174] ibid.

been carried on with intent to defraud creditors of the company or creditors of any other person, or for any fraudulent purpose.[175] In *Morris v Bank of India*,[176] Patten J stated that this requires three elements to be proven:

1. that the business of the company has been carried on with intent to defraud creditors of the company or creditors of any other person, or for any fraudulent purpose;
2. that the defendant participated in the business being carried on in that manner; and
3. that the defendant did so knowingly.

Looking at the first element, in *R v Kemp*,[177] the Court upheld the view of the trial judge that fraudulent trading covers three separate practices, namely carrying on the business of the company:

1. with an intent to defraud creditors of the company;
2. with an intent to defraud the creditors of any other person; or
3. for any fraudulent purpose.

Three basic points should be noted. First, despite the fact that the word 'creditors' is used, the courts have held that an intent to defraud a single creditor can amount to fraudulent trading.[178] Second, as the phrase '*any* fraudulent purpose' is used, it follows that the fraudulent purpose does not need to be a dominant purpose for the carrying on of the business.[179] Third, as the provisions refer to 'any business' of the company, the Supreme Court has held that ss 213 and 246ZA can apply to the business of a company that occurs outside the jurisdiction of the English courts.[180]

The key issue is what amounts to an 'intent to defraud' or 'fraudulent purpose'. No statutory definition exists, so the issue has been left to the courts, who have stated that these phrases 'connote actual dishonesty involving, according to current notions of fair trading among commercial men, real moral blame'.[181] This is clearly a broad, flexible approach that means that each case will turn on its own facts, but the need to prove actual dishonesty does mean that successful fraudulent trading claims are rare (which led to the creation of wrongful trading, discussed at 23.3.4).

The second element requires that the defendant 'participated in' the business being carried on in a fraudulent manner, which has been taken to mean 'no more than "participates in," "takes part in" or "concurs in"'.[182] Accordingly, this must involve:

> some positive steps of some nature. I do not think it can be said that someone is party to carrying on a business if he takes no positive steps at all. So in order to bring a person within the section you must show that he is taking some positive steps in the carrying on of the company's business in a fraudulent manner.[183]

This broadens the scope of potential defendants and could include persons within the company (e.g. the directors or company secretary), persons outside the company (e.g.

---

[175] ibid ss 213(1) and 246ZA(1). Originally, fraudulent trading under the IA 1986 only applied in relation to companies in the course of a winding up. Section 246ZA, which was inserted into the IA 1986 by the Small Business, Enterprise and Employment Act 2015 (SBEEA 2015), now provides that it also applies to companies in administration.

[176] [2003] EWHC 1868 (Ch), [2003] BCC 735.   [177] [1988] QB 645 (CA).

[178] *Re Gerald Cooper Chemicals Ltd* [1978] Ch 262 (Ch).   [179] *R v Philippou* (1989) 5 BCC 665 (CA).

[180] *Bilta (UK) Ltd v Nazir* [2015] UKSC 23, [2016] AC 1.

[181] *Re Patrick and Lyon Ltd* [1933] Ch 786 (Ch) 790 (Maugham J).

[182] *Re Maidstone Building Provisions Ltd* [1971] 1 WLR 1085 (Ch) 1092 (Pennycuick VC).   [183] ibid.

outside financiers), or even the company itself. However, not all persons can be liable. For example, an employee of the company can only be found liable if he exercised 'a controlling or managerial function . . .'[184]

The third element is that the defendant was 'knowingly' a party to the business being carried on in a fraudulent manner. In *Morris v Bank of India*,[185] Patten J provided the following guidance on what level of knowledge is required:

- The defendant need not know 'every detail of the fraud or the precise mechanics of how it would be carried out',[186] but he would need to know, either from his own observation or from what he was told, that the company was intent on a fraud.

- Knowledge means an 'actual realisation'[187] that fraudulent conduct was occurring or likely to occur. A failure to recognize the truth of what was going on, no matter how obvious, is not enough to establish liability.

- Knowledge must be contemporaneous with the conduct in question. Subsequent knowledge, based on hindsight, is not enough to establish liability.

- Knowledge includes 'so-called blind-eye knowledge, which exists when the party in question shuts its eyes to the obvious because of a conscious fear that to enquire further will confirm a suspicion of wrongdoing which already exists'.[188]

If these three elements are proven, then liability can be established. Only a liquidator or administrator has standing to make an application to the court under ss 213 or 246ZA.[189] If such an application succeeds, then the court may declare that the defendant is liable to make such contributions to the company's assets as the court thinks proper.[190] This power is compensatory not punitive—as Chadwick LJ stated:

> the principle on which that power [to order the defendant to make a contribution] should be exercised is that the contribution to the assets in which the company's creditors will share in the liquidation should reflect (and compensate for) the loss which has been caused to those creditors by the carrying on of the business in the manner which gives rise to the exercise of the power. Punishment of those who have been party to the carrying on of the business in a manner of which the court disapproves . . . seems to me foreign to that principle.[191]

In addition, where the defendant is a director, then he can be disqualified for up to 15 years.[192]

23.3.3.2 Fraudulent trading under the CA 2006

Section 993(1) of the CA 2006 provides that '[i]f any business of a company is carried on with intent to defraud creditors of the company or creditors of any other person, or for any fraudulent purpose, every person who is knowingly a party to the carrying on of the business in that manner commits an offence'. Clearly, s 993 is very similar to the fraudulent trading provisions found in the IA 1986 (and so much of the above discussion also applies here), but there are two key differences:

1. Fraudulent trading under the CA 2006 is a criminal offence, whilst fraudulent trading under the IA 1986 imposes civil liability only.

---

[184] *R v Miles* [1992] Crim LR 657 (CA) (Watkins LJ).   [185] [2004] EWHC 528 (Ch), [2004] BCC 404.
[186] ibid [13].   [187] ibid.   [188] ibid.   [189] IA 1986, ss 213(2) and 246ZA(2).
[190] ibid.   [191] *Morphitis v Bernasconi* [2003] EWCA Civ 289, [2003] Ch 552 [55].
[192] Company Directors Disqualification Act 1986 (CDDA 1986), s 10.

2. The fraudulent trading provisions in the IA 1986 only apply in relation to companies in liquidation or administration. Conversely, s 993 of the CA 2006 applies irrespective of whether the company has been, or is in the course of being wound up.[193] The Law Commission did consider confining s 993 to cases involving companies in liquidation,[194] but the Company Law Review Steering Group (CLRSG) disagreed, stating that '[t]he offence provides a valuable weapon in countering corporate crime. It enables the whole of the defendant's conduct to be examined and thus a proper picture of the defendant's criminality to be given. We believe that this is important in the context of regulating commercial activities.'[195]

Despite these differences, it is possible for both sets of provisions to apply and for criminal and civil liability to be imposed.

23.3.4 **Wrongful trading**

At the time of the Cork Report, civil and criminal liability for fraudulent trading was imposed by s 332 of the Companies Act 1948 (CA 1948), but establishing both types of liability was difficult due to the need to prove dishonesty and the strict standard of proof required. Accordingly, the Cork Report recommended that a new civil remedy should be introduced, under which civil liability could be imposed without proof of fraud or dishonesty and without requiring the criminal standard of proof.[196] This resulted in s 214 of the IA 1986, which created a new civil wrong entitled 'wrongful trading'. Section 214 only applies in relation to companies in insolvent liquidation, but the Small Business, Enterprise and Employment Act 2015 (SBEEA 2015) inserted a new s 246ZB into the IA 1986 which provides for wrongful trading to also apply to companies in insolvent administration.

It is worth noting at the outset that, in terms of the number of reported cases, the wrongful trading provisions have been somewhat underwhelming,[197] largely because other remedies (e.g. summary remedy, transactions at an undervalue, preferences) are easier to establish. As Milman notes, 'wrongful trading rarely occurs in a vacuum but usually in the context of other managerial shortcomings which are easier to prove through legal action.'[198]

A person will have engaged in wrongful trading if three conditions are met:

1. the company has gone into insolvent liquidation or insolvent administration;

2. at some time before the commencement of the winding up of the company or before the company entered administration, that person knew or ought to have concluded that there was no reasonable prospect that the company would avoid going into insolvent liquidation or entering insolvent administration; and

3. that person was a director[199] of the company at that time.[200]

---

[193] CA 2006, s 993(2).

[194] Law Commission, *Legislating the Criminal Code: Fraud and Deception* (Law Com CP No 155, 1999) para 9.2.

[195] CLRSG, 'Modern Company Law for a Competitive Economy: Completing the Structure' (DTI, 2000) para 13.31.

[196] *Report of the Review Committee on Insolvency Law and Practice* (Cmnd 8558, HMSO 1982) para 1778.

[197] Although, they have had a major impact in relation to the directors' general duty of care and skill as s 174(2) is identical to ss 214(4) and 246ZB(4).

[198] David Milman, 'Improper Trading: Can It Be Effective Regulated?' (2004) 4 CLN 3.

[199] Sections 214(7) and 246ZB(7) provide that 'director' will include a shadow director.

[200] IA 1986, ss 214(2) and 246ZB(2).

The second condition is the key condition because it establishes the standard required in order for liability for wrongful trading to be imposed.

23.3.4.1 The objective/subjective standard

The second condition for imposing liability for wrongful trading is that the director 'knew or ought to have concluded that there was no reasonable prospect that the company would avoid going into insolvent liquidation or entering insolvent administration'. Accordingly, a key task for the courts is determining what the director knew and what he ought to have known, but determining what a director 'ought to have concluded' can be a difficult task. Accordingly, the IA 1986 establishes a standard, namely that the facts which a director of a company ought to know or ascertain, and the conclusions which he ought to reach, are those which would be known, ascertained, or taken by a reasonably diligent person having both:

(a) the general knowledge, skill, and experience that may reasonably be expected of a person carrying out the same functions as are carried out by that director[201] in relation to the company; and

(b) the general knowledge, skill, and experience that that director has.[202]

It can be seen that a dual objective/subjective standard is imposed. The standard in (a) is largely objective as it based on 'the general knowledge, skill and experience that may reasonably be expected'. As such, it sets a minimum objective level of knowledge and skill that applies to all directors, but this will differ depending on the functions that the director carries out in relation to the company. For example, the court may expect an executive director to demonstrate a different level of knowledge and skill than a non-executive director (NED). Company size and type of business activity may also be important factors—as Knox J noted:

> the requirement to have regard to the functions to be carried out by the director in question, in relation to the company in question, involves having regard to the particular company and its business. It follows that the general knowledge, skill and experience postulated will be much less extensive in a small company in a modest way of business, with simple accounting procedures and equipment, than it will be in a large company with sophisticated procedures.[203]

The standard in (b) is subjective as it based on 'the general knowledge, skill and experience that that director has'. As (a) provides a minimum standard, it follows that (b) only applies where the standard expected of the director is higher than that which may be reasonably expected (e.g. the director is especially experienced, or has some special skill or qualification). The standard in (a) will not be decreased if the director lacks sufficient skill or knowledge—as Weeks J stated, '[p]atently, [the defendants'] own knowledge, skill and experience were hopelessly inadequate for the task they undertook. That is not sufficient to protect them.'[204] The first reported case under s 214 provides a good example of this standard in action.

---

[201] This will include any functions that he does not carry out, but which have been entrusted to him (IA 1986, ss 214(5) and 246ZB(5)).

[202] IA 1986, ss 214(4) and 246ZB(4).   [203] [1989] 5 BCC 569 (Ch) 594–5.

[204] *Re DKG Contractors Ltd* [1990] BCC 903 (Ch) 912.

Re Produce Marketing Consortium Ltd (No 2) [1989] 5 BCC 569 (Ch)

FACTS: Produce Marketing Consortium Ltd ('PMC') was incorporated in 1964 and was involved in importing fruit. It was profitable until 1980, when its performance started to decrease. By 1984, it had an overdraft of £91,756, and its liabilities exceeded its assets due to several loss-making years. The decline was evident from its audited accounts. The accounts for the 1984/85 financial year should have been available by July 1986, but were only made available in January 1987. These accounts revealed that PMC was insolvent, but the company continued trading until October 1987, when it was wound up with debts of £317,694. The liquidator alleged that the company's directors had engaged in wrongful trading.

HELD: Knox J stated that, although the directors did not receive the 1984/85 financial accounts until January 1987, the level of knowledge required includes 'not only what was actually there but what, given reasonable diligence and an appropriate level of general knowledge, skill and experience, was ascertainable'.[205] Accordingly, the financial results for the 1984/85 financial year should have been known to the directors by July 1986. They knew that this financial year had been a poor one and should have concluded that it placed PMC in an 'irreversible decline'.[206] In addition, the directors ought to have known the extent of PMC's deficit and that there was no way the company could make good on it. Knox J therefore held that the two directors ought to have concluded that in July 1986 that there was no reasonable prospect of PMC avoiding insolvent liquidation, and ordered them to contribute £75,000 to PMC's assets.

23.3.4.2 Timing and trading whilst insolvent

One of the key issues in terms of determining the extent of a director's liability is determining the exact moment that a director started to engage in wrongful trading. This 'moment of truth'[207] as it has been referred to occurs when the director 'knew or ought to have concluded that there was no reasonable prospect that the company would avoid going into insolvent liquidation or entering insolvent administration'.[208] From this, it follows that trading whilst insolvent is not per se wrongful trading. As Chadwick J stated:

> The companies legislation does not impose on directors a statutory duty to ensure that their company does not trade while insolvent; nor does that legislation impose an obligation to ensure that the company does not trade at a loss. . . . Directors may properly take the view that it is in the interests of the company and of its creditors that, although insolvent, the company should continue to trade out of its difficulties. They may properly take the view that it is in the interests of the company and its creditors that some loss-making trade should be accepted in anticipation of future profitability. They are not to be criticised if they give effect to such views, properly held.[209]

The following case provides an example of a situation where wrongful trading had not occurred despite the fact that the company was insolvent.

---

[205] [1989] 5 BCC 569 (Ch) 595.   [206] ibid 596.

[207] Geoffrey Morse, *Palmer's Company Law* (Sweet & Maxwell 2018) para 15.599.29.

[208] IA 1986, ss 214(2)(b) and 246ZB(2)(b).

[209] *Secretary of State for Trade and Industry v Taylor* [1997] 1 WLR 407 (Ch) 414.

Re Cubelock Ltd [2001] BCC 523 (Ch)

FACTS: Cubelock Ltd was incorporated in July 1994. The directors expected the company to make a loss in its first year, to break even in its second year, and make a profit in its third year (these expectations appeared to be realistic). Cubelock made a loss in its first year and the accounts for the first five months of its second year showed a loss too. However, the directors were cautiously optimistic that performance would improve as they anticipated acquiring a large contract. In January 1996, the directors heard that Cubelock had lost this lucrative contract and they placed Cubelock into liquidation the same month. The liquidator reported to the Department of Trade and Industry (DTI) that the directors should be disqualified, *inter alia*, on the ground that they had engaged in wrongful trading. The Secretary of State applied for the directors to be disqualified.

HELD: Park J noted that it is common for a company to trade whilst insolvent 'particularly in a company's early months when it is seeking to get itself established and may have anticipated an initial period of losses before turning the corner and moving into profit'.[210] The cautious optimism that the directors had shortly before losing the Glasgow contract was reasonable and so they did not know nor ought they to have concluded that there was no reasonable prospect of avoiding insolvent liquidation. Accordingly, the Secretary of State's application was dismissed.

23.3.4.3 The 'minimizing loss' defence

Even if a director has engaged in wrongful trading, he can avoid liability if he can successfully raise the defence in ss 214(3)/246ZB(3). These sections provide that the court will not make a declaration if it is satisfied that the director 'took every step with a view to minimising the potential loss to the company's creditors as . . . he ought to have taken'. When deciding what steps the director ought to have taken, the court will apply the objective/subjective standard discussed in section 23.3.4.1, namely to ascertain the steps that would have been taken by a reasonably diligent person having both:

(a) the general knowledge, skill, and experience that may reasonably be expected of a person carrying out the same functions as are carried out by that director in relation to the company; and

(b) the general knowledge, skill, and experience that that director has.

Guidance on the application of the defence came in the following case.

Brooks v Armstrong [2015] EWHC 2289 (Ch)

FACTS: Robin Hood Centre plc ('RHC') ran a Robin Hood-themed tourist attraction. It owed sums to a number of trade creditors. In 2006, VAT rules changed, resulting in RHC owing HMRC £130,000 in VAT. The following year, following a rent review, the rent paid by RHC for the premises it occupied increased by £63,500 per year (the landlord was Tesco). RCH continued to trade. It paid off its trade creditors, but it was not paying Tesco any rent, nor was it paying its VAT liabilities. RHC entered liquidation in February 2009, owing considerable sums to HMRC and Tesco. The liquidator alleged that the directors had engaged in wrongful trading. The directors argued that, in paying off the trade creditors, they had taken every step to minimize the potential loss to RHC's creditors.

See Charlotte Jenner, 'Wrongful Trading: The Elements of a Successful Claim' (2015) 28 Insolv Int 124.

---

210 [2001] BCC 523 (Ch) 540.

> **HELD**: The court held that the directors had engaged in wrongful trading. As to whether the defence was successfully raised, the court started by stating that the onus was upon the directors to prove this defence on the balance of probabilities. The court stated that RHC 'was only able to continue to trade because they adopted a policy of discriminating against Tesco and HMRC. They paid trade creditors whilst allowing the debts of those two creditors to increase . . .'[211] The statutory defence to s 214:
>
> > must be judged by reference to the body of creditors as a whole because it is they as a class who are protected by Section 214, not individual creditors. . . . The requirement to take 'every step' . . . needed the Directors to aim to minimise loss for all not just for some.[212]
>
> Accordingly, the directors' defence failed and they were ordered to make a contribution.

What steps will prove sufficient will depend on the facts of the case, but Hicks has provided some useful broad guidance:

> First, a director cannot take appropriate steps without keeping himself adequately informed of company affairs. Secondly, if an individual director fears the worst, his responsibility is to raise the matter with board members at a meeting or individually and to attempt to institute the response that the board ought to take; a full review of the position with professional assistance and properly recorded decision-making probably leading to insolvency proceedings. . . . In the process of attempting to minimise loss the director should therefore generate and preserve evidence that he has done so. He should put pressure on the board to act appropriately not only orally but in writing. Discussion should be minuted as proof of responsible decision-making. Records of professional advice should be kept. It is useless to be proven right after the event if solid evidence of appropriate action is not available to the court.[213]

23.3.4.4 The application and remedies

Only a liquidator or administrator (as applicable) may apply to the court for a declaration under the wrongful trading provisions.[214] If the application is successful, the court may declare that the defendant is liable to make such contribution to the company's assets as the court thinks proper.[215] This contribution can then be used to help pay off the company's debts. Money paid under s 214 must go to the company—it cannot be paid directly to the company's creditors.[216]

The general approach to calculating the amount of the contribution was set out by Knox J, who stated that the jurisdiction of the wrongful trading provisions is 'primarily compensatory rather than penal. Prima facie the appropriate amount that a director is declared to be liable to contribute is the amount by which the company's assets can be discerned to have been depleted by the director's conduct . . .'[217] However, he then went on to state that 'Parliament has indeed chosen very wide words of discretion and it

---

[211] [2015] EWHC 2289, [2015] BCC 661 [275] (Registrar Jones).   [212] ibid [276].

[213] Andrew Hicks, 'Advising on Wrongful Trading: Part 2' (1993) 14 Co Law 55, 58.

[214] IA 1986, ss 214(1) and 246ZB(1).   [215] ibid.   [216] *Re Purpoint Ltd* [1991] BCC 121 (Ch).

[217] *Re Produce Marketing Consortium Ltd (No 2)* [1989] 5 BCC 569 (Ch) 597.   [218] ibid.

would be undesirable to seek to spell out limits on that discretion, more especially since this is . . . the first case to come to judgment under this section'.[218] Consequently, the courts' approach has not been entirely consistent and some cases have appeared to take on board more the directors' level of culpability[219] and others have calculated the contribution via a different measure to that stated by Knox J.[220] As a result of this:

> [t]he bite of the wrongful trading provisions is . . . diminished not merely by the legal uncertainties that liquidators [and administrators] face on seeing widely varying judicial rulings, but also on the propensity of the judiciary to look to culpability (rather than pure compensation) as a factor of relevance in deciding both whether to declare a liability to contribute and subsequent issues of quantum.[221]

In addition to a declaration, the court may also give such further directions as it thinks proper for giving effect to the declaration.[222] A director that has engaged in wrongful trading can also be disqualified for up to 15 years.[223]

23.3.5 Restriction on re-use of company names

Sections 216 and 217 of the IA 1986 are primarily, though not exclusively, designed to combat what has become known as the 'Phoenix syndrome', which is demonstrated via the following example.

 Eg   The Phoenix syndrome

Dragon Tools Ltd is insolvent and unable to pay its debts. The directors (who are also its members) decide to voluntarily wind up the company, leaving many of its creditors unpaid. A few days later, the directors set up a new company, Dragon Tool Ltd. This new company acquires the assets of Dragon Tools (at a knock-down price) and engages in exactly the same business as Dragon Tools.

This practice was highlighted as a concern by the Cork Committee, which noted:

> the ease with which a person trading [through a company] can allow such a company to become insolvent, form a new company, and then carry on trading much as before, leaving behind him a trail of unpaid creditors, and often repeating the process several times. The dissatisfaction is greatest where the director of an insolvent company has set up business again, using a similar name for the new company, and trades with assets purchased at a discount from the liquidator of the old company.[224]

The new company essentially continues business as normal, trading on the goodwill acquired by the liquidated company, but it is no longer burdened by the debts of the liquidated company. Conversely, the unpaid creditors of the liquidated company will

---

[219] See e.g. *Re Sherborne Associates Ltd* [1995] BCC 40 (QB).

[220] See e.g. *Re DKG Contractors Ltd* [1990] BCC 903 (Ch), where the contribution was determined based on the trade debts that the company acquired due to directors' wrongful trading.

[221] Vanessa Finch, *Corporate Insolvency Law: Perspectives and Principles* (2nd edn, Cambridge 2009) 702.

[222] IA 1986, s 215(2).   [223] CDDA 1986, s 10.

[224] *Report of the Review Committee on Insolvency Law and Practice* (Cmnd 8558, HMSO 1982) para 1813.

understandably feel aggrieved. The law needs to strike a balance. One the one hand, the majority of companies that fail do not do so because of director wrongdoing, so it is important that directors of failed companies should be free to create other companies (subject to limitations). On the other hand, the practice described by the Cork Committee should be restricted to ensure that creditors' interests are not unduly prejudiced. As Milman stated, s 216 seeks 'to maintain a balance between giving entrepreneurs a second chance to maximise the goodwill attached to a business or company name while, at the same time, reassuring the public and creditors that the director is fit to do this'.[225]

Section 216 aims to strike this balance by regulating the re-use of company names. It applies to a person where a company (known as the 'liquidating company') has gone into insolvent liquidation and that person was a director or shadow director of that company at any time in the 12-month period leading up to the date of liquidation.[226] Unless that person obtains the leave of the court, he cannot, for a period of five years beginning on the date of the company's liquidation:

- be a director of any other company that is known by a prohibited name;
- in any way, whether directly or indirectly, be concerned or take part in the promotion, formation, or management of a company with a prohibited name; or
- in any way, whether directly or indirectly, be concerned or take part in the carrying on of a business carried on (otherwise by a company) under a prohibited name.[227]

A 'prohibited name' is:

(a) a name by which the liquidating company was known at any time in the 12-month period prior to its liquidation; or

(b) a name which is so similar to a name falling within (a) as to suggest an association with that company[228] (this would clearly apply to Dragon Tool Ltd in the above example).

A person who contravenes s 216 commits a criminal offence.[229] Additionally, s 217 imposes personal liability for the debts of the company upon (i) a person who is involved in the management of a company in contravention of s 216; or (ii) a person who is involved in the management of the new company, and who acts or is willing to act on instructions given by a person whom he knows at the time is contravening s 216.[230] A person liable under s 217 is jointly and severally liable for the company's debts along with the company and any other person liable who is liable for the company's debts (whether through s 217 or otherwise).[231]

23.3.5.1 Exceptions

Section 216(3) provides that the s 216 restriction will not apply in two broad instances. First, s 216 will not apply where a person obtains the leave of the court to use a prohibited name. Second, s 216 will not apply 'in such circumstances as may be prescribed'. Three such circumstances have been prescribed in subordinate legislation, namely:

1. where the business (or substantially the whole of it) is to be acquired from the insolvent company under arrangements made by its liquidator, or made before the insolvent

---

[225] David Milman, 'Curbing the Phoenix Syndrome' [1997] JBL 224, 226.   [226] IA 1986, s 216(1).
[227] ibid s 216(3).   [228] ibid s 216(2).   [229] ibid s 216(4).
[230] ibid s 217(1).   [231] ibid s 217(2).

company entered into insolvent liquidation by an officeholder acting as administrator, administrative receiver, or supervisor of a company voluntary arrangement (CVA);[232]

2. where a director or shadow director applies for permission from the court not later than seven business days from the date on which the company went into liquidation;[233]

3. where the company is using a prohibited name, but it (i) has been known by that name for the whole of the 12-month period ending on the day before the company went into liquidation; and (ii) it has not, at any time in those 12 months, been dormant.[234]

23.4 Adjustment of prior transactions

The directors of a company that is to be liquidated or placed into administration may enter into certain transactions or agreements, the effect of which is to prejudice the company's creditors (e.g. by selling off corporate assets prior to liquidation). The Cork Committee was aware of this problem, stating that:

> Most advanced systems of law recognise the need to enable certain transactions between a debtor and other parties to be set aside in appropriate circumstances, so that the assets disposed of by the debtor may be recovered and made available to meet the claims of his creditors.[235]

Accordingly, ss 238–46 of the IA 1986 empower certain persons to invalidate certain transactions or to require a contribution to be paid to offset the effects of certain transactions. These transactions basically attempt to extract value from the company, thereby leaving fewer assets in order to pay the company's creditors. The government has announced that it intends to examine whether the law relating to such transactions is in need of reform.[236]

23.4.1 Transactions at an undervalue

A company may seek to place assets outside the control of a liquidator or administrator by giving them away or selling them for much less than they are worth (often the gift or sale is to a person connected with the company, such as a director). Section 238, which applies only to companies in liquidation or administration,[237] aims to combat such a scenario by providing a remedy where a company enters into a transaction at an undervalue. A transaction at an undervalue occurs where:

- the company makes a gift to a person or otherwise enters into a transaction with a person on terms that provide for the company to receive no consideration; or
- the company enters into a transaction with a person for a consideration the value of which, in money or money's worth, is significantly less than the value, in money or money's worth, of the consideration provided by the company.[238]

---

[232] IR 2016, r 22.4.

[233] ibid r 22.6. Note that this exception will only last for six weeks. After this period has expired, if the court has not granted permission, the s 216 restriction will again apply.

[234] ibid r 22.7. A 'dormant company' is defined in s 1169 of the CA 2006.

[235] *Report of the Review Committee on Insolvency Law and Practice* (Cmnd 8558, HMSO 1982) para 1200.

[236] BEIS, 'Insolvency and Corporate Governance: Government Response' (BEIS 2018) paras 3.1–3.11.

[237] IA 1986, s 238(1).   [238] ibid s 238(4).

When determining whether a transaction was at an undervalue, the approach adopted by the court was set out by Millet J, who stated that s 238:

> requires a comparison to be made between the value obtained by the company for the transaction and the value of consideration provided by the company. Both values must be measurable in money or money's worth and both must be considered from the company's point of view.[239]

The value of the asset sold by the company is 'prima facie, not less than the amount that a reasonably well-informed purchaser is prepared, in arms' length negotiations, to pay for it'.[240]

23.4.1.1 Relevant time

Not all transactions at an undervalue are subject to legal proceedings under s 238—only those that are entered into by a company at the 'relevant time', which is two years ending with the onset of the company's insolvency.[241] However, even if the transaction at an undervalue takes place within this period, s 240(2) provides that it will only be regarded as occurring at a relevant time if:

- when the company entered into the transaction, it was unable to pay its debts; or
- the company became unable to pay its debts as a consequence of the transaction.

Where the company enters into the transaction with a person connected to the company, then the conditions in s 240(2) will be presumed to be satisfied, unless the contrary is shown.[242]

23.4.1.2 Person connected with the company

The concept of a 'person connected with the company' is of relevance not only to s 238, but to other sections related to the adjustment of prior transactions. A person will be connected to the company if (i) he is a director or shadow director of the company, or an associate of such a person; or (ii) he is an associate of the company.[243]

The concept of an 'associate' is complex and numerous persons can constitute associates. Section 435 defines when a person (A) will be an associate of another person (B) and includes:

- where A is the husband, wife, civil partner, or relative of B;
- where A and B are in partnership;
- where A is an employee of B or vice versa (for these purposes, a director or officer of the company is to be treated as being employed by the company);
- where A is a company and B has control of it (or B and his associates have control of it);
- where A and B are companies, then A will be an associate of B if the same person has control of both companies.

23.4.1.3 The application and remedies

If a company enters into a transaction at an undervalue at the relevant time, then a liquidator or administrator (as applicable) can apply to the court.[244] If the application is

---

[239] *Re MC Bacon Ltd (No 1)* [1990] BCC 78 (Ch) 92.
[240] *Phillips v Brewer Dolphin Bell Lawrie Ltd* [2001] UKHL 2, [2001] 1 WLR 143 [30] (Lord Scott).
[241] IA 1986, s 240(1)(a). When the 'onset of insolvency' occurs is set out in s 240(3).
[242] ibid s 240(2).   [243] ibid s 249.   [244] ibid s 238(2).

successful, the court shall[245] make such order as it thinks fit for restoring the company to the position it would have been in if the company had not entered into the transaction.[246] Section 241 provides a non-exhaustive list of the types of order that can be made (e.g. an order requiring the property to be transferred back to the company). However, the court shall not make an order if it is satisfied that:

- the company entered into the transaction in good faith and for the purpose of carrying on its business; and
- at the time it entered into the transaction, there were reasonable grounds for believing that the transaction would benefit the company.[247]

The existence of these exceptions indicates that some transactions at an undervalue may be legitimate. For example, if a company is close to insolvency, it may sell off certain assets cheaply in order to raise sufficient capital to continue trading and rescue itself. If this tactic failed and the company were to be liquidated, the court may feel that the transaction was entered into in good faith and was designed to benefit the company.

23.4.2 Preferences

Consider the following example.

Eg **Preferences**

Dragon Goods Ltd ('DG') is close to insolvency. It has reached the limit of its overdraft facility and its bank is refusing to provide any more credit. Accordingly, Sophie, one of DG's directors, lends the company £20,000. DG is unable to avoid insolvency and the directors decide to wind up the company. However, before the company enters liquidation, the directors cause DG to repay the £20,000 it borrowed from Sophie. The effect of this is that, upon DG's liquidation, there are not sufficient assets to pay off the other creditors (some of whom had debts that held priority over Sophie's).

The difficulty evidenced in this example was described by the Cork Committee as follows:

> the payment of a debt lawfully due, even if made by a debtor in contemplation of his impending bankruptcy, and with the deliberate intention of preferring the creditor to whom the payment is made over his other creditors, is neither illegal nor fraudulent. Where, however, the expected bankruptcy supervenes shortly afterwards, such a payment has the effect of preventing the proper distribution of the bankrupt's estate *pari passu* among the creditors.[248]

Accordingly, since the CA 1862, the law has sought to provide a remedy for where a company grants a preference, and the relevant law can now be found in s 239 of the IA

245 Despite the use of the word 'shall', it appears that the court is free to not make an order even if a transaction at an undervalue is present (*Re MDA Investment Management Ltd (No 1)* [2003] EWHC 2277, [2005] BCC 783).
246 IA 1986, s 238(3).   247 ibid s 238(5).
248 *Report of the Review Committee on Insolvency Law and Practice* (Cmnd 8558, HMSO 1982) para 1241.

1986. Section 239 only applies to companies in administration or liquidation,[249] and s 239(4) provides that a company gives a preference to a person if:

- that person is one of the company's creditors or a surety or guarantor for any of the company's debts or other liabilities; and
- the company does anything or suffers anything to be done which (in either case) has the effect of putting that person into a position which, in the event of the company going into insolvent liquidation, will be better than the position he would have been in if that thing had not been done.

23.4.2.1 Relevant time

A preference will only be subject to an application under s 239 if it is given at a 'relevant time',[250] which is:

(a) in the case of a preference which is given to a person connected with the company, within a period of two years ending on the date of the onset of insolvency;

(b) in the case of a preference which is not also a transaction at an undervalue and which is not given to a connected person, within a period of six months ending on the date of the onset of insolvency.[251]

In addition, the preference will only be regarded as being given at a relevant time if, at the time it was given, the company was unable to pay its debts, or it became unable to pay its debts as a consequence of the preference.[252] However, unless the contrary is shown, this condition will be presumed to be satisfied if the preference was given to a person connected with the company.[253]

23.4.2.2 Desire to prefer

A preference will not be actionable against a person unless the company that gave the preference was influenced in deciding to give it by a desire to put that person into a position which, in the event of the company going into insolvent liquidation, will be better than the position he would have been in if that thing had not been done[254] (i.e. the company must have desired to give the person a preference). This desire must be present at the time the preference was given.[255] The following case demonstrates this in practice, and the approach taken by the court in determining whether a desire to prefer exists.

Re MC Bacon Ltd (No 1) [1990] BCC 78 (Ch)

FACTS: MC Bacon Ltd ('Bacon') was profitable until it lost its principal customer in 1986. The directors considered liquidating Bacon but, after taking legal advice, decided to carry on trading. In May 1987, Bacon secured its overdraft by granting a debenture to its bank. In August 1987, Bacon was liquidated, owing its unsecured creditors £329,435, and its overdraft with the bank stood at £235,530. Bacon's liquidator alleged that the debenture granted to the bank was a preference.

---

[249] IA 1986, s 239(1).   [250] ibid s 239(2).   [251] ibid s 240(1).   [252] ibid s 240(2).
[253] ibid.   [254] ibid s 239(5).   [255] *Wills v Corfe Joinery Ltd* [1997] BCC 511 (Ch).

> **HELD:** Millett J stated that 'there must have been a desire to . . . improve the creditor's position in the event of an insolvent liquidation'.[256] There is no need to provide direct evidence of this desire as it may be inferred from the circumstances of the case.[257] However, 'the mere presence of the requisite desire will not be sufficient by itself. It must have influenced the decision to enter into the transaction. . . . It need not have been the only factor or even the decisive one'.[258] Applying this and looking at the available evidence, the court held that the debenture was not a preference. If the debenture was not granted, the bank would have called in the overdraft and Bacon would have been forced into immediate liquidation. Accordingly, the desire behind granting the debenture was not to improve the bank's position, but to enable Bacon to continue trading.

Where the preference is given to a person connected with the company, it will be presumed that a desire to prefer exists, unless the contrary is shown.[259]

23.4.2.3 **The application and remedies**

Where a preference is given at a relevant time, a liquidator or administrator (as applicable) may apply to the court.[260] The court shall make such an order as it thinks fit for restoring the position to what it would have been if the company had not given the preference.[261] Where the preference involves the company repaying a loan (which is most cases), the court will usually order that the creditor return the repaid sum to the company.

23.4.3 **Extortionate credit transactions**

Section 244 applies to companies in liquidation or administration that are, or have been, a party to a transaction for, or involving, the provision of credit to the company.[262] Providing that the credit transaction was entered into in a three-year period ending on the date on which the company entered liquidation or administration, the liquidator or administrator (as applicable) can apply to the court for an order if the transaction was extortionate.[263] The transaction is extortionate if, having regard to the risk accepted by the person providing the credit:

- the terms of it are or were such as to require grossly exorbitant payments to be made (whether unconditionally or in certain contingencies) in respect of the provision of the credit; or
- it otherwise grossly contravened ordinary principles of fair dealing.[264]

Unless the contrary is proved, it shall be presumed that the transaction is extortionate[265] (i.e. a s 244 application places the burden of proof upon the credit provider to prove that the transaction was not extortionate). Examples of what the order may provide include a provision (i) setting the transaction aside (in full or in part); (ii) varying the terms of the transaction; or (iii) requiring a party to the transaction to pay to the liquidator or administrator any sums paid by the company.[266]

---

[256] [1990] BCC 78 (Ch) 87.   [257] ibid 88.   [258] ibid.   [259] IA 1986, s 239(6).
[260] ibid s 239(2).   [261] ibid s 239(3).   [262] ibid s 244(1).   [263] ibid s 244(2).
[264] ibid s 244(3).   [265] ibid.
[266] ibid s 244(4). The court may include one or more of these provisions in the order.

In practice, very few claims are brought under s 244, and the government has stated that it will work with stakeholders to see whether s 244 can be better framed to capture situations where creditors are unfairly disadvantaged by credit transactions.[267]

23.4.4 Avoidance of certain floating charges

Section 245, which only applies to companies in liquidation or administration, serves to invalidate certain floating charges granted prior to insolvency. Before looking at the operation of s 245, it is worth noting why the Cork Committee recommended that only floating charges can be invalidated, and not fixed charges:

> The floating charge is an excessive security because, unlike a fixed charge, it extends to future assets not paid for by the company. It is one thing to permit a prudent creditor, fearing for the solvency of his debtor, to insist either upon payment of the debt due to him or a fixed charge upon existing assets of his debtor instead. . . . It is quite another matter to permit a creditor, concerned for the solvency of his debtor, to take a security which will allow the debtor to trade and acquire further assets on credit with which to swell the security at the expense of the unpaid vendors.[268]

Floating charges will be invalid if they were created at a 'relevant time', which is:

- in the case of a charge which is created in favour of a person connected with the company, within a period of two years ending on the date of the onset of insolvency;
- in the case of a charge which is created in favour of any other person, within a period of twelve months ending on the date of the onset of insolvency.[269]

Section 245(4) goes on to provide that the charge will not be created at a relevant time in this instance unless, at the time the company created the charge, it was unable to pay its debts or it became unable to pay its debts due to the transaction under which the charge was created.

Even if a floating charge was created at the relevant time, s 245(2) provides that it may remain valid in part (e.g. the charge will remain valid to the extent of the aggregate of the value of so much of the consideration for the creation of the charge as consists of money paid, or goods or services supplied, to the company at the same time as, or after, the creation of the charge).

The avoidance of the charge does not affect the validity of the debt that the charge secures—this debt will still be owed but, to the extent that the charge is invalidated, it will become an unsecured debt.

23.5 Dissolution

Liquidation does not bring the company to an end (although it often is the penultimate step). A company's existence will only come to an end when it is removed from the register at Companies House, and this is known as 'dissolution.' In 2017/18, 466,347 companies were dissolved in the UK.[270] Dissolution can occur in a number of different ways:

---

[267] BEIS, 'Insolvency and Corporate Governance: Government Response' (BEIS 2018) para 3.6.
[268] *Report of the Review Committee on Insolvency Law and Practice* (Cmnd 8558, HMSO 1982) para 1553.
[269] IA 1986, s 245(3).

- The registrar of companies may strike a company off the register if he has reasonable cause to believe that it is not carrying on any business or operation[271] (i.e. it is defunct).

- A company can voluntarily apply to the registrar to be struck off the register and dissolved.[272]

- Three months after the registrar has been notified that a winding up has been completed, the company will be deemed to be dissolved.[273]

- If the administrator of a company thinks that the company has no property which might permit a distribution to its creditors, he shall inform the registrar of this.[274] The registrar will register this notice[275] and, three months after the notice is registered, the company will be deemed to be dissolved.[276]

- The registrar's decision to register a company is subject to judicial review, and so may be challenged. In *R v Registrar of Companies ex parte Attorney General*,[277] a company's objects involved it entering into contracts for prostitution. As such contracts are illegal and unenforceable, the registrar's decision to register the company was judicially reviewed. The court granted judicial review and the company was removed from the register.

⌘ This case is discussed at 3.2.5.

- A company may be dissolved by an Act of Parliament (e.g. the HSBC Investment Banking Act 2002, which dissolved HSBC Investment Bank plc).[278]

A company's dissolution terminates its existence and therefore brings its separate personality to an end. Any relationships involving the company (notably that between the company and its members) are terminated. All property belonging to, or rights vested in, the company are deemed to be *bona vacantia* and will belong to the Crown,[279] but can be purchased from the Bona Vacantia Division of the Government Legal Department.

23.6 Restoration

It is possible for a dissolved company to be resurrected and placed back onto the register of companies, and this is known as 'restoration'. In 2017/18, 7,586 companies were restored in the UK. There are a number of reasons why this may be necessary, but the most common is to enable legal proceedings to be brought against the company, or to allow the company to bring proceedings against others (e.g. those who have wronged the company, but this wrong only coming to light following the company's dissolution).

The general effect of restoration is that the company is regarded as if it continued in existence and was never struck off.[280] The company will be restored with the name it had prior to its dissolution,[281] unless another company with that name has since been registered. In such a case, the restored company must specify another name.[282]

23.6.1 **Administrative restoration**

If a company has been dissolved due to being defunct, then a former director or former member of that company may apply to the registrar to have the company restored to the

---

[270] Companies House, 'Companies Register Activities 2017 to 2018' (Companies House 2018) Table A9.
[271] CA 2006, s 1000(1). [272] ibid ss 1003–11. [273] IA 1986, ss 201 and 205.
[274] ibid Sch B1, para 84(1). [275] ibid Sch B1, para 84(3). [276] ibid Sch B1, para 84(6).
[277] [1991] BCLC 476 (DC). [278] HSBC Investment Banking Act 2002, s 11(1).
[279] CA 2006, s 1012(1). [280] ibid ss 1028(1) and 1032(1). [281] ibid s 1033(1).
[282] ibid s 1033(2).

register.[283] Following this application, the registrar must restore the company if the following three conditions are met:

1. the company was carrying on business or in operation at the time of its striking off[284] (i.e. it was not defunct);

2. if any property or right vested in the company vested as *bona vacantia*, the Crown representative has consented in writing to the company being restored;[285] and

3. the applicant has delivered specified documentation to the registrar.[286]

23.6.2 **Restoration by the court**

An application can be made to the court to restore a company to the register. Section 1029(2) provides a lengthy list of persons who have standing to bring an application, including the Secretary of State, a former director or member of the company, any person with a potential legal claim against the company, any former liquidator of the company, or any other person appearing to the court to have an interest in the matter.

CHAPTER SUMMARY

- There are two types of winding up, namely voluntary winding up and compulsory winding up.

- A voluntary winding up occurs where the members voluntarily wind up the company by passing a special resolution.

- Where a declaration of solvency is made, the winding up will be a members' voluntary winding up. If no such declaration is made, it will be a creditors' voluntary winding up.

- Compulsory winding up occurs where a person petitions the court for an order winding up the company, and the courts grants such an order. Only specified persons can petition the court and only on specified grounds. Most petitions are made by a creditor on the ground that the company is unable to pay its debts.

- The liquidator's role is to gather, realize, and distribute the assets of the company to its creditors and, if there is a surplus, to persons so entitled.

- The order of distribution of assets upon insolvency is (i) liquidation expenses; (ii) preferential debts; (iii) debts secured by floating charge; (iv) unsecured debts; (v) deferred debts; and (vi) any remaining assets are distributed to the members.

- The assets of the company can be augmented, or criminal liability can be imposed, by commencing proceeding against certain persons who have engaged in malpractice before and during liquidation.

- Certain persons can invalidate certain transactions that occurred prior to the company being liquidated.

- The process by which a company's existence is ended is known as 'dissolution'. A dissolved company can be restored in certain circumstances.

---

[283] ibid s 1024(1) and (3). The application must be made within six years of the company's dissolution (s 1024(4)).

[284] ibid s 1025(2).   [285] ibid s 1025(3).   [286] ibid s 1025(5).

FURTHER READING

Andrew Keay, 'Wrongful Trading and the Liability of Company Directors: A Theoretical Perspective' (2005) 25 LS 431.

- Discusses the arguments for and against the wrongful trading provisions, and discusses whether companies and their creditors should be able to opt out of these provisions.

Vanessa Finch, *Corporate Insolvency Law: Perspectives and Principles* (2nd edn, Cambridge 2009) chs 14 and 15.

- Provides a detailed (if slightly ageing) discussing of the *pari passu* principle, its exceptions, and how to bypass it.

Report of the Review Committee on Insolvency Law and Practice (Cmnd 8558, HMSO 1982).

- The report of the Cork Committee established the foundations for our current system of corporate insolvency law. Despite its age, it still provides an extremely useful discussion of a range of insolvency law issues.

www.gov.uk/government/organisations/insolvency-service accessed 10 January 2019.

- The website of the Insolvency Service. Provides a range of accessible guidance and updates relating to insolvency law.

SELF-TEST QUESTIONS

1. Define the following terms:

- liquidation;
- *pari passu*;
- preferential debts;
- prescribed part;
- deferred debts;
- wrongful trading;
- Phoenix company;
- a preference;
- dissolution;
- restoration.

2. State whether each of the following statements is true or false and, if false, explain why:

- The process by which a company's existence is brought to an end is called liquidation.
- A voluntary winding up begins by the company passing a special resolution.
- The directors will vacate office upon a winding up order being made.
- *Pari passu* means that all the creditors receive the same amount of money.
- The liquidator must first pay off the debts of those creditors whose debts are secured by a fixed charge.
- Crown debts are ranked as preferential debts.
- A portion of the debt owed to floating chargeholders must be set aside and kept for the unsecured creditors.
- Wrongful trading occurs where the directors carry on trading even though the company is insolvent.
- A liquidator can set aside any charge entered into by the company within a period of 12 months, ending on the date of the company's liquidation.

3. 'The wrongful trading provisions have proven to be confusing and largely ineffective.' Discuss this statement.

4. Alison and Lyndsey incorporated Dragon Consultancy Services Ltd ('DCS') in January 2012. Alison and Lyndsey are the company's only directors and members, with each holding 100 £1 shares.

Despite several years of excellent financial performance, the company began to experience financial difficulties. In February 2017, DCS had reached the overdraft limit it had agreed with Welsh Bank plc. In return for increasing the overdraft limit to £100,000, Welsh Bank took a floating charge over all DCS's assets. The business continued to deteriorate and, in January 2018, DCS's accountant told Alison and Lyndsey that it was unlikely that DCS would be able to avoid liquidation. Alison and Lyndsey were of the opinion that DCS could trade its way out of its financial difficulties by having a sale, but this proved ineffective and, in January 2019, DCS was wound up. At this time, DCS's overdraft with Welsh Bank had reached £90,000.

You have been appointed as DCS's liquidator and have discovered the following: (i) in March 2018, Lyndsey had lent £10,000 to DCS and the company had repaid this loan in August 2018; (ii) in addition to the money owed to Welsh Bank, DCS owes £10,000 in unpaid taxes, £20,000 to employees in unpaid wages, and £40,000 to various unsecured creditors. The total assets of DCS amount to around £60,000 and the cost of liquidation DCS will be £3,000.

Carry out the role of liquidator and (i) discuss any ways in which the pool of assets can be augmented; and (ii) work out the amount that each creditor will be paid.

 ONLINE RESOURCES

This book is accompanied by online resources to better support you in your studies. Visit www.oup.com/uk/roach-company/ for:

- answers to the self-test questions;
- further reading lists;
- multiple-choice questions;
- glossary.

Updates to the law can be found on the author's Twitter account (@UKCompanyLaw) and further resources can be found on the author's blog (www.companylawandgovernance.com).

Index

Note: Tables, figures, and boxes are indicated by an italic *t*, *f*, and *b* following the page number.